Architectural GRAPHIC Standards

John Wiley & Sons

Peggy Burns
Publisher

Robert J. Fletcher IV
Production Director

Amanda Miller
Senior Editor

Meg Hudak Day
Senior Marketing Manager

The American Institute of Architects

Janet Rumbarger
Managing Editor

Richard J. Vitullo, AIA
Consulting Editor

Anthony Lewandowski
Computer Consultant

Molly Cutting
Production Coordinator

Pamela James Blumgart
Copy Editor

Virginia Vitzthum
Copy Editor

Elizabeth Laking
Editorial Associate

Jenifer Tennant Dwyer
Administrative Assistant

SECTION EDITORS
Ralph Bennett, AIA
McCain McMurray
Darrel Rippeteau, AIA

COMPUTER GRAPHICS ASSOCIATES
Liza Albano
Samir Ali
Kenneth R. Baetz
Gary Corey
Lawrence Dick
James M. Duda
Luke Fox
Gordon M. Jensen
David Larson
Ann Lassetter
Michael Lundberg
Jeffery Madsen
Camille Mendez-Hordatt
Tamra Ottesen
Scott Peterson, AIA
David Salela
Jerry L. Smith
Chuck Taylor
Antonio Vercillo
James V. Vose
Kenton Wesley Wingfield
Bradley E. Workman, AIA

AGS MENTORS
Ralph G. Allen, FAIA
Lee Hewlett Askew III, FAIA
Richard R. Bergmann, FAIA
Rebecca L. Binder, FAIA
Peter Bohlin, FAIA
Lawrence Cook, FAIA
Charles Eley, FAIA
Douglas K. Engebretson, FAIA
Peter Forbes, FAIA
Robert J. Frasca, FAIA
Steven M. Goldberg, FAIA
David L. Hoffman, FAIA
Bobbie Sue Hood, FAIA
John M. Johansen, FAIA
Thomas L. Kerns, FAIA
Robert P. Ludden, FAIA
William N. Morgan, FAIA
Eric Owen Moss, FAIA
Jefferson B. Riley, FAIA
Albert W. Rubeling, Jr., FAIA
Michael M. Sizemore, FAIA
Walter H. Sobel, FAIA
Laurinda H. Spear, FAIA
Jane Stansfeld, FAIA
Stanley Tigerman, FAIA
Jane Weinzapfel, FAIA

JOHN WILEY & SONS, INC.
New York • Chichester • Brisbane • Toronto • Singapore

RAMSEY/SLEEPER

Architectural GRAPHIC Standards

Ninth Edition

1996 Cumulative Supplement

JOHN RAY HOKE, JR., FAIA
EDITOR IN CHIEF

THE AMERICAN INSTITUTE OF ARCHITECTS

SUBSCRIPTION NOTICE

Architectural Graphic Standards is updated on a periodic basis to reflect important changes in the subject matter. If you purchased this product directly from John Wiley & Sons, Inc., we have already recorded your subscription for this update service.

If, however, you purchased this product from a bookstore and wish to receive future updates or editions billed separately with a 15-day examination review, please send your name, company name (if applicable), address, and the title of this product to:

Supplement Department
John Wiley & Sons, Inc.
One Wiley Drive
Somerset, NJ 08875
1-(800)-225-5945

This book is printed on acid-free paper.

The drawings, tables, data, and other information in this book have been obtained from many sources, including government organizations, trade associations, suppliers of building materials, and professional architects or architecture firms. The American Institute of Architects (AIA), the Architectural Graphic Standards Task Force of the AIA, and the publisher have made every reasonable effort to make this reference work accurate and authoritative, but do not warrant, and assume no liability for, the accuracy or completeness of the text or its fitness for any particular purpose. It is the responsibility of users to apply their professional knowledge in the use of information contained in this book, to consult the original sources for additional information when appropriate, and, if they themselves are not professional architects, to consult an architect when appropriate.

Copyright © 1995, 1996 by John Wiley & Sons, Inc.

All rights reserved. Published simultaneously in Canada.

Reproduction or translation of any part of this work beyond that permitted by Section 107 or 108 of the 1976 United States Copyright Act without the permission of the copyright owner is unlawful. Requests for permission or further information should be addressed to the Permissions Department, John Wiley & Sons, Inc., 605 Third Avenue, New York, NY 10158-0012.

ISBN 0-471-15342-7

Printed in the United States of America
10 9 8 7 6 5 4 3 2 1

CONTENTS

The following pages supplement ten of the twenty chapters in the ninth edition of *Architectural Graphic Standards*.

PUBLISHER'S NOTE	vii
FOREWORD	viii
PREFACE	ix

3 CONCRETE

Concrete Formwork	1
Concrete Reinforcement	6
Cast-in-Place Concrete	7
Precast Concrete	15

5 METALS

Metal Materials, Finishes, and Coatings	22
Structural Metal Framing	26
Metal Joists	32
Cold-Formed Metal Framing	34
Metal Fabrication	41
Ornamental Metal	43

6 WOOD AND PLASTICS

Fasteners and Adhesives	47
Rough Carpentry	49
Heavy Timber Construction	67
Wood Treatment	69
Architectural Woodwork	72

7 THERMAL AND MOISTURE PROTECTION

Introduction	80
Insulation	83
Shingles and Roofing Tiles	84
Membrane Roofing	86
Flashing and Sheet Metal	97
Roof Specialties and Accessories	103
Skylights	110

9 FINISHES

Metal Support Systems	114
Gypsum Board	116
Stone Facing	118
Acoustical Treatment	119
Special Wall Surfaces	121
Special Ceiling Surfaces	122
Wood Flooring	124
Stone Flooring	125
Unit Masonry Flooring	126
Special Flooring	127
Special Coatings	128
Painting	130
Wall Coverings	135

10 SPECIALTIES

Wall and Corner Guards	137
Fireplaces and Stoves	140
Flagpoles	142
Identifying Devices	143
Fire Protection Specialties	144
Protective Covers	145
Partitions and Operable Partitions	147

11 EQUIPMENT
Audiovisual Equipment	149
Food Service Equipment	152
Residential Equipment	160

13 SPECIAL CONSTRUCTION
Air-Supported Structures	163
Special Purpose Rooms	164
Pre-Engineered Structures	165
Fire Suppression and Supervisory Systems	167

16 ELECTRICAL
Wiring and Related Materials	168
Service and Distribution	173
Lighting	177

20 BUILDING TYPES AND SPACE PLANNING
Justice Facilities	186
Housing	191

INDEX	201

PUBLISHER'S NOTE

As publisher of Ramsey/Sleeper's *Architectural Graphic Standards* since 1932, John Wiley & Sons, Inc., is deeply committed to providing the design community with current, reliable information sources. We have witnessed landmark changes in the field, from the integration of the computer in the design office to new zoning and building code regulations that govern the industry. After publishing the eighth edition of *Architectural Graphic Standards*, our readers encouraged us to provide more frequent updates to keep them apprised of these important changes. In response to these requests and our own assessment of the field, we developed the supplement program for *Architectural Graphic Standards*. The intent of the program is to provide design professionals with essential new information annually—information that otherwise would remain inaccessible until the publication of the new edition.

The *1996 Architectural Graphics Standards Cumulative Supplement* is the second supplement published since the release of the ninth edition in 1994. We will continue to review and update the ninth edition through annual supplementation until the tenth edition of *Architectural Graphic Standards* is launched in the year 2000. Our goal is to keep the cumulative supplement, and the professional community it serves, as up to date as possible.

The *1996 Supplement* contains important new information and standards concerning concrete, metals, specialities, equipment, special construction, electrical issues, and building types and space planning. We have also included a complete index that integrates material from the ninth edition with material from the cumulative supplement.

We are proud to publish the *1996 Architectural Graphic Standards Cumulative Supplement* and welcome your comments and suggestions for future updates.

PEGGY BURNS
Publisher
John Wiley & Sons, Inc.

FOREWORD

What does it mean to be identified as a member of The American Institute of Architects? If the initials "AIA" after a member's name are to mean anything, we must commit ourselves to increasing the core competence of our members. We must do this all the while we are adding to their competitive advantage and promoting their professional status. This is the only way I know to ensure their future prosperity. Accomplishing these goals is the ultimate measure of whether a professional society of architects united under the title "AIA" really has value.

Historically, the AIA has been uniquely positioned to gather and disseminate information to the construction industry. One consequence has been the creation of such outstanding resources as the AIA Documents and *The Architect's Handbook of Professional Practice*.

Since 1964 *Architectural Graphic Standards* has been a key resource on this shelf of indispensable professional resources. A strategic joint venture between the AIA and its publishing partner, John Wiley & Sons, Inc., has yielded four editions of *Architectural Graphic Standards* and two cumulative supplements to the ninth edition. This volume is the second supplement to the ninth edition.

America's architects have been well served by the AIA in these core publications, which encourage members to share their knowledge of practice and design. In many ways, our greatest assets as an organization are defined in the pages of these essential published works. With respect to *Architectural Graphic Standards*, this book stands as one of the Institute's brightest stars; it truly delivers "the right stuff."

TERRENCE M. McDERMOTT
Chief Executive Officer
The American Institute of Architects

PREFACE

The American Institute of Architects and John Wiley & Sons, Inc., are delighted to offer the second supplement to the ninth edition of *Architectural Graphic Standards*. For many architects, this annual supplement of 100 new pages has become a useful companion to the main edition. Our mission for the supplement program is to provide architects and other members of the building team with current design data and to keep them abreast of the rapidly changing construction industry. Thoughts and ideas from readers about how the AIA can improve this product are always welcome.

The book features a comprehensive index, which covers the entire ninth edition as well as the supplement pages. This combined index should save the reader time in cross-referencing and should better integrate the supplement with the main edition.

It is our intention with this and subsequent supplements to build on whole *AGS* chapters rather than to revise or produce isolated pages. This approach should bring more balance and editorial coordination to the tenth edition, scheduled for publication in 2000. For this supplement, we have developed new and revised pages in seven chapters: Concrete (Chapter 3), Metals (Chapter 5), Specialties (Chapter 10), Equipment (Chapter 11), Special Construction (Chapter 13), Electrical (Chapter 16), and Building Types and Space Planning (Chapter 20).

I would like to draw your attention to some of the new information in this supplement. In Chapter 3 you will find pages on concrete formwork hardware; concrete admixtures; concrete floor systems; defect prevention for concrete surfaces; repair, coatings, and treatments of concrete; precast concrete wall panel tolerances; and precast concrete connections. In Chapter 5 look for pages on properties of metals; metal finishes; cold-formed metal framing; fixed metal ladders; ornamental ironwork details; perforated metals; sheet metals; steel sheets, coils, and plates.

Chapter 10 focuses on metal solid-fuel heaters, metal louvers, operable walls and partitions, and modular wall systems. In Chapter 11 you will find pages on multimedia, audiovisual, and videoconference equipment; office computer equipment; and commercial bar and food-service equipment. Chapter 13 contains pages on pre-engineered metal building details, and Chapter 16 concentrates on residential electrical wiring, lamp types, and lightning protection. The pages in Chapter 20 focus on the design of justice facilities.

At Wiley, I would like to thank Peggy Burns, publisher; Amanda Miller, senior editor; Robert J. Fletcher IV, production director; and Meg Hudak Day, senior marketing manager, all of whom contribute their vast talent and craftsmanship to making these supplements the very best source of technical information available to design professionals.

At the AIA, I am delighted with the dedication of our gifted professionals. My special thanks go to consulting editor Richard J. Vitullo, AIA, for his good work in researching and developing these fine pages.

Our fantastic production team consisted of Janet Rumbarger, managing editor; Anthony Lewandowski, computer consultant; Molly Cutting, production coordinator; Pamela James Blumgart and Virginia Vitzthum, copy editors; Elizabeth Laking, editorial associate; and Jenifer Tennant Dwyer, editorial assistant. I am very fortunate to have them as my associates.

This year a distinguished group of architects—all members of the AIA's College of Fellows—reviewed and commented on new pages in this supplement. I want to extend my appreciation for the excellent work of the following *AGS* mentors: Ralph G. Allen, FAIA; Lee Hewlett Askew III, FAIA; Richard R. Bergmann, FAIA; Rebecca L. Binder, FAIA; Peter Bohlin, FAIA; Lawrence Cook, FAIA; Charles Eley, FAIA; Douglas K. Engebretson, FAIA; Peter Forbes, FAIA; Robert J. Frasca, FAIA; Steven M. Goldberg, FAIA; David L. Hoffman, FAIA; Bobbie Sue Hood, FAIA; John M. Johansen, FAIA; Thomas L. Kerns, FAIA; Robert P. Ludden, FAIA; William N. Morgan, FAIA; Eric Owen Moss, FAIA; Jefferson B. Riley, FAIA; Albert W. Rubeling, Jr., FAIA; Michael M. Sizemore, FAIA; Walter H. Sobel, FAIA; Laurinda H. Spear, FAIA; Jane Stansfeld, FAIA; Stanley Tigerman, FAIA; and Jane Weinzapfel, FAIA.

The CAD graphics on these pages were admirably performed by associates Liza Albano; Samir Ali; Kenneth R. Baetz; Gary Corey; Lawrence Dick; James M. Duda; Luke Fox; David Larson; Ann Lassetter; Jeffery Madsen; Camille Mendez-Hordatt; Tamra Ottesen; Scott Peterson, AIA; David Salela; Jerry Smith; Chuck Taylor; Antonio Vercillo; James V. Vose, and Kenton Wesley Wingfield.

I am also grateful for three technology partnerships that contributed to this year's supplement. Michael Lundberg and Gordon M. Jensen, senior project manager, of Cambric Graphics, Inc., helped improve the CAD documents for use in this supplement and as vector drawings in the new AGS CD-ROM to be released later this year. Bradley E. Workman, AIA, of Bentley Systems, Inc., the developers of MicroStation, provided valuable support for our CAD work. And finally I thank David A. Jordani, FAIA, president of Jordani Multimedia, developers of the AGS CD-ROM, for his wise counsel.

As always, our greatest debt is to the AIA firms, members, and other contributors for their tremendous efforts on this book. Their valuable service and dedication to excellence is apparent on every page. I would also like to thank Terrence M. McDermott, chief executive officer, and Fred DeLuca, Hon. AIA, chief financial officer, for their trust and support of this important AIA program.

The American Institute of Architects and John Wiley & Sons, Inc., hope you will keep alive Ramsey and Sleeper's vision of *Architectural Graphic Standards* as a publication with no limit on what might be included in future volumes.

JOHN RAY HOKE, JR., FAIA
Editor in Chief

Economy of Concrete Formwork

GENERAL

Formwork costs are a substantial part of the total cost of putting concrete in place—anywhere from 35 to 60 percent. Thus, by developing design elements and details that simplify or standardize form requirements, the architect can help contain overall costs:

1. Reuse forms: This is crucial to economy of construction. The designer can facilitate form reuse by standardizing the dimensions of windows, columns, beams, and footings, using as few different sizes of each as possible. Where columns must change size, hold one dimension (e.g., width) constant, while varying the other (depth). This enables at least half of the form panels to be used many times. Repeat the same floor and column layout from bay to bay on each floor and from floor to floor. This improves labor productivity and permits reuse of many forms.
2. Use a preconstruction mockup: The architect and builder should agree on the location and desired appearance of architectural surfaces before any of the exposed concrete work begins. Specify a full-scale preconstruction mockup to help achieve this and to avoid postconstruction disagreements.
3. Handle forms in large panels: This also reduces construction costs. Wherever possible, make uninterrupted formed areas the same size. Increasing the size of such areas enables the builder to combine form panels into gangs for efficient crane use.
4. Simplify design details: Intricacies and irregularities cost more and often do not add proportionately to the aesthetic effect.

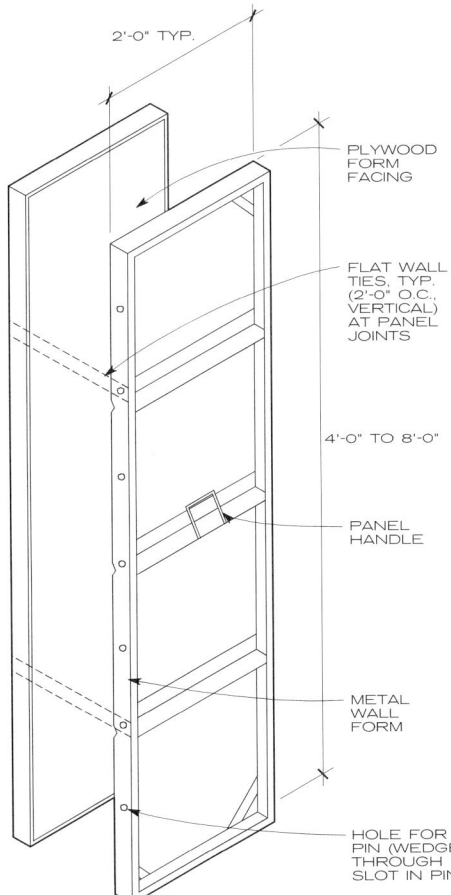

NOTES

1. Commonly made of steel-framed plywood, panels are also available in aluminum. Wall ties (typically flat ties) and wall forms are held together by slotted pins that run through adjoining holes. A wedge pushed down into the slot alongside the wall form tightens the joint. Service life can be extended by turning or replacing the plywood face.
2. Reusable plastic liners may be attached to inner surfaces to produce patterned concrete.
3. For maximum economy, panels can be assembled in large gangs and set in place by crane.

HAND-SET MANUFACTURED WALL FORMS

Mary K. Hurd; Engineered Publications; Farmington Hills, Michigan

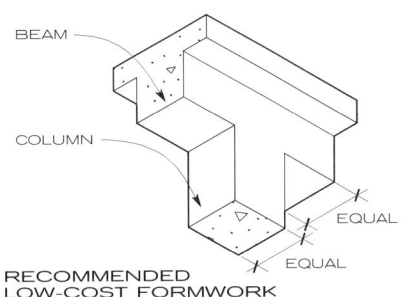

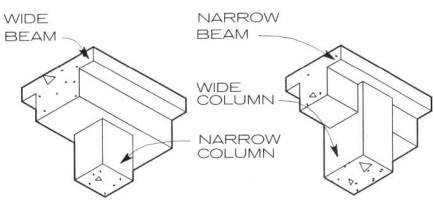

NOTE

In general, the least costly design to form has columns the same width or narrower than the beams they support, allowing the beam form to be erected in a continuous line. In mid-cost formwork design, the beam bottom forms are cut to fit around the column tops. In high-cost formwork design, the beam forms are fitted into pockets on both sides of the column forms.

BEAM-TO-COLUMN FORMWORK ECONOMIES

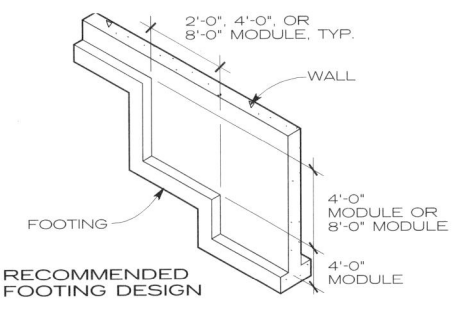

NOTE

When stepped footings are required, use fewer steps and design them to standard lumber and plywood dimensions or modular divisions of these dimensions.

WALL FOOTINGS

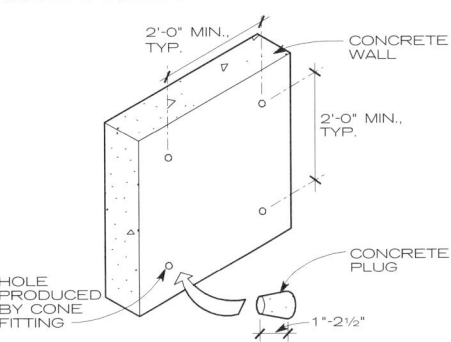

NOTE

Installing and removing ties and patching tie holes are some of the most labor-intensive operations in forming walls. Also, getting a durable, inconspicuous patch often proves difficult. Avoid this problem by specifying smooth cone fittings at the tie ends, then either leaving the resulting uniform tie holes exposed or plugging them with preformed concrete plugs and a bonding agent. Leave no exposed corrodible metal within 1½ in. of concrete surface. Contractors may propose tie spacing wider than 2 ft o.c. to reduce the total number of ties to save money, but this calls for stronger ties and heavier form supports.

FORM TIE PATTERN

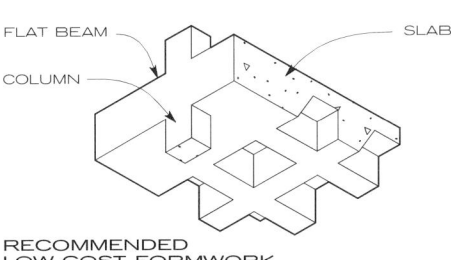

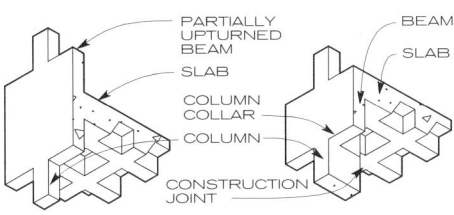

NOTE

Flat beams designed to be equal in depth to the floor assembly are the least costly, since they most efficiently accommodate flying form construction. Deeper, narrower beams cost more, but if deeper beams are needed, costs can be controlled by making the beam the same thickness as the column depth and at least partially upturned. The most costly option is a column thicker than the beam, since this requires a column collar with construction joint.

SPANDREL BEAM FORMWORK ECONOMIES

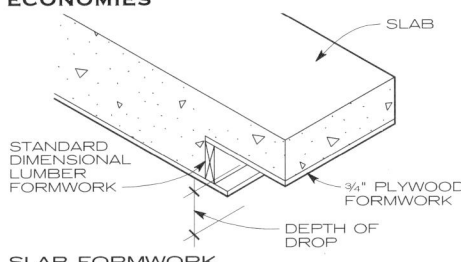

SLAB FORMWORK

NOTE

Adapting design elements to the modular sizes of formwork lumber and plywood and dimensioning parts of the structure to fit the modules can save the expense of custom formwork. For example, to save the waste and time of sawing and piecing together the edge form, make the depth of the drop in a slab equal to the actual size of standard lumber plus ¾ in. for the plywood's thickness.

STANDARD LUMBER FORMS

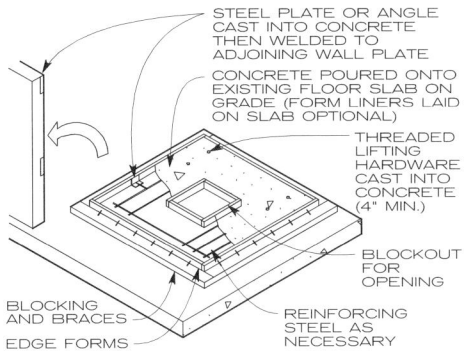

TILT-UP WALL FORMWORK

NOTE

In tilt-up construction, walls are cast on the completed floor slab, which must be level, smoothly finished, and treated with a bond-breaking agent to permit easy separation. The wall is then tilted or lifted into vertical position and fastened to the adjoining wall piece. This method reduces formwork and labor and eliminates transportation requirements that may limit panel size.

TILT-UP WALLS

Concrete Formwork for Columns and Footings

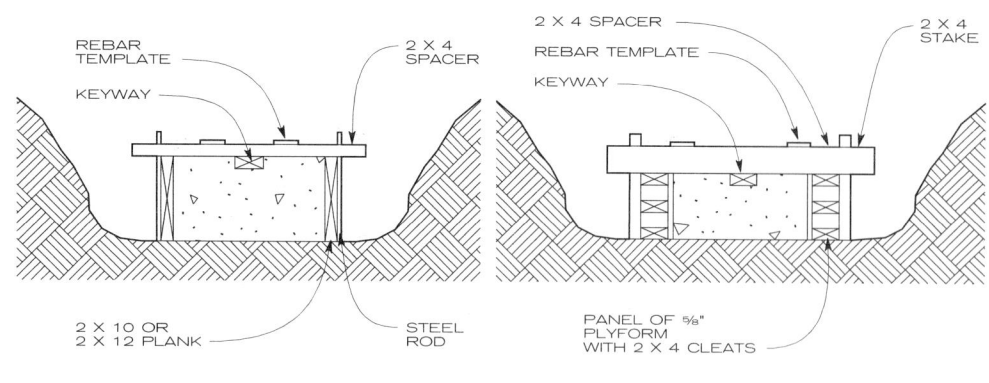

WALL FOOTINGS

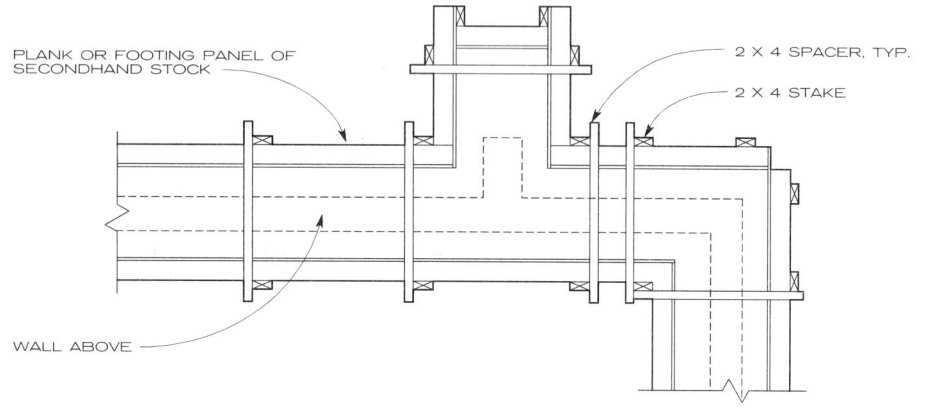

WALL FOOTING PLAN

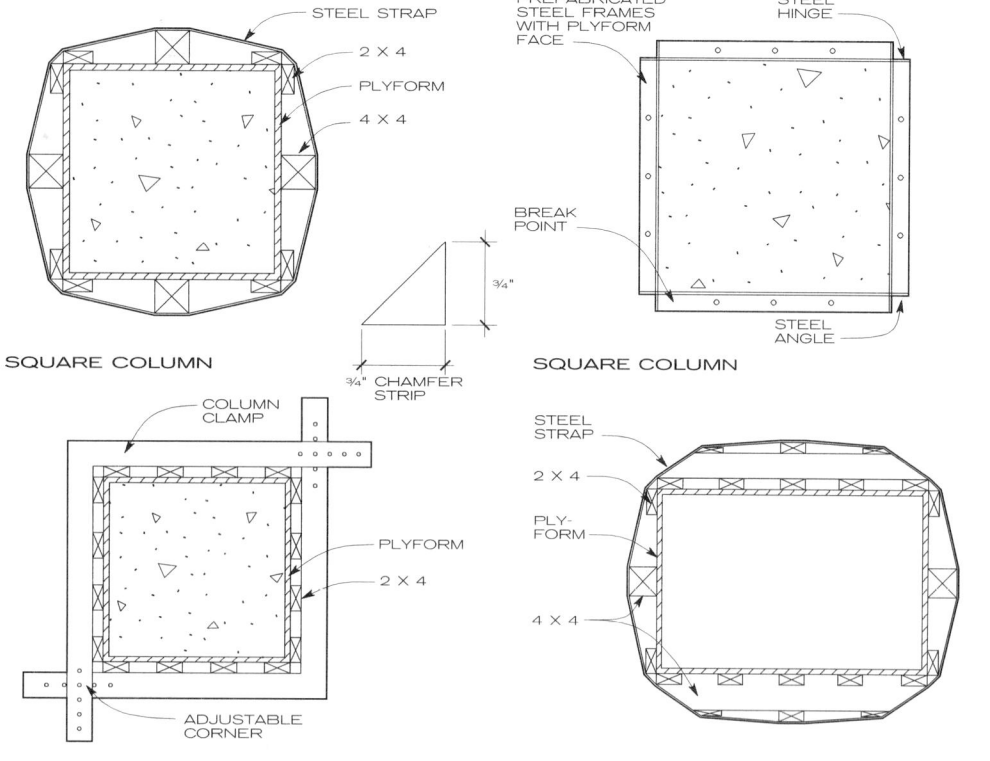

SQUARE COLUMN

SQUARE COLUMN

LARGE COLUMN PLAN

SQUARE COLUMN

NOTE
It is recommended that chamfer strips be used at all outside corners to reduce damage to concrete when forms are removed. Consult manufacturers' guides and catalogs for ideal materials, pour rate (ft/hr), and outside temperature (°F).

COLUMN PLANS

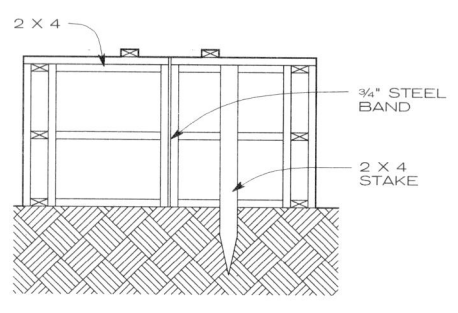

PLAN

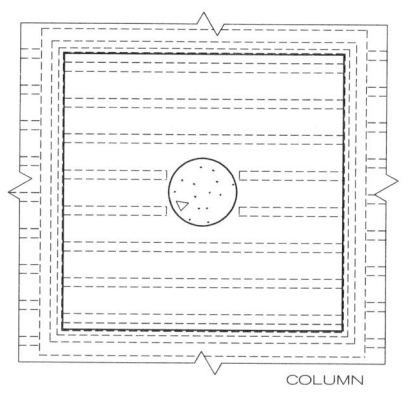

ELEVATION

COLUMN FOOTINGS

PLAN

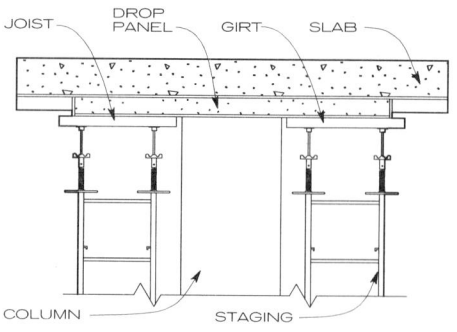

SECTION

DROP PANELS AT COLUMN TOPS

Tucker Concrete Form Company; Stoughton, Massachusetts

CONCRETE FORMWORK

Concrete Formwork for Walls

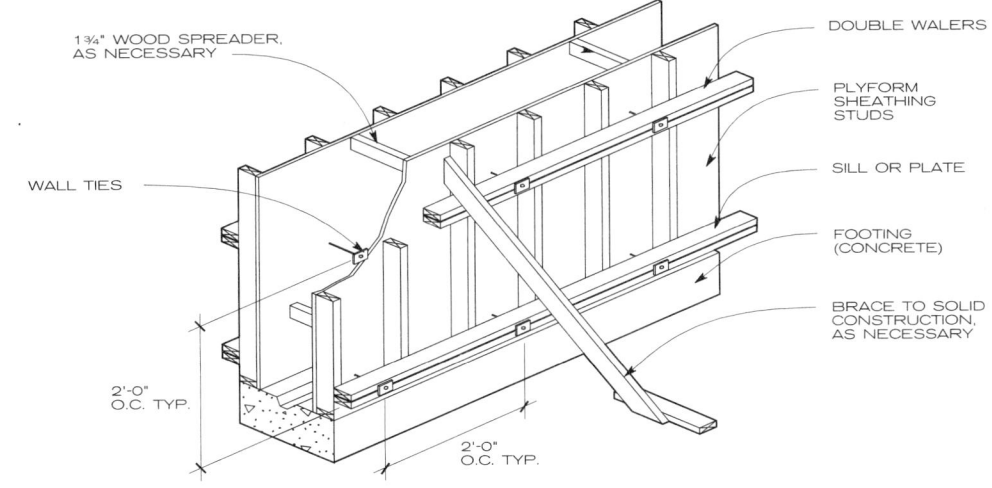

TYPICAL SITE-BUILT WALL FORMWORK

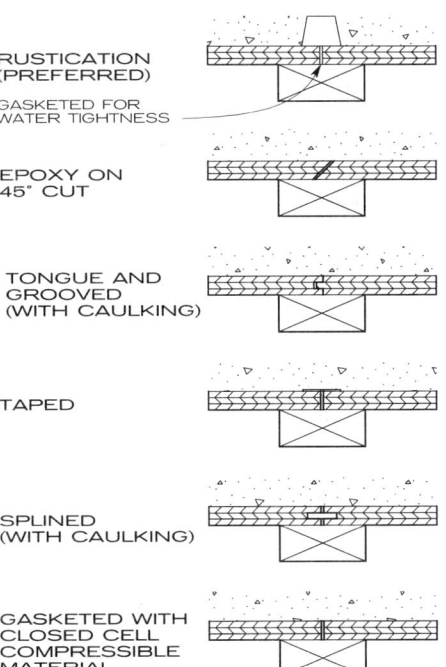

FORM SHEATHING JOINT DETAILS

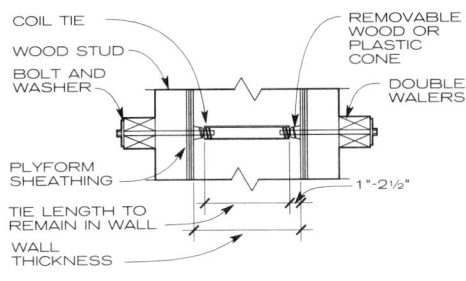

SITE-BUILT WALL FORMS
SECTION AT WALL TIE

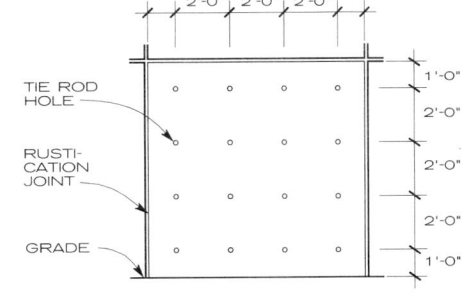

TYPICAL EXPOSED CONCRETE ELEVATION

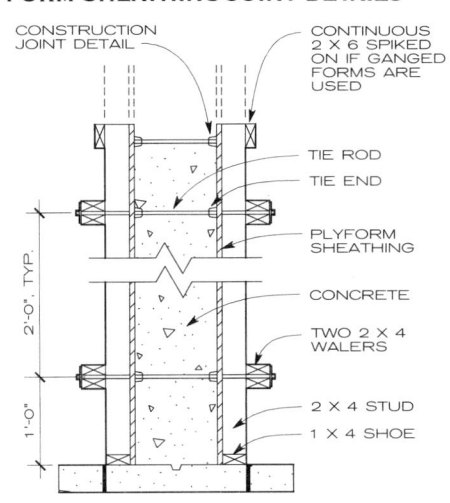

NOTE
Verify size and spacing of components for each job. The combination of plyform sheathing, studs, walers, and ties must be chosen carefully to safely resist concrete pressure and limit deflection of the form face. Steel and aluminum studs and walers may be used in place of wood.

TYPICAL JOB-BUILT WALL SECTION

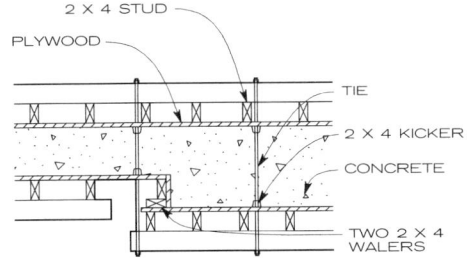

TYPICAL CORNER

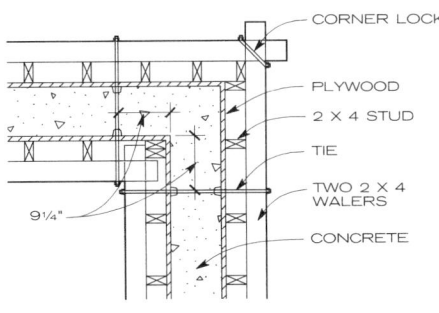

PLAN
TYPICAL WALL WITH OFFSET

NOTES
1. The typical wood and plywood framing details shown must be modified as necessary to accommodate the lateral pressure of fresh concrete on the forms. Studs and walers of aluminum or steel are frequently used. Lateral pressure varies depending on the rate at which the form is filled, the temperature of the concrete, vibration procedures, and the type of admixtures used in the concrete.
2. Consult manufacturers' recommendations for safe working loads on ties. Consult the American Concrete Institute's *Formwork for Concrete* (SP-4) for detailed design recommendations.
3. A great variety of form ties are commercially available (see AGS page on concrete formwork hardware). For architectural surfaces exposed to weather, choose a tie that leaves no corrodible metal closer than $1\frac{1}{2}$ in. from the concrete surface. Ties should be tight fitting and sealed as necessary to prevent leakage at holes in the forms.
4. Ties fitted with wood or plastic cones should leave depressions at least as deep as the surface diameter of the cone. The holes may be filled with recessed plugs or left unfilled if noncorroding ties are used.
5. Provide cleanout doors at the bottom of wall forms.

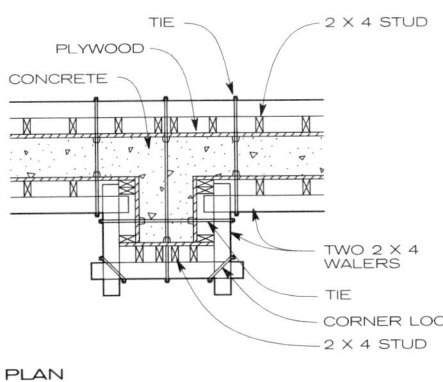

PLAN
PILASTER

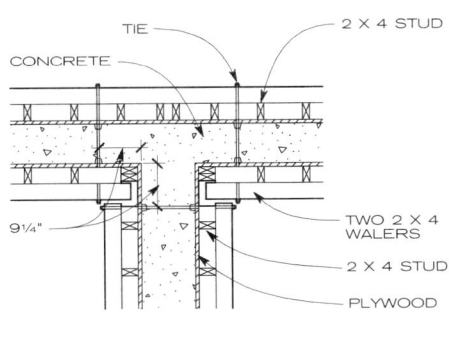

PLAN
TYPICAL T WALL JUNCTION

Tucker Concrete Form Company; Stoughton, Massachusetts
Mary K. Hurd; Engineered Publications; Farmington Hills, Michigan

Concrete Formwork for Slabs and Beams

GENERAL NOTES

1. Scaffolding, steel shores, or wood posts may be used under stringers depending on loads and height requirements.
2. For flat slabs of flat plate forming, metal "flying forms" are commonly used.
3. Patented steel forms or fillers can be special ordered for unusual conditions; see manufacturers' catalogs. Fiber forms are also on the market in similar sizes. Plyform deck is required for forming.
4. Plyform is usually $5/8$ in. minimum thickness, Exposure 1.

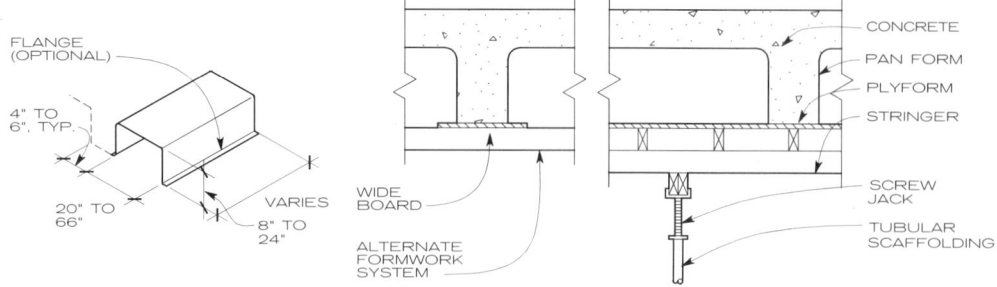

TYPICAL PAN FORM FOR ONE-WAY SLAB

NOTES

1. Forms are available in steel and lightweight fiberglass. Consult manufacturers for forms with different dimensions and rib-form variations. Typically three types are available: nail-down flange (simplest, but produces rough, nonarchitectural surface); slip-in type (based on nail-down form but with board insert for smooth appearance); and adjustable (without flanges; produces smooth rib).
2. Consult ANSI A48.1-1986 for complete pan form standards.

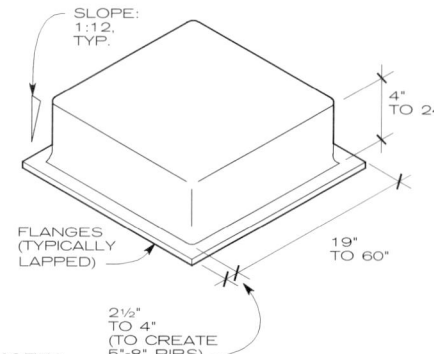

NOTES

1. Standard waffle slab forms are square for ease of use and economy. Dimensions vary slightly from manufacturer to manufacturer. Consult ANSI A48.2-1986 for complete dome form standards.
2. Forms are available in steel and lightweight fiberglass. Consult form manufacturer for options in material, textures, and dimensions.

TYPICAL DOME FORM FOR WAFFLE OR TWO-WAY SLAB

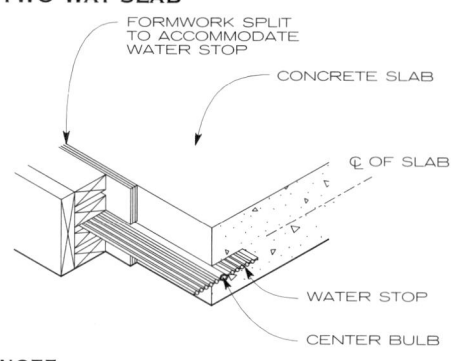

NOTE

Waterstops are flexible barriers used to prevent the passage of liquids and gasses under pressure through joints in concrete slabs. Waterstops are typically made of polyvinyl chloride, and their shapes vary according to application. If a center bulb is specified, it must remain unembedded in the center of the joint.

SLAB FORMWORK WITH WATER STOP

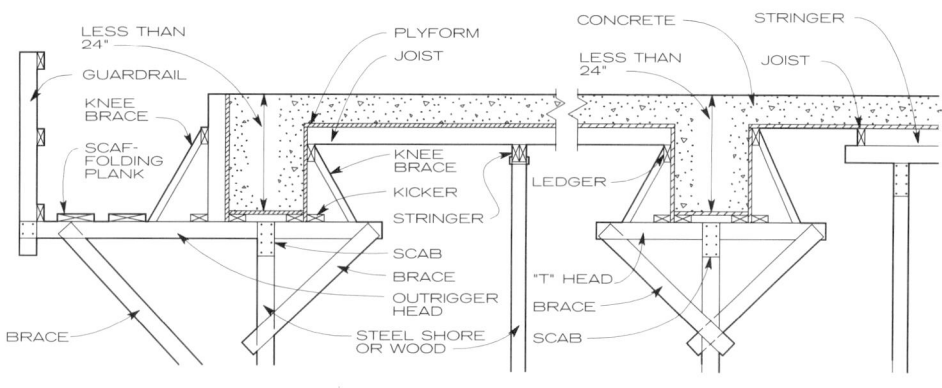

TYPICAL SLAB AND SHALLOW BEAM FORMING

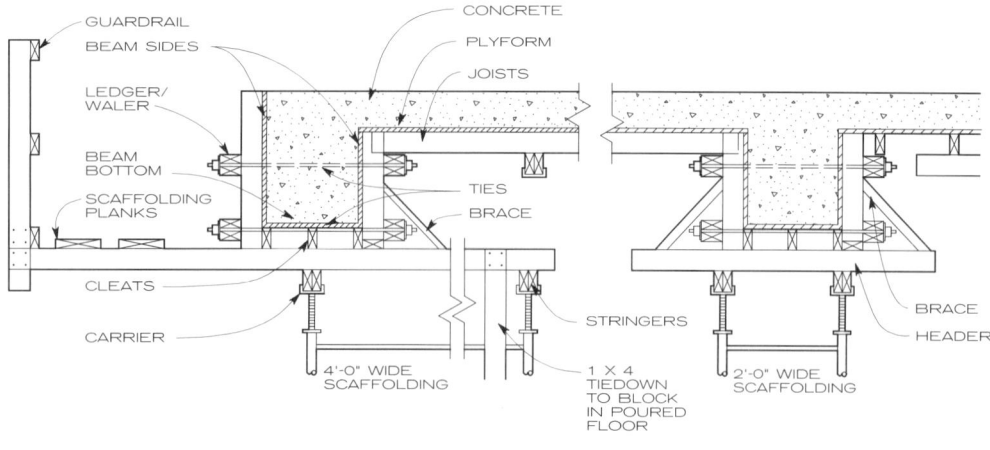

TYPICAL SLAB AND HEAVY BEAM FORMING

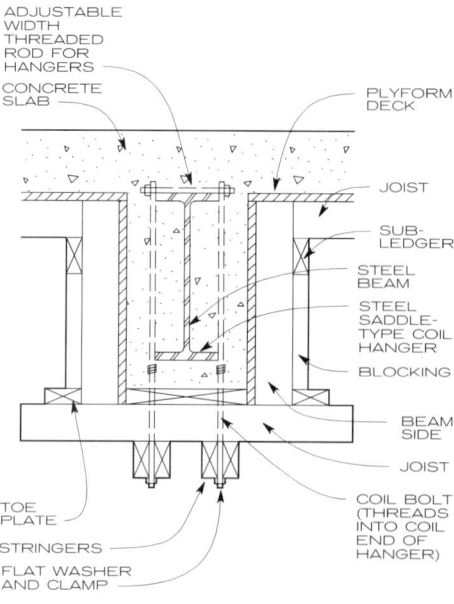

NOTE

This type of formwork is used to fireproof structural steel beams by wrapping them in concrete.

TYPICAL SUSPENDED FORM WITH COIL SADDLE-TYPE HANGERS

Tucker Concrete Form Company; Stoughton, Massachusetts

CONCRETE FORMWORK

Concrete Formwork Hardware

GENERAL

Concrete formwork hardware includes ties, anchors, hangers, and spacers used to hold forms and reinforcements in place against the forces of unhardened concrete and other loads applied during construction. Concrete ties are tensile units adapted to hold concrete forms together and may be classified by use or by load-carrying capacity. Classified by use are two main concrete tie types: "continuous single member," in which the entire tie rod extends through the wall and through both sides of the formwork (this can be a pull-out tie or a snap-off tie), and "internal disconnecting," in which the tensile unit has an inner part with threaded connections to removable external members. Classified by load-carrying capacity are light-duty (safe working loads of up to 3750 lb) and heavy-duty (loads of more than 3750 lb) concrete ties. Safe working load should be set at no more than half the tie's ultimate strength. Other hardware systems and configurations may be available; consult manufacturers for complete details.

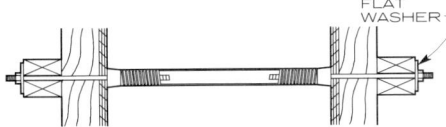
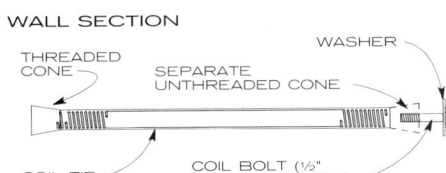

NOTE

Coil ties are medium- to heavy-duty ties fabricated to accept a threaded bolt, which passes through the formwork lumber.

COIL TIES

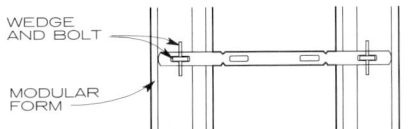
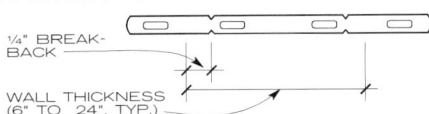

NOTE

Flat ties are light-duty ties used with a wedge and bolt to secure and space modular wall forms.

FLAT TIE

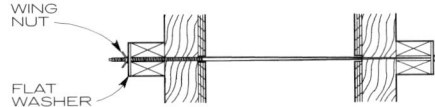
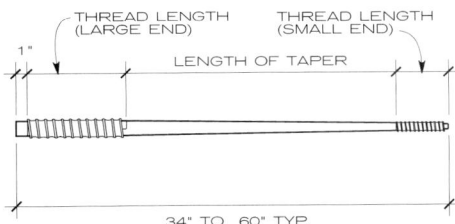

NOTE

Generally used for heavy-duty loads of up to 50,000 lb, the taper tie system is a versatile forming system whose parts are removed after the concrete sets and may be reused. Ties may be installed after forms are in place.

STEEL TAPER TIE

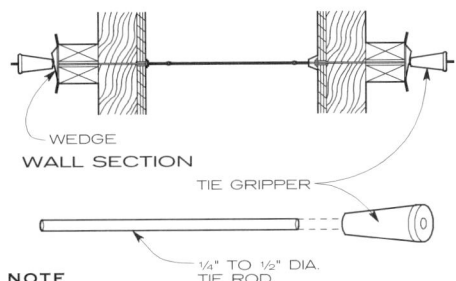

NOTE

Fiberglass form ties, straight rods secured with reusable external metal grippers, have safe working loads ranging from 2250 to 25,000 psi. The ties are readily broken off or cut at the concrete surface, then ground flush.

FIBERGLASS FORM TIE

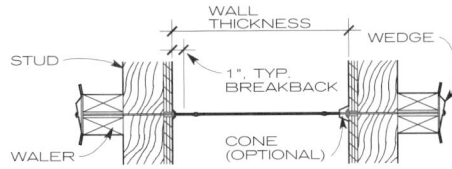

NOTE

Snap ties are a type of through tie for light-duty use, fabricated so the exposed ends of the tie can be snapped off at the breakback (a notch in the rod). The antiturn device makes it easier to break off the exposed end.

SNAP TIES

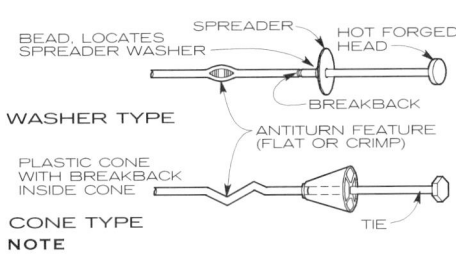

NOTE

Rock anchors are used with coil ties to facilitate one-side forming of walls.

ROCK ANCHOR

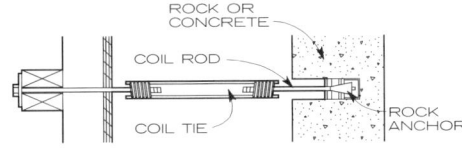
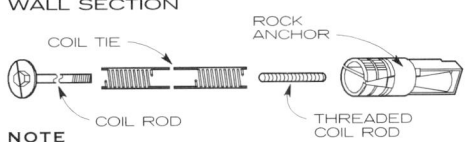

NOTE

Steel wedges are placed at the outside threaded ends of pull-out or snap tie rods, holding the formwork in place. Plastic or wood cones may be placed on the tie rod at the formwork wall surface, so that when the formwork is removed the tie rod ends are set back for subsequent finishing (with plugs, etc.).

TIE ROD ACCESSORIES

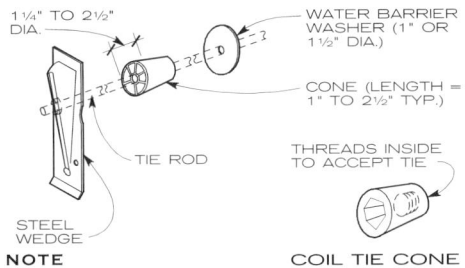

NOTE

This light-duty system is suitable for job-set forms.

CAM LOCK BRACKET/TIE SYSTEM

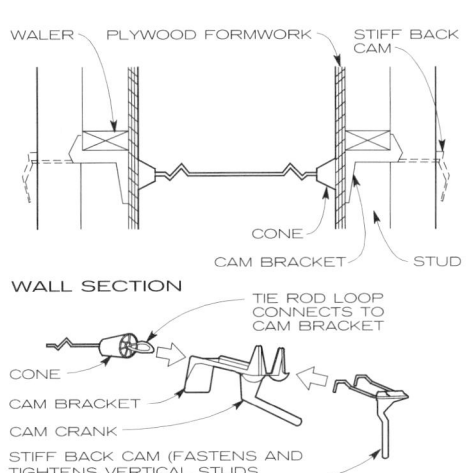

NOTE

The coil anchor is embedded near the top of a concrete lift to support the formwork of the succeeding lift. The reusable he-bolt is threaded into the coil.

HE-BOLT WITH COIL ANCHOR

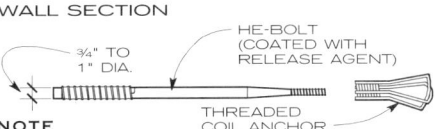

NOTE

She-bolts are reusable heavy-duty tie components threaded onto an internal tie rod permanently embedded in the concrete. They are typically used with crane-handled forms.

SHE-BOLT/TIE ROD

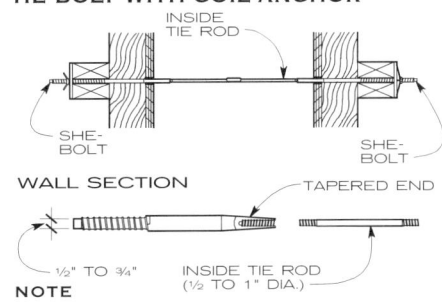
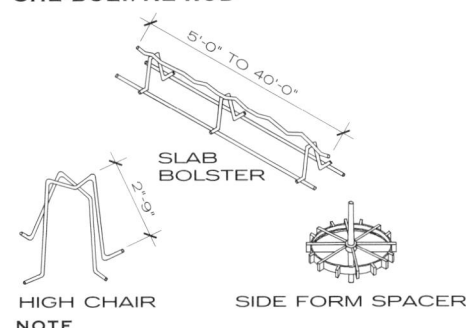

NOTE

Bar supports are used to maintain the reinforcement's design distance from the wall sides or slab bottom. They are typically made of stainless steel or epoxy- or plastic-coated steel.

REINFORCING BAR AND MESH SUPPORTS

Mary K. Hurd; Engineered Publications; Farmington Hills, Michigan

Reinforcing Bars and Wire

GENERAL

Steel reinforcement for concrete consists of reinforcing bars and welded wire fabric. Bars are manufactured by hot-roll process as round rods with lugs, or deformations, which inhibit longitudinal movement of the bar in the surrounding concrete. Bar sizes are indicated by numbers. For sizes #3 through #8, the numbers are the number of eighths of an inch in the nominal diameter of the bars. Numbers 9, 10, and 11 are round and correspond to the former 1 in., $1\frac{1}{8}$ in., and $1\frac{1}{4}$ in. square sizes. Sizes #14 and #18 correspond to the former $1\frac{1}{2}$ in. and 2 in. square sizes. The nominal diameter of a deformed bar is equal to the actual diameter of a plain bar with the same weight per foot as the deformed bar. Epoxy-coated, zinc-coated (galvanized), and stainless steel reinforcing bars are used when corrosion protection is needed; stainless steel also has non-magnetic properties. In some instances, a fiber-reinforced plastic (FRP) rebar is used for highly specialized concrete reinforcement because of its high tensile strength and light weight, corrosion resistance, and dielectric (nonconductive) properties. FRP rebars are manufactured in the same sizes as steel rebars and also have deformations on the surface. Consult manufacturers for further information.

Welded wire fabric is used in thin slabs, shells, and other designs in which available space is too limited to give proper cover and clearance to deformed bars. Welded wire fabric, also called mesh, consists of cold drawn wire (smooth or deformed) in orthogonal patterns; it is resistance welded at all intersections.

Wire in the form of individual wire or groups of wires is used in the fabrication of prestressed concrete.

ASTM STANDARD REINFORCING BAR SIZES

ASTM SIZE DESIGNATION	AREA (SQ IN., ACTUAL)	WEIGHT (LB/FT, ACTUAL)	DIAMETER (IN., ACTUAL)
#18	4.00	13.600	2.257
#14	2.25	7.650	1.693
#11	1.56	5.313	1.410
#10	1.27	4.303	1.270
#9	1.00	3.400	1.128
#8	0.74	2.670	1.000
#7	0.60	2.044	0.875
#6	0.44	1.502	0.750
#5	0.31	1.043	0.625
#4	0.20	0.668	0.500
#3	0.11	0.376	0.375

NOTE

Metrication of reinforcing bars is being considered in the United States; as of October 1995, a decision had not been made about what metric rebar sizes would apply in the United States. Metrication may result in a reengineering of reinforced concrete structures using the new bar sizes.

SHRINKAGE AND TEMPERATURE REINFORCEMENT FOR STRUCTURAL CONCRETE

GRADE	TYPE	PERCENT OF CROSS-SECTIONAL AREA OF CONCRETE, ONE WAY
40/50	Deformed bars	0.20
—	Welded wire fabric	0.18
60	Deformed bars	0.18

COMMON STOCK STYLES OF WELDED WIRE FABRIC

NEW DESIGNATION (W-NUMBER)	OLD DESIGNATION (WIRE GAUGE)	STEEL AREA (IN./SQ FT) LONG.	STEEL AREA (IN./SQ FT) TRANS.	WEIGHT (LB/100 SQ FT)
SHEETS AND ROLLS				
6 x 6 - W1.4 x W1.4	6 x 6 - 10 x 10	.028	.028	21
6 x 6 - W2.0 x W2.0	6 x 6 - 8 x 8	.040	.040	29
6 x 6 - W2.9 x W2.9	6 x 6 - 6 x 6	.058	.058	42
6 x 6 - W4.0 x W4.0	6 x 6 - 4 x 4	.080	.080	58
4 x 4 - W1.4 x W1.4	4 x 4 - 10 x 10	.042	.042	31
4 x 4 - W2.0 x W2.0	4 x 4 - 8 x 8	.060	.060	43
4 x 4 - W2.9 x W2.9	4 x 4 - 6 x 6	.087	.087	62
4 x 4 - W4.0 x W4.0	4 x 4 - 4 x 4	.120	.120	85

METHOD OF DESIGNATION FOR WELDED WIRE FABRIC

REINFORCING BAR GRADE MARK IDENTIFICATION

NOTE

Steel type grade marks: S—billet (A615), I—rail (A616), IR—rail meeting supplementary requirements, S1 (A616), A—axle (A617), W—low alloy (A706).

STANDARD STEEL WIRE SIZES AND GAUGES

PLAIN WIRE NUMBER	DEFORMED WIRE NUMBER	ASW GAUGE NUMBER	FRACTIONAL DIAMETER (IN.)	DECIMAL DIAMETER (IN.)	AREA (SQ IN.)	WEIGHT (LB/LIN. FT)
W20	D20	—	1/2	.505	.200	.680
—	—	7/0	31/64	.490	.189	.642
W18	D18	—	15/32	.479	.180	.612
—	—	6/0	5/32	.462	.168	.571
W16	D16	—	29/64	.451	.160	.544
—	—	5/0	7/16	.431	.146	.496
W14	D14	—	13/32	.422	.140	.476
—	—	4/0	13/32	.394	.122	.415
W12	D12	—	25/64	.391	.120	.408
W11	—	—	3/8	.374	.110	.374
W10.5	—	—	3/8	.366	.105	.357
—	—	3/0	23/64	.363	.103	.350
W10	D10	—	23/64	.357	.100	.340
W9.5	—	—	11/32	.348	.095	.323
W9	D9	—	11/32	.338	.090	.306
—	—	2/0	11/32	.331	.086	.292
W8.5	—	—	21/64	.329	.085	.289
W8	D8	—	21/64	.319	.080	.272
W7.5	—	—	5/16	.309	.075	.255
—	—	1/0	5/16	.307	.074	.251
W7	D7	—	19/64	.299	.070	.238
W6.5	—	—	19/64	.288	.065	.221
—	—	1	19/64	.283	.063	.214
W6	D6	—	9/32	.276	.060	.204
W5.5	—	—	17/64	.265	.055	.187
—	—	2	17/64	.263	.054	.183
W5	D5	—	1/4	.252	.050	.170
—	—	3	15/64	.244	.047	.160
W4.5	—	—	15/64	.239	.045	.153
W4	D4	—	7/32	.226	.040	.136
W3.5	—	—	7/32	.211	.035	.119
—	—	5	13/64	.207	.034	.115
W3	—	—	3/16+	.195	.030	.102
W2.9	—	—	3/16+	.192	.029	.098
W2.5	—	6	3/16	.178	.025	.085
W2.1	—	7	11/64	.162	.021	.071
W2	—	8	5/32	.160	.020	.068
—	—	9	5/32	.148	.017	.058
W1.4	—	—	9/64	.124	.014	.048

REINFORCING BAR GRADES AND STRENGTHS

ASTM SPEC	MIN. YIELD STRENGTH (PSI)	MIN. TENSILE STRENGTH (PSI)	STEEL TYPE
Billet steel ASTM A 615			
Grade 40	40,000	70,000	
Grade 60	60,000	90,000	S
Grade 75	75,000	100,000	
Rail steel ASTM A 616			
Grade 50	50,000	80,000	R
Grade 60	60,000	90,000	
Axle steel ASTM A 617			
Grade 40	40,000	70,000	A
Grade 60	60,000	90,000	
Low-alloy ASTM A 706			
Grade 60	60,000	80,000	W
Deformed wire ASTM A 496			
Welded fabric	70,000	80,000	—
Plain wire ASTM A 82			
Welded fabric < W 1.2	56,000	70,000	—
Size ≥ W 1.2	65,000	75,000	

Concrete Reinforcing Steel Institute; Schaumburg, Illinois
Gordon B. Batson, P.E.; Potsdam, New York

CONCRETE REINFORCEMENT

Concrete Construction: Introduction

CAST-IN-PLACE CONCRETE

Concrete is basically a mixture of two components: aggregates and paste. The paste is composed of portland cement, water, and entrapped air or purposely entrained air. This paste binds the aggregates (sand, gravel, or crushed stone) into a rocklike mass as the paste hardens. (The term "portland cement" refers to a calcarious hydraulic cement produced by heating the oxides of silicon, calcium, aluminum, and iron.) Cement paste ordinarily constitutes about 25 to 40% of the total volume of concrete; of this, the absolute volume of cement is usually between 7 and 15%, water between 14 and 21%, and air content up to 8%.

Reinforced concrete consists of concrete and reinforcing steel. The concrete resists the compressive stresses and the reinforcing steel resists the tensile stresses. (See AGS pages on reinforcing bars and wire for a complete review of reinforcing steel.)

LIGHTWEIGHT CONCRETES

Normal-weight concrete contains regular sand, gravel, or crushed stone and has a dry density in the range of 130 to 155 lb/cubic ft (pcf).

Structural lightweight concrete is similar to normal-weight concrete except that it has a lower density, being made from lightweight aggregates (all-lightweight concrete) or with a combination of lightweight and normal-weight aggregates. Structural lightweight concrete has an air-dry density in the range of 85 to 115 pcf and a 28-day compressive strength in excess of 2500 lb/sq in. (psi). It is used primarily to reduce the dead-load weight in concrete members such as floors in high-rise buildings.

Aggregates for structural lightweight concrete include rotary kiln expanded clays, shales, and slates; sintering grate expanded shales and slates; pelletized or extruded fly ash; expanded slags; pumice; and scoria. These aggregates have densities ranging from 35 to 70 pcf compared to 75 to 110 pcf for normal-weight aggregates.

Moderate-strength lightweight concrete weighs about 50 to 120 pcf oven-dry and has a compressive strength of 1000 to 2500 psi. At lower densities, it is used as fill for thermal and sound insulation of floors, walls, and roofs and is referred to as "fill concrete." At higher densities, it is used in cast-in-place walls, floors, and roofs and precast wall and floor panels.

Low-density concrete, also called insulating concrete, is a lightweight concrete with an oven-dry unit weight of between 15 and 50 pcf, with a 28-day compressive strength between 100 and 1000 psi. Cast-in-place low-density concrete is used primarily for thermal and sound insulation, roof decks, fill for slab-on-grade subbases, leveling courses for floors and roofs, firewalls, etc.

For further discussion of lightweight concrete and other concrete information, consult *Design and Control of Concrete Mixtures*, 13th ed. (Portland Cement Association, Skokie, Ill.).

TYPES OF CEMENT

Five types of portland cement are manufactured to meet ASTM standards:

Type I is a general purpose cement for all uses. It is the most commonly used type.

Type II cement provides moderate protection from sulfate attack for concrete in drainage structures and a lower heat of hydration for concrete used in heavy retaining walls, piers, and abutments where heat buildup in the concrete can cause problems.

Type III cement achieves high strength at an early stage, after a week or less. It is used when rapid removal of forms is desired and in cold weather to reduce the time for controlled curing conditions.

Type IV cement has a low heat of hydration and is used for massive concrete structures such as gravity dams.

Type V cement is sulfate-resisting for use where the soil and groundwater have a high sulfate content.

Other cementitious materials, including fly ash, ground granulated blast furnace slag, and silica fume, are sometimes used in conjunction with portland cement. (Fly ash is a powdery residue resulting from combustion in coal-fired electric generating plants. It reacts chemically with calcium hydroxide produced by hydration to form cementitious compounds.) Depending on the application, these cementitious materials may be used to replace a portion of the cement or as a supplementary material. They are used to modify fresh or hardened concrete properties (for example, to increase the amount of fine aggregate in the concrete mixture to improve workability, to limit the initial heat of hydration of the concrete, or to produce high-strength, low-permeability concretes).

Adjusting mixture proportions is more complicated than simply replacing portland cement either by weight or volume. For example, silica fume mixes typically need a high-range water-reducing admixture to be workable and may have finishing characteristics different from those of conventional concretes. Mixtures with these cementitious materials require entrained air for durability, just as mixtures with only portland cement do. For concrete subjected to freezing and thawing and de-icers, the contents of ash, slag, and silica fume are limited to a specified percentage of the total cementitious materials because the scaling behavior of these concretes is not fully understood.

Although ASTM C150 specifies five cement types, all may not be available in a given market. In some cities Type II is routinely substituted for Type I. Type IV may be available only in quantities prohibitively large for most applications.

AGGREGATES

Normal-weight concrete (135 to 165 pcf) can contain both fine and coarse aggregates. The fine aggregate is generally sand particles less than $3/8$ in. in size. The coarse aggregate is crushed rock or gravel. Lightweight aggregate is manufactured from expanded shale, slate, clay, or slag, and the concrete weighs between 85 and 115 pcf. Recycled concrete, or crushed concrete, is a feasible source of aggregate and an economical alternative when other aggregates are scarce.

Normal-weight aggregates must meet ASTM Specification C33. Lightweight aggregates must meet ASTM Specification C330. The aggregate represents 60 to 80% of the concrete volume, and the gradation (range of particle sizes) affects the amount of cement and water required in the mix, physical properties during placing and finishing, and compressive strength. Aggregates should be clean, hard, strong, and free of surface materials.

ADMIXTURES

Admixtures are various compounds other than cement, water, and aggregate that are added to a mixture to modify the properties of fresh or hardened concrete. Refer to pages on concrete admixtures for more information.

CYLINDER TEST

A standard compression test is made by placing three layers of concrete in a cardboard cylinder 6 in. in diameter and 12 in. high. Each layer is tamped 25 times with a $5/8$ in. diameter steel rod. At the end of the test curing time, usually 7 to 28 days, the concrete cylinder is removed from its form and placed under increasing pressure. The load at which the cylinder breaks is registered on a gauge in pounds, and the strength of the concrete is calculated in lb/sq in.

A major problem with these tests is that the compressive strength—the most important characteristic of concrete—cannot be determined until after curing has begun. Thus deficient concrete occasionally must be removed several weeks after it was placed.

PLACING CONCRETE

Concrete should be placed as near its final position as possible, and it should not be moved horizontally in forms because the mortar may separate from the coarser material. Concrete should be placed in horizontal layers of uniform thickness, with each layer thoroughly consolidated before the next layer is positioned.

RECOMMENDED SLUMPS FOR VARIOUS CONSTRUCTION TYPES

CONCRETE CONSTRUCTION	MAXIMUM*	MINIMUM
Reinforced foundation walls and footings	3	1
Plain footings, caissons, and substructure walls	3	1
Beams and reinforced walls	4	1
Building columns	4	1
Pavement and slabs	3	1
Mass concrete	2	1

* May be increased by 1 in. for consolidation by hand methods such as rodding and spading.

Concrete can be consolidated either by hand tamping or by mechanical internal or external vibration. The frequency and amplitude of an internal vibration should be appropriate for the plastic properties (stiffness or slump) and space in the forms to prevent segregation of the concrete during placing. External vibration can be accomplished by surface vibration for thin sections (slabs) for which internal vibration is not practical. Surface vibrators may be used directly on the surface of the slab or with plates attached to the concrete form stiffeners. External vibration must be sustained longer (1 to 2 minutes) than internal vibration (5 to 15 seconds) to achieve the same consolidation.

SLUMP TEST

The ASTM standard slump cone test is only for determining the consistency among batches of concrete of the same mix design; it should not be used to compare concrete made from different mix proportions. A slump test mold is a funnel-shaped sheet metal form. It is filled from the top in three layers, and at each level the concrete is tamped 25 times with a $5/8$ in. diameter rod. The mold is removed slowly, allowing the concrete to slump down from its original height. The difference between the top of the mold and the top of the molded concrete is the slump. There is no "right" slump consistency for all concrete work: It can vary from 1 in. to 6 in., depending on the specific requirements of the job. The accompanying table lists recommended slumps for various types of construction.

Workability is the ease or difficulty of placing, consolidating, and finishing the concrete. Concrete should be workable, but not so much so that it segregates or bleeds excessively before finishing.

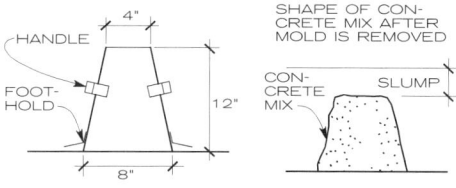

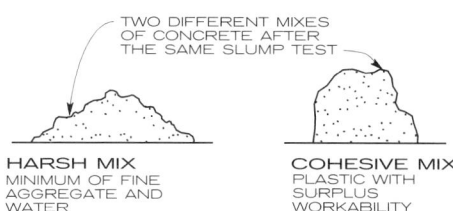

SLUMP TEST

ACCEPTED MAXIMUM AGGREGATE SIZE FOR VARIOUS TYPES OF CONCRETE CONSTRUCTION[1]

MINIMUM DIMENSION OF SECTION OF CONCRETE TO BE POURED (IN.)	MAXIMUM SIZE OF AGGREGATE (SQUARE SCREEN OPENINGS)[2]		
	REINFORCED WALLS, BEAMS, AND COLUMNS	HEAVY REINFORCED CONCRETE SLABS	LIGHTLY REINFORCED OR PLAIN CONCRETE SLABS
5 or less (127 mm)	—	$3/4$ to $1 1/2$ in. (19-38 mm)	$3/4$ to $1 1/2$ in. (19-38 mm)
6–11 (152 to 279 mm)	$3/4$ to $1 1/2$ in. (19-38 mm)	$1 1/2$ in. (38 mm)	$1 1/2$ to 3 in. (38-76 mm)
12–29 (205 to 737 mm)	$1 1/2$ to 3 in. (38-76 mm)	3 in. (76 mm)	3 to 6 in. (76-152 mm)
30 or more (762 mm)	$1 1/2$ to 3 in. (38-76 mm)	3 in. (76 mm)	6 in. (152 mm)

[1] Aggregate size should always be checked in relation to the spacing of reinforcement rods, bars, etc., and to the size of reinforcing mesh.

[2] For pumping concrete, the aggregate size is controlled by the height of pumping, air entrainment, and reinforcement and mesh spacing.

Robert W. Shuldes, P.E.; Portland Cement Association; Skokie, Illinois

Concrete Construction: Introduction

PROPERTIES OF CONCRETE

Concrete design strength generally is stated as a minimum compressive strength of concrete after 28 days of curing. The normal 28-day compressive strength for commercial ready-mix concrete is 3000 to 4000 psi; however, strengths of 5000 to 7000 psi generally are required for pre- or posttensioned concrete. Concrete design strengths of 10,000 to 12,000 psi have been used for columns in high-rise buildings, and a design strength of 20,000 psi has been used for concrete columns confined in a steel tube or pipe.

Compressive strength depends primarily on the type of cement, the aggregate quality, and the water-cement ratio; the latter is the most important. The lower the water-cement ratio, the greater the compressive strength for workable mixes.

Concrete gains strength by hydration, a chemical reaction independent of drying, in which water, cement, and aggregate are mixed. Concrete does not require air to cure; it sets up under water (thus the term "hydraulic cement"). Concrete sets or becomes firm hours after it has been mixed, but curing, the process of attaining strength, takes considerably longer. For 28-day design strengths of less than 10,000 psi, most of the strength is achieved in a few days; approximately 50% is reached in three days; and 70% is reached in seven days. The remaining 30% is gained mostly during the last 21 days; but strength can continue to increase beyond the 28 days.

It can take from 56 to 90 days for concrete to achieve a design strength of greater than 12,000 psi. The cylinders used to test the compressive strength of this very high-strength concrete are usually 4 x 8 in. rather than 6 x 12 in. Making such strong concretes requires close coordination among the concrete mix vendor, contractor, and concrete inspection service.

CURING AND PROTECTION

Two physical conditions profoundly affect concrete's final compressive strength and curing: temperature and the rate at which water used in mixing is allowed to leave the concrete. If moisture for curing is adequate, concrete gains strength faster at higher temperatures. However, if the temperature is too high, long-term strengths may not develop properly. Excellent quality concrete can be made at lower temperatures, but it will take longer to reach a specified strength level, since the cement hydrates more slowly. Freezing concrete during curing greatly reduces its compressive strength and weather resistance.

Proper curing is essential to obtain design strength. Moisture, at temperatures above 50°F, must be available for hydration, but concrete must be protected against temperatures below 40°F during early curing. The longer water is in the concrete, the stronger it becomes.

Moisture conditions can be maintained by spreading wet burlap or mats, waterproof paper, or plastic sheets over the concrete; by placing plastic sheets on the ground before the slab is poured; by spraying liquid curing compound on the surface of fresh concrete; and by leaving the concrete in forms for a longer time.

HOT AND COLD WEATHER CONSTRUCTION

Additional precautions are needed in extreme weather to ensure proper curing of concrete. High temperatures accelerate hardening. More water is needed to maintain the mix consistency; more cement is required to prevent reduced strength from the additional water. Chilled water or ice reduces the temperature of the aggregates, and admixtures can retard the initial set.

Temperatures ranging from 75 to 90°F are considered hot weather construction conditions. Weather that is dry as well as hot is especially problematic for finishing newly placed concrete as it causes the concrete to dry too rapidly and crack. Special care in finishing and curing must be taken to achieve a good quality finish.

In cold weather concrete must be heated to above 40°F during placing and early curing (the first seven days). Protection against freezing may be necessary for up to two weeks. This is accomplished by covering the concrete with plastic sheets and heating the interior space with a portable heater. Concrete floors should be protected from carbon dioxide with specially vented heaters that conduct the exhaust away from the concrete. The time concrete must be protected can be reduced by using Type III or IIIA cement, by maintaining a low water-cement ratio, by using accelerator admixtures, and by steam curing. Never place concrete directly on frozen ground. Fresh concrete that has frozen during curing should be replaced because frozen concrete containing ice crystals has very little strength.

PROPORTION OF STRUCTURAL ELEMENTS

Rules of thumb for approximating proportions of solid rectangular beams and slabs are one inch of depth for each foot of span, and beam width about two-thirds of the depth. The area of steel varies from 1 to 2% of the cross-sectional area of the beam and less than 1% for slabs. Columns usually have higher steel percentages than beams. The maximum for columns is 8% of the cross-sectional area; however, common range is 3 to 6%.

DEFLECTIONS

Deflection of a reinforced concrete member is affected by shrinkage, duration of sustained loads, and creep. Creep is the continuous deformation of the concrete due to sustained loads. Creep and shrinkage may double the initial (instantaneous) deflection in five years under sustained loads. The American Concrete Institute Building Requirements for Reinforced Concrete (ACI 318) set minimum length-to-depth ratios for concrete members (see the table om minimum thickness). When members meet or exceed these minimums, deflections usually are not a problem and do not need to be calculated.

SAMPLE CONCRETE MIXTURES[1]

MIXTURE CHARACTERISTICS	BUILDING INTERIOR	HIGH-STRENGTH INTERIOR COLUMN	POSTTENSIONED PARKING STRUCTURE
Compressive strength F'_c (psi)	3500	8000	7500 [2]
Air content (percent)	1.5	2.0	6
Water-to-cement ratio	0.55	0.38 [3]	0.37 [3]
Max. aggregate size (in.)	1	$3/4$	$3/4$
Slump (in.)	3 to 4	3 to 5	6 to 8 [4]
Admixtures	0	Conventional water reducer	Air-refreshing agent and high-range water reducer[5]

MIX PROPORTIONS, LB/CU YD			
Water	258	315	263
Cement	470	729	658
Other cementitious material	0	100 (fly ash)	53 (silica fume)
Fine aggregate	1190	1250	1200
Coarse aggregate	2100	1695	1660

[1] These mixtures are only examples to illustrate differences in proportioning. Local materials and experience should guide proportioning mixtures for specific projects.

[2] Structural requirements are about 5000 psi. Actual strength is higher due to early strength required for posttensioning and durability limits on water–cementitious materials ratio.

[3] Calculated using all cementitious materials: cement, fly ash, silica fume, etc.

[4] Reduce slump for steep ramps.

[5] Use of silica fume typically increases dosing requirements of high-range water reducer by 50 to 100%.

MINIMUM THICKNESS (IN.) OF NONPRESTRESSED BEAMS AND ONE-WAY SLABS

	SIMPLY SUPPORTED	ONE END CONTINUOUS	BOTH ENDS CONTINUOUS	CANTILEVER
Solid one-way slabs	Span length/20	Span length/24	Span length/28	Span length/10
Beams or ribbed one-way slabs	Span length/16	Span length/18.5	Span length/21	Span length/8

NOTE

Span length is in inches. Values given are for members with normal weight concrete and Grade 60 reinforcement in construction that does not support or connect to partitions or other construction likely to be damaged by large deflection. See ACI 318 for more information.

MAXIMUM WATER–CEMENT RATIOS FOR VARIOUS EXPOSURES

EXPOSURE CONDITION	NORMAL WEIGHT CONCRETE, ABSOLUTE WATER-CEMENT RATIO BY WEIGHT
Concrete protected from exposure to freezing and thawing or application of de-icer chemicals	Water-cement ratio based on strength, workability, and finishing needs
Watertight concrete* In fresh water In sea water	0.50 0.45
Frost-resistant concrete* Thin sections; any section with less than 2 in. cover over reinforcement and any concrete exposed to de-icers All other structures	0.45 0.50
Exposure to sulfates* Moderate Severe	0.50 0.45

* Contain entrained air within the limits of the minimum thickness table.

FORMWORK

Forming costs can account for 30 to 50% of a concrete structure. Reusing forms saves money; it is cheaper, for example, to use one column size throughout a structure than it is to vary column sizes.

In sizing individual floor members, it is usually more economical to use wider girders that are as deep as the joists of beams they support than to use narrow, deeper girders. Using wall pilasters, lugs, and openings increases forming costs. Size all members for use of readily available standard forms rather than custom job-built forms.

SHORING

Floor framing forms are supported by temporary columns and bracing called shoring. Concrete must be cured for a certain time or reach a specified percentage of its design strength before shores and forms can be removed. Reshoring is normally required for several floors if the cycle time for formwork is to be minimized.

MAXIMUM PERMISSIBLE WATER–CEMENT RATIOS

SPECIFIED COMPRESSIVE STRENGTH F'_c (PSI)[1]	MAXIMUM ABSOLUTE PERMISSIBLE WATER-CEMENT RATIO, BY WEIGHT	
	NON-AIR-ENTRAINED CONCRETE	AIR-ENTRAINED CONCRETE
2500	0.67	0.54
3000	0.58	0.46
3500	0.51	0.40
4000	0.44	0.35
4500	0.38	[2]
5000	[2]	[2]

[1] 28-day strength. For most materials, the water-cement ratios shown will provide average strengths greater than required.

[2] For strengths above 4500 psi (non-air-entrained concrete) and 4000 psi (air-entrained concrete), proportions should be established by the trial batch method.

NOTE

1000 psi = 7 MPa.

Robert W. Shuldes, P.E.; Portland Cement Association; Skokie, Illinois

CAST-IN-PLACE CONCRETE

Concrete Admixtures

GENERAL

Admixtures are those ingredients in concrete other than portland cement, water, and aggregates that are added to the mixture immediately before or during mixing. Admixtures can be classified by function as follows: air-entraining admixtures; water-reducing admixtures; retarding admixtures; accelerating admixtures; superplasticizers; finely divided mineral admixtures; miscellaneous admixtures that aid workability, bonding, dampproofing, gas-forming, grouting (nonshrink), and coloring and help reduce permeability and inhibit corrosion.

Concrete should be workable, finishable, strong, durable, watertight, and wear-resistant. These qualities can usually be achieved by selecting suitable materials or by changing the mix proportions. Sometimes air-entraining admixtures are necessary, but in most cases admixtures can be forgone. No admixture can substitute for good concreting practice.

The major reasons for using admixtures are to reduce the cost of concrete construction; to achieve certain properties in concrete more effectively; to ensure the quality of concrete during mixing, transporting, placing, and curing in adverse weather conditions; and to overcome certain emergencies during concreting operations.

NOTES

1. The effectiveness of an admixture depends on such factors as type, brand, and amount of cement; water content; aggregate shape, gradation, and proportions; mixing time; slump; and concrete and air temperatures.
2. Trial mixtures should be made with the admixture and the job materials at temperatures and humidities anticipated on the job to ensure compatibility with other admixtures and job materials and to allow observation of how the properties of the fresh and hardened concrete are affected by local conditions.
3. The cost of using admixtures should be compared with the cost of changing the basic concrete mixture. Determine how using an admixture will affect the cost of transporting, placing, finishing, curing, and protecting the concrete.
4. Recommended total air contents for different exposure conditions are shown for different aggregate sizes in the table below.

TOTAL TARGET AIR CONTENT FOR CONCRETE[1]

NOMINAL MAXIMUM AGGREGATE SIZE (IN.)	AIR CONTENT (PERCENT)[2]		
	SEVERE EXPOSURE[3]	MODERATE EXPOSURE[3]	MILD EXPOSURE[3]
3/8	7 1/2	6	4 1/2
1/2	7	5 1/2	4
3/4	6	5	3 1/2
1	6	4 1/2	3
1 1/2	5 1/2	4 1/2	2 1/2
2 1/2	5	4	2
3	4 1/2	3 1/2	1 1/2

[1] Experience shows that hardened concrete with the air contents specified in this table, as sampled and tested in the plastic state, performs satisfactorily. The air content of hardened concrete may be somewhat different.

[2] Project specifications often allow the air content of the delivered concrete to be within several percentage points of the table target values.

[3] Severe exposure is an environment in which concrete is exposed to wet freeze-thaw conditions, de-icers, or other aggressive agents. Moderate exposure is an environment in which concrete is exposed to freezing but will not be continually moist, not exposed to water for long periods before freezing, and will not be in contact with de-icers or aggressive chemicals. Mild exposure is an environment in which concrete is not exposed to freezing conditions, de-icers, or aggressive agents.

CONCRETE ADMIXTURES BY CLASSIFICATION

TYPE OF ADMIXTURE	DESIRED EFFECT	MATERIAL
Accelerators (ASTM C 494, Type C)	Accelerate setting and early-strength development	Calcium chloride (ASTM D 98); Triethanolamine, sodium thiocyanate, calcium formate, calcium nitrate, calcium nitrite
Air detrainers	Decrease air content	Tributyl phosphate, dibutyl phthalate, octyl alcohol, water-insoluble esters of carbonic and boric acid, silicones
Air-entraining admixtures (ASTM C 260)	Improve durability in environments of freeze-thaw, de-icers, sulfate, and alkali reactivity; Improve workability; segregation and bleeding are reduced or eliminated	Salts of wood resins (Vinsol resin); some synthetic detergents; salts of sulfonated lignin; salts of petroleum acids; salts of proteinaceous material; fatty and resinous acids and their salts; alkylbenzene sulfonates; salts of sulfonated hydrocarbons
Alkali-reactivity reducers	Reduce alkali-reactivity expansion	Pozzolans (fly ash, silica fume), blast-furnace slag, salts of lithium and barium, air entraining agents
Bonding admixtures	Increase bond strength	Rubber, polyvinyl chloride, polyvinyl acetate, acrylics, butadiene-styrene copolymers
Coloring agents	Colored concrete	Modified carbon black, iron oxide, phthalicyanine, umber, chromium oxide, titanium oxide, cobalt blue (ASTM C 979)
Corrosion inhibitors	Reduce steel corrosion activity in a chloride environment	Calcium nitrite, sodium nitrite, sodium benzoate, certain phosphates of fluosilicates, fluoaluminates
Dampproofing admixtures	Retard moisture penetration into dry concrete	Soaps of calcium or ammonium stearate or oleate; butyl stearate; petroleum products
Finely divided mineral admixtures		
Cementitious	Hydraulic properties; partial cement replacement	Ground granulated blast-furnace slag (ASTM C 989); natural cement; hydraulic hydrated lime (ASTM C 141)
Pozzolans	Pozzolanic activity; improve workability, plasticity, sulfate resistance; reduce alkali reactivity, permeability, heat of hydration; partial cement replacement; filler	Diatomaceous earth, opaline cherts, clays, shales, volcanic tuffs, pumicites (ASTM C 618, Class N); fly ash (ASTM C 618, Class F and C), silica fume
Pozzolanic and cementitious	Same as cementitious and pozzolan categories	High calcium fly ash (ASTM C 618, Class C); ground granulated blast-furnace slag (ASTM C 989)
Nominally inert	Improve workability; filler	Marble, dolomite, quartz, granite
Fungicides, germicides, and insecticides	Inhibit or control bacterial and fungal growth	Polyhalogenated phenols; dieldrin emulsions; copper compounds
Gas formers	Cause expansion before setting	Aluminum powder; resin soap and vegetable or animal glue; saponin; hydrolyzed protein
Grouting agents	Adjust grout properties for specific applications (i.e., nonshrink grout for setting steel on masonry or concrete, fill reglets and cracks)	See air-entrained admixtures, accelerators, retarders, workability agents
Permeability reducers	Decrease permeability	Silica fume; fly ash (ASTM C 618); ground slag (ASTM C 989); natural pozzolans; water reducers; latex
Pumping aides	Improve pumpability	Organic and synthetic polymers; organic flocculents; organic emulsions of paraffin, coal tar, asphalt, acrylics; bentonite and pyrogenic silicas; natural pozzolans (ASTM C 618, Class N); fly ash (ASTM C 618, Classes F and C); hydrated lime (ASTM C 141)
Retarders (ASTM C 494, Type B)	Retard setting time to offset effect of hot weather, to delay initial set for difficult placement, or for special finishing, such as exposed aggregate	Lignin; borax; sugar; tartaric acids and salts
Superplasticizers * (ASTM C 1017, Type 1)	Flowing concrete; reduce water-cement ratio	Sulfonated melamine formaldehyde condensates; sulfonated naphthalene formaldehyde condensates; lignosulfonates
Superplasticizer * and retarder (ASTM C 1017, Type 2)	Flowing concrete with retarded set; reduce water	See superplasticizers and water reducers
Water reducer (ASTM C 494, Type A)	Reduce water demand at least 5%	Lignosulfonates; hydroxylated carboxylic acids; carbohydrates (also tend to retard set so accelerator is often added)

* Superplasticizers are also referred to as high-range water reducers or plasticizers. These admixtures often meet both ASTM 494 and C 1017 specifications simultaneously.

Robert W. Shuldes, P.E.; Portland Cement Association; Skokie, Illinois

Concrete Floor Systems

GENERAL NOTES

1. The information presented on these pages is intended only as a preliminary design guide. All structural dimensions for slab thickness, beam and joist sizes, column sizes, etc., should be calculated and analyzed for each project condition by a licensed professional engineer.

2. Spans shown are approximate and are based on use of mild reinforcing steel. Spans may be increased 25 to 50% with the use of prestressing. For spans greater than 40 ft, consider posttensioning.

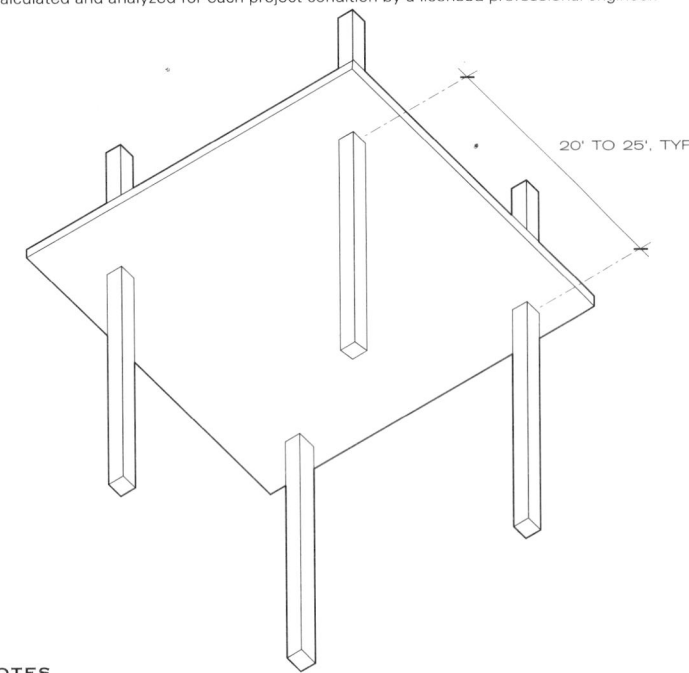

NOTES

1. Advantages: Inexpensive formwork; ceilings may be exposed; minimum thickness; fast erection; flexible column location.
2. Disadvantages: Excess concrete for longer spans; low shear capacity; greater deflections.
3. Appropriate building types: Hotels, motels, dormitories, condominiums, hospitals.
4. A flat plate is best for moderate spans because it is the most economical floor system and has the lowest structural thickness. Avoid penetrations for piping and ductwork through the slab near the columns. Spandrel beams may be necessary.

FLAT PLATE

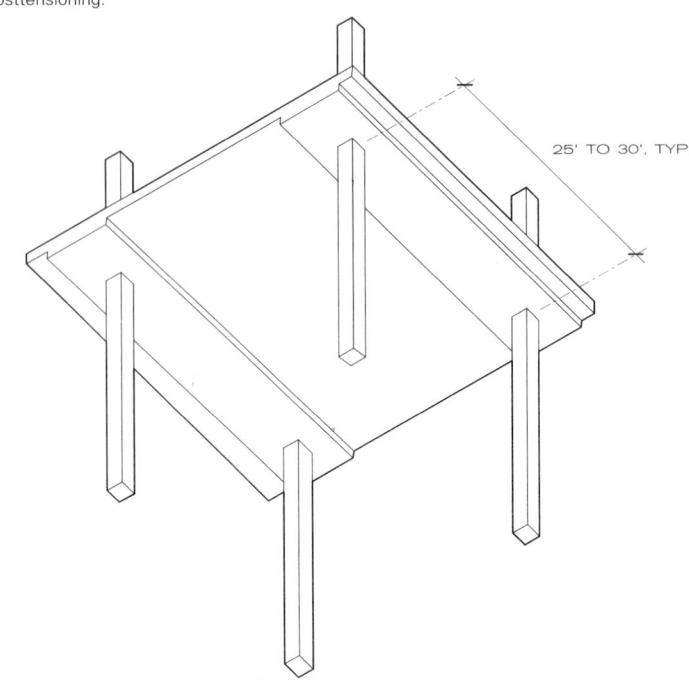

NOTES

1. Advantages: Longer spans than flat plate; typically posttensioned; minimum thickness.
2. Disadvantages: Must reuse formwork many times to be economical.
3. Appropriate building types: High-rise buildings; same use as flat plates if flying forms can be used more than 10 times.
4. A banded slab has most of the advantages of a flat plate but permits a longer span in one direction. It can resist greater lateral loads in the direction of the beams.

BANDED SLAB

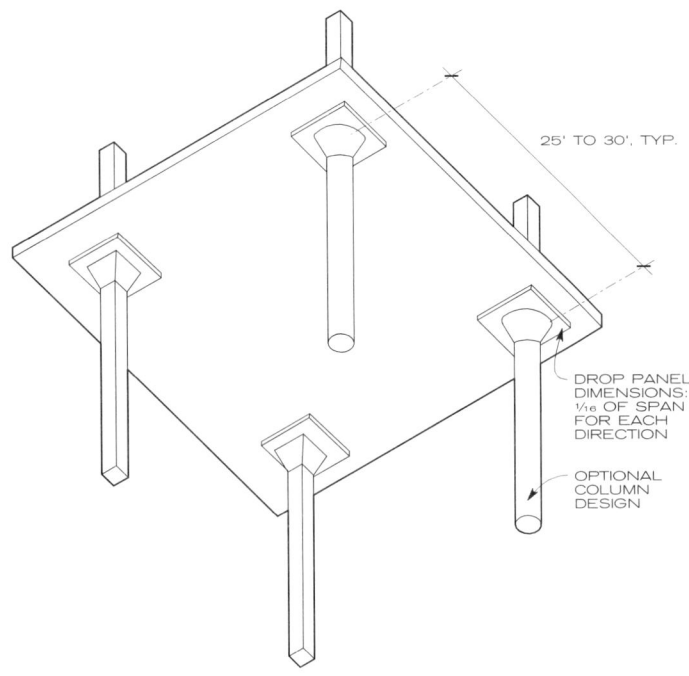

NOTES

1. Advantages: Economical for design loads greater than 150 psf.
2. Disadvantages: Formwork is costly.
3. Appropriate building types: Warehouses, industrial structures; parking structures
4. Flat slabs are most commonly used today for buildings supporting very heavy loads. When live load exceeds 150 lb per sq ft, this scheme is by far the most economical.

FLAT SLAB

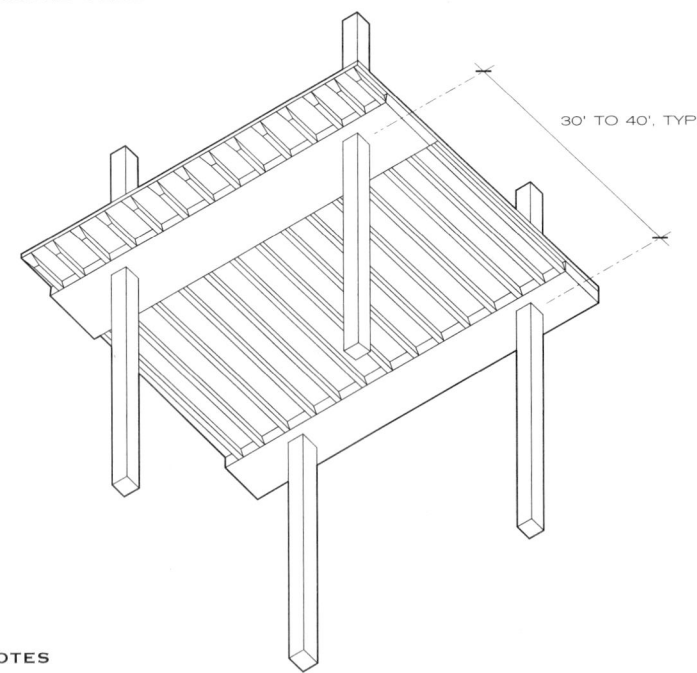

NOTES

1. Advantages: Minimum concrete and steel; minimum weight, hence reduced column and footing size; long spans in one direction; accommodates poke-through electrical systems.
2. Disadvantages: Unattractive for a ceiling; formwork may cost more than flat plate.
3. Appropriate building types: Schools, offices, churches, hospitals, public and institutional buildings, buildings with moderate loadings and spans.
4. This is the best scheme if slabs are too long for a flat plate and the structure is not exposed. The slab thickness between joists is determined by fire requirements. Joists are most economical if beams are the same depth as the joists. Orient joists in the same direction throughout the building and in the long direction of long rectangular bays.

JOIST SLAB

Russell S. Fling, P.E., Consulting Engineer; Columbus, Ohio

CAST-IN-PLACE CONCRETE

Concrete Floor Systems

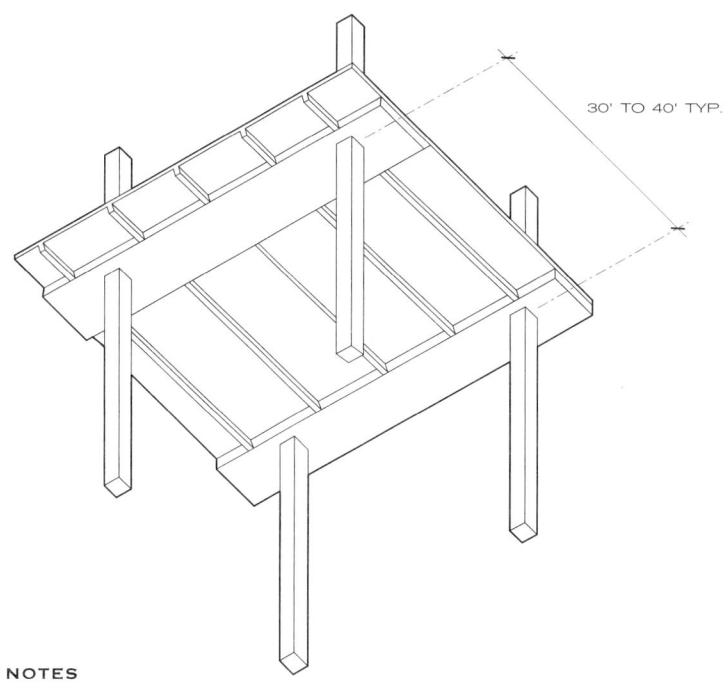

NOTES

1. Advantages: Uses less concrete than joist slab; lower rebar placing costs; joist space used for mechanical systems. Permits lights and equipment to be recessed between joists.
2. Disadvantages: Similar to joist slab; joists must be designed as beams; forms may require special order.
3. Appropriate building type: Same as for joist slabs, especially for longer fire ratings.
4. Ensure the availability of formwork before specifying skip joists. For larger projects, a skip joist slab should be less expensive than a joist slab, and it

SKIP JOIST

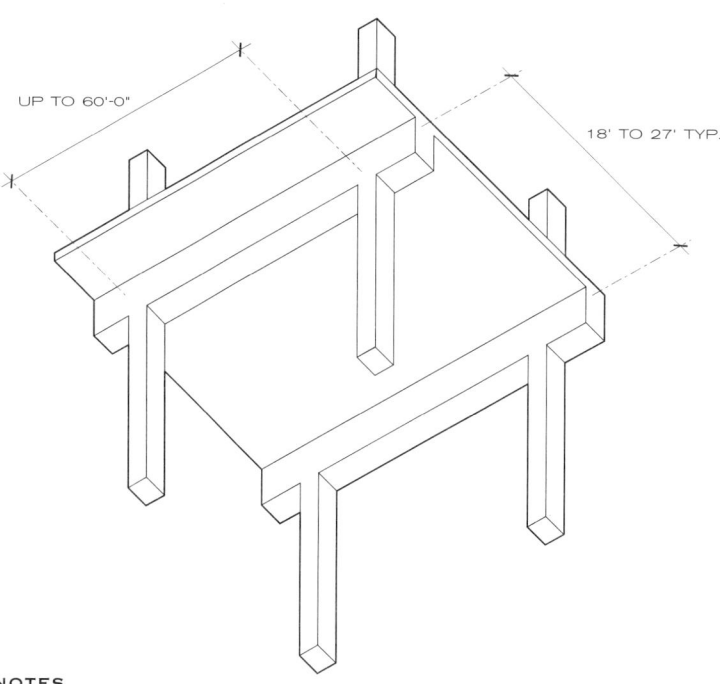

NOTES

1. Advantages: Long span in one direction.
2. Disadvantages: Beams interfere with mechanical services; more expensive forms than flat plate.
3. Appropriate building types: Parking garages, especially with posttensioning.
4. This scheme is most favored for parking garages, but the long span of about 60 ft must be prestressed unless beams are quite deep. Shallow beams will deflect excessively.

ONE-WAY BEAM AND SLAB

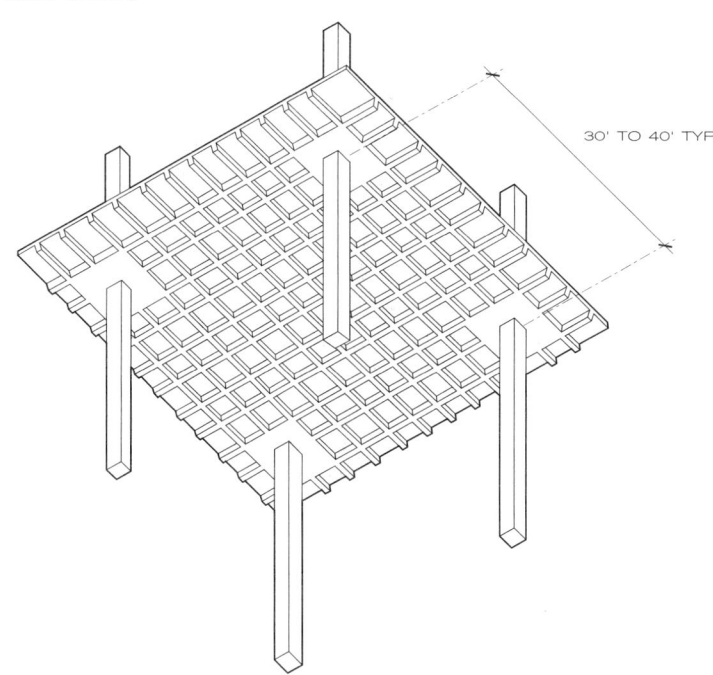

NOTES

1. Advantages: Longer two-way spans; attractive exposed ceilings; heavy load capacity.
2. Disadvantages: Formwork costs more and uses more concrete and steel than a joist slab.
3. Appropriate building types: Prominent buildings with exposed ceiling structure; same types as are suitable for flat slab but with longer spans.
4. Column spacing should be multiples of pan spacing to ensure uniformity of drop panels at each column. Drop panels can be diamond-shaped, square, or rectangular.

WAFFLE SLAB

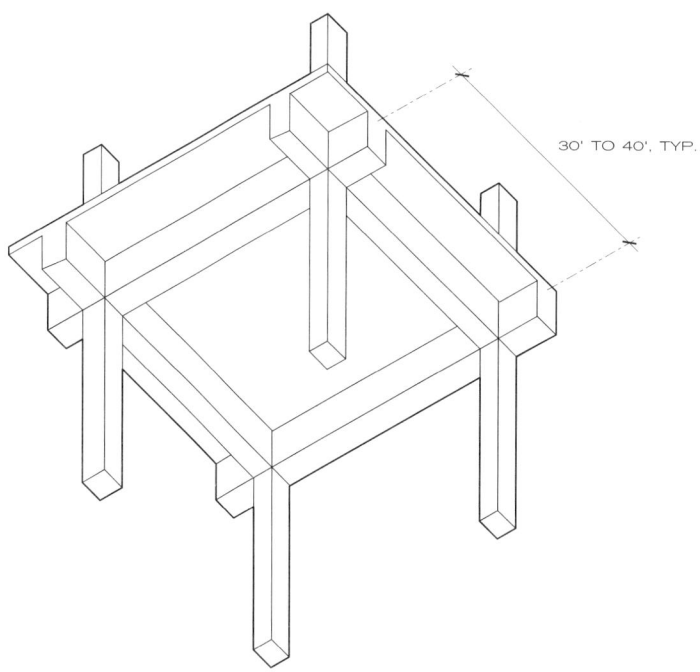

NOTES

1. Advantages: Long span in two directions; small deflection; can carry concentrated loads.
2. Disadvantages: Same as for one-way beams, only more so.
3. Appropriate building types: Portions of buildings in which two-way beam framing is needed for other reasons; industrial buildings with heavy concentrated loads.
4. The high cost of the formwork and structural interference with mechanical systems make this scheme unattractive unless heavy concentrated loads must be carried.

TWO-WAY SLAB AND BEAM

Russell S. Fling, P.E., Consulting Engineer; Columbus, Ohio

CAST-IN-PLACE CONCRETE

Concrete Surfaces, Finishes, and Integral Color

GENERAL

Architectural concrete and structural concrete are both made from portland cement, aggregate, and water, but they have entirely different concrete mix designs. A variety of architectural finishes and colors can be achieved by changing the mix of these three simple ingredients. The cost of production usually determines the limit of finish choices. There are three basic ways to change the appearance of a concrete surface finish:

MATERIAL VARIATION involves changing the size, shape, texture, and color of the coarse and fine aggregate, particularly in exposed aggregate concrete, and choosing white or gray cement.

MOLD OR FORM VARIATION involves changing the texture or pattern of the concrete surface by means of form design, form liners, or joint/edge treatments.

SURFACE TREATMENT involves treating or tooling the surface after the concrete has cured.

Design drawings for architectural concrete should show form details, including openings, joints (contraction, construction, and rustication), and other important specifics. Other factors that affect concrete surfaces are mixing and placing techniques, slump control, curing methods, and release agents.

NOTES

1. Choosing a placing technique (pumping vs. bottom drop or other bucket type) is an important step toward achieving a desired architectural concrete surface and finish. Evaluate whether architectural concrete forms can also be used for structural concrete. Verify that the vibrators used are of the proper size, frequency, and power.
2. Shop drawings should be carefully checked to determine form quality and steel reinforcement placement. Require approval of forms and finishes; field mockup is advised to evaluate the appearance of the concrete panel and the quality of workmanship.
3. Release agents are chemical treatments applied to the liner or face of the form that react with the cement to prevent it from sticking to the form. The safest way to select a release agent is to evaluate several products on a test panel under actual job conditions. The curing compound, used to retard or reduce evaporation of moisture from concrete or to extend curing time, is typically applied immediately after final finishing of the concrete surface. Consult manufacturers and the American Concrete Institute for more detailed information about the compatibility of these treatments and the form surface material or other finishes and surfaces to be applied to the concrete.

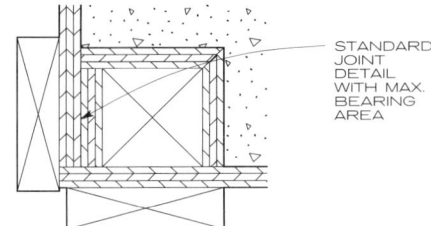
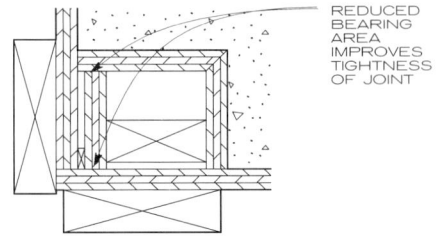

ARCHITECTURAL FEATURE AT CORNER

EXPOSURE METHODS FOR ARCHITECTURAL CONCRETE SURFACES

METHOD	FINISH EFFECT	COLOR SOURCE	FORM SURFACE	CRITICAL DETAILS
1. As cast	Remains as is after form removal, usually exhibits board marks or wood grain	Cement first influence, fine aggregate second influence	Smooth and textured	Slump = $2^{1}/_{2}$ to $3^{1}/_{2}$" Joinery of forms Proper release agent Point form joints to avoid marks
2. Abrasive blasted surfaces				
a. Brush blast	Uniform scour cleaning	Cement and fine aggregate have equal influence	All smooth	Scouring after 7 days Slump = $2^{1}/_{2}$ to $3^{1}/_{2}$"
b. Light blast	Blasted to expose fine and some coarse aggregate (sand blast, water blast, air blast, ice blast)	Fine aggregate primary, coarse aggregate and cement secondary	All smooth	10% more coarse aggregate Slump = $2^{1}/_{2}$ to $3^{1}/_{2}$" Blasting between 7 and 45 days Water and air blasting used where sand blasting prohibited 1500 PSI concrete compressive strength, min.
c. Medium exposed aggregate	Blasted to expose coarse aggregate (sand blast, water blast, air blast, ice blast)	Coarse aggregate	All smooth	Higher than normal coarse aggregate Slump = 2 to 3" Blast before 7 days
d. Heavy exposed aggregate	Blasted to expose coarse aggregate (sand blast, ice blast) 80% visible	Coarse aggregate	All smooth	Special mix coarse aggregate Slump = 0 to 2" Blast within 24 hours Use high-frequency vibrator
3. Chemical retardation of surface set	Chemicals expose aggregate Aggregate can be adhered to surface	Coarse aggregate and cement	All smooth, glass fiber best	Chemical grade determines etch depth Stripping scheduled to prevent long drying between stripping and washoff
4. Mechanically fratured surfaces, scaling, bush hammering, jack-hammering, tooling	Varied	Fine and coarse cement and aggregate	Textured	Aggregate particles $^{3}/_{8}$" for scaling and tooling $2^{1}/_{2}$" minimum concrete cover over reinforced steel 4000 PSI concrete compressive strength, minimum
5. Combination/fluted	Striated/abrasive blasted/irregular pattern Corrugated/abrasive Vertical rusticated/abrasive blasted Reeded and bush hammered Reeded and hammered Reeded and chiseled	The shallower the surface, the more influence fine aggregate and cement have	Wood or rubber strips, corrugated sheet metal, or glass fiber	Depends on type of finish desired Wood flute kerfed and nailed loosely
6. Grinding and polishing	Terrazzo-like finish	Aggregate and cement	All smooth	Surface blemishes should be patched 5000 PSI concrete compressive strength, minimum

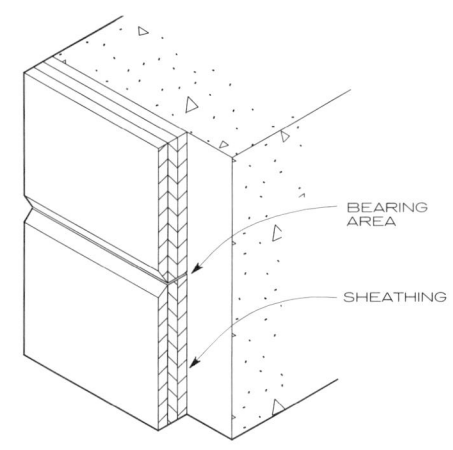

HORIZONTAL FORMWORK JOINT

NOTE

A notch at the joint between two form members reduces the bearing area at the point of contact, improving the tightness of the joint. A non-notched joint is acceptable, but a notch is recommended.

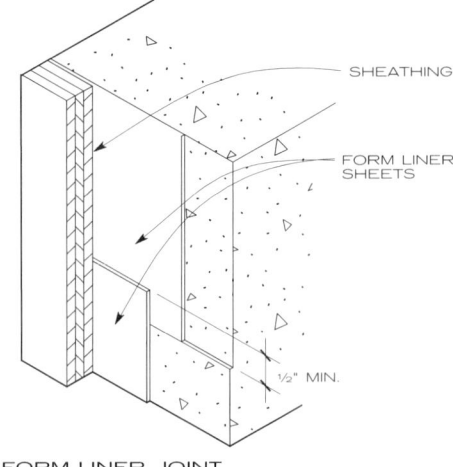

FORM LINER JOINT

NOTE

Placing the inner sheet above the outer sheet reduces shadows, particularly on smooth surfaces.

JOINTS IN FORMWORK

D. Neil Rankins; RGA/Virginia; Richmond, Virginia

CAST-IN-PLACE CONCRETE

Concrete Surfaces, Finishes, and Integral Color

AGGREGATE

Aggregate is one of three components of concrete and greatly affects the final appearance of the concrete surface. Aggregate should be selected on the basis of color, hardness, size, shape, gradation, method of exposure, durability, availability, and cost. Aggregate hardness and density must be compatible with structural requirements and weathering conditions.

Sources for coarse and fine aggregates should be kept the same for an entire job to avoid variations in the final surface appearance, particularly in light-toned concrete. Following are the common types of aggregate available:

QUARTZ is available in clear, white, yellow, green, gray, and light pink or rose. Clear quartz is used as a sparkling surface to complement other colors and pigmented cements.

GRANITE is known for its durability and beauty and is available in shades of pink, red, gray, dark blue, black, and white. Traprock such as basalt can be used for gray, black, or green.

MARBLE probably offers the widest selection of colors—green, yellow, red, pink, gray, white, and black.

LIMESTONE is available in white and gray.

MISCELLANEOUS GRAVEL, after being washed and screened, can be used for brown and reddish-brown finishes. Yellow ochers, umbers, buff shades, and pure white are abundant in riverbed gravels. Check local supplies.

CERAMIC exhibits the most brilliant and varied colors when vitreous materials are used.

EXPANDED LIGHTWEIGHT SHALE may be used to produce reddish-brown, gray, or black aggregate. Porous and crushable, this shale produces a dull surface with soft colors. It should be tested for iron staining characteristics and must meet ASTM C 330.

RECYCLED CONCRETE aggregate is produced when old concrete is crushed. Primarily used in pavement work, this material generally has a higher absorbsion rate and lower density than conventional aggregate. It should be tested for durability, gradation, and other properties, as with any new aggregate source.

EXPOSED AGGREGATE

An exposed aggregate surface is a decorative finish for concrete work achieved by removing the surface cement to expose the aggregate. Aggregates suitable for exposure may vary from 1/4 in. to a cobblestone more than 6 in. in diameter. The extent to which the pieces of aggregate are revealed is largely determined by their size. Size is generally selected on the basis of the distance from which it will be viewed and the appearance desired.

Aggregates with rough surfaces have better bonding properties than those with smoother surfaces; bind is important, particularly when small aggregate is used. For better weathering and appearance, the area of exposed cement matrix between pieces of aggregate should be minimal, which makes the color of cement in exposed aggregate concrete less important.

SUGGESTED VISIBILITY SCALE

AGGREGATE SIZE, IN. (MM)	DISTANCE AT WHICH TEXTURE IS VISIBLE, FT (M)
1/4–1/2 (6–13)	20–30 (6–9)
1/2–1 (13–25)	30–75 (9–23)
1–2 (25–50)	75–125 (23–38)
2–3 (50–75)	125–175 (38–53)

MISCELLANEOUS CONCRETE JOINT/EDGE SHAPES

SURFACE TEXTURE/FORM LINER

Patterned forms and liners make it possible to simulate in concrete the textures of wood, brick, and stone at a lower cost. The texture and resulting shadow patterns conceal minor color variations or damage that would be conspicuous and unacceptable on a smooth surface. Use of rustication strips at joints in textured liners simplifies form assembly work.

NOTES

1. The choice of liner material may depend on whether the work is precast, cast-in-place, or tilt-up. Thin liners that work well for horizontal casting may wrinkle and sag in vertical forms, where sturdier liner materials are required. Form liners such as plastic foams can usually be used only once, while many elastomeric liners are good for 100 or more uses with reasonable care.
2. Reusable aluminum wall forms, textured with various patterns, can also be used; sections are held together with metal pins. Typical sizes are 3 x 8 ft and larger.
3. Making a preconstruction mock-up is helpful in choosing patterned liner materials. If built on site, the mock-up can be used as a reference standard for inspectors and workers. If ribbed liners are specified, the largest aggregate particle should be smaller than the rib.
4. Typical form liner materials are:
   a. Plyform: Sandblasted, wire-brushed, or striated plyform can be used as form sheathing or as a liner inside other structurally adequate forms.
   b. Unfinished sheathing lumber: Used to produce rough, board-marked concrete, this lumber can be used as form sheathing or liner. Ammonia spray on wood will raise grain and accentuate the wood pattern.
   c. Rigid plastics: ABS, PVC, and high-impact polystyrene sheets can be molded or extruded to produce nearly any pattern or texture. Although typically supplied in sheets of 4 x 8, 4 x 10, and 4 x 12 ft, they can be special ordered in lengths up to 30 ft or longer.
   d. Glass fiber-reinforced plastics (GFRP): These look much like other plastics but are stronger and more durable, particularly laminated GFRP. Extruded GFRP is less expensive (and less durable). Custom lengths up to 40 ft are available.
   e. Elastomeric plastics: These rubbery liners, typically polyurethane, are the most costly, but they are very strong and durable and flexible enough to accommodate finer details. Standard sheets in sizes up to 4 x 12 ft arer available, as are larger custom sheets. Typically attached to form sheathing with adhesive, they are sensitive to temperature change and may deform; consult manufacturers.
   f. Polystyrene foam: Single-use liners are used to produce unique patterns for specific jobs.
5. Joints in the forms and liners must be executed carefully and the liners handled properly to achieve high-quality workmanship. Check liners for compatibility with release agents and adhesives.

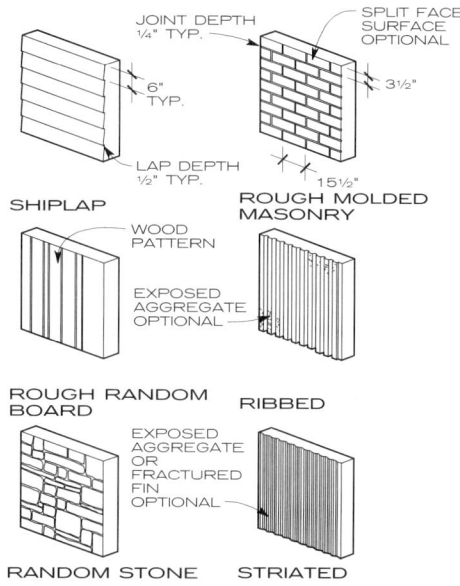

NOTE
Consult manufacturers for other available patterns.

REUSABLE FORM LINER PATTERNS

INTEGRALLY COLORED CEMENT

Colored concrete can provide a cost-effective simulation of natural stone or other building materials. Two standard types of cement are available, offering different shades of color: standard gray portland cement and white cement. Integrally colored concrete is made by adding mineral oxide pigments to concrete mixes made with one of these two types. Fine aggregates should be selected carefully, since they can enhance the color effect. The amount of coloring material should not exceed 10% by weight of the cement; any excess pigment may reduce concrete strength, and strong colors can be achieved with less than 10% pigment. White cement is used when lighter, more delicate shades of concrete are desired, although it is more expensive; darker hues can be produced using gray cement.

NOTES

1. Variations in all components of the concrete mix make color formulas only approximate. After a basic color is selected, the exact shade may be determined by preparing a number of small panels, varying the ratio of pigment to cement, with aggregate playing a more important role in exposed aggregate mixes. To evaluate panels properly, store them for about five days under conditions similar to those on the construction site. Panels lighten as they dry.
2. Batching, mixing, placing, and curing practices must be uniform, and accurate measurement of ingredients must be constant throughout a job to maintain color uniformity. Avoid admixtures that contain calcium chloride, since it can cause discoloration. Clean forms and nonstaining release agents are vital. Consult pigment manufacturers' recommendations.
3. Pigments should meet the quality standards of ASTM C979. Finely ground iron oxides are the most widely used pigments for coloring concrete. Colors and their sources include blue (cobalt oxide), brown (brown iron oxide), buff (yellow iron oxide), green (chromium oxide), red (red iron oxide), gray/slate (black iron oxide).
4. Color-conditioning admixtures offer integral color and have additives that improve workability, better disperse color and cement, and reduce color bleeding for improved uniformity. Consult manufacturers.

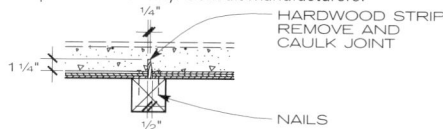

WOOD FORM INSERT

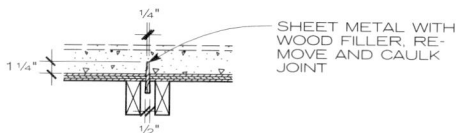

SHEET METAL FORM INSERT

NOTE
In flat concrete work, a rotary saw may be used to make a contraction joint.

CONTRACTION JOINTS

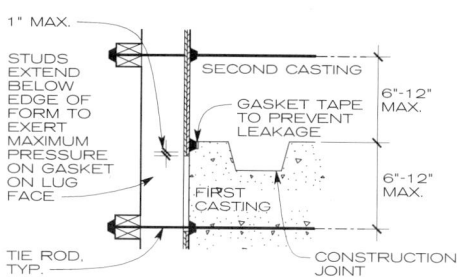

TYPICAL CONSTRUCTION JOINT

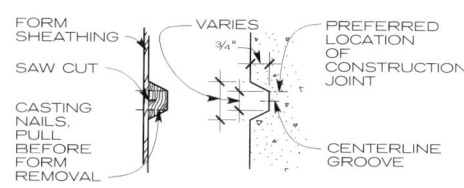

RUSTICATION AT CONSTRUCTION JOINT

D. Neil Rankins; RGA/Virginia; Richmond, Virginia

Concrete Surfaces: Defect Prevention, Repair, Coatings, Treatments

CONCRETE REPAIR

Damage or deterioration of concrete can occur at any time during service life. Minor repairs may be required during initial construction, for example, filling form tie holes; patching lifting loops on precast concrete; or repairing broken edges on beams, walls, and columns. Distress may result from inadequate design or construction, or deterioration, natural effects, or exposure to aggregate chemicals. Most repairs improve appearance, blending adjacent surfaces by matching texture and color. The repair area should be permanently bonded to the adjacent concrete and sufficiently impermeable to liquid penetration to keep it from shrinking or cracking. Repairs should withstand freeze/thaw cycles as well as surrounding concrete does.

The American Concrete Institute defines generally acceptable architectural concrete surfaces as those with minimal color and texture variation and minimal surface defects when viewed at 20 ft. Most architectural concrete contains some irregularities, such as blowholes or bugholes. Criteria for acceptability should be defined in advance, but patches should match the surrounding area as much as possible.

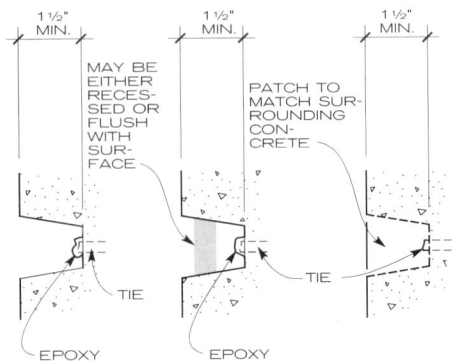

NOTE

Solid plugs may be made of precast mortar, plastic, or lead. Mortar of a drytamp consistency will be less likely to smear on surrounding concrete. If surrounding concrete is smooth, recess plug or patch.

TIE HOLE TREATMENT OPTIONS

REPAIR MATERIALS

Prepackaged cementitious and latex-modified cementitious repair materials are available, with formulations for thin or thicker repairs. Where aesthetics are important, use the same cement and aggregates as in the surrounding work. Most types of Portland cement are acceptable, but match the original type, if possible. Certain prepackaged mixes must conform to ASTM C 928. Aggregates should match the existing concrete aggregate, if possible. For exposed aggregate, matching the texture and color may require special mixtures to meet the specifications. Any admixture used in concrete work can be used in repair mixtures. Bonding agents may be required for some repairs, especially thin ones; they are typically either cement-based, latex-based (ASTM C 1059), or epoxy-based (ASTM C 881). Acrylics, methyl methacrylates, and polymers are less expensive than epoxy bonding agents but are more likely to shrink. Repaired areas should be sealed or coated to the same specifications as the surrounding concrete work to protect against natural forces, corrosives, and chemicals.

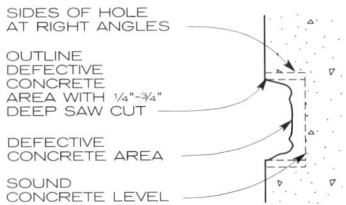

NOTE

Larger and thicker patches should be anchored mechanically to the surrounding concrete.

PATCHING OF DEFECTIVE CONCRETE SURFACES

GUIDELINES FOR PATCHING

1. Design patch mix to match original, with small amount of white cement; may eliminate coarse aggregate or hand-place it. Trial and error, the only reliable match method, should be performed on a mock-up first.
2. Remove defective concrete down to sound concrete; for exposed aggregate concrete, chip slightly deeper than maximum size of aggregate.
3. Clean area; saturate with water and apply bonding agent to base of hole and to water of patch mix.
4. Pack patch mix to density of original.
5. Place exposed aggregate by hand.
6. Bristle-brush after setup to match existing material.
7. Moist-cure to minimize shrinking.
8. Use form or finish to match original.

PROTECTIVE AND DECORATIVE COATINGS

Concrete surfaces may require a sealer or coating to protect against severe weather, chemicals, or abrasions; to prevent dusting of the surface layer; to harden the surface layer; or to add a decorative finish.

Sealers are usually clear and are expected to penetrate the surface without leaving a visible film. Coatings are clear or opaque and, while they may have some penetration, they leave a visible film on the surface. Sealers and coatings should allow vapor emission from the concrete but at the same time keep moisture from penetrating after curing.

Decorative coatings usually protect as well and are formulated in a wide selection of colors. Decorative coatings include water-based acrylic emulsion; elastomeric acrylic resin; liquid polymer stain; solvent-based acrylic stain; portland cement-based finish coating; and water-based acidic stain (a solution of metallic salts).

PROTECTIVE COATINGS AND SEALERS

FINISH	USE
Cementitious acrylic polymeric coating	Aesthetic treatment
2-component epoxy coating	Protects damp or underwater surfaces
Solvent-based aliphatic urethane coating	Resists graffiti, chemicals, abrasion
Epoxy coal tar-based coating	Waterproof, resists corrosion
Coal tar-modified epoxy resin coating	Nonskid waterproof surface membrane
Water-based epoxy coating	Chemical, abrasion resistance for interiors
Vinyl ester-based coating	High chemical resistance
Aliphatic urethane coating	Chemical, abrasion
Solvent-based acrylic methacrylate copolymer sealer	Reduces water penetration
Silane/siloxane sealer penetrating water repellent	Protects from deicers and freeze/thaw damage

NOTES

1. Floor-hardening agents are applied to reduce dusting and increase hardness slightly at the surface.
2. Consult a qualified specialist to determine the correct coating or sealer for a particular application.
3. There may be restrictions on the use of solvent-based coatings and sealers in some areas due to the presence of VOCs (volatile organic compounds).

CRACKING IN CONCRETE CONSTRUCTION

	SLABS ON GRADE					BEAMS, WALLS, COLUMNS, AND STRUCTURAL SLABS		
	SURFACE CRAZING	PLASTIC SHRINKAGE	EARLY CONCRETE VOLUME CHANGES	OTHER CRACKING		SETTLEMENT CRACKS		OTHER CRACKING
Cause	Shrinkage of cement paste at exposed concrete surfaces due to concrete mix, too-wet excessive bleeding, overtroweling surface, rapid drying of surface	Water at the concrete surface evaporates too rapidly due to job site conditions such as low humidity, high wind speeds, high concrete temperatures, high to moderate air temperatures	As concrete cools and hardens, concrete volume shrinks; cracking will occur if slab is restrained at any point	Subgrade settlement	Premature excessive loading on slab	Same as for slabs on grade; also, heavier amounts of reinforcement and nature of formed or shored construction	Flexible forms and insufficient vibration can increase likelihood	Subgrade or formwork settlement, early volume changes, construction overloads, errors in design and detailing
Effect	Unsightly cracking of surface layer although surface is probably sound	Parallel cracking, fairly wide at the exposed surface but shallow; doesn't typically extend to slab edge; crack spacing and length vary greatly	Random or regularly spaced cracks, usually passing completely through slab; during sawcutting of joints, crack may jump ahead of sawcut	Slab will bend and crack	Punch-through at edge by heavy equipment, etc.	Longitudinal cracks develop over reinforcement bars; can cause reinforcement bar corrosion		General cracking
Preventive measures	Reduce amount and rate of shrinkage at concrete surface by avoiding wet mixes, limiting bleeding by increasing sand or air content, limiting troweling/not troweling too early, curing as soon as possible	Reduce rate at which surface moisture evaporates by erecting windbreaks or building walls before slab, avoiding wet mixes, dampening subgrade before concrete pour, curing as soon as possible, avoiding vapor barrier under slab unless necessary	Not always preventable; careful joint design or reinforcement may help; other measures: tool or sawcut joints $1/4$ of slab thickness, min., time sawcut according to concrete curing rate; locate contraction joints at column lines, min.; for unreinforced slabs, space joints at 24 to 36 times slab thickness, max.; posttension at slab; isolate slabs from adjoining structures with preformed joint filler or if continuity is required, increase slab reinforcement	Compact subgrade well	Generally, curing periods of 4 to 7 days, followed by 1 to 2 days of drying	Proper form design and sufficient vibration or revibration: use lowest possible slump, increase concrete cover		Consult with structural concrete engineer or consultant to prevent

NOTE

Expect some cracking in concrete construction. Generally, cracking is controlled with joints and reinforcement; however, not all cracks indicate errors or performance problems, and not all cracks need to be repaired.

Grant Halvorsen, S.E., P.E.; Wheaton, Illinois

CAST-IN-PLACE CONCRETE

Precast Concrete Decks and Slabs

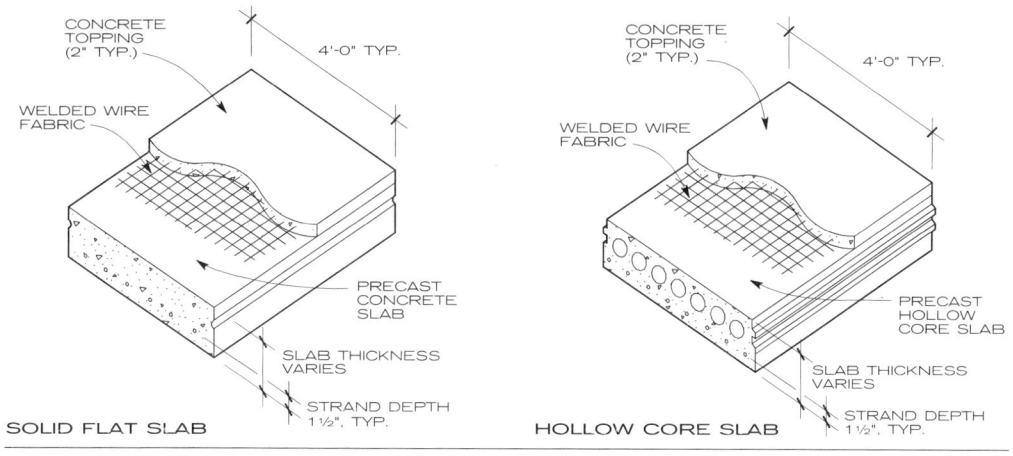

NOTES

1. Normal weight (150 pcf) or lightweight concrete (115 pcf) is used in standard slab construction. Topping concrete is usually normal weight concrete with a cylinder strength of 3000 psi. All units are prestressed with strand release when concrete strength is 3500 psi.
2. Strands are available in various sizes, strengths and placements according to individual manufacturers.

   Strand designation code (SDC):
   78 - S
   - straight
   - diameter of strands in sixteenths
   - number of strands

3. Camber varies substantially depending on slab design, span, and loading. Nonstructural components attached to members may be affected by camber variations. Calculations of topping quantities should recognize camber variations.
4. Safe superimposed surface loads include a dead load of 10 psf for untopped concrete and 15 psf for topped concrete. The remainder is live load.

FLAT DECK MEMBERS

SAFE SUPERIMPOSED SERVICE LOADS (PSF) FOR SOLID FLAT SLABS (4-FT WIDTH, 5000 PSI)

SLAB THICKNESS (IN.) (150 PCF CONCRETE)	SLAB DESIGNATION	TOPPING THICKNESS (IN.)	SPAN (FT)																					
			10	11	12	13	14	15	16	17	18	19	20	21	22	23	24	25	26	27	28	29	30	31	32
4" S.D.C.: 68-S	FS4	None	300	252	214	180	152	127	105	88	73	60	50	40	32										
	FS4+2	2				335	268	213	169	132	101	74	52	32											
6" S.D.C.: 78-S	FS6	None					396	351	303	261	225	195	168	146	126	109	94	81	69	59	49	41	33		
	FS6+2	2								371	323	281	239	201	169	140	115	93	73	56	40				
8" S.D.C.: 68-S	FS8	None								358	311	271	237	207	182	159	138	120	103	88	75	63	53	43	34
	FS8+2	2									395	344	301	264	231	199	167	140	115	94	74	57	41		

SAFE SUPERIMPOSED SERVICE LOADS (PSF) FOR 6- AND 8-IN. HOLLOW-CORE SLABS (4-FT WIDTH, 5000 PSI)

SLAB THICKNESS (IN.) (150 PCF CONCRETE)	SLAB DESIGNATION	TOPPING THICKNESS (IN.)	SPAN (FT)																					
			15	16	17	18	19	20	21	22	23	24	25	26	27	28	29	30	31	32	33	34	35	36	37
6" S.D.C.: 78-S	4HC6	None	364	317	277	243	214	189	168	150	134	120	107	96	87	78	70	62							
	4HC6+2	2				382	335	294	260	231	205	181	157	137	119	102	88	75	63						
8" S.D.C.: 88-S	4HC8	None	360	335	311	290	272	256	242	229	215	205	188	170	154	141	128	117	106	97	89	81	74	67	
	4HC8+2	2				346	325	306	286	271	252	227	205	186	168	152	138	124	111	98	86	76	66	56	

SAFE SUPERIMPOSED SERVICE LOADS (PSF) FOR 10- AND 12-IN. HOLLOW-CORE SLABS (4-FT WIDTH, 5000 PSI)

SLAB THICKNESS (IN.) (150 PCF CONCRETE)	SLAB DESIGNATION	TOPPING THICKNESS (IN.)	SPAN (FT)																					
			20	21	22	23	24	25	26	27	28	29	30	31	32	33	34	35	36	37	38	39	40	41	42
10" S.D.C.: 97-S	4HC10	None	298	278	264	248	237	223	214	203	193	179	164	150	138	126	116	106	98	90	82	75	69	63	57
	4HC10+2	2				295	278	265	250	239	226	218	201	184	168	154	138	124	111	98	87	77	67	58	49
12" S.D.C.: 78-S	4HC12	None							194	185	177	169	162	155	148	142	137	131	126	121	120	112	104		
	4HC12+2	2				280	264	249	236	223	212	201	195	185	177	169	161	154	147	141	135	129	126	116	107

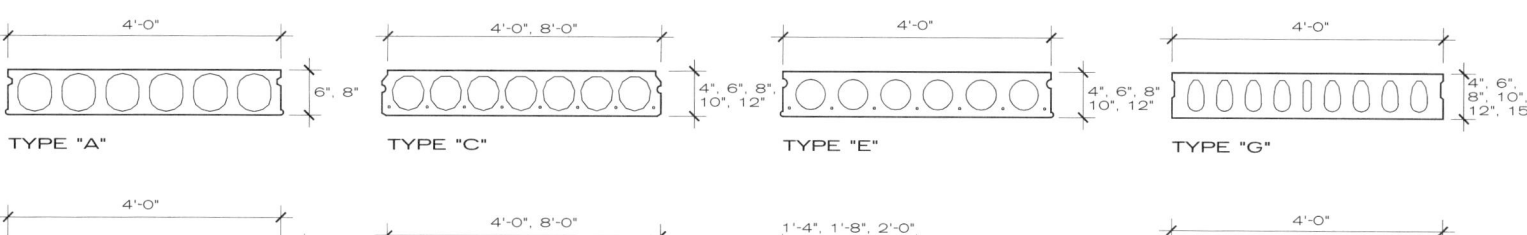

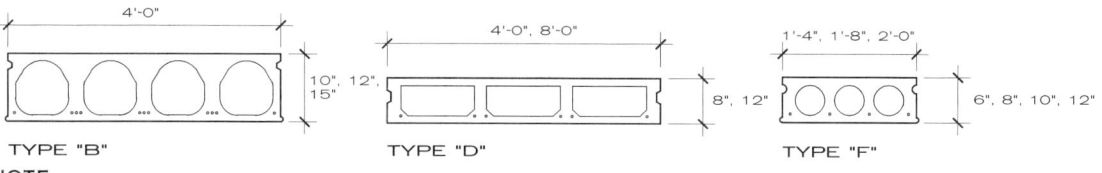

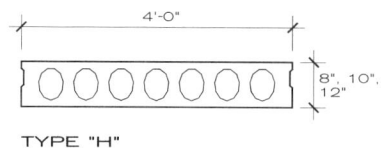

NOTE

All sections are not available from all producers; check availability with local manufacturers.

HOLLOW CORE SLAB TYPES

Sidney Freedman; Precast/Prestressed Concrete Institute; Chicago, Illinois

Precast Long-Span Decks, Girders, and Beams

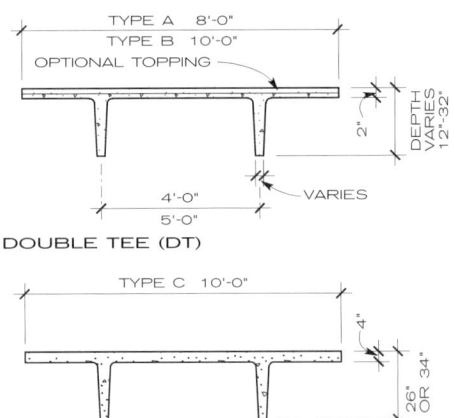

DOUBLE TEE (DT)

PRETOPPED DOUBLE TEE

NOTES

1. Safe loads shown indicate dead load of 10 psf for untopped members and 15 psf for topped members. Remainder is live load.
2. Contact manufacturers in the geographic area of the proposed structure to determine availability, exact dimensions, and load tables for various sections.
3. Check camber for its effect on nonstructural members (partitions, folding doors, etc.), which should be placed with adequate allowance for error. Calculations for topping quantities should also recognize camber variations.
4. Normal-weight concrete is assumed to be 150 lb/cu ft; lightweight concrete is assumed to be 115 lb/cu ft.

STEMMED DECK MEMBERS

APPROXIMATE MAXIMUM SPAN FOR STEMMED DECK SECTIONS

DECK TYPE	DEPTH (IN.)	CONCRETE WEIGHT	DESIGNATION	TOPPING DEPTH (IN.)	STRAND DESIGNATION	MAX. SPAN (FT)	SAFE LOAD (PSF)
A	12	Normal weight	8DT12	0	88 D1	44	32
			8DT12+2	2	68 D1	34	50
		Lightweight	8LDT12	0	68 D1	42	33
			8LDT12+2	2	68 D1	38	33
A	18	Normal weight	8DT18	0	108 D1	60	34
			8DT18+2	2	88 D1	48	47
		Lightweight	8LDT18	0	108 D1	64	34
			8LDT18+2	2	88 D1	52	39
A	24	Normal weight	8DT24	0	148 D1	74	45
			8DT24+2	2	128 D1	64	49
		Lightweight	8LDT24	0	148 D1	80	42
			8LDT24+2	2	108 D1	68	46
A	32	Normal weight	8DT32	0	228 D1	94	52
			8DT32+2	2	208 D1	80	72
		Lightweight	8LDT32	0	228 D1	100	50
			8LDT32+2	2	208 D1	86	65
B	32	Normal weight	10DT32	0	228 D1	88	53
			10DT32+2	2	208 D1	76	66
		Lightweight	10LDT32	0	228 D1	98	42
			10LDT32+2	2	208 D1	82	58
C	26	Normal weight	10DT26	0	148 D1	68	33
		Lightweight	10LDT26	0	148 D1	72	37
C	34	Normal weight	10DT34	0	228 D1	90	34
		Lightweight	10LDT34	0	228 D1	90	51

NOTE

Strand pattern designation:
208 D1
- Number of strands (20)
- S = straight, D = depressed
- Number of depression points
- Diameter of strand in sixteenths

Topping concrete = 3000 psi

150 lb/cu ft fc = 5000 psi for normal or lightweight deck

SAFE SUPERIMPOSED SERVICE LOAD (PLF)* FOR PRECAST BEAM SECTIONS

TYPE	DESIGNATION	NO. STRAND	H (IN.)	H1/H2 (IN.)	16	18	20	22	24	26	28	30	32	34	36	38	40	42	44	46	48	50
RECTANGULAR	12RB24	10	24		8884	6957	5578	4558	3782	3178	2699	2312	1996	1734	1514	1328	1170	1033				
	12RB32	13	32						8238	6859	5785	4933	4246	3683	3217	2826	2495	2213	1970	1760	1576	1415	1272
	16RB24	13	24			9278	7439	6079	5044	4239	3600	3084	2662	2313	2020	1772	1560	1378	1220	1082	961	
	16RB32	18	32					9145	7713	6577	5661	4911	4289	3768	3327	2951	2627	2346	2010	1886	1697	
	16RB40	22	40								9010	7839	6867	6054	5365	4777	4271	3832	3449	3113	2817	
L-SHAPED	18LB20	9	20	12/18	6675	5211	4164	3389	2800	2341	1978	1684	1444	1245	1080							
	18LB28	12	28	16/12			8387	6857	5694	4789	4071	3491	3017	2624	2295	2017	1781	1578	1402	1249	1114	995
	18LB36	16	36	24/12				9617	8117	6927	5966	5180	4529	3983	3521	3126	2787	2493	2236	2011	1813	
	18LB44	19	44	28/16							9039	7866	6893	6078	5389	4800	4293	3854	3471	3153	2838	
	18LB52	23	52	36/16									9798	8658	7694	6871	6162	5548	5012	4542	4127	
	18LB60	27	60	44/16													9292	8349	7532	6819	6193	5641
INVERTED TEE	24IT20	9	20	12/8	7078	5515	4404	3582	2957	2470	2084	1773	1518	1307	1130	980						
	24IT28	13	28	16/12				8874	7247	6013	5053	4292	3677	3175	2758	2409	2113	1861	1644	1456	1292	1147	1020
	24IT36	16	36	24/12						8594	7327	6305	5469	4776	4199	3710	3293	2934	2623	2352	2114	1904
	24IT44	20	44	28/16								9554	8306	7272	6409	5680	5057	4520	4056	3650	3295	2981
	24IT52	24	52	36/16											9164	8137	7261	6507	5853	5283	4786	4348
	24IT60	28	60	44/16													9863	8857	7986	7226	6559	5970

* Safe loads shown indicate 50% dead load and 50% live load; 800 psi top tension has been allowed, therefore additional top reinforcement is required.

Sidney Freedman; Precast/Prestressed Concrete Institute; Chicago, Illinois

PRECAST CONCRETE

Precast Concrete Wall Panels

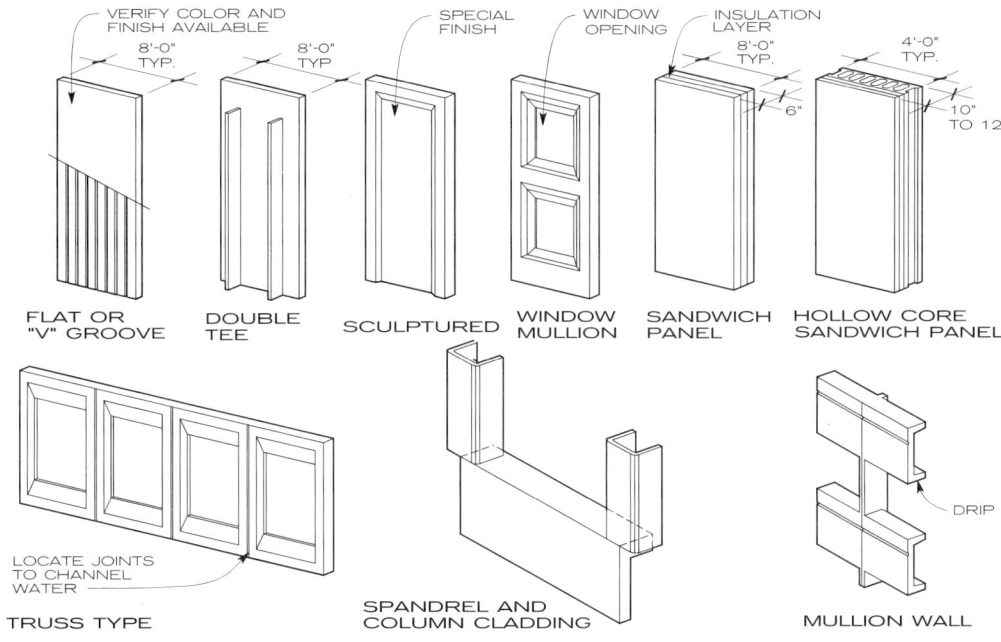

PANEL VARIATIONS

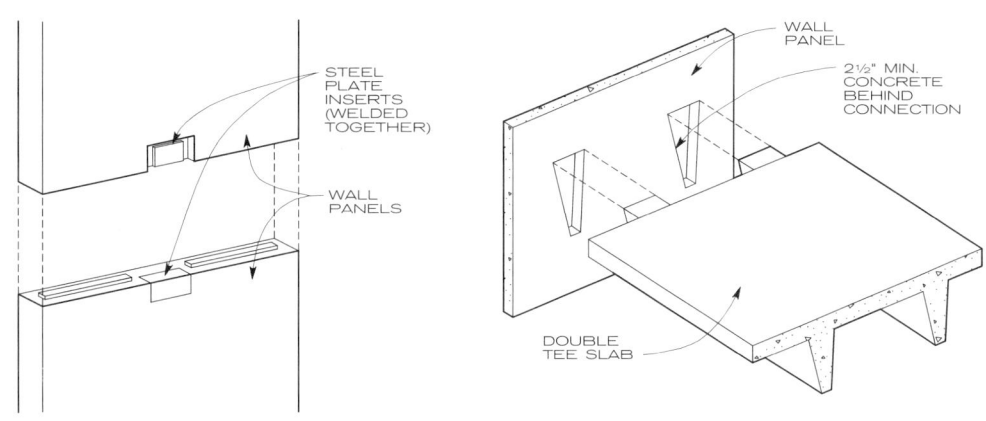

NOTE
Pocket connection may be at top of panel.

BEARING PANEL CONDITIONS

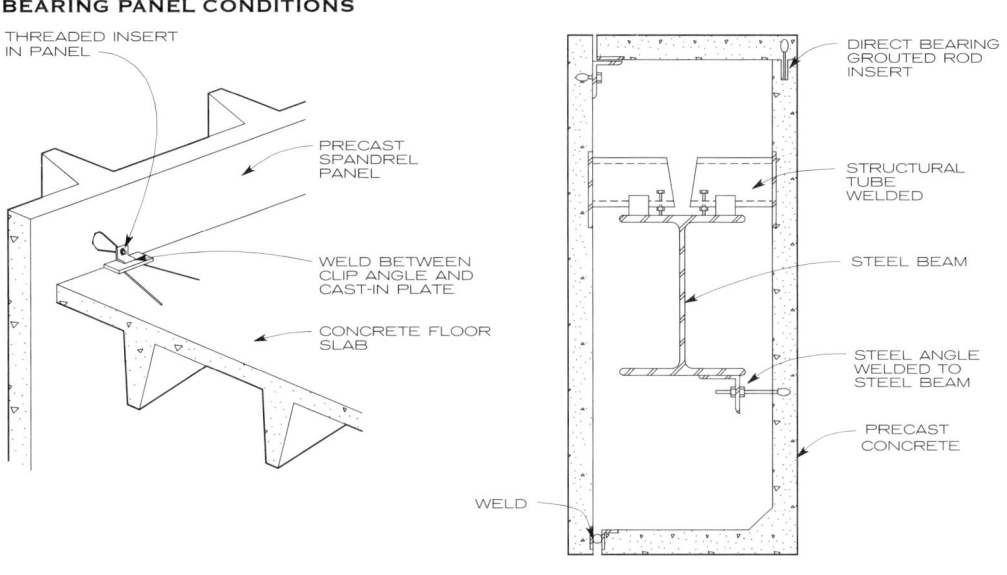

SPANDREL CONDITIONS

Sidney Freedman; Precast/Prestressed Concrete Institute; Chicago, Illinois

WALL PANELS

Carefully distinguish between the more specialized architectural wall panel and the structural wall panel that is a derivative of floor systems. Always work with manufacturers early in the design process. Careful attention must be given to manufacturing and joint tolerance during design. Thoroughly examine joint sealants for adhesion and expected joint movement.

FINISHES

Form liner molds provide a wide variety of smooth and textured finishes. Finishes after casting but prior to hardening include exposed aggregate, broom, trowel, screed, float, or stippled. After hardening, finishes include acid-etched, sandblasted, honed, polished, and hammered rib.

COLORS

Select a color range, as complete uniformity cannot be guaranteed. White cement offers the best color uniformity; gray cement is subject to color variations even when supplied from one source. Pigments require high-quality manufacturing and curing standards. Fine aggregate color requires control of the mixture graduation; coarse aggregate color provides the best durability and appearance.

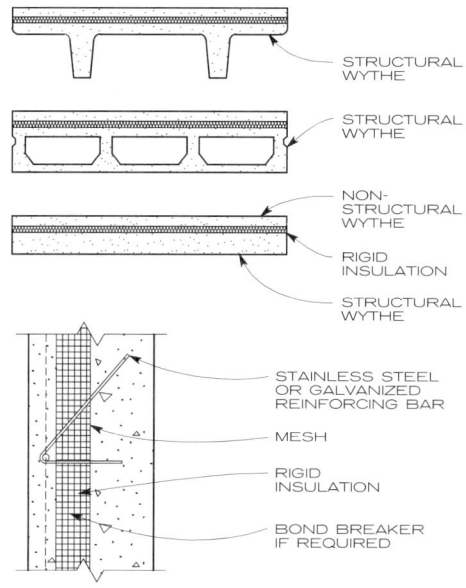

NOTE
Panel requires accurate location of ties and reinforcement and established concrete quality control.

SANDWICH WALL CONSTRUCTION

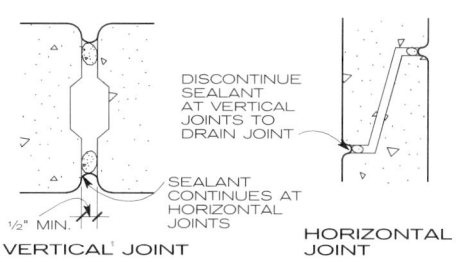

TWO-STAGE SEALANT JOINTS

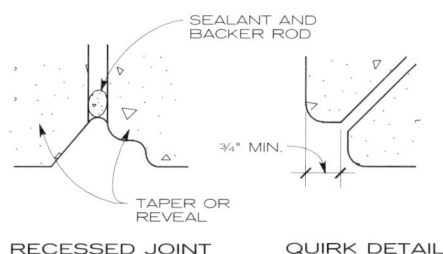

JOINT DETAILS

PRECAST CONCRETE

Precast Concrete Wall Panel Tolerances

GENERAL

Architectural precast concrete is subject to the same erection and manufacturing tolerances as other building materials. When such tolerances are considered in the design stage, the task of determining and specifying them is simpler. By requiring realistic tolerances, architects strengthen and simplify their standards for acceptance. Unrealistic, close tolerances are costly, particularly for custom-produced elements.

Tolerances set the limits of size and shape for precast concrete units. Three groups of tolerances should be established in precast concrete design: product (manufacturing) tolerances, erection tolerances, and interfacing tolerances. Product and erection tolerances usually do not cause site problems. Tolerances are most problematic at the interface of precast concrete and other building materials.

Tolerances should be established for the following reasons:

STRUCTURAL: To ensure that structural design properly accounts for factors sensitive to variations in dimensional control. Examples include eccentric loading condition, bearing areas, hardware and hardware anchorage locations, and locations of reinforcing or prestressing steel.

FEASIBILITY: To ensure acceptable performance of joints and interfacing materials in the finished structure.

VISUAL: To ensure that the variations will be controllable and result in a structure that is visually acceptable.

ECONOMIC: To ensure ease and speed of production and erection by having agreed-upon dimensions for precast concrete products.

LEGAL: To avoid encroaching on property lines and to establish a standard against which the work can be compared in event of a dispute.

CONTRACTUAL: To establish a known acceptability range and responsibility for developing, achieving, and maintaining mutually agreed-upon tolerances.

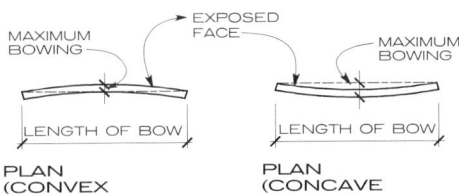

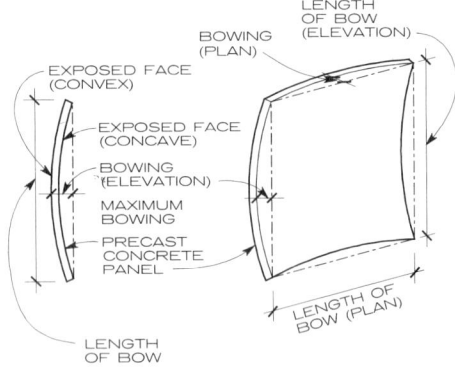

BOWING DEFINITIONS FOR PANELS

GUIDELINES FOR PANEL THICKNESS[1]

PANEL DIMENSIONS[2]	8 FT	10 FT	12 FT	16 FT	20 FT	24 FT	28 FT	32 FT
4 ft	3 in.	4 in.	4 in.	5 in.	5 in.	6 in.	6 in.	7 in.
6 ft	3 in.	4 in.	4 in.	5 in.	6 in.	6 in.	6 in.	7 in.
8 ft	4 in.	5 in.	5 in.	6 in.	6 in.	7 in.	7 in.	8 in.
10 ft	5 in.	5 in.	6 in.	6 in.	7 in.	7 in.	8 in.	8 in.

[1] This table should not be used for panel thickness selection.
[2] This table shows a relationship between overall flat panel dimensions and thicknesses below which suggested bowing and warpage tolerances should be reviewed and possibly increased. For ribbed panels, the equivalent thickness should be the overall thickness of such ribs if continuous from one end of the panel to the other.

PLAN

ELEVATION

A = Plan location from building grid datum ±$1/2$ in.[1]
A_1 = Plan location from centerline of steel ±$1/2$ in.[2]
B = Top elevation from nominal top elevation: exposed individual panel ±$1/4$ in.; nonexposed individual panel ±$1/2$ in.; exposed relative to adjacent panel $1/4$ in.; nonexposed relative to adjacent panel $1/2$ in.
C = Support elevation from nominal elevation: maximum low $1/2$ in.; maximum high $1/4$ in.
D = Maximum plumb variation over height of structure or 100 ft, whichever is less 1 in.[1]
E = Plumb in any 10 ft of element height $1/4$ in.
F = Maximum jog in alignment of matching edges $1/4$ in.
G = Joint width (governs over joint taper) ±$1/4$ in.
H = Joint taper max. $3/8$ in.
H_{10} = Joint taper over 10 ft length $1/4$ in.
I = Max. jog in alignment of matching faces $1/4$ in.
J = Differential bowing or camber as erected between adjacent members of the same design $1/4$ in.

[1] For precast buildings taller than 100 ft, tolerances A and D can increase at the rate of $1/8$ in. per story to a maximum of 2 in.
[2] For precast concrete erected on a steel frame building, this tolerance takes precedence over tolerance on dimension A.

ERECTION TOLERANCES FOR WALL PANELS

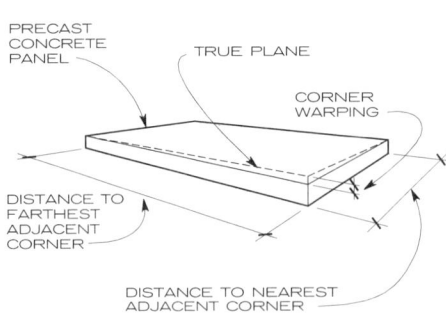

WARPING DEFINITIONS FOR PANELS

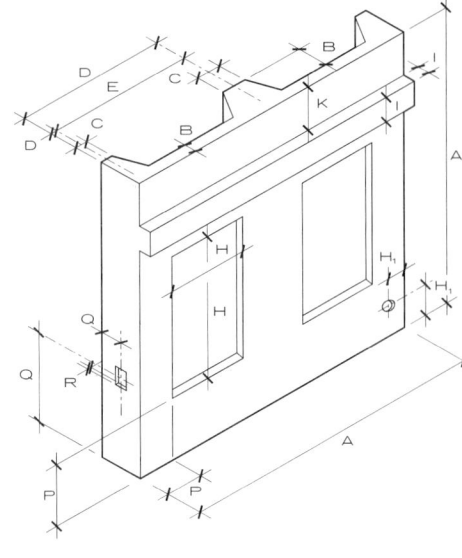

A = Overall length and width (measured at neutral axis of ribbed members): 10 ft or under ±$1/8$ in.; 10 to 20 ft +$1/8$ in., -$3/16$ in.; 20 to 40 ft ±$1/4$ in.; each additional 10 ft ±$1/16$ in. per 10 ft.
B = Total thickness or flange thickness -$1/8$ in., +$1/4$ in.
C = Rib thickness ±$1/8$ in.
D = Rib to edge of flange ±$1/8$ in.
E = Distance between ribs ±$1/8$ in.
F = Angular variation of plane of side mold ±$1/32$ in. per 3 in. of depth or ±$1/16$ in., whichever is greater.
G = Variation from square or designated skew (difference in length of the two diagonal measurements) ±$1/8$ in. per 6 ft of diagonal or ±$1/2$ in., whichever is greater.*
H = Length and width of blockouts and openings within one unit ±$1/4$ in.
H_1 = Location and dimensions of blockouts hidden from view and used for HVAC and utility penetrations ±$3/4$ in.
H_2 = Some types of window and equipment frames require more accurate types of openings. When this is the case, the minimum practical tolerance should be defined with input from the producer.
I = Dimensions of haunches ±$1/4$ in.
J = Haunch bearing surface deviation from specified plane ±$1/8$ in.
K = Difference in relative position of adjacent haunch bearing surfaces from specified relative position ±$1/4$ in.
L = Bowing ±L/360 max. 1 in.
M = Differential bowing between adjacent panels of the same design $1/2$ in.
N = Local smoothness $1/4$ in. in 10 ft. (does not apply to visually concealed surfaces).
O = Warping of distance from nearest adjacent corner $1/16$ in. per ft.
P = Location of window opening within panel ±$1/4$ in.
Q = Position of plates ±1 in.
R = Tipping and flushness of plates ±$1/4$ in.

* Applies both to panel and to major openings in the panel.

Position tolerance for cast-in items measured from datum line location as shown on approved erection drawings: weld plates ±1 in.; inserts ±$1/2$ in.; handling devices ±3 in.; reinforcing steel and welded wire fabric where position has structural implications or affects concrete cover ±$1/4$ in., otherwise ±$1/2$ in.; tendons ±$1/8$ in.; flashing reglets ±$1/4$ in.; flashing reglets at edge of panel ±$1/8$ in.; reglets for glazing gaskets ±$1/16$ in.; groove width for glazing gaskets ±$1/16$ in.; electrical outlets, hose bibs, etc. ±$1/2$ in.; haunches ±$1/4$ in.

TOLERANCES FOR PANELS, SPANDRELS, AND COLUMN COVERS

Sidney Freedman; Precast/Prestressed Concrete Institute; Chicago, Illinois

Precast Concrete Connections

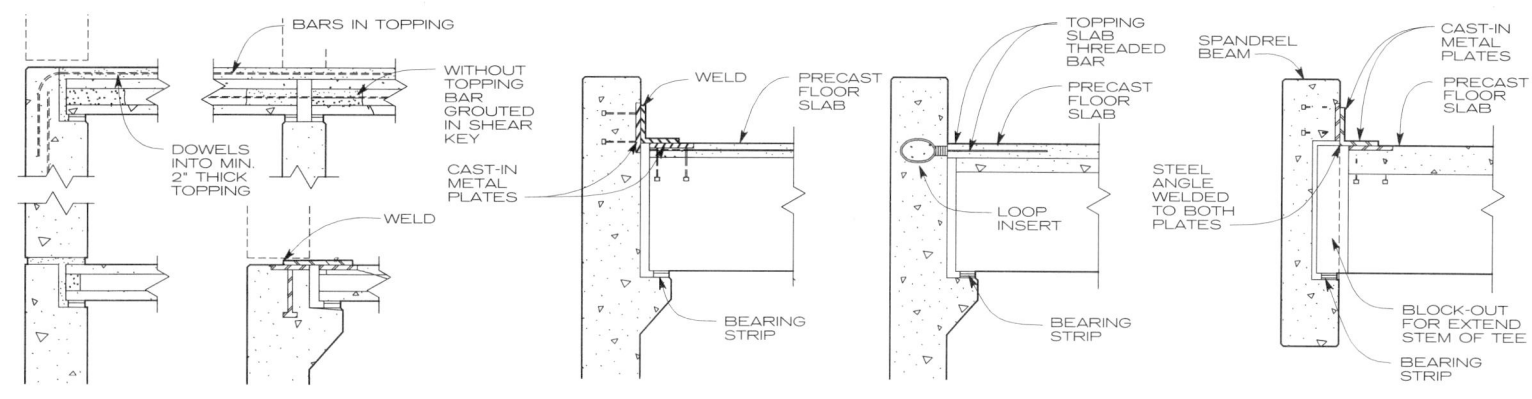

HOLLOW CORE SLAB DETAILS FLOOR-TO-BEARING WALL CONNECTIONS SPANDREL CONNECTION

FLOOR-TO-WALL CONNECTIONS

GENERAL

To fasten members to foundations, set them on shims, tighten nuts to level, then fill space with nonshrink grout.

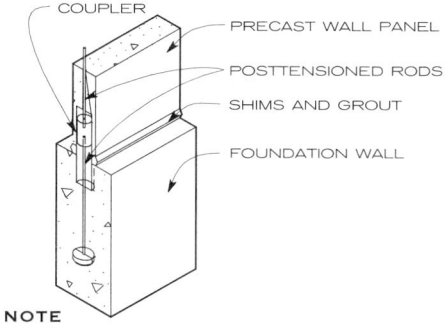

NOTE

Vertical posttensioning can be used to resist uplift forces; moment resistance is achieved.

POSTTENSIONED WALL-TO-FOUNDATION CONNECTION

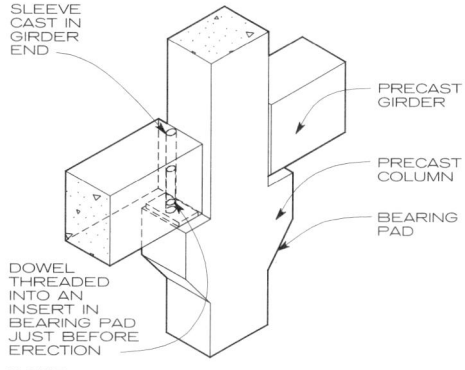

NOTE

The girder sits on the bearing pad, which provides uniform bearing and accommodates small movements due to shrinkage, creep, and temperature changes.

DOWELED BEAM-TO-COLUMN CONNECTION

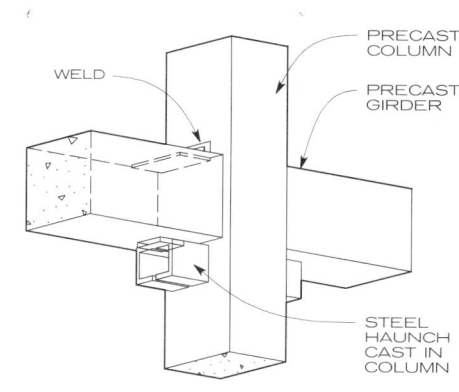

NOTE

Steel haunches are smaller than concrete bearing pads, which is important if headroom is critical.

HAUNCHED BEAM-TO-COLUMN CONNECTION

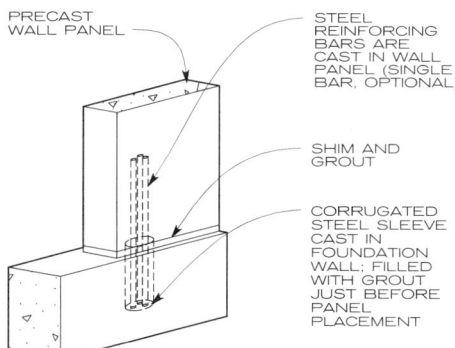

GROUTED WALL-TO-FOUNDATION CONNECTION

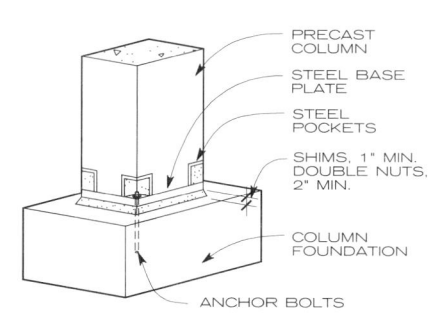

COLUMN–BASE CONNECTION

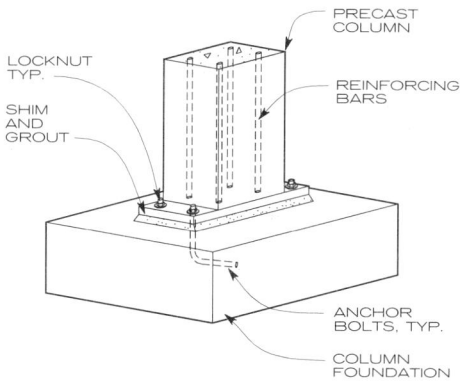

OVERSIZED BASE PLATE AT COLUMN–BASE CONNECTION

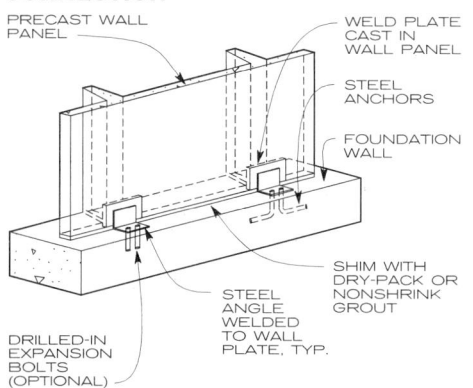

BOLTED WALL-TO-FOUNDATION CONNECTION

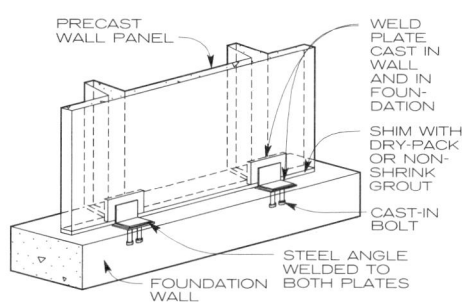

NOTE

Two connections per panel are typical.

WELDED WALL-TO-FOUNDATION CONNECTION

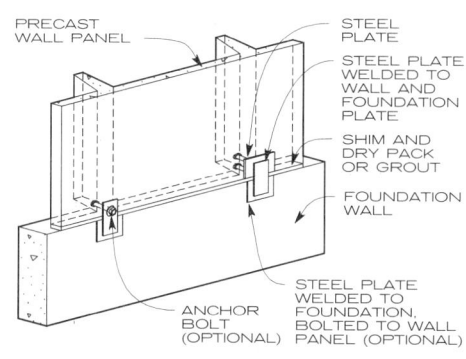

WELDED PLATE-TO-FOUNDATION CONNECTION

Sidney Freedman; Precast/Prestressed Concrete Institute; Chicago, Illinois

PRECAST CONCRETE

Precast Concrete Connections

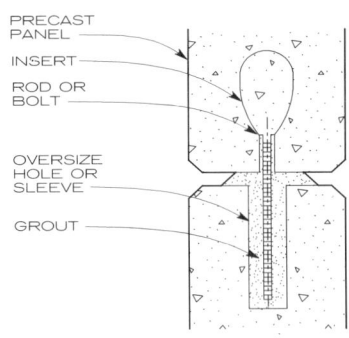

NOTE
Shim stacks occur at two points per panel adjacent to connection.

DIRECT BEARING CONNECTION

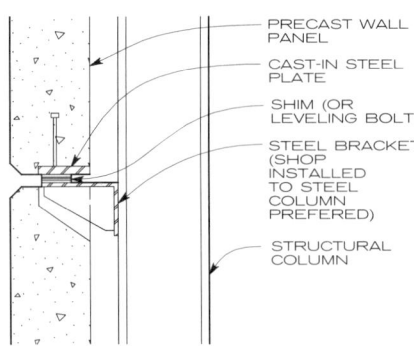

DIRECT BEARING CONNECTION

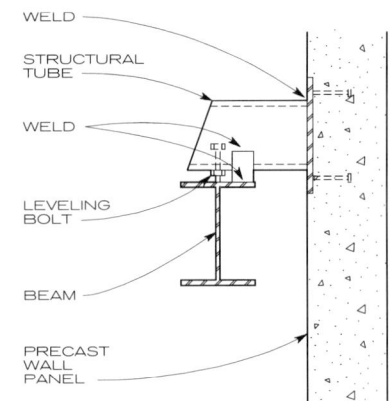

ECCENTRIC BEARING CONNECTION

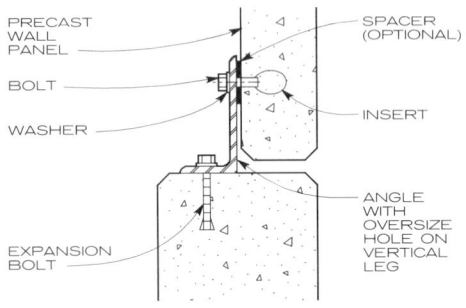

NOTE
Accommodates large tolerance with expansion bolts.

BOLTED TIE-BACK

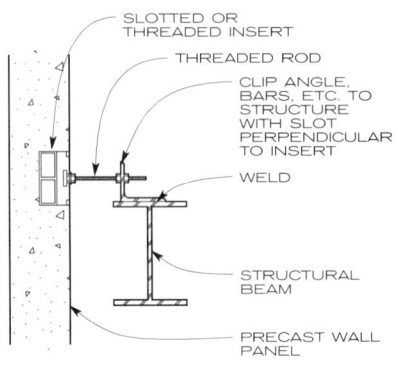

BOLTED TIE-BACK CONNECTION

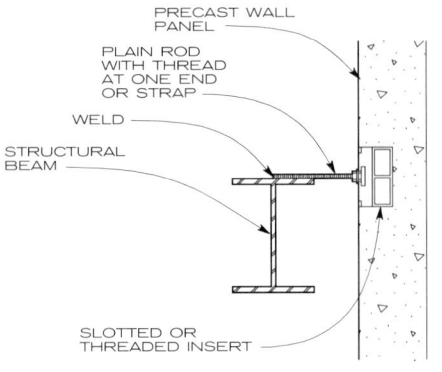

WELDED TIE-BACK CONNECTION

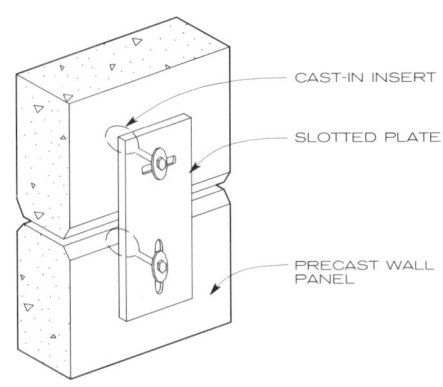

BOLTED ALIGNMENT

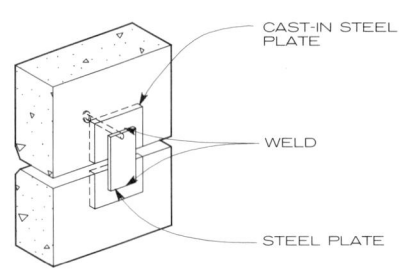

NOTES
1. Good shear transfer.
2. Rigid connection.
3. Possible volume change restraint problems.

WELDED ALIGNMENT

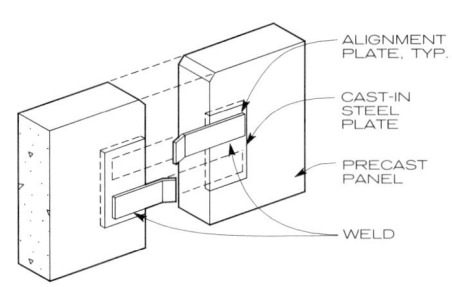

NOTE
Alignment plate is welded to one plate only to allow for possible volume change of panels.

WELDED ALIGNMENT

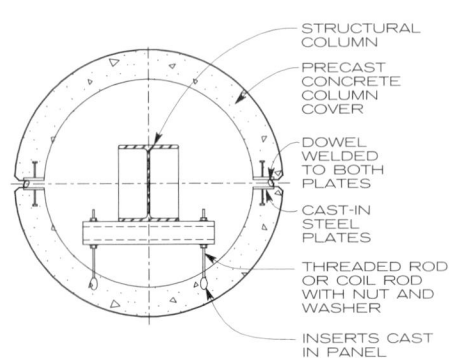

COLUMN COVER CONNECTION

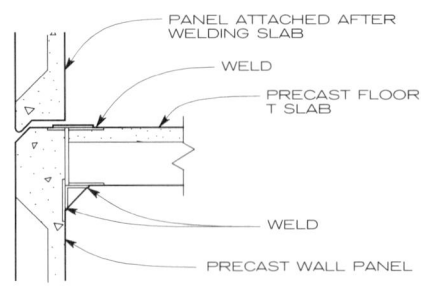

NOTES
1. Avoid use of this detail at both ends of slab to prevent excessive restraint.
2. Rotation of wall elements and effects on bracing wall connections and volume changes must be considered.

SLAB-TO-WALL CONNECTION

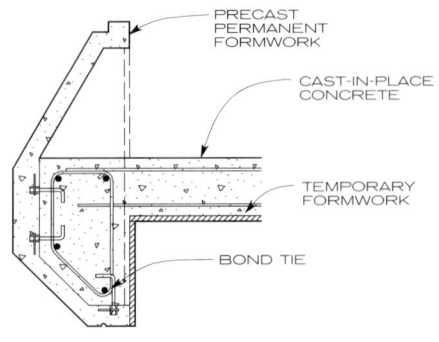

NOTE
One-piece spandrels may require support and restrict placement of concrete.

PRECAST PERMANENT FORMWORK

Sidney Freedman; Precast/Prestressed Concrete Institute; Chicago, Illinois

PRECAST CONCRETE

Tilt-up Concrete

GENERAL

Tilt-up concrete construction is a fast, economical method of enclosing a building with durable, load-bearing walls. The wall panel units are formed and cast horizontally at the job site, on either the building slab floor or on a temporary casting slab. Since the panels do not have to be transported, there are fewer restrictions on panel size. Wood formwork is typically used to define the edges, reveals, details, and openings in the panel. Once the concrete has reached sufficient strength, the panels are lifted, or tilted up, by crane and placed on isolated or continuous foundations (usually grade beams). The panels are braced against the floor slab or a brace foundation until they are tied to the roof and floor system and become an integral part of the completed structure. Although tilt-up concrete construction is mainly restricted to buildings of one story, walls up to four stories tall have been cast and lifted into position.

DESIGN

Panel thickness varies from $5\frac{1}{2}$ to $11\frac{1}{4}$ in. depending on height, loads, span, depth of reveals, surface finish, local codes, and construction practices. Full-height panel widths of 20 ft and weights of 30,000 to 50,000 lb are typical. Spans of 30 ft are common for spandrel panels, as are cantilevers of 10 to 15 ft. Panels are designed structurally to resist lifting stresses, which frequently exceed in-place loads. Floor slab design must accommodate panel and crane loads.

FINISH

Most of the finishes used for factory precast concrete are possible in tilt-up construction. Panels can be cast either face down or face up, depending on desired finish and formwork methods. The face-down method, however, is usually easier to erect. Casting method, desired finish, and available aggregates affect concrete mix design. Control of the concrete mix design and placement of the concrete in the forms are more difficult than with factory-cast units. Discoloration occurs if cracks and joints in the casting are not sealed. Commonly used finishes are as follows:

1. Sandblasting (light, medium, or heavy exposure)
2. Fracture (similar to bushhammered)
3. Form liner (metal deck, plastic, fiberglass, EPS)
3. Paint (usually textured)
4. Brick or tile veneer
5. Aggregate (cast face down in sand bed)

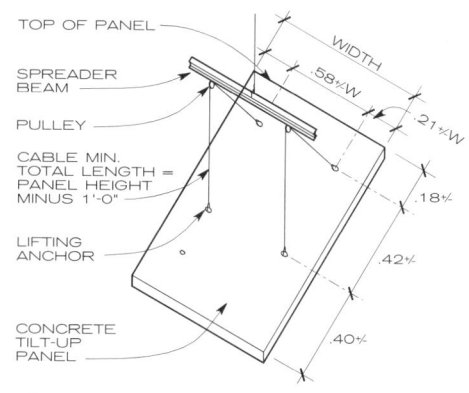

NOTE

The rigging and anchor configuration shown is the most common for tilt-up construction for plain panels without openings. Other configurations may be required depending on the size and shape of the panel; consult a tilt-up construction specialist.

TILT-UP PROCEDURE

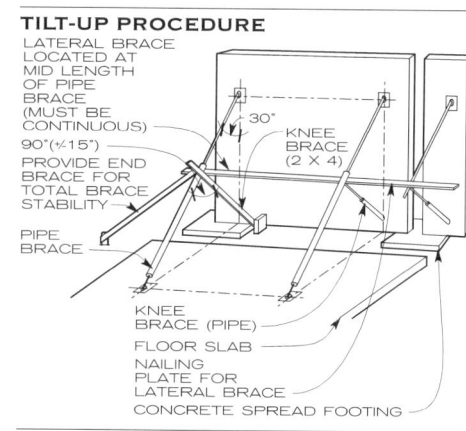

TEMPORARY CONSTRUCTION BRACING

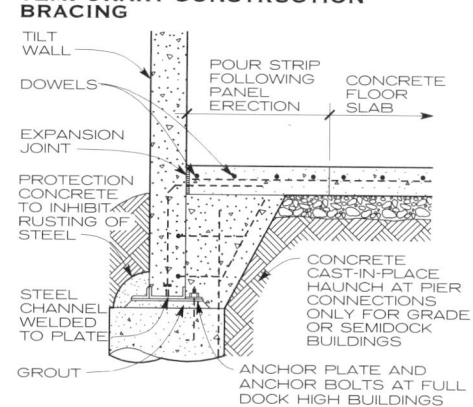

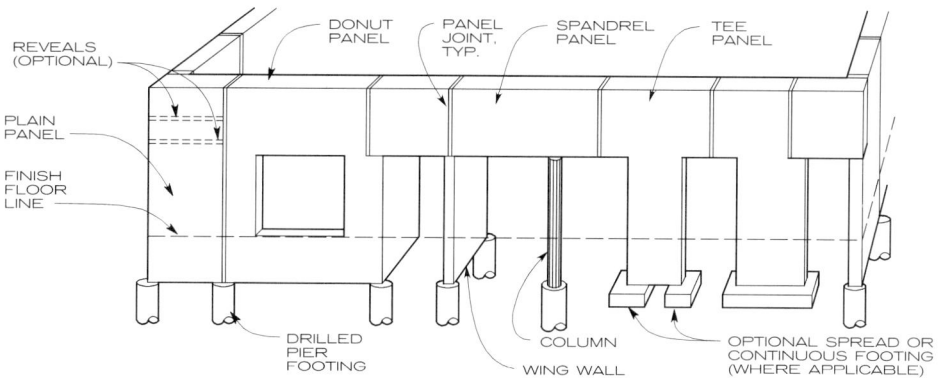

PANEL TYPES

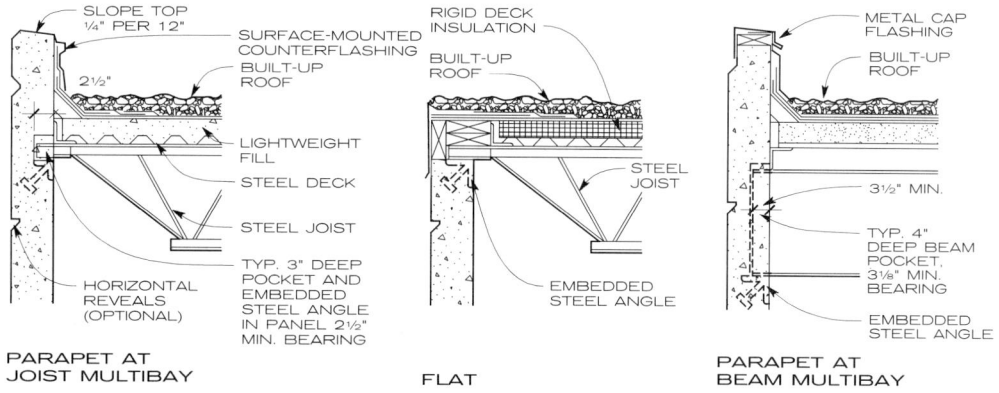

PARAPET AT JOIST MULTIBAY   **FLAT**   **PARAPET AT BEAM MULTIBAY**

LOAD-BEARING PANEL CONNECTIONS AT ROOF (SECTIONS)

PIER CONNECTION (SECTION)

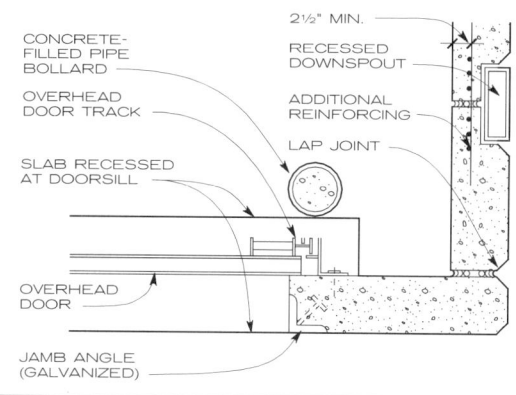

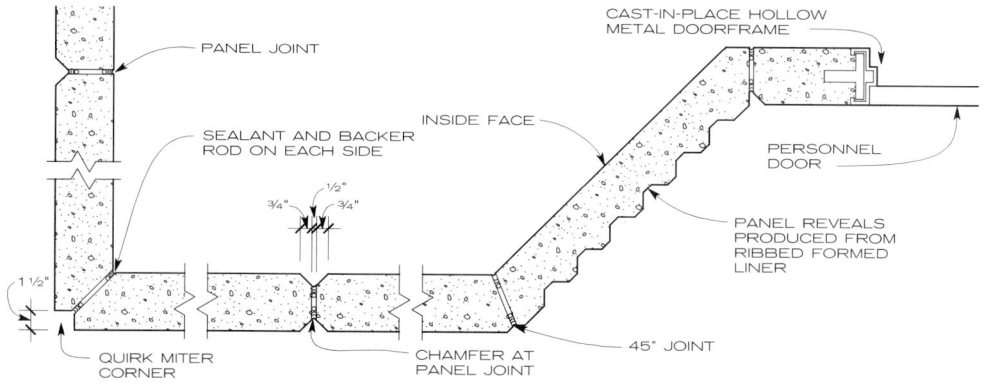

PANEL DETAILS (PLAN)

Haynes Whaley Associates, Structural Engineers; Houston, Texas
Robert P. Foley, P.E.; Con/Steel Tilt-up Systems; Dayton, Ohio

PRECAST CONCRETE

PROPERTIES OF METALS

Basic metals and their alloys are classified in two broad categories, ferrous and nonferrous. Ferrous metals are mainly iron, and nonferrous metal alloys normally contain no iron.

FERROUS METALS

Iron, steel, and their alloys are usually the most cost-effective metal choices for structural applications.

Iron that contains no trace of carbon is soft, ductile, and easily worked, but it rusts in a relatively short time and is susceptible to corrosion by most acids.

The characteristics of the many types of cast iron vary widely among six basic groups: gray, malleable, ductile, white, compacted graphite, and high alloy iron. All cast irons have high compressive strengths, but tensile and yield strengths vary widely depending on basic type. Cast iron is relatively corrosion-resistant but cannot be hammered or beaten into shapes.

Gray irons are rather brittle because they have a high carbon and silicon content. Castings of gray iron possess excellent for damping (absorbing vibrations) and are produced in eight ASTM classes or grades with tensile-strength ratings from 20,000 to 60,000 psi. Applications include decorative shapes, such as fences and posts, gratings, and stair components, as well as utility uses such as manhole covers and fireplugs.

Malleable iron, which is more expensive than gray iron, has been used for decades in applications that require great toughness and high ductility. This low-carbon white iron is cast, reheated, and slowly cooled, or annealed, to improve its workability.

Ductile iron is made by adding magnesium to molten iron shortly before the metal is poured into molds. The magnesium alters the surface-tension mechanism of the molten iron and precipitates the carbon out as small spheres instead of flakes, which make the iron casting more ductile. Ductile iron is less brittle, stiffer, stronger, and more shock-resistant than gray iron. Ductile iron castings are more expensive than gray iron but usually less than malleable iron. Ductile iron is the fastest growing segment of the metal casting industry.

Ductile irons are produced in strength ratings from 55,000 to 130,000 psi. Ductile castings using a special austempering heat-treating process offer much higher tensile strengths, ranging from 125,000 to 230,000 psi. Called ADI castings, they rival or surpass certain alloy steel castings in tensile and yield strengths.

White iron castings, which are extremely hard and brittle, are used primarily in industrial machinery parts that experience high wear and require abrasion resistance.

The characteristics of compacted graphite iron fall between those of gray and ductile iron. The properties of this metal are so difficult to control during production that very few metal casters manufacture it.

High alloy irons are gray, ductile, or white irons with an alloy content of 3 to more than 30%. Their properties are significantly different from those of unalloyed irons.

Wrought iron or steel is relatively soft, corrosion- and fatigue-resistant, and machinable. It is easily worked, making it ideal for railings, grilles, fences, screens, and various types of ornamental work. It is commercially available in bars, rods, tubing, sheets, and plates.

Carbon steel is iron that contains low to medium amounts of carbon. A higher carbon content increases metal strength and hardness but reduces its ductility and weldability. The corrosion resistance of carbon steels is improved by galvanizing, which is a hot zinc dipping process, or applying an organic coating. Some architectural uses include structural shapes such as welded fabrications or castings, metal studs and joists, fasteners, wall grilles, and ceiling suspension grids.

High strength, low alloy (HSLA) steels have better corrosion resistance than carbon steels, and they are chosen when weight is a consideration and higher strength is specified. Low alloy steels are seldom used in exterior architectural applications that involve water runoff because adjacent materials could become stained with rust.

Typical elements used to modify steel include the following:

1. Aluminum for surface hardening.
2. Chromium for corrosion resistance.
3. Copper for atmospheric corrosion resistance.
4. Manganese in small amounts for additional hardening, in larger amounts for better wear resistance.
5. Molybdenum, combined with other metals such as chromium and nickel, to increase corrosion resistance and raise tensile strength without reducing ductility.
6. Nickel to increase tensile strength without reducing ductility; in high concentrations, nickel improves corrosion resistance.
7. Silicon to strengthen low alloy steels and improve oxidation resistance; larger amounts produce hard, brittle castings that are resistant to corrosive chemicals.
8. Sulfer for free machining, especially.
9. Titanium to prevent intergranular corrosion of stainless steels.
10. Tungsten, vanadium, and cobalt for hardness and corrosion resistance.

Stainless steels are at least 11.5% chromium. Nickel is added to boost atmospheric corrosion resistance; molybdenum is added when maximum corrosion resistance is needed, such as when iron will come into contact with sea water. Stainless steel is used in construction for flashing, coping, fasciae, wall panels, floor plates, gratings, handrails, hardware, fasteners, and anchors. Decorative shapes and statuary can be cast in stainless steel.

NONFERROUS METALS

Nonferrous metals and their alloys can be categorized into seven major groups for architectural applications: those based on aluminum, copper (pure copper, brasses, and bronzes), lead, zinc, tin, nickel, and magnesium. Another approach is to divide nonferrous alloys into two groups: heavy metals (copper-, zinc-, lead-, and nickel-based) and light metals (aluminum- and magnesium- based).

ALUMINUM

The nonferrous metal workhorse for architectural applications is aluminum. It has good forming and casting characteristics and offers good corrosion resistance. When exposed to air, aluminum does not oxidize progressively because a hard, thin oxide coating forms on the surface and seals the metal from its environment.

Aluminum and its alloys, numbering in the hundreds, are widely available in common commercial forms. Aluminum alloy sheets can be formed, drawn, stamped, or spun. Many wrought or cast aluminum alloys can be welded, brazed, or soldered, and aluminum surfaces readily accept a wide variety of finishes, both mechanical and chemical.

Although it is light in weight, commercially pure aluminum has a tensile strength of about 13,000 psi. Most aluminum alloys lose strength at elevated temperatures. At subzero temperatures, on the other hand, aluminum is stronger than at room temperature but no less ductile. Cold-working the metal may nearly double its tensile strength. Aluminum can be further strengthened by alloying it with elements such as manganese, silicon, copper, magnesium, zinc, or lithium. The manganese-based aluminum alloy 3003 is used for roofing, sheet metal, siding, and electrical conduit.

BRASS, COPPER, AND BRONZE

Good thermal and electrical conductivity, corrosion resistance, and easy forming and joining all make copper and its alloys useful in construction. However, copper and many of its alloys have relatively low strength-to-weight ratios, and their strength is even further reduced at elevated temperatures. These metals are offered in rod, plate, strip, sheet, and tube shapes; forgings; castings; and electrical wire.

These metals can be grouped according to composition in several general categories: copper, high-copper alloys, and many types of brass and bronze. Monel metal is a copper-nickel alloy that offers excellent corrosion resistance; it is often used for corrosion-resistant fasteners.

Bronze originally was a copper-tin alloy, but today there are aluminum bronzes, silicon bronzes, and leaded phosphor bronzes, among others. Phosphor bronze is a copper-tin-phosphorus alloy; and leaded phosphor bronze is composed of copper, lead, tin, and phosphorus.

Brass is copper with zinc as its principal alloying element. It is important to know that some brass alloys may be called bronzes even though they have little or no tin in them. Some common nonbronze brass alloys are commercial bronze (90% copper, 10% zinc), naval brass (60% copper, 29% zinc, and 1% tin), Muntz metal (60% copper, 40% zinc), and manganese bronze (58% copper, 39% zinc, and 1% tin and iron). When a metal is identified as bronze, the alloy cannot contain zinc or nickel; if it does, it is probably brass. Architectural brasses and bronzes are actually all brasses; they are used for doors, windows, door and window frames, railings, trim and grilles, and finish hardware. Muntz metal, also called malleable brass, is a bronze alloy resembling extruded architectural bronze in color. It is available in sheet and strip and is used in flat surfaces in architectural compositions in connection with extruded architectural bronze.

Copper-based alloys characteristically form adherent films that are relatively impervious to corrosion and protect the base metal from further attack. Certain alloy systems darken rather rapidly from brown to black outdoors. Under most outdoor weather conditions, however, copper surfaces, such as roofs or statuary, develop a blue-green patina. Lacquer coatings can help retain the original alloy color.

LEAD

An extremely dense metal, lead is corrosion-resistant and easily worked. Alloys are added to it to improve properties such as hardness and strength. Typical applications of lead include waterproofing, sound and vibration isolation, and radiation shielding. It can be combined with tin alloy to plate iron or steel, which is commonly called "terneplate." Care should be taken how and where lead is used because lead vapors and lead dust are toxic if ingested.

ZINC

Although it is corrosion-resistant in water and air, zinc is brittle and low in strength. Its major use is in galvanizing (dipping hot iron or steel in molten zinc), although zinc is also used to create sand-cast or die-cast components. Major building industry uses are roofing, flashing, nails, plumbing hardware, structural parts, and decorative shapes.

TIN

Key properties of tin are its low melting point (450° F), relative softness, good formability, and readiness to form alloys. Principal uses for tin are as a constituent of solder, a coating for steel (tinplate, terneplate), and an alloy with other metals that can be cast, rolled, extruded, or atomized. Tin is most popular as an alloy for copper, antimony, lead, bismuth, silver, and zinc. Pewter alloys contain 1 to 8% antimony and 0.5 to 3% copper. Alloy metal in tin solders ranges from 40% lead to no lead and 3.5% silver.

NICKEL

Whitish in color, nickel is used for plating other metals or as a base for chromium plating. Nickel polishes well and does not tarnish. It is also widely applied as an additive in iron and steel alloys as well as other metal alloys. Nickel-iron castings are more ductile and more resistant to corrosion than conventional cast iron. Adding nickel makes steel more resistant to impact.

CHROMIUM

A hard, steel-gray metal, chromium is commonly used to plate other metals, including iron, steel, brass, and bronze. Plated cast shapes can be brightly polished and do not tarnish. Several steel alloys, such as stainless plate, contain as much as 18% chromium. Chromium does not rust, which makes chromium alloys excellent for exterior uses.

MAGNESIUM

Lightest of all metals used in construction, pure magnesium is not strong enough for general structural functions. (For comparison, if a block of steel weighs 1,000 lb, equal volumes of aluminum and magnesium weigh 230 lb and 186 lbs respectively.) Combining other metals such as aluminum with magnesium results in lightweight alloy materials used in ladders, furniture, hospital equipment, and wheels for automobiles.

Robert C. Rodgers, P.E.; Richmond Heights, Ohio

Properties of Metals

METAL CORROSION

Corrosion, which is caused by galvanic action, occurs between dissimilar metals or between metals and other material when sufficient moisture is present to carry an electrical current. The galvanic series shown in the table below is a useful indicator of corrosion susceptibility caused by galvanic action. The metals listed are arranged in order from the least noble (most reactive to corrosion) to the most noble (least reactive to corrosion). The farther apart two metals on the list are, the greater the deterioration of the less noble one will be if they come in contact under adverse conditions.

Metal deterioration also occurs when metals come in contact with chemically active materials, particularly when moisture is present. For example, aluminum corrodes when in direct contact with concrete or mortar, and steel corrodes when in contact with certain treated woods.

Pitting and concentration cell corrosion are other types of metal deterioration. Pitting takes place when particles or bubbles of gas are deposited on a metal surface. Oxygen deficiency under these deposits sets up anodic areas, which cause pitting. Concentration cell corrosion is similar to galvanic corrosion; the difference is in the electrolytes. Concentration cell corrosion can be produced by differences in ion concentration, oxygen concentration, or foreign matter adhering to the surface.

SHAPING AND FABRICATION OF METALS

Many different manufacturing processes are applied to metal to produce structural forms and shapes required in the construction and ornamentation of buildings.

Rolling hot or cold metal between pressurized rollers produces most of the readily available, standard construction material shapes. Baked enamel-coated aluminum is cold rolled to make siding and gutters.

In the extruding process, heated metal ingots or bars are pushed through a die orifice to produce a wide variety of simple and complex shapes. Sizes are limited only by the size or capacity of the die.

Casting is a process in which molten metal is poured into molds or forced into dies and allowed to solidify in the shape of the mold or die. The casting process is used with virtually all metals; however, surface quality and physical characteristics are greatly affected by the metal alloy and casting process selected. Almost all metals can be cast in sand molds. Only aluminum, zinc, and magnesium are ordinarily cast in metal dies in what is called either a die-casting or permanent-mold process. Round, hollow building products such as cast-iron pipe for plumbing and sewer applications are made by centrifugal casting machines.

In the drawing process, either hot or cold metal is pulled through dies that alter or reduce its cross-sectional shape to produce architectural product configurations. Common drawn products are sheets, tubes, pipes, rods, bars, and wires. Drawing can be used with all metals except iron.

Forging is hammering hot metal or pressing cold metal to a desired shape in dies of a harder metal. The process usually improves the strength and surface characteristics of the metal. Aluminum, copper, and steel can be forged.

Machining is used to finish areas of castings or forgings requiring highly precise fits or contours. Shapes can also be machined from heavy plate or solid blocks of metal.

Bending produces curved shapes in tubing, pipe, and extrusions.

Brake forming of metal plate or sheet metal is a process of successive pressings to achieve shapes with straight-line angles.

In the spinning process, ductile types of sheet metal (usually copper or aluminum) are shaped with tools while being spun on an axis.

Embossing and coining are stamped metal with textured or raised patterns.

Blanking is shearing, sawing, or cutting metal sheets with a punch press to achieve a desired configuration.

Perforating is punching or drilling holes through flat plate or sheet metal.

Piercing punches holes through metal without removing any of the metal.

Fusion welding is used to join metal pieces by melting filler metal (welding rod) and the adjacent edges briefly with a torch and then allowing the molten metal to solidify. Two common types of fusion welding are electric-arc and gas. Electric-arc or metallic-arc welding normally uses metal welding rods as electrodes in the welding tool.

Gas welding is also known as oxyacetylene welding because it uses a mixture of oxygen and acetylene to fuel the flames produced by the blowtorch. Oxyacetylene blowtorches are widely used in construction work to cut through metal structural beams and metal plates.

Soldering is a metal joining process that uses either hard or soft solder. The metal pieces being joined together do not melt as they do in the welding process because solders melt at much lower temperatures. Soft solders consist of tin with a high percentage of lead and melt at temperatures of 360° to 370°F. Hard solders are composed of tin and a low content of antimony or silver and melt at temperatures ranging from 430 to 460°F.

Brazing, which is sometimes called hard soldering, also joins two pieces of metal together by torch melting a filler rod material between them. The filler has a high content of copper and melts between 800 and 900°F.

THE GALVANIC SERIES

Anode (least noble) +	Magnesium, magnesium alloys
	Zinc
	Aluminum 1100
	Cadmium
	Aluminum 2024-T4
	Steel or iron, cast iron
	Chromium iron (active)
	Ni-Resist
	Type 304, 316 stainless (active)
	Hastelloy "C"
	Lead, tin
Electric current flows from positive (+) to negative (−)	Nickel (Inconel) (active)
	Hastelloy "B"
	Brasses, copper, bronzes, copper-nickel alloys, monel
	Silver solder
	Nickel (Inconel) (passive)
	Chromium iron (passive)
	Type 304, 316 stainless (passive)
	Silver
	Titanium
Cathode (most noble) −	Graphite, gold, platinum

WEIGHTS OF METALS FOR BUILDINGS

MATERIAL	SPECIFIC GRAVITY	DENSITY (LB/CU FT)	DENSITY (LB/CU IN.)
Magnesium	1.76	110	0.064
Aluminum	2.77	173	0.100
Zinc	7.14	446	0.258
Cast iron	7.22	450	0.260
Wrought iron	7.70	480	0.278
Steel	7.85	490	0.283
Brass	8.47	529	0.306
Copper and bronze	8.92	556	0.322
Lead	11.35	708	0.410

MELTING TEMPERATURES OF METALS

BASE METAL	DEGREES C	DEGREES F
Aluminum	660	1220
Antimony	631	1168
Cadmium	321	610
Chromium	1857	3375
Cobalt	1495	2723
Copper	1083	1981
Gold	1064	1947
Iron	1535	2795
Lead	328	622
Magnesium	649	1200
Manganese	1244	2271
Nickel	1453	2647
Silver	962	1764
Tin	232	450
Zinc	420	788
Zirconium	1852	3366

TYPES AND PROPERTIES OF BRASS

NAME	ARCHITECTURAL BRONZE	COMMERCIAL BRONZE	MUNTZ METAL
Composition (%) Copper (Cu)	56.5	90.0	60.0
Zinc (Zn)	41.25	10.0	40.0
Lead (Pb)	2.25		
Color	Bronze	Bronze	Light yellow
Cold workability	Very poor	Excellent	Fair
Machinability	Good	Poor	Good
Weldability	Poor	Gas, carbon arc, metal arc	Gas, carbon arc, metal arc, spot and seam welding for thin sheets
Hot workability (and soldering and polishing)	Very good	Very good	Very good
Other properties	Excellent forging and free-machining	Very ductile	High strength; low ductility

Robert C. Rodgers, P.E.; Richmond Heights, Ohio

Finishes on Metals

GENERAL

The finishes commonly used on architectural metals fall into three categories:

MECHANICAL FINISHES are the result of physically changing the surface of the metal through mechanical means: the forming process itself or a subsequent procedure performed either before or after the metal is fabricated into an end-use product.

CHEMICAL FINISHES are achieved by means of chemicals, which may or may not have a physical effect on the surface of the metal.

COATINGS are applied as finishes, either to the metal stock or the fabricated product. These coatings either change the metal itself, through a process of chemical or electrochemical conversion, or they are simply applied to the metal surface.

Application environments, service requirements, and aesthetics together determine which metal finish or coating is best to specify. Finishes are usually selected for both appearance and function: Chromium plating on metal bathroom water faucets and handles or baked enamel on sheet metal lighting fixtures, for example, must be attractive as well as functionally protective.

For structural and exterior metal building products, such as steel framing products, metal siding, and outdoor lighting fixtures, function and operating environments are more important criteria. From a design standpoint, it is important to recognize how various finishes and coatings resist wear, corrosion, and erosion. To choose the right coating or finish, architects must know which material or process is best suited for a specific application.

MECHANICAL FINISHES

AS-FABRICATED FINISHES are the texture and surface appearance given to a metal by the fabrication process.

BUFFED FINISHES are produced by successive polishing and buffing operations using fine abrasives, lubricants, and soft fabric wheels. Polishing and buffing improve edge and surface finishes and render many types of cast parts more durable, efficient, and safe.

PATTERNED FINISHES are available in various textures and designs. They are produced by passing an as-fabricated sheet between two matched-design rollers, embossing patterns on both sides of the sheet, or between a smooth roll and a design roll, embossing or coining on one side of the sheet only.

DIRECTIONAL TEXTURED FINISHES are produced by making tiny parallel scratches on the metal surface using a belt or wheel and fine abrasive, or by hand rubbing with steel wool. Metal treated this way has a smooth, satiny sheen.

PEENED FINISHES are achieved by firing a stream of small steel shot at a metal surface at high velocity. The primary aim of shot peening is increasing the fatigue strength of the component; the decorative finish is a by-product. Other nondirectional textured finishes are produced by blasting metal, under controlled conditions, with silica sand, glass beads, and aluminum oxide.

CHEMICAL FINISHES

CHEMICAL CLEANING cleans the metal surface without affecting it in any other way. This finish is achieved with chlorinated and hydrocarbon solvents and inhibited chemical cleaners or solvents (for aluminum and copper) and pickling, chlorinated, and alkaline solutions (for iron and steel).

ETCHED FINISHES produce a matte, frosted surface with varying degrees of roughness by treating the metal with an acid (sulfuric and nitric acid) or alkali solution.

The BRIGHT FINISH process, not used widely, involves chemical or electrolytic brightening of a metal surface, typically aluminum.

CONVERSION COATING is typically categorized as a chemical finish, but since a layer or coating is produced by a chemical reaction, it could be considered a coating as well. Conversion coatings typically prepare the surface of a metal for painting or for receiving another type of finish but are also used to produce a patina or statuary finish. A component is treated with a dilute solution of phosphoric acid or sulfuric acid and other chemicals that convert the surface of the metal to an integral, mildly protective layer of insoluble crystalline phosphate or sulphate or the like. Such coatings can be applied by either spray or immersion and provide temporary resistance to a mildly corrosive environment. They can be specified for gray, ductile, and malleable iron castings as well as steel castings, forgings, or weldments, such as railings and outdoor furniture.

COATINGS

ORGANIC COATINGS on metal can provide protection only or serve both protective and decorative functions. The former category includes primers or undercoats, pigmented topcoats in hidden areas, and clear finishes. Organic coatings serving double duty include pigmented coatings in visible areas, clear finishes used for gloss, and transparent or translucent clear finishes with dyes added.

Organic coatings usually fall under the general categories of paints, varnishes, enamels, lacquers, plastisols, organisols, and powders. Literally hundreds of different organic coating formulations offer an almost unlimited range of properties. Many organic coatings are applied with brushes and rollers, but dipping and spraying of paints account for most industrial and commercial building projects. Dipping is useful for coating complex metal parts, but spraying is used for most architectural applications. Spraying is fast and inexpensive, and new computer-controlled guns can follow even complex curvatures. Conventional spraying, however, has two disadvantages. For one thing, there is no easy, inexpensive way to collect and re-use the coating material. And when solvent-based paints are used, there is the added problem of meeting environmental restrictions.

ELECTRODEPOSITION, an increasingly popular alternative to spraying, is similar to electroplating, except that organic resins are deposited instead of metal. Electrodeposition is based on the principles of electrophoresis—the movement of charged particles in a liquid under the influence of an applied voltage.

Electrodeposition offers several advantages: The coating builds up to a uniform thickness without runs or sags; very little paint is wasted; low levels of volatile organic compounds (VOCs) are emitted; and coatings can be deposited even into deeply recessed areas of a complex shape. Electrodeposition also has disadvantages. Coating thickness is limited, and because only one coat can be applied this way, subsequent coats must be sprayed.

POWDER COATING is perhaps the best known environmentally acceptable painting process. Powder coatings offer several advantages. Because the paints are solventless, they are safer and "greener." In addition, the paints cost less and last a long time.

Powdered paints are formulated in much the same way as solvent-based paints, with the same pigments, fillers, and extenders, but are dry at room temperatures. Heat-reactive or "heat-latent" hardeners, catalysts, or cross-linkers are used as curing agents.

Powder coatings are either thermoplastic or thermosetting. As the term implies, thermoplastic coatings, which include vinyl, polyethylene, and certain polyesters, are melted by heat during application. Before such coatings are applied, the surface must be primed to ensure good adhesion. Thermosetting paints undergo a chemical change; they cannot be remelted by heat. The thermosets do not require a primer. Coating powders include epoxies, polyurethanes, acrylics, and polyesters.

COMPARATIVE APPLICABILITY OF VARIOUS FINISHES FOR ARCHITECTURAL APPLICATIONS

TYPE OF FINISH OR TREATMENT	METAL			
	ALUMINUM	COPPER ALLOYS	STAINLESS STEEL	CARBON STEEL AND IRON
MECHANICAL FINISHES				
As fabricated	Common to all of the metals (produced by hot rolling, extruding, or casting)			
Bright rolled	Commonly used (produced by cold rolling)			Not used
Directional grit textured	Commonly used (produced by polishing, buffing, hand rubbing, brushing, or cold rolling)			Rarely used
Nondirectional matte textured	Commonly used (produced by sand or shot blasting)			Rarely used
Bright polished	Commonly used (produced by polishing and buffing)			Not used
Patterned	Available in light sheet gauges of all metals			
CHEMICAL FINISHES				
Nonetch cleaning	Commonly used on all of the metals			
Matte finish	Etched finishes widely used	Seldom used	Not used	Not used
Bright finish	Limited uses	Rarely used	Not used	Not used
Conversion coatings	Widely used as pretreatment for painting	Widely used to provide added color variation	Not used	Widely used as pretreatment for painting
COATINGS				
Organic	Widely used	Opaque types rarely used; transparent types common	Sometimes used	Most important type of finish
Anodic	Most important type of finish	Not used	Not used	Not used
Vitreous	Widely used	Limited use	Not used	Widely used
Metallic	Rarely used	Limited use	Limited use	Widely used
Laminated	Substantial uses	Limited use	Not used	Substantial uses

NOTE

For more information, see the "Metal Finishes Manual for Architectural and Metal Products," published by the Architectural Metal Products Division of the National Association of Architectural Metal Manufacturers.

Robert C. Rodgers, P.E.; Richmond Heights, Ohio

METAL MATERIALS, FINISHES, AND COATINGS

Finishes on Metals

GENERAL

The two most common methods of applying powdered finishes to metal are spraying and dipping, the same as those used for solvent-based paint. Electrostatic spraying is used to apply powder films from 1 to 5 mil thick. A mixture of air and powder moves from a hopper to a spray gun. The mixture is charged electrostatically as it passes through the spray gun, causing it to stick to any grounded metal object. Powder that falls to the floor is recycled.

For coatings thicker than 5 mil, fluidized-bed dipping is used. The powder is placed in a special tank into which air is blown, turning the powder into a fluid-like mass. Parts are dipped in the "fluid" and baked to cure the finish.

ANODIC COATINGS

Anodic oxides are widely used to protect aluminum and many of its alloys from corrosion. When the metal is anodized in one of a variety of acids, a protective oxide is formed on the surface. Depending on the acid, the oxide may range from thin and nonporous to thick and porous. Three types of anodizing are used for aluminum: chromic, sulfuric, and hardcoat.

CHROMIC ANODIZING results in a relatively soft coating and is the least used of the three types, but it does offer several advantages. It has excellent corrosion resistance, so rinsing is not as important. It is suitable for complex cast parts and offers a coating of the most consistently uniform thickness and the most enduring fatigue strength.

SULFURIC ANODIZING, the most widely used method, produces a harder coating than chromic anodizing, but it can be scratched. It offers a pleasing appearance and can be dyed in several colors. Corrosion resistance is good.

HARDCOAT ANODIZING produces a relatively thick, extremely hard coating that can be dyed in a range of colors. Corrosion resistance is good. Hardcoats are porous, making them suitable as a base for paints and adhesives.

Since all anodic processes produce porous aluminum-oxide coatings, sealing is usually desirable. The coating is immersed in hot water, the oxide is hydrated, and the pores swell shut. Several manufacturers claim that their sealing agents do the same thing through catalytic action at lower temperatures. Chromic- and sulfuric-anodized coatings nearly always are sealed, but hardcoats are not.

VITREOUS COATINGS are composed of inorganic glossy materials (glass). Porcelain enamels are the most commonly used vitreous coating for architectural applications. Although one of the hardest and most durable finishes, they are brittle. Deformation of metal surfaces can cause cracking and splitting. Porcelain enamel coatings come in a wide range of colors and finishes and are typically applied to steel and aluminum (bathtubs, sinks, column covers). Embossed patterns and textures may be applied by altering the metal backing surface or the coating itself.

HOT DIPPING of ferrous metal objects consists of immersing clean parts into a molten bath of the desired coating metal. In general, molten aluminum, lead, zinc, and some alloys can be applied as hot-dip coatings to irons. Each offers specific advantages. Hot-dip coatings are particularly suitable for intricately shaped cast ferrous items such as metal roofing components and nails and other fasteners.

METALLIC PLATING is done by either electrodeposition or electroplating.

In electrodeposition, an electrical current is carried across an electrolyte and an organic resin substance deposited on an electrode (the metal object being painted). In electroplating, the "substance" is a metal, such as chromium, in an electrolyte. Water usually serves as the solvent in the electrolyte. Although chromium is commonly used for plating, many metals can be deposited on the substrate.

Similarly, a wide range of plating quality is available. For example, a thin coating of zinc will protect a metal component from rust or corrosion for a short time. Chromium plating, on the other hand, protects longer and looks better.

Materials widely used to plate complex metal components include bronze, brass, chromium, cadmium, chromates, copper, lead, lead-tin, nickel, phosphates, silver, tin-nickel, and tin-zinc. Not all of these materials can be deposited on all metal substrates. For example, zinc electroplate can be used on steel but not on cast iron. Therefore, coating/substrate compatibility is a crucial consideration in matching coating performance to application requirements. Typical applications for plating include food servicing areas, plumbing fixtures, exterior metal, and architectural products.

LAMINATED COATINGS

Lamination involves bonding preformed plastic films to metals with adhesives. Laminated coatings provide finishes for products such as interior paneling, partitions, and exterior metalwork. Three types of plastic film are widely used: polyvinyl chloride (PVC), polyvinyl fluoride (PVF), and acrylic.

PVC films provide excellent stain and abrasion resistance. Available in five or six colors, these laminates may come with graining or embossing to simulate wood grain, leather, or fabric. Film thicknesses range from 0.004 in. to 0.041 in., but most common and most economical are those from 0.008 and 0.014 in.

PVF films are usually laminated in a thickness of 0.002 in. and have a smooth, medium gloss surface. Despite their thinness, they are very strong, tough, and weather resistant, making them particularly suited to exterior applications such as siding materials. Their color range is limited, but they resist staining and chemical damage well.

Acrylic films are low cost products that stand up well to weather and are widely used for exterior metalwork. They resist UV radiation and yellowing and retain their flexibility with aging. They are usually applied in a thickness of 0.003 in. and are reasonably priced.

REPRESENTATIVE ARCHITECTURAL USES AND COMPARATIVE PROPERTIES OF COATINGS

BINDER TYPE	TYPICAL USES[1]	COST	OUTDOOR LIFE (YEARS)	COLOR STABLE, EXTERIOR	GLOSS RETENTION, EXTERIOR	STAIN RESISTANCE	WEATHER RESISTANCE	ABRASION AND IMPACT RESISTANCE	FLEXIBILITY	WATER REDUCIBLE AVAILABLE	CLEAR AVAILABLE	WELDABLE AS PRIMER
Acrylics												
Solvent-reducible		M	10	yes	G	F	G	G	G	—	yes	yes[2]
Water-reducible:	Residential siding and similar products; cabinets and implements; clear topcoats											
air dried		M	5–10	yes	F	F	G	G	G	yes	yes	yes[2]
baked		M	15–20	yes	G–E	F	G–E	G	G	yes	yes	yes[2]
Alkyds	Exterior primers and enamels	L–M	5–9	no	G	F	F	F	F–G	yes	yes	yes[2]
Cellulose (acetate or butyrate)	Decorative high-gloss finishes	M	NA	yes	G	F	G	G	G	no	yes	no
Chlorinated rubber	Corrosion-resistant paints; swimming pool coatings; protection of dissimilar metals	M	10	yes	F	F	G	G	G	no	no	no
Chloro sulfonated polyethylene	Paints for piping, tanks, valves, etc.	VH	15	yes	NA	F	E	F–G	E	no	no	no
Epoxy	Moisture- and alkali-resistant coatings; non-decorative interior uses requiring high chemical resistance	H–VH	15–20	no	P	G	G–E	E	G	no	no	yes[2]
Fluorocarbons	High-performance exterior coatings; industrial siding; curtain walls	VH	20+	yes	E	E	E	E	G	no	no	no
Phenol formaldehyde	Chemical- and moisture-resistant coatings	M	10	no	F	F	G–E	G–E	G	no	yes	yes[2]
Polyester	Cabinets and furniture; ceiling tile; piping	H	15	some versions	G–E	G–E	G	G–E	yes	yes	no
Polyvinyl chloride	Residential siding; plastisols; industrial siding; curtain walls	H	15	yes	G	F	G–E	G	G–E	yes	no	yes[2]
Silicates (inorganic)	Corrosion-inhibitive primers; solvent-resistant coatings	H	NA	NA	NA	NA	NA	G	G	no	no	yes
Silicone-modified polymers	High-performance exterior coatings; industrial siding; curtain walls	H–VH	15–20	yes	G–E	G	G–E	G–E	G	yes	no	no
Urethane (aliphatic-cured)	Heavy-duty coatings for stain chemical, abrasion, and corrosion resistance	VH	20+	some versions	E	G–E	G–E	G–E	E	yes	yes	yes[2]

L–low; M–moderate; H–high; VH–very high; NA–not applicable or not available; P–poor; F–fair; G–good; E–excellent

[1] All coatings may be shop applied; all may be field applied except solvent reducible acrylics, baked acrylic, cellulose, and fluorocarbons.

[2] For light nonstructural welding only.

Robert C. Rodgers, P.E.; Richmond Heights, Ohio

Economy of Steel

STRUCTURAL ECONOMY OF STEEL FRAMING

The steel industry is in transition from a 36,000 psi (36 ksi) yield strength steel (ASTM A36) base to a 50,000 psi (50 ksi) yield strength steel (ASTM A 572 grade 50) base. The higher yield strength is currently the most common for structural members, while most connection materials, such as angles and plates, are of 36,000 psi yield strength.

The American Institute of Steel Construction *Manual of Steel Construction* maintains column and beam load tables for both 50,000 and 36,000 psi yield strengths.

Several grades of structural carbon steel are available, including "weathering steel," which offers improved atmospheric corrosion resistance. The table below lists the characteristics of the commonly specified structural carbon steels.

STRUCTURAL STEEL DATA

ASTM DESIGNATION	STRENGTH GRADES KSI	ATMOSPHERIC CORROSION RESISTANCE	REMARKS
A 36	36	*	Common in connecting elements
A 572	42, 50, 60, 65	Same as A36	Common in structural members
A 588	42, 46, 50*	4 times that of carbon steel	Most commonly specified "weathering steel"
A 242	42, 46, 50*	5 to 8 times that of carbon steel	Used exposed as "weathering steel"

* 50 ksi normally provided, but reduced for material thicker than 4 in. for A 588, 3/4 in. for A 242.

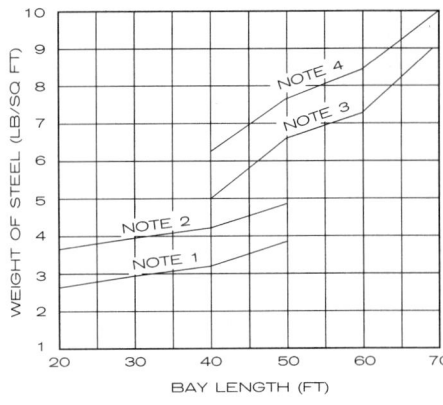

NOTES

1. The roof of a 15-ft high, one-story structure, H-series open-web joists on continuous A572 grade 50 girders (weight of A572 grade 50 columns included). Joist span equals 30 ft.
2. Same as note 1 except that joist span equals 45 ft.
3. Typical level of five-story garage, A572 grade 50 steel throughout (weight of columns included), bay width equals 20 ft.
4. Same as note 3 except that bay width equals 30 ft.

WEIGHT OF NONCOMPOSITE STRUCTURAL STEEL FLOOR OR ROOF

GENERAL NOTES

1. The weight of structural steel per square foot of floor area increases with bay size, as does the depth of the structure. Cost of structural steel may not rise as rapidly as the weight if the number of pieces to be fabricated and erected can be reduced. The improved space utilization afforded by larger bay sizes may be offset by increases in wall area and building volume necessary when structure depth is increased.
2. Steel frame economy can be improved by incorporating as many of the following into the layout and design of a structure as architectural requirements permit:
   a. Keep columns in line in both directions, and avoid offsets or omissions of columns.
   b. Design for maximum repetition of member sizes within each level and from floor to floor.
   c. Reduce the number of beams and girders per level to reduce fabrication and erection time and cost.
   d. Maximize the use of simple beam connections by bracing the structure at a limited number of moment-resisting bents or by the most efficient method, cross-bracing.
   e. Consider composite design and the effects of in-slab electric raceways or other discontinuities.
   f. Consider open-web steel joists, especially for large roofs of one-story structures and for floor framing in many applications.
3. An analysis of alternate framing schemes for a 20 x 40 ft interior bay appears in the table to the left.
4. One constant relationship illustrated in the alternate framing table is the decrease in girder depth when long beams and short girders are used. Steel for roofs or lightly loaded floors is generally the lightest when long beams and short girders are used. For heavier loadings, long girders and short filler beams should result in less steel weight. The most economical framing type (composite, noncomposite, continuous, simple spans, etc.) and arrangement must be determined for each structure, considering such factors as structure depth, building volume, wall area, mechanical system requirements, deflection or vibration limitations, and wind or seismic load interaction between floor systems and columns or shear walls.

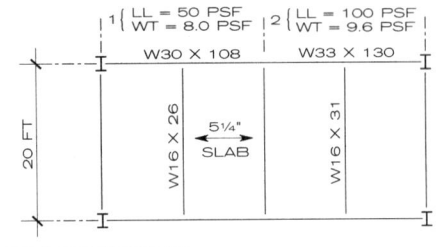

NONCOMPOSITE

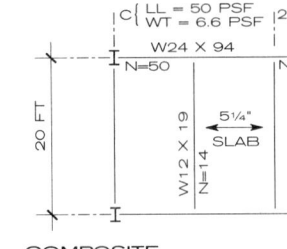

COMPOSITE

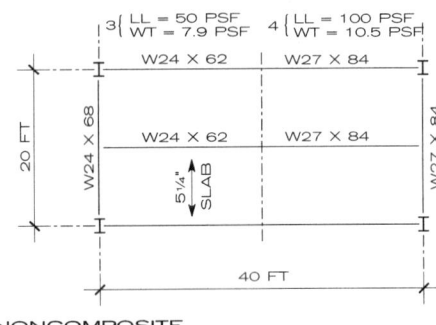

NONCOMPOSITE

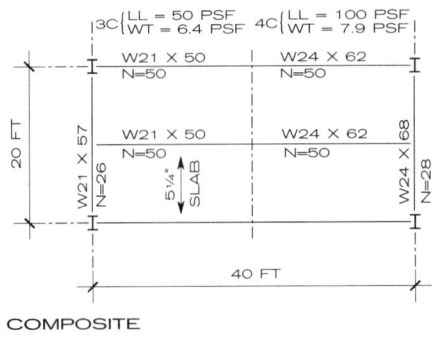

COMPOSITE

STEEL FRAMING LAYOUTS

ALTERNATE FRAMING

	SHORT BEAMS, LONG GIRDERS				LONG BEAMS, SHORT GIRDERS			
	LL = 50 PSF		LL = 100 PSF		LL = 100 PSF		LL = 100 PSF	
	1	1C	2	2C	3	3C	4	4C
Girder depth	30 in.	24 in.	33 in.	30 in.	24 in.	21 in.	27 in.	24 in.
Steel weight per bay (lb)	6400	5280	7680	6080	6320	5140	8400	6320
Weight ratio—Noncomposite: composite	1.21 : 1		1.26 : 1		1.23 : 1		1.33 : 1	
Number of shear studs	0	106	0	154	0	126	0	128
Cost ratio (see note 5)	1.16 : 1		1.19 : 1		1.16 : 1		1.27 : 1	

NOTES

1. Floor slab: 3 1/4 in. lightweight concrete over 2 in. composite metal deck (5 1/4 in. total thickness), all schemes. This provides a 2 hr fire rating without spraying the deck.
2. Additional dead load allowance for finishes, etc.: 30 psf, all schemes.
3. All steel ASTM A572 grade 50.
4. Shear studs: 3/4 in. diameter x 3 1/2 in. long. N=50 means 50 studs per beam.
5. The cost ratio between noncomposite and composite floor steel is approximately 95% of the weight ratio. The cost of studs accounts for the difference.
6. Vibration of floor beams should be analyzed.

American Institute of Steel Construction; Chicago, Illinois

Steel Beams and Columns: Load Table

SAFE TOTAL UNIFORMLY DISTRIBUTED LOAD (KIPS) FOR BEAMS LATERALLY SUPPORTED—ASTM A 572 GRADE 50 STEEL, ALLOWABLE STRESS DESIGN[1]

SPAN LENGTH (FT)	DEPTH[2] WEIGHT	W 6			W 8							W 10				W 10				W 12							W 14		M 14
		9	12	16	10	13	15	18	21	24	28	31	12	15	17	19	22	26	30	33	14	16	19	22	26	30	35	40	22	26	18
6		20	27	37	28	36	43	56	67	77	89	91	40	51	59	69	85	102	119	113	55	63	78	93	112	128	150		106	129	77
8		15	20	28	21	27	32	42	50	57	67	76	30	38	45	52	64	77	89	96	41	47	59	70	92	106	125	141	80	97	58
10		12	16	22	17	22	26	33	40	46	53	60	24	30	36	41	51	61	71	77	33	38	47	56	73	85	100	114	64	78	46
12		10	13	19	14	18	22	28	33	38	45	50	20	25	30	34	43	51	59	64	27	31	39	47	61	71	84	95	53	65	39
14		8.7	11	16	12	16	19	24	29	33	38	43	17	22	25	30	36	44	51	55	23	27	33	40	52	61	72	82	46	55	33
16					11	14	16	21	25	29	33	38	15	19	22	26	32	38	45	48	20	24	29	35	46	53	63	71	40	49	29
18						9	12	14	19	22	26	30	34	13	17	20	23	28	34	40	43	18	21	26	31	41	47	56	63	35	43	26
20							9	11	13	17	20	23	27	30	12	15	18	21	26	31	36	39	16	19	23	28	37	42	50	57	32	39	23
22													11	14	16	19	23	28	32	35	15	17	21	25	33	39	46	52	29	35	21
24													10	13	15	17	21	26	30	32	14	16	20	23	31	35	42	48	27	32	19

[1] For capacity of beams not shown see *AISC Manual of Steel Construction*, 2d ed. (load and resistance factor design) and 9th ed. (allowable stress design).

[2] Depth = steel designation (in.); weight = lb/ft; kip = 1000 lb.

NOTES

1. Consult structural engineer to verify lateral support.
2. Multiply loads by 1.5 to obtain approximate capacities for load and resistance factor design method.

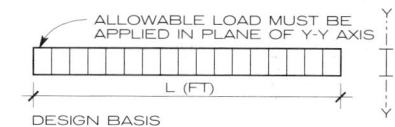

DESIGN BASIS

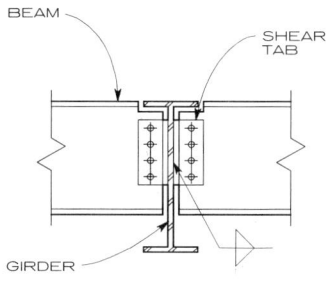

SHOP WELDED TAB FIELD HIGH STRENGTH BOLTED

SHEAR CONNECTION BEAM TO GIRDER

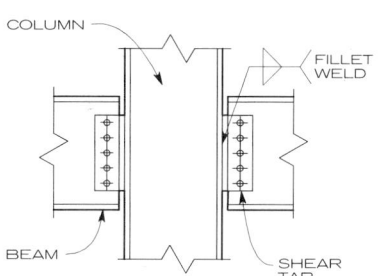

SHOP WELDED TAB FIELD HIGH STRENGTH BOLTED

NONMOMENT CONNECTION BEAM TO COLUMN FLANGE

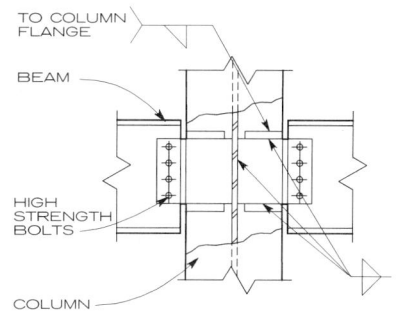

SHOP WEDED TAB TO COLUMN WEB AND PLATES FIELD H.S. BOLTED

NONMOMENT CONNECTION BEAM TO COLUMN WEB

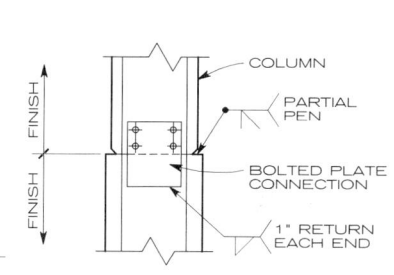

WEB-FIELD H.S. BOLTED FLANGE—PARTIAL PENETRATION

COLUMN SPLICE FLANGE AND WEB

CONNECTIONS AND SPLICES

SAFE TOTAL CONCENTRIC LOAD (KIPS) FOR COLUMNS—ASTM A 572 GRADE 50 STEEL (W SHAPES) AND ASTM A 500 STEEL (TS-SHAPES AND PIPE, 46 KSI), ALLOWABLE STRESS DESIGN*

DESIGNATION	**	6	7	8	9	10	11	12	13	14	15	16	17	18	19	20	22	24
W4	13	79	70	60	49	40	33	28	24	20	18	16						
W6	15	108	102	96	89	82	74	66	57	49	43	38	33	30	27	24	20	17
	20	145	137	129	121	112	102	92	81	70	61	54	47	42	38	34	28	24
	25	182	173	163	152	141	129	117	103	90	78	69	61	54	49	44	36	31
W8	24	178	170	161	152	142	132	121	109	97	85	74	66	59	53	48	39	33
	28	208	198	188	178	166	154	142	128	114	100	88	78	69	62	56	46	39
	31	241	234	226	217	208	199	189	179	168	156	145	132	119	107	97	80	67
Pipe 3", 3.5" O.D.	0.216	38	36	34	31	28	25	22	19	16	14	12	11	10	9			
	0.300	52	48	45	41	37	33	28	24	21	18	16	14	12	11			
	0.600	91	84	77	69	60	51	43	37	32	28	24	22					
Pipe 3.5", 4" O.D.	0.226	48	46	44	41	38	35	32	29	25	22	19	17	15	14	12	10	
	0.318	66	63	59	55	51	47	43	38	33	29	25	23	20	18	16		
Pipe 4", 4.5" O.D.	0.237	59	57	54	52	49	46	43	40	36	33	29	26	23	21	19	15	13
	0.337	81	78	75	71	67	63	59	54	49	44	39	35	31	28	25	21	17
	0.674	147	140	133	126	118	109	100	91	81	70	62	55	49	44	40	33	
Pipe 5", 5.563" O.D.	0.258	83	81	78	76	73	71	68	65	61	58	55	51	47	43	39	32	27
	0.375	118	114	111	107	103	99	95	91	86	81	76	70	65	59	54	44	37
	0.750	216	209	202	195	187	178	170	160	151	141	130	119	108	97	87	72	61
Pipe 6", 6.625" O.D.	0.280	110	108	106	103	101	98	95	92	89	86	82	79	75	71	67	59	51
	0.432	166	162	159	155	151	146	142	137	132	127	122	117	111	105	99	86	73
	0.864	306	299	292	284	275	266	257	247	237	227	216	205	193	181	168	142	119
TS 4 x 4	0.250	83	79	75	70	65	60	55	49	43	38	33	29	26	24	21	18	15
TS 5 x 5	0.250	111	108	104	100	96	92	87	82	77	72	66	60	54	49	44	36	31
TS 6 x 6	0.250	140	137	133	130	126	122	117	113	108	104	99	94	88	83	77	65	55
TS 5 x 3	0.250	76	70	64	58	51	43	36	31	28	23	20	18	16	15			
TS 6 x 4	0.250	107	103	98	92	87	81	75	68	61	54	48	42	38	34	30	25	21
TS 8 x 4	0.250	132	126	120	114	108	101	94	86	79	70	62	55	49	40	33		

* For additional columns and actual dimensions of tubing, see *AISC Manual of Steel Construction*, 2d ed. (load and resistance factor design) and 9th ed. (allowable stress design).

** Weight per ft for W columns. Wall thickness for tubing. kip = 1000 lb; K = effective length factor (verify with structural engineering consultant).

NOTE

Multiply loads by 1.5 to obtain approximate capacities for load and resistance factor design method.

American Institute of Steel Construction; Chicago, Illinois

STRUCTURAL METAL FRAMING

W and M Steel Shapes

W SHAPES— DIMENSIONS FOR DETAILING

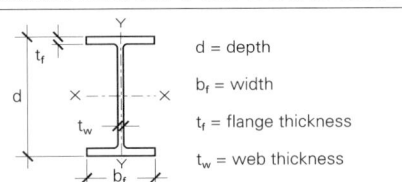

d = depth
b_f = width
t_f = flange thickness
t_w = web thickness

DESIG-NATION	DEPTH (IN.)	FLANGE WIDTH (IN.)	FLANGE THICKNESS (IN.)	WEB THICKNESS (IN.)
W36 x 300	36 3/4	16 5/8	1 11/16	15/16
x 280	36 1/2	16 5/8	1 9/16	7/8
x 260	36 1/4	16 1/2	1 7/16	13/16
x 245	36 1/8	16 1/2	1 3/8	13/16
x 230	35 7/8	16 1/2	1 1/4	3/4
W36 x 210	36 3/4	12 1/8	1 3/8	13/16
x 194	36 1/2	12 1/8	1 1/4	3/4
x 182	36 3/8	12 1/8	1 3/16	3/4
x 170	36 1/8	12	1 1/8	11/16
x 160	36	12	1	5/8
x 150	35 7/8	12	15/16	5/8
x 135	35 1/2	12	13/16	5/8
W33 x 241	34 1/8	15 7/8	1 3/8	13/16
x 221	33 7/8	15 3/4	1 1/4	3/4
x 201	33 5/8	15 3/4	1 1/8	11/16
W33 x 152	33 1/2	11 5/8	1 1/16	5/8
x 141	33 1/4	11 1/2	1 5/16	5/8
x 130	33 1/8	11 1/2	7/8	9/16
x 118	32 7/8	11 1/2	3/4	9/16
W30 x 211	31	15 1/8	1 5/16	3/4
x 191	30 5/8	15	1 3/16	11/16
x 173	30 1/2	15	1 1/16	5/8
W30 x 132	30 1/4	10 1/2	1	5/8
x 124	30 1/8	10 1/2	15/16	9/16
x 116	30	10 1/2	7/8	9/16
x 108	29 7/8	10 1/2	3/4	9/16
x 99	29 5/8	10 1/2	11/16	1/2
W27 x 178	27 3/4	14 1/8	1 3/16	3/4
x 161	27 5/8	14	1 1/16	11/16
x 146	27 3/8	14	1	5/8
W27 x 114	27 1/4	10 1/2	15/16	9/16
x 102	27 1/8	10	13/16	1/2
x 94	26 7/8	10	3/4	1/2
x 84	26 3/4	10	5/8	7/16
W24 x 162	25	13	1 1/4	11/16
x 146	24 3/4	12 7/8	1 1/16	5/8
x 131	24 1/2	12 7/8	15/16	5/8
x 117	24 1/4	12 3/4	7/8	9/16
x 104	24	12 3/4	3/4	1/2
W24 x 94	24 1/4	9 1/8	7/8	1/2
x 84	24 1/8	9	3/4	1/2
x 76	23 7/8	9	11/15	7/16
x 68	23 3/4	9	9/16	7/16
W24 x 62	23 3/4	7	9/16	7/16
x 55	23 5/8	7	1/2	3/8
W21 x 147	22	12 1/2	1 1/8	3/4
x 132	21 7/8	12 1/2	1 1/16	5/8
x 122	21 5/8	12 3/8	15/16	5/8
x 111	21 1/2	12 3/8	7/8	9/16
x 101	21 3/8	12 1/4	13/16	1/2
W21 x 93	21 5/8	8 3/8	15/16	9/16
x 83	21 3/8	8 3/8	13/16	1/2
x 73	21 1/4	8 1/4	3/4	7/16
x 68	21 1/8	8 1/4	11/16	7/16
x 62	21	8 1/4	5/8	3/8
W21 x 57	21	6 1/2	5/8	3/8
x 50	20 7/8	6 1/2	9/16	3/8
x 44	20 5/8	6 1/2	7/16	3/8
W18 x 119	19	11 1/4	1 1/16	5/8
x 106	3/4	11 1/4	15/16	9/16
x 97	18 5/8	11 1/8	7/8	9/16
x 86	18 3/8	11 1/8	3/4	1/2
x 76	18 1/4	11	11/16	7/16
W18 x 71	18 1/2	7 5/8	13/16	1/2
x 65	18 3/8	7 5/8	3/4	7/16
x 60	18 1/4	7 1/2	11/16	7/16
x 55	18 1/8	7 1/2	5/8	3/8
x 50	18	7 1/2	9/16	3/8
W18 x 46	18	6	5/8	3/8
x 40	17 7/8	6	1/2	5/16
x 35	17 3/4	6	7/16	5/16
W16 x 100	17	10 3/8	1	9/16
x 89	16 3/4	10 3/8	7/8	1/2
x 77	16 1/2	10 1/4	3/4	7/16
x 67	16 3/8	10 1/4	11/16	3/8
W16 x 57	16 3/8	7 1/8	11/16	7/16
x 50	16 1/4	7 1/8	5/8	3/8
x 45	16 1/8	7	9/16	3/8
x 40	16	7	1/2	5/16
x 36	15 7/8	7	7/16	5/16
W16 x 31	15 7/8	5 1/2	7/16	1/4
x 26	15 3/4	5 1/2	3/8	1/4
W14 x 730	22 3/8	17 7/8	4 15/16	3 1/16
x 665	21 5/8	17 5/8	4 1/2	2 13/16
x 605	20 7/8	17 3/8	4 3/16	2 5/8
x 550	20 1/4	17 1/4	3 13/16	2 3/8
x 500	19 5/8	17	3 1/2	2 3/16
x 455	19	16 7/8	3 3/16	2
W14 x 426	18 5/8	16 3/4	3 1/16	1 7/8
x 398	18 1/4	16 5/8	2 7/8	1 3/4
x 370	17 7/8	16 1/2	2 11/16	1 5/8
x 342	17 1/2	16 3/8	2 1/2	1 9/16
x 311	17 1/8	16 1/4	2 1/4	1 7/16
x 283	16 3/4	16 1/8	2 1/16	1 5/16
x 257	16 3/8	16	1 7/8	1 3/16
x 233	16	15 7/8	1 3/4	1 1/16
x 211	15 3/4	15 3/4	1 9/16	1
x 193	15 1/2	15 3/4	1 7/8	7/8
x 176	15 1/4	15 5/8	1 5/8	13/16
x 159	15	15 5/8	1 3/8	3/4
x 145	14 3/4	15 1/2	1 1/16	11/16
W14 x 132	14 5/8	14 3/4	1	5/8
x 120	14 1/2	14 5/8	15/16	9/16
x 109	14 3/8	14 5/8	7/8	1/2
x 99	14 1/8	14 5/8	3/4	1/2
x 90	14	14 1/2	11/16	7/16
W14 x 82	14 1/4	10 1/8	7/8	1/2
x 74	14 1/8	10 1/8	13/16	7/16
x 68	14	10	3/4	7/16
x 61	13 7/8	10	5/8	3/8
W14 x 53	13 7/8	8	11/16	3/8
x 48	13 3/4	8	5/8	5/16
x 43	13 5/8	8	1/2	5/16
W14 x 38	14 1/8	6 3/4	1/2	5/16
x 34	14	6 3/4	7/16	5/16
x 30	13 7/8	6 3/4	3/8	1/4
W14 x 26	13 7/8	5	7/16	1/4
x 22	13 3/4	5	5/16	1/4
W12 x 336	16 7/8	13 3/8	2 15/16	1 3/4
x 305	16 3/8	13 1/4	2 11/16	1 5/8
x 279	15 7/8	13 1/4	2 1/2	1 1/2
x 252	15 3/8	13	2 1/4	1 3/8
x 230	15	12 7/8	2 1/8	1 5/16
x 210	14 3/4	12 3/4	1 7/8	1 3/16
W12 x 190	14 3/8	12 5/8	1 3/4	1 1/16
x 170	14	12 5/8	1 9/16	15/16
x 152	13 3/4	12 1/2	1 3/8	7/8
x 136	13 3/8	12 3/8	1 1/4	13/16
x 120	13 1/8	12 3/8	1 1/8	11/16
x 106	12 7/8	12 1/4	1	5/8
x 96	12 3/4	12 1/8	7/8	9/16
x 87	12 1/2	12 1/8	13/16	1/2
x 79	12 3/8	12 1/8	3/4	1/2
x 72	12 1/4	12	11/16	7/16
x 65	12 1/8	12	5/8	3/8
W12 x 58	12 1/4	10	5/8	3/8
x 53	12	10	9/16	3/8
W12 x 50	12 1/4	8 1/8	3/8	5/8
x 45	12	8	5/16	9/16
x 40	12	8	5/16	1/2
W12 x 35	12 1/2	6 1/2	5/16	1/2
x 30	12 3/8	6 1/2	1/4	7/16
x 26	12 1/4	6 1/2	1/4	3/8
W12 x 22	12 1/4	4	7/16	1/4
x 19	12 1/8	4	3/8	1/4
x 16	12	4	1/4	1/4
x 14	11 7/8	4	1/4	3/16
W10 x 112	11 3/8	10 3/8	1 1/4	3/4
x 100	11 1/8	10 3/8	1 1/8	11/16
x 88	10 7/8	10 1/4	1	5/8
x 77	10 5/8	10 1/4	7/8	1/2
x 68	10 3/8	10 1/4	3/4	1/2
x 60	10 1/4	10 1/8	11/16	7/16
x 54	10 1/8	10	5/8	3/8
x 49	10	10	9/16	5/16
W10 x 45	10 1/8	8	5/8	3/8
x 49	9 7/8	8	1/2	5/16
x 33	9 3/4	8	7/16	5/16
W10 x 30	10 1/2	5 3/4	1/2	5/16
x 26	10 3/8	5 3/4	7/16	1/4
x 22	10 1/8	5 3/4	3/8	1/4
W10 x 19	10 1/4	4	3/8	1/4
x 17	10 1/8	4	5/16	1/4
x 15	10	4	1/4	1/4
x 12	9 7/8	4	3/8	3/16
W8 x 67	9	8 1/4	15/16	3/8
x 58	8 3/4	8 1/4	13/16	1/2
x 48	8 1/2	8 1/8	11/16	3/8
x 40	8 1/4	8 1/8	9/16	3/8
x 35	8 1/8	8	1/2	5/16
x 31	8	8	7/16	5/16

M SHAPES— DIMENSIONS FOR DETAILING

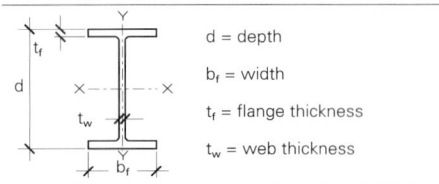

d = depth
b_f = width
t_f = flange thickness
t_w = web thickness

DESIG-NATION	DEPTH (IN.)	FLANGE WIDTH (IN.)	FLANGE THICKNESS (IN.)	WEB THICKNESS (IN.)
M14 x 18	14	4	1/4	3/16
M12 x 11.8	12	3 1/8	1/4	3/16
x 10.8	12	3 1/8	1/4	3/16
x 10	12	3 1/4	3/16	3/16
M10 x 9	10	2 3/4	3/16	3/16
x 8	10	2 3/4	3/16	3/16
x 7.5	10	2 3/4	3/16	1/8
M8 x 6.5	8	2 1/4	3/16	1/8
M6 x 4.4	6	1 7/8	3/16	1/8
M5 x 18.9	5	5	7/16	5/16

American Institute of Steel Construction; Chicago, Illinois

STRUCTURAL METAL FRAMING

S, HP, C, MC, and L Steel Shapes

ANGLES — DIMENSIONS FOR DETAILING

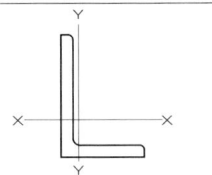

SIZE AND THICKNESS (IN.)		WEIGHT PER FT (LB)	SIZE AND THICKNESS (IN.)		WEIGHT PER FT (LB)
L8 × 8 ×	1 1/8	56.9	L4 × 4 ×	3/4	18.5
	1	51.0		5/8	15.7
	7/8	45.0		1/2	12.8
	3/4	38.9		7/16	11.3
	5/8	32.7		3/8	9.8
	9/16	29.6		5/16	8.2
	1/2	26.4		1/4	6.6
L8 × 6 ×	1	44.2	L4 × 3 1/2 ×	1/2	11.9
	7/8	39.1		7/16	10.6
	3/4	33.8		3/8	9.1
	5/8	28.5		5/16	7.7
	9/16	25.7		1/4	6.2
	1/2	23.0	L4 × 3 ×	1/2	11.1
	7/16	20.2		7/16	9.8
L8 × 4 ×	1	37.4		3/8	8.5
	3/4	28.7		5/16	7.2
	9/16	21.9		1/4	5.8
	1/2	19.6	L3 1/2 × 3 1/2 ×	1/2	11.1
L7 × 4 ×	3/4	26.2		7/16	9.8
	5/8	22.1		3/8	8.5
	1/2	17.9		5/16	7.2
	3/8	13.6		1/4	5.8
L6 × 6 ×	1	37.4	L3 1/2 × 3 ×	1/2	10.2
	7/8	33.1		7/16	9.1
	3/4	28.7		3/8	7.9
	5/8	24.2		5/16	6.6
	9/16	21.9		1/4	5.4
	1/2	19.6	L3 1/2 × 2 1/2 ×	1/2	9.4
	7/16	17.2		7/16	8.3
	3/8	14.9		3/8	7.2
	5/16	12.4		5/16	6.1
L6 × 4 ×	7/8	27.2		1/4	4.9
	3/4	23.6	L3 × 3 ×	1/2	9.4
	5/8	20.0		7/16	8.3
	9/16	18.1		3/8	7.2
	1/2	16.2		5/16	6.1
	7/16	14.3		1/4	4.9
	3/8	12.3		3/16	3.71
	5/16	10.3	L3 × 2 1/2 ×	1/2	8.5
L6 × 3 1/2 ×	1/2	15.3		7/16	7.6
	3/8	11.7		3/8	6.6
	5/16	9.8		5/16	5.6
L5 × 5 ×	7/8	27.2		1/4	4.5
	3/4	23.6		3/16	3.39
	5/8	20.0	L3 × 2 ×	1/2	7.7
	1/2	16.2		7/16	6.8
	7/16	14.3		3/8	5.9
	3/8	12.3		5/16	5.0
	5/16	10.3		1/4	4.1
L5 × 3 1/2 ×	3/4	19.8		3/16	3.07
	5/8	16.8	L2 1/2 × 2 1/2 ×	1/2	7.7
	1/2	13.6		3/8	5.9
	7/16	12.0		5/16	5.0
	3/8	10.4		1/4	4.1
	5/16	8.7		3/16	3.07
	1/4	7.0	L2 1/2 × 2 ×	3/8	5.3
L5 × 3 ×	5/8	15.7		5/16	4.5
	1/2	12.8		1/4	3.62
	7/16	11.3		3/16	2.75
	3/8	9.8	L2 × 2 ×	3/8	4.7
	5/16	8.2		5/16	3.92

American Institute of Steel Construction; Chicago, Illinois

MISCELLANEOUS CHANNELS — DIMENSIONS FOR DETAILING

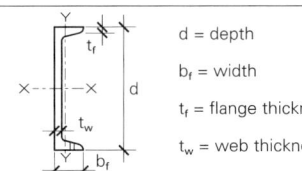

d = depth
b_f = width
t_f = flange thickness
t_w = web thickness

DESIGNATION	DEPTH (IN.)	FLANGE WIDTH (IN.)	FLANGE AVG. THICKNESS (IN.)	WEB THICKNESS (IN.)
MC 18 × 58	18	4 1/4	5/8	11/16
× 51.9	18	4 1/8	5/8	5/8
× 45.8	18	4	5/8	1/2
× 42.7	18	4	5/8	7/16
MC 13 × 50	13	4 3/8	5/8	13/16
× 40	13	4 1/8	5/8	9/16
× 35	13	4 1/8	5/8	7/16
× 31.8	13	4	5/8	3/8
MC 12 × 50	12	4 1/8	11/16	13/16
× 45	12	4	11/16	11/16
× 40	12	3 7/8	11/16	9/16
× 35	12	3 3/4	11/16	1/2
× 31	12	3 5/8	11/16	3/8
MC 12 × 37	12	3 5/8	5/8	5/8
× 32.9	12	3 1/2	5/8	1/2
× 30.9	12	3 1/2	5/8	7/16
MC 12 × 10.6	12	1 1/2	5/8	3/16
MC 10 × 41.1	10	4 3/8	9/16	13/16
× 33.6	10	4 1/8	9/16	9/16
× 28.5	10	4	9/16	7/16
× 25	10	3 3/8	9/16	3/8
× 22	10	3 3/8	9/16	5/16
MC 10 × 8.4	10	1 1/2	1/4	3/16
MC 10 × 6.5	10	1 1/8	3/8	1/8
MC 9 × 25.4	9	3 1/2	7/16	9/16
× 23.9	9	3 1/2	3/8	9/16
MC 8 × 22.8	8	3 1/2	7/16	1/2
× 21.4	8	3 1/2	3/8	1/2
MC 8 × 20	8	3	3/8	1/2
× 18.7	8	3	3/8	1/2
MC 8 × 8.5	8	1 7/8	3/16	5/16

HP SHAPES — DIMENSIONS FOR DETAILING

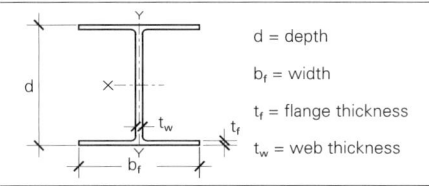

d = depth
b_f = width
t_f = flange thickness
t_w = web thickness

DESIGNATION	DEPTH (IN.)	FLANGE WIDTH (IN.)	FLANGE AVG. THICKNESS (IN.)	WEB THICKNESS (IN.)
HP 14 × 117	14 1/4	14 7/8	13/16	13/16
× 102	14	14 3/4	11/16	11/16
× 89	13 7/8	14 3/4	5/8	5/8
× 73	13 5/8	14 5/8	1/2	1/2
HP 13 × 100	13 1/8	13 1/4	3/4	3/4
× 87	13	13 1/8	11/16	11/16
× 73	12 3/4	13	9/16	9/16
× 60	12 1/2	12 7/8	7/16	7/16
HP 12 × 84	12 1/4	12 1/4	11/16	11/16
× 74	12 1/8	12 1/4	5/8	5/8
× 63	12	12 1/8	1/2	1/2
× 53	11 3/4	12	7/16	7/16
HP 10 × 57	10	10 1/4	9/16	9/16
× 42	9 3/4	10 1/8	7/16	7/16

S SHAPES — DIMENSIONS FOR DETAILING

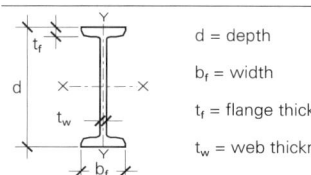

d = depth
b_f = width
t_f = flange thickness
t_w = web thickness

DESIGNATION	DEPTH D (IN.)	FLANGE WIDTH BF (IN.)	FLANGE AVG. THICKNESS TF (IN.)	WEB THICKNESS TW
S24 × 121	24 1/2	8	1 1/16	13/16
× 106	24 1/2	7 7/8	1 1/16	5/8
S24 × 100	24	7 1/4	7/8	3/4
× 90	24	7 1/8	7/8	5/8
× 80	24	7	7/8	1/2
S20 × 96	20 1/4	7 1/4	15/16	13/16
× 86	20 1/4	7	15/16	11/16
S20 × 75	20	6 3/8	13/16	5/8
× 66	20	6 1/4	13/16	1/2
S18 × 70	18	6 1/4	11/16	11/16
× 54.7	18	6	11/16	7/16
S15 × 50	15	5 5/8	5/8	9/16
× 42.9	15	5 1/2	5/8	7/16
S12 × 50	12	5 1/2	11/16	11/16
× 40.8	12	5 1/4	11/16	7/16
S12 × 35	12	5 1/8	9/16	7/16
× 31.8	12	5	9/16	3/8
S10 × 35	10	5	1/2	5/8
× 25.4	10	4 5/8	1/2	5/16
S8 × 23	8	4 1/8	7/16	7/16
× 18.4	8	4	7/16	1/4

AMERICAN STANDARD CHANNELS — DIMENSIONS FOR DETAILING

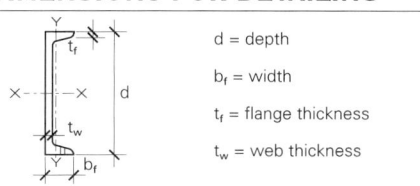

d = depth
b_f = width
t_f = flange thickness
t_w = web thickness

DESIGNATION	DEPTH (IN.)	FLANGE WIDTH (IN.)	FLANGE AVG. THICKNESS (IN.)	WEB THICKNESS (IN.)
C 15 × 50	15	3 3/4	5/8	11/16
× 40	15	3 1/2	5/8	1/2
× 33.9	15	3 3/8	5/8	3/8
C 12 × 30	12	3	1/2	1/2
× 25	12	3	1/2	3/8
× 20.7	12	3	1/2	5/16
C 10 × 30	10	3	7/16	11/16
× 25	10	2 7/8	7/16	1/2
× 20	10	2 3/4	7/16	3/8
× 15.3	10	2 5/8	7/16	1/4
C 9 × 20	9	2 5/8	7/16	7/16
× 15	9	2 1/2	7/16	5/16
× 13.4	9	2 3/8	7/16	1/4
C 8 × 18.75	8	2 1/2	3/8	1/2
× 13.75	8	2 3/8	3/8	5/16
× 11.5	8	2 1/4	3/8	1/4
C 7 × 14.75	7	2 1/4	3/8	7/16
× 12.25	7	2 1/4	3/8	5/16
× 9.8	7	2 1/8	3/8	3/16
C 6 × 13	6	2 1/8	5/16	7/16
× 10.5	6	2	5/16	5/16
× 8.2	6	1 7/8	5/16	3/16
C 5 × 9	5	1 7/8	5/16	5/16
× 6.7	5	1 3/4	5/16	3/16

STRUCTURAL METAL FRAMING

STRUCTURAL TEES CUT FROM W SHAPES— DIMENSIONS FOR DETAILING

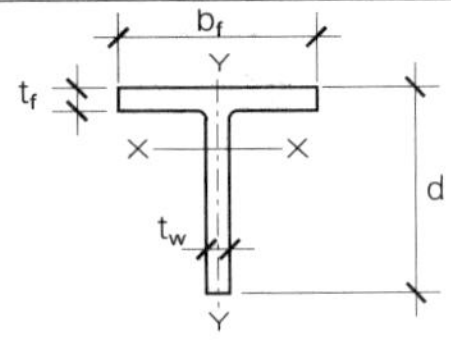

d = depth

b_f = width

t_f = flange thickness

t_w = stem thickness

DESIGNATION		DEPTH OF TEE (IN.)	FLANGE WIDTH (IN.)	FLANGE THICKNESS (IN.)	STEM THICKNESS (IN.)
WT 16.5	x 177	17 3/4	16 1/8	2 1/16	1 3/16
	x 159	17 9/16	16	1 7/8	1 1/16
	x 145.5	17 7/16	15 7/8	1 3/4	1
	x 131.5	17 1/4	15 3/4	1 9/16	7/8
	x 120.5	17 1/8	15 7/8	1 3/8	13/16
	x 110.5	17	15 3/4	1 1/4	3/4
	x 100.5	16 7/8	15 3/4	1 1/8	11/16
WT 16.5	x 84.5	16 15/16	11 1/2	1 1/4	11/16
	x 76	16 3/4	11 5/8	1 1/16	5/8
	x 70.5	16 5/8	11 1/2	15/16	5/8
	x 65	16 1/2	11 1/2	7/8	9/16
	x 59	16 3/8	11 1/2	3/4	9/16
WT 15	x 117.5	15 5/8	15	1 1/2	13/16
	x 105.5	15 1/2	15 1/8	1 5/16	3/4
	x 95.5	15 3/8	15	1 3/16	11/16
	x 86.5	15 1/4	15	1 1/16	5/8
WT 15	x 74	15 5/16	10 1/2	1 3/16	5/8
	x 66	15 1/8	10 1/2	1	5/8
	x 62	15 1/8	10 1/2	15/16	9/16
	x 58	15	10 1/2	7/8	9/16
	x 54	14 7/8	10 1/2	3/4	9/16
	x 49.5	14 7/8	10 1/2	11/16	1/2
WT 13.5	x 108.5	14 3/16	14 1/8	1 1/2	13/16
	x 97	14 1/16	14	1 5/16	3/4
	x 89	13 7/8	14 1/8	1 3/16	3/4
	x 80.5	13 3/4	14	1 1/16	11/16
	x 73	13 3/4	14	1	5/8
WT 13.5	x 64.5	13 13/16	10	1 1/8	5/8
	x 57	13 5/8	10 1/8	15/16	9/16
	x 51	13 1/2	10	13/16	1/2
	x 47	13 1/2	10	3/4	1/2
	x 42	13 3/8	10	5/8	7/16
WT 12	x 88	12 5/8	12 7/8	1 5/16	3/4
	x 81	12 1/2	13	1 1/4	11/16
	x 73	12 3/8	12 7/8	1 1/16	5/8
	x 65.5	12 1/4	12 7/8	15/16	5/8
	x 58.5	12 1/8	12 3/4	7/8	9/16
	x 52	12	12 3/4	3/4	1/2
WT 12	x 51.5	12 1/4	9	1	9/16
	x 47	12 1/8	9 1/8	7/8	1/2
	x 42	12	9	3/4	1/2
	x 38	12	9	11/16	7/16
	x 34	11 7/8	9	9/16	7/16
WT 12	x 31	11 7/8	7	9/16	7/16
	x 27.5	11 3/4	7	1/2	3/8
WT 10.5	x 83	11 1/4	12 3/8	1 3/8	3/4
	x 73.5	11	12 1/2	1 1/8	3/4
	x 66	10 7/8	12 1/2	1 1/16	5/8
	x 61	10 7/8	12 3/8	15/16	5/8
	x 55.5	10 3/4	12 3/8	7/8	9/16
	x 50.5	10 5/8	12 1/4	13/16	1/2
WT 10.5	x 46.5	10 3/4	8 3/8	15/16	9/16
	x 41.5	10 3/4	8 3/8	13/16	1/2
	x 36.5	10 5/8	8 1/4	3/4	7/16
	x 34	10 5/8	8 1/4	11/16	7/16
	x 31	10 1/2	8 1/4	5/8	3/8
WT 10.5	x 28.5	10 1/2	6 1/2	5/8	3/8
	x 25	10 3/8	6 1/2	9/16	3/8
	x 22	10 3/8	6 1/2	7/16	3/8
WT 9	x 71.5	9 3/4	11 1/4	1 5/16	3/4
	x 65	9 5/8	11 1/8	1 3/16	11/16
	x 59.5	9 1/2	11 1/4	1 1/16	5/8
	x 53	9 3/8	11 1/4	15/16	9/16
	x 48.5	9 1/4	11 1/8	7/8	9/16
	x 43	9 1/4	11 1/8	3/4	1/2
	x 38	9 1/8	11	11/16	7/16
WT 9	x 35.5	9 1/4	7 5/8	13/16	1/2
	x 32.5	9 1/8	7 5/8	3/4	7/16
	x 30	9 1/8	7 1/2	11/16	7/16
	x 27.5	9	7 1/2	5/8	3/8
	x 25	9	7 1/2	9/16	3/8
WT 9	x 23	9	6	5/8	3/8
	x 20	9	6	1/2	5/16
	x 17.5	8 7/8	6	7/16	5/16
WT 8	x 50	8 1/2	10 3/8	1	9/16
	x 44.5	8 3/8	10 3/8	7/8	1/2
	x 38.5	8 1/4	10 1/4	3/4	7/16
	x 33.5	8 1/8	10 1/4	11/16	3/8
WT 8	x 28.5	8 1/4	7 1/8	11/16	7/16
	x 25	8 1/8	7 1/8	5/8	3/8
	x 22.5	8 1/8	7	9/16	3/8
	x 20	8	7	1/2	5/16
	x 18	7 7/8	7	7/16	5/16
WT 8	x 15.5	8	5 1/2	7/16	1/4
	x 13	7 7/8	5 1/2	3/8	1/4
WT 7	x 365	11 1/4	17 7/8	4 15/16	3 1/16
	x 332.5	10 7/8	17 5/8	4 1/2	2 13/16
	x 302.5	10 1/2	17 3/8	4 3/16	2 5/8
	x 275	10 1/8	17 1/4	3 3/16	2 3/8
	x 250	9 3/4	17	3 1/2	2 3/16
	x 227.5	9 1/2	16 7/8	3 13/16	2
	x 213	9 3/8	16 3/4	3 1/16	1 7/8
	x 199	9 1/8	16 5/8	2 7/8	1 3/4
	x 185	9	16 1/2	2 11/16	1 5/8
	x 171	8 3/4	16 3/8	2 1/2	1 9/16
	x 155.5	8 1/2	16 1/4	2 1/4	1 7/16
	x 141.5	8 3/8	16 1/8	2 1/16	1 5/16
	x 128.5	8 1/4	16	1 7/8	1 13/16
	x 116.5	8	15 7/8	1 3/4	1 1/16
	x 105.5	7 7/8	15 3/4	1 9/16	1
	x 96.5	7 3/4	15 3/4	1 7/16	7/8
	x 88	7 5/8	15 5/8	1 5/16	13/16
	x 79.5	7 1/2	15 5/8	1 3/16	3/4
	x 72.5	7 3/8	15 1/2	1 1/16	11/16
WT 7	x 66	7 3/8	14 3/4	1	5/8
	x 60	7 1/4	14 5/8	15/16	9/16
	x 54.5	7 1/8	14 5/8	7/8	1/2
	x 49.5	7 1/8	14 5/8	3/4	1/2
	x 45	7	14 1/2	11/16	7/16
WT 7	x 41	7 1/8	10 1/8	7/8	1/2
	x 37	7 1/8	10 1/8	13/16	7/16
	x 34	7	10	3/4	7/16
	x 30.5	7	10	5/8	3/8
WT 7	x 26.5	7	8	11/16	3/8
	x 24	6 7/8	8	5/8	5/16
	x 21.5	6 7/8	8	1/2	5/16
WT 7	x 19	7	6 3/4	1/2	5/16
	x 17	7	6 3/4	7/16	5/16
WT 7	x 13	7	5	7/16	1/4
	x 11	6 7/8	5	5/16	1/4
WT 6	x 168	8 3/8	13 3/8	2 15/16	3/4
	x 152.5	8 1/8	13 1/4	2 11/16	1 5/8
	x 139.5	7 7/8	13 1/8	2 1/2	1 1/2
	x 126	7 3/4	13	2 1/4	1 3/8
	x 115	7 1/2	12 7/8	2 1/16	1 5/16
	x 105	7 3/8	12 3/4	1 7/8	1 3/16
	x 95	7 1/4	12 5/8	1 3/4	1 1/16
	x 85	7	12 5/8	1 9/16	15/16
	x 76	6 7/8	12 1/2	1 3/8	7/8
	x 68	6 3/4	12 3/8	1 1/4	13/16
	x 60	6 1/2	12 3/8	1 1/8	11/16
	x 53	6 1/2	12 1/4	1	5/8
	x 48	6 3/8	12 1/8	7/8	9/16
	x 43.5	6 1/4	12 1/8	13/16	1/2
	x 39.5	6 1/4	12 1/8	3/4	1/2
	x 36	6 1/8	12	11/16	7/16
	x 32.5	6	12	5/8	3/8
WT 6	x 29	6 1/8	10	5/8	3/8
	x 26.5	6	10	9/16	3/8
WT 6	x 25	6 1/8	8 1/8	5/8	3/8
	x 22.5	6	8	9/16	5/16
	x 20	6	8	1/2	5/16
WT 6	x 17.5	6 1/4	6 1/2	1/2	5/16
	x 15	6 1/8	6 1/2	7/16	1/4
	x 13	6 1/8	6 1/2	3/8	1/4
WT 6	x 11	6 1/8	4	7/16	1/4
	x 9.5	6 1/8	4	3/8	1/4
	x 8	6	4	1/4	1/4
	x 7	6	4	1/4	3/16
WT 5	x 56	5 5/8	10 3/8	1 1/4	3/4
	x 50	5 1/2	10 3/8	1 1/8	11/16
	x 44	5 3/8	10 1/4	1	5/8
	x 38.5	5 1/4	10 1/4	7/8	1/2
	x 34	5 1/4	10 1/8	3/8	1/2
	x 30	5 1/8	10 1/8	11/16	7/16
	x 27	5	10	5/8	3/8
	x 24.5	5	10	9/16	5/16
WT 5	x 22.5	5	8	5/8	3/8
	x 19.5	5	8	1/2	5/16
	x 16.5	4 7/8	8	7/16	5/16
WT 5	x 15	5 1/4	5 3/4	1/2	5/16
	x 13	5 1/8	5 3/4	7/16	1/4
	x 11	5 1/8	5 3/4	3/8	1/4

STRUCTURAL TEES CUT FROM S SHAPES— DIMENSIONS FOR DETAILING

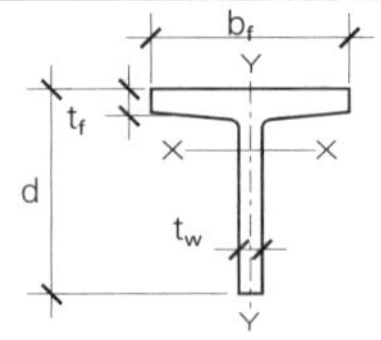

d = depth

b_f = width

t_f = flange thickness

t_w = web thickness

DESIGNATION		DEPTH OF TEE (IN.)	FLANGE WIDTH (IN.)	FLANGE THICKNESS (IN.)	STEM THICKNESS (IN.)
ST 10	x 48	10 1/8	7 1/4	15/16	13/16
	x 43	10 1/8	7	15/16	11/16
ST 10	x 37.5	10	6 3/8	13/16	5/8
	x 33	10	6 1/4	13/16	1/2
ST 9	x 35	9	6 1/4	11/16	11/16
	x 27.35	9	6	11/16	7/16
ST 7.5	x 25	7 1/2	5 5/8	5/8	9/16
	x 21.4	7 1/2	5 1/2	5/8	7/16
ST 6	x 25	6	5 1/2	11/16	11/16
	x 20.4	6	5 1/4	11/16	7/16
ST 6	x 17.5	6	5 1/8	9/16	7/16
	x 15.9	6	5	9/16	3/8
ST 5	x 17.5	5	5	1/2	5/8
	x 12.7	5	4 5/8	1/2	5/16
ST 4	x 11.5	4	4 1/8	7/16	7/16
	x 9.2	4	4 1/8	7/16	1/4
ST 3.5	x 10	3 1/2	3 7/8	3/8	7/16
	x 7.65	3 1/2	3 5/8	3/8	1/4

American Institute of Steel Construction; Chicago, Illinois

Space Frames

GENERAL

A space frame is a three-dimensional truss with linear members that form a series of triangulated polyhedrons. It can be seen as a plane of constant depth that can sustain fairly long spans and varied configurations of shape.

NOTES

1. The prime attributes of space frame structural systems are their light weight; inherent rigidity; their wide variety of form, size, and span; and compatible interaction with other building support systems, primarily HVAC.
2. Most systems are designed for specific applications, and a structural engineer with space frame experience should always be consulted. Manufacturers can provide the full range of capabilities—loading, spans, shapes, specific details—for their products. Standardized systems in 4- and 5-ft modules are available.
3. Metal space frames are classified as noncombustible construction and can usually be exposed when 20 ft above the floor. However, an automatic fire extinguishing system or a rated ceiling may be required. Consult applicable building and fire codes.
4. The finishes commonly available are paint, thermoset polyester, galvanizing, stainless steel, or metal plating.

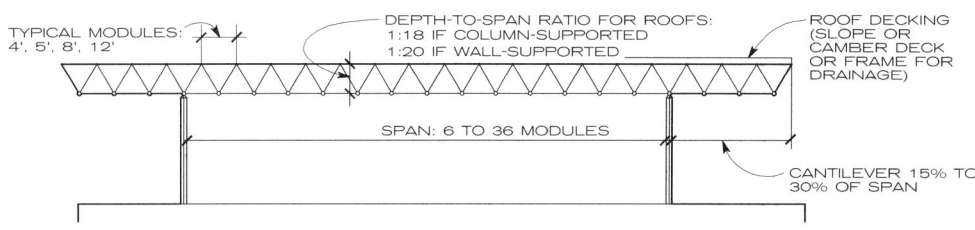

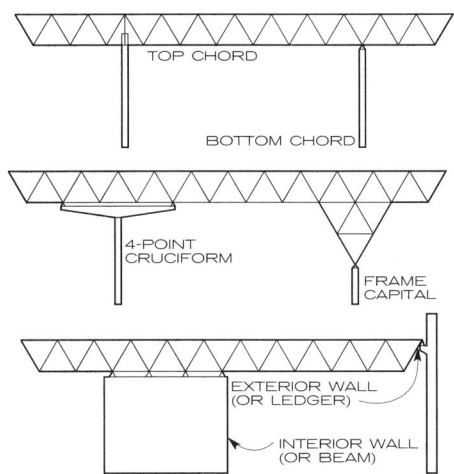

SUPPORT TYPES

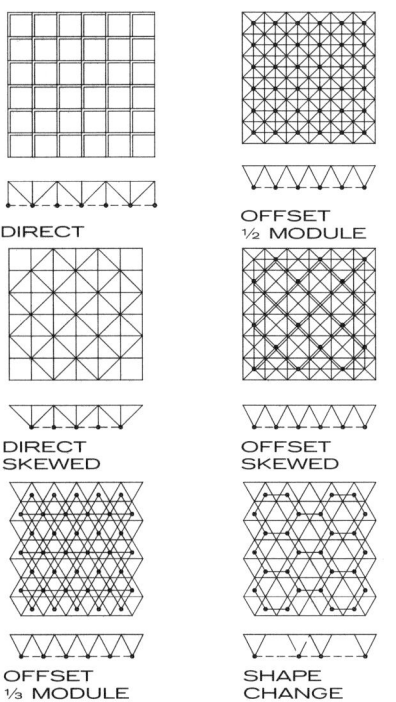

NOTE

Many proprietary node systems are available for specific applications and budgets. Keep field connections to a minimum; welded connections often eliminate joint pieces.

COMMON PATTERNS

NOTE

Select a space frame module that is compatible with the building planning module in shape (e.g., a square module with orthogonal plan) and size (a multiple of the planning module); is consistent with the limitations of the interfacing systems (e.g., the maximum span of the roof deck or mullion spacing of the glazing system); and satisfies the spatial and aesthetic effects in scale and form.

MODULE SELECTION AND CHARACTERISTICS

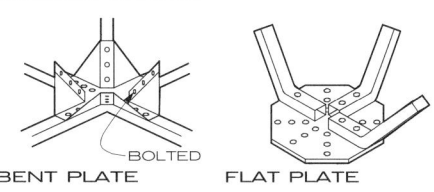

NOTE

Square tubes or angles within their span range are often the most economical.

MEMBER SHAPES

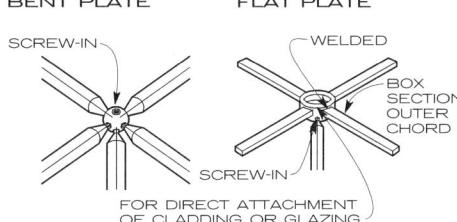

NOTE

Space frame supports are at panel joints only, not along members.

NODE CONNECTIONS

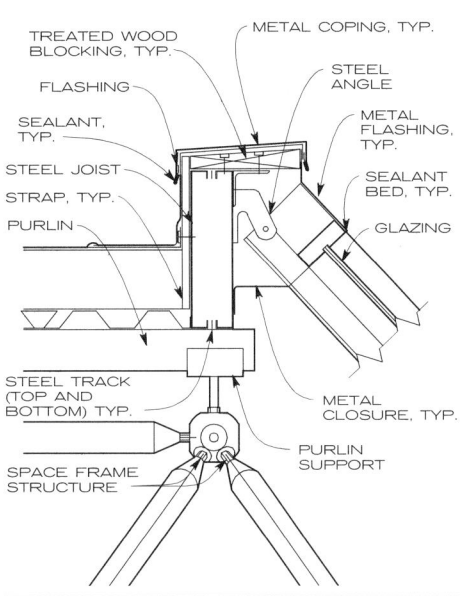

SLOPED GLAZING

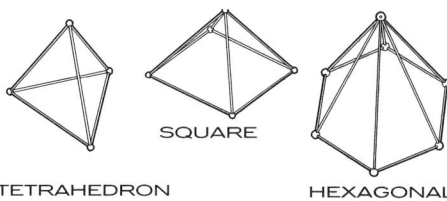

GRID SHAPES

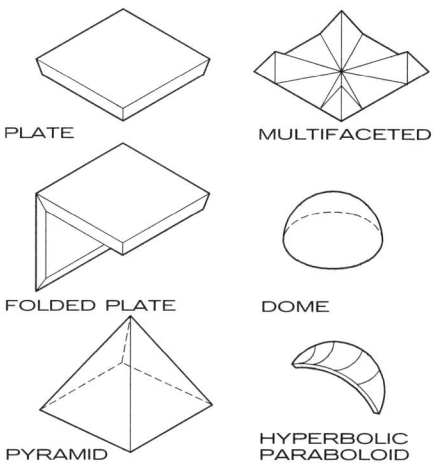

SPACE FRAME FORM TYPES

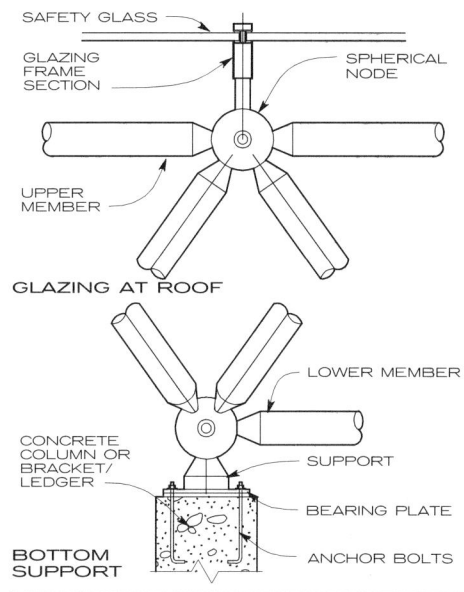

ROOF AND FLOOR CONNECTIONS

Severud Associates; New York, New York

STRUCTURAL METAL FRAMING

Open-Web Steel Joists

PRELIMINARY JOIST SELECTION

The accompanying tables are not to be used for final joist design but are intended as an aid in selecting steel joists for preliminary design and planning. Determining the final design must be a separate and thorough process, involving a complete investigation of pertinent conditions; this page is not intended to support that effort. Consult a structural engineer.

An example of how to use the information presented here follows: Assume a particular clear span. By assuming a joist spacing and estimating the total load, a joist can immediately be selected from the table. Then proceed with preliminary design studies.

NOTES

1. Total safe load = live load + dead load. Dead load includes the weight of the joists. For dead loads and recommended live loads, see pages on weights of materials. Local codes will govern.
2. Span should not exceed a depth 24 times that of a nominal joist.
3. For more information, refer to the standard specifications and load tables adopted by the Steel Joist Institute.

NOTE

The following information applies to both open-web and long-span steel joists.

JOIST DESIGNATION:

```
25  K  10
 |  |   |___ Chord
 |  |_____ K-Series
 |_____ Nominal depth (in.)
```

For greater economy, the K-series joist replaced the H-series joist in 1986.

ROOF CONSTRUCTION: Joists are usually covered with steel decking topped with either rigid insulation board or lightweight concrete fill and either a roof of built-up felt and gravel or single-ply roofing with ballast. Plywood, poured gypsum, or structural wood fiber deck systems can also be used with a built-up roof.

CEILINGS: Ceiling supports can be suspended from or mounted directly to the bottom chords of joists, although suspended systems are recommended because of dimensional variations in actual joist depths.

FLOOR CONSTRUCTION: Joists are usually covered by $2\frac{1}{2}$ to 3 in. of concrete on steel decking. Concrete thickness may be increased to accommodate electrical conduit or electrical/communications raceways. Precast concrete, gypsum planks, or plywood can also be used for the floor system.

VIBRATION: Objectionable vibrations can occur in open web joist and $2\frac{1}{2}$ in. concrete slab designs for open floor areas at spans between 20 and 40 ft, especially at 28 ft. When a floor area cannot have partitions, objectionable vibrations can be prevented or reduced by increasing slab thickness or modifying the joist span. Attention should also be given to support for framing beams, which can magnify a vibration problem when unsupported.

OPENINGS IN FLOOR OR ROOF SYSTEMS: Small openings between joists are framed with angles or channel supported on the adjoining two joists. Larger openings necessitating interruption of joists are framed with steel angle or channel headers spanning the two adjoining joists. The interrupted joists bear on the headers.

ROOF DRAINAGE: On level or near level roofs, especially those with parapet walls, roof drainage should be carefully considered. Roof insulation can be sloped, and joists can be sloped or obtained with top chords that slope in one or both directions. Overflow scuppers should be provided in parapet walls. If roof slope is less than $\frac{1}{4}$ in. per ft, the roof system should be investigated to ensure stability under ponding conditions.

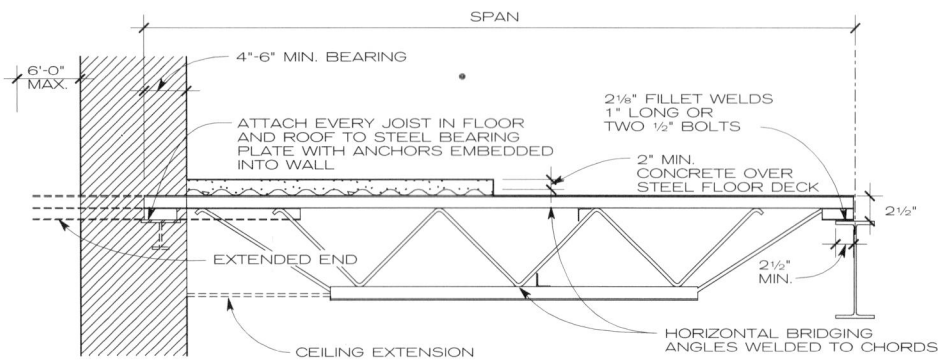

SECTION THROUGH JOIST BEARING

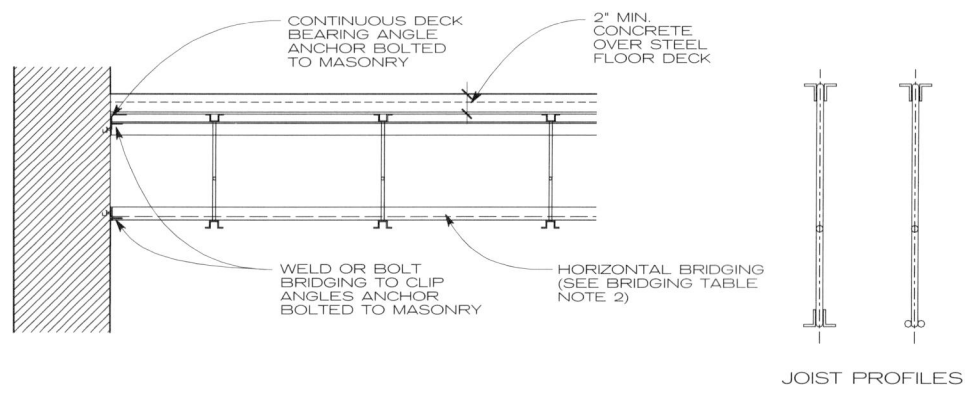

SECTION THROUGH JOISTS

JOIST PROFILES

SELECTED LOAD TABLES: K SERIES—TOTAL SAFE UNIFORMLY DISTRIBUTED LOAD (LB/FT)

JOIST DESIGNATION		8	12	16	20	24	28	32	26	42[1]	48[1]	54[1]	60[1]
K SERIES = 30,000	8K1	550	444	246									
	10K1		550	313	199								
	12K3		550	476	302	208							
	14K4			550	428	295	216						
	16K5			550	550	384	281	214[2]					
	18K6				550	473	346	264	208[2]				
	20K7				550	550	430	328	259				
	22K9					550	550	436	344	252[2]			
	24K9					550	550	478	377	276	211[2]		
	26K10						550	549	486	356	272		
	28K10						550	549	487	384	294	232[2]	
	30K11							549	487	417	362	285[2]	231[2]
	30K12							549	487	417	365	324[2]	262[2]

SPAN (FT)

[1] All joists 40 ft or longer require a row of bolted bridging in place before hoisting lines are slackened.

[2] Where the designed joist span is equal to or greater than this span, the row of bridging nearest the midspan of the joist shall be installed as bolted diagonal bridging. Hoisting cables shall not be released until this bolted diagonal bridging is completely installed.

NUMBER OF ROWS OF BRIDGING

CHORD SIZE[1]	1 ROW[2]	2 ROWS[2]	3 ROWS[2]	4 ROWS[2]	5 ROWS[2]
#1	up to 16	16-24	24-28		
#2	up to 17	17-25	25-32		
#3	up to 18	18-28	28-28	38-40	
#4	up to 19	19-28	28-38	38-48	
#5	up to 19	19-29	29-39	39-50	50-52
#6	up to 19	19-29	29-39	39-51	51-56
#7	up to 20	20-33	33-45	45-58	58-60
#8	up to 20	20-33	33-45	45-58	58-60
#9	up to 20	20-33	33-46	46-59	59-60
#10	up to 20	20-37	37-51	51-60	
#11	up to 20	20-38	38-53	53-60	
#12	up to 20	20-39	39-53	53-60	

[1] Last digit(s) of joist designation shown in accompanying load table.

[2] Check maximum joist span for required midspan bolted diagonal bridging.

NOTE

Distances are clear span dimensions (ft).

Kenneth D. Franch, P.E., AIA; Aguirre, Inc.; Dallas, Texas

METAL JOISTS

Long-Span Steel Joists

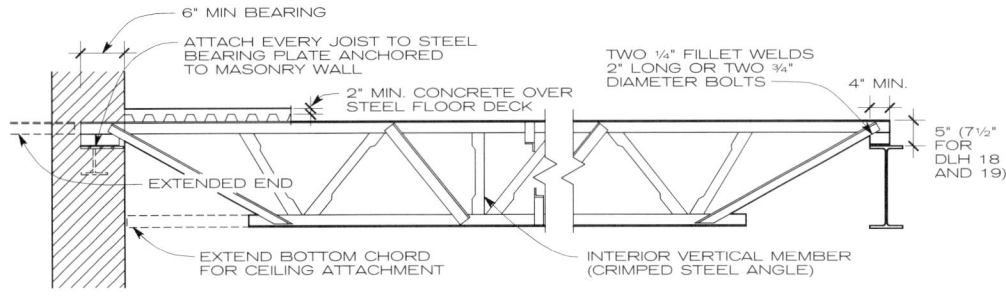

NOTE
Web member type depends on span and load characteristics.

SECTION THROUGH JOIST BEARING

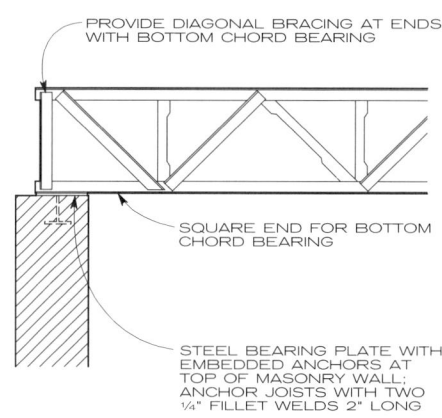

BOTTOM CHORD BEARING AT SQUARE END

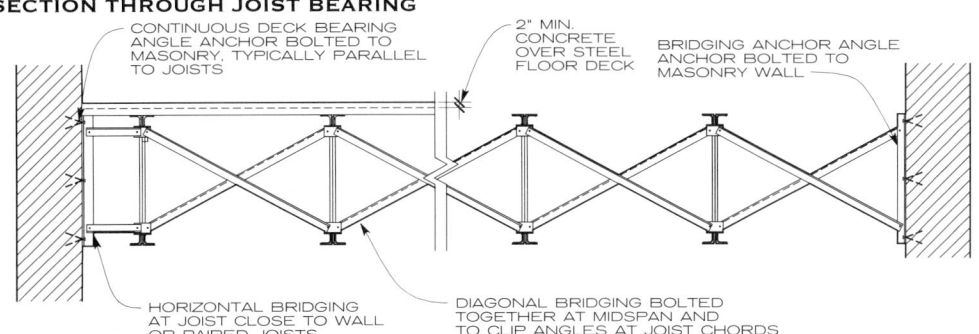

SECTION THROUGH JOISTS

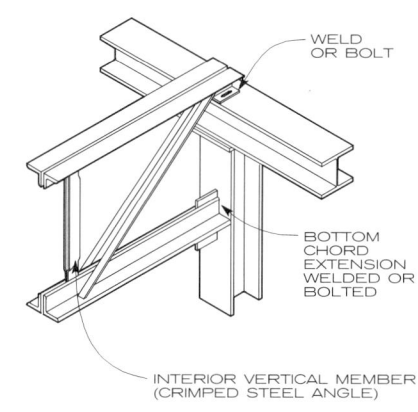

BOTTOM CHORD EXTENSION DETAIL

FIRE RESISTANCE RATING

TIME (HR)	FLOOR/CEILING ASSEMBLIES	TIME (HR)	ROOF/CEILING ASSEMBLIES
1	2½ in. reinforced concrete, listed ⅝ in. gypsum plaster on metal lath attached to bottom chord of joist	1	Built-up roofing on listed 1 in. wood with cement binder fiberboard over 1½ in. metal deck with listed ¾ in. gypsum plaster ceiling on metal lath attached to furring channels hung from joist
	2 in. reinforced concrete, listed ⅝ in. cement plaster over metal lath attached to bottom chord of joist		Built-up roofing on listed 1 in. wood fiberboard over 1½ in. metal deck with listed ¾ in. gypsum plaster ceiling on metal lath attached to furring channels supported from joist
2	2½ in. reinforced concrete, listed ¾ in. gypsum plaster on metal lath attached to bottom chord of joist	2	Built-up roofing on listed 1⅞ in. wood with cement binder fiberboard over 1½ in. gypsum plaster ceiling on metal lath attached to furring channels supported from joist
	2½ in. reinforced concrete, listed ⅝ in. type X wallboard attached to furring channels tied to bottom chord of joist		Built-up roofing on listed 1½ in. wood fiberboard over 1½ in. metal deck with listed ⅞ in. gypsum plaster ceiling on metal lath attached to furring channels supported from joist
	2½ in. reinforced concrete, listed ¾ in. wood fiber gypsum plaster over metal lath on channels secured to joist		Built-up roofing on listed 1 in. expanded perlite board over 1½ in. metal deck with listed ⅞ in. gypsum-vermiculite plaster on metal lath attached to runner channels supported from joist

NOTE
These are abbreviated assembly descriptions. Table 7-C of the Uniform Building Code gives complete descriptions. Underwriters Laboratories and Factory Mutual provide additional system, material, and approval guidelines.

SELECTED LOAD TABLES: LH AND DLH SERIES—TOTAL SAFE UNIFORMLY DISTRIBUTED LOAD (LB/FT)

JOIST DESIGNATION		CLEAR SPAN (FT)											
		28	32	36	42	48	54	60	66	72	78	84	90	96
LH Series $f_f^2 = 30{,}000$ psi	18LH05	581	448	355										
	20LH06	723	560	444										
	24LH07			588	446	343								
	28LH09				639	499	401							
	32LH10					478	389							
	26LH11						451	378	322					
	40LH12							472	402	346				
	44LH13									423	369			
	48LH14										444	390	346	

		90	96	102	108	114	120	126	132	138	144
DLH Series $f_f = 30{,}000$ psi	52DLH13	433	381	338							
	56DLH14			411	368						
	60DLH15				442	398	361				
	64DLH16					466	421	382			
	68DLH17						460	420			
	72DLH18							505	463	426	

NOTE
Number preceding letter is joist depth (32LH10 is 32 in. deep).

PRELIMINARY JOIST SELECTION

The accompanying tables should not be used for final joist design but are intended to speed selection of steel joists for preliminary design and planning.

Determining the final design must be a separate, thorough process, involving a complete investigation of pertinent conditions; this page is not to be used for that purpose. Consult a structural engineer.

An example of how to use the information presented here follows: Assume a particular clear span. By assuming a joist spacing and estimating the total load, a joist can immediately be selected from the table. Then proceed with preliminary design studies.

NOTES
1. Total safe load = live load + dead load. Dead load includes the weight of the joist. For dead loads and recommended live loads, see pages on weights of materials. Local codes will govern.
2. Span should not exceed 24 times the depth of a nominal joist for roofs, 20 times the depth of a nominal joist for floors.
3. For more information, refer to standard specifications and load tables adopted by the Steel Joist Institute.

LH AND DLH BRIDGING

BRIDGING SPACING (FT)	
CHORD SIZE	MAXIMUM SPACING (FT)
02–04	11
05–06	12
07–08	13
09–10	14
11–14	16
15–17	21
18–19	26

NOTE
Welded horizontal bridging is used for typical joist spans. Check joist bridging requirements when joist spans require midspan bolted diagonal bridging. For spans of more than 60 ft, all bridging should be bolted diagonal bridging.

Charles M. Ault; Setter, Leach & Lindstrom, Architects & Engineers; Minneapolis, Minnesota

ALLOWABLE SPANS FOR SINGLE-SPAN FLOOR JOISTS

NOMINAL JOIST SIZE (WITH MIL THICKNESS)	10 PSF DEAD LOAD + 30 PSF LIVE LOAD SPACING O.C. (IN.)			10 PSF DEAD LOAD + 40 PSF LIVE LOAD SPACING O.C. (IN.)		
	12	16	24	12	16	24
2 x 6 x 33	11 ft 7 in.	10 ft 7 in.	9 ft 1 in.	10 ft 7 in.	9 ft 7 in.	8 ft 1 in.
2 x 6 x 43	12 ft 8 in.	11 ft 6 in.	10 ft 0 in.	11 ft 6 in.	10 ft 5 in.	9 ft 1 in.
2 x 6 x 54	13 ft 7 in.	12 ft 4 in.	10 ft 9 in.	12 ft 4 in.	11 ft 2 in.	9 ft 9 in.
2 x 6 x 68	14 ft 6 in.	13 ft 2 in.	11 ft 6 in.	13 ft 2 in.	12 ft 0 in.	10 ft 6 in.
2 x 6 x 97	16 ft 1 in.	14 ft 7 in.	12 ft 9 in.	14 ft 7 in.	13 ft 3 in.	11 ft 7 in.
2 x 8 x 33	15 ft 8 in.	13 ft 3 in.	8 ft 10 in.	14 ft 0 in.	10 ft 7 in.	7 ft 1 in.
2 x 8 x 43	17 ft 1 in.	15 ft 6 in.	13 ft 7 in.	15 ft 6 in.	14 ft 1 in.	12 ft 3 in.
2 x 8 x 54	18 ft 4 in.	16 ft 8 in.	14 ft 7 in.	16 ft 8 in.	15 ft 2 in.	13 ft 3 in.
2 x 8 x 68	19 ft 8 in.	17 ft 11 in.	15 ft 7 in.	17 ft 11 in.	16 ft 3 in.	14 ft 2 in.
2 x 8 x 97	21 ft 10 in.	19 ft 10 in.	17 ft 4 in.	19 ft 10 in.	18 ft 0 in.	15 ft 9 in.
2 x 10 x 43	20 ft 6 in.	18 ft 8 in.	15 ft 3 in.	18 ft 8 in.	16 ft 8 in.	13 ft 1 in.
2 x 10 x 54	22 ft 1 in.	20 ft 1 in.	17 ft 6 in.	20 ft 1 in.	18 ft 3 in.	15 ft 11 in.
2 x 10 x 68	23 ft 8 in.	21 ft 6 in.	18 ft 10 in.	21 ft 6 in.	19 ft 7 in.	17 ft 1 in.
2 x 10 x 97	26 ft 4 in.	23 ft 11 in.	20 ft 11 in.	23 ft 11 in.	21 ft 9 in.	19 ft 0 in.
2 x 12 x 43	23 ft 5 in.	20 ft 3 in.	14 ft 1 in.	20 ft 11 in.	16 ft 10 in.	11 ft 3 in.
2 x 12 x 54	25 ft 9 in.	23 ft 4 in.	19 ft 7 in.	23 ft 4 in.	21 ft 3 in.	17 ft 6 in.
2 x 12 x 68	27 ft 8 in.	25 ft 1 in.	21 ft 11 in.	25 ft 1 in.	22 ft 10 in.	19 ft 11 in.
2 x 12 x 97	30 ft 9 in.	27 ft 11 in.	24 ft 5 in.	27 ft 11 in.	25 ft 4 in.	22 ft 2 in.

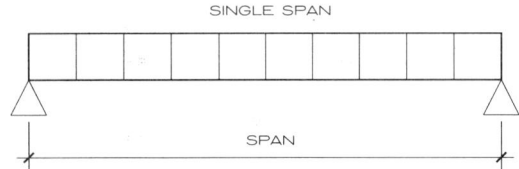

SINGLE SPAN

ALLOWABLE SPANS FOR MULTIPLE-SPAN FLOOR JOISTS

NOMINAL JOIST SIZE (WITH MIL THICKNESS)	10 PSF DEAD LOAD + 30 PSF LIVE LOAD SPACING O.C. (IN.)			10 PSF DEAD LOAD + 40 PSF LIVE LOAD SPACING O.C. (IN.)		
	12	16	24	12	16	24
2 x 6 x 33	12 ft 10 in.	10 ft 6 in.	7 ft 10 in.	11 ft 0 in.	9 ft 0 in.	6 ft 7 in.
2 x 6 x 43	15 ft 8 in.	13 ft 6 in.	11 ft 0 in.	14 ft 0 in.	12 ft 1 in.	9 ft 10 in.
2 x 6 x 54	17 ft 7 in.	15 ft 3 in.	12 ft 5 in.	15 ft 9 in.	13 ft 8 in.	11 ft 2 in.
2 x 6 x 68	19 ft 6 in.	17 ft 2 in.	14 ft 0 in.	17 ft 8 in.	15 ft 4 in.	12 ft 6 in.
2 x 6 x 97	21 ft 7 in.	19 ft 7 in.	16 ft 8 in.	19 ft 7 in.	17 ft 10 in.	14 ft 11 in.
2 x 8 x 33	12 ft 9 in.	10 ft 2 in.	7 ft 1 in.	10 ft 9 in.	8 ft 6 in.	5 ft 8 in.
2 x 8 x 43	19 ft 5 in.	16 ft 8 in.	12 ft 6 in.	17 ft 5 in.	14 ft 3 in.	10 ft 8 in.
2 x 8 x 54	23 ft 0 in.	19 ft 11 in.	16 ft 3 in.	20 ft 6 in.	17 ft 9 in.	14 ft 6 in.
2 x 8 x 68	25 ft 10 in.	22 ft 5 in.	18 ft 3 in.	23 ft 2 in.	20 ft 0 in.	16 ft 4 in.
2 x 8 x 97	29 ft 4 in.	26 ft 7 in.	21 ft 11 in.	26 ft 7 in.	24 ft 0 in.	19 ft 7 in.
2 x 10 x 43	20 ft 3 in.	16 ft 5 in.	12 ft 1 in.	17 ft 3 in.	13 ft 11 in.	10 ft 7 in.
2 x 10 x 54	25 ft 6 in.	22 ft 1 in.	18 ft 0 in.	22 ft 10 in.	19 ft 9 in.	15 ft 6 in.
2 x 10 x 68	30 ft 6 in.	26 ft 5 in.	21 ft 7 in.	27 ft 4 in.	23 ft 8 in.	19 ft 3 in.
2 x 10 x 97	35 ft 4 in.	31 ft 9 in.	25 ft 11 in.	32 ft 1 in.	28 ft 5 in.	23 ft 2 in.
2 x 12 x 43	19 ft 8 in.	15 ft 9 in.	11 ft 3 in.	16 ft 7 in.	13 ft 3 in.	9 ft 0 in.
2 x 12 x 54	27 ft 8 in.	23 ft 9 in.	17 ft 10 in.	24 ft 9 in.	20 ft 4 in.	15 ft 2 in.
2 x 12 x 68	32 ft 7 in.	28 ft 3 in.	23 ft 0 in.	29 ft 2 in.	25 ft 3 in.	20 ft 7 in.
2 x 12 x 97	41 ft 3 in.	36 ft 7 in.	29 ft 10 in.	37 ft 5 in.	32 ft 9 in.	26 ft 9 in.

NOTES

1. The tables above provide maximum joist spans, in feet and inches. For multiple spans, span is either to the right or left of the interior support.
2. Interior bearing supports for multiple span joists should consist of structural (bearing) walls or beams.
3. Bearing stiffeners should be installed at all support points and concentrated loads. End bearing stiffeners are not required for floor joists 54 mil or thicker, spanning 14 ft or less, for one-story houses (walls and roof only) in areas with maximum ground snow load of 30 psf or less.
4. Joists supporting a roof and single wall only may cantilever up to a maximum of 24 in. measured from the centerline of the bearing point, provided that bearing stiffeners are installed at the end of the cantilever and the bearing point and no punchouts are allowed in the cantilevered section. Hole reinforcements may be used to cover up holes.
5. Deflection criteria: L/480 for live loads; L/240 for total loads.

TWO EQUAL SPANS

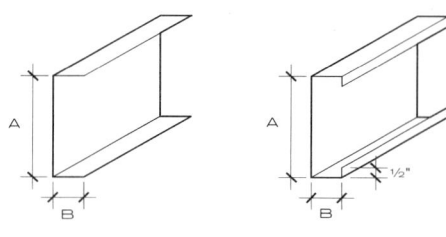

CHANNEL STUDS		C MEMBER	
A (IN.)	B (IN.)	A (IN.)	B (IN.)
2 1/2	1	3 1/2	1 5/8
3 1/4	1 3/8	5 1/2	
3 5/8		8	
4		10	
6		12	

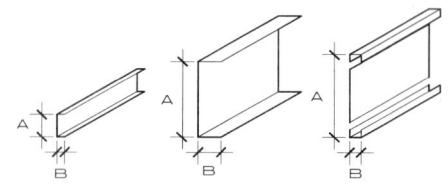

FURRING CHANNEL		C JOIST CLOSURE		NESTABLE JOIST	
A (IN.)	B (IN.)	A (IN.)	B (IN.)	A (IN.)	B (IN.)
3/4	1/2	5 1/2	1 1/4	7 1/4	1 3/4 in.
1 1/2	17/32	6		7 1/2	
		7 1/4		8	
		8		9 1/4	
		9 1/4		9 1/2	
		10		11 1/2	
		12		13 1/2	

Normally available in all joist sizes

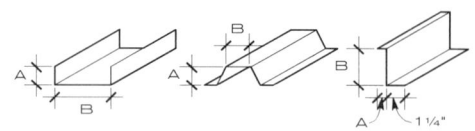

RUNNER CHANNEL		FURRING HAT CHANNEL		Z FURRING	
A (IN.)	B (IN.)	A (IN.)	B (IN.)	A (IN.)	B (IN.)
3/4	2 11/16	7/8	1 3/8	3/4	1
1	3 13/16	1 1/2	1 1/4		1 1/2
1 3/8	3 7/16				2
1 1/4	4 3/16				3
1 1/2	6 3/16				
1 3/4	8 3/16				
3 1/2					

NOTE

Members available in dimensions of 33 through 97 mil.

LIGHT-GAUGE FRAMING MEMBERS

American Iron and Steel Institute; Washington, D.C.

COLD-FORMED METAL FRAMING

Cold-Formed Steel Framing Materials

COLD-FORMED STEEL—MINIMUM MATERIAL THICKNESS

Designation (mil)*	18	27	33	43	54	68	97
Minimum delivered uncoated thickness inches (mm)	0.018 (0.455)	0.027 (0.683)	0.033 (0.836)	0.043 (1.087)	0.054 (1.367)	0.068 (1.720)	0.097 (2.454)
Reference gauge number	25	22	20	18	16	14	12

* 1 mil = 1/1000 in.

CEILING JOISTS ALLOWABLE SPANS—SINGLE SPANS, WITHOUT ATTIC STORAGE

NOMINAL JOIST SIZE	UNBRACED SPACING (IN.)			MID-SPAN BRACING SPACING (IN.)			THIRD-POINT BRACING SPACING (IN.)		
	12	16	24	12	16	24	12	16	24
2 x 4 x 33	9 ft 10 in.	9 ft 2 in.	8 ft 3 in.	11 ft 4 in.	10 ft 4 in.	9 ft 0 in.	11 ft 4 in.	10 ft 4 in.	9 ft 0 in.
2 x 4 x 43	10 ft 8 in.	9 ft 11 in.	8 ft 10 in.	12 ft 4 in.	11 ft 2 in.	9 ft 9 in.	12 ft 4 in.	11 ft 2 in.	9 ft 9 in.
2 x 4 x 54	11 ft 7 in.	10 ft 8 in.	9 ft 6 in.	13 ft 2 in.	12 ft 0 in.	10 ft 6 in.	13 ft 2 in.	12 ft 0 in.	10 ft 6 in.
2 x 4 x 68	12 ft 8 in.	11 ft 7 in.	10 ft 4 in.	14 ft 1 in.	12 ft 10 in.	11 ft 2 in.	14 ft 1 in.	12 ft 10 in.	11 ft 2 in.
2 x 4 x 97	14 ft 11 in.	13 ft 7 in.	12 ft 1 in.	15 ft 6 in.	14 ft 1 in.	12 ft 4 in.	15 ft 6 in.	14 ft 1 in.	12 ft 4 in.
2 x 6 x 33	11 ft 2 in.	10 ft 5 in.	9 ft 5 in.	15 ft 9 in.	14 ft 5 in.	10 ft 0 in.	16 ft 2 in.	14 ft 8 in.	10 ft 0 in.
2 x 6 x 43	12 ft 1 in.	11 ft 2 in.	10 ft 1 in.	16 ft 10 in.	15 ft 7 in.	13 ft 10 in.	17 ft 7 in.	15 ft 11 in.	13 ft 11 in.
2 x 6 x 54	13 ft 0 in.	12 ft 0 in.	10 ft 9 in.	17 ft 11 in.	16 ft 7 in.	14 ft 9 in.	18 ft 10 in.	17 ft 1 in.	14 ft 11 in.
2 x 6 x 68	14 ft 0 in.	12 ft 11 in.	11 ft 7 in.	19 ft 2 in.	17 ft 8 in.	15 ft 10 in.	20 ft 2 in.	18 ft 4 in.	16 ft 0 in.
2 x 6 x 97	16 ft 3 in.	14 ft 11 in.	13 ft 2 in.	21 ft 6 in.	19 ft 10 in.	17 ft 8 in.	22 ft 4 in.	20 ft 3 in.	17 ft 8 in.
2 x 8 x 33*	12 ft 7 in.	11 ft 8 in.	10 ft 6 in.	17 ft 8 in.	16 ft 5 in.	14 ft 9 in.	21 ft 5 in.	19 ft 5 in.	16 ft 7 in.
2 x 8 x 43	13 ft 6 in.	12 ft 6 in.	11 ft 3 in.	18 ft 10 in.	17 ft 6 in.	15 ft 10 in.	23 ft 0 in.	21 ft 2 in.	17 ft 9 in.
2 x 8 x 54	14 ft 4 in.	13 ft 4 in.	11 ft 11 in.	20 ft 0 in.	18 ft 7 in.	16 ft 9 in.	24 ft 4 in.	22 ft 7 in.	20 ft 0 in.
2 x 8 x 68	15 ft 5 in.	14 ft 3 in.	12 ft 9 in.	21 ft 3 in.	19 ft 8 in.	17 ft 8 in.	25 ft 9 in.	23 ft 11 in.	21 ft 4 in.
2 x 8 x 97	17 ft 8 in.	16 ft 2 in.	14 ft 5 in.	23 ft 8 in.	21 ft 10 in.	19 ft 6 in.	28 ft 4 in.	26 ft 3 in.	23 ft 6 in.
2 x 10 x 43*	14 ft 5 in.	13 ft 4 in.	12 ft 1 in.	20 ft 2 in.	18 ft 9 in.	16 ft 11 in.	24 ft 8 in.	22 ft 11 in.	20 ft 6 in.
2 x 10 x 54	15 ft 4 in.	14 ft 2 in.	12 ft 9 in.	21 ft 4 in.	19 ft 10 in.	17 ft 10 in.	26 ft 0 in.	24 ft 2 in.	21 ft 9 in.
2 x 10 x 68	16 ft 5 in.	15 ft 2 in.	13 ft 7 in.	22 ft 8 in.	21 ft 0 in.	18 ft 11 in.	27 ft 6 in.	25 ft 6 in.	23 ft 0 in.
2 x 10 x 97	18 ft 7 in.	17 ft 1 in.	15 ft 2 in.	25 ft 1 in.	23 ft 2 in.	20 ft 9 in.	30 ft 2 in.	27 ft 11 in.	25 ft 1 in.
2 x 12 x 43	15 ft 2 in.	14 ft 1 in.	12 ft 8 in.	21 ft 4 in.	19 ft 10 in.	17 ft 11 in.	26 ft 1 in.	24 ft 3 in.	21 ft 6 in.
2 x 12 x 54	16 ft 1 in.	15 ft 0 in.	13 ft 5 in.	22 ft 7 in.	20 ft 11 in.	18 ft 11 in.	27 ft 6 in.	25 ft 7 in.	23 ft 1 in.
2 x 12 x 68	17 ft 3 in.	15 ft 11 in.	14 ft 4 in.	23 ft 11 in.	22 ft 2 in.	19 ft 11 in.	29 ft 0 in.	27 ft 0 in.	24 ft 4 in.
2 x 12 x 97	19 ft 5 in.	17 ft 10 in.	15 ft 11 in.	26 ft 4 in.	24 ft 4 in.	21 ft 10 in.	31 ft 8 in.	29 ft 4 in.	26 ft 5 in.

* Bearing stiffeners shall be installed at all support points and concentrated loads.

CEILING JOISTS ALLOWABLE SPANS—SINGLE SPANS, WITH ATTIC STORAGE (20 PSF)

NOMINAL JOIST SIZE	UNBRACED SPACING (IN.)			MID-SPAN BRACING SPACING (IN.)			THIRD-POINT BRACING SPACING (IN.)		
	12	16	24	12	16	24	12	16	24
2 x 4 x 33	8 ft 8 in.	8 ft 0 in.	6 ft 0 in.	9 ft 7 in.	8 ft 8 in.	6 ft 0 in.	9 ft 7 in.	8 ft 8 in.	6 ft 0 in.
2 x 4 x 43	9 ft 4 in.	8 ft 8 in.	7 ft 8 in.	10 ft 5 in.	9 ft 5 in.	8 ft 3 in.	10 ft 5 in.	9 ft 5 in.	8 ft 3 in.
2 x 4 x 54	10 ft 0 in.	9 ft 3 in.	8 ft 3 in.	11 ft 2 in.	10 ft 1 in.	8 ft 10 in.	11 ft 2 in.	10 ft 1 in.	8 ft 10 in.
2 x 4 x 68	10 ft 11 in.	10 ft 0 in.	8 ft 11 in.	10 ft 11 in.	10 ft 0 in.	8 ft 11 in.	1 ft 11 in.	10 ft 0 in.	8 ft 11 in.
2 x 4 x 97	12 ft 8 in.	11 ft 7 in.	10 ft 3 in.	13 ft 1 in.	11 ft 11 in.	10 ft 5 in.	13 ft 1 in.	11 ft 11 in.	10 ft 5 in.
2 x 6 x 33*	9 ft 10 in.	9 ft 0 in.	6 ft 0 in.	12 ft 0 in.	9 ft 0 in.	6 ft 0 in.	12 ft 0 in.	9 ft 0 in.	6 ft 0 in.
2 x 6 x 43	10 ft 7 in.	9 ft 10 in.	8 ft 10 in.	14 ft 7 in.	13 ft 4 in.	11 ft 6 in.	14 ft 10 in.	13 ft 5 in.	11 ft 8 in.
2 x 6 x 54	11 ft 3 in.	10 ft 5 in.	9 ft 5 in.	15 ft 7 in.	14 ft 4 in.	12 ft 6 in.	15 ft 11 in.	14 ft 5 in.	12 ft 7 in.
2 x 6 x 68	12 ft 2 in.	11 ft 3 in.	10 ft 0 in.	16 ft 8 in.	15 ft 4 in.	13 ft 5 in.	17 ft 0 in.	15 ft 5 in.	13 ft 6 in.
2 x 6 x 97	13 ft 11 in.	12 ft 9 in.	11 ft 4 in.	18 ft 7 in.	17 ft 1 in.	14 ft 11 in.	18 ft 10 in.	17 ft 1 in.	14 ft 11 in.
2 x 8 x 33	11 ft 0 in.	10 ft 3 in.	9 ft 3 in.	15 ft 6 in.	14 ft 4 in.	12 ft 6 in.	17 ft 10 in.	15 ft 11 in.	13 ft 4 in.
2 x 8 x 43	11 ft 11 in.	10 ft 11 in.	9 ft 10 in.	16 ft 7 in.	15 ft 5 in.	10 ft 8 in.	19 ft 9 in.	16 ft 0 in.	10 ft 8 in.
2 x 8 x 54	12 ft 7 in.	11 ft 8 in.	10 ft 6 in.	17 ft 6 in.	16 ft 33 in.	14 ft 7 in.	21 ft 2 in.	19 ft 3 in.	16 ft 8 in.
2 x 8 x 68	13 ft 5 in.	12 ft 5 in.	11 ft 2 in.	18 ft 7 in.	17 ft 3 in.	15 ft 6 in.	22 ft 6 in.	20 ft 7 in.	18 ft 0 in.
2 x 8 x 97	15 ft 2 in.	13 ft 11 in.	12 ft 5 in.	20 ft 6 in.	18 ft 11 in.	17 ft 0 in.	24 ft 8 in.	22 ft 9 in.	20 ft 1 in.
2 x 10 x 43*	12 ft 7 in.	11 ft 9 in.	10 ft 7 in.	17 ft 9 in.	16 ft 6 in.	14 ft 10 in.	21 ft 7 in.	19 ft 10 in.	17 ft 1 in.
2 x 10 x 54	13 ft 5 in.	12 ft 52 in.	11 ft 2 in.	18 ft 9 in.	17 ft 5 in.	15 ft 8 in.	22 ft 10 in.	21 ft 1 in.	16 ft 9 in.
2 x 10 x 68	14 ft 3 in.	13 ft 3 in.	11 ft 10 in.	19 ft 10 in.	18 ft 5 in.	16 ft 7 in.	24 ft 1 in.	22 ft 4 in.	19 ft 11 in.
2 x 10 x 97	16 ft 0 in.	14 ft 9 in.	13 ft 2 in.	21 ft 9 in.	20 ft 2 in.	18 ft 1 in.	26 ft 3 in.	24 ft 4 in.	21 ft 10 in.
2 x 12 x 43	13 ft 4 in.	12 ft 5 in.	11 ft 2 in.	18 ft 9 in.	17 ft 5 in.	15 ft 8 in.	22 ft 9 in.	20 ft 9 in.	18 ft 0 in.
2 x 12 x 54	14 ft 1 in.	13 ft 1 in.	11 ft 9 in.	19 ft 9 in.	18 ft 5 in.	16 ft 7 in.	24 ft 2 in.	22 ft 5 in.	20 ft 1 in.
2 x 12 x 68	15 ft 0 in.	13 ft 11 in.	12 ft 6 in.	20 ft 11 in.	19 ft 5 in.	17 ft 6 in.	25 ft 6 in.	23 ft 8 in.	21 ft 3 in.
2 x 12 x 97	16 ft 9 in.	15 ft 5 in.	13 ft 10 in.	22 ft 11 in.	21 ft 2 in.	19 ft 0 in.	27 ft 8 in.	25 ft 8 in.	23 ft 1 in.

* Bearing stiffeners shall be installed at all support points and concentrated loads.

NOTES
1. The tables above provide the maximum ceiling joist span in feet and inches.
2. Deflection criteria: L/240 for total loads.
3. Ceiling dead load = 5 psf (0.24 kPa)
4. 1 in. = 25.4 mm, 1 ft = 304.8 mm, 1 psf = 48 Pa.

American Iron and Steel Institute; Washington, D.C.

Cold-Formed Steel Framing—Opening Details

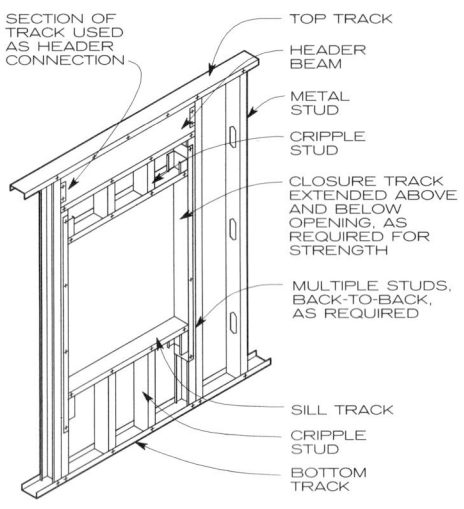

WINDOW OPENING

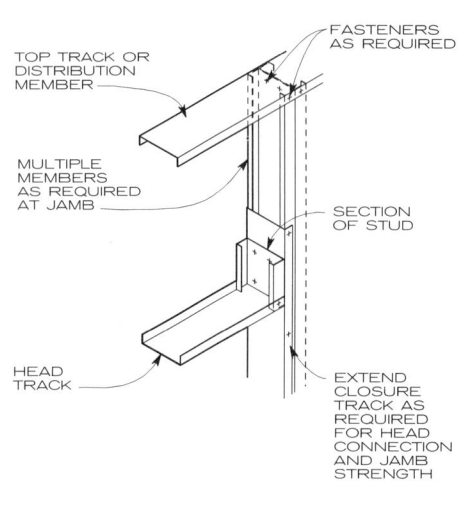

DOORJAMB BASE AT FLOOR FRAMING

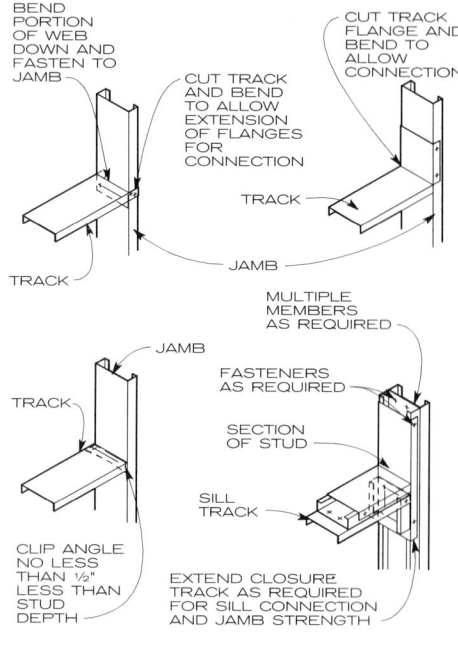

DOOR OPENING

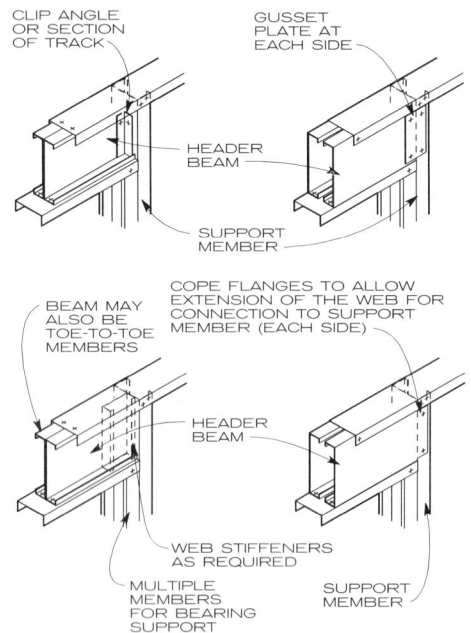

HEADER BEAMS FOR WIDE OPENINGS

NOTE
Detail may be applicable to larger openings in interior partitions. For nonaxial loads.

HEAD AT OPENING LESS THAN 4 FEET (LOAD-BEARING WALL)

SILL CONNECTIONS AT JAMB

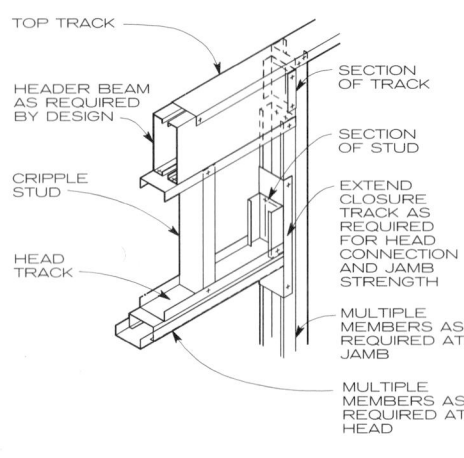

NOTE
For axial loads.

OPENING GREATER THAN OR EQUAL TO 4 FEET (LOAD-BEARING WALL)

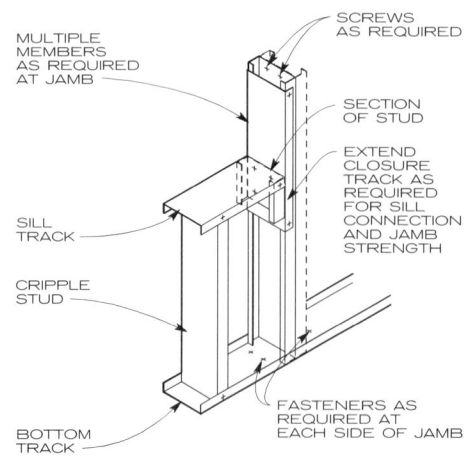

JAMB AND SILL AT OPENING LESS THAN 4 FEET

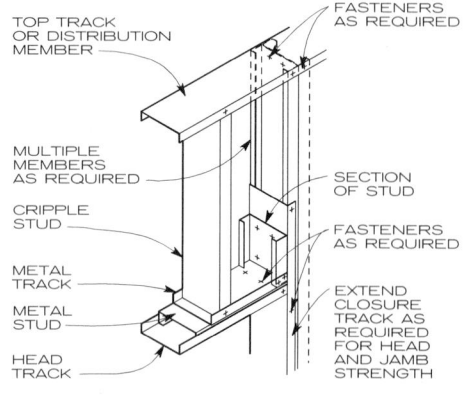

NOTE
For nonaxial loads.

OPENINGS GREATER THAN OR EQUAL TO 4 FEET (LOAD-BEARING WALL)

American Iron and Steel Institute; Washington, D.C.

COLD-FORMED METAL FRAMING

Cold-Formed Steel Framing and Bracing Details

GENERAL

Lightweight steel framing is cold-formed, which means the components are manufactured by brake-forming and punching galvanized coil and sheet stock. Steel framing members consist of two basic types of components that are C-shaped in section: one type has 1/4-in. flanges folded inward and the other has no flanges. Studs, joists, and rafters are made with flanges to stiffen them so they will more readily stand vertically. Components without flanges, called tracks, have unpunched solid webs. For added strength, tracks are sized slightly larger than the flanged members so the tracks will fit snugly inside them as sill or top plates or as part of posts or headers.

Steel framing is strong and versatile. The strength (and load-carrying capacity) of a member can be increased simply by increasing the thickness, or gauge, of the metal; the dimensions of the member, or the spacing, do not necessarily have to be increased. There is little limitation on the length of steel framing members; joists or studs may be fabricated in lengths up to 40 ft. If handled with care, steel framing is straight and consistent; also, it is not affected by moisture content.

Disadvantages of steel framing include lack of insulating qualities, difficulty in cutting compared to wood, and dangerously sharp edges. Consult the American Iron and Steel Institute (AISI) for further information.

BRACING

Buildings must be properly braced to resist racking under wind and seismic loads. Diagonal strap bracing is sloped to resist racking forces in tension and fastened by screws or welds to studs and plates. Properly spaced lateral steel bracing resists stud rotation and minor axis bending under wind, seismic, and axial loads; it is especially critical during construction, before sheathing or finishes are installed.

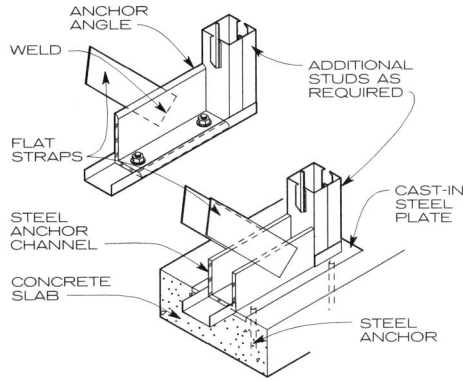

NOTE

The top detail is for one-to-two story buildings and the bottom detail for buildings greater than two stories. Steel channel, plate, and anchor size depend on applied uplift and horizontal shear forces.

DIAGONAL STABILITY BRACING ANCHORAGE DETAILS

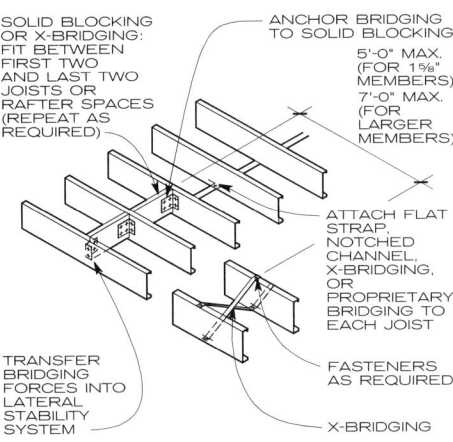

NOTE

If sheathing is not installed on members, bridging is required on both flanges.

JOIST OR RAFTER BRIDGING

American Iron and Steel Institute; Washington, D.C.

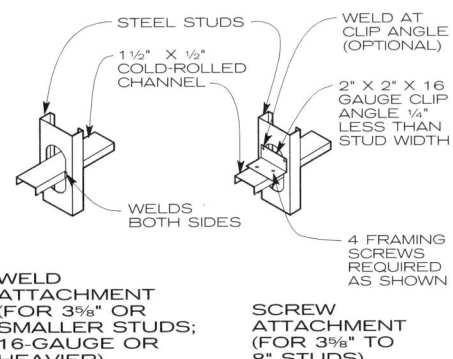

WELD ATTACHMENT (FOR 3 5/8" OR SMALLER STUDS; 16-GAUGE OR HEAVIER)

SCREW ATTACHMENT (FOR 3 5/8" TO 8" STUDS)

NOTE

Channels to be spaced as required by design.

LATERAL BRACING ATTACHMENT

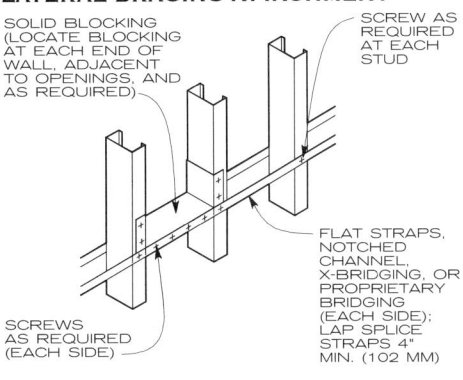

NOTE

Number of rows of bridging as required by design.

WALL BRIDGING

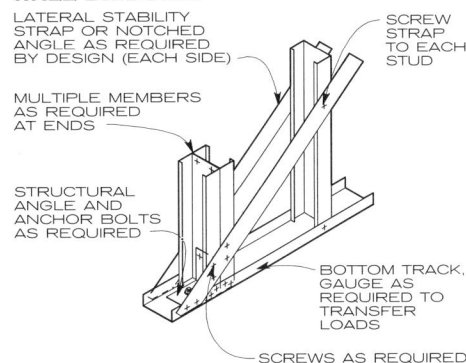

NOTE

Strap forces may require additional stiffening of the bottom track or structural angle.

DIAGONAL STABILITY BRACING ANCHORAGE

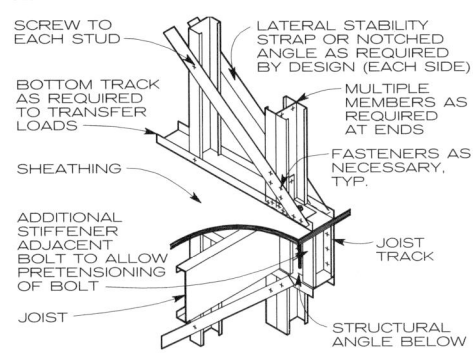

NOTE

Strap forces may require additional stiffening of top and bottom track or structural angle.

DIAGONAL STABILITY BRACING AT INTERMEDIATE FLOOR

LIMITING HEIGHT TABLES FOR INTERIOR PARTITIONS AND CHASE WALL PARTITIONS

STUD WIDTH	STUD SPACING	ALLOW DEFL.	PARTITION ONE LAYER	PARTITION TWO LAYERS

LIMITING HEIGHT 18 MIL STEEL STUD ASSEMBLIES

STUD WIDTH	STUD SPACING	ALLOW DEFL.	ONE LAYER	TWO LAYERS
1 5/8"	16"	1/120	10' 9" d	10' 9" d
		1/240	9' 6" d	10' 6" d
	24"	1/120	8' 9" f	8' 9" f
		1/240	8' 3" f	8' 9" f
2 1/2"	16"	1/120	14' 3" f	14' 3" f
		1/240	12' 6" d	13' 6" d
	24"	1/120	11' 6" f	11' 6" f
		1/240	10' 9" d	11' 6" d
3 5/8"	16"	1/120	18' 3" f	18' 3" f
		1/240	16' 0" d	17' 0" d
	24"	1/120	15' 0" f	15' 0" f
		1/240	14' 0" d	14' 9" d
4"	16"	1/120	19' 6" f	19' 6" f
		1/240	17' 3" f	18' 3" d
	24"	1/120	16' 0" f	16' 0" f
		1/240	15' 0" f	15' 9" d

33 MIL STEEL STUD ASSEMBLIES

STUD WIDTH	STUD SPACING	ALLOW DEFL.	ONE LAYER	TWO LAYERS
2 1/2"	16"	1/120	17' 9" d	18' 6" d
		1/240	14' 0" d	14' 9" d
	24"	1/120	15' 6" d	16' 3" d
		1/240	12' 3" d	13' 0" d
3 5/8"	16"	1/120	23' 0" d	24' 0" d
		1/240	18' 3" d	19' 0" d
	24"	1/120	20' 0" d	20' 9" f
		1/240	16' 0" d	16' 6" d
4"	16"	1/120	24' 9" d	25' 9" d
		1/240	19' 6" d	20' 3" d
	24"	1/120	21' 6" d	22' 0" f
		1/240	17' 3" d	17' 9" d

LIMITING HEIGHT 18 MIL CHASE WALL PARTITIONS

STUD WIDTH	STUD SPACING	ALLOW DEFL.	ONE LAYER	TWO LAYERS
1 5/8"	16"	1/120	15' 3" f	15' 3" f
		1/240	13' 3" d	14' 6" d
	24"	1/120	12' 6" f	12' 6" f
		1/240	11' 6" f	12' 6" f
2 1/2"	16"	1/120	90' 3" f	20' 3" f
		1/240	17' 6" d	19' 0" d
	24"	1/120	16' 6" f	16' 6" f
		1/240	15' 6" f	16' 6" f
3 5/8"	16"	1/120	25' 9" f	25' 9" f
		1/240	22' 9" d	24' 3" d
	24"	1/120	21' 0" f	21' 0" f
		1/240	19' 9" d	21' 0" f
2 1/2"*	16"	1/120	24' 3" f	25' 9" d
		1/240	19' 3" d	20' 6" d
	24"	1/120	21' 3" f	22' 6" f
		1/240	17' 0" d	18' 0" d

* 33 mil chase wall partitions.

NOTE

Limiting height for 1/2 or 5/8 in. thick panels and 5 psf uniform load perpendicular to partition or furring. Use one-layer heights for unbalanced assemblies. Consult local code authority for limiting criteria (d—deflection, f—bending stress).

COLD-FORMED METAL FRAMING

Cold-Formed Steel Framing Joist Details

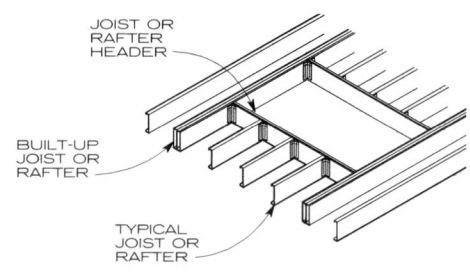

TYPICAL OPENING IN JOISTS/RAFTERS

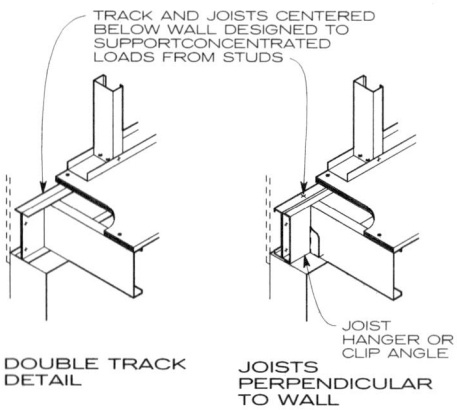

RIM JOIST DETAILS

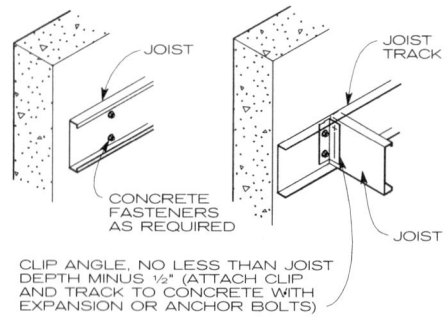

NOTE
Provide solid blocking and bridging as required.

FLOOR JOISTS AT CONTINUOUS WALL

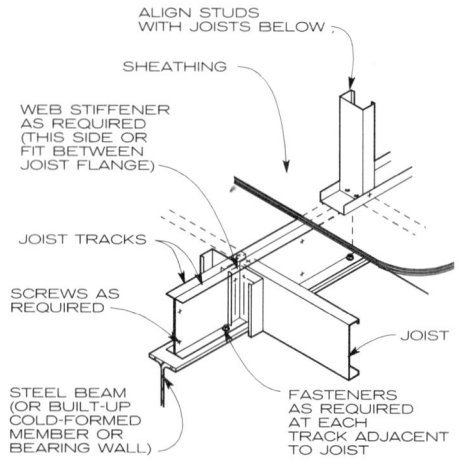

JOISTS SUPPORTED BY BEAM OR BEARING WALL

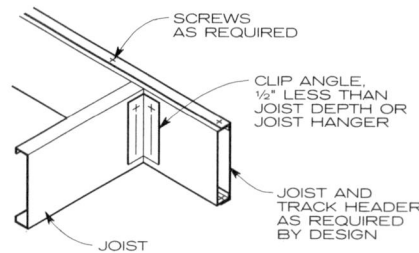

JOIST-TO-JOIST HEADER

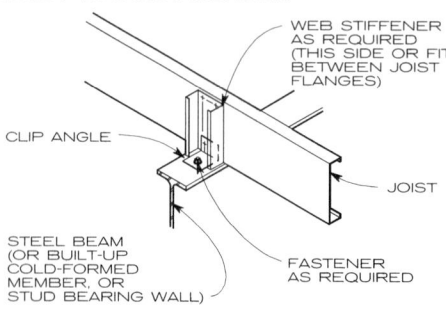

NOTES
1. Continuous bridging is required between each joist above a beam. Solid blocking in every other space may be used in lieu of bridging.
2. When a bearing wall is above, the studs must align with the joists below.
3. Web stiffeners are not required when continuous solid blocking is used.

JOISTS OVER BEAM OR BEARING WALL (CONTINUOUS SPAN)

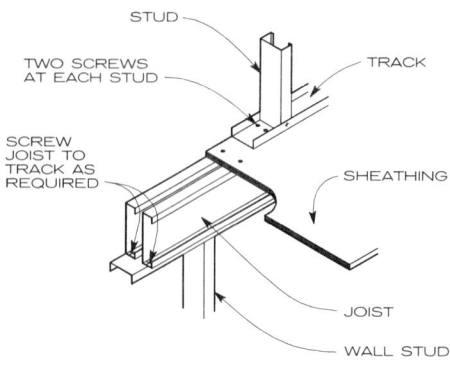

FLOOR JOISTS PARALLEL TO EXTERIOR WALL

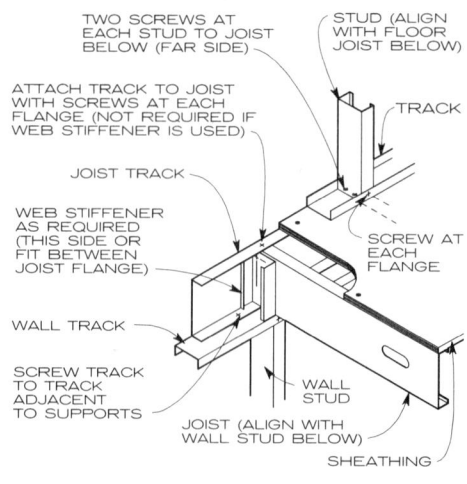

FLOOR FRAMING AT EXTERIOR WALL

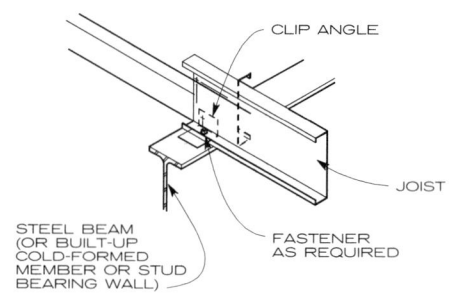

NOTES
1. Continuous bridging is required between each joist above a beam. Solid blocking in every other space may be used in lieu of bridging.
2. When a bearing wall is above, studs must align with joists below.

FLOOR JOISTS SUPPORTED BY BEAM OR BEARING WALL (OVERLAPPED)

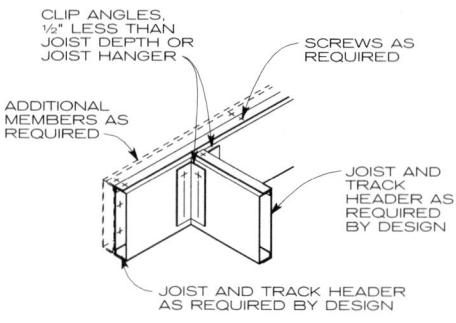

JOIST HEADER TO BUILT-UP JOISTS

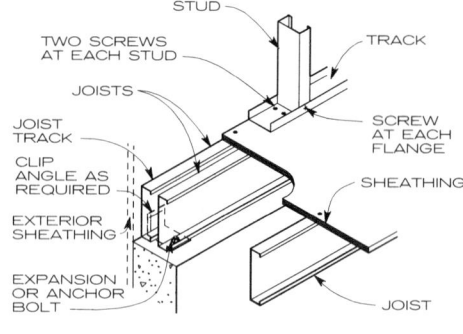

NOTE
Provide solid blocking and bridging as required.

FLOOR JOISTS PARALLEL TO FOUNDATION

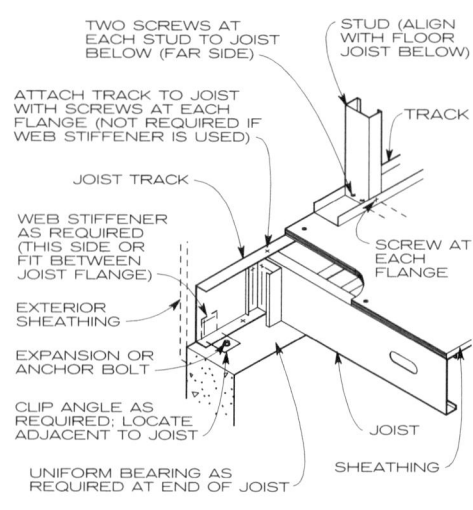

FLOOR JOISTS BEARING ON FOUNDATION

American Iron and Steel Institute; Washington, D.C.

COLD-FORMED METAL FRAMING

Cold-Formed Steel Framing Details

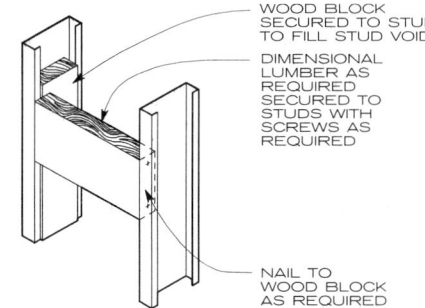

HEAVY FIXTURE ATTACHMENT

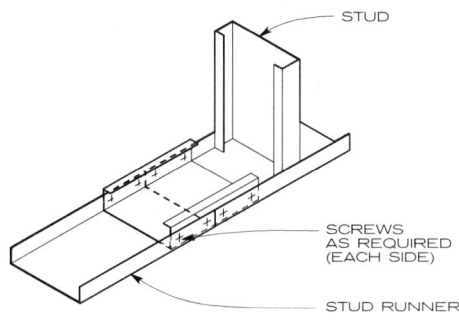

TOP AND BOTTOM TRACK SPLICE

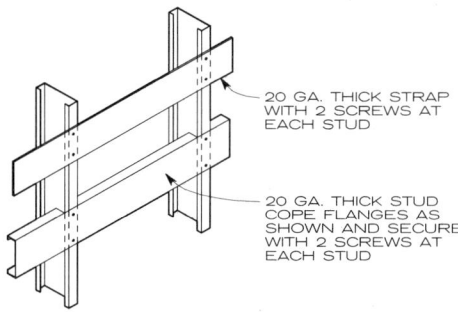

NOTE
Dimensional lumber may also be used for backing.

BACKING FOR CABINETS

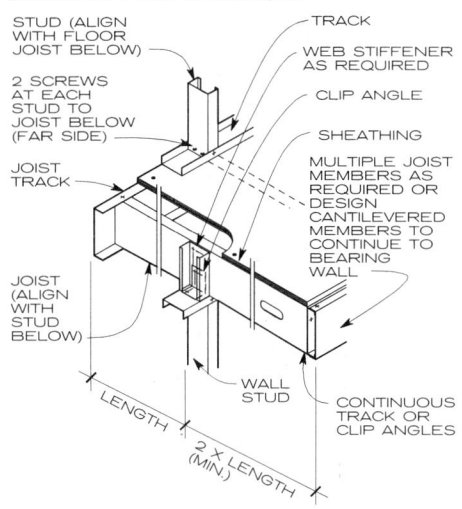

NOTES
1. Provide continuous bridging between each joist at the lower wall.
2. Solid blocking in every other space may be used in lieu of bridging.
3. Where axial load-bearing members do not align vertically, provide top track distribution members at wall below.

FLOOR CANTILEVER

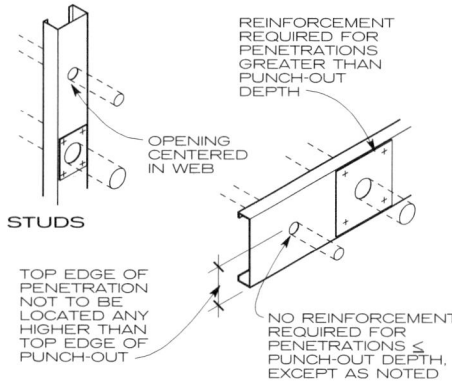

NOTES
1. Do not notch or cut flanges.
2. Capacity verification by design is required for any openings located at concentrated loads and bearing ends.
3. For unpunched members, consult the manufacturer.

JOIST, STUD, OR RAFTER WEB PENETRATIONS

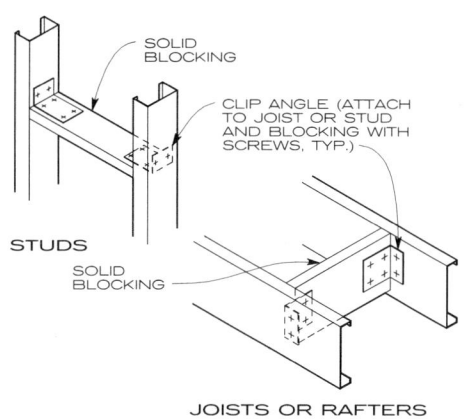

NOTES
1. Where blocking material thickness allows, notch and bend track 90 degrees for connection.
2. Where provisions are made for transfer of flange forces to solid blocking, blocking need not be in the full depth of the member.

SOLID BLOCKING

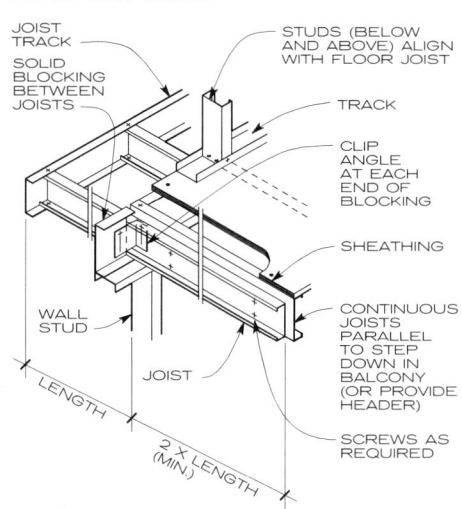

NOTES
1. Balconies require special detailing and protection against moisture and thermal bridging.
2. Where axial load-bearing members do not align vertically, provide top track distribution members at wall below.

BALCONY WITH STEP DOWN

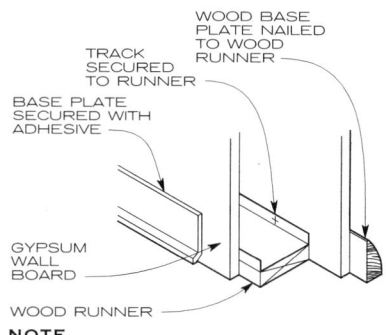

NOTE
This detail is optional depending on contractor preference.

NAILABLE BASE PLATE

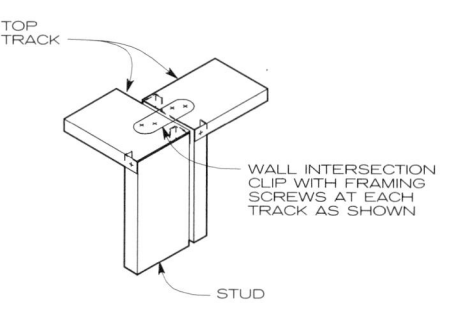

TOP PLATE INTERSECTION

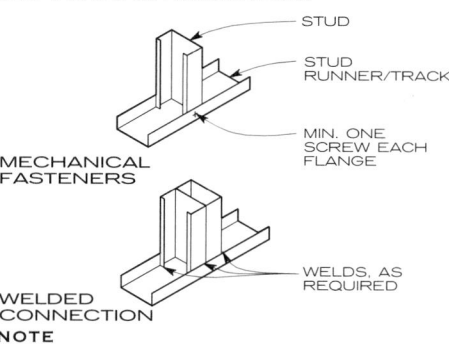

NOTE
Load-bearing studs must be seated tight to track web.

STUD-TO-TRACK CONNECTION

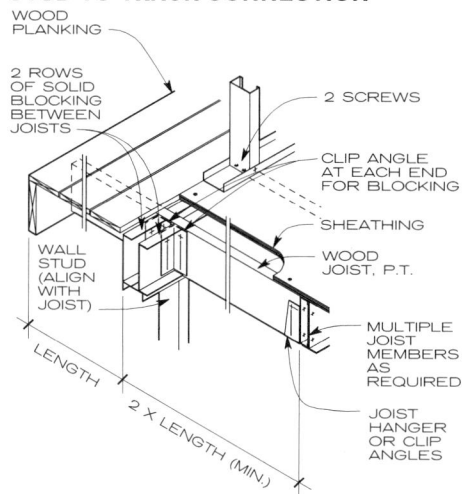

NOTES
1. Balconies require special detailing and protection against moisture and thermal bridging.
2. Where axial load-bearing members do not align vertically, provide top track distribution members at top of wall below.

WOOD DECK BALCONY

American Iron and Steel Institute; Washington, D.C.

40 Cold-Formed Steel Framing Details

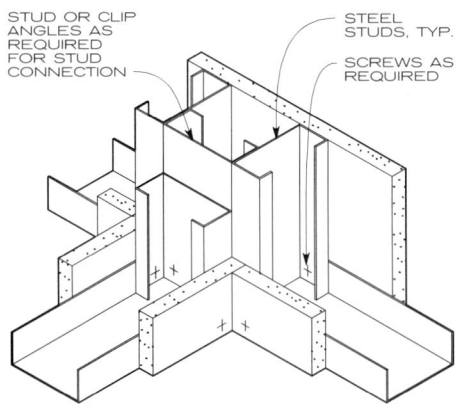
WALL INTERSECTION FRAMING

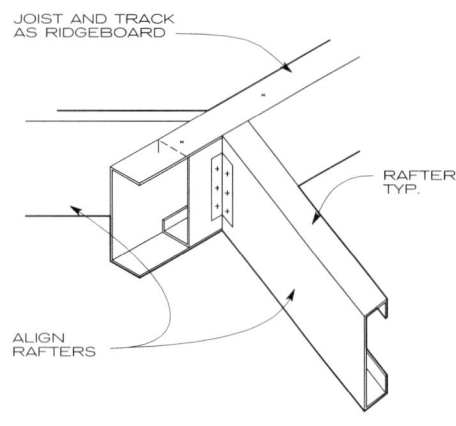
RIDGEBOARD

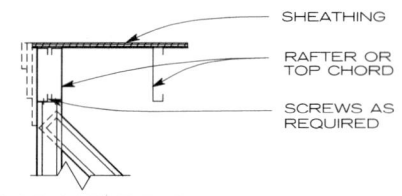
ROOF GABLE END

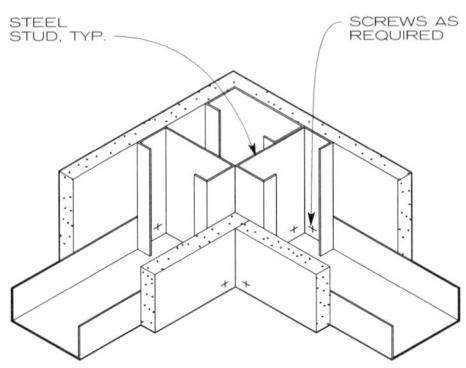
CORNER FRAMING

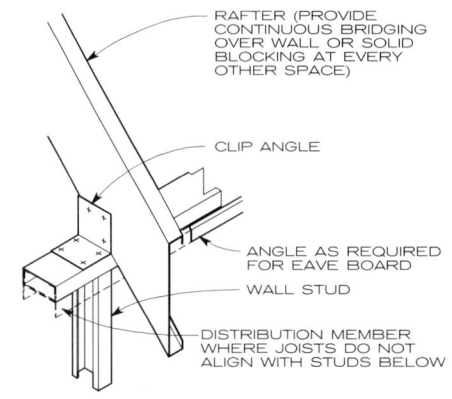
ROOF EAVE AT CATHEDRAL CEILING

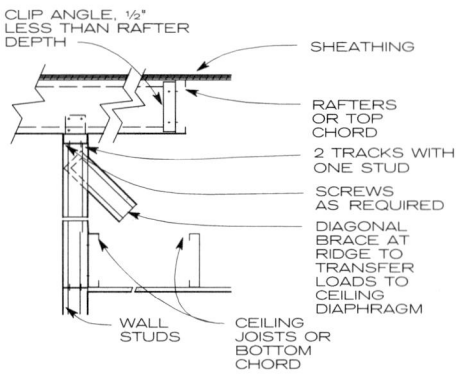
CANTILEVERED ROOF GABLE END

NOTE
Provide bridging at ceiling joists and roof rafters and continuous bridging between rafters at wall.

ROOF END DETAILS

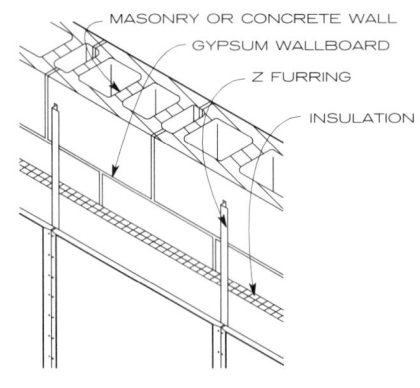
FURRING CHANNELS

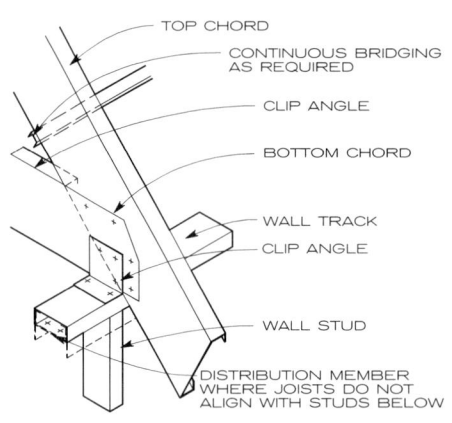
ROOF TRUSS EAVE DETAIL

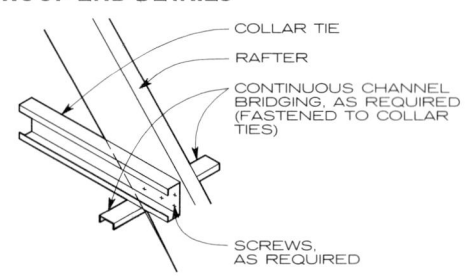
COLLAR TIE DETAIL

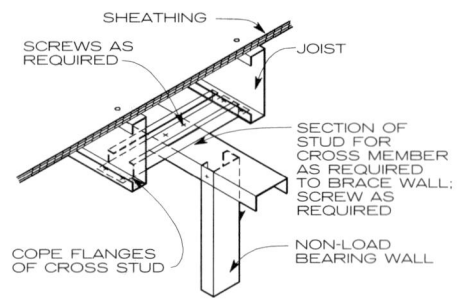
TOP OF NON-LOAD BEARING WALL PARALLEL TO JOISTS

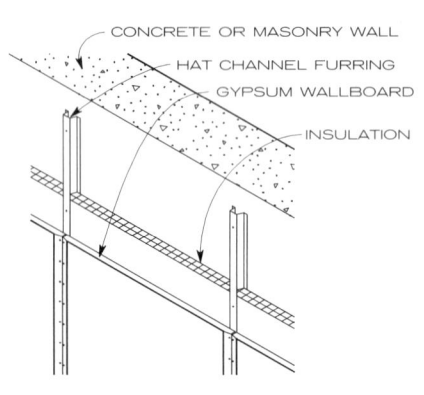
FURRING CHANNELS

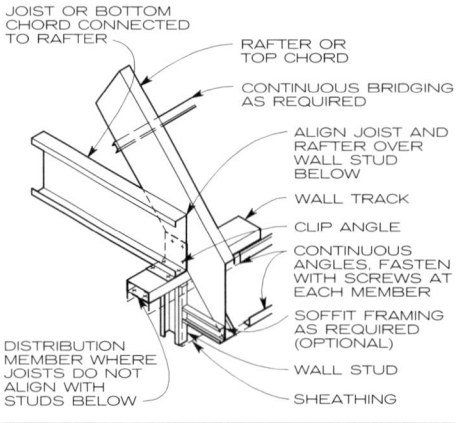
ROOF EAVE DETAIL

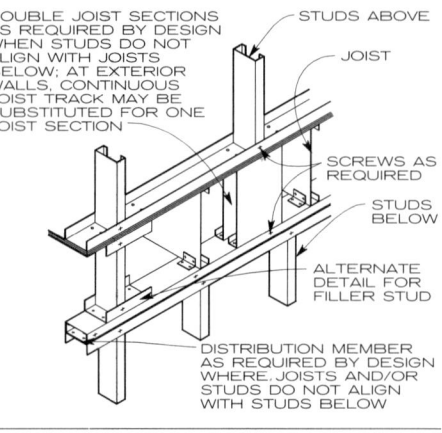
TOP TRACK DISTRIBUTION MEMBER

American Iron and Steel Institute; Washington, D.C.

5 COLD-FORMED METAL FRAMING

Steel Stairs

GUIDELINES

1. Width of stair:
   a. Dwelling stairs: minimum 36 in. treads.
   b. Public exit stairs: minimum 44 in. treads.
   c. Rescue assistance area (ADA): 48 in. between handrails.
2. Treads:
   a. Dwellings: 9 in. minimum (nosing to nosing).
   b. Other (ADA): 11 in. minimum (nosing to nosing).
   c. Uniform width within one flight.
3. Risers:
   a. Dwellings: 8 1/4 in. maximum.
   b. Other (ADA): minimum 4 in., maximum 7 in.
   c. Uniform height within one flight.
4. Nosing: maximum 1 1/2 in. with 60° under nosing; maximum 1/2 in. radius at edge.
5. Stair rails:
   a. Height in dwellings: 36 in.
   b. Height in exit stairs: 42 in.
   c. Rails should be arranged so that a sphere 4 in. in diameter cannot be passed through.
   d. Rails should be arranged to discourage climbing.
   e. Concentrated load nonconcurrently applied at the top rail shall be 200 lb per ft in vertical downward and horizontal direction. The test loads are applicable for railings with supports not more than 8 ft apart.
6. Handrails:
   a. Dwellings: on one side only, required.
   b. Other (ADA): required on both sides.
   c. Height: 34 to 38 in.
   d. Grip surface: 1 1/4 to 1 1/2 in.
   e. Clearance at wall: 1 1/2 in.
   f. Projecting or recessed.
   g. Extension at top of run: 12 in.
   h. Extension at bottom of run: 12 in. plus width of tread.
   i. When a guardrail more than 38 in. high is used, a separate handrail should be installed (ASTM).
   j. Nothing should interrupt the continuous sliding of hands.
7. Regulators and standards: building codes, ADA, ASTM, ANSI, NFPA, and OSHA.

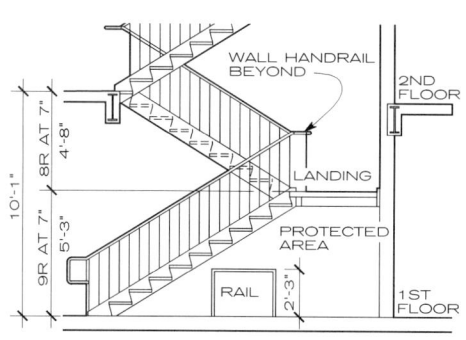

STAIR SECTION

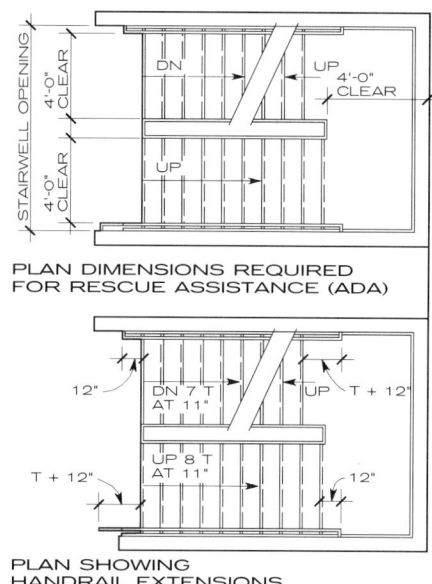

PLAN DIMENSIONS REQUIRED FOR RESCUE ASSISTANCE (ADA)

PLAN SHOWING HANDRAIL EXTENSIONS

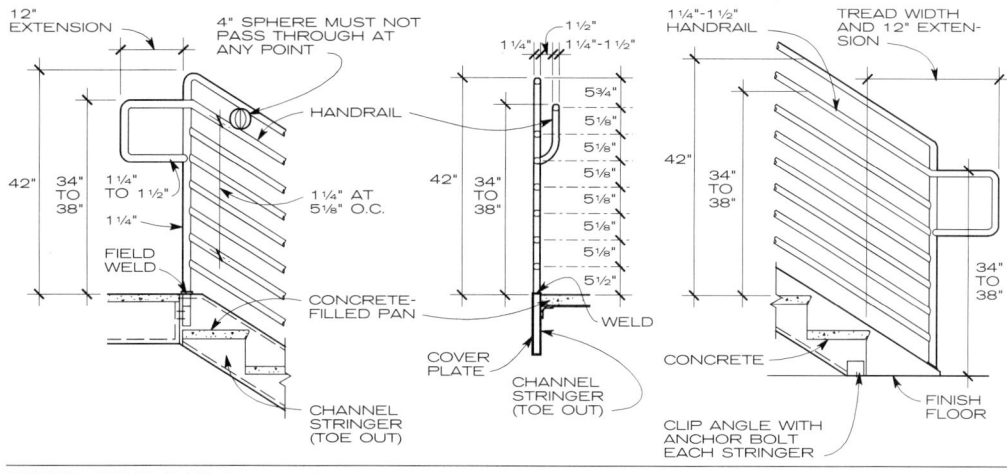

STEEL STAIR RAILS

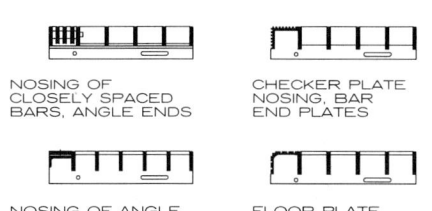

TREADS

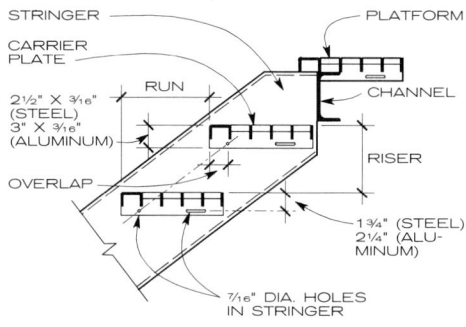

NOTE
This stair is not suitable for persons with disabilities.

INDUSTRIAL AND SERVICE STAIRS

PAN-TYPE STAIR CONSTRUCTION

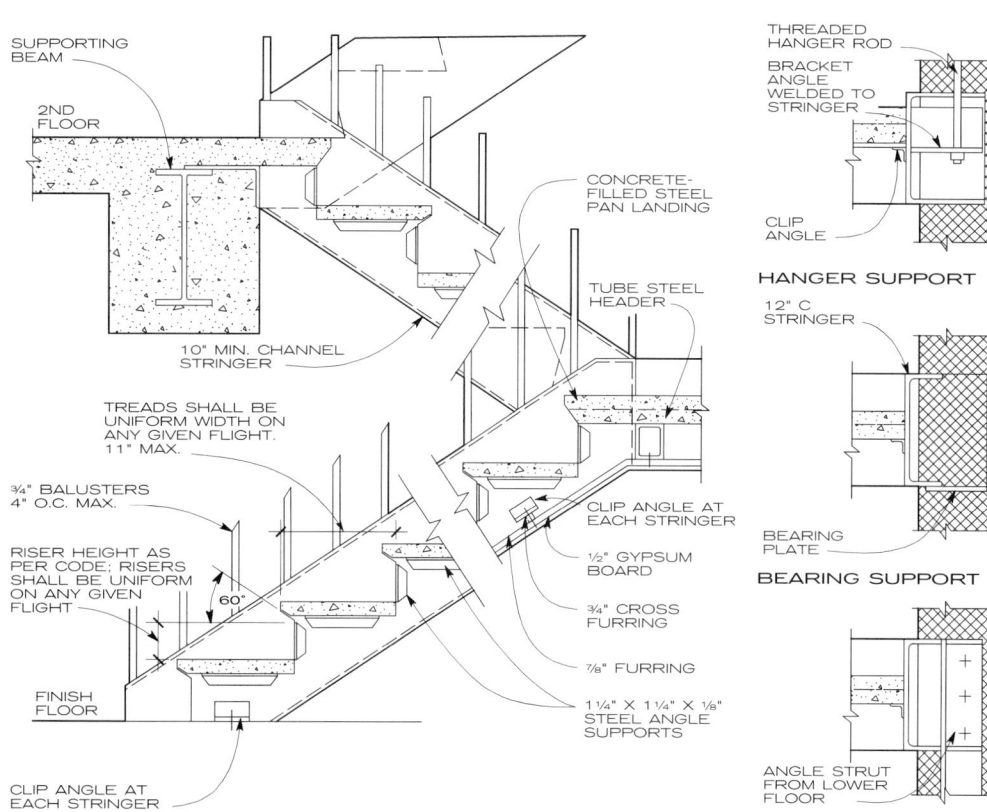

HANGER SUPPORT

BEARING SUPPORT

STRUT SUPPORT

Charles A. Szoradi, AIA; Washington, D.C.

METAL FABRICATION

Fixed Metal Ladders

GENERAL NOTES

1. Materials for ladders and supports include galvanized steel and aluminum. Galvanized steel ladders are fastened to the wall with galvanized steel fasteners; aluminum ladders are fastened with stainless steel fasteners.
2. All fixed wall ladders must conform to OSHA/ANSI A14.3 standards. Also consult local codes for design requirements.

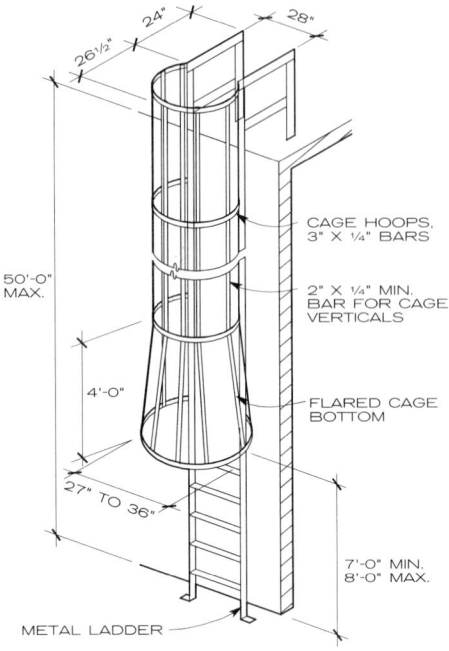

NOTE

Cages should be used on ladders at hazardous locations or on short ladders at high locations.

FIXED VERTICAL LADDER (50 FEET OR LESS)

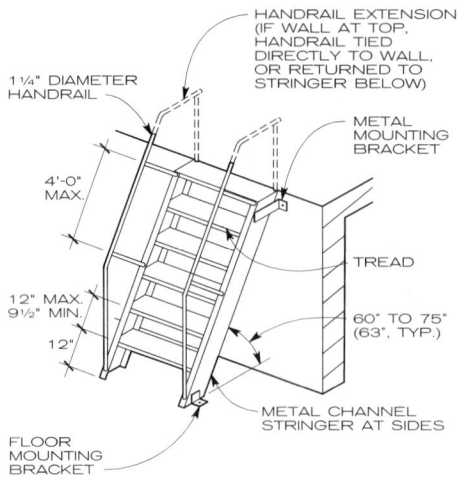

NOTE

The maximum rise between treads depends on exact ladder height and angle.

SHIP'S LADDER

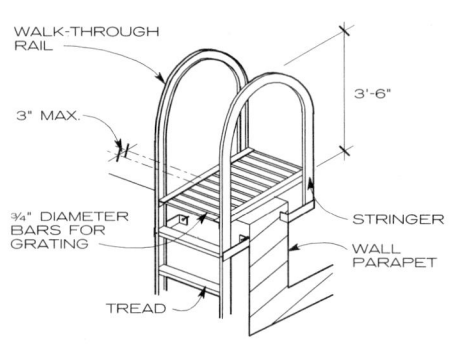

ALTERNATE VERTICAL LADDER WALK THROUGH

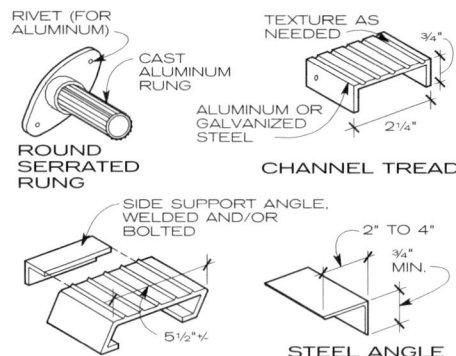

TREADS AND RUNGS

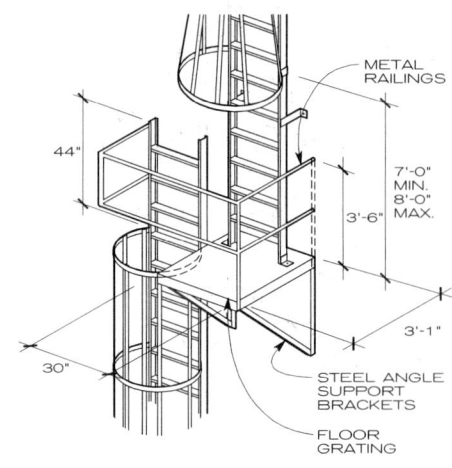

NOTE

Cages and rest platforms are required for climbing heights of more than 50 ft.

REST PLATFORM

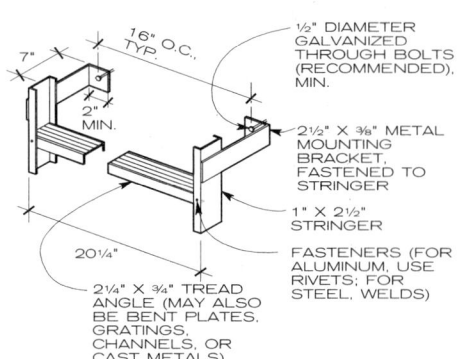

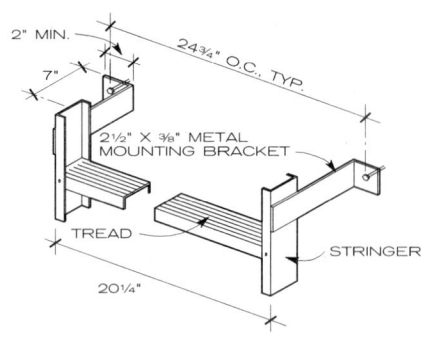

SIDE RAIL MOUNTING BRACKET DETAILS

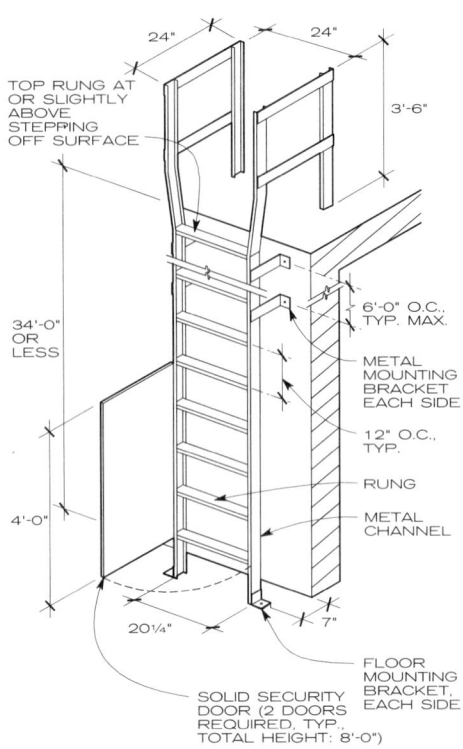

FIXED VERTICAL LADDER (UP TO 24 FEET)

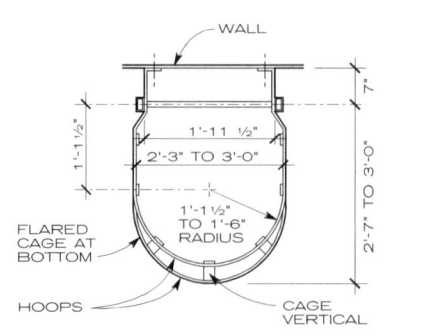

SAFETY CAGE

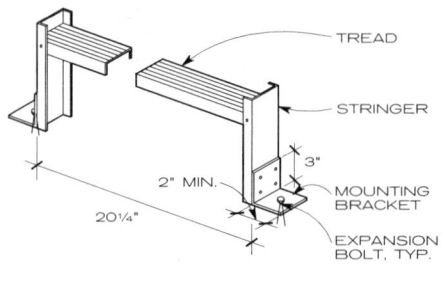

FLOOR-MOUNTING BRACKET DETAIL

Richard J. Vitullo, AIA; Oak Leaf Studio; Crownsville, Maryland

METAL FABRICATION

Ornamental Ironwork Details

GENERAL

Wrought iron is a commercial form of iron with a relatively soft and malleable fibrous structure. The term literally means "fashioned" or "formed" iron and is widely associated with ironwork details. ASTM A 186 defines wrought iron as iron with a carbon content between 0.03 and 0.05%, a material prevalent up to the 19th century. Iron with such a low carbon content is scarce today, so most fabricators use steels containing combinations of iron with a higher percentage of carbon for ornamental details. Low carbon steel or mild steel is the most desirable of these.

NOTES

1. Steel and iron are the metals most frequently used for ornamental structures. Other popular metals are aluminum (favored for its light weight and rust resistance), polished bronze, brass, and copper. Blacksmiths primarily produce custom work today; a smaller proportion of their work is restoration.
2. Working with iron is a craft not readily mastered by generalists; low bidders may not be qualified to deliver a high-quality product. Check references for similar types of jobs performed or jobs at similar costs. Consult the National Ornamental and Miscellaneous Metal Association (NOMMA) and the Artists-Blacksmiths Association of North America for more information on references and lists of blacksmith shops in the United States.
3. NOMMA publishes voluntary guidelines for joint finishes in ornamental work. They are Finish #1 (no evidence of a welded joint); Finish #2 (completely sanded joint, some undercutting and pinholes); Finish #3 (partially dressed weld with splatter removed); and Finish #4 (good quality, uniform undressed weld with minimal splatter).

TYPICAL SIZES AND WEIGHTS (LB PER FT) FOR SOLID IRON AND CARBON STEEL BARS

DIAMETER OR THICKNESS (IN.)		1/8	3/16	1/4	5/16	3/8	7/16	1/2	5/8	3/4	7/8	1	1 1/4	1 1/2
ROUNDS (DIAMETER IN.)		.042	.094	.167	.261	.376	.511	.668	1.04	1.50	2.04	2.67	4.17	6.01
Flat bars (width)	1/8 in.	0.053												
	3/16 in.	0.080	0.120											
	1/4 in.	0.106	0.160	0.213										
	5/16 in.	0.133	0.200	0.266	0.322									
	3/8 in.	0.159	0.239	0.399	0.398	0.478								
	7/16 in.	0.186	0.279	0.372	0.464	0.558	0.651							
	1/2 in.	0.212	0.319	0.425	0.531	0.637	0.744	0.850						
	5/8 in.	0.266	0.398	0.531	0.664	0.797	0.930	1.062	1.328					
	3/4 in.	0.319	0.478	0.637	0.797	0.956	1.116	1.275	1.594	1.912				
	7/8 in.	0.372	0.558	0.748	0.930	1.116	1.302	1.487	1.859	2.231	2.603			
	1 in.	0.425	0.637	0.850	1.062	1.275	1.487	1.700	2.125	2.550	2.975	3.400		
	1 1/4 in.	0.531	0.797	1.062	1.328	1.594	1.859	2.125	2.656	3.187	3.719	4.250	5.312	
	1 1/2 in.	0.638	0.956	1.275	1.594	1.913	2.231	2.550	3.188	3.825	4.463	5.100	6.375	7.650
	1 3/4 in.	0.744	1.116	1.488	1.859	2.231	2.603	2.975	3.719	4.463	5.206	5.950	7.438	8.925
	2 in.	0.850	1.275	1.700	2.125	2.550	2.975	3.400	4.250	5.100	5.950	6.800	8.500	10.200
	2 1/2 in.	1.063	1.594	2.125	2.656	3.188	3.719	4.250	5.313	6.375	7.438	8.500	10.625	12.750

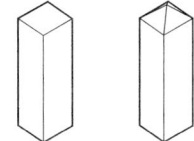 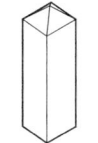 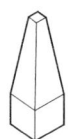 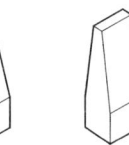 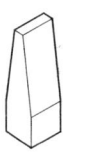   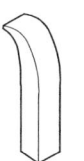 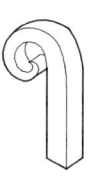

BAR ENDS

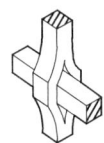 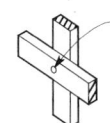  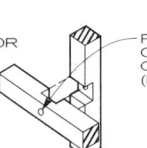  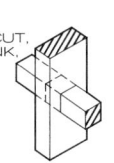

INTERSECTING MEMBERS

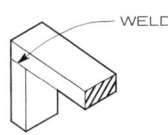 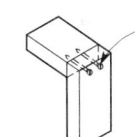 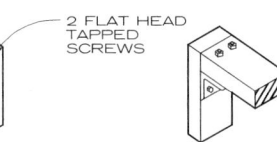 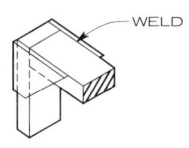

CORNER CONDITIONS

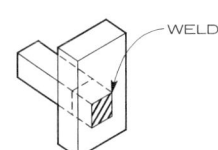 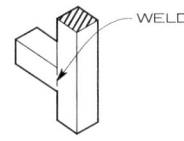 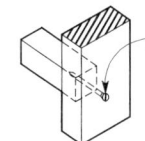 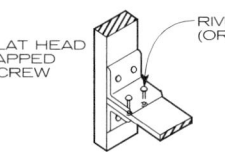

EDGE CONDITIONS

Richard J. Vitullo, AIA; Oak Leaf Studio; Crownsville, Maryland

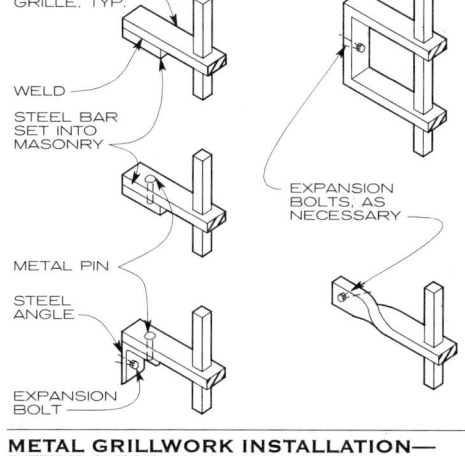

METAL GRILLWORK INSTALLATION—DETAILS FOR MASONRY OPENINGS

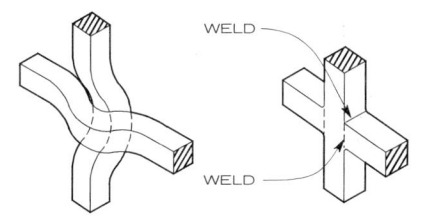

CRIMPED AND WELDED MEMBERS

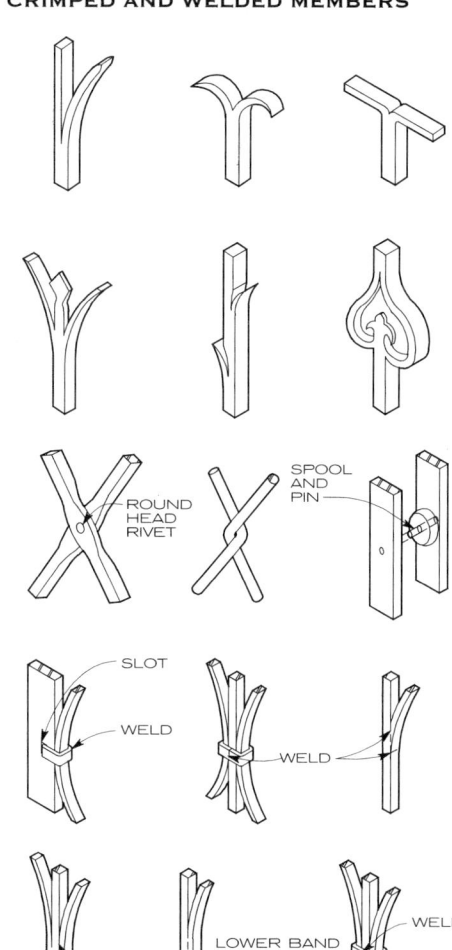

MISCELLANEOUS CONNECTIONS

ORNAMENTAL METAL

Perforated Metals

GENERAL

Perforated metals were initially created to fulfill industrial needs such as minimizing the weight of a particular component or controlling the passage of fluids or gasses. As an architectural component, perforated metals can be used as control devices or simply as decoration. They can serve as sound suppression acoustical devices in ceilings, walls, and grilles; when incorporated into light fixtures, grilles, or ceiling and wall components, they can filter light and obscure views. Since perforated metals retain a great deal of their strength and also ventilate well, they are often employed in furniture and other designs. Because they can bend and interrupt wavelengths of many types, perforated metals are used to contain microwave radiation and the EMI/RFI radiation emitted by electrical devices.

NOTES

1. Metal is typically perforated with hole-punching machines, which work best on sheets .008 in. to 3/4 in. thick. Specialized equipment is available for thicker metal.
2. The intended use of the perforated metal sheet determines the size, shape, and pattern of the holes punched. The strength and stiffness required vary according to use. Since perforated materials can be used in different applications involving a wide range of geometries, materials, and loading conditions, design data are given in very general form.
3. The enormous number of perforating patterns possible with round holes, squares, slots, and other special perforations make it impractical to list every pattern combination. The numbered perforations listed by the Industrial Perforators Association (IPA) are considered standard.
4. For design and tolerances of perforated metals, consult the IPA.
5. Round holes from .020 in. to more than 6 in. in diameter make up the majority of all perforated metal sheets produced. This is because round holes can be produced with greater efficiency and less expense and are generally stronger than other hole shapes.
6. Nonstandard end patterns may require special dies. Unperforated borders may cause distortions of the finished sheet. Roller leveling may be used to correct some of these distortions but may not always work. To calculate the (round) holes per square inch:

$$\frac{\% \text{ Open area}}{78.54 \times D \times D}$$

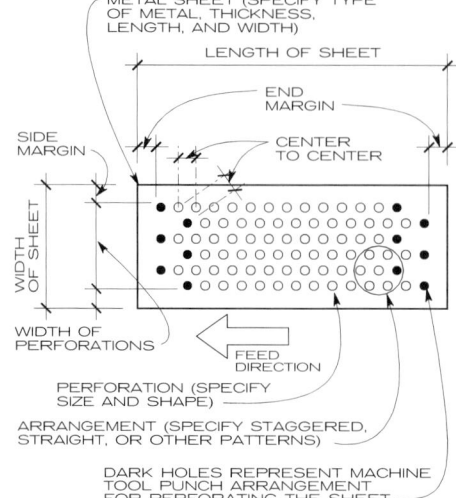

NOTE
Spacing can be specified as a center-to-center dimension, a percentage of open area, or holes per square inch.

TYPICAL TERMS FOR SPECIFYING PERFORATED METAL

CHECKLIST OF PERFORATING COST INFLUENCES

1. Material type: The least expensive material may not save money; a higher strength alloy may allow thickness to be reduced.
2. Material thickness: Thinner materials can be perforated easier and faster.
3. Hole shape and pattern: Round holes are the most economical; the 60° staggered round hole pattern is the strongest, most versatile, and most common.
4. Hole size: Do not go below of hole size to 1-to-1 ratio of hole size to sheet thickness; stay with a 2-to-1 ratio or larger if possible.
5. Bar size: Do not use bars with less than a 1-to-1 ratio with sheet thickness.
6. Center distance: This controls the feed rate and thus the conduction rate. If possible, choose a pattern with longer center distance.
7. Open areas: Extreme open area proportions tend to increase distortion; if possible, stay under 70 percent.
8. Margins: Keep side margins to a minimum to reduce distortion. Use standard unfinished end margins if possible.
9. Blank areas: Consider the die pattern when determining blank areas; consult the metal supplier.
10. Standardization: Specify standard hole patterns, material dimensions, and tolerances when possible. Before specifying a "special," ask the perforator what can be done with existing tooling.
11. Accept normal commercial burrs unless otherwise specified.

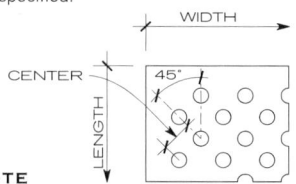

NOTE
This standard IPA option is stronger than straight row patterns but not as strong as a 60° staggered arrangement. It is also not as versatile in providing compact hole spacing and high open areas as the 60° arrangement.

45° STAGGERED ROUND HOLE PATTERN

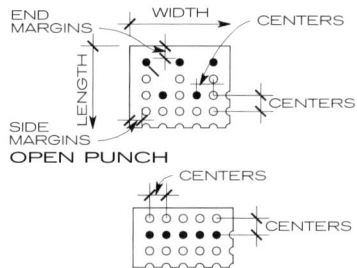

NOTE
A straight line pattern of holes is weaker than a staggered arrangement and can stretch the material more. Dark holes in the drawings above indicate the punch patterns.

STRAIGHT LINE ROUND HOLE PATTERN

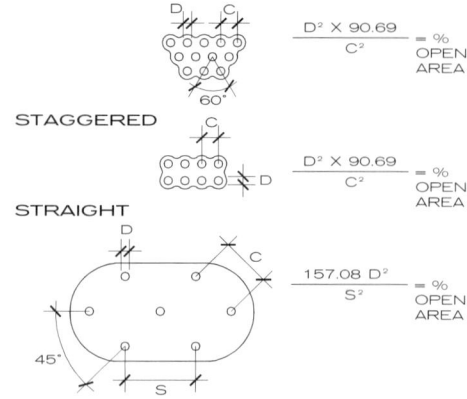

ROUND HOLE OPEN AREAS

ROUND HOLES

IPA NUMBERS	PERFORATIONS (IN.)	CENTERS (IN.)	HOLES PER SQ IN.	% OPEN AREA	LINE	S*/S, STRENGTH WIDTH DIRECTION	S*/S, STRENGTH LENGTH DIRECTION
100	.020		625	20	Staggered	.530	.465
101	.023		576	24	Straight		
102	.027		400	23	Straight		
103	.032		324	26	Straight		
104	.040		225	30	Straight		
105	.045		224	37	Straight		
106	1/16	1/8		23	Staggered	.500	.435
107	5/64	7/64		46	Staggered	.286	.225
108	5/64	1/8		36	Staggered	.375	.310
109	3/32	5/32		32	Staggered	.400	.334
110	3/32	3/16		23	Staggered	.500	.435
111	3/32	1/4		12	Staggered		
112	1/10	5/32		36	Staggered	.360	.296
113	1/8	3/16		40	Staggered	.333	.270
114	1/8	7/32		29	Staggered	.428	.363
115	1/8	1/4		23	Staggered	.500	.435
116	5/32	7/32		46	Staggered	.288	.225
117	5/32	1/4		36	Staggered	.375	.310
118	3/16	1/4		51	Staggered	.250	.192
119	3/16	5/16		33	Staggered	.400	.334
120	1/4	5/16		58	Staggered	.200	.147
121	1/4	3/8		40	Staggered	.333	.270
122	1/4	7/16		30	Staggered	.428	.363
123	1/4	1/2		23	Staggered	.500	.435
124	3/8	1/2		51	Staggered	.250	.192
125	3/8	9/16		40	Staggered	.333	.270
126	3/8	5/8		33	Staggered	.400	.334
127	7/16	5/8		45	Staggered	.300	.239
128	1/2	11/16		47	Staggered	.273	.214
129	9/16	3/4		51	Staggered	.250	.192
130	5/8	13/16		53	Staggered	.231	.175
131	3/4	1		51	Staggered	.250	.192

S* = yield strength of perforated material
S = yield strength of unperforated material (strength for 60° standard staggered pattern)
Length direction = parallel to straight row of holes
Width direction = direction of stagger

Industrial Perforators Association; Milwaukee, Wisconsin

ORNAMENTAL METAL

Perforated and Sheet Metals

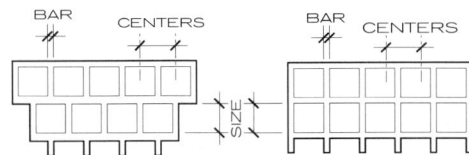

SQUARE PERFORATIONS STAGGERED   SQUARE PERFORATIONS STRAIGHT LINES

SQUARES

IPA NUMBER	PERFORATIONS (IN.)	CENTERS (IN.)	OPEN AREA	LINE
200	2/10	1/4	64%	Straight
201	1/4	3/8		Straight
202	3/8	1/2	56%	Straight
203	1/2	11/16	53%	Straight
204	3/4	1	56%	Straight
205	1	1 1/4		Straight
206	1	1 3/8		Straight

SQUARE HOLE OPEN AREAS

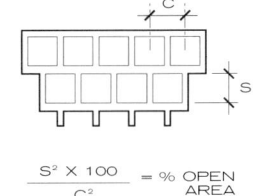

$$\frac{S^2 \times 100}{C^2} = \% \text{ OPEN AREA}$$

NOTE

Square holes, principally used for grilles and machine guards, offer optimal visibility and throughput. Typically punched in a straight line, in either straight or staggered patterns, square holes make for weaker perforated sheets than round hole patterns and are generally more expensive. Sharp corners make square hole tooling wear out faster than round hole tooling.

SQUARE HOLES

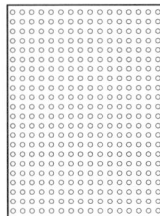

NO. 105, .045" DIA., 37% OPEN AREA

NO. 108, 5/64" DIA., 36% OPEN AREA

NO. 120, 1/4" DIA., 58% OPEN AREA

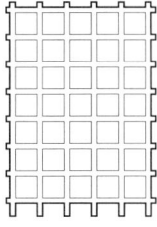

NO. 200, 1/8", 64% OPEN AREA

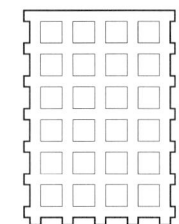

NO. 201, 1/4" OPENNING

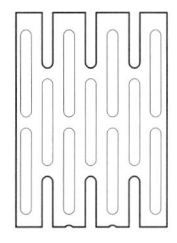

NO. 208, 1/8" X 1" OPENING, 43% OPEN AREA

MISCELLANEOUS PERFORATION PATTERNS

HEXAGONAL HOLES   ROUND CANE

OCTAGONAL CANE   GRECIAN

NOTE

A broad assortment of nonstandard hole shapes and patterns is available; consult metal perforator. Also available are indented holes, collared holes, and louvered holes.

MISCELLANEOUS NONSTANDARD PERFORATION PATTERNS

NOTE

These three types of slots are IPA standard types. Non-standard square-end slots are also available. Consult manufacturers for other open area calculations for slots.

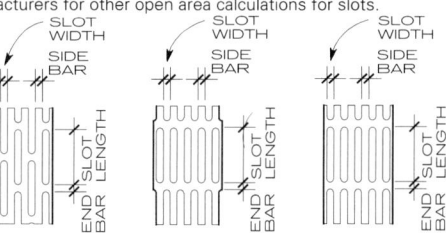

SLOTS SIDE STAGGER   SLOTS END STAGGER   SLOTS STRAIGHT LINES

SLOTS

IPA NUMBER	PERFORATIONS	OPEN AREA	LINE
207	1/8" x 3/4"	41%	Side staggered
208	1/8" x 1"	43%	Side staggered

SLOTS

GAUGES AND WEIGHTS OF SHEET METALS*

	STEEL		GALVANIZED STEEL		LONG TERNE		STAINLESS-USS GAUGE			MONEL	
	USS GAUGE REV.		USS GAUGE		USS GAUGE			LB/SQ FT		USS GAUGE	
GAUGE	DECIMAL THICKNESS	LB/SQ FT	DECIMAL THICKNESS	LB/SQ FT	DECIMAL THICKNESS	LB/SQ FT	DECIMAL THICKNESS	CHROME ALLOY	CHROME NICKEL	DECIMAL THICKNESS	LB/SQ FT
32	.0100		.0130	.563			.0100	.418	.427		
31	.0110		.0140	.594			.0109	.450	.459		
30	.0120	.500	.0157	.656	.012	.518	.0125	.515	.525		
29	.0135	.563	.0172	.719	.014	.581	.0140	.579	.591		
28	.0149	.625	.0187	.781	.015	.643	.0156	.643	.656		
27	.0164	.688	.0202	.844	.017	.706	.0171	.708	.721		
26	.0179	.750	.0217	.906	.018	.768	.0187	.772	.787	.0187	.827
25	.0209	.875	.0247	1.031	.021	.893	.0218	.901	.918	.0218	.965
24	.0239	1.000	.0276	1.156	.024	1.018	.0250	1.030	1.050	.0250	1.148
23	.0269	1.125	.0306	1.281	.027	1.143	.0281	1.158	1.181	.0281	1.286
22	.0299	1.250	.0336	1.406	.030	1.268	.0312	1.287	1.312	.0312	1.424
21	.0329	1.375	.0366	1.531	.033	1.393	.0343	1.416	1.443	.0343	1.562
20	.0359	1.500	.0396	1.656	.036	1.518	.0375	1.545	1.575	.0375	1.700
19	.0418	1.750	.0456	1.906	.042	1.768	.0437	1.802	1.837	.0437	1.975
18	.0478	2.000	.0516	2.156	.048	2.018	.0500	2.060	2.100	.0500	2.297
17	.0538	2.250	.0575	2.406	.054	2.268	.0562	2.317	2.362	.0562	2.572
16	.0598	2.500	.0635	2.656	.060	2.518	.0625	2.575	2.625	.0625	2.848
15	.0673	2.812	.0710	2.969	.068	2.831	.0703	2.896	2.953	.0703	3.216
14	.0747	3.125	.0785	3.281	.075	3.143	.0781	3.218	3.281	.0781	3.583
13	.0897	3.750	.0934	3.906	.090	3.768	.0937	3.862	3.937	.0937	4.272
12	.1046	4.375	.1084	4.531	.105	4.393	.1093	4.506	4.593	.1093	5.007
11	.1196	5.000	.1233	5.156	.120	5.018	.1250	5.150	5.250	.1250	5.742
10	.1345	5.625	.1382	5.781	.135	5.643	.1406	5.793	5.906	.1406	6.431
9	.1494	6.250	.1532	6.406			.1562	6.437	6.562	.1562	7.166
8	.1644	6.875	.1681	7.031			.1718	7.081	7.218	.1718	7.855
7	.1793	7.500					.1875	7.590	7.752	.1875	8.590

*Gauges and weights have been computed subject to standard commercial tolerances.

Industrial Perforators Association; Milwaukee, Wisconsin

ORNAMENTAL METAL

Steel Sheets, Coils, and Plates

GUIDE FOR SELECTING CARBON STEEL FOR PERFORATING APPLICATIONS

TYPE	DESCRIPTION	SHEETS TH	SHEETS W	SHEETS L	COILS TH	COILS W	CARBON CONTENT	TENSILE PSI	YIELD, PSI	% ELONG. 2 IN.	HARD-NESS	COST SHEETS	COST COILS
HOT-ROLLED STEELS													
Commercial quality (SAE or AISI 1008; ASTM A 569)	A low-cost sheet steel with moderate drawing and forming qualities for use when finish is unimportant. For best perforating results specify pickled and oiled for removal of oxides.	7 to 16 ga.	up to 60 in.	up to 144 in.	7 to 16 ga.	up to 60 in.	0.10 max.	45,000 to 60,000	30,000 to 40,000	28 to 38	55 to 70	100 pickled and oiled-104	95 99
Drawing quality (SAE or AISI 1008; ASTM A 621)	This quality is intended for use when forming requirements are too severe for commercial quality. Pickling and oiling to remove oxides is recommended. In-stock availability is not as great as commercial quality.	7 to 16 ga.	up to 60 in.	up to 144 in.	7 to 16 ga.	up to 60 in.	0.10 max	45,000 to 60,000	30,000 to 40,000	28 to 38	55 to 70	103	98
High-strength, low alloy (USS Cor-Ten or equivalent; ASTM A 375)	Good formability because of low carbon content in combination with relatively high Yield and Tensile properties permit these steels to be used in lighter gauges to reduce weight in applications in which strength in important. Readily available.	7 to 16 ga.	up to 60 in.	up to 144 in.	11 to 14 ga.	up to 60 in.	0.12 max	70,000 min	50,000 min	22 min	80 to 90	132	126
Abrasion-resisting (C .35-.50; Mn 1.50-2.00; P .050 max.; S .055 max.; Si .15-.35)	High manganese content in combination with intermediate carbon greatly enhances resistance to abrasion; can improve part life 2 to 10 times. Moderate formability.	7 to 16 ga.	up to 60 in.	up to 144 in.	N.A.	N.A.	.35 to .50	100,000 to 120,000	55,000 to 70,000	10 to 20	210 to 225 (Bhn.)	118	N.A.
COLD-ROLLED STEELS													
Commercial quality (SAE or AISI 1008; ASTM A 366)	Cold rolled steels have improved surface finishes and tighter size tolerances than hot rolled steels. They are available in two classes: Class 1 is intended for exposed applications; Class 2 is for unexposed use. Three finishes can be specified: Matte is the standard finish. It is uniformly dull and suitable for painting. Commercial bright finish is a relatively bright, intermediate finish. Luster finish is smooth and bright and most suitable for plating. Because perforating alters surface appearance, surface preparation after perforating may be required before application of the final finish.	7 to 28 ga.	up to 60 in.	up to 18 ft	11 to 28 ga.	up to 60 in.	0.10 max	40,000 to 50,000	25,000 to 35,000	30 to 40	45 to 60	119 (16 ga.)	113
Drawing quality (ASTM A 619)	Recommended for use when forming requirements are too severe for commercial quality. Can be supplied (Class 1) free of fluting or stretcher straining when intended for use in a reasonably short time. Available in mill quantities.	7 to 28 ga.	up to 60 in.	up to 18 ft	11 to 28 ga.	up to 60 in.	0.10 max	40,000 to 50,000	20,000 to 30,000	38 to 40	40 to 50	125 (16 ga.)	120
Drawing quality special milled (ASTM A 620)	For use when the material must be free of surface disturbances without roller leveling immediately before use and essentially free from significant changes in mechanical properties over an extended period of time. Available in mill order quantities.	7 to 28 ga.	up to 60 in.	up to 18 ft	11 to 28 ga.	up to 60 in.	0.10 max	40,000 to 50,000	20,000 to 30,000	38 to 40	40 to 50	127 (16 ga.)	122
CORROSION-RESISTANT STEELS													
Galvanized (ASTM 525)	A versatile, low-cost, corrosion-resistant steel with a zinc coating applied in a continuous hot-dip process. Available in commercial, drawing, and other qualities.	10 to 20 ga.	up to 60 n.	up to 18 ft	12 to 28 ga.	up to 60 in.	0.10 max	45,000 to 55,000	35,000 to 45,000	25 to 35	50 to 65	147 (20 ga.)	145
Mill-bonderized galvanized	Galvanized sheet with a coating of mill-bonderized phosphate for immediate painting without flaking or peeling.	16 to 26 ga.	up to 60 in.	up to 18 ft	16 to 26 ga.	up to 60 in.	0.10 max	45,000 to 55,000	35,000 to 45,000	25 to 35	50 to 65	149 (20 ga.)	N.A.
Galvanealed (coating designation A 60)	Heat-treated galvanized sheet, dull gray without spangles with a rough texture well suited to painting. Can withstand temperatures to 750° without flaking. Less ductile than regular galvanized coating.	14 to 26 ga.	up to 48 in.	up to 18 ft	14 to 26 ga.	up to 48 in.	0.10 max	40,000 to 55,000	32,000 to 42,000	25 to 35	50 to 65	150 (20 ga.)	147
Electro-galvanized (ASTM A 591)	A thin zinc coating is applied to cold rolled steel by electroplating so as not to appreciatively affect the weight-thickness relationship. Smooth, without spangles, it is recommended as an undercoat for painted finishes. Available in commercial and drawing qualities.	14 to 26 ga.	up to 60 in.	up to 18 ft	14 to 26 ga.	up to 60 in.	0.10 max	40,000 to 50,000	25,000 to 35,000	30 to 40	45 to 60	146 (20 ga.)	144
Aluminized, type 1 (ASTM 463)	Sheet steel coated on both sides with aluminum combines the properties of both metals. Type 1 is provided in two weights, regular and light, and is available in commercial and drawing qualities. If the heaviest Type 2 aluminized coating is desired, consult with a supplier or the steel manufacturer.	14 to 26 ga.	up to 60 in.	up to 18 ft	14 to 26 ga.	up to 60 in.	0.10 max	50,000 to 60,000	35,000 to 45,000	18 to 28	60 to 70	162 (20 ga.)	157

Note: APPROXIMATE RELATIVE COST (10-GA. H.R. STEEL = 100)

Industrial Perforators Association; Milwaukee, Wisconsin

ORNAMENTAL METAL

Wood Adhesives

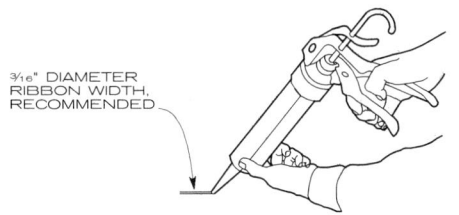

ADHESIVE GUN

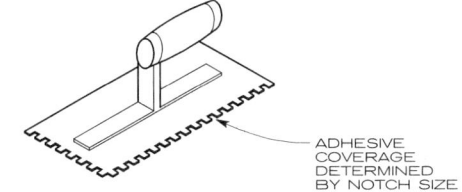

NOTCHED TROWEL (TO SPREAD ADHESIVE OVER LARGE AREAS)

ADHESIVE APPLICATIONS

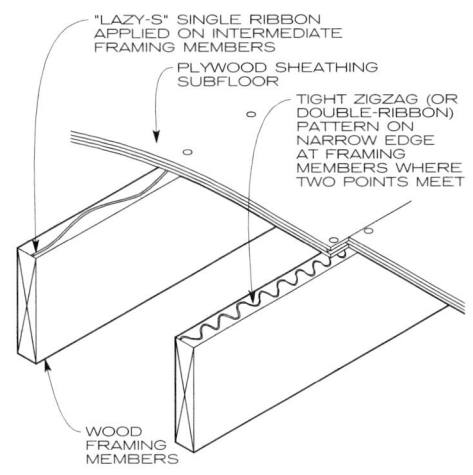

NOTE
Adhesive is applied to one surface only.

RECOMMENDED ADHESIVE BEAD PATTERNS

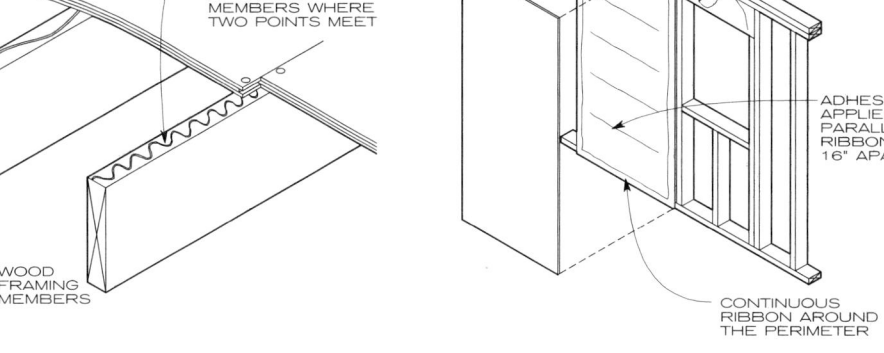

ADHESIVES SUMMARY

CLASS	FORM	PROPERTIES	TYPICAL USES
Urea resin	Dry powders or liquids; may be blended with melamine or other resins	High strength under both wet and dry conditions; moderately durable under damp conditions; moderate to low resistance to temperatures above 120°F; white or tan color	Hardwood plywood for interior use and furniture; interior particleboard; flush doors; furniture core stock
Phenol resin*	Dry powders or liquids	High strength under both wet and dry conditions; very resistant to moisture and damp conditions; dark red in color	Primary adhesive for exterior softwood plywood and flakeboard
Resorcinol resin and phenol-resorcinol resins	Liquid; hardener supplied separately	High strength under both wet and dry conditions; very resistant to moisture and damp conditions; dark red color	Primary adhesive for laminated timbers and assembly joints to withstand severe service conditions
Polyvinyl acetate resin emulsions	Liquid; ready to use	Generally high strength in dry conditions; low resistance to moisture and elevated temperatures; joints tend to yield under continued stress; white or yellow color	Furniture assembly, flush doors, bonding of plastic laminates, architectural woodworking
Cross-linkable polyvinyl acetate resin emulsions	Similar to polyvinyl acetate resin emulsions but includes a resin capable of forming linkage	Improved resistance to moisture and elevated temperatures; improved long-term performance in moist or wet environment; color varies	Interior and exterior doors, molding and architectural woodworking
Contact adhesives	Typically an elastomer base in organic solvents or water emulsion	Initial joint strength develops immediately upon pressing, increases slowly over a period of weeks; dry strength generally lower than those of conventional woodworking glues; water resistance and resistance to severe conditions variable; color varies	For some nonstructural bonds; high-pressure decorative laminates to substrates. Useful for low-strength metal and some plastic bonding.
Mastics (elastomeric construction adhesives)	Puttylike consistency, synthetic or natural elastomer base, usually in organic solvents	Gap filling; develops strength slowly over several weeks; water resistance and resistance for severe conditions vary; color varies	Lumber and plywood to joists and studs; gypsum board; styrene and urethane foams
Thermoplastic synthetic resins (hot melts)	Solid chunks, pellets, ribbons, rods, or films; solvent-free	Rapid bonding; gap filling; lower strength than conventional woodworking adhesives; minimal penetration; moisture resistant; white to tan color	Edge banding of panels; films and paper overlays
Epoxy resins	Chemical polymers, usually in two parts, both liquid; completely reactive, no solvents	Good adhesion to metals, glass, certain plastics, and wood products; permanence in wood joints not adequately established; gap-filling	Used in combination with other resins for bonding metals, plastics, and materials other than wood; fabrication of cold-molded wood panels
Protein glues (casein and hide)	Dry powders or reconstituted liquid	Bonds extremely well to wood; moisture resistant	Interior applications; laminating beam

*Most types used in the U.S. are alkaline-catalyzed. The general statements refer to this type.

Data: Adapted from Table 100-G-12, *Architectural Woodwork Quality Standards* (6th ed., version 1.1, 1994)

GENERAL

Adhesives have been used for bonding wood for centuries, but until the 1930s they were limited to only a few naturally derived substances–those based on animal or vegetable proteins, gums, or resins. Stepped-up materials research efforts during World War II spurred the development of synthetic adhesives for bonding metals, concrete, glass, rubber, plastics, and wood.

Many of these synthetic adhesives are used to manufacture products such as plywood, oriented-strand board (OSB), and laminated timbers. They can also be used during construction to attach plywood subfloors to floor joists, adhere ceramic tiles to floors or walls, attach drywall, and the like. In addition to their structural use, adhesives also can be used to eliminate squeaks in floors and for some mechanical fastening.

Adhesives are composed of a base component, dispersion medium, and various additives that impart specific properties. The elastomeric base of a construction-type adhesive accounts for 30 to 50% of its weight. Depending on its intended application, this base is made of natural rubber (isoprene) or synthetic rubbers such as neoprene, butyl, polyurethane, polysulfide, nitrile, styrene-butadiene, or butadiene acrylonitrile. Additives include tackifiers, flow and extrusion modifiers, curing agents, antioxidants, and fillers. Together, the base and the additives are dispersed (or dissolved) in a liquid, typically an organic solvent or water.

Currently, most adhesives use organic solvents, but water-based adhesives are gaining in popularity because they do not emit harmful vapors, are easy to clean up, and can be discarded as regular trash. During the specification process, disposal of the containers from organic solvents must be considered. Many jurisdictions are enacting clean air statutes in which organic solvents are targeted as air pollutants. In addition, organic solvents can have adverse affects on the workers who apply them as well as future building occupants. One drawback to most water-based adhesives is that they tend only to resist water, while the solvent-based adhesives are waterproof.

CONSTRUCTION ADHESIVES

Construction adhesives are defined as elastomer-based extrudable mastics, which means that the main adhesive component is elastic and will continue to maintain some of its flexibility indefinitely. Mastics are a type of adhesive with high viscosity, or resistance to flow. A construction adhesive is a substance capable of holding materials together by surface attachment.

Adhesives used for building have been formulated to tolerate many of the often adverse conditions that exist at most job sites, such as extreme temperatures and temperature fluctuations. They are excellent for filling gaps, and thus work on both smooth and rough surfaces. Because they form bond lines up to $1/4$ in. thick, they can bridge gaps between ill-fitting pieces. The degree of adhesion depends on the surface conditions of the materials; ice, dirt, grease, or other contaminants will all have a negative effect.

Many of the characteristics of modern adhesives are described in the table. Note that most adhere to wood, but performance depends on careful consideration of physical and chemical compatibility of glue and wood, processing requirements, mechanical properties, and durability under design conditions.

Richard J. Vitullo, AIA; Oak Leaf Studio; Crownsville, Maryland

FASTENERS AND ADHESIVES

Structural Wood Fasteners

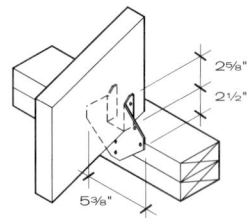

NOTE: For tying unnotched 2x rafters to top wall plates; for uplift and lateral load resistance.
TWO-SIDED RAFTER TIE

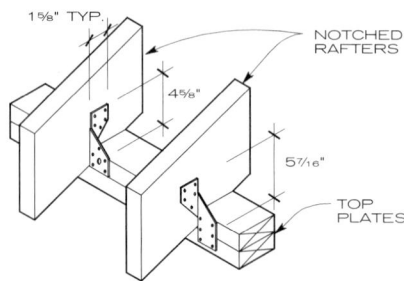

NOTE: Ties one or two top plates to notched rafters for tension cord connections.
ONE-SIDED RAFTER TIES

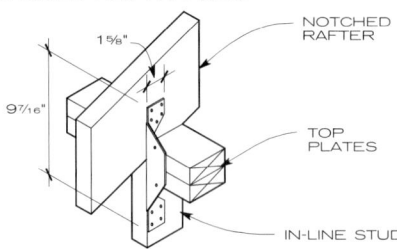

NOTE: Ties notched rafter to stud on same plane as rafter for tension load connection.
RAFTER-TO-STUD TIE

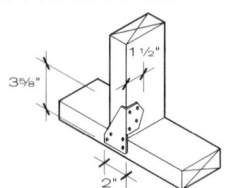

NOTE: Ties stud to bottom plate for tension load connection.
STUD TIE

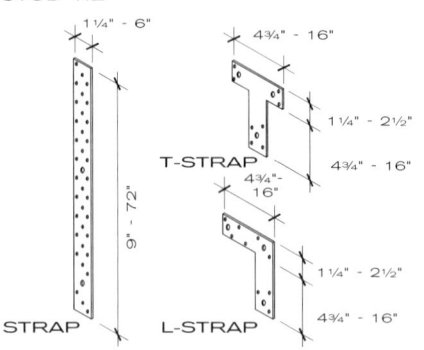

STRAP: For tying varied tension load connections, e.g., joists at ridge, wall-to-floor connections, etc.
T- AND L-STRAPS: For varied vertical to horizontal connections.
TIES

NOTES

1. For utmost rigidity, strength, and service, each type of fastener requires joint designs adapted to wood strength along and across the grain and to dimensional changes that may occur with variations in moisture content.
2. For forces such as wind uplift and lateral loads (wind and earthquake), the foundation, floor-to-floor, and roof connections are the main areas of concern, although, in varying degrees, all connections taken together will resist these forces. In some joints, the fastener or connector is the only resistor to the applied load.
3. Most fasteners used to join wood framing or to attach metal connectors to framing are made of steel, with a hot-dipped galvanized coating the most typical finish used. Stainless steel, or finishes such as a corrosion-resistant primer or a copolymer coating, can also be used. In the presence of moisture, metals used for nails

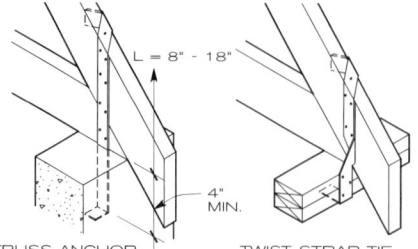

NOTE: Provides tension for wood-to-wood or wood-to-masonry connections for wood trusses and joists.
TRUSS ANCHORS

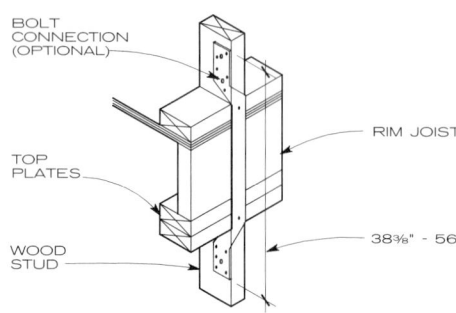

NOTE: Provides floor-to-floor tension connection; for nailed or bolted connections.
FLOOR TIE ANCHOR

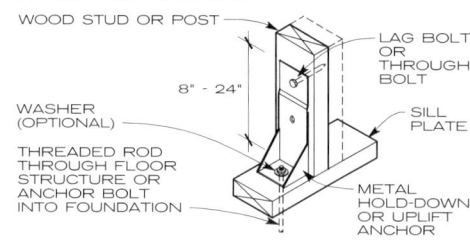

NOTE: Transfers tension loads between floors; ties studs/posts to foundation.
METAL HOLD-DOWN/UPLIFT ANCHOR

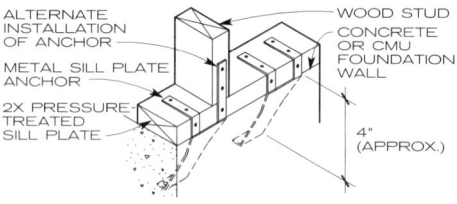

NOTE: Anchors sill plate to concrete or CMU foundation wall and/or studs.
SILL PLATE ANCHORS/SIDE INSTALLATION

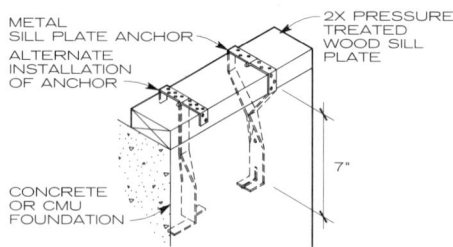

NOTE: Anchors sill plate to concrete or CMU foundation wall.
SILL PLATE ANCHORS/CENTERLINE INSTALLATION

ANCHORS

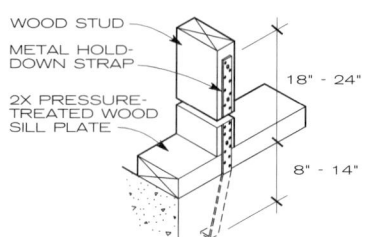

NOTE: Anchors sill plate and stud to concrete or CMU foundation wall.
METAL HOLD-DOWN/UPLIFT STRAP

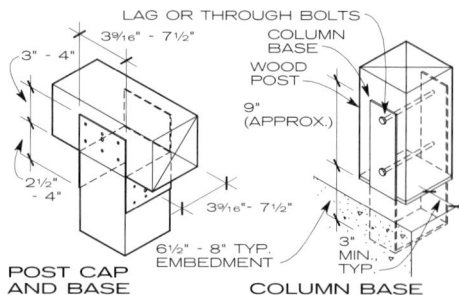

POST CAP/BASE: For varied post cap or base connections.
COLUMN BASE: Attaches wood post to concrete embedment to resist high uplift loads.
COLUMN CAPS AND BASES

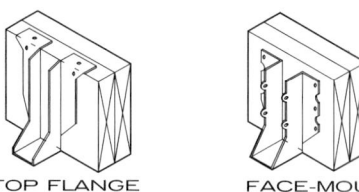

NOTE: Joist connector (in wide variety of sizes).
JOIST HANGERS

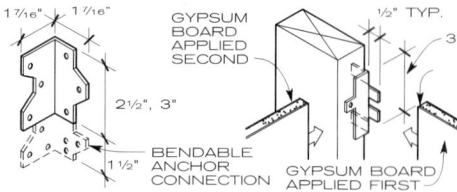

FRAMING ANCHOR: For varied wood-to-wood two-way connections; optional bendable extensions allow three-way connections.
BACK-UP CLIP: To provide back-up support for gypsum board in lieu of wood framing; can save wood material.

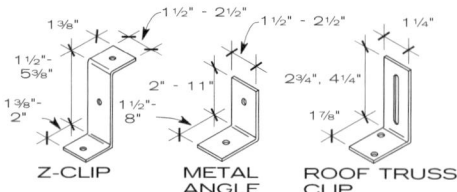

Z-CLIP: Secures 2x blocking between joists and/or trusses.
METAL ANGLE: Provides varied wood-to-wood or wood-to-concrete anchorage.
ROOF TRUSS CLIP: Provides alignment control between roof truss and nonbearing walls; slot permits load-induced truss movement.
VARIOUS CLIPS AND ANCHORS

and other fasteners may corrode when in contact with material treated with certain preservatives. Fasteners made of hot-dipped galvanized steel, copper, silicon bronze, and 304 and 316 stainless steel have performed well in wood treated with ammoniacal copper arsenate (ACA) and chromated copper arsenate (CCA), the most common preservatives for wood. Of course, provision should always be made to avoid galvanic action between dissimilar metals.

Richard J. Vitullo, AIA; Oak Leaf Studio; Crownsville, Maryland

FASTENERS AND ADHESIVES

Treated Wood Foundations

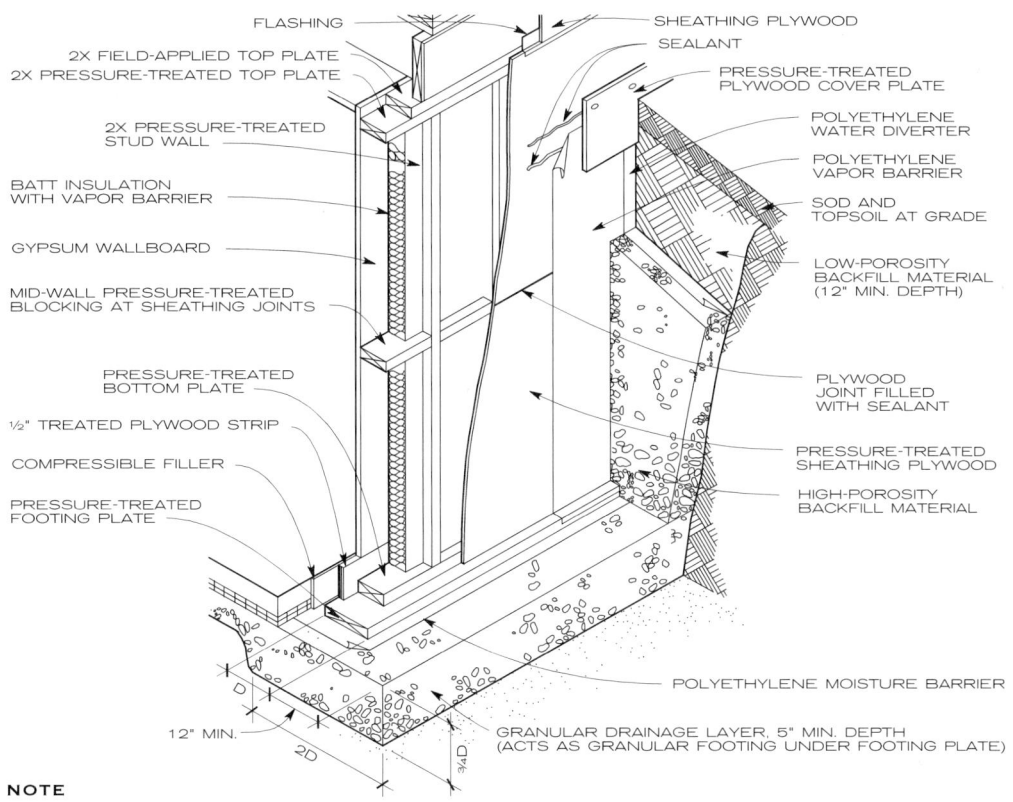

TYPICAL BASEMENT WALL

NOTE
1. Geotextile material may be used under and around drainage layers and backfill if soil conditions warrant.
2. Stud size and spacing vary with material grade and backfill depth. In general, 42 in. backfill requires 2x4 at 12 in. o.c., 64 in. requires 2x6 at 16 in. o.c., and 84 in. requires 2x6 at 12 in. o.c..

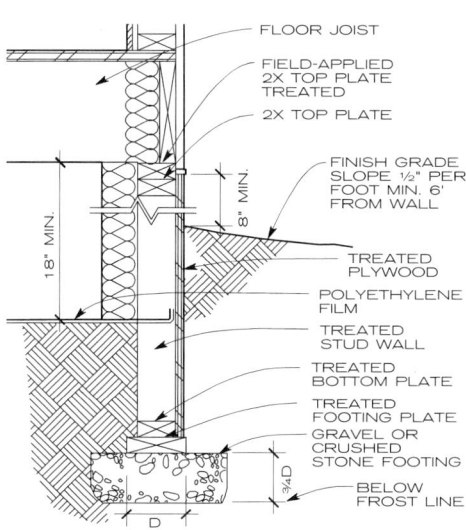

CRAWL SPACE WALL

MINIMUM SOIL COVER ON SHALLOW FOOTINGS

BASEMENT WALL WITH EXTERIOR KNEE WALL

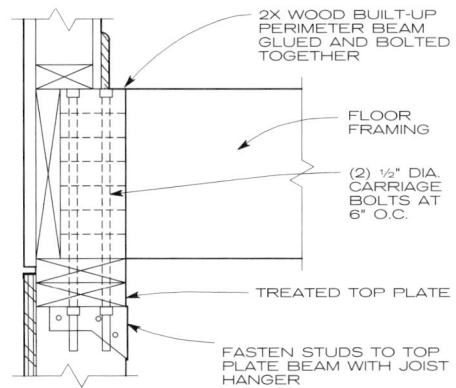

BUILT-UP PERIMETER BEAM AT STAIRS

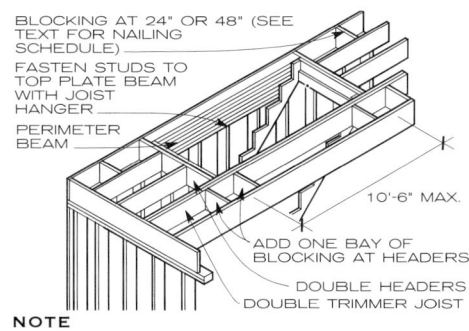

NOTE
For less than 48 in. backfill, use standard framing methods and fasten stairwell header to top plate with three 10d toenails.

STAIR OPENING AT PERIMETER WALL

INTRODUCTION

The construction of treated wood foundations is similar to the construction of standard wood light-frame walls except for two factors: (1) the wood used is pressure treated with wood preservatives, and (2) the extra loading and stress requirements caused by below-grade conditions must be accommodated in the design and detailing of the fasteners, connections, blocking, wall corners, and the like.

As with standard masonry or concrete foundation systems, treated wood foundations require a good drainage system in order to maintain dry basements and crawl spaces. However, the drainage system typically used with treated wood foundations is different from that used with masonry or concrete systems. The components of a drainage system suitable for use with a treated wood foundation are

1. A highly porous backfill material, which directs water down to a granular drainage layer.
2. A porous granular drainage layer under the entire foundation and floor system to collect and discharge water.
3. Positive discharge of water by means of a sump system designed for the soil type. This drainage system, developed for treated wood foundations, takes the place of the typical porous backfill over a perimeter drain tile.

NOTES

1. Characteristics of a treated wood foundation system:
   a. All framing is standard 2x construction.
   b. Can be erected in any weather and when site access for concrete or masonry is a problem.
   c. Deep wall cavities allow use of high R-value insulation without loss of interior space.
   d. Wiring and finishing are easily achieved.
2. Treated wood foundations are not appropriate for all sites. Selection of the proper foundation system for a project depends on site conditions, including soil types, drainage conditions, ground water, and other factors. Wet sites in low areas, especially areas with coarse-grained soil, should be avoided if a full basement is desired, although a crawl space-type foundation can be used in these cases. Consult a soils engineer to determine the viability of any foundation system.
3. Lumber and plywood used in treated wood foundations must be grade-stamped for foundation use and are typically pressure treated with chromated copper arsenate. Treated wood products used in foundation construction are required to contain more preservative than treated wood used in applications such as fencing and decking. Codes generally call for hot-dipped galvanized fasteners above grade and stainless steel fasteners below grade.
4. Avoid skin contact and prolonged or frequent inhalation of sawdust when handling or working with any pressure-treated wood product.
5. Consult applicable building codes and the American Forest & Paper Association's "Permanent Wood Foundation System—Design, Fabrication, Installation Manual" for requirements and design guidelines. In the early stages of a project, consult with the building code officials for the area or jurisdiction to assess their familiarity with and willingness to approve this type of system.
6. The vertical and horizontal edge-to-edge joints of all plywood panels used in these systems should be sealed with a suitable sealant. Consult the American Plywood Association Source List "Caulks and Adhesives for Permanent Wood Foundation System, Form H405" for a list of high-performance caulking compounds.
7. Correct materials and details of construction are very important for treated wood foundations. If the contractor to be used for the installation is unfamiliar with this foundation system, the design should include the use of prefabricated foundation panels. Most problems with treated wood foundations can be traced to improper installation by inexperienced workers.
8. Since this type of foundation system depends especially on the first floor deck to absorb and distribute any backfill loads, backfilling cannot occur until the first floor deck is complete.

Richard J. Vitullo, AIA; Oak Leaf Studio; Crownsville, Maryland
American Forest & Paper Association; Washington, D.C.

ROUGH CARPENTRY

Treated Wood Foundations

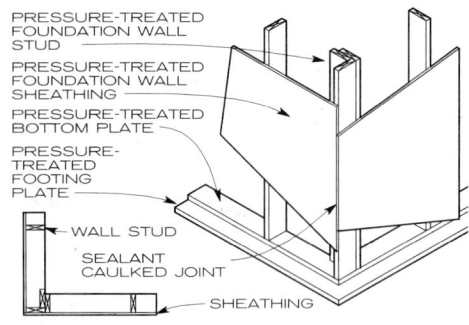

OUTSIDE CORNER DETAILS

NOTES
1. At an outside corner, soil pressures tend to force the wall sections together, making reinforcement unnecessary.
2. Three studs should be used at the corner to support interior finishes.

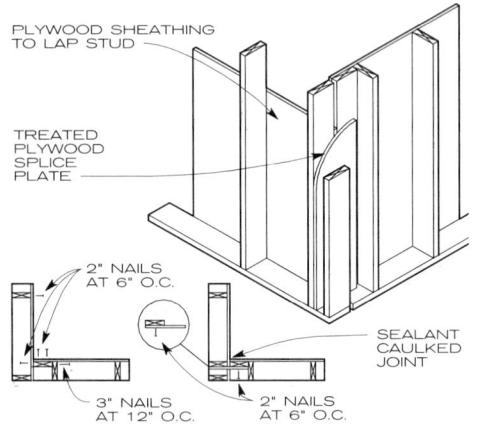

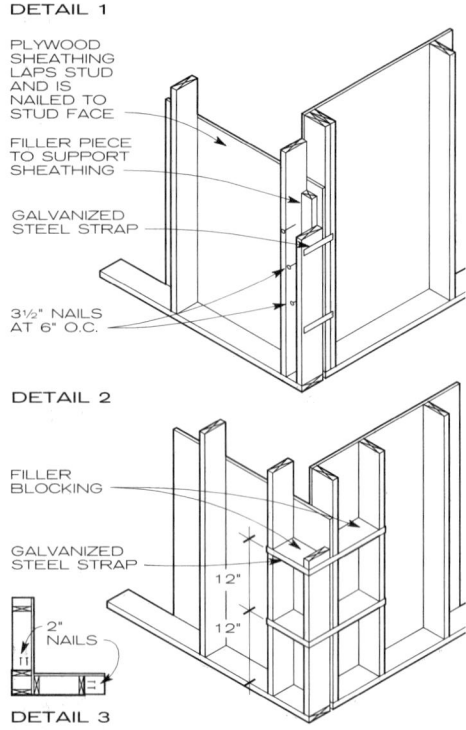

INSIDE CORNER DETAILS

NOTES
1. At inside corners, soil pressures tend to force the wall panels apart, making additional structural reinforcement necessary.
2. Detail no. 1 provides the required additional reinforcement with a treated plywood splice plate and additional nailing below grade.

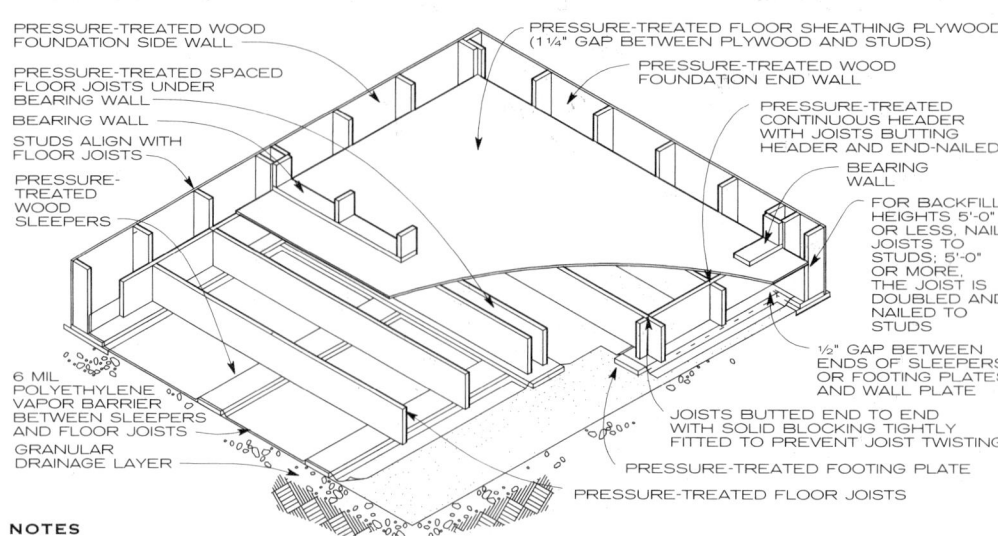

WOOD SLEEPER FLOOR SYSTEM

NOTES
1. Joists to be butted end to end over pressure-treated wood sleepers.
2. Floor stiffness will be increased by blocking between every joist above each sleeper.

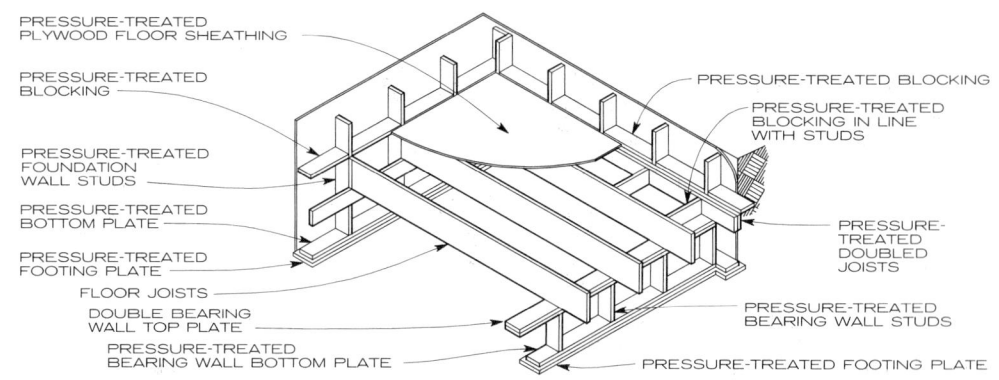

SUSPENDED WOOD FLOOR

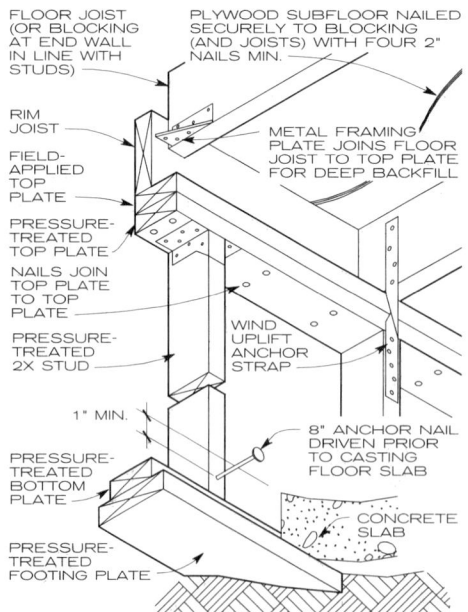

WALL ANCHORAGE DETAIL

NOTES
1. Fasteners and connector plates transfer soil pressure thrust from wall sheathing and studs to floor system; type and amount of fasteners and connectors depend on height of backfill.
2. Wind uplift anchor straps and anchor nails spaced as required by code.

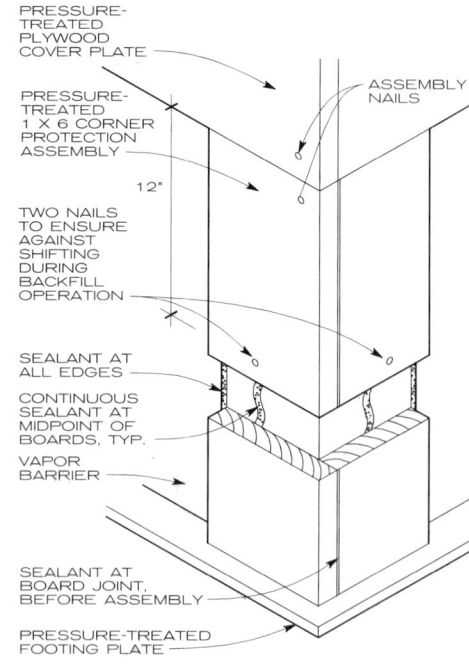

OUTSIDE CORNER PROTECTION DETAIL

NOTE
All wood members within 18 in. of the ground should be bottom treated.

Richard J. Vitullo, AIA; Oak Leaf Studio; Crownsville, Maryland
American Forest & Paper Association; Washington, DC

Treated Wood Foundations

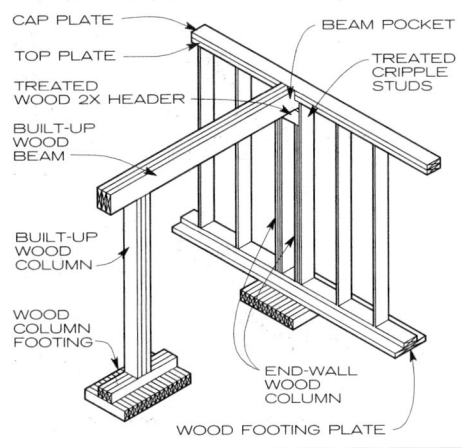

MAIN BEAMS AND COLUMNS

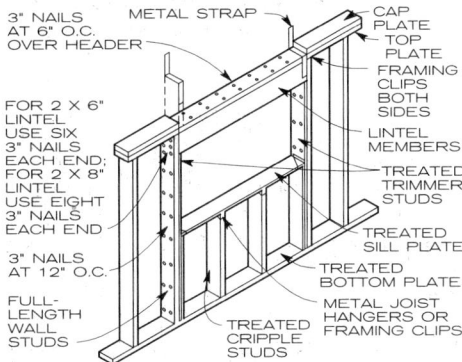

NOTES

1. For backfill heights up to 4 ft 6 in. and if width of opening is 4 ft 0 in. to 5 ft 6 in., use double sill plates and double full-length wall studs.
2. For backfill heights up to 4 ft 6 in. and if width of opening is 6 ft 0 in. to 9 ft 0 in., use triple sill plates and triple full-length wall studs.
3. For backfill heights of 48 in. or less, nailing and fastening can conform to the appropriate building code.
4. For backfill heights greater than 4 ft 6 in. or openings wider than 9 ft 0 in., contact engineer for design.

WINDOW FRAMING DETAIL

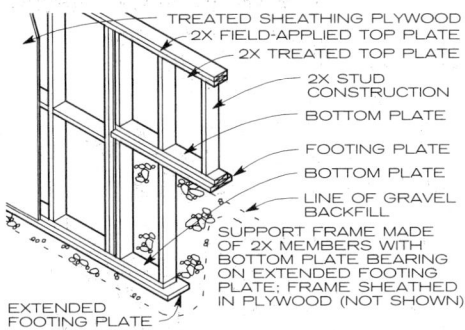

STEPPED FOOTING DETAIL

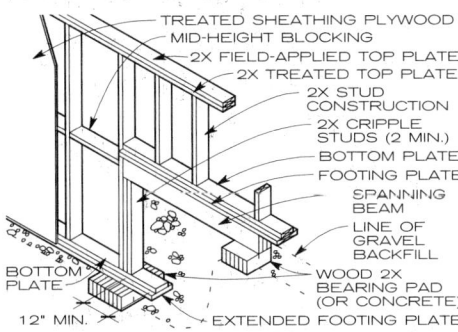

SPANNING BEAM DETAIL

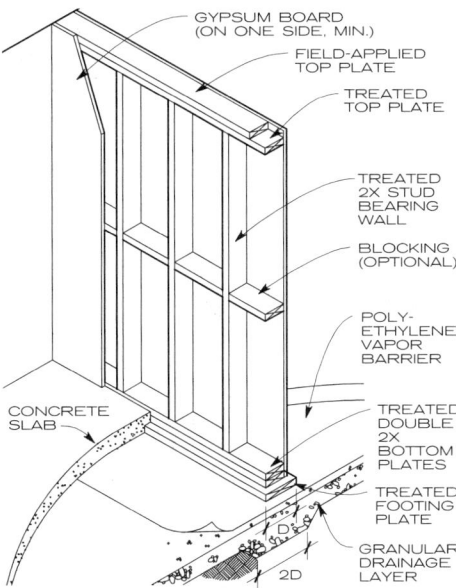

BEARING WALL AT CONCRETE SLAB

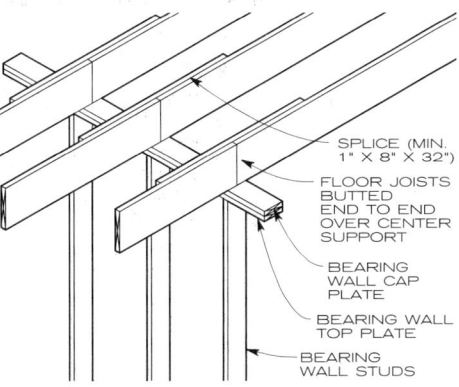

INTERIOR BEARING WALL—FLOOR JOIST SUPPORT

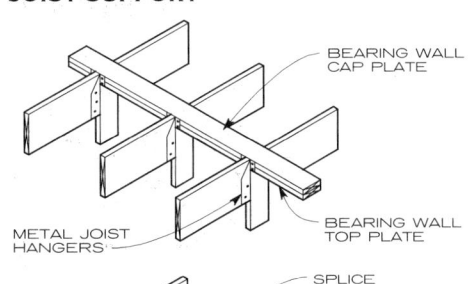

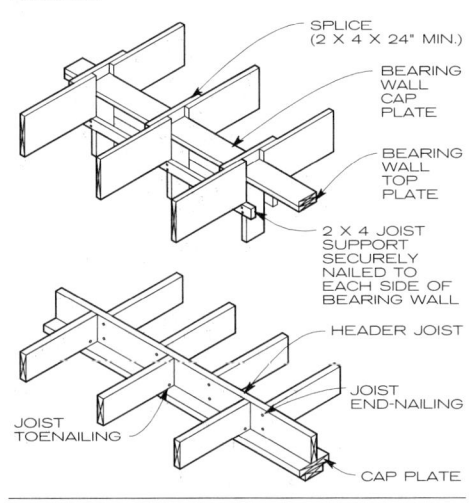

INTERIOR BEARING WALL—FLOOR JOIST SUPPORT (ALTERNATIVES)

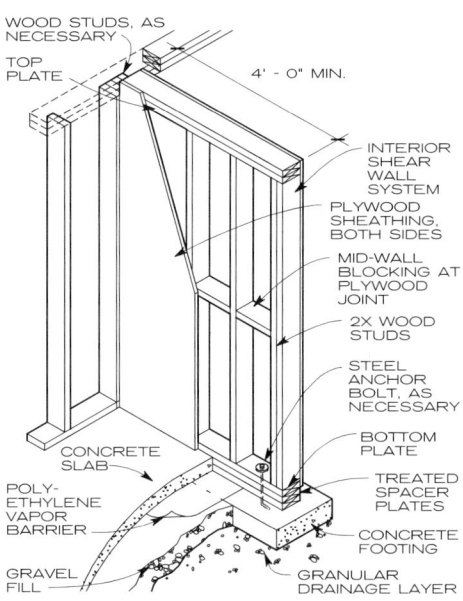

NOTE

Interior shear wall material does not need to be treated with wood preservatives.

INTERIOR SHEAR WALL DETAIL

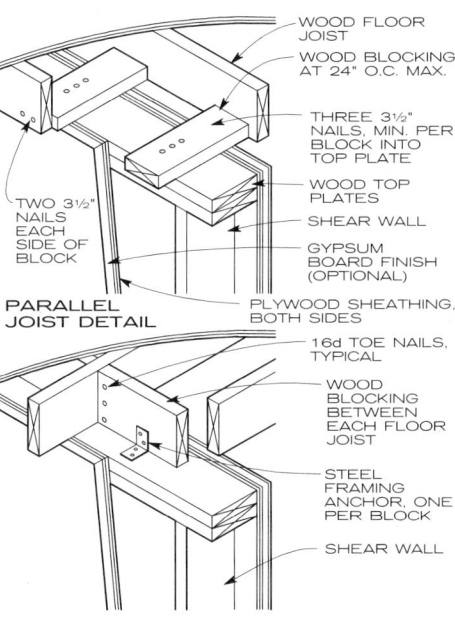

SHEAR WALL ANCHORAGE

SHEAR WALLS AS RACKING RESISTANCE

Foundation walls may be subject to racking loads, which occur parallel to a wall and can cause shearing forces along the plane of the wall. Racking loads are caused by soil pressure and other lateral forces such as earthquake and wind. Walls, connections, and fasteners must be designed to resist these forces. Generally, soil pressure comes into play for backfill greater than 24 in. in height; check anticipated wind and earthquake forces to determine how best to accommodate them.

Check long shear walls or those with a length-to-width ratio greater than 2:1 for diaphragm deflection, particularly if the structure is built on a slope. The unequal heights of the backfill on a slope apply unequal loads to the end walls or walls parallel to the floor joist system. These walls, having received these loads by the diaphragm action of the floor system, then act as shear walls. Internal shear walls, accommodated within interior partitions, also may be needed.

The strength of a diaphragm or shear wall depends on careful nailing of the plywood to the structural members. Plywood joints should be staggered to increase stiffness.

Richard J. Vitullo, AIA; Oak Leaf Studio; Crownsville, Maryland
American Forest & Paper Association; Washington, D.C.

ROUGH CARPENTRY

Timber Frame Construction

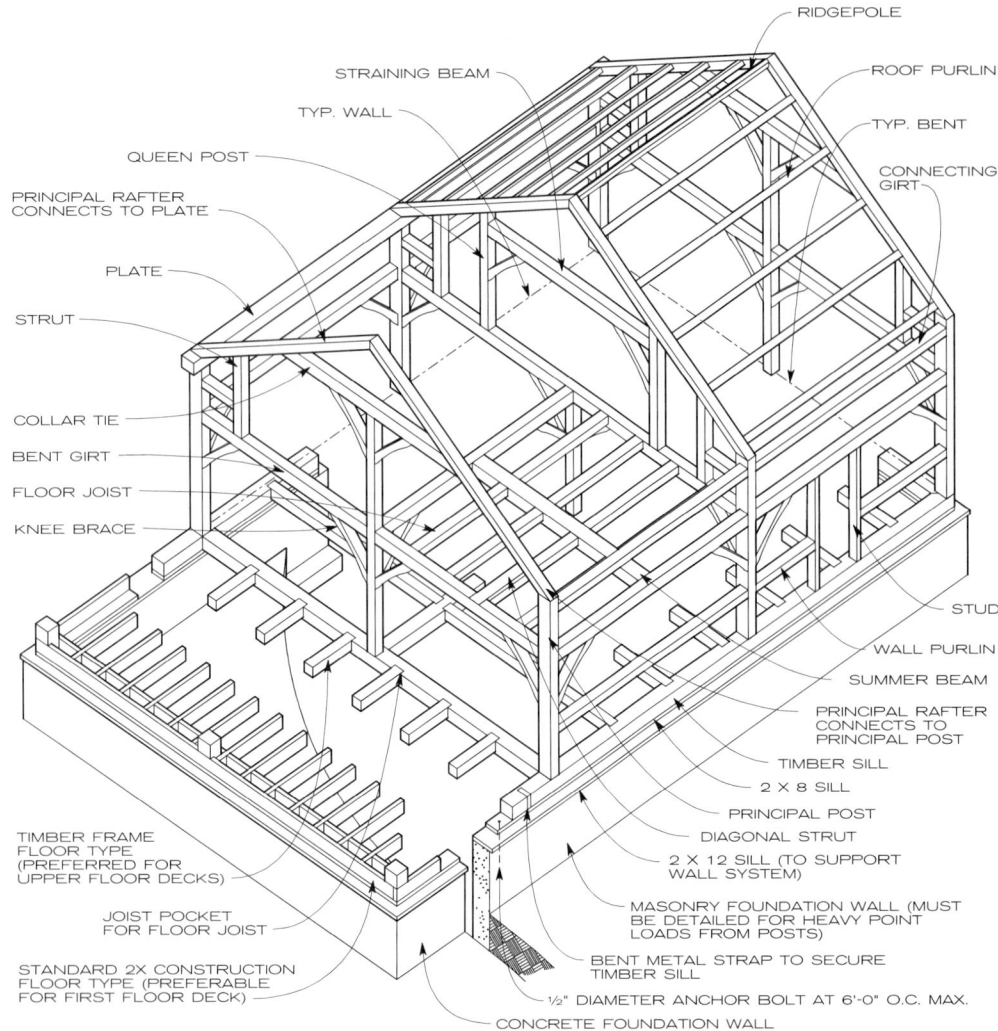

TYPICAL TIMBER FRAME (SHOWING TWO ROOF AND FLOOR TYPES)

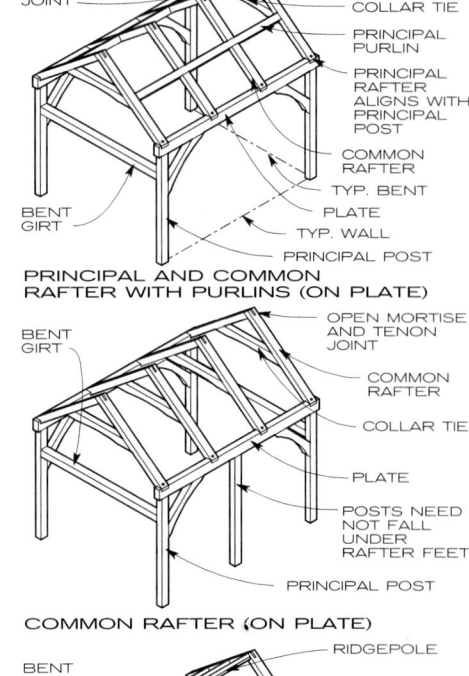

TIMBER FRAME ROOF TYPES

GENERAL

Timber frame buildings are characterized by large, exposed timber structural members. The distinction between timber framing and other types of heavy timber construction is somewhat subjective, but in a true timber frame, the posts, beams, and braces are connected to one another with elegant, largely all-wood joints based on very old traditions. Sound timber frame construction requires high standards of design, engineering, and workmanship. It can be compared to the craftsmanship of cabinetmaking, rather than to conventional wood frame construction.

One of the reasons timber frame construction faded from popularity around 1900, after centuries of dominance, was the cost of its labor-intensive building methods. During the past twenty years, techniques have been developed that offset this drawback: the frame can be prefabricated in shops with heavy tools, and structural, insulated wall panels can be used to build the walls. Connection details in true timber frame construction are still rooted in the ancient wood-pegged, mortise-and-tenon joint. More modern wood connectors of steel can be used, depending on budget and aesthetics, but many would say the resulting structure would not be a true timber frame.

Typically, posts in timber-framed buildings are spaced in a grid, 8 to 16 ft apart. These relatively large posts support beams, girts, connectors, plates, and principal rafters. In turn, those members support rafters, purlins, summer beams, and joists, which are spaced at 2 to 6 ft centers. The relatively large timbers make timber frame construction inherently fire resistant, qualifying as Class IV construction under most building codes.

The walls and roof in a timber frame, freed of the task of supporting great loads, can be made of materials that need to function only as a rain screen and curtain walls. These materials are attached to the outside of the larger, structural members, enclosing the space while exposing the timbers to the interior and protecting the frame from deterioration.

Nonstructural foam-core panels with an exterior layer of wood sheathing, a foam core, and an interior drywall finish layer are extremely energy efficient and cost-effective for use in wall and roof construction in a timber frame. Sometimes it is preferable to use structural foam-core panels, with oriented-strand board (OSB) or plywood sheathing on both sides, as they better resist warping and lateral forces and provide a better nailing surface for attaching interior trim, cabinets, artwork, etc. These structural panels are typically installed outside a layer of gypsum board that is back-screwed to the inner OSB skin.

ANATOMY OF A TIMBER FRAME BUILDING

In the design process, the general layout of timbers is determined first, based on the rough program and layout of spaces. Once the wood species has been selected, each timber is sized individually. Next, the connection details, or joinery, and the embellishments and finishes are designed.

A typical timber frame can be divided into four major systems: walls, floors, roof, and bents. Walls, in the terminology of timber framing, are planar compositions of timbers parallel to the walls and are often the primary preassembled sections of the building. Usually, bents include the principal structural posts of the frame and the major supporting rafters. The space between two bents is called a bay and is generally between 10 and 16 ft wide. If the roof structure is not included in the bent system, a large timber plate is set at the top of the bent or wall for the roof framing to rest on.

ROOF SYSTEMS

More than any other factor, the arrangement of timbers in the roof determines whether the walls or the bents will be the principal structural unit. Frames are often defined by the type of roof they support, since the roof is usually the most difficult aspect of the frame to design, detail, and erect. The choice of roof system most appropriate to a particular building depends on the shape and pitch of the roof, the loading, wood species, available timber length, floor plan, and personal aesthetic preferences.

NOTES

1. Wood shrinks considerably across the grain but very little along the grain, and all dimensions based on sections through plates and sills must account for this shrinkage. Bents that connect principal rafters directly to the posts and are not interrupted by plates will have negligible differential movement between roof and wall joints.

2. Timber systems that rely on full-length plates, sills, ridgepoles, or tie beams tend to require timbers of considerable length, which are scarce. Therefore, these long lengths must be assembled from shorter members tied together with scarf joints. Since most sawmills cannot obtain timbers longer than 30 ft, it is important to consult with a structural engineer and local sawmill to determine the most practical dimensions for the timbers before the design is completed.

3. Depending on budget or aesthetic priorities, hybrid systems can be devised, such as timber frame walls with conventional roof framing or conventional stud walls with a timber frame roof. Consult a structural engineer about the design, detailing, and integration of these systems.

Richard J. Vitullo, AIA; Oak Leaf Studio; Crownsville, Maryland
Tedd Benson and Ben Brungraber, Ph.D., PE; Benson Woodworking Co., Inc.; Alstead, New Hampshire

ROUGH CARPENTRY

Timber Frame Construction

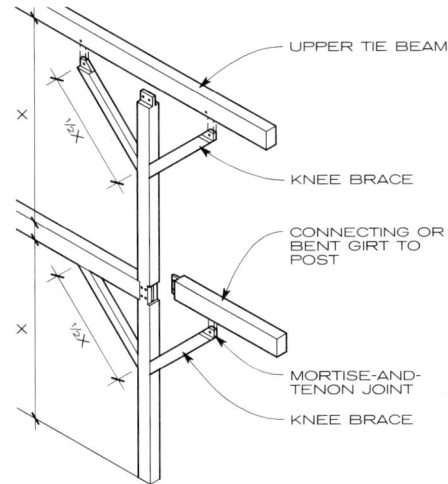

NOTE

For basic structural rigidity within a timber frame, the knee brace is a critical component. It is typically used between the upper ends of vertical posts and horizontal beams, but may also be used at the base of a post or to brace an inclined member, such as a rafter. Rigidity in a frame can be achieved by using a few well-placed long braces or several shorter braces. Braces typically should not be shorter than half the length of the beam-to-beam span of the post.

KNEE BRACE

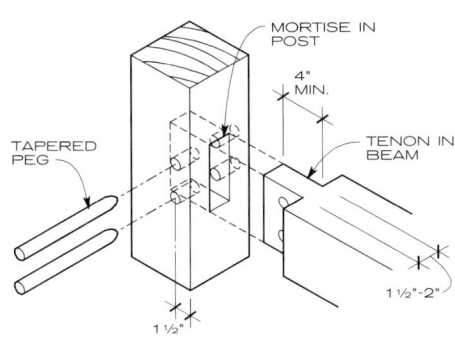

NOTE

The basic mortise-and-tenon joint can be very effective in resisting both tension and compression forces. To increase tensile strength, increase the depth and thickness of the tenon and use additional pegs if the width and length of the tenon allow.

BASIC MORTISE-AND-TENON JOINT

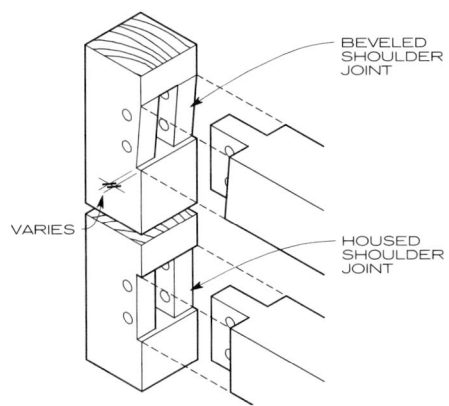

NOTE

A beveled shoulder or housed joint is used to connect all load-bearing beams, such as bent and connecting girts and summer beams, to posts. Angled variations can be used when principal rafters join to posts or for diagonal braces. The depth of the shoulder depends on loading, torsion, other joinery in the area, and wood species.

SHOULDERED MORTISE-AND-TENON JOINTS

Richard J. Vitullo, AIA; Oak Leaf Studio; Crownsville, Maryland
Tedd Benson and Ben Brungraber, Ph.D., PE; Benson Woodworking Co., Inc.; Alstead, New Hampshire

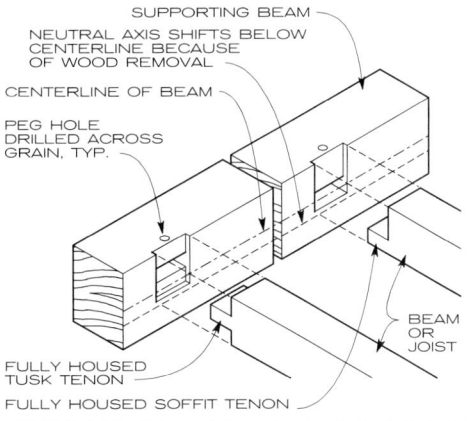

TUSK AND SOFFIT TENON JOINTS

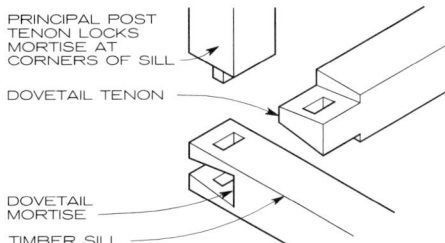

DOVETAIL MORTISE AND TENON

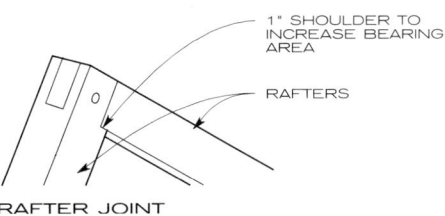

RAFTER JOINT

OPEN MORTISE-AND-TENON JOINTS

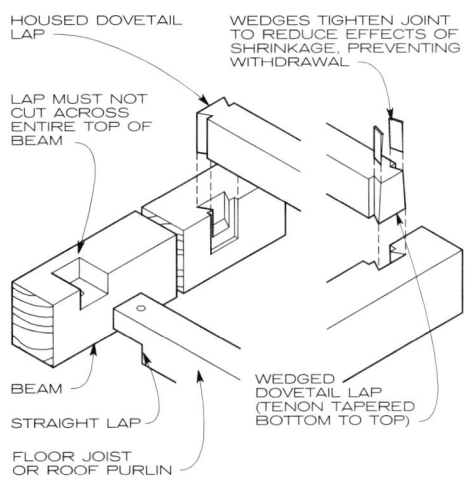

LAP JOINTS

WOOD JOINERY

Most timber framing joints are variations on the mortise and tenon, in which a tongue on one timber is received by a slot in the other and locked with rounded pegs driven through holes drilled through both parts of the joint. The simplest version of this joint is used in compression situations or for situations with minimal loading. Knee braces and collar ties generally use an angled variation.

Spline joints are similar to a mortise and tenon, except that a third member, called a spline or "free tenon" (usually hardwood), is introduced to connect between mortised timbers and to serve as the tie. Spline joints are an effective way to achieve minimum end and edge distances without being dependent on the size and capacity of the receiving post or beam.

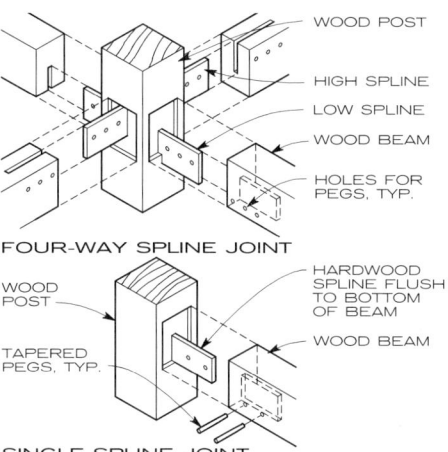

SPLINE JOINTS

NOTE

Using through-splines made of hardwood leaves all the pegs loaded parallel to the grain, with plenty of available end-grain distance, and avoids loaded edges in the posts. Spline edges often are left prominent to achieve a decorative effect.

SPLINE JOINTS

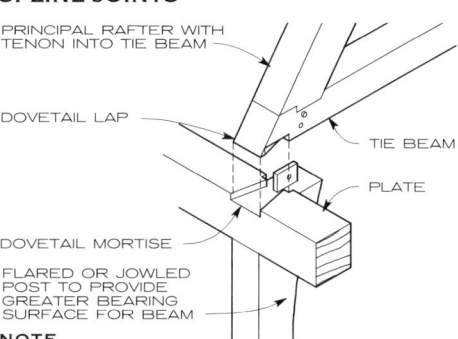

NOTE

A tying joint is a combination of joints used to connect several members. The intersection of a principal post, a plate, a tie beam, and a rafter is known as a tying joint.

TYING JOINT

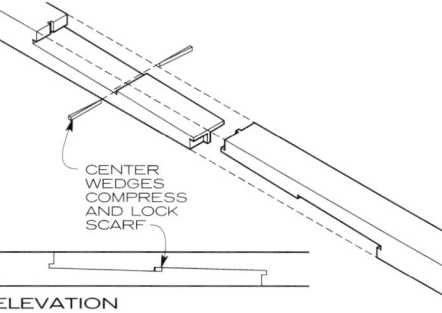

SCARF JOINT

NOTE

Scarf joints are lap joints used to splice two or more shorter timbers into one long timber. Although there are many variations, scarf joints are used primarily for plates and sills that demand long continuous timber.

SCARF JOINT

Lap joints, such as simple overlaps or dovetails, constitute the other broad category of joints used in timber frames. Scarfs, used to splice timbers along their length, are variations of the lap joint.

Joints are chosen on the basis of the tasks they are to fulfill, including locking the frame together, bearing weight, and transferring forces and building loads from one timber to another.

Compound joinery, such as where two timber valley rafters meet at a purlin, is one of the difficult aspects of timber framing. The complex geometry and the precision required demand master-level craftsmanship.

ROUGH CARPENTRY

Timber Frame Construction

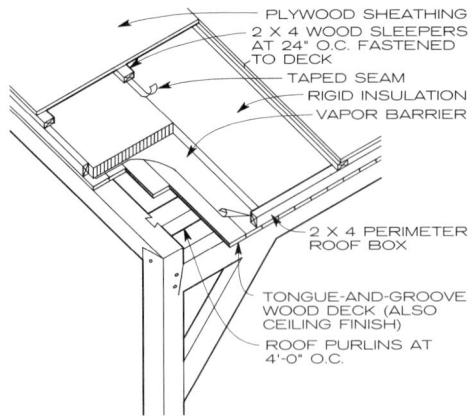

WOOD SLEEPERS AND TONGUE-AND-GROOVE CEILING ON ROOF PURLINS

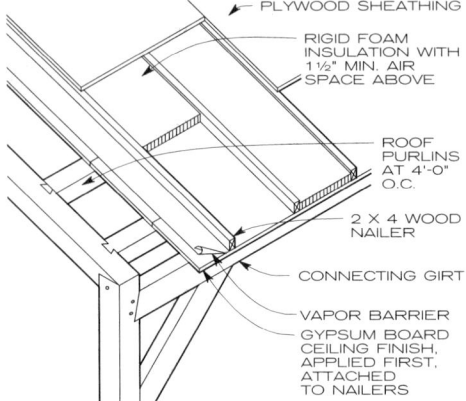

WOOD NAILERS ON ROOF PURLINS

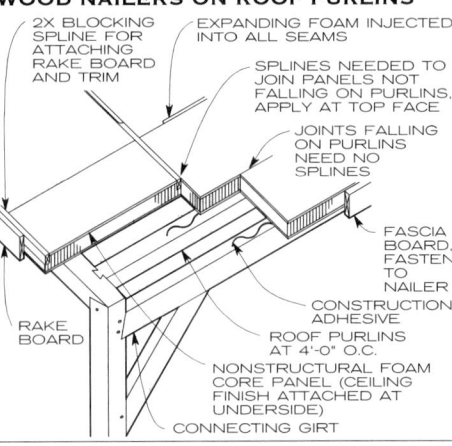

NONSTRUCTURAL FOAM CORE PANELS ON ROOF PURLINS

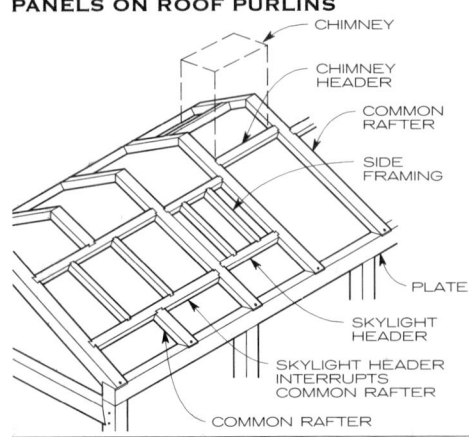

ROOF FRAMING HEADERS

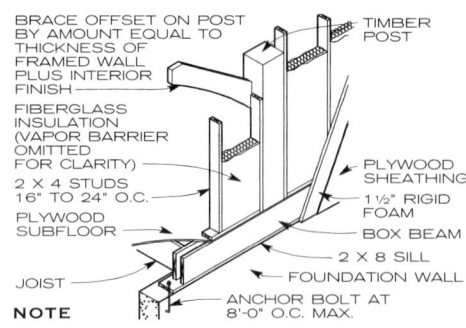

NOTE

This system reduces the exposure of the timber frame by partially concealing the frame in the wall system. It allows air infiltration due to shrinkage and movement and requires an exterior rigid foam insulation layer to minimize the potential for air movement and condensation.

INFILL WOOD STUD SYSTEM

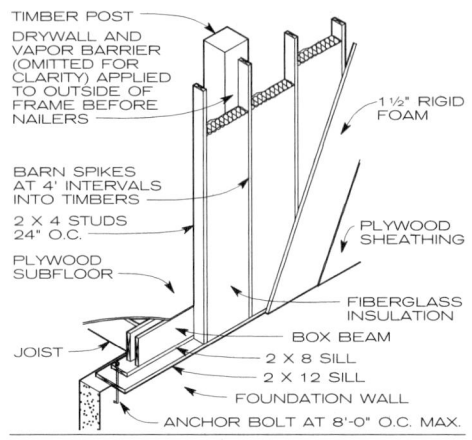

EXTERIOR WOOD STUD SYSTEM

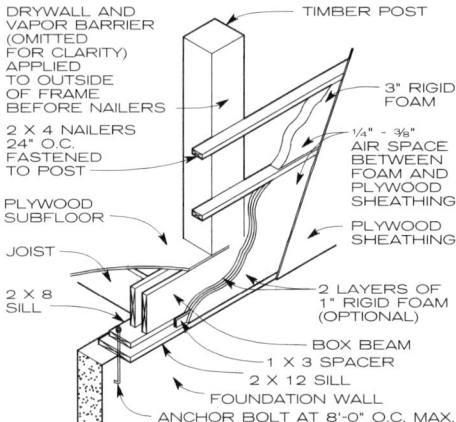

HORIZONTAL NAILER WALL SYSTEM

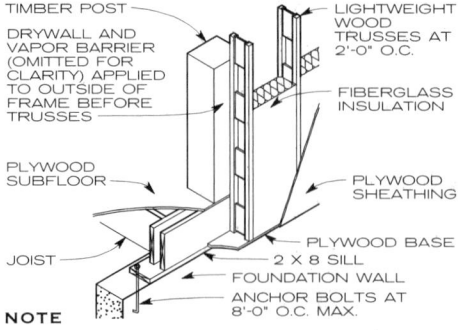

NOTE

This system allows a great deal of insulation to be packed into the nonstructural wall cavity between trusses. The foundation wall may be offset to the outside of the truss system (with pilasters added on the inside to support timber posts) to avoid the appearance of excess overhang.

EXTERIOR LIGHTWEIGHT WOOD TRUSS SYSTEM

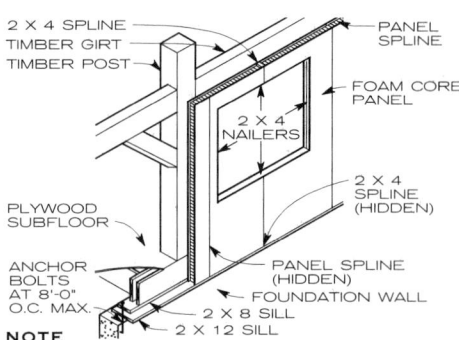

NOTE

Structural foam core panels (with wood sheathing on both sides of the foam core) may be needed at areas that may have excess stress or loading with interior finish attached to the frame before the panels are attached.

FOAM CORE PANEL WALL SYSTEM

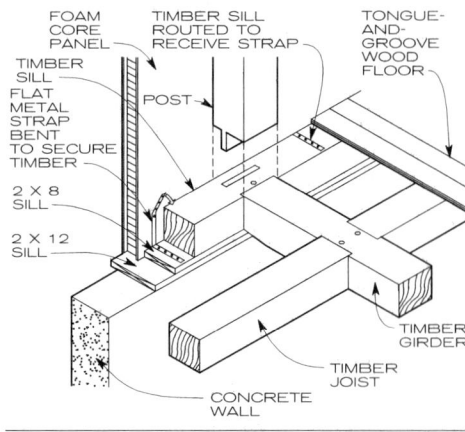

TIMBER SILL AND JOIST SYSTEM

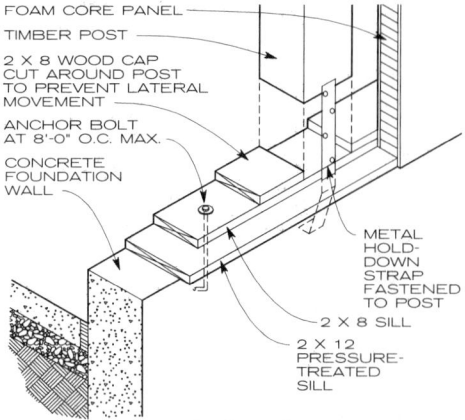

STANDARD 2X LUMBER SILL

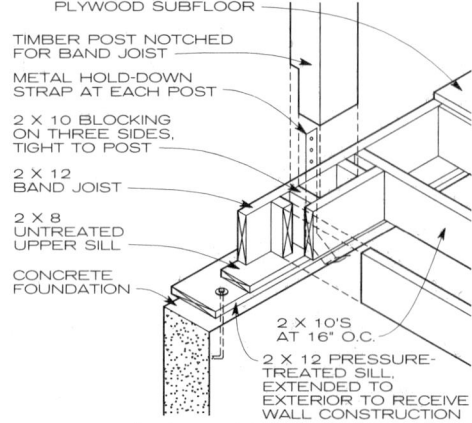

STICK FRAME SILL AND FLOOR DECK

Richard J. Vitullo, AIA; Oak Leaf Studio; Crownsville, Maryland
Tedd Benson and Ben Brungraber, Ph.D., PE; Benson Woodworking Co., Inc.; Alstead, New Hampshire

ROUGH CARPENTRY

Timber Frame Construction

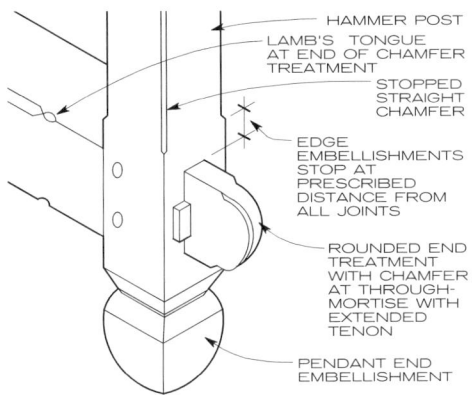
END AND EDGE EMBELLISHMENTS

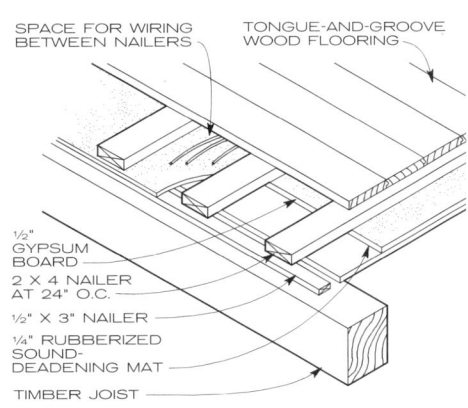
UNDER FLOOR SERVICE CHASE

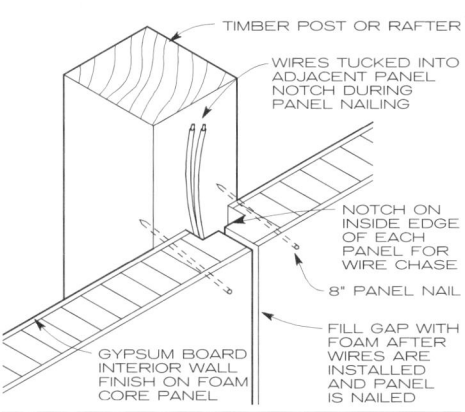
TIMBER POST OR RAFTER AT FOAM CORE PANEL WIRE CHASE DETAIL

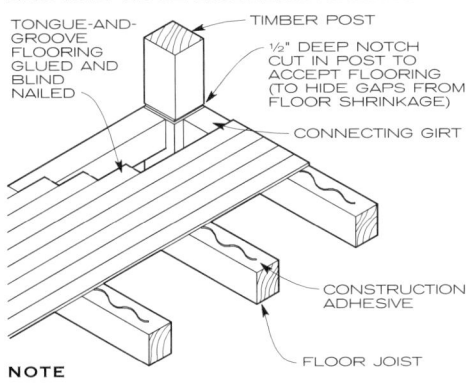
NOTE
Maintain 5/8 in. gap between flooring edge and wall for expansion and contraction.

STANDARD TONGUE-AND-GROOVE FLOOR

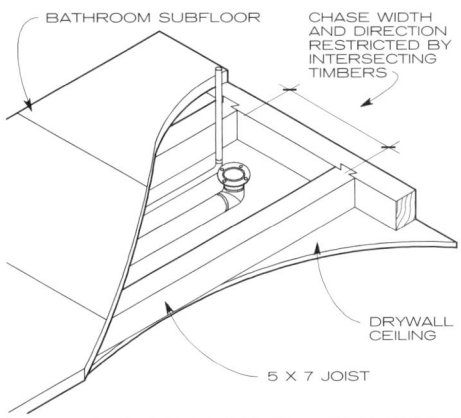
UNDER FLOOR SERVICE CHASE BETWEEN TIMBER JOISTS

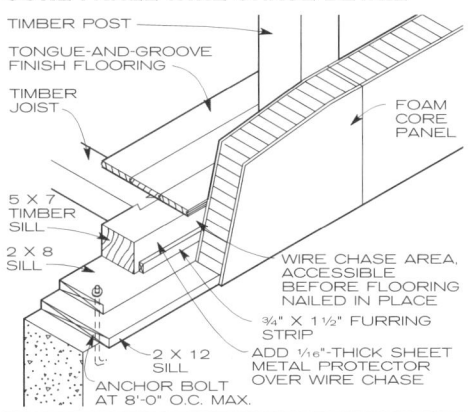
TIMBER-SILL WIRE CHASE DETAIL

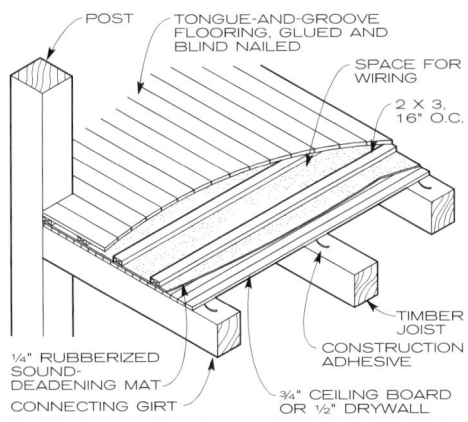
SOUND-RESISTANT FLOOR DETAIL

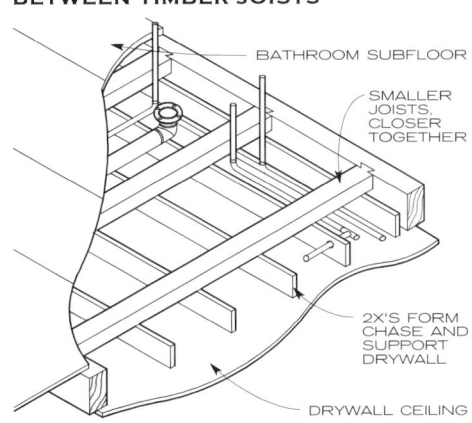
UNDER FLOOR SERVICE CHASE WITH DROPPED CEILING DETAIL

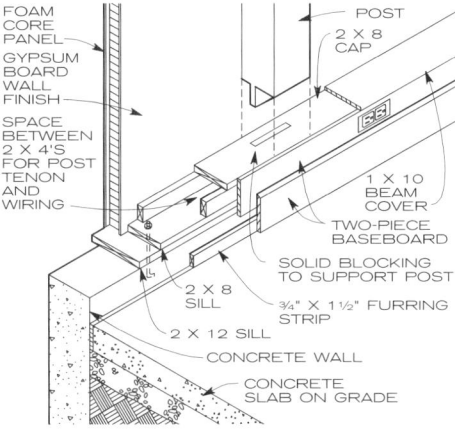
BOX BEAM SILL WIRE CHASE DETAIL

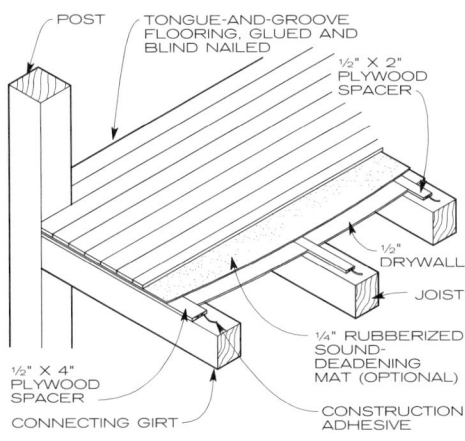
GYPSUM BOARD CEILING WITH SPACERS

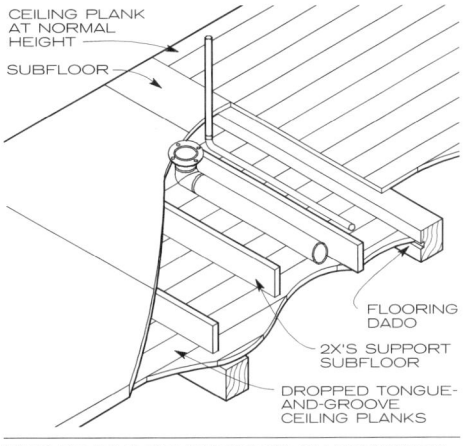
UNDER FLOOR SERVICE CHASE WITH DROPPED FLOOR DETAIL

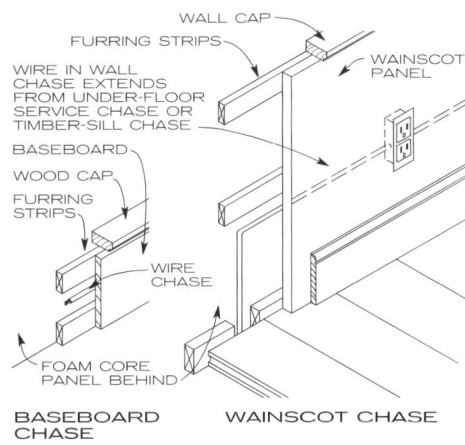
SURFACE-MOUNTED WIRE CHASES AT FOAM CORE PANEL

Richard J. Vitullo, AIA; Oak Leaf Studio; Crownsville, Maryland
Tedd Benson and Ben Brungraber, Ph.D., PE; Benson Woodworking Co., Inc.; Alstead, New Hampshire

ROUGH CARPENTRY

Wood Truss Construction

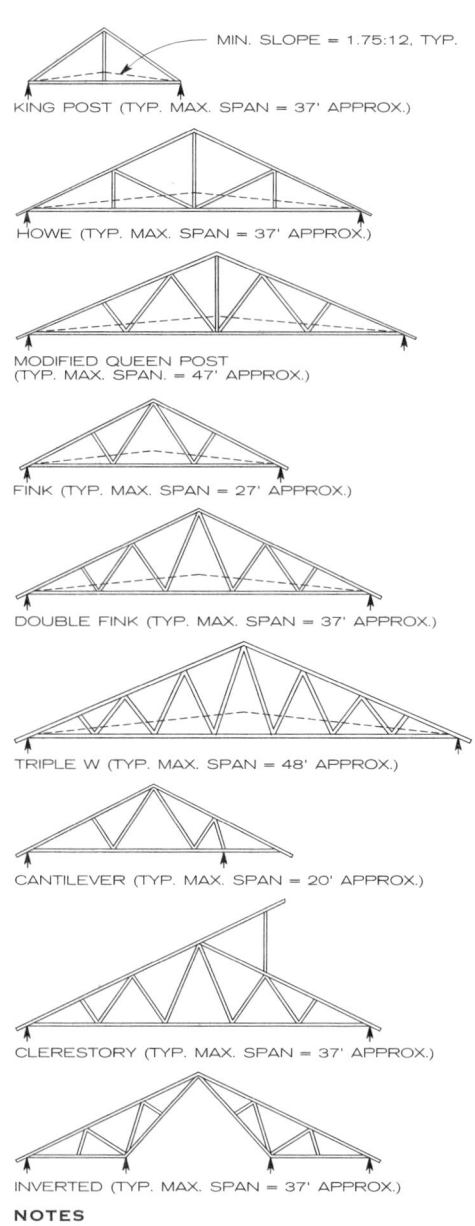

NOTES

1. The average spacing for light trusses (trussed rafters) is 2 ft o.c. but varies up to 4 ft. The average combined dead and live loads is 45 lb per sq ft. Spans are usually between 20 and 32 ft but can be as much as 50 ft.
2. Early in the design process, consult an engineer or truss supplier for pre-engineered truss designs to establish the most economical and efficient truss proportions. The supplier may provide final truss engineering design.
3. Permanent and temporary erection bracing must be installed as specified to prevent failure of properly designed trusses.
4. Some locales require an engineer's stamp when prefab trusses are used. Check local codes.
5. Member forces in a truss rise rapidly as the lower chord is raised above the horizontal.

PITCHED CHORD TRUSSES

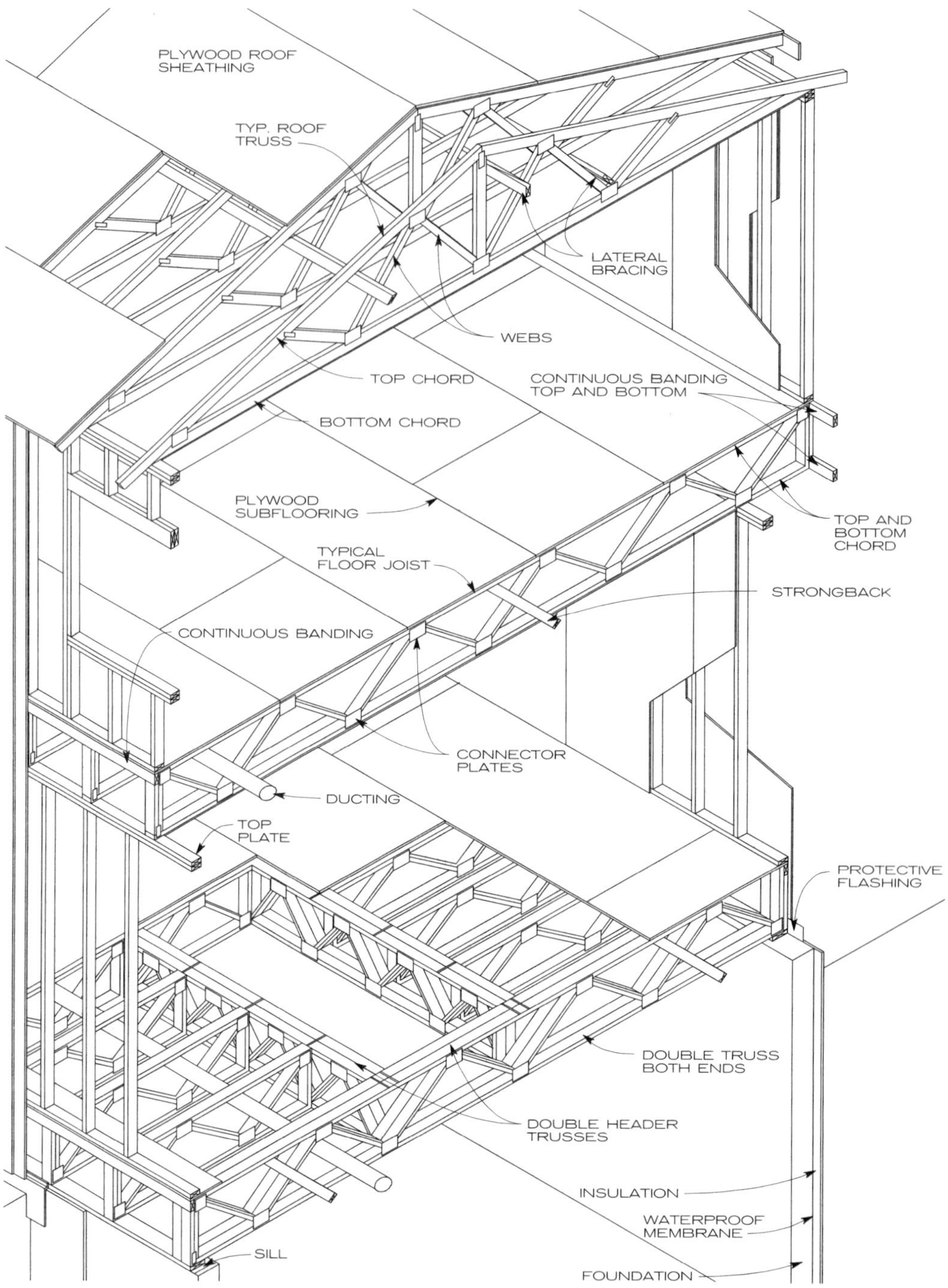

PLATE TOOTH PUNCHED THROUGH PLATE HAS PARTICULAR LENGTH, SHAPE, AND TWIST; ALL AFFECT WITHDRAWAL STRENGTH (TOOTH LATERAL RESISTANCE)

GAUGE NET AREA OF STRUCTURAL STEEL LEFT IN PLATE AFTER PUNCHED TEETH ARE FORMED; RESIDUAL STRENGTH OF THIS UNPUNCHED STEEL IS USED TO TRANSFER FORCES IN TRUSS JOINT

PLATE CONNECTOR PRESSED BY PNEUMATIC, HYDRAULIC, OR ROLLER PRESS INTO BOTH SIDES OF TRUSS

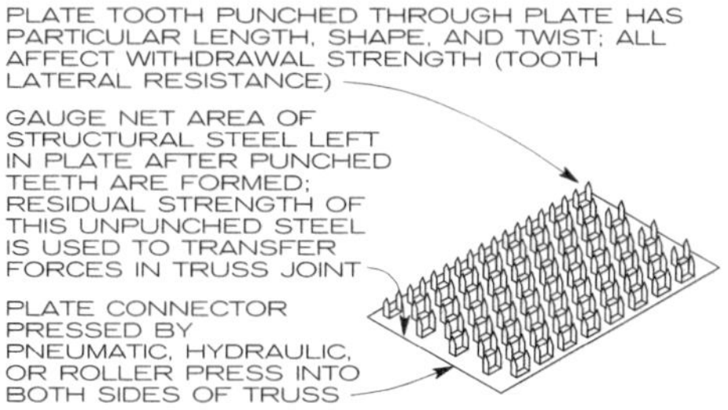

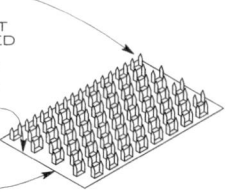

TYPICAL METAL PLATE CONNECTOR

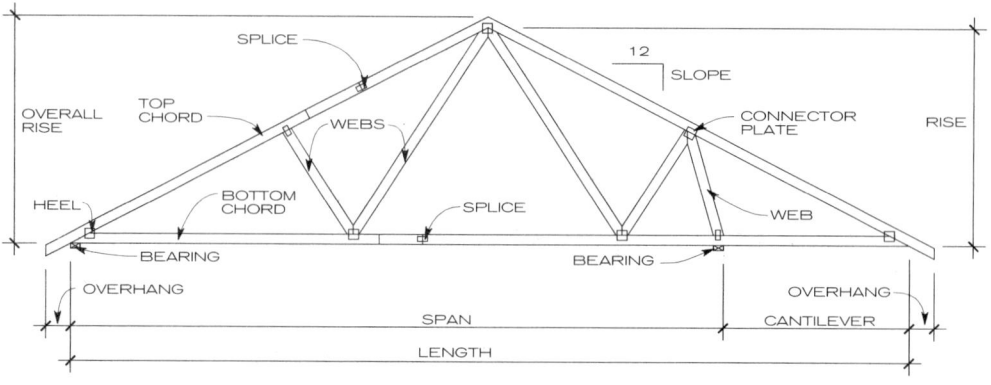

TRUSS FRAMING

TYPICAL PITCHED CHORD ROOF TRUSS

Richard J. Vitullo, AIA; Oak Leaf Studio; Crownsville, Maryland

ROUGH CARPENTRY

Wood Truss Construction

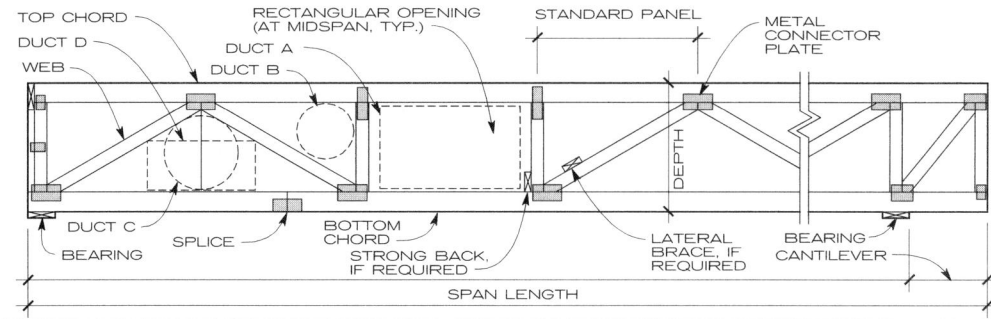

TYPICAL PARALLEL CHORD FLOOR AND ROOF TRUSS

DEPTH OF TRUSS AND SIZE OF DUCTWORK (IN.)

DEPTH	A	B	C	D		
10	6 ½ x 22	5 ½	5	3 x 25	4 x 15	5 x 9
12	8 ½ x 22	6 ½	7	5 x 20	6 x 14	7 x 7
14	10 ½ x 22	7 ½	9	6 x 23	7 x 16	8 x 11
16	12 ½ x 22	9	11	7 x 22	8 x 18	9 x 14
18	14 ½ x 22	10	12	8 x 24	9 x 20	10 x 16
20	16 ½ x 22	11	14 ½	8 x 28	9 x 24	10 x 21
22	18 ½ x 22	12	16	8 x 30	10 x 25	12 x 19

NOTE: The relative ease of running electrical and mechanical components through framing is a major advantage of a truss roof system. Sizes given here are approximate; verify individual sizes carefully. Duct sizes are based on maximum panel sizes allowable by prior arrangement.

PARALLEL CHORD TRUSS—SPANS FOR PRELIMINARY DESIGN

TRUSSED RAFTERS SPACING (C TO C)(IN.)—RESIDENTIAL LOADS

	FLOORS			ROOFS					
	A. 55 PSF			B. 40 PSF		C. 55 PSF		C. 55 PSF*	
DEPTH (IN.)	12	16	24	16	24	16	24	16	24
12	23-6	21-0	17-1	24-0	21-4	21-11	18-2		
13	24-11	22-0	17-11						
14	26-4	22-11	18-8	27-5	23-3	24-5	19-10		
15	27-7	23-10	19-5						
16	28-7	24-9	20-1	30-3	25-0	26-4	21-4	31-10	27-10
18	30-6	26-4	21-5	32-11	26-9	28-1	22-9	35-1	30-7
20	32-4	27-11	22-8	34-8	28-0	29-7	23-11	38-1	33-1
22	34-0	26-9	23-11						
24	35-8	30-10	25-0	38-3	30-11	32-7	26-4	43-10	36-7
28				41-6	33-6	35-5	28-7	49-2	39-11
32				44-3	35-7	37-8	30-4	52-9	42-9
36				47-0	37-10	40-1	32-3	56-3	45-7
48								60-0	53-3

TRUSSED RAFTERS SPACING (C TO C)(IN.)—COMMERCIAL FLOOR LOADS

	D. 80 PSF			E. 100 PSF			F. 120 PSF		
DEPTH (IN.)	12	16	24	12	16	24	12	16	24
12	19-0	17-3	15-1	17-3	15-8	13-7	16-0	14-7	12-4
14	21-4	19-4	16-6	19-4	17-7	14-9	18-0	16-4	13-6
16	23-6	21-5	17-10	21-5	19-5	15-11	19-10	17-11	14-6
18	25-8	23-4	19-0	23-4	21-0	17-0	21-8	19-2	15-6
20	27-8	24-10	20-2	25-2	22-3	18-0	23-4	20-3	16-5
24	31-6	27-5	22-2	28-5	24-6	19-10	25-11	22-4	18-1
16*	27-7	25-1	21-11	25-1	22-9	19-11	23-2	21-2	18-5
24*	38-0	34-6	30-1	34-6	31-4	27-4	32-0	29-1	25-1
32*	47-1	42-9	36-1	42-9	38-10	32-3	39-8	36-1	29-5

LOAD	A (PSF)	B (PSF)	C (PSF)	D (PSF)	E (PSF)	F (PSF)
Top chord live load	40	20	35	60	80	100
Top chord dead load	10	10	10	10	10	10
Bottom chord dead load	5	10	10	10	10	10
TOTAL LOAD	55	40	55	80	100	120

* indicates a double-chorded truss, top and bottom.

NOTES

1. Spans are clear, inside to inside, for bottom chord bearing. Values shown would vary only slightly for a truss with top chord loading.
2. Designed deflection limit under total load is $l/240$ for roofs, $l/360$ for residential floors, and $l/480$ for commercial floors.
3. Spans should not exceed 24 in. x depth of truss.
4. Roof spans include a +15% short-term stress.
5. Spans shown are for only one type of lumber; in this case—#2 Southern pine, with an f_b value of 1550. Charts are available for other grades and species. Lumber and grades may be mixed in the same truss, but chord size must be identical. Repetitive member bending stress is used in this chart.

Richard J. Vitullo, AIA; Oak Leaf Studio; Crownsville, Maryland

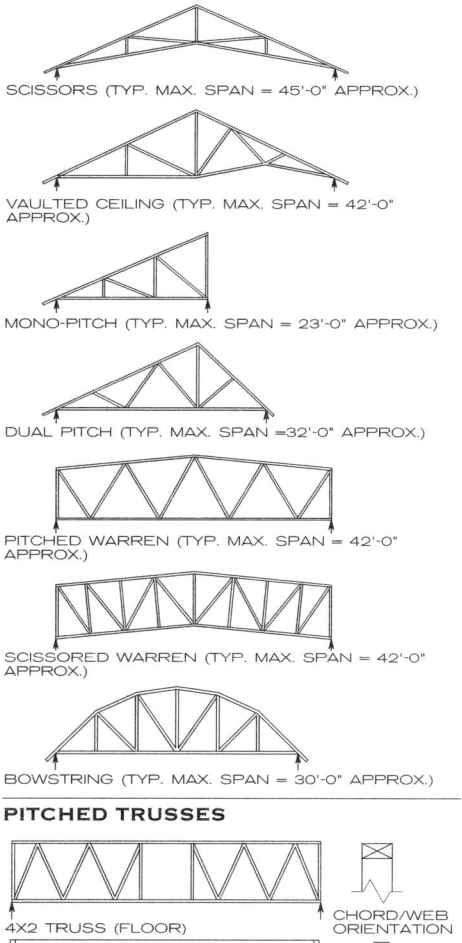

PITCHED TRUSSES

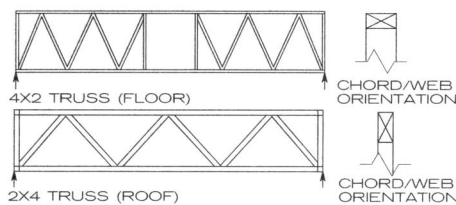

PARALLEL TRUSSES

GENERAL

Metal plate-connected wood trusses have been used in building construction since 1953, when the metal connector plate was invented. These proprietary metal plates are available in a range of styles and tooth orientations. The metal plates are punched with barbs that grab onto the wood truss, thus reducing the hand nailing required to fabricate a structure. Plate size for a given truss is based on a combination of the tooth withdrawal strength of the plate, the tensile and shear strength of the steel, and the net sectional area of the lumber.

This system is primarily used for roofs with either pitched or parallel chord trusses. It is occasionally employed for floors with parallel chord trusses. Individual trusses are cut from 2 x 4 in. or 2 x 6 in. lumber and can be spaced 24 in. or 48 in. o.c. For typical residential construction, 24 in. o.c. is used. Exceptionally long spans are possible with metal plate-connected trusses, allowing the large, unencumbered interior spaces often required in commercial, agricultural, and other nonresidential building types.

Camber is designed for dead load only:
  Camber (in.) = Length (ft)/60

BRACING

Providing adequate bracing for trusses is essential, both during installation and in the overall roof design. Truss members must be held in place with supports that meet them at right angles. Truss chords and web members are placed in a vertical, plumb position and maintain that position, resisting applied design loads, throughout the life of the structure. Permanent bracing and anchorage are expected to be an integral part of construction, and strongbacks are often used for this purpose.

Movement by crane can damage trusses. Crane spreader bars are used to avoid this "out-of-plane" buckling. Special stiffening may be applied to trusses during erection.

ROUGH CARPENTRY

Wood Floor Truss Details

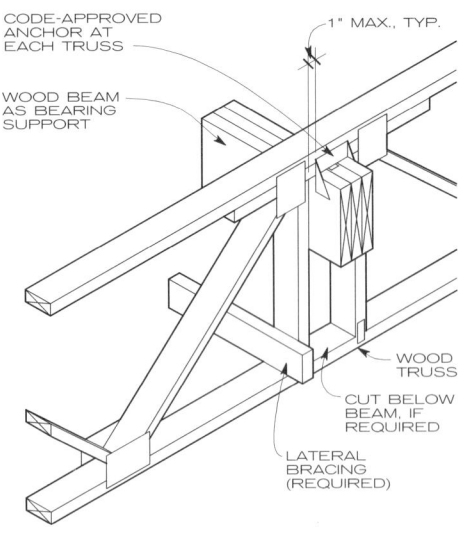

TOP CHORD SUPPORT DETAIL AT WOOD BEAM

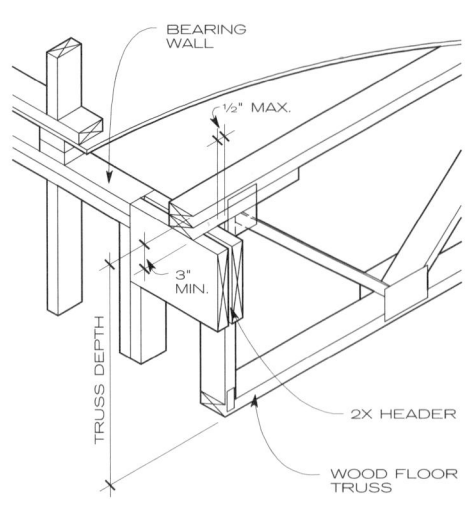

TOP CHORD SUPPORT DETAIL AT EXTERIOR BEARING WALL

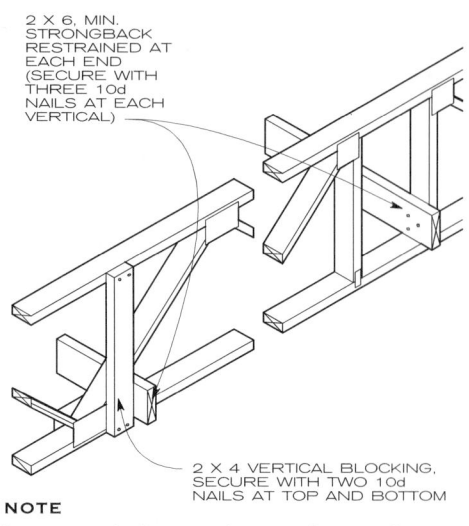

NOTE
Locate strongbacks at maximum 10 ft o.c. at free-span trusses.

STRONGBACK DETAILS

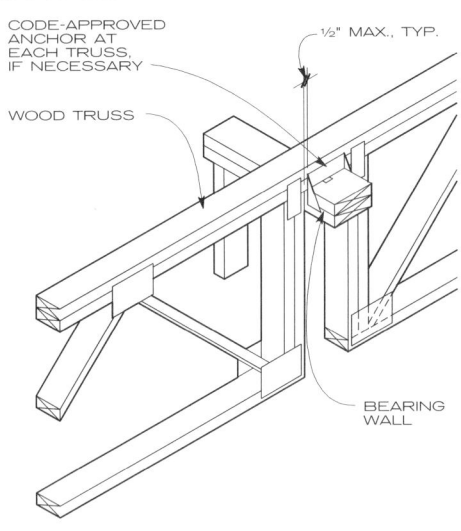

TOP CHORD SUPPORT DETAIL AT INTERIOR BEARING WALL

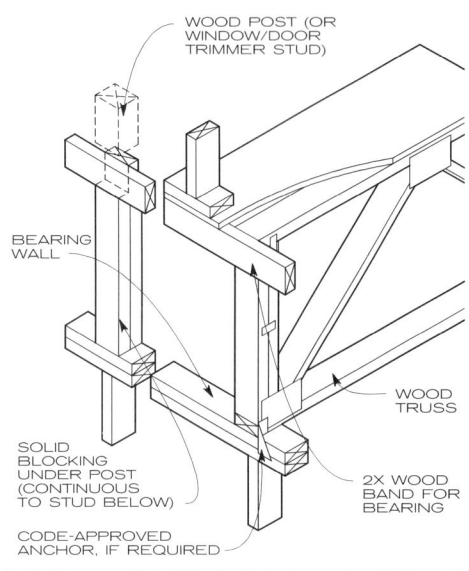

EXTERIOR WALL BEARING DETAIL

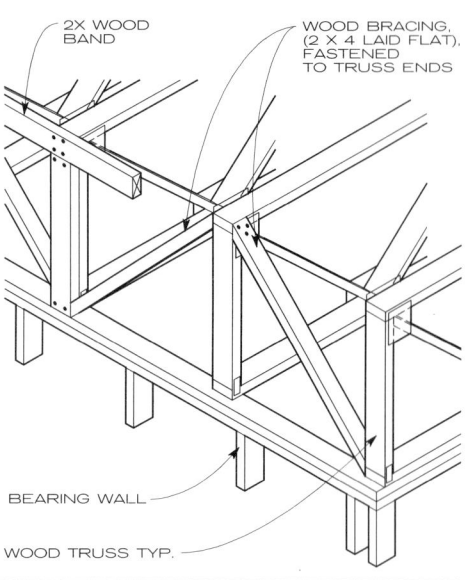

DIAGONAL BRACING AT BEARING END

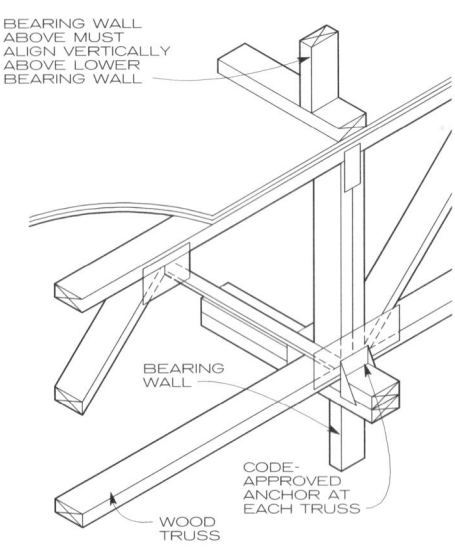

BOTTOM CHORD SUPPORT AT BEARING WALL

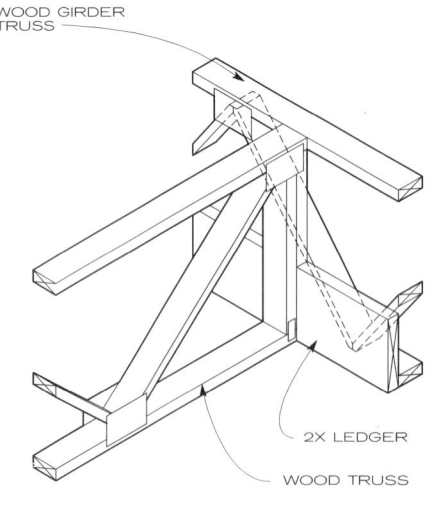

LEDGER DETAIL

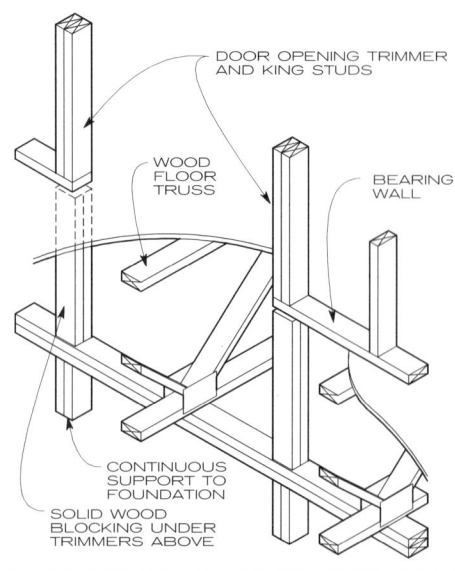

BLOCKING DETAIL AT INTERIOR BEARING WALL

Richard J. Vitullo, AIA; Oak Leaf Studio; Crownsville, Maryland

ROUGH CARPENTRY

Wood Roof Truss Details

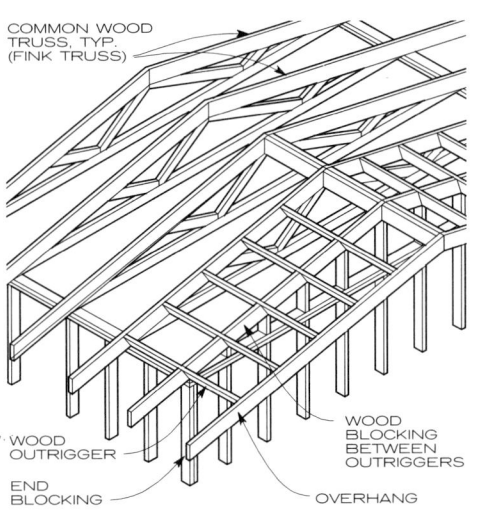

GABLE ROOF OVERHANG DETAIL

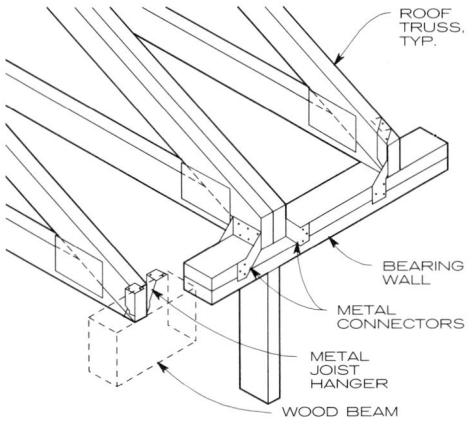

END-BEARING ROOF TRUSS WITH METAL CONNECTORS

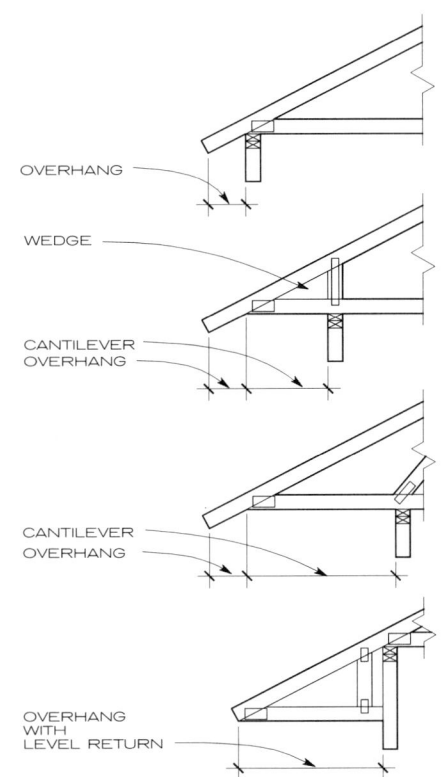

OVERHANG DETAILS

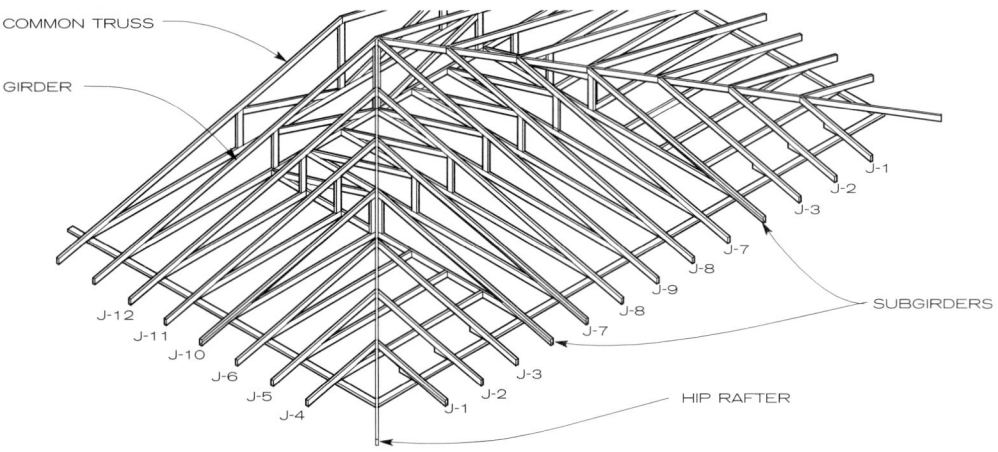

JACK TRUSS SYSTEM

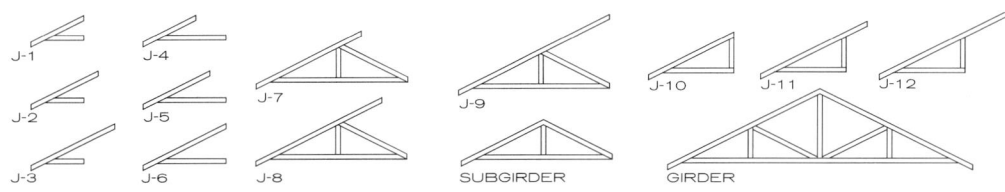

JACK TRUSS COMPONENTS

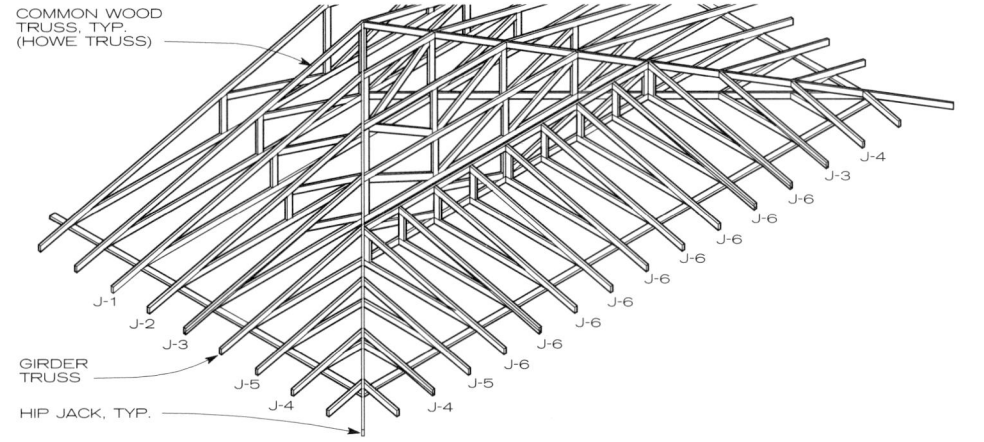

STEP-DOWN TRUSS SYSTEM

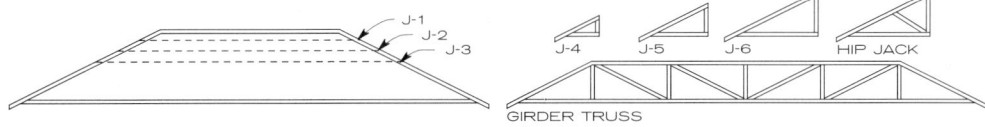

STEP-DOWN COMPONENTS

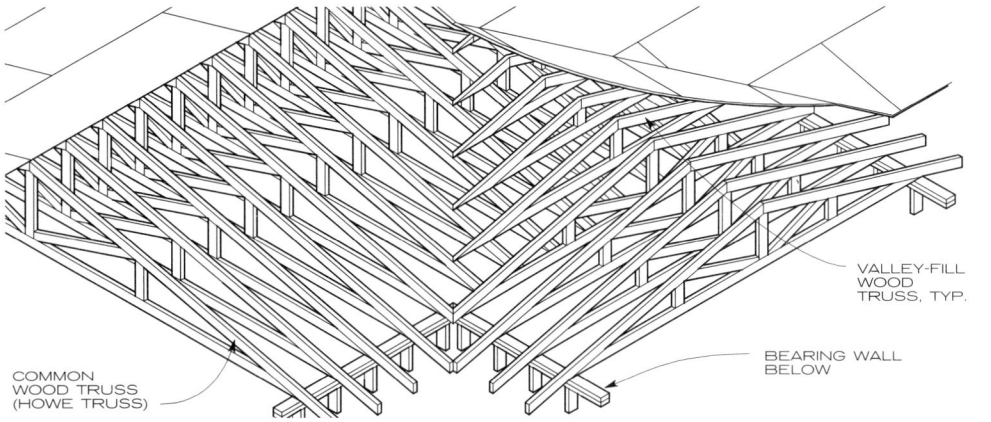

ROOF INTERSECTION WITH VALLEY FILL

Richard J. Vitullo, AIA; Oak Leaf Studio; Crownsville, Maryland

ROUGH CARPENTRY

Framing Details

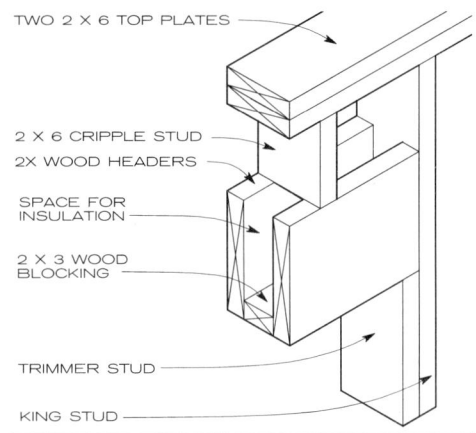

2X6 BEARING WALL—HEADER DETAIL

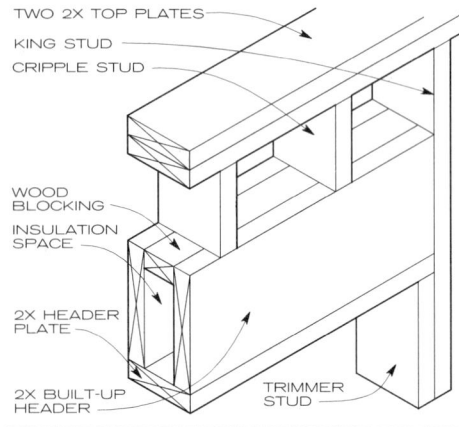

2X BEARING WALL—HEADER DETAIL

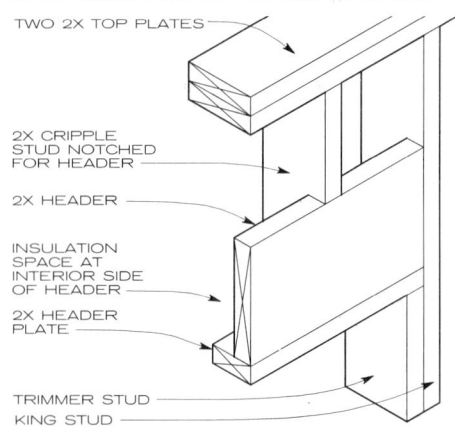

2X BEARING WALL—HEADER DETAIL

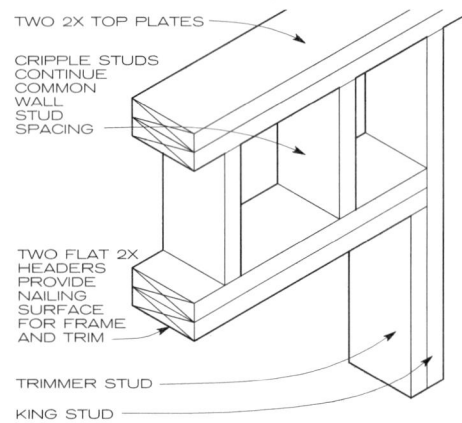

2X PARTITION WALL—HEADER DETAIL

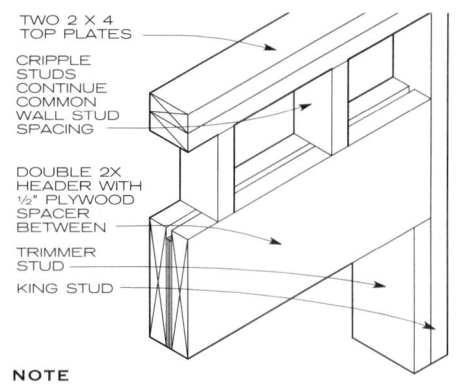

NOTE
Provides maximum nailing surface on interior and exterior walls.

2X4 BEARING WALL—HEADER DETAIL

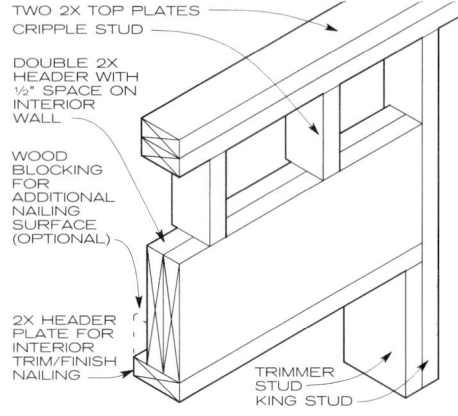

2X BEARING WALL—HEADER DETAIL

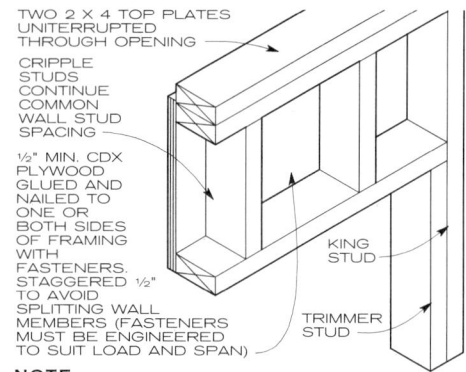

NOTE
Interior plywood face must be smooth for finishing with gypsum board.

2X4 BEARING WALL—OPEN BOX PLYWOOD—HEADER DETAIL

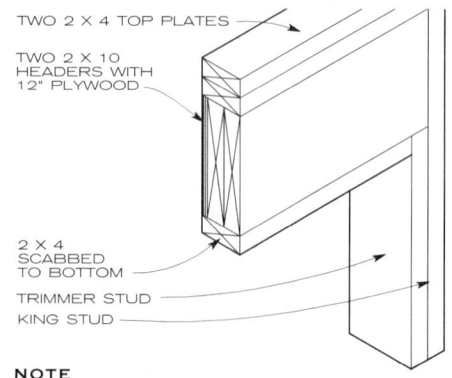

NOTE
This detail eliminates cripple studs above opening.

2X BEARING WALL—HEADER DETAIL

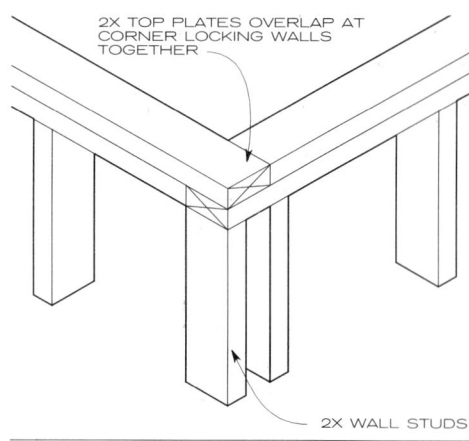

TOP PLATE FRAMING DETAIL

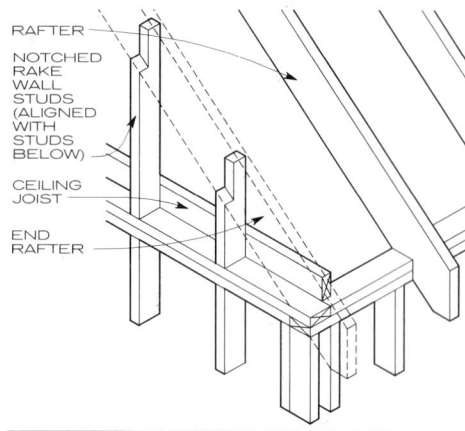

RAKE WALL DETAIL—PLATFORM FRAMING

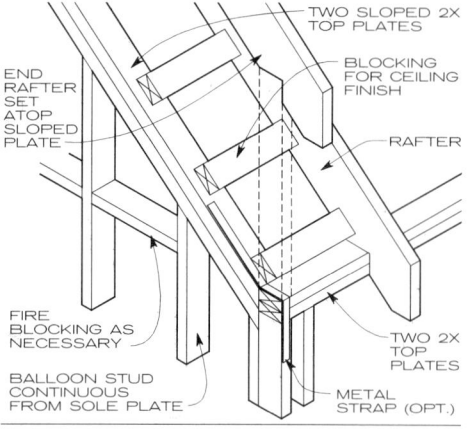

RAKE WALL DETAIL—BALLOON FRAMING

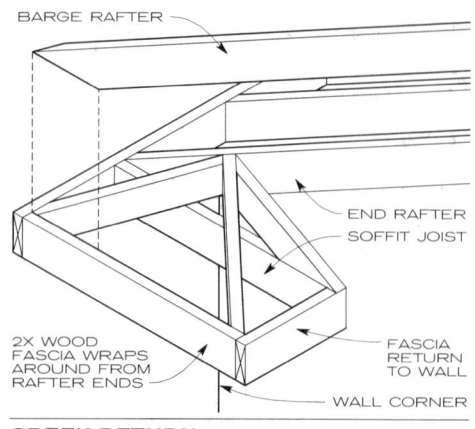

GREEK RETURN

Richard J. Vitullo, AIA; Oak Leaf Studio; Crownsville, Maryland

ROUGH CARPENTRY

Framing Details

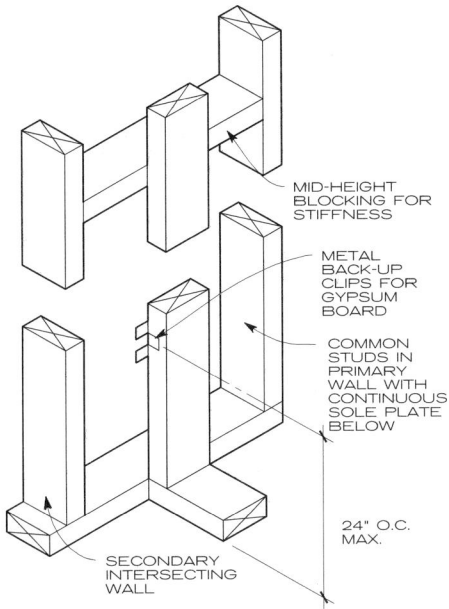

INTERSECTING WALLS WITH METAL GYPSUM BOARD CLIPS

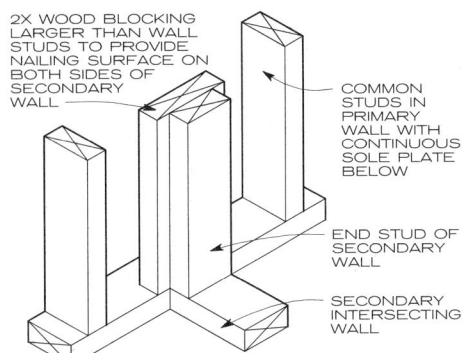

INTERSECTING WALLS WITH BLOCKING

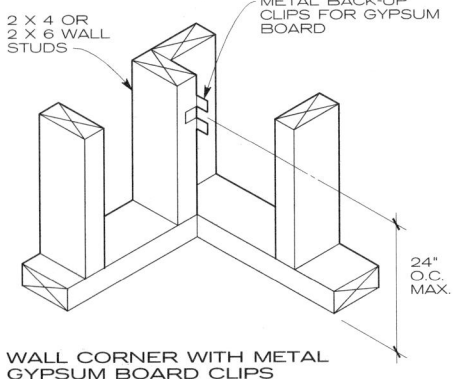

WALL CORNER WITH METAL GYPSUM BOARD CLIPS

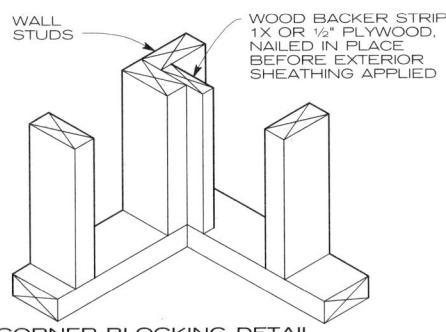

CORNER BLOCKING DETAIL

INSULATED WALL DETAILS

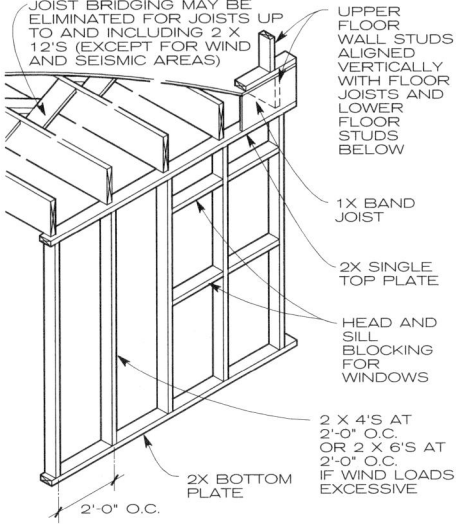

IN-LINE FRAMING

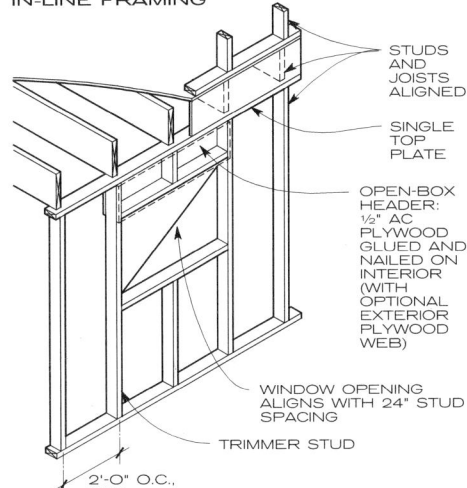

IN-LINE FRAMING WITH WIDE OPENING

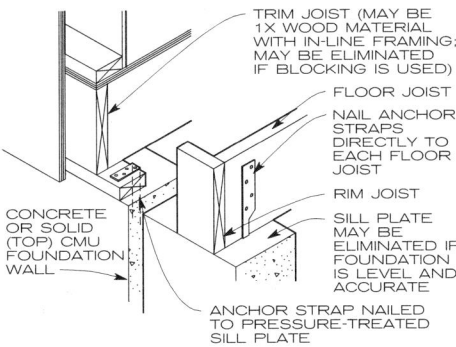

REDUCED SILL PLATE AND RIM JOIST DETAILS

NOTES

1. Some framing details rely on techniques that reduce the amount of lumber in wood construction. Among these are in-line framing details and corner details with metal framing clips for gypsum board. These types of details were developed to conserve wood resources, reduce material cost and job-site waste, and enhance energy efficiency by reducing thermal bridging across wall systems and increasing insulation cavities. When wood levels are to be reduced, a structural engineer should first be consulted.

2. Gypsum board installed at inside corners with metal clips or wood backers does not get fastened to either. The sheet resting against the backer or clips is installed first so the second sheet (which is nailed to the stud) will lock the first sheet in place. The "floating joint" that results is recommended to reduce cracks in the corner.

REDUCED WOOD FRAMING DETAILS

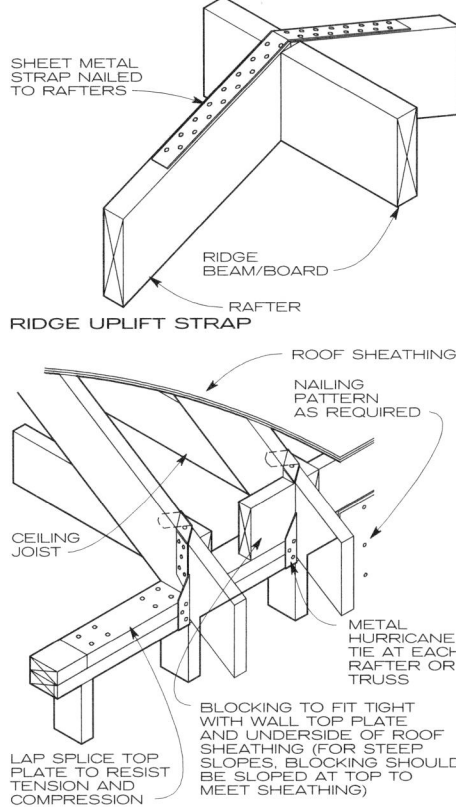

RIDGE UPLIFT STRAP

ROOF DIAPHRAGM PERIMETER

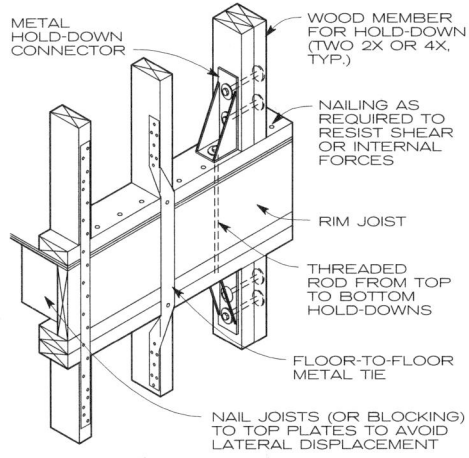

TIES BETWEEN FLOORS

NOTE

It is essential to provide a continuous path of resistance from roof to foundation in order to dissipate both lateral and uplift forces. Connections along this load path will guarantee uninterrupted resistance. Seismic and wind forces are transferred from the roof diaphragm to shear walls and through the walls into the ground at the foundation. Shear walls resist horizontal forces in the roof and floor diaphragms and so must be connected to them. It is important to apply wall sheathing to the full wall height, nailing it to the top plate, blocking, or rim joist and also to the mud sill or bottom plate. Shear wall height/width ratios are an important consideration; consult a structural engineer for their design. The details illustrated show several connection paths; for each specific design, a structural engineer familiar with seismic and wind resistant construction should be consulted. Many of the requirements for high wind situations apply to seismic loading as well, except in shear wall design.

Ties between floors: Wood members (studs) must be sized for the load-carrying capacity at the critical net section.

WIND AND SEISMIC CONNECTOR FRAMING

Richard J. Vitullo, AIA; Oak Leaf Studio; Crownsville, Maryland

ROUGH CARPENTRY

Structural Building Panels

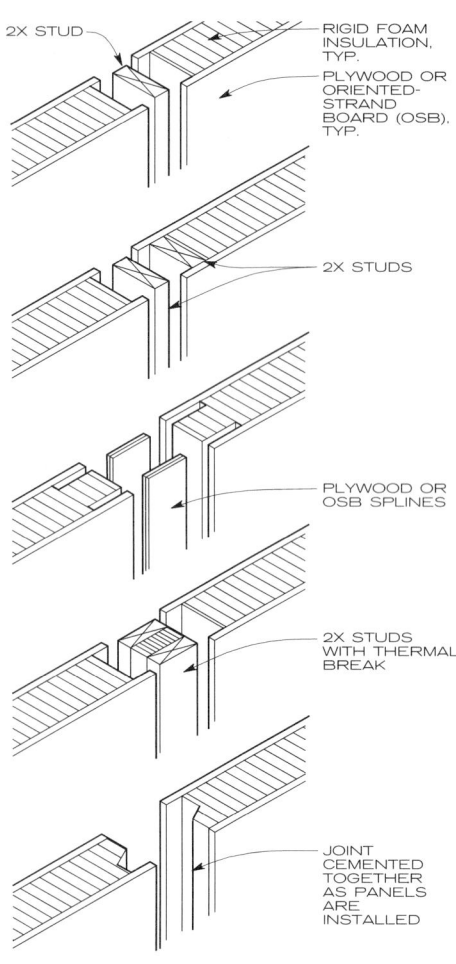

NOTE

Studs and splines are screwed (and usually glued) to panels from both sides. Consult manufacturer's specifications. Joints are typically sealed with expanding foam.

TYPICAL INTERMEDIATE PANEL SPLINE DETAILS

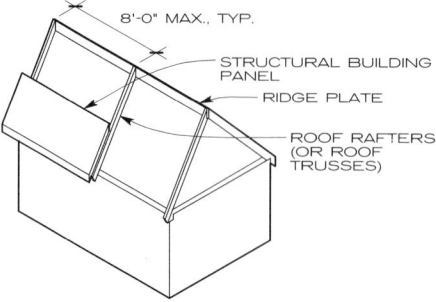

ROOF FRAMING WITH RAFTERS AND TRUSSES

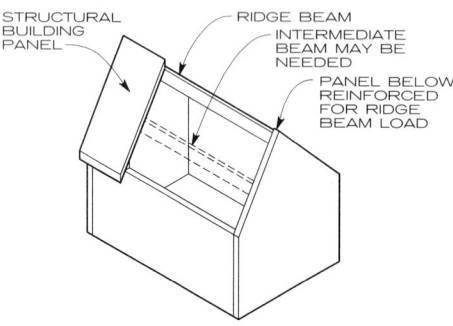

ROOF FRAMING WITH RIDGE BEAM

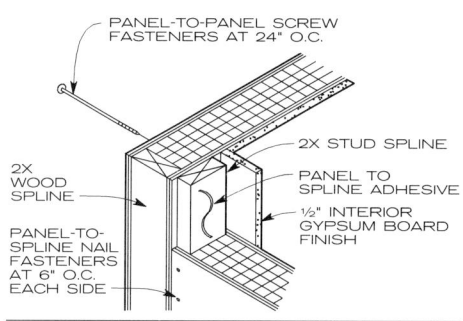

TYPICAL CORNER DETAIL

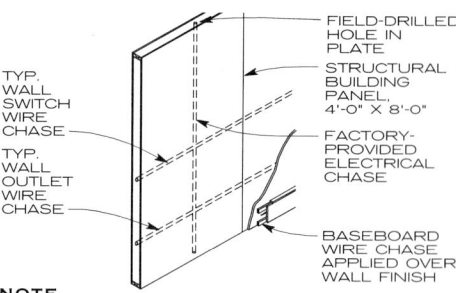

NOTE

Consult local codes for all electrical installations.

TYPICAL WIRE CHASE LOCATIONS IN PANELS

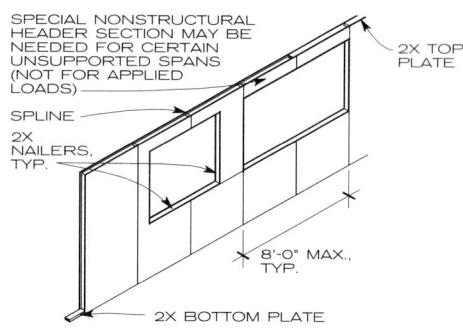

TYPICAL WINDOW DETAILS

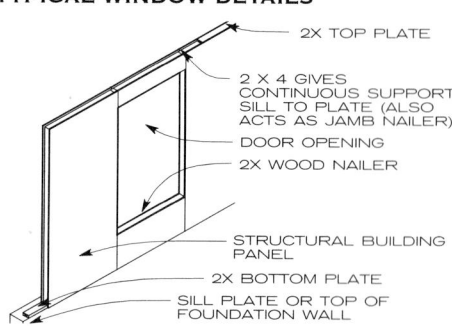

TYPICAL REINFORCED DOOR OPENING DETAIL

GENERAL

Structural building panels are factory-assembled composite panels ready for installation as a complete structural and/or insulating wall section. The material of each component of the panel system is very important when selecting a panel manufacturer. Components include the skin, foam core, adhesive, and optional exterior or interior finish. The application for which the panel is intended determines the materials used. Consult manufacturers for specifications.

Sizes vary from 4 by 8 ft panels weighing about 100 lb to 8 by 28 ft panels that must be installed using a crane.

PANEL TYPES

There are two main types of structural building panels—stress-skin panels and foam core panels:

STRESS-SKIN PANELS are manufactured by gluing and nailing plywood skins to both sides of a wood frame, resulting in a unit that performs like an I-beam. Stress-skin panels are not necessarily insulated.

STRUCTURAL FOAM CORE PANELS fall into two groups: sandwich panels and unfaced panels. Sandwich panels are rigid-foam panels faced with two structural-grade skins, usually made of oriented-strand board (OSB) or plywood. Depending on the application and the manufacturer, these foam core panels may or may not include framing members within the core. Unfaced structural foam core panels look like panels of stick-framing with rigid foam between the members instead of fiberglass batt insulation. Interior and exterior finishes are applied to these panels in the field.

The skins of structural building panels (like I-beam flanges) resist tension and compression, while the wood frame or core (like an I-beam web) resists shear and prevents buckling of the skins.

Richard J. Vitullo, AIA; Oak Leaf Studio; Crownsville, Maryland

All structural foam core panels are insulated with a core of expanded polystyrene (EPS), extruded polystyrene, or urethane foam, from $3\frac{1}{2}$ to $11\frac{1}{4}$ in. thick. Urethane panels are either glue-laminated like polystyrene or foamed in place (either in the factory or in the field). Urethane has an R-value of 6 or 7 per inch versus R-5 for extruded polystyrene and R-4 for EPS foam. Urethane is about twice as strong in compression as polystyrene and has a perm rating of less than one, which technically qualifies it as a vapor barrier. EPS has a perm rating of from 1 to 3 and may require a vapor barrier. EPS, however, is inert, nontoxic (if ingested), and resilient; it doesn't feed microorganisms and is generally cheaper than urethane. Consult manufacturers on CFC and formaldehyde content in the foam core and skin material as it varies among manufacturers. Regarding flammability of both foam core types, consult with the manufacturer about the individual product.

APPLICATIONS

In above-grade applications, the most common materials for exterior facings are plywood OSB or finish materials like T-111 plywood, tongue-and-groove pine, and other wood siding material. For below-grade situations, pressure-treated plywood skins and splines are used. Generally, structural building panels should not be used for plumbing walls, as the spaces needed for plumbing runs would compromise the insulation and structural integrity of the panel.

For roof applications it is best to use a vented structural foam panel, either integral or field-installed. Many asphalt-shingle manufacturers will not warrant their product when it is installed on unvented panels because of overheating, which accelerates deterioration.

CHARACTERISTICS

Using structural building panels generally enhances the speed of construction because the panels replace three different steps in standard construction: framing, sheathing, and insulation. Panel systems offer superior energy performance compared to a stick-frame house of similar cost and standard of construction. This is largely because the rigid insulation has higher R-values, there are fewer seams to seal, and conductive heat is not lost through air infiltration around the framing. Structural building panels also offer good resistance to lateral loads.

Panels can be susceptible to infestation by insects such as carpenter ants and termites, which eat through wood and tunnel through the foam core material, reducing insulation value and even compromising structural integrity. Use of termite shields, foam cores treated with insect repellent, and other strategies should be considered.

NOTES

1. Since structural building panels are a relatively new building system, code officials should be consulted early and often to prevent any misunderstandings or delays in the code approval process. Also, check with manufacturers to determine whether their product has received compliance approval with BOCA, ICBO, SBCCI, or HUD.
2. The seams are the part of a structural building panel system most prone to infiltration and weakness and most likely to show the results of expansion and contraction. Tight spline connections with sealant at all edges–top, bottom, and sides–can greatly increase thermal efficiency.

ROUGH CARPENTRY

Structural Building Panels

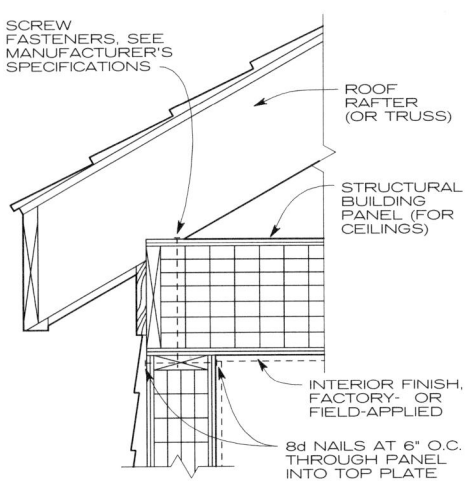
ROOF EAVE DETAIL WITH PANEL CEILING

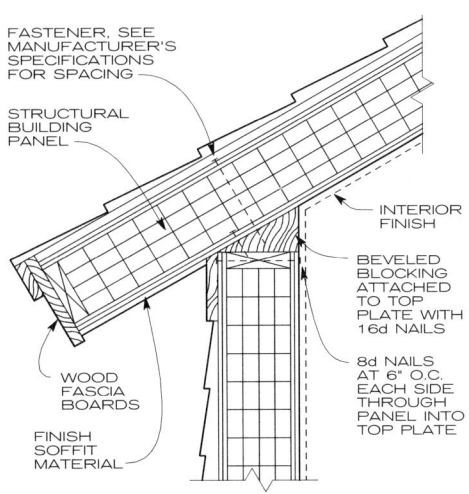
ROOF EAVE DETAIL WITH SLOPED CEILING

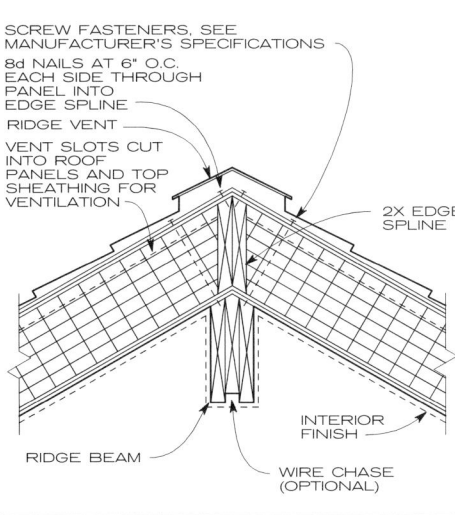
PANEL AT RIDGE CONNECTION

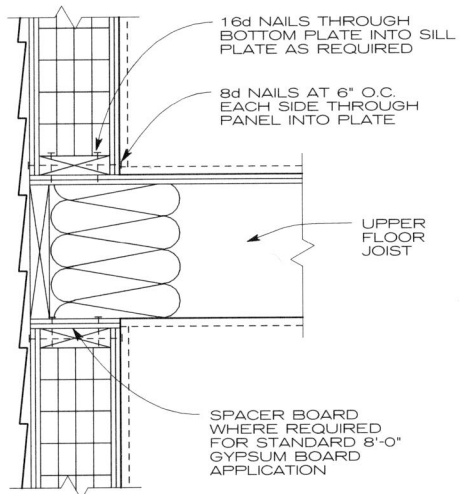
PANEL AT UPPER FLOOR CONNECTION WITH FLOOR JOIST BETWEEN

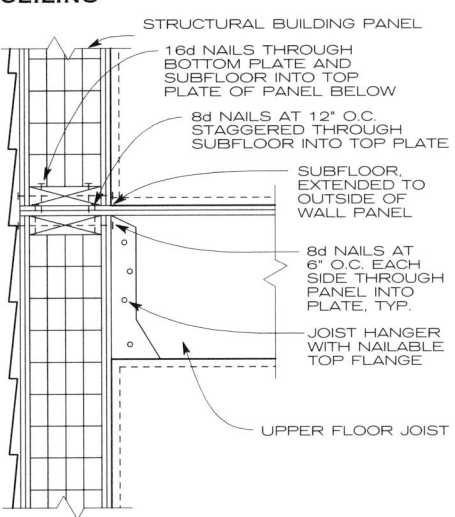
PANEL AT UPPER FLOOR CONNECTION WITH FLOOR JOIST ADJACENT

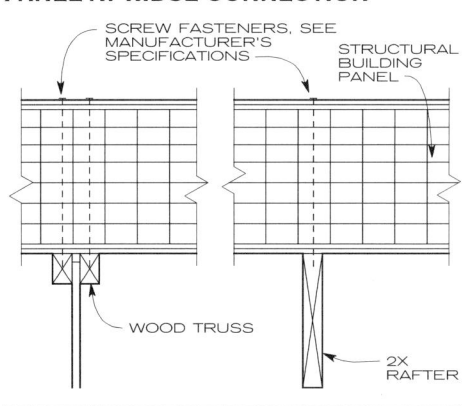
CONTINUOUS PANEL DETAIL AT ROOF

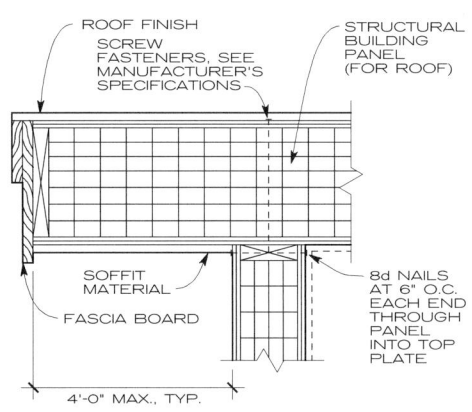
GABLE END OVERHANG AT ROOF PANEL DETAIL

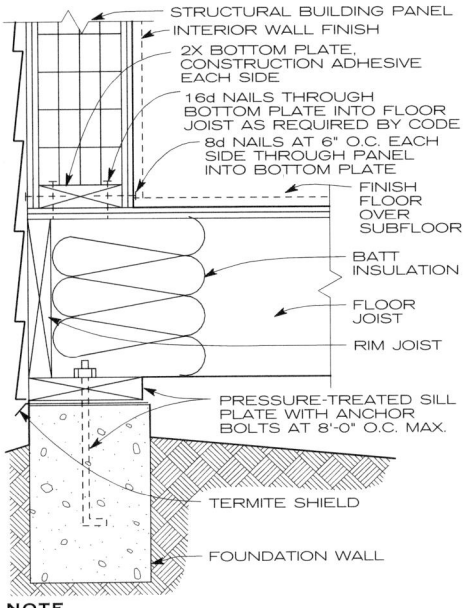

NOTE
Check perm rating of foam core insulation to determine whether additional vapor barrier is required. Consult local codes.

PANEL AT SILL WITH FLOOR JOIST BELOW CONNECTION

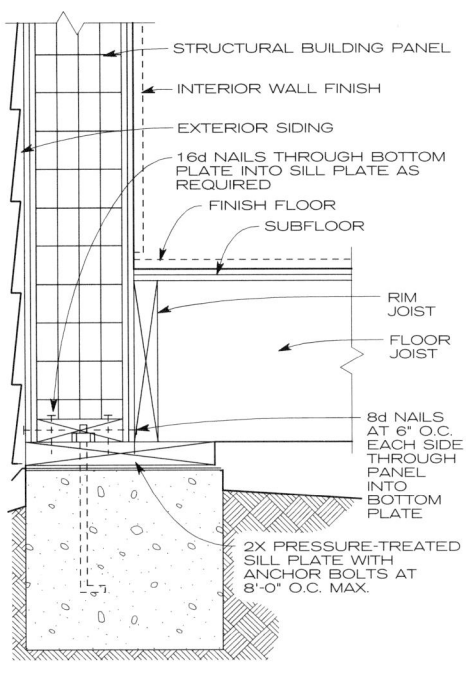
PANEL AT SILL CONNECTION WITH FLOOR JOIST ADJACENT

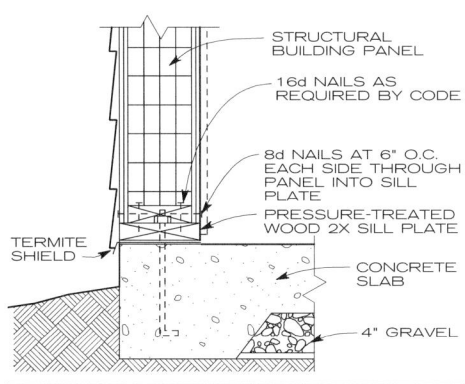
PANEL AT SILL ON SLAB-ON-GRADE

Richard J. Vitullo, AIA; Oak Leaf Studio; Crownsville, Maryland

ROUGH CARPENTRY

Wood I-Joist Construction Details

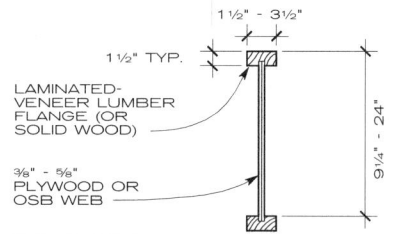
TYPICAL WOOD I-JOIST

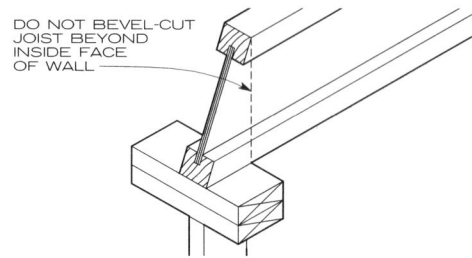
TYPICAL BEVEL-CUT JOIST

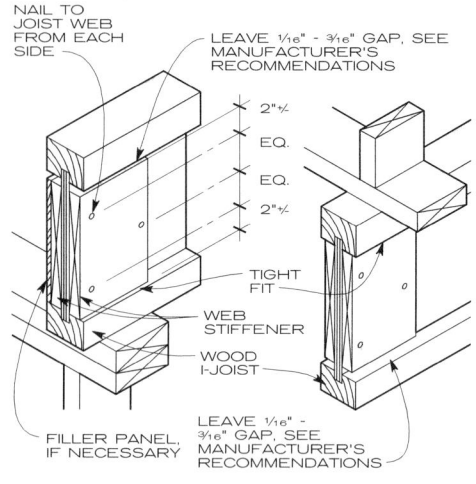

| BEARING WALL BELOW | BEARING WALL ABOVE |

WEB STIFFENER DETAILS

GENERAL

A wood I-joist is made of a web with top and bottom flanges. It is similar in shape and profile to the steel I-beam, but while the steel component is forged from a single ingot, the wood member is a composition. Plywood or oriented strand board (OSB) is used for the web of the wood I-joist, and either solid lumber or laminated-veneer lumber for the flanges. Many manufacturers produce wood I-joists under different trade names, and each differs in its dimensions, as well as span and deflection, loading, and performance characteristics. Consult manufacturers for details and performance criteria.

Compared to solid lumber, wood I-joists have both relative advantages and disadvantages:

ADVANTAGES

1. Easier to handle and lighter weight, with about 50% less wood material per joist than an equivalent solid wood member.
2. Makes efficient use of a natural resource–the I-joist can be made from second and third growth timber stands, with no need for old growth trees.
3. Available in lengths up to 60 ft, priced per linear foot.
4. Greatest strength when loaded parallel to plane of web.
5. A high degree of uniformity, with no crowns, checks, or loose knots.
6. Plumbing and HVAC can easily be run through web structure (based on the manufacturer's guidelines).
7. Starts with dry materials, so there is much less shrinkage than with solid lumber.
8. Wood I-joists can generally be set at wider on-center spacing, thus reducing installation time.

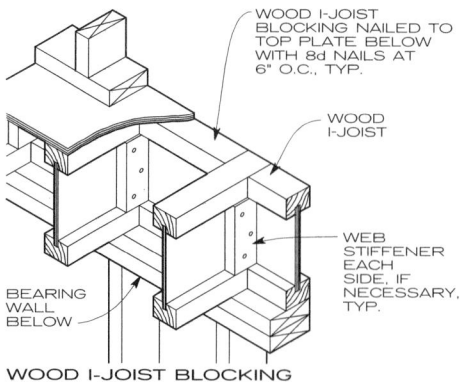
WOOD I-JOIST BLOCKING

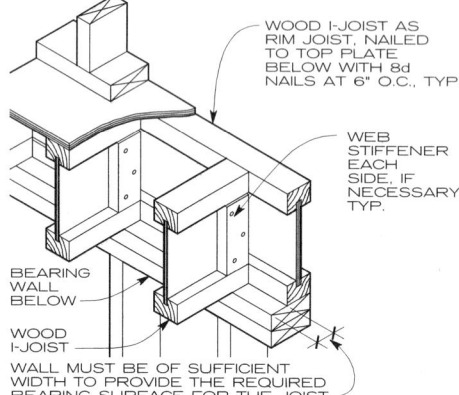
WOOD I-JOIST AS RIM JOIST

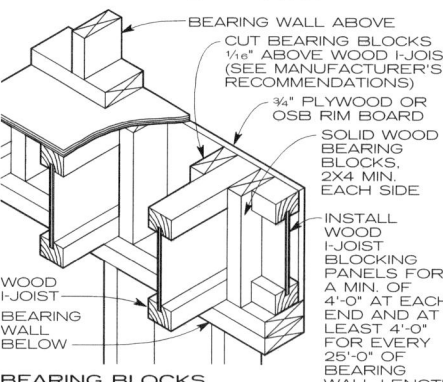
BEARING BLOCKS

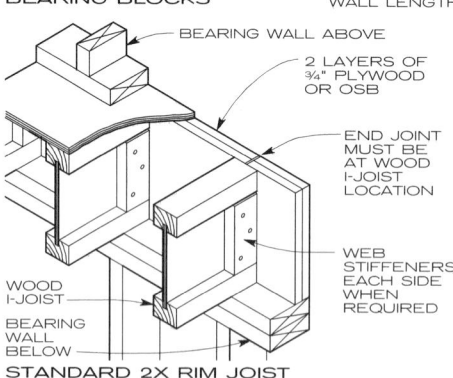
STANDARD 2X RIM JOIST

NOTE
Check building code for appropriate detail in areas of high lateral load.

STUD BEARING WALL DETAILS

DISADVANTAGES

1. Material costs are generally more (per linear foot) than for solid lumber (for standard residential floor joist dimensions and spans).
2. Contractors are less familiar with wood I-joists and can create problems by cutting holes into webs and weakening the member.

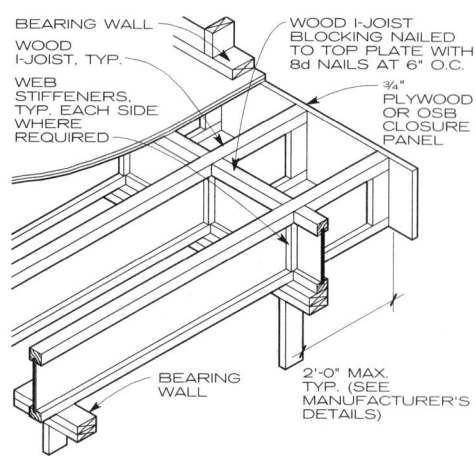
NOTE
Joist must be designed to carry the load-bearing wall.
LOAD-BEARING CANTILEVER DETAIL

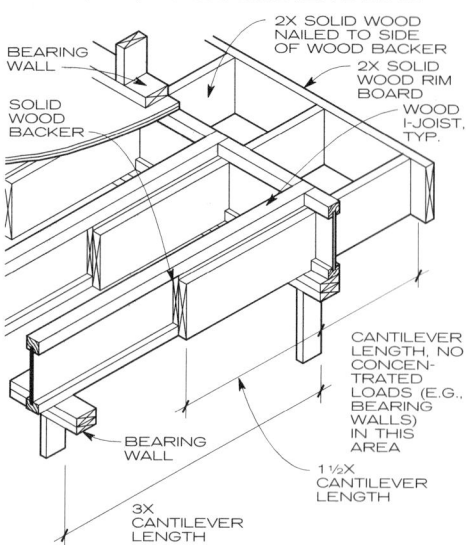
NON-LOAD-BEARING DROPPED CANTILEVER DETAIL

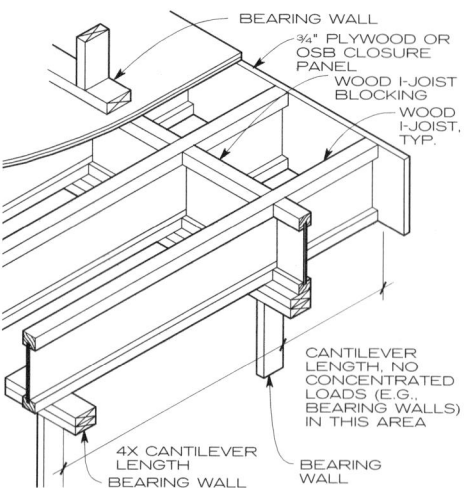
NON-LOAD-BEARING CANTILEVER DETAIL

CANTILEVER DETAILS

3. Less lateral stiffness than solid lumber.
4. Can be shifted by winds during construction due to light weight.
5. Some adhesives used in laminated-veneer components may pose indoor air-quality problems.

Richard J. Vitullo, AIA; Oak Leaf Studio; Crownsville, Maryland

ROUGH CARPENTRY

Wood I-Joist Construction Details

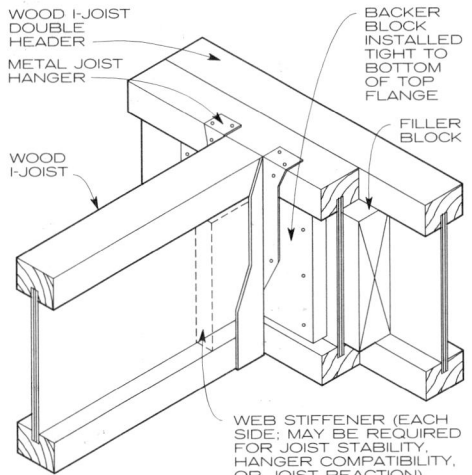

NOTE
Connection between joists must provide adequate load transfer between members.

WOOD I-JOIST CONNECTION TO WOOD I-JOIST HEADER

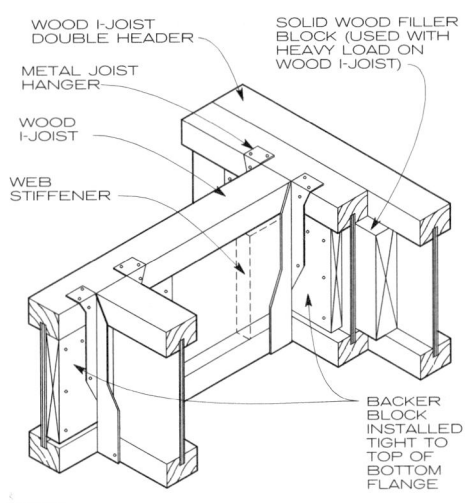

NOTE
Connection between joists must provide adequate load transfer between members.

WOOD I-JOIST CONNECTION TO WOOD I-JOIST HEADER (HEAVY LOAD)

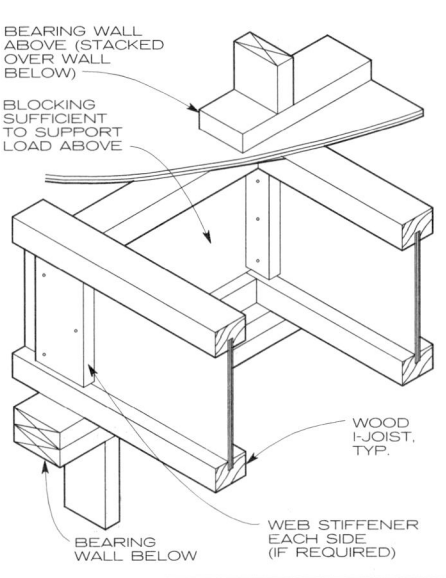

BEARING WALL ABOVE AND BELOW

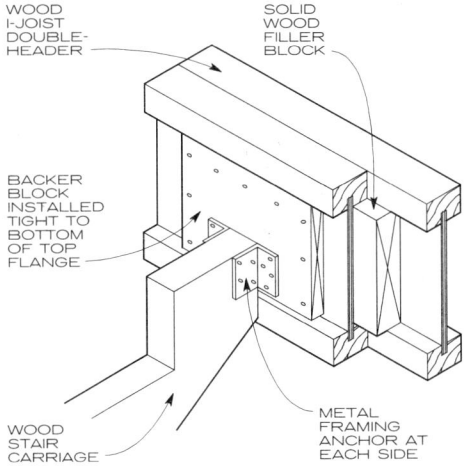

NOTE
Connection between joists must provide adequate load transfer between members.

STAIR CARRIAGE CONNECTION DETAIL

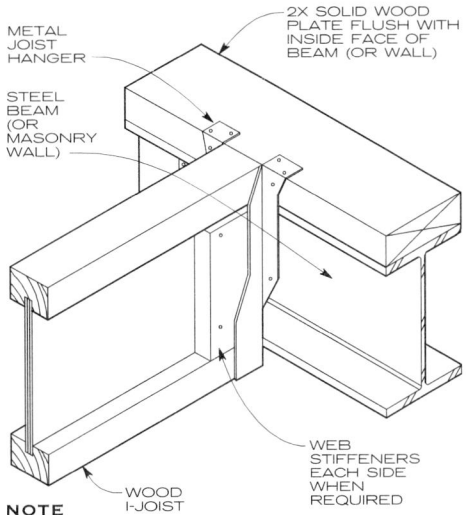

NOTE
Thicker wood plate over beam may be required; check hanger manufacturer's top flange nailing requirements.

WOOD I-JOIST SUPPORTED AT TOP OF BEAM (OR WALL)

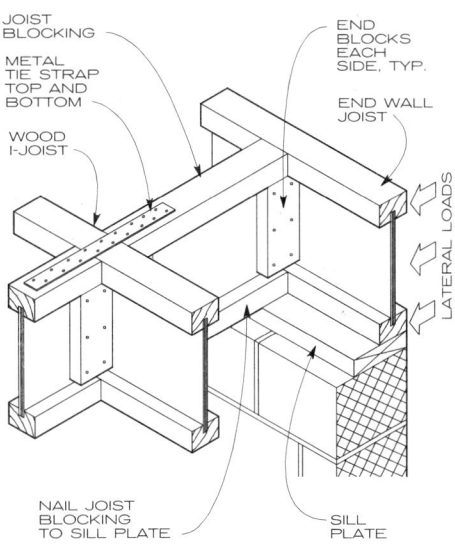

LATERAL LOAD BLOCKING AT END WALL

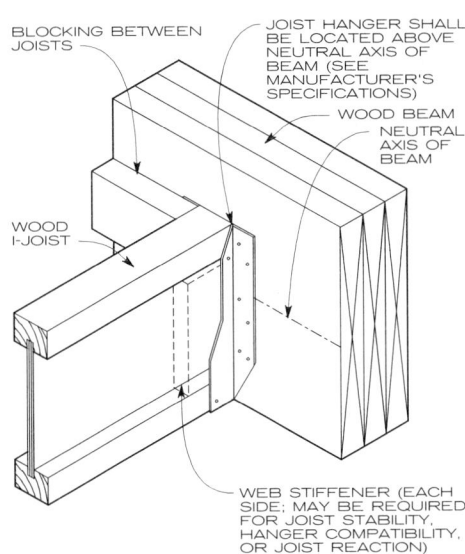

JOIST HANGER DETAIL

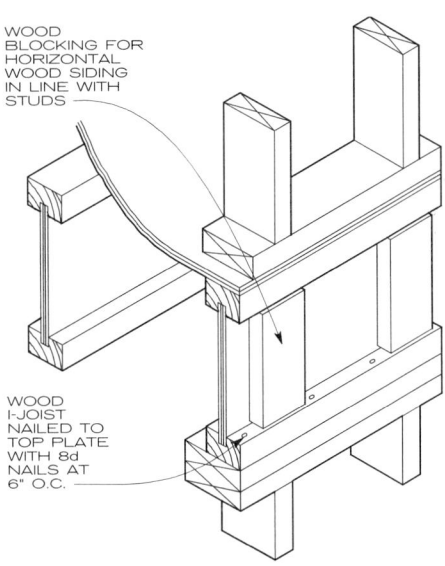

TYPICAL WOOD BLOCKING AT EXTERIOR WALL

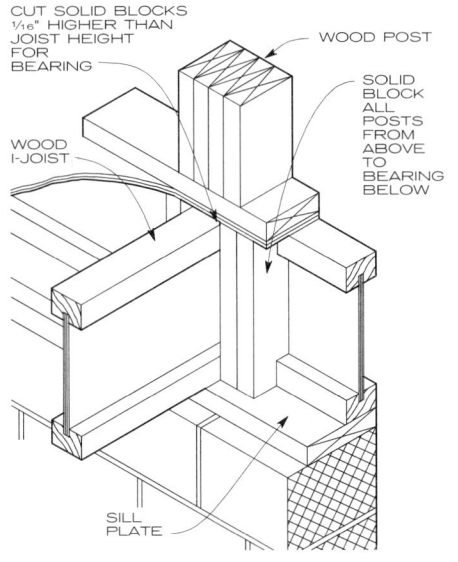

COLUMN LOAD TRANSFER

Richard J. Vitullo, AIA; Oak Leaf Studio; Crownsville, Maryland

ROUGH CARPENTRY

Wood I-Joist Construction Details

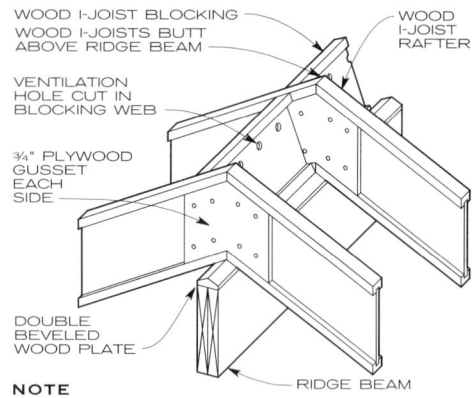

NOTE
Uplift connections may be required.

WOOD I-JOIST RAFTER AT RIDGE BEAM DETAIL

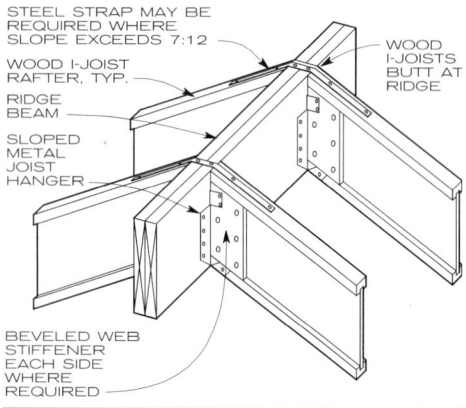

NOTE
Uplift connections may be required.

WOOD I-JOIST RAFTER AT RIDGE BEAM DETAIL

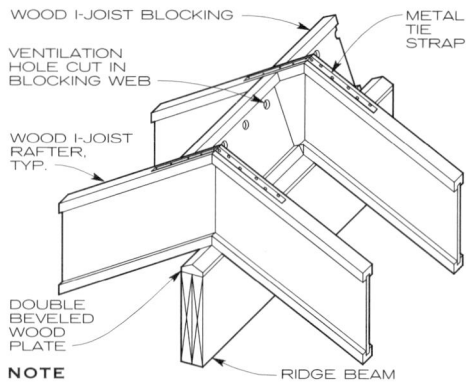

NOTE
Uplift connections may be required.

WOOD I-JOIST RAFTER AT RIDGE BEAM DETAIL

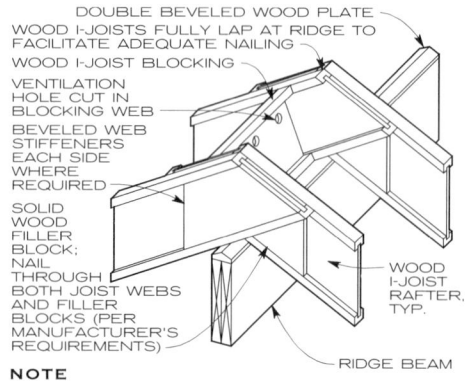

NOTE
Uplift connections may be required.

LAPPED WOOD I-JOIST RAFTER AT RIDGE BEAM

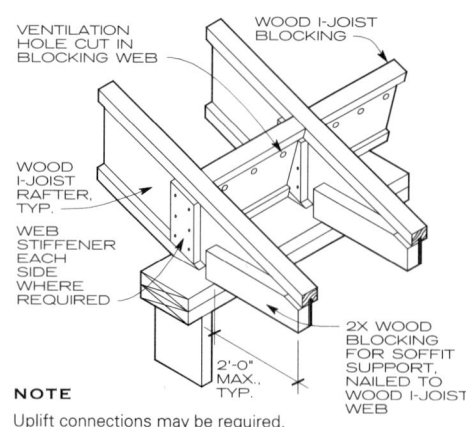

NOTE
Uplift connections may be required.

WOOD I-JOIST RAFTER AT OVERHANG

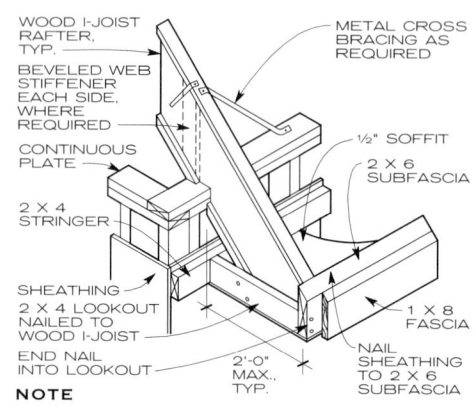

NOTE
Uplift connections may be required.

WOOD I-JOIST RAFTER AT OVERHANG

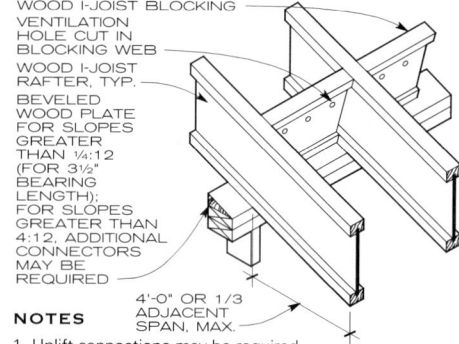

NOTES
1. Uplift connections may be required.
2. Special sloped seat-bearing metal connectors can be used in lieu of beveled wood plate in some sloped applications. See manufacturer's recommendations.

WOOD I-JOIST RAFTER AT OVERHANG

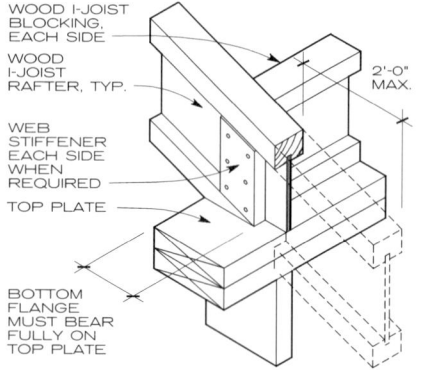

NOTE
Uplift connections may be required.

TYPICAL BIRD'S MOUTH I-JOIST CUT DETAIL

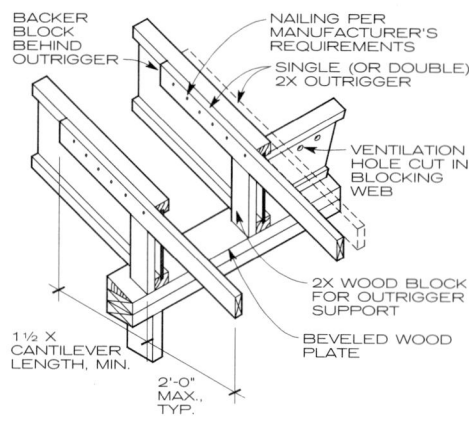

NOTE
Uplift connections may be required.

WOOD I-JOIST RAFTER WITH OUTRIGGER

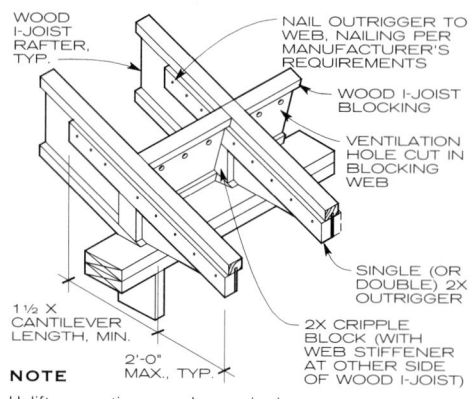

NOTE
Uplift connections may be required.

WOOD I-JOIST RAFTER AT OUTRIGGER

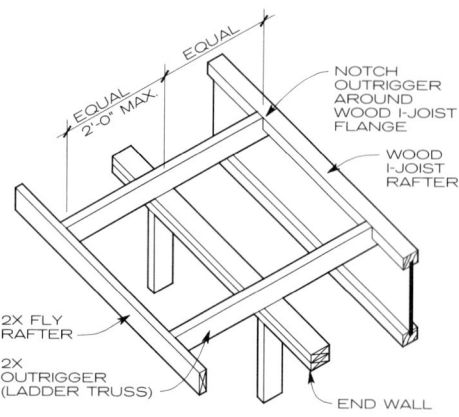

FLY RAFTER DETAIL

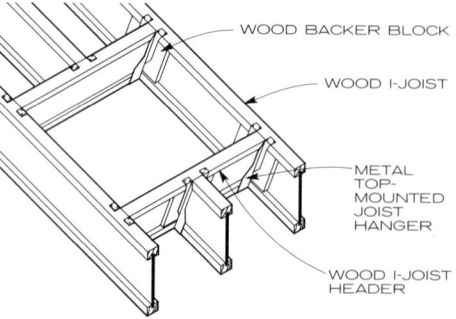

WOOD I-JOIST SKYLIGHT FRAMING DETAIL

NOTE
Check code and manufacturer's requirements for all ventilation hole sizes cut in blocking web.

Richard J. Vitullo, AIA; Oak Leaf Studio; Crownsville, Maryland

ROUGH CARPENTRY

Timber Bridges

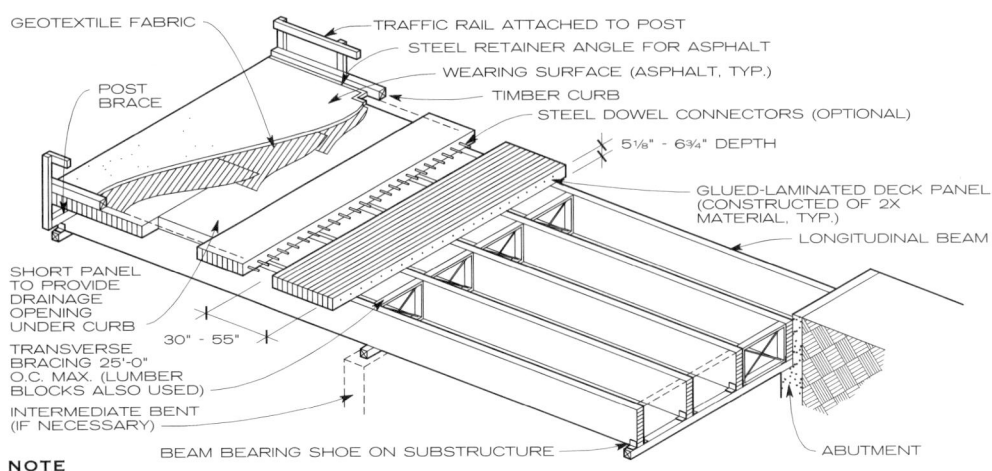

NOTE
Clear spans for glued-laminated longitudinal beams are from 20 to 100 ft. For sawn lumber beams, clear spans can be made up to 25 ft. Wood species used are generally Douglas fir-larch or Southern pine.

TYPICAL LONGITUDINAL BEAM BRIDGE

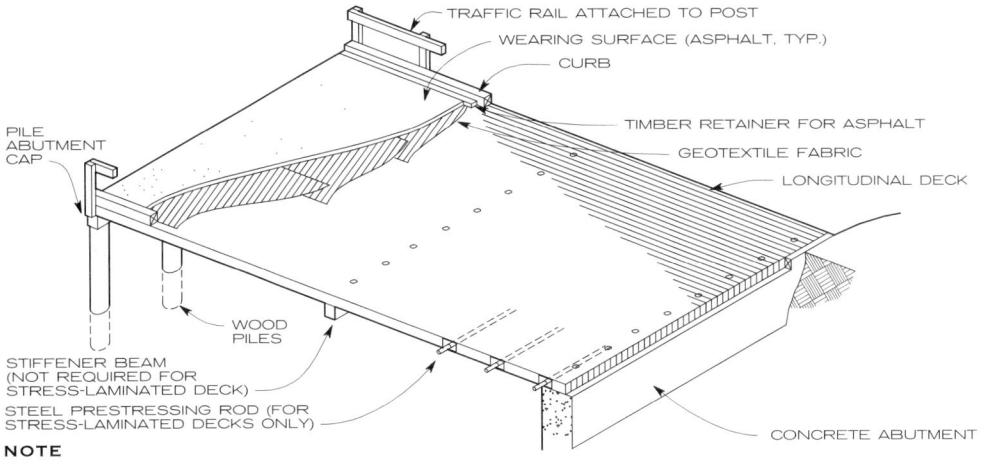

NOTE
Clear spans for glued-laminated decks are approximately 35 ft.

TYPICAL LONGITUDINAL DECK SUPERSTRUCTURE

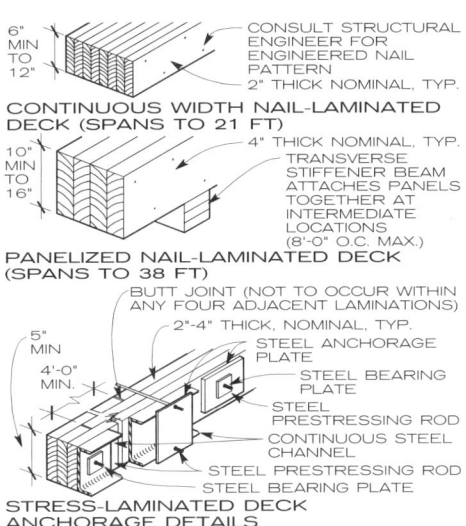

LONGITUDINAL DECK DETAILS

DECK (SPAN UP TO 24 FT)

BOX SECTION (SPAN UP TO 70 FT)

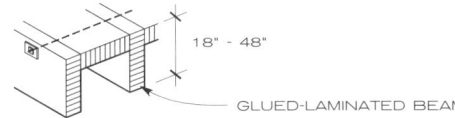
T-SECTION (SPAN UP TO 63 FT)

NOTE
T-section may be preferable over box section for long spans because of ease of inspection and maintenance.

TYPICAL STRESS-LAMINATED TIMBER SUPERSTRUCTURES

INTRODUCTION

Although wood was probably the first material used to construct a bridge, in the 20th century concrete and steel have became the major bridge construction materials. Wood is still widely used for short- and medium-span bridges. The strength, light weight, and energy absorption properties of timber make it a desirable material for bridge construction. Timber can carry short-term overloads without adverse effects. Large wood members are fire resistive, impervious to continuous freezing and thawing, and resist the harmful effects of de-icing agents.

In modern applications, the life of timber bridges is extended to forty years or longer through the use of preservative-treated wood, which requires little or no maintenance. The specifications and standards for the preservative treatment of wood maintained by the American Wood Preservers Association (AWPA) are the most widely used and comprehensive documents covering treatment procedures for sawn lumber, glued-laminated timber (glulam), piling, and poles used for timber bridges.

STRUCTURAL CHARACTERISTICS

All timber bridges consist of two basic components—the superstructure and the substructure. The superstructure is the framework of the bridge span and includes the deck, floor system, main supporting members, railings, and other incidental components. The five basic types of superstructure are beam, deck (slab), truss, arch, and suspension. The substructure is the portion of the bridge that transmits loads from the superstructure to the supporting rock or soil. Timber substructures include abutments and bents. Abutments support the two bridge ends, while bents provide intermediate support for multiple-span crossings.

TIMBER SUPERSTRUCTURES

LONGITUDINAL BEAM (in bridge design, the longitude is measured in the direction of traffic flow): The simplest and most common timber bridge superstructure, the longitudinal beam type consists of a deck system supported by a series of timber beams between two or more supports. Beams are constructed from logs, sawn lumber, glued-laminated timber (glulam), or laminated veneer lumber (LVL).

LONGITUDINAL DECK: Longitudinal deck or slab superstructures are constructed of glulam, nail-laminated sawn lumber, or stress-laminated lumber decks placed longitudinally between supports, with the wide dimension of the lamination vertical. In this type of superstructure, the deck is designed to resist all applied loads and deflection without additional supporting members or beams. Nonetheless, transverse distributor beams are usually attached to the underside of the deck to help distribute the load. Maximum clear spans are approximately 35 ft.

TRUSS: Trusses are structural frames consisting of straight members connected to form a series of triangles. Trusses can span distances of up to 250 ft. In bridge applications, a typical truss superstructure consists of two main trusses, a floor system, and bracing. This type is classified as a deck truss (in which the deck is at or above the level of the top chord) or a through truss (in which the deck is near the bottom chord). When the height of a through truss is insufficient for overhead bracing, it is called a half-through or pony truss. Timber trusses are constructed in many geometric configurations, but two of the most popular are the bowstring truss and parallel chord truss.

ARCH: Arches used in clear span timber bridge construction have glued-laminated timbers for the main members. This type of superstructure, called a glulam deck arch, probably best shows the versatility of glulam in bridge construction. The glulam arches are manufactured in segmental, circular, or parabolic shapes. Two basic arch types are used: the two-hinge arch (for short spans of 80 ft or less) and the three-hinge arch (for long spans of between 80 and 200 ft). The roadway for deck arch bridges is supported by glulam post bents connected to the arches with steel gusset plates. Use of this design is most practical when considerable height is required and when foundations can be constructed to resist horizontal end reactions. It is particularly suitable for deep crossings because long clear spans result in substantial substructure cost savings.

SUSPENSION: Timber suspension bridges consist of a timber deck structure suspended from flexible steel cables or chains supported by timber towers. This superstructure type is capable of spanning clear distances of more than 500 ft and is normally used only when span requirements make other bridge types impractical or when it is not feasible to use intermediate bents.

TIMBER SUBSTRUCTURES

ABUTMENTS: Abutments support the bridge ends and contain roadway embankment material. The simplest timber abutment is a sawn lumber or glulam spread footing placed directly on the surface of the embankment if foundation materials permit. Another type is the post abutment, in which the superstructure is supported on sawn lumber or glulam posts connected to a spread footing. Pile abutments may be used if soils cannot hold footings.

BENTS: Bents are intermediate supports between abutments used for multiple-span bridges. They are made from timber piles or sawn lumber frames, depending on height requirements and soil conditions.

GENERAL DESIGN CRITERIA

For design criteria and specifications for timber bridges, refer to the current edition of the American Association of State Highway and Transportation Officials (AASHTO) Standard Specifications for Highway Bridges and "Timber Bridges: Design, Construction, Inspection, and Maintenance," U.S. Department of Agriculture, August 1992.

Richard J. Vitullo, AIA; Oak Leaf Studio; Crownsville, Maryland
Michael A. Ritter, PE, Structural Engineer; Forest Products Lab, USDA; Madison, Wisconsin

HEAVY TIMBER CONSTRUCTION

Timber Bridges

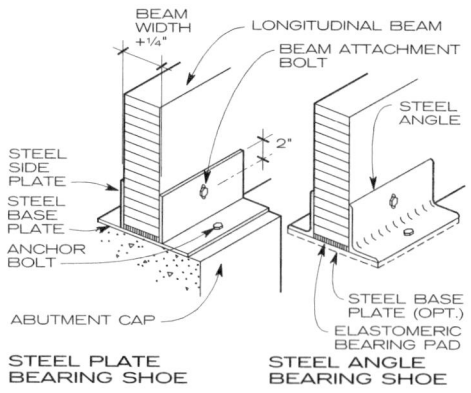

TYPICAL BEARING SHOE DETAILS

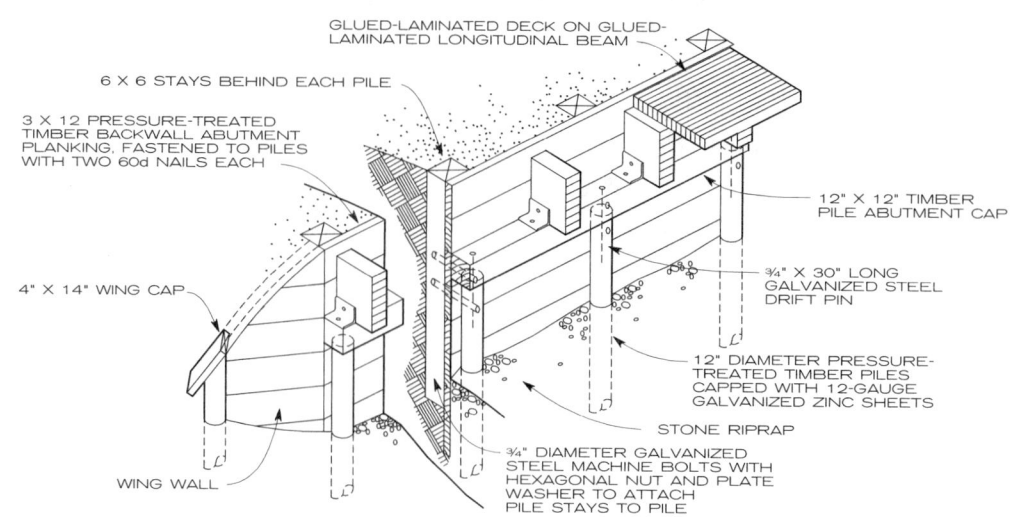

TYPICAL PILE ABUTMENT DETAIL

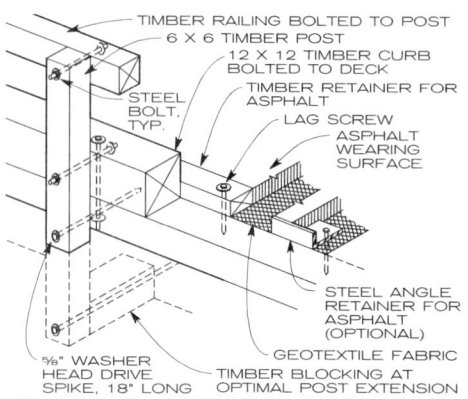

BRIDGE EDGE CONDITION

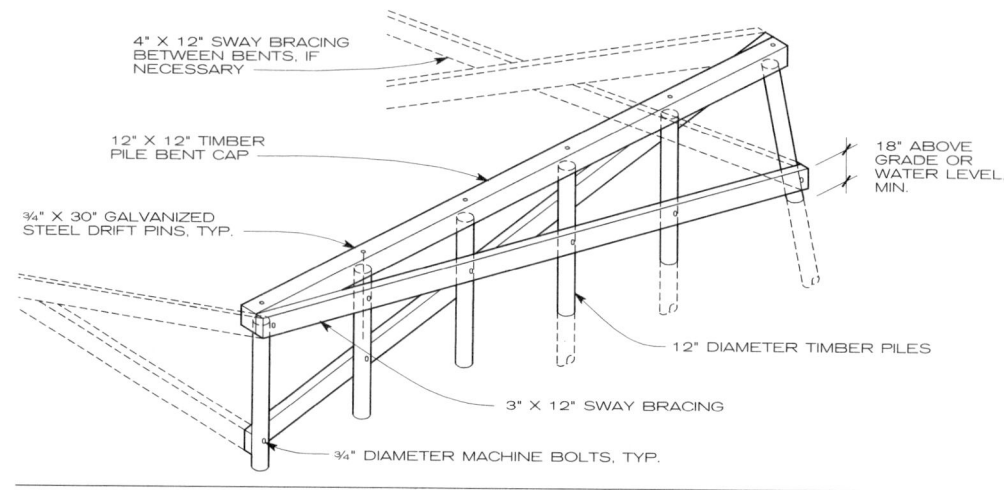

TYPICAL PILE BENT DETAIL

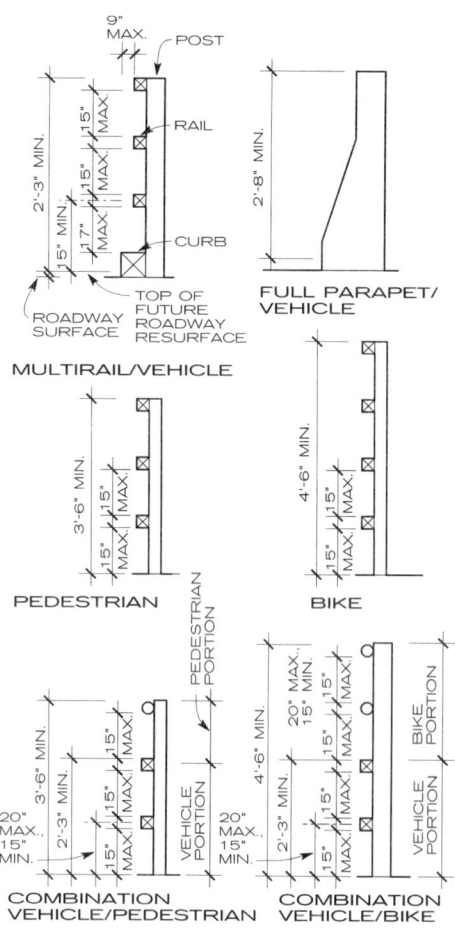

TYPICAL RAIL SYSTEMS

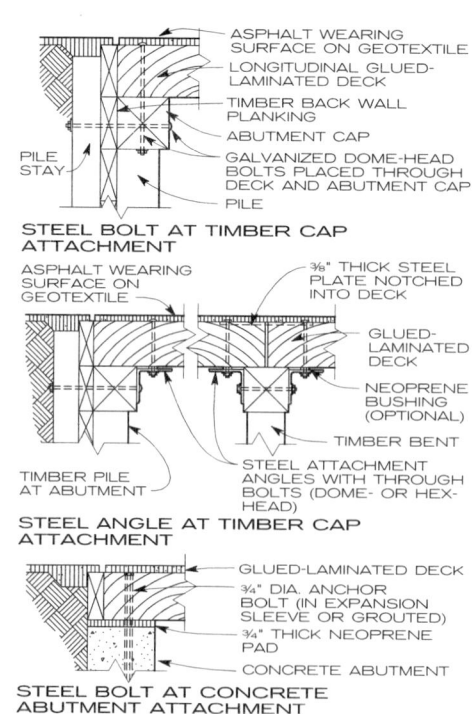

TYPICAL LONGITUDINAL DECK ATTACHMENT DETAILS

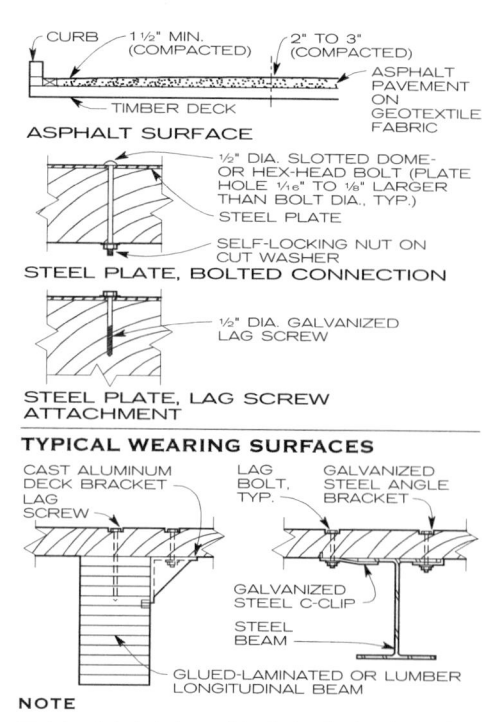

TYPICAL WEARING SURFACES

TYPICAL GLUED-LAMINATED DECK ATTACHMENT DETAILS

Richard J. Vitullo, AIA; Oak Leaf Studio; Crownsville, Maryland
Michael A. Ritter, PE, Structural Engineer; Forest Products Lab, USDA; Madison, Wisconsin

HEAVY TIMBER CONSTRUCTION

Wood Preservatives

RELATIVE TREATABILITY OF SELECTED DOMESTIC SPECIES

HEARTWOOD LEAST DIFFICULT TO PENETRATE	HEARTWOOD MODERATELY DIFFICULT TO PENETRATE	HEARTWOOD DIFFICULT TO PENETRATE	HEARTWOOD VERY DIFFICULT TO PENETRATE
Bristlecone pine, pinyon pine, redwood	Bald cypress, California red fir, Douglas fir (coast), Eastern white pine, jack pine, loblolly pine, longleaf pine, ponderosa pine, red pine, shortleaf pine, sugar pine, Western hemlock	Eastern hemlock, Engelmann spruce, grand fir, lodgepole pine, noble fir, sitka spruce, Western larch, white fir, white spruce	Alpine fir, corkbark fir, Douglas fir (Rocky Mountain), Northern white cedar, tamarack, Western red cedar

RELATIVE HEARTWOOD DECAY RESISTANCE OF NATURALLY RESISTANT UNTREATED WOODS*

RESISTANT OR VERY RESISTANT	MODERATELY RESISTANT	SLIGHTLY OR NONRESISTANT
Bald cypress (old growth), cedar, white oak, redwood	Bald cypress (new growth), Douglas fir, Western larch, Eastern white pine, Southern yellow pine (longleaf, slash), tamarack	Pines other than longleaf, slash, and Eastern white, spruces, true firs

* Source: U.S. Forest Products Laboratory Wood Handbook

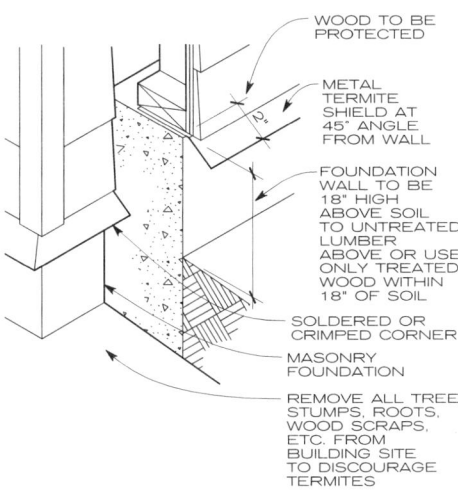

TERMITE PROTECTION DETAILS

GENERAL

Wood may be destroyed by decay fungi; by insects like carpenter ants and termites; and by marine borers in saltwater exposures. Four conditions must exist before these organisms can destroy wood: (1) a free oxygen supply; (2) a moisture level in the wood above the fiber saturation point (20%); (3) a temperature in the range of 50 to 90°F; (4) the presence of a food source, in this case, the wood.

In most indoor environments, where moisture levels are generally low, wood will last for a very long time. In certain indoor environments, however, and in many exterior environments, wood cannot be kept dry out of the proximity of moisture. Most building codes recognize this by requiring the use of pressure-treated wood or naturally resistant wood species where building components come into contact with concrete, masonry, or exposed soil. This requirement also covers floor joists and crawl space support members within 12 to 18 in. of exposed soil.

DECAY-RESISTANT WOOD

When specifying a wood that will resist decay, the choice is between naturally decay-resistant wood or wood treated with preservatives. The first requires use of the heartwood of naturally decay-resistant woods such as Western red cedar, bald cypress, redwood, and others that contain natural poisons called extractives, which are not palatable to decay-causing organisms. However, not all grades or species of these woods are suitable for some structural situations. Treating wood with preservatives is a process that impregnates wood with chemicals through a pressure-treatment process. Use of nonpressure treatments such as spraying, dipping, and brushing is mostly limited to field treatment of wood during construction or remedial treatment of existing wood in place.

PRESSURE-TREATED WOOD

There are two processes commonly used for pressure treating wood, the full cell and modified full cell processes. In both, the wood is placed in a large, cylindrical tank and the preservative forced under pressure into its cells.

In the modified full-cell process the preservative coats the walls of the wood cells and is absorbed when the process is finished the wood cell cavities are empty of preservatives. Most over-the-counter pressure-treated wood is treated with this process. In the full-cell process, a vacuum is introduced at the beginning to force the air out of the wood cell cavities, which then remain filled with preservative after treatment. The full-cell process is used in most creosote and pentachlorophenol treating for wood used in severe environments, including applications such as utility poles, railroad ties, saltwater piles, and timber bridges. Regardless of which process is used, the wood is generally dried to a 20% moisture content prior to treatment to promote maximum penetration of the preservative.

PENETRATION AND RETENTION OF PRESERVATIVES

Penetration and retention are the two measures that define the effectiveness of preservation methods. Penetration depends on the species of wood and the size of the lumber member being treated. Some species that resist preservative penetration, such as Douglas fir, are incised with small slits to make treatment more effective. Others, such as Southern yellow pine, are easily treated without incisions. While the sapwood of some species is readily penetrated, the heartwood of most resists penetration (although the heartwood of all species naturally resists decay). While the penetration of preservatives is hard to determine without damaging the wood, retention of the preservative can be measured directly by weighing the wood, stated in terms of pounds (of the chemical retained) per cubic foot (pcf). Retention standards are set by the American Wood Preservers' Association and enforced through chemical analysis of treated wood by an independent third-party agency approved by the American Lumber Standard Committee (ALSC). A quality mark outlining pertinent information can be found on complying wood stock.

PRESERVATIVE TYPES

Three classes of preservatives are in use today: creosote, oil-borne (organic), and waterborne (inorganic).

CREOSOTE is a coal-tar product that is dissolved in a distilled solution or petroleum oil. It is an effective preservative in applications with extreme exposure to decay or insect attack (marine borers in saltwater environments, such as marine piles or bridge timbers). Wood treated with the full-cell process is more effective in these applications, but the creosote may bleed into the surroundings, causing contamination. Most utility poles, freshwater piles, and fenceposts are treated with the empty-cell process, which yields a clean, nonbleeding surface. Creosote-treated products cannot be painted, but epoxy shellac and coal-tar pitch are acceptable sealants. This type of preservative can last from thirty to sixty years. Clean air standards prohibit the use of creosote in many areas.

ORGANIC OIL-BORNE PRESERVATIVES are carried in organic solvents such as liquefied isobutane and are used to treat most softwoods and hardwoods. These preservatives include pentachlorophenol (penta), copper naphthenate, tributyl tinoxide (TBTO), and copper 8-quinolinolate.

Penta extends the service life of wood by twenty to forty years and is used to treat utility poles, fenceposts, and highway timbers. Tinted light to dark brown, penta-treated wood accepts adhesives and finishes reasonably well once the oil medium has evaporated. Polyurethane, shellac, varnish, and latex enamel are effective as sealants. Penta can migrate to the surface of wood, leach into the surrounding soil, and contaminate groundwater. Only slowly does it break down into biodegradable compounds..

Plywood and other wood treated with copper-8-quinolinilate can be used in applications where food is harvested, transported, or stored. The chemical is dissolved in liquid petroleum gas or light hydrocarbon solvents so the surface is clean and free of solvent odor. Consult with the treatment company regarding applicable FDA and USDA acceptances.

INORGANIC WATERBORNE PRESERVATIVES are the most popular and commonly available types used for treating wood. They include chromated copper arsenate (CCA), ammoniacal copper arsenate (ACA), and ammoniacal copper zinc arsenate (ACZA). These preservatives are related chemically and have a lot in common. Chromium holds the other components in the wood and prevents leaching; ammonia helps carry copper, zinc, and arsenic deeper into the wood; arsenic guards against attack by termites and fungi. Southern yellow pine is usually treated with CCA, and Douglas fir and other western woods with ACA and ACZA. The various formulations of CCA vary in the amount of chromium, copper, and arsenic they contain. The oxide form of CCA, type C, is widely preferred for most construction. During the treatment process, CCA is water soluble, but air drying for a few days renders it insoluble. This is because the chromium reacts chemically with the wood, permanently bonding itself and the copper and arsenic to the cell walls, preventing leaching during its service life. CCA-treated wood can last up to forty years.

Another waterborne preservative is borax, which has promise due to its effectiveness against fungi and insects and its low-toxicity to people and animals. However, it leaches out when the wood gets wet.

FINISHING OF PRESERVATIVE-TREATED WOOD

Waterborne preservatives are recommended when clean, odorless, and paintable wood products are required. Wood treated with such preservatives may be used indoors if sawdust and construction debris are cleaned up. Painting wood treated with creosote or oil-borne pentachlorophenol is not recommended, as it is difficult to use, requiring extensive care and an aluminum-based paint. Paintable waterborne pentachlorophenol treatments are available. For certain interior applications in commercial, industrial, or farm buildings, creosote- or penta-treated wood may be used if exposed surfaces are sealed with two coats of urethane or epoxy paint or shellac. Guidelines for precautions in these cases are outlined in an EPA-approved consumer information sheet for each preservative treatment.

FASTENERS

CCA, ACA, and ACC are corrosive to uncoated metals. For aboveground construction, hot-dipped or hot-tumbled galvanized steel and stainless steel fasteners are recommended. Joist hangers and framing anchors should also be corrosion resistant. For below-grade construction, such as treated wood foundation systems, types 304 and 316 stainless steel Type H silicon bronze, ETP copper, and monel fasteners are required. Adhesives work well with CCA-treated wood. Phenolresorcinol, resorcinol, and melemine-formaldehyde structural adhesives are used in glulam beams made from treated wood members. On job sites, use adhesives recommended for use with treated wood.

PRECAUTIONS FOR USE AND HANDLING

The chemical formulations used for preservative treatment of wood are registered with the EPA, which has approved guidelines for the use of pressure-treated wood to ensure safe handling and avoid environmental or other health hazards. Some guidelines for use and handling follow:

1. Dispose of treated wood by ordinary trash collection or burial. Treated wood should never be burned in open fires or in stoves, fireplaces, or residential boilers.
2. Avoid frequent inhalation of sawdust from treated wood. Whenever possible, sawing and machining of treated wood should be done outdoors.
3. Avoid frequent or prolonged skin contact with penta- or creosote-treated wood.
4. After handling treated wood products, wash exposed areas thoroughly before eating or drinking.

Richard J. Vitullo, AIA; Oak Leaf Studio; Crownsville, Maryland
American Plywood Association; Tacoma, Washington

Wood Preservatives

SOUTHERN PINE PRESERVATIVE RETENTIONS AND APPLICABLE AWPA STANDARDS[1]

WOOD USES	APPLICATIONS		WATERBORNE PRESERVATIVES[2]			AWPA STANDARDS	CRESOTE AND OILBORNE PRESERVATIVES[3]			
			AMMONIACAL COPPER ARSENATE (ACA)	AMMONIACAL COPPER ZINC ARSENATE (ACZA)	CHROMATED COPPER ARSENATE (CCA)		CREOSOTE	CREOSOTE-PETROLEUM	CREOSOTE SOLUTIONS	PENTA-CHLORO-PHENOL (PENTA)
LUMBER, TIMBERS, AND PLYWOOD	Aboveground		0.25	0.25	0.25	C2/C9	8[5]	8[5]	8[5]	0.40
	Soil and freshwater use		0.40	0.40	0.40	C2/C9	10[5]	10[5]	10[5]	0.50
	Permanent wood foundation (PWF)		0.60	0.60	0.60	C22	NR*	NR	NR	NR
	Saltwater use		2.5	2.5	2.5	C2/C9	25	NR	25	NR
PILES	Land or freshwater use and foundations		0.80	0.80	0.80	C3	12	12	12	0.60
	Marine One prevalent marine organism	Teredo only	2.5[4] and 1.5	2.5[4] and 1.5	2.5[4] and 1.5	C18	20	NR	20	NR
		Pholads only	NR	NR	NR	C18	20	NR	20	NR
		Limnoria tripunctata only	2.5[4] and 1.5	2.5[4] and 1.5	2.5[4] and 1.5	C18	NR	NR	NR	NR
	Marine Sphaeroma terebrans or combination of pholads and limnoria tripunctata (use a dual treatment)	First treatment	1.0	1.0	1.0	C18	—	—	—	—
		Second treatment	—	—	—	C18	20	—	20	—
POLES	Utility	Normal	0.60	0.60	0.60	C4	7.5	7.5	7.5	0.38
		Severe service conditions (high incidence of decay and termite attack)	0.60	0.60	0.60	C4	9.0	9.0	9.0	0.45
	Building construction	Round	0.60	0.60	0.60	C23	9.0[5]	NR	NR	0.45
POSTS	Commercial-residential fence	Round, half-round, and quarter-round	0.40	0.40	0.40	C5	8[5]	8[5]	8[5]	0.40
		Sawn four sides	0.40	0.40	0.40	C2	10[5]	10[5]	10[5]	0.50
	Highway construction: Fence, guide, sign, and sight	Round, half-round, and quarter-round	0.40	0.40	0.40	C14	8	8	8	0.40
		Sawn four sides	0.40	0.40	0.40	C14	10	10	10	0.50
	Highway construction: Guardrail and spacer blocks	Round	0.50	0.50	0.50	C14	10	10	10	0.50
		Sawn four sides	0.50	0.50	0.50	C14	12	12	12	0.60

* NR = not recommended

[1] American Wood Preservers' Association (AWPA) Standards detail plant operating procedures for pressure treatment of wood. These standards include minimum vacuum, pressure, and penetration requirements and maximum steaming parameters. AWPA also details minimum retention requirements, sampling zones for assay and maximum redrying temperature allowances for each preservative, commodity, and wood species. For a copy of the AWPA standards booklet, write to the American Wood Preservers' Association, P.O. Box 286, Woodstock, MD 21163-0286. For other wood species, contact the relevant organization.

[2] ACA, ACZA, and CCA are the most commonly available waterborne preservatives. Ammoniacal copper quat (ACQ) is also approved by AWPA as a waterborne preservative for Southern pine, Western hemlock, Hem-fir, and Douglas fir as lumber, timbers, plywood, and fenceposts.

[3] Copper naphthenate is also approved by AWPA as an oilborne preservative for specific wood species and applications excluding saltwater use.

[4] Assay retentions are based on two assay zones—0 to 0.5 in. and 0 to 2.0 in.

[5] Not recommended where cleanliness and freedom from odor are necessary.

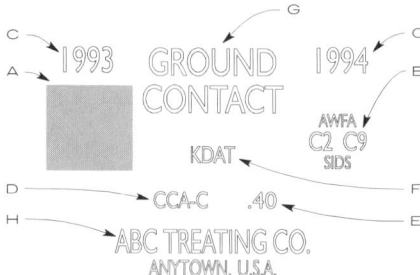

A: Trademark of inspection agency certified by the American Lumber Standard Committee (ALSC); contact the Southern Pine Council (SPC) or ALSC for a list of certified inspection agencies.
B: Applicable American Wood Preservers' Association (AWPA) standard
C: Year of treatment
D: Preservative used for treatment
E: Retention level
F: Dry or KDAT (kiln-dried after treatment), if applicable
G: Proper exposure conditions
H: Treating company and location

TYPICAL QUALITY MARK FOR TREATED LUMBER

USE PRECAUTIONS FOR PRESSURE-TREATED WOOD[1]

APPLICATIONS	ORGANIC PRESERVATIVES		INORGANIC PRESERVATIVES
	CREOSOTE	PENTACHLORO-PHENOL	ARSENICALS
1. Skin contact applications	Okay[2]	Okay[2]	Okay
2. Residential interiors	No	No	Okay
3. For interior components of industrial and farm buildings that are in ground contact and subject to decay or insect attack (also see #5 below)	Okay[2]	Okay[2]	Okay
4. Laminated beams for commercial or industrial buildings	No	Okay[2]	Okay
5. Interiors of farm buildings when animals can crib (bite) or lick the treated wood	No	No	Okay
6. Agricultural farrowing or brooding facilities	No	No	Okay
7. Applications in which preservatives may become a component of food or animal feed, such as structures or containers for storing silage or food	No	No	No
8. Cutting boards or countertops for preparing food	No	No	No
9. Decks, patios, and walkways if surface is visibly clean and free from residues	Okay	Okay	Okay
10. Portions of beehives that may come into contact with honey	No	No	No
11. Applications in which treated wood can come into direct or indirect contact with drinking water for public or animal consumption	No[3]	No[3]	No[3]

[1] Based on EPA-approved consumer information sheets
[2] Must be painted with two coats of recommended sealer
[3] Okay for incidental contact such as bridges or docks

Richard J. Vitullo, AIA; Oak Leaf Studio; Crownsville, Maryland
Southern Pine Council; Kenner, Louisiana
American Plywood Association; Tacoma, Washington

WOOD TREATMENT

Fire-Retardant Treated Wood

GENERAL

Building construction materials are tested for four criteria related to performance during a fire: fire resistance, flame spread, fuel contributed, and smoke developed. Fire resistance is the material's ability to resist burning while retaining its structural integrity. Flame spread measures the rate at which flames travel along the surface of a material. Fuel contributed is a measure of how much combustible matter a material furnishes to a fire. Smoke developed is a measure of the surface burning characteristics of a material.

How fire spreads through wood structures depends on the size and arrangement of wood members and the details that restrict or encourage air movement around them. Larger cross sections take longer to burn. As wood burns, it develops an outer layer of charcoal, which insulates the wood beneath and slows burning. This "char" layer proceeds through the burning wood at an average rate of 1 1/2 in. per hour. Various design strategies can be used to resist fire damage to a wood structure and its spread to adjacent areas, but the most important is to protect the wood members by means of coverings, coatings, or treatments.

FIRE-RETARDANT TREATMENT

Modern fire-retardant treatment (FRT) of wood consists of pressure treatment with aqueous solutions of various organic and inorganic chemicals, followed by kiln drying to reduce moisture content to 19% or less for lumber under 2 in. thick and 15% or less for plywood. All proprietary FRTs must conform to UL classifications. FRT wood is commonly used in plywood sheathing, roof trusses, rafters, floor joists, studs, staging, and shingles and shakes. Fire-retardant chemical combinations include zinc chloride, ammonium sulfates, borax or boric acid, and lesser amounts of sodium dichromate. Ammonium phosphates are no longer used because they cause rapid disintegration of wood.

Fire retardants work when fire-retardant chemicals react with the tars and gases normally produced by burning wood. The resultant carbon char acts as thermal insulation (greater than on untreated wood), slowing the rate of burning. Gases released from the FRT wood are diluted with carbon dioxide and water vapor, lessening the chance of flashover, in which wood gases are ignited by high temperatures and then explode.

FRT STANDARDS AND CLASSIFICATIONS

Interior fire retardants meet Class I ratings, which are required by code for vertical exit ways and special areas. Class II ratings are required for horizontal exit ways, but this rating is rarely reached with untreated wood. FRT lumber and plywood are recognized substitutes for noncombustible materials for insurance purposes. Many codes accept FRT wood products for a variety of applications.

Both the flame spread index and smoke-developed index give numerical scales for a material's fire classification. The flame spread index is the primary test for fire performance, according to ASTM E-84, which mandates a flame spread rating of 25 or less. In the Model Building Codes, flame spread ratings are classified as 0-25 (Class I or A), 26-75 (Class II or B), and 76-200 (Class III or C).

A smoke-developed index of 450 or less is permitted for FRT wood. The UL FR-S listing applies only to treated products with a UL-723 (ASTM E-84) flame and smoke classification not exceeding 25 in a 30-min. test. The classification applies to the species tested and does not pertain to the structures in which the materials are installed.

Fire retardants come in interior and exterior types. Interior fire retardants are used on wood trusses and studs; exterior retardants protect exterior lumber, siding, roof shakes and shingles, and scaffold planking. The latter type offers durable, nonleachable, long-term fire protection in outdoor or moist (relative humidity of 95% or greater) conditions.

Some codes count Class C or Class B FRT shingles and shakes as noncombustible materials. For wood exposed to the weather, specify exterior-type retardants that retain their protective properties under the standard rain test.

Interior Type A wood is appropriate for interior and weather-protected applications with less than 95% relative humidity. In rare instances, when relative humidity is less than 75%, Type B can be specified. Interior Type A is used where a wood with low hygroscopicity (the rate at which the chemical draws moisture from the air) is required.

FRT INTERIOR WOODWORK

Instead of solid lumber, it is often desirable to build members of treated cores clad with untreated veneers 1/28 in. thick or less. Most codes discount this narrow finishing in determining the flame spread index of the wood, permitting use of untreated wood in about 10% of the combined wall and ceiling surface area. Sizes and species currently being treated (flame spread index less than 25) include red oak and Western red cedar up to 4/4 and yellow poplar up to 8/4. Color and finishes are affected by FRTs.

FINISHING AND FINISHES

FRT lumber and plywood can be lightly sanded for cosmetic cleaning after treatment. Painting and staining are possible but not always successful, particularly transparent finishes. Test finishes for compatibility before application.

Treated lumber may be end cut, but ripping and extensive surfacing will normally void the UL label. To the extent possible, materials should be precut before treatment, otherwise a wood treater should be consulted. Treated plywood can be cut in either direction without loss of fire protection.

Intumescent coatings are sometimes used to reduce flammability of wood surfaces in both opaque and transparent finishes. Under high heat, these coatings expand or foam, creating an insulating effect that reduces flame spread.

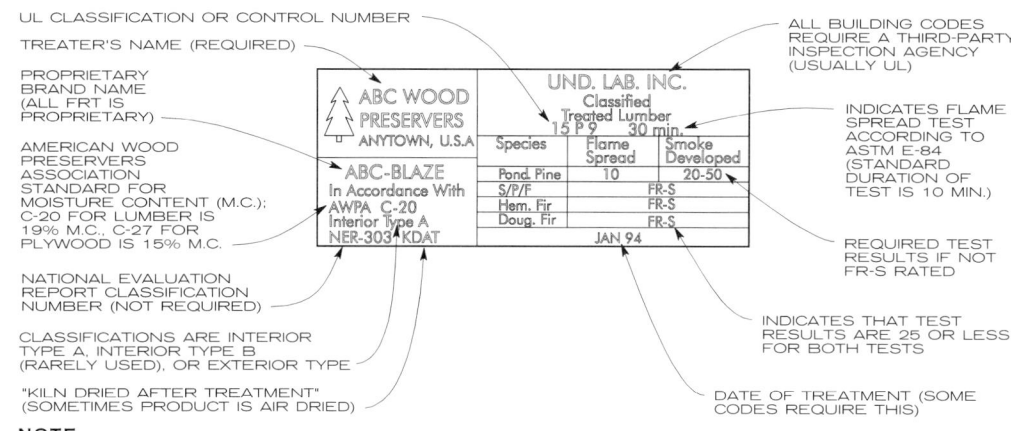

NOTE

Wood shakes and shingles are further classified as class B or C. Rather than stamp each piece, each bundle is tagged with an identification mark.

TYPICAL FIRE-RETARDANT TREATED WOOD IDENTIFICATION MARK

Check local codes before specifying these coatings because they tend to be less durable, softer, and more hygroscopic than standard finishes.

NOTES

1. These standards apply to FRT wood: ASTM E-84, ASTM D-2898, ASTM D-3201, ASTM E-108, AWPA C-20, AWPA C-27, and ULI Building Materials Directory (current edition). For more information, contact the American Wood Preservers' Association (AWPA), American Wood Preservers' Institute, USDA Forest Service, Southern Forest Products Association, Western Wood Preservers Institute, and American Forest and Paper Association.

2. FRT wood has increased weight and decreased strength; consult a structural engineer and the wood treater for actual design values for structural applications.

3. FRT wood fasteners must be hot-dipped, zinc-coated galvanized stainless steel, silicon bronze, or copper; other materials deteriorate upon contact with FRT chemicals.

4. The smoke-developed index for the products listed in the flame spread index remained below 450, the limiting value used in most building codes.

FLAME SPREAD INDEX

MATERIAL[1]		ASTM E-84 FLAME SPREAD	SOURCE[2]
Lumber	Birch, yellow	105-110	UL
	Cedar, Western red	70	HPMA
	Douglas fir	70-100	UL
	Maple (flooring)	104	CWC
	Oak, red or white	100	UL
	Pine, Ponderosa	105-230[3]	UL
	Pine, Southern yellow	130-195	UL
	Poplar	170-185	UL
	Redwood	65	CRA
	Spruce, Northern	65	UL
Softwood plywood (Exterior glue)	Douglas fir, 1/4"	118	CWC
	Douglas fir, 5/8"	95	APA
	Southern pine, 1/4"	95-110	APA
Hardwood plywood	Lauan, 1/4"	150	HPMA
Particleboard	1/2", 47 lb/cu ft	156	NBS
	5/8", 44 lb/cu ft	153	NBS
Flakeboard	Red oak, 1/2", 42-47 lb/cu ft (four types)	71-189	FPL
Shakes	Western red cedar, 1/2"	69	HPMA
Shingles	Western red cedar, 1/2"	49	HPMA

[1] Unless indicated, thickness of material is 1 in. nominal.

[2] Sources: APA—American Plywood Association; CRA—California Redwood Association; CWC—Canadian Wood Council; FPL—USDA Forest Products Laboratory; HPMA—Hardwood Plywood Manufacturers Association; NBS—National Bureau of Standards; UL—Underwriters Laboratories.

[3] Average of 18 tests was 154 with three values over 200.

[4] Hardwood Plywood Manufacturers Association test records

FLAME SPREAD INDEX OF FACTORY-FINISHED PRODUCTS

MATERIAL			ASTM E-84 FLAME SPREAD[4]
Particleboard	1/32"	Factory finish printed	118-178
	1/2"	Paper overlay	175
	5/8"	Vinyl overlay	100
Medium-density fiberboard (MDF)	3/16"	Factory finish printed	167
Hardboard	1/8"	Factory finish printed	158-194
		Paper overlay	155-166
Flakeboard	Aromatic cedar, 3/16"		156
Hardwood plywood	Aspen, 1/4"	Factory finished	196
	Birch, 5/32"	Factory finished	160-195
	Cherry, 1/4"	Factory finished	160
	Hickory, 1/4"	Factory finished	140
	Lauan, 1/4"	Factory finish printed	99-141
	Maple, 1/4"	Factory finished	155
	Oak, 1/4"	Factory finished	125-185
	Pine, 1/4"	Factory finished	120-140
	Walnut, 1/4"	Factory finished	138-160

Richard J. Vitullo, AIA; Oak Leaf Studio; Crownsville, Maryland

WOOD TREATMENT

Wood Ornaments

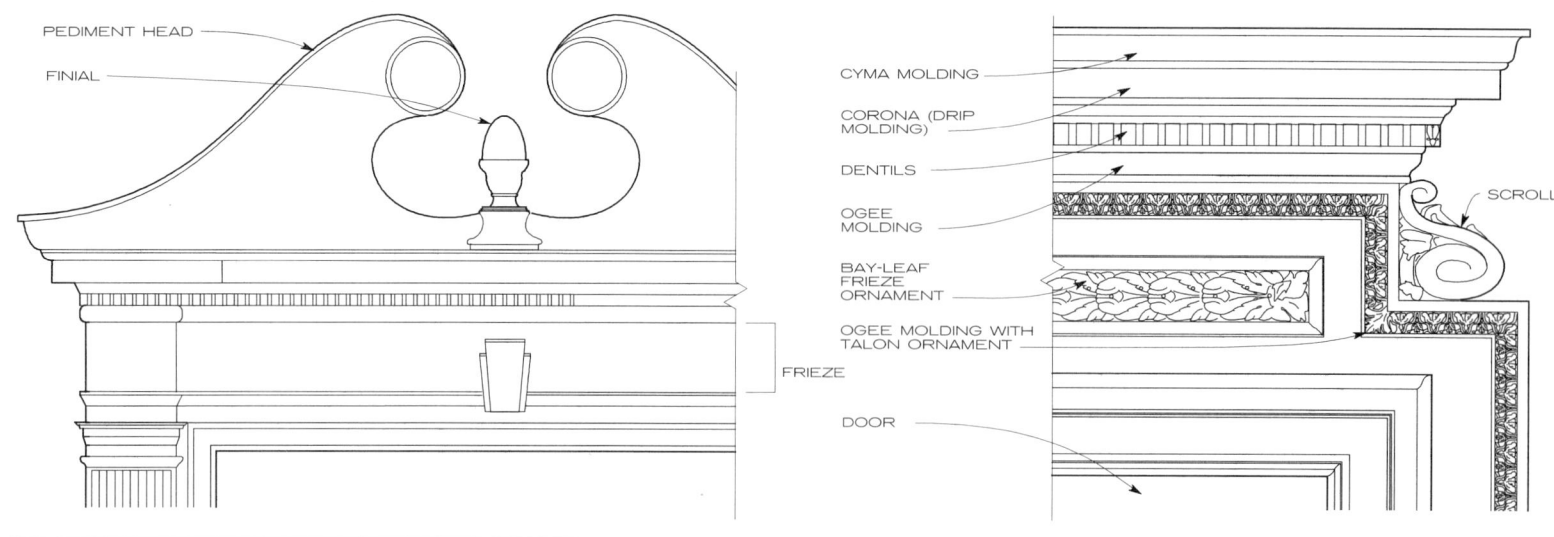

OVERDOOR DETAILS

WOOD CORBELS

GENERAL

Woodwork is considered an ornament when it has a special or unique design that does not fall within the standard categories of architectural woodwork as defined by the Architectural Woodwork Institute.

Some typical uses for ornamental wood include pediment heads, mantels, ornamental grilles, fluted pilasters, cupolas, finials, medallions, corbels, balusters, posts, and columns. Within the classification of ornamental wood are combinations of flat or molded solid lumber, or cored lumber components with wood veneer faces with, or without, the addition of moldings. All joinings between ornamental members should be designed for functional as well as decorative purposes.

Wood ornamentation is an art that can take shape in an almost infinite number of forms and designs, limited only by the mechanical production constraints of woodworking shops. "Wood" ornaments can also be produced in larger quantities (in molds) with the synthetic material polyurethane. Once cured, the polyurethane can be painted and substituted for the wood ornaments.

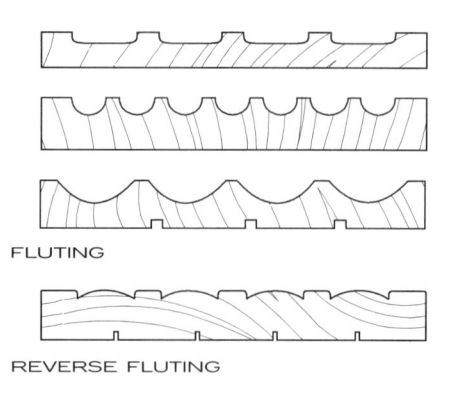

FLUTING

REVERSE FLUTING

FLUTING SECTIONS

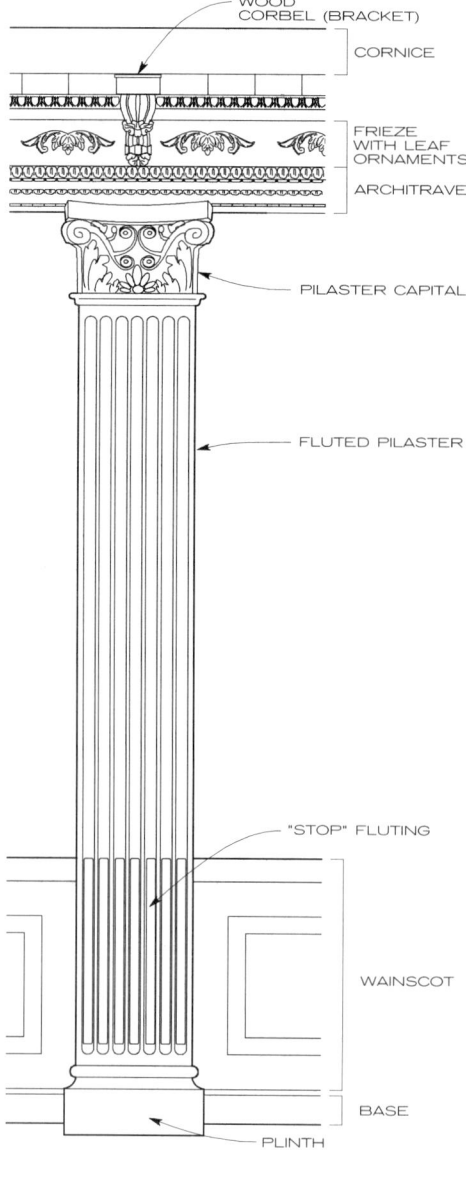

ORNAMENTAL WOOD PILASTER

Richard J. Vitullo, AIA; Oak Leaf Studio; Crownsville, Maryland

ARCHITECTURAL WOODWORK

Wood Ornaments

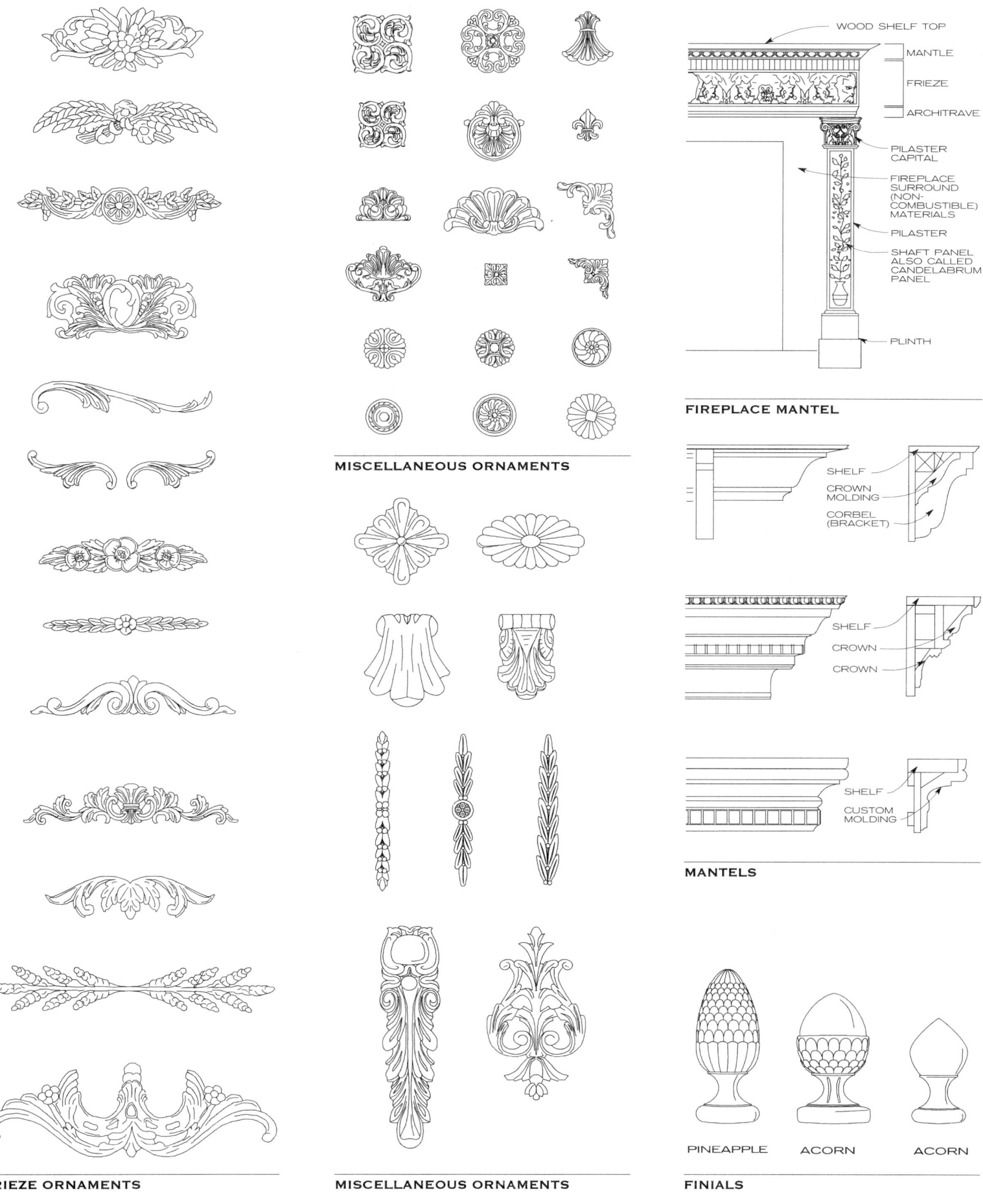

FRIEZE ORNAMENTS

MISCELLANEOUS ORNAMENTS

MISCELLANEOUS ORNAMENTS

FIREPLACE MANTEL

MANTELS

FINIALS

Richard J. Vitullo, AIA; Oak Leaf Studio; Crownsville, Maryland

ARCHITECTURAL WOODWORK

Interior Wood Trim and Moldings

GENERAL

Interior trim is a generally decorative treatment applied after wall, floor, and ceiling finishes have been installed. It can be made of flat or molded wood from single pieces of wood or built-up pieces that give a more complex and decorative appearance. Interior trim conceals joints between different materials and blocks air infiltration through walls, which typically is greatest at material joints. Interior trim also frames wall and ceiling openings (door and window/skylight trim), defines planar edges (crown and base molding), and acts as a visual divider between dissimilar materials (chair rail).

The Architectural Woodwork Institute differentiates wood trim according to its length. Standing wood trim is trim that can be accommodated easily with single lengths of wood (depending on species), such as crown moldings, fascias, soffits, chair rails, baseboards, and shoe moldings. Running trim is usually made up of finger-jointed wood to achieve the lengths customarily needed for this type of trim.

NOTES

1. Blocking that receives moldings should be set plumb, level, true, and straight, with no distortion, and should be provided for full surface contact. Attach blocking to substrates with nails, screws, or bolts.
2. Woodwork should be stored in a dry, ventilated space. If this is not possible, seal the ends of all pieces as soon as possible. Moldings should be at optimum moisture content at the time of installation and should be allowed to acclimate to project conditions before installation.
3. Joints in adjacent and related members should be staggered. Cope at inside corners and miter at outside corners to produce tight-fitting joints with full surface contact throughout the length of the joint; use scarf joints (face mitered) for end-to-end joints in trim.
4. Blind nail where possible, and use finishing nails in exposed areas. Predrill as required to eliminate splitting; set exposed nail heads for filling.
5. Most flat trim like baseboards and casing has a ploughed or relieved back, which gives wide trim a degree of flexibility, allowing it to fit snugly against a wall surface.
6. The molding profiles illustrated are a small sampling of those available from most millwork shops. Custom profiles should be shown on drawings full size. Dimensions given are for typical stock molding profiles.

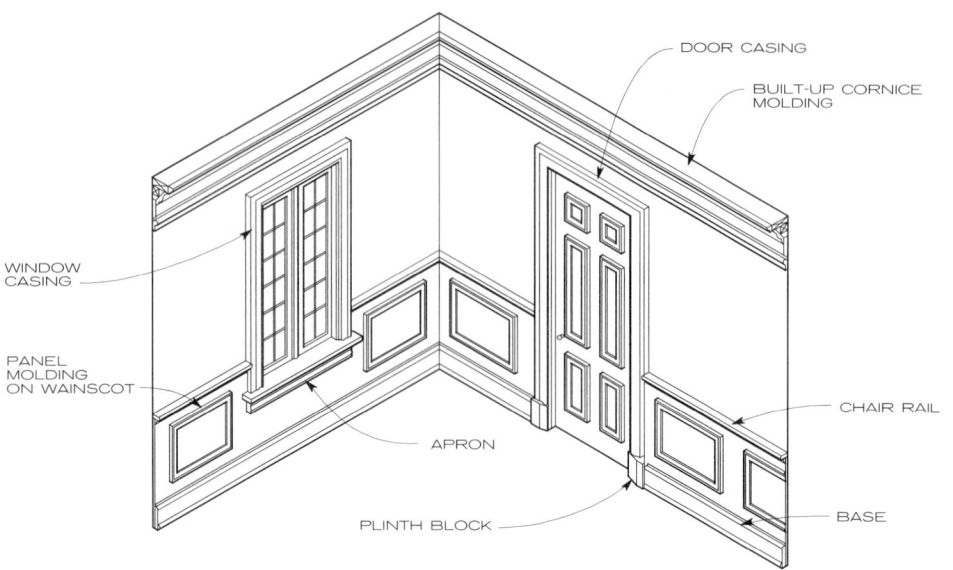

TYPICAL WOOD TRIM AND MOLDINGS

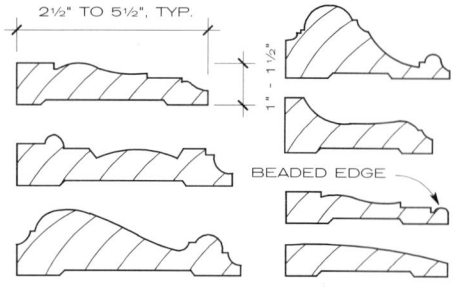

NOTE

Casings are used to finish the joint between the window or door head and side jambs and wall finish. Often a casing used at windows is also used as apron material, with the wide side toward the stool.

CASINGS

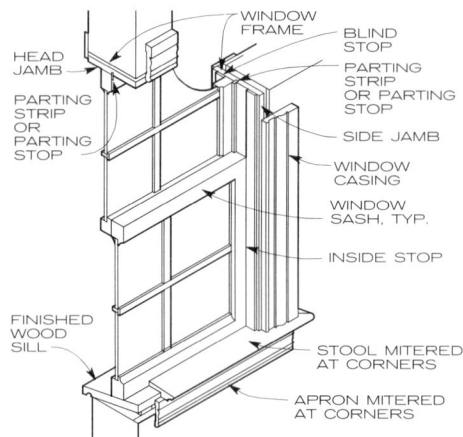

TYPICAL WINDOW TRIM

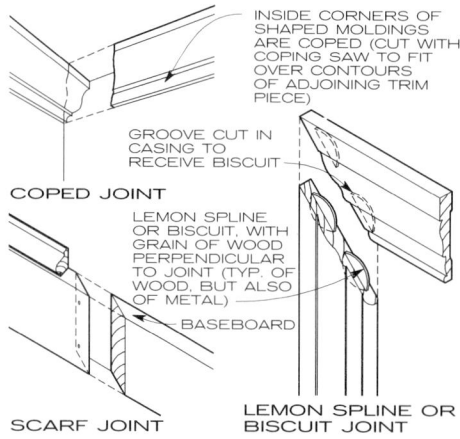

MOLDING CONNECTION DETAILS

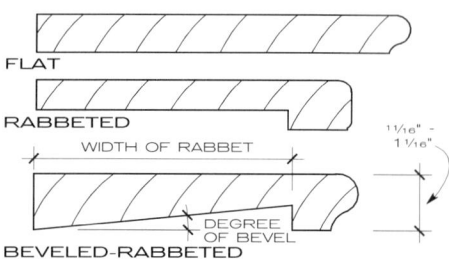

NOTE

Stools are used as interior caps on windowsills and receive casing from above and apron below. They are specified by width of rabbet and degree of bevel.

STOOLS

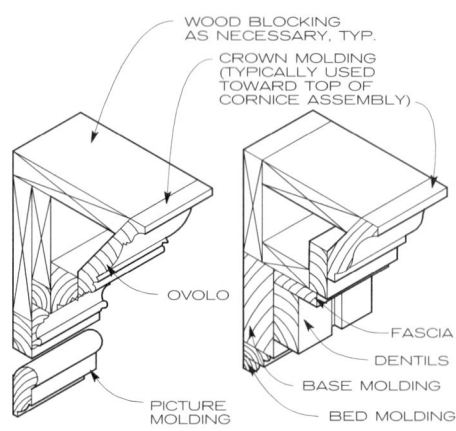

TYPICAL CORNICE TRIM

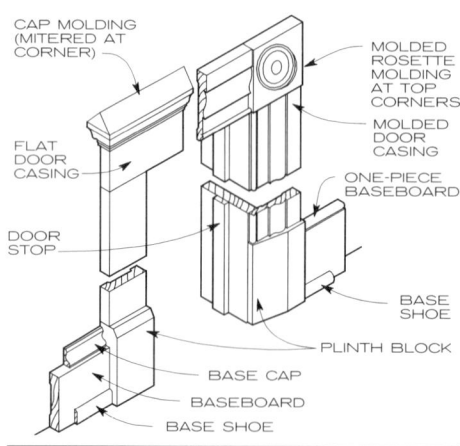

TYPICAL DOOR AND BASE TRIM

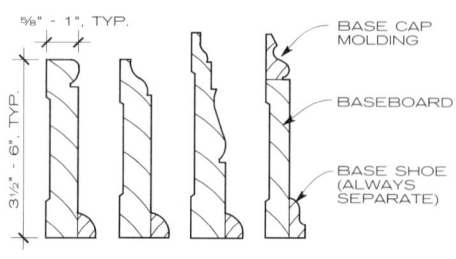

NOTE

Baseboards and base moldings are used at the juncture of wall and floor exclusively. Baseboard may be one piece (with integral base cap) or flat with optional base cap. Separate caps and shoes are flexible and facilitate a close fit to uneven wall and floor surfaces.

BASEBOARD AND BASE MOLDINGS

Richard J. Vitullo, AIA; Oak Leaf Studio; Crownsville, Maryland

ARCHITECTURAL WOODWORK

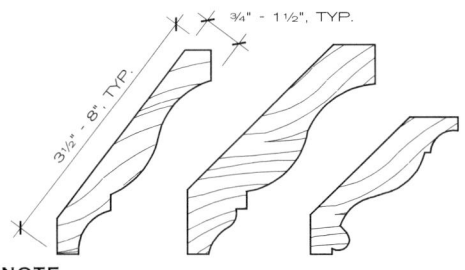

NOTE
Crown moldings are applied alone at the joint between wall and ceiling or together with other moldings in a built-up cornice, typically toward the top of the cornice assembly; measured edge to edge.

CROWN MOLDINGS

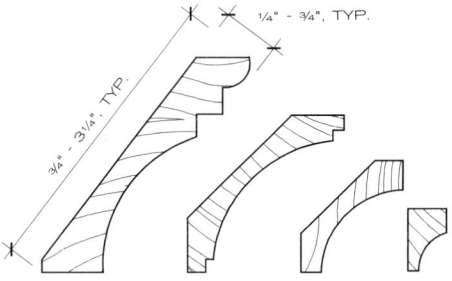

NOTE
Cove moldings are used at inside corners, such as wall-to-wall or ceiling-to-wall.

COVE MOLDINGS

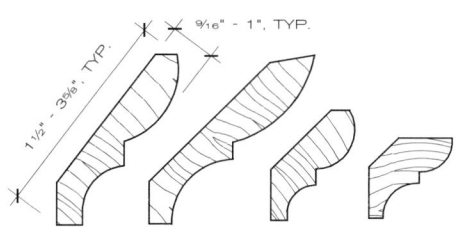

NOTE
Bed moldings are used at the bottom of built-up cornices and at other vertical-to-horizontal junctures.

BED MOLDINGS

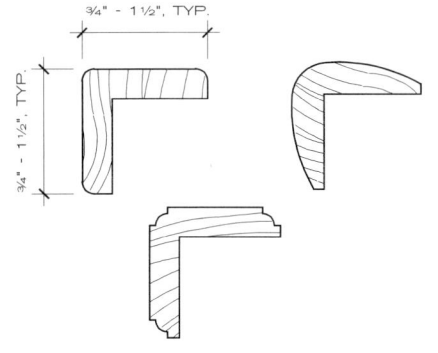

NOTE
This molding is used on outside corners.

CORNERS

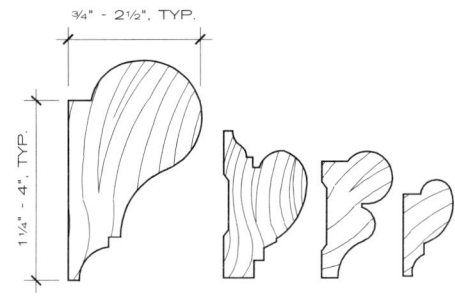

NOTE
Often integrated with cornices, picture moldings are used as continuous projecting supports for picture hooks. Custom-made hooks are available to fit these profiles.

PICTURE MOLDINGS

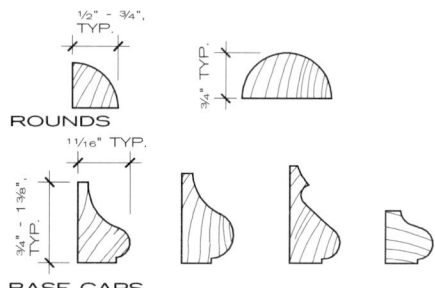

ROUNDS

BASE CAPS

NOTES
1. Half-rounds are used to conceal vertical and horizontal joints. Quarter-rounds are used at inside corners and as base shoe.
2. Base caps are applied at the top of the baseboard, flush against the wall.

BASE CAPS AND ROUNDS

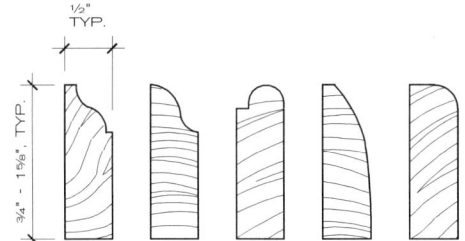

NOTE
Stops are used at jambs to guide windows and stop doors.

STOPS

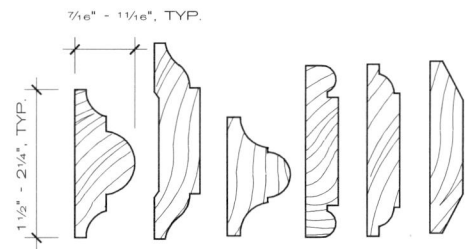

NOTE
These moldings are used in panels to conceal joints, over window jamb edges in a multiple-opening window, and as astragals at middle joints of double-leaf doors.

PANEL STRIPS, BATTENS, AND ASTRAGALS

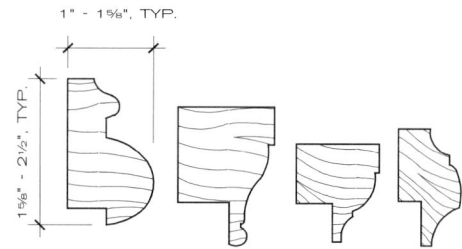

NOTE
Backbands are applied as trim at the outer edge of door jamb and head, among other uses.

BACKBANDS

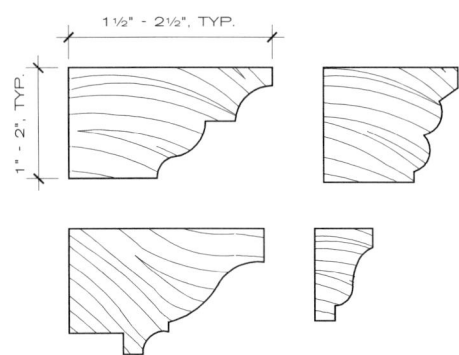

NOTE
Cap or rake moldings are used at head of door and window trim and at top of wainscots.

CAP OR RAKE MOLDINGS

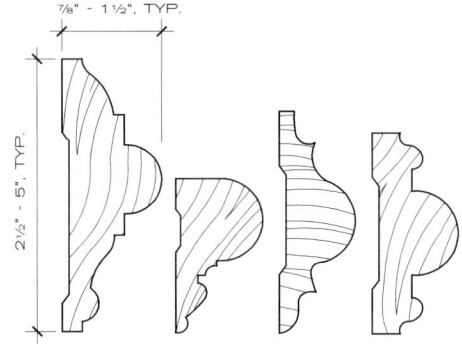

NOTE
Chair rails were originally meant to protect the wall surface from chair backs; applied typically $1/3$ up from the floor, either alone or atop wainscot paneling.

CHAIR RAILS

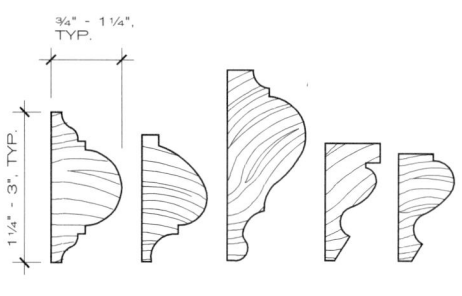

NOTE
Panel moldings are typically used as door and wainscot trim, mitered together and arranged in rectangles.

PANEL MOLDINGS

Richard J. Vitullo, AIA; Oak Leaf Studio; Crownsville, Maryland

Panel Products and Wood Veneers

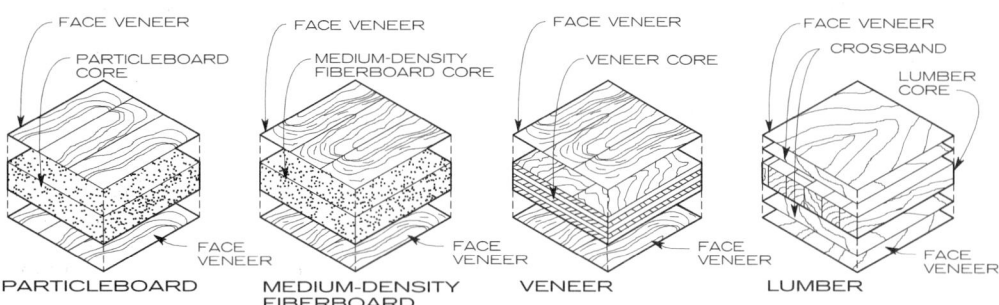

HARDWOOD PLYWOOD CORE TYPES

GENERAL

Architectural wood panels are made from wood material that is cut or formed into sheet products that are referred to as the "panel core." These sheets are used alone (with or without a finish) or laminated together with other veneer products to make plywood. A great variety of panels are manufactured using different core materials and adhesives or binders and various forming techniques and surface treatments. The characteristics of the panels vary with these differences in material and construction.

PANEL CORE TYPES

Panel cores, which serve as the substrate for laminates and veneers on the outer surface, are classified by ingredients and methods of manufacture. The following types of panel cores are suitable for architectural use:

INDUSTRIAL GRADE PARTICLEBOARD CORE

This core type is made by using heat and pressure to bond together synthetic resin or binder and wood particles of various sizes. Employed in a wide variety of architectural woodwork applications, industrial grade particleboard is especially well suited as a substrate for high-quality veneers and decorative laminates. When used as panels without any surface layers, the product is called particleboard. When used with wood veneer on the surface, the panels are referred to as particle-core plywood. Particleboard core classified by density or weight per cubic ft falls into three categories:

1. Low density—less than 40 lb per cubic ft (640 kg per cubic meter)
2. Medium density—40 to 50 lb per cubic ft (640 to 800 kg per cubic meter)
3. High density—more than 50 lb per cubic ft (800 kg per cubic meter)

MOISTURE-RESISTANT PARTICLEBOARD CORE

Some medium-density industrial particleboard is bonded with phenolic resins, which makes it more resistant to swelling when exposed to moisture. Phenolic resins, unlike urea resins, do not emit significant quantities of formaldehyde. The most common grades are type 2-M-2 (M-2 exterior glue) and 2-M-3 (M-3 exterior glue).

FIRE-RETARDANT PARTICLEBOARD CORE

Medium-density industrial particleboard may be treated during manufacture to carry a UL Class 1 fire rating stamp (flame spread 20, smoke developed 25). This material can be used as substrate for paneling requiring a Class 1 rating.

MEDIUM-DENSITY FIBERBOARD (MDF) CORE

MDF is made from wood particles reduced to fibers in a moderate-pressure steam vessel, combined with resin, and bonded together under heat and pressure. The surface is flat, smooth, uniform, dense, and free of knots or grain pattern. MDF is useful as a substrate for paint, thin overlay materials, veneers, and decorative laminates. The homogeneous edge allows machining and paint finishes. MDF is one of the most stable mat-formed panel products and is widely used as an architectural panel.

MOISTURE-RESISTANT MDF CORE

Some MDF is bonded with an exterior resin to produce a highly water-resistant product.

VENEER CORE (PLYWOOD)

This panel product is made up of alternating layers of thin veneer and is commonly known as plywood. Adhesive is placed between the layers, and the panels are pressed until the adhesive is set; heat is often used to speed the cure. The two outside layers, often selected for species, grain, and appearance, are called the face veneers.

HARDBOARD CORE

Hardboard is made of interfelted fibers consolidated under heat and pressure to a density of 31 lb per cubic ft or more. Available with either one side (S1S) or two sides (S2S) smooth, hardboard is often used for casework backs, drawer bottoms, and divider panels. Architectural woodworkers typically use two types of hardboard core: standard (untempered) and tempered, which is standard hardboard that has been subjected to a curing treatment to increase its stiffness, hardness, and weight.

PLYWOOD TYPES

The term "plywood" means a panel product made of three or more layers (plies) of wood or wood products (veneers or overlays and/or core materials) that have been laminated into a single sheet (panel). Plywood falls into two groups according to materials and manufacturing:

HARDWOOD PLYWOOD panels are made from hardwood or decorative softwood veneers over a core material such as medium-density particleboard, medium-density fiberboard, or low-density lumber.

SOFTWOOD PLYWOOD panels are made with softwood face veneers and are seldom incorporated into finished architectural woodworking projects because of the instability of the core material and core voids.

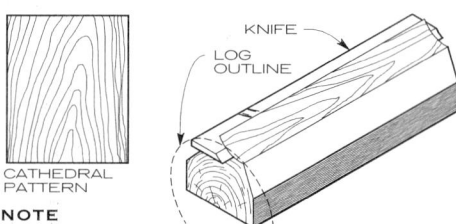

NOTE

This is the slicing method most often used to produce veneers for high-quality architectural woodworking. Slicing is done parallel to a line through the center of the log. A combination of cathedral and straight-grain patterns results, with a natural progression of pattern from leaf to leaf.

PLAIN-SLICED (FLAT-SLICED) VENEER

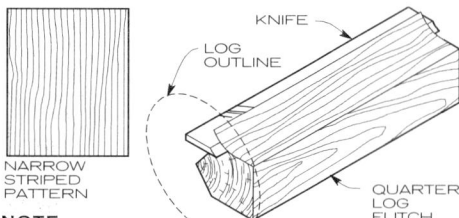

NOTE

Quarter slicing, roughly parallel to a radius line through the log segment, simulates the quarter-sawing process used with solid lumber. In many species the individual leaves are narrow as a result. A series of stripes is produced, varying in density and thickness among species. "Flake" is a characteristic of this slicing method in red and white oak.

QUARTER-SLICED VENEER

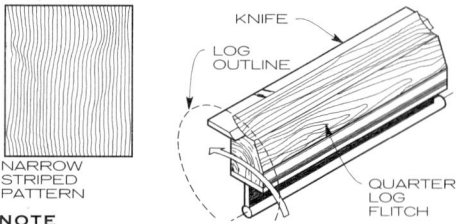

NOTE

Rift veneers are produced most often in red and white oak, rarely in other species. Note that rift veneers and rift-sawn solid lumber are produced so differently that a "match" between them is highly unlikely. In both cases the cutting is done slightly off the radius lines, minimizing the "flake" associated with quarter slicing.

RIFT-SLICED (RIFT-CUT) VENEER

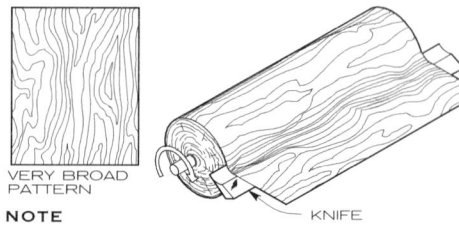

NOTE

To create rotary-cut veneers, the log is center mounted on a lathe and "peeled" along the path of the growth rings, like unwinding a roll of paper. This provides a bold, random appearance. Rotary-cut veneers vary in width, and matching at veneer joints is extremely difficult. Almost all softwood veneers are cut this way. Rotary-cut veneers are the least useful in fine architectural woodwork.

ROTARY-CUT VENEER

CHARACTERISTICS OF CORE MATERIAL PERFORMANCE

PANEL TYPE	FLATNESS	VISUAL EDGE QUALITY	SURFACE UNIFORMITY	DIMENSIONAL STABILITY	SCREW HOLDING	BENDING STRENGTH	AVAILABILITY
Industrial particleboard core (medium-density)	Excellent	Good	Excellent	Fair	Fair	Good	Ready
Medium-density fiberboard core (MDF)	Excellent	Excellent	Excellent	Fair	Good	Good	Ready
Veneer core–all hardwood	Fair	Good	Good	Excellent	Excellent	Excellent	Ready
Veneer core–all softwood	Fair	Good	Fair	Excellent	Excellent	Excellent	Ready
Lumber core–hardwood or softwood	Good	Good	Good	Good	Excellent	Excellent	Limited
Standard hardboard core	Excellent	Excellent	Excellent	Fair	Good	Good	Ready
Tempered hardboard core	Excellent	Good	Good	Good	Good	Good	Limited
Moisture-resistant particleboard core	Excellent	Good	Good	Fair	Fair	Good	Limited
Moisture-resistant MDF core	Excellent	Excellent	Good	Fair	Good	Good	Limited
Fire-resistant particleboard core	Excellent	Fair	Good	Fair	Fair	Good	Limited

NOTE

Characteristics of core material performance are influenced by the grade and thickness of the core and specific gravity of the core species. Visual edge quality is rated before treatment with edge bands or fillers and, for lumber core, assumes the use of "clear edge" grade. Surface uniformity is directly related to the performance of fine veneers placed over the surface. Dimensional stability is usually related to exposure to wide variations in relative humidity. Screw holding and bending strength are influenced by proper design and engineering.

Richard J. Vitullo, AIA; Oak Leaf Studio; Crownsville, Maryland
Architectural Woodwork Institute; Centreville, Virginia

Panel Products and Wood Veneers

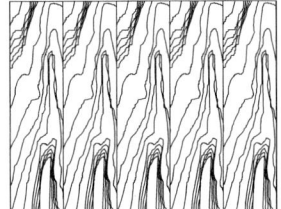
SLIP MATCH

BOOK MATCH

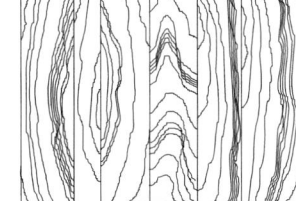
RANDOM MATCH

RUNNING MATCH

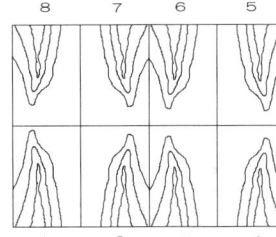
PANEL END MATCH   ARCHITECTURAL END MATCH

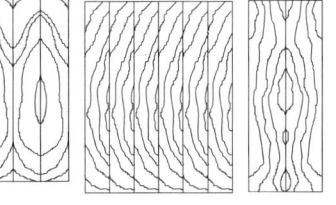
BALANCE AND CENTER MATCH

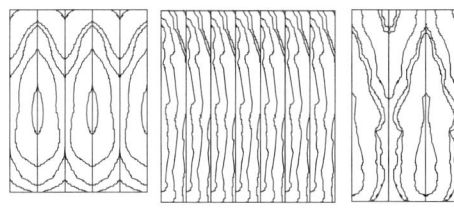
BALANCE MATCH

VENEER MATCH TYPES

GENERAL CHARACTERISTICS OF WOOD VENEER SPECIES

SPECIES		WIDTH TO (IN.)	LENGTH (FT)	FLITCH SIZE	COST[1]	AVAILABILITY
Mahogany	Plain sliced Honduras mahogany	18	12	Large	Moderate	Good
	Quartered Honduras mahogany	12	12	Large	High	Moderate
	Plain sliced African mahogany	18	12	Large	Moderate	Moderate
	Quartered African mahogany	12	12	Large	High	Good
Ash	Plain sliced American white ash	12	10	Medium	Moderate	Good
	Quartered American white ash	8	12	Small	High	Good
	Quartered or plain sliced European ash	6, 10	10	Medium	High	Limited
Anegre	Quartered or plain sliced anegre	6, 12	12	Large	High	Good
Avodire	Quartered avodire	10	10	Large	High	Limited
Cherry	Plain sliced American cherry	12	11	Medium	Moderate	Good
	Quartered American cherry	4	10	Very small	High	Moderate
Birch	Rotary cut birch (natural)	48	10	Large	Low	Good
	Rotary cut birch (select red or white)	36	10	Medium	Moderate	Moderate
	Plain sliced birch (natural)	10	10	Small	Moderate	Limited
	Plain sliced birch (select red or white)	5	10	Small	High	Limited
Butternut	Plain sliced butternut	12	10	Medium	High	Limited
Makore	Quartered or plain sliced makore	6, 12	12	Large	High	Good
Maple	Pl. sl. (half round) American maple	12	10	Medium	Moderate	Good[2]
	Rotary bird's-eye maple	20	10	Medium	Very high	Good
Oak	Plain sliced English brown oak	12	10	Medium	Very high	Limited
	Quartered English brown oak	10	10	Medium	Very high	Limited
	Plain sliced American red oak	16	12	Large	Moderate	Good
	Quartered American red oak	8	10	Small	Moderate	Good
	Rift sliced American red oak	10	10	Medium	Moderate	Good
	Comb grain rift American red oak	8	10	Small	Very high	Limited
	Plain sliced American white oak	16	12	Medium	Moderate	Good
	Quartered American white oak	8	10	Small	Moderate	Good
	Rift sliced American white oak	8	10	Medium	High	Good
	Comb grain rift American white oak	8	10	Small	Very high	Limited
Hickory or Pecan	Plain sliced American hickory or pecan	12	10	Small	Moderate	Good
Sapele	Quartered or plain sliced sapele	6, 12	12	Large	High	Good
Sycamore	Plain sliced English sycamore	10	10	Medium	Very high	Limited
	Quartered English sycamore	6	10	Medium	Very high	Limited
Teak	Plain sliced teak	16	12	Large	Very high	Limited[3]
	Quartered teak	12	12	Medium	Very high	Limited[3]
Walnut	Plain sliced American walnut	12	12	Medium	Moderate	Good
	Quarter sliced American walnut	6	10	Very small	High	Rare

[1] Cost reflects raw veneer costs weighted for waste or yield characteristics and degree of labor difficulty.
[2] Seasonal factors may affect availability.
[3] Availability of blond teak is very rare.

NOTE

When quartered or plain sliced are listed on the same line, the width dimensions are listed with quartered first and plain sliced second.

MATCHING BETWEEN ADJACENT VENEER LEAVES

It is possible to achieve certain visual effects by the manner in which the leaves are arranged. Rotary cut veneers are difficult to match, therefore most matching is done with sliced veneers. Matching of adjacent veneer leaves must be specified. Consult your AWI woodworker for choices.

BOOK MATCHING

Book matching is the most commonly used match in the industry. In it, every other piece of veneer is reversed so adjacent pieces (leaves) are "opened" like the pages of a book. Because the "tight" and "loose" faces alternate in adjacent leaves, they reflect light and accept stain differently. The veneer joints match, creating a symmetrical pattern that yields maximum continuity of grain.

SLIP MATCHING

Adjoining leaves are placed (slipped out) in sequence without being turned, thus all the same face sides are exposed. The grain figure repeats but joints do not show grain match. All faces have some light refraction.

END MATCHING

End matching is often used to extend the apparent length of available veneers for high wall panels and long conference tables. End matching occurs in two types:

ARCHITECTURAL END MATCH: Leaves are individually book or slip matched, alternating end-to-end and side-to-side. Architectural end matching yields the best continuous grain patterns for length as well as width.

PANEL END MATCH: Leaves are book or slip matched on panel subassemblies, with sequenced subassemblies end matched, resulting in some modest cost savings on projects where applicable. For most species, panel end matching yields a pleasing, blended appearance and grain continuity.

RANDOM MATCHING

Veneer leaves are placed next to each other in a random order and orientation, producing a casual board-by-board effect in many species. Conscious effort is made to mismatch the grain at joints.

RUNNING MATCHING

Each panel face is assembled from as many veneer leaves as necessary. This often results in an asymmetrical appearance, with some veneer leaves of unequal width.

BALANCE MATCHING

Each panel face is assembled from an odd or even number of veneer leaves of uniform width before edge trimming.

BALANCE AND CENTER MATCHING

Each panel face is assembled from an even number of veneer leaves of uniform width before edge trimming. Thus, there is a veneer joint in the center of the panel, producing horizontal symmetry.

Richard J. Vitullo, AIA; Oak Leaf Studio; Crownsville, Maryland
Architectural Woodwork Institute; Centreville, Virginia

ARCHITECTURAL WOODWORK

Panel Products and Wood Veneers

8-PIECE SUNBURST

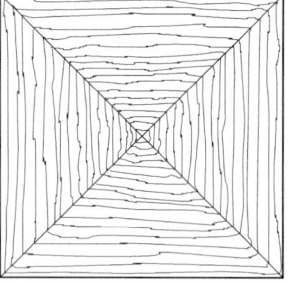
BOX MATCH

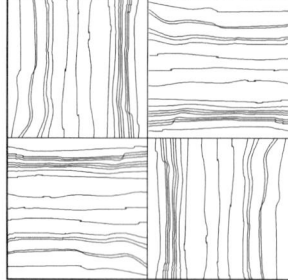
PARQUET MATCH

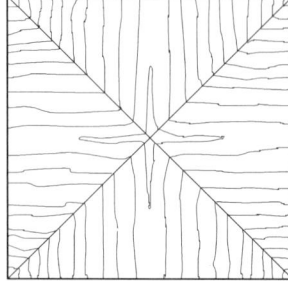
REVERSE OR END GRAIN BOX

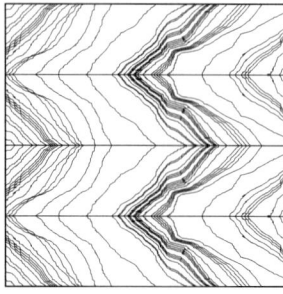
HERRINGBONE

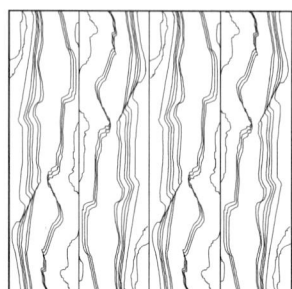
SWING MATCH

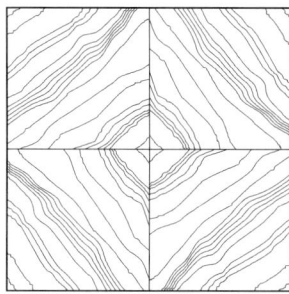
DIAMOND

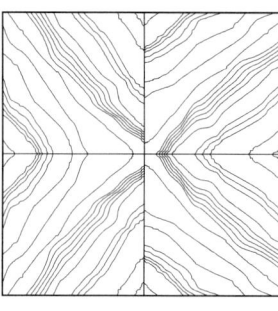
REVERSE DIAMOND

SKETCH FACE

NOTE
During specification, use both names and illustrations to define the desired effect, as names vary by region for these matching techniques.

SPECIAL WOOD VENEER MATCHING OPTIONS

FACING MATERIAL TYPES

Wood product substrates are classified in two main facing material categories: decorative laminates/overlays and wood veneers.

DECORATIVE LAMINATES/OVERLAYS

This finish surface category can be broken down into the following broad groups:

HIGH-PRESSURE DECORATIVE LAMINATES are formed under heat and pressure from resin-impregnated kraft paper substrates with decorative plastic face materials and a clear protective top sheet. This assembly, commonly called plastic laminate, offers resistance to wear and many stains and chemicals. Common uses include casework exteriors, countertops, and wall paneling.

THERMALLY FUSED DECORATIVE PANELS are flat pressed from a thermoset polyester or melamine resin-impregnated web, and most have been prelaminated to industrial particleboard or medium-density fiberboard substrates when they arrive at the woodwork fabricator. Performance is similar to that of high-pressure decorative laminates. Common uses include casework interiors, furniture, shelving, display materials, and decorative paneling.

MEDIUM-DENSITY OVERLAYS are made from pressed resin-impregnated paper overlays and are highly resistant to moisture. They are available applied to cores suitable for both interior and exterior uses. The seamless panel face and uniform density offer a sound base for opaque finishes and paint.

VINYL FILMS, FOILS, AND LOW BASIS WEIGHT PAPERS are decorative facing materials that, although they have limited use in custom architectural woodworking, are suitable for some installations.

WOOD VENEERS

Wood veneers are produced in a variety of industry standard thicknesses. The slicing process is controlled by a number of variables, but the thickness of the veneer has little bearing on the quality of the end product.

There are two types of veneers, hardwood and softwood. Hardwood veneers are available in many domestic and imported wood species and are normally plain sliced, but certain species can be rift sliced, quarter sliced, or rotary cut. Softwood veneers are usually sliced from Douglas fir, but pine and other softwoods are available. Most softwood veneer is rotary cut, but plain-sliced and rift-sliced (vertical grain) softwoods can be obtained with a special order.

Most veneers are taken from large trees, but some are sliced from fast-growing trees, dyed, and reglued in molds to create "grain" patterns. The color of these reconstituted veneers is established during manufacture because the high percentage of glue line resists later staining.

The manner in which a log segment is cut with relation to the annual rings of the tree determines the appearance of the veneer. Individual pieces of veneer, referred to as "leaves," are kept in the order in which they were sliced for reference during installation. The group of leaves from one slicing is called a "flitch" and is identified by a number and the gross square feet it contains. The faces of the leaves with relation to their position in the log are identified as the "tight face" (toward the outside of the log) and the "loose face" (toward the inside or heart of the log).

NOTES

1. To achieve balanced construction, panel products should be absolutely symmetrical from the center line. Materials used on either side should contract and expand or exhibit moisture permeability at the same rate as the veneer.

2. In panel construction, the thinner the facing material, the less force it can generate to cause warping. The thicker the substrate, the more it can resist a warping movement or force.

3. Wood veneer standards: For hardwood plywood, the face veneer characteristics of the Hardwood Plywood and Veneer Association (HPVA) have generally been adapted for use. These face grades apply to custom architectural woodwork.

4. Flame spread factors: The fire rating of the core material determines the rating of the assembled panel. Fire-retardant veneered panels must have a fire-retardant core. Particleboard core is available with a Class I (Class A) rating, but MDF is not currently available with a fire rating. Existing building codes, except where locally amended, provide that facing materials $1/28$ in. or thinner are not considered in determining the flame spread rating of the panel. For more information, refer to the Architectural Woodwork Institute guide "Fire Code Summary."

COMMON FACE VENEER PATTERNS OF SELECTED COMMERCIAL SPECIES

PRIMARY COMMERCIAL HARDWOOD SPECIES	FACE VENEER PATTERNS[1]			
	PLAIN SLICED (FLAT CUT)	QUARTER CUT	RIFT CUT AND COMB GRAIN	ROTARY CUT
Ash	Yes	Yes	—	Yes
Birch	Yes	—	—	Yes
Cherry	Yes	Yes	—	Yes
Hickory	Yes	—	—	Yes
Lauan	—	Yes	—	Yes
Mahogany (African)	Yes	Yes	—	Yes
Mahogany (Honduras)	Yes	Yes	—	Yes
Maple	Yes	Yes	—	Yes
Meranti	—	Yes	—	Yes
Oak (red)	Yes	Yes	Yes	Yes
Oak (white)	Yes	Yes	Yes	Yes
Pecan	Yes	—	—	Yes
Walnut (black)	Yes	Yes	—	Yes
Yellow poplar	Yes	—	—	Yes
Typical methods of cutting[2]	Plain slicing or half-round on rotary lathe	Quarter slicing	Offset quarter on rotary lathe	Rotary lathe

[1] The headings above refer to the face veneer pattern, not to the method of cutting. Face veneer patterns other than those listed are obtainable by special order.

[2] The method of cutting for a given face veneer pattern shall be at mill option unless otherwise specified by the buyer in an explicit manner to avoid the possibility of misunderstanding. For example, plain-sliced veneer cut on a vertical slicer or plain-sliced veneer cut on a half-round rotary lathe could be specified.

Richard J. Vitullo, AIA; Oak Leaf Studio; Crownsville, Maryland
Architectural Woodwork Institute; Centreville, Virginia
Chart reprinted with permission from the Hardwood Plywood and Veneer Association

Screens, Blinds, and Shutters

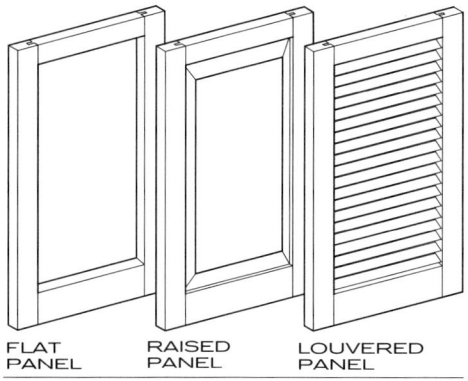

FLAT PANEL — **RAISED PANEL** — **LOUVERED PANEL**

SHUTTER TYPES

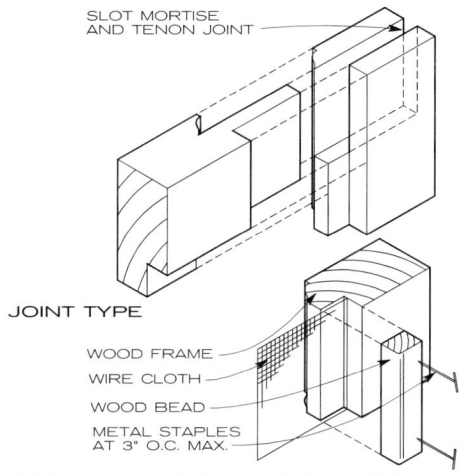

JOINT TYPE

WIRE CLOTH INSTALLATION DETAIL

CUSTOM WORKMANSHIP GRADE SCREEN DETAILS

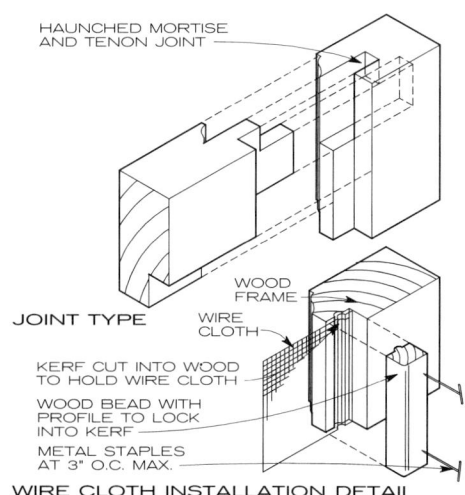

JOINT TYPE

WIRE CLOTH INSTALLATION DETAIL

PREMIUM WORKMANSHIP GRADE SCREEN DETAILS

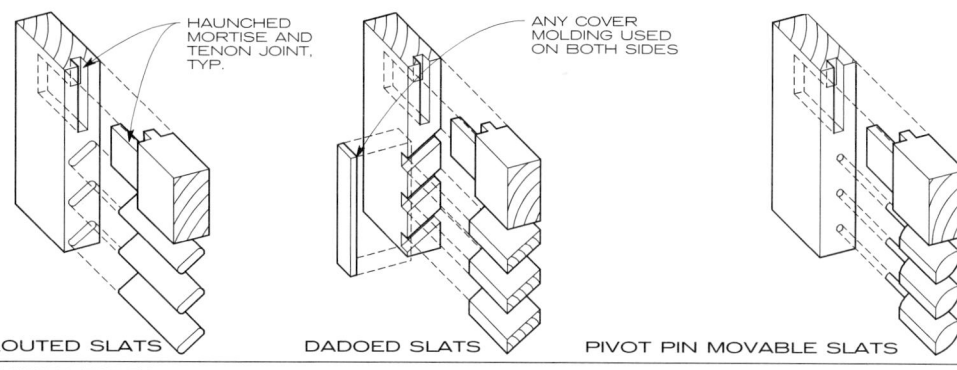

ROUTED SLATS — **DADOED SLATS** — **PIVOT PIN MOVABLE SLATS**

LOUVER TYPES

SCREEN MATERIALS

WORKMANSHIP LEVEL	CUSTOM		PREMIUM		ECONOMY	
APPLIED FINISH	TRANSPARENT FINISH	OPAQUE FINISH	TRANSPARENT FINISH	OPAQUE FINISH	TRANSPARENT FINISH	OPAQUE FINISH
AWI lumber grade	II	II	I	II	II	II
Screen frame parts, any of the listed species unless otherwise specified	Ponderosa pine, sugar pine, Idaho white pine, northern white pine, mahogany, Douglas fir	Unless otherwise specified, same as transparent	Teak, South American mahogany, African mahogany	Unless otherwise specified, same as transparent	Any pine, fir, hemlock, larch	Unless otherwise specified, same as transparent
Wire cloth, any of the listed materials unless otherwise specified	Aluminum wire, bronze wire (18 x 14 mesh)		Bronze wire (18 x 14 mesh)		Nylon or fiberglass mesh	

BLIND AND SHUTTER MATERIALS

MATERIALS		CUSTOM WORKMANSHIP		PREMIUM WORKMANSHIP		ECONOMY WORKMANSHIP	
		TRANSPARENT FINISH	OPAQUE FINISH	TRANSPARENT FINISH	OPAQUE FINISH	TRANSPARENT FINISH	OPAQUE FINISH
AWI grade lumber	Stiles, rails, slats and mullions / Applied moldings	II plus compatibility of color between veneer and lumber	II	I plus compatibility of grain and color between veneer and lumber	II	II with no selection for grain or color	II
	Flat panels	II permitted for panels less than 14 in. across the grain		not permitted		II permitted for panels in any dimension	
	Raised panels	II used to rim panel product centers and permitted for panels less than 14 in. across the grain		I used to rim panel product centers	II used to rim panel product centers	II permitted for panels in any dimension	
Panel products	Veneered stiles, rails, and mullions	particleboard or fiberboard (veneer only by direct specification)	particleboard or fiberboard recommended (veneer permitted)	particleboard or fiberboard (veneer only by direct specification)		not applicable	
	Flat and raised panel core	particleboard or fiberboard (veneer only by direct specification)	particleboard or fiberboard recommended (veneer permitted)	particleboard or fiberboard (veneer only by direct specification)		particleboard or fiberboard recommended (veneer permitted)	particleboard, fiberboard, or veneer
	Face: veneer grade for transparent finish and material for opaque finish	"A" face plus compatibility of color between veneer and lumber	"B" veneer, plain fiberboard, or medium-density overlay	"AA" face plus compatibility of grain and color between veneer and lumber	"A" veneer, plain fiberboard, or medium-density overlay	"B" face veneer	"B" veneer, plain fiberboard, or medium-density overlay
Minimum panel products thickness	Veneered stiles and rails	3/4" (19 mm)		3/4" (19 mm)		1/2" (13 mm)	
	Flat panels	1/2" (13 mm)		1/2" (13 mm)		1/4" (6 mm)	
	Raised panels	3/4" (19 mm)		3/4" (19 mm)		1/2" (13 mm)	

NOTES

1. For additional information, refer to Architectural Woodwork Quality Standards, 6th edition (version 1.1), 1994, Architectural Woodwork Institute (AWI).
2. Lumber grades indicated in the charts on this page are according to AWI quality standards:
   Grade I: Pieces are selected for uniform grain and color on exposed faces and edges.
   Grade II: Pieces are selected for uniform grain on exposed faces and edges.
   Grade III: No matching for grain or color is required.
3. AWI recognizes three levels of workmanship for wood screens, blinds, and shutters:
   CUSTOM GRADE: Most conventional architectural woodwork falls within this grade. High-quality workmanship, materials, and installation are required for work with this designation.
   PREMIUM GRADE: This specification requires careful oversight to guarantee the highest quality workmanship, materials, installation, and execution of design intent. It is typically reserved for special projects or project features.
   ECONOMY GRADE: This grade indicates the minimum expectations for quality, materials, and installation within the scope of AWI standards.
4. All exterior screens and shutters must be treated with a wood preservative in accordance with AWI Quality Standards, Section 100.
5. Pivot pins for use in damp or coastal areas must be manufactured of nylon, stainless steel, or brass.
6. Exterior grade panel products are recommended for blinds and shutters because once installed they are typically kept open, with one face constantly exposed to the sun and other weathering (and drying) conditions, while the other face is likely to retain moisture.

Richard J. Vitullo, AIA; Oak Leaf Studio; Crownsville, Maryland

Roofing Overview

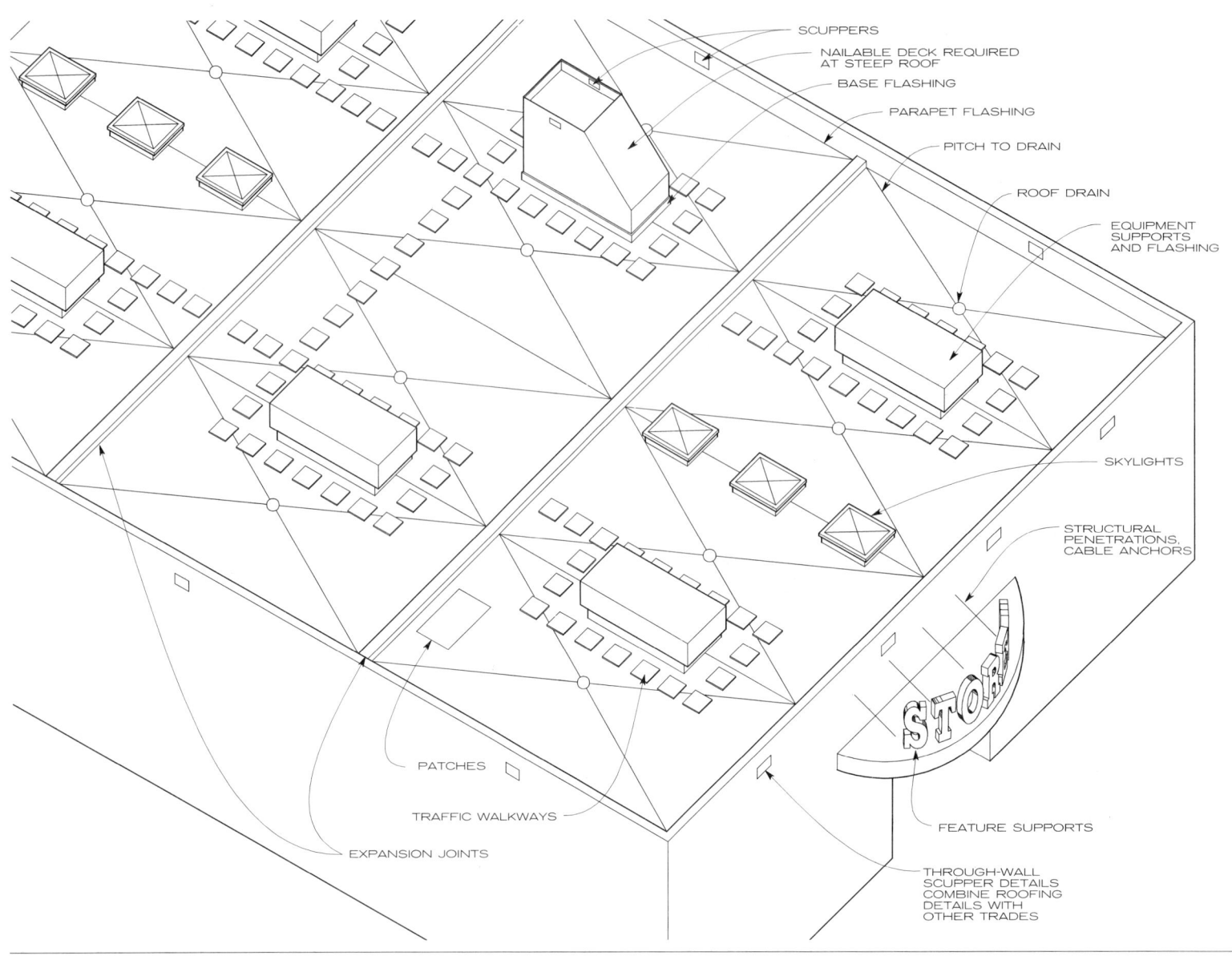

LOW-SLOPE MEMBRANE ROOFING

MEMBRANE PRINCIPLES

The membrane is the weatherproofing component of a roof. All roof membranes serve at least three functions: waterproofing, reinforcement, and surfacing; some membrane materials can perform more than one of these roles. The waterproofing agent is the most important element within the roof membrane. In built-up and modified bitumen roofing, the waterproofing agent is bitumen. In single-ply roofing, the waterproofing agent is synthetic rubber or plastic.

REINFORCEMENT

Reinforcement stabilizes the roof membrane, holds the waterproofing agent in place, and provides tensile strength to the membrane. In built-up roofing, reinforcement is provided by organic or glass fiber roofing felts. In modified bitumen roofing, the reinforcement is generally glass fiber felt or polyester scrim, which is factory-fabricated into the finished sheet. Reinforcement for single-ply membranes, if required, consists of polyester and other woven fabrics.

SURFACING AND AGGREGATE

Most membranes require some type of wearing surface. Surfacing materials protect the waterproofing and reinforcement elements from the effects of sunlight and weather exposure and provide other properties, such as fire resistance, traffic protection, and reflectivity. Membranes may be field or factory surfaced with aggregates or other coatings. Gravel, slag, marble chips, or mineral granules are used as aggregates; asphalt and liquid coatings are used on smooth surfaced roofs.

ROOF MEMBRANE SELECTION

Low-slope roofing membranes are manufactured from a wide variety of materials. A conventional built-up roofing system is fabricated on site from bitumen and saturated felt plies. Factory-modified bitumen sheets are available, which improve the resistance of the system to various factors; these are installed in layers similar to built-up roofing. Single-sheet systems include elastomeric (EPDM) and plastomeric (PVC) roofing, both of which have improved resistance to chemical or other hazards. For unusually high traffic situations, protected (inverted) membrane roofing can protect the waterproof membrane with a top layer of insulation or other material.

Complex surfaces may require liquid or spray foam roofing for adequate waterproofing coverage. Manufactured low-slope metal panel systems are also used as roofing membranes. The roof membrane is produced by combining a number of components to form a waterproof barrier for the building. The characteristics of each component must be considered when specifying the roof system.

The roof membrane is subjected to the stresses of expansion and contraction, weathering from moisture and sunlight, abrasion from foot traffic, wind forces, and live and instantaneous loading factors. ASTM standards outline the minimum requirements for manufacturing materials used for moisture proofing.

Four factors must be given primary consideration in selecting the roofing system: the membrane material, slope of the roof, roof substrate on which the membrane will be installed, and method of attaching the roof membrane to the substrate. Other critical factors include proper design and installation of flashing, expansion joints, and roof penetrations. Regardless of the type of roof membrane, insulation, or roof deck, proper drainage of the roof system is the single most important design consideration for ensuring the performance of the roofing system. Premature failure of a roof system that is improperly drained is virtually assured.

Valerie Eickelberger; Rippeteau Architects, PC; Washington, D.C.
National Roofing Contractors Association; Rosemont, Illinois

Roofing Overview—Low Slope

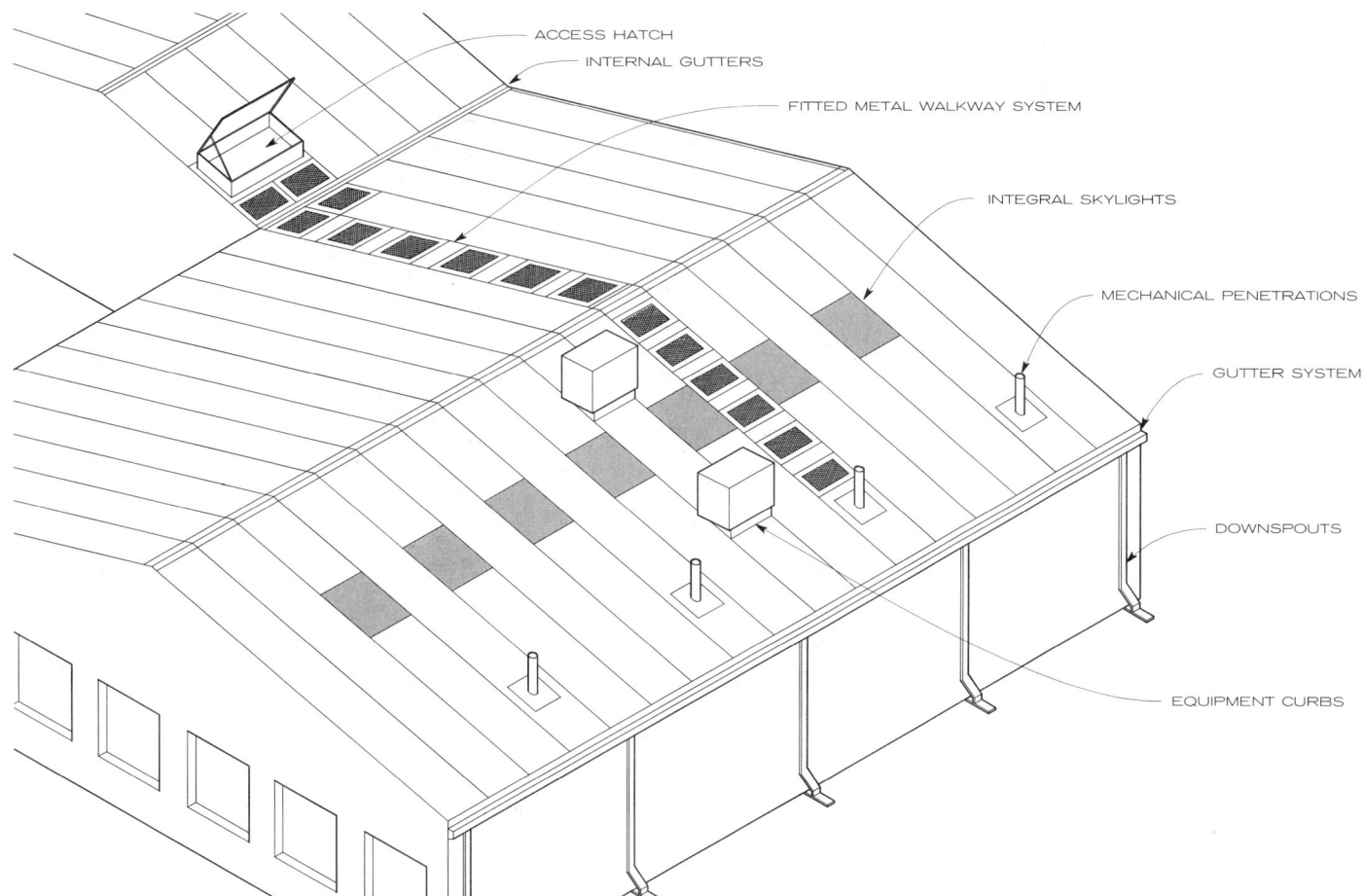

LOW-SLOPE MANUFACTURED METAL ROOFING

LOW-SLOPE ROOFING COMPONENTS

ROOF SUBSTRATE

The roof substrate (or deck) determines the membrane system to be selected for a building. The roof deck should provide positive drainage; this can be accomplished by sloping the structural deck, installing tapered board insulation, or installing insulating fill. Drains should be located at low points in the roof, not at columns or bearing walls. Some roof decks and insulation substrates require special precautions or may be unsuitable for use with certain roof membrane systems.

NAILABLE AND NON-NAILABLE DECKS

The roof deck may be nailable, non-nailable, or insulated. Nailable roof decks include those made of cement-wood fiber panels, lightweight insulating concrete, poured gypsum concrete, metal bound gypsum planks, and wood planks and plywood. Non-nailable roof decks include those made of precast concrete panels, prestressed concrete, reinforced concrete, steel, and thermosetting insulating fill. Many roof decks have at least one layer of insulation on the top side, which the fasteners must penetrate to reach the insulation substrate and the roof deck below.

In general, roof membranes are not fully attached directly onto a nailable deck surface. Rather, for nailable decks, the first layer of material (i.e., base sheet, slip sheet, insulation, or membrane base ply) generally is mechanically fastened to the deck. Non-nailable roof decks may require the installation of a base sheet or insulation separator, to be either spot or channel mopped in place before installation of a fully adhered single-ply or built-up roof membrane. Some roof membranes may be attached directly to a non-nailable roof deck.

FLASHING

Most roof leaks occur at points where the horizontal roof deck joins a vertical surface. Proper installation of composition (base) flashing and metal counterflashing can prevent leaks. Base flashing should be installed 8 to 14 in. above the finished roof surface and fastened to the base flashing at the top edge. Since the bending radius of present composition roofing materials is limited to 45 degrees, cant strips are installed between the roof and any vertical surface to protect the base flashing. Metal counterflashing must extend low enough to protect the top of the base flashing from wind-driven snow or rain. Varying expansion/contraction characteristics make it inadvisable to connect sheet metal to the roof membrane, which can tear or crack.

ROOF EXPANSION JOINTS

Roof expansion joints accommodate movement of the roof assembly that results from thermal expansion and contraction. These joints are also designed to prevent membrane splitting and ridging and to accommodate movement within the building itself. Roof expansion joints should be provided at expansion or contraction joints in the structural system, places where joints or the structural framing system change direction or material, intersections between the building and wings and additions, junctions where interior heating conditions change, and sites where movement between walls and roof deck may occur.

MECHANICAL EQUIPMENT AND PENETRATIONS

Mechanical equipment and piping on or through the roof should be curb-mounted with cant strips at the base of the curb and provision for attachment of base flashing. Two-piece metal counterflashing should be installed over the base flashing. Units using curbs with built-in metal base flashing flanges should not be used. Short pipe projections may be flashed into the membrane by using soft metal or lead flashing with integral flashing flanges stripped into the membrane, but pitch pockets should be avoided.

LIQUID MEMBRANE ROOFING AT DOME

COMPLEX SURFACES

Liquid or spray foam membranes may be used on complex or curved surfaces such as domes to provide moisture protection. These types of membranes are also commonly used for reroofing and for areas that would otherwise be difficult to waterproof. Liquid membranes consist of a liquid basecoat, reinforcing fabric, and a liquid topcoat. Spray foam membranes have a high insulating value and consist of foam sprayed on the deck surface and covered with a protective coating of aggregate or elastomeric material.

Valerie Eickelberger; Rippeteau Architects, PC; Washington, D.C.
National Roofing Contractors Association; Rosemont, Illinois

INTRODUCTION

Roofing Overview—Steep Slope

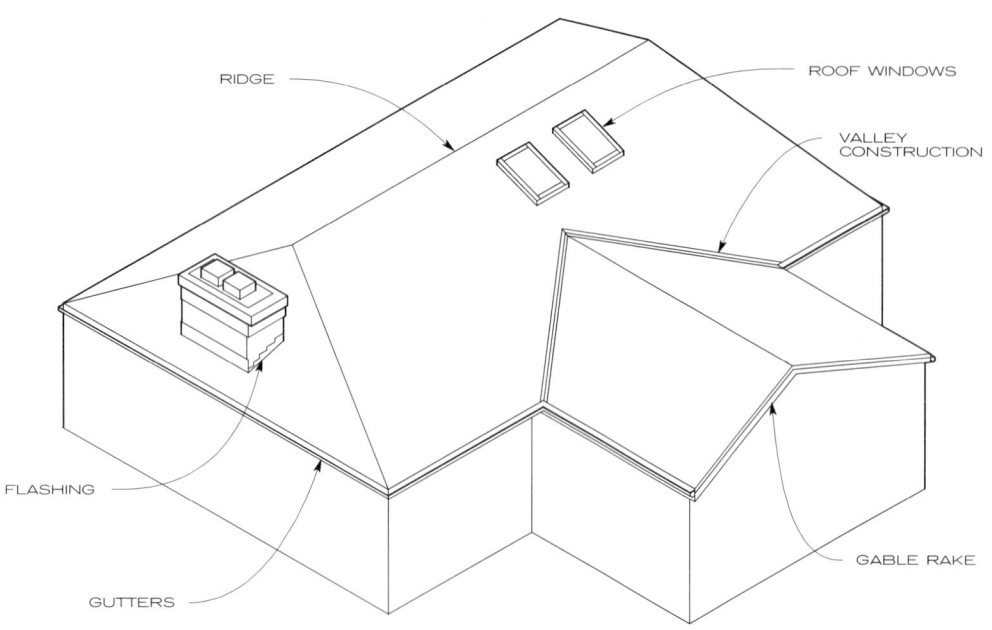

PITCHED ROOF WITH LOW SLOPE

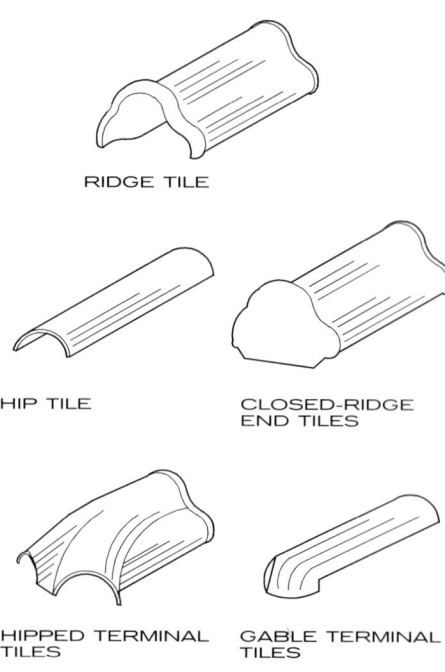

SPECIAL TILES

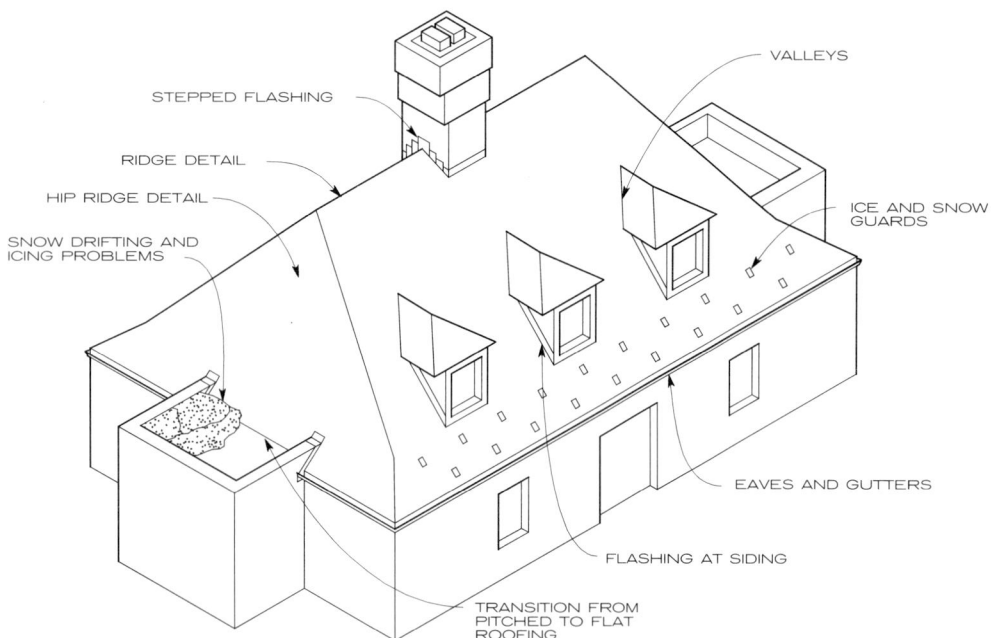

PITCHED ROOF WITH STEEP SLOPE

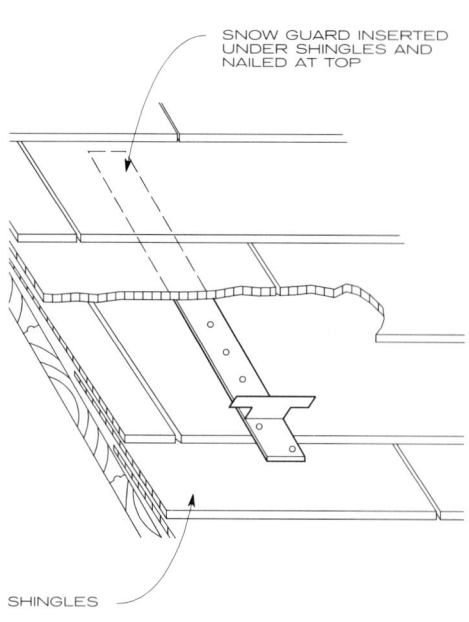

SNOW GUARD

STEEP ROOFING

Steep roofs have a slope that is generally 3 in. per ft or greater. Roofing materials suitable for steep roofs include asphalt rolls or shingles, clay and concrete tiles, composition roofing tiles, metal shingles or panels, wood shingles and shakes (split from logs), and slate. Steep roofs often have complicated roof intersections. Step flashing, crickets, and valleys keep moisture away from these intersections. Crickets are formed at an upward angle to prevent the accumulation of snow and ice and to deflect water. Where sloping roofs join at a downward angle, valleys concentrate water runoff and are highly vulnerable to leakage. Transitional details may be necessary to prevent snow and ice accumulation where roof surfaces join. Flashing should be installed at eaves wherever a possibility exists of ice forming along the eaves and causing a backup of water. Manufactured ice shields for eaves are also available. Damage to persons or property from sliding ice and snow may be prevented with snow guards.

TILE ROOF TYPES

Traditional types of roofing tile are made from clay, concrete, and metal. Contemporary tile roofing materials include composite materials, fiber cement, cement wood, and ceramic slate. Tile offers a wide range of design possibilities because of the large variety of types and shapes available, including roll tiles (barrel or mission tile), S shapes, flat tile, and ridge tiles of various shapes. Graduated tiles (tiles of diminishing widths) are required for round towers, circular bays, and porches. Tile manufacturers furnish graduated tiles in all popular shapes. Some manufacturers also offer special valley tile, manufactured in an angular or round form, and other special shapes for particular applications.

RESISTANCE TO WIND

If tiles are nailed too tightly, they lift up at the butt, allowing high winds to blow them off the roof or rainwater to be driven under them. Tiles should be nailed individually, and nails should be driven in until the nail head just clears the tile and the tile hangs on the nail. Building officials have designated some localities with high-wind conditions as wind hazard areas. In these areas, the nose ends of all eaves-course tiles should be secured with hurricane clips, which are available in different shapes to suit the type of roof sheathing used. Tiles should be laid with a 3 in. minimum headlap.

Valerie Eickelberger; Rippeteau Architects, PC; Washington, D.C.
National Roofing Contractors Association; Rosemont, Illinois

Roof, Eave, Attic, Crawl Space Ventilation

VENTILATION REQUIREMENTS TO PREVENT CONDENSATION

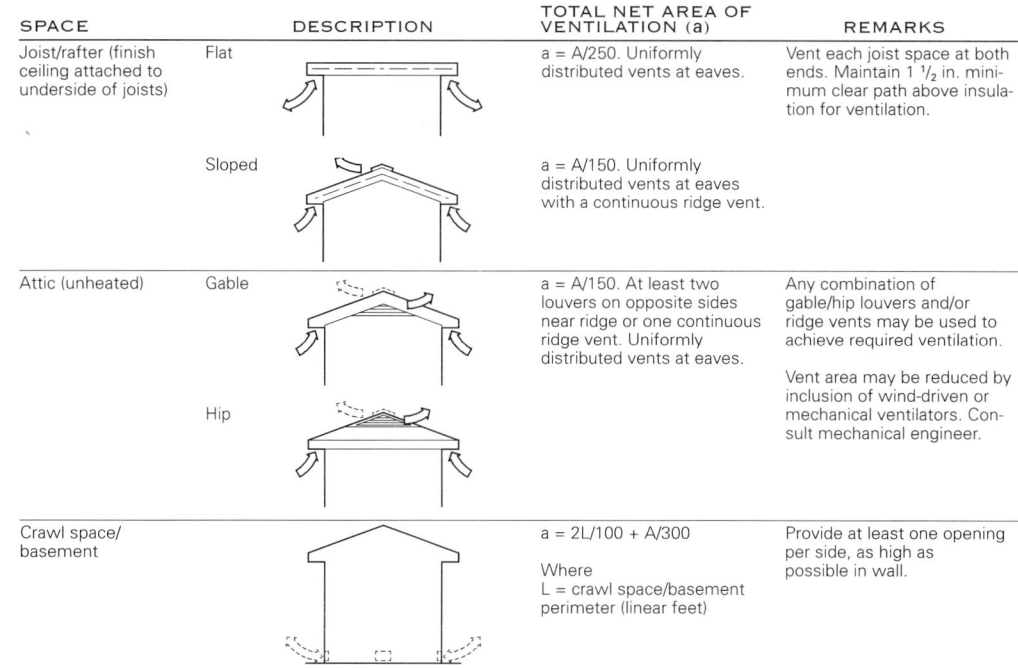

SPACE	DESCRIPTION		TOTAL NET AREA OF VENTILATION (a)	REMARKS
Joist/rafter (finish ceiling attached to underside of joists)	Flat		a = A/250. Uniformly distributed vents at eaves.	Vent each joist space at both ends. Maintain 1 1/2 in. minimum clear path above insulation for ventilation.
	Sloped		a = A/150. Uniformly distributed vents at eaves with a continuous ridge vent.	
Attic (unheated)	Gable		a = A/150. At least two louvers on opposite sides near ridge or one continuous ridge vent. Uniformly distributed vents at eaves.	Any combination of gable/hip louvers and/or ridge vents may be used to achieve required ventilation. Vent area may be reduced by inclusion of wind-driven or mechanical ventilators. Consult mechanical engineer.
	Hip			
Crawl space/ basement			a = 2L/100 + A/300 Where L = crawl space/basement perimeter (linear feet)	Provide at least one opening per side, as high as possible in wall.

NOTES
1. A = area of space to be ventilated, in square feet.
2. For insect screening, the openings therein shall not exceed 1/4 in. (6 mm). The effective net area of ventilation is reduced by screening; consult manufacturers of screening materials for percentage of "free air" flow reduced by the amount of solid material in screening.

VENT APPLICATIONS
GENERAL

Attics and crawl spaces must be ventilated to remove moisture and water vapor that has entered the spaces from surrounding air or soil or that has been created by human activity. Generally, crawl spaces (and basements) require a greater amount of ventilation than an equivalent area of attic. The quantity of water vapor depends on the building type (e.g., residence, school, etc.), activity (e.g., bathroom, kitchen, etc.), air temperature, and relative humidity. If the temperature of the ventilated space falls below the dew point temperature, condensation will occur which will deteriorate insulation, framing, etc. This can be avoided by proper detailing to limit moisture infiltration and increase ventilation to remove it if it does enter the space.

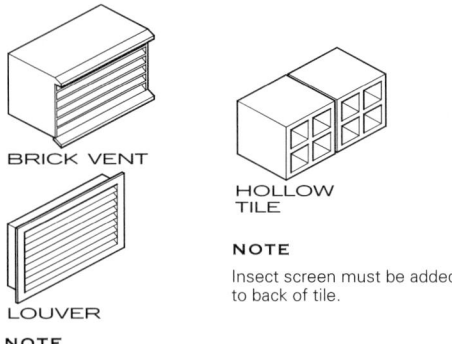

NOTE
Insect screen must be added to back of tile.

NOTE
Most vents for crawl spaces are set into unit masonry (and are sized accordingly) or concrete. Consult manufacturers. Metal louvers and vents have integral insect screens.

CRAWL SPACE VENTILATION MATERIALS

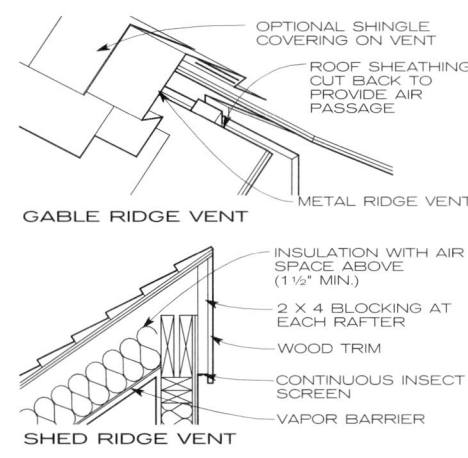

RIDGE VENTS

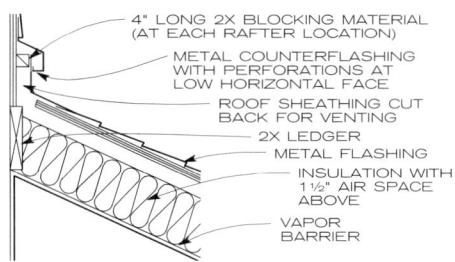

VENT FOR SHED ROOF AT WALL

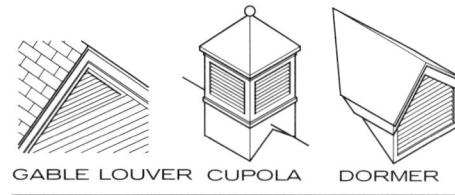

ROOF LOUVER TYPES

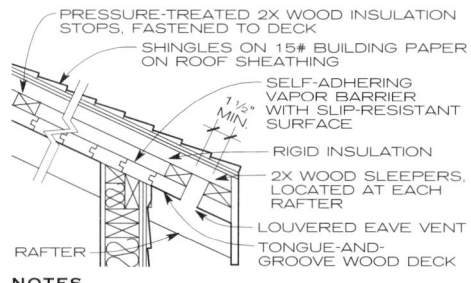

INSULATED TONGUE-AND-GROOVE ROOF VENTILATION DETAIL

NOTES
1. Provide ridge vent to complete cavity ventilation detail.
2. Fasteners should be carefully selected and located to secure insulation, stops, sleepers, sheathing, etc. to structural tongue-and-groove deck.

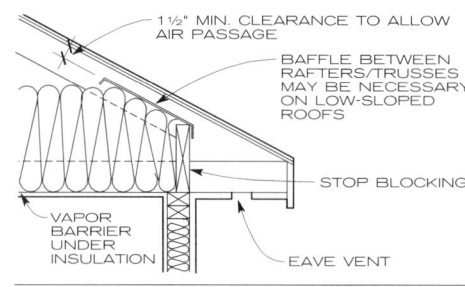

INSULATION BLOCKING AND BAFFLE

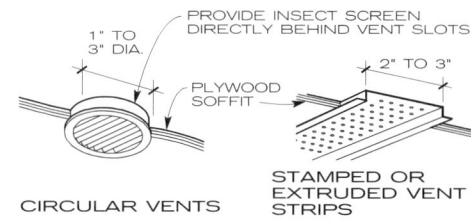

EAVE VENTILATION TYPES

Richard J. Vitullo, AIA; Oak Leaf Studio; Crownsville, Maryland
Erik K. Beach; Rippeteau Architects, PC; Washington, D.C.

INSULATION

Concrete Tile Roofing

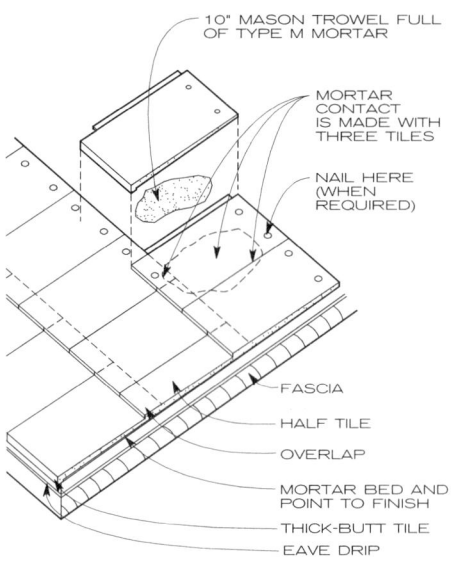

FLAT TILE

NOTE

Mortar contact is made with 3 tiles.

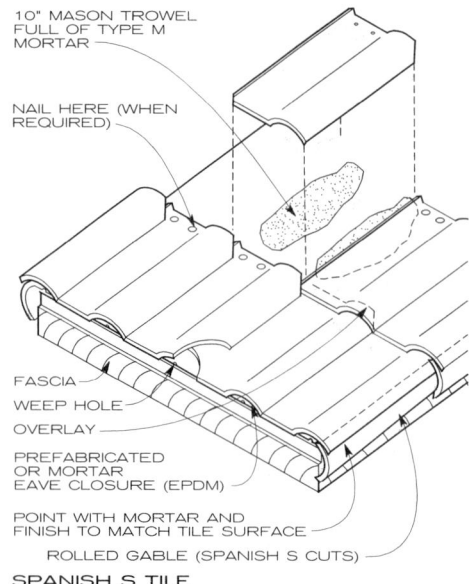

SPANISH S TILE

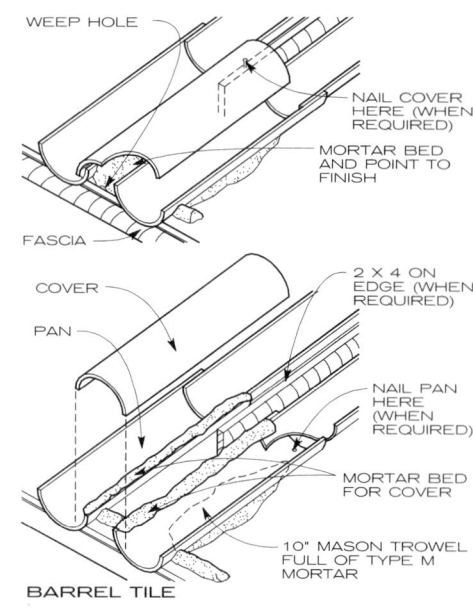

BARREL TILE

MORTAR AND TILE PLACEMENT

GENERAL

Concrete tile is manufactured by extruding a mixture of portland cement, sand, and water on individual molds under high pressure. The finish surface of the tile is covered with a cementitious material that has been colored with synthetic oxides. The tiles are cured to required strengths in chambers where humidity and temperature are controlled. Moisture absorption by concrete tiles can lead to structural roof problems, and particular care should be given to specifying the correct concrete tile for a given environment.

For both categories of concrete tile—roll or flat—it is important to adhere to minimum slope requirements as follows:

1. Roll tile and flat tile can be installed on roof decks with slopes of 4 in. per ft or more when at least one layer of 30-lb felt underlayment is applied horizontally and tiles are nailed or wired with a minimum 3 in. headlap. Use of spaced sheathing is not recommended.
2. Any concrete tile can be used on solid-sheathed roof decks with slopes less than 4 in. per ft as long as two or more layers of No. 30 or No. 40 asphalt-saturated (nonperforated) felt are set in hot asphalt or mastic to serve as the underlayment. A single layer of modified bitumen-coated roofing systems roll-good sheet with laps either torched or heat welded is acceptable. Vertical lath stringers with horizontal battens are installed over the underlayment, creating a supporting surface for the tile, which must be installed with at least 4 in. headlap. Do not use spaced sheathing.
3. Regardless of slope, in localities where the January mean temperature is less than 30°F, stricter minimum requirements apply. Refer to the National Roofing Contractors Association manual.

FLAT TILE

When using flat roof tiles, a metal eave-riser with weep holes should be installed at the eave line. During installation, adjust tile spacing to provide uniform exposure, with a minimum 3 in. headlap.

ROLL TILE

When using roll, or mission, tile, apply the first course above a metal bird-stop with weep holes. Fit the underside of the tile with specially formed eave closure strips, fastened inside the tile cover. The heads of all remaining tiles should be aligned with the horizontal guide lines. Adjust roll tile spacing to provide uniform exposure, with at least a 3 in. headlap. Jamming interlocking tiles together (side to side) will restrict movement and result in broken corners.

ROOF SLOPE

For roof slopes 5 in. in 12 and less, solid sheathing may be used with or without battens. Nailing is not required with battens, but every tile should be nailed if battens are not used. In either case, perimeter nailing is required for 3 ft or three courses, whichever is greater, from all eaves, rakes, ridges, hips, or valleys. (Do not nail into valley metal.)

For roof slopes between 5 and 7 in. in 12, nail every other tile over solid sheathing with battens and every tile if battens are not used. For slopes between 7 and 12 in. in 12, every other tile should be nailed over solid sheathing with battens. Perimeter nailing is required in all these situations.

For slopes 12 in. in 12 and greater, nail every tile over solid sheathing with battens; perimeter nailing is necessary.

TILES SET IN MORTAR

The practice of installing cement tiles with mortar over a built-up subroof evolved in high-wind and high-moisture areas of the southeastern United States. In this system, the built-up subroof provides the moisture barrier, and the tiles protect the subroof from solar ultraviolet rays, high winds, and external damage. This concrete tile system can also be used on low-slope roofs, but the minimum is 2 in. in 12. On slopes between 5 in. in 12 and 7 in. in 12, additional mechanical fastening is required for the first three courses of tile in areas subject to high winds. For roofs with steeper slopes, tile should be mechanically fastened.

TYPICAL ROLL TILES

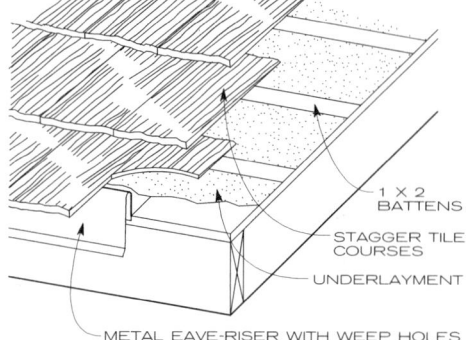

NOTE

This detail is for pitches 4:12 and greater.

FIELD INSTALLATION OF FLAT TILES

ATTACHMENT PROCEDURES FOR CONCRETE ROOF TILES

ROOF SLOPE	FIELD TILE NAILING		NAILING FOR PERIMETER TILE AND TILE ON CANTILEVERED AREAS[2]
	SOLID SHEATHING WITH BATTENS	SOLID SHEATHING WITHOUT BATTENS[1]	
3:12 to and including 5:12	Not required	Every tile	Every tile
Above 5:12 to less than 12:12	Every other tile	Every tile to 7:12	Every tile
12:12 and over	Every tile	N/A	Every tile

NOTES

1. For slopes exceeding 7:12, battens are required.
2. Perimeter nailing areas include three tile courses but not less than 36 inches from either side of hips or ridges and from edges of eaves and gable rakes. In special wind areas designated by the building official, additional fastenings may be required.

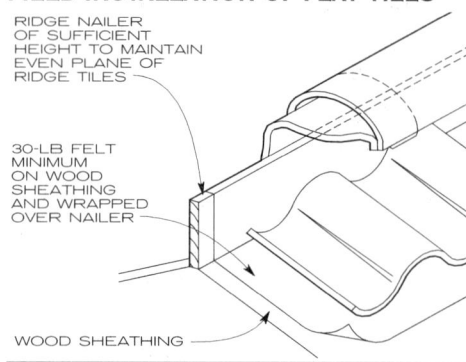

HIP AND RIDGE DETAIL

National Roofing Contractors Association; Rosemont, Illinois
Grace S. Lee; Rippeteau Architects, PC; Washington, D.C.

Miscellaneous Roofing Tiles

COMPOSITE ROOFING TILES

Fiber cement, cement wood, galvanized steel with acrylic coating, and ceramic slate roofing tiles are popular alternatives to clay or concrete roofing tiles. These composite tiles have been designed to be lighter, stronger, and easier to install than traditional, "natural" tiles. Their strength and combination of materials make them more fire retardant and wind resistant than conventional tiles.

FIBER CEMENT

Fiber cement tiles combine organic fiber with cement, silica, water, and other additives. The resulting product is a roof slate that is lightweight, strong, versatile, and easy to install. The tiles can be made in a variety of distinctive shapes, colors, and textures that mimic natural materials such as slate and patterned wood shingles. Fiber cement tiles resist deterioration and moisture penetration and are immune to pests and fungal growth. They are well-suited for coastal regions and other areas with high humidity.

Fiber cement tiles should be applied to nailable decks only. For plywood decks with rafters spaced 20 in. or less, the plywood should be at least $1/2$ in. thick. If rafters are spaced greater than 20 in., $5/8$ in. plywood is recommended. To fasten, use standard $1 1/2$ in. galvanized 11-gauge flat-head roofing nails with a $3/8$ in. head. Flashing should be of a noncorrosive metal not lighter than 28 gauge.

CERAMIC SLATE

Ceramic slate tiles combine the look of natural slate with the fired-in strength and durability of ceramic tile. Such tiles have the thickness, texture, and appearance of older slate but at a fraction of the weight and cost. They are impervious to freeze-thaw cycles, fire, moisture, and efflorescence.

CEMENT WOOD TILES

Cement wood tiles are lightweight tiles that can be used for reroofing as well as for new construction. They have excellent impact resistance and are easily sawn and nailed. As a richly textured, composite product, cement wood tiles create an aesthetic similar to that of heavy cedar shakes yet provide the fire protection associated with cementitious products. Cement wood tiles, with their composite of portland cement and wood fiber, are long lasting. The portland cement is noncombustible and allows for Class A fire ratings, and the wood fibers provide excellent tensile strength and a light weight when compared to standard concrete tiles.

METAL ROOFING TILES

The advantage of metal roofing tiles over traditional clay or concrete tiles is that they are lightweight. They are easier to handle, quicker to install, and, because they require fewer building components, are less costly. Minimum recommended roof pitch for use of metal roofing tiles is a slope of 3 in 12. Roofs with shallower slopes require sealant in all side laps.

Metal roofing tiles usually come in sheets and have a base material of roll-formed 24- to 26-gauge prepainted galvanized or galvalume steel. A layer of crushed and graded stone granules is bonded to the steel panels with an acrylic resin formula and then a clear acrylic overglaze is applied. Slow oven curing completes the process, and the underside of the tile is protected with a final coat of polyester paint. Panels can be installed quickly and are secured to either wood or steel battens, creating a strong, weatherproof construction. The panels can be installed directly over existing roofs, unlike clay or concrete tiles, and are thus ideally suited for retrofitting roofs.

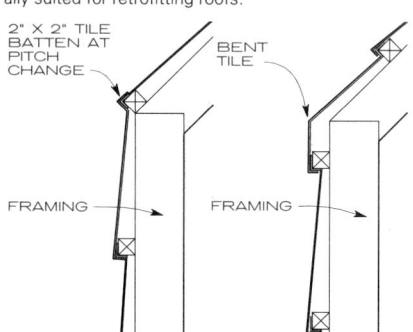

NOTE
When an equal number of full courses cannot be accommodated at the pitch change, a full panel can be bent to suit. When the roofline changes dramatically, install a batten at the pitch change.

METAL ROOFING AT PITCH CHANGE

Grace S. Lee; Rippeteau Architects, PC; Washington, D.C.

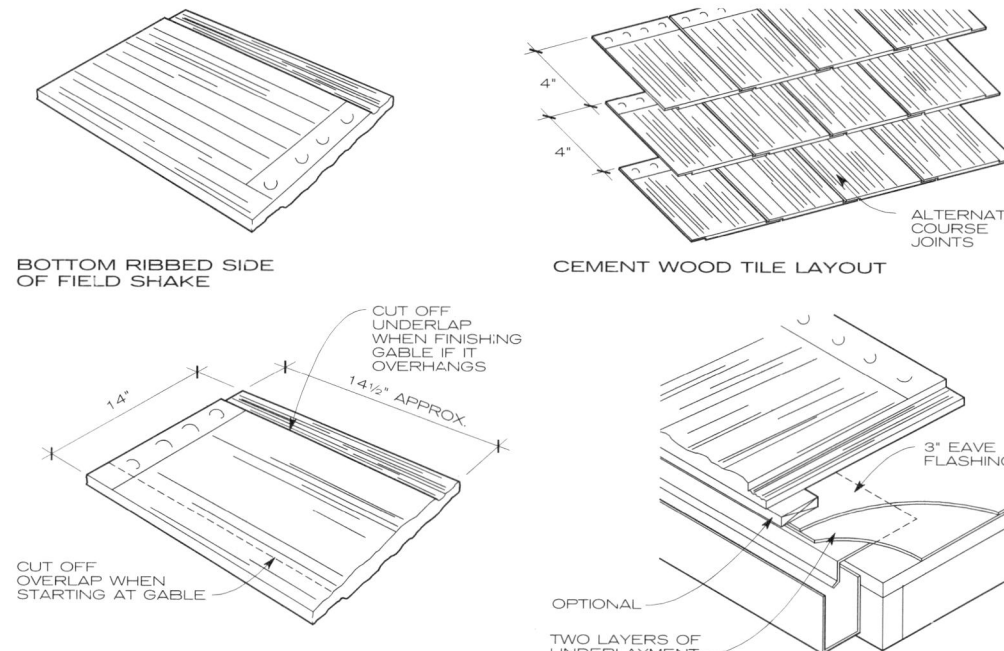

CEMENT WOOD TILES

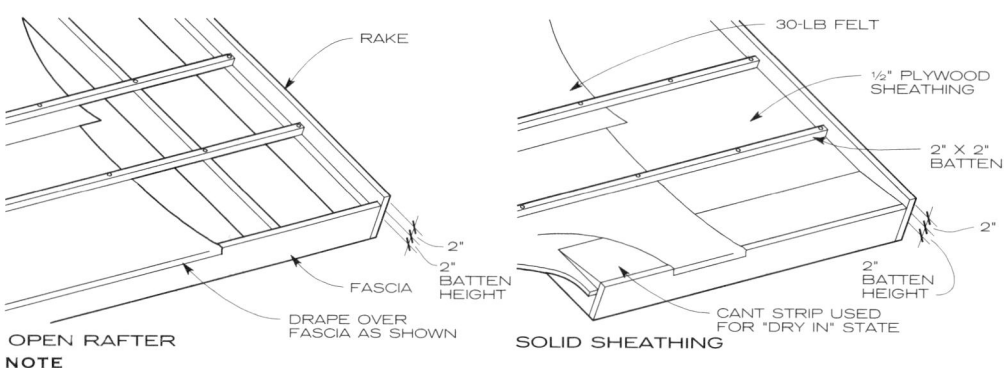

NOTE
Metal roofing panels can be applied directly over solid plywood sheathing or over open rafters if a self-supporting underlayment is used.

METAL ROOFING TILE UNDERLAYMENT

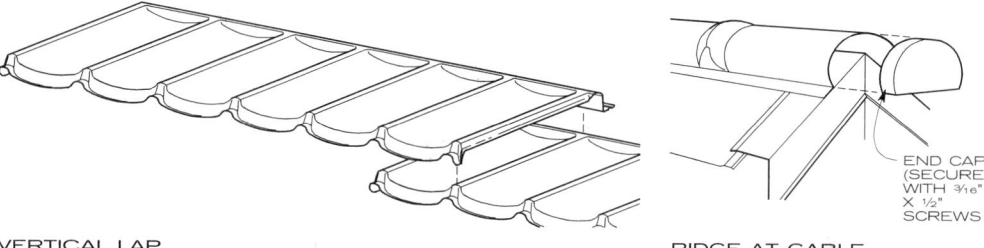

METAL ROOFING TILES

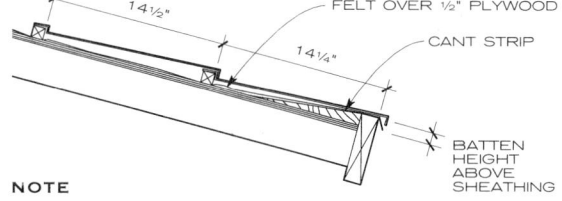

NOTE
The fascia must be positioned above the roof deck sheathing or rafters by the height of the batten. The fascia becomes the first panel batten.

METAL ROOFING DETAILS AT EAVE AND RIDGE

SHINGLES AND ROOFING TILES

Built-up Roofing

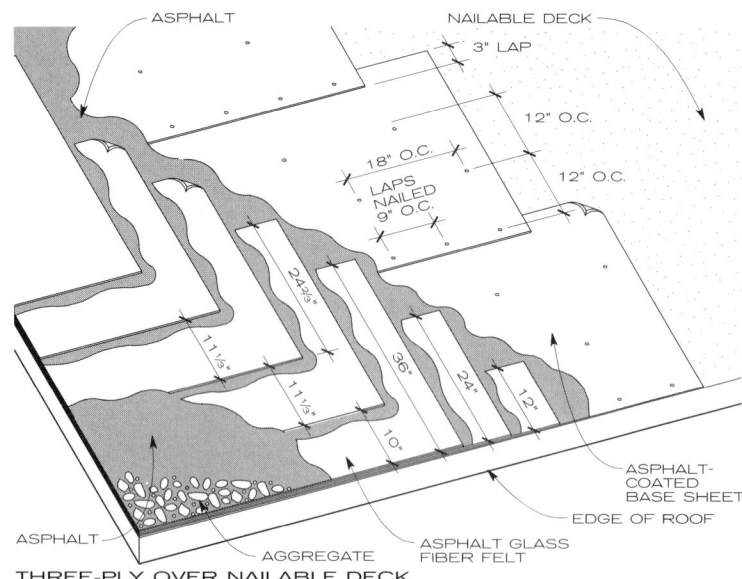

THREE-PLY OVER NAILABLE DECK

NOTES
1. If applied over sheathing panels, add rosin-sized sheathing paper between the deck and base sheet.
2. In lieu of asphalt, coal tar is an acceptable product.

AGGREGATE SURFACE BUILT-UP ROOFING

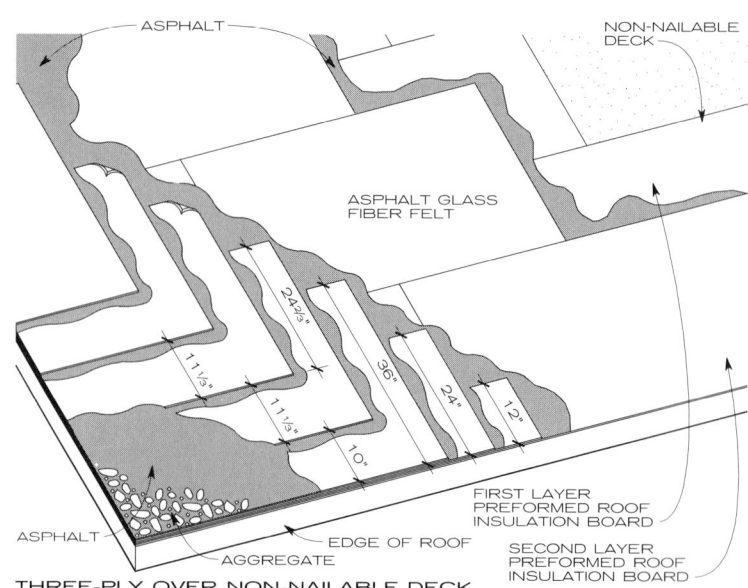

THREE-PLY OVER NON-NAILABLE DECK

NOTES
1. For a more conservative system, specify four plies rather than three.
2. In lieu of asphalt, coal tar is an acceptable product.

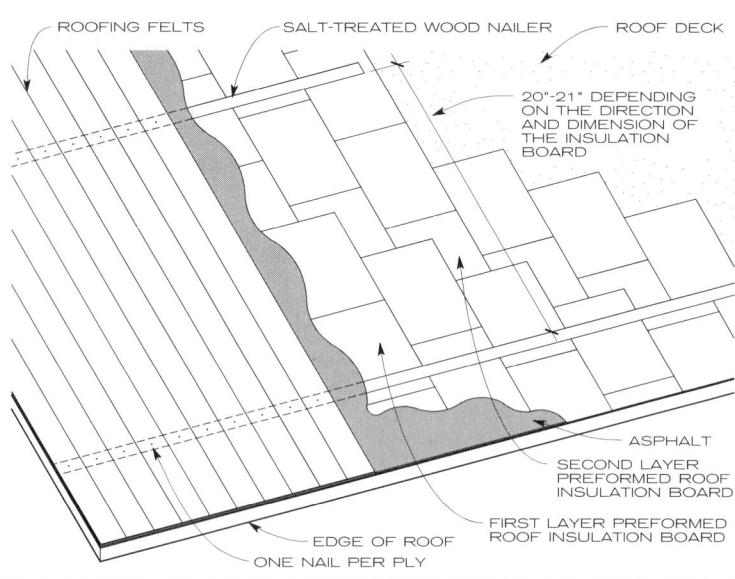

WOOD NAILER BACKNAILING SYSTEM

COAL TAR TYPES

ASTM D-450 TYPE NO.	KIND OF COAL TAR	SOFTENING POINT (°F) MIN.	SOFTENING POINT (°F) MAX.
I	Coal-tar pitch	126	140
II	Waterproofing pitch	106	126
III	Coal-tar bitumen	133	147

ASPHALT TYPES

TYPE	KIND OF ASPHALT	SOFTENING POINT (°F) MIN.	SOFTENING POINT (°F) MAX.	MAX. TEMP. (°F)
I	Dead level asphalt	151	135	475
II	Flat asphalt	176	158	500
III	Steep asphalt	205	185	525
IV	Special steep asphalt	225	210	525

GENERAL

A built-up roofing (BUR) system is composed of a base sheet attached to the roof substrate, two or more reinforcing felt ply sheets, and a surfaced cap sheet. Asphalt and coal tar are the bitumens used for built-up roofing. As the heated mopping bitumen fuses with the saturating bitumen in the roofing felts, the layers are welded together. Surfacings include aggregate, minerals, protective or reflective coatings, and smooth surface.

Four types of asphalt and two types of coal tar are presently used as bitumens in built-up roofing systems. The grade of asphalt used for BUR systems should be appropriate for the slope of the roof. Backnailing of felts is recommended for built-up roofing whenever the roof slope exceeds 1/2 in. per ft. Aggregate-surfaced built-up roofing should not be used on slopes exceeding 3 in. per ft.

Reinforcing felts for BUR may be saturated, coated, or impregnated with bitumen and are manufactured from both organic and inorganic materials. Organic felts are manufactured from the fiber of paper, wood, or rags. Saturated felts are saturated with asphalt or coal tar bitumen. Impregnated roofing felts are generally lighter in weight and termed impregnated because their surface is not completely covered (coated) with asphalt. Saturated and coated roofing felts are generally factory coated on both sides and surfaced on one or both sides with fine mineral sand or other release agents to prevent adhesion inside the roll prior to application.

Prepared roofing materials are saturated and coated felts with talc, mica, sand, or ceramic granules incorporated into the weather surface of the felts, both to provide weather protection and for decorative purposes. Reinforced flashing membrane consists of a glass-fiber base felt that is laminated with cotton or glass-fiber fabric and coated with asphalt. Rosin-sized sheathing paper is a rosin-coated building paper generally used in built-up roofing to separate felts from wood plank roof decks.

TEMPERATURE

Proper application temperatures are vital to the creation of a quality roof membrane system. Temperatures that are too high can lead to incomplete coverage, voids, and a lack of waterproofing qualities. Temperatures that are too low can lead to poor adhesion, high expansion properties, and low tensile strength.

Bitumens can be heated at high temperatures for short periods of time without damage and must be heated at high temperatures in order to achieve complete fusion and strong bonding of the plies. There is an optimum viscosity range and an optimum temperature range at the point of application that allow complete fusion, optimum wetting and mopping properties, and the desirable interply bitumen weight. The equiviscous temperature (EVT) is defined as the temperature at which the viscosity of roofing asphalt is 125 centistokes, plus or minus 25°F, at the mop bucket or felt layer immediately prior to application to the substrate. A centistoke is a unit that measures the kinematic viscosity.

Centistokes = [Dynamic Viscosity/Density] x Centipoise

The recommended EVT range for roofing asphalt, Types I, II, III, and IV, is the temperature at which a viscosity of 75 centipoise is attained, plus or minus 25°F. The recommended EVT range for coal tar products, types I and III, is the temperature at which a viscosity of 25 centipoise is attained, plus or minus 25°F. One consequence of a change in EVT from 125 centistokes to 75 centipoise, plus or minus 25°F, is the potential need to increase the temperature at which bitumen is heated in the kettle or tanker. Excessive and prolonged heating of asphalt and coal tar products may have a deleterious effect on the quality of the product.

National Roofing Contractors Association; Rosemont, Illinois
Valerie Eickelberger; Rippeteau Architects, PC; Washington, D.C.

Built-up Roofing

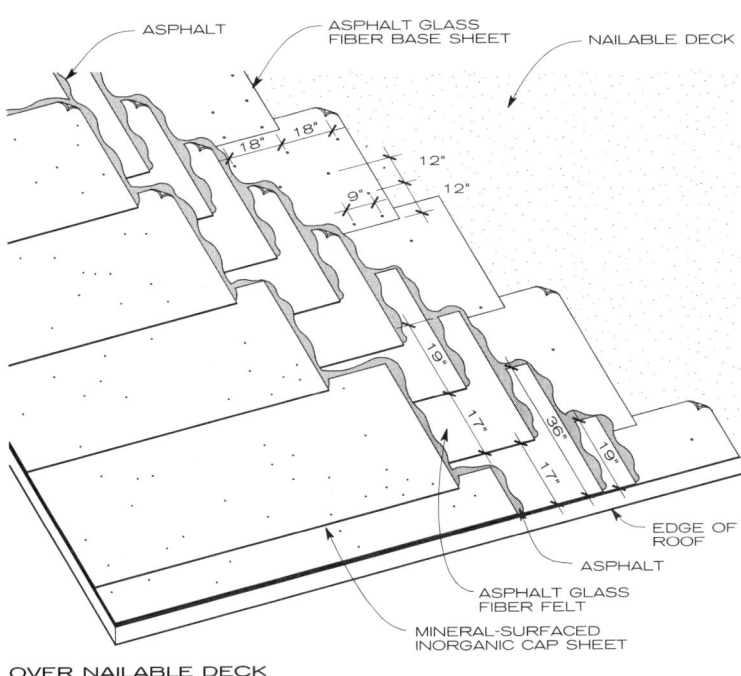

OVER NAILABLE DECK

NOTE

If applied over nailable deck sheathing panels, add a rosin-sized sheathing paper between the deck and base sheet.

MINERAL-SURFACED CAP SHEET BUILT-UP ROOFING

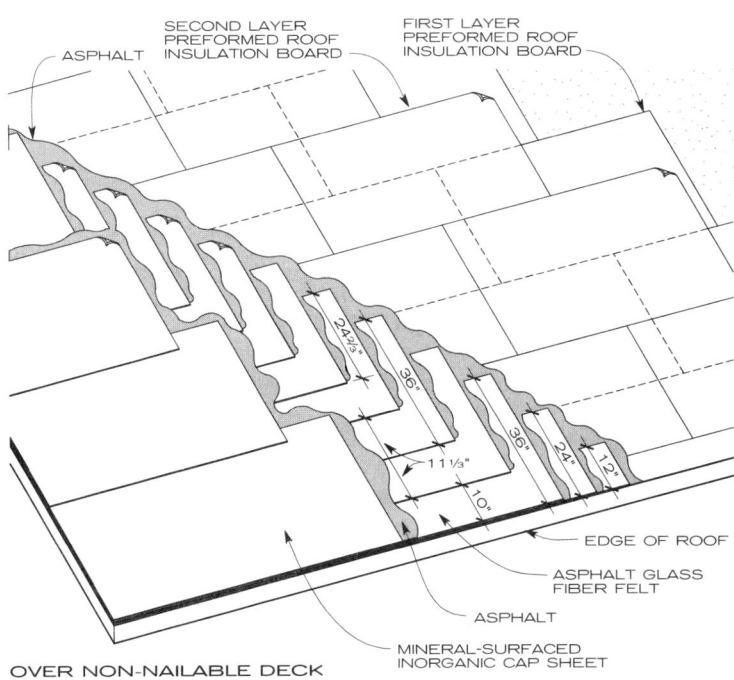

OVER NON-NAILABLE DECK

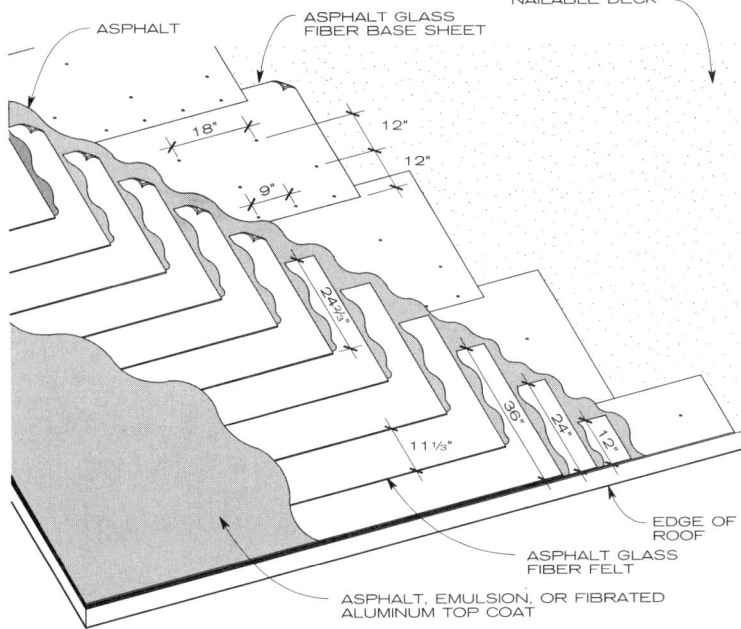

THREE-PLY OVER NAILABLE DECK

NOTE

If applied over sheathing panels, add a rosin-sized sheathing paper between the deck and base sheet.

THREE-PLY OVER NON-NAILABLE DECK

NOTE

For a more conservative system, specify four plies rather than three.

SMOOTH SURFACE BUILT-UP ROOFING

BUILT-UP ROOF SURFACING

Surfacing protects the bitumen and felts of a built-up roof from direct sunlight and weather exposure, and may provide other properties such as fire resistance or reflectivity. Surfacing types include aggregate, smooth surfacing, and mineral cap sheet.

AGGREGATE SURFACING

The aggregate in roofing serves as an opaque covering that improves the appearance and fire resistance of the roof and helps resist premature aging and damage from weather, temperature fluctuations, and ultraviolet rays. Aggregate also increases the wind uplift resistance of the roof membrane and permits much heavier pourings of bitumen than would otherwise be possible.

SMOOTH SURFACING

Built-up roof membranes may be left smooth, surfaced with a top coating of hot asphalt. Smooth surfacing should not be confused with a built-up membrane left unsurfaced (exposed felts). Smooth surfaced built-up roofing should be specified only in those circumstances where aggregate-surfaced built-up roofing is impractical, such as when the roof surface exceeds 3 in. per ft, where the proximity of an air-intake or exhaust equipment may cause loose aggregate, or where appropriate aggregate is not available.

MINERAL SURFACED (CAP SHEET)

Some areas of the country, particularly the far western and southern states, use mineral-surfaced cap sheets as the final surfacing for built-up roofing membranes. These specifications are similar to aggregate and smooth-surfaced specifications except that a final layer of prepared roofing material is installed on top of the multiply built-up roof assembly. This specification is not popular in colder climates, primarily because it requires phased construction of the final layer of roofing material.

National Roofing Contractors Association; Rosemont, Illinois
Valerie Eickelberger; Rippeteau Architects, PC; Washington, D.C.

Modified Bitumen Membrane Roofing

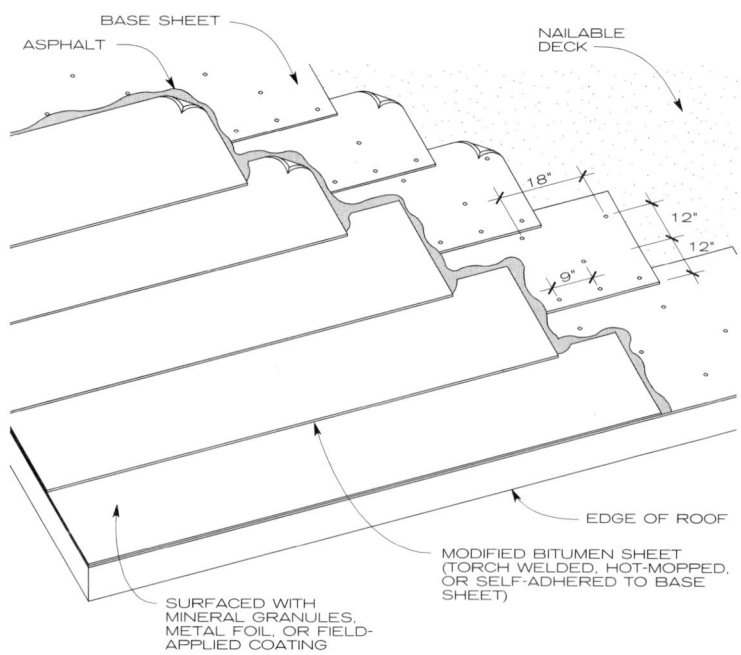

TWO-PLY MODIFIED BITUMEN MEMBRANE

NOTE
If applied over-sheathing panels when the cap sheet is hot-mopped, add a rosin-sized sheathing paper between the deck and base sheet.

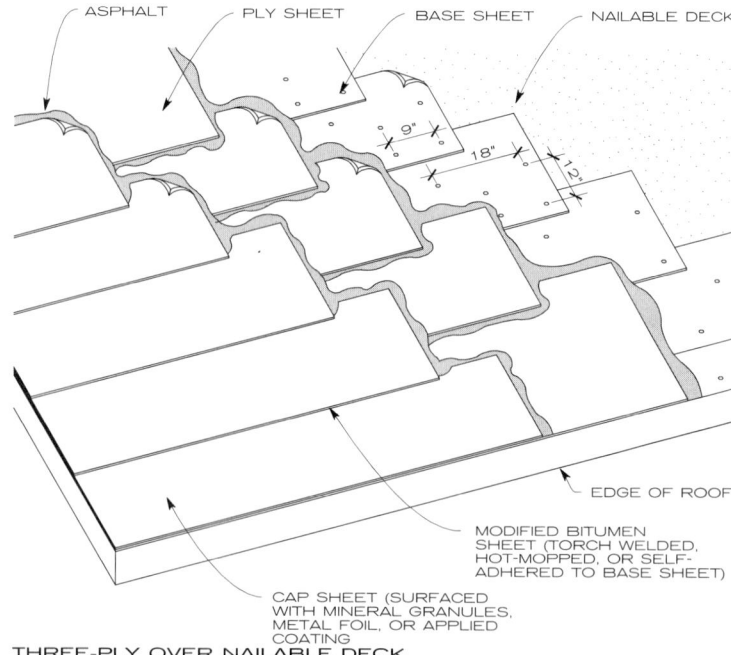

THREE-PLY MODIFIED BITUMEN MEMBRANE

NOTE
If applied over-sheathing panels when the cap sheet is hot-mopped, add a rosin-sized sheathing paper between the deck and base sheet.

MODIFIED BITUMEN MEMBRANES

Polymer-modified bitumen membranes couple bitumen and polymers with various reinforcements to form a membrane system with improved properties. Modifiers include atactic polypropylene, styrene-butadiene-styrene, and styrene-butadiene-rubber. The modifying compounds impart improved flexibility, cohesive strength, toughness, and resistance to flow at high temperatures. The seams are sealed by torch welding or with hot asphalt. Thickness ranges from 40 to 160 mils.

For some systems a base sheet is fastened to the deck as an underlayment. In the hot-mopped system, the membrane is constructed similar to a built-up roof with hot asphalt mopped between the plies. Self-adhered sheets have a factory-applied asphalt-adhesive coating on the underside. The protective sheet is peeled away to stick the membrane to the roof deck. Torch-applied membrane systems have a factory-applied coating of modified asphalt on the underside of the sheet, which is melted with a propane torch to make the sheet adhere.

Reinforcing materials for polymer modified bitumen membranes include plastic film, polyester mat, glass fiber, felt or fabric, and metal foils, embedded within or laminated onto the modified bitumen sheet. Membranes may be surfaced with liquid coatings, metallic laminates, or ceramic or mineral granules to enhance resistance to weathering, ultraviolet rays, or fire or to improve appearance. Terminations at roof edges, parapets, and other flashings may be torch-applied, hot-mopped, or self-adhered. Laps are formed as the sheet is being applied.

National Roofing Contractors Association; Rosemont, Illinois
Valerie Eickelberger; Rippeteau Architects, PC; Washington, D.C.

MEMBRANE ROOFING

Built-up and Modified Bitumen Details

GENERAL

In general, the details for installation of bitumen roofing, whether built-up roofing or modified bitumen roofing, are similar in many respects. Details for both types of roofing are included where applicable. The details show typical conditions that occur at bitumen roofs, such as roof edge conditions, piping penetrations, and equipment supports.

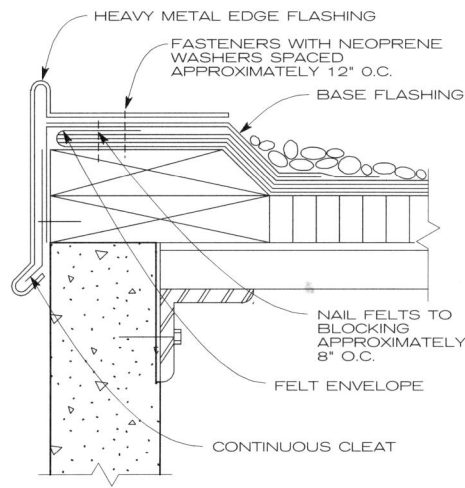

HEAVY METAL ROOF EDGE

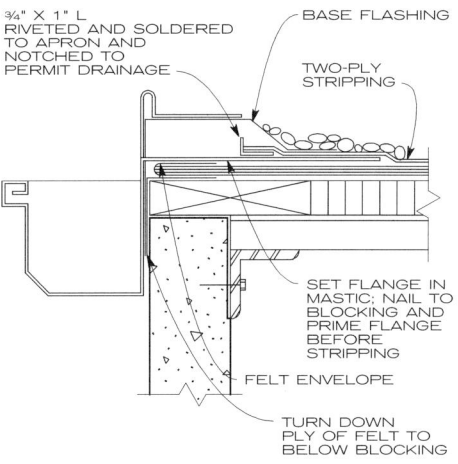

SCUPPER THROUGH ROOF EDGE

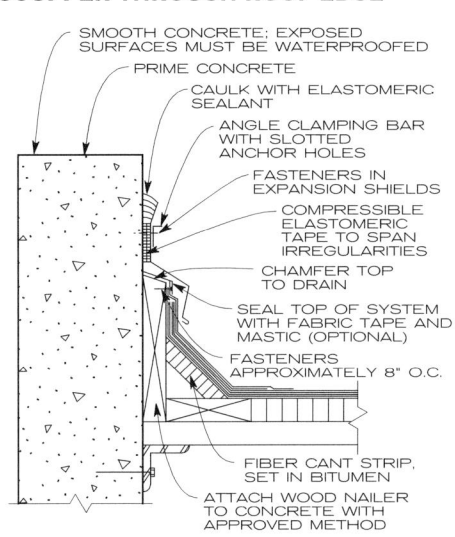

COUNTERFLASHING CONCRETE PARAPET

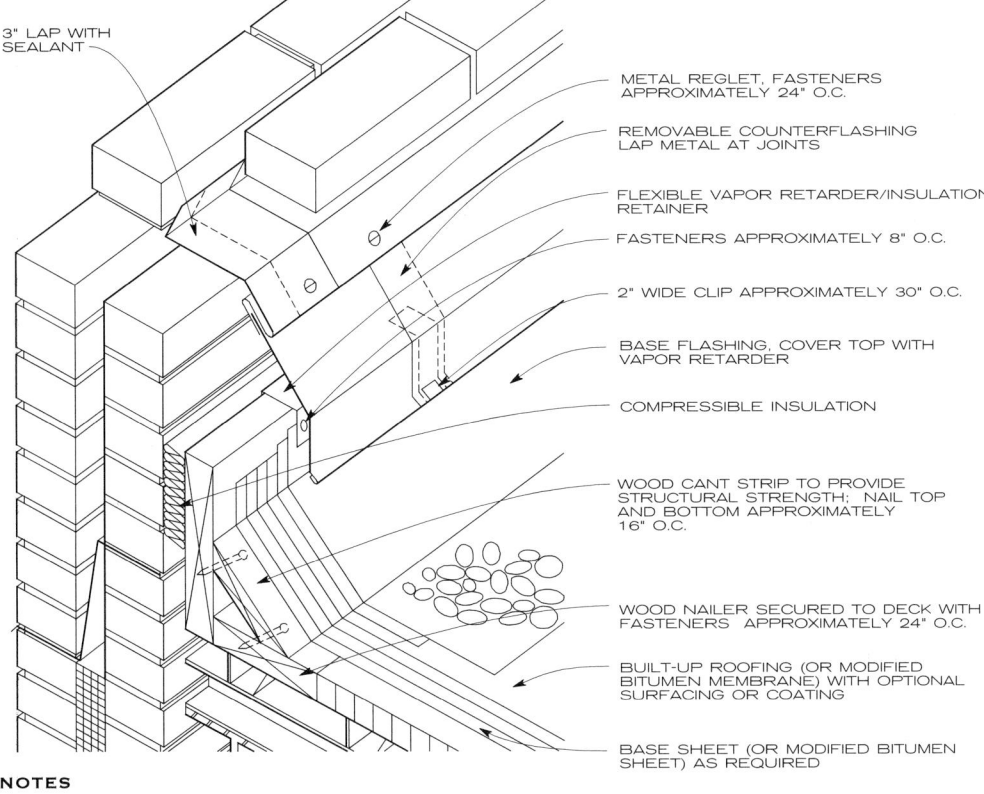

BASE FLASHING FOR WALL-SUPPORTED DECK

NOTES
1. This detail should be used only when the deck is supported by the wall.
2. The joints in the two pieces of flashing should not be soldered. Breaks in soldered joints could channel water behind the flashing. Clips at the bottom of the flashing are not necessary on flashings of 6 in. or less.

BASE FLASHING FOR NON-WALL-SUPPORTED DECK

NOTES
1. This detail allows wall and deck to move independently.
2. This detail should be used where there is any possibility that differential movement will occur between the deck and a vertical surface, such as at a penthouse wall. The vertical wood member should be fastened to the deck only. This is one satisfactory method of joining the two-piece flashing system. Other methods may be used.

National Roofing Contractors Association; Rosemont, Illinois
Valerie Eickelberger; Rippeteau Architects, PC; Washington, D.C.

MEMBRANE ROOFING

Built-up and Modified Bitumen Details

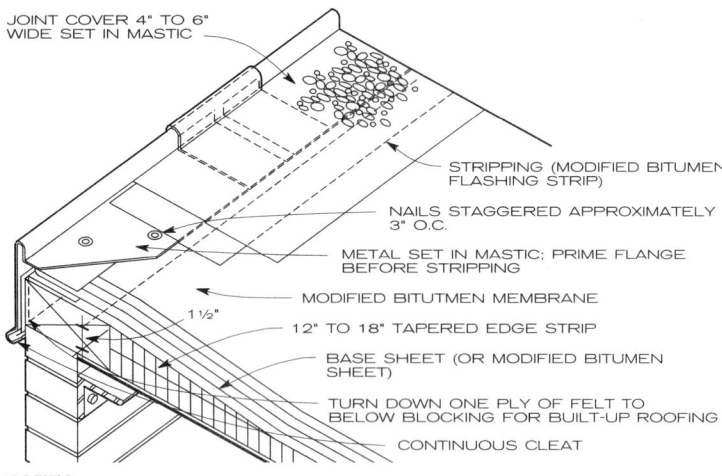

NOTES
1. Envelope shown is for coal tar pitch and low-slope asphalt.
2. Attach nailer to masonry wall.
3. This detail should be used only where the deck is supported by the outside wall.
4. This detail should be used with light-gauge metals, such as 16 oz. copper, 24-gauge galvanized metal, or 0.040 in. aluminum. A tapered edge strip is used to raise the gravel stop. Frequent nailing is necessary to control thermal movement.
5. Wood blocking may be slotted for venting where required.

GRAVEL STOP

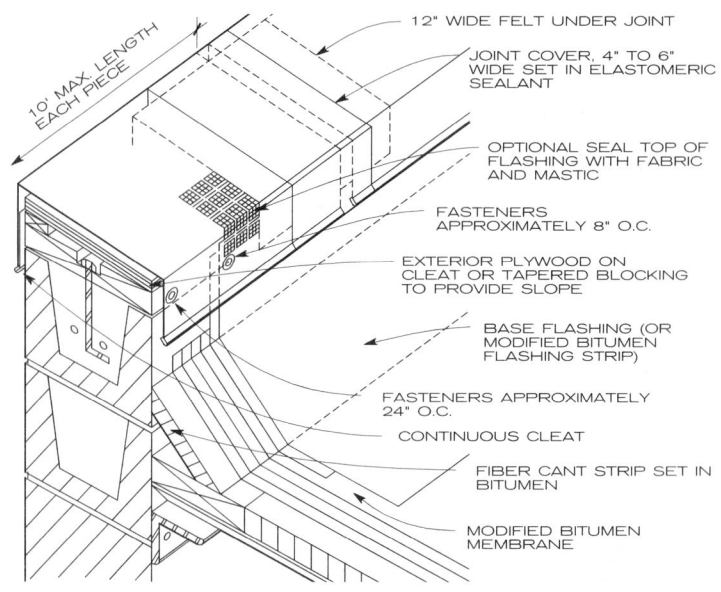

NOTE
This detail should be used only when the deck is supported by the wall. An expansion joint detail should be used for a deck not supported by a wall.

LIGHT METAL PARAPET CAP

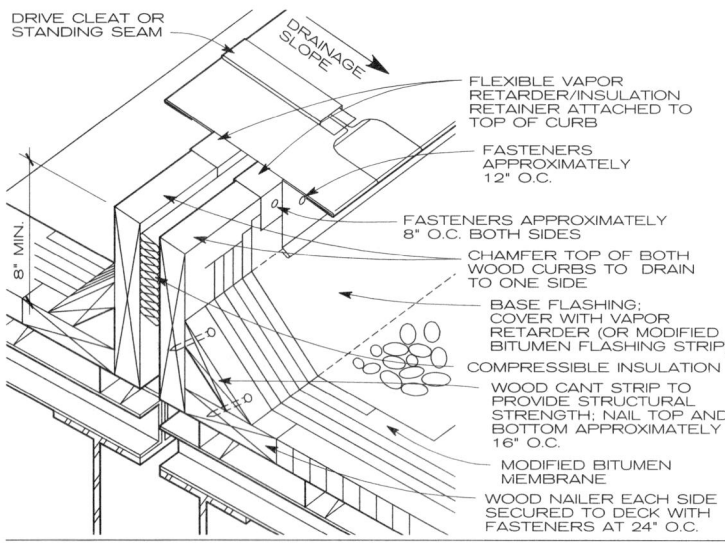

EXPANSION JOINT

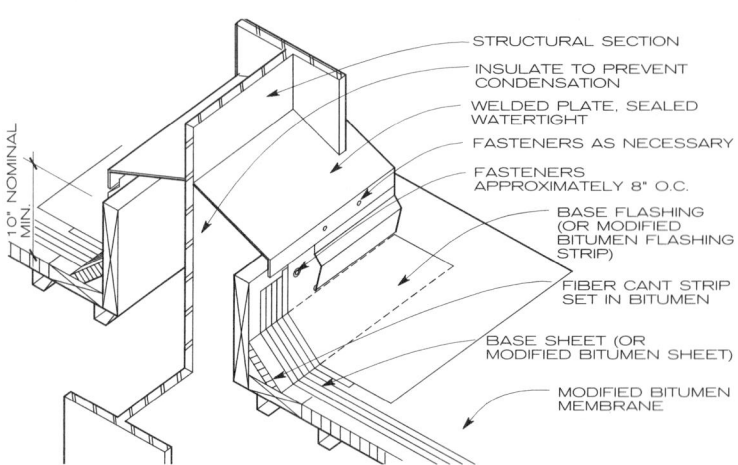

NOTE
This detail illustrates one method of eliminating pitch pockets. The curbed system allows for movement in the structural member without disturbing the roof system.

STRUCTURAL MEMBER THROUGH ROOF

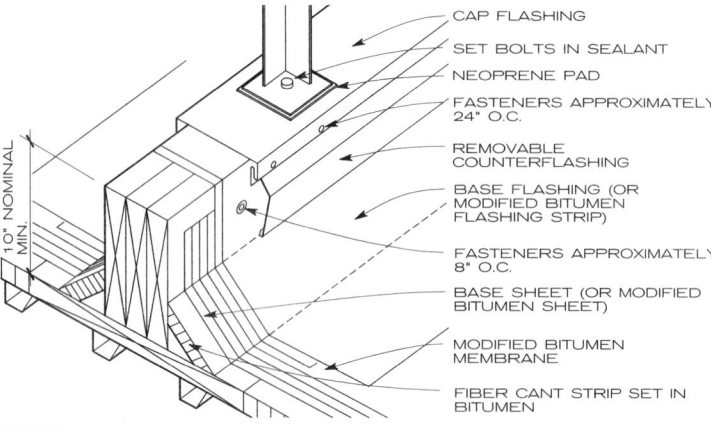

NOTE
This detail allows for roof maintenance around the equipment support. Continuous support is preferred in lightweight roof systems because equipment weight can be spread over two or more supporting members. Clearance must be provided for removal and replacement of roofing and flashing between parallel supports.

EQUIPMENT SUPPORT ON LIGHT ROOF DECK

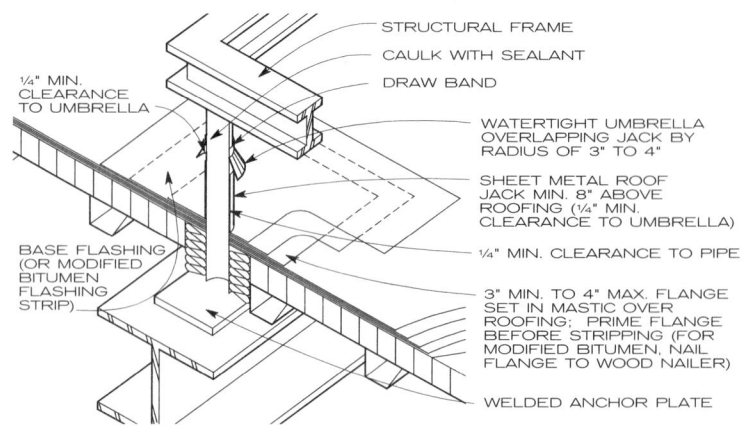

NOTE
This detail depicts site-fabricated construction. Many manufacturers now offer prefabricated flashing pieces or permit the use of materials for flashing purposes other than those shown here. Proprietary designs vary widely; consult individual manufacturers about use.

INSULATED DECK STEEL FRAME SUPPORT

National Roofing Contractors Association; Rosemont, Illinois
Valerie Eickelberger; Rippeteau Architects, PC; Washington, D.C.

MEMBRANE ROOFING

Built-up and Modified Bitumen Details

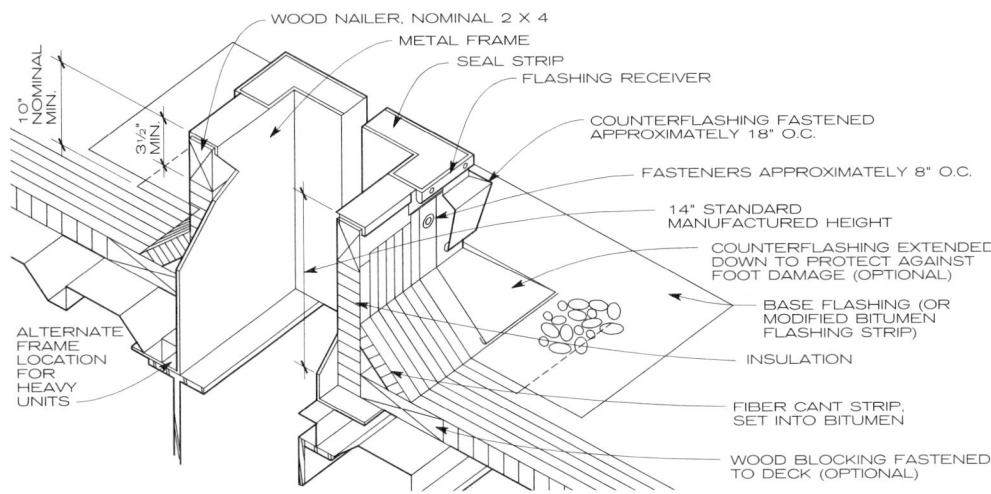

EQUIPMENT CURB

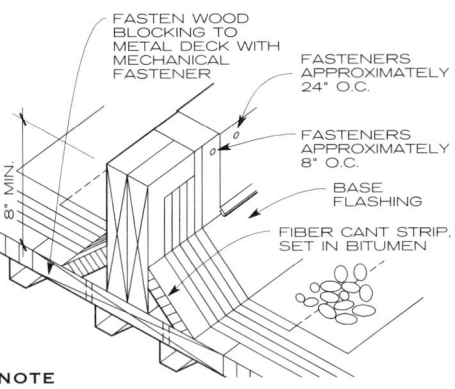

NOTE

An area divider is designed simply as a raised double wood member attached to a properly flashed wood base plate that is anchored to the roof deck. Area dividers should be located between the roof's expansion joints at 150 to 200 ft intervals, depending upon climatic conditions and area practices. They should never restrict the flow of water.

AREA DIVIDER

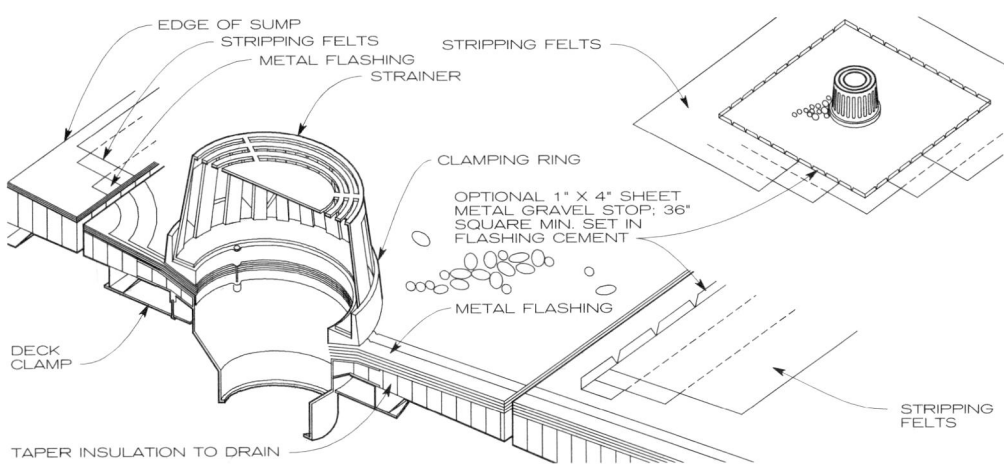

NOTES

1. Minimum 30 in. square, $2\frac{1}{2}$ to 4 lb lead or 16 oz soft copper flashing set on finished roof felts set in mastic. Prime top surface before stripping.
2. Membrane plies, metal flashing, and flash-in plies extend under the clamping ring.
3. Stripping felts extend 4 in. and 6 in. beyond edge of flashing sheet, but not beyond edge of sump.
4. The use of metal deck sump pans is not recommended.

ROOF DRAIN

NOTE

This detail allows for expansion and contraction of pipes without roof damage.

PIPE ROLLER SUPPORT

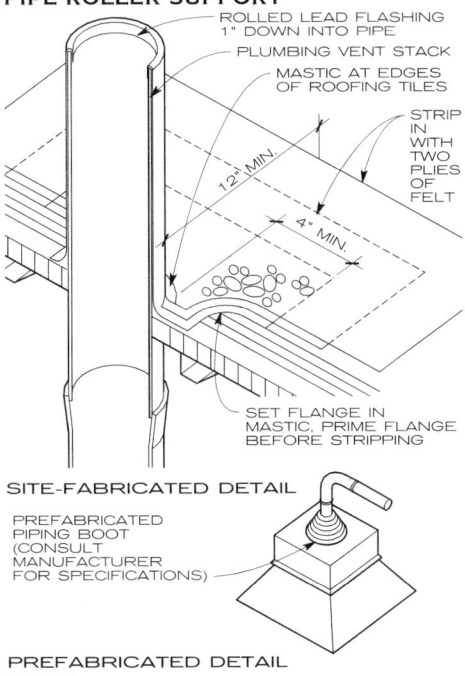

PREFABRICATED DETAIL

NOTES

1. Sheet lead minimum of $2\frac{1}{2}$ lb per sq ft.
2. Minimum clearance of 12 in. from cant strips and other curbs or pipes.

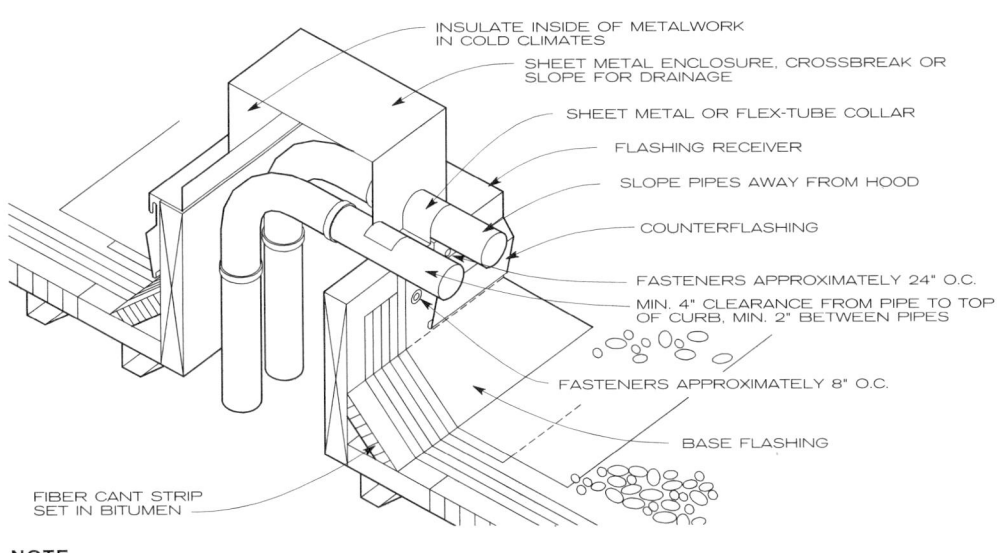

NOTE

This detail illustrates another method of eliminating pitch pockets and a satisfactory method of grouping piping that must come up above the roof surface.

MULTIPLE PIPE PENETRATION

SINGLE PIPE PENETRATION

National Roofing Contractors Association; Rosemont, Illinois
Valerie Eickelberger; Rippeteau Architects, PC; Washington, D.C.

MEMBRANE ROOFING

EPDM SINGLE-PLY ROOFING

Ethylene propylene diene monomer (EPDM) membranes are 30 to 60 mil thick, single-sheet roofing materials. They are available either nonreinforced or reinforced with fabric. Seams in the membrane are spliced and cemented. EPDM membranes are highly resistant to degradation from certain chemicals, ozone, and ultraviolet radiation and have excellent resilience, tensile strength, abrasion resistance, hardness, and weathering properties.

EPDM membranes may be laid loose, mechanically fastened, or fully adhered to either nailable or non-nailable decks. For loose-laid systems, ballast provides resistance against wind uplift forces. Some membranes require field application of surfacings or coatings to provide weather resistance, aesthetics, or other properties. Specifications for formulation and installation of EPDM membranes vary with the individual manufacturer.

Separation layers of asphalt-saturated organic felt or board-type roof insulation permit the membrane to move relative to the deck without abrasion. Membrane terminations at roof edges, parapets, and other flashings employ material identical to the roof membrane material shaped to conform to the substrate and area being flashed. Standards for EPDM membranes are maintained by ASTM and the Rubber Manufacturers Association.

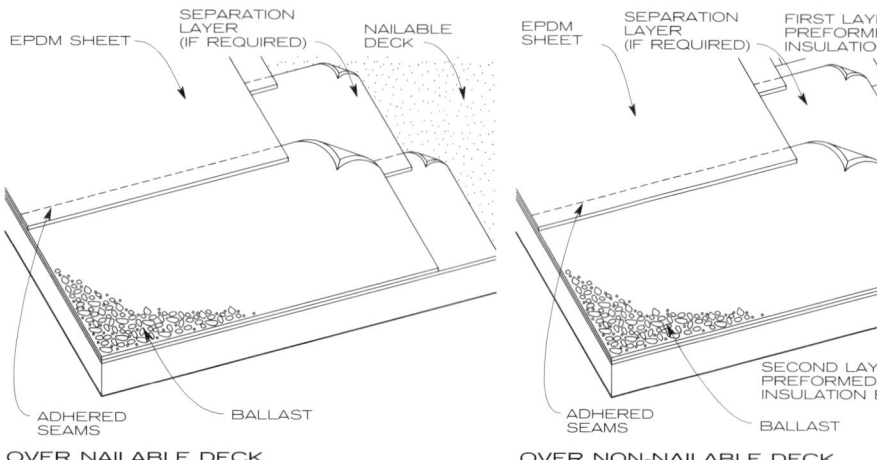

LOOSE-LAID EPDM ROOFING

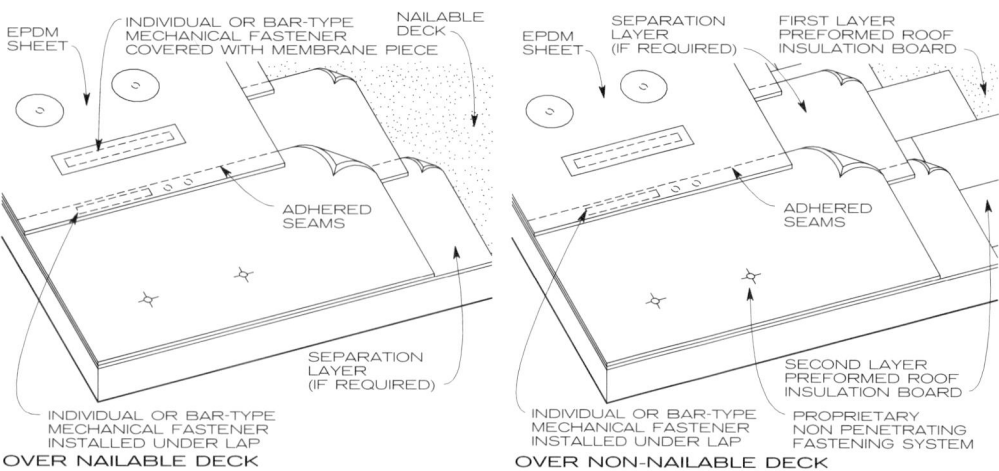

MECHANICALLY FASTENED EPDM ROOFING

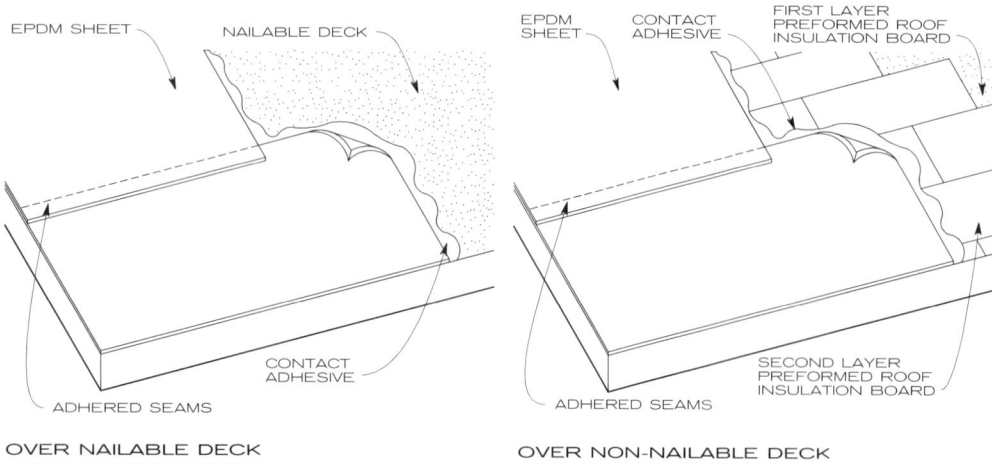

FULLY ADHERED EPDM ROOFING

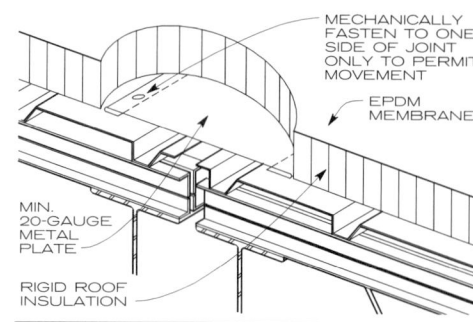

LOOSE-LAID EXPANSION JOINT

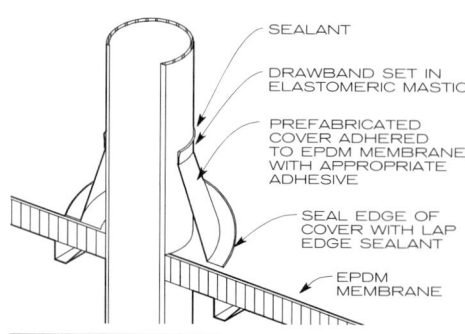

PREFABRICATED PIPE FLASHING

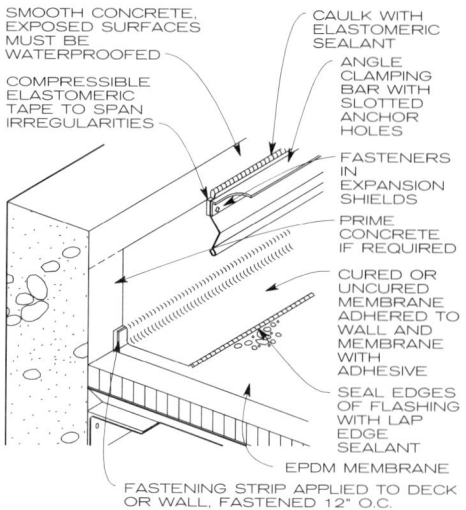

PARAPET COUNTERFLASHING

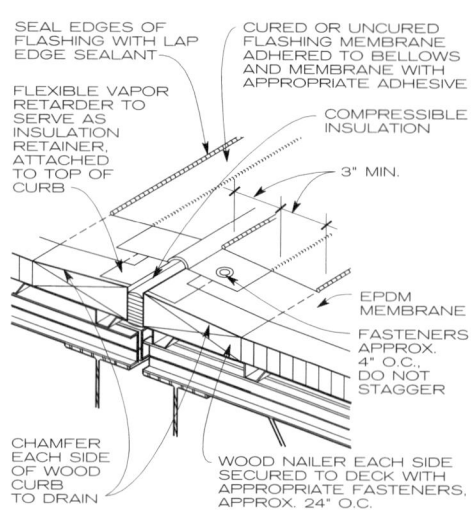

EXPANSION JOINT

National Roofing Contractors Association; Rosemont, Illinois
Valerie Eickelberger; Rippeteau Architects, PC; Washington, D.C.

Single-Ply PVC Roofing

SINGLE-PLY PVC ROOFING

Polyvinyl chloride (PVC) membranes may be nonreinforced or reinforced with glass fibers or polyester fabric 45 to 60 mils thick. Seams are formed by heat or chemical welding, and may require additional caulking. PVC membranes are resistant to bacterial growth, industrial chemical atmospheres, root penetration, and extreme weather conditions. PVC membranes have excellent fire resistance and seaming capabilities.

ASTM Standard D-4434 classes PVC materials into several types and classes depending upon the construction of the sheet material:

TYPE I: Unreinforced sheet
TYPE II, CLASS I: Unreinforced sheet containing fibers
TYPE II, CLASS II: Unreinforced sheet containing fabrics
TYPE III: Reinforced sheet containing fibers or fabrics

PVC membranes may be laid loose, mechanically fastened, or fully adhered to either nailable or non-nailable decks. For loose-laid systems, ballast provides resistance against wind uplift forces. Some PVC membranes have a factory-applied coating to provide weather resistance, aesthetics, or other properties to the membrane. Some membranes may require field application of surfacings or coatings to provide these properties.

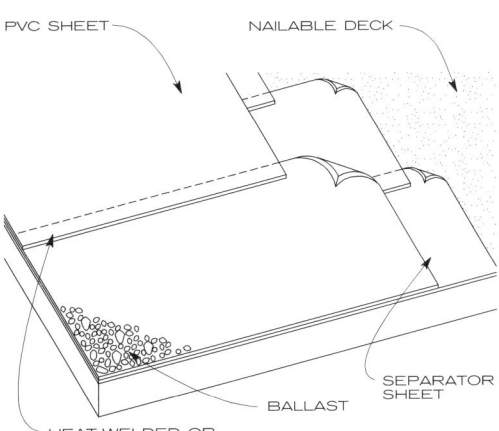
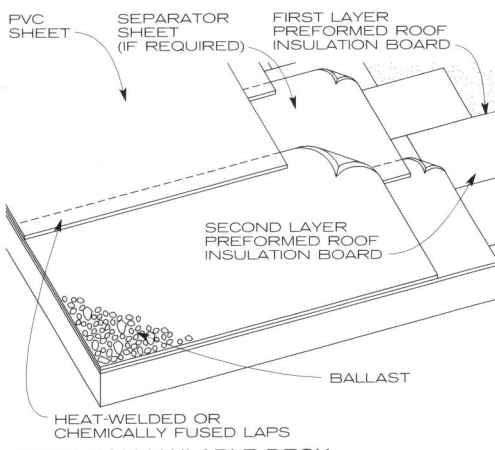

LOOSE-LAID PVC ROOFING

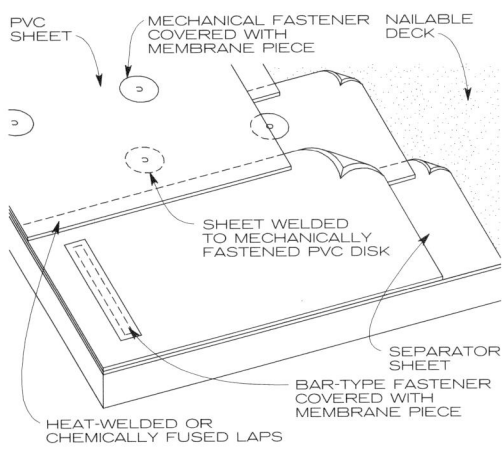
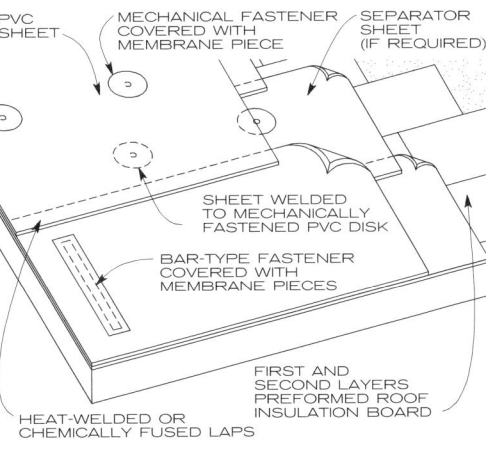

MECHANICALLY FASTENED PVC ROOFING

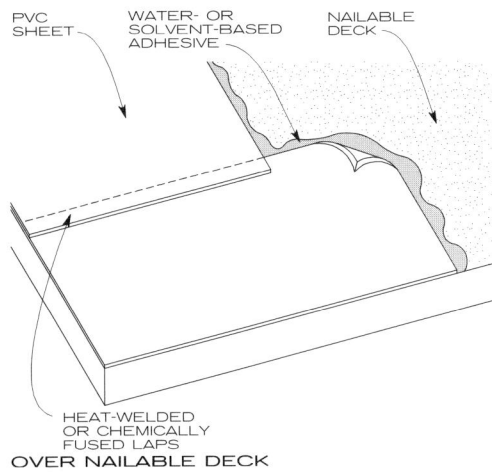
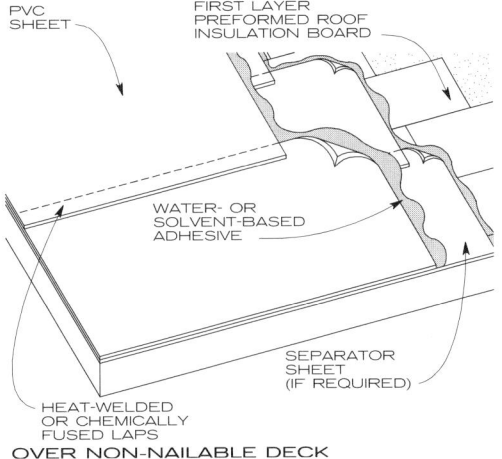

FULLY ADHERED PVC ROOFING

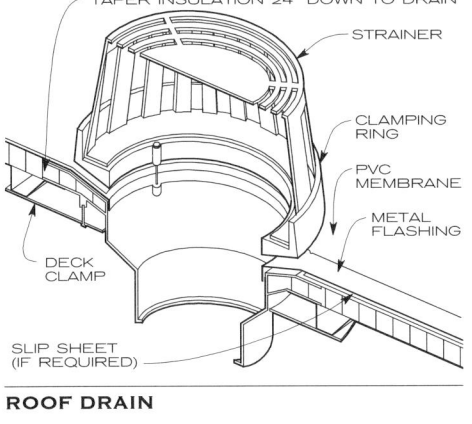

ROOF DRAIN

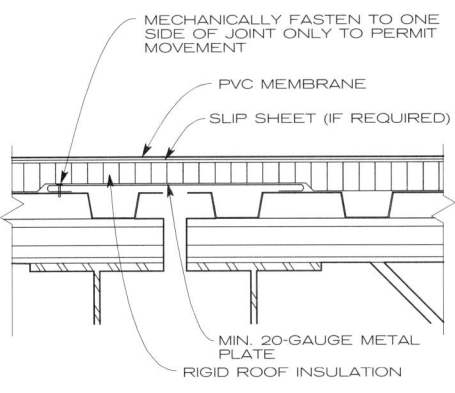

LOOSE-LAID EXPANSION JOINT

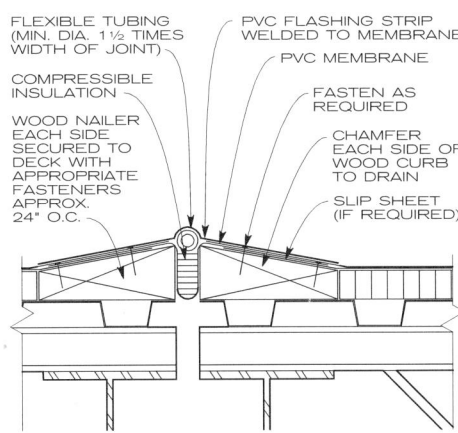

EXPANSION JOINT

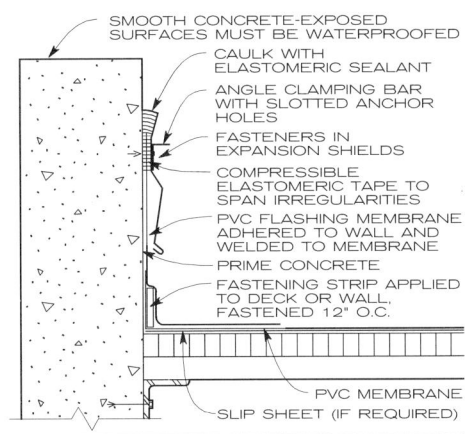

PARAPET COUNTERFLASHING

National Roofing Contractors Association; Rosemont, Illinois
Valerie Eickelberger; Rippeteau Architects, PC; Washington, D.C.

MEMBRANE ROOFING

Liquid-Applied Roofing

GENERAL

Liquid-applied roofing systems are systems primarily applied as liquids at ambient temperatures. Most of them have some sort of reinforcing fabric that is applied along with the liquid component. Liquid-applied roofing applied over existing roofs is not generally accepted as a "membrane" but as a coating.

Acrylic latex and urethane are the two main types of liquid-applied roofing. Acrylic latex refers to a family of products that use water-based polymers and cure by water evaporation. Liquid-applied urethane roof coatings are chemically cured to form an elastomeric membrane. Because these coatings are applied as liquids, installation is relatively simple, even for roofs with irregular geometries or multiple penetrations. For systems using a reinforcing fabric, a coating is applied to an acceptable surface. While the coating is still wet, a layer of polyester or fiberglass is laid into it followed by an additional layer of coating. Subsequent layers may be added as desired or necessary.

Liquid-applied roofing systems are appropriate for new construction but are most commonly used as enhancements or for repairs to existing roofs, including modified bitumen roofs and built-up roofs.

Advantages of liquid-applied roofing are that it conforms very well to irregular surfaces, is easily applied, and comes in various colors. However, it does cause marginal ponded water performance and is best used in sloped roof situations.

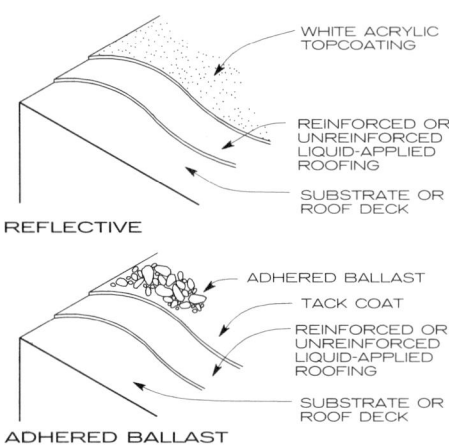

NOTE

Liquid-applied roofing systems may also be used under rigid insulation and ballast for further protection. Refer to "Protected Membrane Roofing" for further details.

LIQUID-APPLIED ROOFING SYSTEMS

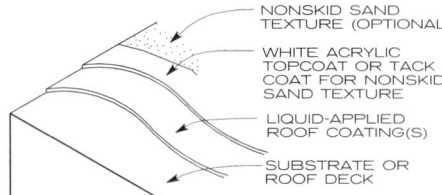

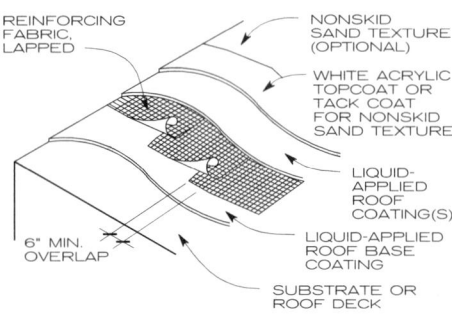

LIQUID-APPLIED MEMBRANE TYPES

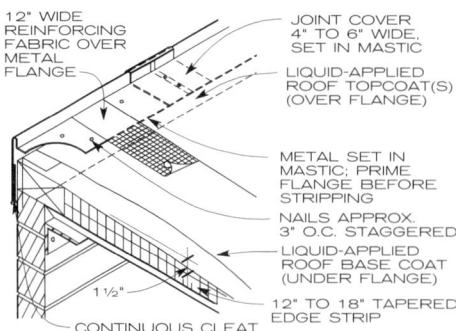

NOTES

1. Attach nailer to masonry wall. Refer to Factory Mutual data sheet # 1-49.
2. This detail should be used only when the deck is supported by the outside wall.
3. This detail should be used with light-gauge metals such as a 16-oz copper, 24-gauge galvanized metal, or 0.04-in. aluminum. A tapered edge strip is used to raise the gravel stop. Frequent nailing is necessary to control thermal movement.

GRAVEL STOP

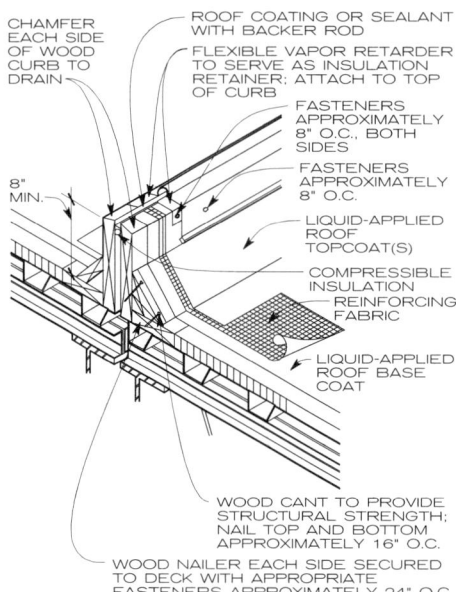

EXPANSION JOINT

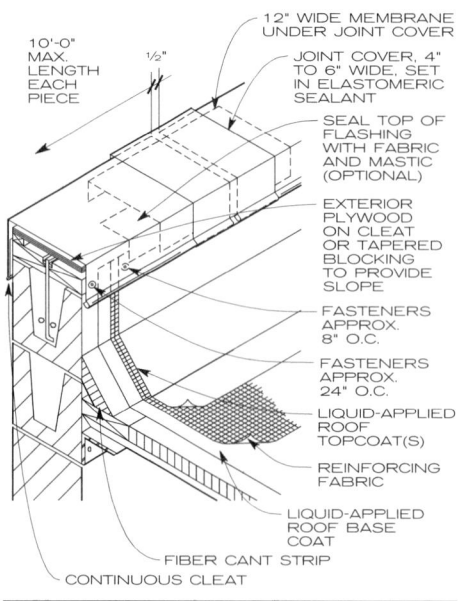

LIGHT METAL PARAPET CAP

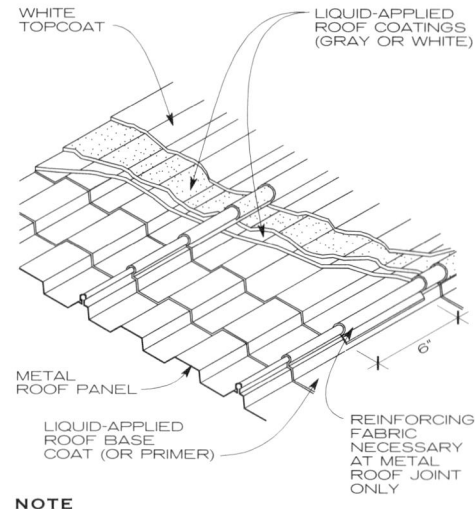

NOTE

Roof slope minimum is $1/4$ in. in 12 or 2%; no maximum.

RETROFIT LIQUID-APPLIED ROOFING OVER EXISTING METAL ROOF

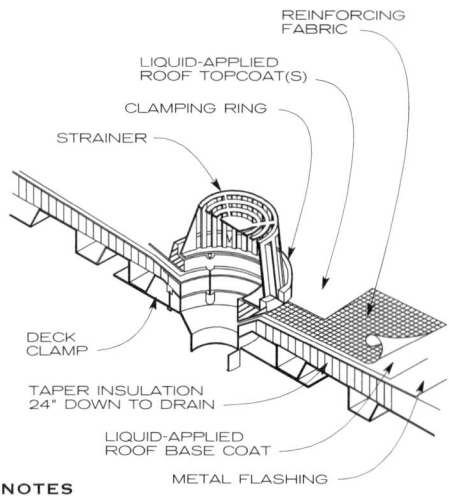

NOTES

1. Use minumum 30-in. sq, $2 1/2$ lb to 4 lb lead flashing. Set in mastic. Prime top surface before stripping.
2. Liquid-applied roof coatings, reinforcing fabric, and metal flashing (optional) extend under clamping ring.

ROOF DRAIN

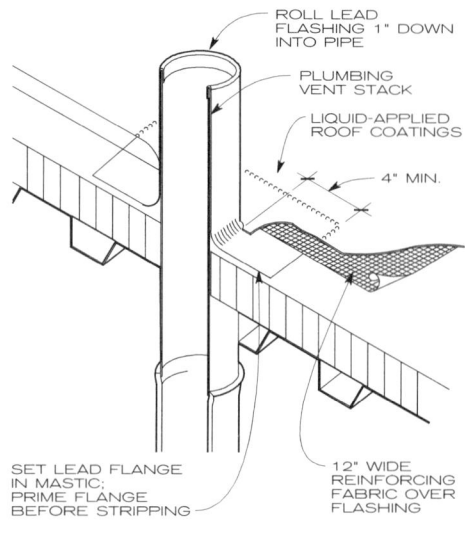

NOTE

Sheet lead minimum of $2 1/2$ lb per sq ft.

SINGLE PIPE PENETRATION

Richard J. Vitullo, AIA; Oak Leaf Studio; Crownsville, Maryland
Rich Boon; The Roofing Industry Educational Institute; Englewood, Colorado

Protected Membrane Roofing

GENERAL

In a typical roofing system, the waterproof membrane system (built-up, modified bitumen, or single-ply) is applied on top of the insulation, which lies on top of the substrate and/or structural deck. The membrane in this situation is exposed to temperature extremes and wear and tear from people walking or working on the roof. In a protected membrane roof (sometimes called the inverted or insulated roof membrane assembly, or IRMA), a layer of extruded polystyrene insulation board protects the membrane. Extruded polystyrene is the only material generally approved for this application because it does not absorb moisture. This roofing system is best used in extreme climates, where it is important to protect the membrane from the elements, or where the rooftop will receive heavy use (e.g., plaza or parking deck applications).

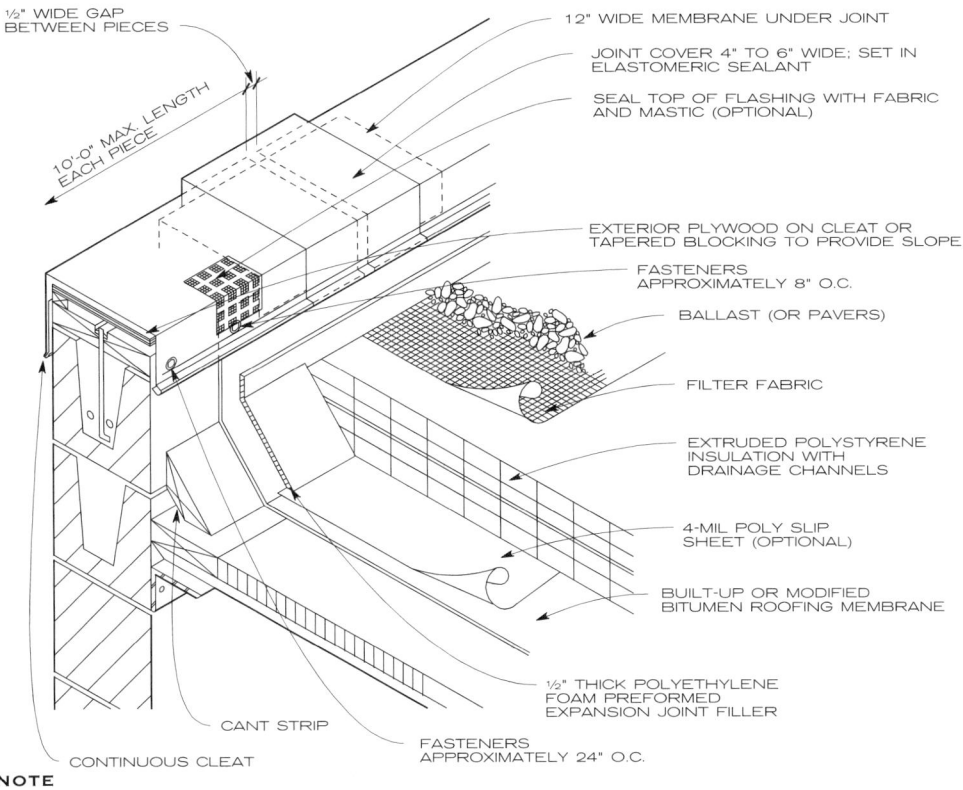

NOTE

Membrane may be built-up, modified bitumen, or single-ply. If thermoplastic membrane is specified, provide slip sheet between insulation and membrane.

LIGHT METAL PARAPET CAP AT BUILT-UP OR MODIFIED BITUMEN ROOF

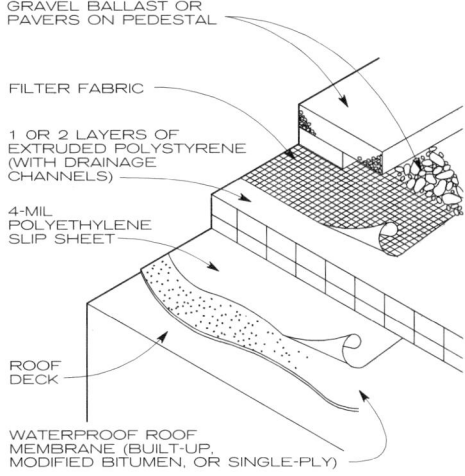

NOTES

1. Ballast weight is a minimum of 10 lb per square foot.
2. Refer to ANSI/SPRI/RMA RP-4 for wind design guidance.
3. In lieu of aggregate or concrete ballast, proprietary insulation boards with concrete topping are available. These boards weigh between 4.5 lb per square foot and 10 lb per square foot, depending on the product selected.

TYPICAL PROTECTED MEMBRANE ROOF SYSTEM

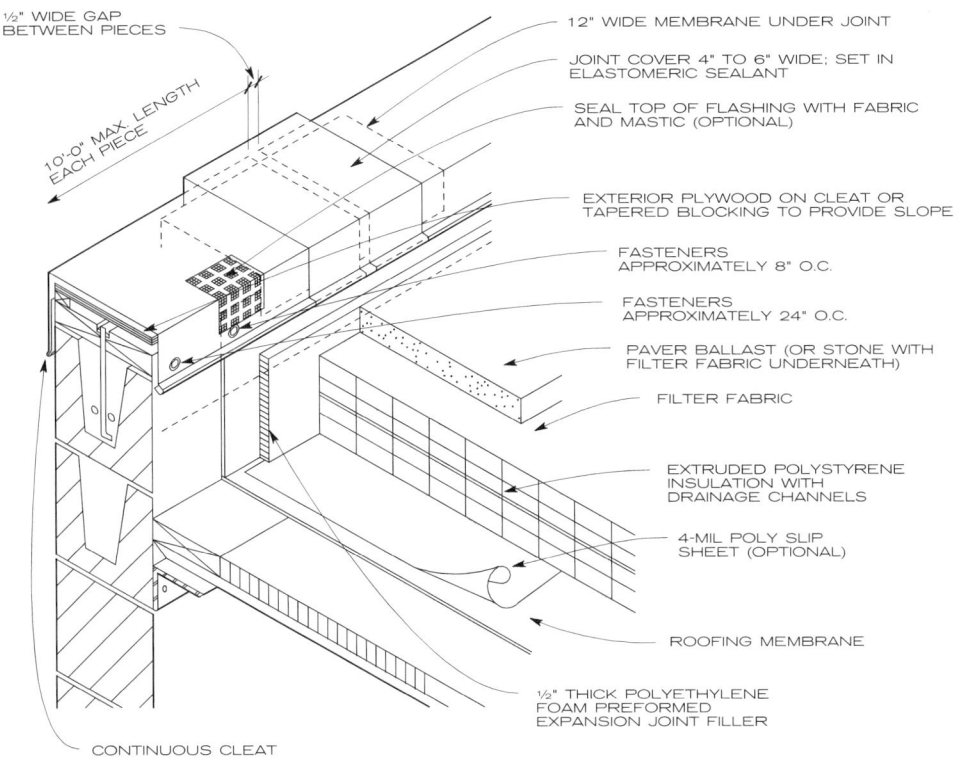

NOTES

1. Membrane must be single-ply. If thermoplastic membrane is specified, provide slip sheet between insulation and membrane.
2. Set pavers on pedestals or specify that the top layer of insulation boards have ribs on the top side to facilitate drying.

LIGHT METAL PARAPET AT SINGLE-PLY ROOF

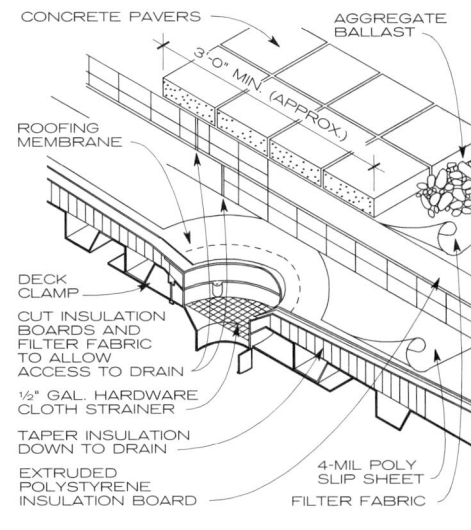

NOTES

1. Standard weight concrete pavers should be used to mark drain locations and to facilitate access to drains.
2. To facilitate placement of insulation boards, etc., the clamping ring and strainer are to be removed from metal drains. A ½ in. hardware cloth strainer should be laid at the bottom of the drain bowl.
3. For a thermoplastic membrane, use a 4-mil polyethylene slip sheet between the membrane and the insulation boards. Cut a hole in the sheet at the drain, approximately 2 in. larger than the diameter of the drain bowl.

ROOF DRAIN

Richard J. Vitullo, AIA; Oak Leaf Studio; Crownsville, Maryland
Rich Boon; The Roofing Industry Educational Institute; Englewood, Colorado

MEMBRANE ROOFING

Spray-Applied Polyurethane Foam Roofing

GENERAL

Polyurethane foam roofing is spray-applied, seamless, and fully adhered. The foam is made by mixing isocyanate and resin components at a 1:1 ratio. Spray polyurethane foam is a closed-cell foam that provides good insulation and water resistance. These systems are used with a protective coating or stone ballast covering system, which protects the foam roofing from ultraviolet rays and mechanical damage.

These systems can be applied in varying thicknesses to eliminate ponding, to improve drainage, and to meet specified R-values (approximately R-6.25 per inch). Some advantages of spray foam systems are that they can be used over highly irregular surfaces, unusual geometries, or existing sloped metal systems. They are also inherently lightweight and offer good wind uplift resistance.

NOTES

1. Before spray polyurethane foam is applied, all surfaces must be clean, free of contaminants, securely fastened to the substrate, and completely dry. Moisture-sensitive indicators may be needed to detect any moisture within the existing roof assembly. Vapor retarders may be necessary; consult with the manufacturer to coordinate a specific roofing condition with foam application.
2. Most polyurethane foam manufacturers produce three seasonal grades: winter (fast), regular, and summer (slow).
3. If wind speed affects foam quality, use wind screens or discontinue spraying. The surface texture of sprayed foam can vary due to wind, equipment adjustment, spray technique, and characteristics of the system used. Foam that will be elastomeric coated should have a smooth texture resembling orange peel. For an aggregate covering, the texture should be no rougher than popcorn.

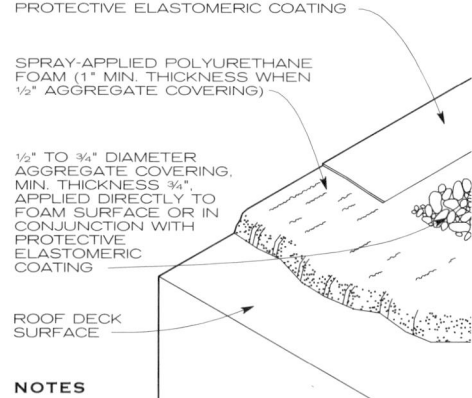

NOTES

1. Protection systems fall into two general classifications, protective elastomeric coatings and aggregate. There are seven generic types of elastomeric protective coatings: acrylic, silicone, urethane, butyl, hypalon, neoprene, and modified asphalt. The physical properties of these coatings may vary, and the coating manufacturer should be consulted for recommendations on specific needs.
2. Granules may be applied to the wet uncured protective topcoat to enhance the resistance of the coating systems to UV or mechanical damage.

SPRAY-APPLIED POLYURETHANE FOAM ROOFING SYSTEM

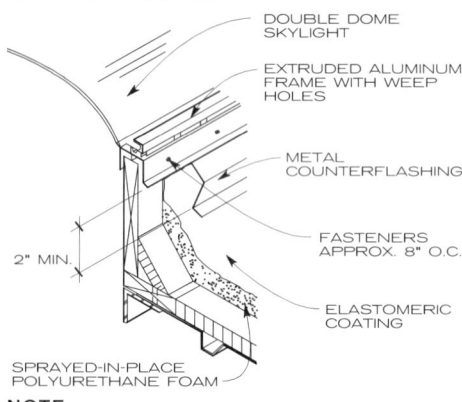

NOTE

On skylights, do not cover weep holes with polyurethane foam or coating.

SKYLIGHT, SCUTTLE, OR VENT CURB

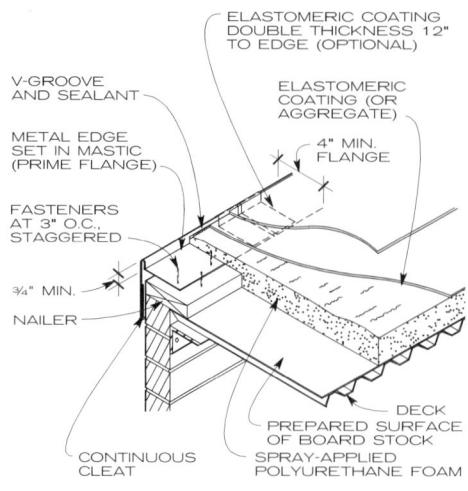

METAL ROOF EDGE

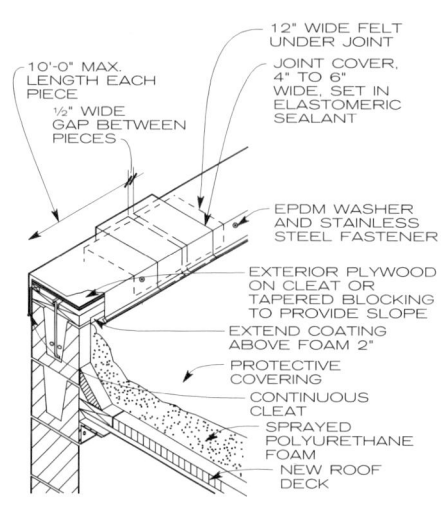

NOTE

This detail should be used only when the deck is supported by the wall. An expansion joint detail should be used for non-wall-supported decks.

LIGHT METAL PARAPET CAP

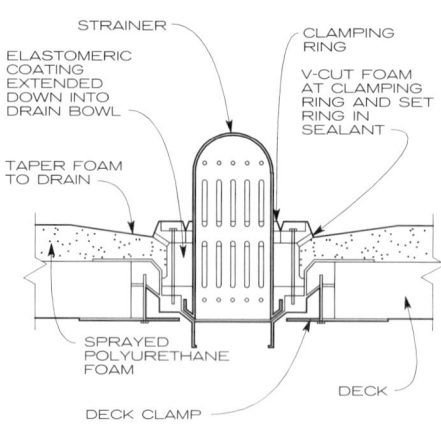

NOTES

1. Remove clamping ring prior to foam application. Place protective covering over drain bowl opening to prevent overspray from filling bowl.
2. Taper foam toward drain bowl to provide positive drainage.
3. The use of metal deck sump pans is not recommended.

ROOF DRAIN

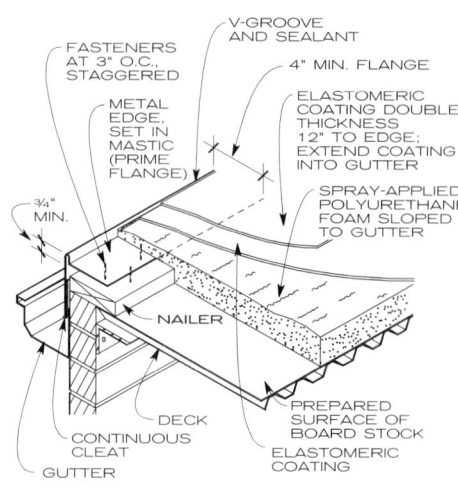

ROOF EDGE AT GUTTER

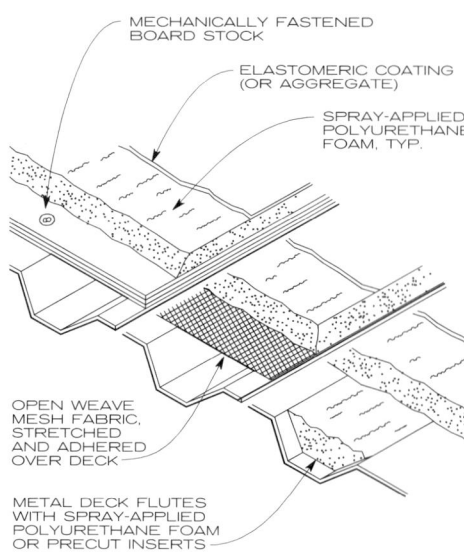

METAL DECK DETAILS

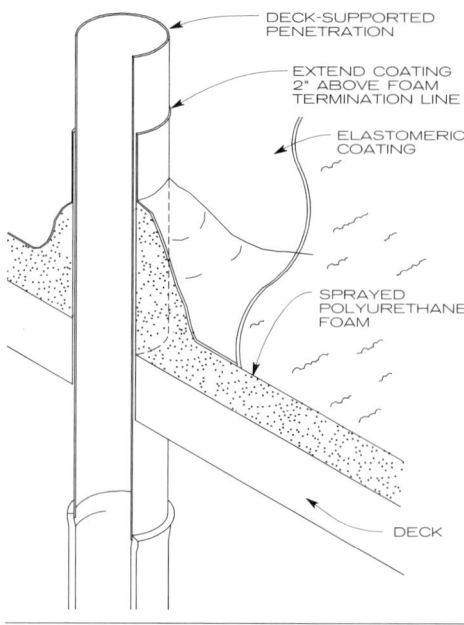

SINGLE PIPE PENETRATION

Richard J. Vitullo, AIA; Oak Leaf Studio; Crownsville, Maryland
Rich Boon; The Roofing Institute Educational Institute; Englewood, Colorado

MEMBRANE ROOFING

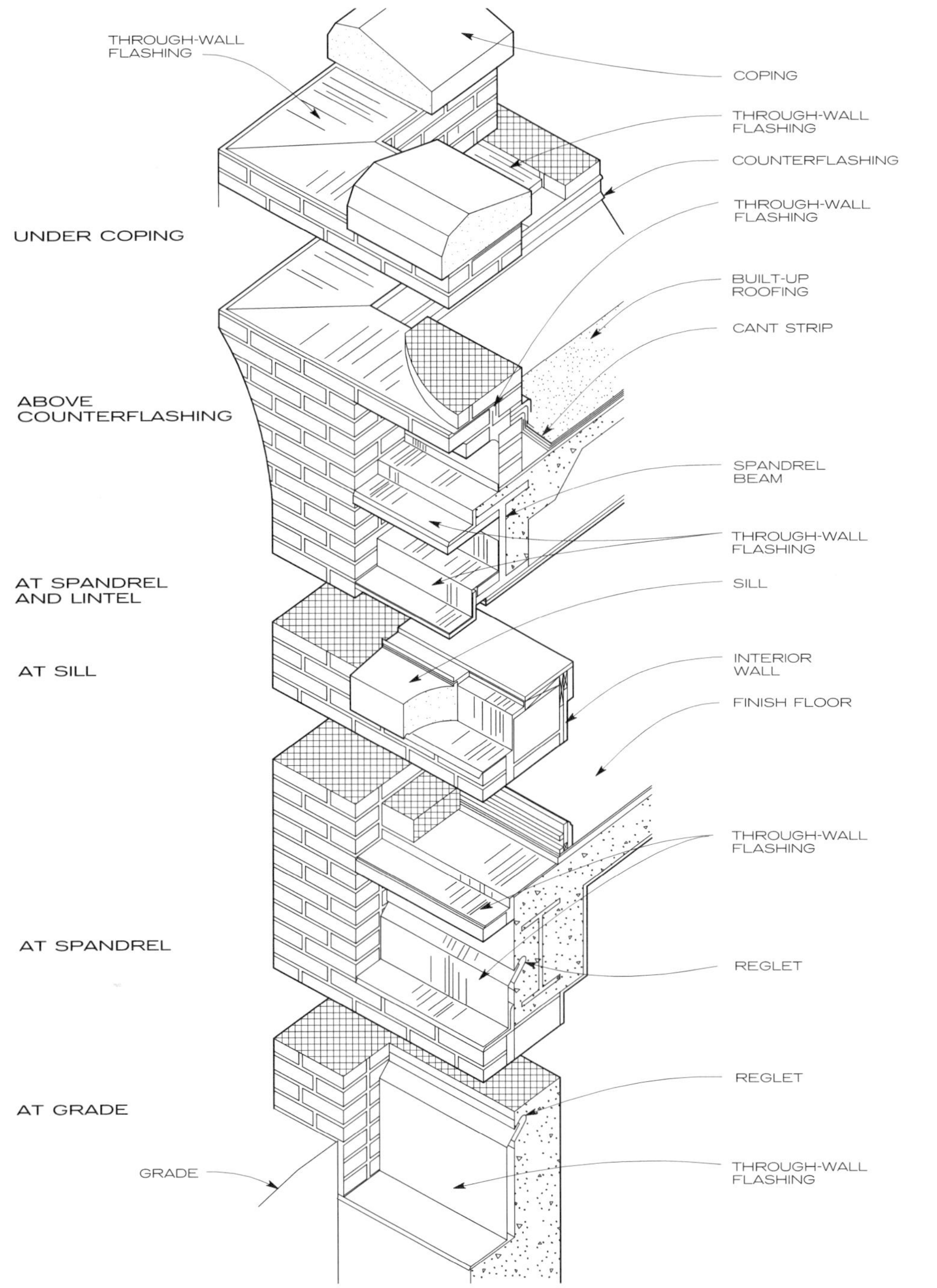

Through-Wall Flashing

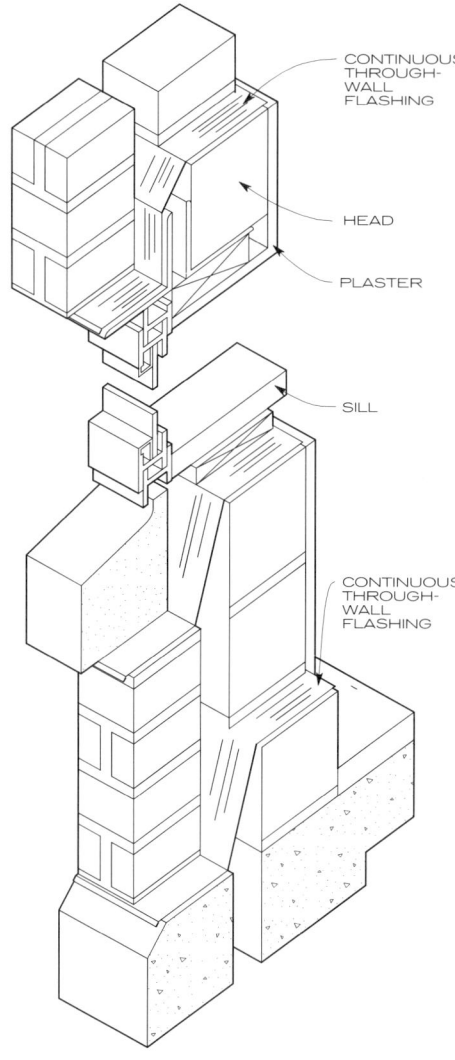

THROUGH-WALL FLASHING AT CAVITY WALL

THROUGH-WALL FLASHING INSTALLATION

GENERAL

Modern building materials are often waterproof, but they are not permanently impervious to wind-driven moisture. Gradual shrinkage of some materials and the natural movement of buildings can eventually cause leaks. When moisture enters walls it tends to form pockets of water, which eventually drain into the interior of the building, sometimes by gravity, other times by capillary action. This water will damage interiors, deface exteriors, disintegrate mortar and masonry, and rust steel spandrels, lintels, etc.

Flashings should be used wherever there is any possibility of water entering a structure. Through-wall flashing is the most successful method of permanently preventing leaks, except in areas exposed to earthquakes, where through-wall flashing is not recommended. Through-wall flashing is made of many different materials, including metals, plastics, and combinations of metals with paper, fabric, or rubber. Materials that are in contact must be compatible without deterioration.

Joints in flashings must be durable and waterproof and should usually lap 4 in. When the flashing is metal, joints should be soldered. Flashing should be extended to within $1/2$ in. of the exterior face. End- and edge-formed dams should be used where necessary to control drainage direction. Metal flashing that extends below grade is installed in reglets after the surface waterproofing has been applied below-grade.

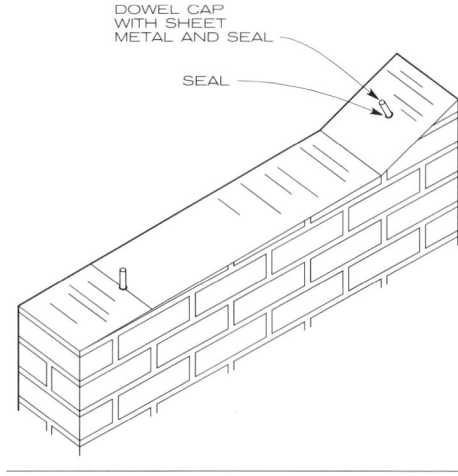

THROUGH-WALL FLASHING UNDER COPING

SMACNA, Inc., from the SMACNA Architectural Sheet Metal Manual, 5th ed., with permission
Valerie Eickelberger; Rippeteau Architects, PC; Washington, D.C.

Counterflashing Systems

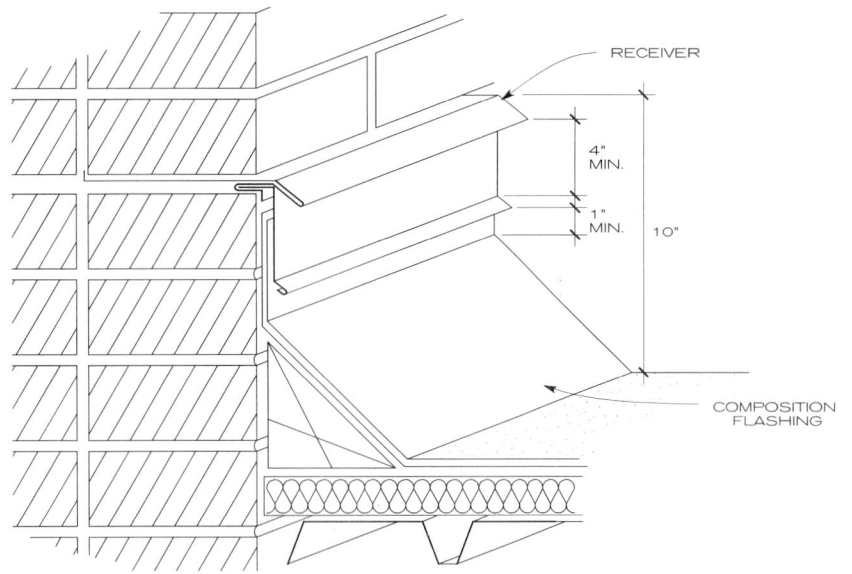

COUNTERFLASHING INSTALLATION

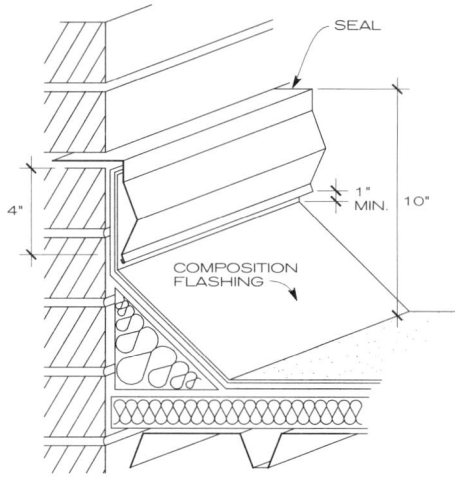

COUNTERFLASHING WITH RECEIVER

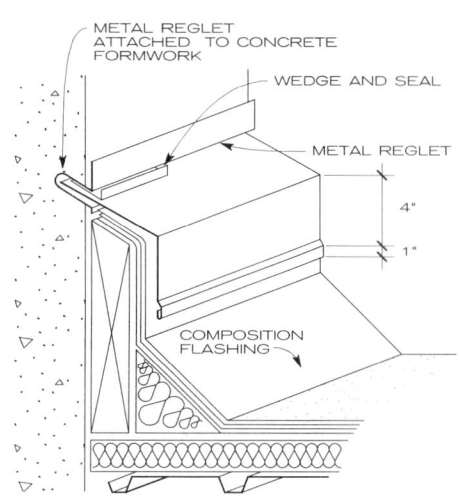

COUNTERFLASHING WITHOUT RECEIVER

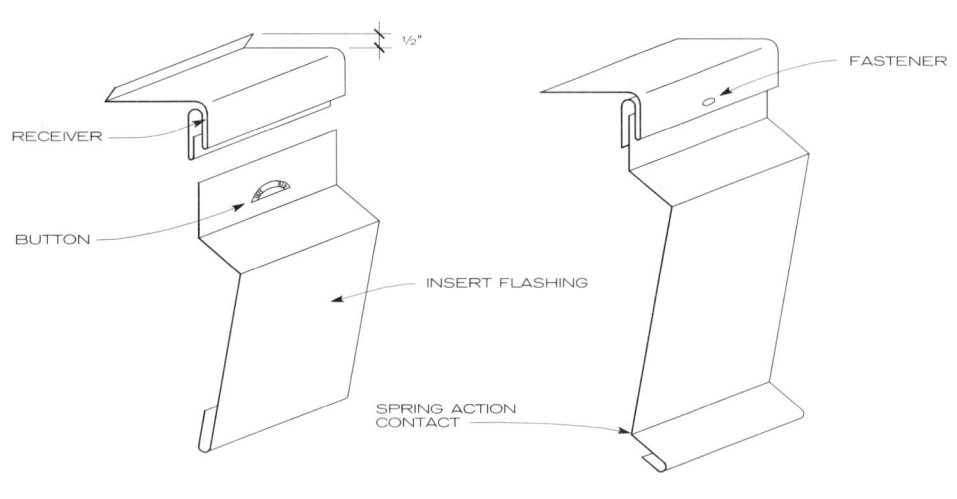

TWO-PIECE COUNTERFLASHING

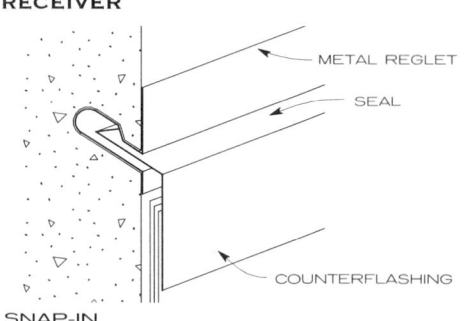

SNAP-IN

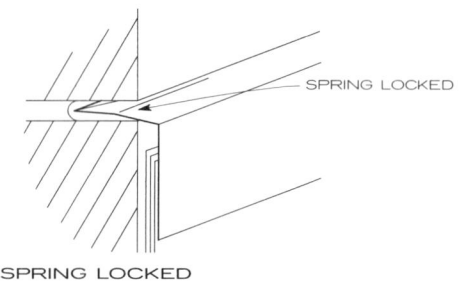

SPRING LOCKED

INSERT FLASHING DETAIL

GENERAL

Careful consideration must be given to flashing systems where a roof and wall meet. The base flashing system must keep water from entering the building and must allow for building movement. Counterflashing turns water away from a wall onto the roof or base flashing. The base flashing is usually inserted into a reglet, which must be capable of supporting the flashing. In high wind areas, clips can be specified for the lower edge of the counterflashing. Counterflashing that is removable is cost effective for the work installation sequence and for repair of roofing systems.

All membrane roofing should have removable counterflashing. Metal counterflashing should be used in conjunction with composition base flashing. Metal base flashings are used with shingle or metal roofs, but are not recommended for use with membrane roofing systems. A metal base flashing may be used over a composition flashing as a protective cover in locations where the base flashing may be abused by traffic. It is recommended that base flashings be applied over a cant and be extended up the wall a minimum of 10 in. above the roofline.

Receivers for counterflashing should be elevated 10 in. above the finished roof. Install metal counterflashing to cover a minimum of 4 in. of the base flashing. After the counterflashing is installed, the receiver is bent 45 degrees to provide a drip edge. The lower edge of metal counterflashing should be a minimum of 1 in. above a cant. The counterflashing is notched and lapped at inside corners and joints, and seamed at outside corners. The flashing receiver is notched and lapped 4 in. at corners and joints.

SMACNA, Inc., from the SMACNA Architectural Sheet Metal Manual, 5th ed., with permission
Valerie Eickelberger; Rippeteau Architects, PC; Washington, D.C.

FLASHING AND SHEET METAL

Counterflashing Systems

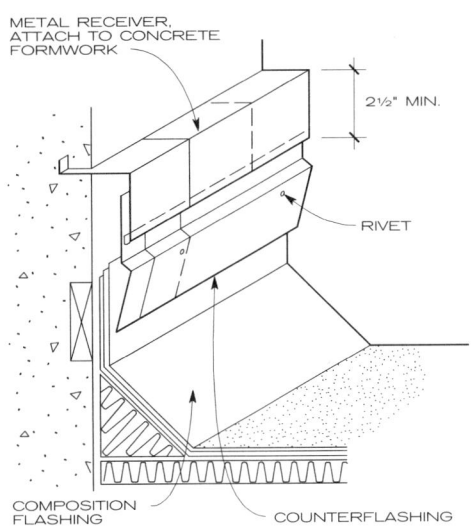
COUNTERFLASHING FOR CONCRETE

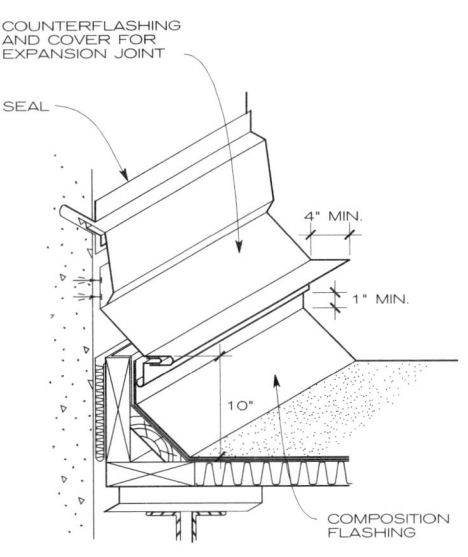
COUNTERFLASHING EXPANSION JOINT

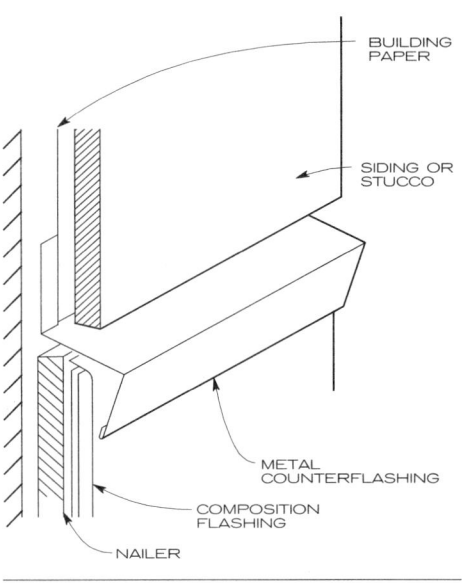
COUNTERFLASHING FOR NONMASONRY WALL

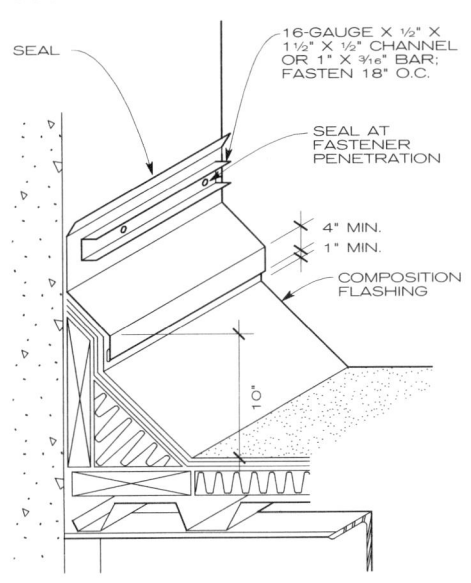
COUNTERFLASHING AT EXISTING WALL

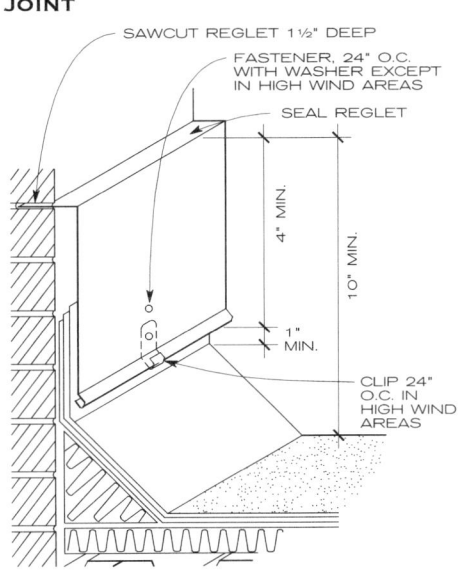
COUNTERFLASHING WITHOUT RECEIVER

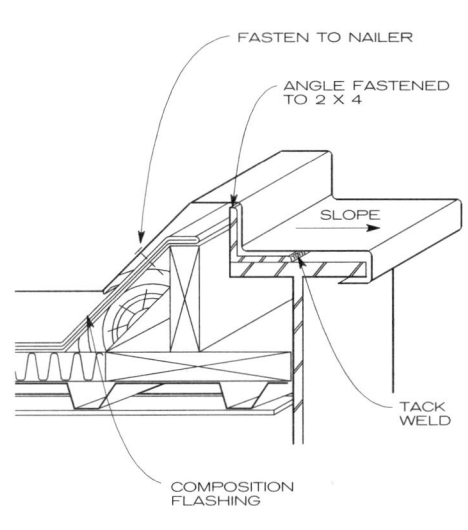
COUNTERFLASHING OVER STRUCTURAL STEEL

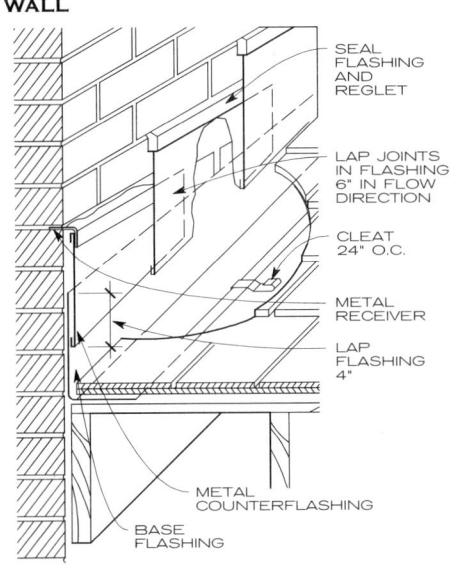
COUNTERFLASHING AT SLOPED ROOF

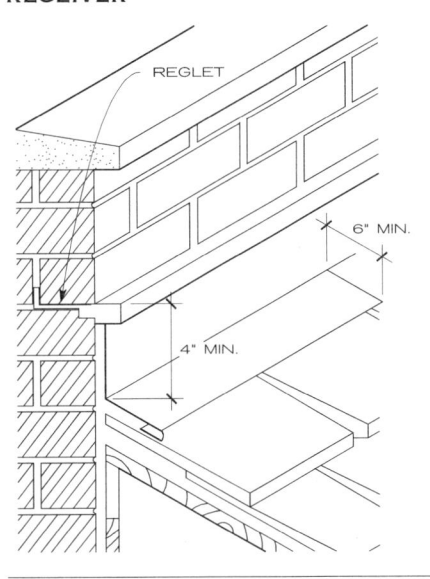
COUNTERFLASHING AT SLOPED ROOF

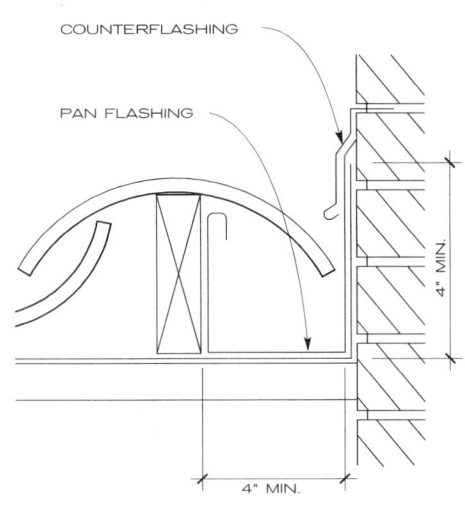
COUNTERFLASHING AT TILE ROOF

SMACNA, Inc., from the SMACNA Architectural Sheet Metal Manual, 5th ed., with permission
Valerie Eickelberger; Rippeteau Architects, PC; Washington, D.C.

FLASHING AND SHEET METAL

100 Flashing Specialty Details

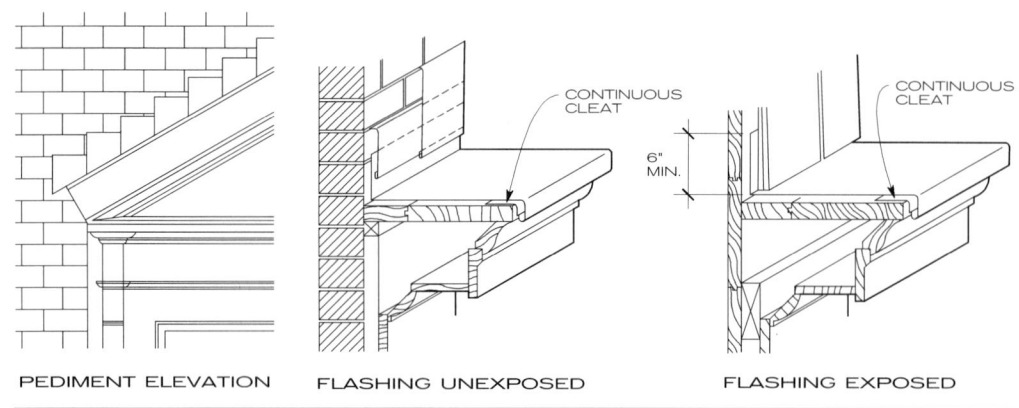

WOOD PEDIMENT LEDGE FLASHING

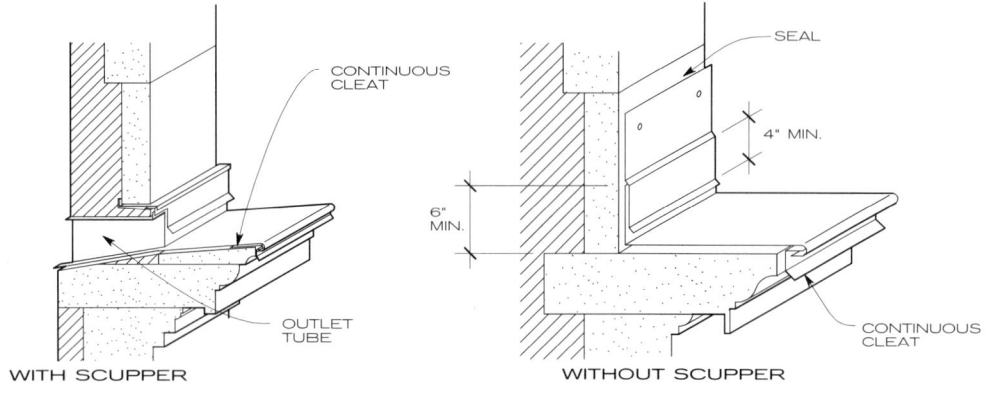

STONE LEDGE FLASHING

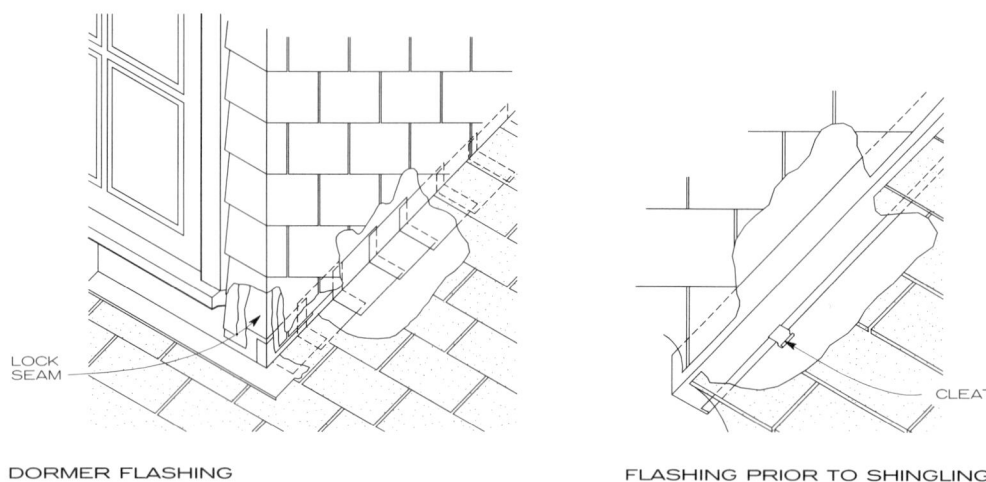

DORMER FLASHING

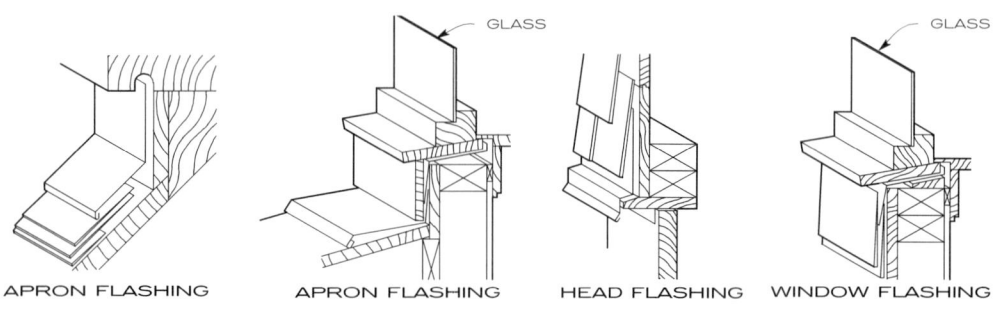

DORMER FLASHING DETAILS

FOUNDATION WALL

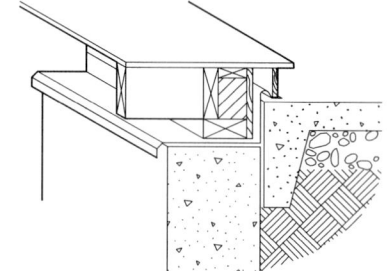

FOUNDATION WALL WITH PORCH FLOOR

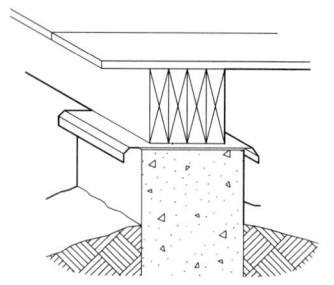

INTERNAL SUPPORT WALL

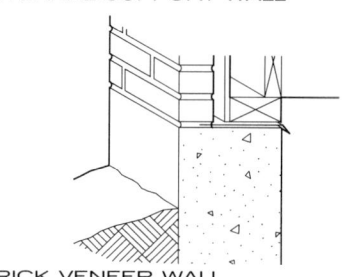

BRICK VENEER WALL

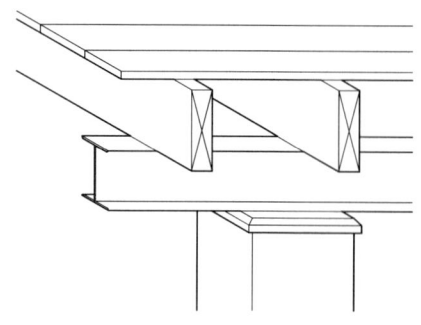

INTERNAL FLOOR SUPPORT

NOTES

1. Termite shields may be fabricated of copper or galvanized steel. Aluminum may be used except where masonry is above the termite shield.
2. Joints should be lapped 3/4 in. and soldered or flat locked. Corners should be notched, filled, and soldered.

TERMITE SHIELDS

SMACNA, Inc., from the SMACNA Architectural Sheet Metal Manual, 5th ed., with permission
Valerie Eickelberger; Rippeteau Architects, PC; Washington, D.C.

FLASHING AND SHEET METAL

Mansard-Type Metal Roofing

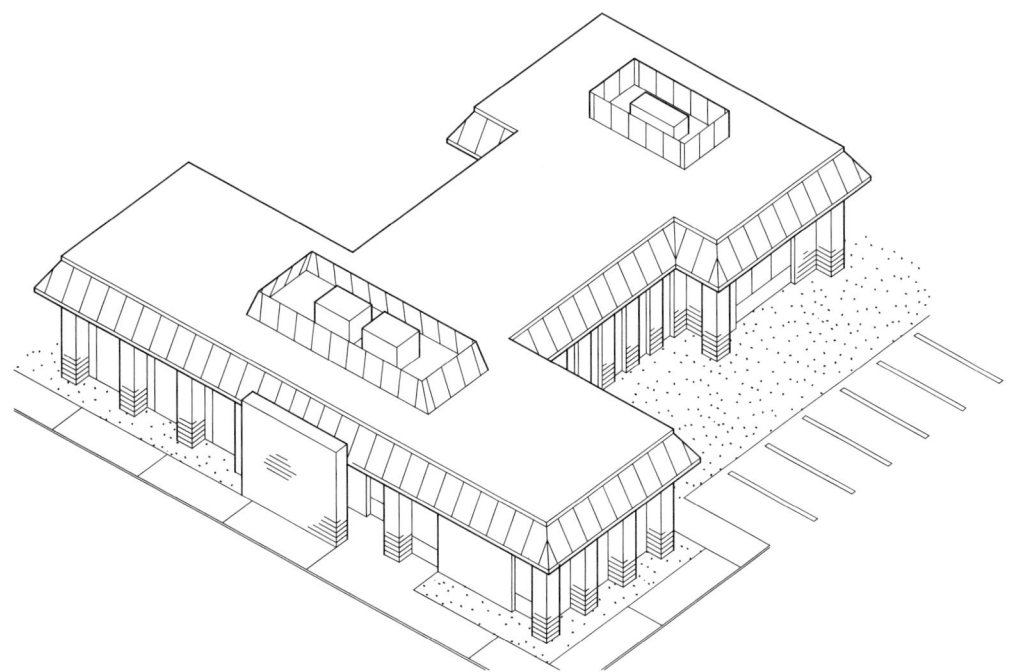

TYPICAL MANSARD ROOF

SELF-SUPPORTING ROOF

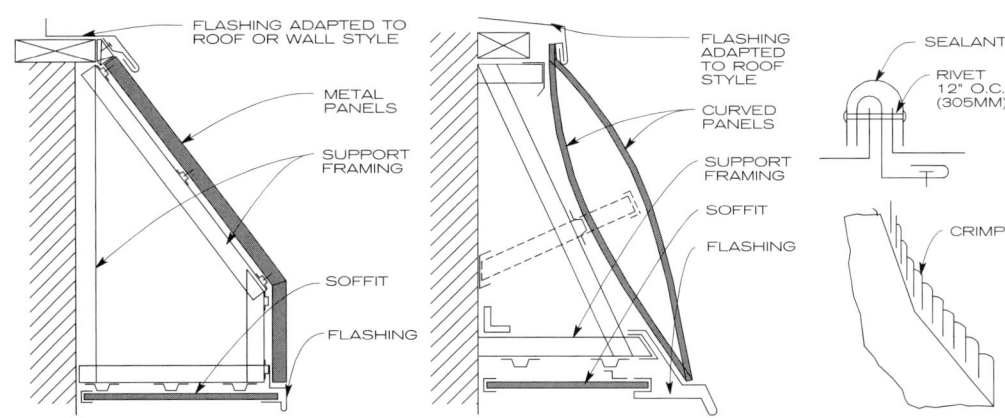

CONTINUOUSLY SUPPORTED ROOF

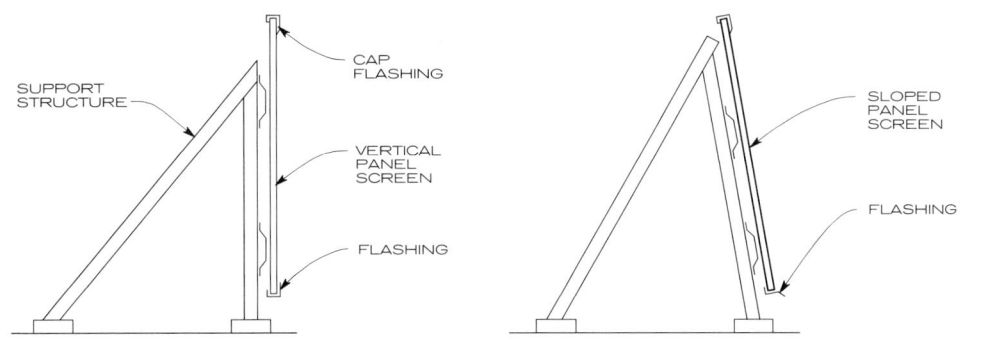

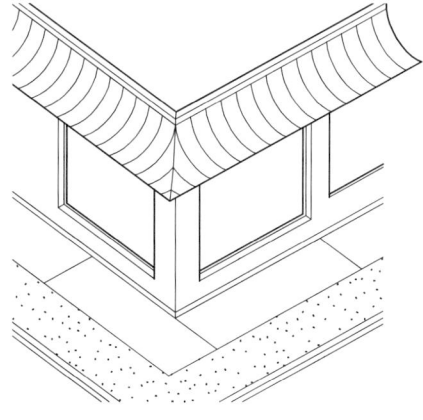

ORNAMENTAL ROOF CANOPY

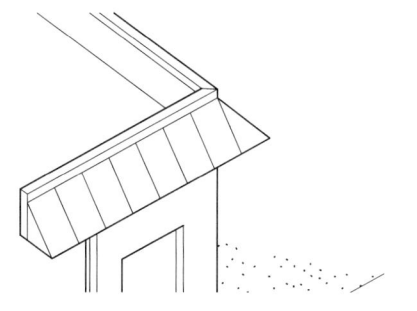

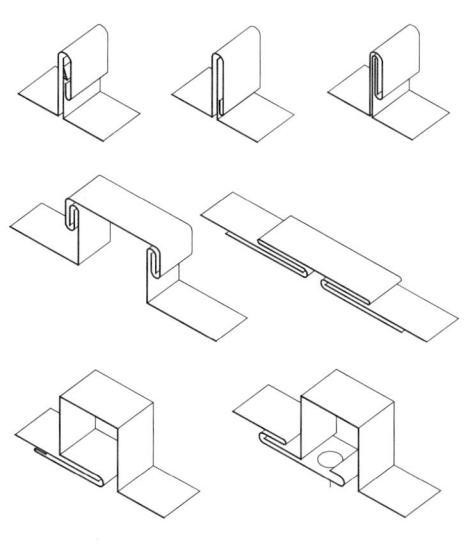

SEAM PROFILES

METAL MANSARD ROOFS

Metal mansard roofs are typically used on one-story commercial structures. Often they conceal rooftop equipment, using batten screens or louvered enclosures. Metal mansard roofs are also used for flat or curved ornamental roofs or canopies for the front of buildings.

Aluminum, copper, stainless steel, galvanized steel, or prefinished metals may be used for metal mansard roofs. The metal can be prefabricated for several styles of field connection using various seam configurations. Prefinished metals used in curved applications typically have a 15-ft radius limit. Concave or convex panels normally have a 24-in. minimum radius for standing seams and a 72-in. minimum radius for batten seams. Soft metals are used when the metal must be stretched.

Metal mansard roofs may be continuously supported or self-supporting. Continuously supported roofs have a continuous sheathing substrate. Self-supporting roofs have structural framing with vertical and horizontal members located where needed for metal panel attachment. Mansard roofs require cap and sill flashing.

SMACNA, Inc., from the SMACNA Architectural Sheet Metal Manual, 5th ed., with permission
Valerie Eickelberger; Rippeteau Architects, PC; Washington, D.C.

FLASHING AND SHEET METAL

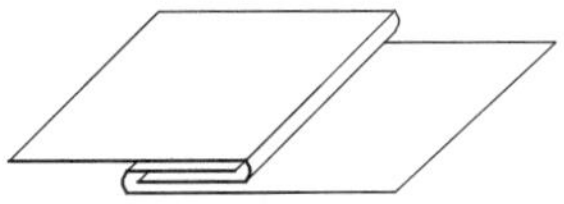

Metal Roofing—Locks and Seams

COMMON (CLINCH) LOCK, HOOK SEAM

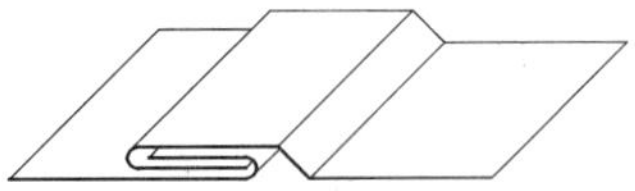

FLAT LOCK SEAM

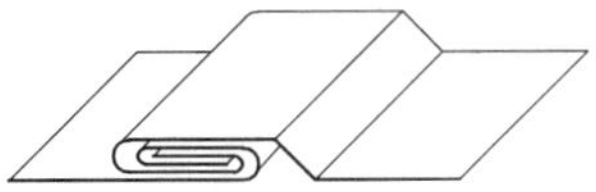

DOUBLE FLAT LOCK SEAM

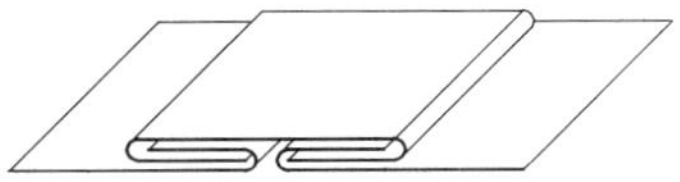

DRIVE CLEAT OR LOCK

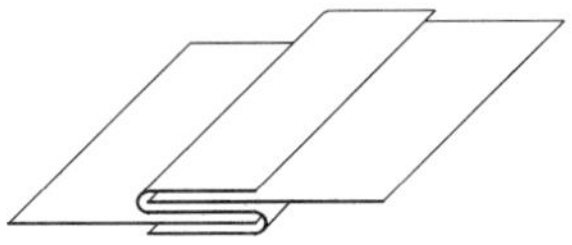

S CLEAT OR LOCK

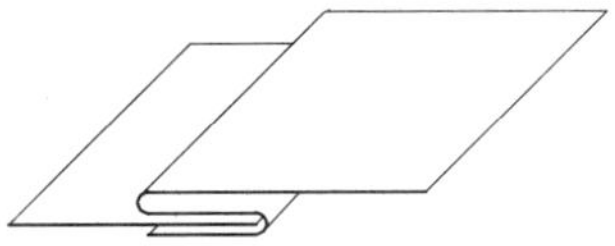

S POCKET

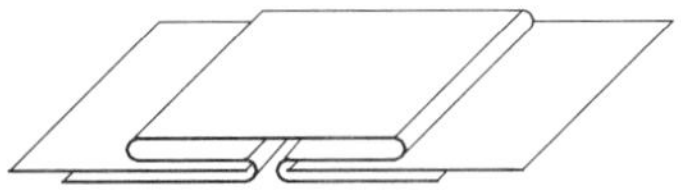

DOUBLE S SEAM

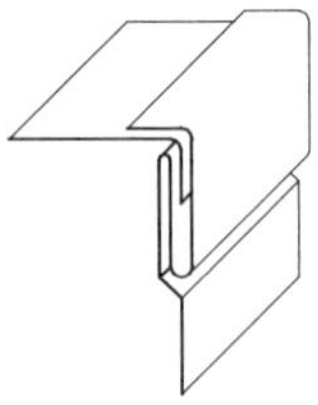

PITTSBURGH LOCK

SINGLE CORNER SEAM

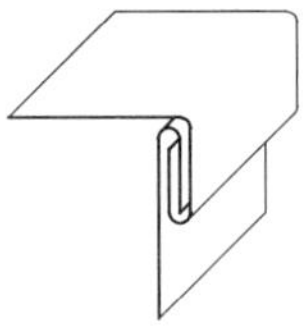

DOUBLE CORNER SEAM

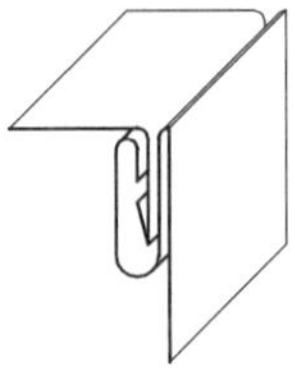

BUTTON LOCK CORNER SEAM

LOCK SEAM

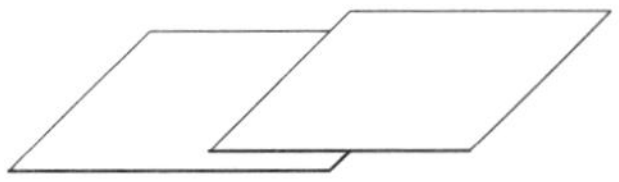

LAP SEAM

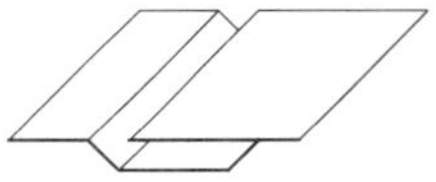

JOGGLE LAP

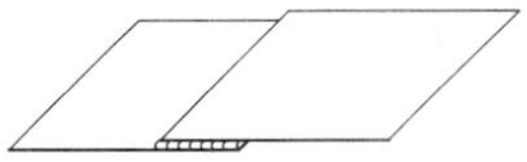

SOLDERED LAP SEAM

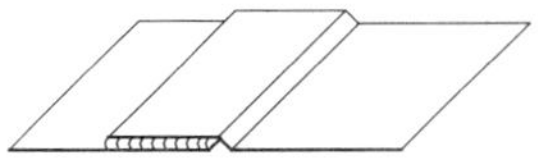

SOLDERED LAP SEAM FOR HEAVY-GAUGE METAL

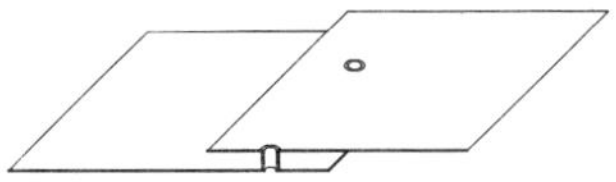

RIVETED LAP SEAM

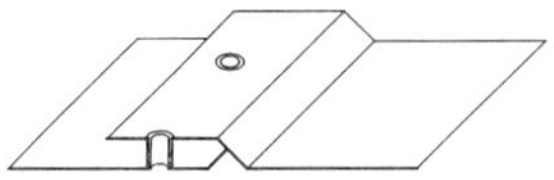

RIVETED LAP SEAM FOR HEAVY-GAUGE METAL

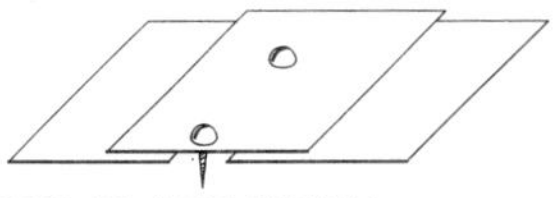

COVERED PLATE SEAM

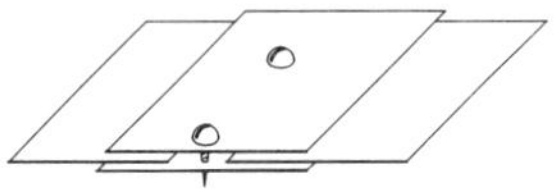

COVERED PLATE WITH BACKUP PLATE

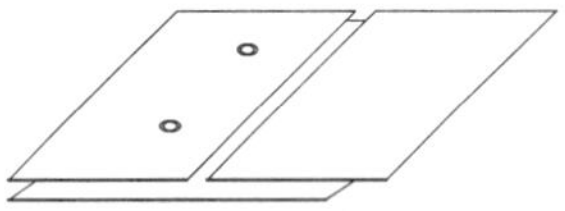

BUTT SEAM WITH BACKUP PLATE, FASTENED ONE SIDE

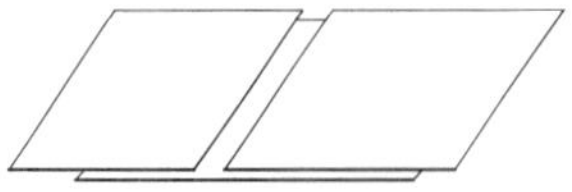

BUTT SEAM WITH BACKUP PLATE, FASTENING OPTIONAL

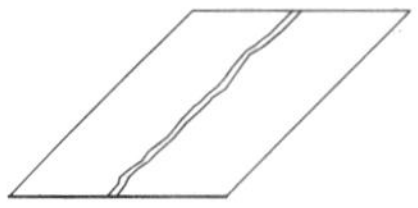

WELDED JOINT

FLAT SEAM

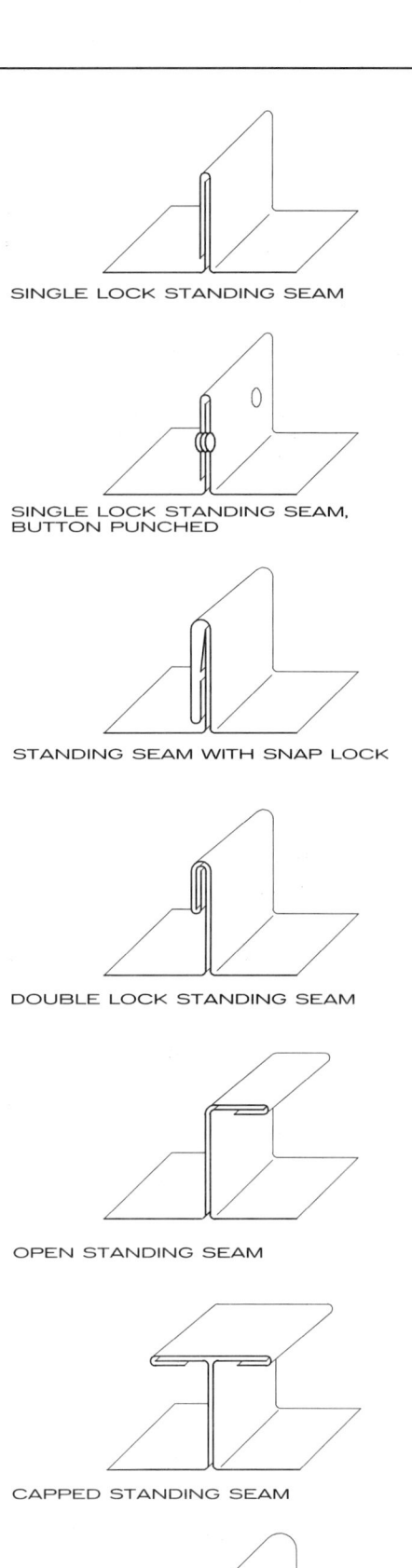

SINGLE LOCK STANDING SEAM

SINGLE LOCK STANDING SEAM, BUTTON PUNCHED

STANDING SEAM WITH SNAP LOCK

DOUBLE LOCK STANDING SEAM

OPEN STANDING SEAM

CAPPED STANDING SEAM

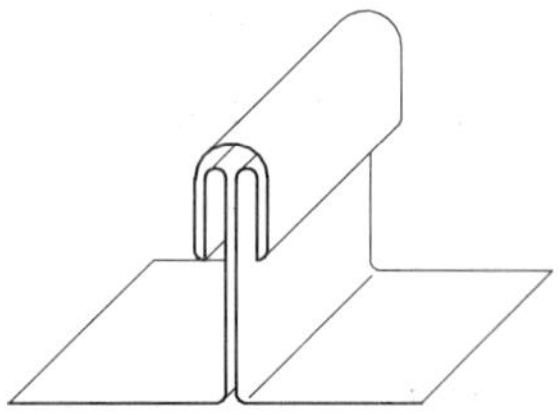

SNAP CAP STANDING SEAM

STANDING SEAM

SMACNA, Inc., from the SMACNA Architectural Sheet Metal Manual, 5th ed., with permission
Valerie Eickelberger; Rippeteau Architects, PC; Washington, D.C.

FLASHING AND SHEET METAL

Metal Roofing Retrofit for Problematic Flat Roof

GENERAL

Structural metal panels are used in roofing applications when removal of the existing roof membrane is too costly or undesirable. Metal panel roofs are durable, have good wind and fire resistance ratings, and require little maintenance. The panels are manufactured either from steel or aluminum and are mechanically seamed on the job site. Sealants in tape or gel form are used as a gasket between metal connections. The sealant, applied in the female corrugation to make the roof more weathertight, allows the panels to expand and contract independently of the insulation and structural systems.

Two-part clips concealed inside the standing seams accommodate thermal expansion and eliminate the need for fasteners in the flat parts of the panel. The top part of the clip holds the metal panel, while the base of the clip is fastened to the structural member. A slot between the two parts of the clips allows independent movement. The concealed clip also provides the attachment necessary for wind uplift ratings.

Structural metal roofs can be used with slopes as low as 1/4 in. per ft but may also be used in a steep slope configuration. The panels are available in a wide variety of colors and typically have corrosion-resistant coatings.

Before adding the weight of structural metal roof panels to a building, it is important to verify the load-bearing capacity of the existing roof structure.

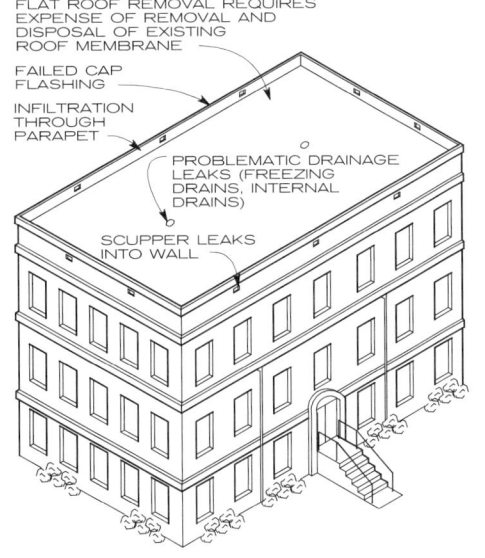

EXISTING PROBLEMATIC FLAT ROOF

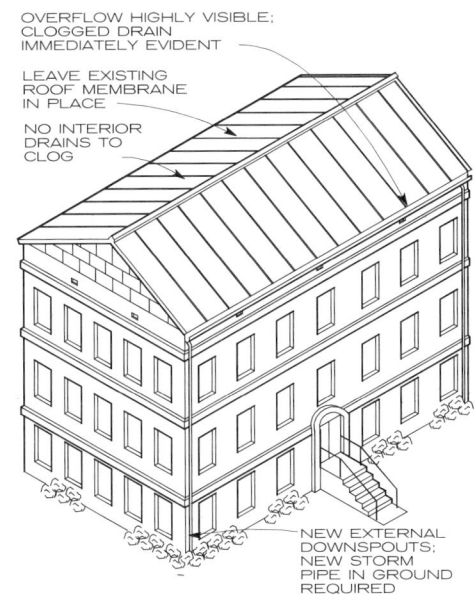

RETROFIT WITH METAL PANEL ROOF

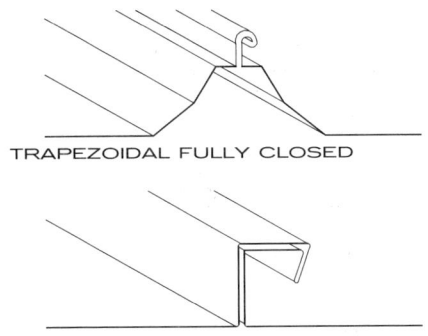

SEAM TYPES FOR METAL ROOFING PANELS

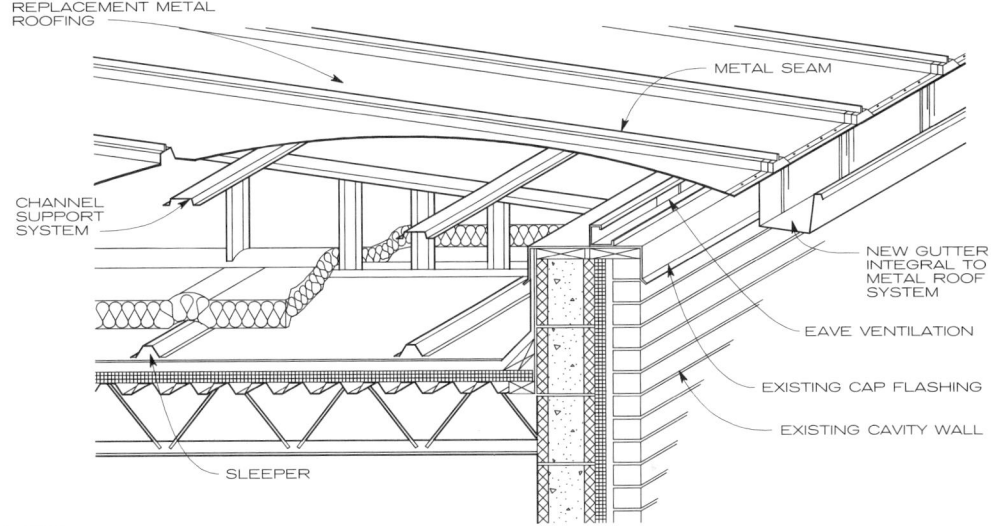

NOTE
Design sleeper to distribute roof load adequately over the roof surface. Consider compressibility of insulation and condition of membrane. Provide bearing plates and hold-down clips as necessary.

BUILDING SECTION THROUGH ROOF SYSTEM

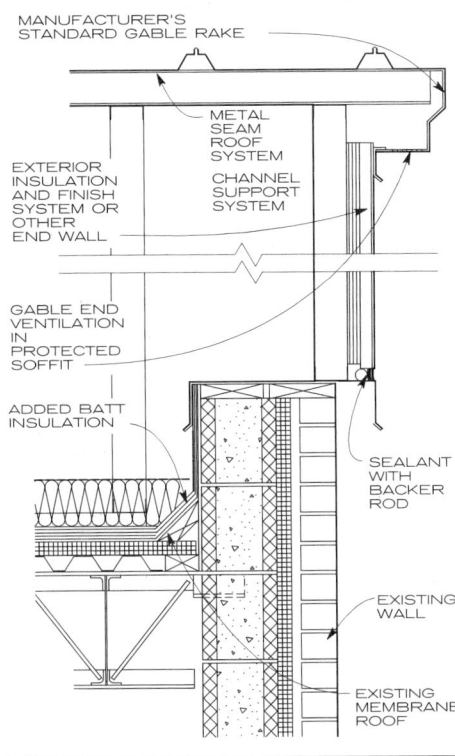

GABLE END WALL

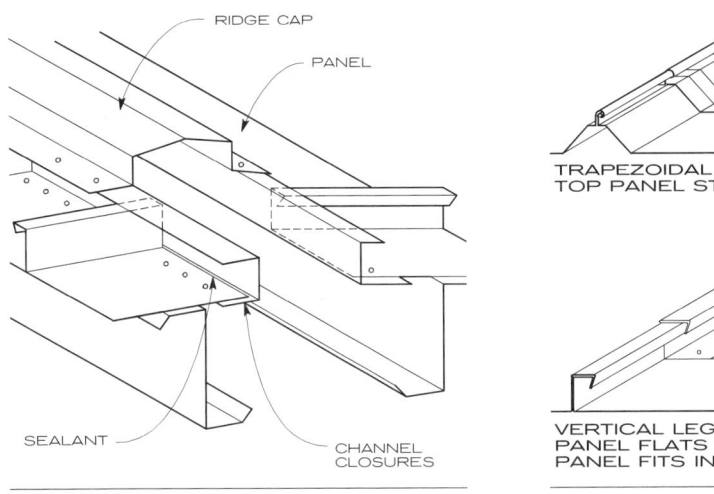

RIDGE CAP FOR METAL ROOFING PANELS

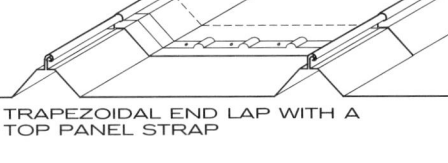

TRAPEZOIDAL END LAP WITH A TOP PANEL STRAP

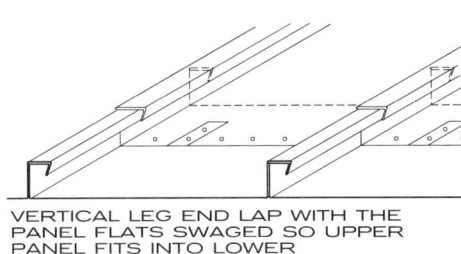

VERTICAL LEG END LAP WITH THE PANEL FLATS SWAGED SO UPPER PANEL FITS INTO LOWER

END LAPS FOR METAL ROOFING PANELS

Valerie Eickelberger; Rippeteau Architects, PC; Washington, D.C.
Paul Nimitz; PDN Associates; Blue Springs, Montana

Roof and Parapet Expansion Joints

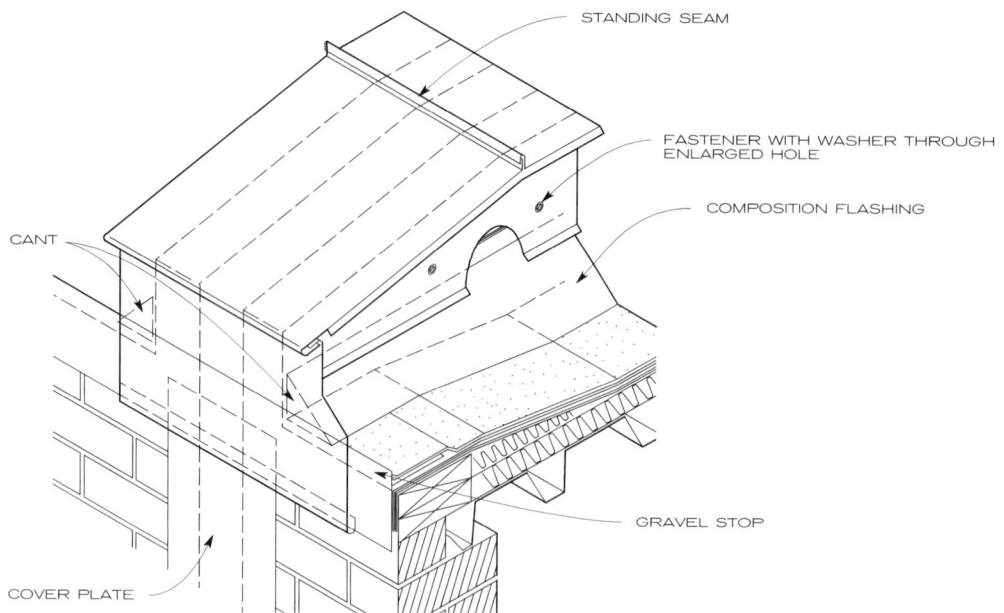

EXPANSION JOINT AT GRAVEL STOP

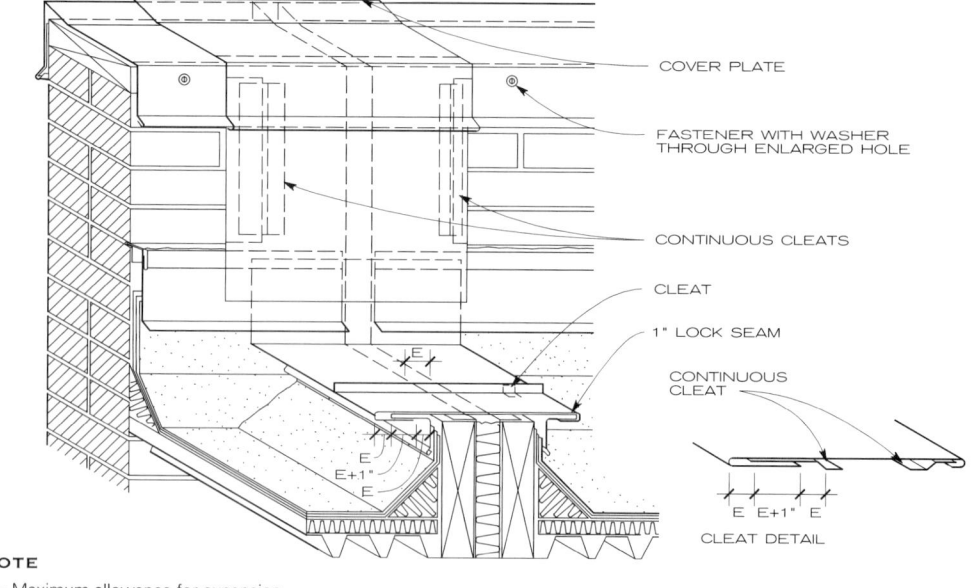

NOTE
E = Maximum allowance for expansion.

EXPANSION JOINT AT PARAPET

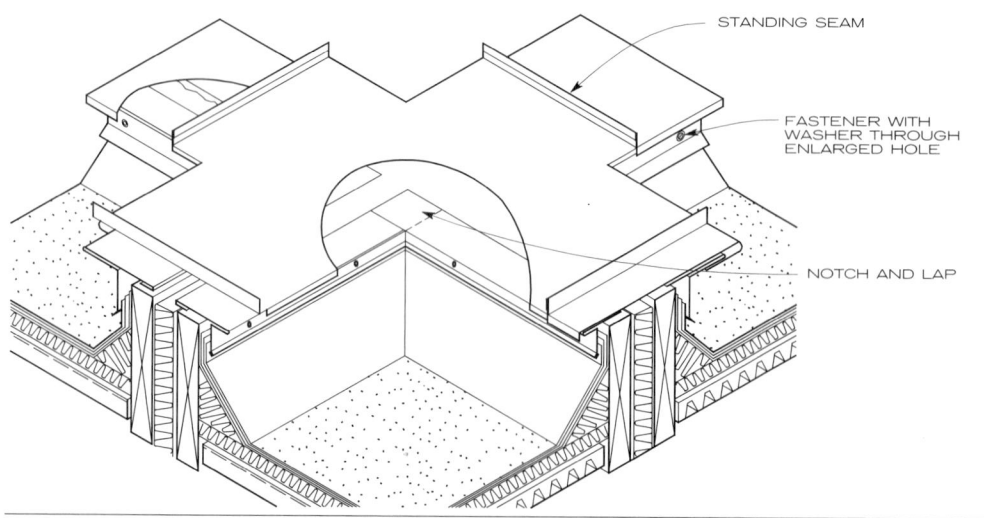

EXPANSION JOINT INTERSECTION

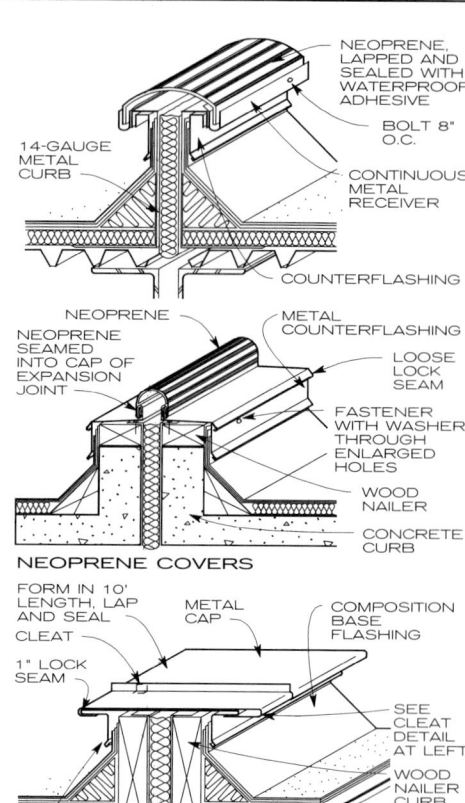

NEOPRENE COVERS

METAL COVER

NOTES

1. The minimum recommended gauge for the expansion joint shown is 24-gauge stainless steel, 16 oz copper, 22-gauge galvanized steel, or 0.050 in. aluminum.
2. Expansion joints allow independent movement of the roof structure.

ROOF EXPANSION JOINT

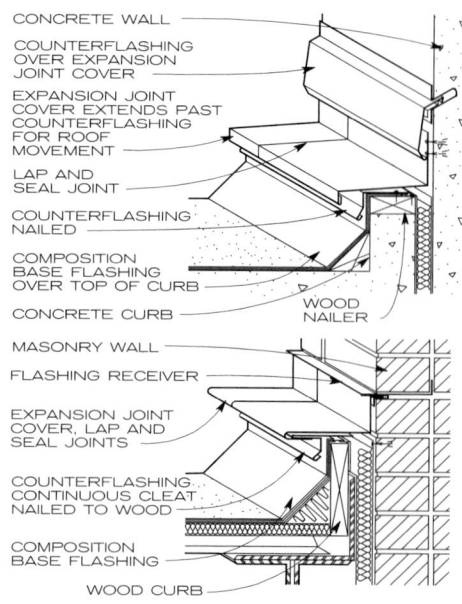

ROOF-TO-WALL EXPANSION JOINT

NOTES

1. The minimum recommended gauge for the expansion joint shown is 24-gauge stainless steel, 16 oz copper, 22-gauge galvanized steel, or 0.050 in. aluminum.
2. Expansion joints allow independent movement of the roof structure.

SMACNA, Inc., from the SMACNA Architectural Sheet Metal Manual, 5th ed., with permission
Valerie Eickelberger; Rippeteau Architects, PC; Washington, D.C.

ROOF SPECIALTIES AND ACCESSORIES

Scuppers

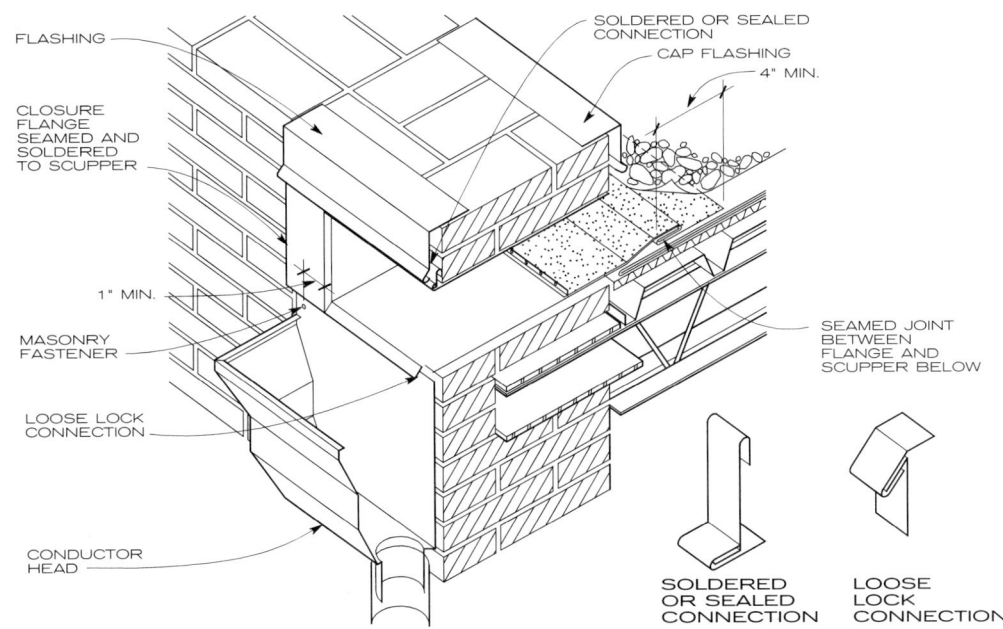

SCUPPER DETAIL AT PARAPET WALL (CONDUCTOR HEAD SIDE)

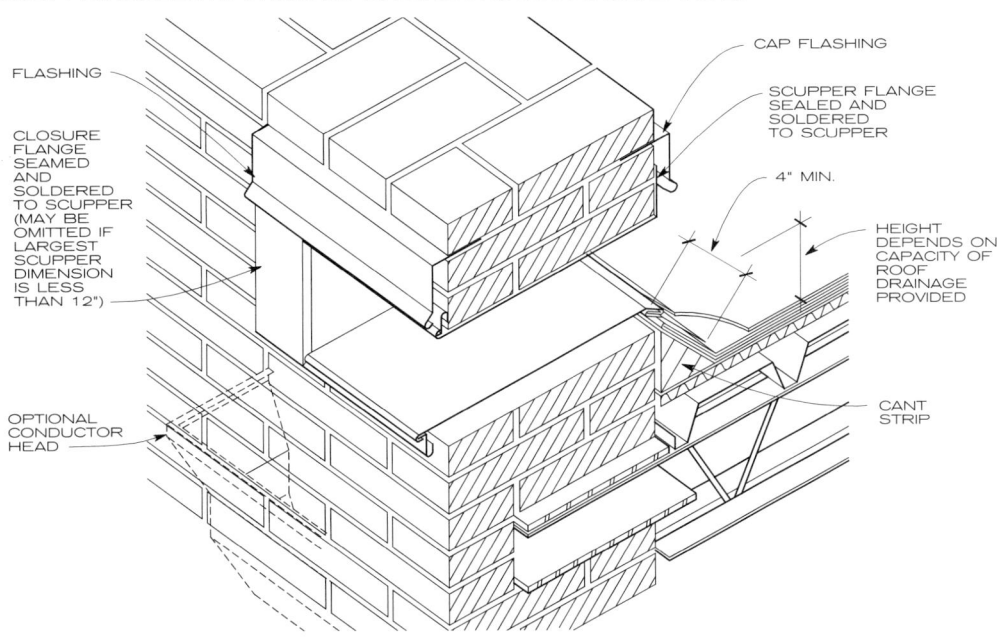

NOTES

1. Use overflow scuppers when roof is completely surrounded by parapets and drainage depends on scuppers or internal damage.
2. Precast concrete panels with scuppers do not need closure flanges on face; all penetrations should be seated.

OVERFLOW SCUPPER DETAIL AT PARAPET WALL

SCUPPER CAPACITY IN GPM*

HEAD (H)(IN.)	LENGTH (L) OF WEIR (IN.)									
	4	6	8	10	12	18	24	30	36	48
1	11.0	17.4	23.40	29.3	35.4	53.4	71.5	89.5	107.5	143.2
2	30.5	47.5	64.4	81.4	98.3	149.1	200.0	251.1	302.0	403.4
3	52.9	84.1	115.2	146.3	177.5	270.9	364.3	457.7	551.1	737.9
4	76.7	124.6	172.6	220.5	269.0	412.3	556.1	700.0	843.7	1133.3
6	123.3	211.4	299.4	387.5	475.5	739.7	1003.9	1268.1	1532.3	2060.7

*Based on the Francis formula: $Q = 3.33 (L - 0.2H) H^{1.5}$, in which

Q = Flow rate, cubic ft per second

L = Length of scupper opening, ft (should be 4 to 8 times H)

H = Head on scupper, ft (measured 6 ft back from opening)

1 GPM = 448.8 CFS

GENERAL

The size and number of scuppers should be carefully determined to control ponding on roofs. Rectangular shapes convey more water (per inch of water depth on the roof) than round shapes. The performance of rectangular shapes approximates that of a broad-crested weir. Standard equations for channel flow are based on test models larger than typical roof scuppers. While downspout sizes normally are based on draining a given area of roof, that flow rate may not pass through a scupper that has been sized to have a cross-sectional area equal to the downspout area.

SCUPPER SIZING PROCEDURES

1. Determine the head (H) in inches of water (typically 1 in. minimum by code) at a point 6 ft back from the scupper opening.
2. Determine the roof drainage area in sq ft (SF).
3. Using rainfall intensity in inches per hour (IPH) from a rainfall data table, determine discharge capacity in gallons per minute (GPM). GPM = SF of room area x IPH x 0.0104. The constant is 7.48 gallons per cubic foot divided by 12 inches per foot divided by 60 minutes per hour:

   GPM = (0.0104) IPH x SF
4. Using H and the GPM, find the aggregate scupper length (L) in the scupper capacity table (below).
5. Select enough individual scuppers to satisfy the total GPM requirement and locate them proportionately.

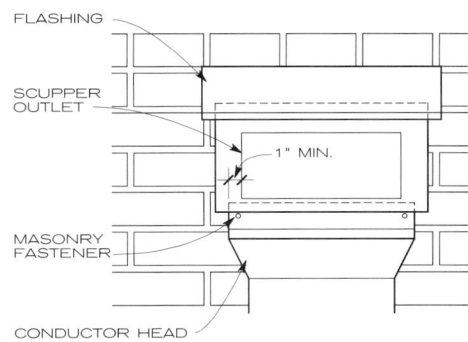

NOTE

Scupper assemblies from top to bottom (flashing to scupper outlet to conductor head) should be overlapped to ensure that water will be directed away from the wall.

SCUPPER ASSEMBLY ELEVATION

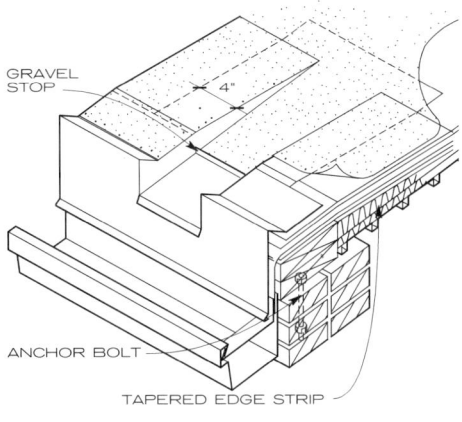

NOTE

Scuppers that empty into a gutter may be integrated with a roof edge. The scuppers are soldered into a formed gravel stop-fascia system. The suggested maximum scupper interval is 10 ft. The front rim of the gutter must be 1 in. below the back edge, and it should be below the nailers used to elevate the roof edge. The drip edge on the fascia should lap the back edge of the gutter a minimum of 1 in. The gutter must be free to move behind the fascia.

COMBINATION SCUPPER AND GUTTER

SMACNA, Inc., from the SMACNA Architectural Sheet Metal Manual, 5th ed., with permission
Grace S. Lee; Rippeteau Architects, PC; Washington, D.C.

Special Roofing Details

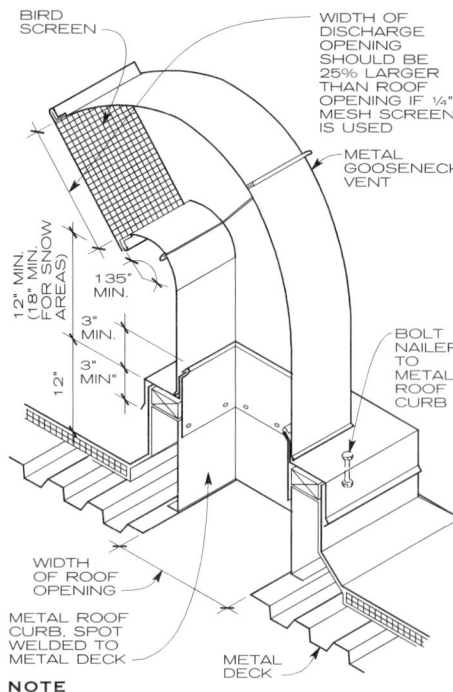

NOTE

This ventilator may be used for either intake or exhaust with gravity flow.

GOOSENECK GRAVITY VENTILATOR

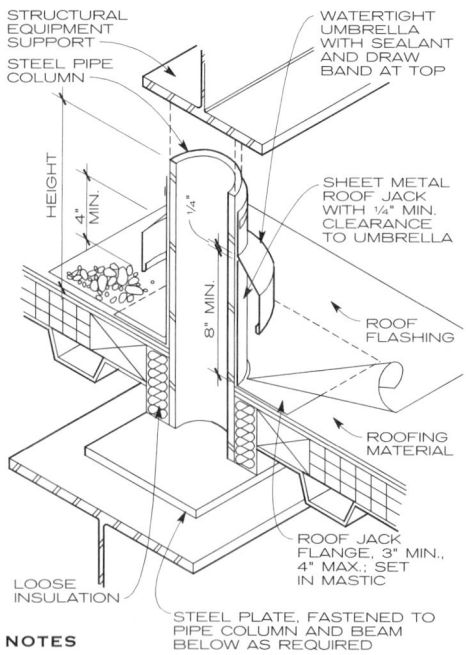

NOTES

1. This detail can be adapted for other uses, such as sign supports.
2. Many roofing manufacturers offer prefabricated flashing pieces or permit the use of materials other than those shown here for flashing. Specifications on these proprietary designs vary; consult the manufacturers.
3. For access to areas underneath equipment, vary pipe column height as shown in the accompanying chart.

COLUMN EQUIPMENT SUPPORT

PIPE COLUMN HEIGHT

EQUIPMENT WIDTH (IN.)	COLUMN HEIGHT (IN.)
Up to 24	14
25 to 36	18
37 to 48	24
49 to 60	30
61 and wider	48

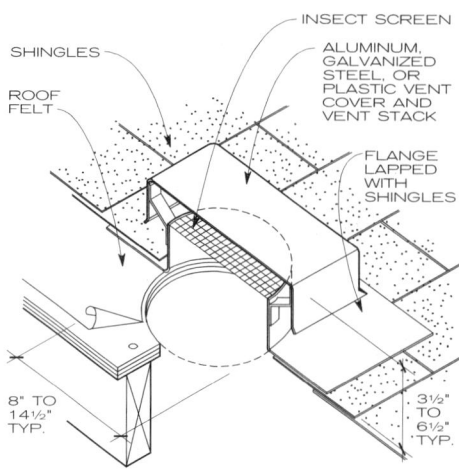

ROOF VENT IN SLOPED ROOF

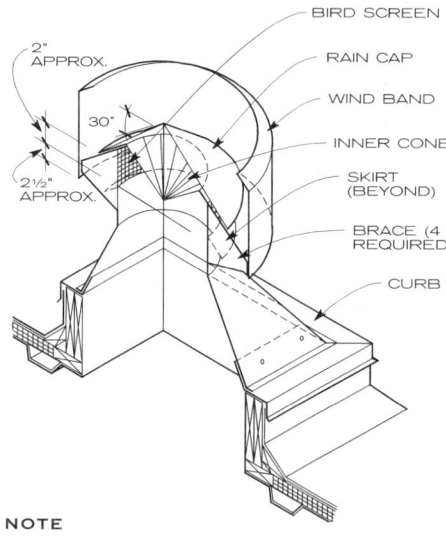

NOTE

All sloped partial or full conical shapes should be based on the same angle (generally 30°).

STATIONARY GRAVITY ROOF VENTILATOR

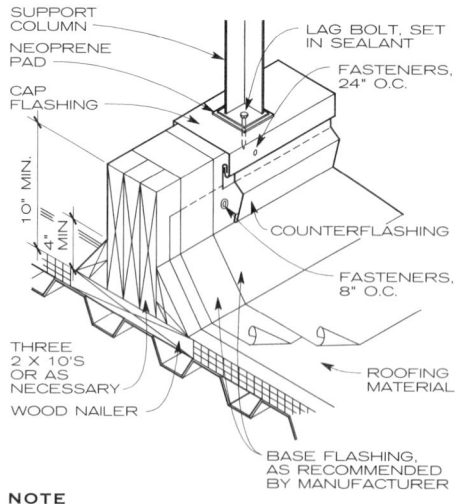

NOTE

This detail allows for roof maintenance around the equipment or sign. The continuous support, in contrast to the point load of a pipe column support, is preferred for lightweight roof systems. Clearance must be provided for removal and replacement of roofing and flashing between parallel supports.

CONTINUOUS EQUIPMENT SUPPORT CURB

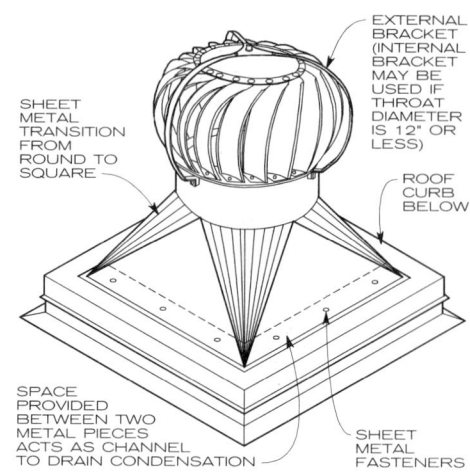

NOTE

This ventilator may be used on a sloped roof.

ROTATING VENTILATOR

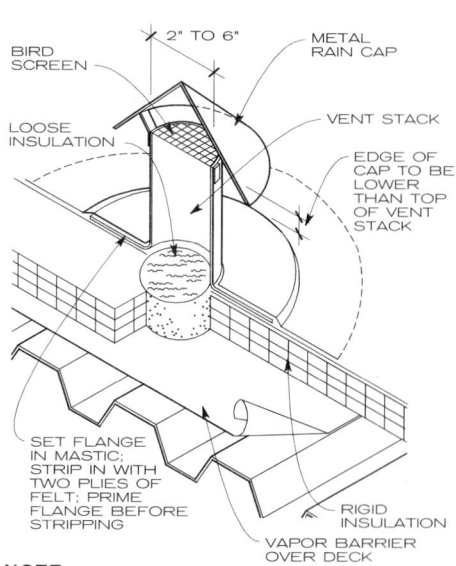

NOTE

This detail allows moisture due to leaks, faulty vapor barriers, or construction work to escape from the roof system.

ROOF RELIEF VENT

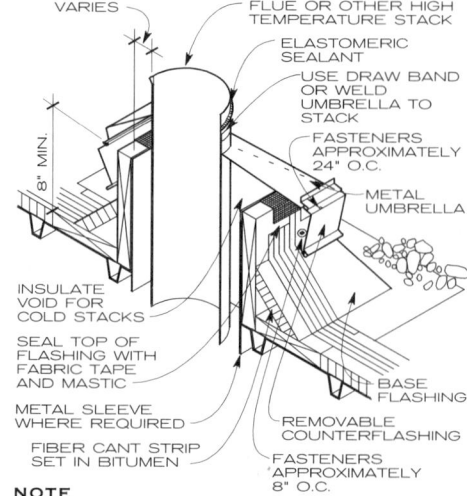

NOTE

This detail allows the opening to be completed before the stack is placed. The metal sleeve and the clearance necessary will depend on the temperature of the material handled by the stack.

FLUE STACK ROOF PENETRATION

Richard J. Vitullo, AIA; Oak Leaf Studio; Crownsville, Maryland

Special Roofing Details

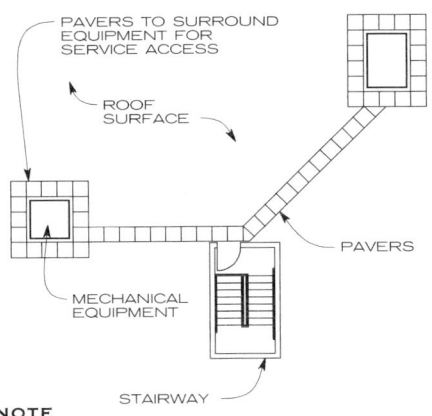

NOTE

Roof pavers provide a stable walking service on any flat roof surface and protect the roof membrane from wear and tear. Service walkways should follow the most direct route to equipment to avoid shortcuts by maintenance personnel. Consult mechanical engineer about access needed to mechanical equipment.

SERVICE WALKWAYS ON ROOFS

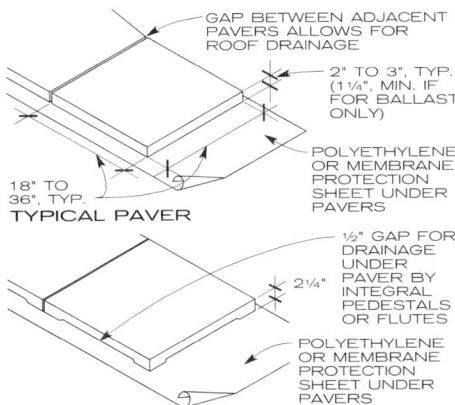

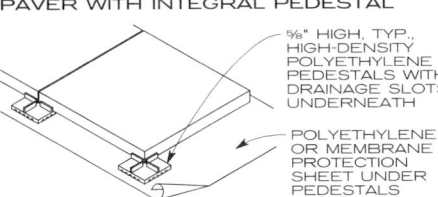

NOTE

Ballast pavers are typically made from precast concrete with a non-skid texture on the surface.

BALLAST PAVERS

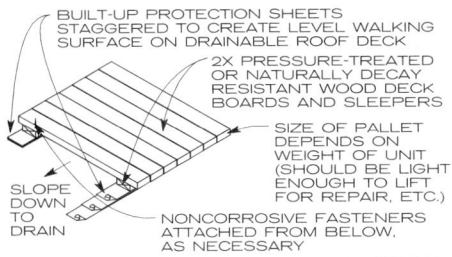

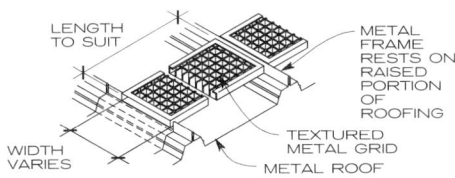

MISCELLANEOUS ROOF WALKING SURFACES

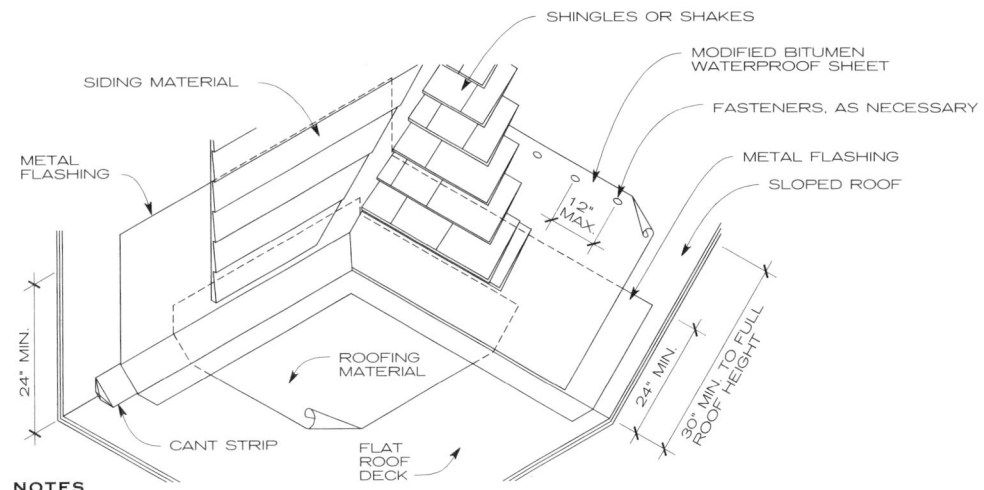

NOTES

1. Modified bitumen sheet specified to provide self-sealing around fastener.
2. Height of flashing and waterproof sheet depends on local snow probabilities and codes and on the roof slope.

WATERPROOFING AT ROOF TRANSITIONS

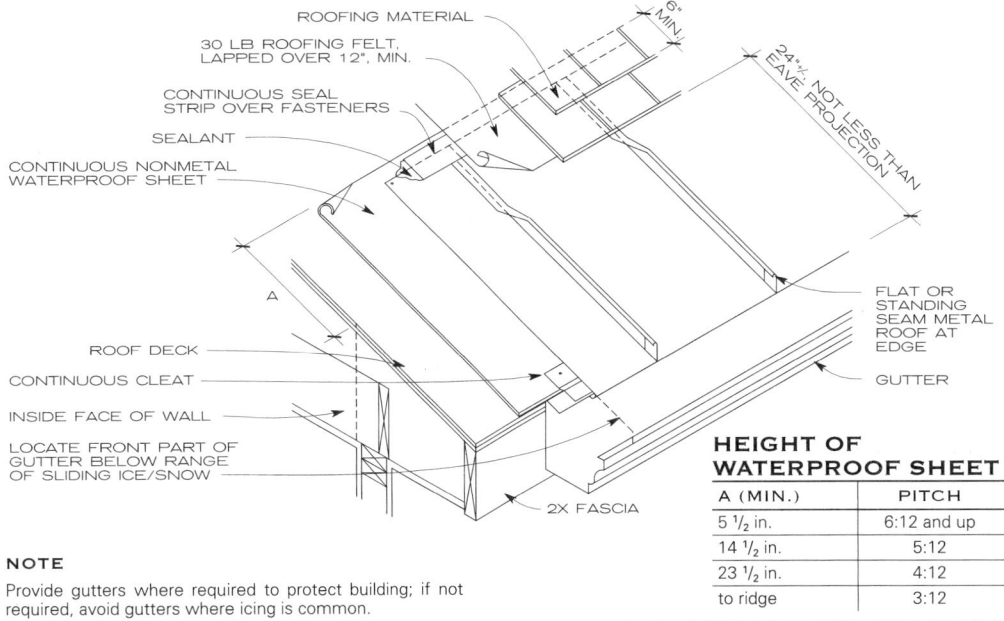

HEIGHT OF WATERPROOF SHEET

A (MIN.)	PITCH
5 1/2 in.	6:12 and up
14 1/2 in.	5:12
23 1/2 in.	4:12
to ridge	3:12

NOTE

Provide gutters where required to protect building; if not required, avoid gutters where icing is common.

ICE DAM DETAILING AT EAVE WITH GUTTER

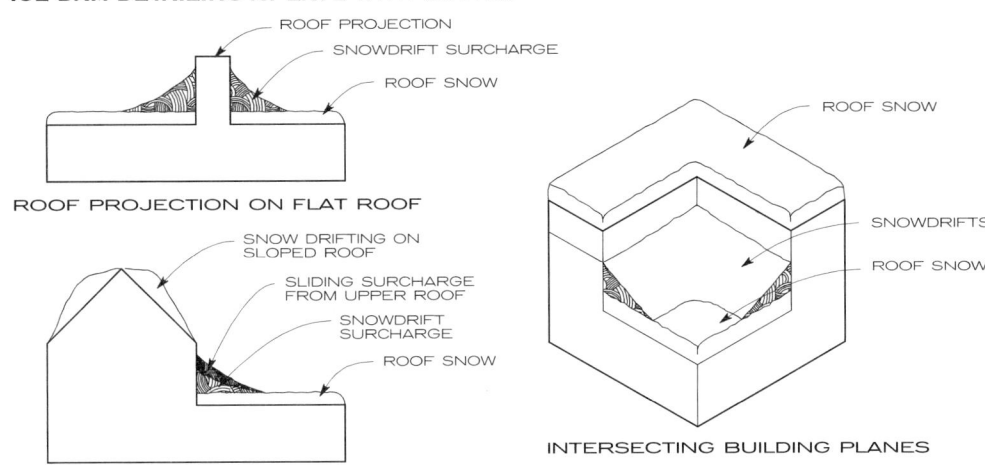

NOTES

1. Consult codes for projected local snow heights.
2. Snow accumulation on roofs is generally unequal due to wind action. The resulting unequal load distribution might be aggravated by unequal melting of accumulated snow.

SNOW TENDENCIES ON BUILDING SURFACES

Richard J. Vitullo, AIA; Oak Leaf Studio; Crownsville, Maryland

ROOF SPECIALTIES AND ACCESSORIES

Roof Repair Strategies

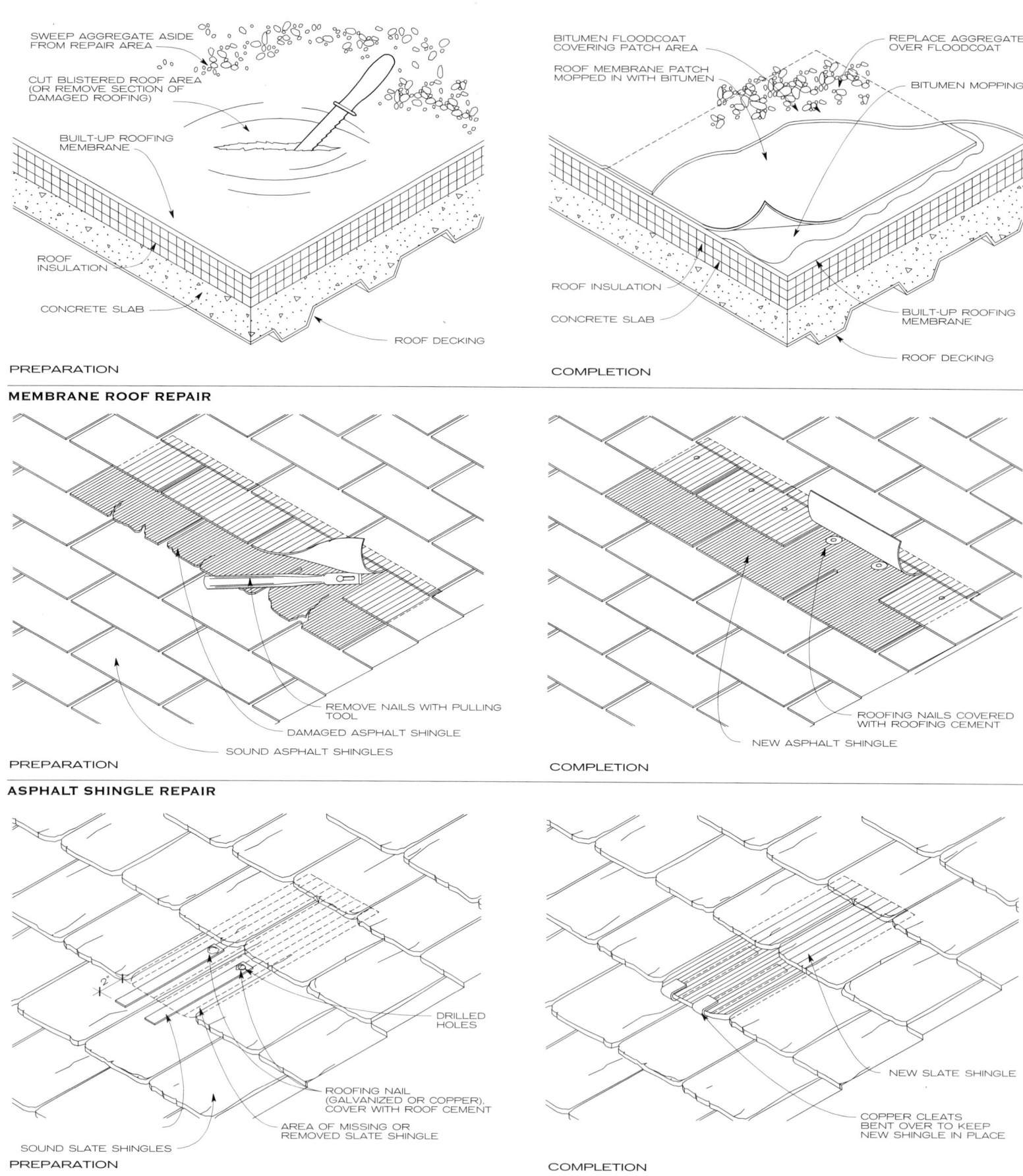

MEMBRANE ROOF REPAIR

ASPHALT SHINGLE REPAIR

SLATE SHINGLE REPAIR

Valerie Eickelberger; Rippeteau Architects, PC; Washington, D.C.

7 ROOF SPECIALTIES AND ACCESSORIES

Wind Uplift

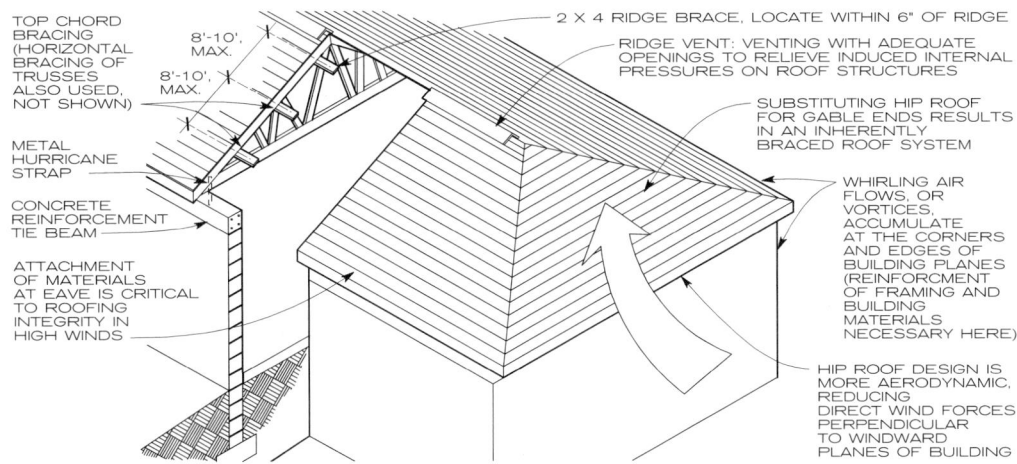

RECOMMENDED WOOD FRAME ROOF DESIGN

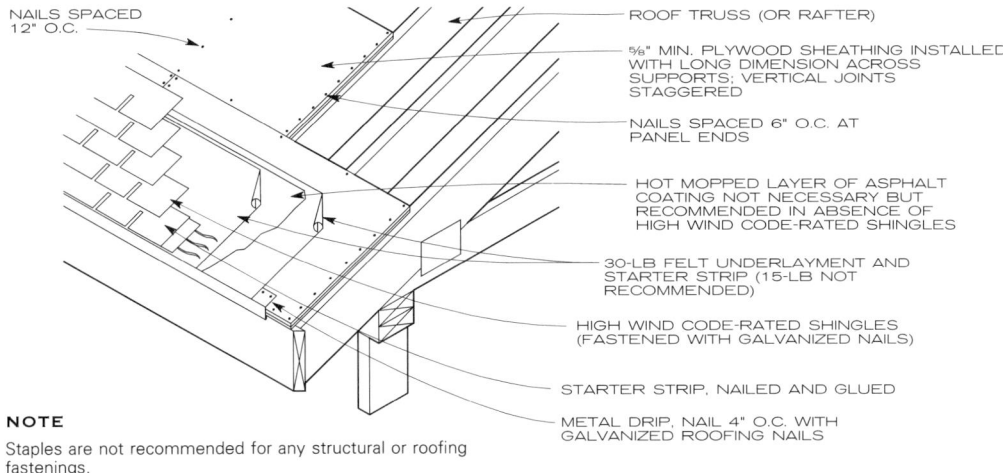

NOTE
Staples are not recommended for any structural or roofing fastenings.

HIGH WIND RESISTANCE DETAIL—COMPOSITION AND ASPHALT SHINGLES

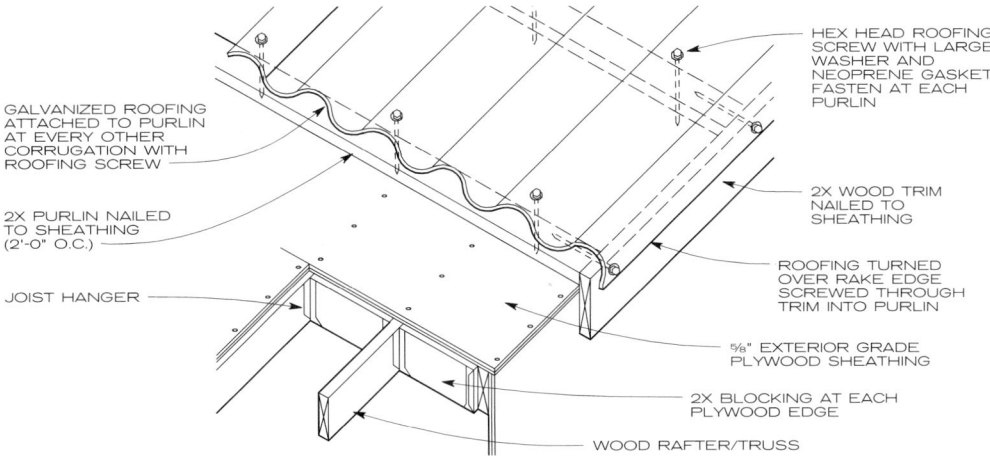

HIGH WIND RESISTANCE DETAIL—GALVANIZED METAL ROOFING

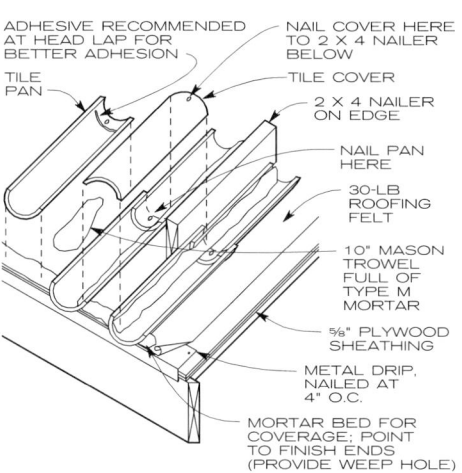

HIGH WIND RESISTANCE DETAIL—BARREL TILE ROOFING

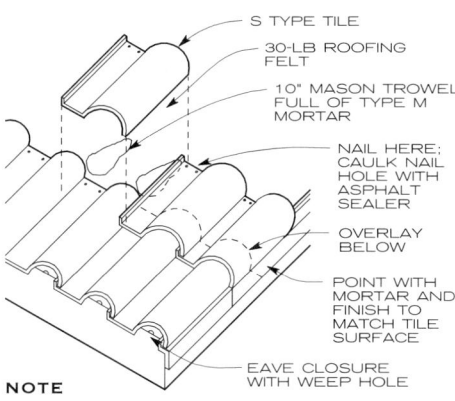

NOTE
After tile roofs are laid up completely, traffic should not be allowed on roof and no work that creates vibration in framing or roof sheathing should be allowed for 72 hours, minimum (24 hours is needed to ensure proper set).

HIGH WIND RESISTANCE DETAIL—S TYPE TILE ROOFING

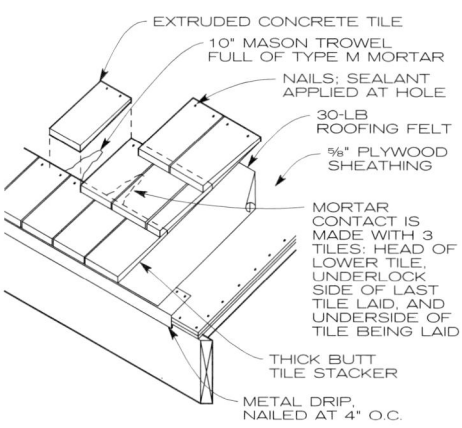

HIGH WIND RESISTANCE DETAIL—EXTRUDED CONCRETE

GENERAL

Roofing materials are particularly susceptible to damage from wind uplift and debris borne by high winds. Contributing to this problem is the use of inferior roofing materials and fasteners, substandard workmanship practices, and poor design choices for areas known for frequent or potentially severe high winds. Use of design practices that resist wind uplift and lateral forces can protect the total building system from damage due to high winds and/or hurricanes. Anchoring framing members to the foundation system, tying together all framing, and bracing members, particularly roof trusses, are practices that strengthen and brace the entire building. Only when that has been accomplished are good roofing design and details relevant.

ROOFING FAILURES IN HIGH WIND

Some of the main reasons for roofing material failure caused by high winds are described here:

1. Roof sheathing—Inadequate reinforcement at the edges causes sheathing to separate from the roof truss or rafter. Wafer board, composite board, oriented strand board, or structural particleboard used as sheathing does not provide sufficient wind resistance.
2. Composition shingle and felt underlayment—Use of shingles, attachment adhesives, and/or fasteners not rated for high winds or fasteners used in insufficient numbers, locations, and/or orientation can lead to wind damage.
3. Extruded concrete or clay tile—Poor nailing and/or mortar connections and underlayment failure due to lack of bonding between the underlayment and mortar or mortar and tile can cause failure of the roof. As well, clay tile may shatter when hit with flying debris.
4. Sheet metal—Inadequately adhered and fastened eave flashing, drips, and metal gravel stops can cause failure.

Richard J. Vitullo, AIA; Oak Leaf Studio; Crownsville, Maryland

GENERAL

Roof openings such as skylights, scuttles, and vents must be detailed with care, considering they will be exposed to the same external factors as the roof assembly itself. These factors include wind pressure—both positive and negative—which acts on the framing and/or glazing; rainwater penetration; live loads from snow and ice; dynamic loads from impact; daily cycles of thermal expansion and contraction; drainage of water and melting snow; and abuse from maintenance personnel. In addition, measures must be specified to keep people from falling through these openings.

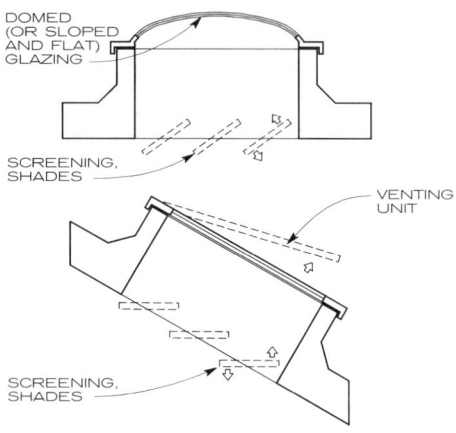

NOTE

In determining the desired form and size of the skylight unit/assembly, consideration should be given to

1. Environmental conditions, including orientation and winter and summer solar penetration angles at the site
2. Prevailing wind direction and patterns
3. Precipitation quantity and patterns
4. Adjacent topography and landscaping (shade trees, etc.)
5. Coordination with HVAC system
6. Use of shading, screening, or light reflecting/bouncing devices
7. Views desired relative to view obstructions, streetlights, etc.

SKYLIGHTS

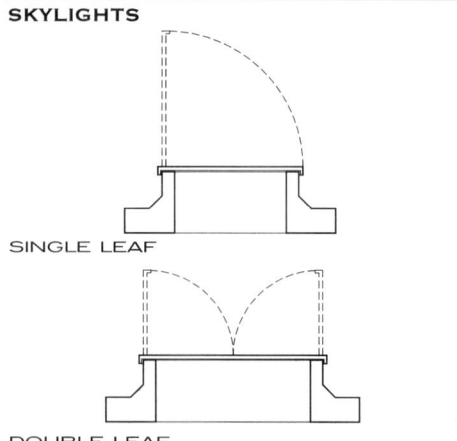

SCUTTLES

SCUTTLES

Scuttles, often referred to as roof hatches, provide roof access for maintenance personnel using ladders, a built-in ship's ladder, or stairs; an emergency escape route in the event of a fire; and access for moving large equipment into or out of the building, possibly eliminating the need for extra-large doors in rooms and corridors below.

Scuttles come as preassembled units, often with integral curbs, and are usually made with spring-assisted openings. When glazing is introduced, scuttles can function as skylights as well. For use as smoke/fire vents, scuttles must have automatic opening capability.

If scuttles are to serve as a required means of egress, consult building codes for number, size, and location required; type of access permitted (ship's ladder, stair, etc.); and type of operation permitted (manual force required to open unit or powered opening).

SKYLIGHTS

Skylights provide daylight to interior spaces and can reduce dependence on electrical lighting. In passive solar designs, skylights are used to admit direct solar radiation, enhancing space heating, and, when vented properly, to induce convective airflow, reducing cooling loads through natural ventilation.

Skylights are available as preassembled units, which are shipped to the site ready to be installed, or as framed assemblies of stock components, which arrive prefabricated for site assembly. Both fixed and hinged skylights are manufactured. The hinged variety can be opened manually or by remote control devices for venting. Frames are typically mounted on a built-up prefabricated or site-built curb, with integral counterflashing; they can be assembled with or without insulation.

Self-flashing skylight units are available with or without curbs. Those without curbs are intended only for pitched roof assemblies and are not recommended for roof assemblies with finished spaces below.

Framed skylight assemblies are custom designed by manufacturers to meet the necessary wind, roof, and dead loads of the assembly itself. When a skylight is pitched beyond a certain angle, it must be designed to resist environmental factors as does a curtain wall assembly. Roof drainage for rain- and storm water can limit skylight dimensions. Condensate gutters are needed in the body of the skylight assembly and around its perimeter.

FRAMING, GLAZING, AND GASKETS

The heart of a well-designed skylight unit or skylight framed assembly is the detailing of frames, glazing, and sealant systems. Thickness, size, and geometric profile of all glass and acrylic glazing materials should be carefully selected for compliance with building codes and manufacturers' recommendations. The following glazing materials are considered resistant to impact and breakage and are generally approved by codes (listed in descending order of cost):

1. Formed acrylic with mar-resistant finish
2. Formed acrylic
3. Polycarbonates
4. Flat acrylic
5. Laminated glass
6. Tempered glass
7. Clear polished wire glass
8. Textured obscure wire glass

Framed skylights require somewhat greater mullion widths when glazed with acrylics in order to accommodate the expansion and contraction characteristics of plastics. When glazed with glass, framed skylight mullions are spaced according to the standard glass widths: laminated glass (48 in., maximum), wire glass (60 in., maximum), and tempered glass (72 in., maximum). High-performance insulating glass is generally used in preassembled units (and sometimes framed assemblies) and provides important energy savings.

For economy, tinted acrylics should be limited to $1/4$ in. thickness. A combination fiberglass sheet and aluminum frame system with high insulating value and good light diffusion can be a cost-effective alternative. Domed acrylic glazing is almost self-cleaning, as the sloped shapes facilitate rain washing of the surface.

Frame systems must be engineered to carry the total resultant forces of the loads imposed on the skylight in accordance with all building codes. Framing, glazing, and gaskets also must be able to resist exposure to airborne pollutants. Frames with thermal breaks incorporated have better energy performance.

Finishes for aluminum frame components are available as mill finish, clear anodized, duranodic bronze or black, acrylic enamel, and fluorocarbon.

Gaskets are especially subject to degradation from solar ultraviolet rays. Excessive expansion and contraction of acrylic glazing can cause "rolling" of the gasket between metal framing. Small valleys created at the bottom of the sloped glazing and the horizontal glazing cap will hold water, which increases the chance of gasket breakdown and subsequent water infiltration.

SECURITY AND SAFETY

Frames or screens to protect glazing from impact, fire brands, or forced entry can be designed into the skylight system. To avoid forced entry, a framed skylight should include deterrents to disassembling the framing, removing the snap-on cover, and melting the glazing (acrylics can easily be burned with a torch). Metal security screens may be required.

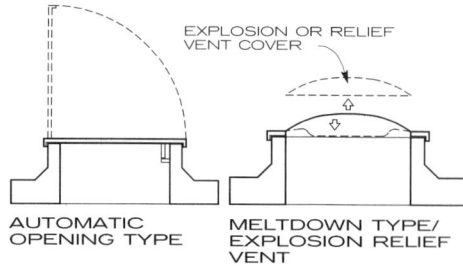

FIRE AND SMOKE VENTS

FIRE AND SMOKE VENTING

In certain building types and occupancies, such as those with large expanses of unobstructed space, fire and smoke vents that open automatically with a fire-induced temperature increase are required. Roof vents are often required over stairs, elevator hoistways, high-hazard occupancy areas (to offer explosion relief), and in areas behind the proscenium in theaters. The vents permit smoke, heat, and volatile gases to escape, lower the temperature at floor level, and reduce water damage by limiting active sprinkler heads to those in the immediate area of the fire.

There are two basic types of fire and smoke vents, both commonly available with integral curbs and flashing:

1. Meltdown: plastic glazing that softens and drops out of the frame when exposed to high temperatures (unit must be replaced once exposed to fire).

2. Automatic opening: solid or glazed cover with springs held by a fusible link that melts when the temperature rises, releasing the springs and opening the vent.

Enough vents must be distributed over the entire roof area to ensure early venting of a fire, regardless of its location. The size and spacing of the vents must be determined for each building according to its size and use and the degree of hazard involved. When UL- or FM-listed vents are required, choice of size is generally limited to stock sizes. Venting is based on moving a specific number of cubic feet of air per minute through the vents. Consult building codes for required capacity, size, and spacing.

PERCENTAGE OF ROOF AREA REQUIRED FOR SKYLIGHTING

LIGHT ZONE	LIGHT DESIGN LEVELS (FC)		
	30	60	120
1	3.3	5.2	13.3
2	2.8	4.3	10.8
3	1.8	3.2	6.9
4	1.5	2.8	4.0

Typical roof vent area requirements are 0.67% roof area for low heat release occupancies, 1% roof area for moderate heat release occupancies, and 2% roof area for high heat release occupancies.

Generally, several small units satisfy the total venting area requirement better than a few larger ones (NFPA #204). Roof scuttles are available that may also serve as fire and smoke vents. Consider the spacing of vents relative to interior spaces and their uses, proximity to exits, and, if glazed, their role in daylighting.

Explosion relief vents are a type of fire and smoke vent that opens automatically when interior pressure rises above a predetermined level. Plastic glazed units deform under higher than normal air pressure and are released from their frame.

Richard J. Vitullo, AIA; Oak Leaf Studio; Crownsville, Maryland

Skylights, Scuttles, and Vents

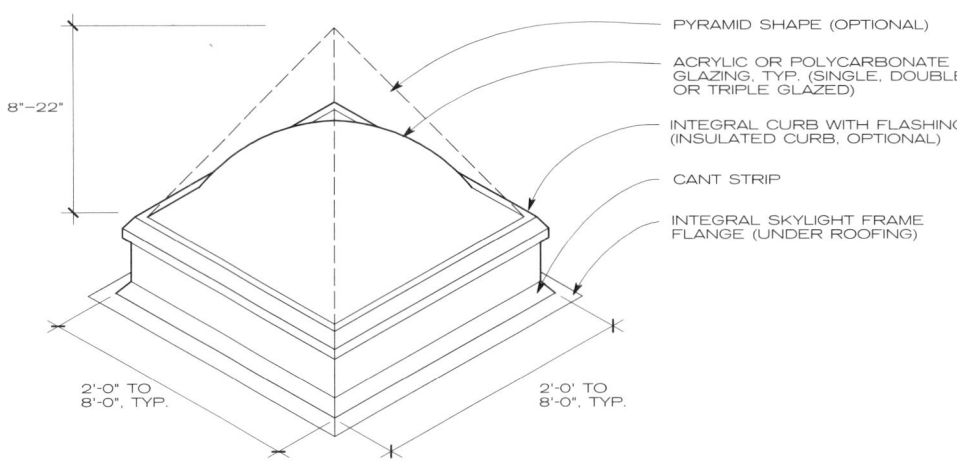

NOTE
Glazing may be clear, tinted transparent, or white translucent.

DOME UNIT SKYLIGHT—FLAT ROOF

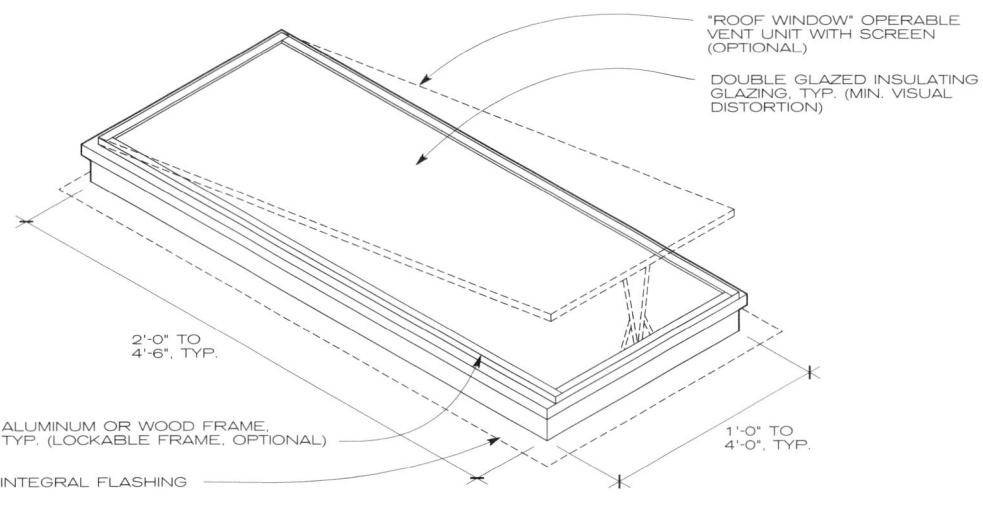

NOTE
1. Clear and tinted transparent glass, typical; tempered, laminated, and wire glass available.
2. Manual and powered vent operation, venetian blinds, shades, and exterior awnings available. Consult manufacturer.

FLAT PANEL UNIT SKYLIGHT—SLOPED ROOF

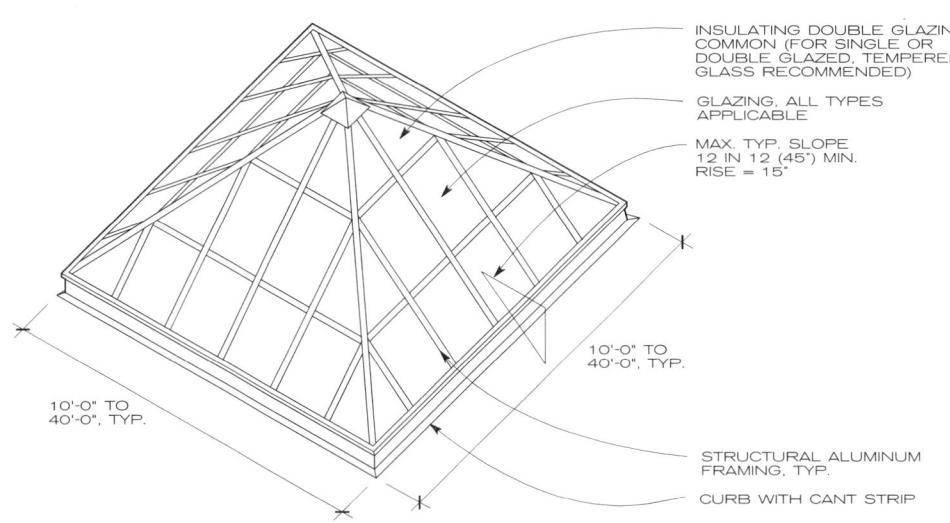

PYRAMID FRAMED SKYLIGHT ASSEMBLY

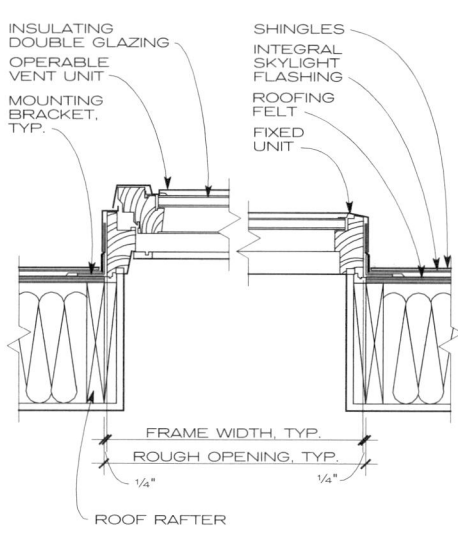

INSULATED CURB

WOOD CURB

UNIT SKYLIGHT SECTION

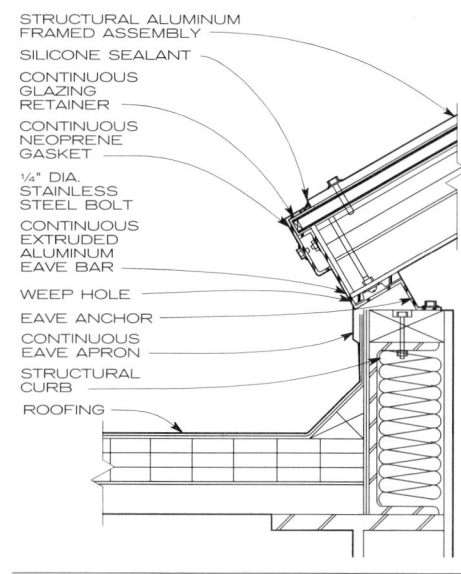

FLAT PANEL UNIT SKYLIGHT SECTION

CURB DETAIL AT SLOPED FRAMED ASSEMBLY

Richard J. Vitullo, AIA; Oak Leaf Studio; Crownsville, Maryland

SKYLIGHTS

Skylights, Scuttles, and Vents

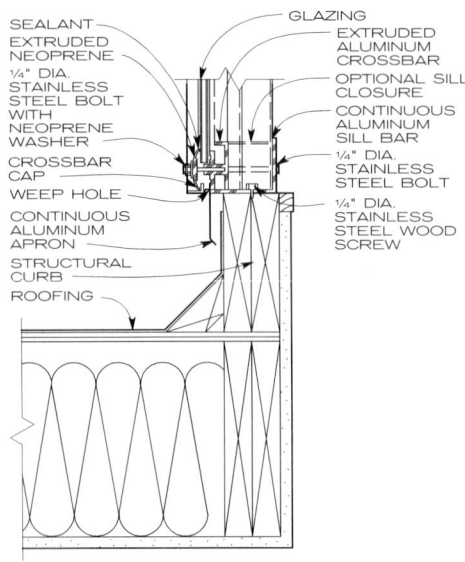

VERTICAL FRAME CURB DETAIL (WOOD FRAME)

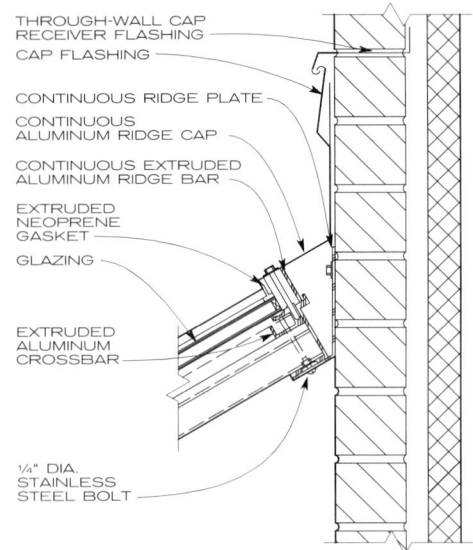

SINGLE-PITCH BACK WALL DETAIL AT TOP (MASONRY WALL)

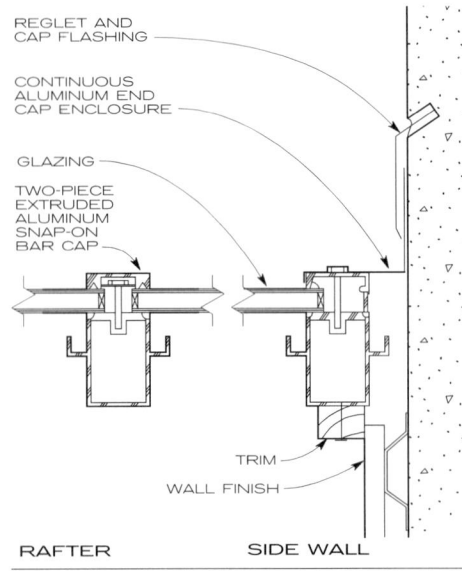

SINGLE-PITCH RAFTER AND SIDE WALL DETAIL (CONCRETE WALL)

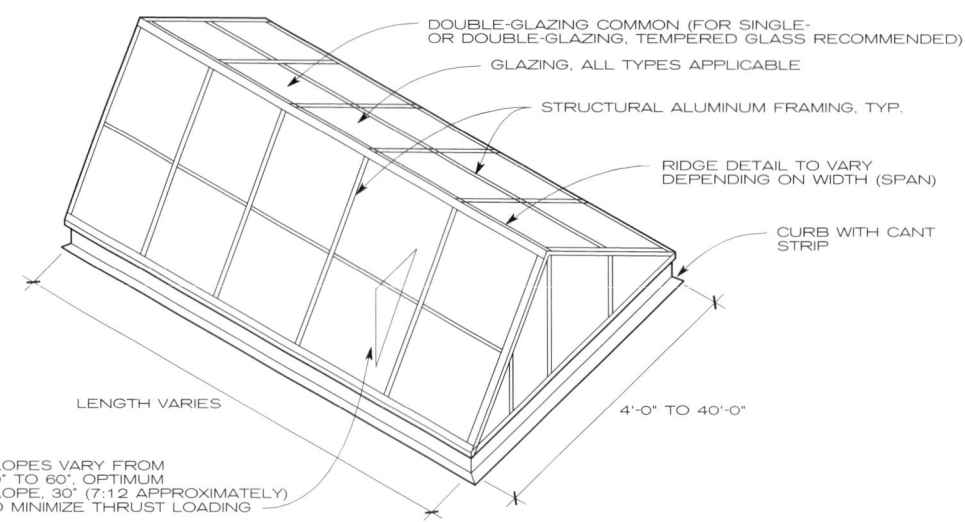

NOTE

Options for a pitched skylight include (1) integration of skylight with roof structure at ridge, slope of skylight to match slope of roof, no end glazing; (2) hip end glazing; and (3) vaulted framing; minimum rise is 22%.

DOUBLE-PITCH FRAMED SKYLIGHT ASSEMBLY

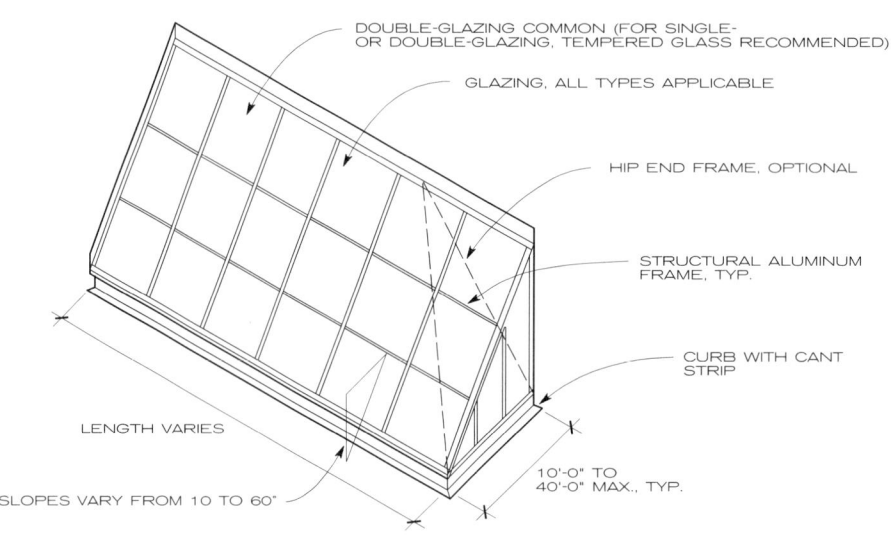

NOTE

Sloped aluminum frame may be segmented or curved.

SINGLE-PITCH FRAMED SKYLIGHT ASSEMBLY

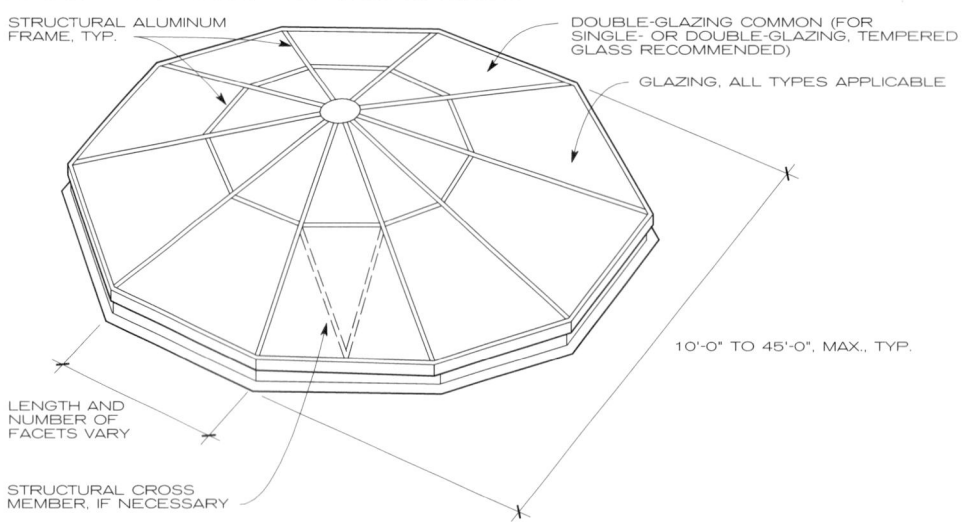

POLYGONAL FRAMED SKYLIGHT ASSEMBLY

Richard J. Vitullo, AIA; Oak Leaf Studio; Crownsville, Maryland

SKYLIGHTS

Skylights, Scuttles, and Vents

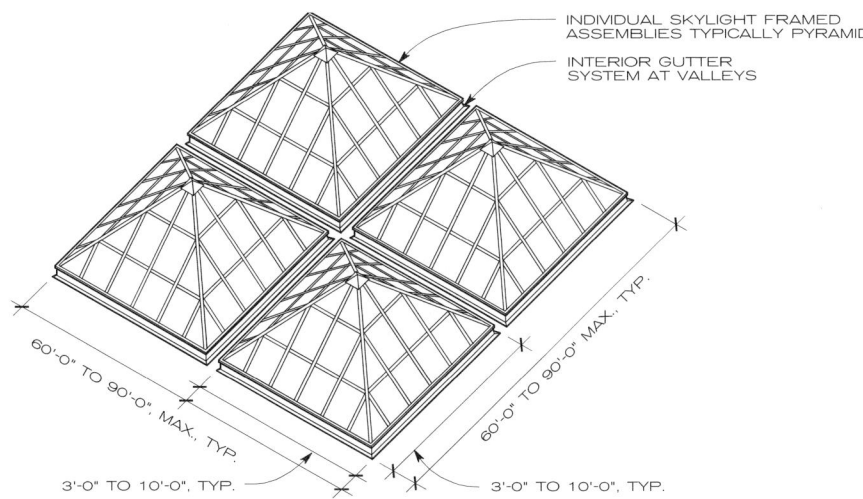

NOTES

1. Individual skylights for unit skylights may be pyramids or domes for flat roofs or flat panels for sloped roofs.
2. The number of multiples of individual skylights depends only on the structural frame system below, although the larger the grid assembly, the more water runoff must be accommodated.

MULTIPLE-GRID SKYLIGHTS—UNIT AND FRAMED ASSEMBLIES

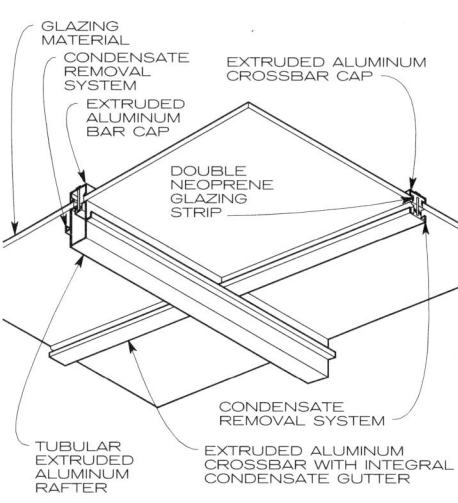

TYPICAL TUBULAR ALUMINUM FRAME DETAIL

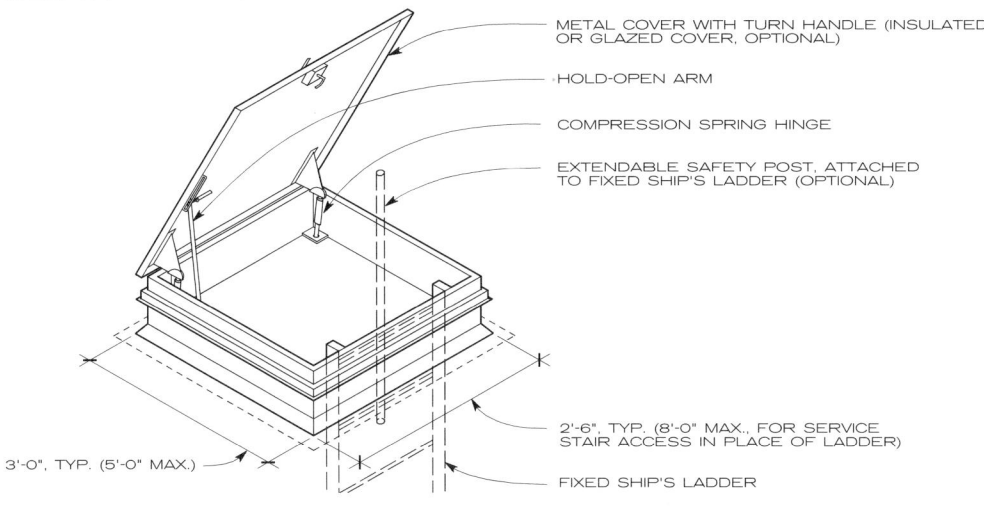

NOTE

Double leaf scuttles are typically specified for larger openings.

ROOF SCUTTLE

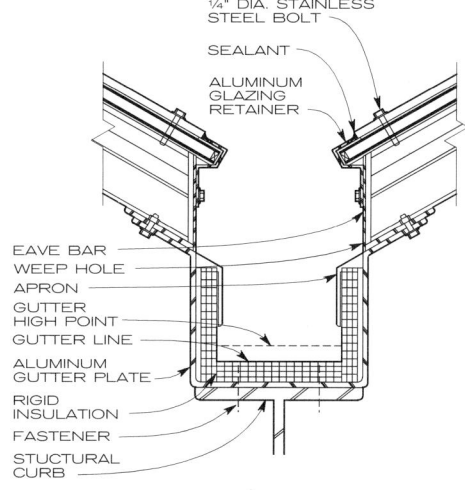

NOTE

Structural gutter system available for multiple and grid network systems of ridge- and pyramid-type enclosures.

MULTIPLE GRID GUTTER SECTION DETAIL

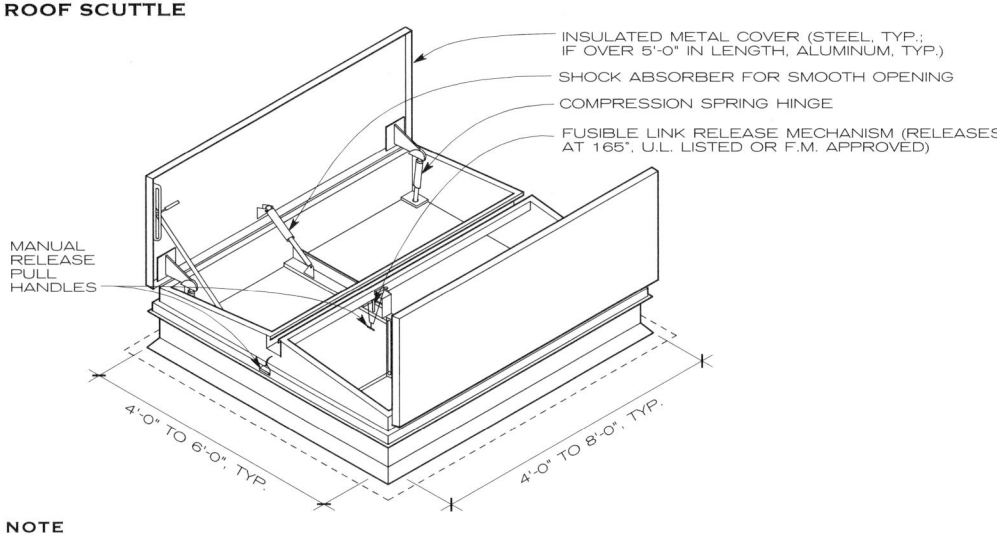

NOTE

Vents are manufactured both with and without labels. Consult codes for vent requirements. Fire and smoke vents can be adapted for use as explosion vent.

FIRE AND SMOKE VENT

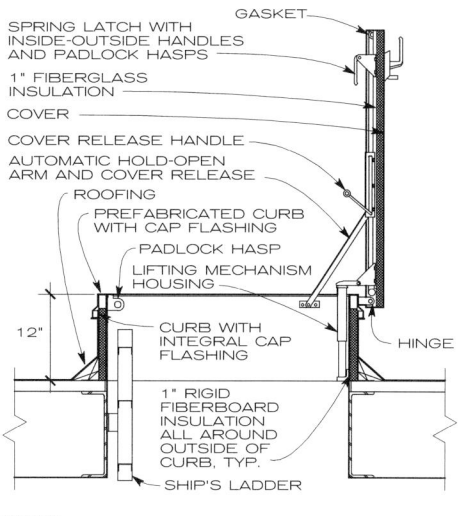

NOTE

Fire and smoke vent section is similar in construction, hardware, and integration with roof assembly. Consult manufacturer for all additional hardware.

SCUTTLE SECTION DETAIL

Richard J. Vitullo, AIA; Oak Leaf Studio; Crownsville, Maryland

Ornamental Plaster Fabrications

TYPES OF ORNAMENTAL PLASTER

RUN-IN-PLACE: This type of ornament is mounded or applied in its final position while in its plastic state using a three-coat plaster system. This method requires installation of the furring, lath, base plaster coats, and finish plaster ornament and surfaces on site, a time-consuming process that results in relatively heavy assemblies. It is typically used to repair or replace sections of damaged existing and historic plaster ornament.

CAST PLASTER ORNAMENT: This type of ornament, which can be made in panels, is run, cast, or fabricated in a shop and installed after hardening. Joints between sections of ornament are finished in the field. Typically gypsum plaster reinforced with glass fibers, cast plaster is fabricated by laying or spraying the material into a mold. Castings are reinforced with jute rope, burlap, wood lath, or metal framing, depending on the casting size and installation methods. Controlled shop fabrication processes, reduced on-site time, and the ability to fabricate thinner, lighter sections often make this method less costly than run-in-place.

NOTES

MODELS: Models are the "positive" form of the cast ornament and can be fabricated from clay, plaster, or wood as necessary to achieve the desired appearance. When existing ornament is being matched, it can serve as the model.

MOLDS: Typically made of urethane or silicone rubber, molds from which ornament is cast are "negative" forms produced from models. Molds for run-plaster ornament are sheet metal templates cut to the profile of the molding and attached to a wood backing called a "slipper."

ATTACHMENT: Small cast ornament is typically applied using a plaster "slip" made of plaster and water as an adhesive. Large sections of cast plaster ornament are attached with screws or hung with metal hangers.

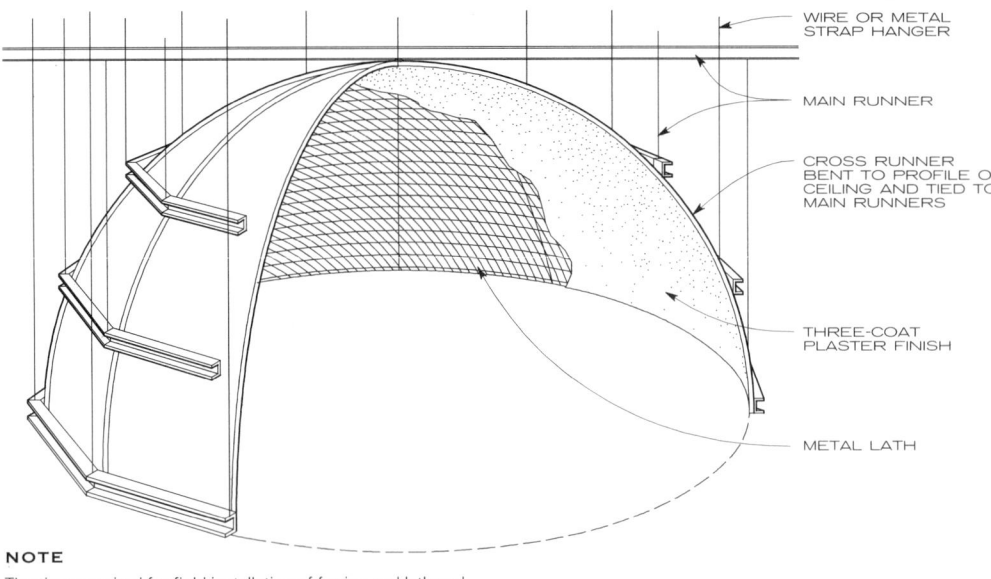

NOTE
The time required for field installation of furring and lath and the weight of a three-coat plaster finish are factors to consider when designing this system.

PLASTER DOME BUILT IN PLACE (VAULTS CONSTRUCTED SIMILARLY)

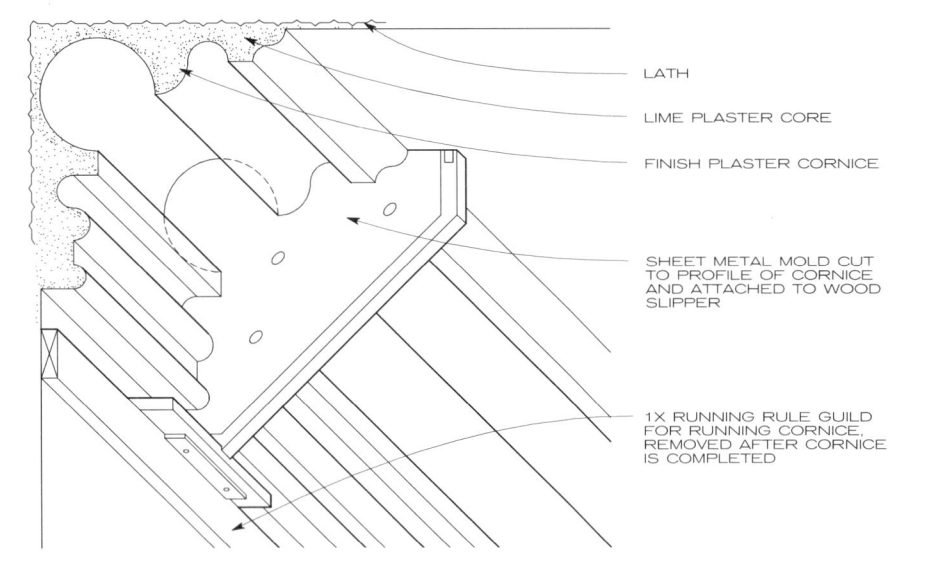

RUN-IN-PLACE CORNICE

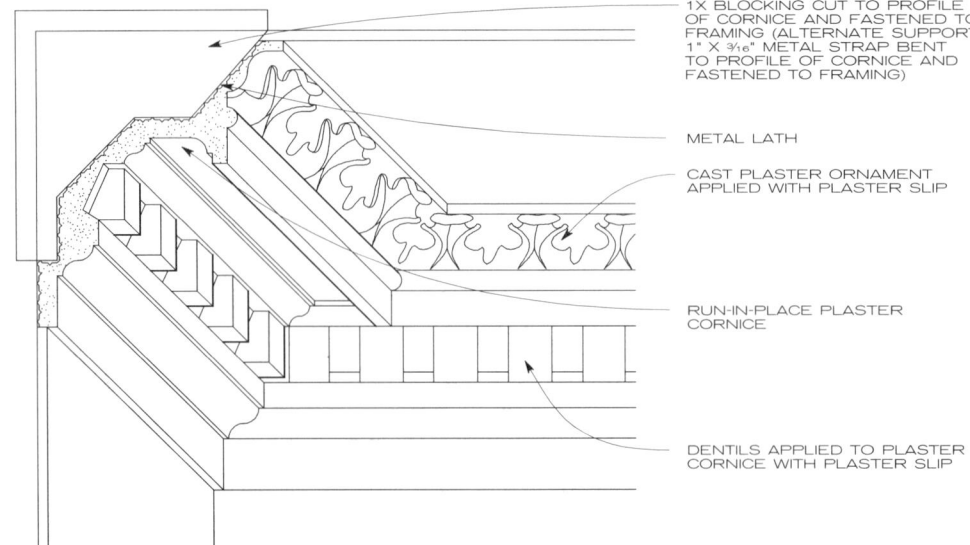

BRACKETED CORNICE RUN IN PLACE WITH STUCK-ON ORNAMENT

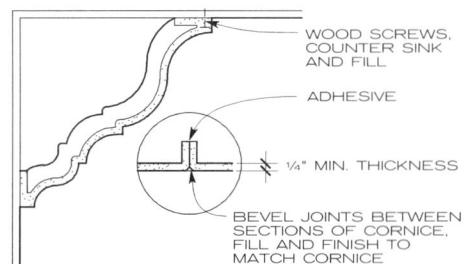

GLASS FIBER-REINFORCED GYPSUM CORNICE

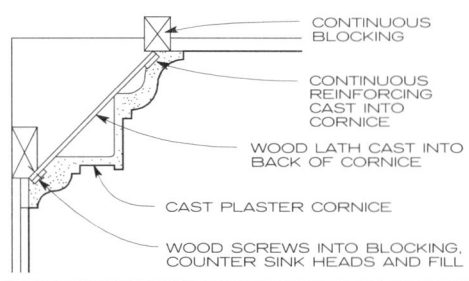

CAST PLASTER ORNAMENT ATTACHED WITH SCREWS

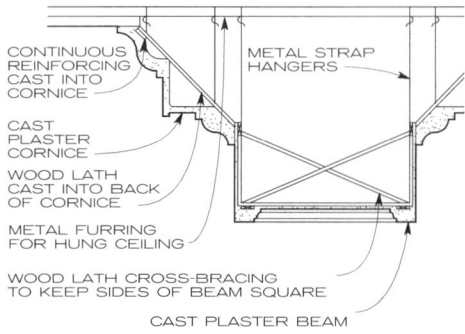

CAST PLASTER CORNICE AND BEAM SCREWED AND HUNG

Reed A. Black; Oehrlein & Associates; Washington, D.C.

METAL SUPPORT SYSTEMS

Ornamental Plaster Fabrications

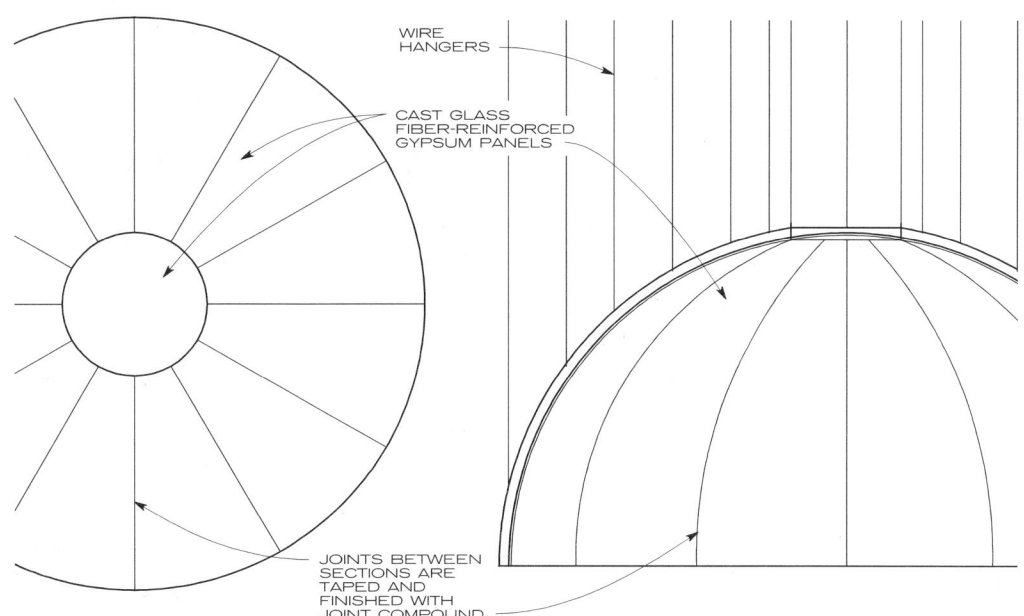

REFLECTED CEILING PLAN   SECTION

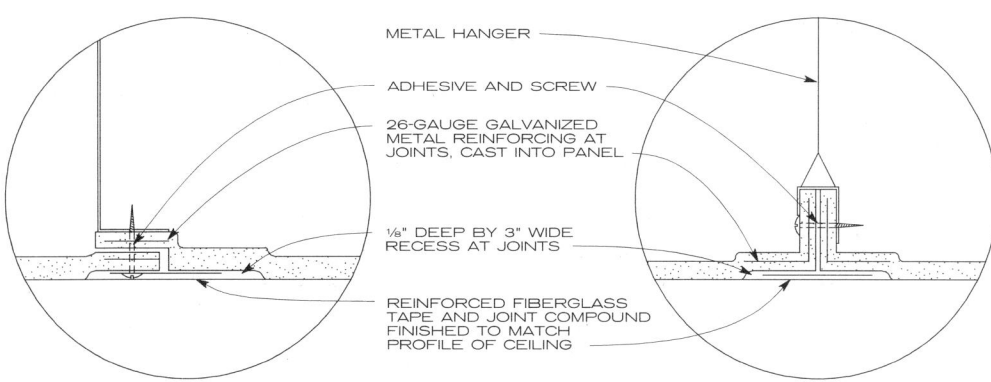

ALTERNATE JOINT DETAIL WHEN PANELS ARE NOT ACCESSIBLE FROM THE BACK   JOINT DETAIL

NOTE

Cast fabrications are typically lighter and require less on-site construction time than built-in-place plaster systems.

Large cast sections may require structural reinforcing and special cradles for fabrication, shipping, and erection.

CAST GLASS FIBER-REINFORCED GYPSUM DOME (VAULTS ARE SIMILAR)

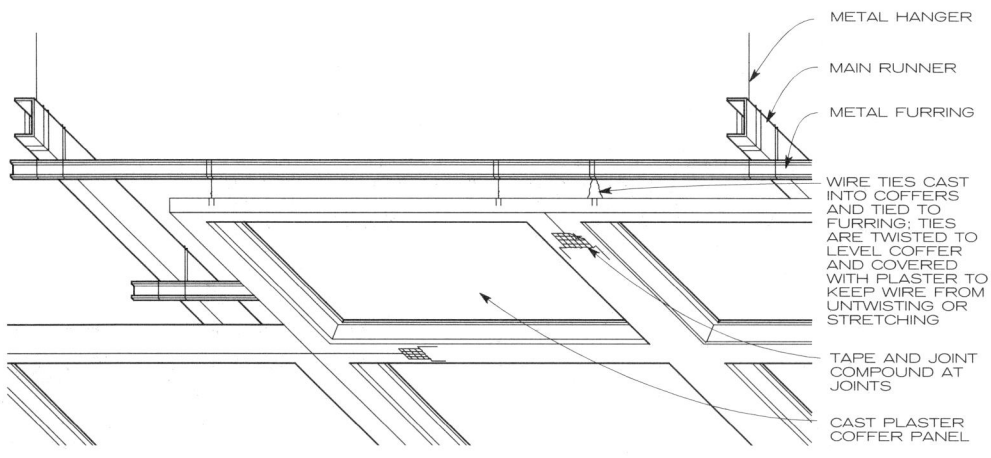

COFFERED CEILING

Reed A. Black; Oehrlein & Associates; Washington, D.C.

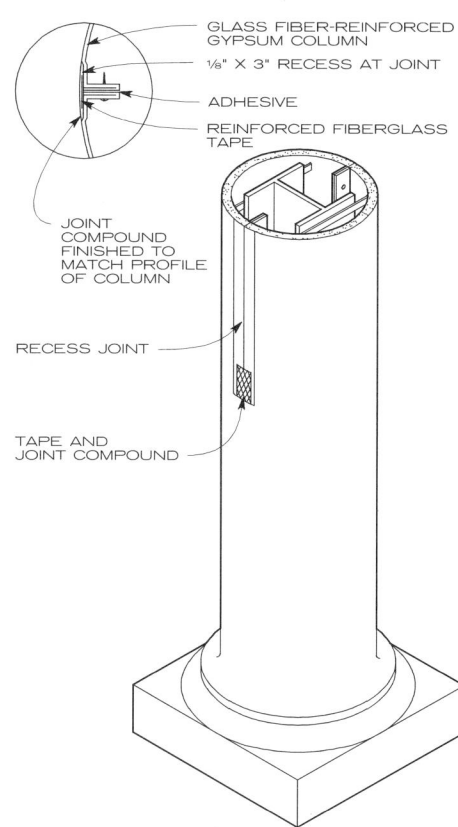

TWO-PIECE GLASS FIBER-REINFORCED GYPSUM COLUMN

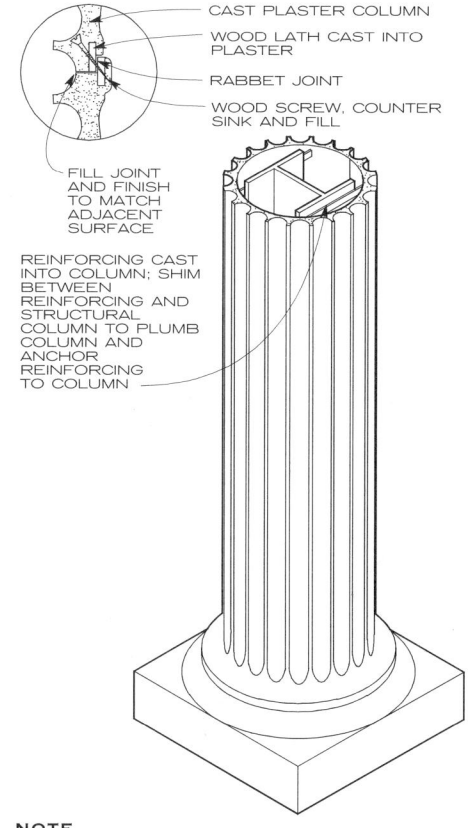

NOTE

Columns may be fabricated in one piece without joints and seams when they do not have to fit around the building structure.

TWO-PIECE CAST PLASTER COLUMN

METAL SUPPORT SYSTEMS

116 Special Conditions

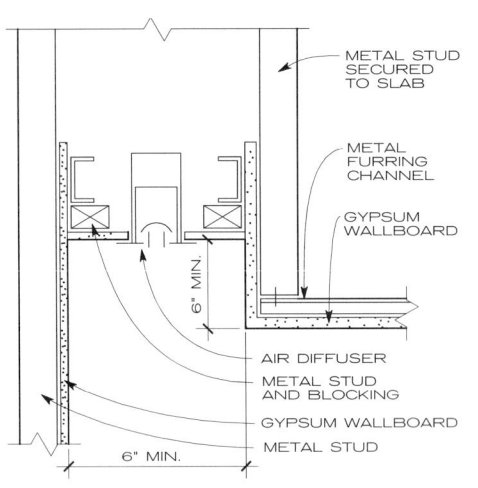
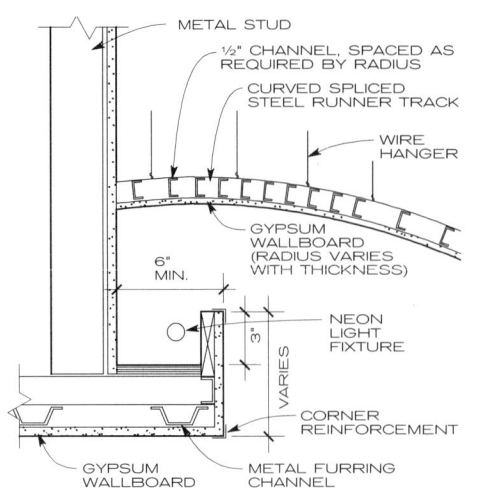
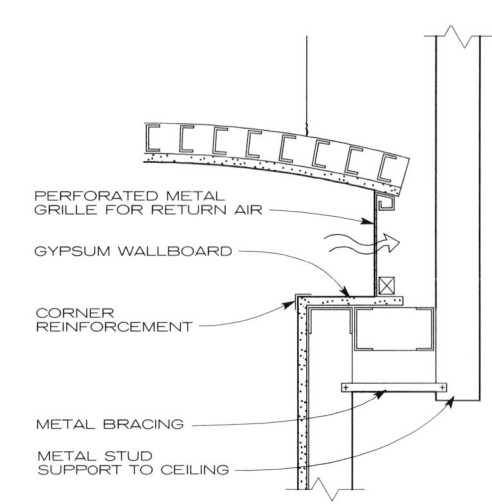

CEILING COVES

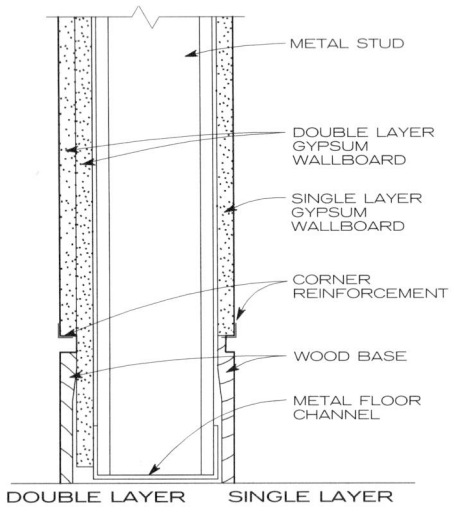
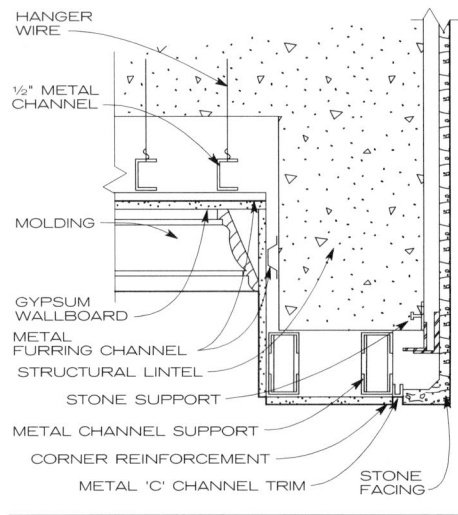
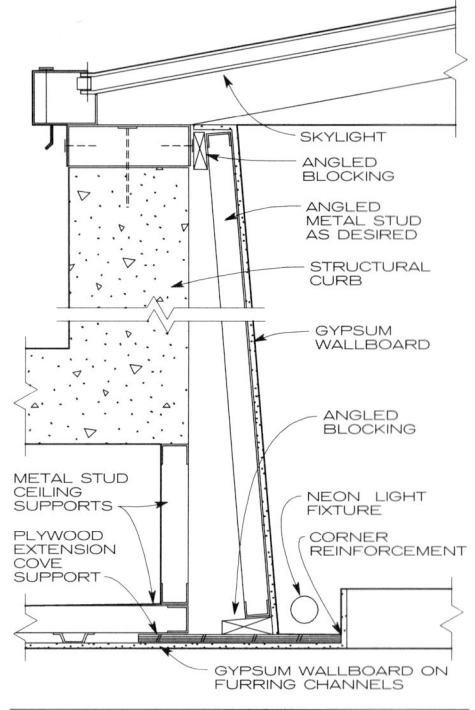

WALL AT WOOD BASE   **CEILING SOFFIT AT LINTEL**   **SKYLIGHT**

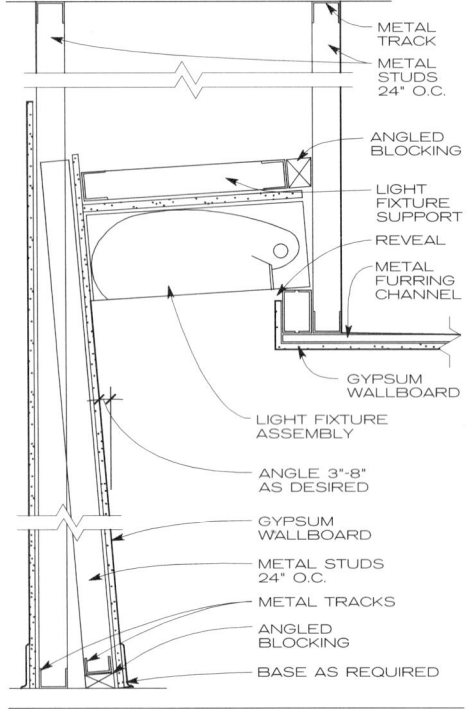
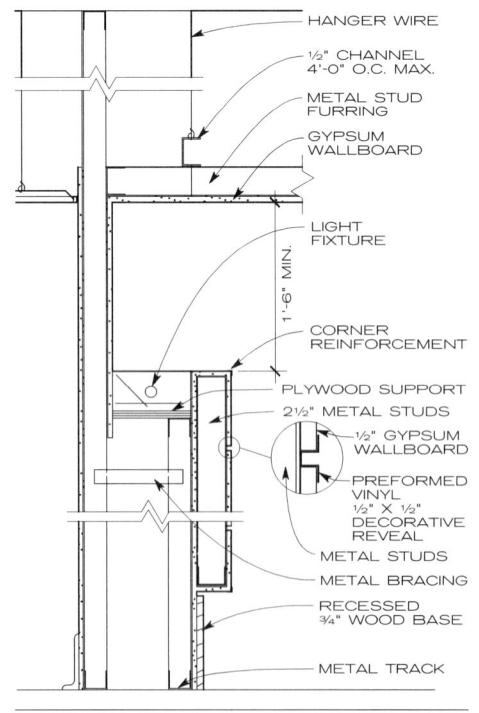

CANTED WALL WITH LIGHT COVE   **FEATURE WALL WITH LIGHT COVE**   **PARTIAL HEIGHT PARTITION**

Thomas R. Krizmanic, AIA; Studios Architecture; Washington, D.C.

GYPSUM BOARD

NEW WALL ASSEMBLIES

FIRE RATING	STC	WALL THICKNESS (IN.)	CONSTRUCTION DESCRIPTION	WALL SECTIONS
1 Hour	40	Varies	**EXTERIOR WALL FURRING:** One layer ⁵⁄₈ in. aluminum foil-backed gypsum wallboard applied to ³⁄₄ x 1 ¹⁄₂ in. Z furring channel 24 in. o.c., vertically applied with method appropriate to exterior wall. Use 1 in. type S drywall screws 8 in. o.c. to edges and 12 in. o.c. to intermediate Z channel flange. Insulate cavity with 24 x 1 ¹⁄₂ in. rigid foam.	
1 Hour	40	8 ¹⁄₈	**SECURITY WALL (15 minute):** One base layer of 13-gauge steel expanded metal mesh with nominal 1 x 2 ¹⁄₂ in. grid-spacing under one layer of ³⁄₄ in. plywood applied to one side of 6 in. metal studs 8 in. o.c. with 1 ¹⁄₂ in. screws. One face layer of ⁵⁄₈ in. type X gypsum wallboard applied to each side with 1 in. type S drywall screws 12 in. o.c. Stagger joints 16 in. o.c. each layer and side.	
1 Hour	52	10 ³⁄₄	**CAVITY WALL:** One layer ⁵⁄₈ in. type X gypsum wallboard applied to outside face of two rows of 1 ⁵⁄₈ in. metal studs (air space 9 ¹⁄₂ in. between inside wallboard faces) 24 in. o.c. with 1 in. type S drywall screws 8 in. o.c. to edges and 12 in. o.c. to intermediate studs. Crossbrace at third points vertically with ⁵⁄₈ in. wallboard gussets 9 ¹⁄₂ x 12 in. Use 3 ¹⁄₂ in. fiberglass insulation in cavity.	
1 Hour	47	3 ¹⁄₂	**PREFINISHED GYPSUM WALL PANELS:** One layer, ¹⁄₂ in. type X prefinished vinyl surface gypsum wall panels (prebowed) applied vertically at joints to each side of 2 ¹⁄₂ in. metal studs 24 in. o.c. with 1 in. type S drywall screws 30 in. o.c. Attach to intermediate studs with ³⁄₈ in. bead of adhesive. Attach at top and bottom with 1 ³⁄₈ inch matching finish nails 12 in. o.c. Attach aluminum batten retainer to panels at studs with 1 in. type S drywall screws 12 in. o.c. Install matching finish batten over retainers and 2 in. glass fiber insulation in cavity. Stagger joints 24 in. o.c. each side.	
1 Hour	45	5	**PREFINISHED GYPSUM WALL PANELS:** Base layer ¹⁄₄ in. regular gypsum wallboard nailed to 2 x 4 wood studs 16 in. o.c. with 1 ³⁄₈ in. 4d coated nails, 12 in. o.c., fire stopped at mid-height. Face layer ¹⁄₂ in. type X prefinished vinyl surface gypsum wall panels (prebowed) applied vertically to each side with laminating compound and ⁷⁄₈ in. drywall screws, 12 in. o.c., at top and bottom. Stagger joints 24 in. o.c. each layer and side. Cover exposed fasteners with suitable molding.	
2 Hour	50	5 ³⁄₄	**WATER-RESISTANT WALL (ONE SIDE):** One layer ⁵⁄₈ in. water-resistant gypsum wallboard applied to wet side of 3 ⁵⁄₈ in. 20-gauge metal studs 16 in. o.c. with 1 in. type S drywall screws 12 in. o.c. Opposite side, two layers ⁵⁄₈ in. gypsum wallboard installed vertically. Use 3 in. fiber insulation in cavity. Stagger joints 24 in. o.c. each layer and side.	
2 Hour	45	8 ¹⁄₄	**BULLET-RESISTANT WALL (ONE SIDE):** Base layer of ¹⁄₄ in. steel plate bolted to each side of steel tube framed wall with 4 x ¹⁄₄ in. steel tube at top, bottom, and 4 ft o.c., horizontally. Two layers each side ⁵⁄₈ in. type X gypsum wallboard on ⁷⁄₈ in. furring channels 24 in. o.c. applied with 1 in. type S drywall screws. Stagger joints 24 in. o.c. each layer and side.	

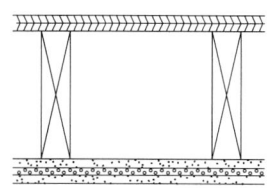

2 HR/STC EST. 50

NOTE

One layer ⁵⁄₈ in. type X gypsum wallboard applied with 1 in. type S drywall screws perpendicular to the cross tees of a drywall suspension system suspended from a steel deck. Concrete floors 2 ¹⁄₂ in. thick.

DRYWALL SUSPENSION SYSTEM

2 HR/STC EST. 45

NOTE

Base layer ⁵⁄₈ in. type X gypsum wallboard applied at right angles to 2 x 10 wood joists with 1 in. type S drywall screws 16 in. o.c. Resilient furring channels spaced 24 in. o.c. and nailed through baseboard into and at right angles to joists. Face layer ⁵⁄₈ in. same type wallboard screwed to furring channel with same type screws. Tongue-and-groove sub- and finish floor.

DOUBLE LAYER RESILIENT (WOOD FRAME)

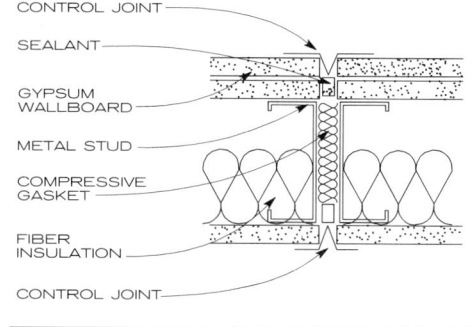

SOUND-ISOLATED INTERRUPTED CEILING

WALL CONTROL JOINT

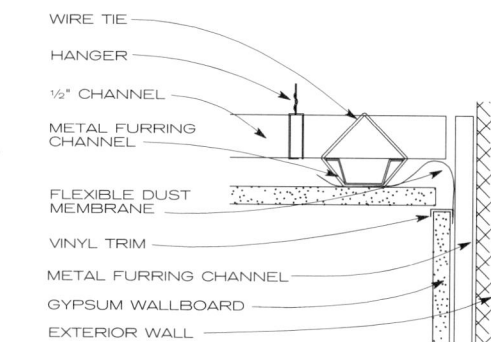

EXTERIOR WALL INTERSECTION

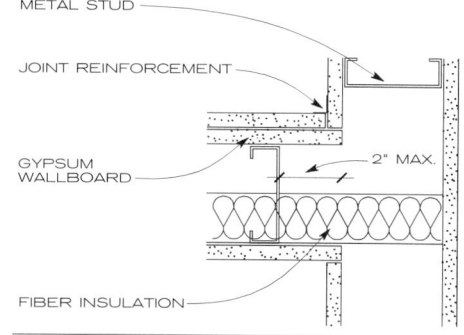

SOUND-ISOLATED PARTITION INTERSECTION

Thomas R. Krizmanic, AIA; Studios Architecture; Washington, D.C.

Stone Wall Facing Patterns

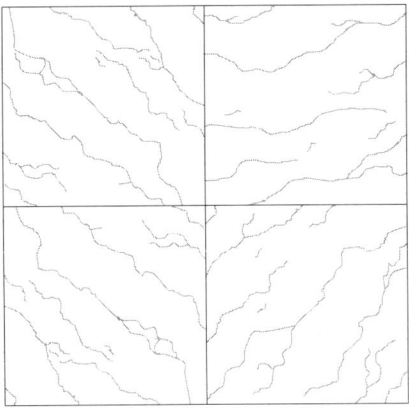

BLEND PATTERN

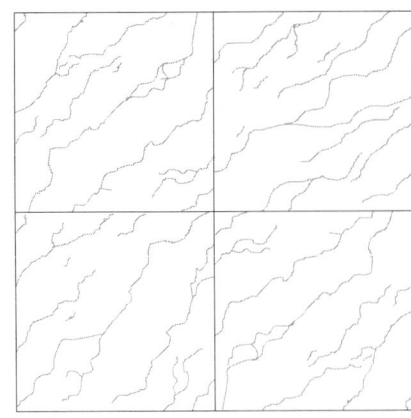

SIDE-SLIP OR END PATTERN

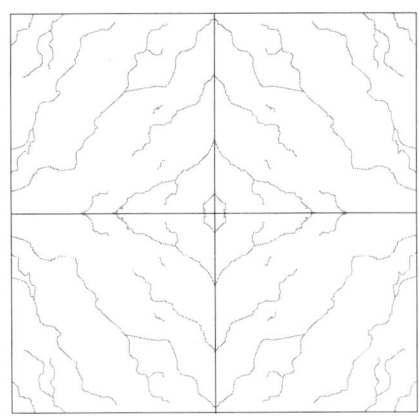

END-MATCH, BOOK-MATCH, OR QUARTER-MATCH PATTERNS

MARBLE WALL FACING PATTERN

MARBLE WALL FACING PATTERNS

Stone with distinctive texture and markings, such as certain marbles, lends itself to specific pattern arrangements. The markings vary depending on whether the marble veneer is cut with or across its setting bed.

BLEND PATTERN: Panels of the same variety of stone, but not necessarily from the same block, are arranged at random.

SIDE-SLIP OR END-SLIP PATTERN: Panels from the same block are placed side by side or end to end in sequence to give a repetitive pattern and blended color in the horizontal or vertical.

END-MATCH OR BOOK-MATCH PATTERNS: In an end-match pattern, the adjacent faces of panels A and B are finished and panel B is inverted above panel A. In a book-match pattern, panel B is placed next to panel A.

VENEER CUTTING

Quarry blocks are reduced to slabs by a gang saw. The gang saw consists of a series of parallel steel blades in a frame that moves forward and backward. The most productive and precise gang saws use diamond-tipped blades with individual hydraulic blade tensioners; others are fed a cutting abrasive in a stream of water.

Marble blocks can be sawn either parallel or perpendicular to the bedding plane. The perpendicular cut is referred to as an across-the-bed or vein cut. The parallel cut is a with-the-bed or Fleuri cut. Other marbles produce a pleasing surface only when sawn in one direction and are generally available only in that variety.

VENEER PATTERNS

Only certain marbles lend themselves to specific pattern arrangements, such as a side-slip or end-slip pattern, which require a constant natural marking trend throughout the marble block. Formal patterns require selectivity, which usually increases the installed cost of the marble veneer. Usually, material sawn for a vein cut can be matched; Fleuri cuts can only be blended.

NOTE

Although the above arrangements of matched panels indicate an almost perfect match of veining lines, such perfection is impossible because a portion of the marble block is lost during the sawing process and because the vein shifts. Ideally, jointing should be planned for groupings of four panels of equal size.

TYPICAL FINISHES AND COMMON SIZES OF STONE WALL PANELS FOR INTERIOR USE

STONE	GRADE	FINISH	MIN. THICKNESS (IN.)	MAX. FACE DIMENSION (IN.)	NOTES
Granite	Building (exterior) Veneer Masonry	Polished Honed	3/4 - 1 1/4 *	5 x 5	• This very hard and durable surface is not likely to stain. • Many colors and grains are available.
Marble	Group A (exterior) Group B Group C Group D	Polished Honed	1/2 - 7/8 *	4 x 7	• The most colorful and interesting marbles are in groups B, C, and D; however, some filling of natural voids may be required. • Many colors and patterns are available.
Limestone	Select Standard Rustic Variegated	Smooth Tooled Polished	7/8 - 3	4 x 9	• Soft and easy to shape, limestone shows wear and may discolor over time. • Colors range in the buffs and grays.
Slate	Ribbon Clear	Natural cleft Sand rubbed Honed	1 - 1 1/2	2 - 6 x 5	• Ribbon stock is distinguished by its ornamental, integral bands, which are usually darker than the rest of the stone. • Colors range in the pastel hues.

* 1/4 - 1/2 in. tiles (usually a face dimension of 12 in. x 12 in.) available. Tiles can be directly applied to a wall with adhesive or thin-set mortar similar to flooring applications. Tiles are not recommended for walls over 8 ft high.

NOTES

1. Sizes and thicknesses shown are only indicative of some of the common sizes and thicknesses used. Intended use and size generally dictate minimum thickness.

2. Joint width between panels should be specified. Traditionally, it has been 1/16 in. minimum.

Mark Forma; Leo A. Daly Company; Washington, D.C.

STONE FACING

Acoustical Wall Treatment

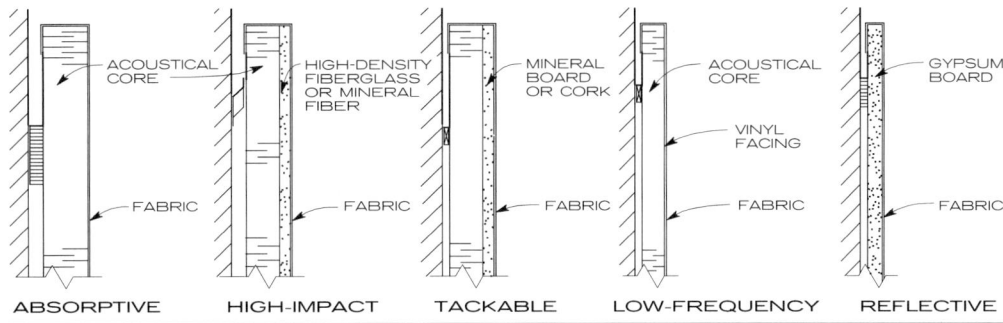

PANEL TYPES

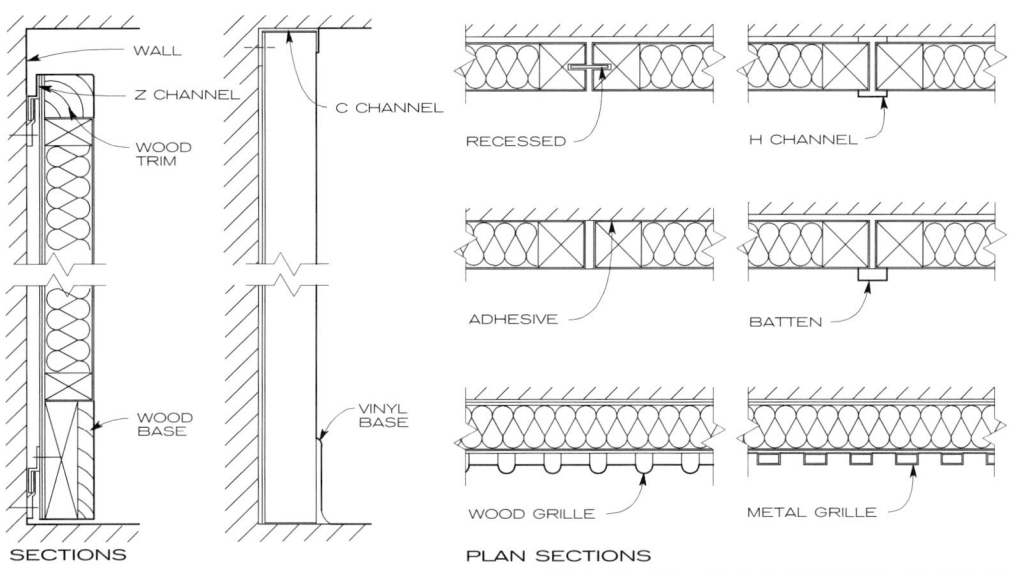

SECTIONS — PLAN SECTIONS

WALL TREATMENT

ACOUSTICAL MASONRY UNITS

1. USE: sound absorption and diffusion.
2. MATERIALS: concrete masonry units 4, 6, 8, or 12 in. thick, with fiberglass or metal baffle in the slotted area for sound absorption; quadratic residue sequence shaped surface for sound diffusion.
3. N.R.C.: 0.45 to 0.85.

NOTE

Acoustical masonry units are available with glazed, split rib, and ground face masonry finishes. The units offer better sound absorption at low frequencies than at middle to high frequencies and can be used as load-bearing structural walls. Painting slightly reduces the N.R.C. rating of these units.

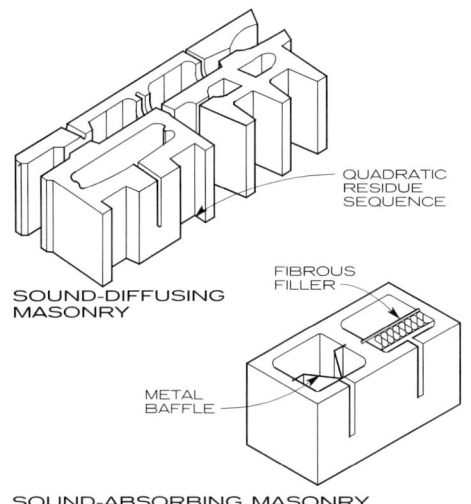

ACOUSTICAL MASONRY UNITS

DIFFUSIVE WALL TREATMENT

1. USE: sound diffusion/scattering.
2. MATERIALS: factory-assembled wood, fiberglass, or fiberglass-reinforced gypsum panels with integrally shaped surfaces.
3. N.R.C.: typically less than 0.30.
4. THICKNESS: up to 18 in. depending on panel shape.

NOTE

Wall panels may be used individually or grouped to form a monolithic wall system. Panels function best if they are installed 4 ft. above the floor surface (ear height) and extend to a minimum of 8 ft. above the floor surface. Maximum panel size varies with the manufacturer up to 4 x 8 ft.

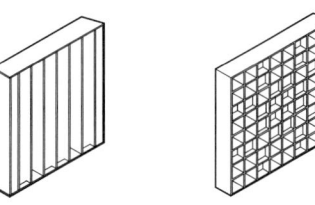

QUADRATIC RESIDUE SEQUENCES

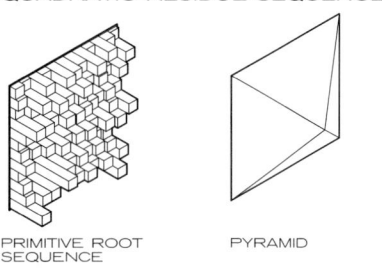

DIFFUSIVE WALL TREATMENT

ABSORPTIVE WALL TREATMENT

1. USE: sound absorption.
2. MATERIALS: factory- or field-assembled fabric wrapped glass fiber or mineral wood panels.
3. N.R.C.: 0.55 to 1.0.
4. THICKNESS: one, two, or four inches.
5. PANEL TYPES: absorptive, high-impact, tackable, and special acoustical characteristics.
6. EDGE PROFILES: square, bevel, radius, and chamfer.
7. EDGE REINFORCEMENT: chemical treatment, metal, plastic, and wood.
8. INSTALLATION HARDWARE: mechanical clips, impaling pins, magnetic fasteners, hook and loop tape, and adhesives (the last two require installation of a metal angle at panel bottom to carry the weight of the panel).

NOTE

Wall panels may be used individually or grouped to form a monolithic wall system. The N.R.C. coefficient varies with the thickness of the material, the acoustical transparency of the fabric, and the installation mounting. Panels are more effective at absorbing mid- and high-frequency sound. Vinyl facing over an acoustical core increases low-frequency absorption and decreases mid- and high-frequency absorption. Panels are not recommended for installation in high abuse areas unless perforated metal or high-density scrim facing protects the acoustical core. Maximum panel size varies with the manufacturer up to 4 x 12 feet.

SPRAY-ON ACOUSTICAL MATERIAL

1. USE: sound absorption.
2. MATERIALS: aerated concrete, mineral, or cellulose fibers spray-applied to metal lath or directly to hard surfaces such as concrete, steel, masonry, or gypsum wallboard.
3. N.R.C.: 0.35 to 1.0.

NOTE

This material is available in thicknesses of $1/2$ to $1\;1/2$ in. with abuse-resistant surfaces and fire protection ratings. Applying spray-on acoustical material to lath increases low-frequency sound absorption and makes it possible to accommodate irregular shapes. The N.R.C. rating of this material depends on how it is mounted and the thickness of the material.

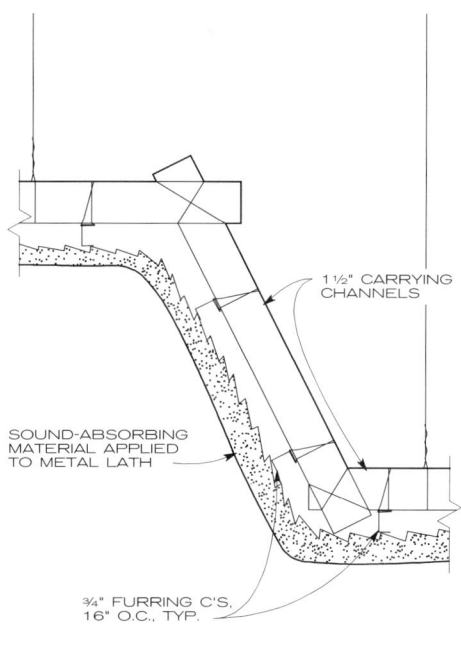

SPRAY-ON ACOUSTICAL MATERIAL

Michael G. Lawrence, AIA; M Lawrence Architects; Washington, D.C.
Neil Thompson Shade; Acoustical Design Collaborative, Ltd.; Falls Church, Virginia

ACOUSTICAL TREATMENT

Acoustical Insulation and Barriers

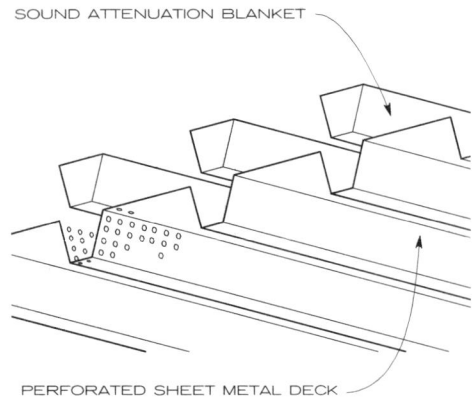

METAL ACOUSTICAL ROOF DECK

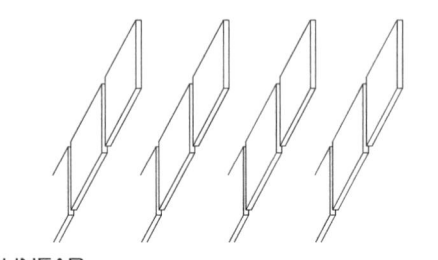

LINEAR

EGGCRATE

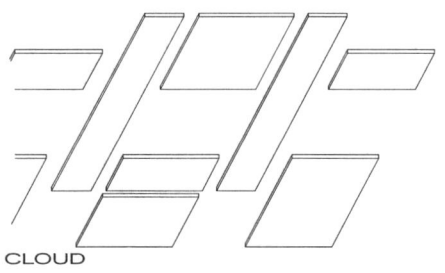

CLOUD

SUSPENDED PANELS

ACOUSTICAL ROOF DECKS

Acoustical roof decks are commonly used in industrial, gymnasium, and similar facilities where the underside of the roof serves as the exposed ceiling surface of the space below. Typically comprised of perforated metal roof deck panels, with fiberglass or mineral fiber infill, acoustical form boards, or structural roof insulation, these decks provide sound absorption and structural support for the exterior roofing material. NRC ratings range from 0.55 to 0.85.

SUSPENDED PANELS

Sound is absorbed through vertical suspension fiberglass blankets wrapped in fabric, vinyl, or perforated metal. Fiberglass or mineral fiber blankets can be used horizontally with perimeter framing. Typically 2 x 4 ft in size, panels can be suspended from the structure or attached directly to the ceiling grid, but installation patterns vary. NRC ratings, often greater than 1.0 due to sound exposure on both sides, depend on panel density and layout geometry. In general, one panel is required per 8 to 10 sq ft of floor area.

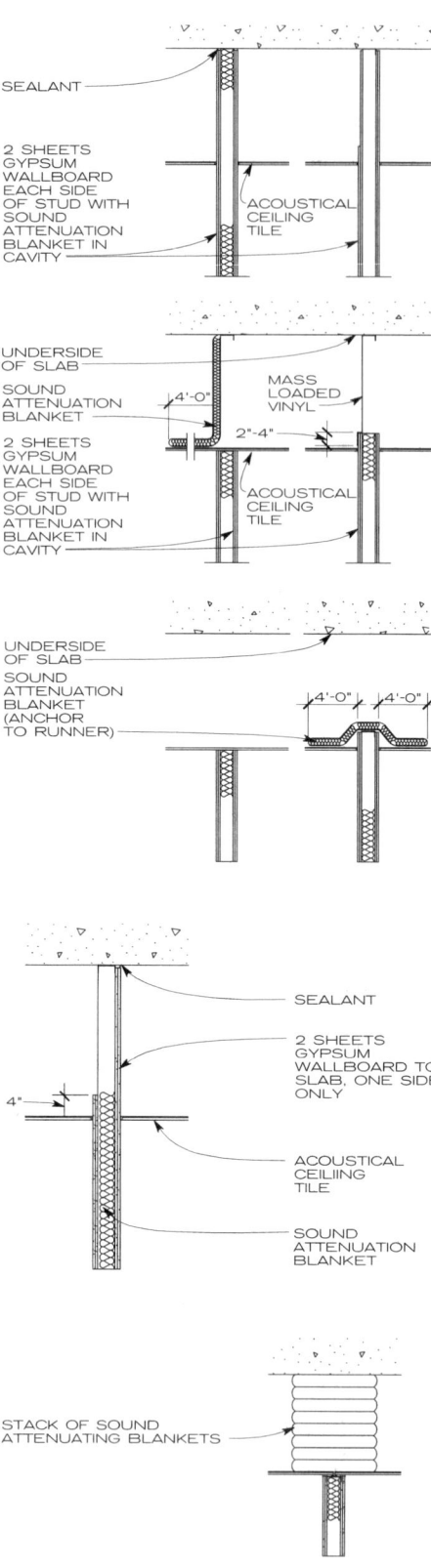

PLENUM BARRIER DETAILS

PLENUM BARRIERS

These products are used to reduce sound transmission through the plenum space above partitions. Materials are mass-loaded vinyl, fiberglass, or mineral fiber batts and gypsum board. All openings through the barrier for pipes, ducts, etc. must be closed off for the barrier to be effective. STC rating is improved from 5 to 40 dB.

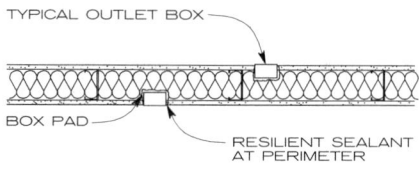

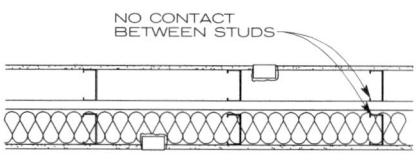

PARTITION PLANS

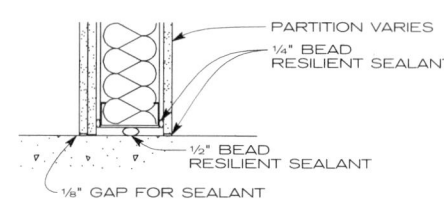

PARTITION SECTION

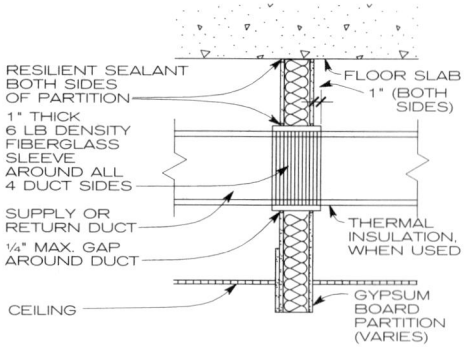

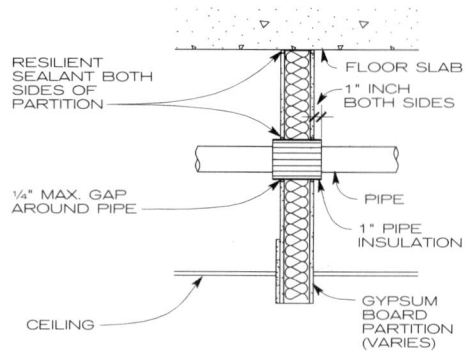

ACOUSTICAL SEALS AND CLOSURES DETAILS

ACOUSTICAL SEALS AND CLOSURES

These seals and closures, usually made of resilient sealant material or fiberglass, are used to close off sound leaks. All penetrations around partitions must be filled with resilient sealant, while pipes and ducts should be isolated from partitions with fiberglass. Use of these materials improves the STC from 5 to 15 dB.

Michael G. Lawrence, AIA; M Lawrence Architects; Washington, D.C.
Neil Thompson Shade; Acoustical Design Collaborative, Ltd; Falls Church, Virginia

ACOUSTICAL TREATMENT

Fiber-Reinforced Plastic-Coated Panels

SURFACE CHARACTERISTICS

CHARACTERISTIC	ADVANTAGES
High performance/durability	Resistant to abuse Abrasion resistant Weather resistant
Nonporous surface	Germ inhibition
Low maintenance	Ease of cleaning
Installation	Lightweight panels Common installation procedures
Versatility	New construction Renovation Demountable Projection/marker surface
Chemical resistance	Resistant to chemical attack*
Fire resistance	Class A fire rating*
Color/texture/pattern availability	Standard/custom color, graphics textures

* Refer to specific manufacturer's literature.

PANEL CONSTRUCTION GUIDE

PANEL COMPONENT	MATERIALS	ADVANTAGES
Face	Ceramic on steel Anodized aluminum Painted aluminum Stainless steel Painted steel Fiberglass-reinforced	Variety of finishes Matching adjacent metals Polished finish
Stabilizer panel	Tempered hardboard Asbestos-free board Mineral fiberboard Plywood* Gypsum board* Fire-rated fiberboard Polystyrene foam*	Lower cost, lighter weight Additional fire protection
Back	Ceramic on steel Galvanized sheet steel Aluminum sheet Exposed stabilizer panel	Attractive finished back May be finished in field
Anchors	Screws Concealed trim Exposed trim Plastic/metal rivets* Stainless steel nails*	

* Applicable to fiberglass panels only.

PANEL SIZE LIMITATIONS

PANEL	CERAMIC/STEEL (IN.)	FIBERGLASS (IN.)
Maximum width	60*	48*
Maximum length	144*	144*

* Custom size, color, and thickness available. Consult manufacturer.

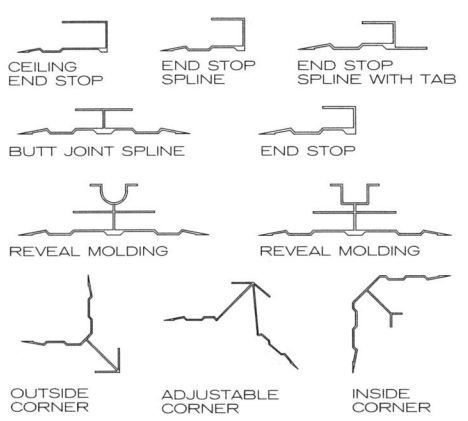

CERAMIC STEEL TRIM COMPONENTS

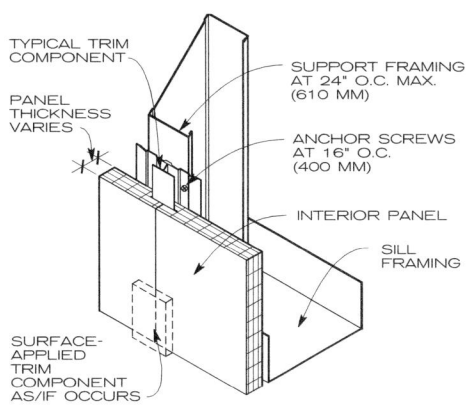

TYPICAL VERTICAL BUTT JOINT

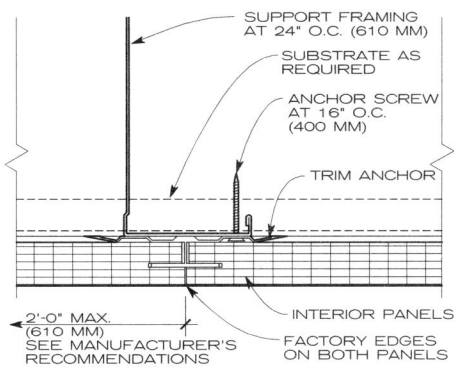

VERTICAL BUTT JOINT WITH CONCEALED TRIM

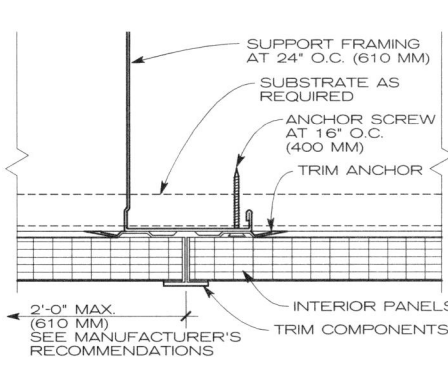

VERTICAL BUTT JOINT WITH EXPOSED TRIM

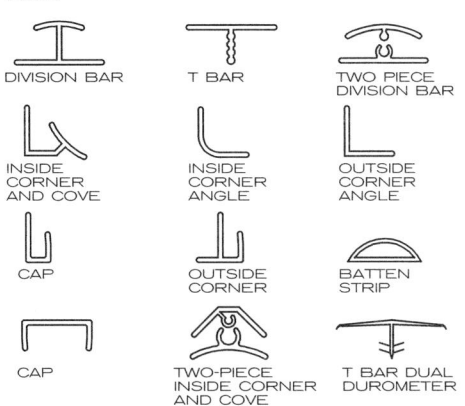

FIBERGLASS/VINYL TRIM COMPONENTS

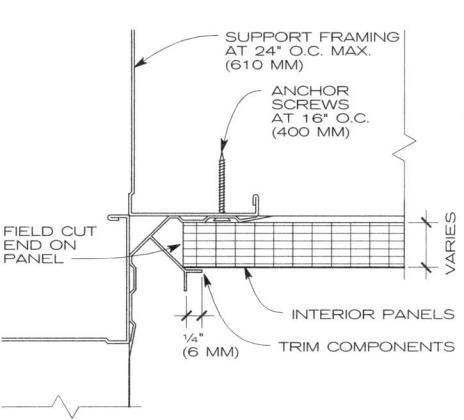

INSIDE CORNER

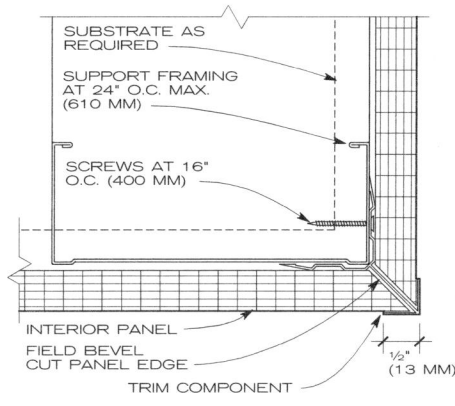

OUTSIDE CORNER DETAIL

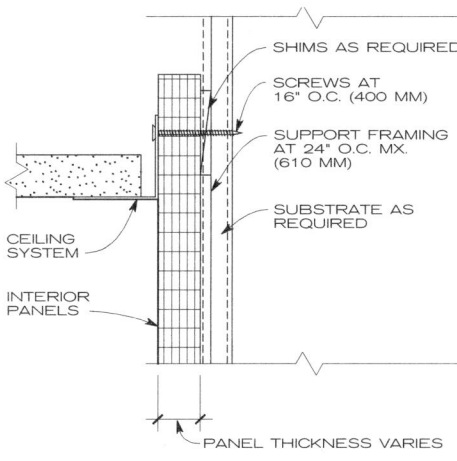

DETAIL AT CEILING

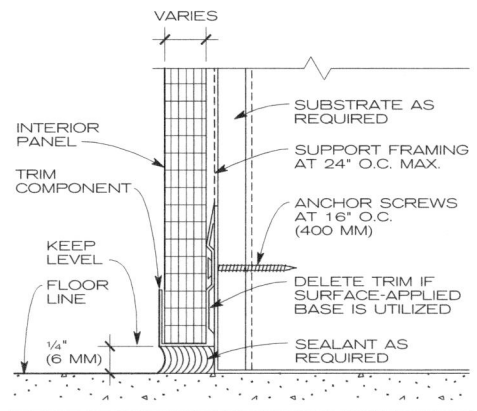

PANEL AT SILL

Kevin R. McDonald, AIA; HNTB Corporation; Alexandria, Virginia
Alliance America; Norcross, Georgia

SPECIAL WALL SURFACES

Linear Ceilings

LINEAR METAL CEILINGS

PANS

Dimensions: Typical widths range from 4 to 8 inches (100 to 200 mm).

Materials: Roll-formed sheet steel is for interior applications only; roll-formed aluminum can be used for interior or exterior applications.

Surface: Surfaces can be smooth, perforated or unperforated, or textured.

Finish: Baked polyester enamels, metallic coatings, and brushed or polished aluminum with a clear coating are available.

CARRIERS

Material: Roll-formed sheet steel is for interior use only, while roll-formed aluminum is suitable for interior or exterior applications.

Finish: The finish is flat black baked polyester enamel.

ACCESSORIES

Possible accessories include integral light fixtures and air diffusers, trim channels, splices, and end caps.

OPTIONS

Fire-rated and acoustically rated systems are available.

EXTERIOR APPLICATIONS OF LINEAR METAL CEILINGS

Wind loads must be factored in when exterior applications of linear metal ceilings and soffits are planned. Wind loads are determined by geographic conditions and a building's height above the ground. Linear metal systems must be engineered to withstand uplift pressure. Rigid bracing is used instead of suspension wires to support these systems.

LINEAR BAFFLE CEILINGS

Steel or aluminum baffles hung from a suspended ceiling framework mask exposed plenum areas. Baffles are available in a variety of profiles and depths ranging from 4 to 12 inches (100 to 300 mm).

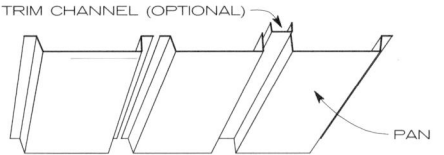

LINEAR METAL CEILING—OPEN REVEAL

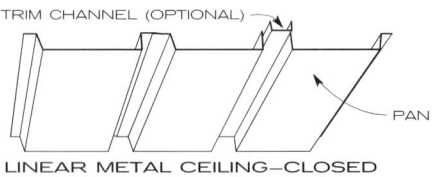

LINEAR METAL CEILING—CLOSED REVEAL

TYPICAL PAN CONFIGURATIONS

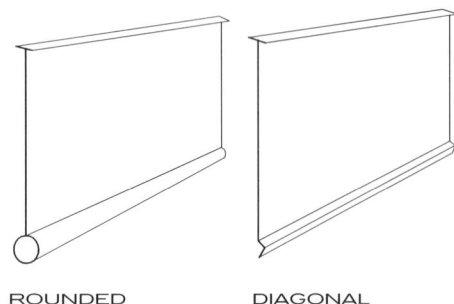

ROUNDED DIAGONAL

TYPICAL BAFFLE PROFILES

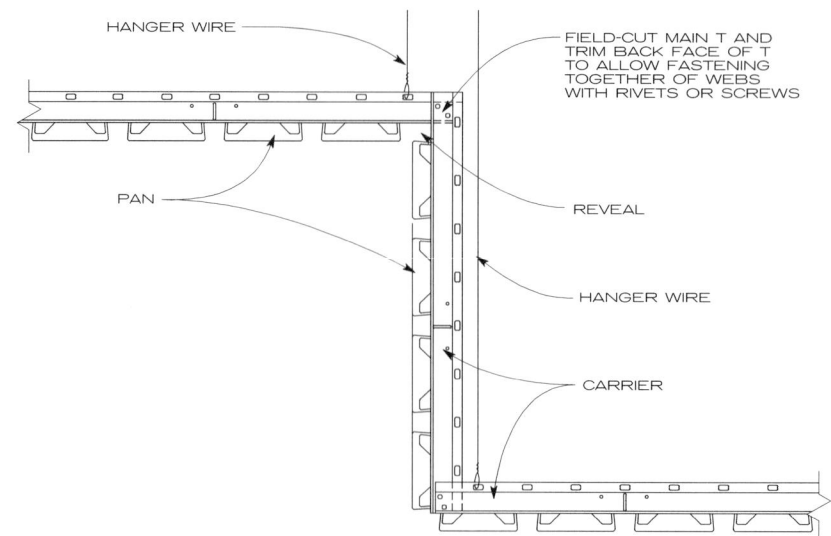

LINEAR METAL CEILING SYSTEM

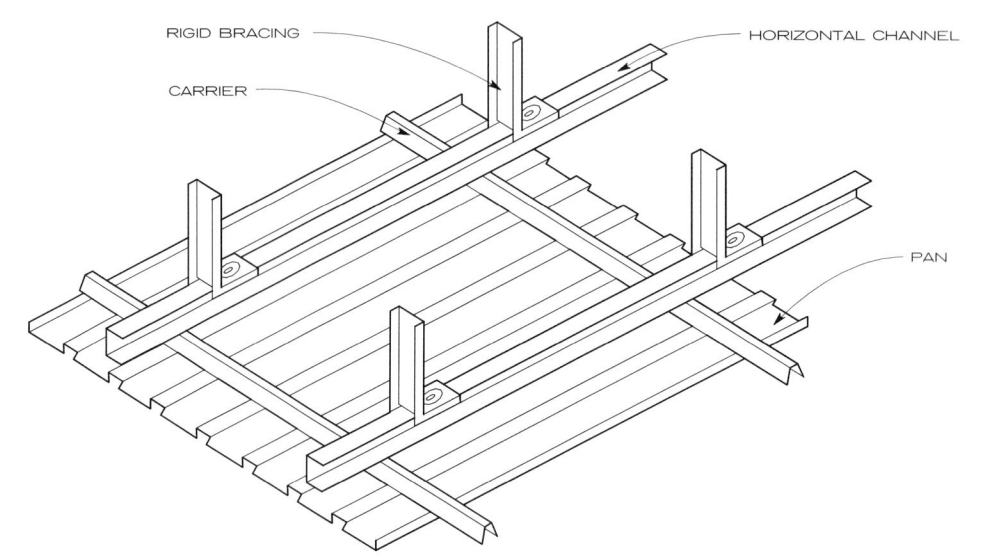

EXTERIOR LINEAR METAL CEILING SYSTEM

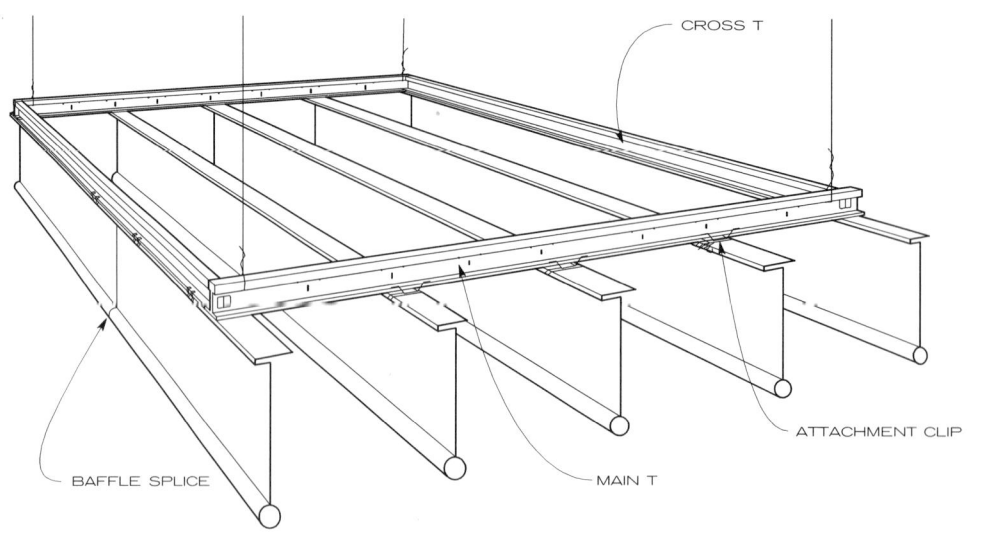

LINEAR BAFFLE CEILING SYSTEM

Keith McCormack, CCS, CSI; RTKL Associates; Baltimore, Maryland
USG Interiors, Inc., Chicago, Illinois

SPECIAL CEILING SURFACES

Textured Ceiling Panels

TYPES OF ACOUSTICAL CEILING UNITS

ACOUSTICAL TILE
These prefabricated, sound-absorbing ceiling units are installed in a concealed suspension system or directly attached to the substrate with adhesive or staples. Typical size is 12 by 12 inches (305 by 305 mm).

ACOUSTICAL PANEL
These prefabricated, sound-absorbing ceiling units are installed in a suspension system. Typical sizes are 24 by 24 inches (610 by 610 mm) and 24 by 48 inches (610 by 1210 mm).

CONSTRUCTION OF ACOUSTICAL CEILING UNITS

CAST (MOLDED)
These ceiling units are composed of mineral fibers, fillers, binders, and water mixed together to form a slurry. The slurry is cast on trays and heat cured. The pattern and sound-absorbing qualities are created by the treatment of the material face in the wet stage. After drying, acoustical units are painted; if color is added to the slurry, the unit will be colored throughout.

NODULAR
Nodular tiles are composed of mineral fibers, perlite, fillers, binders, and water mixed together to form a dry slurry. The slurry is formed into sheets, dried, and cut. The surface is inherently porous and is subsequently textured by mechanical fissuring and embossing; ceiling units are then painted.

WET-FELTED
Wet-felted tiles are composed of mineral fibers, fillers, binders, and water mixed together to form a slurry. The slurry is poured onto felts, drained, compacted, dried, and cut. Textures are created by mechanical perforation, fissuring, and stippling. Surface finishes include paint, fabric, polyester film, and vinyl-coated aluminum.

GLASS FIBER WITH FACING
This type of tile consists of nonwoven fiberglass insulation with a fabric or vinyl film surface finish.

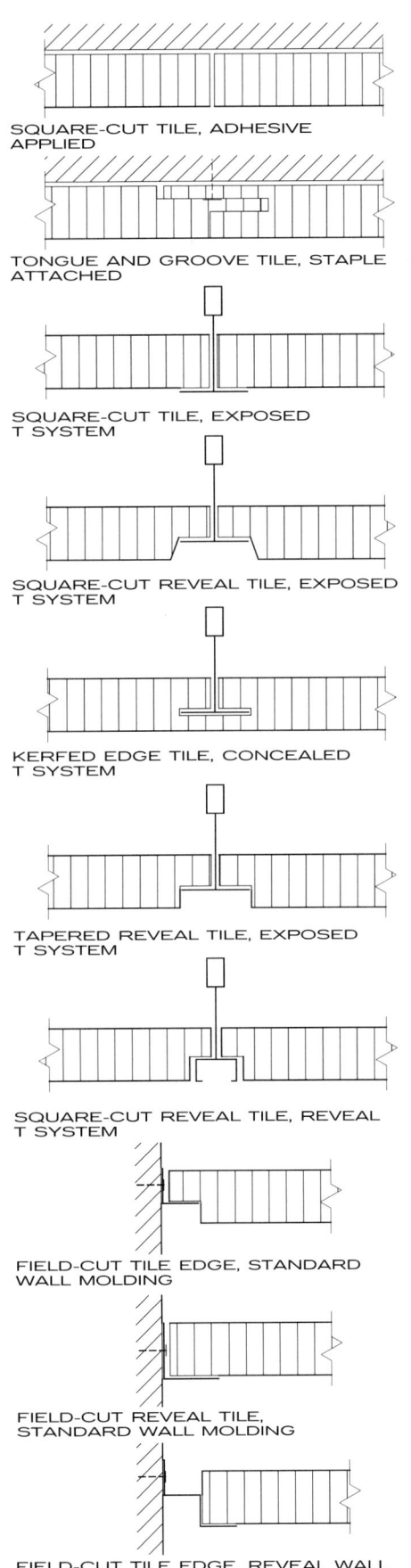

EDGE CONDITIONS AND SUPPORT SYSTEMS

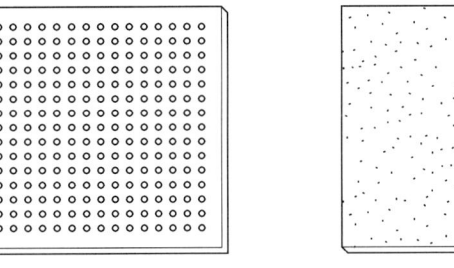
PERFORATED, REGULARLY SPACED HOLES

PERFORATEED, RANDOMLY SPACED HOLES

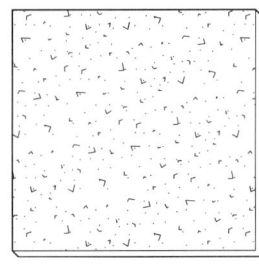
FISSURED

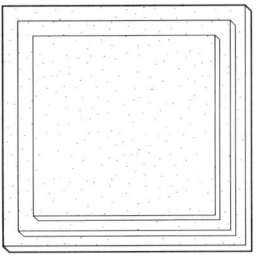
REVEAL EDGE, STIPPLE FINISH

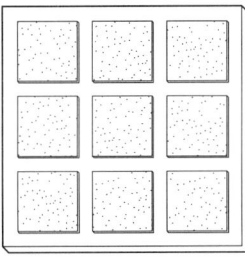
ROUTED PATTERN, PERFORATED FINISH

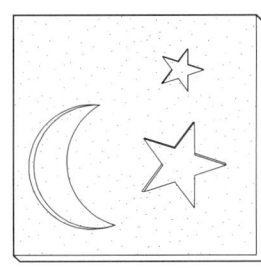
EMBOSSED DESIGN, STIPPLE FINISH

TWO-SQUARE, STIPPLE FINISH

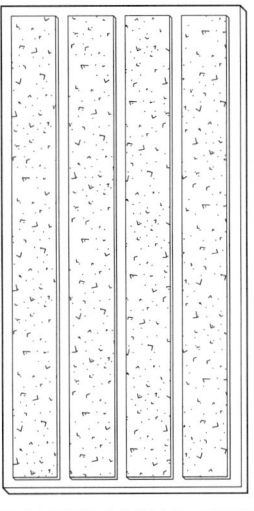
ROUTED LINEAR, FISSURED FINISH

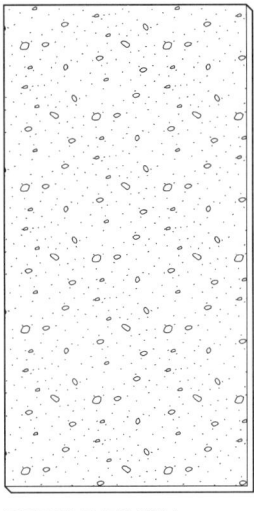
PEBBLE FINISH

ACOUSTICAL CEILING UNIT TEXTURES AND DESIGNS

Keith McCormack, CCS, CSI; RTKL Associates; Baltimore, Maryland

SPECIAL CEILING SURFACES

Resilient Wood Flooring Systems

GENERAL

The wood flooring types shown on this page are those most commonly used for sports facilities. The specifics of each floor system differ from manufacturer to manufacturer. Some flooring systems are proprietary and protected by patents. Manufacturers can custom configure flooring systems for special uses.

The type of wood sports flooring chosen for a particular situation depends on the following criteria:

1. Cost
2. The performance of the floor
3. Sport(s) to be played on the floor
4. Other uses to which floor will be put
5. Durability
6. The environment in which the floor will be used

GRADES OF WOOD SPORTS FLOORING

Maple is the wood most commonly used for sports flooring in the United States. Maple sports flooring is available in three grades, which designate only the appearance of the floor and not its performance or durability.

FIRST GRADE: nearly free of defects; least color variation, with very little dark hardwood; used in premier sports venues where appearance is of primary concern.

SECOND AND BETTER: may have tight, sound knots and other slight imperfections and some color variation; floor has a generally light appearance.

THIRD GRADE: all defects and color variations permitted; floor is mostly dark heartwood; used when cost is a consideration.

MAPLE FLOOR SYSTEM CHARACTERISTICS

SYSTEM	COST	PERFORMANCE	DURABILITY	STABILITY
Proprietary	High	High	High	High
Sprung	High	High	Medium	High
Sleeper	Medium	Medium	Medium	High
Cushioned	Low	Medium	High	Medium
Channel	Low	Low	High	High
Mastic	Low	Low	High	Medium

FINISHES AND GAME LINES

Wood sports floors are sanded, sealed, and finished with at least two coats of sealer and two coats of finish.

Game lines are painted between the last coat of sealer and the first coat of finish. Game line paint must be compatible with sealer and finish.

REFERENCE

Maple Flooring Manufacturers Association
60 Revere Drive, Suite 500
Northbrook, IL 60062

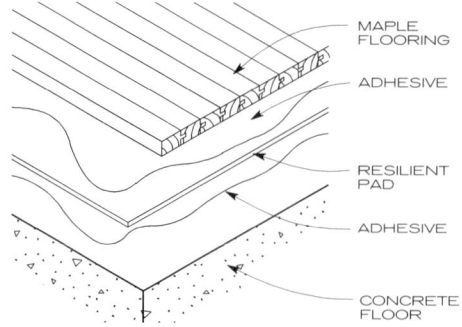

NOTES
1. Lowest cost
2. Easy to install
3. Suitable for multipurpose applications
4. Use where floor performance is not critical

MASTIC APPLIED SYSTEM

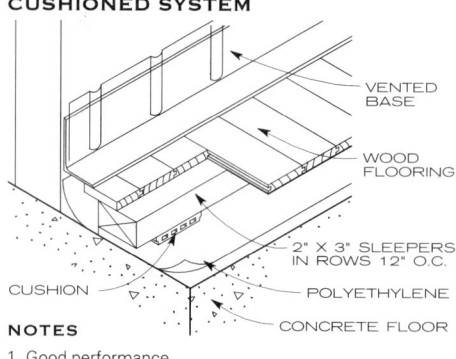

NOTES
1. Good performance characteristics
2. Relatively low cost
3. Susceptible to moisture damage

CUSHIONED SYSTEM

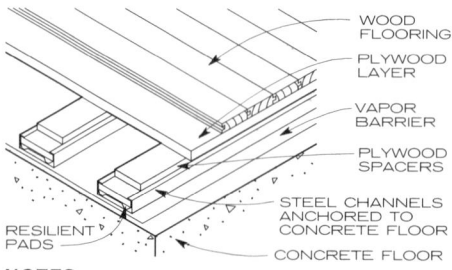

NOTES
1. Good performance
2. Can have dead spots
3. Susceptible to moisture damage
4. More difficult installation

SLEEPER SYSTEM

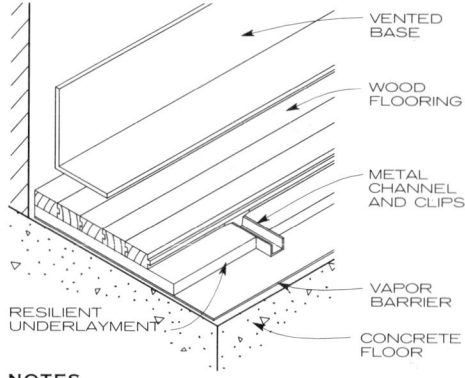

NOTES
1. Dimensionally stable in all environments
2. Good multipurpose floor
3. Limited performance characteristics

CHANNEL AND CLIP SYSTEM

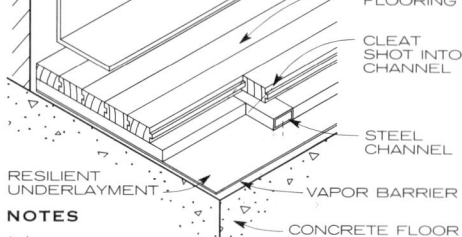

NOTES
1. Low cost
2. Fast installation
3. Dimensionally stable in all environments
4. Good multipurpose floor
5. Limited performance characteristics

NAIL-IN-CHANNEL SYSTEM

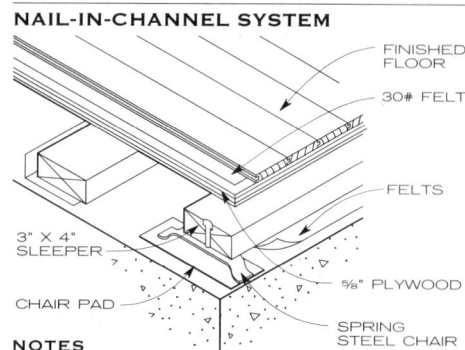

NOTES
1. Superior performance
2. High cost
3. Susceptible to moisture damage
4. More difficult installation

SPRUNG SYSTEM

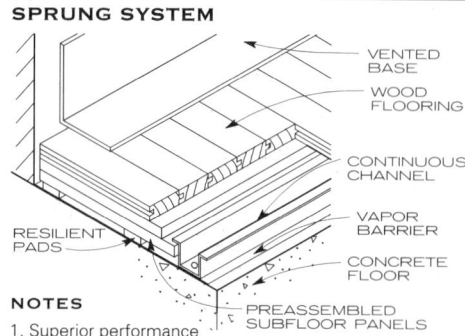

NOTES
1. Superior performance
2. Dimensionally stable
3. Suitable for multipurpose applications
4. A higher cost system

PROPRIETARY FLOATING SYSTEM— ROBBINS BIO-CHANNEL®

NOTES
1. Superior performance
2. Dimensionally stable
3. Suitable for multipurpose applications
4. A higher cost system

PROPRIETARY SYSTEM— CONNOR/AGA REZILL CHANNEL®

Jim Swords; HOK Sports Facilities Group; Kansas City, Missouri
Connor/AGA Sports Flooring Corporation; Amasa, Michigan

WOOD FLOORING

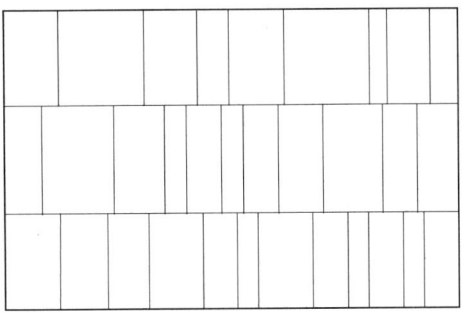
COURSED

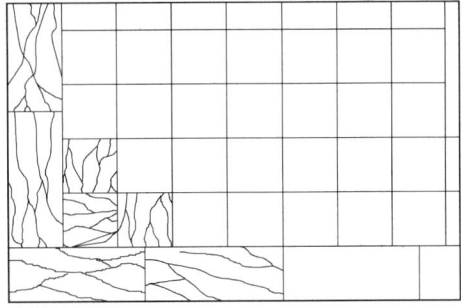
SQUARES

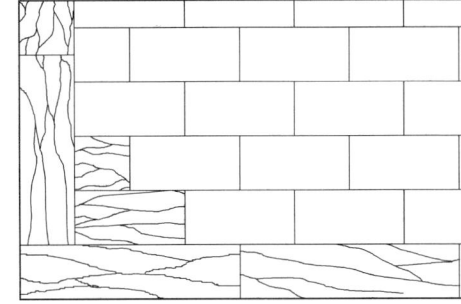
COURSED

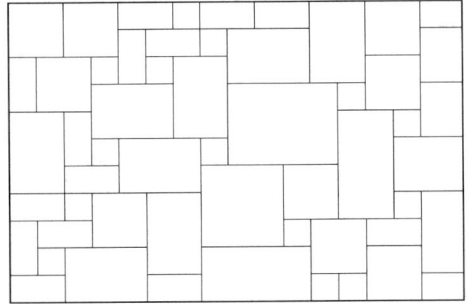
RANDOM RECTANGULAR

GEOMETRIC

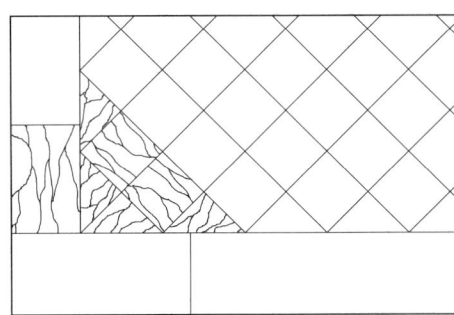
DIAMOND

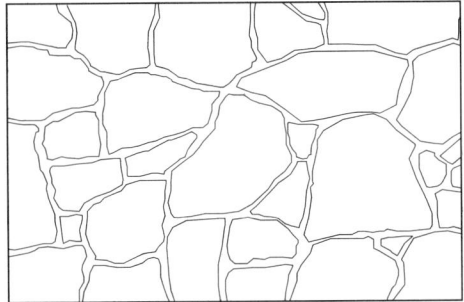
RANDOM IRREGULAR

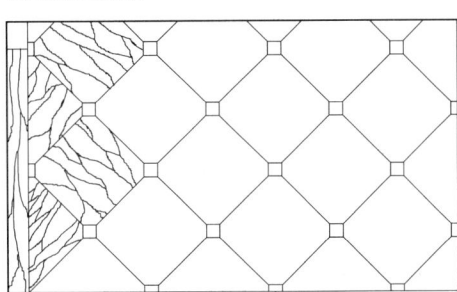

OCTAGON-SQUARE

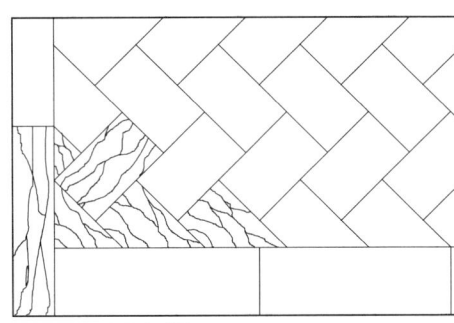
HERRINGBONE

FLAGSTONE AND SLATE PATTERNS

MARBLE AND GRANITE PATTERNS

FINISHES

POLISHED: A glossy surface that brings out the full color of the stone. Generally, polished finishes can only be used on hard, dense material such as granite or marble.

HONED: A satin smooth surface with little or no gloss.

THERMAL: A planar surface with flame finish applied by mechanically controlled means to ensure uniformity. Surface coarseness varies depending on the grain structure of the stone. Generally, thermal finishes are used on granite.

RUBBED: A planar surface with occasional slight scratches.

TYPICAL FINISHES AND COMMON SIZES OF STONE TILES AND PAVERS

STONE	FINISH	THICKNESS (IN.)(MIN.)	FACE DIMENSION (IN.)(MAX.)	Ha
Granite	polished honed thermal	$3/8$, $1/2$ (tiles) $1 1/4$ - 4 (pavers)	12 x 12 (tiles) 15 x 30 (pavers)	N/A
Marble	polished honed	$1/4$ - $1/2$ (tiles) $1 1/4$ (pavers)	12 x 12 (tiles) 24 x 24 (pavers)	10
Limestone	smooth	$1 3/4$ - $2 1/2$ (pavers)	24 x 36 (pavers)	10
Slate	natural cleft sand-rubbed	$1/4$ - 1	12 x 12 to 24 x 54	8
Flagstone	natural cleft semirubbed	$1/2$ - 4	12 x 12 to 24 x 36	8

NOTES

1. *Ha*, the abrasive hardness value, is the reciprocal of the volume of the material abraded multiplied by ten. A minimum value of 10 is recommended for flooring. Stones with a difference of 5 or more in *Ha* value should not be used together because they will wear differently.
2. Joint width should always be specified; $1/16$ to $1/8$ in. is considered standard.
3. Only attempt to set stone flooring over a wood subfloor after the subfloor has been reinforced to ensure against deflection.
4. Lippage is a condition that occurs when tiles are installed with a thin-bed method over an uneven surface. Tiles may "lip," one edge higher than their neighbors, giving the finished surface a ragged appearance. In some conditions, a certain amount of lippage is unavoidable. As a general rule, the recommended maximum variation of the finished surface should be no more than $3/16$ in. cumulative over a 10 ft. 0 in. lineal measurement, with no more than $1/32$ in. variation between individual tiles.

Mark Forma; Leo A. Daly Company; Washington, D.C.

Brick and Pressed Concrete Unit Flooring

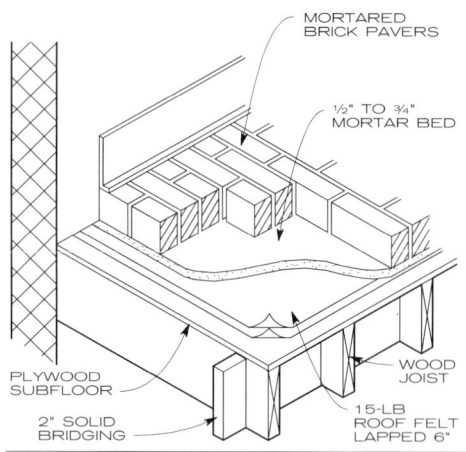

MORTARED BRICK PAVERS ON WOOD FRAMING

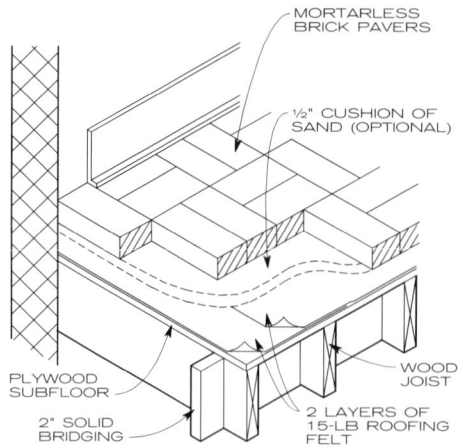

MORTARLESS BRICK PAVERS ON WOOD FRAMING

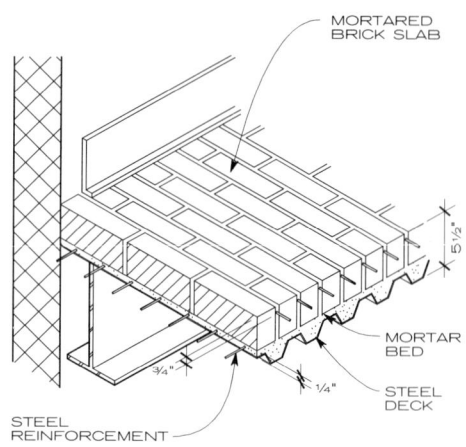

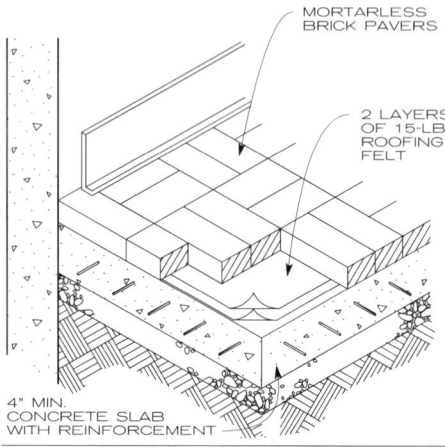

MORTARLESS BRICK PAVERS ON CONCRETE SLAB

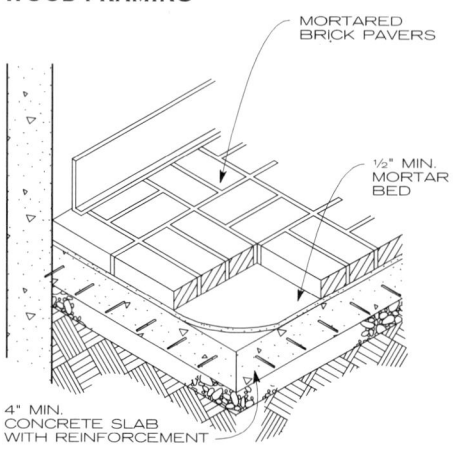

MORTARED BRICK PAVER ON CONCRETE SLAB

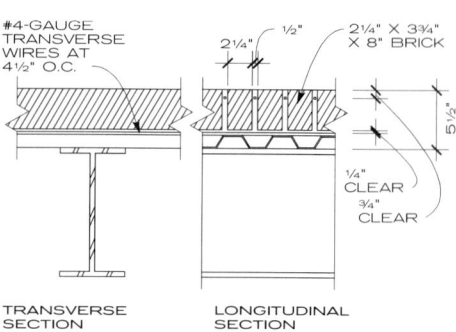

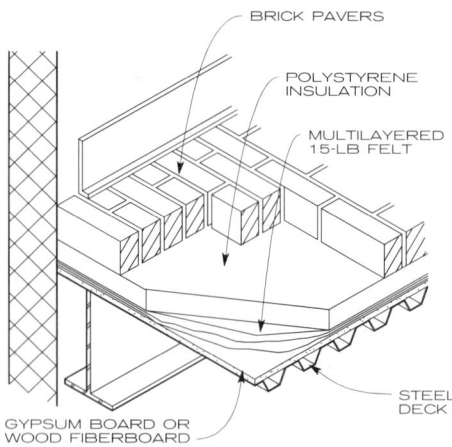

BRICK PAVERS ON STEEL DECK

TYPICAL BRICK AND CONCRETE PAVER TYPE AND NOMINAL SIZE

Brick pavers: 4 × 4 in., 4 × 8 in., 4 × 12 in.; 1/2 to 2 1/4 in. thick. Concrete pavers: 12 × 12 in., 12 × 24 in., 18 × 18 in., 18 × 24 in., 2 3/8 to 3 in. thick.

NOTES

1. Brick paving assemblies are classified by type of paving surface and type of base supporting the surface. Interior brick paving may be adapted to suspended diaphragm bases, reinforced brick structural slabs with mortar joints, and conventional concrete slabs on grade.

2. In residential wood joist design, the additional weight of brick pavers must be considered to ensure selection of a suitable grade and joist size. For mortared paving, deflection and diaphragm action must be considered in order to maintain the integrity of the mortar joints.

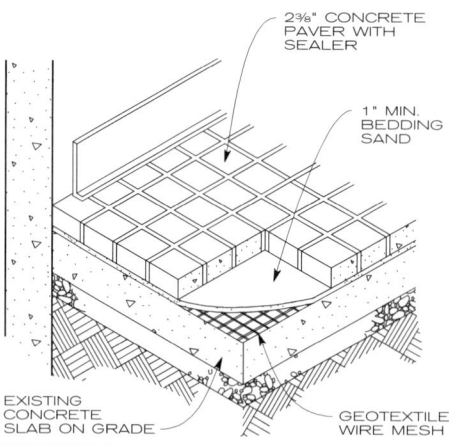

CONCRETE PAVERS ON CONCRETE SLAB

3. Reinforcement of brick masonry paving can eliminate the need for a separate reinforced concrete slab or other rigid base. Reinforced brick paving can be used to span an open space and is a practical system for relatively short spans. For continuous span application, an assembly combining both reinforced brick masonry and steel decking can be used.

4. Maintenance: Brick floors are abrasion resistant and hard-wearing. Coatings and waxes are desirable on interior brick floors, where they enhance appearance and make surfaces easier to clean. Prewaxing brick pavers on the exposed face facilitates cleaning, and applying a sealer locks in loose sand particles and provides an impervious finish.

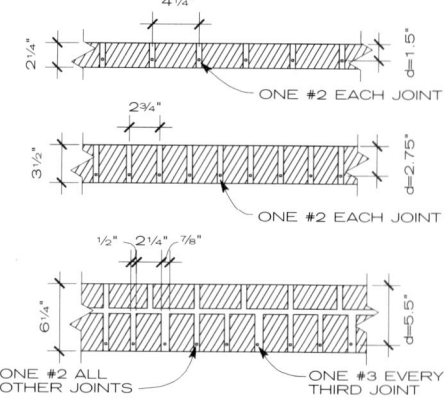

REINFORCED BRICK MASONRY

REINFORCED BRICK MASONRY SLABS

LIVE LOAD (PSF)	MAXIMUM CLEAR SPAN		
	$t = 2\,1/4$ IN. 1 #2 EACH JOINT	$t = 3\,1/2$ IN. 1 #2 EACH JOINT	$t = 6\,1/4$ IN. 1 #3 EVERY 3RD JOINT 1 #2 OTHER JOINTS
30	6'- 10"	10'- 5"	14'- 5"
40	6'- 3"	9'- 9"	13'- 8"
50	5'- 10"	9'- 2"	13'- 1"
100	4'- 6"	7'- 3"	10'- 11"
250	1'- 10"	5'- 0"	7'- 10"

NOTES

1. Design parameters for the table above: The compressive strength average of the brick is 8000 psi. The mortar is type M (1:1/4:3), portland cement:lime:sand. Reinforcement steel is ASTM A 82-66, $f_s = 20,000$ psi. A simple span loading condition was assumed.

$$M = \frac{wl^2}{8}$$

2. All mortar joints are 1/2 in. thick for the slabs shown, except as noted.

Mark Forma; Leo A. Daly Company; Washington, D.C.

UNIT MASONRY FLOORING

Special Flooring and Floor Treatment

SPECIAL FLOORING

Special flooring manufacture is a constantly changing industry with myriad products and companies. Choose products to meet the requirements of a specific application after consultation with manufacturers. Select a well-established, reputable manufacturer with a tested and proven product. Have the product installed by experienced, factory-trained personnel.

RESINOUS FLOORING

EPOXY RESIN FLOORING: This abrasion- and impact-resistant, broadcast and/or trowel-applied, two-component epoxy resin floor is made of graded aggregates and mineral oxide pigments. Typical thicknesses are $1/8$ and $1/4$ in. Epoxy resin flooring can be applied to a variety of substrates and usually cures overnight, depending on the humidity. It is chemical resistant, fire retardant, and odor free and may be made slip resistant with a satin finish.

ACRYLIC RESIN FLOORING: This two- or three-component system is based on methyl methacrylate acrylic (MMA) resins; it has a low VOC. Four types are available in varying thicknesses: primer/sealers (8-10 mils), coatings ($1/16$ in.), toppings ($1/16$ - $3/16$ in.), and overlays ($3/16$ - $3/8$ in.). The system comprises graded aggregates, mineral oxide pigments, and pigmented topcoats. Typically, a $1/8$ in. thick floor is sufficient for light loads and pedestrian traffic and a $1/4$ in. thick floor is required for normal to heavy loads. Heavy-duty loads require a floor $1/2$ in. thick or thicker. Uses include animal housing/runs, industrial, institutional, coolers/freezers, cafeterias, food preparation, and multipurpose recreational facilities.

LATEX RESIN FLOORING: This trowel-applied, jointless floor offers low absorption and good chemical resistance. Chemical-resistant types are available to handle a variety of anticipated chemical spills. A waterproof membrane may be used to make the floor entirely waterproof, and it may be turned up at the base to form an integral coved base. Uses include showers, laboratories, animal research housing, pharmaceutical plants, and TV studios.

MAGNESIUM OXYCHLORIDE FLOORING

This is a fireproof, trowel-applied, seamless, hard surface floor that is slip resistant in both wet and dry locations. Durable and simple to install, it is used primarily in commercial kitchens and manufacturing locations such as welding shops. Its use is not recommended when standing water or mineral corrosives will be present. The standard color is red, although some earth tones may be available.

EPOXY MARBLE CHIP FLOORING AND SEAMLESS QUARTZ FLOORING

This seamless decorative flooring consists of ceramic-coated quartz or colored quartz aggregates in clear epoxy. It may be broadcast or trowel-applied in thicknesses of $1/16$, $1/8$, or $1/2$ in. Available in a wide range of aggregate colors, it may be slip resistant and is typically installed over concrete substrate. It is used in laboratories, locker rooms, and light manufacturing and institutional locations.

ELASTOMERIC LIQUID FLOORING

Conductive elastomeric liquid flooring—a multiple- or single-part system applied over concrete, metal, or wood substrates—consists of elastomeric resins, nonsparking aggregates, and a carbon or metallic conductive agent. Typically applied in thicknesses of $1/4$ or $1/2$ in., it may be applied to a wide variety of substrates and in a series of coats to achieve a smooth finish. Durable, easy to install, jointless (no divider strips), and waterproof are characteristics of this type of floor.

Elastomeric liquid flooring is designed to provide static control and spark resistance that can prevent electrostatic damage to electronic products as well as the conductivity required to prevent fire or explosions in high-hazard environments. The slab and conductive surface must be grounded and the floor well maintained in order for the floor to keep the required conductivity and static dissipative properties. Typical installations requiring these qualities include clean rooms and electronic manufacturing and assembly facilities. Typical installations requiring the conductive capabilities of elastomeric liquid flooring include arsenals, ammunition plants, chemical processing facilities, and hazardous explosive areas. End user static control and spark resistance must be clearly specified to ensure appropriate levels of resistance. People working in these environments must wear conductive footwear.

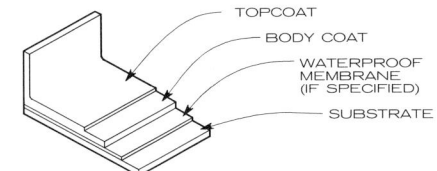
EPOXY RESIN FLOORING

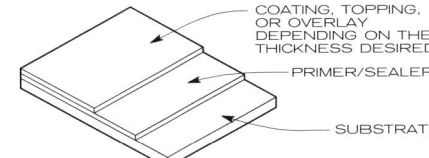
ACRYLIC RESIN FLOORING

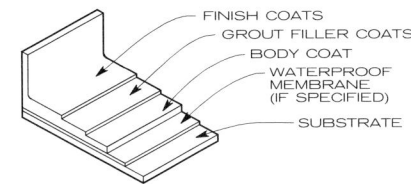
LATEX RESIN FLOORING

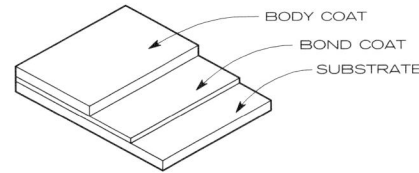
MAGNESIUM OXYCHLORIDE FLOORING

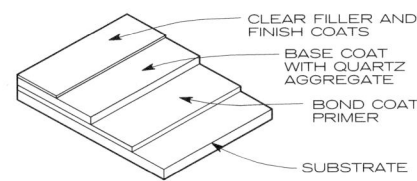
EPOXY MARBLE CHIP/ SEAMLESS QUARTZ FLOORING

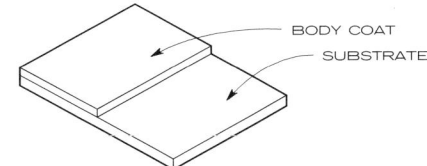
ELASTOMERIC LIQUID FLOORING

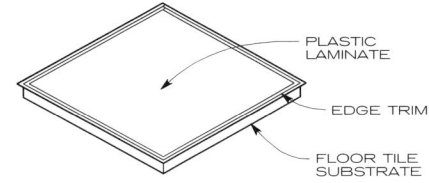
PLASTIC LAMINATE FLOORING

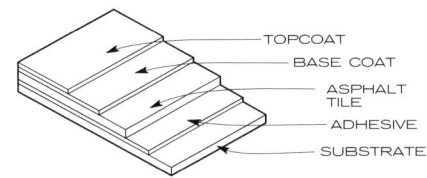
ASPHALT TILE FLOORING

FLOOR COATINGS

PLASTIC LAMINATE FLOORING

Plastic laminate flooring generates and retains low static levels. It has a low sheen, matte finish. Durable, flexible, and easily maintained, it is used exclusively as the top finish surface for access flooring. Applied to access floor substrates of steel, aluminum, wood, or particleboard with moisture-resistant adhesives, this type of flooring consists of a formulated, washable, surface sheet over a melamine-impregnated printed pattern sheet with core layers of phenolic-impregnated kraft paper. Typical tile size is 24 x 24 in., with standard thicknesses of $1/16$, $5/64$, and $1/8$ in., depending on load. Three quality grades are available. Floors must meet or exceed ANSI, NEMA, and NFPA codes and criteria.

ASPHALT PLANK FLOORING

A smooth, heavy-duty, comfortable, long-lasting, low maintenance tile floor, asphalt plank flooring is used in post offices, warehouses, and industrial locations. Tiles are set in adhesive troweled over a concrete substrate. An acrylic protective base coat is applied in two to three layers after the tiles have been set. A topcoat of two to three layers is applied to give the floor a high gloss for easier maintenance. Standard tile size is $1/2$ x 12 x 24 in. Other available thicknesses are $1/4$ - 3 in. Standard available colors are black and red.

MASTIC FILLS

Products described in other categories may also be considered in this one. Examples include self-adhering floor or deck coatings, traffic toppings, and underlayments that also fill cracks or uneven surfaces. Taken literally, this heading can include "mud set" mortar for tile over uneven substrates.

FLOOR TREATMENT

METALLIC-TYPE STATIC-DISSEMINATING AND SPARK-RESISTANT FINISH

This product is designed to provide static-control properties and spark-resistance capabilities that can prevent electrostatic damage to electronic products, as well as the conductivity required to prevent fire or explosions in high-hazard environments. The slab and conductive surface must be grounded. Maintenance of the floor is critical in order to keep the required conductivity and static-dissipative properties. Typical installations requiring static-dissipative products include clean rooms and electronic manufacturing and assembly facilities. Typical installations requiring conductive products include arsenals, ammunition plants, and chemical processing and other explosive hazardous areas. End user static control and spark resistance must be clearly specified to ensure appropriate levels of resistance. People working in these environments must wear conductive footwear.

Dry-shake metallic floor hardener is blended with plasticizing agents and conductive binders. This blend is applied to the surface of plastic concrete and becomes an integral part of the floor surface. It can be applied with a mechanical spreader, by hand, or with a shovel. Concrete admixture, air content, and floor finish requirements are strictly defined by metallic floor hardener manufacturers in terms of compatibility and amount, etc.

SLIP-RESISTANT FLOOR TREATMENT

These cementitious or noncementitious coatings are specifically designed to provide a nonskid finish for interior or exterior floors. Silica or synthetic aggregates provide the nonskid capability. The treatment is formulated for use on concrete or masonry surfaces and may be brushed or rolled on or trowel- or fluid-applied.

Chip Baker; Sverdrup Facilities Inc.; Arlington, Virginia

SPECIAL FLOORING

Special Coatings

DEFINITION

Special coatings are adhesive materials that have been developed for specific purposes such as resisting severe or corrosive environments or other forms of abuse. Special skills and techniques are usually required to mix, handle, and apply these materials.

A "special coating system" includes applied materials used in prime, intermediate, and finish coats. Factors that influence the choice of a system include

1. Substrates
2. Environmental conditions and surroundings
3. Cost

Prime and finish coats should be specified from the same manufacturer to eliminate many compatibility problems.

Proper substrate preparation, priming, and spread rate thickness are important for successful application of special coatings. Application is made by spray, brush, roller, or trowel.

SURFACE PREPARATION

The major reason coatings fail is poor surface preparation, which impairs adhesion. No coating is better than the surface over which it is applied. Surfaces must be prepared by a method suited to how they will be used and the exposure they will receive, in accordance with manufacturers' recommendations and the Steel Structures Painting Council (SSPC).

METAL SURFACES

Before a coating is applied, metal surfaces must be thoroughly cleaned, eliminating all visible deposits of surface dirt, grease, oil, and other deposits. Loose mill scale, rust, paint, and other detrimental foreign matter must also be removed. Grind rough welds and sharp edges, and remove weld spatter.

The SSPC recommends a variety of methods for preparing steel surfaces before application of a coating:

SSPC-SP-1 Solvent Cleaning
SSPC-SP-2 Hand Tool Cleaning
SSPC-SP-3 Power Tool Cleaning
SSPC-SP-5 White Metal Blast Cleaning
SSPC-SP-6 Commercial Blast Cleaning
SSPC-SP-7 Brush-off Blast Cleaning
SSPC-SP-8 Pickling
SSPC-SP-10 Near White Blast Cleaning

CONCRETE AND MASONRY SURFACES

Coatings adhere best to clean and slightly rough substrates. Grease, dirt, oils, efflorescence, laitance, and other surface deposits must be removed before additional surface preparation begins. Cleaning may be achieved by methods such as mechanical abrasion, abrasive blast, high pressure water wash, or acid etching. If cleaning solutions are applied, they must be completely removed before the coating is applied. Surfaces must be dry. If the surface is very smooth, it must be abraded or roughened slightly.

TYPES OF SPECIAL COATINGS

CEMENTITIOUS COATINGS

Polymer-modified, inorganic coatings can be ideal on concrete and masonry substrates. These coatings are primarily used on vertical surfaces above or below grade, on the exterior or interior, and on new construction or restoration and renovation work for aesthetics, permeability, and moisture resistance. They are also useful for walls subject to positive or negative hydrostatic pressure.

ABRASION-RESISTANT COATINGS

Epoxy or elastomeric seamless coating may be used over substrates of brick, stucco, concrete, block, drywall, and plywood in both interior and exterior applications. These coatings may be weatherproof and resist chemicals. Abrasion resistance may be inherent or achieved through an additional topcoat.

ELASTOMERIC COATINGS

Acrylic polymer coatings may be used over exterior concrete, masonry, and stucco surfaces. These thick, dirt-resistant, membranelike coatings are flexible in a range of temperatures, displaying an ability to follow expansion and contraction of surfaces without rupturing or wrinkling. They are very high-build materials that bridge small cracks and protect against deterioration from moisture penetration of the substrate. Like other special coatings, these typically should not be used to bridge building expansion joints. Acrylic polymer coatings are available in smooth and textured finishes.

HIGH-BUILD GLAZED COATINGS

Acrylic resin, elastomeric, or epoxy coatings may be suitable for use over exterior or interior concrete, block, masonry, plaster, stucco, wood, and metal surfaces in vertical or horizontal applications. Applied in multiple coats or thick single coats, these coatings usually provide resistance to chemicals and abrasion. These high-performance coatings provide good adhesion and hardness, producing a tile-like gloss finish. Some systems may be reinforced with fiberglass mesh between base and seal coats to increase maximum impact resistance.

FIRE-RESISTANT PAINTS

Fire-resistant paints are able to withstand fire and protect the substrate for short periods of time, usually less than one hour. They will not support combustion and do not deteriorate readily under fire conditions. They will reduce or prevent the spread of flame over a combustible surface. In some cases they may be used as one component of a fire-rated assembly. The products of such an assembly are noncombustible, and the coating, which prevents oxygen from reaching the substrate, contains chemicals that inhibit the release of volatile gases necessary for combustion.

To be eligible for listing as a fire-retardant paint, a coating must either reduce the flame spread of the surface to which it is applied by at least 30% or have a flame spread rating of 70 or less as tested under current ASTM E-84 guidelines. Manufacturers may recommend a three- to five-year schedule for reapplying the coating in order to maintain its fire-resistant capability. Fire-resistant paints can be used to coat wood, drywall, plaster, and metal.

INTUMESCENT PAINTS

Intumescent paint is a type of fire-resistant paint that behaves differently than typical such products in a fire condition. When subjected to flame or intense heat, intumescent paints liquefy, allowing escaping gases to form an insulating layer of char, which forms a protective layer around the substrate. Fire-resistant designs have been tested by independent laboratories to establish application requirements and the extent of protection available. Incompatible paints used as a topcoat with intumescent paints may prevent the chemical reactions necessary to form the intumescent char, thereby reducing or negating the fire-resistant property.

GRAFFITI-RESISTANT COATINGS

Graffiti-resistant coatings permit the easy removal of graffiti without damage to the substrate. The system comprises a multicoat base system that increases the hardness of the substrate and a sacrificial, multicoat topcoat system. Cleaners can be nontoxic and do not require sandblasting, solvents, or toxic materials. Additional topcoats can be added after cleaning, if desired, to reinforce the sacrificial protection layer.

COATING SYSTEMS FOR STEEL

Selection of steel coating systems for tanks and piping are primarily governed by substrate and service conditions. Industry specific standards also affect specifications. Water treatment, food processing, energy production, and chemical processing industries have different requirements and standards that should be verified prior to specification. Water tanks in most U.S. jurisdictions must meet very stringent National Sanitary Foundation (NSF) requirements for potable water storage.

EXTERIOR COATING SYSTEM FOR STEEL STORAGE TANKS

Choice of coating for steel storage tank exteriors depends on tank condition and location, the weather during application, and the service conditions. A number of two-part epoxy systems and urethane systems have been formulated to address these concerns. Coatings may possess rust-inhibitive qualities, the ability to cure at low-temperatures, and excellent weathering ability and may offer galvanic protection. Dry-fall ability may be desirable in some instances and is available from alkyd products. Compatible products can be used as metal fillers and to accelerate curing rates. Local regulations regarding the content of volatile organic compounds (VOCs) will influence product selection and application techniques.

INTERIOR COATING SYSTEM FOR STEEL STORAGE TANKS

Choice of coatings for steel storage tank interiors is affected by tank condition and location and service conditions. A number of two-part epoxy systems and phenolic systems have been formulated to address these concerns. These products are designed to provide sustained immersion service in food processing, petrochemical, and water treatment industries for use in freshwater, saltwater, and severe chemical environments. National Sanitation Foundation (NSF) approvals may be necessary in certain applications.

COATING SYSTEM FOR STEEL PIPING

Coatings for steel piping are subject to many of the same conditions as coatings for steel tanks. Coatings for piping used for chemical service must be selected to match the level of chemical exposure expected. Mild exposures may permit the use of an acrylic coating, while aggressive chemical and moisture exposure may require the use of chlorinated rubber coatings. Severe chemical exposures typically require a two-part epoxy system.

The American Society of Mechanical Engineers and ANSI publish standardized color codes for pipe identification. For example, red means fire protection equipment; yellow, dangerous materials; blue, protective materials; green, safe materials; yellow with a black legend or stripe, radioactive materials.

Isabel Ramirez and Ted Hallinan; Sverdrup Facilities Inc.; Arlington, Virginia

CHEMICAL-RESISTANT COATINGS

EXPOSURE	TYPE OF COATING	APPLICATIONS	ALCOHOLS	ALIPHATIC HYDROCARBONS	ALKALI SOLUTIONS	AROMATIC HYDROCARBONS	FRESHWATER	KATONES	MINERAL ACIDS	MINERAL OILS	ORGANIC ACIDS	OXIDIZING AGENTS	SALT SOLUTIONS	VEGETABLE OILS	WASTEWATER	WEATHERING
Rural, urban light industrial	Alkyd primer and alkyd topcoat	Warehouses, manufacturing plants, schools, storage tank exteriors	O	O	N	N	O	N	N	C	N	N	N	N	N	G
Mild chemical	High-build epoxy, polyamide-cured, and urethane topcoat	Wood yards, plywood plants, sawmills	C	C	C	O	C	N	O	C	O	O	C	C	C	E
Fresh and salt water immersion; moderate chemical exposure	Coal tar epoxy, polyamide-cured	Pilings, waste treatment pits, pulp and paper mills, marine structures and barges, cogeneration	C	C	C	C	I	N	O	C	O	O	I	C	I	F
Fresh and potable water immersion	High-build epoxy, amine-cured	Water storage, tank interiors, locks and water control gates	C	C	C	C	I	O	O	C	O	O	I	I	I	F
Severe chemical	High-build epoxy, polyamide-cured, and urethane topcoat	Pulp and paper mills, coal-handling, chemical pits, sour crude refineries, fertilizer plants	C	C	C	O	C	O	O	C	O	O	C	C	C	E
Severe chemical—acid resistance	High-build epoxy, amine-cured	Pulp and paper mills, dockside exposures, fertilizer pits, acid loading docks, dye plants	C	C	C	C	I	O	O	C	C	C	I	I	I	F
Severe chemical—alkali and solvent resistance	Organic zinc-rich epoxy primer and high-build epoxy, polyamide-cured, topcoat	Pulp and paper mills, coal-handling facilities, dockside exposures	C	C	C	C	I	O	O	C	O	O	C	C	I	F
Severe chemical—alkali resistance	Organic zinc-rich epoxy primer and high-build epoxy, polyamide-cured, and urethane topcoat	Capital structures where color and gloss retention are needed	C	C	C	O	C	O	O	C	O	O	C	C	C	E
Severe chemical—solvent and alkali resistance	Inorganic zinc-rich primer and high-build epoxy polyamide-cured topcoat	New construction, pulp and paper mills, power pits, coal liquefaction, cogeneration	C	C	C	C	I	O	O	C	O	O	C	C	I	F
Severe chemical	Zinc-rich primer and urethane topcoat	Where gloss retention and color are important	C	C	C	O	C	C	O	C	O	O	C	C	E
High temperature (up to 1200°F)	Heat-resistant silicone aluminum	Stacks, incinerators, superheated steam lines, boiler casings and drums	O	O	N	N	N	N	N	C	N	N	N	N	N	E
Immersion, severe exposures	Coal tar epoxy polyamide-cured	Waste treatment pits, pulp and paper mills, cogeneration, power pits, sour crude exposures	C	C	C	O	I	N	O	C	O	O	I	C	I	F

I—immersion   C—frequent contact   O—occasional contact   N—not recommended   F—fair   G—good   E—excellent

CHEMICAL-RESISTANT COATINGS

Chemical-resistant coatings are selected according to substrate type and actual chemical exposure. Formulations of this product type vary widely from manufacturer to manufacturer and are subject to changes caused by technological advances and environmental legislation. Dry-film thicknesses, cure rates, and application methods also vary among product types and manufacturers. End user program requirements and consultation with manufacturers is recommended before specifying these products. In-place or laboratory testing may be advisable in critical conditions.

Isabel Ramirez and Ted Hallinan; Sverdrup Facilities Inc.; Arlington, Virginia

Paints and Coatings

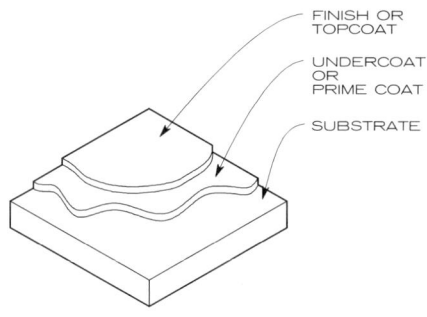

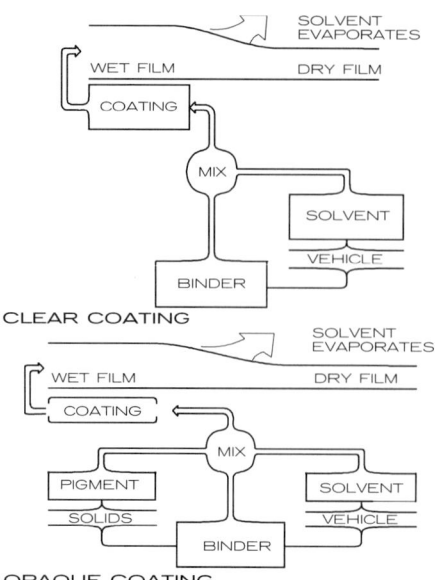

TYPES OF COATINGS

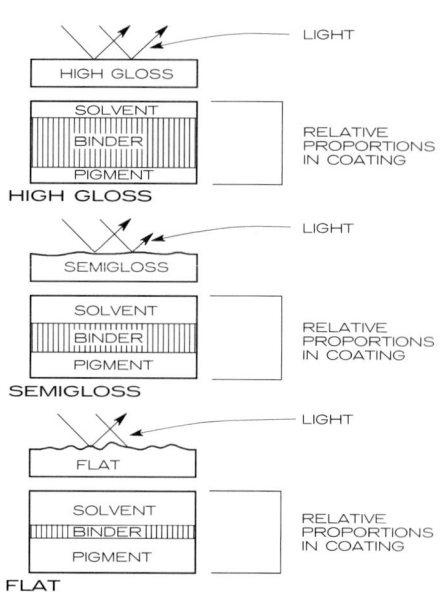

EFFECT OF PIGMENT CONTENT ON GLOSS OF COATING

COMPOSITION OF COATINGS

GENERAL

Coatings are thin surface facings applied in liquid form which solidify to protect building components from harmful exposure. Appropriate coating selection depends upon performance, appearance, cost, and rate of deterioration of the substrate should the coating fail. Coatings are made up of the prepared substrate, prime coats or undercoats, and finish or topcoats, all of which should be compatible for adhesion and resistance to deterioration.

DESIGN CONSIDERATIONS

Environmental and ambient conditions affect coating performance. Resistance to sun, moisture, pollution, chemicals, extremes of temperature, soiling, and abrasion will determine a set of coatings, from which a selection is made based on remaining criteria. Design considerations should also include:

1. Flow, or ease of application.
2. Leveling or smoothing after application.
3. Drying time, of which two factors are important: (a) set-to-touch or surface drying, when surface resists contaminants, and (b) through-dry, when all layers are dry and ready to recoat.
4. Permeability: moisture migration through coating.
5. Wetting: penetration of coating to a lower level. Lower wetting ability requires greater surface preparation.
6. Film thickness: amount of protection provided by coating.
7. Adhesion between layers.
8. Flexibility: accommodation to changes in moisture and temperature.
9. Abrasion, impact, and stain resistance and ease of cleaning.

TYPES

Coatings are classified by appearance—clear, semitransparent, or opaque, and are water-based or organic solvent-based. Coatings are composed of a vehicle—alone when clear, or with pigments when semitransparent or opaque. The vehicle is in turn composed of binder and solvent. The binder is the nonvolatile part of the vehicle which forms the film of the coating and which bonds pigments when they are used. Additives for special properties, such as driers, stabilizers, plasticizers, and thinners, are included in the binder. The solvent is the volatile part of the vehicle which dissolves the binder to adjust viscosity, and which evaporates as the coating changes from liquid to solid state. Pigment adds opacity and/or color to the vehicle.

Clear coatings only slightly obscure the surface of the substrate. They are used when it is important to preserve appearance, such as the grain of wood or the color of an exposed concrete aggregate. Clear coatings are composed of a vehicle only, solvent and binder, with no pigment added. Sealers, waterproofing, and varnishes are typical examples of clear coatings.

Semitransparent coatings partially obscure the substrate surface. They can modify the appearance of the substrate by changing the color of wood without hiding its grain. Semitransparent coatings are composed of solvent, binder, and limited pigment. Stains are exemplary of this group.

Opaque coatings completely obscure the surface of the substrate. The color and/or texture of the substrate are changed; the original appearance unimportant or undesirable. Opaque coatings are made up of pigment, solvent, and binder. Paints are opaque coatings.

Coating properties are determined by the binder, which forms the surface film and bonds to the substrate. A combination of binders will alter the properties displayed by a coating, as will additives that modify the formation of the coating. Binders composed of small molecules (e.g., drying oils) penetrate rough surfaces and adhere well but dry slowly and are not chemically resistant. Binders composed of large molecules, built-up or polymerized of smaller molecules, yield strong, chemically resistant films but are susceptible to dissolution in the same solvent when formulated for solvent evaporation only. Large molecules may be formed by reaction between small molecules as in linseed oil; they may be made before application and dissolved in solvent to lower viscosity; or they may be formed by a combination of these two methods.

Pigments hide the substrate by adding opacity and color, but may also increase durability and protective characteristics by screening UV radiation, controlling transmission of moisture and gases, and inhibiting degradation or corrosion of the substrate. Colored pigments absorb some light rays while reflecting others, and white pigments absorb little light, so their hiding efficacy depends on the ability to scatter and reflect incident light. Scattering and reflecting ability in turn depends upon the size, distribution, and refractive index of the pigment particles. Pigment also determines the gloss of the coating finish through its relative proportion to binder and solvent in the vehicle.

Environmental exposure concurrent with or following application of the coating may affect the coating or the substrate. Some types of exposure to consider are atmospheric contamination, such as sulfurous or marine air which may discolor coatings and accelerate chalking and deterioration; mildew in humid environments; and sudden drops or rises in temperature at the time of application, which may flatten or blister a freshly applied coating.

EXTERNAL FACTORS

A number of external factors affect the stability of a coating.

SOLAR RADIATION/UV RADIATION can fade colored pigments, cause chemical reaction in some binders or solvents, and degrade the substrate if the coating is not UV opaque. It may be necessary for the coating to reflect, scatter, or absorb visible light to avoid this problem.

TEMPERATURE: Solar radiation raises the temperature of the coating, causing expansion and accelerating solvent evaporation. Exposure to heat through convection of hot air or other gases, or by conduction through the substrate (as through accidental exposure to fire) may also affect coating performance. Freezing temperatures hinder proper curing of some vehicles.

RAIN: A heated coating can undergo thermal shock when exposed to rain. Rainwater can also be absorbed and cause swelling of the coating or leach pigments from the coating. Rain may also penetrate through cracks or checks and freeze, causing damage to the coating and the substrate.

WATER VAPOR: Vapor may be required to properly cure some coatings. Under some conditions water vapor should be allowed to permeate the coating to prevent condensation, while at other times permeation must be prevented to protect the substrate.

CHEMICAL FUMES: Generated by chemical processes or by burning fossil fuels, chemical fumes can leave deposits on the coating, by reacting directly with it or by entering solution with rainwater or condensation.

DUST, DIRT: Dust penetrates porous coatings, collects airborne pollutants, and can stain or degrade the coating in reaction with rainwater. Marring of the coating may also be intentional, as with graffiti.

ABRASION, IMPACT: Coatings can be abraded by high-velocity flow of gaseous or liquid substances, by traffic, vandalism, or airborne dust. Impact may be through natural causes such as hailstones, may be accidental, or may be intentional, as with vandalism.

SURFACE WATER: External fresh or sea water can rise and fall, exposing normally submerged portions of the surface to solar radiation and oxygen and subjecting the coating and substrate to differential thermal expansion between the exposed and submerged portions of the surface.

CHEMICAL SOLUTIONS: Coatings may be submerged in chemical solutions such as sea water, sewage, oils, lubricants, or solvents and some of these may react with specific constituent parts of the coating, degrading or dissolving it.

SELECTION CONSIDERATIONS

Coating selection should be based on external or environmental factors (see above), type and degree of exposure to these factors, including an estimate of speed of substrate deterioration should the coating fail. Conditions met by the coating may vary over time, across a surface, or within the substrate, and contingencies should be planned. The possibility of an alkaline substrate such as concrete becoming moist through penetration or condensation should be considered before a non-alkaline-resistant coating is applied. Differential wear on walking or other surfaces should be considered, as well as applications of higher performance coatings.

The in-place cost of a coating accounts for surface preparation and application as well as the coating itself. Failure may result in permanent damage to the substrate, or may require complete removal and preparation for a new coating. The properties of the principal binder should determine the selection of a coating, with modifications and additions to the formulation made for specific job requirements.

SAFETY AND HEALTH CONSIDERATIONS

Hazards associated with coating application and surface preparation include toxic fumes from strong solvents; toxic dust from sandblasting, grinding, or fire; and toxicity of coating solvents when absorbed through skin or inhaled. In addition, use of photochemically reactive solvents may be limited or restricted by air-pollution controlling ordinances.

James W. Laffey; Washington, D.C.

PAINTING

PAINTS AND COATINGS: PROPERTIES

TYPE	PRINCIPAL BINDER	BASE/ CURE	TYPICAL USES	COMPARATIVE COST RANGE	IN-SERVICE LIFE RANGE IN YEARS	GLOSS RETENTION	STAIN RESISTANCE	WEATHER RESISTANCE	ABRASION IMPACT RESISTANCE	FLEXIBILITY
Clear	Acrylic, methyl methacrylate copolymer	solvent; water	Waterproofing and surface sealer against dirt retention, graffiti; for vertical surfaces of concrete, masonry, stucco; may be pigmented.	moderate to high	5 to 10	excellent to good	fair	excellent to good	good	good
	Alkyd, spar varnish	solvent	For interior and protected exterior wood surfaces. Also as vehicle for aluminum pigmented coatings.	moderate	up to 1 exterior	fair to good	poor	poor	fair	good
	Phenolic, spar varnish	solvent	Exterior wood surfaces subject to moisture. May be used in marine environments. Also vehicle for aluminum pigment.	moderate to high	up to 2 exterior	fair to good	fair	good	good	good
	Silicone	solvent	Waterproofing and surface sealer against dirt retention for vertical surfaces of concrete, masonry, stucco.	moderate	5 to 7	flat	fair	good	penetrating coating	
	Urethane, one-part	moist cure[1]	Surfaces subject to chemical attack; abrasion, graffiti, heavy or concentrated traffic, such as gymnasium floors.	moderate to high	up to 15	excellent to good	good to excellent	good to excellent	good to excellent	excellent
Stain	Acrylic	solvent; water	Pigmented translucent or semi-opaque exterior surface sealers; solvent based for masonry, concrete; water based for wood.	moderate to low	3 to 5	flat finish	not a factor	good to fair	penetrating coatings—resistance same as for substrate	
	Alkyd	solvent; water	Pigmented exterior or interior surface sealer for wood surfaces such as shingles, does not impart sheen to surface.	moderate	3 to 5	flat finish		fair		
	Oil	solvent	Pigmented exterior or interior surface sealer for wood such as shingles, trim, opaque or semitransparent.	moderate	3 to 5	fair		fair		
Opaque	Acrylic	water	For exterior/interior vertical surfaces of wood, masonry, plaster, gypsum board, metals. Good color retention. Permeable to vapor.	moderate to low	5 to 8	good to fair	fair	good	good to fair	good to excellent
	Acrylic, epoxy modified, two-part	water	High performance coating for interior vertical surfaces subject to graffiti, stains, heavy scrubbing. May be used in food preparation areas.	high	10 to 15	good	good	good to excellent	good to excellent	good to excellent
	Alkyd	solvent; water	For exterior/interior vertical and horizontal surfaces, such as wood, metals, masonry. Poor permeability to vapor.	moderate	5 to 8	good to excellent	fair	fair to good	fair to good	fair to good
	Chlorinated rubber	solvent	Swimming pool coatings. Corrosion protection; isolating dissimilar metals.	high to very high	up to 10	fair	fair	good	fair to good	good
	Chlorosulfonated polyethylene	solvent	Protective coating for tanks, piping, valves, elastomeric roofing membranes.	very high	up to 15	not applicable	fair	excellent	fair to good	excellent
	Epoxy, two-part; epoxy ester, one part	solvent cure; solvent	Moisture/alkali resistant. Two-part for nondecorative interior uses highly resistant to chemicals. Esters in wide choice of colors.	high to very high	15 to 20; up to 10	poor to good	excellent for two-part	good to excellent	excellent	good to excellent
	Phenolic	solvent	Chemical- and moisture-resistant coatings. May be used over alkaline surfaces.	moderate to high	up to 10	fair	fair	good to excellent	good to excellent	good
	Polychloroprene	solvent[2]	Marketed as "Neoprene"; resistant to chemicals, moisture, ultraviolet radiation. Also used as roofing membrane; generally covered with Hypalon.	very high	up to 25	not applicable		good	excellent	excellent	good
	Polyester	solvent	Limited application in field; over cementitious surfaces, metal, plywood for exterior exposures.	high	up to 15	good to excellent	good to excellent	good to excellent	good	good to excellent
	Silicone	solvent	Surfaces with temperatures up to 1200°F. Often with aluminum pigments. Corrosion and solvent resistant.	very high	varies	not applicable, special purpose coating			good	good
	Silicone; modified acrylic, alkyd, epoxy	solvent	High-performance exterior coatings. Industrial siding, curtain walls, when shop-applied baked-on.	high to very high	15 to 20	good to excellent	good	good to excellent	good	good
	Styrene, butadiene	water	Interior coating for gypsum board, plaster, masonry. Limited exterior use over cementitious substrate, as filler over rough porous surfaces.	moderate to low	4 to 6	poor to fair	fair	poor	fair	good
	Urethane, one or two part	moist or chemical cure[3]	Heavy-duty wall and floor coatings. Resistance to stains, chemicals, graffiti, scrubbing, solvents, impact, abrasion.	high to very high	15 to 20	excellent	good to excellent	good to excellent	good to excellent	excellent
	Vinyl, polyvinyl chloride-acetate	solvent	Residential metal siding and trim, gutters, leaders, baseboard heating covers, when shop-applied, baked-on.	high	up to 15	good	fair	good	good	good to excellent
	Vinyl, polyvinylidene chloride	water	Metal and concrete surfaces in contact with dry and wet food, potable water, wastewater, jet and diesel fuels.	high	up to 10	good	good	good	good	good
	Vinyl, polyvinyl acetate	water	Exterior and interior vertical surfaces, such as masonry, concrete, wood, plaster, gypsum board, metals. Permeable to vapor.	moderate to low	5 to 8	good to fair	fair	good	good to fair	good
	Bituminous, coal tar pitch, asphalt; emulsions, cutbacks	solvent	Waterproofing of metals, concrete, masonry, portland cement plaster, piping when below grade or immersed.	low	10 to 15 protected	not a factor		good	poor	fair
	Cement	water	Leveling coat over porous masonry or concrete not subject to abrasion or scrubbing. Cement and oil used as primers for metal surfaces.	low	varies	flat finish	poor	poor for color	good	poor

[1] Solvent-based, oil-modified urethane is also available; for use on interior/exterior vertical and horizontal wood surfaces. Cost is moderate.
[2] May be obtained as water-reducible coating; use as field-applied coating very limited; generally used as tank linings.
[3] Solvent base, oil-modified urethane is also available; for use on vertical and horizontal surfaces. Cost is moderate, but durability is lower than for other types.

NOTES

1. Solvent-based acrylic is impermeable to water vapor, high gloss.
2. Water-based acrylic is semigloss, water vapor permeable.
3. Phenolic varnish has a dark tint; will darken with age; may be topcoated with clear alkyd.
4. Clear varnishes are not recommended for exterior wood because of limited durability.
5. Urethane may be formulated to yield hard, glossy surface so that graffiti can be removed with strong solvents.
6. Fillers may be required when using clear coatings over hardwood, such as oak; abraded wood may limit choice; consult manufacturer's literature.
7. Stains may be used as surface sealers to change color of wood and then be topcoated with clear coatings.
8. Stains over exterior wood surfaces generally will provide better protection than clear coatings, but usually will not last as long as opaque coatings.
9. Alkyd may be modified with silicone for better color retention.
10. Epoxy-esters have intermediate properties between two-part epoxies and alkyds and phenolics.
11. Bitumen-epoxy formulations are available for use as heavy-duty waterproofing of underground piping, structural members.
12. Phenolic may chalk upon exterior exposure; high degree of resistance to acids, alkalis, and solvents; some formulations available for surface temperatures of up to 300-350°F.
13. Polyesters available glass fiber reinforced; also used widely for baked-on factory applied finishes for formed metal wall panels.
14. Silicone for high temperature applications generally with aluminum pigment.
15. Polyvinyl chloride film is used for factory-applied finishes for formed metal wall panels.
16. Cement paint will absorb rainwater and will darken until water evaporates; requires moist curing after application; if not properly cured will tend to dust and rub off.
17. For high performance coatings under severe conditions, life expectancy may be less.

James W. Laffey; Washington, D.C.

Paints and Coatings: Substrate Conditions

GENERAL

Paints and coatings are in liquid form before and during application, after which they cure to form a non-self-supporting film. They cannot exist without a solid, generally rigid substrate to receive and support them. Since a coating bonds itself firmly and continuously to the substrate, the exposure, condition, and properties of the substrate, as well as its surface characteristics and defects, directly affect the coating during and after application.

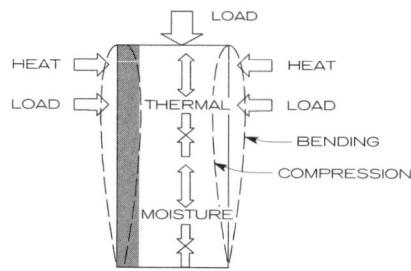

NOTES

Movement in the substrate, which may crack the coating, may result from

1. Thermal expansion/contraction due to exposure to solar radiation; sources of heat outside the substrate, such as heat-generating equipment adjacent to it; and heat-generating processes contained by the substrate.
2. Differential thermal movement between the substrate and the coating it supports, caused by variations in exposure. For example, rain may suddenly cool a coating over a hot substrate or solar radiation may heat a coating over a cold substrate.
3. Shrinking/swelling due to changes in the internal moisture content of the substrate. Under extreme conditions, variations may be as much as 5% or more across the grain in wood.
4. Deflection under load, vertical or horizontal, which induces tensile and compressive stresses in the substrate that may affect the coating.
5. Restrained end conditions of the substrate, which may cause bending stresses. Vibration in the substrate will result in cyclical stress reversals.

SUBSTRATE MOVEMENT

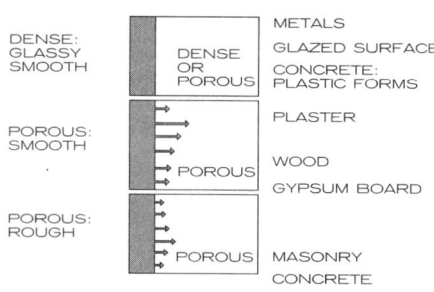

NOTES

Absorption at the surface of the substrate and that of the substrate itself may vary and affect the choice of coating or its performance characteristics:

1. Glassy dense surfaces, even applied over a porous substrate, will prevent absorption of a coating. Such surfaces may require roughening by sandblasting or acid etching to ensure proper adhesion of coatings.
2. Porous substrates may have varying degrees of absorption within a continuous surface (for example, different rates of absorption in bands of spring and summer growth of wood). Different rates of absorption will result in different degrees of adhesion and may cause a coating to crack along junction lines between such bands.
3. The rough surface of a porous substrate may cause varying degrees of absorption in an application, even though the absorption of the substrate does not vary significantly. For instance, when the roughness of a surface prevents the application of a film of uniform thickness over it, different rates of absorption may result. This will cause changes in the gloss of the coating, overpigmentation in areas of excessive absorption of the vehicle, and varying degrees of adhesion.

SUBSTRATE ABSORPTION

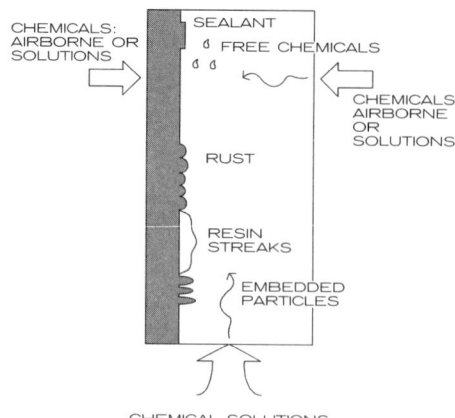

NOTES

Chemicals may be contained within the substrate or absorbed by it:

1. Soluble alkaline salts in concrete or mortar may be dissolved and crystallize on the surface.
2. Resin streaks in wood may react with the coating and bleed through, or old coatings may react chemically with new ones.
3. Rust deposits may stain some coatings and may impair adhesion.
4. Sealants used in joints may stain the substrate and/or coating.
5. Fasteners may corrode; loose particles of metal may lodge themselves in the substrate and corrode after the coating is applied.
6. Admixtures, form oils, curing agents, and antifreeze solutions used when concrete is cast may prevent proper adhesion of coatings or may react with them.
7. If cleaning solutions used during surface preparation are not completely removed before the coating is applied, they may react with the coating or impair its absorption and/or adhesion.

CHEMICALS IN SUBSTRATE

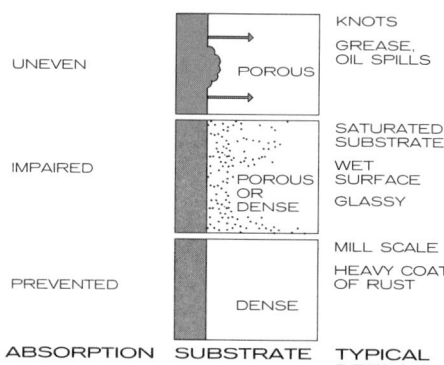

NOTES

Uneven or impaired adhesion results in coating failure. Adhesion of the coating to the surface of a substrate is affected by

1. Surface defects such as knots, resin streaks in the wood, or surface contaminants such as oil, grease, or salt deposits over any type of substrate. Such defects impair bonding of the coating to the substrate, creating weak spots where vapor may condense. When the vapor expands, it breaks or lifts the film.
2. Moist or wet surfaces. These may impair adhesion of certain coatings. In particular, moisture collection at the bonding surface of coatings may result in blistering or lifting of the film.
3. Use over glassy surfaces. Incomplete adhesion to glassy surfaces may result in flaking and peeling of the film.
4. Deposits of mill scale, heavy coats of rust, and salts. These prevent adhesion.
5. Surface defects and contaminants that have not been corrected or removed before a coating is applied.

ADHESION TO SUBSTRATE

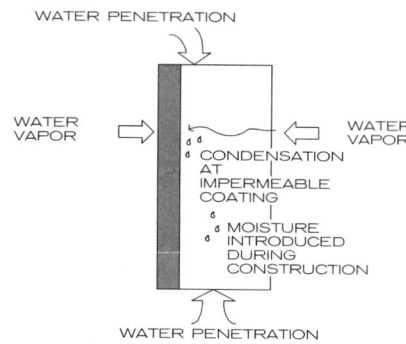

NOTES

Moisture may penetrate a porous substrate as

1. Water vapor migrating from high vapor pressure areas, such as warm, humid interior spaces, to low vapor pressure areas, such as cold, dry outdoors. If the dew point occurs within the substrate, vapor will condense, especially if the coating is of low permeability and blocks its free passage to the outdoors.
2. Water vapor penetrating a permeable coating to condense on a cold impermeable substrate such as metal
3. Rain penetrating into the substrate through faulty joints, damaged or faulty flashings, or cracks in the coating
4. Water absorbed when the substrate was exposed to rain or ground moisture while improperly stored before or during construction
5. Water that was a constituent part of the substrate during construction and has not yet evaporated. Generally a slow process, this condition often occurs in concrete, mortar, or gypsum plaster since more water is generally used than is required by the hydration process.
6. Moisture in the substrate when the coating is applied, which may prevent proper adhesion
7. Moisture penetrating the substrate after application of a coating, which may destroy the bond between substrate and coating.

MOISTURE IN SUBSTRATE

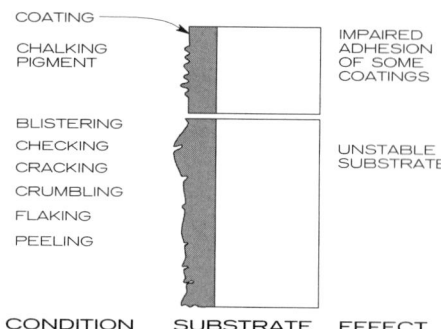

NOTES

When new coatings are applied over previously coated substrate, the surface stability of the old coating may affect the performance of the new coating. All coatings deteriorate over a period of time, and deterioration of a coating may result in

1. Chalking, which leaves behind loose pigment. Chalking occurs when the vehicle is broken down by weathering, particularly solar radiation. Suitable coatings may be applied to surfaces that are chalking with little or no surface preparation, although loose chalk should always be removed as a minimal measure.
2. Checking and cracking. Breaks can develop in coatings as they lose flexibility with age. These occur when stresses imposed on the coating by thermal or moisture movements in the substrate exceed the strength of the coating.
3. Crumbling, flaking, and peeling. Generally caused when moisture and airborne pollutants penetrate the coating, crumbling, flaking, and peeling may follow checking and cracking.

Coatings that have deteriorated until extensive checking is evident generally should not be used as a receiving surface for new coatings. Cracked, crumbling, flaking, or peeling surfaces should never be used, and the old coating must be completely removed from the substrate before application of a new coating.

COATINGS AS SUBSTRATE

McCain McMurray; Washington, D.C.

Paints and Coatings: Types and Uses

EXTERIOR

SUBSTRATE		COATING SYSTEM TOPCOAT; TYPE AND BASE		PRINCIPAL BINDER	COATING GLOSS	COLOR RETENTION	SUBSTRATE SURFACE CONDITION	NOTES TO DESIGNER OR SPECIFIER
Wood Dry, Vertical	SIDING, vertical/horizontal • recommended moisture content not over 12% • protected from moisture or limited occasional exposure to water Typical components: • veneered plywood siding • MDO plywood siding • hardboard siding • redwood siding • cedar siding, shingles, and shakes	clear; solvent	topcoat	phenolic, tung oil	gloss semigloss	poor	dry only	1. Clear coatings are not recommended for plywood. 2. Light color stains have shorter durability than heavily pigmented ones. 3. PVA is used on yellow pine and red cedar. 4. Acrylic is resistant to ultraviolet rays, thus doesn't become brittle or yellowed. 5. No coating for wet wood has been recommended; wood should be dry before any coating is applied. 6. Opaque stains hide surface imperfections and will last longer but will also hide the wood grain. 7. Wood requires primer to equalize absorption; hardboards require filler to smooth out grain. 8. Always use oil-based primer under any coating on cedar and redwood. 9. Backprime and edge seal wood in locations subject to occasional moisture penetration or to water vapor migration and/or condensation. Unless properly sealed, only permeable coatings such as acrylic should be used; even then, they may peel. 10. Clear phenolic coatings may be protected with alkyd-type clear coatings for better color retention. 11. All knots and pitch streaks should be sealed with shellac and all nails set and nail holes filled. 12. Even galvanized, ferrous metal nails may corrode and stain water-based coatings because such coatings allow water vapor to penetrate to the nails, increasing the possibility of rusting. 13. Alkyds may react with chemicals in previous coatings. 14. Clear finishes for trim and doors may be pigmented to stain the wood, or a staining primer may be used. 15. Extensive surface preparation, when required, applies to both previously coated and uncoated surfaces but principally to previously coated ones.
			primer	self-priming, topcoat, or shellac			dry only	
		stain; water, or solvent	topcoat	alkyd, oil base, self-priming (solvent)	flat	fair	dry only	
		opaque; solvent	topcoat	alkyd	gloss semigloss	good	dry only	
			primer	alkyd, oil base			dry only	
		opaque; water	topcoat	acrylic	semigloss flat	excellent	may be damp	
			primer	alkyd, oil base acrylic, emulsion			dry only	
	TRIM • recommended moisture content not over 12% • occasional exposure to moisture or water Typical components: • shutters • doors • accent areas of limited size • railings	clear; solvent	topcoat	urethane, one part oil modified	gloss semigloss	fair	dry only	
			primer	self-priming			dry only	
		stain; solvent	topcoat	none recommended				
		opaque; water or solvent	topcoat	alkyd, oil base (solvent)	gloss semigloss	good	dry only	
			primer	alkyd, oil base			dry only	
Wood Floors Dry	• recommended moisture content not over 12% • exposed to moisture or water • subject to light to moderate traffic Typical components: • porch decking • exterior stairs	clear; solvent	topcoat	none recommended				1. Clear coatings for exterior floors are not recommended because ultraviolet radiation may degrade not only the coating but the substrate as well. Once the substrate fails, it has to be completely refinished before it can receive another coating; clear coatings may last one to two years and may require yearly maintenance. 2. Pigmented coatings only are recommended for wood exposed to sunlight; pigments used should block penetration of ultraviolet radiation to the substrate. 3. Water-based coatings generally are porous and not sufficiently abrasion resistant for use on surfaces subject to abrasion. 4. Urethane has excellent resistance to abrasion, alkali, acids, solvents, strong detergents, and fuels. Clear urethane is not recommended for exterior exposure due to possible degradation of the substrate by ultraviolet radiation.
			primer	not applicable				
		clear; solvent	topcoat	urethane, one part moist cure	gloss semigloss	fair	dry only	
			primer	self-priming; follow for hardwood recommended			dry only	
		clear; solvent	topcoat	urethane, one part, moisture cure	gloss, semigloss	fair	dry only	
			primer	self-priming			dry only	
Concrete, Masonry, and Stucco Dry, Vertical	• aged over 90 days • no visible signs of efflorescence • protected from moisture entry • limited water vapor diffusion Typical components: • precast concrete panels • concrete, clay masonry • stucco, cement-bound mineral fiber	clear; solvent	topcoat	silicone (min. 5% solution)	flat	N/A	dry only	1. Solvent-based coatings are not recommended for use over exterior concrete or masonry surfaces as such coatings form an impermeable film, preventing the escape of any moisture that may still be present in or may later penetrate the substrate. Condensation at the interface of coating and substrate may also contain soluble alkaline salts; either one or both may cause blistering or peeling. Solvent-based coatings should only be used when the substrate is completely dry and there is no possibility of substantial moisture penetration. 2. Water-based coatings generally allow water vapor to escape to the outside and do not present the same problem as solvent-based coatings. 3. Silicone should be considered more as a water repellent than a coating film. 4. Heavy-bodied, water-based coatings are available as fillers for rough surface masonry units.
		clear; water	topcoat	acrylic, methyl methacrylate	semigloss	good	may be damp	
		opaque; solvent	topcoat	alkyd	gloss semigloss flat	good	dry only	
			primer	styrene-butadiene				
		opaque; water	topcoat	acrylic	semigloss flat	excellent		
			primer	self-priming				

Table continues on following page

McCain McMurray; Washington, D.C.

134 Paints and Coatings: Types and Uses

EXTERIOR (CONTINUED)

SUBSTRATE		COATING SYSTEM TOPCOAT; TYPE AND BASE		PRINCIPAL BINDER	COATING GLOSS	COLOR RETENTION	SUBSTRATE SURFACE CONDITION	NOTES TO DESIGNER OR SPECIFIER
Concrete floors, Dry	• aged over 90 days • light to moderate traffic • surface intact, dusty	clear; solvent	topcoat	epoxy ester	gloss	fair	dry only	1. Sealers-hardeners are preferably applied to fresh concrete. 2. Epoxy is a high-performance, high-cost coating suitable for floors exposed to heavy wear, chemical spills, and moisture. It may be used to resurface worn floors after proper patching. 3. No coating will perform well over a poor quality substrate. 4. The compatibility of coating with bond breakers, curing agents, and hardeners that may have been used over the substrate should be checked.
			primer	self-priming			dry only	
	• aged over 90 days • light to moderate traffic • surface worn, dusty	opaque; solvent	topcoat	urethane, one-part moisture cure	gloss semigloss	fair	dry only	
			primer	self-priming, substrate to be patched			dry only	
Concrete, Wet	• aged under 30 days or when subject to water penetration or condensation • surfaces cleaned to remove efflorescence Typical components: • concrete walls • concrete floors	clear, or opaque; solvent	topcoat	hardening sealing compounds				1. Epoxy may be used over damp surfaces; it is a high-performance, high-cost coating. 2. Application of coatings should be delayed as long as possible to allow the substrate to dry out. 3. Coatings considered should be water vapor permeable. 4. Bleeding of alkaline salts to the surface may result in brown spots over permeable coatings. If impermeable coatings are used over permeable primer, such coatings are likely to blister and peel.
			primer					
		opaque; water	topcoat	none recommended				
			primer	not applicable				

INTERIOR

SUBSTRATE		COATING SYSTEM TOPCOAT; TYPE AND BASE		PRINCIPAL BINDER	COATING GLOSS	COLOR RETENTION	SUBSTRATE SURFACE CONDITION	NOTES TO DESIGNER OR SPECIFIER
Gypsum Board Walls, Ceilings	Subject to • light scrubbing • mild detergents	opaque; water or solvent	topcoat	alkyd (solvent)	gloss semigloss flat	good	must be dry	1. Epoxy-modified acrylic is suitable for severe exposure in food preparation areas; it is available USDA-approved when required. 2. Solvent-base coatings should not be used directly over gypsum board as they tend to raise the nap of the paper facing. 3. Joints in gypsum board should be taped and spackled; absorption over spackled areas may differ from that of paper facing. 4. When fire resistance is required, intumescent coatings, either solvent or water based, may be selected.
			primer	vinyl, polyvinyl acetate; water			may be damp	
	Subject to • periodic scrubbing • occasional splatter of grease; food stains	opaque; water	topcoat	acrylic	semigloss flat	excellent	may be damp	
			primer	self-priming			may be damp	
Wood Dry, Vertical, Horizontal	Doors, wood veneered Trim Paneling	clear; solvent	topcoat	alkyd; may be over stain	flat	good	dry only	1. Single-component urethane may be applied over stain. 2. Abraded or rough surfaces may restrict use of some coatings; consult manufacturers' literature. 3. Fillers are recommended for open grain wood, such as oak, to smooth out the surface; stain may be added to filler when required. 4. Edges of doors should be sealed to prevent absorption of moisture. 5. Particleboard is generally finished with opaque coatings; for clear use filler and stain; absorption may be uneven. 6. Hardboard is generally finished with opaque coatings only; primers are required. 7. Alkyd for wood veneer and trim may be self-priming.
	Doors, hardboard veneer Doors, wood veneer Trim	opaque; water or solvent	topcoat	alkyd (solvent)	gloss semigloss	good	dry only	
			primer	alkyd (solvent)			dry only	
	Floors, light to moderate use	clear; solvent	topcoat	alkyd, self-priming	gloss semigloss	good	dry only	
	Floors, heavy use	clear; solvent	topcoat	urethane, one part moisture cure	gloss semigloss	good	dry only	
	Floors, moderate to high use	opaque; solvent	topcoat	alkyd, self-priming	gloss	good	dry only	
Concrete, Masonry, Portland Cement Plaster	Dry, not exposed to moisture penetration such as ground moisture Typical components: • concrete and concrete masonry walls and partitions	opaque; water	topcoat	vinyl, polyvinyl acetate	semigloss flat	good	may be damp	1. Cement-water paints may be used in damp areas such as on basement walls; colors generally are limited to light tints; moisture is required during curing period, usually 24 to 48 hours. 2. Use of coatings is not recommended over alkaline substrate; coating of fresh concrete, masonry, or plaster should be delayed for as long as possible. 3. Heavy-bodied primers/fillers are recommended for rough, porous surfaces.
			primer	self-priming or styrene-butadiene			may be damp	
		opaque; solvent	topcoat	alkyd	semigloss flat	good	dry only	
			primer	styrene-butadiene			may be damp	
Concrete floors	Dry, not exposed to ground moisture penetration Light to moderate use	opaque; solvent	topcoat	urethane, one part moisture cure	gloss semigloss	good	dry only	1. Dusting surfaces should be sealed first.
			primer	self-priming			dry only	
Gypsum plaster	Dry, fully cured, no signs of efflorescence, protected from moisture penetration	opaque; water or solvent	topcoat	acrylic (water)	semigloss flat	excellent	may be damp	1. Substrate may be alkaline; therefore, primers/coatings should be alkali resistant. 2. Coating of plaster should be delayed for as long as possible to allow it to dry out.
			primer	self-priming			may be damp	

McCain McMurray; Washington, D.C.

PAINTING

Wall Coverings

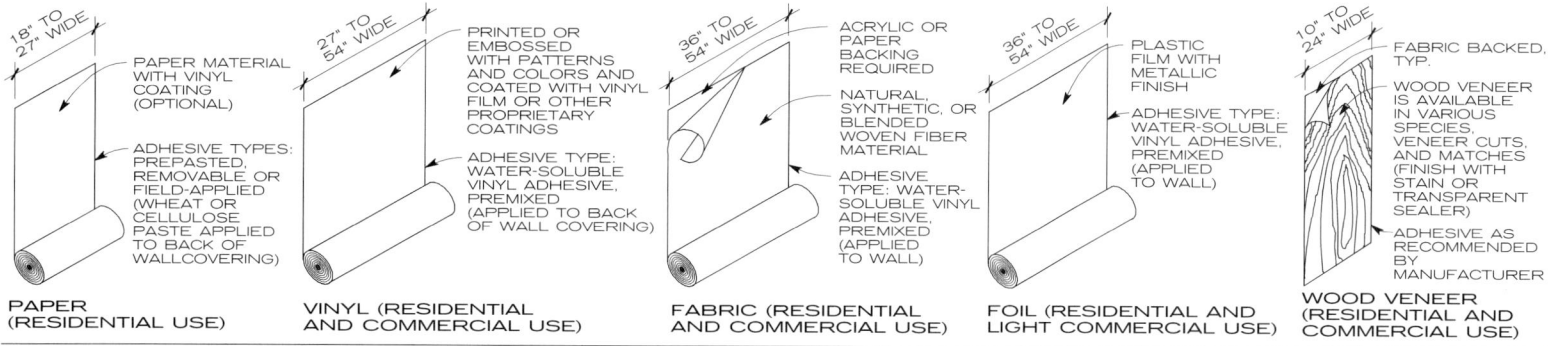

WALL-COVERING MATERIALS

NOTES

1. In some installations, fabric-wrapped panel systems have advantages over standard adhesive-applied wall coverings. There is generally less damage to the original wall surface, less surface preparation is needed, and an acoustical or tackable wall panel (which improves the STR or NRC rating of a wall) can be added to a room and concealed behind the fabric wrapping. In addition, the fabric or backing panel can be easily changed.
2. For wrapped panels, fabric or other wall covering should cure to room temperature and humidity conditions before installation.
3. Instruct installer to cut and hang three test panels for architect's inspection and approval before cutting other material from the roll.
4. The following terms apply to wall coverings:
   a. Bolt: typically three continuous rolls of wall covering
   b. Double cutting: trimming method that overlaps edges and forms a butt joint with a single cut
   c. Single roll: from 30 to 36 sq ft wall covering
   d. Double roll: from 60 to 72 sq ft wall covering
   e. Railroading: installing wall covering in horizontal direction
   f. Underlayment: any paper, fabric, or other liner material used to prepare a wall for installation of a wall covering
5. Avoid exposed wall-covering edges. Specify continuous metal or plastic edge trim where required; wrap covering into any reveals that occur.

FIBER CHARACTERISTICS FOR FABRIC WALL COVERINGS (RATING SCALE OF 1–5)

FIBER/FABRIC	TYPE	DESCRIPTION/SOURCE	GENERAL PROPERTIES							
			DIMENSIONAL STABILITY	RESILIENCY AND ELASTICITY	STRENGTH	ELECTRICAL CONDUCTIVITY	HEAT CONDUCTIVITY	ABSORBENCY	MOISTURE REGAIN	SPECIFIC GRAVITY
Cotton	Natural	Soft, fibrous matter from seed pod of cotton plant	5	2	3	5	5	5	7 to 11%	1.54
Linen	Natural	Strong, lustrous yarn or fabric from the flax plant	5	1	4	5	1	5	8 to 12%	1.52
Wool	Natural	Protein fiber of hair taken from sheep	1	5	1	2	2	5	15%	1.32
Silk	Natural	Single filament protein fiber extruded from silkworm	5	4	4	2	2	4	11%	1.25
Acetate	Man-made	Modified cellulosic fibers	2	1	1	3	3	2	6%	1.32
Viscose rayon	Man-made	Regenerated cellulosic fiber made from wood or other pulp	3	1	1	4	4	5	11 to 14%	1.50 to 1.53
Olefin	Man-made	Synthetic polymers including polypropylene (or polyethylene)	4[f]	5	5	1	1	1[i]	0	0.92
Acrylic	Man-made	Synthetic polymer	5[h]	4	3	1	1	1	1.0 to 2.5%	1.14 to 1.19
Nylon	Man-made	Petroleum-based synthetic polyamide fiber (some natural sources exist)	5[f]	5	5	2	1	1	4.0 to 4.5%	1.14
Polyester	Man-made	Petroleum-based synthetic polymer	5[h]	5	5	1	1	1[i]	0.2 to 0.8%	1.38

NOTES

1. The ratings for these charts use the following numerical system of 1 to 5, "1" meaning the property or resistance level is least applicable and "5" meaning the property or resistance level is most applicable. Also the following notes apply to the charts:
   a. Hydrogen peroxide below 90°F will harm fiber.
   b. Petroleum products safe; acetone harmful to fiber.
   c. Will degrade if wet.
   d. Carpet beetles will attack fabric.
   e. Hydrogen peroxide is not harmful to fiber.
   f. Fabric may shrink at high temperatures.
   g. Long exposure will degrade fabric.
   h. May shrink at high temperatures if not heat set.
   i. Fabric will wick moisture.
   j. Fabric is resistant if behind glass.
   k. Will harm at high temperatures and concentrations.
2. These charts are a general guide to the most significant performance-related properties of common untreated or natural fibers. There are many other properties associated with fibers and, particularly, fabrics, which can have many fiber-blend permutations. Consult the fabric manufacturer for those properties (and ASTM results) relevant to the individual installation.
3. Care must be taken in cleaning any fabric used in an architectural installation. Consult fabric manufacturer for recommended cleaning procedures.
4. The following are definitions of various terms used in the charts:
   Strength—evaluated in terms of breaking, tearing, or bursting strength.
   Electrical conductivity—the ability of a fiber or fabric to carry or transfer electrical charges. Low conductivity fabrics build up static electrical charge.
   Heat conductivity—the ability of a fiber or fabric to carry or transfer heat.
   Specific gravity—related to the weight of a fiber, expressed as the density of the fiber in relation to the density of an equal volume of water at 4°C.
5. Consult standards developed by the Association for Contract Textiles, the American Society for Testing and Materials, and the American Association of Textile Chemists and Colorists to establish performance guidelines for commercially installed textiles:
   VERTICAL APPLICATION—Direct glue wall coverings
   a. Flammability: ASTM E84 rated (see local code for building occupancy ratings).
   b. Colorfastness to light: AATCC 16A or E/class 4 minimum at 40 hours.
   c. Colorfastness to wet and dry crocking: AATCC 8 class 3 minimum.
   VERTICAL APPLICATION—Panel or upholstered applications
   a. Flammability: ASTM E84 rated (see manufacturer and local code for specific applications).
   b. Breaking/tensile strength: ASTM D3597, 50 pounds minimum/warp and weft directions.
   c. Yarn/seam slippage: ASTM D3597, 25 pounds minimum/warp and weft directions.
   d. Colorfastness to light: AATCC 16A or E/class 4 minimum at 40 hours.
   e. Colorfastness to wet and dry crocking: AATCC 8/class 3 minimum.

RESISTANCE LEVELS OF FIBER/FABRIC (RATING SCALE OF 1–5)

FIBER/FABRIC	RESISTANCE LEVEL OF FIBER/FABRIC TO				
	INSECTS AND MICROORGANISMS	OXIDIZING AGENTS (CHLORINE BLEACHES)	ORGANIC DRY CLEANING SOLVENTS (NAPTHA, ETC.)	SUNLIGHT	AGE
Cotton	5[c]	1	5	2	5
Linen	5[c]	1	5	1	4
Wool	1	1	5	2	5
Silk	5[d]	2[e]	5	1	2
Acetate	4	5[a]	5[b]	2	4
Viscose rayon	not applicable	2	5	2	5
Olefin	5	not applicable	1	2	5
Acrylic	5	5[k]	5	5	5
Nylon	5	not applicable	1	4[g]	5
Polyester	5	5	5	4[j]	5

Richard J. Vitullo, AIA; Oak Leaf Studio; Crownsville, Maryland
Kristie Strasen; Strasen Frost Associates; New York, New York

Wall Coverings

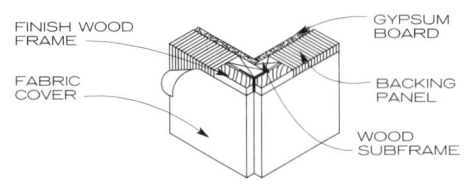

ACOUSTICAL/TACKABLE PANEL

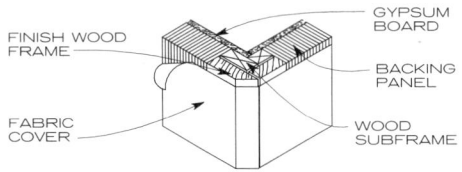

HIGH-IMPACT PANEL

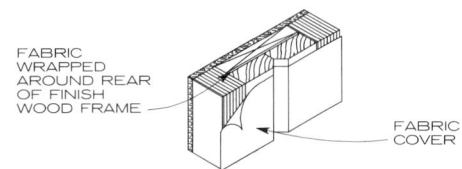

PLENUM PANEL

NOTES

1. In these types of fabric panels the fabric is permanently bonded to the substrate and/or core material. Panels can be manufactured to any size or shape with any corner or edge details; aluminum edge frames can be added for extra stiffness.
2. Panels are fastened to wall surfaces with magnets, foam tape, hook and loop, liquid adhesive, mechanical metal strip, or clip, with optional base support brackets.

PREFABRICATED FABRIC-WRAPPED PANELS

WALL COVERING INSTALLATION

When selecting a wall covering, it is necessary to consider the installation location, traffic patterns, light sources (both natural and man-made), and acoustical requirements. Consider the following when preparing a wall:

1. Wall covering weights vary from 7 to 12 oz per square yard (Type I); 13 oz per square yard (Type II); and 22 or more oz per square yard (Type III). The limited thickness and opacity of Type I and II materials may make wall surface imperfections and colors visible.
2. Before fabrics or other pervious wall coverings are installed, they are usually backed with a paper layer or liquid-applied acrylic coating to prevent seam slippage and adhesive bleed-through, as well as to increase stability and provide a neutral background for light-colored wall coverings. Backings allow the wall covering to be applied with conventional paper-hanging techniques.
3. Wall surfaces should be clean, smooth, dry, and structurally intact. Low spots should be filled and sanded, loose paint and other coverings removed, glossy surfaces sanded to roughen them slightly, and all dust removed.
4. The proper wall primer should be used on wall surfaces, particularly new gypsum wallboard. Not all water-based adhesives can be used over latex paint primer. Consult manufacturers for compatibility of adhesives and primer materials.
5. There are three basic adhesive types: wheat-based (the traditional paste, no longer popular), clay-based (traditionally used for heavy-duty applications), and vinyl (formulated for improperly prepared or problem wall surfaces).
6. When specifying adhesives, ask manufacturers and installers for recommendations to prevent buckling, sagging, delamination, and environmental considerations such as off-gassing.

ESTIMATING WALL COVERING MATERIALS

Wall coverings can be estimated by two methods:

Square Foot Method (no pattern repeat):

1. Measure the length of all walls and calculate the total.
2. Multiply the total combined length of the walls by the greatest wall height rounded up to the nearest foot to determine the total wall area.
3. Add 15% to the total area to account for waste.
4. Find the total area of all doors and windows wider than the width of a strip of wall covering.
5. Subtract total door and window area from total wall area. This will be the approximate square foot amount of wall covering required.
6. Divide the approximate square foot amount of wall covering by the number of square feet in each roll or bolt (refer to manufacturer's literature) to determine the number required for each job.

Panel Method (patterns and materials with highly visible seams):

1. Determine the trimmed width of material (54 in. wide becomes 52 in. wide).
2. On a scaled floor plan, place vertical seams in locations not less than 6 in. from inside and outside corners.
3. Adjust seam locations as necessary for desired seam arrangement, then count the panels. Count partial-width panels as whole widths.
4. Determine the panel height by measuring the floor-to-ceiling height and adding one pattern repeat for vertical patterns.
5. Multiply the number of panels by the adjusted panel height to determine the total material length required.
6. For wall coverings sold by linear yard, divide total length by three to determine the number of yards needed to complete the work. For wall coverings sold by the square foot, convert the total length of material into square feet and divide by the number of square feet in each roll or bolt (check with manufacturer).

QUIRK MITER CORNER

45° BEVELED CORNER

45° BEVELED BUTT JOINT

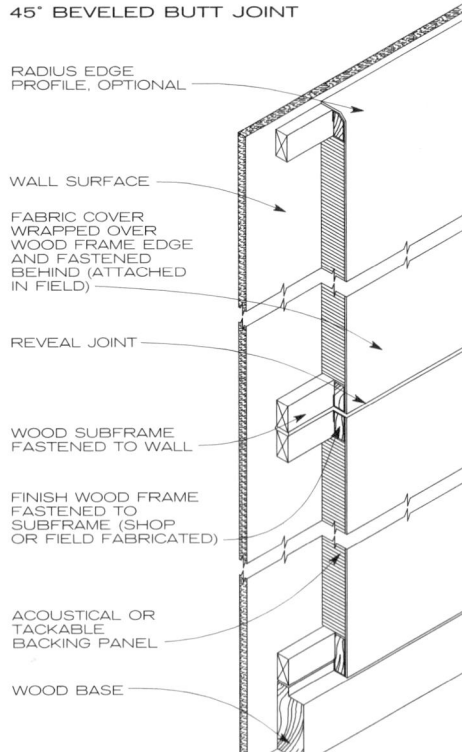

FABRIC-WRAPPED PANELS—WOOD FRAME SYSTEM

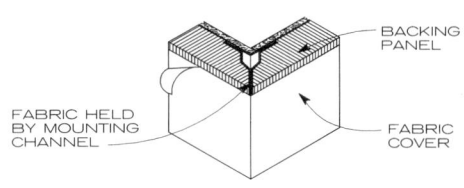

OUTSIDE CORNER

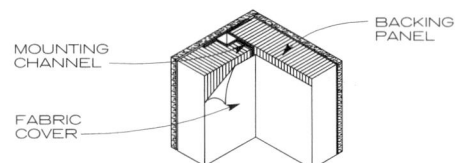

INSIDE CORNER

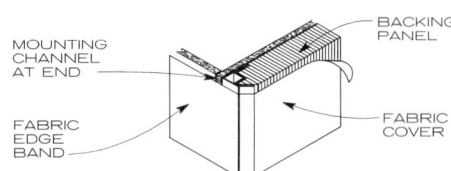

45° BEVELED CORNER

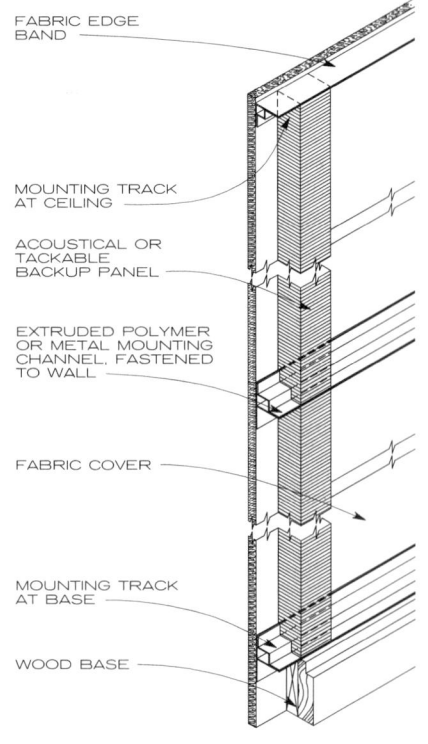

FABRIC-WRAPPED PANELS—TRACK SYSTEM

Richard J. Vitullo, AIA; Oak Leaf Studio; Crownsville, Maryland
Kristie Strasen; Strasen Frost Associates; New York, New York

Wall and Corner Guards

GENERAL NOTES

1. Wall guards, panels, and trim are typically attached to a finished wall surface with adhesive or screws. Panels are typically made of high-density fiberglass and covered with vinyl acrylic claddiing, but they may also have fabric coverings in low impact areas.
2. Most wall and corner guard manufacturers supply inside and outside connector trim pieces, as well as end caps. Consult manufacturers.
3. For all wall and corner guard installations, it is important to provide backup blocking behind areas where fasteners are attached, particularly for handrail-type guards.

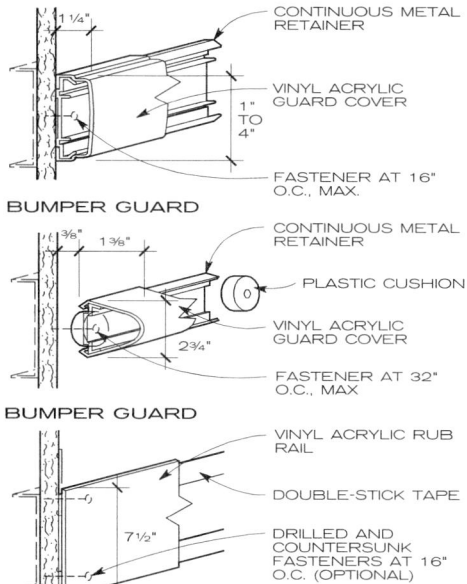

BUMPER GUARDS

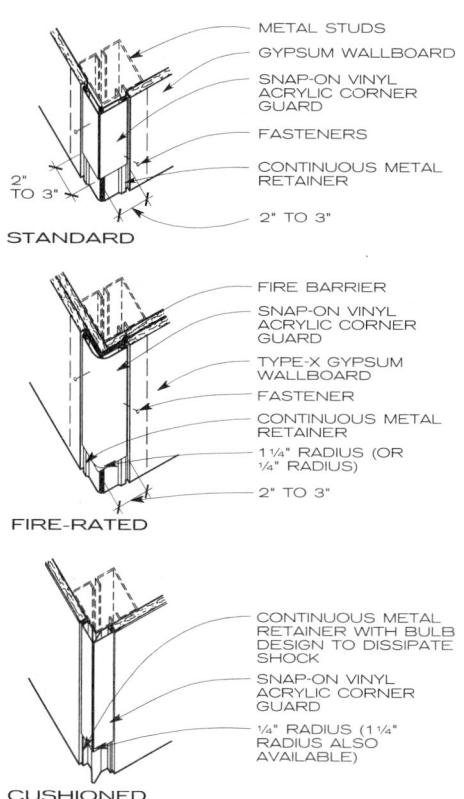

NOTE
Depending on the design of the retainer, corner guards can be mounted to almost any wall angle intersection up to 135 degrees.

FLUSH-MOUNTED CORNER GUARDS

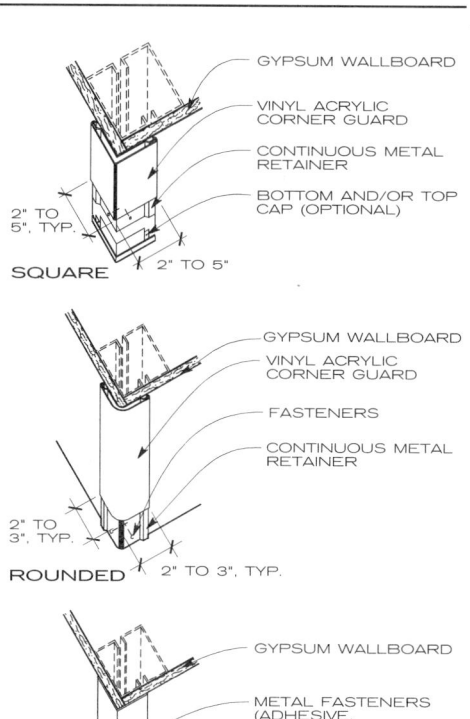

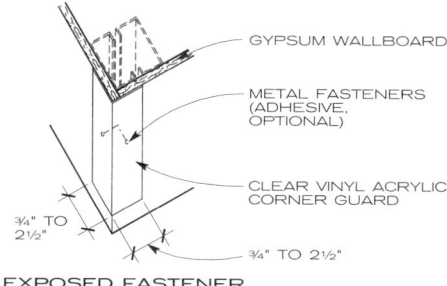

SURFACE-MOUNTED CORNER GUARDS

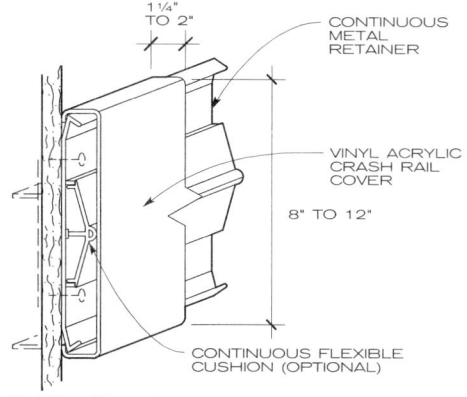

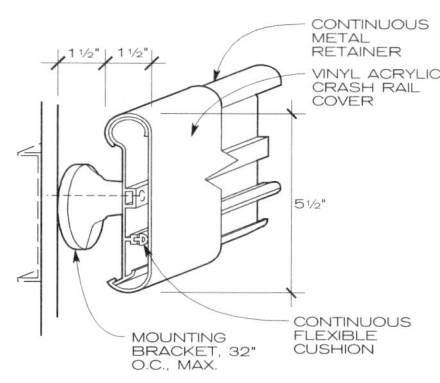

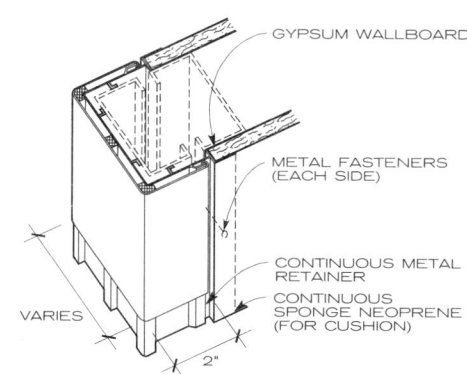

WALL-END GUARD

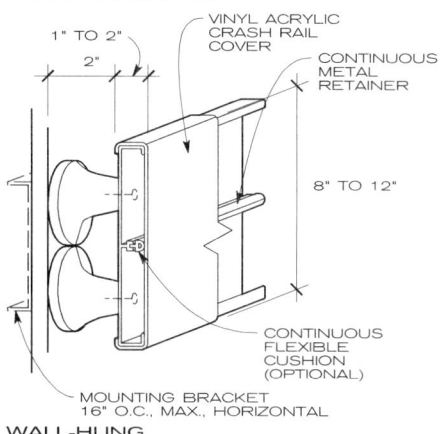

CRASH RAILS

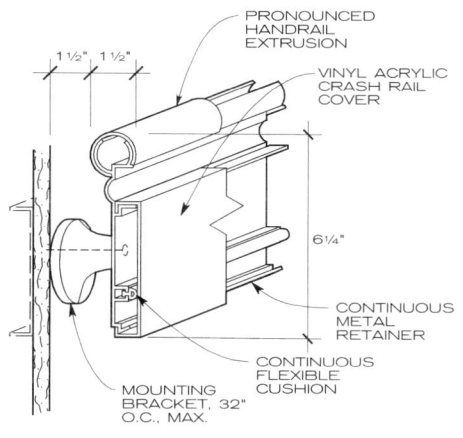

HANDRAIL WITH BUMPER CUSHION

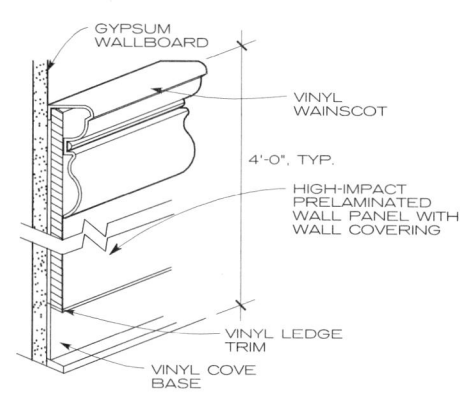

WAINSCOT PANEL WALL GUARD

Richard J. Vitullo, AIA; Oak Leaf Studio; Crownsville, Maryland

Column and Beam Covers

GENERAL NOTES

1. Column and beam covers are designed to conceal and protect structural and mechanical components, although they also have aesthic value. They are installed according to the manufacturers' designs, which may differ from one company to the next. Some are designed with one section of the cover permanently fixed in place and the other section removable. In other designs, more than one section of the cover is removable. Column and beam covers can be used in interior and exterior locations.

2. The most common materials used for the cover superstructure are base metals of extruded aluminum (.063 to .25 in. thick), stainless steel (18 to 11 gauge), and galvanized steel (18-gauge base with finish cover). Factory-applied mechanical finishes include anodized (for aluminum); satin or mirror finish (on brass, aluminum, or stainless steel); Kynar coating (on galvanized steel); and embossed patterns on any base metal. Other factory-applied finishes include baked enamel, powder coat, and primer (for field painting). Clear lacquer coatings are sometimes applied in the field to preserve mirror or other finishes. For high-traffic and highly vulnerable areas where protection from graffiti is also a concern (e.g., mass transit facilities), use of factory-applied ceramic/porcelain veneer on steel is recommended.

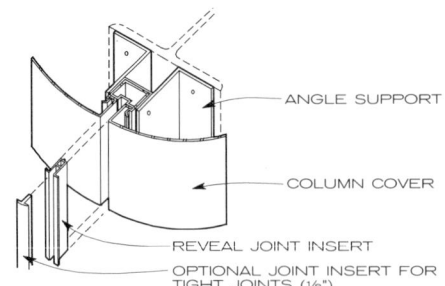

NOTE
This detail is used to protect joint edges at ceramic-coated steel seams.

COLUMN COVER WITH INSERTS

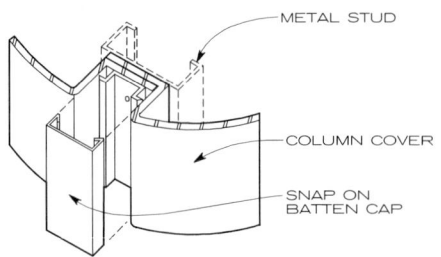

NOTE
Batten caps are available in a wide variety of sizes, colors, and materials. Consult manufacturers.

COLUMN COVER JOINT WITH BATTEN CAP

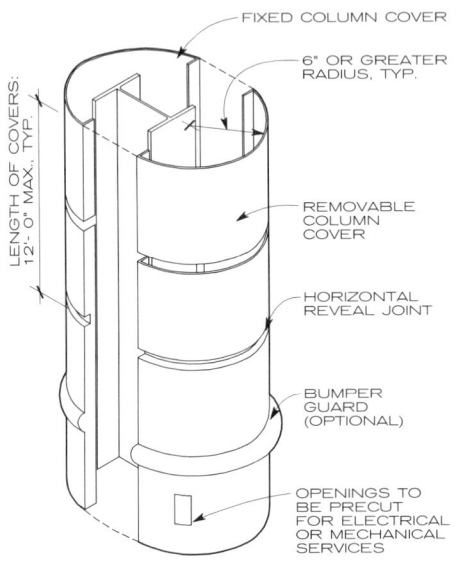

TYPICAL FREESTANDING COLUMN COVER

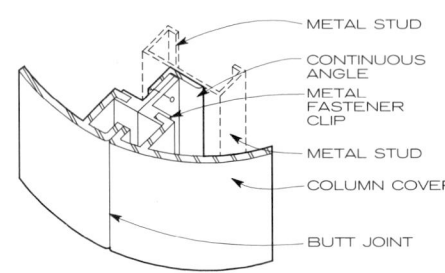

BUTT JOINT COLUMN COVER WITH FASTENER CLIP

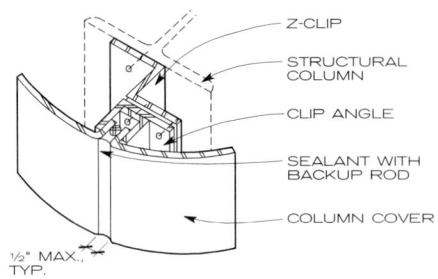

COLUMN COVER WITH SEALANT JOINT

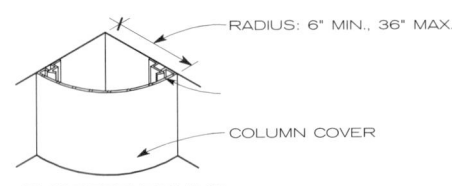

QUARTER-ROUND

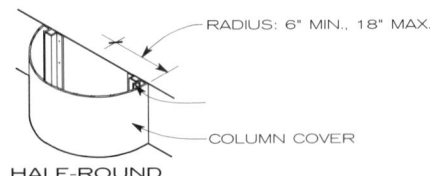

HALF-ROUND

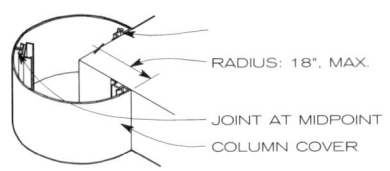

THREE-QUARTER ROUND

TYPICAL COLUMN COVERS

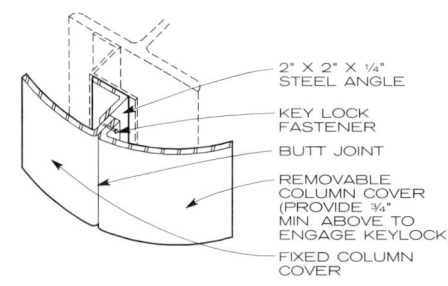

BUTT JOINT COLUMN COVER WITH KEY LOCK

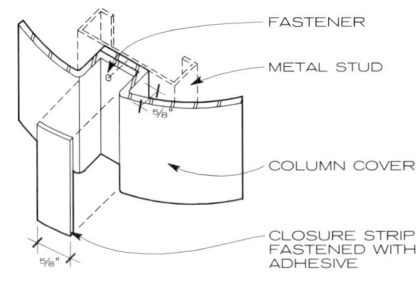

COLUMN JOINT WITH CLOSURE STRIP

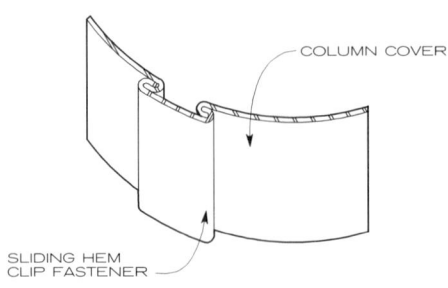

SLIDING HEM CLIP

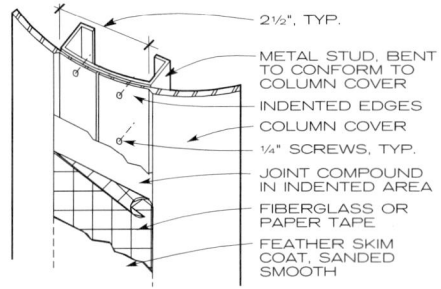

COLUMN COVER WITH STANDARD JOINT COMPOUND DETAIL

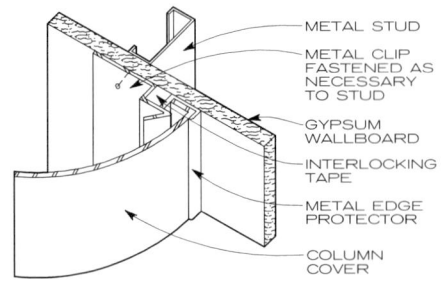

PARTIAL COLUMN COVER—WALL MOUNT DETAIL

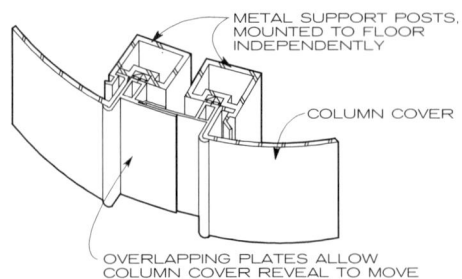

COLUMN COVER AT EXPANSION JOINT

Richard J. Vitullo, AIA; Oak Leaf Studio; Crownsville, Maryland

10 WALL AND CORNER GUARDS

Column and Beam Covers

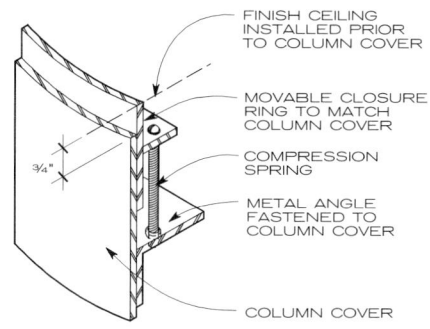

NOTE
This type of column cover can be installed flush with a finished ceiling.

SPRING-ACTIVATED COLUMN COVER CLOSURE

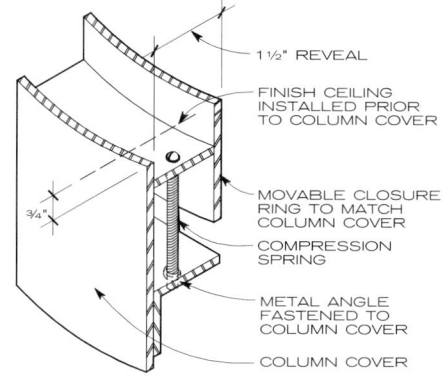

SPRING-ACTIVATED COLUMN COVER CLOSURE WITH REVEAL

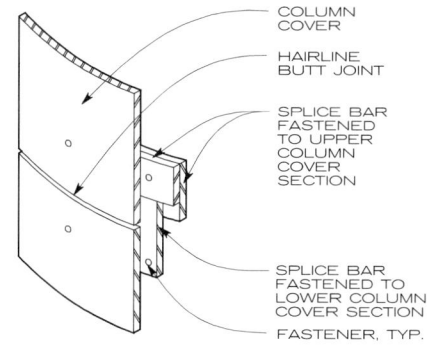

HORIZONTAL SPLICE WITH BUTT JOINT

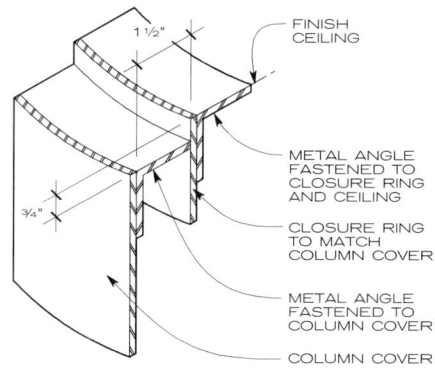

CEILING-FASTENED CLOSURE RING WITH REVEAL

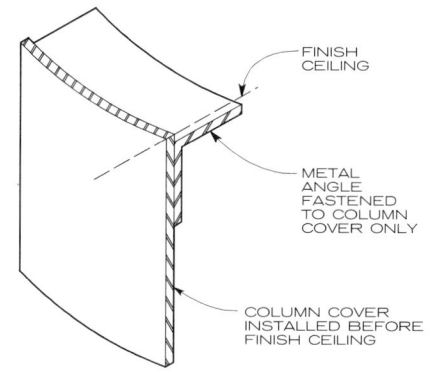

CEILING DETAIL WITH FLUSH COLUMN COVER

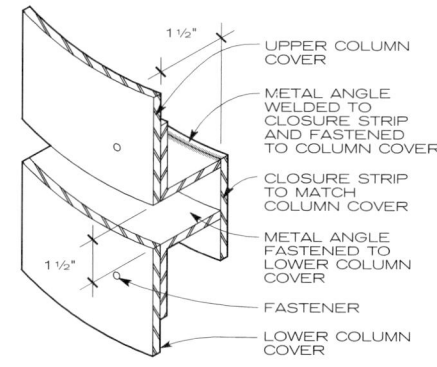

HORIZONTAL REVEAL JOINT

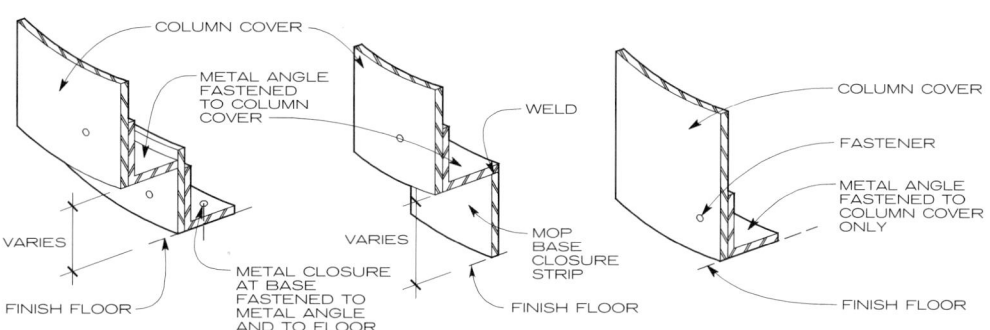
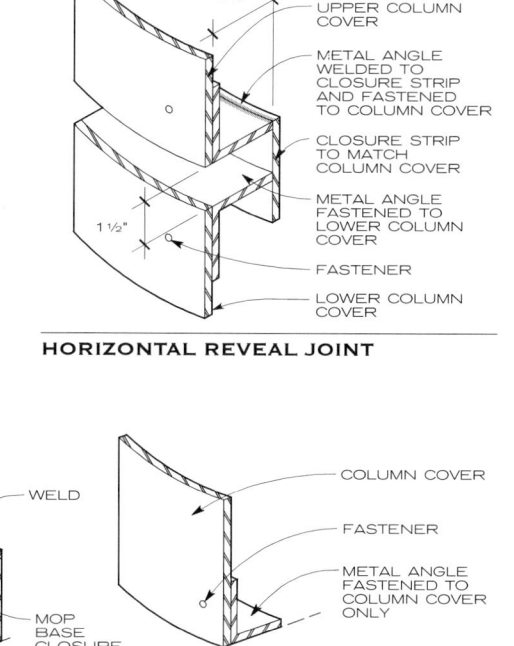

FLOATING MOP BASE   FIXED MOP BASE   FLUSH BASE

NOTE
Column cover base assemblies are not fastened to floors but only to vertical supports (metal studs, etc.).

COLUMN COVER BASE DETAILS

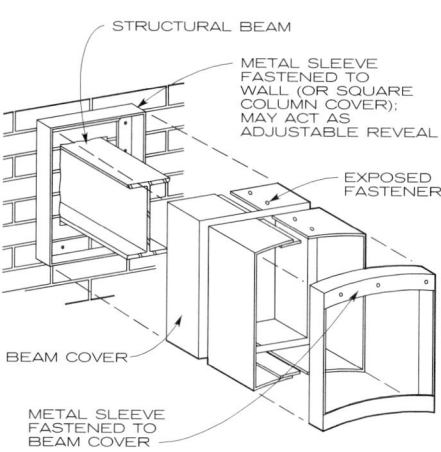

NOTE
Dimensions and joint configurations vary according to design requirements or preference. Consult manufacturers.

BEAM COVER AT WALL

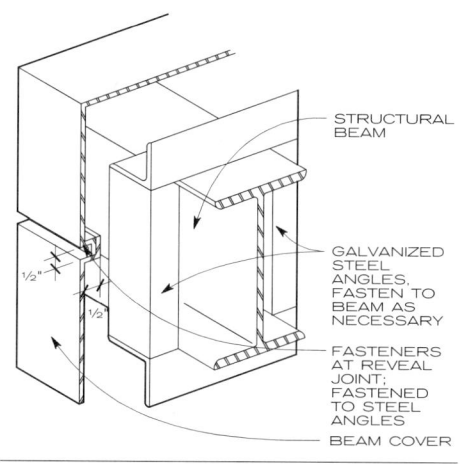

BEAM COVER FASTENING DETAIL

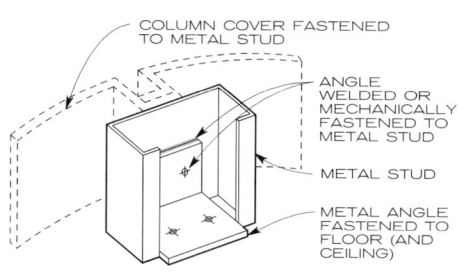

DETAIL AT METAL STUD

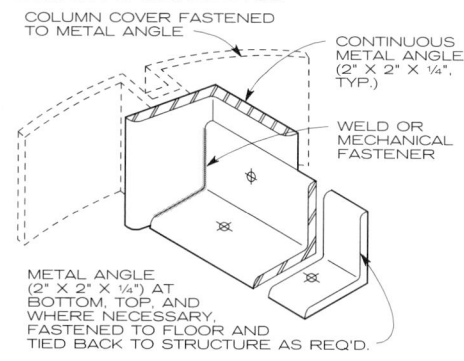

DETAIL AT METAL ANGLE

COLUMN COVER SUBFRAME ATTACHMENTS

Richard J. Vitullo, AIA; Oak Leaf Studio; Crownsville, Maryland

Metal Solid-Fuel Heaters

GENERAL NOTES

1. **APPLIANCE CLASSIFICATIONS:** Metal solid-fuel heaters efficiently heat areas ranging in size from a single room to an entire house. They are classified according to the fuel that powers them: woodstoves (cordwood) or pellet stoves (densified biomass). Woodstoves manufactured today burn both softwood and hardwood species of cordwood, which have variable moisture and Btu content but are readily accessible and manually prepared for use.

2. **BURNING TECHNOLOGIES:** Current EPA regulations for solid-fuel appliances have resulted in woodstoves significantly more efficient than those produced before. The key to efficiency is igniting and burning the smoke and gases released during combustion, particularly during extended and reduced fuel burns. Burning smoke and gases reduces fuel consumption, polluting emissions, and the frequency of chimney maintenance. Woodstoves must meet EPA standards for efficiency and cleanliness of burning. EPA standards differ for catalytic and noncatalytic technology, and within the latter category, for wood-burning and pellet-burning stoves.

3. **APPLIANCE CONFIGURATIONS:** Both woodstoves and pellet stoves can be freestanding, a fireplace insert, or built in. Freestanding appliances are often chosen in new construction or for renovation when no chimney exists. Fireplace inserts are often used to retrofit an open fireplace to increase efficiency and heat output. Built-in heaters are chosen to achieve the look and performance of the fireplace insert without the expense of building a masonry fireplace and chimney. Instead, the built-in uses a high temperature metal chimney, usually concealed in a chase. Noncombustible materials such as brick, stone, or ceramic tile are applied around the appliance face to give the look of a traditional fireplace.

4. **HEAT DISTRIBUTION, APPLIANCE PLACEMENT, AND SIZING:** The design of an appliance determines how it distributes heat. If the outside walls of the firebox are directly exposed to living space, the appliance is primarily a radiant heater. The heat created when waves of infrared energy from a stove strike solid objects is very comfortable in large open areas but may not be able to reach remote areas of a house.

   Convection heaters feature double-wall construction. Radiant energy is converted to currents of warm air in the space between the firebox and the surrounding metal cabinet. Natural convection currents of warm air moving through the house, cooling, and returning to the heater distribute heat gradually or with the assistance of an electric blower.

   With the advent of clean glass technology, purely convection heaters completely surrounded by cabinets became rare. Much more common is a third type of heater, which combines the heat distribution qualities of the first two. A combination radiant/convection heater employs a cabinet around part of the heater for convection, but radiant energy is emitted from exposed parts of the firebox wall and the ceramic glass of the loading door. The combination offers even distribution of heat, delivering the radiant energy that heats immediate rooms comfortably and the convection currents that gradually deliver heat to more distant areas. Glass cleaning air wash technology and high-efficiency burning give the user a clear view of the fire and make the stove easier to operate.

   Although a central location and open spaces provide optimum heat distribution, both radiant and combination stoves distribute heat satisfactorily if they are placed in a room of adequate size. Placement is often determined by how the living space is used and by the location of the chimney.

   The performance of EPA-certified appliances on low burns allows some tolerance for oversizing an appliance for a heating area. However, appliances much too large for the area to be heated makes operation in mild weather difficult. Also important are heating expectations: A stove intended for occasional, recreational, or emergency use can be sized differently from one intended as a primary heat source. Manufacturers' recommendations for heating area capacity may not take into account local climate or the specifics of heat loss; consult a certified dealer.

5. **AESTHETICS:** The material used to construct a stove has little effect on heating performance. Cast iron offers decorative features such as arches, curves, and relief work unattainable with steel. Steel stoves may come in styles varied through a choice of legs or pedestals, arched door frames, and brass or gold-plated accents. Stoves with soapstone panels are another option. Air wash technology, which keeps the glass clean, is perhaps the most popular design feature in all stoves.

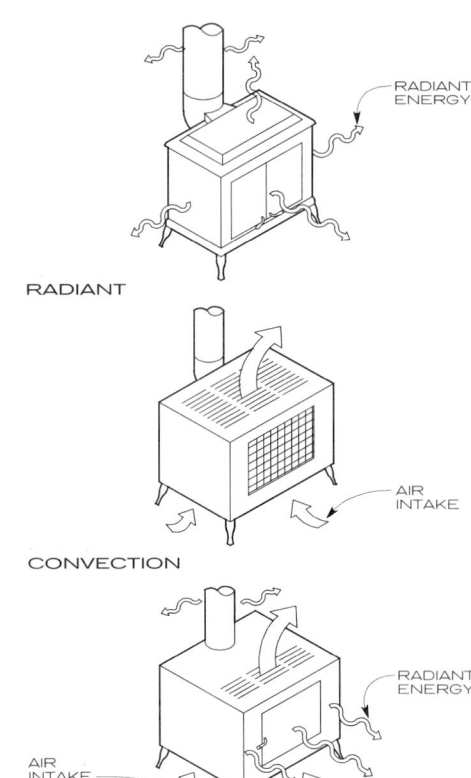

RADIANT

CONVECTION

COMBINATION RADIANT/CONVECTION

HEAT DELIVERY SYSTEMS

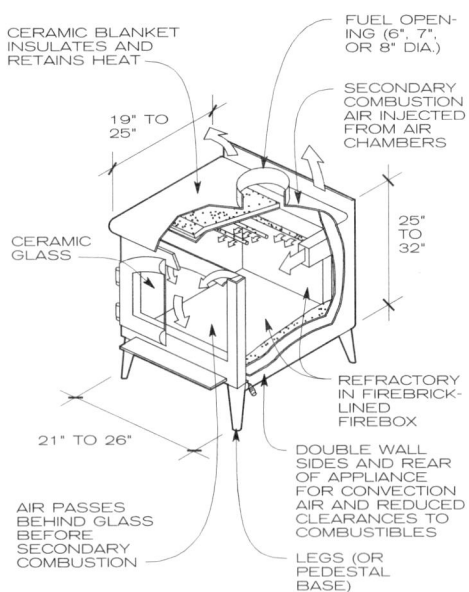

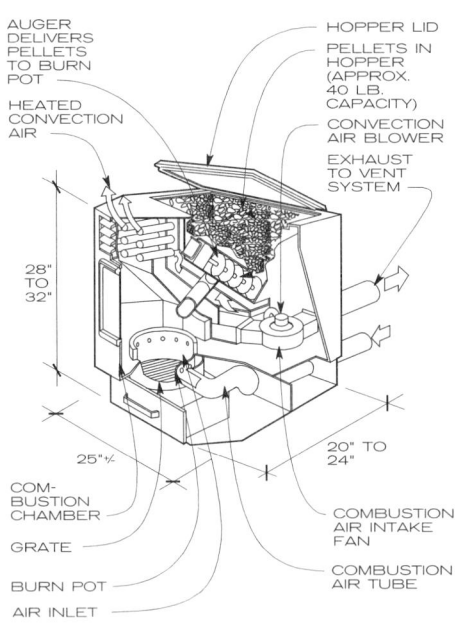

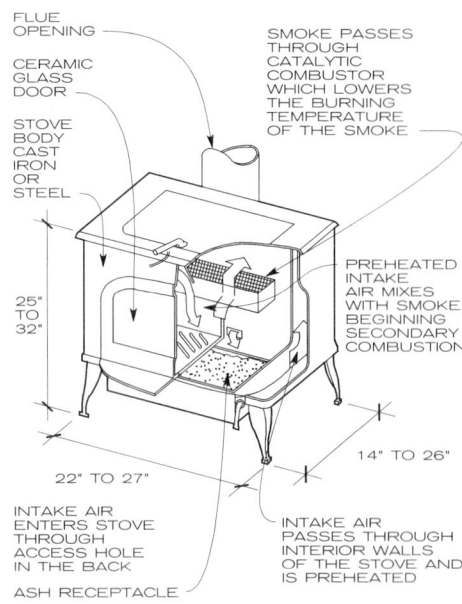

NOTE

Noncatalytic systems create the conditions necessary to burn combustible gases without the use of catalysts. The technology has a number of characteristics: Firebox insulation keeps temperatures high. Devices that reflect heat back into the firebox create the gas turbulence needed for complete combustion and give the gases a long route hot enough for them to burn before being cooled. Heated secondary air supplies ensure that enough oxygen is present. This secondary air is usually fed to the fire above the fuel bed through ducts with small holes.

NONCATALYTIC STOVE SYSTEM

NOTE

Pellets are a consistently low-moisture fuel made from dried ground wood waste or other biomass waste compressed into small cylinders about 6 mm ($1/4$ in.) in diameter and 25 mm (1 in.) long. The pressure and heat used for their production binds the pellets together without the need for additives. Pellets usually burn cleanly because they are fed to the combustion chamber at a controlled rate and are matched with the right amount of combustion air. Pellet-burning stoves generally can operate at lower emission levels than natural firewood appliances. Some pellet stoves also burn corn.

TYPICAL DENSIFIED PELLET APPLIANCE

NOTE

A catalyst is a substance that effects a reaction without being consumed in the process. The catalyst in a catalytic combustion appliance is a coated ceramic honeycomb through which exhaust gas is routed. The catalytic coating, usually palladium and/or platinum, lowers the ignition temperature of the gases from 1000° to 500° F as they pass through, causing them to ignite. This arrangement allows catalytic appliances to operate at low firing rates and still burn cleanly. Because the catalyst restricts gas flow through the appliance, these units always include a bypass damper into the flue. The damper is opened when the appliance is loaded; when a hot fire has been established, it is closed, forcing the gases through the combustor for an extended clean burn.

CATALYTIC SOLID-FUEL APPLIANCE

Walter Moberg Design, Inc.; Portland, Oregon
Hearth Education Foundation; Austin, Texas

Metal Solid-Fuel Heaters

CHIMNEYS AND DRAFT

The woodstove chimney and pellet stove vent are essential components of the solid-fuel heating system. For woodstoves, factory-built metal chimneys offer precise sizing (optimum draft is obtained by matching the cross-sectional area of the flue outlet), safety (heat-tested to 2100°F, according to UL 103), and low maintenance (insulation reduces condensation). Masonry chimneys often need to be downsized with a UL 1777-listed stainless steel, poured or factory-built liner that extends from the appliance to the top of the chimney. Liners improve startup and draft, improve safety, and reduce and simplify maintenance.

Follow code or manufacturers' requirements for chimney clearance and height. For safety, follow the 2 ft/10 ft/3 ft rule: The chimney must terminate at least 2 ft higher than anything within 10 ft and extend at least 3 ft above the roof penetration. High-efficiency stoves may need added height to ensure adequate draft; a minimum height of 14 ft from appliance to chimney top is generally recommended.

Pellet appliances often use lower temperature double-wall pellet venting. Mechanical venting for some appliances can be totally horizontal if clearances to adjacent structures and openings are met, but additional vertical venting is recommended in case of unexpected shutdown. Mechanical draft pellet venting that penetrates the roof can terminate as little as 1 ft above the penetration; natural draft venting must be at least 2 ft higher than anything within 10 ft.

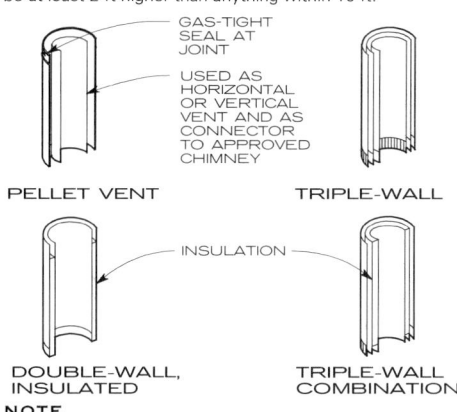

CHIMNEY TYPES FOR WOODSTOVES AND PELLET STOVES

NOTE

Chimneys keep flue gases as warm as possible, keep nearby combustibles at safe temperatures, and exhaust harmful smoke and gases to the outdoors.

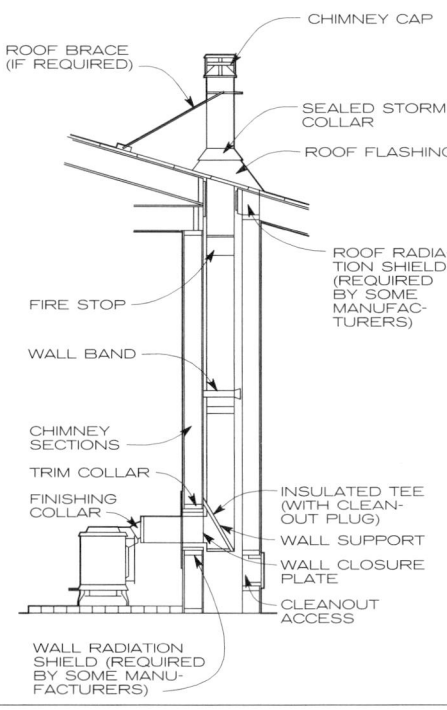

THROUGH-THE-WALL INSTALLATION— FACTORY-BUILT CHIMNEY

INSTALLATION

Underwriters Laboratories tests and lists most woodstoves tested for close clearances to unprotected combustibles. Brick or sheet metal protectors are not usually necessary, and their use in any case cannot reduce required clearance to less than 12 in. Use of double wall connector pipe from the appliance to the chimney may be recommended to reduce clearances for woodstoves, but such pipe must be listed for use with both the appliance and the chimney to which it will be connected.

Pellet appliances are listed by UL (but to a different standard) for very close clearances. They are usually vented with listed pellet venting from the appliance to the outside.

Unlisted appliances should be installed according to the provisions of NFPA 211.

Acceptable floor protection materials and minimum size for these stoves are specified by the manufacturers; if not, follow NFPA 211 or local code requirements.

REFERENCES

HEARTH Education Foundation. *HEARTH Woodstove Specialist Training Manual.* Austin, Tex., 1993.

———. *HEARTH Pellet Appliance Specialist Training Manual.* Austin, Tex., 1995.

National Fire Protection Association. *NFPA 211: Chimneys, Fireplaces, Vent, and Solid-Fuel Burning Appliances.* Quincy, Mass., 1992.

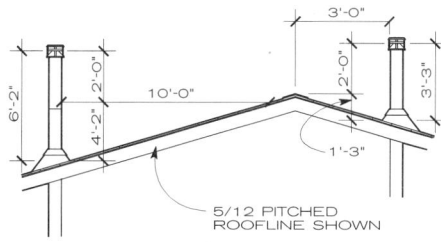

NOTE

Chimney height must meet minimum draft requirements, generally 14 ft from stove to the chimney cap.

CALCULATING CHIMNEY HEIGHTS WITH PITCHED ROOFS

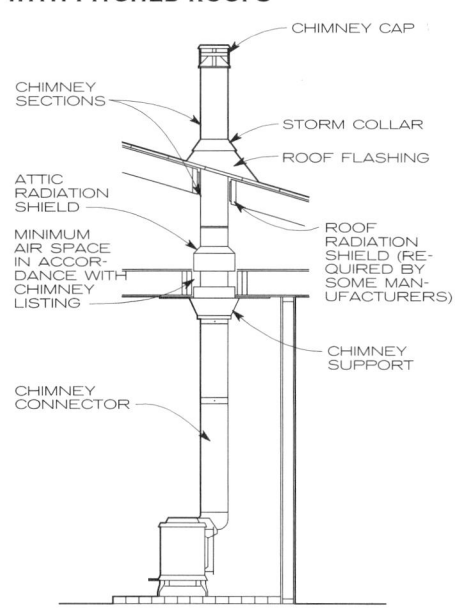

NOTE

Chimney must meet manufacturers' recommendations for minimum height.

STANDARD CEILING INSTALLATION— FACTORY-BUILT CHIMNEY

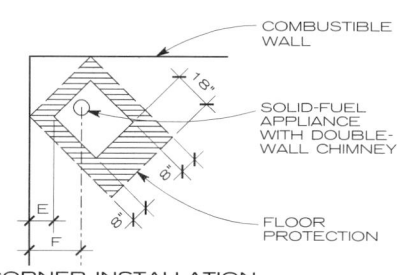

CORNER INSTALLATION

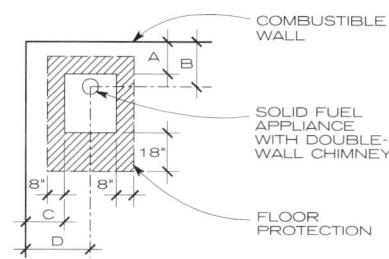

PARALLEL INSTALLATION

NOTE

All clearances shown are subject to change based on manufacturers' specifications, local codes, and any clearance reduction systems used.

MINIMUM CLEARANCES TO COMBUSTIBLES (IN.)

SINGLE WALL CONNECTOR (RESIDENTIAL)

A	B	C	D	E	F
15	21	18	30	11	25

DOUBLE WALL CONNECTOR (LISTED MOBILE HOME OR RESIDENCE, CLOSE CLEARANCE)

A	B	C	D	E	F
8	14	16	28	7	21

NOTE

Floor protection is required as follows: Minimum extension beyond loading door, 18 in.; beyond other sides, 8 in.

TYPICAL LISTED SOLID-FUEL APPLIANCE CLEARANCES

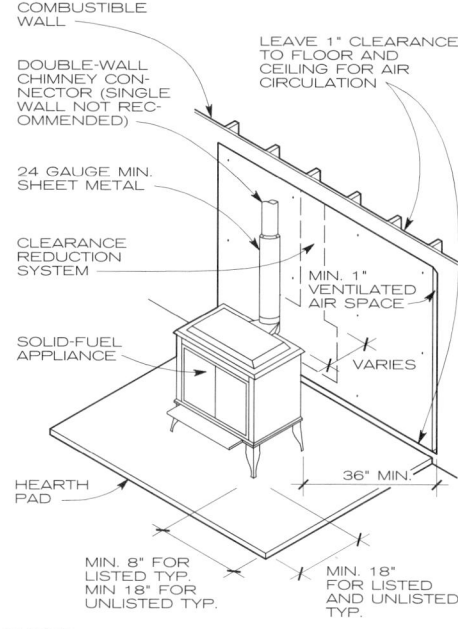

NOTES

1. For stoves with legs 2 to 6 in., hearth pad should be 4-in. hollow masonry with 24-gauge (min.) sheet metal cover.
2. With legs taller than 6 in., hearth pad should be 2-in. solid masonry with 24-gauge (min.) sheet metal cover.
3. Stoves with legs shorter than 2 in. must be installed on a noncombustible floor even if there is a hearth pad.

SOLID-FUEL APPLIANCE WALL CLEARANCE REDUCTION SYSTEM

Walter Moberg Design, Inc.; Portland, Oregon
Hearth Education Foundation; Austin, Texas

FIREPLACES AND STOVES

Flags and Flagpoles

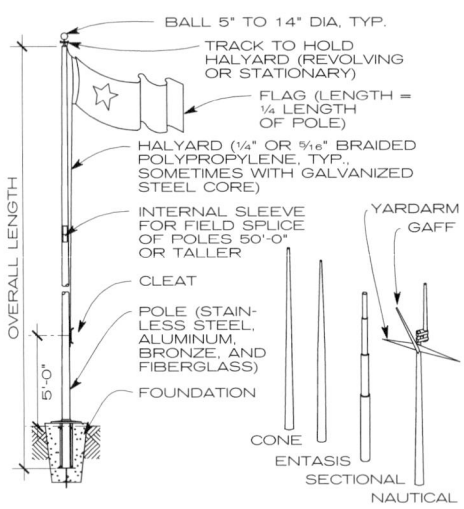

NOTE

Flagpoles must withstand wind loads while the flag is flying. The combination wind load on pole and flag should be considered. Refer to wind load tests by the National Association of Architectural Metal Manufacturers (NAAMM).

FLAGPOLE DESIGN

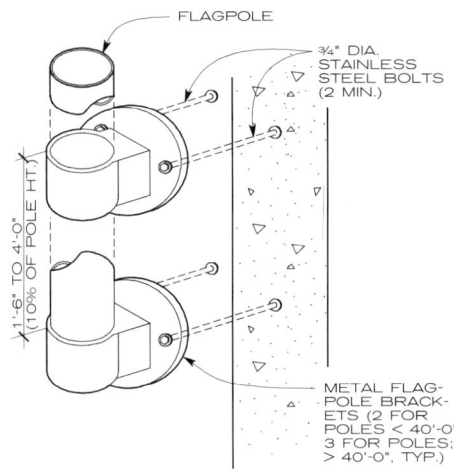

NOTE

Brackets are made of cast aluminum, bronze, and stainless steel; designs vary.

VERTICAL WALL-MOUNTED FLAGPOLE

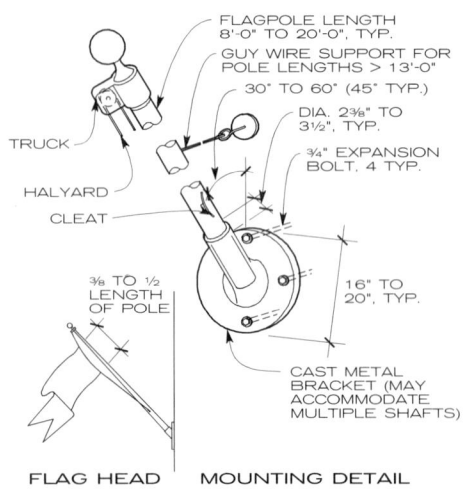

OUTRIGGER WALL-MOUNTED FLAGPOLE

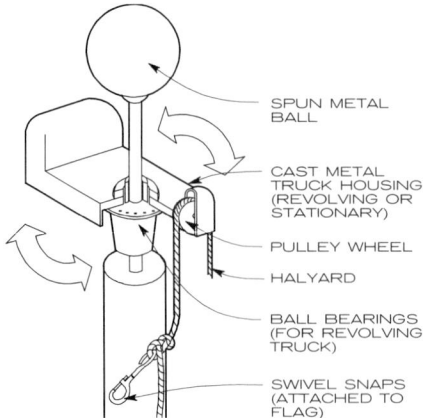

NOTE

A revolving truck allows free movement of the flag while flying; a second truck is typically used as backup only, not simultaneously with the first truck.

DOUBLE TRUCK DETAIL

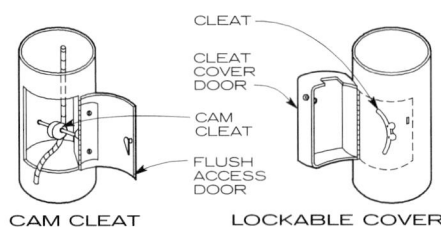

VANDALPROOF CLEAT DETAILS

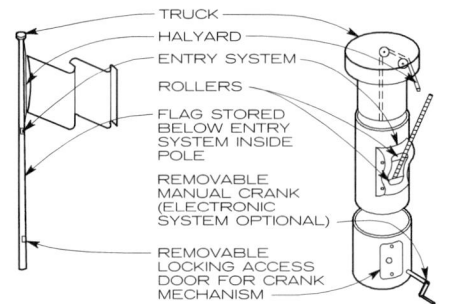

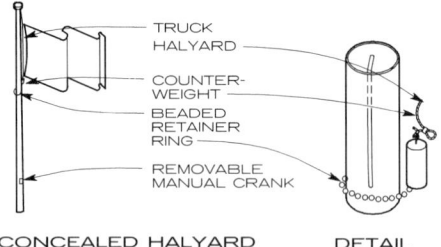

VANDALPROOF FLAGPOLE DESIGN

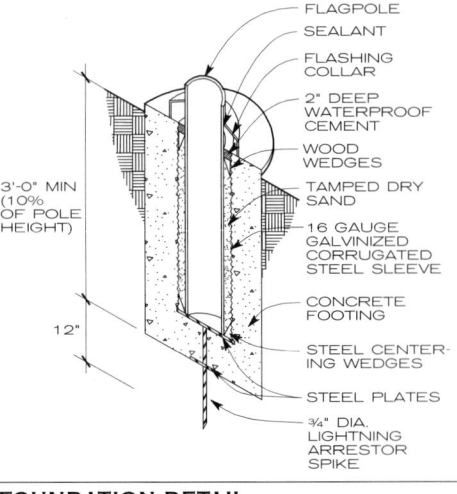

FOUNDATION DETAIL

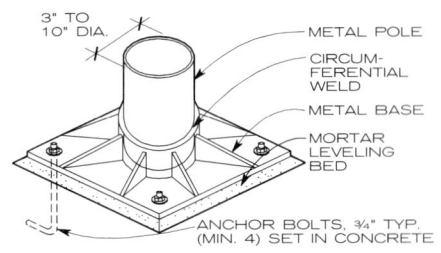

NOTE

Electrical wiring may be threaded through the pole.

SHOE BASE DETAIL

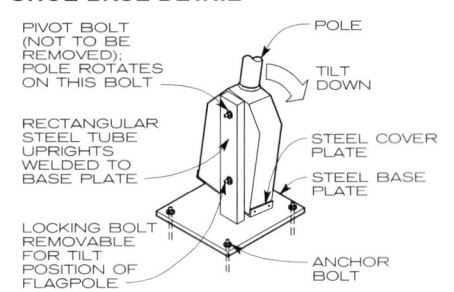

COUNTERBALANCED TILTING POLE

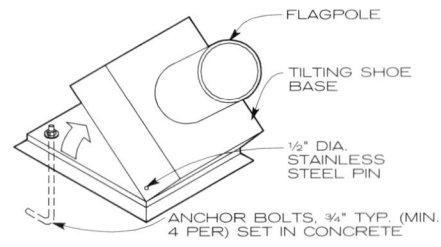

HINGED TILTING POLE

SUGGESTED FLAG SIZES

FOR GROUND-SET POLES		FOR VERTICAL WALL-SET POLES		FOR ROOF-SET POLES		FOR OUTRIGGER POLES	
EXPOSED POLE HEIGHT (FT)	FLAG SIZE (FT)	EXPOSED POLE HEIGHT (FT)	FLAG SIZE (FT)	EXPOSED POLE HEIGHT (FT)	FLAG SIZE (FT)	POLE LENGTH (FT)	FLAG SIZE (FT)
15	3 x 5	12 to 15	4 x 6	15	4 x 6	8	3 x 5
20 or 25	4 x 6	16 or 30	5 x 8	20 to 30	5 x 8	10 to 12	4 x 6
30 or 35	5 x 8	35 or 40	6 x 10	35 or 40	6 x 10	15 to 16	5 x 8
40 or 45	6 x 10	above top of wall		45 to 50	8 x 12	18 to 23	6 x 10
50, 55, or 60	8 x 12			60 to 65	10 x 15		
65 or 70	10 x 15			70 to 75	10 x 15		
80 or 90	10 x 15						
100	12 x 18						

Richard J. Vitullo, AIA; Oak Leaf Studio; Crownsville, Maryland

FLAGPOLES

Common Signs and Symbols 143

 TELEPHONE
 MEN'S RESTROOM
 GIFT SHOP
 SMOKING
 WATER WAY
LOUNGE
 ACCOMMODATION INFORMATION
 LOST AND FOUND
 PARKING

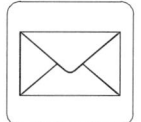 MAIL
 WOMEN'S RESTROOM
 LUGGAGE
 FIRST AID
 EMERGENCY
 TEXT TELEPHONE
 ACCESSIBLE FOR HEARING LOSS
 VOLUME CONTROL TELEPHONE
 INTERNATIONAL ACCESSIBILITY SYMBOL

 DINING
 RESTROOMS
 LOCKERS
 INFORMATION
 BUS STOP
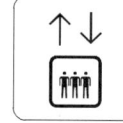 CAR RENTAL
 ELEVATOR
TICKET INFORMATION
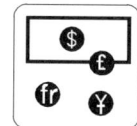 CURRENCY EXCHANGE

 TRAIN STATION
 WOMEN'S RESTROOM
 AIRPORT
 CAFE
 EXIT
 FIRE EXTINGUISHER

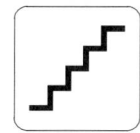 STAIRS
 MEN'S RESTROOM
 RAMP
 DRINKING FOUNTAIN
 WAITING ROOM
 EXIT STAIRS
 PARKING

 COAT ROOM
 ESCALATOR
 TAXI STAND
 BARBER
 LITTER RECEPTACLE
 CHANGING TABLE
BANK / CASH MACHINE
 NO PARKING (24" X 24" RECOMMENDED SIZE)
 NO SMOKING

STANDARD PICTOGRAPHS

 ACCESSIBLE
HANDICAPPED PARKING ONLY
 RESERVED PARKING
VAN ACCESSIBLE
ACCESSIBLE ENTRANCE
BIOLOGICAL HAZARD
RADIATION HAZARD
HIGH VOLTAGE HAZARD

HAZARD PICTOGRAMS

 EXIT
 RESTROOMS
AREA OF RESCUE ASSISTANCE
IN CASE OF FIRE DO NOT USE ELEVATORS USE STAIRS
FIRE EXIT ONLY ALARM SOUNDS WHEN OPENED
AUTHORIZED VEHICLES ONLY

 NO PARKING ANYTIME
 RESERVED PARKING
 VISITOR PARKING
 STOP (24" X 24" RECOMMENDED SIZE)
emergency exit only
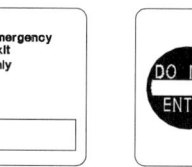 DO NOT ENTER

Proportions of the International Symbol of Accessibility

SYMBOL OF ACCESSIBILITY

EMERGENCY/EGRESS/PROHIBITORY SIGNS

Mark Knapp Crawfis Assoc., Inc.; Mansfield, Ohio

IDENTIFYING DEVICES 10

Fire Extinguisher

GENERAL

Portable fire extinguishers can serve as a first line of defense against fires of limited size, even property equipped with automatic sprinklers or other fixed protection equipment. The following are criteria for selecting fire extinguishers:

1. Type and severity (size, intensity, and speed of travel) of potential fire hazard.
2. Environmental conditions of potential fire hazard (ambient temperature conditions, presence of fumes, etc.).
3. Effectiveness of extinguisher on potential fire hazard.
4. Ease of use.
5. Suitability for its environment.
6. Any anticipated adverse chemical reactions between the extinguishing agent and the burning materials.
7. Any health and operational safety concerns (exposure of operators during fire control efforts).
8. Training and physical capabilities of available personnel to operate extinguisher.
9. Upkeep and maintenance requirements.

NOTES

1. To comply with the Americans with Disabilities Act of 1990, fire extinguishers that protrude more than 4 in. into walks, halls, corridors, passageways, or aisles must be recessed into the wall.
2. The authority with jurisdiction over the location dictates the number, type, and placement of fire extinguishers and fire extinguisher cabinets.
3. All extinguishers without wheels must be installed on hangers or brackets, mounted in cabinets, or set on shelves. Extinguishers weighing up to 40 lb should be no more than 5 ft above the floor. The top of extinguishers with a gross weight greater than 40 lb should be no more than 3 ft 6 in. above the floor.
4. Halon-type extinguishers are no longer manufactured as a result of an international environmental agreement.
5. These standards and classifications are taken from the National Fire Protection Association Publication 10, Portable Fire Extinguishers, 1994 ed. Always check local code requirements before specifying fire extinguishers.

CLASSIFICATION OF OCCUPANCIES BY HAZARD TYPE

1. LIGHT (LOW) HAZARD: Light hazard occupancies have few Class A combustible materials, including furnishings, decorations, and contents. This may include offices, classrooms, churches, or hotels.
2. ORDINARY (MODERATE) HAZARD: Ordinary hazard occupancies have more Class A combustibles and Class B flammables in light hazard occupancies. They include certain dining areas, mercantile shops, and research operations.
3. EXTRA (HIGH) HAZARD: Places with more Class A combustibles and Class B flammables than ordinary hazard occupancies present are extra hazard occupancies. Likely locations include woodworking, vehicle repair, and paint shops and cooking areas.

DISTRIBUTION OF FIRE EXTINGUISHERS

The minimum number of fire extinguishers needed to protect a property from Class A fires is determined by the accompanying tables; frequently, additional extinguishers are installed. Fire extinguishers rated for Class B fires are placed a maximum travel distance of 50 ft from the hazard (smaller rated extinguishers are placed no more than 30 ft from the hazard). Fire extinguishers rated for Class C fires shall be required in locations with energized electrical equipment that would require a nonconducting extinguishing medium. For Class D fires, extinguishers are located not more than 75 ft from the Class D hazard.

FIRE CLASSIFICATIONS FOR SELECTING FIRE EXTINGUISHERS

LETTER SYMBOL AND COLOR	PICTURE SYMBOL	DESCRIPTION
Green		Class A: Fires involving ordinary combustible materials (such as wood, cloth, paper, rubber, and many plastics) that require the heat-absorbing (cooling) effects of water or water solutions, or the coating effects of certain dry chemicals that retard combustion.
Red 		Class B: Fires involving flammable or combustible liquids, flammable gasses, greases and similar materials that are best extinguished by excluding air (oxygen), inhibiting the release of combustible vapors, or interrupting the combustion chain reaction.
Blue 		Class C: Fires involving energized electrical equipment where safety to the operator requires the use of electrically nonconductive extinguishing agents.
Yellow	★D	Class D: Fires involving combustible metals (such as magnesium, titanium, zirconium, sodium, lithium, and potassium).

FIRE EXTINGUISHER SIZE AND PLACEMENT FOR CLASS A HAZARDS

	LIGHT HAZARD OCCUPANCY	ORDINARY HAZARD OCCUPANCY	EXTRA HAZARD OCCUPANCY
Min. rated single extinguisher	2-A[1]	2-A[1]	4-A[2]
Max. floor area per unit of A	3,000 sq ft	1,500 sq ft	1,000 sq ft
Max. floor area for extinguisher	11,250 sq ft	11,250 sq ft	11,250 sq ft
Max. travel distance to extinguisher	75 ft	75 ft	75 ft

[1] Up to two water-type extinguishers with 1-A rating can be used to fulfill the requirements of one 2-A rated extinguisher for light hazard occupancies.
[2] Two 2$\frac{1}{2}$ gallon (9.45 L) water-type extinguishers can be used to fulfill the requirements of one 4-A rated extinguisher.

MULTIPURPOSE DRY CHEMICAL (CLASS A, B, AND C FIRES)

Capacity (lb)	2$\frac{1}{2}$	5	6	10	20
Height (in.)	14	14$\frac{1}{2}$	16	20	24
Diameter (in.)	3	4$\frac{1}{4}$	5	5	7
Class	1A:10B:C	2A:10B:C; 3A:40B:C	3A:40B:C	4A:60B:C	20A:120B:C
Effective range	10 to 20 ft				
Discharge time	5 lb, 10 sec; 10 lb, 11 sec; 20 lb, 15 sec; 30 lb, 15 sec				
Recharge	After use				
Pressure source	Compressed gas				
Temperature effect	Will operate at -65°F				
Electrical conductivity	Will not conduct				

NOTE: Fluidized and siliconized monoammonium phosphate powder is dispersed, smothers and breaks chain reaction of fire.

CARBON DIOXIDE (CLASS B AND C FIRES ONLY)

Capacity (lb)	5	10	15	20
Height (in.)	17$\frac{3}{4}$	24	30	30
Diameter (in.)	5$\frac{1}{4}$	7	7	8
Class	5B:C	10B:C	10B:C	10B:C
Effective range	3 to 8 ft			
Discharge time	2$\frac{1}{2}$ lb, 12 sec; 5 lb, 22 sec; 10 lb, 23 sec; 15 lb, 26 sec; 20 lb, 25 sec			
Recharge	After use			
Pressure source	Compressed gas			
Temperature effect	Will operate at -40°F			
Electrical conductivity	Will not conduct			

NOTE: Pressurized liquid carbon dioxide is released, changed into a gas, and appears as a cloud of white "snow," smothering fire.

REGULAR DRY CHEMICAL (B AND C FIRES)

Capacity (lb)	2$\frac{1}{2}$	5	$\frac{1}{2}$	6	10	20
Height (in.)	14$\frac{3}{8}$ to 14$\frac{5}{8}$	14$\frac{5}{8}$ to 15$\frac{1}{4}$	14$\frac{5}{8}$ to 15$\frac{1}{4}$	15$\frac{1}{2}$ to 16$\frac{1}{4}$	20 to 20$\frac{1}{2}$	23$\frac{1}{4}$ to 24
Diameter (in.)	3	4$\frac{1}{4}$	4$\frac{1}{4}$	5	5 to 6	7
Class	10B:C	10B:C	40B:C	40B:C	60B:C	120B:C
Effective range	10 to 20 ft					
Discharge time	5 lb, 10 sec; 10 lb, 11 sec; 20 lb, 15 sec; 30 lb, 34 sec					
Recharge	After use					
Pressure source	Compressed gas					
Temperature effect	Will operate at -40°F					
Electrical conductivity	Will not conduct					

NOTE: A siliconized sodium bicarbonate base (the traditional dry chemical design) extinguishes fire. A base of potassium bicarbonate is also available.

PRESSURIZED WATER

Capacity (gal)	2$\frac{1}{2}$
Height (in.)	24$\frac{1}{2}$
Diameter (in.)	7
Weight (lb)	28
Class	2A
Effective Range	30 ft
Discharge time	50 seconds
Recharge	Weigh cylinder and check annually; in all cases, follow instructions on label
Pressure source	Compressed air
Temperature effect	Will freeze
Electrical conductivity	Will conduct

NOTE

Water quenches fire and cools area.

SODIUM CHLORIDE

Capacity (lb)	30
Height (in.)	27$\frac{3}{4}$
Diameter (in.)	7
Class	FM
Effective range	4 to 6 ft
Discharge time	28 seconds
Recharge	After use
Pressure source	Compressed gas
Temperature effect	-40 to +120
Electrical conductivity	Will not conduct

NOTES

1. Sodium chloride dry powder is dispersed over a burning combustible metal or alloy; heat from fire causes dry powder to cake and form exterior crust that excludes air and dissipates heat.
2. For lithium and lithium alloy Class D fires, a copper-based extinguishing agent is used.

Mark Conroy; National Fire Protection Association; Quincy, Massachusetts

Metal Louvers

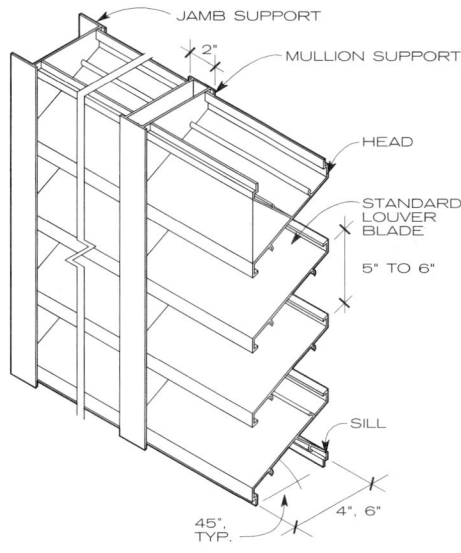

NOTE
Generally, this is the most economical louver type.

EXPOSED MULLION LOUVER

GENERAL NOTES

1. Metal architectural louvers allow airflow through a wall for ventilation, especially of machine exhaust. They protect the interior space from vandalism, weather, insects, or birds and can be used to obscure unsightly views. Louvers can be fabricated in standard rectangles or custom shapes such as circles, triangles, and ellipses. Radiused corners and other details are available from some manufacturers. Penthouses frequently incorporate louvered walls to screen equipment and provide airflow.
2. Standard louver materials are 16-, 18-, or 20-gauge galvanized or cold-rolled steel and 8-, 12-, or 14-gauge extruded aluminum alloy. Other metals can be used for special applications. Translucent fiberglass is a standard blade material when daylighting is desirable. Fasteners are either aluminum or stainless steel. The dimensions shown are the most common; other sizes are available.

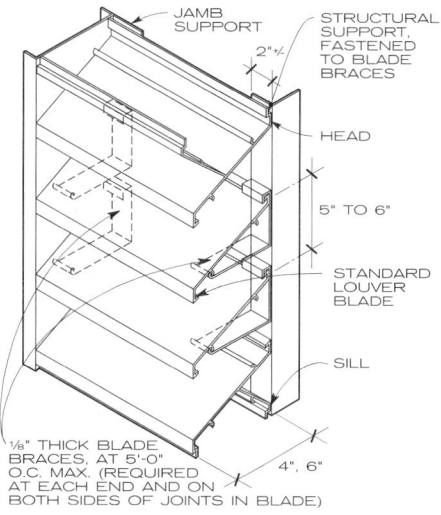

NOTE
This louver type offers a visual line uninterrupted by exposed vertical supports.

CONTINUOUS HORIZONTAL LOUVER

3. Factory finishing is recommended for maximum control of color and durability. The finish for steel louvers is baked enamel, which comes in a variety of colors. Aluminum finishes include mill, clear lacquer, baked enamel, and anodic. Fluorocarbon polymeric finish coatings (kynar), which can be applied to steel or aluminum, resist chalking, ultraviolet deterioration, salts, chemicals, and pollutants.
4. Mechanically assembled extruded aluminum louvers are the most common type of louver assembly on the market. Mechanical fasteners are better than welding in extruded aluminum alloy construction because annealing occurs near the weld, weakening the material along both sides. Also, repairs are easier if mechanical fasteners are used.

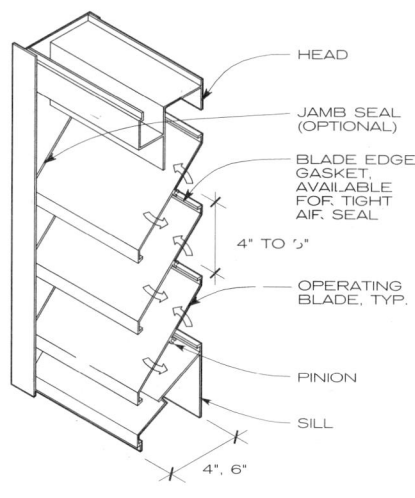

NOTE
Adjustable operating louvers are available with manual, electric, or pneumatic actuators. Free area 38 to 58%.

ADJUSTABLE OPERATING LOUVER

5. With sheet metal, welding an assembly of louvers is easier and less expensive than using clip angles and screws to fasten the blades to the framework.
6. Free area is the net area of free airflow through a louver, generally measured in square feet or as a percentage of the area in the louver type selected. Manufacturers' free area ratings should include the effects of bird or insect screens, which reduce free area.
7. For all louvers servicing mechanical equipment, consult a mechanical engineer for design and specification of the louvers. Louvers are rated for air performance and water penetration and certified through the Air Movement and Control Association. The Building Services Resources and Information Association also rates the performance of metal louvers.

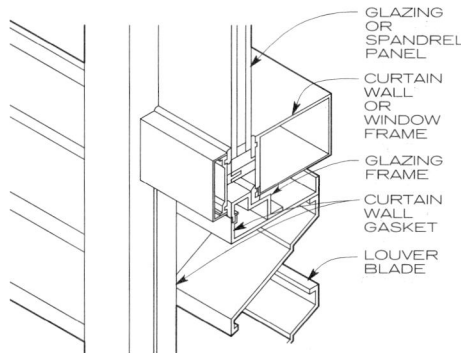

LOUVER INSTALLATION IN CURTAIN WALL

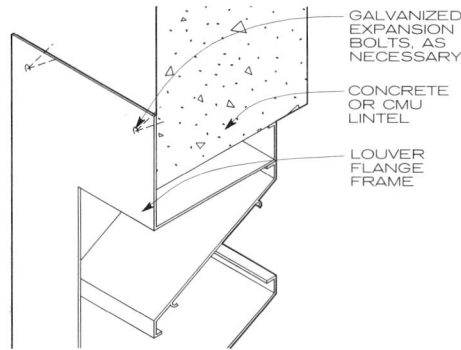

FLANGE MOUNT DETAIL

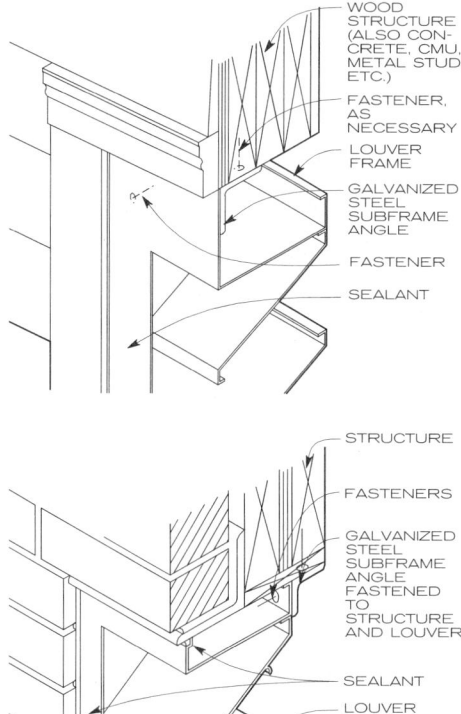

ANGLE SUBFRAME DETAILS

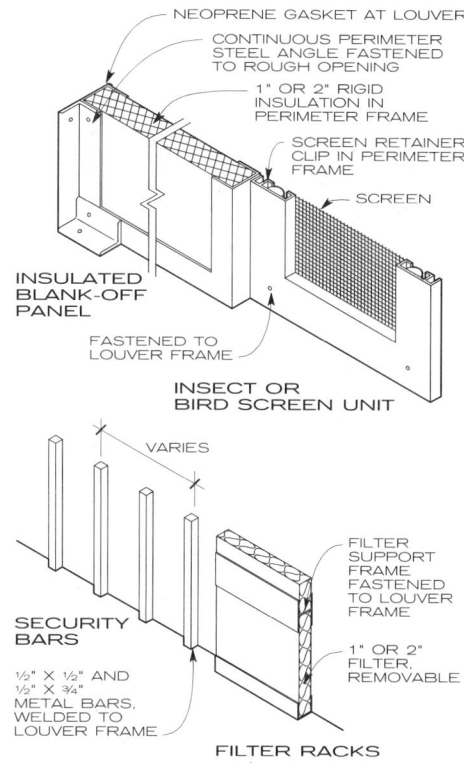

MISCELLANEOUS LOUVER ACCESSORIES

Richard J. Vitullo, AIA; Oak Leaf Studio; Crownsville, Maryland

Metal Louvers

GENERAL

Louver blades come in many shapes, sizes, and performance types that vary with the manufacturer; the blades illustrated here represent the basic types. Some blades are fixed only; others can be opened and shut. The center-to-center dimensions given are approximate; generally, standard blades (not specialty blades such as acoustic, air-foil, etc.) are designed with minimal overlap so they can obstruct views but maximize the free area.

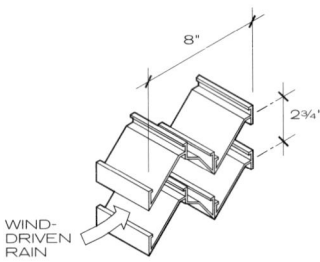

NOTE
Louvers utilizing this blade design completely obscure views and are tamperproof and storm-resistant. This blade prevents nearly 100% of wind-driven rain from entering (generally tested with winds up to 30 mph for one hour).

HORIZONTAL STORM-RESISTANT BLADE

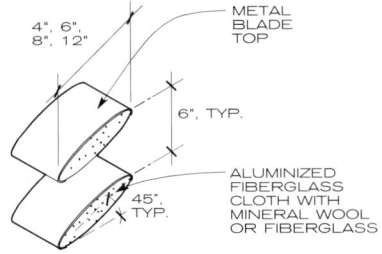

NOTE
Acoustically insulated air-foil blades block sound from inside or out and accommodate high air velocities. Free area is 29%; blades may be fixed or operable.

FIXED AIR-FOIL ACOUSTICAL BLADE

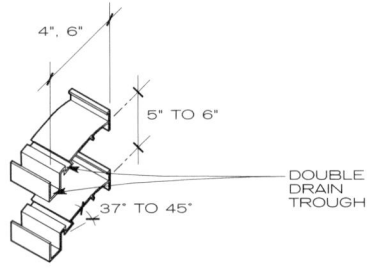

NOTE
This blade type provides high water resistance and a free area of about 50%. Typically employed in louvers with jamb and mullion drains, it is not designed to protect against wind-driven rain.

DOUBLE DRAINABLE LOUVER BLADE

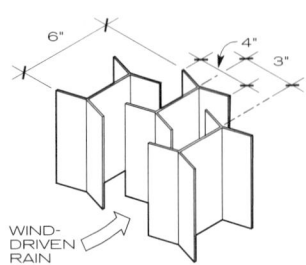

NOTE
Louvers utilizing this blade design completely obscure views and are tamperproof and completely stormproof.

VERTICAL STORM-RESISTANT BLADE

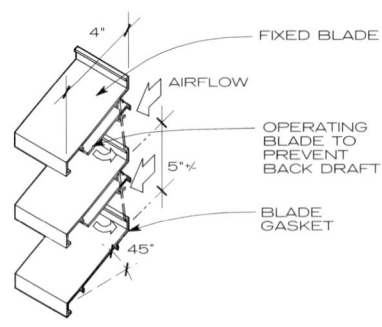

AUTOMATIC EXHAUST DAMPER/LOUVER

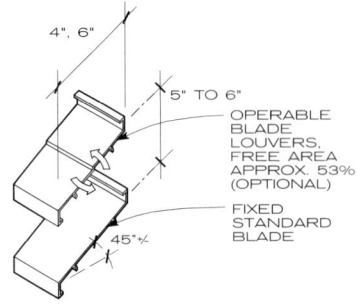

NOTE
Standard blades are suitable for most applications where water infiltration is not a concern. Free area is approximately 48%. Single operating panels should not exceed 48 in. wide x 96 in. high. This blade can be either fixed or operable.

STANDARD BLADE

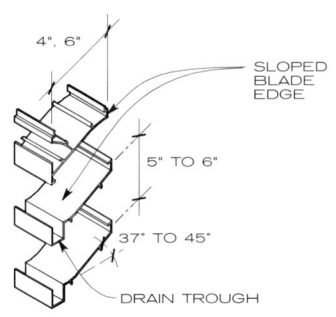

NOTE
Designed to provide high free area (55%) and low water penetration, this blade is not recommended for use with hidden mullions; louvers that employ these blades contain integral drains in their mullions that direct water away from the inside of the louver. All drain troughs must be kept free of debris. Not designed to hinder wind-driven rain.

HIGH-PERFORMANCE DRAINABLE BLADE

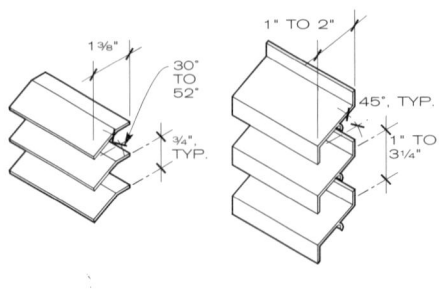

NOTE
These shallow louver blades can allow a very high free area (from 32 to 73%). They are often used when standard-depth louvers are not practical.

SHALLOW AIR CONDITIONING BLADE

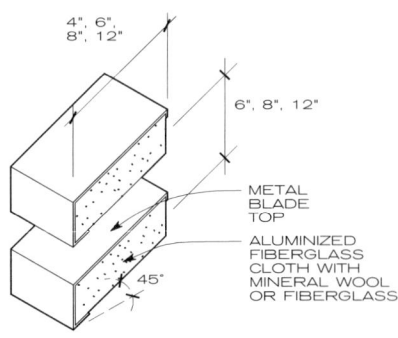

NOTE
Acoustically insulated blades block sound from inside or out and prevent weather infiltration. Free areas range from 21 to 29%. Blades may be fixed or operable.

FIXED ACOUSTICAL LOUVER

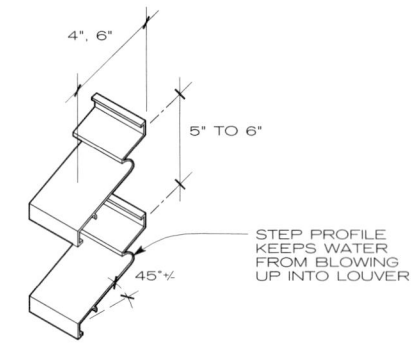

NOTE
Step blades help prevent water infiltration. Free area is approximately 48%.

STEP BLADE PROFILE

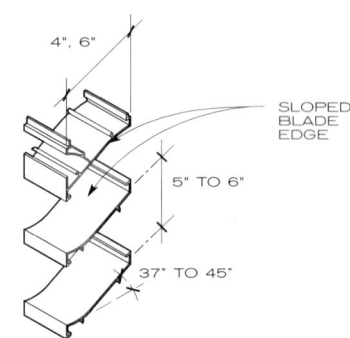

NOTE
Designed to provide a high free area (55%), this blade accommodates high air velocities and protects against wind-blown precipitation.

HIGH-PERFORMANCE STANDARD BLADE

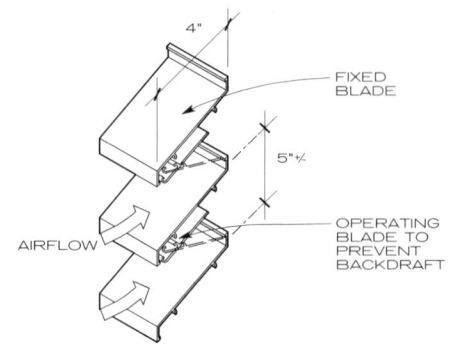

AUTOMATIC INTAKE DAMPER/LOUVER

Richard J. Vitullo, AIA; Oak Leaf Studio; Crownsville, Maryland

10 PROTECTIVE COVERS

Operable Walls and Partitions

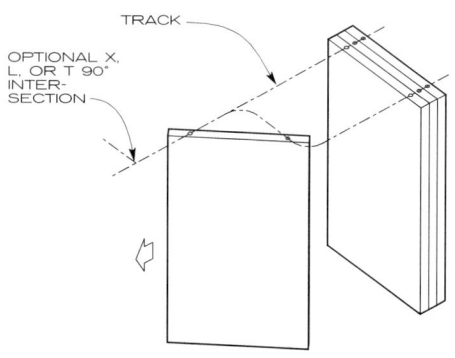

INDIVIDUAL PANELS

NOTE

This manually operated system is for panels more than 16 ft tall (40 ft max. typically), which are supported by two carriers on each panel.

HINGED PAIRS

NOTE

This manually operated system is for panels up to 18 ft in height and typically is used for straight runs only. Each panel has one carrier.

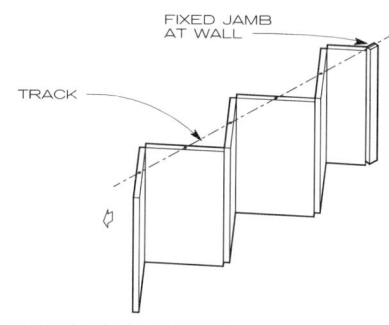

CONTINUOUSLY HINGED

NOTE

Panels are hinged together to form a continuous panel train. This type is manually operated for systems with a total wall weight under 3700 lb and operated with an electric motor for weights exceeding 3700 lb. This type of panel is typically suitable for straight run applications only.

PANEL OPERATION TYPES

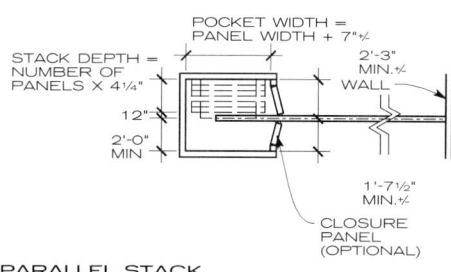

PARALLEL STACK

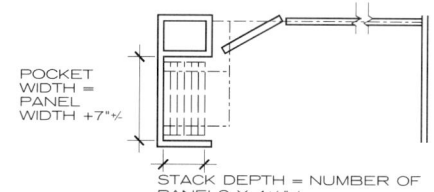

PERPENDICULAR STACK

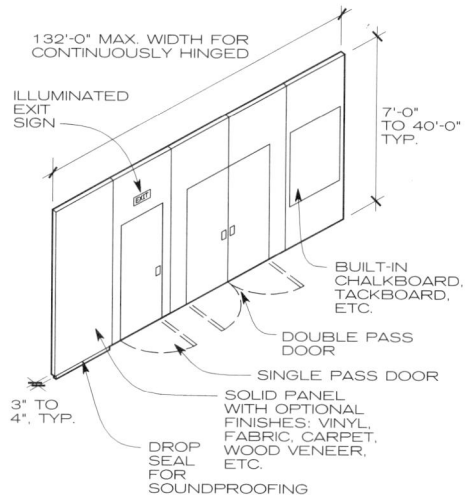

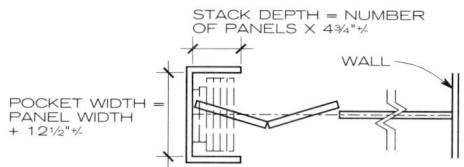

CENTER STACK

REMOTE STACK

NOTE

Dimensions given are for planning purposes only; consult manufacturer for specifics. Panels with automatic bottom seals require a wider stack storage area; dimensions given are for fixed, adjustable, or operable bottom seals.

NOTE

Panel wall width for individual and paired panels is unlimited. Sound transmission coefficient ratings for typical panels are available up to 55.

STORAGE ARRANGEMENTS FOR PANEL STACKS

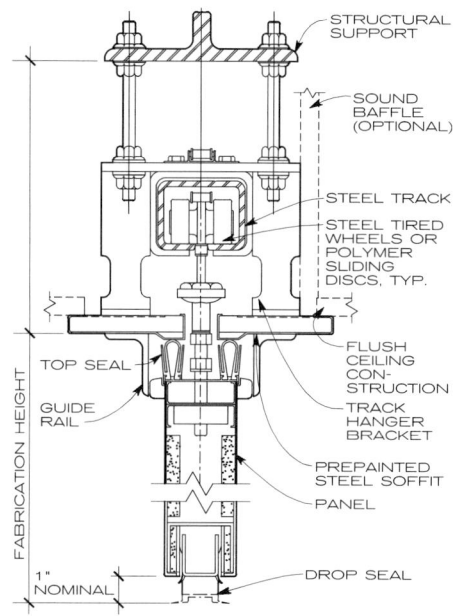

TOP-HUNG FOLDING PARTITION DETAIL

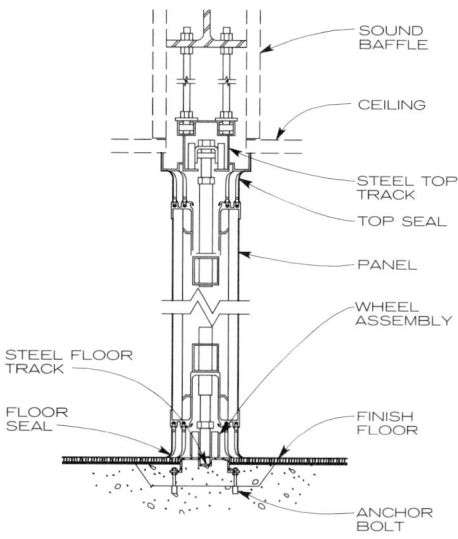

FLOOR-SUPPORTED FOLDING PARTITION DETAIL

NOTE

The bottom carrier handles about 90% of the panel's weight.

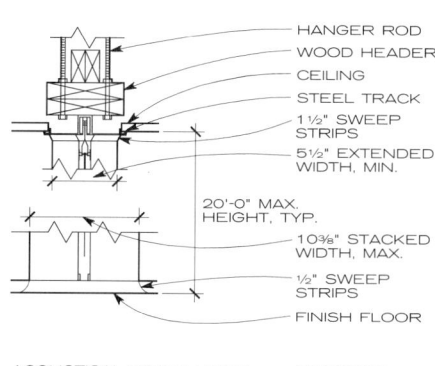

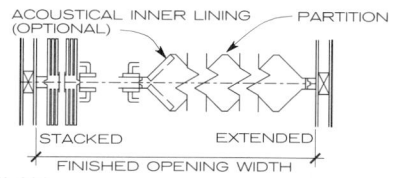

PLAN

NOTE

Acoustical inner liners can be added to these partitions. Typical partitions are either built of laminated panels or individual vinyl-clad steel panels with extruded vinyl hinges.

ACCORDION PARTITIONS

Richard J. Vitullo, AIA; Oak Leaf Studio; Crownsville, Maryland

Modular Wall Systems

GENERAL

Movable wall systems of non-load bearing interior partitions offer flexibility for office environments in which functions and layouts may change quickly or repeatedly. Generally, they are manufactured either as one-piece self-contained panels or as two-piece systems in which structure and cladding are independent of each other. In either case, floor and ceiling tracks are installed on finished (carpeted, etc.) floors and fastened to suspended ceiling grids. Height adjustment and leveling are accomplished with components included in a typical panel assembly. Panels may be attached to each other or independently fixed into floor and ceiling channels, offering more flexibility. Typically, movable wall systems delineate space, provide visual and sound privacy, channel power and telecommunications cable, and support storage and work surface components. Various manufacturers offer different features for electric and telecommunications cable raceways and access, opening treatments, connection details, panel/cladding and finish materials, sound transmission coefficient ratings, fire ratings, and demountability/movability options. Consult manufacturers for specific features.

ONE-PIECE PANELS

One-piece panels are composite panels typically made from sheet steel or aluminum with a core of insulation and structural ribs for stiffness. Panels are typically 2 3/8 to 3 in. thick, although other thicknesses are available.

TWO-PIECE PANELS

These panels are manufactured as separate structural and cladding systems. The structure is made from steel members that are factory-assembled into panel-sized components and then installed. Panel cladding material varies and may include regular and high-impact vinyl-clad gypsum, insulation-filled sound control panels, or sandwich panels (steel sheets with a honeycomb infill), among others. Panel cladding is typically 1/2 to 5/8 in. thick.

GENERAL NOTES

1. Suspended ceilings are usually ineffective as a sound barrier. Consequently, when a series of soundproofed offices are planned under such a ceiling, the chances of sound travel over partitions should be considered. Baffles installed tightly above each run of the slab will eliminate cracks through which sound can easily pass.
2. The perimeter of the partition installation—ceiling, floor, and sides—should be gasketed with a factory-applied sealant. All door frames should be fitted with a factory-applied rubber liner at the head and jambs that compresses when the door is closed.
3. For extra sound control, all doors should have a continuous drop seal and threshold and glazing in doors and partitions should have double lights that are hermetically sealed.

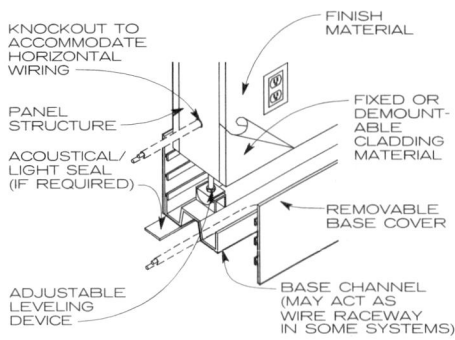

NOTE
Various locking devices fasten panels to the floor. Consult manufacturers.

BASE DETAIL

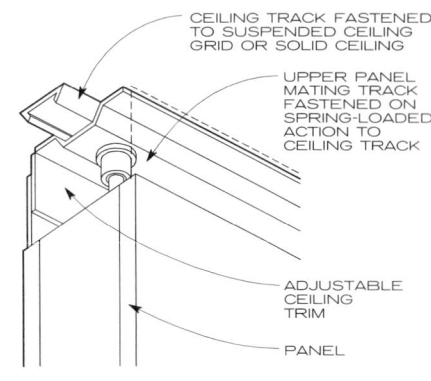

CEILING DETAIL

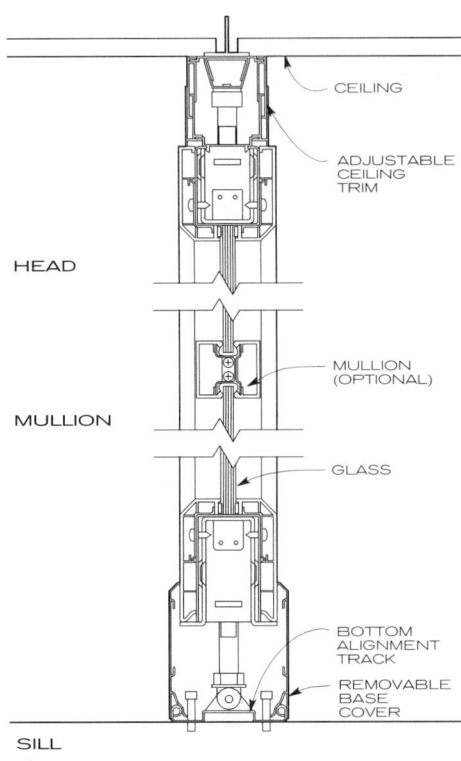

GLAZED WALL SECTION DETAIL

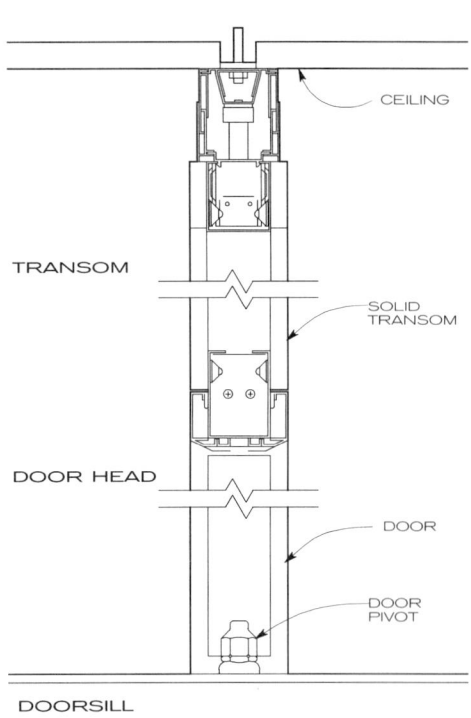

DOOR SECTION DETAIL

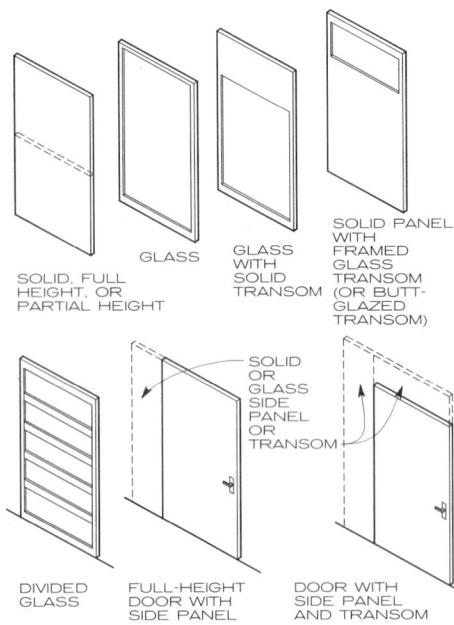

NOTE
Wall panel sizes range from 6 to 60 in. wide, up to a single panel height of 1 ft.

PANEL TYPES

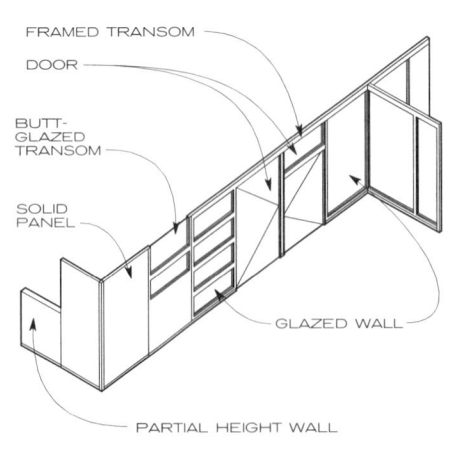

WALL CONFIGURATION SHOWING PANEL TYPES

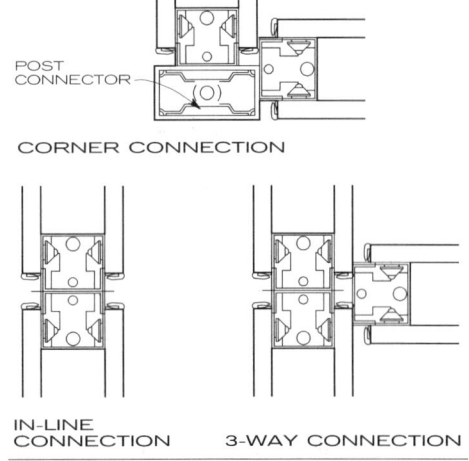

PANEL CONNECTION DETAILS

Richard J. Vitullo, AIA; Oak Leaf Studio; Crownsville, Maryland

10 PARTITIONS AND OPERABLE PARTITIONS

Multimedia Videoconference Equipment

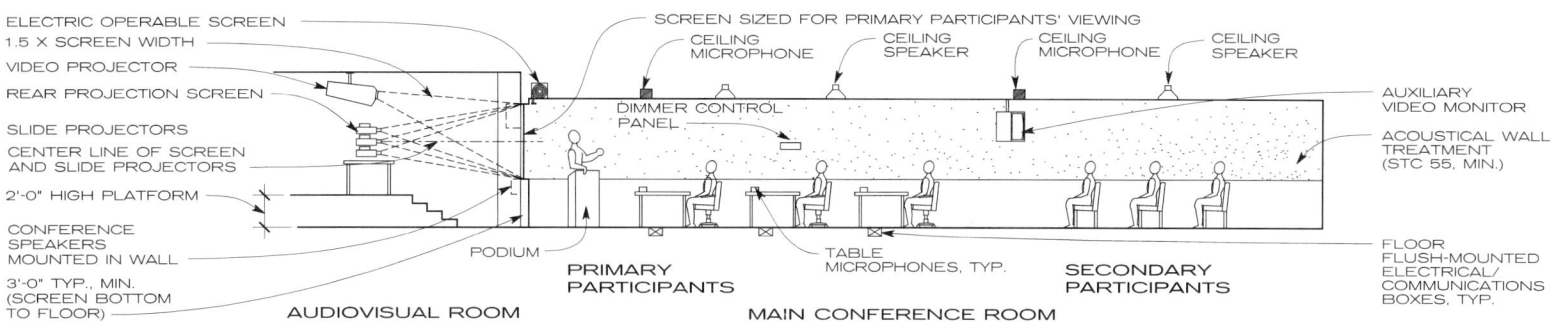

SECTION—MULTIMEDIA CONFERENCE ROOM

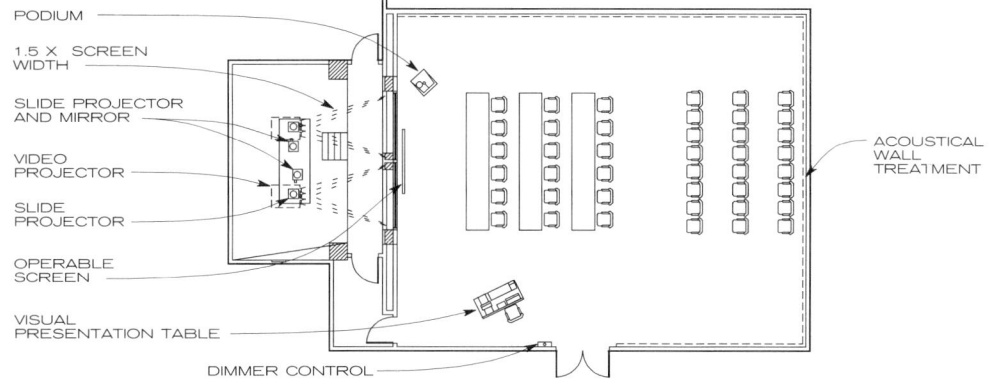

PLAN—MULTIMEDIA CONFERENCE ROOM

GENERAL

Teleconferencing is voice or data communication between remote locations and the origination site. Videoconferencing is teleconferencing with visual images added to voice and data communications. Generally, a videoconference space includes two video screens (with speaker for each), one screen for a video image from a remote location and another for supplementary images, such as those from a visual presenter, computer, or videocassette recorder.

SCREENS

Rear projection screens or large-screen monitors may be used for videoconferencing. When using a rear projection screen, it is possible to use brighter lights in the conference room during viewing than with a regular video monitor. (The forward projection screen may be perforated for sound. Forward projection systems do not need specially dedicated rooms but are usually mounted in a recess in the ceiling. They are not recommended for videoconference rooms since the high light levels required for video cameras tend to wash out forward projection screens.)

PROJECTORS

Slide, video, and overhead projectors are used in multimedia conference rooms. Video projectors are manufactured in three-lens CRT systems and single-lens LCD "light valve" systems. Three-lens projectors are best for screens up to 10 ft wide, a typical size for conference rooms, and are relatively inexpensive. If an audiovisual room is small, mirrors can be used to increase the image size for rear projection. For extra large conference rooms, with screens typically 15 to 25 ft wide, one-lens projectors can be placed any distance from the screen. This setup offers a bright, sharp image but presently is very expensive compared to the three-lens systems.

SPEAKERS AND MICROPHONES

Speaker placement is very important in a videoconference space. Speaker size usually depends on the size and shape of the space to be served.

There are three main types of speakers: Playback speakers, matched with prerecorded audio and video discs and tapes, are the largest speakers and offer the highest quality sound. Teleconference speakers, located below and near the center of the video screen, bring the audio feed from the remote videoconference space. Voice reinforcement speakers amplify voices from microphones in the same space. Microphones are placed at strategic locations in the videoconference space, including on tables, for primary participant involvement; on a stand, for secondary participant involvement; as a wireless or clip-on feature, for moderator/coordinator; and on the ceiling ("choir" microphones) to pick up specific sounds desired (to minimize feedback, these must be kept as far from the speakers as possible).

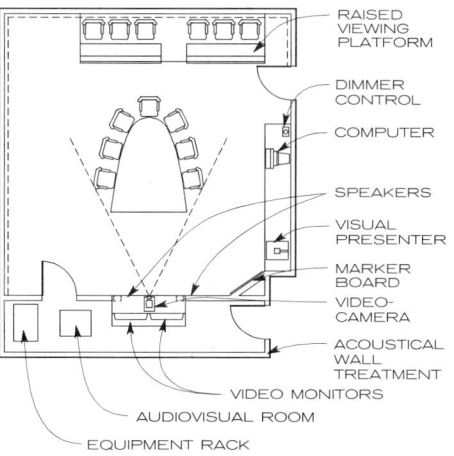

NOTE

A rear projection video camera and projection screen may be used with this arrangement; the room size depends on the screen size and video camera distance preferred.

VIDEOCONFERENCE ROOM

AUXILIARY VIDEO MONITORS

Space used by secondary videoconference participants may need auxiliary monitors to display supplementary video images such as charts or graphics that need close scrutiny. The main videoconference screen usually does not require this backup video screen.

MISCELLANEOUS EQUIPMENT

Some videoconference spaces are equipped with remote control systems, which control all electronic functions, including light and sound, from a central control panel. Some spaces are also equipped with special light fixtures that are tilted away from the screen area, shining more light on participants and less on the screen area.

Other equipment typically includes a videocassette player, an amplifier for speakers, an automatic microphone mixer, compact disc player, audiocassette player, matrix switcher, and coder/decoder equipment to convert analog signals to digital signals for fiber-optic transmission.

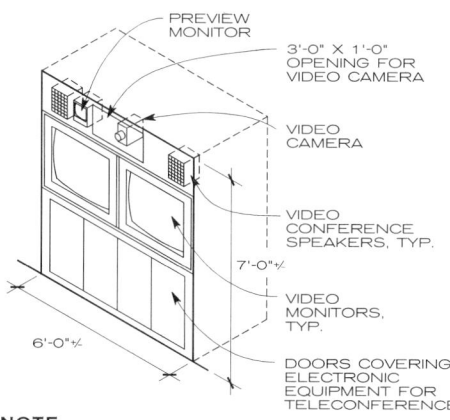

NOTE

This wall unit may be assembled on a portable console for mobility.

TYPICAL VIDEO MONITOR VIDEOCONFERENCE WALL

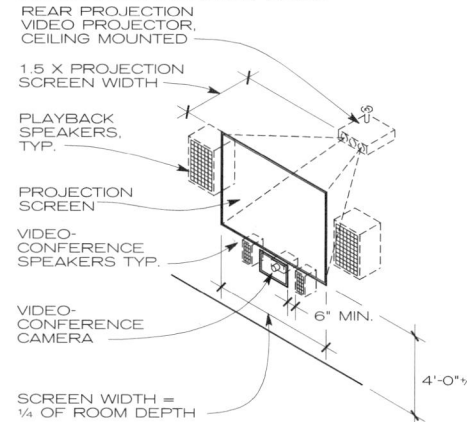

NOTE

Ratio of screen height to width: video 3:4; HDTV, 9:16.

TYPICAL REAR PROJECTION VIDEOCONFERENCE WALL

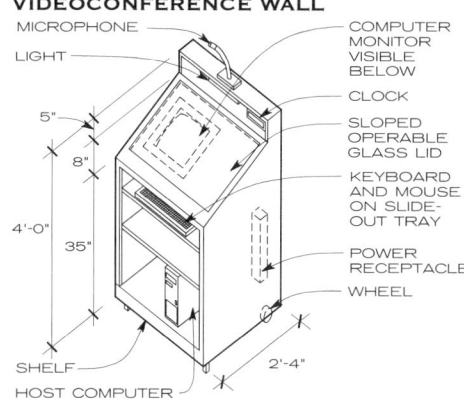

VIDEOCONFERENCE PODIUM

Polysonics; Washington, D.C.

150 Audiovisual Projection Equipment and Screens

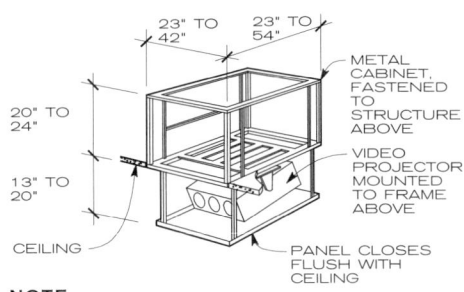

NOTE

This system is typically operated by remote control and may be linked with motorized projection screen operation. Some models are equipped with a trapdoor-type closer.

RETRACTABLE RECESSED VIDEO PROJECTOR MOUNT

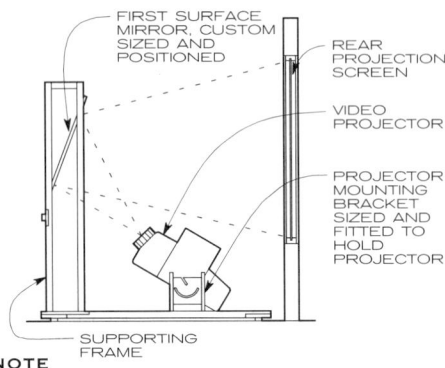

NOTE

This system requires half the space of a direct-projected rear projection system. Rear projection offers the best image quality of all projectors.

REAR PROJECTION VIDEO SCREEN FOR SMALL PROJECTION ROOM

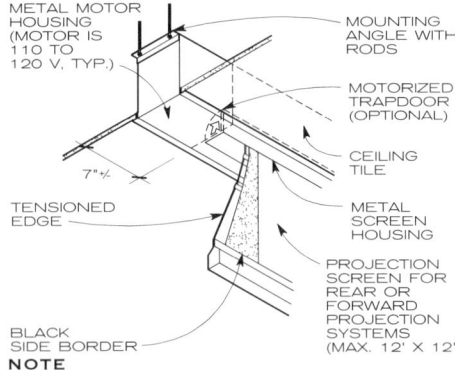

NOTE

Ceiling tile may be installed under the metal housing and cut around a trapdoor with a tile piece attached. The tensioned screen edge keeps it taut, good for three-lens video and data projection, which require perfect convergence.

MOTORIZED RECESSED PROJECTION SCREEN

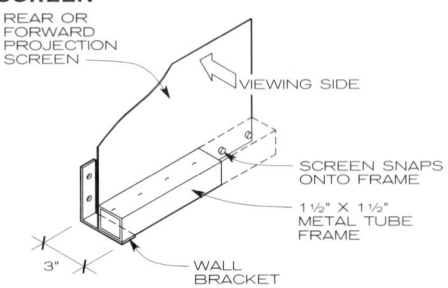

NOTE

This mounting is for forward screens up to 20 ft wide and rear screens up to 12 ft wide.

METAL FRAME SURFACE-MOUNTED PROJECTION SCREEN

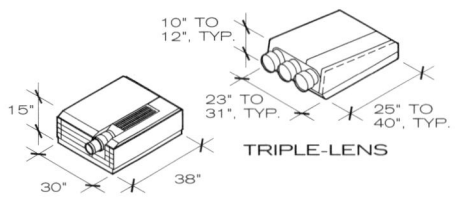

NOTE

Single-lens video projectors do not require a predetermined distance or screen size for placement; they may be placed at any distance and focused like a slide projector. These projectors produce bright, high-resolution images.

VIDEO PROJECTORS

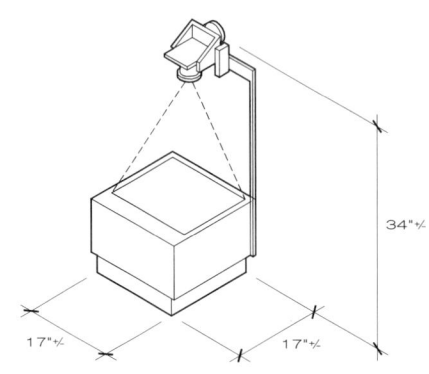

NOTE

This forward projection screen is typically made of silver lenticular fiberglass that is matte white, glass-beaded, and flame and mildew resistant.

SPRING ROLLER-OPERATED PROJECTION SCREEN

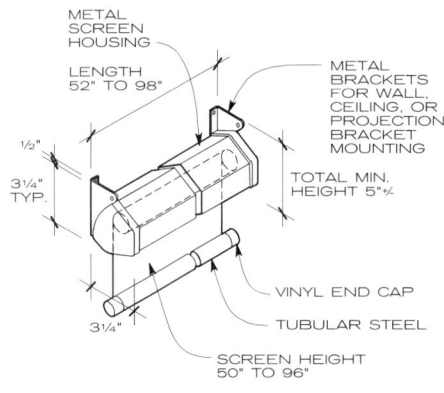

NOTE

This mount is for rear projection screens up to 20 ft wide and forward projection screens up to 30 ft wide.

METAL FRAME/TENSION CABLE PROJECTION SCREEN MOUNT

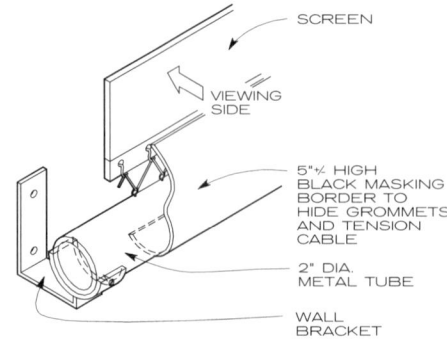

NOTE

The image may be viewed in the room or a remote location.

VISUAL PRESENTER

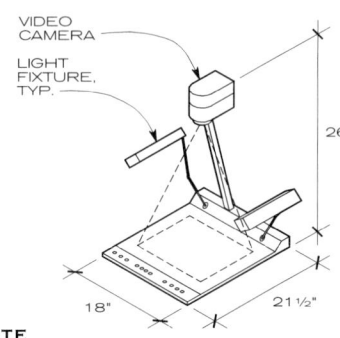

VIDEO MONITOR MOUNTING

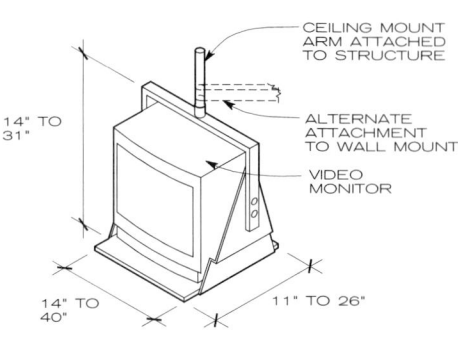

NOTE

This framing detail is for screens approximately 6 ft high by 8 ft wide, maximum.

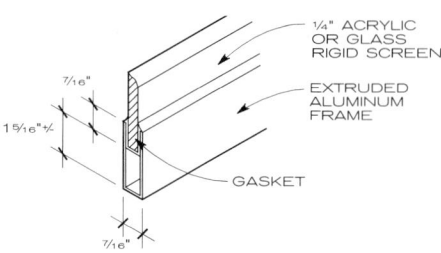

NOTE

This framing detail is for heavy-duty use, for screens up to 10 ft high by 25 ft wide.

REAR PROJECTION SCREEN FRAMING

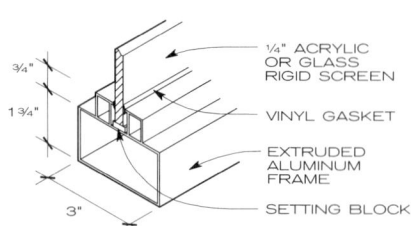

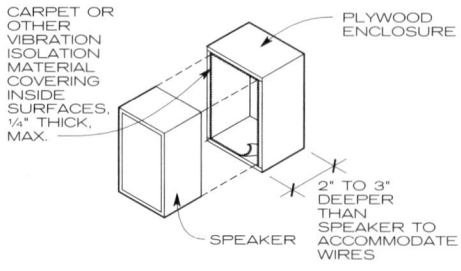

SPEAKER INSTALLATION DETAIL

Polysonics; Washington, D.C.

11 AUDIOVISUAL EQUIPMENT

Office Computer Equipment

GENERAL

A typical computer workstation in the office is equipped with a central processing unit (CPU), monitor, keyboard, and mouse. Various peripheral devices to help store, process, and retrieve data (printers, plotters, scanners, tape backup units, etc.) can be attached.

LOCAL AREA NETWORK (LAN)

LANs have changed the layout of computer equipment in the office. In years past, each workstation had its own printer, modem, scanner, etc. With the introduction of networks, these peripheral devices are now shared among a group of users. For example, one printer/modem/scanner can easily service as many as 20 users.

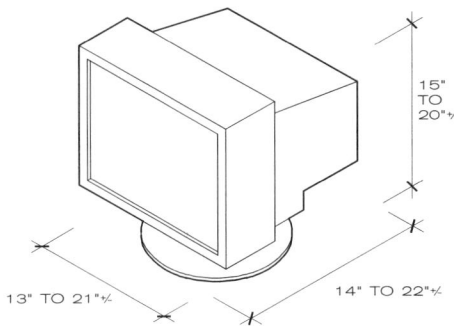

NOTE

Monitors display information to be processed. Available in one of three general types—monochrome, gray-scale, or color—they vary in diagonal screen dimensions from 13 to 21 in. (some are available between 9 and 13 in.).

MONITOR

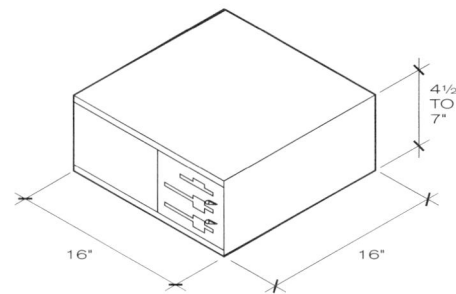

DESK TOP

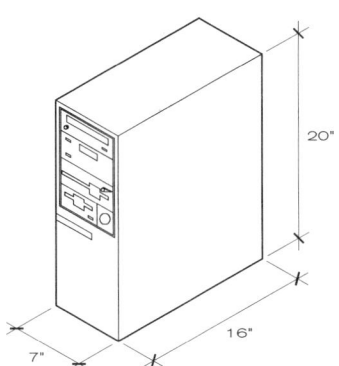

TOWER TYPE

NOTE

The central processing unit (CPU) is where computer data are stored, processed, and retrieved. CPUs are rated by processing speed (megahertz, MHz), hard-disk capacity (megabytes, MB, or gigabytes, GB), and random access memory (RAM).

CENTRAL PROCESSING UNIT (CPU)

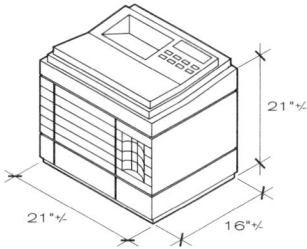

NOTE

Laser printers are typically used in larger business settings where speed, performance, and print quality are important. Most laser printers are rated at 4 to 8 pages per minute (ppm); some may be rated as high as 20 ppm.

LASER PRINTER

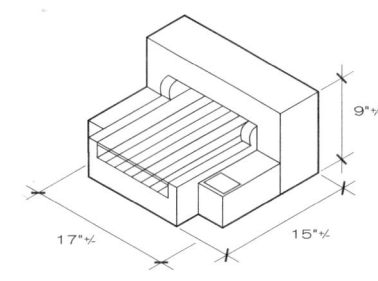

NOTE

Inkjet printers are generally more economical than laser printers. They are typically rated at 2 to 4 pages per minute (some may be as high as 8 ppm) and used in smaller business settings or home offices. The print quality is generally not as crisp as that from a laser printer.

INKJET PRINTER

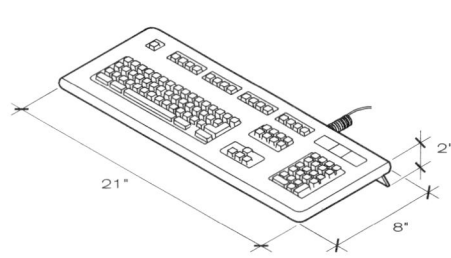

NOTE

The keyboard is a primary computer input device.

KEYBOARD

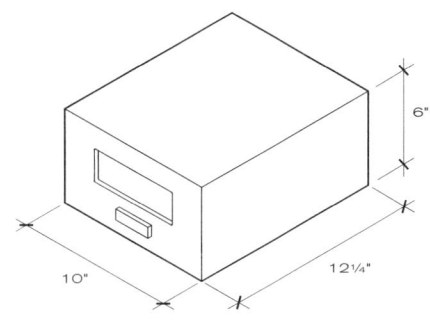

NOTE

A tape backup unit is an external storage device, typically used to copy and save data in case a hard disk crashes.

TAPE BACKUP UNIT

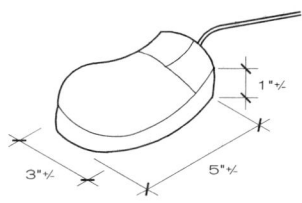

NOTE

A mouse is a pointing device used to move a cursor around a screen. It is helpful in operating a computer with a graphical user interface.

MOUSE

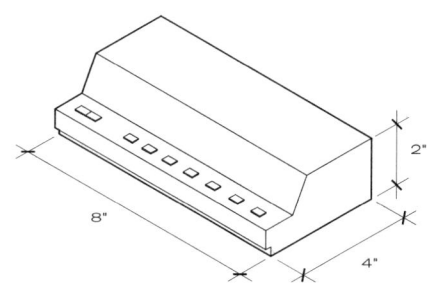

NOTE

A modem is used to transmit data from one computer to another computer or other device, such as a fax machine, via telephone lines.

MODEM

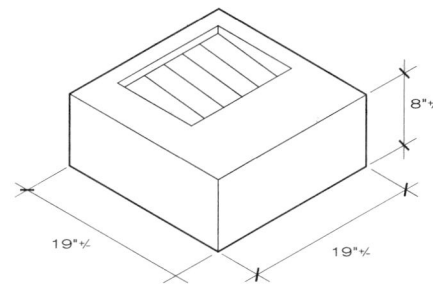

NOTE

Scanners allow a computer to read pictures or words from printed pages. This material is then stored in data files in the computer.

SCANNER

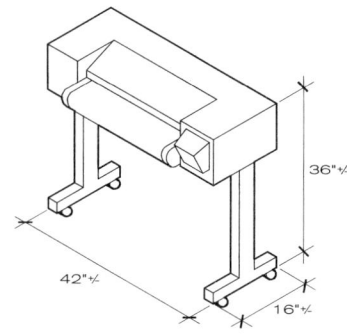

NOTE

A plotter is a device that draws with a plotting pen. It is typically used to plot or print graphics from CAD-type programs.

PLOTTER

Elin Landenburger; Alexandria, Virginia

152 Commercial Food Service Equipment

GENERAL NOTES

1. Food service equipment must meet the sanitation and safety construction standards of the National Sanitation Foundation, an independent nonprofit organization dealing with public health issues. Other organizations involved in standards for food service equipment are Underwriters Laboratories (UL) and the American Society of Mechanical Engineers.
2. Food service equipment is either fabricated from a custom design or selected from a catalog. There are many variations in equipment specifications for such elements as power supply, door swings, finish, metal type, metal gauge, capacity, and accessories. These food service equipment pages show typical layouts and equipment for a mid-sized hotel kitchen that must produce a la carte meals, room service meals, banquets, etc. Equipment size and type will vary according to variables such as dining room size, menu type, and building type.
3. Prefabricated and custom-built walk-in refrigerators and freezers are specified differently. Consult a food service consultant for sizing, since these units can be specified to an infinite variety of sizes and shapes.
4. Food service equipment is primarily gas-powered, unless fumes are a concern, in which case electricity is used. If possible, steam is the preferred energy source because of its economy and efficiency.
5. Confer with a qualified food service consultant to determine the precise equipment and layout for the space to be served.

GAUGE AND USE OF GALVANIZED STEEL

GAUGE	RECOMMENDED USE
12	Support channels and bracing
14	Undershelves and partitions
16	Undershelves and side panels
18	Utensil drawers, hoods, body panels, interior partitions

GAUGE AND USE OF STAINLESS STEEL

GAUGE	TYPICAL USE
8 and 10	Support elements for heavy equiment or at stress points
12	Heavily used tabletops, pot sinks, or other surfaces that will receive a great amount of wear
14	Tabletops, sinks, shelves, and brackets that will be used frequently or that will hold heavy objects
16	Small equipment tops and sides that will carry light objects; shelves under equipment and heavily used side panels
18	Side panels that are not exposed to much wear, equipment doors, hoods, and partitions
20	Covers for supported or insulated panels, such as refrigerators or insulated doors

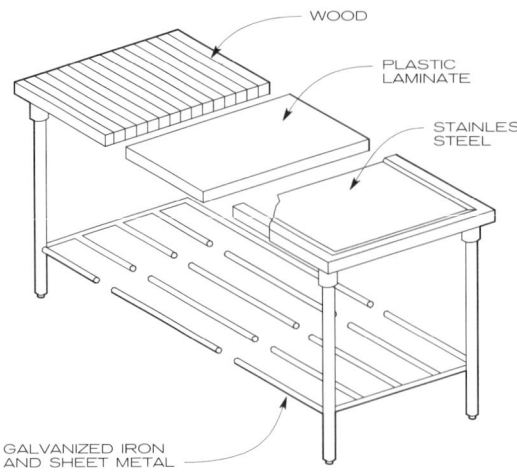

NOTES

1. Wood is used only for dining room or bakery production tables. Hard rock maple and pecan cutting tops are usually specified. Not to be used for nonbakery food production; cracks in wood surface can harbor bacteria.
2. Plastic laminate should not be used where cutting, chopping, or carving will occur. It will not warp or crack; it is an inexpensive substitute for stainless steel for nonfood production or decorative countertops, where codes allow.
3. Stainless steel is the most commonly used material for all areas in a commercial kitchen. Although relatively expensive, it is extremely durable. Cold-rolled steel stock is formed under pressure; welded connections are used only within equipment (bolted connections are used to connect pieces of equipment).
4. Galvanized iron and sheet metal are used as underbracing for equipment and as an inexpensive substitute for stainless steel for legs, tables, and interior shelves.
5. Other materials, including glass, ceramic tile, copper, and brass, may be used for food service equipment, but all surfaces that come into contact with food or the food handler should be smooth and nonporous and resist chipping or wear under frequent use. Surfaces must also resist the corrosive effects of salt, food acids, and oils.

MATERIALS USED IN FOOD SERVICE EQUIPMENT

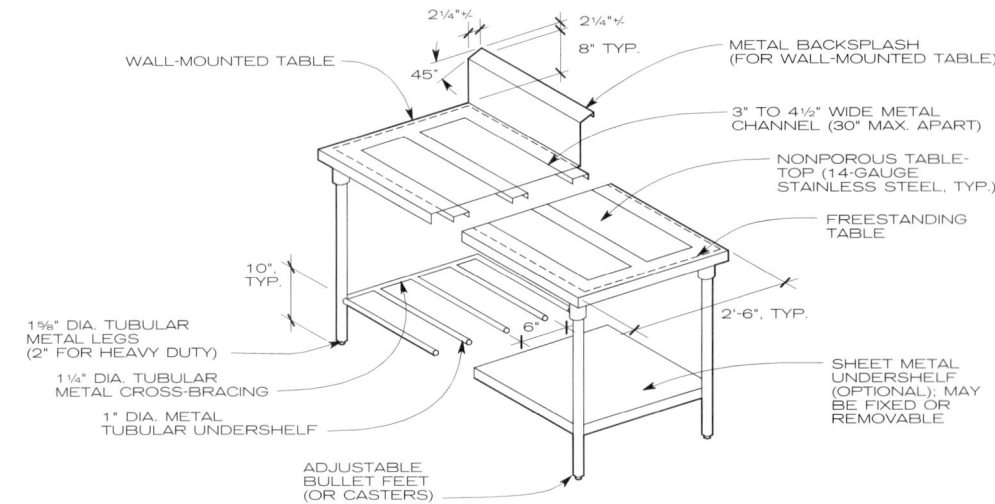

NOTE
Tubular metal pieces should be welded, coved together, and sanded smooth. A layer of cork-based sound-deadening material may be applied to the underside of tabletops and finished with aluminum lacquer. Consult health codes for types of lacquer permitted.

FABRICATED WORKTABLE

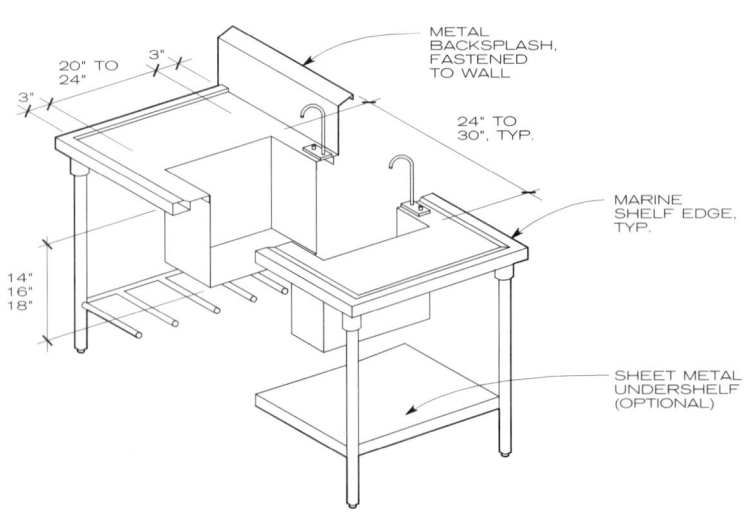

FABRICATED WORKTABLE WITH SINK

John Birchfield; Birchfield Foodsystems, Inc.; Annapolis, Maryland

11 FOOD SERVICE EQUIPMENT

Commercial Food Service Equipment

GENERAL

Exhaust hoods remove air, water vapor, grease, and food odors from the kitchen area and air and water vapor from dish washing areas. Ovens and steam-jacketed kettles only require hoods that remove air, heat, and water vapor, but if large amounts of grease from a broiler, char-broiler, fryer, or grill are present, the hood system must extract this pollutant before the air is drawn outside by fans. This is done with grease "cartridges," or with stainless steel extractors, both of which violently blow the exhausted air around. This flings the grease particles to the sides of the baffles; then they are collected in a trough for easy removal, or run out a drain. The extractors can usually be washed in a standard kitchen dishwasher. Consultation with code officials and food service consultants is of utmost importance when designing exhaust hoods.

NOTES

1. CFM requirements for exhaust hoods are determined by the length of the hood and the equipment types underneath. Typical requirements range from 150 to 450 CFM per linear foot of hood.
2. Some codes may require a higher exhaust rate. To make up this air differential and to prevent more air from being drawn from surrounding areas, introduce air through a supply duct. The supplied air should make up 50 to 85% of the total exhaust.

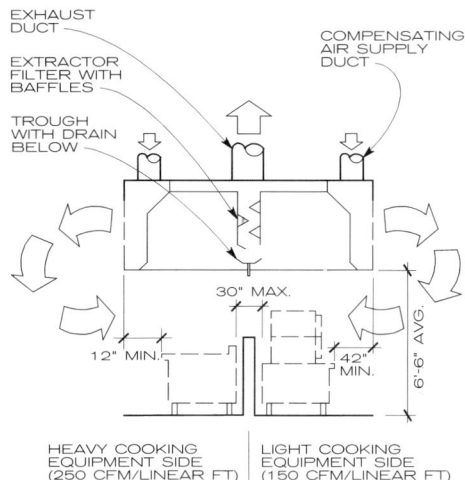

NOTE

Single exhaust hoods are available for single cooking lines. Dimensions and capacities of exhaust hoods vary with particular kitchen cooking requirements.

TYPICAL EXHAUST HOOD REQUIREMENTS

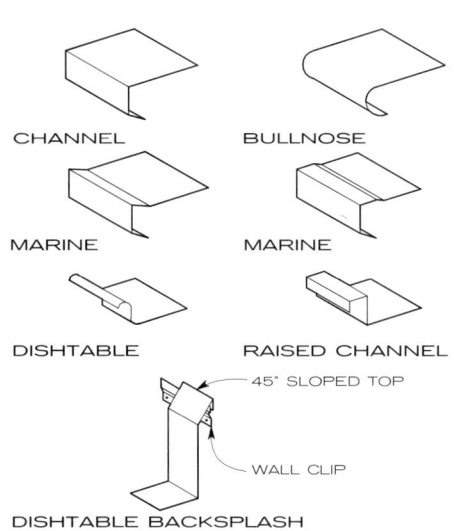

NOTE

Channel edges and bullnose edges are used only when water will not be spilled on the table surface.

TABLE EDGE PROFILES

John Birchfield; Birchfield Foodsystems, Inc.; Annapolis, Maryland

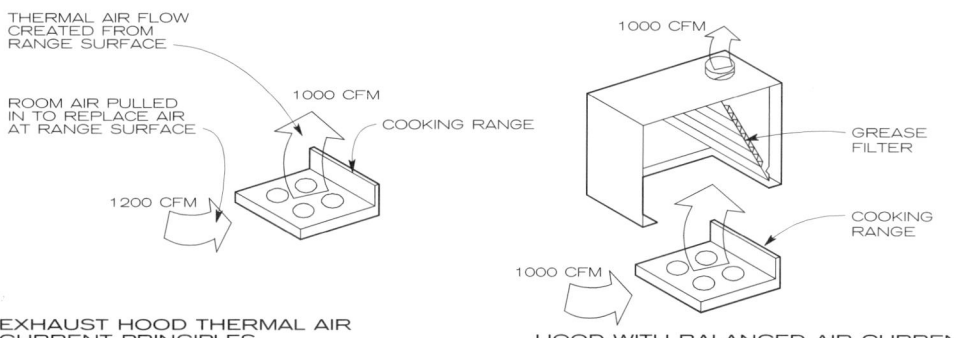

EXHAUST HOOD THERMAL AIR CURRENT PRINCIPLES

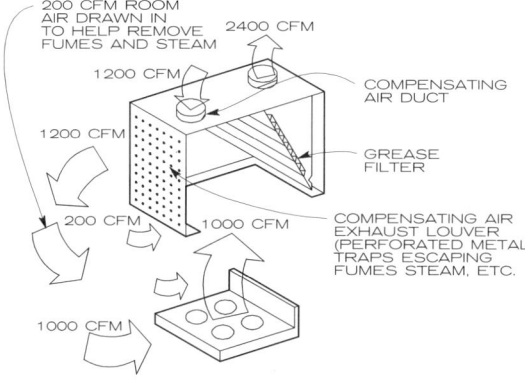

HOOD WITH 20% SAFETY FACTOR

NOTE

Room air drawn in at the front of the hood at the rate of 200 cubic ft per minute (CFM) will create an extra 20% safety margin at the hood to handle thermal surges, crosscurrents, etc.

EXHAUST HOOD CHARACTERISTICS

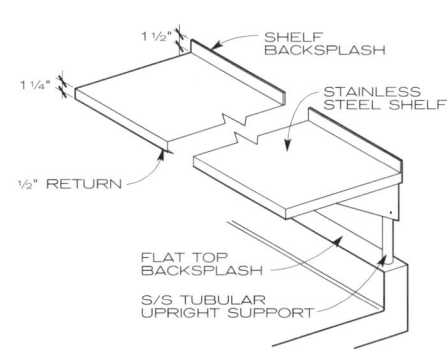

ELEVATED TABLE-MOUNTED SHELF

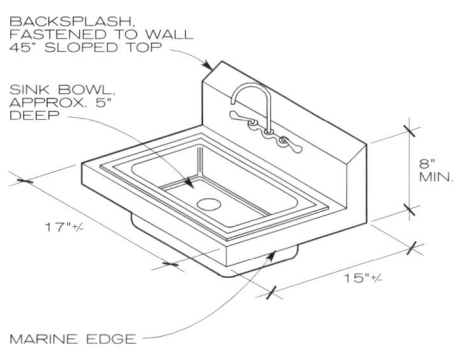

NOTE

Hand sinks are typically required by code near every major work area in the kitchen. Some are equipped with an electronic eye or foot levers to encourage workers to wash their hands.

WALL-MOUNTED HAND SINK

HOOD WITH BALANCED AIR CURRENTS

HOOD WITH 50% COMPENSATING AIR

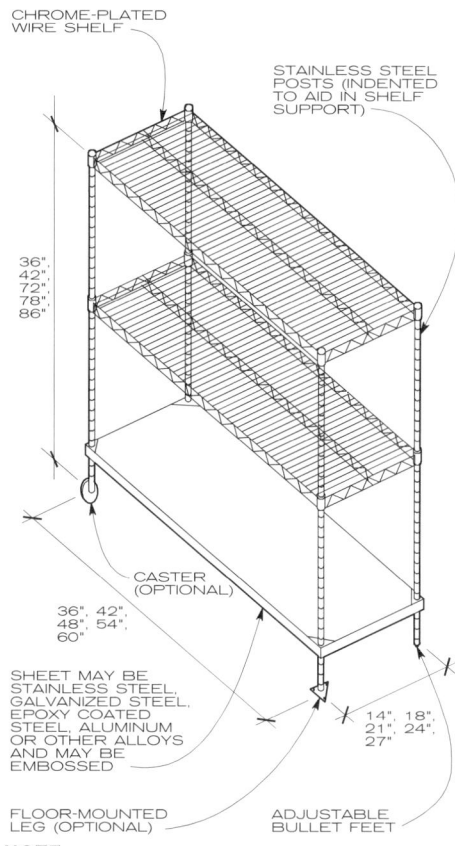

NOTE

This shelf may be used in dry storage rooms and walk-in refrigerators and freezers. Shelving may be mounted to the wall for stability and can be attached to other modular units.

MODULAR WIRE SHELVING UNIT

Commercial Food Service Equipment—Chef

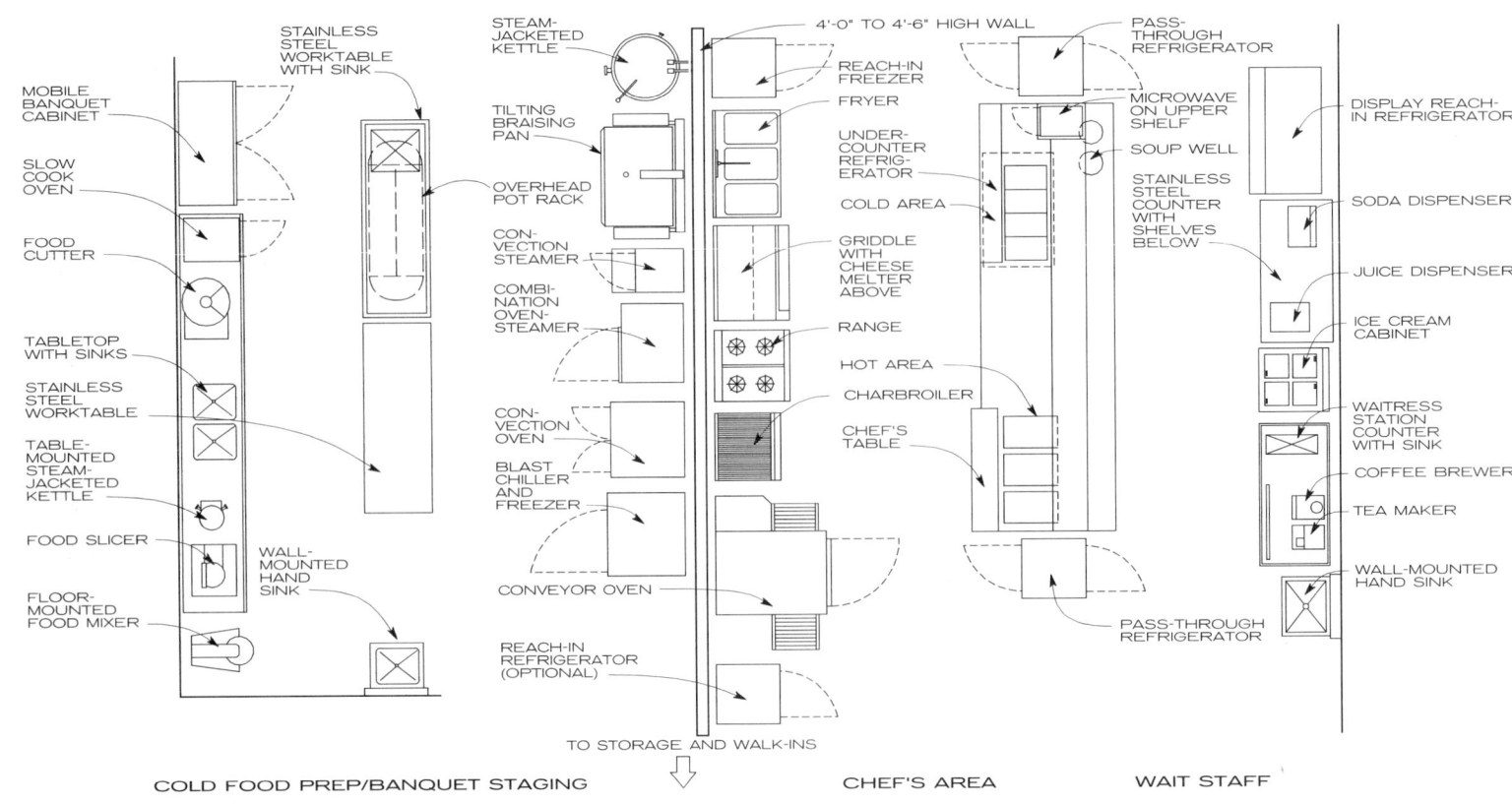

TYPICAL KITCHEN PLAN

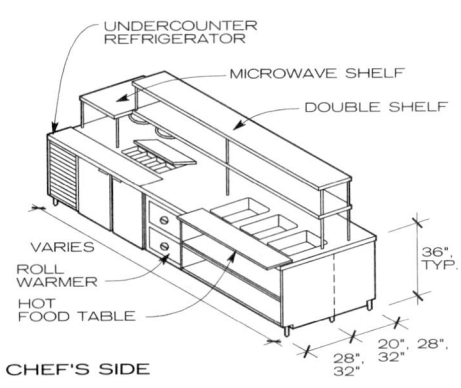

CHEF'S SIDE

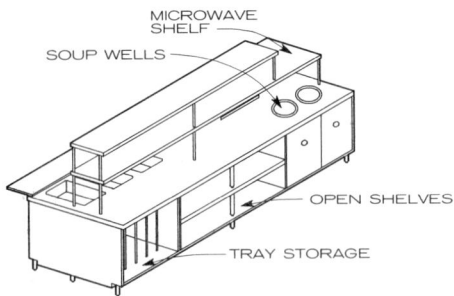

WAIT STAFF PICK-UP SIDE

NOTE

The chef's table is the heart of the kitchen operation; it is here the hot and cold food is arranged on plates for pick-up by the wait staff. Since both kitchen and wait staffs need access, the table is usually placed in an island configuration. Usually custom-built to meet the chef's requirements.

CHEF'S TABLE

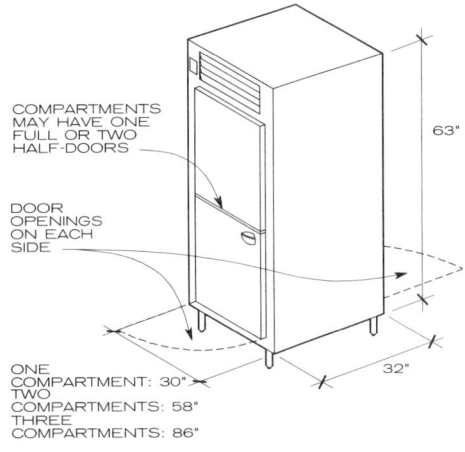

NOTE

This unit is typically placed either at end of the chef's table or in the wall separating the service area from the kitchen.

PASS-THROUGH REFRIGERATOR

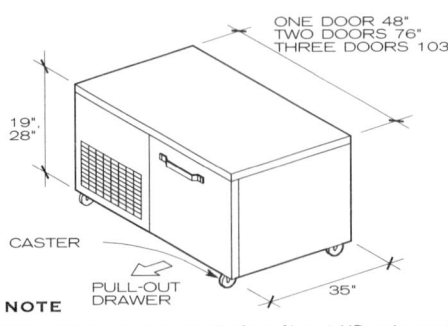

NOTE

This unit has a motor capacity from 1/4 to 1 HP and a maximum load of 500 to 1000 lb.

UNDERCOUNTER REFRIGERATOR FREEZER

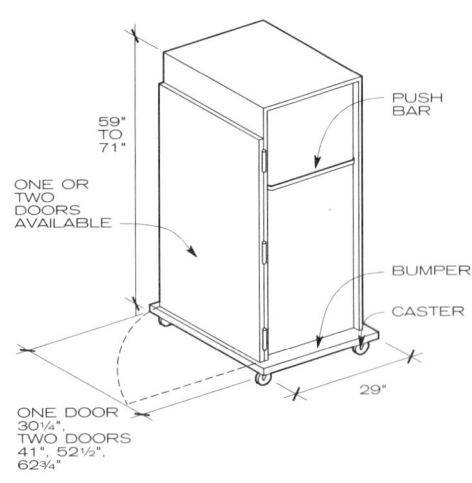

NOTE

This cabinet is used to keep preplated meals hot.

MOBILE BANQUET CABINET

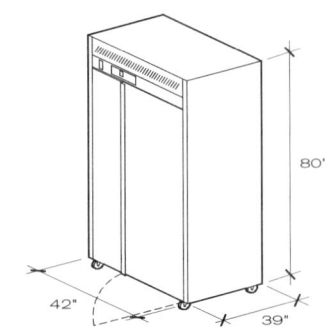

NOTE

This unit provides cook/chill and cook/freeze options.

BLAST CHILLER AND FREEZER

John Birchfield; Birchfield Foodsystems Inc.; Annapolis, Maryland

FOOD SERVICE EQUIPMENT

Commercial Food Service Equipment—Hot and Cold

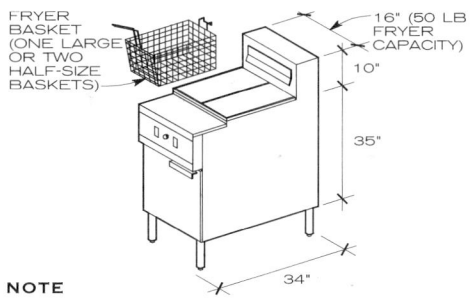

NOTE

Fryers cook food by immersing it in hot fat and are powered by either gas or electricity. Fryers can be either freestanding, table mounted, modular (electric only), or drop-in (electric only). Typical capacities range from 15 to 75 lb of shortening or fat. Two modular units with a filter dump station between them is a common fryer configuration.

FRYER

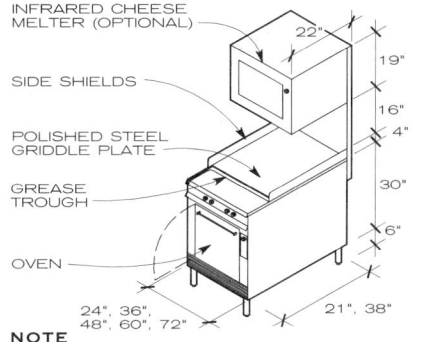

NOTE

Griddles, also called grills, have a flat, heated surface that cooks food quickly. They can be freestanding units, part of a range, table models, or part of a modular unit and are either gas- or electric-powered.

GRIDDLE WITH CHEESE MELTER

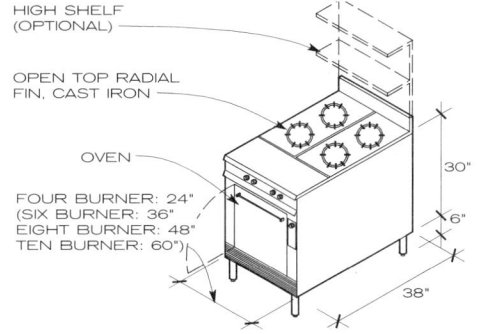

NOTE

The range is often the most heavily used piece of equipment in a food service facility. The open-top gas range is preferred by cooks, especially for sauteing, because the flame is visible and easily adjusted. Electric models are available.

RANGE

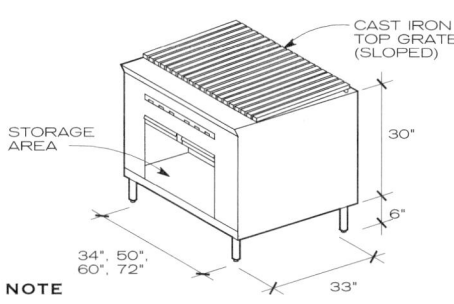

NOTE

A charbroiler cooks food rapidly, one side at a time, usually with radiant heat produced by gas or electricity. There are many types: freestanding top burner broilers, charbroilers, salamanders (small above-the-range broilers for last minute browning), conveyor broilers, and rotisseries.

CHARBROILER

John Birchfield; Birchfield Foodsystems Inc.; Annapolis, Maryland

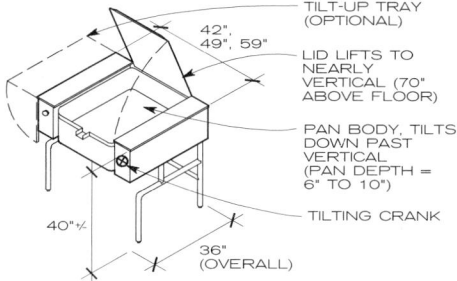

NOTE

Also called a tilting skillet or tilting frying pan, this braising pan can be used for grilling, steaming, braising, sauteing, or stewing. It holds a large volume of food, typically 20 to 40 gallons. The pan body tilts down so that liquids can be poured off, and also to aid in cleaning.

TILTING BRAISING PAN

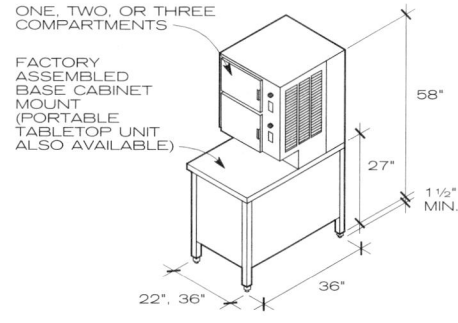

NOTE

Low- (5 lb per sq in.) and no-pressure steamers are used to prepare vegetables, seafood, eggs, rice, and pasta and work very efficiently. They are powered by gas, electricity, direct steam, or a steam coil.

CONVECTION STEAMER

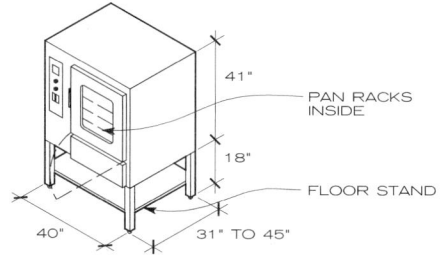

NOTE

Also called a "combi," it combines a convection oven with a steamer in one piece of equipment. It is popular because of its versatility.

COMBINATION OVEN-STEAMER

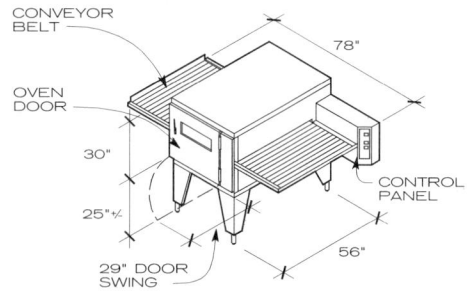

NOTE

A conveyor oven moves food through a heated cavity at a predetermined speed, ensuring even cooking time and allowing high-volume production. Heating is by convection or radiant heat, on one or both sides of the belt. Pizzas, cookies, hamburgers, and seafood all travel this route.

CONVEYOR OVEN

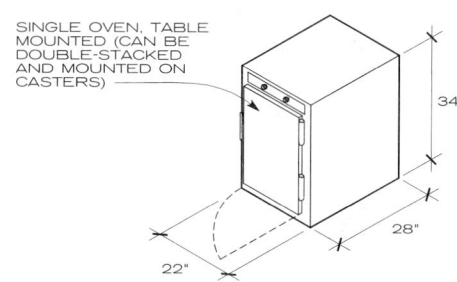

NOTE

Primarily used to roast meats, this oven can also be used to warm hot foods and proof bread or dough. Designed to cook at 200 to 240°F, these ovens reduce shrinkage of roast meats up to 40% and save energy.

SLOW-COOK OVEN

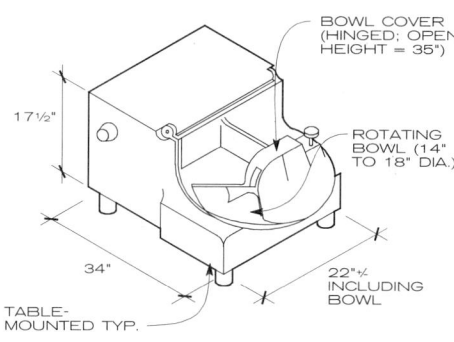

NOTE

Used for chopping meats and vegetables, this machine is similar in function to a food processor. It is also called a "buffalo chopper." Another larger type is a vertical cutter mixer (VCM), with a capacity of 30 to 45 quarts.

FOOD CUTTER

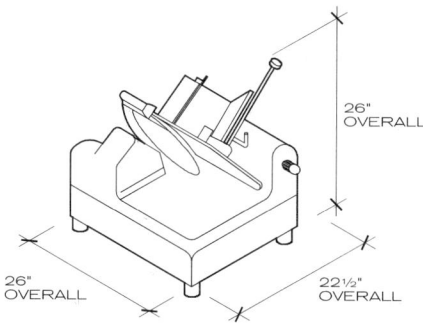

NOTE

Motor capacity varies from $1/5$ to $1/2$ HP.

FOOD SLICER

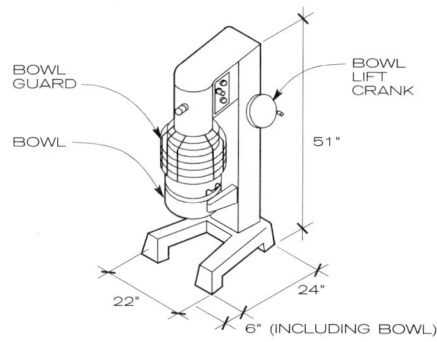

NOTE

This is used to mix/process large quantities of food, especially if a variety of attachments is required.

FOOD MIXER

FOOD SERVICE EQUIPMENT

Commercial Food Service Equipment—Bakery

TYPICAL BAKERY AREA PLAN

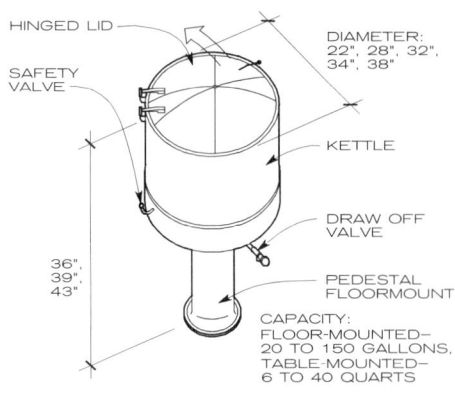

NOTE
A steam-jacketed kettle is used for soups, stews, sauces, boiled meats, etc. The kettle is double-walled; heat comes from an inner jacket that contains the steam. The kettle can be mounted either on a pedestal, on legs, on a yoke (trunnion) for tilting, on the wall, or on a tabletop.

STEAM-JACKETED KETTLE

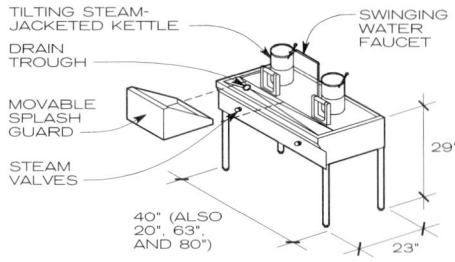

NOTE
This stand can hold up to four steam-jacketed kettles on pinions, or trunnions, which enable tilting and pouring.

TRUNNION STAND

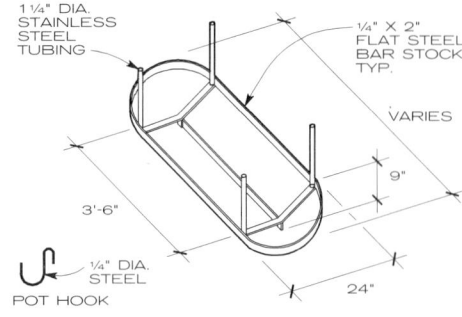

NOTE
Dimensions shown are for medium-use kitchens; review unusual conditions, such as use of extra large pots or need for wider support spans, with a structural engineer.

OVERHEAD POT RACK

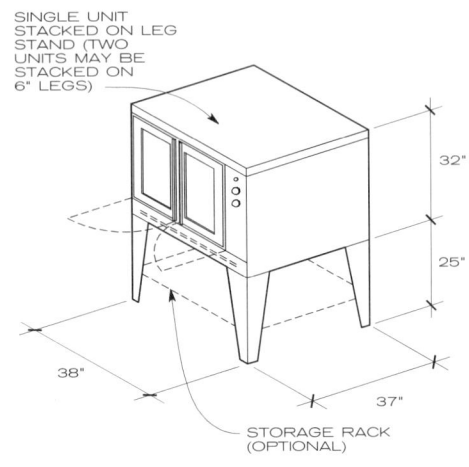

NOTE
Convection ovens need less energy and less space than other commercial kitchen ovens. A fan circulates heat evenly throughout the oven chamber, and the interior shelves can be stacked very close together.

CONVECTION OVEN

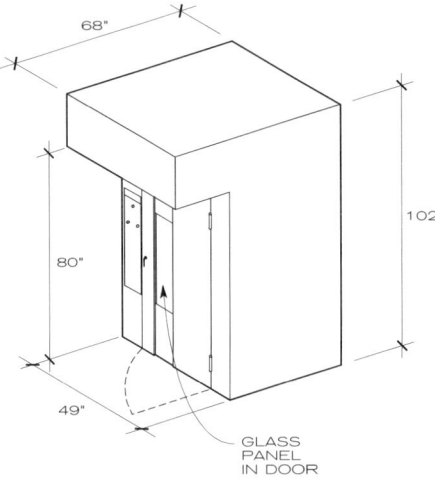

NOTE
The rack is loaded, usually with baked goods, and wheeled into the oven. The rack rotates on a carousel or a ceiling hung bracket, baking food with a steady, even heat. Rack ovens are powered by gas, electricity, or oil.

RACK OVEN

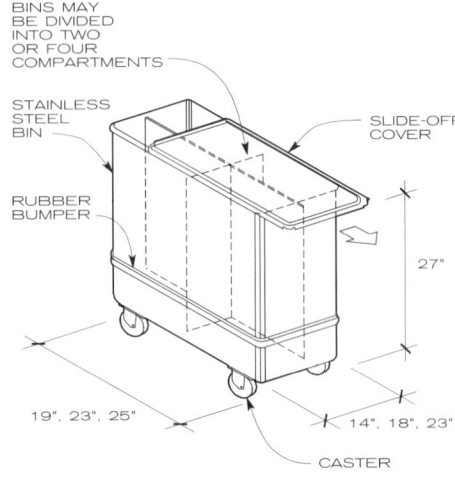

NOTE
Used for storage of baked goods and ingredients like flour, sugar, and rice. Bin can be stored under open-based tables.

ROLLING INGREDIENT BIN

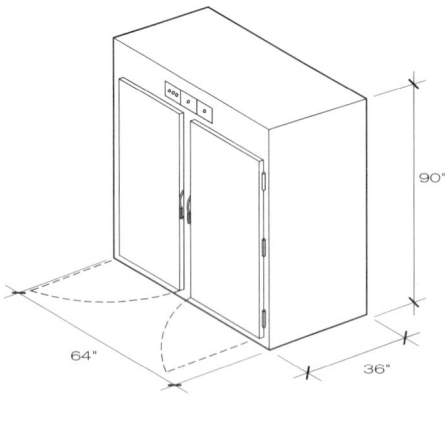

NOTE
This unit proofs bakery items (emits the moist, low heat that dough needs to rise), then, after a specified amount of time, issues cold air to halt the rising.

RETARDER/PROOFER

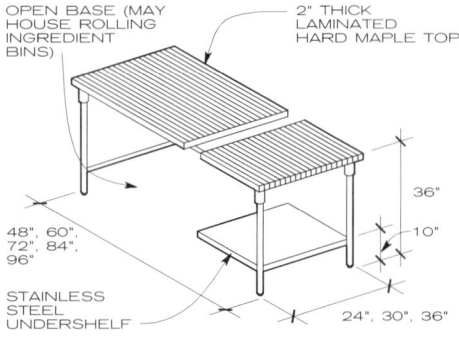

NOTE
Baker's tables are used exclusively for making baked goods. Any other use that could bring bacteria-laden foods into contact with the wood surface is prohibited.

BAKER'S TABLE

John Birchfield; Birchfield Foodsystems Inc.; Annapolis, Maryland

Commercial Food Service Equipment—Wait and Dishwashing

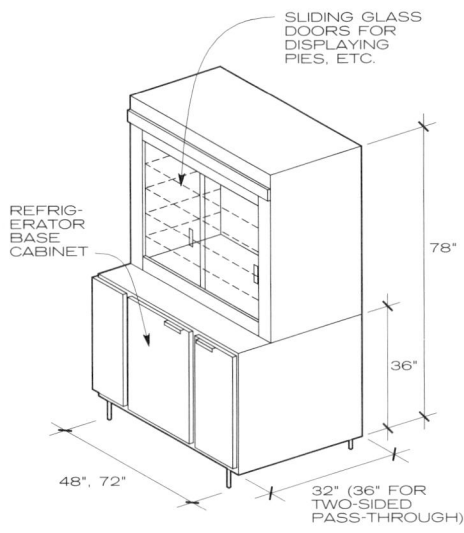

DISPLAY REACH-IN REFRIGERATOR

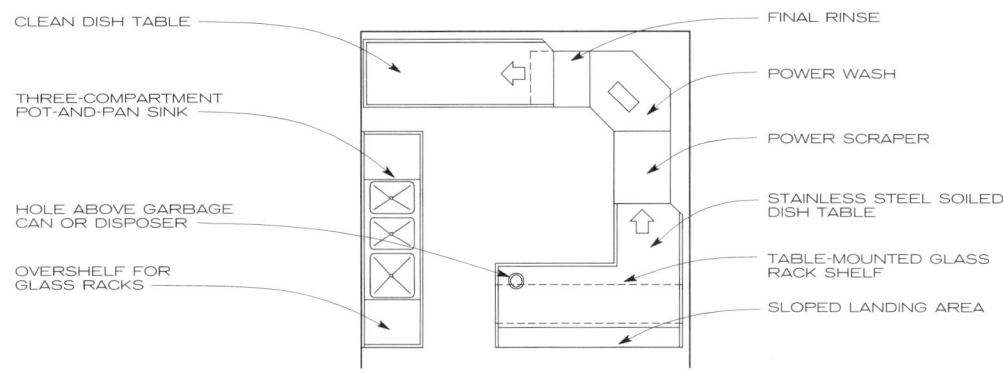

TYPICAL DISHWASHING AREA PLAN

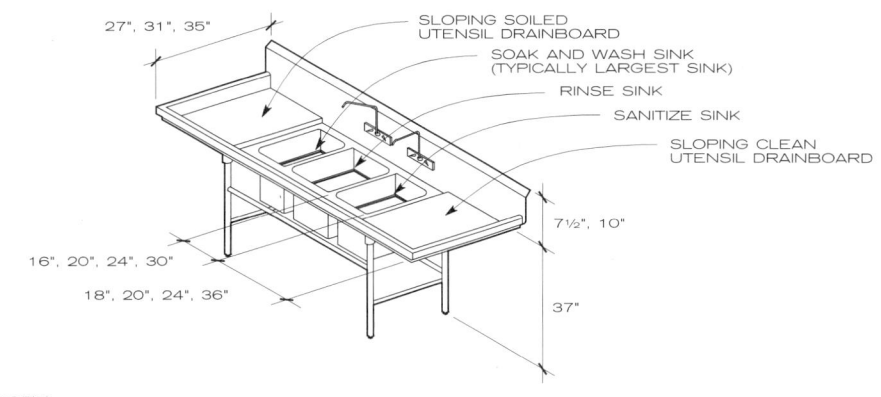

NOTE
The sink illustrated is a fairly common type, but depth of sinks, number of sinks, and size of drainboards can vary.

POT AND PAN SINK

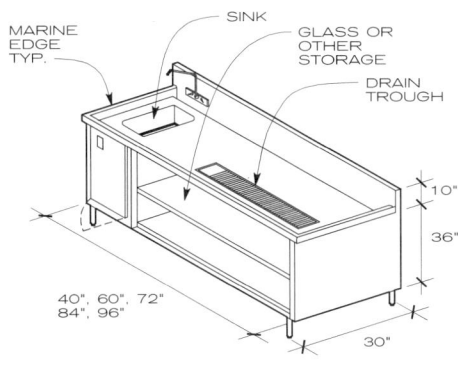

NOTE
Multipurpose table unit used to store cups and glasses and to prepare soft drinks, coffee, tea, and other beverages.

WAITRESS STATION COUNTER

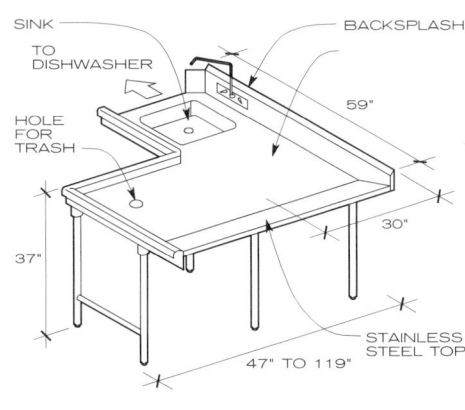

SOILED DISH TABLE

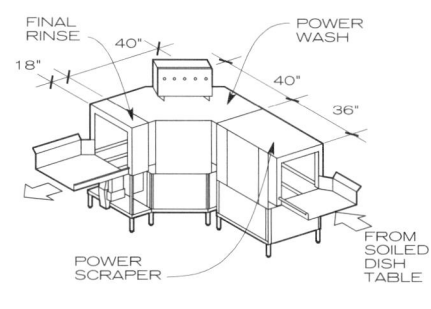

NOTE
A spray of hot water and detergent washes the dishes, followed by a rinse of 180°F water or chemicals to sanitize them. Sometimes an exhaust hood is used; the design of machines varies greatly.

DISHWASHING MACHINE

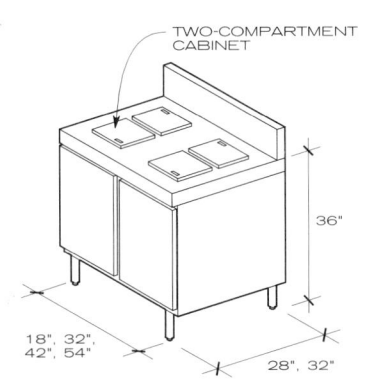

ICE CREAM CABINET

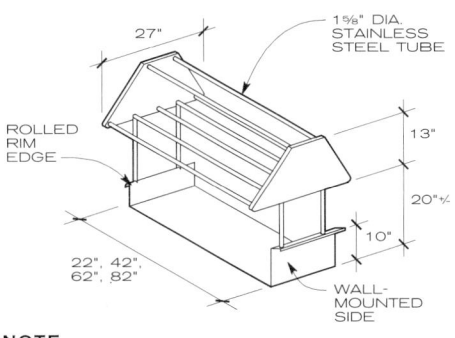

NOTE
Typically this is mounted on the soiled dish table.

TABLE-MOUNTED GLASS RACK SHELF

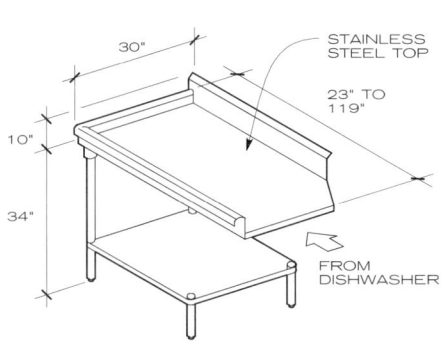

CLEAN DISH TABLE

John Birchfield; Birchfield Foodsystems Inc.; Annapolis, Maryland

FOOD SERVICE EQUIPMENT

Commercial Bar Equipment

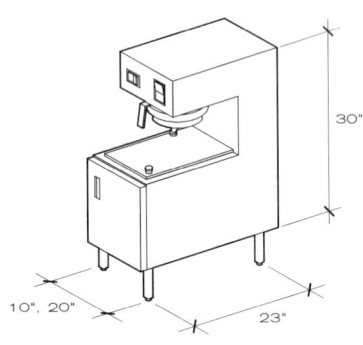

NOTE
This drops into a cutout in the wait staff counter.

DROP-IN SODA DISPENSER

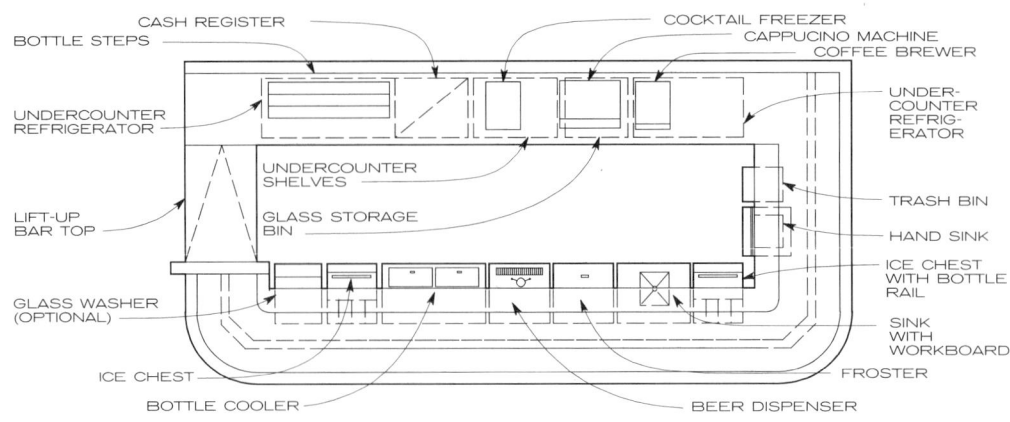

TYPICAL BAR EQUIPMENT LAYOUT

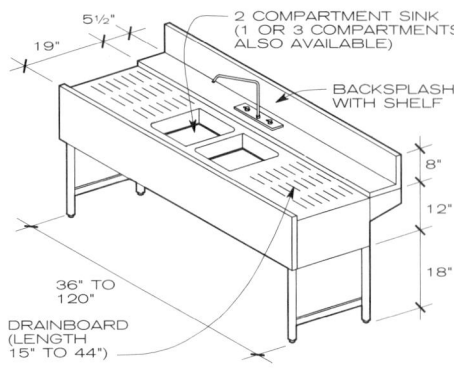

NOTE
A mechanical glass washer may be substituted for this.

SINK WITH WORKBOARD

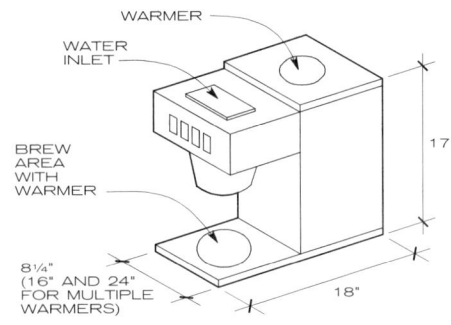

NOTE
Typically tea makers sit on top of the wait staff counter.

TEA MAKER

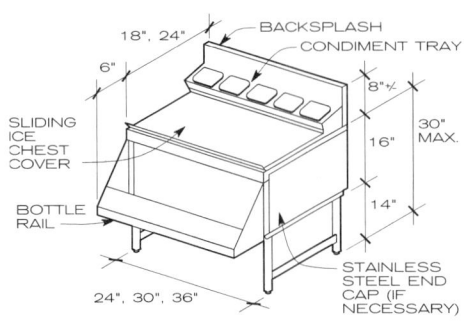

NOTE
These units vary according to use, with different cover opening styles (hinged or sliding), condiment tray configurations, and placement of ice dividers in chest.

ICE CHEST

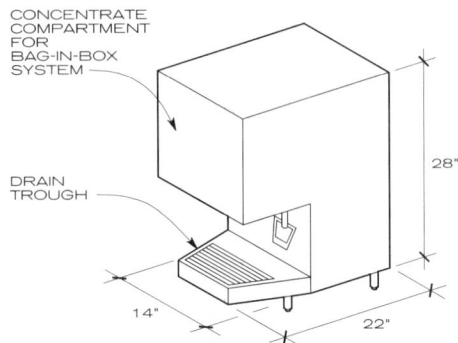

NOTE
Coffee brewers sit on top of the wait staff counter.

COFFEE BREWER

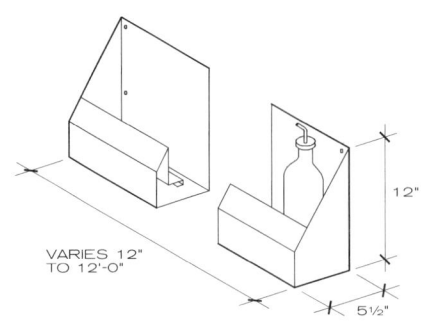

NOTE
Bottle rails are attached to the front of sinks, ice chests, or other bar equipment. Lockable models are available.

BOTTLE RAIL

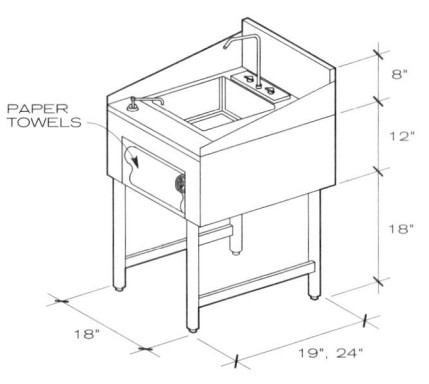

BAR HAND SINK

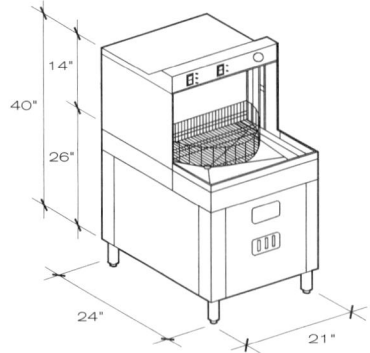

NOTE
Juice dispensers sit on top of the wait staff counter.

JUICE DISPENSER

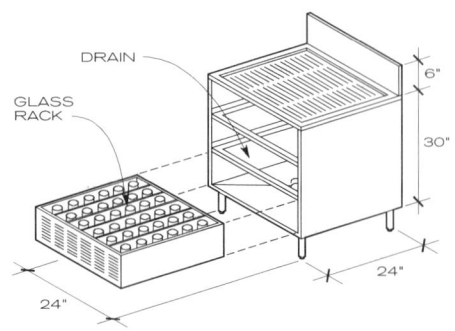

NOTE
A sink with drainboard may be substituted for this.

GLASS WASHER

GLASS STORAGE BIN

Richard J. Vitullo, AIA; Oak Leaf Studio; Crownsville, Maryland

11 FOOD SERVICE EQUIPMENT

Bar and Beverage Equipment

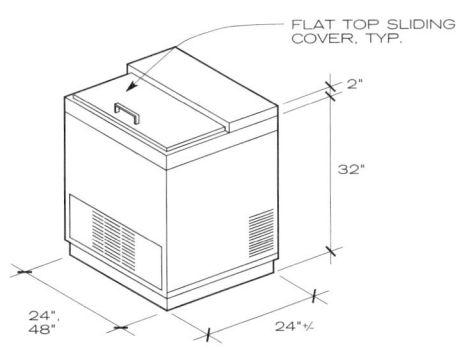

NOTE
Frosters chill mugs, glasses, and plates to minus 10°F on interior shelves. Usually they are placed under the front bar.

FROSTER

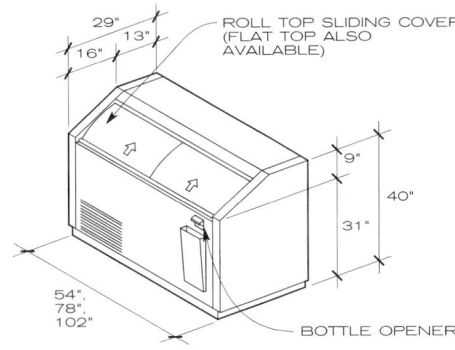

NOTE
These are used to cool beverages to between 34° and 40°F.

BOTTLE COOLER

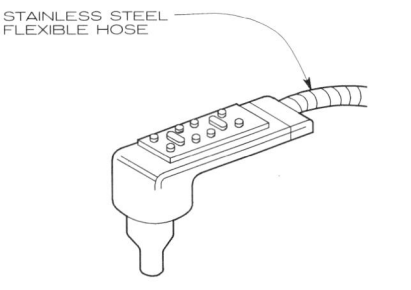

NOTE
This dispenses water, soda, wine, and other drinks.

MECHANICAL POSTMIX BAR DISPENSER

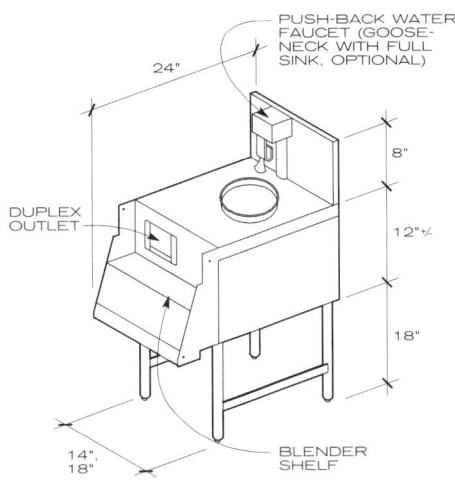

BLENDER STATION

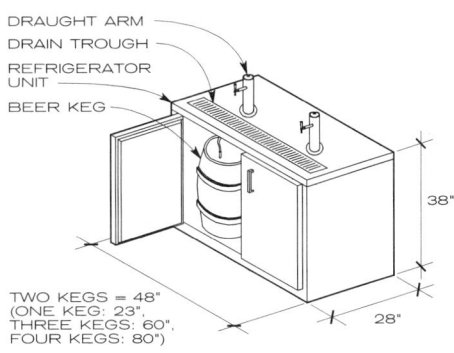

NOTE
The dispenser shown is a direct draw system. Kegs may be up to 300 ft away from the bar (usually in a walk-in cooler).

BEER DISPENSER

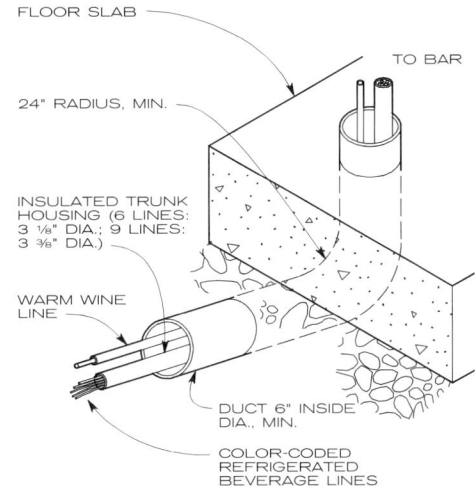

REMOTE BEVERAGE DISPENSER DETAIL

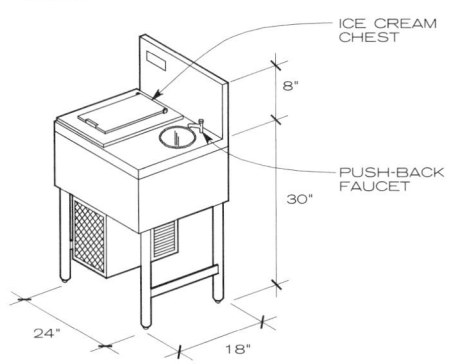

ICE CREAM CABINET

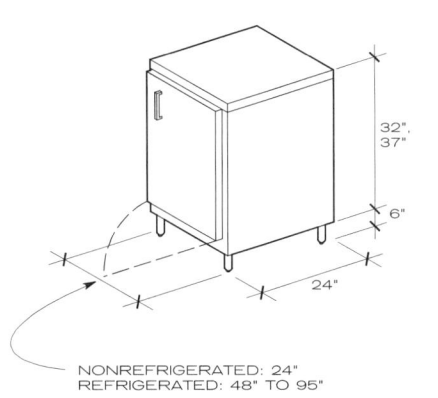

BACK-BAR DRY STORAGE CABINET

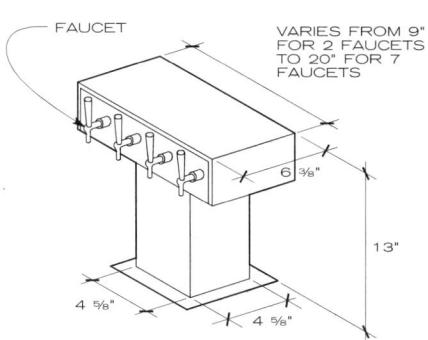

TEE TOWER

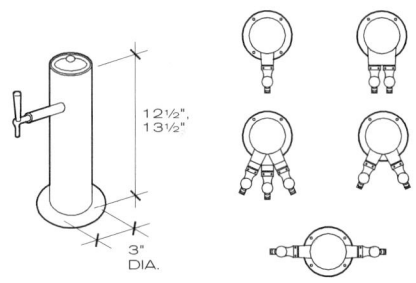

BEER DISPENSING FAUCETS

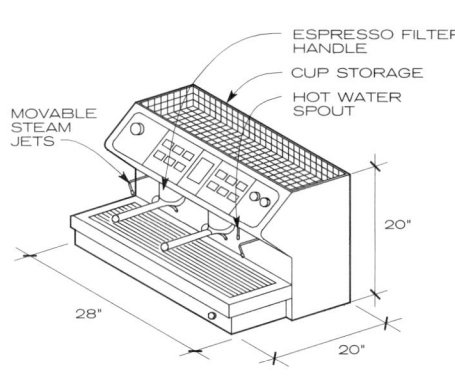

CAPPUCINO/ESPRESSO MACHINE

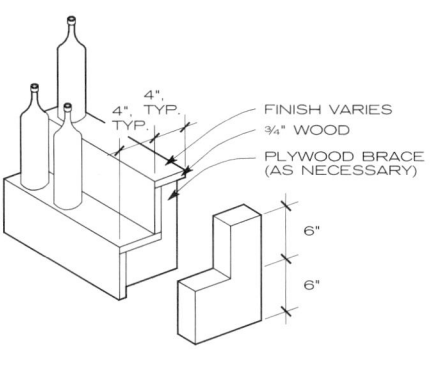

NOTE
These are also called bottle steps.

LIQUOR DISPLAY SHELVES

Richard J. Vitullo, AIA; Oak Leaf Studio; Crownsville, Maryland

FOOD SERVICE EQUIPMENT

Washers, Dryers, Dishwashers, and Trash Compactors

GENERAL NOTES

1. See kitchen and laundry layout pages for locations of washers, dryers, and dishwashers and their respective wall chases for pipes and vents.
2. Check manufacturers' catalogs for "open-door" dimensions if door clearances may be a problem.
3. All dimensions given are actual ones, but certain variations in body design may affect the actual depth of particular models. Check all units for exact voltage. Some units available with gas.

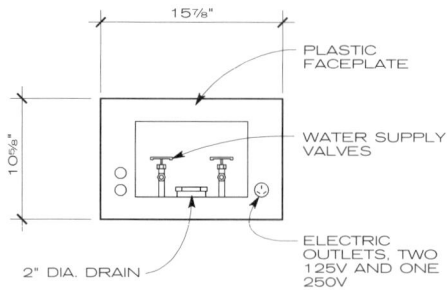

ELEVATION

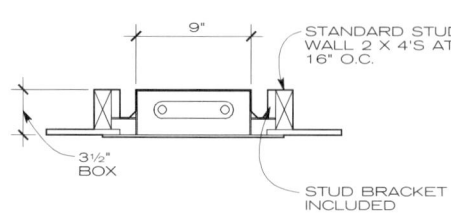

SECTION

UTILITY CONNECTION BOX (RECESSED)

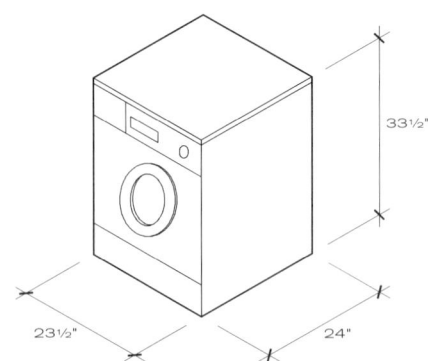

NOTE
Front-loading washers may be equipped with an integral top if not mounted under a counter.

BUILT-IN (UNDERCOUNTER) FRONT-LOADING WASHER

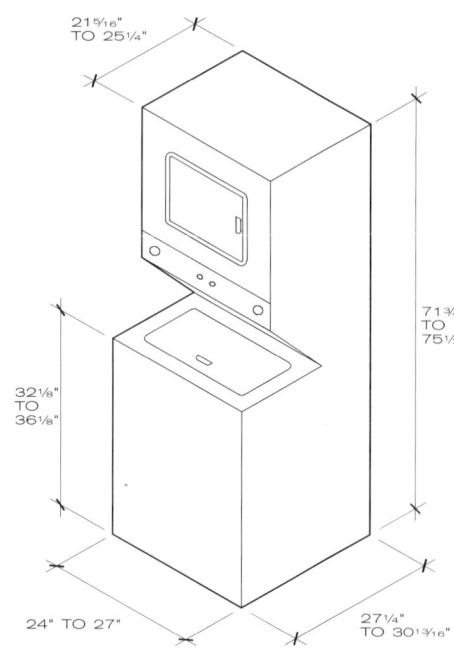

STACKED WASHER-DRYER COMBINATION

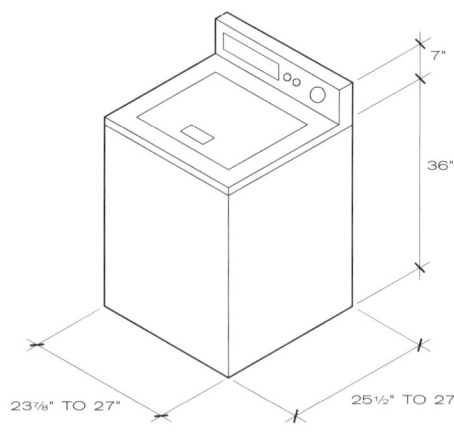

FREESTANDING TOP-LOADING WASHER

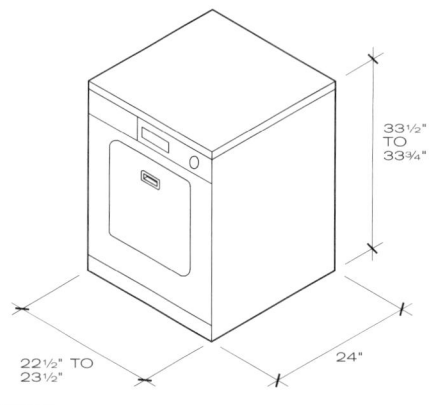

NOTE
Front-loading dryers may be equipped with an integral top if not mounted under a counter.

BUILT-IN (UNDERCOUNTER) FRONT-LOADING DRYER

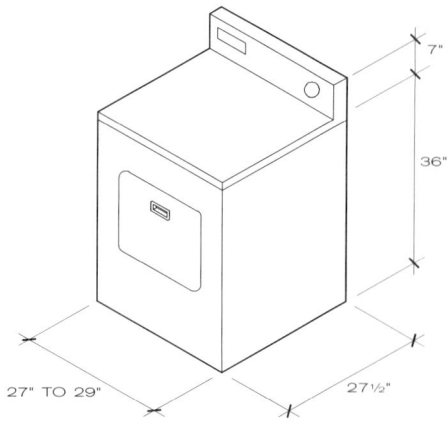

FREESTANDING FRONT-LOADING DRYER

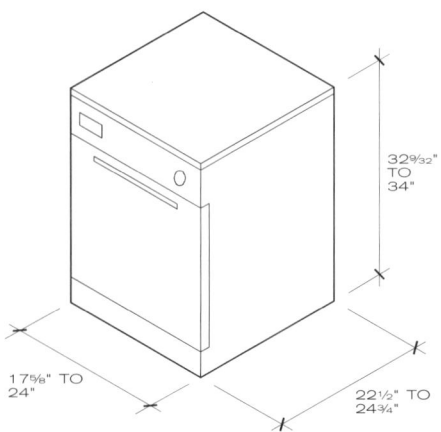

NOTE
Do not place dishwasher farther than 10 ft from sink, typically, for proper drainage.

BUILT-IN DISHWASHER

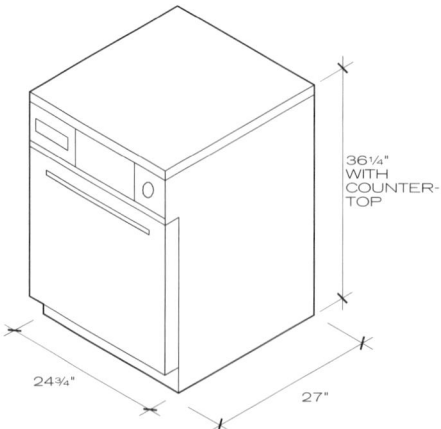

NOTE
Some portable models may be converted to built-in.

PORTABLE DISHWASHER

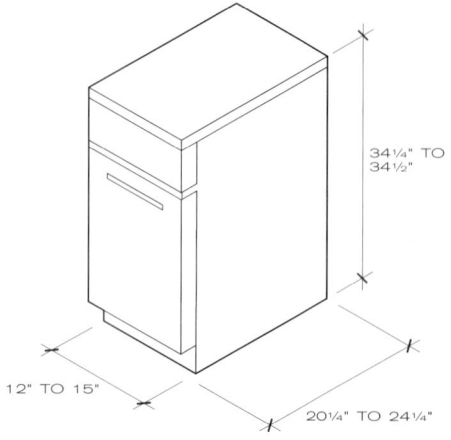

TRASH COMPACTOR

Richard J. Vitullo, AIA; Oak Leaf Studio; Crownsville, Maryland

RESIDENTIAL EQUIPMENT

Ranges, Ovens, Cooktops, and Vent Hoods

GENERAL NOTES

1. Electric and gas ranges are available. Smooth surface electric cooktops have radiant and halogen heating elements or an induction coil below a glass-ceramic top. Radiant heating elements (below surface or surface units, plug-in, coil, or solid plate) provide heat directly from resistance elements. Halogen-type elements usually combine radiant elements with a halogen light source, which allows the element to heat up faster than a radiant element alone. Other range options include griddles and charbroilers. Induction elements consist of a high frequency induction coil beneath a glass-ceramic surface. Metal cooking utensils are heated by magnetic friction without directly heating the cooktop surface. Induction elements are considered energy-efficient.

2. Ovens are available in gas or electric, either as conventional, combination radiant/convection, or microwave models. Convection ovens have a dedicated third element (in addition to the top and bottom elements) surrounding the convection fan at the rear of the oven, which circulates heated air evenly throughout the oven, eliminating any unevenness in temperature.

3. All dimensions shown should be used as general guidelines only; consult manufacturers for specific dimensions.

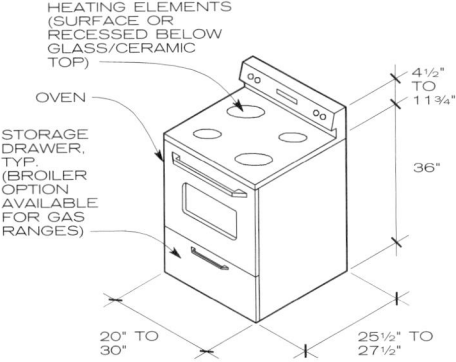

NOTE
Freestanding range/ovens may have front-mounted controls; if so, the backsplash area may be eliminated.

FREESTANDING RANGE/OVEN

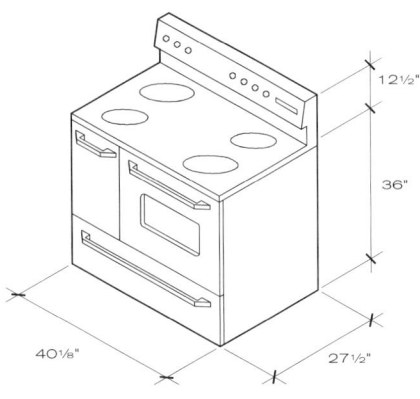

FREESTANDING RANGE WITH LARGE AND SMALL OVENS

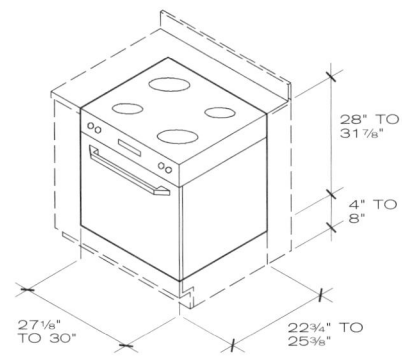

NOTE
Drop-in ranges typically hang from and are supported by the countertop and do not rest on the cabinet or floor below.

DROP-IN RANGE OVEN

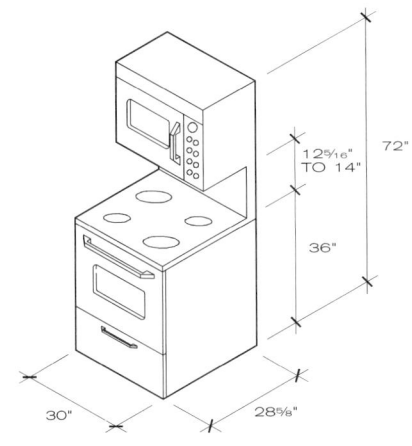

NOTE
Conventional or microwave ovens may be installed above a counter-height range/stove.

FREESTANDING RANGE WITH UPPER AND LOWER OVENS

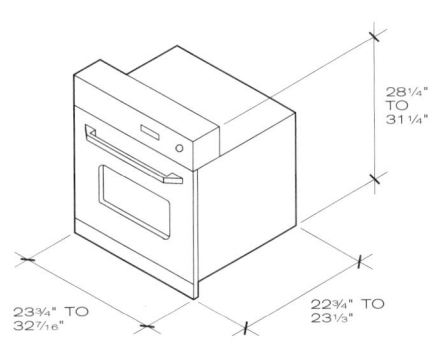

NOTE
Single wall ovens may be installed in a wall cabinet (at eye level) or under the counter in a base cabinet.

BUILT-IN SINGLE WALL OVEN

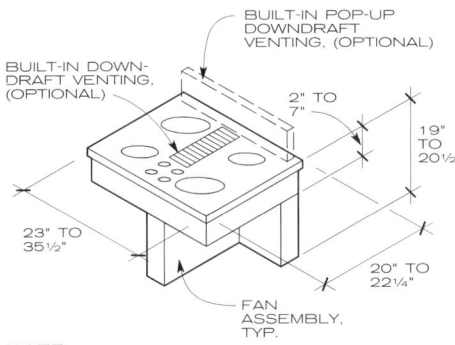

NOTE
Radiant and halogen cooktops typically require a 5 in. min. free area between the countertop and any combustible material below (typically shelving). Downdraft fan assemblies are located directly under a vent (rear pop-up vents offer the best free space under a counter). Available two-element cooktops are approximately 12 in. wide.

DROP-IN RANGE COOKTOP

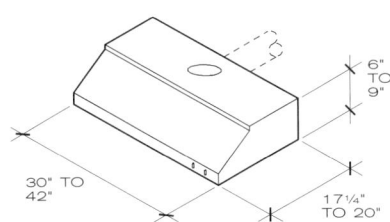

NOTE
Range hoods vent through filters back into the room (self-venting) or through ducts and filters to the outdoors. Accessories such as fans, filters, and lights vary greatly in design configuration. Some ranges and cooktops are equipped with downdraft venting, which may eliminate the need for an overhead range hood. Fans typically vent from 50 to 350 cu ft/min (CFM) of air for standard residential cooktop use. For commercial ranges, consult a design professional for CFM requirements.

RANGE HOOD

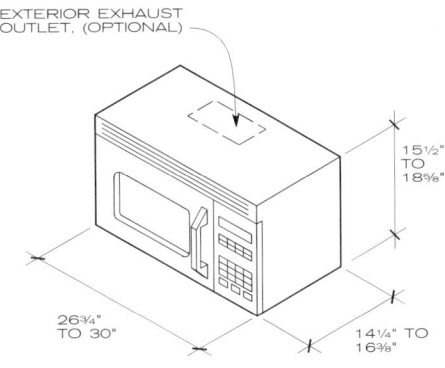

NOTE
Venting may be directed to the outside or recirculated.

BUILT-IN MICROWAVE OVEN

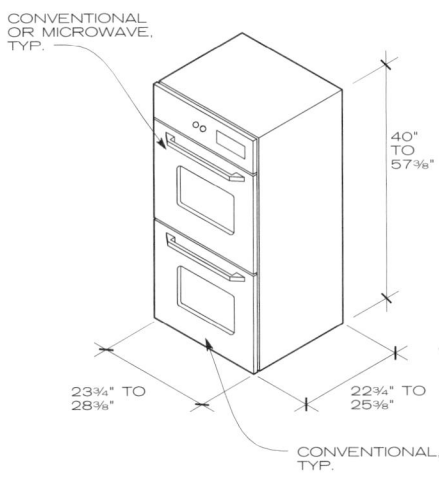

BUILT-IN DOUBLE WALL OVEN

Richard J. Vitullo, AIA; Oak Leaf Studio; Crownsville, Maryland

RESIDENTIAL EQUIPMENT

Refrigerators, Freezers, and Unit Kitchens

GENERAL NOTES

1. Ultra energy-efficient refrigerators/freezers are available in AC models for conventional utility power and DC models for alternative (remote) energy applications. Some models use 60 to 90% less energy than standard energy-efficient models. Many standard refrigerator and freezer manufacturers have CFC-free models, which means no CFCs were used in the insulation or in the coolant system. Consult manufacturers.

2. See manufacturers' catalogs for actual dimensions of specific units, which may include the number of burners, refrigerator size, sink size, finish materials, and options such as garbage disposal, range hood, microwave oven, ice maker, dishwasher, or freezer.

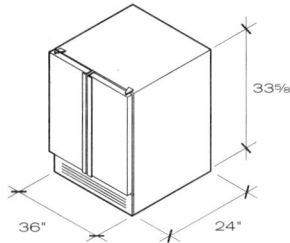

SIDE-BY-SIDE (WITH FREEZER)

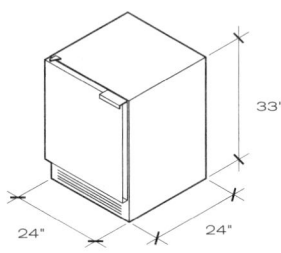

SINGLE DOOR

UNDERCOUNTER REFRIGERATORS

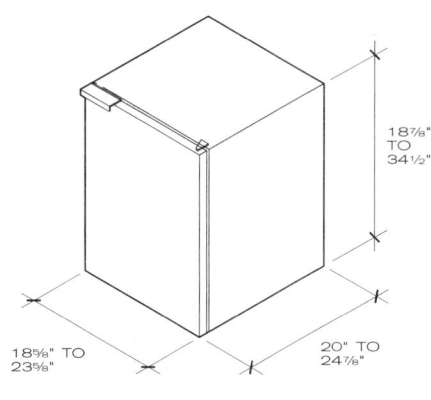

REFRIGERATOR WITH TOP FREEZER

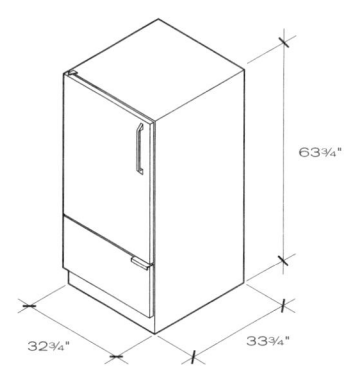

SMALL CAPACITY FREESTANDING REFRIGERATOR

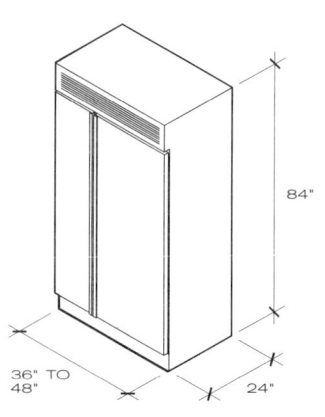

BUILT-IN SIDE-BY-SIDE REFRIGERATOR/FREEZER

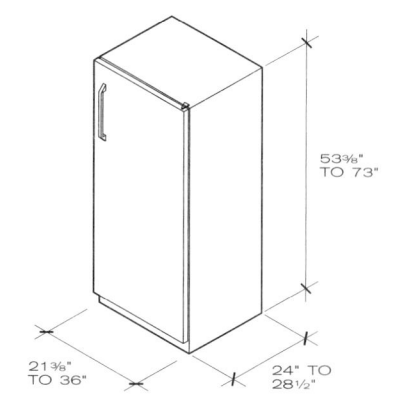

UPRIGHT FREEZER

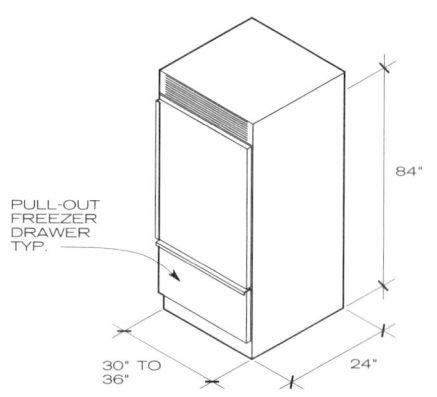

PULL-OUT FREEZER DRAWER TYP.

BUILT-IN REFRIGERATOR WITH BOTTOM FREEZER

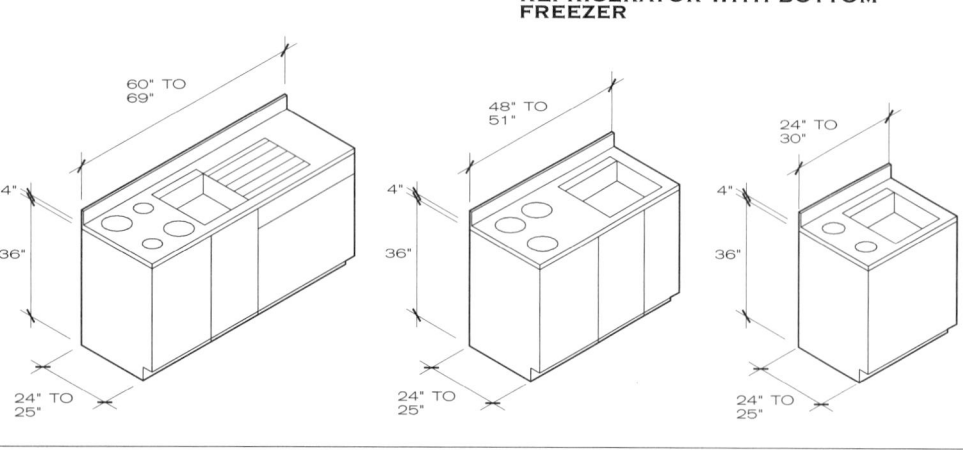

CHEST FREEZER / REFRIGERATOR WITH BOTTOM FREEZER / UNIT KITCHENS

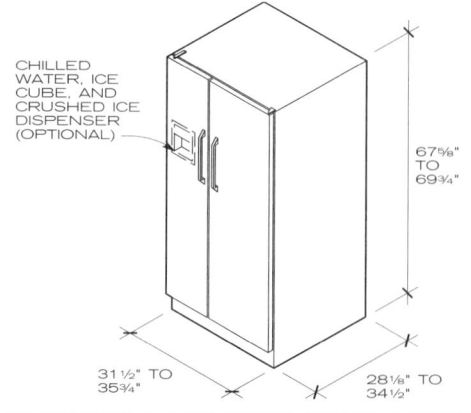

CHILLED WATER, ICE CUBE, AND CRUSHED ICE DISPENSER (OPTIONAL)

SIDE-BY-SIDE REFRIGERATOR

Richard J. Vitullo, AIA; Oak Leaf Studio; Crownsville, Maryland

RESIDENTIAL EQUIPMENT

Air-Supported Structures

GENERAL

Air-supported structures are lightweight, totally free span structures that maintain stability in space and resist loads with a pressure differential between the interior and exterior. This method of support leaves the interior free of support devices that could interfere with the efficient use of space. The roof and side walls can be a single structural element in pure tension, a fabric envelope. The only compression members are the slightly pressurized air inside and the rigid base of the membrane.

STRUCTURAL MEMBRANE

The structural membrane is usually a nylon, fiberglass, or polyester fabric coated with polyvinyl chloride. Such skins have a life span from 7 to 10 years and offer fire retardation that passes NFPA 701. A urethane topcoat will reduce dirt adhesion and improve service life. Fluorocarbon top finishes further enhance characteristics and can double service life. Teflon-coated fiberglass membranes have a life expectancy of more than 25 years. This material is not combustible, passing ASTM E84, with a flame spread rating of 10, smoke developed < 50, and fuel contributed, 10. An acoustical liner (NRC = 0.65) is also available.

NOTES

1. Most air-supported structures are primarily designed to resist wind loads. Mechanical blowers must maintain 3 to 5 psf pressure inside the structure at all times. Architectural elements of the building must be detailed to avoid loss of air pressure.
2. Consult building codes to determine requirements for all air-supported structures.

GROUND-MOUNTED AIR STRUCTURES

The shape of ground-mounted air structures permits the structure to meet the ground vertically, allowing gravity loads to resist the membrane tension. The semicircular cross-section of the membrane structure has a curvature radius large enough to allow the fabric alone to carry wind forces that may affect the building. If lightweight fabrics are used, catenary cables or webbing may be required as well. Webbing is typically sewn into the fabric seams, forming a one-way system; cables are incorporated into pockets in a one-way system or formed into a cable net harness that is placed over the fabric in a two-way system.

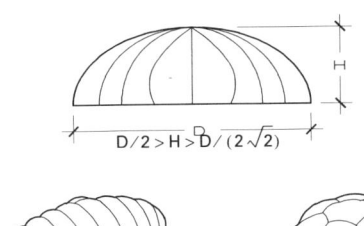

$D/2 > H > D/(2\sqrt{2})$

SPAN LIMITATIONS	VAULT	DOME
Without cables	D = 120 ft	D = 150 ft
With cables	D = 400 ft	D = 600 ft

BASIC CONFIGURATION OF GROUND-MOUNTED AIR STRUCTURES

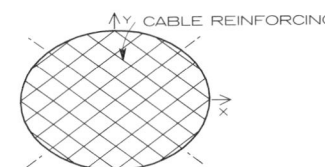

SUPERELLIPSE PLAN

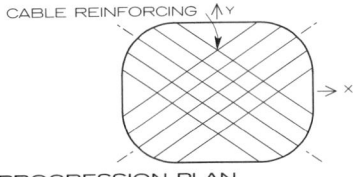

PROGRESSION PLAN

LONG-SPAN DOME STRUCTURE TYPES

Paul Gossen, Geiger Engineers, P.C.; Suffern, New York

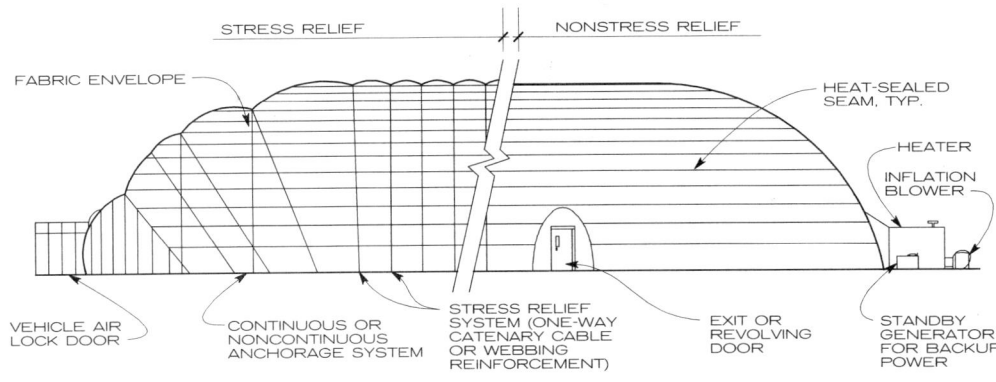

NOTE
For temporary structures, anchorage system may be water tanks, sandbags, earth screw anchors, etc., depending on conditions.

TYPICAL GROUND-MOUNTED AIR-SUPPORTED STRUCTURE

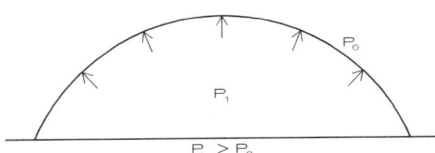

SINGLE MEMBRANE

This is the most common type of air-supported structure. The internal pressure (P_1) is kept approximately 0.03 psi above the external atmospheric pressure (P_0). It is this pressure difference that keeps the dome inflated.

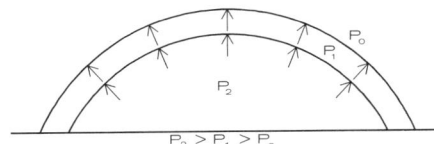

DOUBLE MEMBRANE

The air space between the two membranes is used for insulation and security. If the outer skin is punctured, the inner skin will remain standing. Both single and double membrane air-supported structures require the constant use of blowers to keep them inflated.

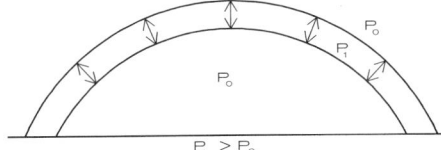

DUAL MEMBRANE

The internal and external pressures are the same in a dual membrane structure. Only the area between the skins is pressurized. This inflated area can be sealed, eliminating the need for constant use of blowers, although blowers are recommended to make up losses from leakage.

AIR-INFLATED STRUCTURES

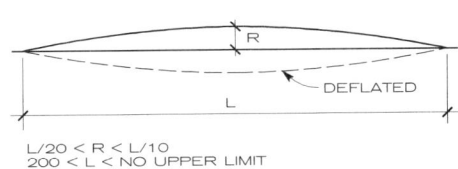

$L/20 < R < L/10$
$200 < L < $ NO UPPER LIMIT

NOTE

The membrane must be patterned to carry loads without wrinkling. Structural behavior is nonlinear with large displacements. The roof shape must be established so that under maximum loads the horizontal components of the cable forces result in minimum bending moment in the compression ring. Consult an air-supported structures specialist to integrate structural and architectural requirements.

LONG-SPAN DOME STRUCTURE

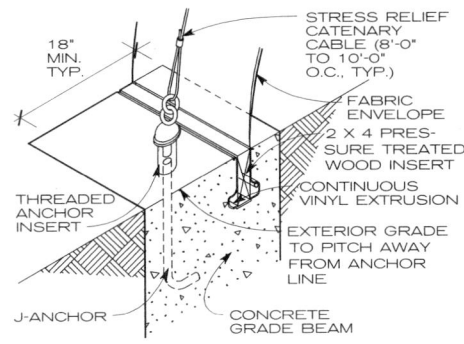

WEDGE INSERT

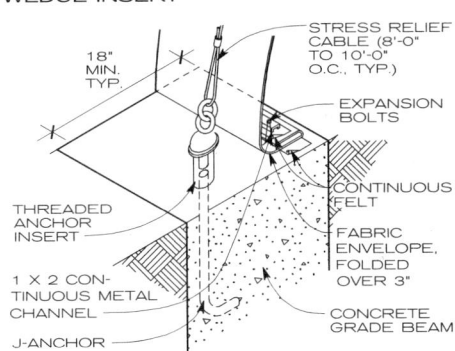

SURFACE-MOUNTED FABRIC ENVELOPE

NOTE
Beam design is based on actual uplift of air structure at the design inflation pressure and wind load.

CONTINUOUS ANCHORAGE DETAILS

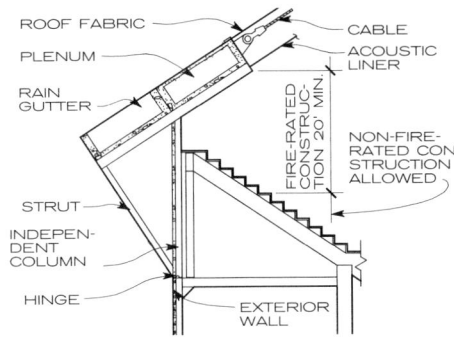

NOTE
The perimeter compression ring must be independent of the support structure to prevent radial restraint.

LONG-SPAN STRUCTURE SUPPORT DETAIL

Cold Storage Rooms

GENERAL NOTES

1. Doors—standard sizes:
   2 ft 6 in., 3 ft 0 in., 3 ft 6 in., 4 ft 0 in., 5 ft 0 in. wide x 6 ft 6 in. high; 4 ft 0 in. or 5 ft 0 in. wide by 6 ft 6 in. or 7 ft 0 in. high.
   Sliding, double action, and display doors are available. ADA requires a 32-in. clear opening. Doors are manually or electrically operated.
2. Prefabricated insulated panels (nominal size)—standard sizes:
   Thickness: 4 in.
   Width: 11.5 in., 23 in., 46 in.
   Height: 7 ft 6 in., 8 ft 6 in., 10 ft 6 in., 11 ft 6 in.
   Finish material: aluminum, galvanized steel, or stainless steel.
3. Walk-in unit sizes:
   Width: 3 ft 11 in., 5 ft 10 in., 7 ft 9 in., 9 ft 8 in., 11 ft 7 in.
   Length: 5 ft 10 in., 7 ft 9 in., 11 ft 7 in., 13 ft 6 in., 15 ft 5 in., 17 ft 4 in., 19 ft 3 in.
   Height: 7 ft 6 in., 8 ft 6 in., 9 ft 6 in., 10 ft 6 in., 11 ft 6 in.
   Available accessories: stationary or mobile shelf units and adjustable cantilevered shelves, windows, interior partitions, meat rails, floor racks, ramps, and walk-ins.
4. Check local codes for drainage requirements.

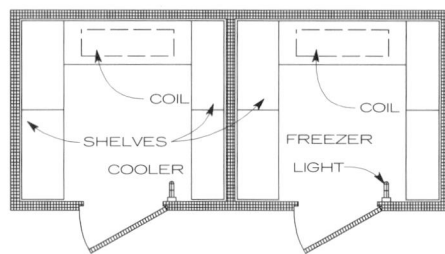

SIDE-BY-SIDE PLAN

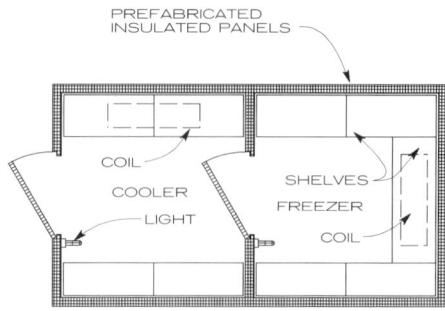

WALK-THROUGH PLAN

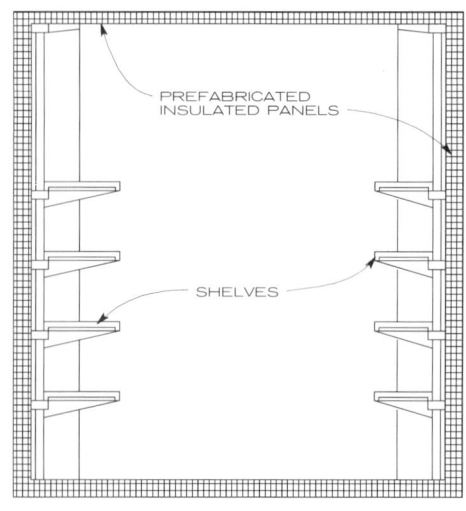

SECTION

TYPICAL WALK-IN UNITS

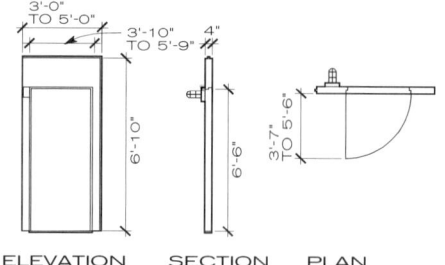

ELEVATION   SECTION   PLAN

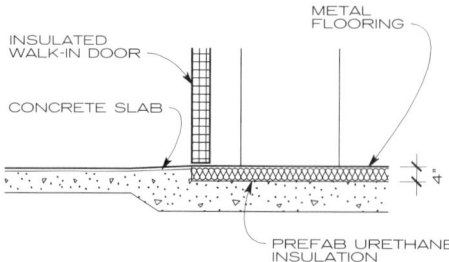

WALK-IN WITH FLUSH METAL FLOOR

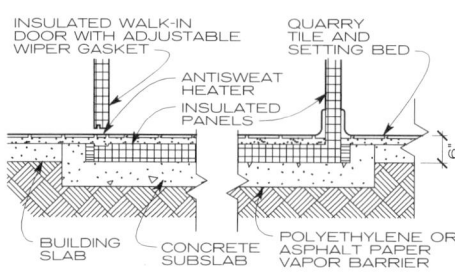

WALK-IN WITH FLUSH TILE

NOTE

Phase service is required for lights and anticondensate heaters on door panels. Connections are made to the junction box at the light, which is always inside the walk-in directly opposite the top hinge.

WALK-IN FLOOR DETAILS IN NEW CONSTRUCTION

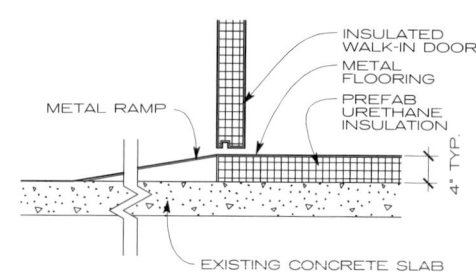

WALK-IN FLOOR OVER BUILDING FLOOR WITH EXTERIOR METAL RAMP

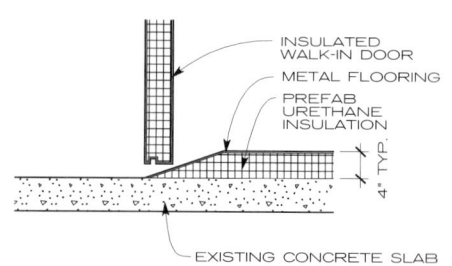

WALK-IN FLOOR OVER BUILDING FLOOR WITH INTERIOR METAL RAMP

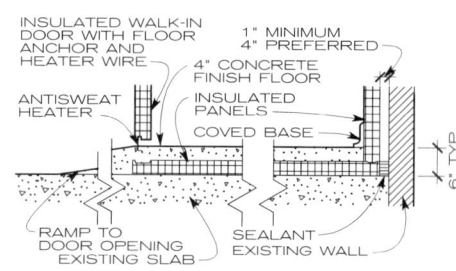

WALK-IN WITH BUILDING FINISH FLOOR AND EXTERIOR RAMP

NOTE

Metal flooring is typically made of galvanized steel, stainless steel, or aluminum grating

WALK-IN DETAILS ON EXISTING SLAB

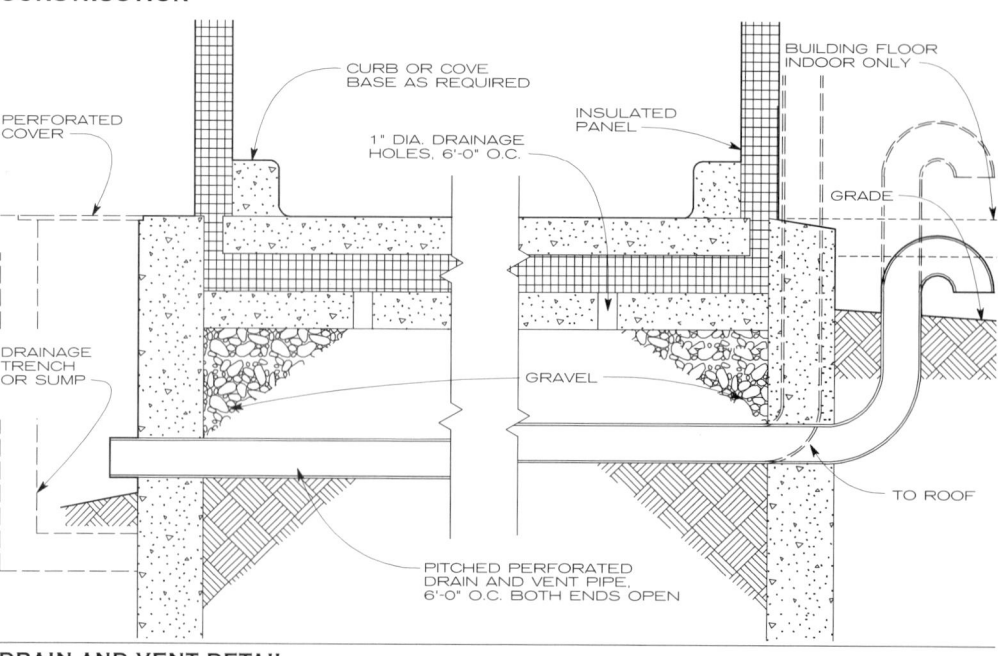

DRAIN AND VENT DETAIL

Cini-Little International, Inc.; Food Service Consultants; Washington, D.C.

SPECIAL PURPOSE ROOMS

Pre-engineered Metal Buildings

BUILDING TYPES AND WIDTHS

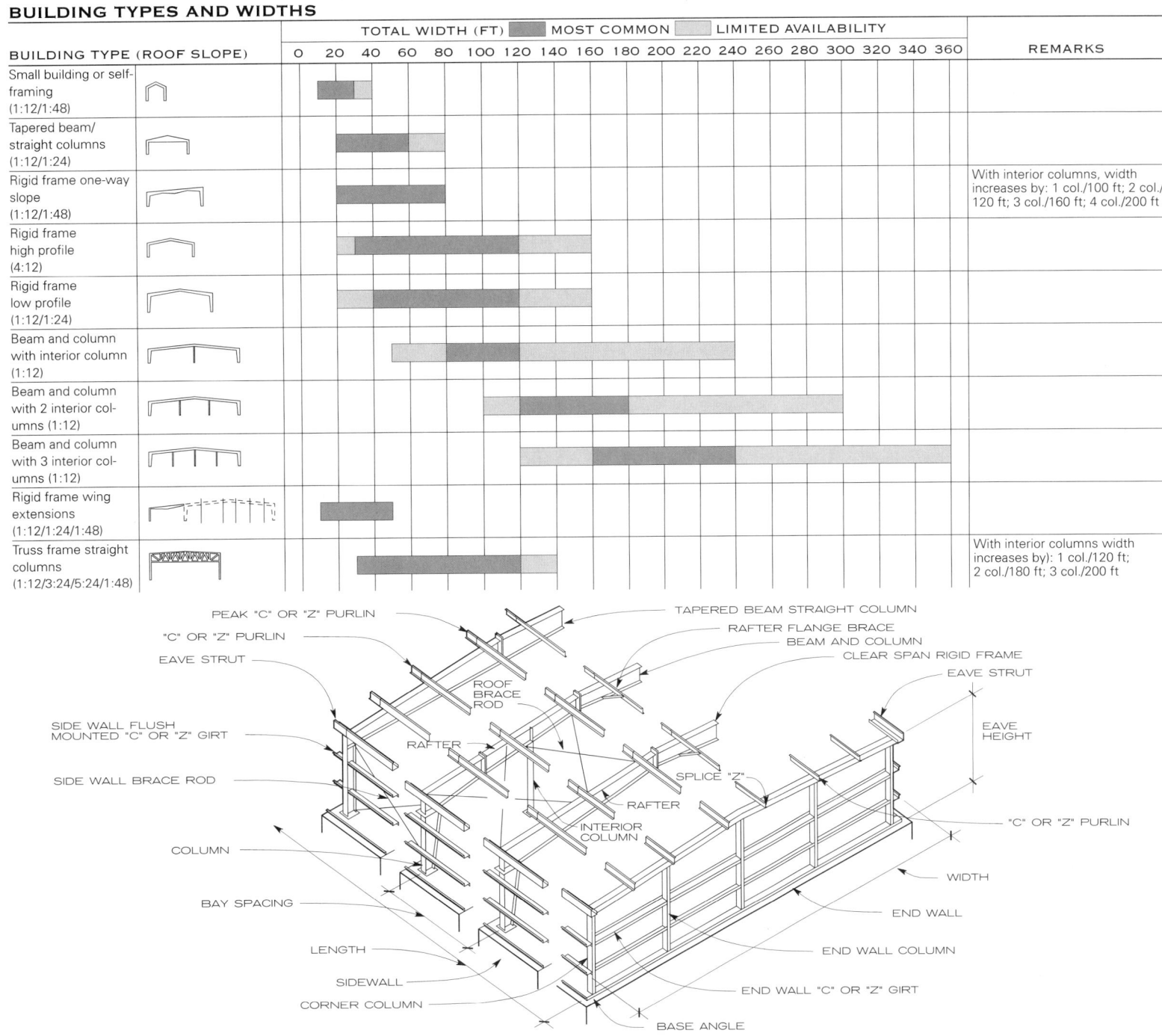

FRAMING SYSTEMS COMPONENTS

DEFINITIONS

Pre-engineered metal buildings are available in standard framing sizes and types from various manufacturers. The following definitions are those used by the metal building industry:

BAY refers to the dimension along a wall between the centerlines of wall columns and the dimension from the outside of an end wall corner column to the centerline of the first adjacent wall column. Spacings range from 18 to 30 ft, with 20 to 25 ft most common.

WIDTH is measured from the surface of the outside wall girts. Inside clearance varies.

EAVE HEIGHT is measured from the bottom of a wall column to the top of an eave strut. Nominal 2-ft increments vary from 10 to 30 ft.

LOADS, other than those provided by the manufacturer, should be specified during the structural design phase. Future additional loads also should be considered. Roof live loads are those loads, including snow load, exerted on a roof except dead, wind, and lateral loads. Commonly available in 12, 20, or 40 psf. Dead load is the weight of all permanent roof framing and covering materials only and varies with the manufacturer.

LATERAL LOADS are dead loads other than the metal building framing, such as sprinklers, mechanical and electrical systems, and ceilings. They are commonly available in 15, 20, or 25 psf.

WIND LOAD is loading caused by the wind blowing from any horizontal direction. Site and atmospheric conditions needing special consideration should be specified.

SEISMIC LOAD is required for earthquake zones and must be specified for individual designs.

AUXILIARY LOADS are dynamic live loads other than basic design loads, such as cranes, materials handling systems, and impact loads.

DIAGONAL BRACING normally is required in the plane of the columns and beams in one or more bays to prevent racking and to resist lateral loading perpendicular to the span of the frames.

GIRTS are horizontal structural members that transmit lateral loads (pressure and suction) from the exterior walls to the columns. Sag rods may be needed to support the girts about the weak axis and to achieve design economy.

ANCHOR BOLTS are necessary to resist reactions at column bases. Foundations must be designed for reactions transmitted by the column bases and anchor bolts.

NOTE

The user should verify that individual manufacturer's standard practice and any special design considerations meet or exceed established engineering principles, local practice, and applicable building codes.

Robert P. Burns, AIA; Burns and Burns, Architects; Iowa City, Iowa

PRE-ENGINEERED STRUCTURES

Pre-engineered Metal Building Details

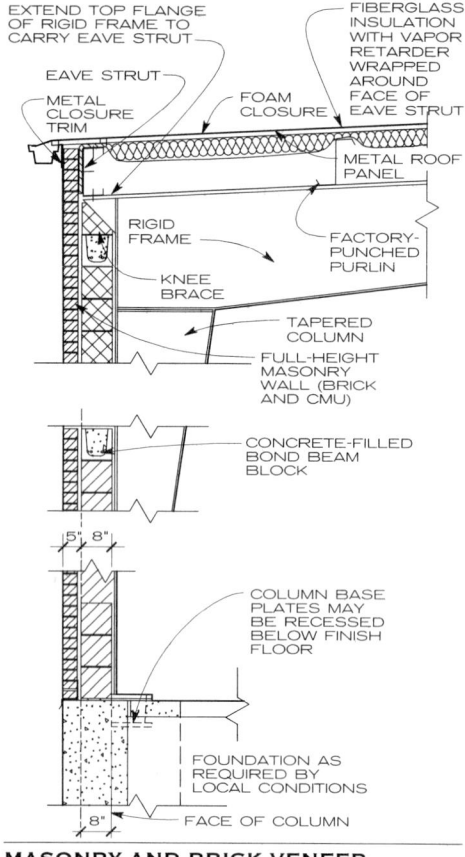

MASONRY AND BRICK VENEER WALL SECTION

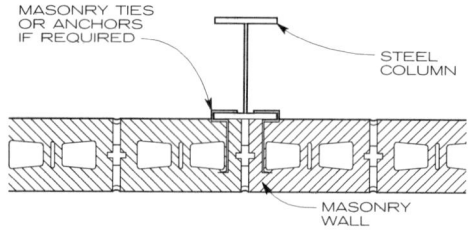

BOND-BEAM BLOCK TO COLUMN CONNECTION

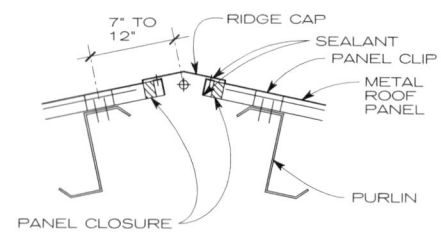

RIDGE DETAIL

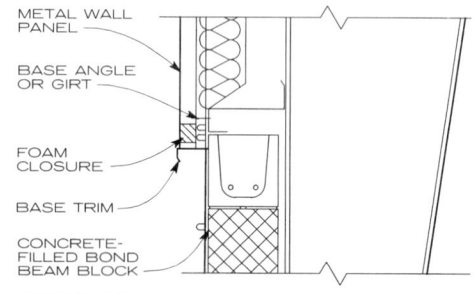

MASONRY WALL AND METAL PANEL CONNECTION

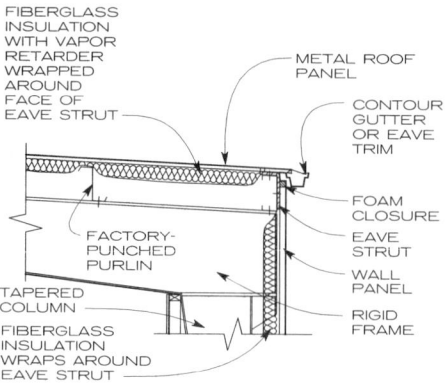

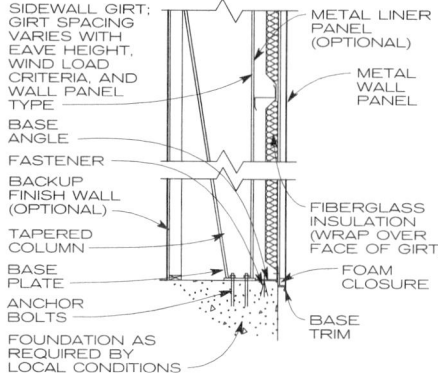

NOTE
A sidewall girt may be inset between columns, attached by clip angles to the steel frame.

METAL WALL PANEL SECTION

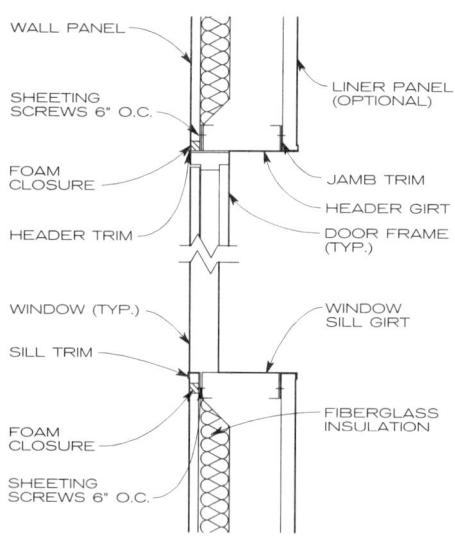

DOOR/WINDOW HEAD AND SILL DETAIL

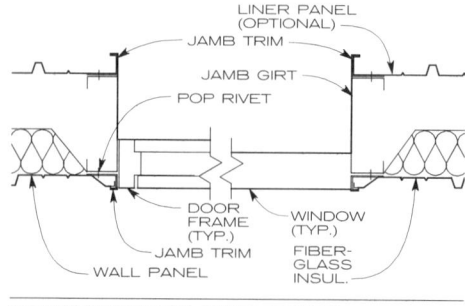

DOOR/WINDOW JAMB DETAIL

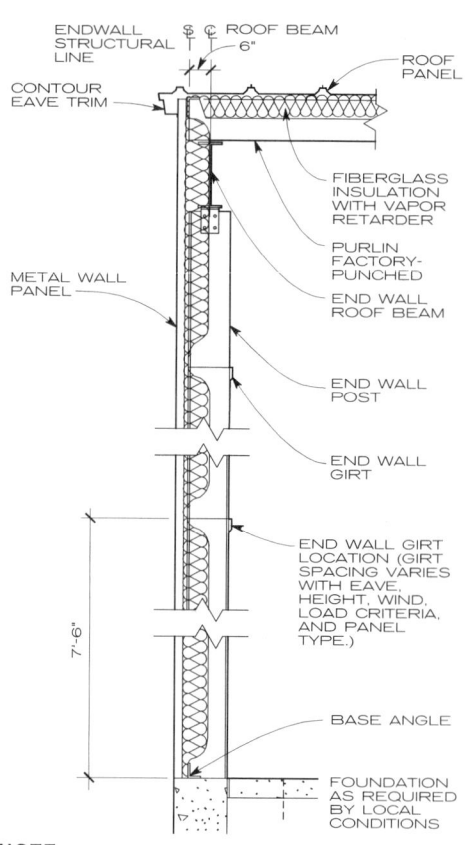

NOTE
Column face is approximately 1 in. inside the structural line.

END WALL CONDITION SECTION

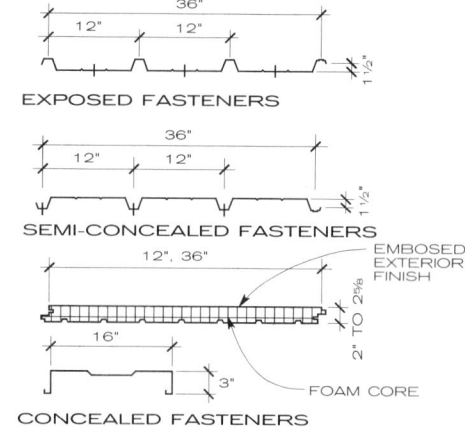

NOTE
Wall panels are installed vertically, in lengths, typically up to 40 ft. Finishes include painted metal with smooth or textured finish.

WALL PANEL TYPES

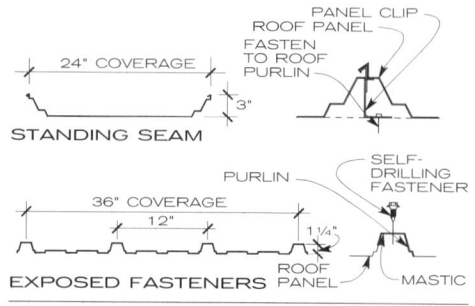

ROOF PANEL TYPES

Robert P. Burns, AIA; Burns & Burns, Architects; Iowa City, Iowa

PRE-ENGINEERED STRUCTURES

Explosion and Fire Suppression Systems

EXPLOSION PREVENTION

Accidental ignition of flammable solids, liquids, and gases can best be prevented by eliminating potential flammable materials and sparks or flames. Use hard-finish surfaces of inert, spark-resistant, nonflammable materials. Dust and debris constitute a hazard: Hooded dust-collection systems and sloping horizontal surfaces, coved bases, and coved indoor corners can help.

Provisions should be made for containing spilled liquids and solids. For flammable gases, provide ventilation for health safety and prevention of concentrated vapors. Provide explosion-proof electrical devices and grounding systems in accordance with the NEC, NFPA, and insurance underwriters' requirements.

EXPLOSION SUPPRESSION

Explosion suppression is a specialized application in which an extinguishing agent snuffs out an explosion in its developing stages. Explosion detection systems detect the pressure rise associated with an explosion and immediately discharge extinguishing or suppression agents.

From start to finish, the entire detection/extinguishing process may take only 65/1000 of a second, which limits application to very small confined areas. Ideal applications include the interiors of tanks, hoppers, ductwork, or other equipment containing explosive concentrations of vapors, dust, and powders. Refer to NFPA 69.

SPECIAL EXTINGUISHING SYSTEMS

Automatic fire suppression and extinguishing systems are permanent building installations that protect a structure, its contents, and its occupants against the hazards of fire and explosion. The nature and magnitude of the hazard dictate the extinguishing agent and system configuration to be used. Extinguishing agents include water, clean agent, carbon dioxide, foam, and dry chemicals. Systems may be either total flooding or local application types.

Total flooding systems consist of an extinguishing agent, distribution piping, discharge nozzles, detection devices, alarms, and controls in sufficient supply to reach a mandated concentration of agent within an enclosed space.

Local application systems consist of those components listed above but are designed to direct extinguishing agents to achieve calculated surface coverages of hazardous areas.

CLEAN AGENT SYSTEMS

Clean agent refers to EPA-approved, electrically nonconducting, volatile, or gaseous fire extinguishment that does not leave a residue upon evaporation.

Clean agent systems extinguish a fire by lowering oxygen content. Since such systems cause no water damage and leave no residue, they are ideal for protecting valuable records and electronic equipment. Clean agent systems can be discharged in occupied areas, allowing time for orderly shutdown of equipment and evacuation.

The relatively high cost of clean agent systems mandates their use to protect confined areas such as storage vaults, tape libraries or computer rooms, and spaces under floors.

A typical total-flooding clean agent installation consists of storage cylinders, distribution piping, discharge nozzles, detectors (heat, smoke, UV), and alarms. Interfaces among the clean agent extinguishing system, HVAC equipment, and electrical equipment are required to ensure adequate shutdown during alarm conditions. Special construction of doors, door closers, partitions, and ceilings is necessary to make space as airtight as possible.

Because clean agent systems are depleted totally upon discharge, backup or redundant storage cylinders may be required while the system is being serviced and recharged. Local codes or underwriting agencies may require sprinkler backup in areas protected by clean agent within sprinklered buildings. Refer to NFPA 2001.

DRY CHEMICAL SYSTEMS

Dry chemical, powderlike products are available for use as extinguishing agents. Although effective against flammable liquid fires and electrical fires, dry chemical systems can cause extensive cleanup problems and may damage sensitive electronic components or equipment. For these reasons, the most common use of dry chemical systems is for local applications over relatively small areas such as cooking surfaces, dip tanks, and spray booths.

CARBON DIOXIDE SYSTEMS

Carbon dioxide (CO_2) is suitable for extinguishing flammable liquid fires and fires involving energized electrical equipment. CO_2 systems extinguish fire by reducing the concentrations of oxygen in the air, the vapor phase of the fuel, or both to the point where combustion stops. These systems are generally used in unoccupied areas or places where an electrically nonconductive medium is essential: electrical equipment rooms, transformers, vaults, or areas containing rotating equipment or flammable liquids. Types include local flooding, local application, hand hose line, and standpipe systems.

Personnel hazards such as suffocation and reduced visibility due to fogging during and after discharge must be considered in the application of total flooding CO_2 systems. Such systems must allow for total evacuation of the area prior to discharge and incorporate audible predischarge alarms. Local application systems usually are installed in confined areas such as restaurant range hoods, open top tanks, and printing presses. Activation of CO_2 systems may be automatic or manual.

In general, large systems requiring a lot of CO_2 use low-pressure storage systems for outside installation, while systems requiring small CO_2 quantities can use high-pressure storage cylinders inside the building.

Natural leakage occurring around doors, windows, and dampers generally provides sufficient venting of CO_2 from rooms, ductwork, and equipment enclosures after discharge; therefore, special venting considerations are required only in gas-tight enclosures. Refer to NFPA 12.

FOAM SYSTEMS

Foaming agents used for fire protection fall into one of three major classes: low-, medium-, and high-expansion foams, as determined by foam-to-solution volume ratios.

Foam provides a unique agent for total flooding of confined spaces, transporting water to otherwise inaccessible places, and for volumetric displacement of vapor, heat, and smoke.

Foam is used principally to form a floating blanket on flammable or combustible liquids, preventing or extinguishing fire by excluding air and cooling the fuel. It also prevents reignition by suppressing formation of flammable vapors. Film coating characteristics of fire-fighting foams also provide a measure of protection from adjacent fires.

Foam-type fire suppression systems may consist of portable foam-generating equipment with hand-held nozzles or may involve fixed applications for the protection of entire facilities. Liquid fuel storage and unloading facilities and aircraft hangars and fueling areas often employ foam systems. High-expansion foams have proved effective in high-rack storage areas. Refer to NFPA Chapters 11 and 11A.

EXPLOSION VENTING

Explosion venting, required in many high-hazard occupancies, provides a relief area to the building exterior, thereby controlling the direction of a blast. The vent relief area is governed by the pressure resistance of the non-relieving portions of the building.

The relief area may be walls of lightweight material, lightly fastened hatch covers, lightly fastened outward swinging doors in exterior walls, and lightly fastened walls or roofs. Venting devices are normally designed to release at a maximum internal pressure of 20 psf, and the remaining walls, roof, and floors are designed to withstand a minimum internal pressure of 100 psf. Refer to building codes, NFPA 68, and insurance underwriters' guidelines for specific requirements and design guidelines.

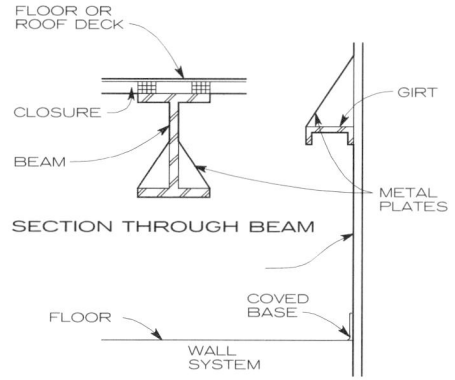

MINIMIZING ACCUMULATION OF FLAMMABLE SOLIDS

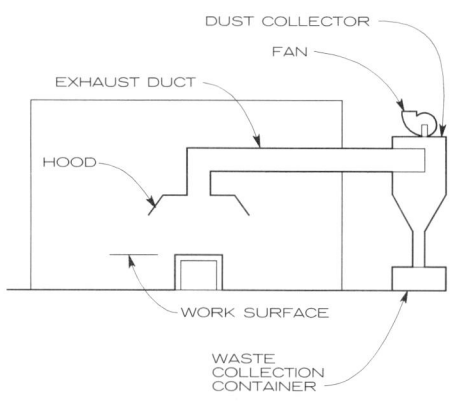

LOCALIZED DUST COLLECTION

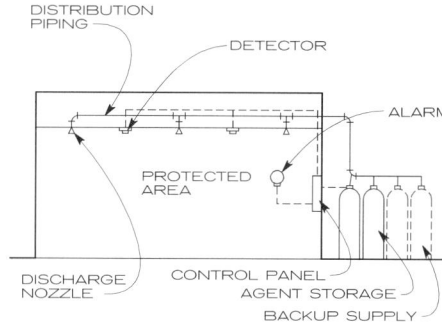

TOTAL FLOODING EXTINGUISHING SYSTEM

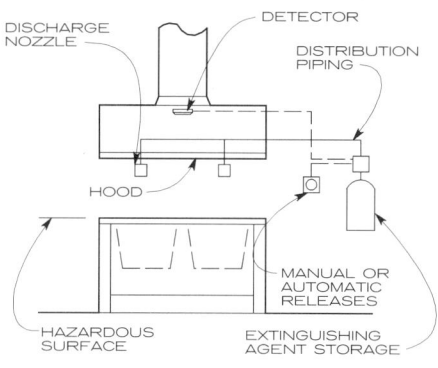

LOCAL APPLICATION EXTINGUISHING SYSTEM

Lockwood Greene; Atlanta, Georgia

FIRE SUPPRESSION AND SUPERVISORY SYSTEMS

168 Residential Electrical Wiring

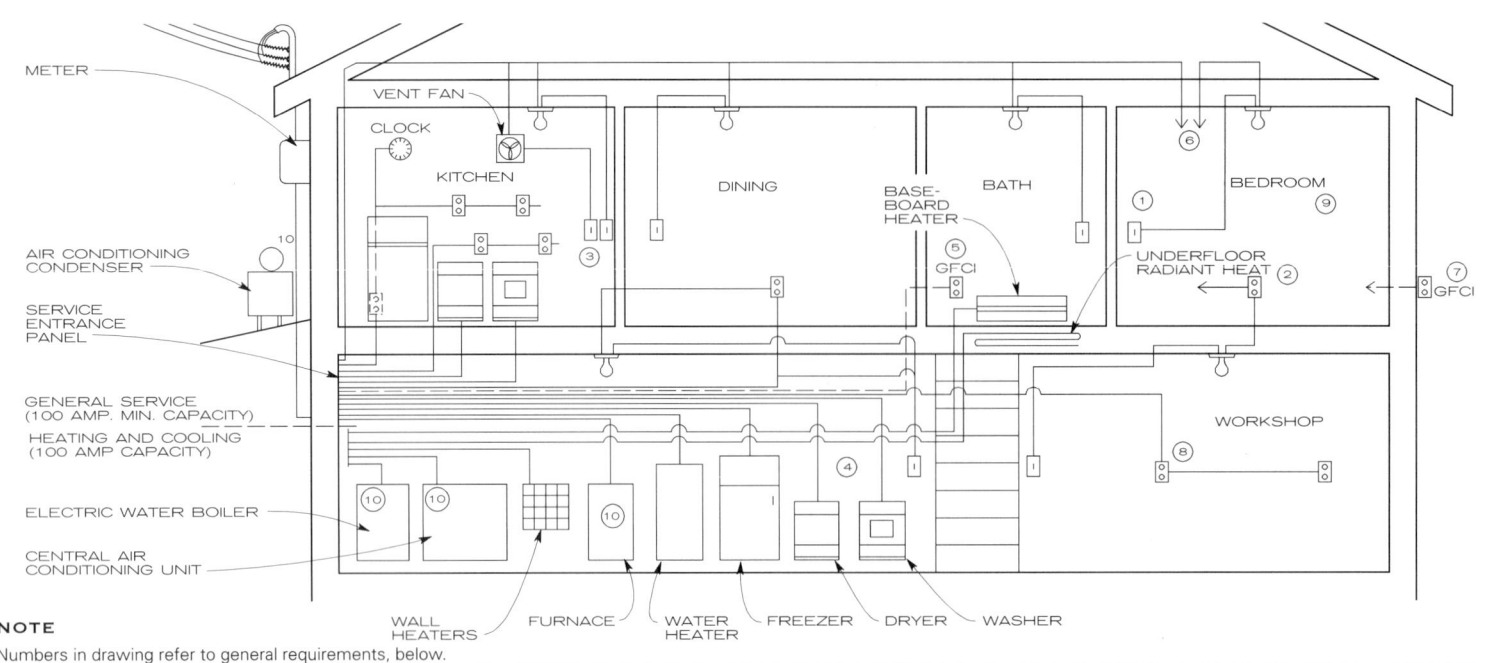

SCHEMATIC DIAGRAM OF TYPICAL RESIDENTIAL ELECTRICAL LAYOUT

NOTE
Numbers in drawing refer to general requirements, below.

GENERAL REQUIREMENTS

1. A minimum of one wall-switch-controlled lighting outlet is required in every habitable room, hallway, stairway, attached garage, and outdoor entrance. Exception: In habitable rooms other than kitchens and bathrooms one or more receptacles controlled by a wall switch are permitted in lieu of lighting outlets.

2. In every kitchen, family room, dining room, den, breakfast room, living room, parlor, sunroom, bedroom, recreation room, and similar rooms, receptacle outlets must be installed so that no point along the floor line is farther than 12 ft, measured horizontally, from an outlet, including any wall space 2 ft or more wide and the wall space occupied by sliding panels in exterior walls.

3. A minimum of two #12 wire 20-A small appliance circuits are required to serve only small appliance outlets, including refrigeration equipment, in the kitchen, pantry, dining room, breakfast room, and family room. Both circuits must extend to the kitchen; the other rooms may be served by one or both of them. No other outlets may be connected to these circuits, except a receptacle installed solely for an electric clock. In kitchen and dining areas, receptacle outlets must be installed at each and every counter space wider than 12 in.

4. A minimum of one #12 wire 20-A circuit must be provided to supply the laundry receptacle(s), and it may have no other outlets.

5. At least one receptacle outlet must be installed in the bathroom near the basin and must be provided with ground fault circuit interrupter protection.

6. Code requires sufficient 15- and 20-A circuits to supply three watts of power for every square foot of floor space, not including garage and open porch areas. Minimum code suggestion is one circuit per 600 sq ft; one circuit per 500 sq ft is desirable.

7. A minimum of one exterior receptacle outlet is required (two are desirable) and must be provided with ground fault circuit interrupter protection.

8. A minimum of one receptacle outlet is required in basement and garage, in addition to the one in the laundry. In attached garages it must be provided with ground fault circuit interrupter protection.

9. Many building codes require a smoke detector in the hallway outside bedrooms or above the stairway leading to upper floor bedrooms.

10. Disconnect switches are required.

NOTE

Refer to the National Electrical Code (NEC) for further information on residential requirements.

LEGEND FOR FIRST FLOOR AND BASEMENT PLANS

A = Mount receptacles at countertop locations 2 in. above backsplash.

B = Mount receptacle 48 in. above finish floor (AFF).

C = Range and oven outlet boxes should be wall mounted, 36 in. AFF. Use flexible connections to units.

D = Switch and outlet for exhaust fan. The switch should be wall mounted above the sink backsplash and the outlet blank cover mounted adjacent to the fan wall opening. A separate switch may be omitted if the fan is supplied with an integral switch.

E = Dishwasher receptacle is wall mounted behind unit, 6 in. AFF.

F = Equipped with self-closing gasketed waterproof cover.

G = Mount 42 in. AFF.

NOTES

1. Wiring shown as exposed indicates absence of finished ceiling in basement level. All BX cable run through framing members. Attachment below ceiling joists is not permitted.

2. Connect to two incandescent porcelain lamp holders with pull chain. Mount two evenly spaced ceiling fixtures in crawl space.

3. Connect to shutdown switch at top of stairs.

4. Boiler wiring safety disconnect switch should have red wall plate, clearly marked "BOILER ON-OFF."

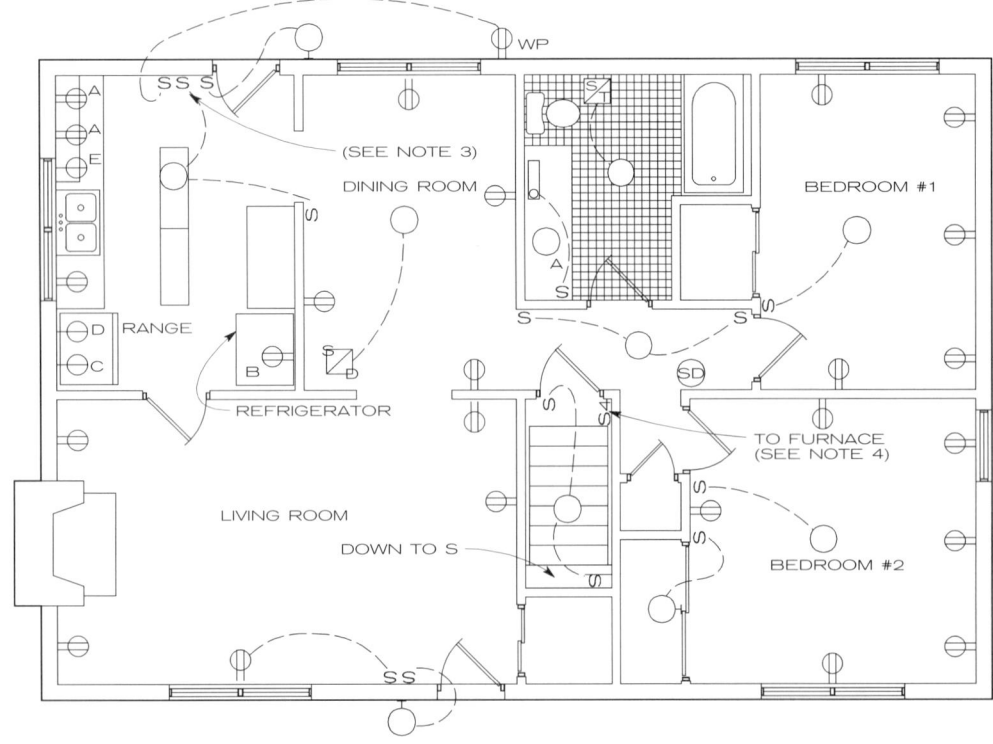

FIRST FLOOR PLAN OF ELECTRICAL EQUIPMENT AND DEVICES

Charles B. Towles, P.E.; TEI Consulting Engineers; Washington, D.C.

WIRING AND RELATED MATERIALS

Residential Electrical Wiring

AVERAGE WATTAGES OF COMMON ELECTRICAL DEVICES

TYPE	WATTS
Air conditioner, central	2500 6000
Air conditioner, room type	800–2500
Blanket, electric	150–200
Clock	2–3
Clothes dryer	4000–6000
Dishwasher	1000–1500
Fan, portable	50–200
Food blender	500–1000
Freezer	300–500
Frying pan, electric	1000–1200
Furnace blower	380–670
Garbage disposal	500–900
Hair dryer	350–1200
Heater, portable	1000–1500
Heating pad	50–75
Heat lamp (infrared)	250
Iron, hand	600–1200
Lamp, incandescent	10 upward
Lamp, fluorescent	15–16
Lights, Christmas tree	30–150
Microwave oven	1000–1500
Mixer	120–250
Power tools	up to 1000
Projector, slide or movie	300–500
Radio	40–150
Range (all burners and oven)	8000–14000
Range top (separate)	4000–8000
Range oven (separate)	4000–5000
Refrigerator	150–300
Refrigerator, frostless	400–600
Sewing machine	60–90
Stereo (solid-state)	30–100
Television	50–450
Vacuum cleaner	250–1200
Washer, automatic	500–800
Water heater	2000–5000

BRANCH CIRCUIT PROTECTION

Lighting (general purpose)	#14 wires	15 A
Small appliances	#12 wires	20 A
Individual appliances	#12 wires	20 A
	#10 wires	30 A
	#8 wires	40 A
	#6 wires	50 A

LOADS, CIRCUITS AND RECEPTACLES FOR RESIDENTIAL ELECTRICAL EQUIPMENT

APPLIANCE	TYPICAL CONNECTED VOLT-AMPERES[1]	VOLTS	WIRES[2]	CIRCUIT BREAKER OR FUSE[3]	OUTLETS ON CIRCUIT	NEMA[11] DEVICE[4] AND CONFIGURATION
KITCHEN						
Range[5]	12000	115/230	3 # 6	60 A	1	14-60R
Oven (built-in)[3]	4500	115/230	3 # 10	30 A	1	14-30R
Range top[3]	6000	115/230	3 # 10	30 A	1	14-30R
Dishwasher[3]	1200	115	2 # 12	20 A	1	5-20R
Waste disposer[3]	300	115	2 # 12	20 A	1	5-20R
Broiler[5]	1500	115	2 # 12	20 A	1 or more	5-20R
Refrigerator[6]	300	115	2 # 12	20 A	1 or more	5-20R
Freezer[6]	350	115	2 # 12	20 A	1 or more	5-20R
LAUNDRY						
Washing machine	1200	115	2 # 12	20 A	1 or more	5-20R
Dryer[3]	5000	115/230	3 # 10	30 A	1	14-30R
Hand iron; ironer	1650	115	2 # 12	20 A	1 or more	5-20R
LIVING AREAS						
Workshop	1500	115	2 # 12	20 A	1 or more	5-20R
Portable heater[7]	1300	115	2 # 12	20 A	1	5-20R
Television[7]	300	115	2 # 12	20 A	1 or more	5-20R
FIXED UTILITIES						
Fixed lighting	1200	115	2 # 12	20 A	1 or more	5-20R
Air conditioner 3/4 hp[8]	1200	115	2 # 12	20 A or 30 A	1	5-20R
Central air conditioner[9]	5000	115/230	3 # 10	40 A	1	
Sump pump[9]	300	115	2 # 12	20 A	1 or more	5-20 R
Heating plant, i.e., forced-air furnace[8][10]	600	115	2 # 12	20 A		
Attic fan[9]	300	115	2 # 12	20 A	1 or more	5-20R

[1] Wherever possible, use actual equipment rating.
[2] Number of wires does not include equipment grounding wires. Ground wire is No. 12 AWG for 20-A circuit and No. 10 AWG for 30-A and 50-A circuits.
[3] May be direct connected. For a discussion of disconnect requirements, see NEC Article 422.
[4] Equipment ground is provided in each receptacle.
[5] Heavy-duty appliances regularly used at one location should have separate circuits. Only one such unit should be attached to a single circuit.
[6] Separate circuit serving only one other outlet is recommended.
[7] Should not be connected to a circuit with appliances or other heavy loads
[8] Separate circuit recommended.
[9] Recommended that all motor-driven devices be protected by a local motor-protection element unless motor protection is built into the device.
[10] Connect through disconnect switch equipped with motor-protection element.
[11] National Electrical Manufacturers Association (NEMA).

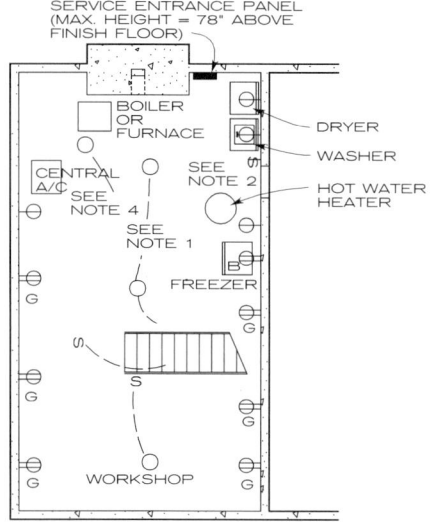

NOTE
See legend on previous page.

BASEMENT PLAN OF ELECTRICAL EQUIPMENT

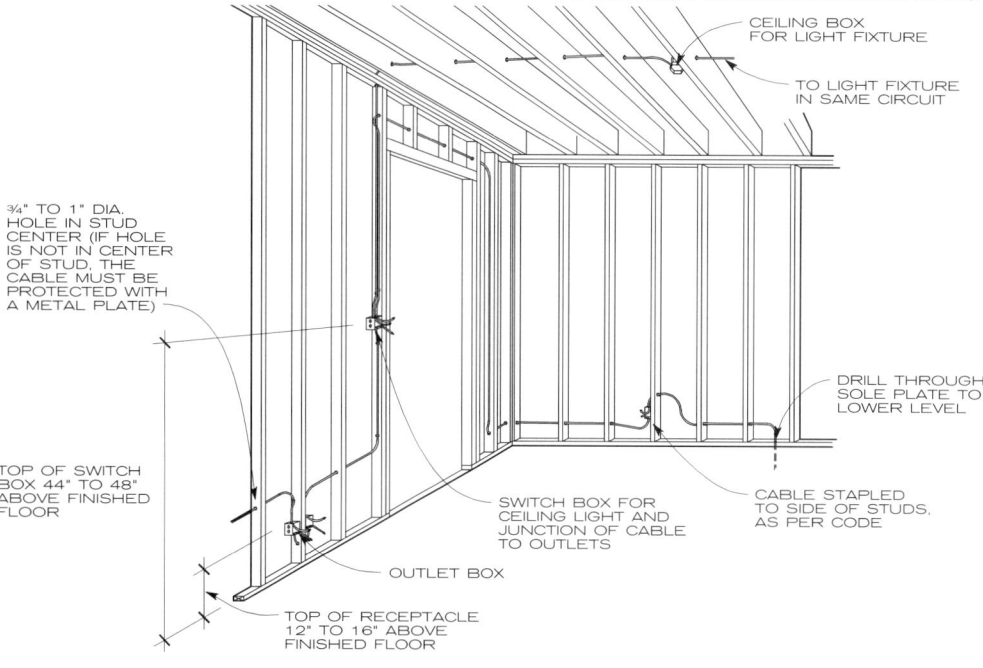

NOTE
In metal stud construction, cables are passed through precut openings in place of field-drilled holes.

TYPICAL WIRING IN WOOD CONSTRUCTION

Charles B. Towles, P.E.; TEI Consulting Engineers; Washington, D.C.

Outlets, Switches, and Plates

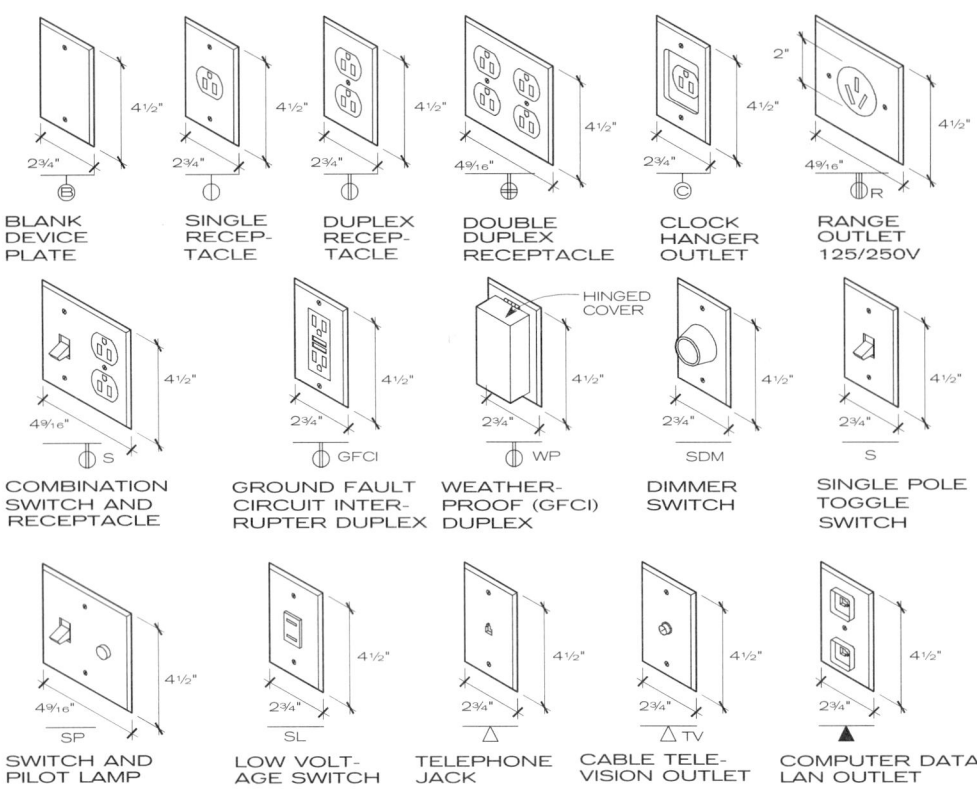

GANG SIZE

GANG	HORIZONTAL (IN.)	
	HEIGHT	WIDTH
2	4 1/2	4 9/16
3	4 1/2	6 3/8
4	4 1/2	8 3/16
5	4 1/2	10
6	4 1/2	11 13/16

NOTES

1. Add 1 13/16 in. for each added gang. Screws are 1 13/16 in. o.c.
2. Plates are made in plastic, brass (.04 to .06 in. thick), stainless steel, and aluminum.
3. All devices to be approved by Underwriters Laboratories and to comply with the National Electrical Code.
4. All devices to be of NEMA configuration.
5. Ground fault circuit interrupter or circuits are required in baths, garages, unfinished basements, outdoors at grade

RECEPTACLES AND SWITCHES

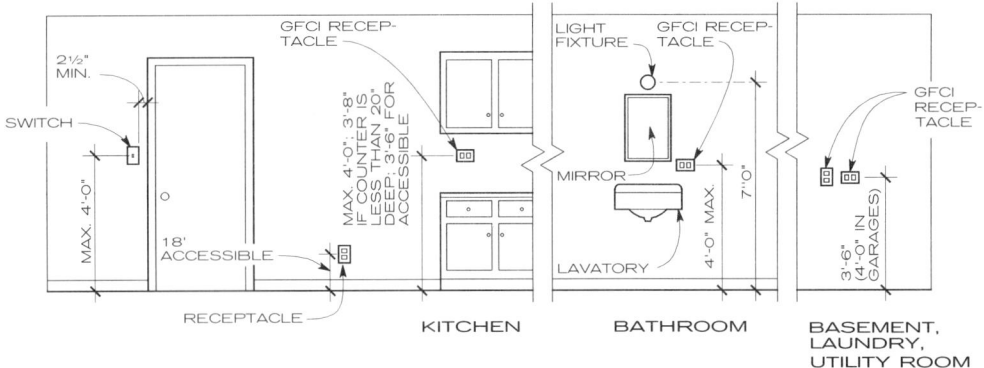

NOTES

1. Outlets and switches shown are those most generally used. Number of gangs behind one wall plate depends on the type of devices used.
2. Symbols used are ASA standard.
3. Interchangeable devices (miniature devices) available in various combinations using any of the following—switch, convenience outlet, radio outlet, pilot light, bell button—in one gang. Combined gangs are available.

SWITCH AND OUTLET LOCATIONS

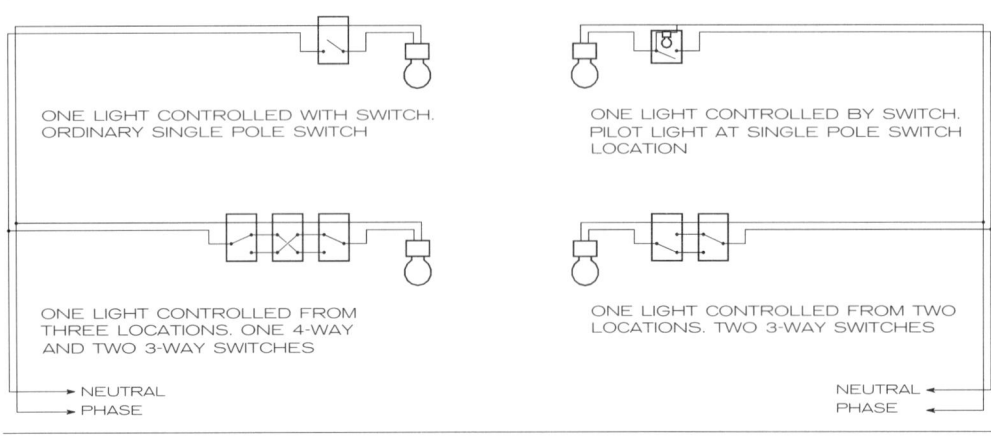

SWITCH WIRING DIAGRAMS

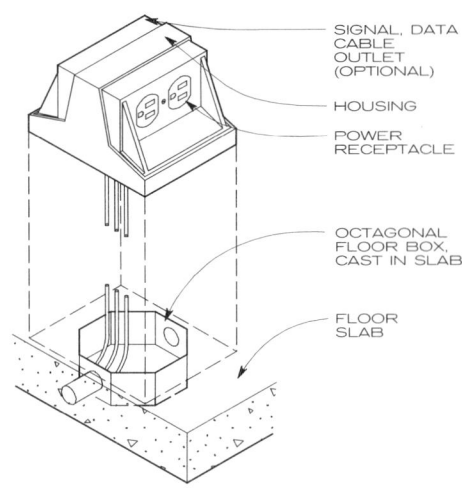

NOTE

Outlets and switches shown are those most generally used. The number of gangs behind one wall plate depends on the type of devices used.

MONUMENT FLOOR OUTLET

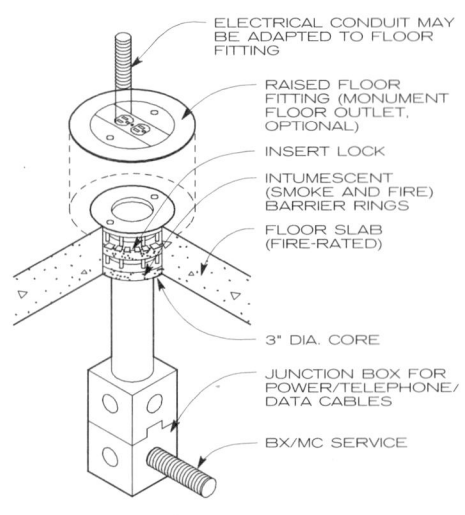

NOTE

Unit is adjustable to accommodate varying floor thicknesses. When abandoned, the floor fitting is replaced with a flat plate.

POKE-THROUGH ELECTRICAL BOX

Charles B. Towles, P.E.; TEI Consulting Engineers; Washington, D.C.

WIRING AND RELATED MATERIALS

Cables, Boxes, and Raceways

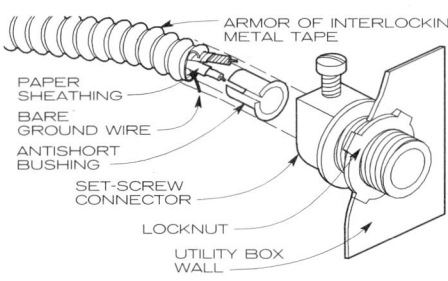

ARMORED (BX)
NOTE

Armored cable is manufactured with 2-, 3-, and 4-conductor insulated wire in sizes 14, 12, 10, 8, 6, 4, 2; its internal bonds help the armor itself serve as a bonding conductor.

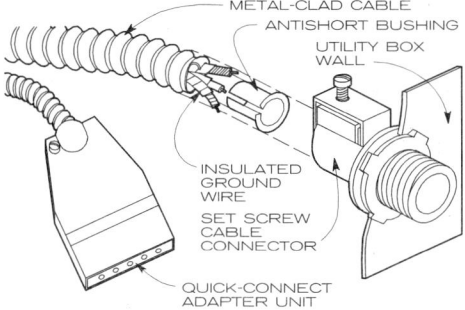

METAL-CLAD (MC)
NOTE

Manufactured in sizes and specs similar to armored cable, metal-clad cable is available with a separate insulated ground conductor and in larger sizes. It may be clad in aluminum or steel, corrugated, smooth, or with metal interlocking tape and may be factory assembled with quick connect adapter units for access floor or ceiling wiring systems. Consult an electrical engineer before installation.

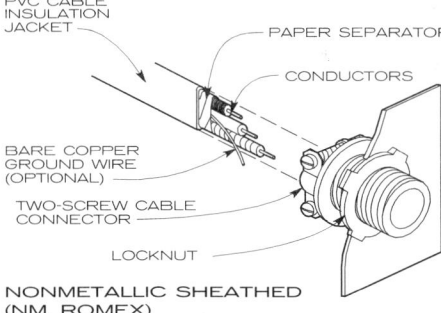

NONMETALLIC SHEATHED (NM, ROMEX)
NOTE

Manufactured in 2- and 3-conductor PVC insulated wire in sizes 14, 12, 10, 8, 6, and 4 with or without ground wire, nonmetallic sheathed cable is permitted in residential and many other building types up to three stories.

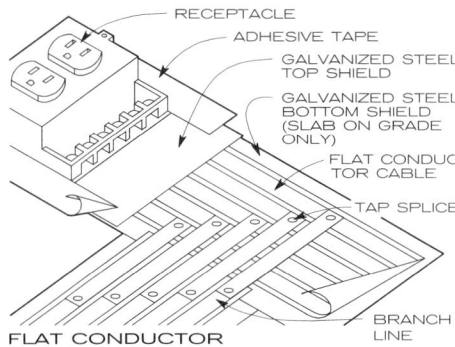

FLAT CONDUCTOR
NOTE

Flat conductor cable has combinations of 3, 4, and 5 conductors for easy access under carpet squares; data, communications, and TV flat cable are available. Consult manufacturers before installation.

CABLES

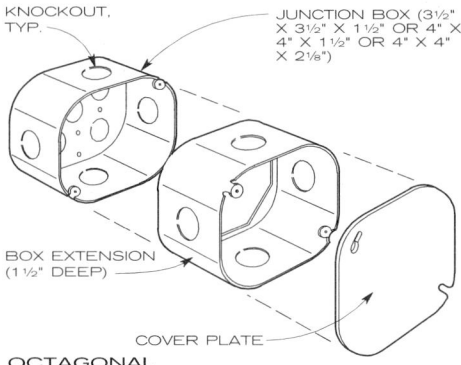

OCTAGONAL
NOTE

Commonly used for flush ceiling outlets, octagonal boxes may also be used as a floor box for monument receptacles.

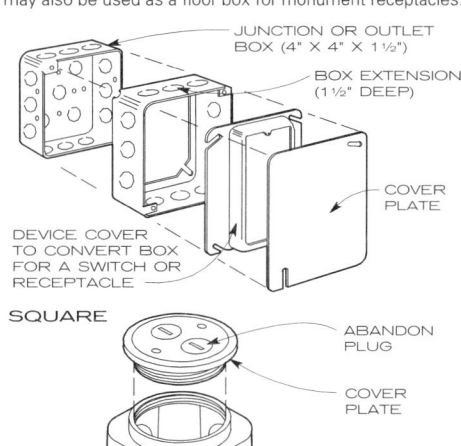

SQUARE

FLUSH FLOOR
NOTE

Boxes are mounted to wood floor structure (nonadjustable) or cast-in-place concrete with leveling screws. Concrete boxes include cast-iron, stamped steel, or nonmetallic materials. This is a heavy-duty box, in comparison to a standard octagonal floor box for monument receptacle.

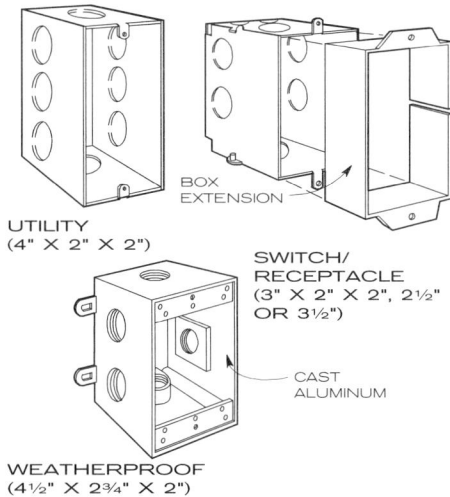

UTILITY (4" X 2" X 2")

SWITCH/RECEPTACLE (3" X 2" X 2", 2½" OR 3½")

WEATHERPROOF (4½" X 2¾" X 2")
NOTE

Metallic and nonmetallic versions; knockout locations vary. Utility and exterior boxes not gangable; switch and masonry boxes may be. Flush mounting in concrete requires a concrete tight box and rigid conduit and tubing; in CMU construction, a raceway or tubing is threaded through the cavities.

ELECTRICAL BOXES

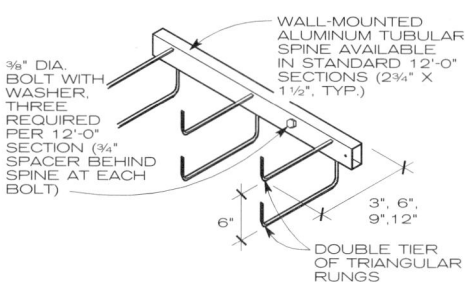

WALL-MOUNT CABLE RACK

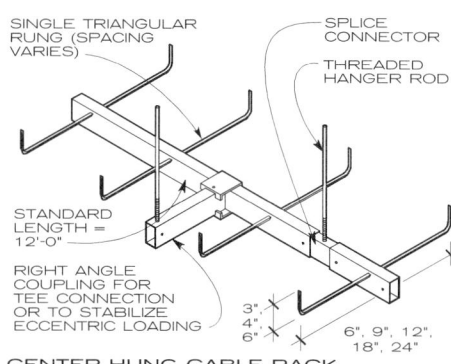

CENTER-HUNG CABLE RACK

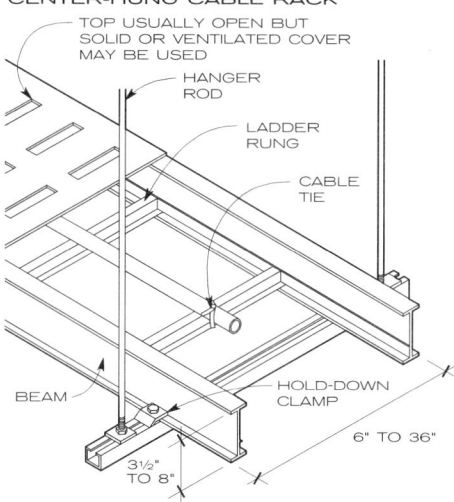

CABLE TRAY SYSTEM
NOTE

Cable trays protect and carry a large number of insulated cables in a limited space. For more protection or where heat buildup is not a problem, perforated or solid bottoms and top covers are available. Many fittings, bends, and tees (horizontal and vertical) are available. Consult manufacturers for materials other than aluminum or steel.

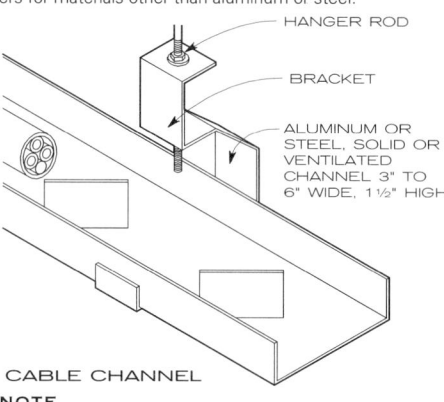

CABLE CHANNEL
NOTE

Cable channel can be used as a branch cable tray to carry a single large cable or conduit or several small ones.

CONDUIT AND CABLE SUPPORTING DEVICES

Charles B. Towles, P.E.; TEI Consulting Engineers; Washington, D.C.

Floor Wiring Systems for Workstations

POKE THROUGH SYSTEMS

Poke-through systems are used in conjunction with overhead branch distribution systems that run in accessible suspended ceiling cavities to outlets in full-height partitions. When services are required at floor locations without adjacent partitions or columns, as in open office planning, they must either be brought down from a wireway assembly (known as a power pole) or up through a floor penetration containing a fire-rated insert fitting and flush or above-floor outlet assembly. To install a poke-through assembly, the floor slab must either be core drilled or contain preset sleeves arranged in a modular grid. Poke-through assemblies are used in conjunction with cellular deck and underfloor duct systems when the service location required does not fall directly above its associated system raceway.

With one floor penetration, the single poke-through assembly can serve all the power, communications, and computer requirements of a work station. Distribution wiring in the ceiling cavity can be run in raceways. The more cost-effective method is to use armored cable (BX) for power and approved plenum-rated cable for communications and data when the ceiling cavity is used for return air. To minimize disturbance to the office space below when a poke-through assembly must be relocated or added, a modular system of prewired junction boxes for each service can be provided, although it is more common to elect this option for power only. A different type of working system must be selected for a floor slab on grade, above a lobby or retail space, above mechanical equipment space, or above space exposed to the atmosphere.

CELLULAR DECK SYSTEMS

The low initial cost of a poke-through system makes it both viable and attractive for investor-owned buildings when tenants are responsible for future changes and for corporate buildings with limited construction budgets. Poke-through systems are effective when office planning includes interconnecting workstation panels containing provisions (base raceways) to extend wiring above the floor, reducing the number of floor penetrations needed for services.

Based on the projected frequency of changes in office furniture layouts, a corporate or government organization may elect to invest in a permanent raceway system to minimize cost and disturbance to occupants when changes or additions are made. When structural design dictates the use of metal decking, a cellular floor raceway system utilizing trench header ducts is the most likely choice.

Cellular raceways come in a variety of sizes and configurations ranging from 1 1/2 to 3 in. high with cells 8 or 12 in. o.c. and 2 or 3 cells per section. An overall floor deck can be full cellular, where bottom plates are provided throughout, or blended as shown.

Trench header ducts come in various sizes and configurations. The height is adjustable for slab depths above cells of 2 1/2 to 4 in. and widths vary from 9 to 36 in. Cover plates are 1/4 in. thick, with lengths from 6 to 36 in., and can either be secured with spring clips or flush, flathead bolts. Two versions of trench design are available: One has a compartmental bottom tray with a grommeted access hole for each cell it crosses; the other has a bottomless trench duct consisting of side rails and a separate wireway in the middle, with grommeted access holes only for the power cells.

When service is needed, the floor is core drilled above the desired cell, the cell top is drilled into, and an afterset insert with above-floor fitting is attached. If data and communication wiring can occupy the same cell, with power wiring in an adjacent cell, two separate service fittings are required for each workstation.

When it is necessary to eliminate or minimize core drilling, a modular pattern of preset service flush outlets can be provided along the cellular sections before the floor is poured (as shown). Upon activation, one flush outlet can serve all the power, communication, and data requirements of a workstation.

The modular grid and frequency of preset locations will determine the convenience of service provisions for the workstations.

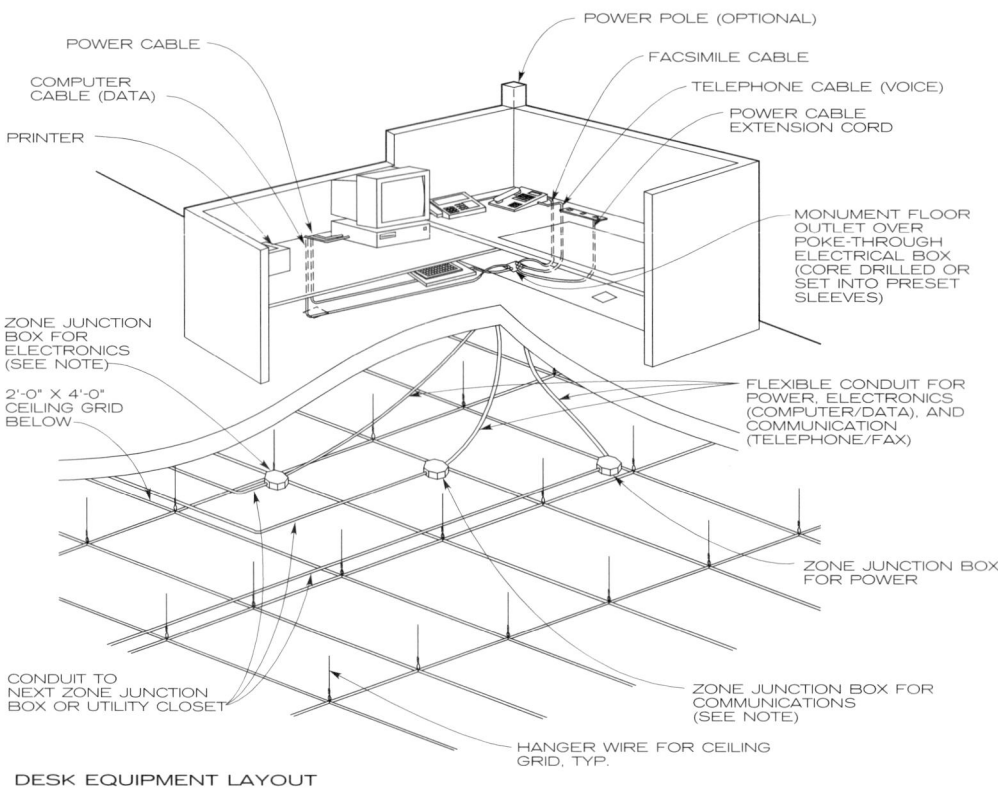

DESK EQUIPMENT LAYOUT

NOTE

Computer and telephone cabling is often combined as an integrated voice/data cabling system, eliminating the need for three raceways except when extra capacity is needed.

POKE-THROUGH HARDWARE SYSTEM/ZONE JUNCTION BOX

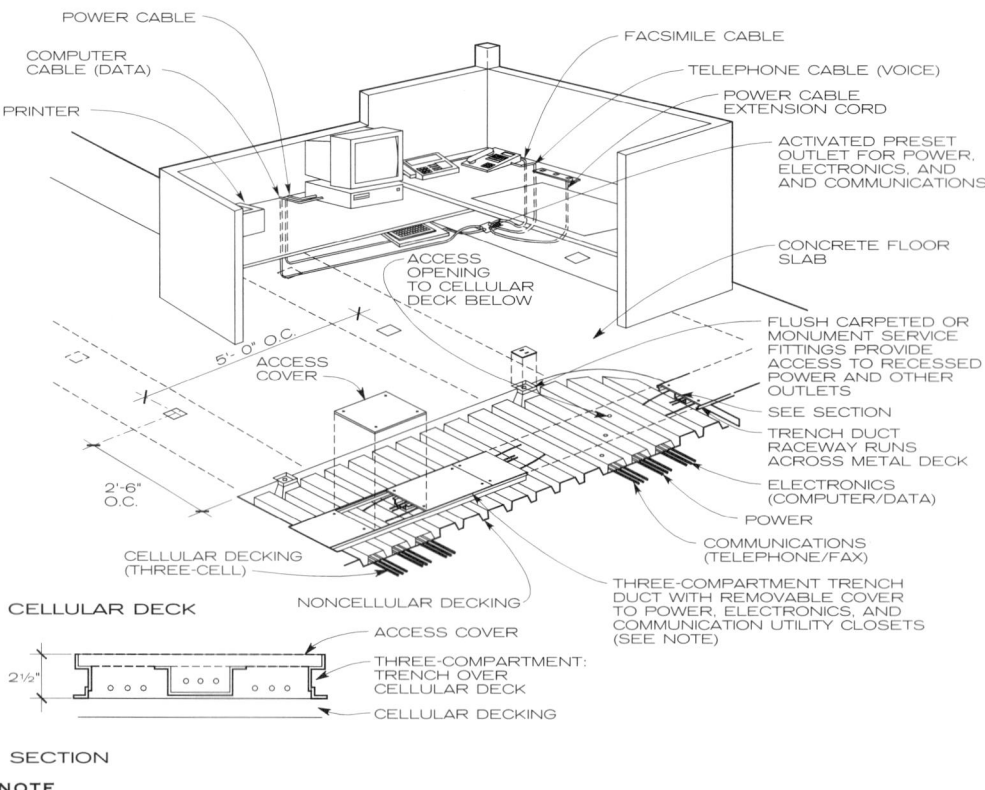

CELLULAR DECK SYSTEM WITH TRENCH HEADER DUCTS

NOTE

Computer and telephone cabling is often combined as an integrated voice/data cabling system, eliminating the need for three raceways except when extra capacity is needed.

Richard F. Humenn, P.E.; Joseph R. Loring & Assoc., Consulting Engineers; New York, New York

Site Electrical Distribution, Service, and Grounding

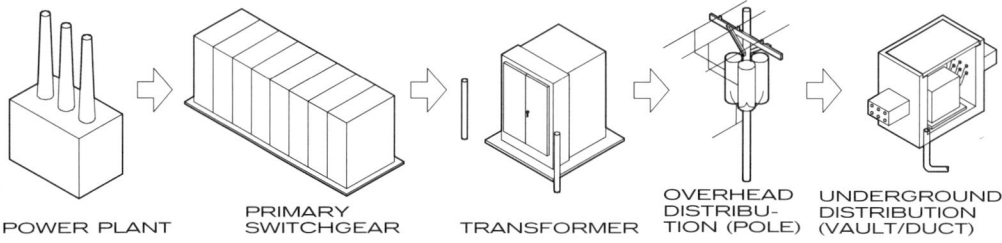

NOTE

Primary high-voltage service is received at a site via various stages, from the formation of electrical energy (water power, turbines, etc.) to substations that receive the electricity at high voltage and distribute this energy at a lower voltage via switchgear to the point of use. At each stage, protective devices (switches or circuit breakers) are installed. Transformers are installed to reduce voltage along the lines for the requirements of the end user.

PRIMARY SERVICE DISTRIBUTION

NOTE

When buildings cover a large area, such as a college campus or medical center, the use of medium voltages of 5 to 34 kV for distribution feeders is usually required. Therefore, the utility company terminates its primary feeders on the owner's metal-clad or metal-enclosed switchgear, which may be inside or of exterior weatherproof construction. Code clearance in front and back of board must be provided in accordance with the National Electrical Code.

PRIMARY SWITCHGEAR WITH PRIMARY POWER FROM TWO SERVICES

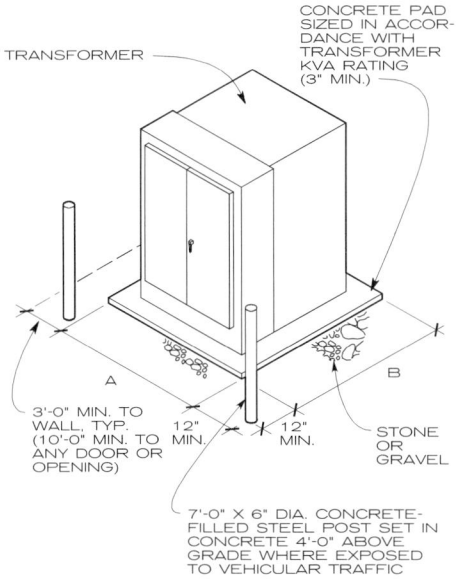

TYPICAL PAD SIZES

POWER	A	B
150 - 300 kVA	75 in.	80 in.
500 - 1500 kVA	84 in.	84 in.

NOTES

1. Pad-mounted transformers with weatherproof, tamperproof enclosures permit installation at ground level without the danger of exposed parts. Three-phase units up to 1500 kVA are normally used with underground primary and secondary feeders. The customer's grounding grids or grounding electrical conductors should not be connected at pad-mounted transformer locations.
2. High voltage compartment requires 10-ft clearance for on-off operation of the insulated stick located on the transformer (known as "hot stick" operation).

PAD-MOUNTED TRANSFORMER

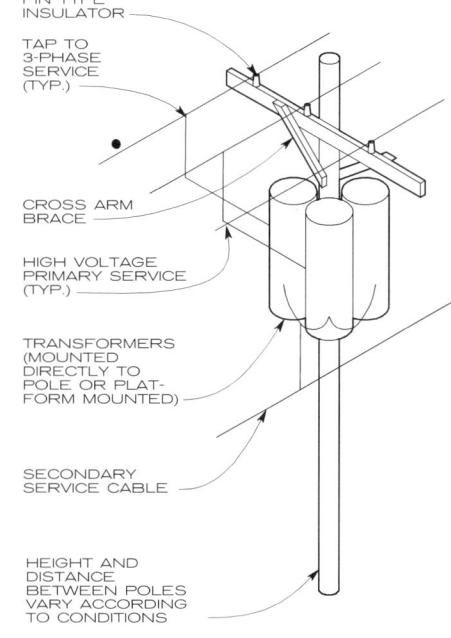

NOTE

Overhead distribution lines are supported by poles from the origin of the electrical service to the termination point. Poles are fabricated out of various kinds of wood (e.g., pine or cedar) or steel, depending on the type of equipment to be supported, weather conditions, and cost of materials. Transformers mounted directly onto the poles or on platforms provide the required low voltage service to the final point. Spacing between the poles, height of the poles, and clearances between electrical lines and the ground depend upon the type of terrain, weather environment, and obstructions (e.g., inhabited area, waterways, railroads, roadways, etc.). See the National Electrical Safety Code for restrictions.

OVERHEAD POLE CONFIGURATION

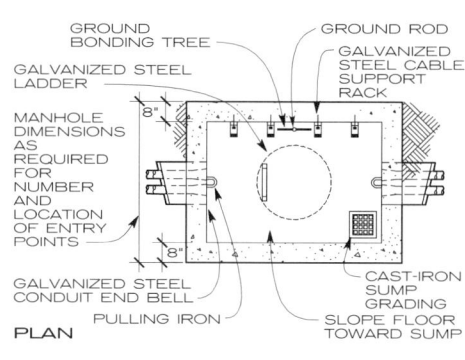

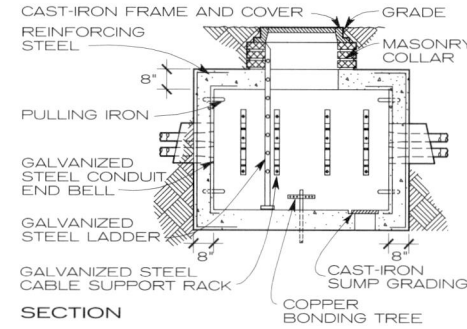

NOTE

Manholes are provided for splicing and pulling of electrical cables for underground distribution. Size ductbanks emanating out of the manhole according to the latest edition of the National Electrical Code.

MANHOLE DETAILS

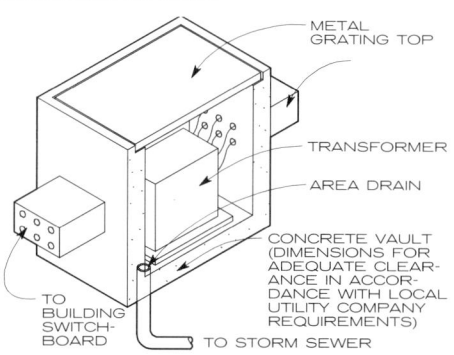

NOTE

Underground vaults are generally used for utility company transformers where all distribution feeders are underground. These systems usually constitute a network or spot network. Vaults are often located below the sidewalks and have grating tops. Transformer is usually liquid filled; if an oil-filled transformer is used, an oil interceptor is recommended before discharge to building storm sewer.

UNDERGROUND VAULT

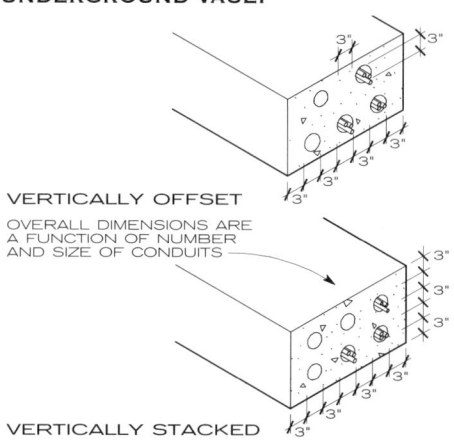

UNDERGROUND DUCT BANK

Charles B. Towles, P.E.; TEI Consulting Engineers; Washington, D.C.

174 Transformers and Voltage Control

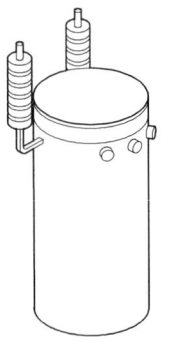 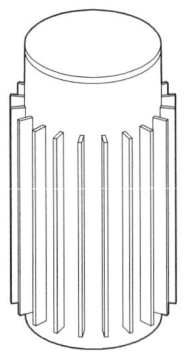

SINGLE-PHASE   THREE-PHASE

NOTE
Rated secondary voltages: 208, 240, or 480. Immersed in oil; self-cooled.

POLE-MOUNTED TRANSFORMERS

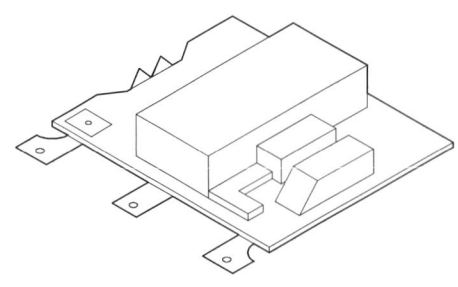

NOTE
Provides convenient control of lighting and power circuits from control stations.

REMOTE CONTROL SWITCH

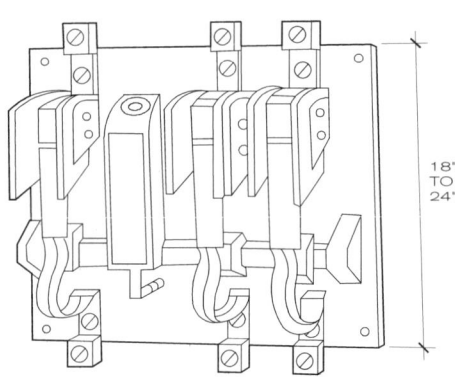

NOTE
Rated voltage: 600 VAC. For circuits that are closed and opened repeatedly, various design combinations are allowed. Used for all classes of magnetically held loads, open or closed.

CONTACTOR

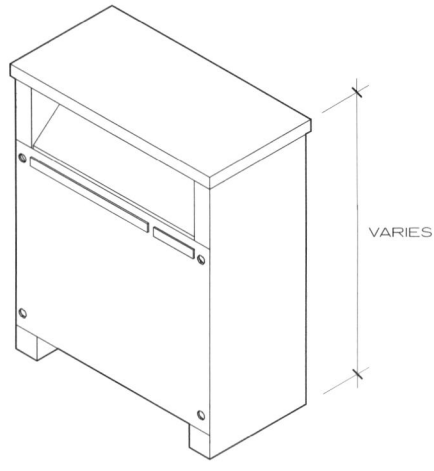

NOTE
Rated secondary voltages: 120/208 or 240 volts or three phase. Primarily mounted on indoor floors and walls.

DRY TRANSFORMER

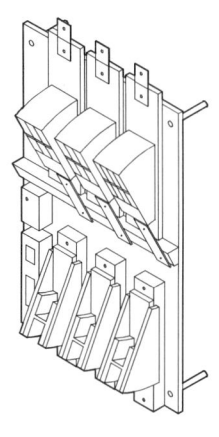

NOTE
Automatically transfers loads from a normal source to the emergency source.

AUTOTRANSFER SWITCH

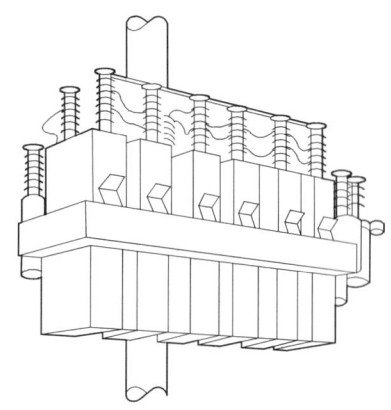

POLE RACK
NOTE
Power factor correction on either low or high voltage systems. Types, indoor or outdoor. Size and voltage as required. Switched or floating.

CAPACITOR

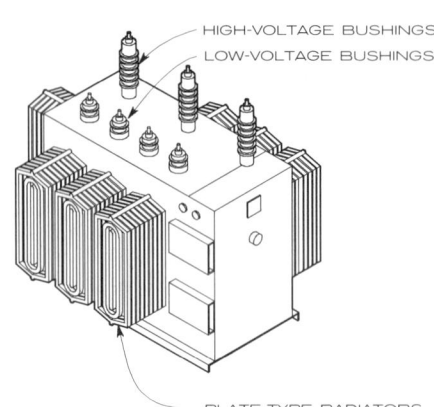

NOTE
Secondary substation transformer with high to low voltage. Primarily a commercial type for the outdoors. Optional external fan cooling.

LIQUID-FILLED TRANSFORMER

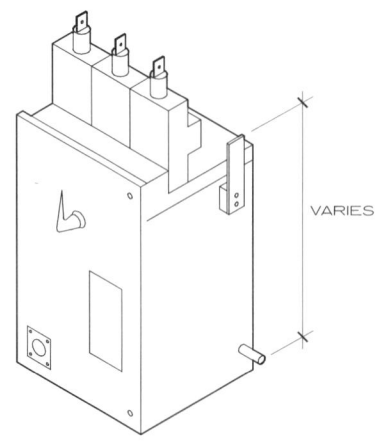

NETWORK TYPE
NOTE
Maximum voltage: 125/216 VAC or 277/480 VAC. Interrupting capacity 30,000 and 60,000 A. RMS. SYM. A fault on primary cable or network transformer will open protector to isolate fault from system.

PROTECTOR

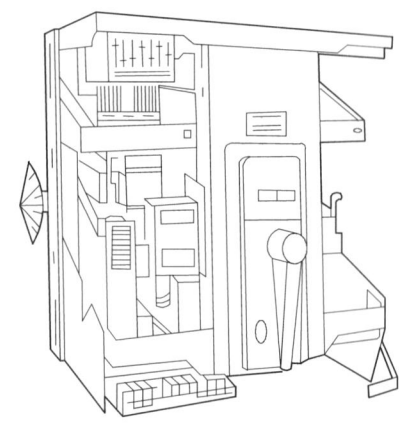

LOW VOLTAGE
NOTE
Rated voltages: 240 VAC, 480 VAC, 600 VAC, and 250 VDC. Manual or electric operation. Electromechanical or solid-state breaker trip devices. Stationary or drawout types.

DISTRIBUTION CIRCUIT BREAKER

Charles B. Towles, P.E.; TEI Consulting Engineers; Washington, D.C.

16 SERVICE AND DISTRIBUTION

Substations, Switchboards, Motor Starters, and Busways

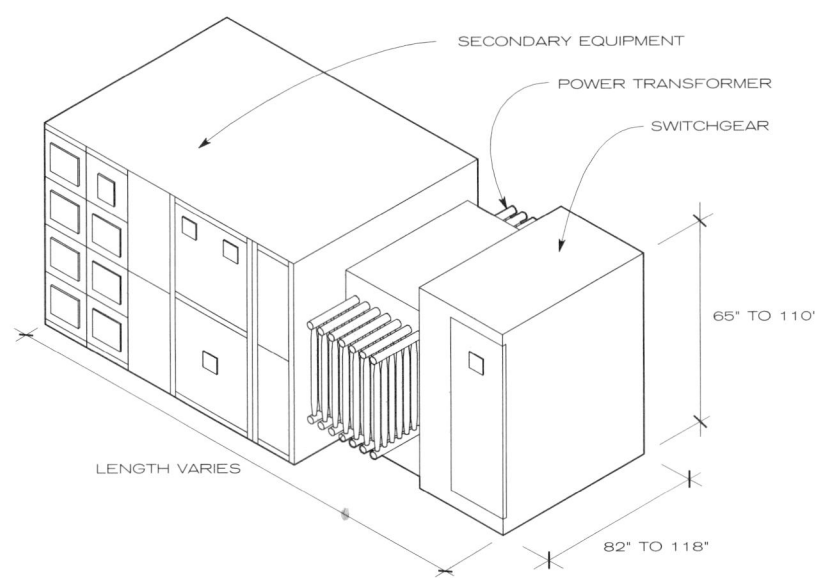

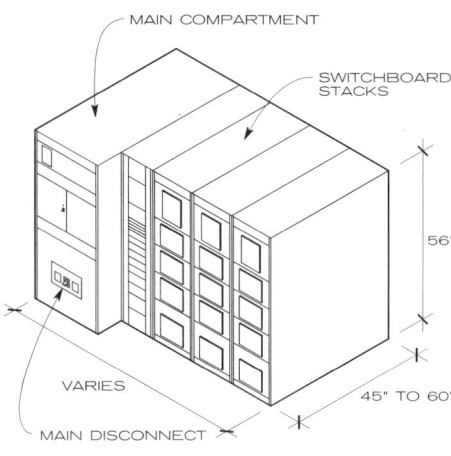

NOTE
Metering compartment, main disconnect, check meters, and low voltage distribution section. See manufacturer's literature for type, size, and arrangements. See National Electrical Code for required aisle space, servicing area, and room layout.

SWITCHBOARD

NOTE
A secondary unit substation, sometimes called a power center, is a close-coupled assembly consisting of three-phase power transformers, enclosed high voltage incoming line sections, and enclosed secondary low voltage outgoing sections encompassing the following electrical ratings:

Transformer kVA: 112.5 through 2500 (self-cooled rating) liquid-filled, dry-type, or cast coil.
Primary voltage: 2.4 kV thru 34.5 kV.
Secondary voltage: 208, 240, 480, or 600 V (max.).

See National Electrical Code for aisle space, ventilation, servicing area, and special building condition requirements.

SECONDARY UNIT SUBSTATION

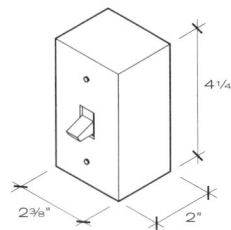

MANUAL
NOTE
Manual single-phase starters are designed to give positive, accurate, trouble-free overload protection to single phase motors rated up to 1 HP. Typical applications are fans, machine tools, motors, HVAC, etc. Maximum voltage is 240 V AC.

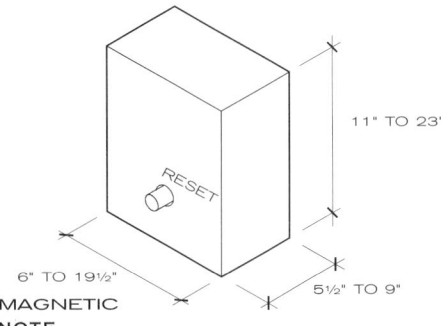

MAGNETIC
NOTE
Magnetic motor starters are designed for across-the-line control of squirrel cage motors or as primary control for wound rotor motors. Starters can be furnished for nonreversing, reversing and two-speed applications. Maximum voltage is 600 V AC; maximum horsepower is 200 HP.

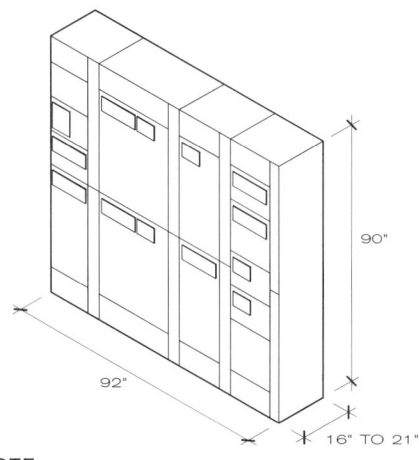

NOTE
Motor control centers provide a method for grouping motor control, associated control, and distribution equipment. It is designed to operate machinery, industrial processes, and commercial building systems.

LOW-VOLTAGE MOTOR CONTROL CENTER

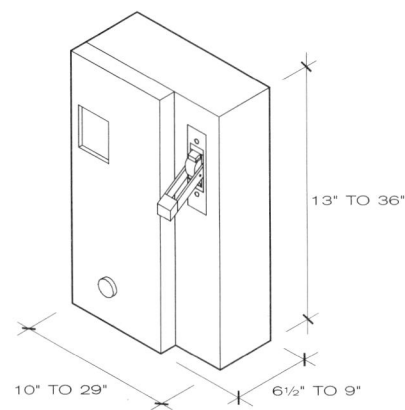

COMBINATION
NOTE
Magnetic combination starters are designed for across-the-line control of squirrel cage motors or as primary control for wound rotor motors. In addition, they provide a disconnect means and short-circuit protection. They are available for nonreversing or reversing applications.

MOTOR STARTERS

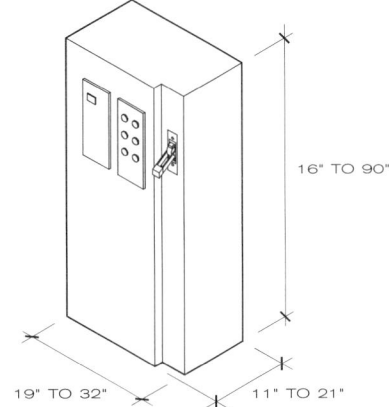

SOLID-STATE
NOTE
This unit is a reduced voltage motor starter, used to reduce starting current and high starting torque. Typical applications for controllers are in motors used in cranes, belt-driven equipment, conveyors, material handling facilities, compressors, and woodworking equipment. Available for AC motors 5 to 900 HP.

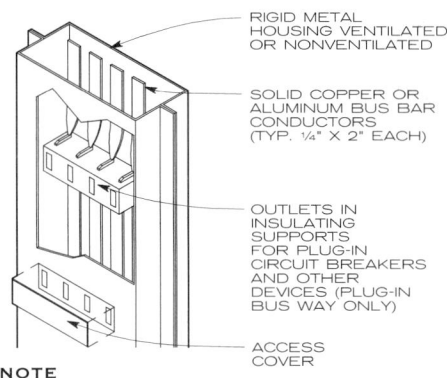

NOTE
Plug-in and feeder busways carry current from 50 to 5000 amps. They are utilized when large blocks of low voltage power (up to 600 V) must be transmitted over long distances or when taps must be made at various points, as in vertical risers in office buildings. Codes limit locations in buildings where different types of busways may be installed. Consult an electrical engineer before using this system. Busway housing may be hung from an overhead support, mounted to a wall, or braced to the structure in vertical riser installation.

BUSWAY SYSTEM

Charles B. Towles, P.E.; TEI Consulting Engineers; Washington, D.C.

Panelboards, Circuit Breakers, Disconnect Switches, and Fuses

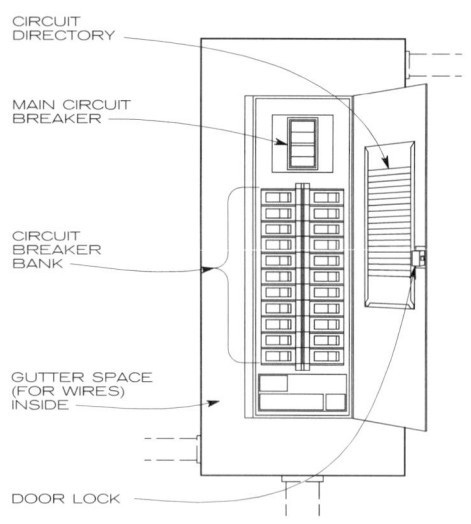

NOTE
Knockout holes allow conduit connections from all sides.

PANELBOARD DIMENSIONS

MAXIMUM NUMBER OF CIRCUITS	BOX DIMENSIONS (IN.)		
	WIDTH	HEIGHT	DEPTH
12	9–15	13–20	$3^3/_4$–$4^5/_8$
20	9–15	$20^1/_4$–24	$3^3/_4$–$4^5/_8$
30	12–15	30–33	$3^3/_4$–$4^5/_8$
40	14–15	34–39	4–$4^5/_8$

RESIDENTIAL AND COMMERCIAL PANELBOARD

PLUG FUSE
1. Rated voltage: 125
2. Ampere rating: 1-30
3. Fuse types: S, T

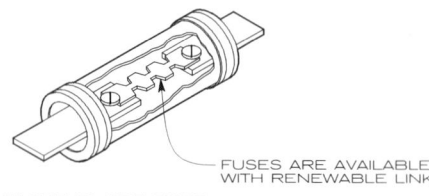

KNIFE BLADE FUSE
1. Rated voltage: 250 and 600
2. Ampere ratings: 70-6000
3. Fuse types: K1, RK1, K5, RK5, J, H, G, and L

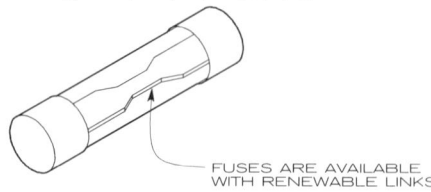

CARTRIDGE FUSE
1. Rated voltage: 250 and 600
2. Ampere rating: $^1/_{10}$-60
3. Fuse types: K1, RK1, K5, RK5, J, H, and G

NOTE
Cartridge and knife blade fuses are available for short circuit protection up to 200,000 A (Rms).

FUSES

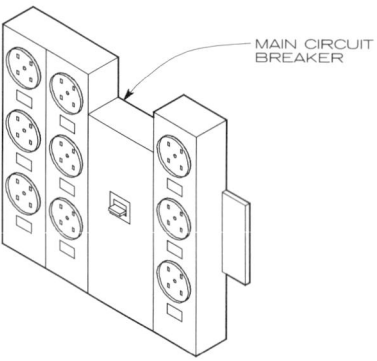

MULTIPLE METER BANK WITH MAIN CIRCUIT BREAKER
1. Rated voltages: 120/240 V, 3-wire, single-phase or 208/120 V, 4-wire, three-phase.
2. Either indoor or outdoor construction.
3. Number of sockets as required by application.

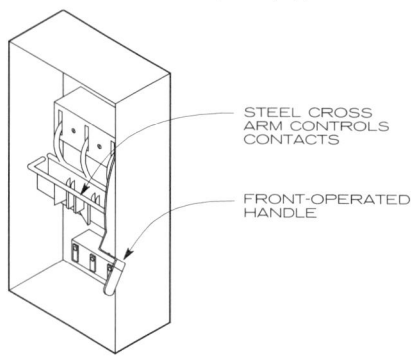

FUSED SAFETY

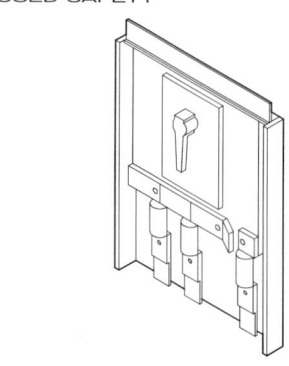

HIGH-PRESSURE CONTACT

NOTE
High-pressure contact switches may be top or bottom feed; 600 V AC max; 800–4000 A.

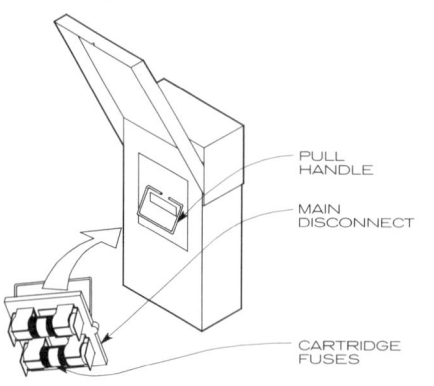

FUSE BOX

DISCONNECT SWITCHES

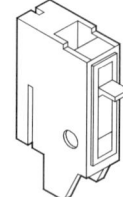

MOLDED CASE
1. Rated voltages: 120 VAC, 240 VAC, 600 VAC, 125 VDC, and 250 VDC.
2. Frame sizes: 100, 150, 225, 400, 600, 800, 1200 A poles, 2 or 3 above 100 A.
3. Current limiting types with fuses.

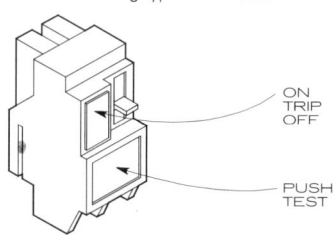

MOLDED CASE WITH GROUND FAULT
1. Rated voltages: 120 VAC or 120/240 VAC.
2. Frame size: 100 A ratings, 15-30 A poles, 1 or 2.

CIRCUIT BREAKERS

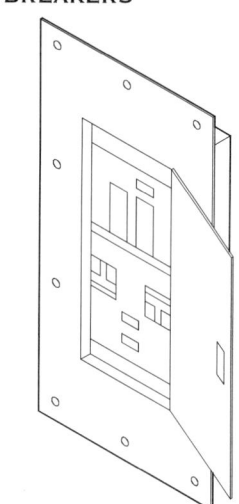

CIRCUIT BREAKER

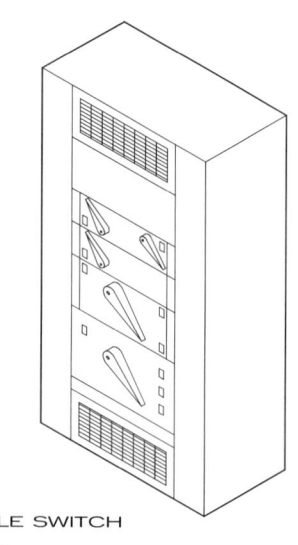

FUSIBLE SWITCH

DISTRIBUTION PANEL BOARDS

Charles B. Towles, P.E.; TEI Consulting Engineers; Washington, D.C.

SERVICE AND DISTRIBUTION

Lamp Characteristics

LAMPS IN THE DESIGN PROCESS

The goal of lighting design is to supply appropriate lighting characteristics to a given environment in an efficient manner. Characteristics such as quality of light, quantity of light, and spatial distribution are dictated by the needs of the users and the requirements of the space.

A lighting system primarily consists of lamps (which supply and regulate the lighting), ballasts, and luminaires. However, other aspects of the design with which the lighting system interacts, such as fenestration, surface treatments, and control systems, are also considered part of the lighting system.

A lamp, commonly known as a lightbulb, is the artificial light source that changes electrical energy into light energy. A ballast supplies the proper electrical characteristics to start and operate a lamp. Ballasts are not needed for lamps that operate directly on line power, such as most incandescent types. A luminaire, commonly known as a fixture, distributes and modifies the light from a lightbulb.

The lighting characteristics required in a space are primarily supplied by the lamp but may be modified by other elements. For instance, the type of ballast dictates flicker, and the luminaire may modify light distribution and color.

COLOR TEMPERATURE

Color temperature is a measure of the color of the light source itself. It is indicated in degrees Kelvin. Some light sources (incandescent and the sun) operate essentially as black-body radiators. Others (fluorescent and high-intensity discharge) must be referred to by their correlated color temperatures (CCT). Lamps with low Kelvin temperatures are "warm" or reddish light sources and emphasize reds, oranges, and yellows. Those with high color temperatures are "cool" or bluish in appearance and emphasize blues and greens. A wide range of color temperatures encompasses "white light" and, without a visual comparison, the human eye sees all of these as white.

COLOR RENDERING

Color rendering refers to how objects appear when illuminated by a light source. It is usually measured by a color rendering index (CRI) with a scale of zero to 100. The higher the CRI, the better a source makes objects appear. At the bottom of the scale, there is no ability to discern colors. At 100, colors are rendered exactly as they appear under a given reference light source, which is the black-body radiator for the same or correlated color temperature. For this reason, color rendering can only be compared among light sources of the same color temperature.

Lamps with good color rendering require a lower illuminance (the amount of light reaching a surface) to achieve judgments of equivalent brightness, visual clarity, and visual satisfaction. Therefore, higher-CRI lamps require fewer lumens, and fewer watts, than lower-CRI lamps.

COLOR TEMPERATURES OF SELECTED LIGHT SOURCES*

DAYLIGHT	
Blue sky	10,000 to 30,000
Overcast sky	7000
Noon sunlight	5250
FLUORESCENT LAMPS	
RE 50 very cool tri-phosphor	5000
Cool white halophosphate	4100
RE 41 cool tri-phosphor	4100
RE 30 warm tri-phosphor	3000
Compact fluorescent (most screw-in types)	2700 or 2800
INCANDESCENT LAMPS	
Halogen low-voltage MR16	3100
Halogen reflector PAR	2800 to 2925
General service 60W–200W	2790 to 2980
CANDLE FLAME	1800

* Degrees Kelvin; approximate, correlated values

ECONOMICS OF ENERGY SAVINGS

SUBSTITUTION FROM	TO	WATTS SAVED	RATED LIFE (HOURS)	DOLLARS SAVED OVER LIFE*	SIMPLE RETURN ON INVESTMENT
90W A19 (incandescent)	23W compact fluorescent	67	10,000	$67	335%
4-34W T12 fluorescent, 2 magnetic ballasts	4-32W T8 fluorescent, 1 electronic ballast	15	20,000	$30	300%
200W A23 incandescent	70W metal halide with fixture	111	6,000	$67	33%

* Figured at 10 cents per kilowatt hour.

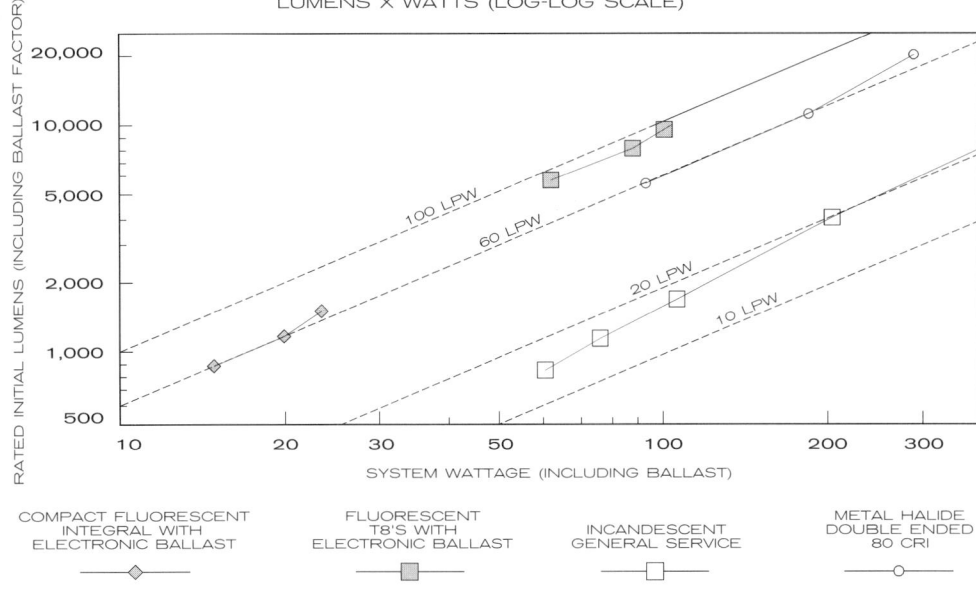

RELATIVE EFFICACIES OF LAMP TECHNOLOGIES

LIGHT OUTPUT

Visible light power radiated in all directions from a lamp is measured in lumens. Rated lumen output for fluorescent lamps should be modified according to the ballast factor of the ballast used. Light emitted by a lamp will be diminished by the reflectance and geometry of the luminaire, dust, age, and other factors. Mean lumens or design lumens take into account the depreciation of light as a result of lamp aging. Further, since light does its useful work only when appropriately reflected off surfaces into the eye, the light output of different lamps cannot be fully compared independent of the rest of the lighting design.

In some specialized situations the lamp itself is the design--for instance, in marquee lighting and some LED signs. The brightness at the surface of a lamp is measured in candle units. This measure of brightness is important in lamps used for directional lighting, such as reflector lamps.

ELECTRICAL INPUT

Electrical power is measured in watts. For ballasted lamps, rated wattage is nominal--it is the power drawn by the lamp alone from a standardized reference ballast. Real input is the combined lamp and ballast wattage of the system.

Power accumulated yields energy, which is measured in watt-hours or kilowatt-hours. For most situations, this can be calculated if it is known how much time the lighting system is on. Some systems, including low-pressure sodium and any one offering dimming, have variable wattage.

EFFICACY

The energy efficiency of a lamp is measured as light output divided by power input, or lumens per watt, or efficacy. For lamps that have ballasts, the wattage of the complete system should be considered. Efficacy is generally determined by technology type: Incandescent is the least efficient electric source type; low-pressure sodium is the most efficient. Subfamilies within technology types may be further differentiated by efficacy. For instance, krypton-fill, halogen, and infrared reflector are all technological improvements within the incandescent category. Among lamps of a given technology type, efficacy increases as input increases. Therefore, two 60-watt incandescent lamps provide about as much light as one 100-watt incandescent.

As shown in the graph below. Lamps vary significantly in their efficacy. At relatively low lumen levels, compact fluorescent technology can provide lumens approximately equivalent to that provided by incandescent technology with approximately four times better efficacy. Among white-color, higher-lumen sources, double-ended metal halide lamps achieve approximately 60 lumens per watt, and T8 fluorescents with electronic ballasts provide almost 100 lumens per watt. High-intensity discharge lamps can achieve even higher efficacies and are appropriate if color quality is not critical.

ENERGY AND ECONOMICS

By incorporating efficiency when appropriate into lamps, ballasts, luminaires, controls, and overall design, lighting systems can consume dramatically less energy. Compared to standard design, decreases in overall energy consumed can be anywhere from 20 to 50% or more. Depending on local electrical rates, an efficient lighting design can save the end user a significant amount in reduced electrical rates. The extra cost of purchasing and installing efficient devices is usually very small compared with the savings that can be achieved.

Fred Davis, C.L.E.P.; Fred Davis Corp., Energy and Lighting; Medfield, Massachusetts

Lamp Characteristics

LIFETIME

Lamps are rated according to the number of hours burned after which half the lamps will no longer light in test conditions with a burn cycle of 3 hours. Since the actual life of a lamp is determined by actual burn cycles and other factors such as temperature and vibration, the actual life of a lamp may not equal its rated life. Generally, the longer the burn cycle, the longer the life of a lamp.

Lamps may be expected to last longer than their rated life if burned on longer cycles; conversely, a shorter life is likely for burn cycles shorter than 3 hours. A rapid-start fluorescent lamp may last 160% of its rated life if burned continuously.

FLICKER

All discharge lamps (fluorescent and HID) flicker, i.e., they turn on and off many times per second. Generally, this is imperceptible except to a small percentage of the population. Caution must be taken, however, to avoid a stroboscopic effect in the presence of moving machinery, which may appear motionless if it is moving in a rhythm synchronous with the lighting flicker. High-frequency electronic ballasts generally eliminate any perceptible flicker.

TEMPERATURE CONDITIONS

The lifetime and light output of a lamp can be affected by temperature. Incandescent and high-intensity discharge (HID) lamps generally perform well in cold outdoor conditions; special jacketed versions of fluorescent lamps are also suited to outdoor use.

SHIELDING

Most lamp types should be shielded from direct precipitation; incandescent PAR lamps are one exception. Some metal halide lamps must be enclosed in fixtures to protect users from ultraviolet radiation or "nonpassive" failures. Electrodeless lamps generally operate at radio frequencies, and shielding users from radiation is essential.

BASE TYPES

The medium screw-base, the most well-known base type for electric lamps, is used with many lamp types. Interchangeability among lamp types is an important feature in many luminaires with this socket.

Most other base types are specific to certain lamp types to ensure correct electrical and positional matches. For example, recessed double contact (RDC) sockets are used with high output and very high output fluorescents, which have RDC bases and require ballasts to supply the proper voltage; many high-wattage incandescents (300-1000W) have mogul screw-bases and will not fit into medium screw sockets; many HID and specialized incandescent lamps have base-socket arrangements that ensure the light center is positioned correctly in a directional luminaire.

There are important exceptions to lamp-base-socket matching. For instance, both T8 and T12 four-foot fluorescent lamps have medium bipin sockets, even though they require different ballast types. Because of this, it is important to avoid an electrical mismatch in a fixture with medium bi-pin bases.

BALLASTED AND SELF-BALLASTED LAMPS

Incandescent lamps generally operate at line voltages, but all other lamp types require ballasts to supply the proper electrical characteristics. Many types of compact fluorescent, and a few high-pressure sodium and mercury vapor lamps, are available in self-ballasted, screw-in versions. Some of these use kits, which consist of a separate screw-in ballast and lamp.

NOMENCLATURE

Lamp designations incorporate references to the shape and size of the lamp. The shape is described with one or more capital letters, for instance "G" stands for globe, "ER" stands for ellipsoidal reflector, and "T" stands for tubular. The size of the lamp is denoted as the diameter in $1/8$ inches. Thus, a G40 lamp has a globe shape and is $40/8$ (or 5) inches in diameter; a T12 lamp is tubular and $12/8$ (or $1 1/2$) inches in diameter.

Fluorescent lamp designations begin with "F." "FB" is used for U-bent lamps and "FO" for T8 (optic) fluorescents. The next number is either the nominal wattage, for preheat and rapid-start lamps, or the length, for slimline and HO lamps. Therefore, F40 is a fluorescent lamp of 40 watts, and F96 is a fluorescent lamp 96 inches long.

MERCURY CONTENT AND DISPOSAL

Almost all non-incandescent lamps contain small quantities of mercury, which becomes an environmental pollutant upon disposal. Nonetheless, using incandescents is actually worse for the environment, given the pollution generated by the power plants producing the much higher quantities of electricity consumed. Given the mix of power plants in the United States in the early 1990s, the net contribution of pollutants to the environment—from disposal and power production—is much less for fluorescent than for incandescent lamps. This is true for each pollutant.

Sgnificant strides have been taken in the 1990s to reduce the mercury content of lamps. In 1995 a mercury-free high-pressure sodium lamp and fluorescents with a very low mercury content were introduced.

Disposal of lamps containing mercury has been a subject of regulatory concern. This is not because a typical disposal causes significant pollution—spent fluorescent lamps, in particular, contain small quantities of mercury, which are quite stabilized at the end of the tube's life. However, regulations may require that spent lamps, especially in large quantities, be treated as hazardous waste.

Consult current state and federal regulations, and consider commercial services for proper disposal. Disposal services available include pickup, reclamation of the mercury, recycling of other lamp components, and proper disposal.

ENERGY POLICY ACT

The U.S. Energy Policy Act of 1992, public law 102-486 (EPAct), was signed into law on October 24, 1992. It outlines energy-efficient standards and other regulations that preclude the manufacture or importation of certain lamps in the United States after certain dates. To comply with the act, lamps must meet minimum efficacy and color rendering requirements. Lamps not intended for general service, such as traffic signal, decorative, and plant-growth lamps, are exempt from the act.

LAMPS AFFECTED BY THE U.S. ENERGY POLICY ACT OF 1992

COMPLIANCE DATE	LAMPS AFFECTED	STANDARDS TO BE DEVELOPED BY
April 1994	8 ft fluorescent	
October 1995	4 ft fluorescent	
October 1995	2 ft. U-bent fluorescent	
October 1995	PAR, R incandescent	
October 1999	High-intensity discharge	October 1996
October 2001	General service fluorescent and incandescent	October 1998
October 2005	General service fluorescent and reflector incandescent	October 2002

IMPACT OF ENERGY POLICY REPRESENTATIVE REPLACEMENT OPTIONS

LAMP TYPE MADE OBSOLETE (AS OF OCT. 1995)	BEST EFFICIENCY SYSTEM SOLUTION 36-73% ENERGY SAVINGS	GOOD EFFICIENCY SUBSTITUTION 12-60% ENERGY SAVINGS
LINEAR FLUORESCENT		
F40T12/CW	FO32T8/RE841	F40T12/RE741/34W
F40T12/WW	FO32T8/RE830	F40T12/RE730/34W
F40T12/D	FO32T8/RE850	F40T12/RE765/34W
FB40/6"/CW	FBO32T8/6"/RE841	FB40T12/RE741/6"/34W
F96T12/CW	FO96T8/RE841	F96T12/RE741/60W
F96T12/CW/HO	FO96T8/HO/RE841	F96T12/HO/RE741/95W
INCANDESCENT REFLECTOR		
75WR30/FL,SP	Triple 18W compact fluorescent in reflector fixture	50WPAR30/FL,SP/HCAP
75WPAR38/FL,SP		45WPAR38/FL,SP/HCAP
150WPAR38/FL	60WPAR38/FL/HCAP IR	90WPAR38/FL/HCAP
150WR40/FL	35W M/PAR30 metal halide fixture	

LAMPS BY FORM AND FUNCTION

Lamps illuminate by radiating light. The geometric form of this radiation and its interaction with surrounding surfaces determine how a space is illuminated. Light sources may be classified by their geometry: area, reflector, linear, and planar. The geometry of light distribution, or photometry, is usually determined, or at least modified, by the luminaire. "Distributed light" systems redirect the output of a lamp in a more radical manner, and source technology no longer limits the geometry of lamps.

AREA LIGHT SOURCES

Area light sources distribute light more or less symmetrical in all directions. A theoretical "point source" would illuminate the interior of a sphere equally at all points. The sun, in space, because of its distance, might be considered a point source, as might a candle. Typically in most modern spaces, light sources are not in the center, and illumination is not desired equally at all points.

The smaller the light source, the greater the brightness and, ability to achieve qualities such as brilliance and sparkle. The common A-19 incandescent is a fairly good approximation of a point source, as the size of its filament, and thus its light center, is fairly small. Incandescent halogen types have even smaller filaments and thus provide greater brightness for a given wattage. Most HID lamps are also area light sources; typically, their brightness is very high for the area they illuminate.

As the components have shrunk, compact fluorescents have come closer to matching the outside shape of an A19 incandescent lamp. Because light is diffused over the surface, compact fluorescents are not able to achieve qualities such as brilliance and sparkle; however, they are very efficient as area lighting sources.

REFLECTOR LIGHT SOURCES

Light distributed from reflector sources is directed and confined, more or less, within a cone. "Flood" and "spot" types are examples, but these terms may be obsolete considering the wide range of beams now available. Limiting light to directional distribution is performed by the lamp, by the luminaire, or by a combination of the two. Optical control is determined by the geometry and reflectivity of the reflector and interactions with the photometry of the light source itself.

Center beam candlepower (CBCP) is the maximum output in the center of the beam, measured in candelas. The size of the cone of light is most often designated as "beam spread," the conical angle at which light output is 50% of the CBCP. How evenly the light is distributed might also be described, as smooth, ringed, etc.

Optical control of a beam is better with smaller light sources. Since a halogen burner is the closest to a true point source, it is often used in reflector applications. Generally, the narrower the beam spread, the more advantageous a small source is. Halogen reflectors are thus more efficient than compact fluorescents for narrow beam spreads. Some HID types are also available in lamp shapes that serve as reflectors.

LINEAR LIGHT SOURCES

The most common linear light source is the straight-tube fluorescent, usually used in ceiling applications, which essentially demand a planar source. To translate the linear source into a planar one requires a combination of longitudinal reflectors behind and flat diffusers in front. Light output is fairly even radially along the length of the tube. Strategies to increase overall efficiency have taken advantage of customized-bend, high-reflectivity retrofit reflectors.

Incandescent lamps are also available in a few linear shapes, such as single-end 20W T-$6 1/2$ for exit signs and double-end 60W T8 for vanity fixtures. However, much more efficient alternatives are available for most such applications.

PLANAR LIGHT SOURCES

Fluorescent lights are available now in many planar shapes: the U-bent, the circline, the long compact fluorescent, the square, and the flat compact fluorescent.

DISTRIBUTED LIGHT

Recent developments in optical reflector and transmissive materials have made it possible to separate light sources physically from their applications. Fiber optics and light pipes have been used for displays, signs, and theatrical effects. Larger cables and more efficient couplings between source and cable provide opportunities for architectural lighting that is reasonably efficient. Lamps that provide efficient input for such systems include a specialized metal halide whose light is very narrowly focused.

Fred Davis, C.L.E.P.; Fred Davis Corp., Energy and Lighting; Medfield, Massachusetts

Fluorescent Lamps

GENERAL

Fluorescent technology offers among the highest efficacies of all lamps for high color quality white light and is three to five times more efficient than incandescent technology. Fluorescent lamps, as well as high-intensity discharge (HID) lamps, work on an electric-discharge principle and require a ballast. Light in a fluorescent lamp is produced when fluorescent powders are activated by ultraviolet energy generated by a mercury arc.

Fluorescent lamps are available in many types. Variations in phosphor chemistry, gas fill, size, and electrical input make possible many colors, efficiencies, sizes, and light outputs.

PHOSPHORS

Phosphors are the chemical powders that line the inside of a fluorescent tube. Their composition is responsible for the color, quality, and efficiency of light emanating from a fluorescent lamp. Among "white" sources, halophosphate phosphors such as cool white and warm white were the most popular types from the 1950s through the 1970s. In the 1980s trichromatic rare earth (RE) phosphors were developed, which offered greater efficiency and improved color rendering. These are now the predominant phosphors available in T10, T8, and compact fluorescent lamps; they are also available in most T12 sizes.

Trichromatic phosphors are available in two grades on the color rendering index (CRI) and a number of color temperatures. So-called "thin-coat" trichromatic phosphors have a CRI in the low to mid 70s; "thick-coat" phosphors have a CRI in the low 80s. By comparison, cool white halophosphate lamps had a CRI of 62. Both triphosphor series are available in a number of color temperatures, including warm–3000K, neutral–3500K, and cool–4100K. Very cool–5000K and 6500K–colors are available in some types.

Other, specialized phosphors are available in some straight-tube fluorescents, although these are usually much less efficient. Some high-CRI white lamps, with CRIs over 90, are available for applications that demand color matching; the lamps highest on the CRI are available at the highest Kelvin temperatures, up to 7500K. Colors, particularly red, blue, and gold, are used for special effects.

FLUORESCENT STRAIGHT TUBES

Fluorescent straight-tube lamps are the predominant lamp type in indoor commercial lighting. Because of their widespread use, much attention has been focused on developing a wide variety and more efficacious versions.

The T12 (1½-in. diameter) was the predominant shape for decades, and by far the most popular of these was the F40T12, rapid-start, 40W, cool white (CW) four-footer. As a requirement of the Energy Policy Act of 1992, manufacturers stopped making this lamp for U.S. use in October 1995.

"Energy-saver" lamps, with krypton added to the gas fill, are direct substitutes for most "standard" or full-wattage lamps. The light output in these lamps is reduced along with the reduction in power input. A 34W lamp is the energy-saver version of the standard 40W F40T12. It is intended for use in environments of 60°F or warmer.

TUBE DIAMETER

Among straight-tube fluorescents, tube diameter is an important determinant of efficacy: Generally, the narrower the tube, the higher the efficacy. In the 1980s lamps of smaller diameter and thus of higher efficacy were developed. Compared to the "standard" F40 CW, the T10 lamp provides increased light output and improved color, with a slight increase in electrical input. The thick-coat triphosphor T8 lamp provides the same light output, improved color, and a significant decrease in electrical input.

T8 lamps use 20% fewer watts than standard F40s and operate even more efficiently when used on electronic ballasts. In 1995 efficient indoor lighting design generally uses a combination of T8 series lamps with electronic ballasts.

The next straight-tube development is the T5 shape, introduced in Europe in 1995. These lamps, which use miniature bi-pin bases, offer further efficacy gains but are manufactured in lengths compatible with European building module dimensions of 600 mm and 1200 mm rather than the 2-ft and 4-ft dimensions standard in the United States. Therefore, T5 lamps need their own, dedicated luminaires.

STRAIGHT TUBE FLUORESCENT SHAPES AND TYPICAL NOMINAL LENGTHS

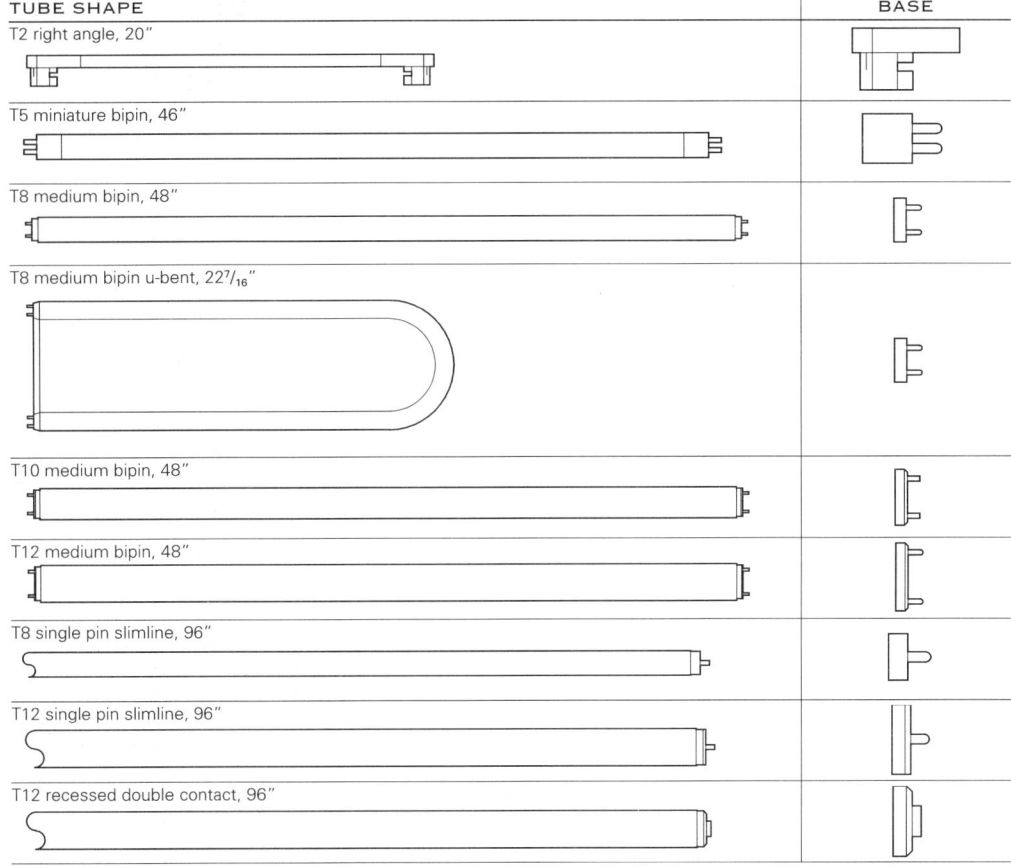

TUBE SHAPE	BASE
T2 right angle, 20"	
T5 miniature bipin, 46"	
T8 medium bipin, 48"	
T8 medium bipin u-bent, 22⁷⁄₁₆"	
T10 medium bipin, 48"	
T12 medium bipin, 48"	
T8 single pin slimline, 96"	
T12 single pin slimline, 96"	
T12 recessed double contact, 96"	

NOTE
Lamps are not to scale; nominal length is from back of socket to back of socket.

LENGTH AND SHAPE

Straight-tube fluorescents are available in a wide range of lengths, from 6 to 96 in. In general, the longer the tube, the higher the efficacy.

A number of variants of the straight-tube shape are available. The U-shaped lamp is essentially a straight-tube lamp bent in half. It comes with center-to-center leg-spacings of 1⁵⁄₈ in. (16, 24, 31W T8), 3⁵⁄₈ in. (35, 40W T12), or 6 in. (32W T8; 34, 40W T12). Circular fluorescents basically are straight tubes bent in a circle. They are available in outside diameters of 6½ in. (20W), 8¼ in. (22W), 12 in. (32W), and 16 in. (40W) T9 shapes. Straight tubes with outer glass jackets are designed for locations outdoors or in other sub-zero temperatures.

REPRESENTATIVE 4-FT AND 8-FT LAMPS AND LAMP/BALLAST COMBINATIONS

	NOMINAL LAMP RATINGS						ACTUAL LAMP/BALLAST COMBINATION			
WATTAGE	LENGTH (IN.)	SHAPE	PHOSPHOR TYPE	START MODE	INITIAL LUMENS	LAMP EFFICACY (LPW)	NUMBER OF LAMPS; BALLAST TYPE: ELECTRONIC/MAGNETIC	BALLAST FACTOR	SYSTEM WATTS	SYSTEM EFFICACY (LPW)
40*	48	T12	Cool White	Rapid	3,050	76	2-L M	0.94	88	65
32	48	T12	RE700	Rapid (Cathode cutout)	2,650	83	2-L M	0.87	67	69
34	48	T12	RE800	Rapid	2,850	84	2-L E	0.88	62	81
42	48	T10	RE800	Rapid	3,700	88	2-L E	0.85	74	85
32	48	T8	RE700	Instant	2,900	91	2-L E	0.95	65	87
32	48	T8	RE800	Instant	3,050	95	2-L E	0.95	63	92
32	48	T8	RE700	Instant	2,900	91	3-L E	0.91	87	91
32	48	T8	RE700	Instant	2,900	91	4-L E	0.89	111	93
75*	96	T12	Cool White	Instant (Slimline)	6,150	82	2-L M	0.94	158	73
59	96	T8	RE800	Instant	6,000	102	2-L E	0.85	105	97

* These lamps are no longer manufactured; shown as base-case reference only.

Fred Davis, C.L.E.P.; Fred Davis Corp., Energy and Lighting; Medfield, Massachusetts

Fluorescent Lamps

BALLASTS AND STARTING MODES

The ballast provides the proper electrical characteristics to start and operate a fluorescent lamp. The starting process occurs in two stages: First, a sufficient voltage between an electrode and ground ionizes the gas (mercury plus an inert gas) in the lamp. Next, a voltage must develop across the lamp sufficient to extend the ionization throughout the lamp and to develop an arc.

The three starting modes for ballasts for fluorescent lamps are preheat, instant-start, and rapid-start. Each ballast type is used only with compatible lamps. Electronic ballasts are available in both instant-start and rapid-start designs.

For the preheat mode, a separate starter button is often used to heat the electrodes before high voltage is applied across the lamp. The instant-start mode applies a high voltage (400 to 1000 V) across the lamp to ionize the gas and initiate arc discharge. This design provides the lowest energy consumption, sometimes at the expense of lamp life. In the rapid-start mode, electrodes (cathodes) are heated continuously by means of low voltage windings built into the ballast, allowing a gentle start. A variation cuts power to the cathodes after the arc is struck. Ballast factor is the percentage of a lamp's rated lumens produced when operated on a specific commercial ballast.

ELECTRONIC BALLASTS

Electronic ballasts improve the efficacy of lamps by driving them at high frequencies, above 15 kHz. Such ballasts eliminate flicker and are much lighter than electromagnetic ballasts. The improvement in efficacy made possible by electronic ballasts alone is approximately 10-12% for 4-ft lamps and 5% for 8-ft lamps, compared to operation at 60 Hz. Electronic ballasts are available that operate one, two, three, or four 4-ft T8 lamps at once.

Like magnetic ballasts, most electronic ballasts are designed so actual lumen output is as close to the rated lumens as possible. However, some electronic ballasts have been designed to deliberately provide higher than rated lumens (ballast factor > 1.0), while others have been designed for lower than rated lumens (ballast factor < 0.9). The ballast factor should be consulted carefully to ensure that the lighting design meets the desired light output.

FLUORESCENT FAMILIES

Fluorescent lamp families differ from each other in base type, starting characteristics, and "loading" (the amount of electrical energy applied per length of lamp). Generally, the most efficacious lamp family is the T8, and it should be used where appropriate. Applications requiring high output may call for multiple fluorescent lamps, efficient high-intensity discharge, or one of the higher loading families. For low light levels, any fluorescents are more efficacious than incandescent lamps.

Subminiature lamps use a T2 bulb with a "right-angle" base. They are available in 8-in. 6W, 12-in. 8W, and 20-in. 13W sizes.

Preheat fluorescent lamps utilize separate starters. These T5, T8, T12, and T17 lamps range in length from 6 to 60 in. The smallest of these uses a miniature bipin base. Lamp lifetime is 6000 to 7500 hours for T5s and T8s, 9000 for T12 and T17. These lamps are not commonly used in commercial general lighting.

The rapid-start T12 lamp, which operates at 430 mA with a medium bipin base, was formerly the mainstay of commercial lighting, even though it is available in only F30 36-in. and F40 48-in. sizes. The Energy Policy Act of 1992 eliminated inefficient halophosphate 4-ft full-wattage (40W) versions, leaving trichromatic phosphor types available for full wattage. Energy savers of all phosphors are available in 25W and 34W. 32W cathode-cutout 4-ft lamps cut electrical input to the cathode after starting, but they should not be used in situations with frequent on and off switching.

T8 lamps, operating at 265 mA, are the lamps of choice for energy-efficiency. They are available in 2-ft 17W, 3-ft 25W, 4-ft 32W, 5-ft 40W, and 8-ft 59W sizes. The 8-ft lamp has single-pin bases, for instant start only. The remainder have medium bipin bases and can operate on instant-start or rapid-start ballasts as long as they are specific to the T8 lamp. Rated life on instant-start ballasts is 15,000 hours, as opposed to 20,000 hours on rapid-start ballasts; however, in typical use, with 8- to 12-hr burn cycles on electronic ballasts, actual life difference is minimal.

Slimline lamps are single-pin based and range from 2 to 8 ft. They operate on instant-start ballasts. The F96 T12 lamp was the standard lamp in 8-ft luminaires.

High output lamps operate at 800 mA and produce approximately 45% more light than slimlines of the same length, although at lower efficacy. They have recessed double contact (RDC) bases and rated life ranges from 9000 to 12000 hours. Very high output lamps operate at 1500 mA and range as high as 215 watts.

COMPACT FLUORESCENTS

Compact fluorescents were developed in the early 20th century to put the efficiency of fluorescent technology into a package small enough to compete with incandescent lamps in some application niches. Technological improvements have provided several generations of ever smaller, brighter glass shapes.

These glass shapes are fitted to either plug-in pin bases, which need a separate ballast, or to screw-in bases with ballasts built in. Compact fluorescents are used in a variety of luminaires, including most types that were historically designed for incandescent. For best efficiency, fixtures should be designed around the photometrics particular to the compact fluorescent.

Lamps with plug-in pin bases are dedicated for a ballast type. Two-pin lamps are preheat types that contain a glow starter in the lamp base, whereas four-pin lamps work with electronic ballasts that incorporate the starting function. As with straight-tubes, when compared to magnetic ballasts, electronic ballasts for compact fluorescents are lighter and more efficacious and eliminate flicker. Base-down operation of some compact fluorescents yields fewer than rated lumens; others have amalgam chemistry that offsets this phenomenon. Optimum output is close to horizontal.

REPRESENTATIVE COMPACT FLUORESCENT CHARACTERISTICS

LAMP	WATTS*	INITIAL LUMENS	MAX. OVERALL LENGTH (IN.)
Tube integral screw-in	18	1100	7.19
Twin lamp alone	13	900	7.50
Quad modular side-mount	22	1200	7.75
Triple integral screw-In	15	900	4.94
Triple integral screw-in	25	1750	6.20
Triple lamp alone	32	2200	5.80
Circline lamp alone	22	1100	8.25 O.D.
Flat lamp alone	36	2800	8.50
Reflector modular screw-in	13	860	6.38
Long CFL lamp alone	18	1250	8.94
Long CFL lamp alone	40	1550	6.95

* Watts exclude ballasts, except for integral units, which use electronic ballasts. All lamps listed have thick-coat trichromatic phosphors.

REPRESENTATIVE COMPACT FLUORESCENT SHAPES

GLASS SHAPES	PLUG-IN VERSION (FOR BALLASTED FIXTURE)			SCREW-IN VERSION (FOR USE IN MEDIUM SOCKET)	
	LAMP ALONE	BASE 2-PIN	BASE 4-PIN	MODULAR ASSEMBLY (LAMP AND BALLAST)	INTEGRAL (ONE-PIECE)
Globe, tube	—	—	—	●	●
Twin	●	●	●	●	—
Quad	●	●	●	●	●
Triple	●	●	●	●	●
Octic	—	—	—	—	●
Helical	●	—	—	—	●
Circline	●	—	●	●	—
2-D	●	●	—	●	—
Flat	●	—	●	—	—
Reflector	—	—	—	●	●
Long CFL	●	●	—	—	—

Fred Davis, C.L.E.P.; Fred Davis Corp., Energy and Lighting; Medfield, Massachusetts

Incandescent Lamps

GENERAL

Incandescent lamps are the least efficient electric lighting sources, converting only 7–12% of electrical input to visible light. They operate on the principle of electric resistance: As electric current flows through a filament, resistance causes it to heat to a temperature high enough to glow, or incandesce.

Despite the many efficient alternatives to incandescents, they remain popular in certain applications because they can be dimmed easily and inexpensively and because they sparkle the most brilliantly. Incandescents have traditionally worked best for low-lumen applications, but LED and electroluminescent technologies now offer low-wattage alternatives. Switching on instantly and interchangeability among a variety of wattages are other advantages of incandescents. Most important, the small filament size of halogen reflector lamps makes them the most efficient type in narrow-beam applications.

The low initial price of incandescent lamps and luminaires can be misleading because their operating costs are relatively high: Such costs include not only electricity, but also the cost of replacing lamps. Another factor to consider is lamp life: As a rule, light output decreases over time. Therefore, if a lower lumen level is acceptable, a lower wattage lamp should be considered.

INCANDESCENT TECHNOLOGY IMPROVEMENTS

Incandescent technology has improved over the years, but the efficacy of the most efficient incandescents—more than 30 lumens per watt for infrared reflecting halogen—is still far lower than that of the least efficient fluorescents.

Early improvements in incandescent technology included the coiled-coil filament and the use of inert gases as fill material in the lamp. For greater efficacy still, krypton gas is used: It is less conductive than the standard argon-nitrogen mixture but more expensive.

Tungsten-halogen lamps use a halogen regenerative cycle to keep the filament from evaporating. A halogen additive in the fill gas, usually iodine or bromine, reacts chemically with tungsten molecules that have evaporated off the filament. The tungsten is then redeposited onto the filament instead of on the bulb wall. The lamp operates at an extremely high temperature, which necessitates that a special glass envelope, usually quartz, surround the filament.

The high temperature of tungsten-halogen lamps also gives them greater efficacy than standard incandescents—their color temperature is 200 to 300° K higher. The small, vertical filaments in tungsten-halogen lamps allow for very efficient reflectors. As a result, some low-wattage halogen reflectors are more energy-efficient than some compact fluorescent types for relatively narrow-beam applications.

A further improvement in halogen lamps involves infrared-reflective (IR) film. A very thin dichroic coating applied to the halogen lamp or capsule reflects infrared (heat) energy back onto the filament, allowing visible light to pass through. The hotter filament increases lumen output, thus improving efficacy.

Lamps whose outside bulb walls are made of quartz require special handling, as oils from bare hands can damage them. Many manufacturers now enclose the halogen capsule in an outer glass envelope, eliminating this problem.

AREA SOURCES

General service area lamps range from a 15-watt A15 to a 1500-watt PS52. They are designed for 120/, 125/, and 130/volt circuits. Besides the most popular A, or arbitrary, shape, other shapes include PS, or pear straight. Halogen capsule versions of A-type shapes provide slightly better efficacy than standard incandescents.

Decorative shapes include FL (flame), B (bulbular), and G (globe). These are usually less efficient than standard incandescents, and efficient design will use low-wattage versions if necessary. The T (tubular shape) has been used in exit signs and for illuminating mirrors and pictures, which can also use linear and compact fluorescents if color is appropriate.

Tungsten halogen lamps are also available in noncapsule versions. Single-ended T3 and T4 tungsten halogen lamps range from 75 to 1500 watts, with the mini-candelabra screw base being the most common base. Double-ended tungsten halogens are linear shapes ranging up to 1500 watts. Small, low-voltage halogen type lamps are often used in reflectorized luminaires; usually under 2 in. in length, they use bipin bases, and range from 5 to 150 watts. IR versions of some linear halogen wattages provide substantial energy savings.

REFLECTOR SOURCES

The most popular flood and spot lamps were R (reflector) shapes, both R30 and R40 sizes. Flood R30 lamps had a beam spread of 130 degrees and much of the light in the outer part of the beam was often trapped in luminaires, especially recessed luminaires. Most are no longer manufactured. The newer ER (ellipsoidal reflector) and BR (bulged reflector) shapes maintain more lumens in the center of the beam than the R design.

PAR (parabolic reflector) lamps use a hard glass outside lens and are available in both "spot" (smooth glass len)/ and "flood" (stippled lens) versions. Halogen versions range from 35 to 120 watts, in PAR16, 20, 30, and 38 shapes, all of which use a medium screw socket. Beam spread ranges from 8 to 50 degrees. Other designations such as FL (flood), SP (spot), V (very), N (narrow), and W (wide) may not be standardized, and rated beam spreads should be verified. Halogen infrared technology is available in some PAR38 versions and affords the highest efficacy among incandescent reflectors.

Small, low-voltage halogen reflector lamps, usually 12 volts, are used in luminaires with transformers for the purpose. MR11 and MR16 shapes, originally used in slide projectors, became popular in display and other accent lighting applications. Wattages range from 20 to 75. Like line-voltage halogen PARs, MRs come in a very wide range of beam spreads.

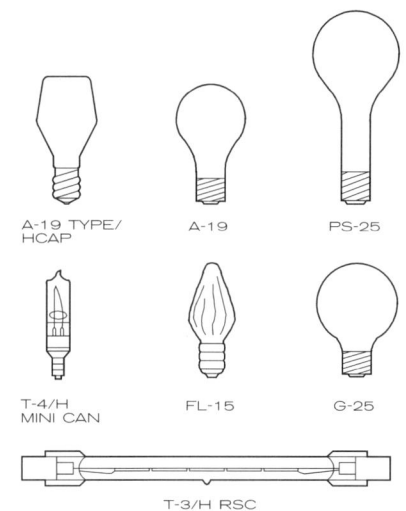

AREA SOURCES

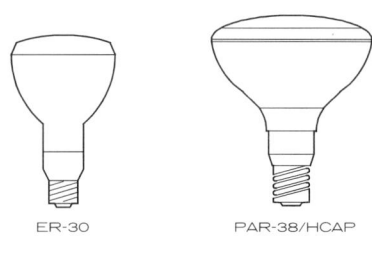

REFLECTOR SOURCES

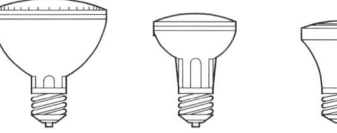

BASES

REPRESENTATIVE INCANDESCENT SHAPES

REFLECTOR INCANDESCENT LAMPS REPRESENTATIVE LAMP RATINGS

SHAPE/BEAM/ HALOGEN	WATTS	CENTER BEAM CANDLE POWER	BEAM SPREAD TO 50% OF MAX.	HOURS LIFE	MAXIMUM OVERALL LENGTH (IN.)
MR16/NSP/H 12V	20	5000	8	2000	1.75
PAR20/ NFL/HCAP	35	900	30	2500	3.25
PAR38/SP/HCAP	45	5500	12	2500	5.31
PAR20/NFL/HCAP	50	1250	30	2500	3.25
PAR30/WFL/HCAP (long-neck)	50	500	50	2500	4.69
PAR38/FL/HCAP IR	60	3650	30	3000	5.31
R30/FL*	75	470	130	2000	5.38
ER30	75	1500	36	2000	6.38
PAR30/FL/HCAP	75	2000	40	2500	3.63
PAR38/FL/HCAP	90	3750	30	2500	5.31
R40/FL*	100	900	120	2000	6.50
PAR38/FL*	150	4000	30	2000	5.31

* These lamps no longer manufactured, shown as reference.

NOTE

All with medium base except MR.

AREA INCANDESCENT LAMPS REPRESENTATIVE LAMP RATINGS

SHAPE/HALOGEN/BASE	WATTS	INITIAL LUMENS	HOURS LIFE	MAXIMUM OVERALL LENGTH (IN.)
A15/medium	15	115	2500	3.50
G25/medium	40	410	1500	4.50
A19 type/HCAP/med.	52	770	3500	4.38
A19/medium	60	860	1000	4.44
A-19/medium	75	1180	750	4.44
A21/medium	100	1690	750	5.25
PS25/medium	150	2650	750	6.94
T4/H/mini-can	150	2800	2000	3.00
T4/H/mini-can	250	5000	2000	3.16
T3 linear/HIR/RSC	350	10,000	2000	4.69
T3 linear/H/RSC	500	11,100	2000	4.69
PS40/mogul	500	9100	1000	9.75

H=halogen; CAP=capsule; IR=infrared reflective film

Fred Davis, C.L.E.P.; Fred Davis Corp., Energy and Lighting; Medfield, Massachusetts

HID and Miscellaneous Lamps

HIGH-INTENSITY DISCHARGE

High-intensity discharge (HID) lamps are the most common electric lights other than incandescent and fluorescent. In rough order of increasing efficacy, the categories of HID lamps include mercury vapor, metal halide, high-pressure sodium, and low-pressure sodium. The highest efficacies among them, however, have the poorest color qualities.

Like fluorescents, HID lamps use a ballast to provide proper starting and operating voltages. Light is produced by an electric arc discharging through a mixture of gases. Unlike fluorescents, HID lamps use a fairly compact arc tube that operates under very high temperature and pressure. The small point source makes HID lamps and luminaires compact and powerful. Most are particularly suited to outdoor applications or large rooms with high ceilings, as long as frequent switching is not needed. Clear lamps offer best optical control; coated lamps offer more diffuse light.

Unlike incandescents and fluorescents, HID lamps require a warmup period to reach full light output. After power is applied, temperature and pressure in the mixture of gases and metals gradually builds, forcing vapors into the arc and releasing light. Depending on lamp type, warmup, ranges from 2 to 15 minutes. If power is extinguished, HID lamps must cool before the arc can restrike. Restrike time lasts from 1 to 15 minutes, depending on lamp type. A few "instant restrike" types are available.

Over time, HID lamps may shift in color and the lumen output of some may drop substantially. For these, lamp change-outs should be planned well before the end of rated life. Rating the life of HID lamps is based on 10-hour cycles, as opposed to the three hours for rating incandescents and fluorescents. As with fluorescents, strobe effects with moving machinery should be avoided. HID lamps may have medium, mogul, or numerous other base types. A very few specialized types may be interchanged with metal halide, high-pressure sodium, and mercury vapor lamps.

METAL HALIDE

Originally developed in 1965, metal halide technology has continually improved. Today, its high efficacy and good color qualities make metal halide the best choice for many indoor and outdoor applications.

Common metal halide lamps have a color temperature of around 3500–4300K, and a CRI of 65–70. In addition, there are warm color lamps, 2700–3200K. In the early 1990s, some metal halide lamps were developed with very high CRIs, up to 93. Wattages range from 32 to 1500 watts, with a large variety of lamp and base configurations.

Metal halide lamps contain various metal halides and mercury. When the halide vapor approaches the high temperature in the central core of the arc, it disassociates into the halogen and the metal, with the metals radiating the appropriate spectra. Most metal halide lamps must be used in luminaires made to withstand an explosive rupture of the arc tube. Many should be used in luminaires that include a device to automatically turn the lamp off if the fixture is opened or broken. Most lamps should be turned off for a minimum of 15 minutes at least once per week.

Varieties of metal halide lamps include universal position burning, lamps optimized for burning in specific positions, cool or warm color temperatures in clear or phosphor coatings, safety lamps that extinguish if the outer envelope breaks, lamps with internal shielding that can withstand a rupture of the arc tube for use in open luminaires, and compact lamps that produce a high CRI in a small arc tube.

Electronic ballasts available for some metal halide types offer lighter weight, increased efficacy of 4–10%, less flicker, improved color and lumen maintenance, and increased life. Metal halide lamps with ceramic arc tubes have recently been introduced. These provide improved color control, more than 80 CRI, and higher efficacy.

HIGH-PRESSURE SODIUM

High-pressure sodium (HPS) lamps are highly efficacious, ranging from 65 to 125 lumens per watt (including ballast losses). They have a gold-pink color, 1900–2100K. CRI is poor, under 25. They are used where color rendering is not critical—in street, security, and industrial lighting.

Using xenon gas as an aid in starting, HPS lamps produce light by electric current passing through vaporized sodium. HPS lamps do not need enclosure (except from precipitation), and are fairly insensitive to operating position. So-called "deluxe" HPS have a CRI of 65. "White" HPS lamps of 2500–2800K have a CRI over 75. These improvements in color quality come at the cost of efficacy.

ALL LAMPS—COMPARISON OF GENERAL CHARACTERISTICS

LAMP TYPE	LAMP LUMENS PER WATT	HOURS LIFE	COLOR RENDITION	RELIGHT TIME
Incandescent	10 – 30	750 – 4000	Excellent	Immediate
Fluorescent	55 – 100	7500 – 24000	Good to excellent	Immediate
Metal halide	80 – 125	3000 – 20000	Good to excellent	10–15 min.
High-pressure sodium	65 – 140	16000 – 24000	Fair	Less than 1 minute
Low-pressure sodium	up to 180	18,000	Nonexistent	0–5 minutes
Mercury vapor	30 – 63	16000 – 24000	Fair to good	3–5 minutes

HID LAMPS—REPRESENTATIVE LAMP RATINGS

HID/SHAPE/BASE*	WATTS	INITIAL LUMENS	HOURS LIFE	CRI	MAX. OVERALL LENGTH (IN.)
M / ED-17 / medium	70	5,200	15000	65	5.44
M / ED-17 / medium	70	6,200	10000	85	5.44
M / T-6 1/2 / RSC	70	5,000	10000	85	—
M / ED-17 / medium	100	8,500	15000	65	5.44
M / ED-17 / medium	100	9,200	10000	85	5.44
M / ED-17 / medium	150	10,800	15000	65	5.44
M / BT-28 / mogul	175	11,600	15000	65	5.44
M / BT-28 / mogul	250	22,000	10000	65	8.31
M / BT-37 / mogul	400	36,000	12000	65	8.31
M / BT-37 / mogul	1000	110,000	12000	65	11.50
S / ED-17 / medium	70	6,300	24000	21	5.44
S / ED-17 / medium	100	9,500	24000	21	5.44
S / ET-23 1/2 / mogul	150	16,000	24000	21	5.44
S / ET-18 / mogul	250	24,000	24000	21	9.75
S / ET-18 / mogul	400	50,000	24000	21	11.50
S / E-25 / mogul	1000	140,000	24000	21	15.06
L / T-17 / BY22d	35	4,800	18000	NA	12.19
L / T-21 / BY22d	90	13,500	18000	NA	20.75
H / A-23 / medium	100	4,300	24000	45	5.44
H / ED-28 / mogul	250	12,100	24000	45	8.31

*M = metal halides; S = high-pressure sodium; L = low pressure sodium; H = mercury.

LOW-PRESSURE SODIUM

Low-pressure sodium (LPS) lamps were first introduced in 1932 and have the highest efficacy of any light source available. However, the most important characteristic of LPS lamps is that they are monochromatic. The starting gas is neon, which emits a reddish glow as the lamp heats up. At full output, light from LPS is monochromatic yellow, and there is no color rendering ability. LPS comes in tubular lamps, from 18 to 180 watts, and is used for security and some roadway lighting.

MERCURY VAPOR

Developed in the early 1900s, mercury vapor is the least efficient of the HID sources. The technology involves excitation of mercury in a vaporized state. It is available in clear or phosphor coatings. The phosphors work much as they do with fluorescents, to convert ultraviolet to visible light and to improve color rendering. Because efficacy and color quality is so much better, metal halide is preferred over mercury vapor in most situations.

OTHER LAMP TYPES

Electrodeless lamps first appeared commercially in the 1990s. These are sources excited by electromagnetic energy passing through the glass lamp without using an electrode. Coupling energy into a lamp at high frequencies forms plasma conditions that allow long life and fairly high efficacies. However, these high-frequency and microwave-powered sources must contain radiation within the lamp. The first products range from 23 to 85 watts, with efficacies from 48 to 70. Prototypes of a high-wattage sulfur lamp have shown the potential for high efficacy.

Other efficient lamp types are used in applications requiring low lumen levels, such as in exit signs. Energy consumption in exit signs is important because they are on continuously. Very low wattages allow an exit sign to use under 2 watts, compared to 20–50 watts with incandescent lamps.

Small light-emitting diodes (LEDs) are p-n junction semiconductor lamps. First used as indicator lights, they are now available in exit sign strips. Electroluminescent lamps are thin, flat area sources in which light is produced by a phosphor excited by a pulsating electric field. Typically, green panels are used in LED exit signs. Radioactive tritium tubes are self-contained sources requiring no power supply.

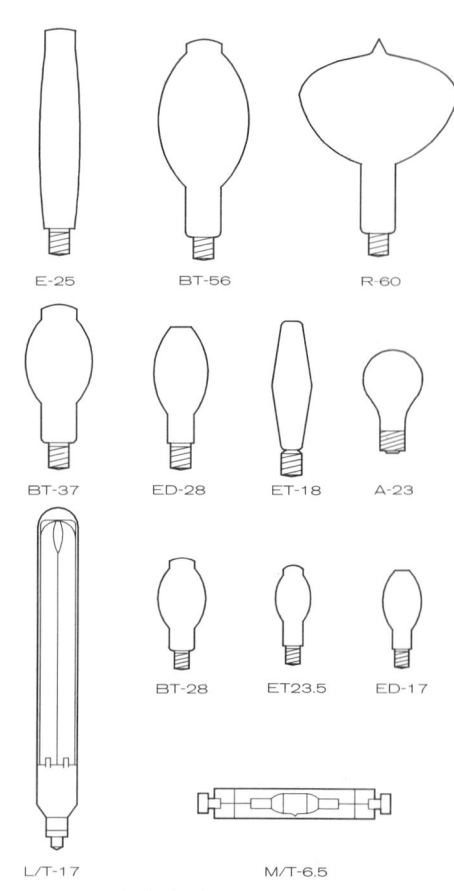

REPRESENTATIVE HID SHAPES

Fred Davis, C.L.E.P.; Fred Davis Corp., Energy and Lighting; Medfield, Massachusetts

Uninterruptible Power Supply Systems

GENERAL

UPS (uninterruptible power supply) is designed to provide continuous power with specific electrical characteristics by conditioning utility company power, battery power, or generator-supplied power.

Uninterruptible power supply (UPS) systems closely control the power supply voltage and frequency to critical equipment such as computers, communications systems, and medical instrumentation.

UPS systems are either on line, with power routing through them continuously, or off line, with power routed through them only when the incoming power is interrupted or departs from the design characteristics. The time required for an off-line, solid-state UPS to automatically switch on varies with the type of switch selected: The quicker the switch, the more expensive the switching equipment in general. The time needs to be matched to the tolerances of the critical equipment being supplied by the UPS to prevent loss of data or other problems.

Battery backup time is selected to allow a controlled shutdown of equipment or to allow a backup generator to be started and stabilize at full power.

Redundant UPS systems may be required if UPS power loss cannot be tolerated for system maintenance or equipment breakdown.

Some equipment can produce electrical disturbances that are fed back into the electrical circuit. This must be prevented through filtering in order to maintain clean power to the other equipment being supplied by the UPS.

The UPS unit and battery should be placed close together. Some UPS cabinets contain sealed batteries; others require separate batteries.

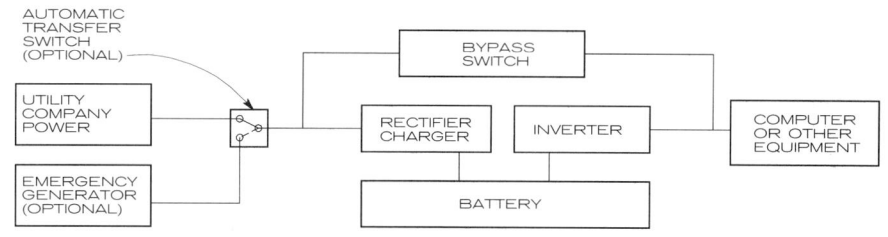

TYPICAL UNINTERUPTIBLE POWER SUPPLY SYSTEM DIAGRAM

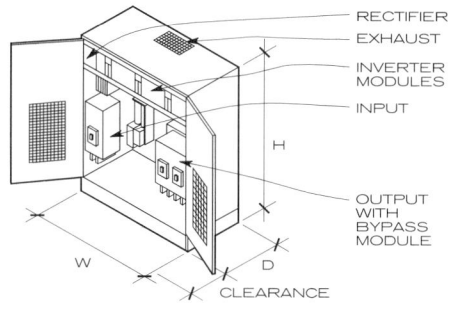

SOLID-STATE UPS

SOLID-STATE UPS SIZES

KVA	W (IN.)	D (IN.)	H (IN.)	WEIGHT (LB)
25	28	32	70	1400
50	72	36	72	4000
125	72	36	72	5600
200	72	36	72	6000
350	168	32	76	12,700
500	168	40	76	14,600

NOTE

Sound level approximately 65–70 dB. Heat rejection approximately 450–700 Btu/hr/kVA at 50 kVA to 250 Btu/hr/kVA at 500 kVA. Maintain room temperature at 70–80°F. Some units require clearance for access.

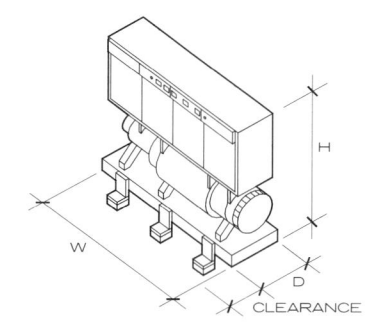

ROTARY UPS

ROTARY UPS SIZES

KVA	W (IN.)	D (IN.)	H (IN.)	WEIGHT (LB)
25	80	24	62	2600
50	80	24	62	3400
125	125	32	74	7000
250	140	32	80	10,000
500	164	60	84	15,000
1000	173	64	98	32,200

NOTE

Sound level approximately 60 to 80 dB. Heat rejection approximately 400 Btu/hr/kVA at 50 kVA to 250 Btu/hr/kVA at 500 kVA. Maintain room temperature at 70–80°F. Some units require front and rear clearance for access.

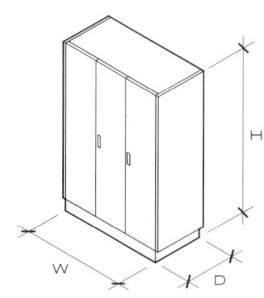

BATTERY CABINET

BATTERY CABINET SIZES

KVA	TIME (MIN)	W (IN.)	D (IN.)	H (IN.)	WGT. (LB)	NUMBER REQUIRED
75	15	40	32	76	2300	2
100	15	40	32	76	2300	3
200	15	48	32	76	2300	4
400	10	40	32	76	2300	8
500	7.5	40	32	76	2300	4

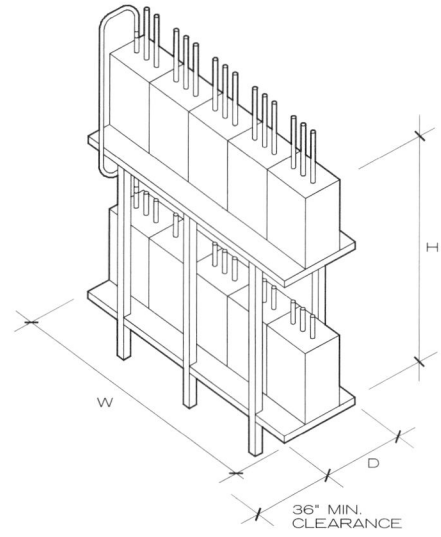

BATTERY RACKS

TWO-TIER RACK SIZES

KVA	TIME (MIN.)	W (IN.)	D (IN.)	H (IN.)	WGT. (LB)	NUMBER REQUIRED
15	30	96	16	54	3100	2
100	15	168	18	52	1000	4
250	15	108	18	52	20,500	6
500	15	156	18	52	34,600	6

THREE-TIER RACK SIZES

KVA	TIME (MIN.)	W (IN.)	D (IN.)	H (IN.)	WGT. (LB)	NUMBER REQUIRED
25	15	108	18	79	4300	1
50	15	108	18	79	5000	1
100	15	108	18	79	10,000	2
250	15	144	18	79	20,500	3
500	15	108	18	79	34,600	6

NOTE

Racks can be placed back to back. Provide shower and eyewash station and ventilation, and maintain approximately 77°F room temperature. Place battery racks close to UPS units. Providing seismic bracing required by code.

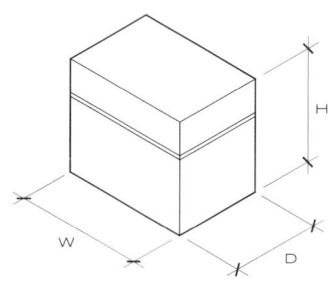

UPS UNDER 10 KVA

UPS UNDER 10 KVA SIZES

WATTS	W (IN.)	D (IN.)	H (IN.)	TIME (MIN.)
200	8	15	6	15–20
800	22	16	9	15–20
1500	22	16	18	15–20
KVA				
3.0	26	19	52	10
5.0	36	19	52	10
10.0	36	19	52	10

NOTE

A wide variety of UPS systems is available for smaller applications, ranging from desktop models for single microcomputers to floor models that can supply several computers or other equipment.

Charles B. Towles, P.E.: TEI Consulting Engineers; Washington, D.C.

184 Standby Engine Generators and Battery Systems

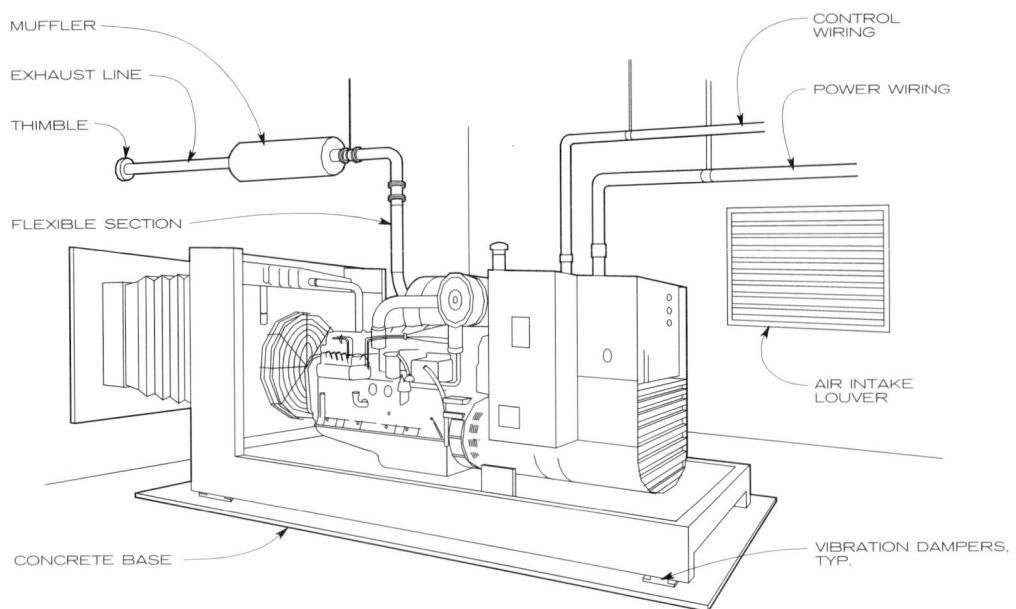

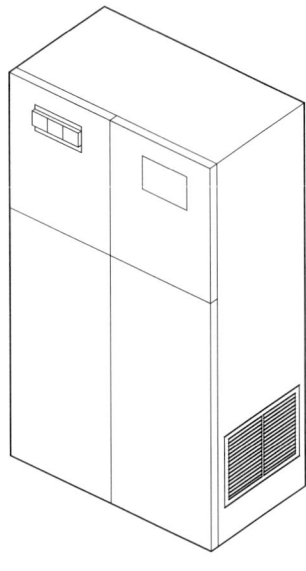

NOTE

Standby generators provide emergency power during power outages, when life safety lighting and/or critical equipment power requirements are beyond the capacity of battery units or when required by code (as in hospitals or high-rise buildings). Engines should be located away from main electrical switchgear. Engine rooms must have adequate ventilation for engine- and generator-radiated heat and must be protected against extreme environments under all conditions of airflow.

There must be enough room around a power generating unit to service it and to remove the unit. Standby generators require frequent inspections, tests under load conditions, and maintenance. Provisions must be made to prevent vibration transmission to nearby occupied areas. In addition to the cooling methods illustrated, cooling by remote radiator, heat exchanger, submerged pipe, cooling tower, and evaporative cooler should be considered. See National Electric Code for working space requirements and proper application.

NOTE

Battery-powered lighting equipment provides the minimal emergency illumination required for personnel safety and evacuation in buildings not requiring standby generator power. It is also used in buildings requiring standby generator power for the central control, telephone switchboard, generator, and electrical switchgear rooms to provide lighting for critical operations and troubleshooting if the generator fails to start. The batteries, which require frequent inspection, tests, and maintenance, are available in lead calcium, nickel cadmium, and wet lead acid.

EMERGENCY ENGINE GENERATOR WITH CONTROL PANEL

EMERGENCY LIGHTING BATTERY SYSTEMS

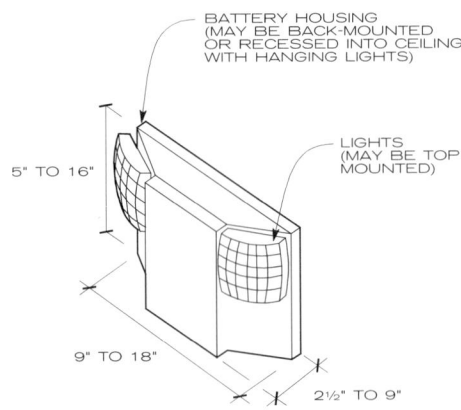

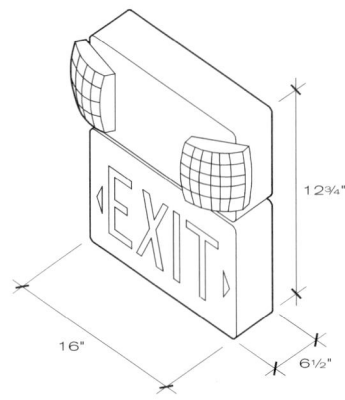

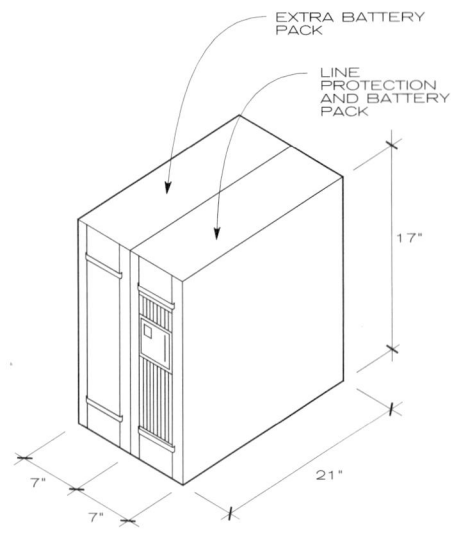

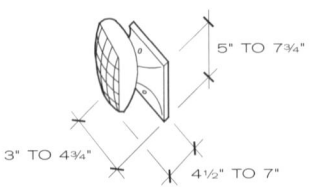

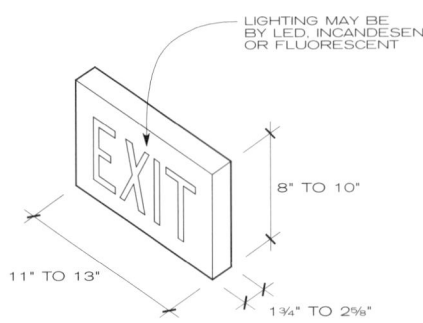

NOTE

Used to light exit passageways during power outages. Typically powered by lead calcium or nickel cadmium batteries.

WITH EMERGENCY LIGHTING

REMOTE FIXTURE

NOTE

Used with an emergency lighting battery system, this remote fixture may have one or two heads.

EXIT AND EMERGENCY LIGHTING

NOTE

Available in solid acrylic, cast aluminum with acrylic letters, steel, or polycarbonate housing, these signs may be side-, top-, or back-mounted or recessed. They can be powered by standard AC or battery pack.

EXIT SIGNS

NOTE

This unit protects network data and telecommunications equipment and eliminates a wide range of potential power problems: spikes, surges and extended overvoltage conditions, noise, sags, extended brownouts, and harmonics and frequency variations common with standby generator operation. Power rating ranges from 1000 to 3000 V.

DATA AND TELECOMMUNICATIONS PROTECTION

Charles B. Towles, P.E.; TEI Consulting Engineers; Washington, D.C.

LIGHTING

Lightning Protection

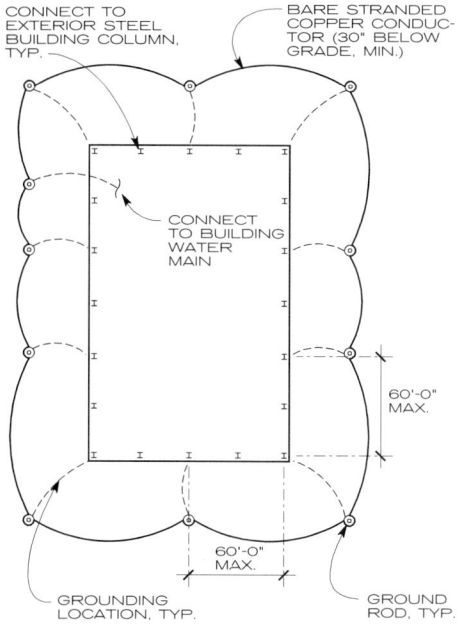

NOTE

All buildings and equipment should be grounded to protect people and equipment from fault currents. A complete interconnected system should be installed according to the requirements of the National Electrical Code and the National Electrical Safety Code. The structural steel of the building is connected to a buried "ground grid" to provide this requirement. All electrical equipment is connected with this system to provide a direct path to earth. Specify the number of ground rods and conductor size according to National Electrical Code requirements.

BUILDING GROUND GRID

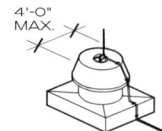

SMALL EQUIPMENT

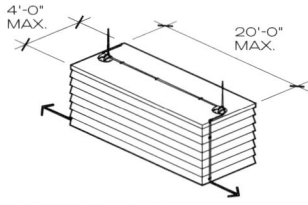

MEDIUM EQUIPMENT

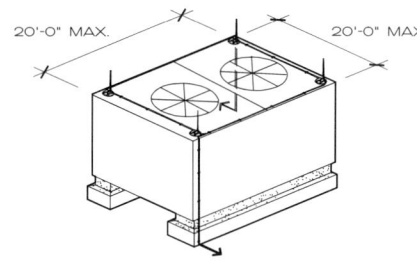

LARGE EQUIPMENT

NOTE

Codes vary slightly regarding bonding requirements for metal bodies on rooftops. Generally, if a metal body is in a zone of protection (lower than adjacent air terminals) and within 6 ft of a calculated bonding distance, it should be bonded to the lightning protection system. Smaller, secondary size materials may be used for these connections. Metal bodies taller than the air terminals and less than $3/16$ in. thick require air terminal protection. Those greater than $3/16$ in. thick are protected if adequately bonded.

ROOFTOP EQUIPMENT BONDING AND PROTECTION

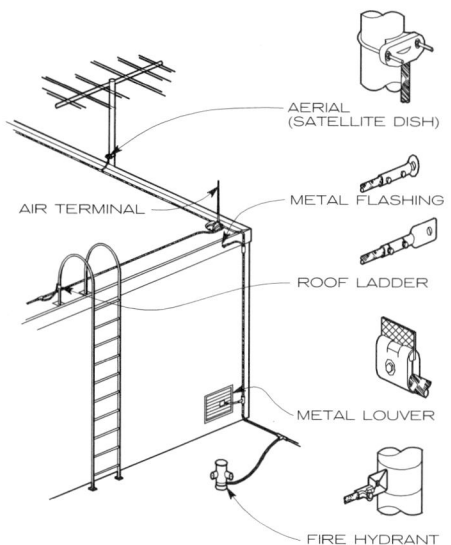

FASTENER TYPES

MISCELLANEOUS ROOFTOP EQUIPMENT

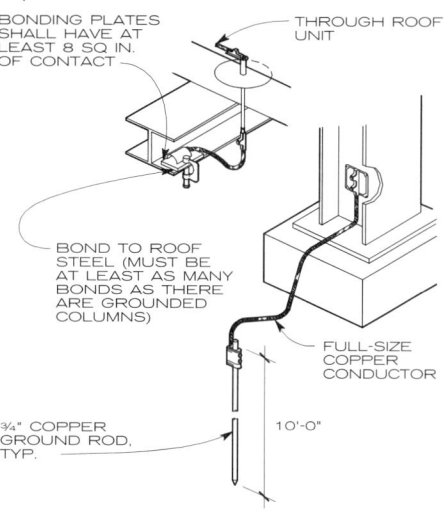

NOTE

In some cases, especially on tall structures, it may be advantageous to substitute the steel frame of a structure for portions of the usual conductor system, normally the downleads. Connections are made to cleaned areas of the building steel, at grade and at roof level, and the columns serve to connect the roof and ground systems.

STEEL FRAME AS CONDUCTOR

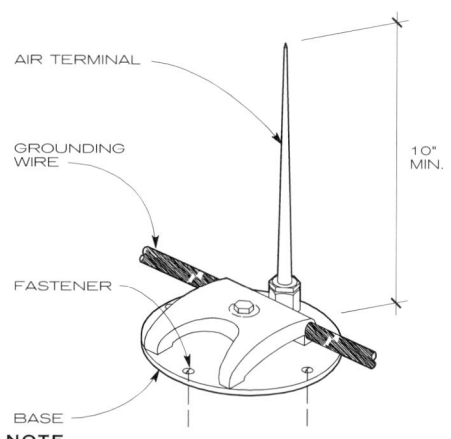

NOTE

Adhesives are typically used for flat roof installation.

TOP-MOUNTED AIR TERMINAL (LIGHTNING ROD) DETAIL

Douglas J. Franklin; Thompson Lightning Protection, Inc.; St. Paul, Minnesota

GENERAL

A lightning protection system is an integrated arrangement of air terminals, bonding connections, arresters, splicers, and other fittings installed on a structure in order to safely conduct to ground any lightning discharge to the structure.

Lightning protection systems and components are grouped into three categories (U.L. classes) based on building height and intended applications. Class I equipment and systems are for ordinary buildings under 75 ft in height, Class II is for those over 75 ft in height, and Class II Modified is a special group covering only large, heavy-duty stacks and chimneys similar to those used at power plants. Each of these system types comprises five or six major groups of components:

1. Air terminals (lightning rods) located on the roof and building projections.
2. Main conductors that tie the air terminals together and connect them with the grounding systems.
3. Bonds to metal roof structures and equipment.
4. Arresters to prevent power line surge damage.
5. Ground terminals, typically rods or plates driven or buried in the earth.
6. Tree protection (usually applicable only to residential work).

Each of these types of equipment and the methods for their installation is covered in the accompanying drawings.

Beyond these material requirements, other factors to be considered relative to lightning protection systems include selection of codes for compliance, inspection criteria (again based on code), criteria to evaluate competence of installing personnel, and requirements for annual inspection and maintenance.

OVERALL SYSTEMS DESIGN NOTES

1. Air terminals should be located around the perimeter of flat roof buildings and along the ridge of pitched roof buildings spaced at 20 ft on center maximum and located not more than 2 ft from ridge ends, outside corners, and edges of building walls.
2. Full-size main conductors should connect all air terminals.
3. Additional air terminals should be located in the center of large open flat spacings not to exceed 50 ft.
4. Cable runs connecting these center roof air terminals should be no longer than 150 ft without a lead back to the perimeter cable.
5. Gently sloping roofs are classed as flat under the rules shown above.
6. Download cables to ground should be connected to the roof perimeter cable at a maximum spacing of 100 ft on center. Buildings with a perimeter of 250 to 300 ft should have three downleads. For each additional 100 ft or fraction thereof add one download.
7. No building or structure should have fewer than two downloads.
8. Arresters should be installed on the electric and telephone services and on all radio and television lead-ins to a structure. Responsibility and jurisdiction for the installation of these devices can vary with locality, so special consideration may have to be given to these items.
9. Trees adjacent to residences pose a special hazard. It is recommended that all trees larger than an adjacent structure and within 10 ft of it be fully protected. Consult codes or manufacturer for recommendations on materials and installation requirements.
10. On-site inspections and certification of completed systems, installer competency certification, and guaranteed inspection/maintenance options are all available under existing standards. Consult codes and standards for specifics.

REFERENCES

The following codes, technical sources, and quality control procedures are standards for lightning protection systems.

Lightning Protection Institute, "Installation Code LPI–175."

National Fire Protection Association, "Lightning Protection Code NFPA 780."

Underwriters Laboratories, master labeled program under "U.L. Installation Requirements 96A."

Justice Facilities

TYPES OF COURTS

There are many different types of courts in the United States, each with its own characteristics and requirements. Federal courts have several levels of jurisdiction, beginning with the magistrate courts and the U.S. district courts. Courts of appeals hear appeals from the district courts, and the U.S. Supreme Court—the court of last resort—hears appeals from the appeals courts. Tax and bankruptcy courts are also part of the federal judiciary.

Each state has its own judicial system. Some states have special jurisdiction courts, such as juvenile or traffic courts. A good source for information on each state's court system is the National Center for State Courts.

Limited jurisdiction courts can be part of a state system or of a smaller municipal entity. They hear only such matters as misdemeanors and traffic offenses. General jurisdiction courts have trial jurisdiction over all matters and may have some authority to renew appeals from limited jurisdiction courts.

SYMBOLISM AND IMAGE

Historically, the American courthouse has been characterized by its size, siting, and specific architectural elements such as columns, domes, clock towers, and grand entrances. The architectural elements of a courthouse should reflect the dignity of the judiciary and its importance in the community.

PLANNING COURTROOM SPACES

The spaces required in a typical trial courthouse vary considerably from state to state and by level of court. Most contain courtrooms, judicial chambers (offices), jury assembly and deliberation rooms (for courts with jury trials), clerks' offices, records rooms, and prisoner holding cells (in criminal courts). Court clerks, law clerks, court reporters, and administrators need offices, and witness waiting rooms and attorney-client conference rooms are needed. Other offices might include those for the prosecutor (district attorney), public defender, and parole officers. Some courts require special courtrooms, or hearing rooms, for arbitration, mediation, high security criminal cases, and juvenile, family, and traffic cases.

The courthouse must be designed with its special circulation patterns in mind. Separate and distinct circulation paths for the public, judges and their staff, and in-custody defendants help ensure efficiency, safety, and security and are a distinctive feature of modern courthouses.

The public circulation area includes all areas used by the public, attorneys, clients, witnesses, and jurors (before selection), such as the main lobby, corridors, public elevators, public restrooms, waiting areas, and clerk of court counters.

The private circulation area allows judges and trial-related court personnel to move between chambers and courtrooms and jurors to move between courtrooms and jury deliberation rooms. Private circulation usually connects secured, private parking facilities for judges to private elevators and corridors leading to courtrooms and chambers.

Secure circulation provides a path for in-custody defendants, who enter the courthouse through a secure vehicular sally port and are taken to a secure central holding and staging area. A secure prisoner elevator serving holding units between two courtrooms is an easy way to move prisoners to courtrooms without crossing private judicial/juror/staff corridors.

INTERNAL LOCATION OF COURT FUNCTIONS

Clerks' offices, windows for paying fines, and other offices that attract heavy visitor traffic should be located near the main entrance. Courtrooms should be located away from the entrance to minimize noise and distractions. Chambers should also be located away from high-volume public areas. Busier traffic, misdemeanor, and other limited jurisdiction courtrooms belong closer to public entrances, while general jurisdiction courtrooms should be less accessible, perhaps on an upper floor. Jury deliberation rooms, courtroom holding facilities, attorney-client conference rooms, witness waiting rooms, and security officers' stations should be near courtrooms.

LEGEND

Don Hardenbergh; Courtworks; Williamsburg, Virginia

OVERVIEW OF COURT TYPES

	FEDERAL	STATE	LOCAL
Appellate	Supreme Court, Court of appeals	Supreme Court, intermediate, and appellate court	
General jurisdiction	District courts	Circuit Superior District	
Limited jurisdiction	Magistrate courts	Justice, district, and county courts	Municipal, city, and town courts
Special courts (examples)	Bankruptcy, tax	Juvenile, traffic, and small claims	
Administrative law courts (examples)	Hearing officers, U.S. Atomic Energy Comm., Federal Maritime Comm.	Workers' comp., public utility commissions, admin. law judges	

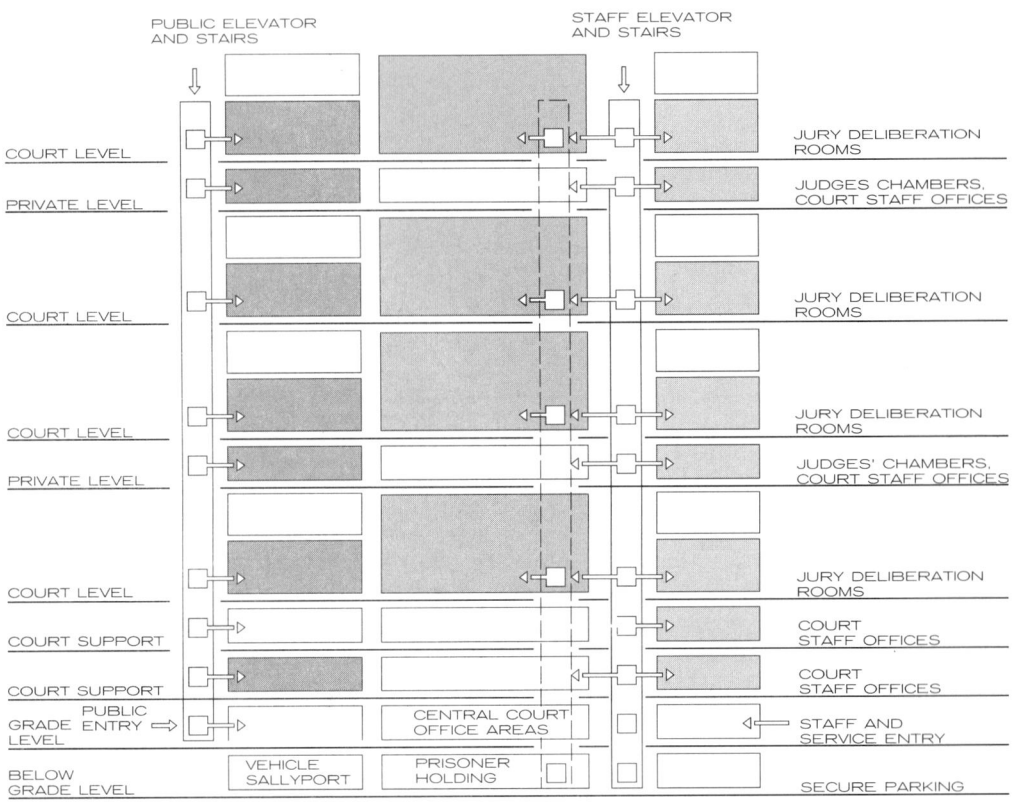

TYPICAL COURTHOUSE STACKING

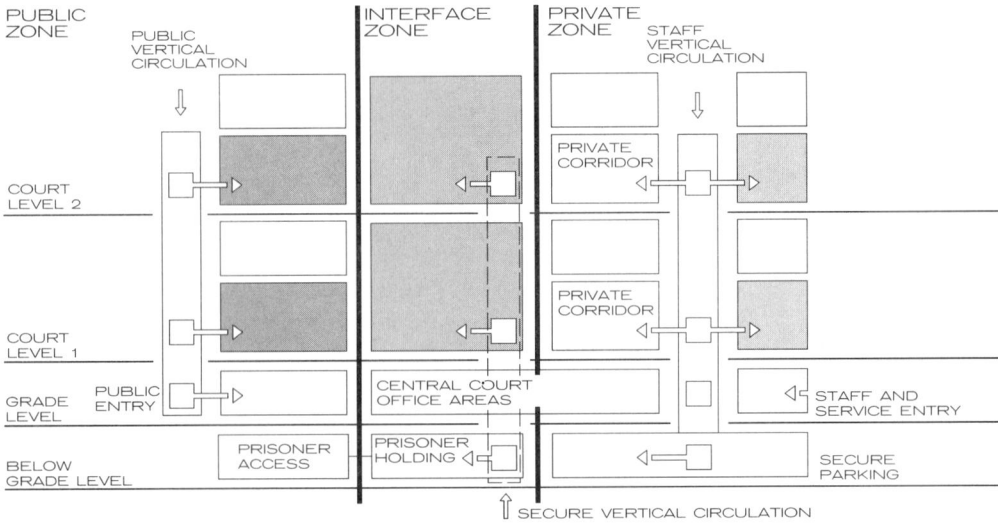

COURTHOUSE CIRCULATION AND ZONING SECTION

JUSTICE FACILITY PLANNING

Justice Facilities

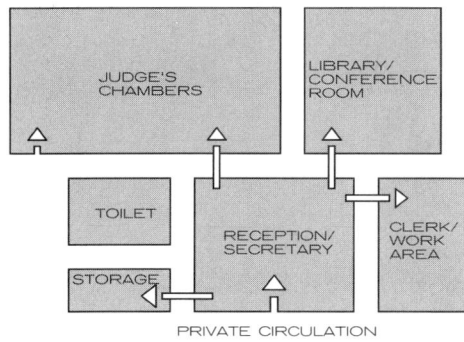

TYPICAL CHAMBER DIAGRAM

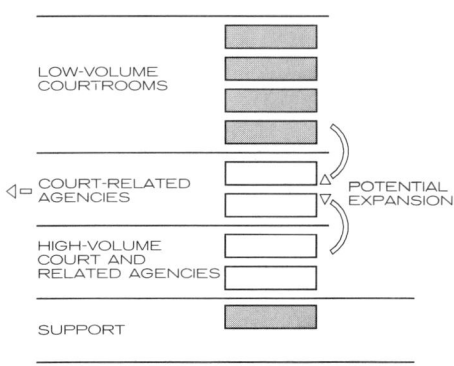

PROVISION FOR FUTURE VERTICAL EXPANSION

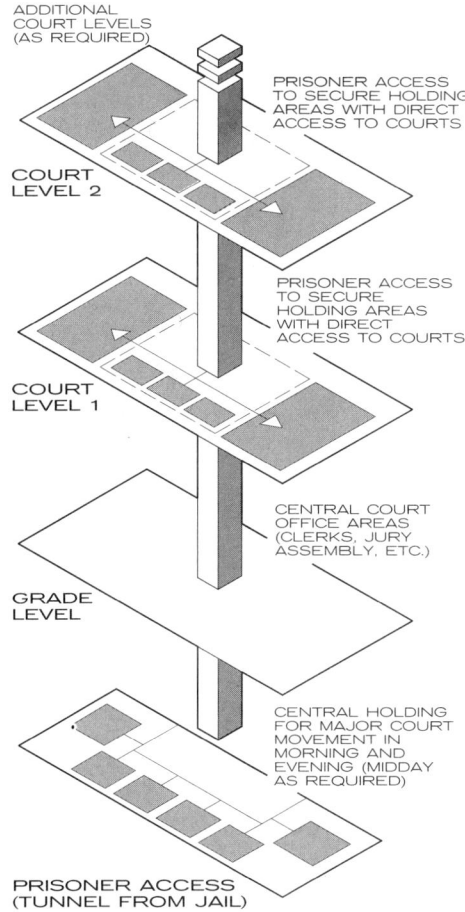

VERTICAL SECURITY CIRCULATION

Don Hardenbergh; Courtworks; Williamsburg, Virginia

COURTROOMS

Courtrooms should be easily accessible to the public. In large multistory facilities, they may be on an upper floor, but in small rural courthouses they may be located near the main entrance. Staff and judges should be able to enter the courtroom through a private corridor, and prisoners should enter directly from a secure holding area adjacent to the courtroom. Prisoners and defendants should not enter the courtroom near the public, jurors, or witnesses. Jurors should not pass near the defendant or the public on their way into the courtroom and should be able to move directly from the courtroom to the deliberation room.

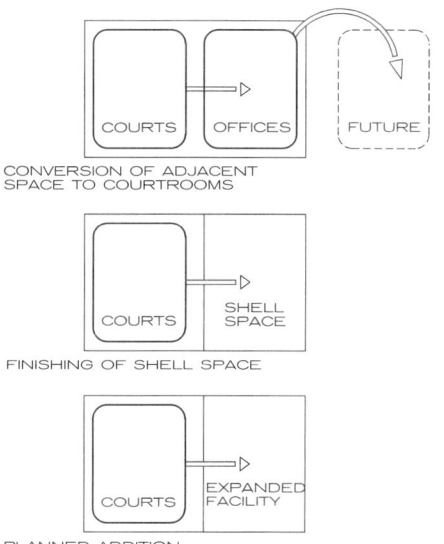

PROVISIONS FOR FUTURE HORIZONTAL EXPANSION

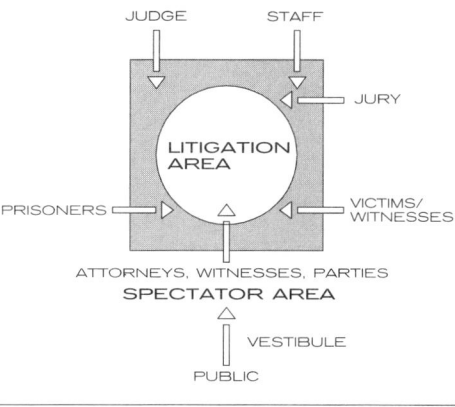

COURTROOM ACCESS

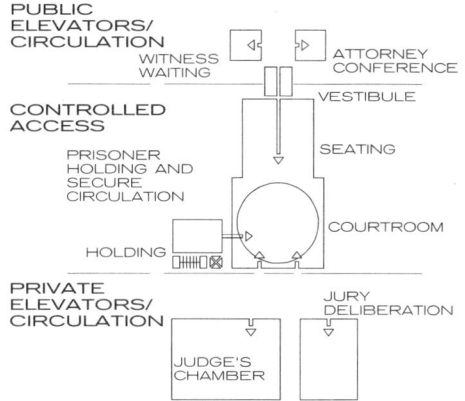

COURT FLOOR ZONING

Judicial chambers contain the judges' private offices and space for judicial staff such as a secretary, court clerk, and law clerk. Chambers may include a conference room and law library. They should be in a private, quiet, and safe area of the courthouse, usually away from the main entrance or on an upper floor. Judges should have quick and easy access to the courtrooms, while persons meeting with them should pass through a reception or screening area.

Traditionally, judicial chambers are adjacent to the judge's courtroom. While this is convenient for the judge, it makes future organizational changes more difficult. In larger courthouses, it is becoming popular to separate judges' chambers from the courtrooms; sometimes they are even on different floors. Such separation permits sharing of common resources such as the law library, conference areas, and court staff rooms; enhances security; and provides flexibility for later adjustments.

GROSSING AND EFFICIENCY FACTORS

Functional courthouses require more space for circulation and building support functions than most other building types. The departmental gross square footage (DGSF) needed for administrative purposes is reasonably consistent with similar requirements in commercial office or government administration buildings. But highly specialized areas such as courtrooms and holding facilities require considerably more internal circulation.

Basic core functions include major public corridors linking departments; private corridors linking courtrooms, judges' chambers, jury deliberation rooms, and other dedicated support spaces; secure corridors linking courtrooms with prisoner detention facilities; public elevators and elevator lobbies; private and secure elevators; stairs; mechanical, electrical, and plumbing chases; public toilet facilities; and the exterior walls of the building.

Because courthouses have unique security and circulation requirements, individual functional areas must be larger than in an office building. To handle the crowds of disparate people, courthouse lobbies, elevator cores and elevator lobbies, and public corridors must be larger than in a typical office building. An appropriate building gross square foot (BGSF) multiplier for courthouses is typically 1.20 to 1.25 of the DGSF.

TYPICAL COURTHOUSE EFFICIENCY FACTORS

Net area	57 to 65%
Departmental gross area	75 to 85%
Building gross area	100%

SECURITY

Effective courthouse security is maintained by combining structural elements, traffic pattern control, security devices, specific security policies, and security staff. The danger of armed violence requires controlled courthouse access; walk-through metal detectors and X-ray devices at the entrance are necessary in larger urban courthouses. The number of public entrances should be limited and lobbies sized and configured to permit queuing at security checkpoints without making people wait outside.

General court floor security should be controlled by a bailiff station in the public area, with access to private corridors restricted by a proximity card access system. Access to private corridors serving judges' chambers, staff, and jury deliberation rooms may be regulated by closed-circuit television (CCTV) and intercom systems or by a receptionist.

Prisoners should move from a secure sally port into a central holding area. Good sight lines in the courtroom are vital to effective control. Bullet-resistant materials should surround the judge's bench, and duress alarms (linked to a CCTV system) are essential for rapid emergency response. Fine and fee payment windows should have security glazing and duress alarms.

FLEXIBILITY AND EXPANSION

Several measures can prolong the operational life of a courthouse. Floor-to-floor heights and bay sizes may be standardized throughout the building to permit future conversion of noncourtroom space into courtrooms. Locating low-to-medium volume office functions on middle floors makes future modifications easier: As these offices outgrow their space they can be moved to adjacent buildings, allowing court functions to expand upward from the high-volume public floors and downward from the trial courtroom floors. Another strategy is to build shell space (an empty floor or room), which can be fitted out and occupied when needed.

Justice Facilities

FUNCTION VS. OPERATION

Courthouses can be organized by function or by type of court. All courtrooms, all chambers, and all clerks' offices are grouped together in a functional organization. An operational arrangement separates different types of courts or departments, such as criminal courts, general jurisdiction trial courts, traffic courts, or family courts. Judges for each court are housed with their clerks and courtrooms on separate floors, or in separate areas, of the building.

COURTROOM DESIGN

Image, symbolism, and functionality are important in courthouse design. The arrangement of the participants and furniture reflects society's view of the relationships between the defendant and judicial authority or, in a civil case, of the relationship between the parties. Furnishings and finishes should reflect the seriousness of the proceedings, yet not be too dark and overbearing.

Courtroom space is needed for the judge, court reporter, clerk, bailiff (security officer); prosecutor or plaintiff and attorney; defendant and attorney; witnesses, jury, and spectators. Other participants include social workers, probation officers, interpreters, police officers, and the press.

The traditional courtroom is rectangular and deeper than it is wide, although some modern courtrooms are round or square. The shape of the courtroom must allow all participants to see and hear one another clearly without having to look back and forth too much.

Functionally, courtrooms are divided into a litigation (well) area and a public (spectator) area, separated by a bar or low railing. The litigation area may be rectangular, with the judge's bench located along the front wall or in the corner of the room.

The depth of the litigation area is determined by whether a jury box is included and the distance needed to separate the judge's bench and attorneys' tables. This separation is necessary both to provide adequate circulation within the litigation area and to give prominence to the judge.

The spectator area in most types of courtrooms should have a minimum seating capacity of 75. Traffic or misdemeanor courts, however, may require a minimum seating of 100 or more depending upon the court's workload.

The height of the courtroom should be proportional to the size of the room and should provide appropriate distance from the ceiling for a judge standing at the bench. The ceiling height over the litigation area may be higher than that over the spectator area.

Acoustics should allow no reverberations or echoes, so that participants are able to hear the proceedings clearly. A public address system is generally recommended.

Soundproofing between courtrooms and surrounding spaces (particularly holding cells), double-door vestibules between the public corridors and courtrooms, and carpeting all reduce noise in the courtroom. Generally, the front wall of the courtroom may be constructed of reflective materials to enhance the sound from the litigation area, while the back wall should be covered with sound-absorptive materials to reduce noise.

Courtrooms with exterior windows can suffer from sunlight shadowing and dappling effects, heating and cooling complications, reduced security, exterior noise, and visual distractions. If the location permits, skylights are an excellent source of natural light without the problems presented by windows.

ACCESS FOR PERSONS WITH DISABILITIES

All courtrooms should comply with the Americans with Disabilities Act Accessibility Guidelines for Buildings and Facilities (ADAAG). Areas of the courtroom that need to be accessible are spectator seating, the witness stand, counsel tables, and the jury box. Space should be provided so that all other workstations can be made accessible in the future. The first tier of the jury box may be at floor level, and so may the witness box (the witness box and first tier of the jury box should be the same height).

Allow 48-in.-wide spaces for wheelchairs in the spectator area. The number of wheelchair accessible spaces must meet the seating requirements for assembly areas. All courtrooms with public seating of 51 or more (to a maximum of 300) require four wheelchair locations.

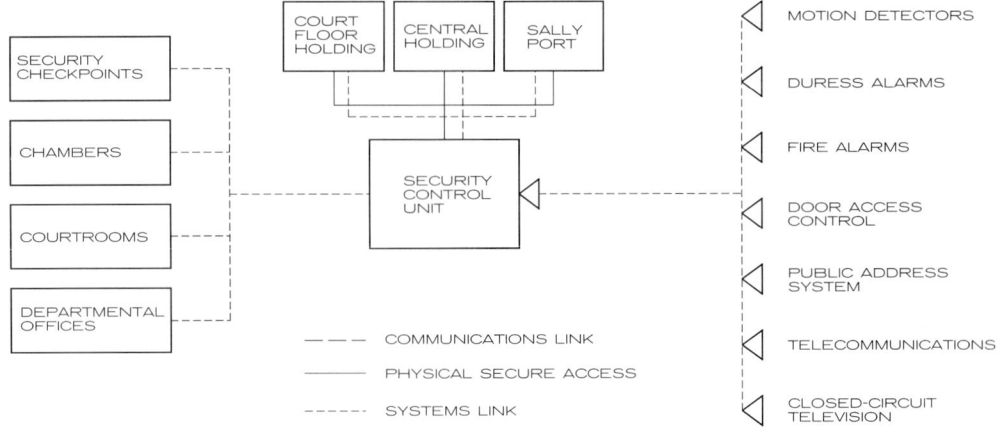

SECURITY CONTROL DIAGRAM

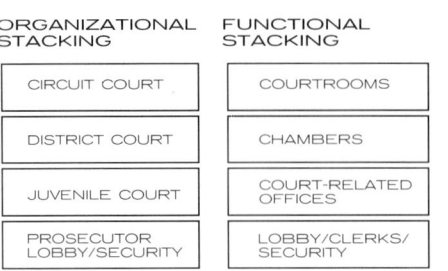

STACKING DIAGRAMS

TYPICAL DIMENSIONS FOR LITIGATION AREAS

TYPE OF COURTROOM	WIDTH (FT)	DEPTH (FT)	TOTAL AREA (SQ FT)
Formal nonjury hearing room	28	30	840
Jury courtroom (1-tier jury box)	32	32	1024
Jury courtroom (2-tier jury box)	36	32	1152
Jury courtroom (3-tier jury box)	38	32	1216
Ceremonial/large courtroom	40	34	1360

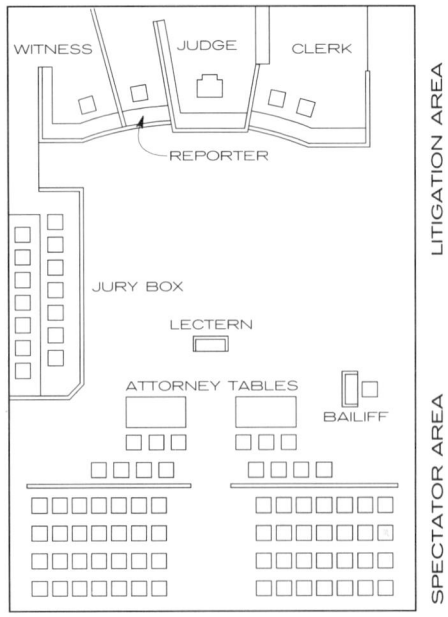

TYPICAL COURTROOM WITH WITNESS ADJACENT TO JURY

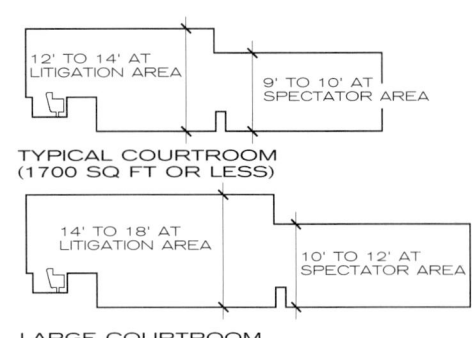

COURTROOM CEILING HEIGHT

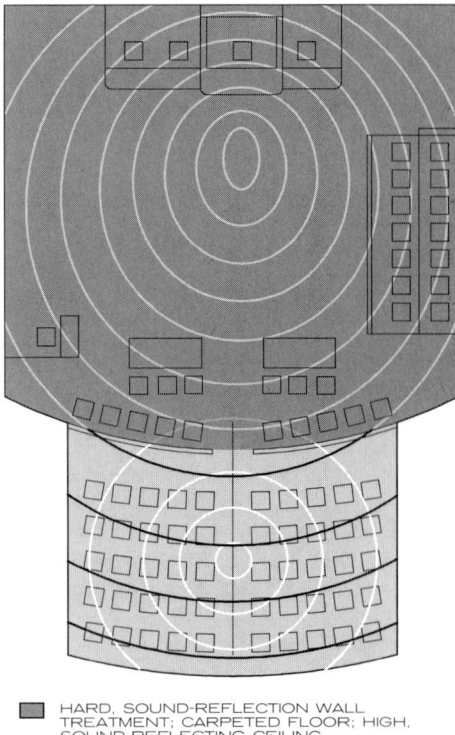

COURTROOM ACOUSTICS

Don Hardenbergh; Courtworks; Williamsburg, Virginia

JUSTICE FACILITY PLANNING

Justice Facilities

Sound amplification for the hearing impaired must be installed and available. At least half of each type of courtroom, hearing room, jury deliberation room, and jury assembly room should have an assistive listening (either FM, audio loop, or infrared) device.

SECURITY

Circulation routes for courtroom participants should be clearly separated, and there should be no spaces where a weapon or bomb might be placed or posts or pillars in the courtroom behind which someone might hide. The judge's bench should be shielded with bullet-absorptive material and equipped with duress alarms connected to the central security station.

FURNISHINGS AND FINISHES

The colors and tones of the walls and ceilings should project dignity and calm. Furnishings and finishes should be comfortable, sturdy, durable, vandal-resistant, and easy to clean. Draperies or other window coverings should be used if the courtroom has windows. Seats, benches, and chairs should be comfortable and easy to maintain.

TECHNOLOGICAL APPLICATIONS

Judges, court staff, and attorneys increasingly need access to audiovisual and video equipment, computer terminals, and information databases. While live court reporters will continue taking the record in the immediate future, electronic sound and video recording and playback equipment is becoming more popular and should be available in courtrooms, both for recording the trial and for videoconferencing and hearing remote testimony.

SOUND AND VIDEO EQUIPMENT

Microphones should be located at the bench, clerk's workstation, witness stand, lectern, jury box, and attorneys' tables. Allow space for video display monitors to be installed at the attorneys' tables, lectern, witness stand, and jury box. Camera locations for potential video court reporting, video arraignment, media coverage, or courtroom security surveillance should be identified. Camera coverage of the court proceedings should avoid coverage of the jurors.

SOUND AMPLIFICATION SYSTEMS

All courtrooms should be equipped with sound amplification equipment for assisting the hearing-impaired and for playing back audio exhibits. The master controls should be located at the bench or clerk's station.

COMPUTER TERMINALS AND OTHER EQUIPMENT

Plan on future installation of computer terminals and monitors for the bench, court clerk's station, and court reporter's station in all courtrooms. If possible, recess the clerk's and judge's monitor into the millwork.

Allow for installation of additional electrical outlets at the attorneys' tables, jury box, clerk's station, bench, and public seating area.

THE COURT

CLERK'S WORKSTATION

The court clerk checks case files and records appropriate case dispositions. The clerk frequently passes files to and from the judge and must be close enough to do so easily. The clerk should generally be elevated on one riser so he or she can see the whole courtroom.

The court clerk's work surface should be approximately 30 to 36 in. deep and 4 ft long in order to accommodate case files and computer equipment. The workstation requires the same task lighting as the judge's bench and the clerk's station may have the same duress alarm/intercom link with the central security station as the judge. There should be desk drawers or pigeonholes for paperwork and an inconspicuous, lockable storage area where evidence and trial materials may be stored during recesses.

The court clerk's station should have flush, floor-mounted electrical receptacles, a telephone jack, and cable conduits for computer terminals and a built-in computer monitor. The computer terminal should be equipped with a silent keyboard and laser printer. The control console for the sound amplification system may be located at the court clerk's station, along with a microphone for the clerk.

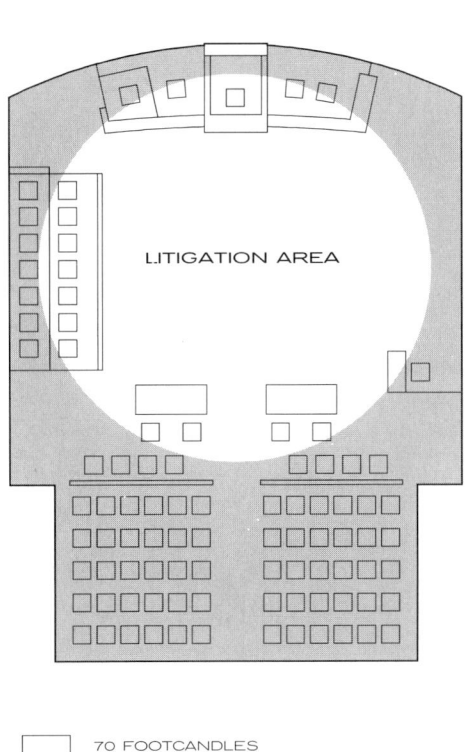

MINIMUM COURTROOM LIGHTING LEVELS

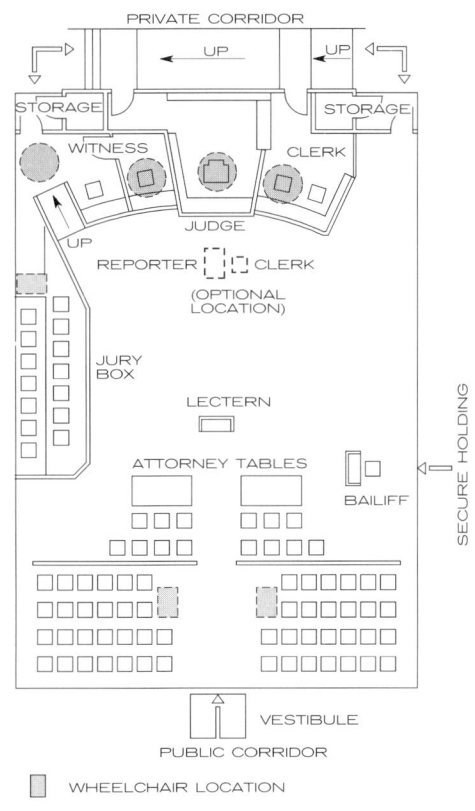

WHEELCHAIR ACCESSIBLE COURTROOM

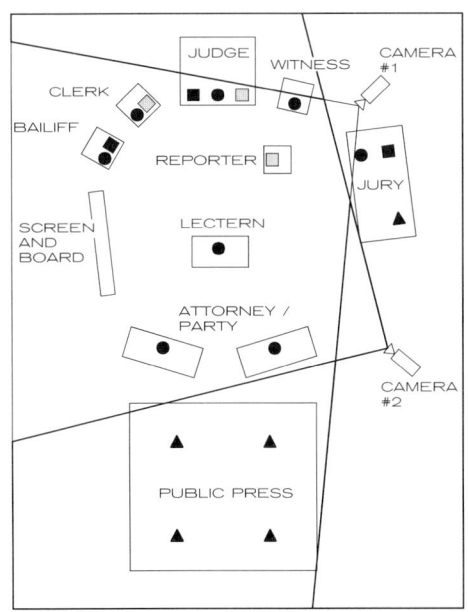

AUDIOVISUAL EQUIPMENT LOCATIONS

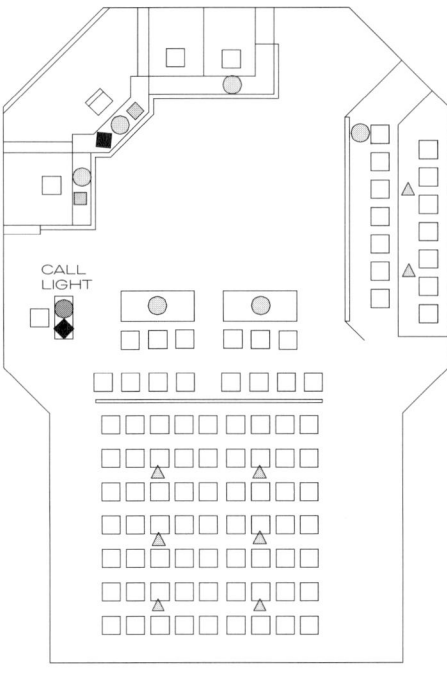

SYSTEM CONTROL LOCATIONS

Don Hardenbergh; Courtworks; Williamsburg, Virginia

JUSTICE FACILITY PLANNING

JUDGE'S BENCH

The judge's bench should convey dignity and authority. From the bench, the judge should be able to see and hear all courtroom participants, exercise a protective influence over witnesses, address all persons in the courtroom, and pass and receive documents from attorneys, the court clerk, and the court reporter.

The size of the judge's bench should be proportionate to the size of the courtroom. There should be at least 4 ft behind the judge's desk so the judge can move freely for sidebar conferences, reach for reference books, and easily enter and exit the bench.

The bench should include several drawers for supplies and personal items, as well as a bookcase at least six ft wide for legal reference books.

The eye level of the judge should be higher than that of a standing person of average height. Generally, the judge's bench should be elevated 21 in. or at least three risers. A barrier such as an ornamental rail along the front of the bench prevents individuals from approaching too close to the bench or reading documents or notes that are on the judge's bench.

Room lighting should be augmented by task lighting directly above the bench. Lighting controls for the entire courtroom should be located at or near the bench or the clerk's station.

Electrical receptacles flush-mounted in the floor and cable conduits for a built-in video display and computer terminal should be installed. The bench should be equipped with a telephone and a microphone connected to an amplifier controlled by the judge or the clerk.

COURT REPORTER

The court reporter's station should be adjacent to the witness stand so the reporter can clearly view and hear voice testimony. The court reporter should also have an unobstructed view of the entire litigation area, including the judge, witness box, jury box, and attorneys' tables.

The court reporter's station is generally at floor level, which accentuates the prominence of the judge's bench and keeps clear the judge's and attorneys' view of the witness. It should have space and comfortable seating appropriate to the recording methods being used. The workstation should have several electrical outlets and enough space for electronic recording equipment and sound reinforcement equipment should be provided. It also should be made ready for computer equipment and video recording technology. A silent printer in the courtroom may be needed for producing transcripts.

WITNESS STAND

All courtroom participants must be able clearly to hear and see the witness. In addition, because many witnesses testify at a personal sacrifice of time, money, and sometimes safety, they deserve the court's courtesy and protection.

The witness stand is traditionally placed between the jury and the judge, but many courts now use a movable witness box that can face the jury box. The witness stand should be no closer than 4 ft to the jury box so the nearest juror is 7 to 8 ft away. There should be a physical barrier between the witness stand and the judge to prevent the witness from seizing objects from the bench.

The witness stand should be 3½ to 4 ft wide and approximately 5 ft deep to allow for easy entry and exit. Witnesses must frequently receive, examine, and return exhibits; a desk area approximately 15 to 18 in. deep for resting files or evidence may extend from the front or side of the stand.

The exhibit area for screens, chalkboards, and computer and video monitors should be close to the witness stand and visible to jurors and witnesses. The exhibit area could be placed between the witness stand and the jury box.

There should be electrical receptacles and cable conduits for built-in video display of recorded evidence and taped depositions and for review of automated case transcripts. A movable microphone should be mounted in the witness stand so that it is both unobtrusive and able to pick up the testimony of children and soft-spoken witnesses.

JURY BOX

Jurors are temporary "officers of the court" and should be afforded the comfort and courtesies appropriate to their role. The front of the jury box should be shielded with a modesty panel. A 9- or 10-in. shelf should be installed as part of the rail around the jury box, both to allow jurors to examine documents and exhibits and to prevent attorneys from getting too close to the jurors. The first row of seating may be at floor level to permit wheelchair access, with the second tier elevated on one riser. The jury box should accommodate 14 jurors (12 jurors and 2 alternates).

Jurors must be able to hear the judge, witnesses, and attorneys clearly, and they should have unobstructed sight lines to the judge, witness, attorneys, and exhibit area.

The jury box should allow 10 to 12 sq ft per juror. A 14-person jury box needs to be 19 to 21 ft long and approximately 8 ft deep. The jury box should be large enough to accommodate a wheelchair. Audio jacks for earphones for the hearing impaired may be installed at one or two positions. Seats should be fastened to the floor and should swivel and have armrests. Many jury boxes have a footrail.

The jury box should be at least 4 ft from the nearest attorneys' table and 6 ft from the nearest attorney's chair. In addition it should be far enough from the spectator area to inhibit any physical or verbal contact. A bailiff's station may be located between the jurors and the spectators to prevent such communication.

The entrance to the jury box should be near the exit to the jury deliberation rooms. Jurors should not have to cross the courtroom or move through the spectator seating area.

The jury box may be equipped with electrical receptacles, cable conduits, and computer and video terminals for display of recorded and automated evidence, taped depositions, and case transcripts. A microphone may be placed near the jury box.

ATTORNEYS' TABLES

Each table should be at least 7 ft long and should seat up to four people. The tabletop should be 3 to 4 ft wide to accommodate books, documents, and other work materials. The area of each attorneys' table, including chairs and 2-ft circulation space behind the chairs, should be approximately 64 sq ft to allow the parties to move freely around the table. The tables should not have drawers or concealed recesses where a weapon or bomb may be placed.

Attorneys should be able to see and hear all courtroom participants clearly. The litigation area lighting above the attorneys' tables may be augmented with direct task lighting if necessary.

Attorneys and litigants should be able to confer in private. To prevent conversations from being overheard, or documents from being read, attorneys' tables should be 4 ft apart and about 6 ft from the nearest juror or spectator.

The front of the judge's bench should be at least 10 ft from the front of the attorneys' tables. This distance conveys judicial objectivity and dignity.

Electrical receptacles and cable conduits for built-in computer display terminals may be provided for accessing legal databases, reviewing taped depositions, and video display of evidence, exhibits, and transcripts. There should be flush floor-mounted electrical outlets, microphones, and a telephone line so that attorneys may be connected to their office computers by modem.

BAILIFF'S STATION

The bailiff, or deputy sheriff, is responsible for the security of the courtroom and all participants. He or she must have access to an alarm connected to the main security office.

The bailiff generally moves about the courtroom but should be provided with a small table and movable swivel chair, which should occupy no more than 15 sq ft. The area surrounding the bailiff's station should be free of obstacles.

The bailiff should be able to see all areas of the courtroom clearly. The bailiff's station should be located near the defendant's table or by the jury box.

SPECTATOR SEATING

Public bench-type seating at floor level allows access by disabled persons and accentuates the raised litigation area and judge's bench. Aisles should be wide enough to allow wheelchair access.

Public entry into the courtroom should be through a vestibule for security purposes and for noise control. The floor should be carpeted and the surrounding walls acoustically treated.

EVIDENCE DISPLAY AND STORAGE

After exhibits are introduced into evidence and marked, they should be displayed in full view of the court. Hazardous exhibits, such as firearms and other objects that could be used as weapons, drugs, and toxic substances should be placed away from the witness, jury box, and defendant's table. Usually, the clerk's station is the most suitable location. Charts and displays are best presented either between the witness box and the jury box, so the witness may point to them, or across from the jury box if their detail is large enough to be seen at a distance. Increasingly, evidence, including videotapes, physical evidence, computer animations, X-rays, and documents, will be displayed on video monitors.

The courtroom should have an inconspicuous evidence closet where the clerk may secure items during recess. In addition, approximately 40 sq ft should be provided for storing such items as projectors, television monitors, chart boards, easel pads, tripods, chalk and markers, cleaning cloths, pins and tape, and pointers. These may be stored behind the courtroom.

ADDITIONAL SOURCES OF INFORMATION

American Bar Association. *Twenty Years of Courthouse Design Revisited, Supplement to the American Courthouse*. Chicago, 1993.

American Institute of Architects. *Justice Facilities Review*. Washington, D.C. (published annually).

Don Hardenbergh. *The Courthouse, A Planning and Design Guide for Courthouse Facilities*. Williamsburg, Va., 1991.

Hunter Hurst. *Shaping a New Order in the Court: Sourcebook for Juvenile and Family Court Design*. Pittsburgh, Pa., 1992.

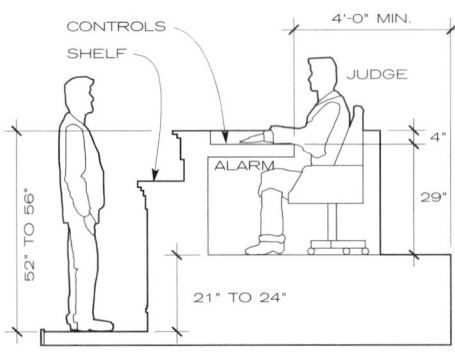

JUDGE'S BENCH

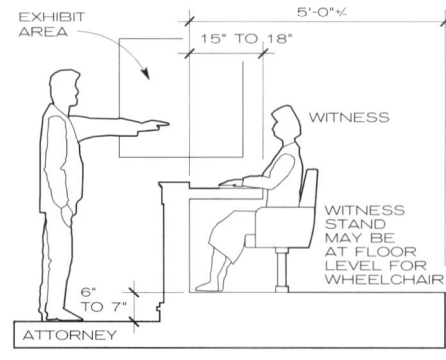

WITNESS STAND

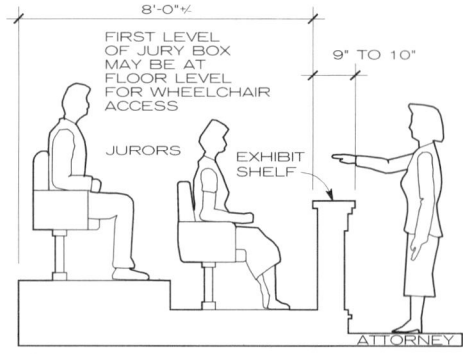

TWO-TIER JURY BOX

Don Hardenbergh; Courtworks; Williamsburg, Virginia

Residential Site Planning

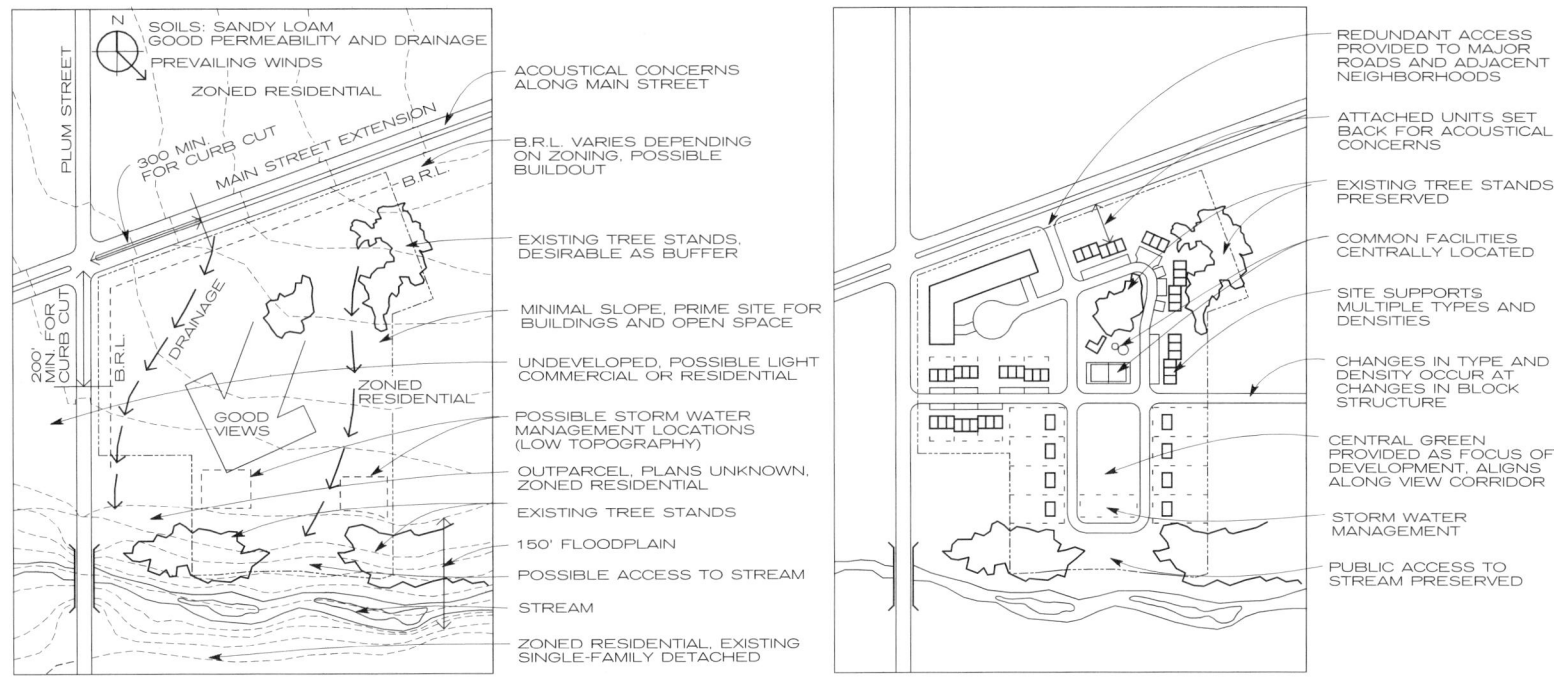

SITE ANALYSIS AND SCHEMATIC SITE PLAN

GENERAL

Residential site planning requires balance among a large number of complex and often competing priorities.

ORIENTATION

No unit should be without sun for at least part of a winter day; south-facing units are premium. Prevailing winds, both regional and local, should be studied so that no building is entirely masked. At the same time, harsh winds should be buffered by plantings, and if buildings are differentiated by side, bedroom and service sides should face the harsh wind.

USE AND ENHANCEMENT OF NATURAL AMENITIES

Too frequently, housing projects are named for amenities that are destroyed during development. Promontories, mature trees, and water features should be incorporated into the design and, if possible, enhanced.

PROVISION FOR VIEWS

Spectacular views can drive the design of a housing project, but every project should strive to provide reasonable views from all units. Although no unit should have a parking area as its only view, many people enjoy views of streets and roadways. Views of green space are important, especially in urban projects.

CONTEXT

The designer must strive to identify valuable off-site resources and influences so that they are recognized in the design.

Such resources include the following:

1. Geometries and alignments
2. Slopes and soils
3. Views of singular objects and natural amenities
4. Recreational facilities
5. Topography and drainage
6. Surrounding and adjoining uses
7. Available infrastructure
8. Market and location

CLEAR DELINEATION OF PRIVATE AND PUBLIC AREAS

Beyond unit design considerations, the site should be organized so that all territory can be clearly allocated to either private custody or public care and maintenance. It is frequently desirable for each unit to control some private open space. However, in higher density developments such space is often limited or filled in unique ways.

REGULATORY REQUIREMENTS

Land available for housing and related uses may face restrictions, including the following:

1. Rights of way for future uses
2. Area required for storm water management and sediment control
3. Mandated unusable areas between projects (called buffers)
4. Building restriction lines: setbacks, build-to lines, height limits, viewsheds, watersheds, separations, rights of way, easements
5. Roadways and parking areas
6. Protection of environmentally sensitive and natural resource areas such as forests, streams, and animal habitats

DENSITY AND BUILDING TYPES

These factors are the most critical to the developed character of the site and are prescribed by zoning and by developer preference—as informed by the architect and others. Zoning density is expressed numerically along with limitations that are often intended to suggest unit type. But any prescribed density can be reached by combining building types with associated parking arrangements. The permitted density may ultimately be reduced through restrictions of various sorts and is rarely achievable on small or irregular sites.

UNITY AND VARIETY

In site design, monotony and excessive repetition are as undesirable as meaningless variation, which can be disorienting and appear chaotic.

EMERGENCY ACCESS

Size and turning radius of emergency equipment, especially fire engines, can mandate street width, turning radius, and access patterns. Access to buildings becomes an issue at higher densities; installation of sprinkler systems can often balance equipment access around buildings. Always consult the fire marshal in the early stages of design.

SECURITY

Because projects are produced and marketed as discrete places, security considerations can reinforce their hermetic character and prevent integration into the larger community. At higher densities, this phenomenon can produce gated communities with limited or single access, card-accessed parking areas, and private police.

Conventional urban patterns can replace costly and artificial surveillance systems: building placement, window location, and resident awareness, together with architectural limitations on free circulation, can enhance neighborhood security.

ACCESS

Although singular access is frequently desired for marketing and control, redundant access from existing automotive and pedestrian networks provides choice and convenience while reducing concentrations of traffic.

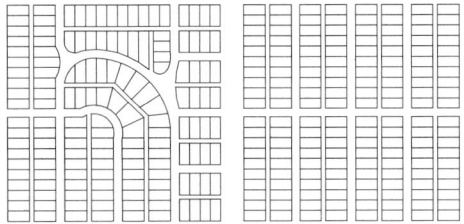

ARBITRARY VARIATION AND MONOTONOUS REPETITION

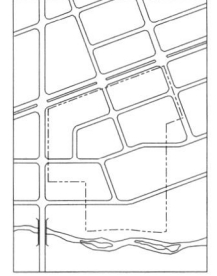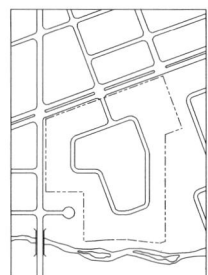

MULTIPLE ACCESS AND SINGLE ACCESS

Ralph Bennett; Bennett Frank McCarthy Architects, Inc.; Silver Spring, Maryland

Residential Density

GENERAL

Numerical definition of density is the most important planning index in housing but it can also be the most misleading. Density numbers frequently become inflammatory in planning debates, so it is important that the architect provide specific images of the actual appearance of planned settlements.

Density appears in two forms: gross and net. Gross density is the index applied to large areas—15 to 20 acres or more—and includes private as well as public improvements such as roads, schools, parks, and residentially oriented retail uses.

Net density is used in relation to project-sized areas—smaller than 15 to 20 acres—and consists of the number of proposed dwelling units divided by the site area. Net density is usually expressed in acres and includes access drives, parking areas, common and buffer areas, and community facilities.

FACTORS AFFECTING DENSITY

1. Dwelling unit size and arrangement.
2. Parking: on grade, in garages, in units, structured in large groups.
3. Passive and active open space.
4. Land use restrictions such as buffers, easements, and setbacks.
5. Land price: the owner's objectives are ultimately formed by this factor, in conjunction with market projections.

TYPICAL DENSITIES

1. SINGLE-FAMILY DETACHED HOUSES: The density in developments of this type is generally 6 dwelling units or fewer per acre. In the example illustrated, the density is 4.5 dwelling units per acre, with on-site parking but no garages and 7,500-sq-ft lots.
2. SINGLE-FAMILY ATTACHED TOWN HOUSES (parking on grade): The density in a development of this type is up to 14 dwelling units per acre.
3. SINGLE-FAMILY ATTACHED TOWN HOUSES WITH GARAGE: Up to 20 dwelling units per acre will fit in a development of this sort.
4. TWO-STORY ATTACHED HOUSES: With carports, these houses are designed at a density of around 10 units per acre.
5. GARDEN APARTMENTS: Parking on grade is provided in a garden apartment complex, which contains up to 18 dwelling units per acre. In the example shown, each apartment building has 36 units, for a density of 18 units per acre.
6. WALK-UP APARTMENTS: Built over one parking level, a walk-up apartment complex could accommodate up to 30 dwelling units per acre.
7. ELEVATOR BUILDINGS: Elevator buildings with structured parking can be built at a density of up to 100 dwelling units per acre. The example shown is a double-loaded corridor slab building with 200 units. With surface parking, it offers a density of 45 units per acre.
8. MIXED NEIGHBORHOODS: A mixed neighborhood encompasses a variety of dwelling types and, correspondingly, a variety of housing unit densities. The example shown includes an 8-unit walk-up apartment building on a 16,000-sq-ft lot, with a density of 16 units per acre, and single-family detached houses with garages on 8,000-sq-ft lots, with a density of 4 units per acre. The overall density in this example is 6.4 units per acre.

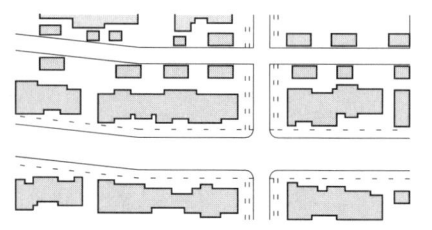
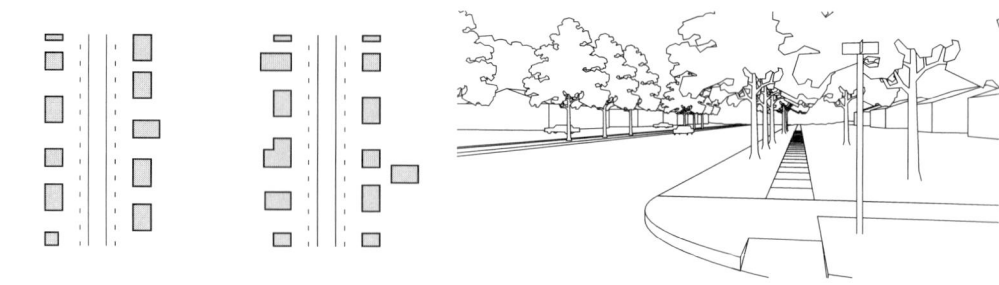

SINGLE-FAMILY DETACHED HOUSES

TWO-STORY ATTACHED HOUSES

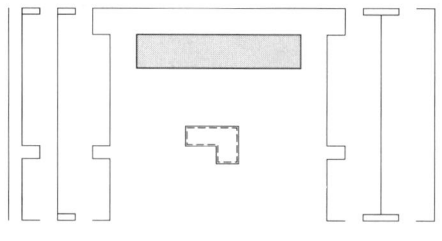

GARDEN APARTMENTS (THREE-STORY WALK-UP BACK-TO-BACK)

ELEVATOR BUILDING

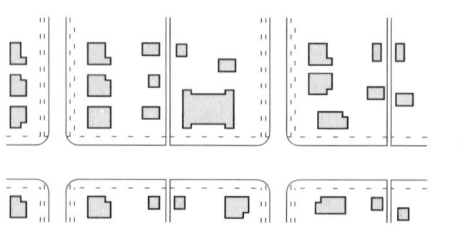

MIXED NEIGHBORHOOD

Ralph Bennett; Bennett Frank McCarthy Architects, Inc.; Silver Spring, Maryland

HOUSING

Single-Family Detached Housing

SITE PLAN CONSIDERATIONS

ACCESS
1. Where possible, access should connect and align with existing systems.
2. Marketing and security considerations frequently dictate single access, but redundant circulation gives choice and improved service.

PEDESTRIAN CIRCULATION
1. Rarely provided at lower densities, pedestrian access is essential at higher densities.
2. Pedestrian walkways usually parallel streets.
3. Connections to mass transit are appropriate.

PARKING
1. Parking arrangements have a significant impact on density and appearance.
2. On-street parking for guests is desirable at lower densities and essential at higher densities.

RELATION TO TOPOGRAPHY
1. ADA and subdivision regulations dictate street and walk grades and mandate site reformation at all but the lowest densities.

SERVICE
1. Trash pickup, mail service, and deliveries depend on street access to individual units.
2. Fire apparatus usually dictates road standards.

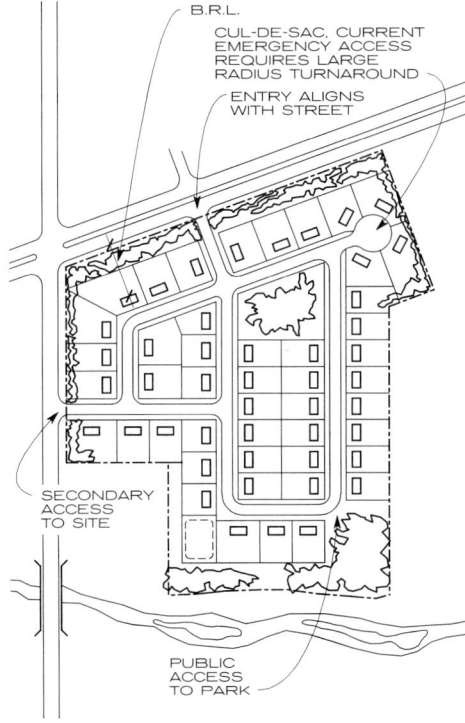

STREET ACCESS

TECHNOLOGY

STRUCTURE
1. Typically wood frame.
2. Fire separation is required for incorporated parking (garage).

MECHANICAL
1. Air, water.
2. Oil, gas heat, or heat pump.
3. Compression refrigeration or heat pump cooling.
4. Exterior condenser for heat pump or air-conditioning. This type has greatest flexibility for solar and other alternative energy systems.
5. Sprinklers are required in some jurisdictions.

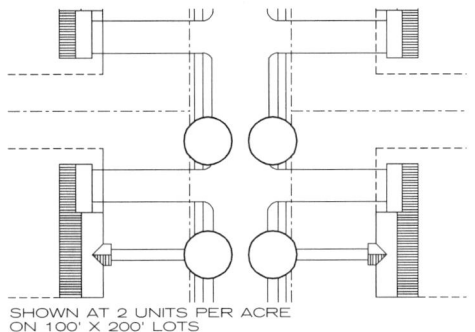

SHOWN AT 2 UNITS PER ACRE ON 100' X 200' LOTS
LARGE LOT SINGLE-FAMILY HOUSES

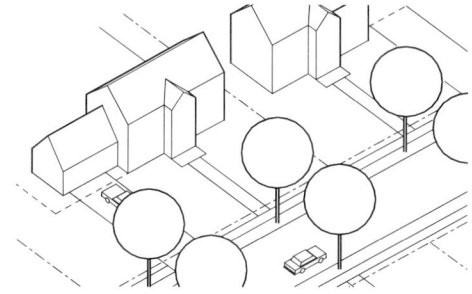

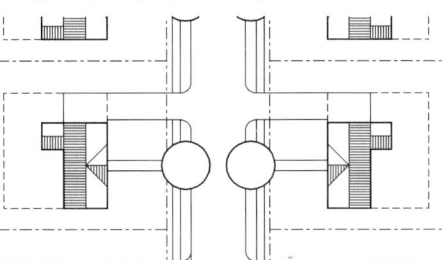

SHOWN AT 5 UNITS PER ACRE ON 75' X 100' LOTS
SMALL LOT SINGLE-FAMILY HOUSES

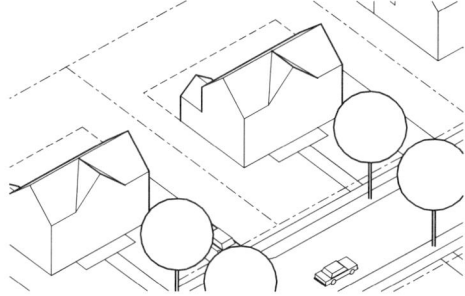

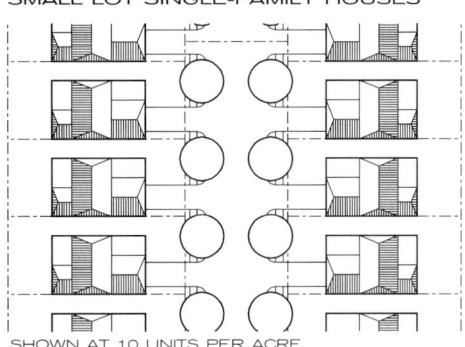

SHOWN AT 10 UNITS PER ACRE ON 40' X 90' LOTS
ZERO LOT SINGLE-FAMILY HOUSES

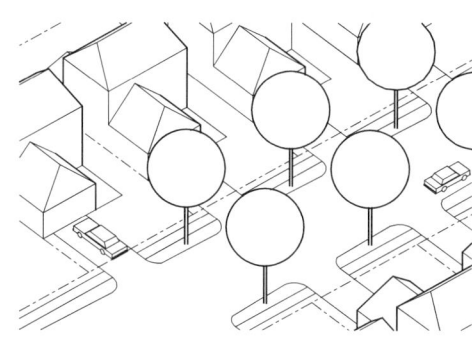

DENSITY CONFIGURATIONS

DETACHED HOUSING CHARACTERISTICS

TYPE	LOT SIZE (SQ FT)	DENSITY RANGE (D.U./ACRE)*	CHARACTERISTICS
Large lot	20,000 and up	0.5 - 5	Flexibility in orientation. Building restriction lines not significant. Expansion simple. Site character can be exploited.
Small lot	5000 - 10,000	4 - 8	Aggregation becomes important. Community planning important. Services important (fire, mail, rubbish). Pedestrian circulation possible and required. Urban design principles apply. Building restriction lines become important. Public sewer and water needed. Clear delineation between public and private space needed.
Zero lot	3000 - 5000	8 - 11.5	Eliminates one sidelot setback. Shallower lots possible. Other side yard usable as private space. Windows on property line reduced or eliminated.
Z-lot	3000 - 5000	8 - 13	Similar to zero lot. Allows more flexible allocation of land. Lot line views over neighboring ownership must be avoided.
Alternating-width lots	3000 - 5000	8 - 11.5	Gives variety along street.

* D.U.—Dwelling units

Ralph Bennett; Bennett Frank McCarthy Architects, Inc.; Silver Spring, Maryland

Single-Family Attached Housing

SITE PLAN CONSIDERATIONS

ACCESS
1. Where possible, should connect and align with existing systems.
2. Many arrangements are possible, including alleys, on-site parking, pooled parking and on-street parking.

PEDESTRIAN CIRCULATION
1. Necessary to connect dwellings to common facilities and off-site facilities.
2. Usually parallels streets.

PARKING
1. Has significant impact on density and appearance.
2. If not pooled, on-street essential for guests and overflow.

RELATION TO TOPOGRAPHY
1. ADA, Fair Housing, and subdivision regulations dictate street and walk grades and mandate site reformation at all but the lowest densities.

SERVICE
1. Trash pickup, mail service, and deliveries rely on access from street to individual units.
2. Fire apparatus usually dictates road standards.

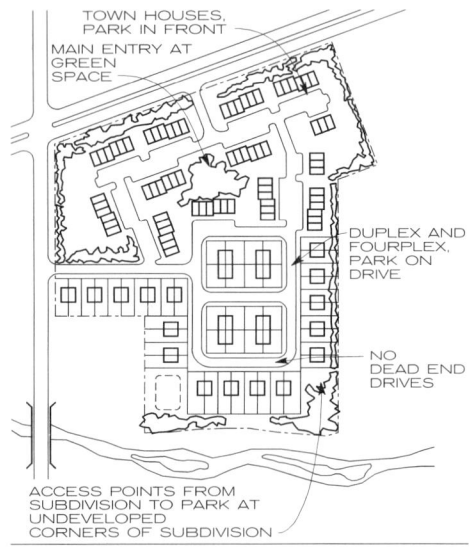

STREET ACCESS

MASSING
Variety and richness can be achieved by massing buildings so that individual units are not diagrammatically identifiable. Scale is given by secondary elements, room sized or smaller. Basic combinations are manipulated to produce complex unit configurations; the resulting composition is very different from basic types.

 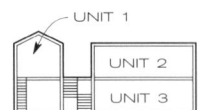

THREE-UNIT BUILDING OF COMBINED TYPES (MANOR)

TECHNOLOGY

STRUCTURE
1. Typically wood frame.
2. Gypsum board walls between units (party walls), 2-hour rating. Some jurisdictions require masonry.
3. Parking must have rated separation if sharing wall or ceiling with unit.

MECHANICAL
1. Air, gas heat, electric baseboard heat, or heat pump.
2. Compression refrigeration or heat pump cooling.
3. Exterior condenser for heat pump or air-conditioning.
4. Sprinklers required in many jurisdictions.

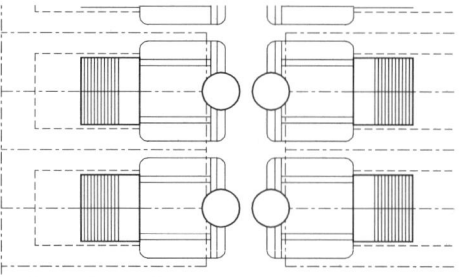

SHOWN AT 9 DWELLING UNITS PER ACRE
DUPLEX HOUSES

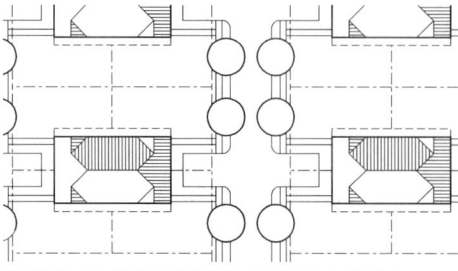

SHOWN AT 10 DWELLING UNITS PER ACRE
FOURPLEX HOUSES

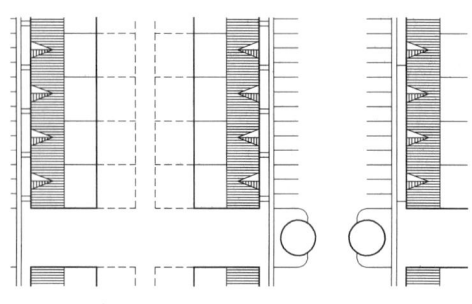

SHOWN AT 13 DWELLING UNITS PER ACRE
ATTACHED HOUSES (TOWN HOUSES)

DENSITY CONFIGURATIONS
ATTACHED HOUSING CHARACTERISTICS

TYPE	LOT SIZE (SQ FT)	DENSITY RANGE (D.U./ACRE)*	CHARACTERISTICS
Duplex	3000 - 5000	8 - 10	Allows grouping of parking, access. Side yard can be used. Houses have three exposures.
Fourplex	2000 - 3000	10 - 15	Houses have two exposures. High level of privacy possible. Masses as larger building.
Townhouse	1000 - 1500	12 - 22	Urban type exported. Public/private clearly delineated. Maximum flexibility for minimum surface. Makes satisfactory streets.

* D.U. = Dwelling units

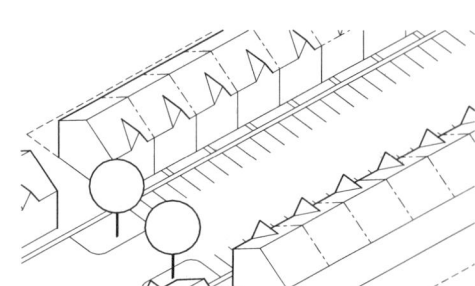

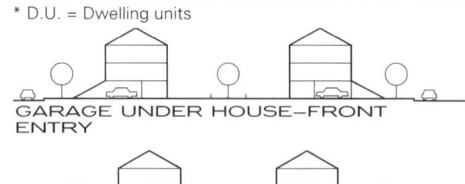

GARAGE UNDER HOUSE—FRONT ENTRY

GARAGE UNDER HOUSE—REAR ENTRY

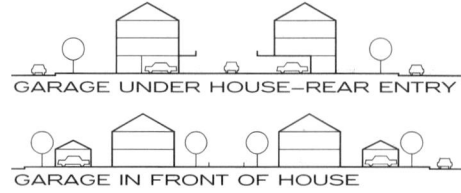

GARAGE IN FRONT OF HOUSE

GARAGE BEHIND HOUSE

NOTE
Attached houses achieve the highest density possible with individual structured parking (garages). Combining this housing type with parking produces many rich variations.

PARKING

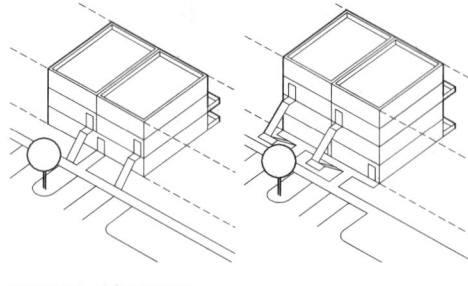

TOWN HOUSES OVER FLATS   TOWN HOUSES OVER TOWN HOUSES

NOTE
Town houses can be stacked upon themselves or on one-story units (flats). Density is increased and fire separations are required horizontally as well as vertically. Individual entries are usually provided.

MULTISTORY VARIANTS

Ralph Bennett; Bennett Frank McCarthy Architects, Inc.; Silver Spring, Maryland

Exterior Space Design

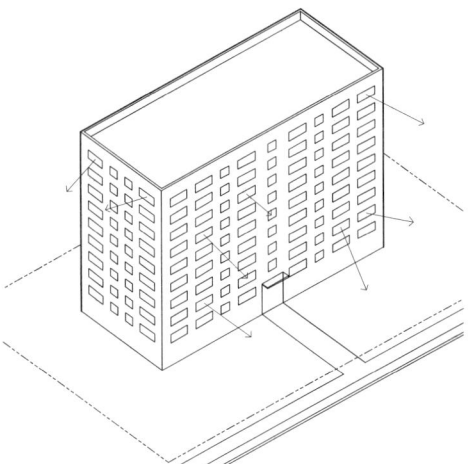

HIGH-RISE BUILDING

NOTES

1. In high-rise, single-entry buildings, the views of most residents are distant from public areas.

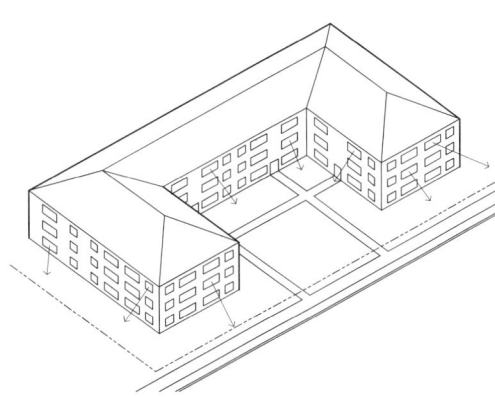

LOW-RISE BUILDING

2. Low-rise, multiple-entry buildings facilitate close supervision of public areas.

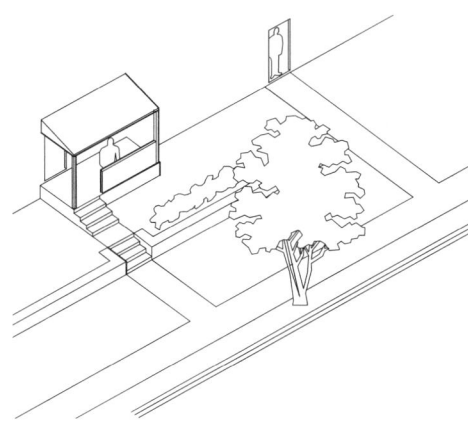

NOTE

Architectural and landscape devices help demarcate private and public spaces between a house front and the street.

DIVISION OF PUBLIC AND PRIVATE SPACE

SUPERVISION OF PUBLIC AREAS

GENERAL

Clear delineation of usable exterior space is essential to the success of any housing design. Proper planning of exterior space improves security, reduces maintenance, enhances appearance, and permits residents to act as responsible citizens.

DESIGN

On traditional city streets, public and private realms are clearly defined.

The street is in the public realm. Semipublic areas—the entry and foyer—open onto the street from a short distance. The semiprivate areas of the house—living, dining, and/or cooking areas—look out onto the public realm but are screened. The private areas of the house—the bedrooms—are a floor or more above the street, looking out but secluded from view. Semiprivate outdoor areas are at the back of the house, visible to neighbors but secluded from the street.

In multifamily buildings, the provision of a supervised public realm is more complicated than in the attached house. In this case, buildings need to be arranged so that unit windows and common circulation space overlook the public areas of the project. This can be accomplished by

1. Keeping buildings in the two- to six-story height range
2. Clustering the dwelling units so their entrances are distributed rather than concentrated
3. Arranging unit windows so no portion of the ground surface is invisible to dwelling units

BUILDING LOCATION

Separation of buildings from parking and minimum distances between buildings are often mandated by zoning and by building codes.

To avoid involuntary eye contact, vertical walls containing windows and balconies should be at least 60 ft apart. This dimension is often reduced; if so, attention must be paid to elements that can provide elective privacy, such as

1. Curtains and blinds
2. Balcony walls with adjustable opacity
3. Deformation of the wall to provide bays and oblique, rather than frontal, views

ADJACENT USES

Location of certain site activities near unit windows can cause conflict. Although common practice often places back-to-back garden apartments overlooking parking, this setup is not optimum. This arrangement can be improved if the parking area is planted, illumination is at a low level, and the building design provides other views.

Recreational uses such as basketball, tennis, and other noisy, large-muscle activities should be kept away from unit windows and balconies.

Play areas for small children ideally are located where they can be seen from dwelling unit windows.

LANDSCAPE DESIGN

The provision of green space is essential for housing, even in intensely urban areas. Street trees and planted courtyards add value to the densest housing site.

Where space permits, passive green space without specific programmatic purpose can be an attractive addition. Such space should not be so large as to be unsupervisable from the dwellings, and dwellings should be located to take advantage of the amenity it provides.

COMMUNITY FACILITIES

Two houses make a community and offer opportunities for elective socialization and joint use.

In small developments, the ordinary activities of daily life offer opportunities for community focus. These activities include picking up mail, putting out trash, doing laundry, and working on cars.

In larger projects, the following activities may provide opportunity for community activity and physical focus:

1. Marketing and management
2. Activities requiring shelter, such as meeting, fitness, day care, and convenience retail
3. Outdoor recreation, such as swimming, tennis, handball, and racquetball

DETAILS

Architectural devices mark and enhance the public and private realms. These devices include fences; walls; changes of level provided by stairs and ramps; zones of planting; and porches, stoops, and terraces.

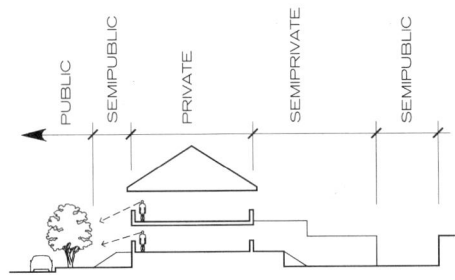

PUBLIC AND PRIVATE ZONES IN A ROW HOUSE

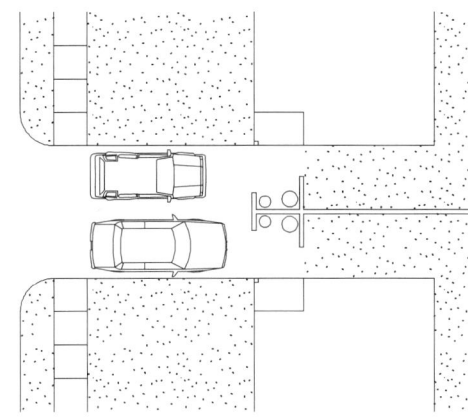

ADJACENT HOUSE ENTRANCES

Ralph Bennett; Bennett Frank McCarthy Architects, Inc.; Silver Spring, Maryland

Fair Housing Requirements

GENERAL

The regulatory climate for housing is complex and ever-changing. Therefore, designers should consult regulatory agencies at all levels of government before initiating planning or detailed design of any housing project.

Information on this page is related to site design, building arrangement, and design of the exterior path to the dwelling unit and other common facilities. Further information related to housing can be found in Chapters 1, 11, and 20 of the ninth edition of *Architectural Graphic Standards.*

FAIR HOUSING AMENDMENTS ACT

The Fair Housing Amendments Act (FHAA) was passed in 1988 and applies to all housing scheduled for first occupancy after March 13, 1991. The act is unusual in that it is a civil rights law, not a building code or standard. Although the U.S. Department of Housing and Urban Development (HUD) developed and promulgates the guidelines, HUD has no plans to review its role and will enforce FHAA primarily based on complaints. Compliance will be achieved through complaints by affected individuals and by professional testers.

FAIR HOUSING ACCESSIBILITY GUIDELINES

The most comprehensive instructions for compliance with the construction provisions of the FHAA are provided by the Fair Housing Accessibility Guidelines (FHAG), which were released in their final form in March 1991.

WHAT PROJECTS ARE COVERED

Any multifamily project with four or more dwelling units is covered by the legislation, but not all parts of all dwelling units in all covered projects must be accessible.

Other standards that supplement or supersede the FHAG are the following:

1. SPACES FOR COMMON USE: ANSI standard A117.1-1986
2. SPACES FOR PUBLIC USE (if any): Americans with Disabilities Act (ADA) Guidelines
3. ANY SPACE: Any local building code standard that HUD deems more restrictive

In buildings equipped with passenger elevators, all units must be accessible. Multistory dwelling units (except loft units) not located in elevator buildings are exempt from this requirement.

In walk-up multistory buildings, FHAA requires all ground floor units to be accessible where practical, based on site considerations. A minimum of 20% of the units must be accessible. FHAA definition of the ground floor in walk-up buildings is unclear, but the intention of the legislation was to avoid the installation of elevators in buildings not otherwise needing them. Because interpretations of the law vary, guidance should be sought.

NOTE
FHAG permits use of both level changes and lofts in dwelling units as long as common areas are accessible.

DESIGN FEATURES PERMITTED IN ACCESSIBLE UNITS

SITE PLANNING ISSUES

Site accessibility for housing is defined as the existence of a continuous accessible route of travel from a suitable automobile or transit drop-off point (called the arrival point) to the dwelling unit. Such a route may include parking access aisles, curb ramps, walks, ramps, and lifts and must meet the requirements of ANSI A117.1-1986.

Sloped walkways, when included, are defined as being no steeper than 5%. Steeper walkways are defined as ramps and must have a maximum slope of 8.5%; ramps require handrails.

All community facilities must be connected to all covered dwelling units by an accessible route. In certain circumstances, use of a private automobile may be considered part of such a route.

SITE PRACTICALITY TESTS

The designer may use either of two tests to determine whether accessibility is practical at a particular site:

1. INDIVIDUAL BUILDING TEST: Locate an arrival point and entrance for each building or entry, and estimate the slope between them. If a line connecting these two points is steeper than 10%, access is deemed impractical. This test must be conducted both before and after regrading.
2. SLOPE ANALYSIS TEST: Calculate the percentage of the site sloped at grades steeper than 10%. This percentage is the percentage of ground floor units (with a minimum of 20%) that must be accessible.

DWELLING UNIT DESIGN

Dwelling units covered by the FHAA must be designed according to the FHAG. The difference between these requirements and the ANSI A117.1-1986 standard is substantial. Under the FHAG, the unit must be usable and include adaptable features but does not have to be fully accessible according to the ANSI standard. Planning decisions such as door and corridor widths and bathroom and kitchen layouts must meet certain standards, some not as restrictive as the ANSI standard. Items such as accessible plumbing fixtures and counters can be provided as required by specific owners and users.

Units covered by the law must have the following characteristics:

1. Usable doors to enter all rooms
2. An accessible route into and throughout the dwelling unit
3. Switches and controls mounted in accessible locations
4. Usable bathrooms with concealed reinforcing installed in the walls
5. Usable kitchens that permit wheelchair access

Certain design features, including level changes, are permitted. Intermediate levels (lofts) are permitted, although they are not precisely defined. In buildings equipped with elevators, multistory units must include a toilet on the accessible (ground) floor.

Changes in floor level are permitted if they can be defined as "design features" that do not interrupt the accessible route through the remainder of the dwelling.

ITEMS THAT TYPICALLY ARE NOT AFFECTED BY FHAG

1. Windows
2. Interior door hardware
3. Doors not used for passage
4. Fireplaces
5. Stairs
6. Upper floor levels
7. Lower floor levels
8. Closet shelving
9. Circuit breakers
10. Mechanical equipment
11. Individual garages
12. Lofts
13. Basements

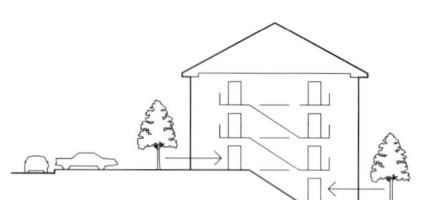

NOTE
The FHAA does not clearly define "ground floor" in requiring that all ground floor units be accessible when practical. For situations such as that shown here, it may be wise to seek guidance regarding accessibility requirements for ground floor units on the lowest level.

GROUND FLOOR UNIT ACCESSIBILITY

Ralph Bennett, Bennett Frank McCarthy Architects, Inc.; Silver Spring, Maryland
Thomas Davies, Jr., AIA; Kim A. Beasley, AIA; Paradigm Design Group; Washington, D.C.

HOUSING

Dwelling Unit Design

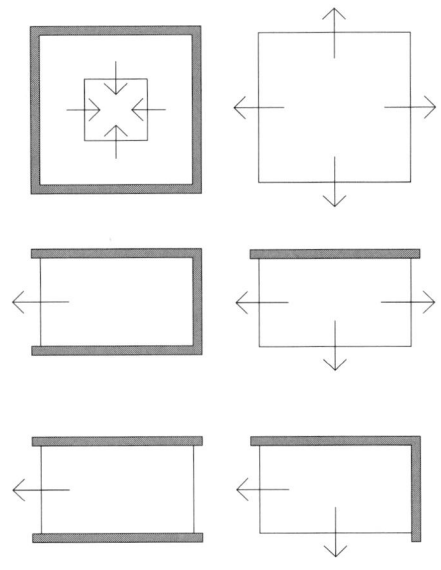

NOTE

The number of sides exposed to light and air and whether they are adjacent can be used to describe all dwelling units.

UNIT DESIGN—POSSIBLE EXPOSURES

GENERAL

Before design of a housing project begins, a unit density and mix of types that suit the site must be determined. Units composing the mix are designed according to standards related to the sales price or monthly rental of the dwelling unit. Unit characteristics can be summarized as follows:

MINIMAL HOUSING: No foyer; combined living and dining; small bedrooms (80 sq ft); one bath.

AFFORDABLE HOUSING: Small foyer; combined living and dining; large bedroom may have private bath; other bedrooms share bath with common rooms; minimal storage.

LUXURY HOUSING: Foyer; living, dining, and family (or great) rooms; circulation in hall, some semiprivate rooms (study/sitting); ample to lavish master bedroom suite; other bedrooms share one or two baths; two- or three-car garage.

CUSTOM HOUSING: Large foyer; separate living, dining, and family rooms; porch; large kitchen and pantry; grand circulation; frequent redundant circulation (H&V); many semiprivate rooms; large bedrooms; multiple bathrooms; ample storage; staff service space.

IDENTITY FROM EXTERIOR

With the possible exception of deeply subsidized housing, all housing must survive in the market. This means the project must not deviate greatly from the demonstrated preferences of its market, although it must also offer an identifiable image or appearance.

This image, often called "curb appeal," is frequently defined for the architect by advertising and marketing specialists. In single-family houses, the house itself constitutes a statement. Attached houses also make individual statements, as well as developing community imagery for the potential tenant or buyer. In multifamily housing, the identity of the dwelling is submerged within the group and the individual unit is distinguished by its internal arrangement. Thus, group and individual identity must be defined and developed.

SIDEDNESS

Dwelling units always benefit when buildings are designed with a clear front or public side and a back or semiprivate side. Sidedness enables the cultivation of other contrasting characteristics such as ceremonial/intimate, open/closed, noisy/quiet, ornamented/plain, and urban/pastoral.

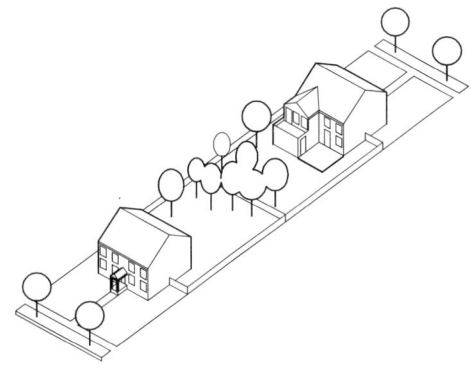

NOTE

Housing design should distinguish between public and semiprivate sides of the dwelling unit.

SIDEDNESS

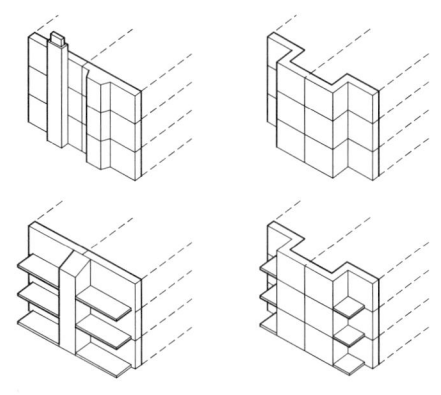

BUILDING MASSING

DWELLING UNIT PLANNING

Dwellings of all sizes have common elements and sequences that must be identifiable.

ENTRANCE

Marketing concerns usually demand a dramatic spatial event at the moment of entry, whether a double-height foyer in a luxury house or a sweep of the living and dining areas in an apartment. However, the architectural organization of this event may require a transitional space, perhaps somewhat enclosed, as compression before expansion into the major semipublic areas of the unit.

CIRCULATION AND ROOMS

In large houses it is possible to separate circulation from the rooms served using devices such as corridors, passageways, foyers, vestibules, and the like. Circulation in smaller units occurs through rooms, most often living and dining rooms.

PLAN BALANCE

In dwelling unit design, all aspects of the plan must be proportional and consistent. A many-bedroom dwelling with living areas too small to accommodate all the occupants is problematic. So is the house with enormous living and dining areas but too few or too small bedrooms. Kitchens, general storage, and circulation must also be sized according to the number of occupants.

FOCUS

All good dwellings offer a hierarchy of experience culminating in a focus, which is commonly the living or living/dining area or family room/kitchen. This spatial focus is often enhanced by spatial definition and/or greater height and by features such as fireplaces (the hearth, of course, is the traditional center of the house), stairs, or access to outdoors.

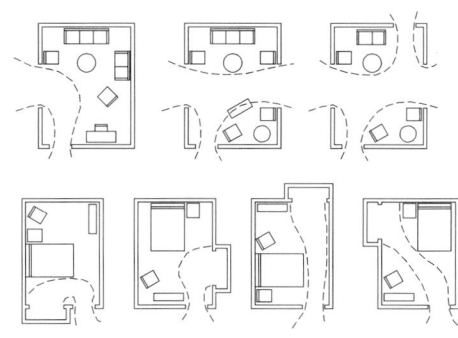

NOTE

In small plans, circulation should occur through no more than two adjacent corners of living and dining rooms. After accounting for circulation, sufficient space should remain for reasonable furniture arrangements.

CIRCULATION

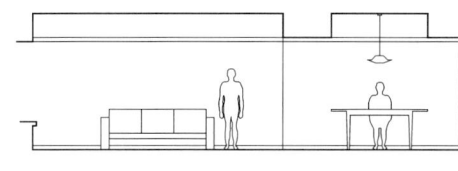

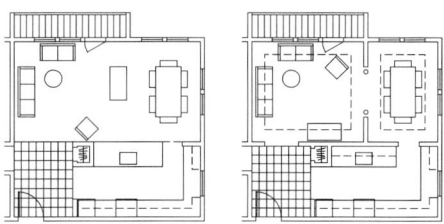

NOTE

Spaces defined by walls can be reinforced by articulation of the ceiling. Even in small units, ceiling drops and soffits can provide reinforcement of activity areas and spaces.

ARTICULATION OF SPACE

ACCESS TO EXTERIOR

Contemporary living requires connection to outdoor space by circulation where possible or at least by view. In apartments, where this connection may take the form of a balcony, it is usually made at the living room. But since a balcony reduces view and light, it may be placed at the bedroom instead, with access from the living room. Bedroom balconies are a luxury amenity.

UNIT PLAN AND BUILDING MASSING

Plan arrangement is related to building massing; by projecting and recessing adjacent rooms or parts of rooms, building mass can be broken down. Similarly, continuous alignment of exterior walls leads to large-scale massing and elevations in which surface elements such as windows and textured and colored surface areas can be used to compose and adjust scale.

Components such as balconies, storage closets, and fireplaces are often useful for composing elevations and massing, particularly when simplified plan geometries produce large, basic massing.

Ralph Bennett; Bennett Frank McCarthy Architects, Inc.; Silver Spring, Maryland

Walk-up Apartments

SITE PLAN CONSIDERATIONS

ACCESS
1. Where possible, points of access should connect and align with existing systems.
2. Many arrangements are possible with streets, courts, and freestanding buildings

PEDESTRIAN CIRCULATION
1. Pedestrian connections are necessary between apartments and common facilities and off-site facilities.
2. Usually parallels streets except where site plan offers rustic walks.

PARKING
1. Parking sites must be pooled or in structures.

RELATION TO TOPOGRAPHY
1. ADA and subdivision regulations dictate street and walk grades and mandate site reformation at all but the lowest densities.
2. Breaks between stairwell groups allow adjustment to the terrain.

COMMON FACILITIES
1. Rental and management offices are common for 50 units or more.
2. Pools and recreation facilities are common in complexes of more than 100 units.
3. Maintenance and storage facilities are common in larger projects.
4. Tot lots and play areas are required for complexes of 20 units or more in many jurisdictions.
5. RV and boat storage are offered in some areas.

SERVICE
1. Mail service and deliveries to stairwells or larger group boxes; trash to Dumpsters distributed in parking lots or other central locations.
2. Fire apparatus usually dictates road standards; sprinklers may permit reduced equipment access.

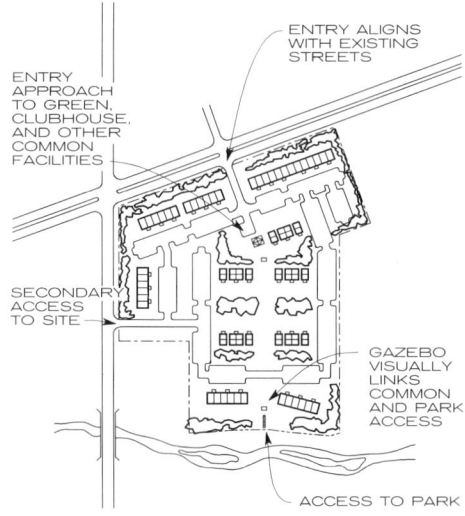

SITE PLAN

TECHNOLOGY

STRUCTURE
1. Wood frame.
2. Walls between stairwell groups must be masonry or heavy gypsum (2-hr rating).
3. Unit wall must be gypsum board on wood or steel studs (1-hr rating).
4. Second stair must be in rated enclosure.

MECHANICAL
1. Forced air, gas heat, or heat pump.
2. Compression refrigeration or heat pump cooling.
3. Larger units (two bedrooms or more) have centrally located furnaces with ducts and exterior condensers for heat pumps and refrigeration; smaller units may have through-the-wall units with no exterior condenser.
4. Sprinklers required in many jurisdictions.

WALK-UP HOUSING CHARACTERISTICS

TYPE	DENSITY RANGE (D.U./ACRE)*	CHARACTERISTICS
Through unit	Up to 17 (including off-street parking)	Permits sided site planning. Two exposures for each unit. Bedrooms or living areas can be oriented toward parking or view.
Back-to-back unit	Up to 20 (including off-street parking)	Efficient: 4 units per floor. As usually deployed, 50% of units face parking, 50% face view and green.

* D.U. = Dwelling units

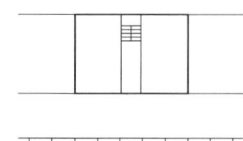

THROUGH UNIT

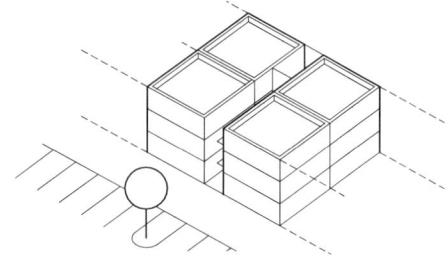

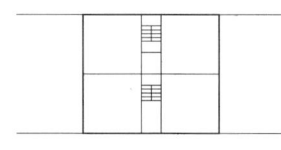

BACK-TO-BACK UNIT

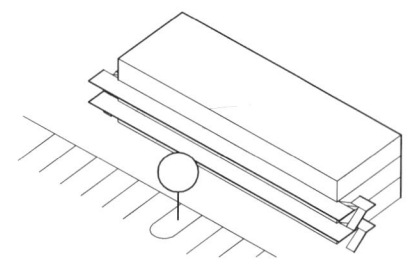

SINGLE-LOADED GALLERY ACCESS

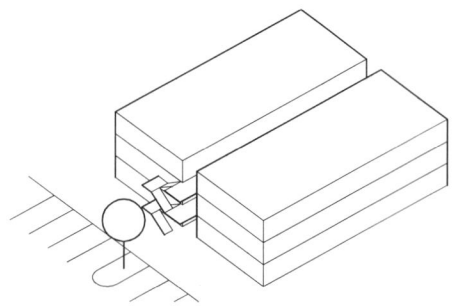

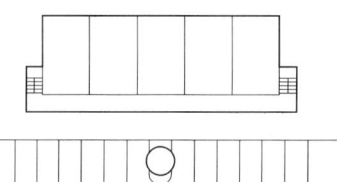

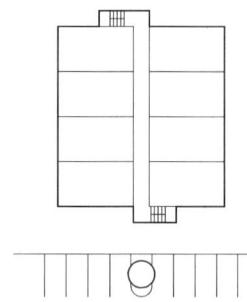

DOUBLE-LOADED GALLERY ACCESS

WALK-UP APARTMENT CONFIGURATIONS

CONFIGURATION

Walk-up apartments are ubiquitous in the United States and come in many varieties. Their appeal lies in the great efficiency of their circulation. Two-story buildings are common and generally require only one stair. Three-story buildings generally require two stairs, one of which must be rated. Buildings higher than three stories present market problems but do exist. Combination walk-up buildings, with elevators going to higher stories, are common in Europe but are uncommon in the United States due to the higher proportional cost of elevators.

Ralph Bennett; Bennett Frank McCarthy Architects, Inc.; Silver Spring, Maryland

Elevator Apartments

SITE PLAN CONSIDERATIONS

ACCESS
1. Entrances should, where possible, connect and align with existing systems.
2. Many arrangements are possible, including alleys, on-site parking, pooled parking, and on-street parking.

PEDESTRIAN CIRCULATION
1. Necessary to connect dwellings to common facilities and off-site facilities.
2. Usually parallels streets.

PARKING
1. Has significant impact on density and appearance.
2. If not pooled, on-street essential for guests, overflow.

RELATION TO TOPOGRAPHY
1. ADA and subdivision regulations dictate street and walk grades, and mandate site reformation at all but the lowest densities.

SERVICE
1. Trash through chutes to compactor in trash room in basement or ground floor; mail to mail room on ground floor; delivery to units or security guard.
2. Fire marshal may request access around building depending on building height and sprinkler system.

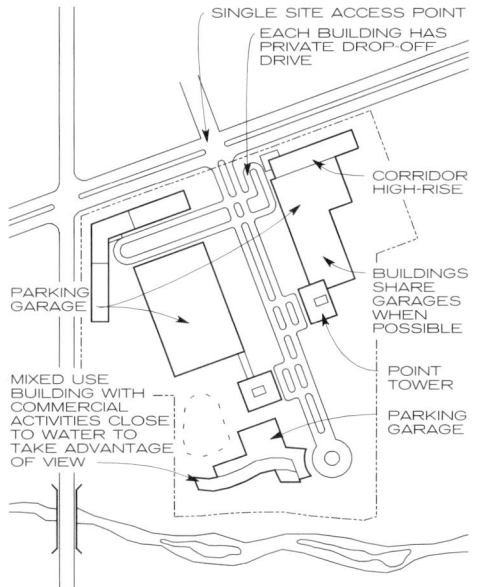

SITE PLAN

TECHNOLOGY

STRUCTURE
1. Masonry or concrete, occasionally fire-protected steel.
2. A full range of high-rise building safety measures are required, especially for structures taller than nine stories, which is generally the maximum reach for rescue equipment.

MECHANICAL
1. Decentralized air, gas heat, or heat pump.
2. Compression refrigeration or heat pump cooling.
3. Larger units (two bedrooms or more) have centrally located furnaces with ducts and exterior condensers for heat pumps and refrigeration; smaller units may have through-the-wall units with no exterior condenser.
4. Large and/or luxury buildings may have central systems with boilers, central chillers, and a condenser and two- or four-pipe systems.
5. Sprinklers are required in many jurisdictions.

GROUND FLOOR PLANNING

Ground floors in elevator buildings are significantly different from ground floors in other housing structures because larger numbers of people pass through on the way to their dwellings and because the ground floor is a smaller proportion of the area of the building. Urban versions of the type offer opportunities for retail and commercial uses that can be accessed directly from the street.

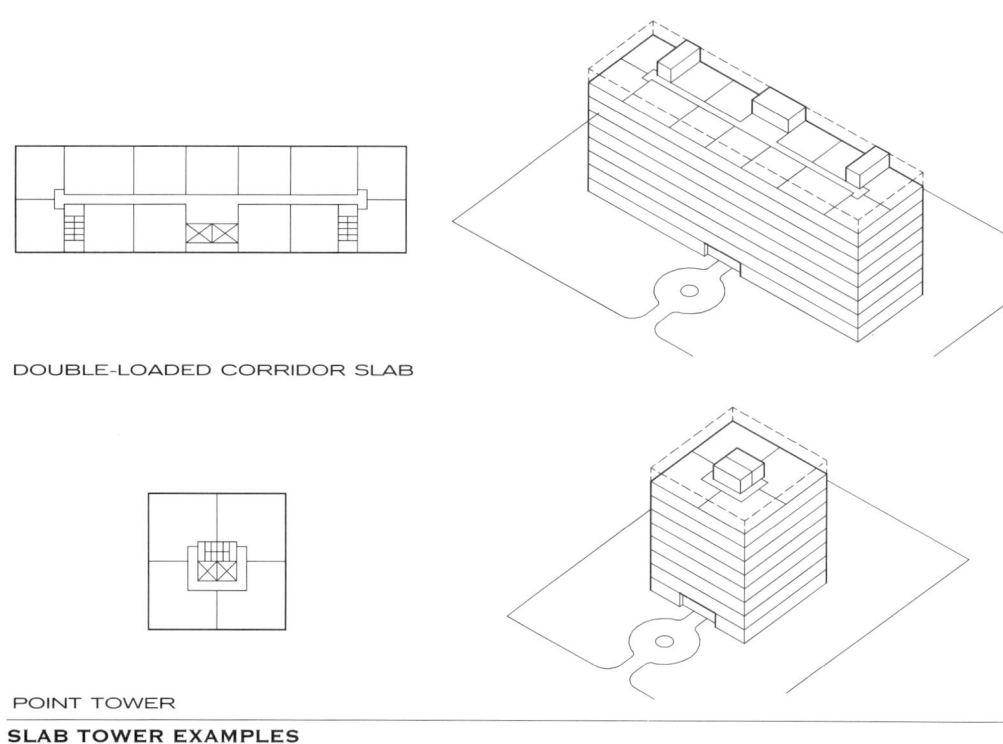

DOUBLE-LOADED CORRIDOR SLAB

POINT TOWER

SLAB TOWER EXAMPLES

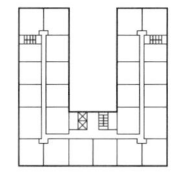 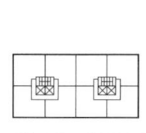 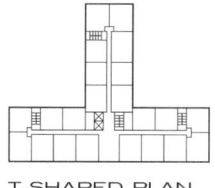 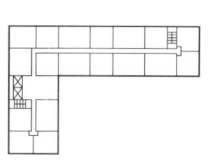

U-SHAPED PLAN WITH SINGLE CORE | SLAB COMPOSED OF TWO TOWERS JOINED | T-SHAPED PLAN WITH SINGLE CORE | L-SHAPED PLAN WITH SINGLE CORE

SLAB TOWER PLAN VARIATIONS

ELEVATOR APARTMENT CHARACTERISTICS

TYPE	CHARACTERISTICS
Double-loaded corridor (slab)	Units have only one exposure. Corridors are interior spaces. Units can be shallow and wide (lengthening corridors, but bringing much light into unit) or narrow and deep (shortening corridors but making a dark zone on the interior). Stairs are required at ends of corridors (limited dead ends allowed).
Single-loaded corridor (slab)	Less efficient than double-loaded corridor. Useful when oriented east-west because all units can face south. Corridor can be naturally illuminated.
Point tower	Efficient circulation because of small number of units/floor; scissors egress stairs can make circulation more efficient. Units can have two exposures. Casts minimal shadow on lower buildings.

Frequently, therefore, the ground floor of elevator buildings is set aside for common spaces and uses. Lobby and security; mail; meeting space; management offices; trash; and mechanical, electrical, and fire equipment frequently are located at grade. In urban situations, retail and commercial uses are appropriate.

If dwelling units are located on the ground floor, they can offer direct access to outdoors.

CIRCULATION VARIATIONS

In the great majority of elevator buildings, the double-loaded corridor is used, which produces a corridor on each floor. By using multifloor units, or by adding stairwell circulation up and down from elevator landings, the number of floors with corridors can be reduced by two-thirds and up to two-thirds of units can have two exposures. Fair Housing Accessibility Guidelines may prohibit some of these variations, especially the skip-stop.

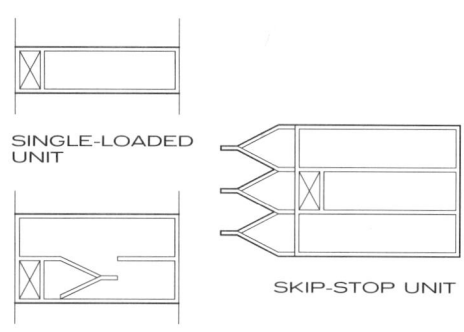

CROSS-SECTION OF VARIATIONS IN CIRCULATION

Ralph Bennett; Bennett Frank McCarthy Architects, Inc.; Silver Spring, Maryland

Special Needs Housing

GENERAL

Special populations require housing forms suited to their needs. Most significantly, small groups of people with special requirements tend to live together so that their needs can be met in a concentrated and efficient way. Facility size is often dictated by financial and operating considerations; the larger the facility, the more difficulty the designer has in making a residentially scaled environment.

Group residences are available for elderly persons, for persons in transition from addiction and psychiatric programs and from incarceration, for persons with terminal illnesses (hospices), and for those who may share another kind of common need.

These facilities typically provide a number of small, simple rooms along with common spaces that include living, dining, and food preparation areas, as well as recreational and administrative facilities.

A more complex group-housing arrangement recently imported from Scandinavia is co-housing—a form of group living that usually features more elaborate individual accommodations along with the common areas found in group homes.

SITE CONSIDERATIONS

1. Direct but controlled access is required from parking and transit facilities to a clearly identifiable entrance.
2. Views from unit windows become especially important in developments where residents spend considerable time in their unit.
3. A variety of views is desirable, from active streets to quiet landscapes. This gives tenants choice in otherwise uniform accommodations.
4. Solar orientation becomes important for such facilities: no unit should be without direct sun at some time during a winter day.
5. Since direct access to outdoors is rarely practical in such housing, exterior access from common spaces becomes more important. Such space should be agreeable for sedentary occupation—sunny but with shade and sheltered from the wind.

TECHNOLOGY

STRUCTURE

1. Single-story buildings can be wood frame in most jurisdictions if properly protected. Two-story or higher buildings must be masonry or protected steel in most jurisdictions.

MECHANICAL

1. Decentralized air, gas heat, or heat pump.
2. Compression refrigeration or heat pump cooling incorporated into through-the-wall units is often used.
3. Common areas have centrally located furnaces with ducts and exterior condensers for heat pumps and refrigeration.
4. Buildings such as hospices, where temperature and humidity control are crucial, use central systems with boilers, central chillers and condenser, and two- or four-pipe systems.
5. Buildings serving persons with special medical needs may require specialized HVAC systems for isolations.
6. Sprinklers are required in most jurisdictions.

SAFETY

1. Systems to announce and report emergencies as well as accommodations for egress are strongly related to the level of assistance required to allow residents to exit the building. The more assistance required, the more extensive the measures required.
2. Building code and fire safety requirements for special needs housing are complex and changing. Protected construction, sprinklers, and supervised fire and smoke alarm systems are generally required.
3. Precautions above this level are dictated by the occupants' ability to perceive danger and act to remove themselves from it. Corridor widths, exit requirements including horizontal exits, separations between dwelling and corridor, and resident staff requirements are all subject to negotiation with local authorities, using model codes as the basis.
4. Local building code authorities should be consulted early in the design process.

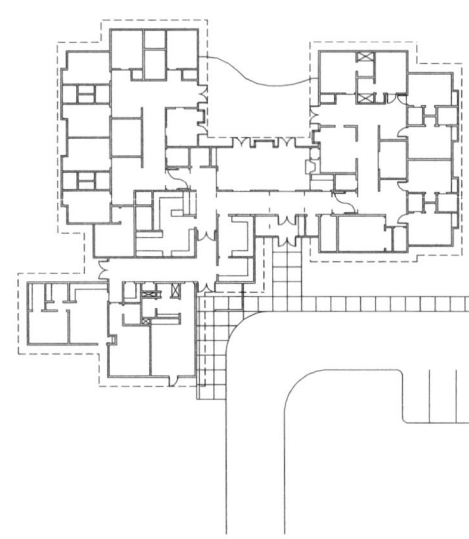

NOTE

This 14-unit facility is divided into two clusters of seven rooms, each cluster is served by a lounge and a spa (a room for bathing and personal care). Common facilities include a large living room, kitchen with snack bar, and administration and staff facilities including a residence for the manager. Rooms offer varying aspects from a busy road to a semi-enclosed garden off the common living room to distant landscape views.

HOSPICE RESIDENCE; MONTGOMERY HOSPICE, INC.; OLNEY, MARYLAND
BENNETT FRANK MCCARTHY ARCHITECTS.

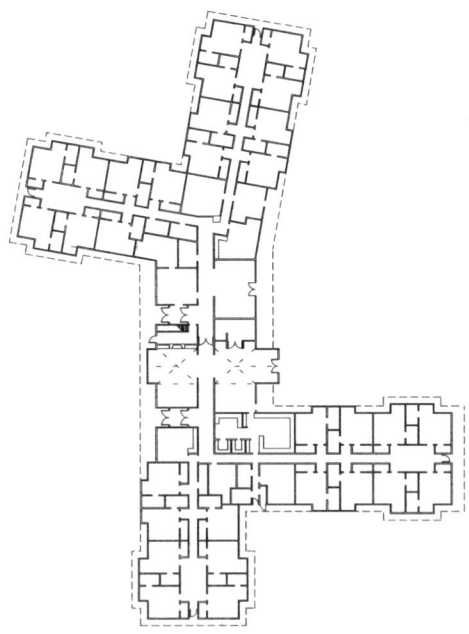

NOTE

This 30-unit group assisted-living facility is divided into two fire-separated buildings to meet subsidy requirements that limit facilities to 15 units. Common areas are linked with openings protected by smoke-actuated doors. Common areas include living room, dining room, institutional kitchen, and laundry.

RAPHAEL HOUSE, VICTORY HOUSING; ROCKVILLE, MARYLAND
BENNETT FRANK MCCARTHY ARCHITECTS, INC.

NOTE

This 36-room group home is designed for elderly persons suffering from Alzheimer's disease and dementia. Each group and subgroup of units has its own vivid and distinct visual identity. Easily accessed outdoor space is controlled to limit wandering. The plan is organized to permit supervision by limited staff.

WOODSIDE PLACE AT PRESBYTERIAN MEDICAL CENTER; OAKMONT, PENNSYLVANIA
PERKINS EASTMAN & PARTNERS

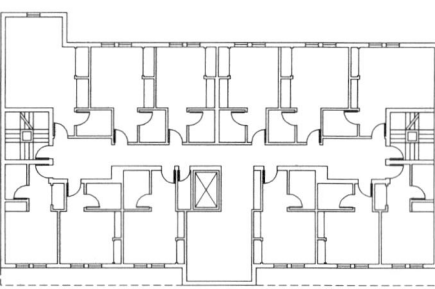

TYPICAL FLOOR

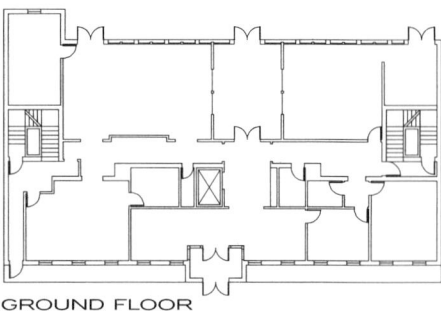

GROUND FLOOR

NOTE

This 36-room single-room-occupancy hotel is designed for emotionally disturbed homeless persons. Social services are offered on the ground floor. Bedrooms are enriched with private bathrooms and mini-kitchens. A private garden for the residents is provided at the rear of the building.

NEW YORK SRO; BROOKLYN, NEW YORK
ARCHITROPE

EXAMPLES OF SPECIAL NEEDS HOUSING

Ralph Bennett; Bennett Frank McCarthy Architects, Inc.; Silver Spring, Maryland

INDEX

This is a cumulative index for the ninth edition of *Architectural Graphic Standards* and the *1996 Supplement*. Page references in **boldface** preceded by **S** indicate *Supplement* pages.

Abitare, 896
Abrasion resistance, of metal, 245
Abutments, bridge, **S67–68**
Access
  basins, 649
  controls, 70, 71, 74, 836
  doors, 415, 416
  to fire apparatus, 93
  floors, 30, 492
  floor supports, 647
  hatches, 415
  panels, 416
  residential sites, **S191, S193, S197**
  roof, **S74–78, S104–109**
  security site selection and planning for, 68, 69
Accessibility, 7, 8–22
  ADA guidelines, **S189**, 11–22, 24, 97, 339, 340, 487, 507, 798
  in courtrooms, **S188–189, S190**
  fair housing guidelines, **S196**
  guidelines for bathrooms/restrooms, 20, 21, 666, 806
  guidelines for buildings and facilities, 8–9
  to historic structures, 762
  human dimensions, 7
  for persons with disabilities, **S189**, 8–9
  sports arena checklist, 666
  swimming pool, 687
  symbol of, **S143**, 495
  universal, 8–22, 522, 666
Accessibility Equipment Manufacturers Association, 592
Acid washing, elastomeric joint sealants, 401
ACM (asbestos-containing materials), 127
Acoustical design, 59–64
  reverberation time, 64
Acoustical Society of America (ASA), 124, 484, 576
Acoustical treatment, **S119–120**, 474–476
  barriers, **S120**
  ceiling units, **S120, S123**
  insulation, **S120**
  masonry units, **S119**
  panels, **S123, S136**
  roof decks, **S120**
  seals, **S120**
  spray-on material, **S119**
  tiles, **S123**
  walls, **S119**
Acrylic
  carpet, 481
  dome skylights, 398
  glazing, 446
  lights, 446

  permeance and permeability to water vapor, 352
  plastic sheets, 446
  plexiglass, 445
  sealants, 399
Acrylic resin flooring, **S127**
Active solar heating, 723, 729–731
Adhesive and Sealant Council (ASC), 402
Adhesives
  bonding, 372
  environmental impact of, 747
  organic, 470, 471
  wood, **S47–48**
Adhesives Manufacturers Association, 402
Adobe, burned, 230
Adobe construction, 230
  historic building preservation, 752
Adult measurements, 2–7
Advisory Council on Historic Preservation, 778
Air barriers, house wrap, 716
Air boots, 561, 562
  fittings, 634
Air conditioning, 614, 618, 628, 636–637
  compressors, 627
  for computer rooms, 628
  in conjunction with thermal storage, 723
  electrical circuits for, 640
  electronic control systems, 636–637
  evaporators, 627
  HVAC systems, 614–619
  indoor air quality, 615
  operations, 627
  outlets and diffusers, 633
  piping symbols, 864
  refrigeration principles, 627
  symbols for, 863
  system types, 614
Air Conditioning and Refrigeration Institute, 638
Air Conditioning and Refrigeration Wholesalers, 638
Air Conditioning Contractors of America, 638
Air diffuser, **S116**
Air Diffusion Council (ADC), 638
Air Distributing Institute, 638
Air distribution systems, 614, 631–635
  duct materials and fittings, 634
  ductwork sizing, 635
  multizone, 631
  thermal boxes and air outlets, 633
  warm air, for small buildings, 632
Airfields, 819
Air filters, 805

Air filtration, trees and, 158
Airflow
  natural, 713
  quantities, 564
Air handling equipment rooms, 805
Air Movement and Control Association (AMCA), 638
  Home Ventilating Institute Division, 638
Air pollution control, 620
  national emission standards, 127
Airports, 819–822
Air quality
  indoor, 615
  trees and, 158
Air-supported structures, **S163**
Air volume systems, variable, 636
Alarms
  bank, 507
  fire, 572
  security, 74
Alleys, 89, 90, 92
Alliance for Historic Landscape Preservation, 778
Allied Stone Industries (ASI), 242
Allowable loads
  for columns, 249, 281
  for laminated decks, 311
  for steel C joints, 260
  for wood joists, 276, 277, 278, 280, 285
  for wood rafters, 286, 287, 288, 289
Altars, 542
Aluminum
  alloy fasteners, 149
  angles, tees, zees, and channels, 264
  coated steel, 361
  coatings, 245
  doors, 422, 521
  finishes for architectural applications, **S24–25**
  flagpoles, 494
  flashing, 377, 393
  frames, **S113**, 398, 433, 445
  gauges and weights, **S45**
  grating, 269
  gutters, 390
  historic use, 757
  life cycle of, 744
  nosings with concrete filler, 28
  pipes, 595
  properties of, **S22**, 244
  roofing, 362, 368
  saddles and thresholds, 440
  sealants, 400
  shapes, 264
  shingles and tiles, 361
  siding, 368

  sliding doors, 414, 423
  structural sealant finishes, 453
  tubing, 265, 595
  tubular, framing, 398
  weather stripping, 442
  windows, 425, 426, 427, 428, 760
Aluminum Association, 272, 456
Aluminum Extruders Council (AEC), 456
Amateur Athletic Union (AAU), 700
  basketball standards, 674
Ambulances, 98
  turning dimensions, 99
Ambulatory care facilities, 828
American Architectural Manufacturers Association (AAMA), 456
American Association of Certified Appraisers, 124
American Association of Cost Engineers, 124
American Association of Homes for the Aging (AAHA), 854
American Association of Museums (AAM), 854
American Association of Nurserymen (AAN), 162, 558, 854
American Association of School Administrators (AASA), 558
American Association of Textile Chemists and Colorists, 558
American Cement Alliance (ACA), 186
American Concrete Institute (ACI), 172, 179, 186
  concrete masonry standards, 133
American Concrete Pipe Association, 162
American Consulting Engineers Council, 592
American Correctional Association (ACA), 854
American Council for an Energy-Efficient Economy (ACEEE), 664
American Floor Covering Association, 484
American Forest and Paper Association, **S49**
American Furniture Manufacturers Association, 558
American Galvanizers Association, 272
American Gas Association, 638
American Hardboard Association, 456
American Hardware Manufacturers Association (AHMA), 456
American Harp Society, 520
American Historical Association, 778
American Hockey League, 700
American Horse Shoe Association, 700
American Hospital Association (AHA), 854

Index

American Institute for Conservation (AIC), 778
American Institute for Hollow Structural Sections (AIHSS), 272
American Institute of Architects (AIA)
  Committee on Historic Resources (CHR), 778
  documents, 886–887
American Institute of Certified Planners (AICP), 124
American Institute of Steel Construction (AISC), 272, 576
  Manual of Steel Construction, 249
American Institute of Timber Construction, 344
American Iron & Steel Institute, 272, 576
American Library Association, 558
American Lighting Association, 558, 664
American Lumber Standards Committee (ALSC), 344
American National Standards Institute (ANSI), 124, 405, 504, 520, 592, 664
  acceptable nosing profiles, 28
  elevator standards, 580
  fire escape standards, 268
  grab bar standards, 487
  iron fitting standards, 595
  kitchen standards, 22
  nosing design standards, 28
  residential bathroom standards, 20, 21
  walkway standards, 416
  wheelchair lift standards, 586
American Planning Association (APA), 124
American Plywood Association (APA), **S49**, 306, 309, 344
  plywood grades, 308
  plywood trademarks, 305
  siding construction recommendations, 330
American Professional Soccer League, 700
American Ski Federation, 700
American Society for Concrete Construction (ASCC), 186
American Society for Hospital Engineering, 854
American Society for Testing and Materials (ASTM), 124, 168, 257, 270, 405, 504, 520, 576, 664
  airborne sound standards, 62
  brick standards, 201
  built-up roofing standards, 358
  concrete paver standards, 138
  control joint spacing standards, 197
  deformed bar and steel wire standards, 133
  elastomeric joint sealant standards, 401
  exterior brick standards, 212
  masonry anchor standards, 194
  PVC roof membrane standards, 371
  reinforcing bar standards, 207
  reinforcing steel standards, 171
  siding construction standards, 330
  specifications, 191
  stone cladding standards, 231
  structure-borne sound standards, 63
  waterproofing standards, 347–349
American Society of Civil Engineers (ASCE), 162
American Society of Consulting Planners, 124
American Society of Furniture Design (ASFD), 558
American Society of Golf Course Architects (ASGCA), 162, 700

American Society of Heating, Refrigerating and Air Conditioning Engineers (ASHRAE), 65, 638, 702, 704, 742
  vapor permeance standards, 352
American Society of Interior Designers (ASFD), 558
American Society of Landscape Architects, 162
American Society of Mechanical Engineers (ASME), 520, 592, 638
American Society of Plumbing Engineers, 638
American Society of Professional Estimators, 124
American Society of Safety Engineers, 124
American Society of Sanitary Engineering (ASSE), 520, 638
American Solar Energy Society, 748
Americans with Disabilities Act Accessibility Guidelines (ADAAG)
  Areas of Rescue Assistance (ARAs), 24
  ATMs, 507
  for bathtubs and showers, 19
  for commercial restrooms, 806
  curb ramps, 14, 97
  detectable warnings, 14
  for doors, 15
  for elevators, telephones, and drinking fountains, 17
  kitchens, 22
  mobility aids, 10
  nosings, 340
  open riser stairs, 340
  for parking, sidewalks, and curb ramps, 14
  parking spaces, 666
  for protruding objects and changes in level, 13
  public restrooms, 666
  for ramps and slopes, 16
  reach dimensions for wheelchairs, 12
  residential bathrooms, 20, 21
  restaurant seating, 798
  sinks, 487
  space requirements for wheelchair use, 11
  for water closets, stalls, urinals, and lavatories, 18
  wood stairs, 339
Americans with Disabilities Act (ADA), 8–9, 20
  building code stairway requirements, 25
Americans with Disabilities Act Information Office, 124, 504, 558, 700
American Tennis Association, 700
American Textile Manufacturers Institute, 558
American Water Ski Association, 700
American Welding Society (AWS), 186, 272, 576
American Wine Association, 520
American Wood Council (AWC), 344
American Wood-Preservers Association, **S67**, 344
  standards, **S70**
American Wood Preservers Bureau (AWPB), 344
American Wood Preservers Institute, 344
Anchors and anchorage, **S48**, 193, 194, 291
  beams, 321, 328
  bolts, 239–240, 261, 262, 291, 294, 473, 479, 569
  bolts, tie-down, 50
  brick, 215
  brick veneer, 214, 301

cast-in-place, 183, 270
compression, 169
concrete construction, 179, 183, 440
construction detailing, 49
dovetail, 206, 208, 211, 212
earth, 129
expansion, 291
fixed arch, 321
flexible, 206
floor tie, **S48**
hinge, 321
lane float, 689
liner, 238
masonry, 190, 193, 194, 207
metal bucks, 407, 408, 409
metal floor and roof decks, 258, 259
post, 313
riveted strap, 28
rock, **S5**
rods, 129, 237, 473
rooftop collector supports, 731
shear wall, **S51**
shields and, 291
sill plate, **S48**
solid rock, 296
split-tail, 236
stone, 232, 235, 239, 240, 473, 479
stone veneer, 237, 238
truss, **S48**
uplift, **S48**
wall details, **S50**
walls, 190, 199, 232
walls, cavity, 211
walls, multiwythe, 208, 209
walls, single wythe, 206
wire, 473
wood, 313
Z-type, 194, 208, 212
Angles
  metal, **S139**
  metal, wood fastener, **S48**
  steel, bearing shoe detail, **S68**
Animal care facilities
  kennels, 846
  shelters, 846
  stables, 847–848
  veterinary hospitals, 844–845
Anodic coatings, **S25**
Anthropometric data
  adults, 2
  children, 3
Antimony
  melting temperature of, **S23**
Apartment houses
  hot water requirements, 611
  laundries, 784
  mailboxes, 502
Apartments
  construction cost estimating, 119
  elevator, **S192**, **S199**
  garden, **S192**
  laundry equipment and dishwashers, 516
  locks, 74
  walk-up, **S192**, **S198**
Appliances, large
  circuits for, 640
  design standards for accessible kitchens, 22
  residential, 516–518
Appliances, small kitchen
  storage, 789–790
Aquatics, 683–694
Aquifer systems, 719
ARAs (areas of rescue assistance), 24
Archery Manufacturers Association, 700
Archery range specifications, 698
Arches
  classical, 115

in glued-laminated construction, 318, 321
lamella, 44
masonry, 216, 217
principles of construction, 217
relieving, 752
segmental brick, 752
stone, 765
timber bridge, **S67**
Architectural Anodizers Council (AAC), 272
Architectural Barriers Act, 8
Architectural Design, 896
Architectural Digest, 558
Architectural Fabric Structures Institute, 576
Architectural Lighting, 558
Architectural Precast Association (APA), 186
Architectural Record, 896
Architectural Review, 896
Architectural Translucent Skylight and Curtain Wall Association, 456
Architectural woodwork, **S72–73**, **S79**, 331–341
  cabinet details, 333–336
  interior wall paneling details, 338
  joints, 331, 332
  molding and trim, 341
  shelving, 337
  stairs, 339, 340
Architectural Woodwork Institute (AWI), 344
  premium grade standards, 339
  quality standards, 338
Architecture, 896
Architecture d'Aujourd'hui, 896
Architecture + Urbanism (A&U), 896
Architraves, 114, 341, 770
Arcs, in geometry, 874
Area
  calculations, 118–123, 873, 878
  thermal expansion of, 881
Area dividers, **S91**
Areas of rescue assistance (ARAs), 24
Armchairs, 543
  contemporary, 552
  dimensions, 544
  folding, 545
Art Glass Suppliers Association, 456
Asbestos abatement, 127, 128
  cost of removal, 128
Asbestos Abatement Council, 162
Asbestos-containing materials (ACM), 127
Asbestos Hazard Emergency Response Act (AHERA), 127
Asbestos Information Association of North America, 162
Ash dumps, 218, 223
Ashlar masonry, 232
Ash pits, 218, 220, 223
Ash urns, 155
Asphalt
  bridge surface, **S68**
  in built-up roofing, **S86**
  curbs, 136
  emulsion, glass blocks, 228
  felts, 359, 365
  glass fiber felt, **S86**
  paving, 136, 137–138
  plank flooring, **S127**
  roll roofing, 358
  shingles, 365, 746
  shingles, high wind resistance detail, **S109**
  shingles, repair, **S103**
  strips, flashings, 393
  surface, rubberized, 673

NOTE: Page references in **boldface** preceded by **S** indicate *Supplement* pages.

Index

Asphalt Institute, 162
Asphalt Roofing Manufacturers Association (ARMA), 402
Assembly facilities, 835-843
   auditorium seating, 841
   grandstands and bleachers, 837
   stadiums, 835-836
   stage lighting, 842-843
   theater design criteria, 838-839
   theater sightlines, 840
Associated Landscape Contractors of America, 162, 558
Associated Pipe Organ Builders of America, 520
Association for Preservation Technology, 751, 778
Association of Edison Illuminating Companies, 664
Association of Energy Engineers, 748
Association of Engineering Firms Practicing in the Geosciences (ASFE), 162
Association of Home Appliance Manufacturers (AHAM), 520
Association of Professional Material Handling Consultants, 520, 592
Association of Specialists in Cleaning & Restoration, 778
Association of State and Territorial Solid Waste Management Officials (ASTSWMO), 520
Association of University Architects (AUA), 854
Association of Wall and Ceiling International, 484
Astragals, **S75**, 341, 437
Athletic facilities, 665-700
   aquatic, 683-694
   arena accessibility checklist, 666
   court sport, 677-681
   equestrian, 695-697
   fencing, 698
   field sport, 667-674
   resources, 700
   target shooting, 698-699
   track and field, 675-676
Atlanta Merchandise Mart, 558
ATMs (automated teller machines), 507, 508
Atrium design
   for energy conservation, 720, 722
   wintergarden, 722
Attics
   framing, 285
   ventilation, **S83**, 394
Audio Engineering Society, 576
Audio recorders, for access control, 74
Audiovisual equipment, **S149-151**
Audiovisual facilities, **S149**
   tables for, in schools, 537
Auditoriums, 823
   reverberation time, 64
   seating, 841
Automated teller machines (ATMs), 507, 508
Automatic Guided Vehicle Systems, 592
Automation systems, building
   energy management, 570
   HVAC control, 636-637
   lighting control, 571
Automobiles, design data, 98-105
   turning dimensions, 99
Aviation Safety Institute, 854
Awnings, 500, 501, 734
Awning windows, 428, 430
AWPA. *See* American Wood Preservers Association

Backsplash, 334
Backstops, 668, 674
Badminton, 674, 681
Baffles, **S122**, 55
   ceiling system, **S122**
   chamber, 220
   insulation, **S83**, 718
Bakery, food service, **S156**
Balcony
   railings, 27, 43
   wood deck, **S39**
Ballast
   paver, **S95**, **S106**
   protected membrane roofing aggregate, **S95**
   PVC roofing, 371
Ballasts, electronic, and compact fluorescent lamps, 656
Ball sports, facilities for
   baseball, 667
   basketball, 678
   football, 669
   polo, 695
   racquetball, 679
   rugby, 671
   soccer, 670
   softball, 667
   tennis, 677
   volleyball, 681
Balusters, 27, 270, 339, 340
Balustrades, 115, 770
   stone, 233
   terra-cotta, 752
Bank equipment, 188, 506-507, 508
Banners (signs), 155
Banquet halls, seating capacities, 798
Baptismal fonts and baptistries, 542
Bargeboards, 303
Barns, 847
Barrier-free design
   in historic buildings, 761-762
   parking lots, 103
   sidewalk ramps, 96
   space layout, 6
Barriers
   acoustical, **S120**
   plenum, **S120**
Bars and night clubs
   equipment, **S158-159**
   seating for, 797, 798
Bars, reinforcing, **S6**, 168, 169
   doors, 435
Bar sports, facilities for, 682
Baseball, 667, 673, 674
   Little League, 668
   Major League, 667
Baseboards, **S74**
   chase behind, **S55**
Basements
   finished, 301
   foundation, 716
   insulation, 355
   unfinished (unheated), 301
   walls, **S49**, 170, 203
   windows, 429
Base plates, steel, 321
Bases
   metal column, **S48**
   moldings, **S74-75**
Basketball, 674, 678
   NBA standards, 678
   NCAA standards, 678
Basket racks and rooms (locker rooms), 497, 799
Bathrooms
   accessible, 6, 20, 21, 487
   accessories, 488, 518
   cabinets, 488

   fixture sizes and clearances, 781
   maneuvering clearances, 806
   piping for, 603
   plumbing fixtures, 606, 609
   residential, 20, 21, 781
   saunas, 565
   toilet compartments, 486
Bathtubs
   accessible, 19, 20, 487
   porcelain enamel, 609
   space requirements, 21
   tile enclosures, 471
Battens, **S75**
   metal roofing, 376
   plywood siding, 330
   wood siding, 329
Batteries
   cabinets and racks for, **S183**
Bays
   loading docks, 513
   truck docks, 107
Beads
   casing, 459
   corner, 459
   quirk, 341
Beams
   anchorage, 179, 214
   bond, 49, 133, 207
   box, **S54**
   box, sill wire chase, **S55**
   cable crash, 151
   cantilever, static loads for, 885
   castellated, 45
   collar, 297
   column connection, 249
   composite, framing, 295
   composite structure, 45
   concrete, and column intersections, 164
   concrete, covers, **S138-139**
   concrete, formwork for, **S1**, **S4**, 167
   concrete, in floor systems, **S11**
   concrete, long-span, precast, 181
   concrete, minimum thickness, 172
   concrete, posttensioned, 179
   concrete, precast, **S16**
   concrete, precast and CMU, 215
   concrete, prestressed, 179
   concrete, reinforcement protection, 168
   concrete, steel reinforcement of, 170
   fixed, static loads for, 884
   flitch, 45
   framing, 295, 315
   framing, header, **S36**
   in glued-laminated construction, 318-319, 322
   gypsum board at, 468
   heavy timber, 765
   load tables, **S27**, 181, 249, 282-284, 883-885
   longitudinal, **S67**
   and plank construction, 314
   pocket, **S51**
   reinforced brick, 215
   ridge, **S66**
   simple, static loads for, 883
   size, spacing, and span, 282-283
   spanning, **S51**
   splices, 322, 374
   steel, **S26**
   steel, load tables, **S27**, 249
   steel, wall anchorage in, 214
   straining, **S52**
   summer, **S52-53**
   tie, 297
   wood, load tables, 282-284
Beds and bedroom furniture, 545
   arrangements, 780
   for disabled, 6

Below/Hook Lifters Association, 592
Benches, 525
   courtroom, **S189**, 801
   outdoor, 526
   schools, 536
Bents, **S67**
   girt, **S52**
   girt, upper, **S53**
Berms, 103
   earth, 720
Bicycle paths, 88, 90, 96
Bidets, 606, 781, 859
Bike rail, **S68**
Billiard and Bowling Institute of America, 700
Billiard tables, 682
Bioclimatic chart, 702
Birthing centers, 828
Bleachers, 837
Blind, accommodations for, 13
Blinds
   integral, 734
   Venetian, 571
   wood window, **S79**
Blocking
   corner, **S61**
   insulation, **S83**
   lateral load, **S65**
   solid, **S39**
Blueprint, 896
Boats
   design data, 109-110
   launching ramps for, 111
Bocce, 671
Boiler rooms, room planning for, 804
Boilers, 620
   flue economizers, 630
   gas-fired, 623
   range, 612
   vents, 625
Bollards, 93, 151, 154
Bolts, 292
   for concrete formwork, **S5**
   corrosion-resistant, 334
   expansion, stone veneer, 237
   extension flush, 434
   high-strength, 249, 253
   lag, shields for, 291
   Lewis, 237
   mortise, 434
   stonework anchoring, 239-240, 473, 479
   toggle, 293
Bond breakers, 401
   sealants, 399
   waterproofing, 347
Bookcases, open classroom furniture, 537
Book shelves, 337
Booths, restaurant, 797, 798
Boston Design Center, 558
Bowling, lawn, 681
Braces, 261, 294, 316, 327
   core system, 254
   corner, 294
   cross, 111, 254, 323
   diagonal, 254
   doors, 405
   excavations, 129
   exterior walls, 294
   knee, **S52-53**, 167
   lateral, wood truss, 323
   metal buildings, 569
   pipes and ducts, 50
   wood decks, 313
   wood framing, 298
   wood trusses, 323, 326
Bracing
   in steel framing, **S37**
   for tilt-up concrete, **S21**

NOTE: Page references in **boldface** preceded by **S** indicate *Supplement* pages.

Index

Brackets
  cam lock, **S5**
  floor mounting, **S42**
  wall, 270
Brass
  gauges and weights, **S23**, **S45**
  pipe, 594
  properties of, **S22**, 244
  saddles and weather stripping, 440
  tubing, 265
Brass and Bronze Ingot Manufacturers, 272
Breeching
  boilers, 625
  insulation, 602
Brick, 188, 189, 200, 201
  adobe, 230
  anchorages, 215
  arches, 216, 752
  ASTM standards, 201
  bonds, 200
  face, cavity walls, 212
  face, grade requirements for exposures, 201
  flooring, **S126**
  historic building preservation, 752
  joints, 192, 200
  masonry, 197, 207, 212, 215, 882
  masonry stoves, 220
  modular work, 200
  paving, 137, 138
  permeance and permeability to water vapor, 352
  pressed concrete, 138
  reinforced beams, columns, and pilasters, 215
  reinforced lintels, 199
  reinforced masonry, **S126**
  rowlocks, 270
  sealants, 400
  sizes, 200
  sizes, standard nomenclature for, 201
  sundried mud, 230
  veneer, 32, 189, 213, 214, 301, 302, 431
  walls, 134, 190, 199, 215
  walls, cavity, 210, 212, 764
  walls, curtain, 215
  walls, grouted hollow, 215
  walls, recess and sill details, 208
  walls, reinforced load-bearing, 207
  walls, retaining, 215
  watertables, 201, 384
Brick Institute of America (BIA), 242
Bridges, timber, **S67–68**
Bridging, 256–257
  floor joists, 294
  joists, **S32**, **S33**, **S37**
  rafters, **S37**
  wall framing, 300
  walls, **S37**
  wood/steel, 299
British thermal unit (Btu), 738
Bronze
  flagpoles, 494
  nosings, 28
  properties of, **S22–23**, 244
  saddles and weather stripping, 440, 442
  stair railings, 757
  weight for buildings, **S23**
Btu (British thermal unit), 738
Bucks, metal, 405, 407–409
Builders Hardware Manufacturers Association (BHMA), 434, 456
Building and Fire Research Laboratory, 576
Building automation systems, 636–637
Building envelope design, 29–36
  climate response and, 714–718
  flat plate concrete, 34
  lightweight steel frame and brick veneer, 32
  posttensioned concrete, 35
  precast concrete frame, 36
  staggered steel truss, 31
  steel bar joist, with bearing wall, 29
  steel frame, with access floor and curtail, 30
  wood roof truss and wood floor truss, 33
Building materials
  corrugated, 140, 141, 362, 390, 758
  embodied energy of, 743
  environmental impact analysis of, 743
  environmental impact of, 746, 747
  fibrous, 354
  flammable, flooring, 483
  heat transmission resistance of, 740
  historic, 750
  insulation, 354
  life-cycle analysis of, 743
  life cycle of, 744
  metallic, 354
  movement of, 196
  nontoxic, 745
  permeance and permeability to water vapor, 352
  recyclable, 851
  recycled, 745
  thermal resistance values of, 739, 740, 856
Building Officials and Code Administrators International (BOCA), 124
  fire alarm system, 572
  National Building Code stairway requirements, 25
  occupant loads, 23
Building panels, structural, **S62–63**
Building papers
  permeance and permeability to water vapor, 352
  thermal resistance, 739
Buildings
  access control, 71
  automation systems, 570–571, 637
  commercial, 720–721
  historic preservation of, 113–114, 749–778
  insulation, 353–354, 740, 741
  loads and calculations, 43, 635
  metal, pre-engineered, **S165–166**, 569
  nonresidential, 720
  orientation of, 705–712
  residential types, **S191**
  security, 66–74
  smart, 720
  timber frame, **S52**
Building Seismic Safety Council (BSSC), 124
Building Stone Institute (BSI), 242
Building structure
  air-supported, 560
  composite elements, 45
  flat plate concrete, 34
  frame construction with cold roof, 715
  historic, 764–765
  integration of, 29–36
  lightweight steel frame and brick veneer, 32
  long-span, 44, 138, 181, 560
  masonry box-frame, 188
  posttensioned concrete, 35
  precast concrete frame, 36
  preengineered, 569
  staggered steel truss, 31
  steel bar joist with bearing wall, 29
  steel frame with access floor and curtain wall, 30
  technologies, 29–36
  tensile, 44
  wood roof truss and wood floor truss, 33
Building systems, 29–45
  comparative, 37–42
  continuous span, 318
  core component guidelines, 810
  energy design, 714, 716–722
  envelope design, 29–36
  flat plate concrete, 34
  integrated, 29–36, 719
  interiors, 29–36
  mechanical systems, 29–36
  posttensioned concrete, 35
  precast concrete frame, 36
  rigid frame, 253, 569
  security planning, 72
  seismic design, 48
  staggered steel truss, 31
  steel bar joist with bearing wall, 29
  steel frame, lightweight, and brick veneer, 32
  steel frame with access floor and curtain wall, 30
  ventilation, 713
  wood roof and floor truss, 33
Building Systems Institute, 124
Building types, 85, 779–854
  airports, 819–822
  child care centers, 812, 813
  churches, 831
  historic, 750
  hospitals, 827–830
  justice facilities, **S186–190**
  low-rise, 31
  mosques, 833
  museums, 815–818
  offices, 808–811
  resources, 854
  school, 823–826
  stadiums, 835, 836
  synagogues, 832
  veterinary hospitals, 844, 845
Bulkheads, 690
Bulletin boards, 496
Bumpers, precast concrete, 136
B.U.R. *See* Modified bitumen membrane
Burglary alarm systems, banks, 507
Busducts, 860
Business and Institutional Furniture Manufacturers Association (BIFMA), 558
Butyl
  joint fillers, 399
  tape, skylights, 398

Cabanas, 799
Cabinets
  bar, dry storage, **S159**
  base, 333–334, 336
  bathroom, 488
  battery, **S183**
  classifications, 333
  coatings, 245
  custom grade, 333–335
  darkroom, 519
  details, 333, 334
  European-style, 336
  filing, 527, 533–535
  fire, 499
  ice cream, **S157**, **S159**
  library, 540
  mobile banquet, **S154**
  open classroom furniture, 537
  wall, 333–334
  wall, kitchen, 336
Cables
  armored, 643
  crash beams, 151
  electrical, 643, 644, 646, 647
  telecommunications distribution, 663
  trays, 644, 645
CAD (computer-aided design) layer guidelines, 871
Cadmium
  melting temperature of, **S23**
Cafeterias, seating capacities, 798
Caissons, 135
Calculations
  of area, 118–123, 873, 878
  cut and fill, 878
  of energy, 711, 712
  structural, 883–885
  of volume, 118
California Redwood Association (CRA), 344
Cameras, surveillance, 507, 508
Campbell Center for Historic Preservation Studies, 778
Campus plan, 823
Canadian Society of Landscape Architects (CSLA), 162
Canadian Wood Council (CWC), 344
Candela, 52
Candlepower (CP), 52
Canes
  clearances for, 13
  walking, 10
Canoes, 109
Canopies, 500–501
  canvas, 734
  roof, ornamental, **S101**
  storefront, 420
Cant, **S104**
Cantilever, **S64**
  overhang with, **S59**
Capacitors, pole-mounted, 650
Capitals, 114
  plaster, 768
Caps
  flashing, **S105**
  mineral-surfaced sheet built-up roofing, **S87**
  parapet, light metal, **S90**, **S94–95**
  rain, **S106**
  snap, **S102**
Card catalogs
  cabinets, 540
  reach dimensions, 12
Card readers, 74
  garages, 100
Carousels, 537
Carpentry
  decks, 312, 313
  doors and frames, 411
  eaves and overhangs, 301
  exterior stairs, 313
  finish, 329–330
  flooring, 477, 478
  framing, 301
  plywood design data, 305
  plywood roof decks and soffits, 310
  plywood subflooring on wood framing, 309
  rough, **S49–66**, 294–304
  stairs, 340
Carpet, 481–482
  environmental impact of, 747
  fiber characteristics, 482
  maintenance programming, 482
Carpet and Rug Institute, 484
Carports, 100, 785
Carriages
  container, 588
  stair framing, 296
  wood stairs, 339
Casings, interior wood, **S74**

NOTE: Page references in **boldface** preceded by **S** indicate *Supplement* pages.

Index

Cast iron
  architectural metals, 757
  bases, 765
  channels, 141
  columns, 763
  pipes, 595
  radiators, 616
  sectional type burner, 620
Cast Iron Soil Pipe Institute (CIPSI), 162, 638
Cast metal
  abrasive surface thresholds, 440
  nosings, 28
  saddles, 440
  uses for, 154–155
Cast plaster
  cornice, S114
  two-piece column, S115
Cast stone, uses for, 155
Cast Stone Institute (CastSI), 242
Catchbasins, 141, 143
Cathedrals, reverberation time, 64
Catwalks, 7, 840, 843
  marine, 111
Caulking, lead wedge, 235
Cavity walls, 199, 210, 211, 212, 232
  angle support, 194
  brick, 764
  flashing, 198
  shelf anchors, 194
Cedar
  fences, 149
  shingles and shakes, 363
Cedar Shake & Shingle Bureau (CSSB), 402
Ceilings, 256
  acoustical materials, 474
  acoustical ratings, 464, 468
  acoustical tile, S120, 271, 474, 475
  acoustical units, S123
  assemblies sound criteria, 61
  baffle system, S122
  cast (molded) units, S123
  cathedral, S40
  cathedral, insulation and, 355
  closure rings, fastened, S139
  closures wood paneling, 338
  coffered, S115
  courtrooms, height in, S188
  coves, S116
  decking, 310
  finishes, S139
  fire protection, 357
  fixtures, 554
  gypsum board, with spacers, S55
  gypsum board at, 468
  integrated systems, 561–562
  joists, 285, 297, 298
  lath and plaster, 460–461
  linear, S122
  metal, 474–475
  modular systems, 561
  nodular units, S123
  panels, 416
  panels, interior wall system, S121
  panels, roof eave with, S63
  panels, textured, S123
  radiant heating, 624
  reflected, 561
  reflected fans, S115
  sloped, roof eave with, S63
  soffits, at lintel, S116
  sound isolated interrupted, S117
  special surfaces, S122–123
  suspended, S122–123, 271, 460, 474–475
  suspended, lath and plaster, 460, 461
  tile coatings, 245
  tongue-and-groove, S54
  types, 474–475
  vaulted, S57
  wet felted units, S123
Ceilings and Interior Systems Construction Association (CISCA), 484, 504
Cellars
  doors, 415
  wine storage, 515
Cellular insulation materials, 354
Cellulose Insulation Standards Enforcement Program (CISEP), 402
Cement
  grout channels, 141
  integrally colored, S13
  mortar, 470
  portland, 191
  and preservation of masonry, 753
  types, S7, 171
  wood tiles, roofing, S85
Cement-water ratios
  concrete, 172
  slab strengths, 175
Center for Accessible Housing (CAH), School of Design, 124
Center for Architectural Conservation, 778
Center for Insulation Technology, 402
Center for Preservation and Rehabilitation Technology, 778
Centralized heating, electric systems, 624
Central processing unit (CPU), S151
Ceramic slate, S85
Ceramic tile, 469–471
  countertops, 471
  expansion joints, 470
  flooring, 471
  grout and mortary types, 470
  installation, 470, 471
  thresholds for, 471
  tub enclosures, 471
  walls, 470
Ceramic Tile Institute, 484
Ceramic veneer, 226
Certified Ballast Manufacturers, 664
Chain link fences, 148
  baseball backstop, 674
Chair rails, S75, 341, 770
Chairs, 544
  anthropometric data, 5
  for children, 538
  church equipment, 542
  classic, 546–550
  contemporary, 551, 553
  folding, 524
  lift, 697
  lounge, 543
  office, 532
  outdoor, 526
  for restaurants/bars, 797
  school, 536
  stacking, 524, 541, 542
  stair lifts, 586
Chaise lounges, outdoor, 526
Channels
  furring, S34, S40, 263, 468
  metal, 264
  runner, S34
  runoff, 130
  slots and anchors, 194
  studs, 260, 462
  surface drainage, 141
  suspension systems, 468
Chases
  baseboard, S55
  service, under floor, S55
  wainscot, S55
  wire, S62
  wire, surface-mounted, S55
  wire, timber-sill, S55
Check dams, 142
Checkroom equipment, 796
Chemical resistance, 245
  coatings for, S129
Child care centers, 812, 813
Children
  anthropometric data, 3
  furniture for, 538
  patient rooms for, 802
Chilled water systems, 619
  air conditioning, 627
  direct gas-fired, 623
  pumps, 804
  terminal units, 629
Chimneys, 218, 221–222, 625
  caps, 221
  clearances, S141, 221
  connector systems, 221
  construction, 222
  downdrafts, 221
  flashings, 381
  flues, 221, 222
  hoods, 221, 625
  industrial, 221
  insulation, 222
  medium heat, 625
  metal, 493
  metal, UL-approved, 221
  pots, 221, 625
  prefabricated, 625
  types, S141
  vent stacks, 625
  wood framing members, 218
Chinking, log construction, 317
Chlorine contact chambers, 146
Chlorpolyvinylchloride (CPVC) pipe, 594
Chords, in geometry, 874
Chromium
  melting temperature of, S23
  properties of, S22, 244
Churches, 831
  chimney requirements, 221
  liturgical equipment, 507, 541–542
  reverberation time, 64
Cities, 80
City blocks, 82
  patterns, 80
  types, 82, 83
City tractors, 106
Cladding, 329–330, 367–369
Clamping ring, S94
Clapboard, historic preservation of, 755
Classical architecture, 112–117
  columns, 113, 114, 117
  details, 113
  doors, windows, pediments, and rustication, 116
  entasis, fluting, volutes, and pilasters, 114
  intercolumnation, superposition, arches, and balustrades, 115
  moldings, 112
  orders, 112, 113–114
  orders, hidden, 117
  use of elements, 117
Classrooms, 823, 826
  child care centers, 813
  early learning equipment, 538
  latches and locks, 435
  open, furniture, 537
Clay
  chimney pot, 221
  flue liners, 218, 219–220, 221, 222
  masonry units, 201
  structural, 207
  tennis court surfaces, 677
  vitrified, pipe, 144
Clay tile
  channels, 141
  drainpipes, 140
  pavers, 137
  roofing, 360, 367, 758
  structural, 225
Cleaning equipment, storage for, 790
Cleaning methods, masonry surfaces, 753–754
Cleanouts, 220, 223
  pipes, 596
  wall-type, 596
Clean room, 564
Cleats, in metal roofs, 374
Clerestories
  solar heating, 726–727
  trusses, S56, 327
Climate, 702–704
  Arctic region map, 714
  bioclimatic chart, 702
  buffering, 720
  and building design, 714–718
  cold, design for, 714, 715
  control strategies, 702, 716–718, 818
  design conditions and strategies, 702–703
  energy and resource conservation, 702
  environmental site analysis, 77
  hot arid, design for, 717
  humid overheated, design for, 718
  terms, 714
  underheated, design for, 716
Climate control systems, 702
Clinch strips, flashings, 379
Clips
  for column covers, S138
  gypsum lath system, 458
  wood fasteners, backup, S48
  wood fasteners, roof truss, S48
  wood fasteners, wood, S48
Clocks, 155, 572
Closers, 438
Closets, 786
  dimensions, 6
  mirrored doors, 545
  reach limits, 12
  storage arrangements, 787
Closures, acoustical, S120
CMS (computerized control and monitoring system), 637
Coat hooks, accessible, 806
Coatings, S130–131
  abrasion-resistant, S128
  ceiling surfaces, special, S122–123
  cementitious, S128
  chemical-resistant, S128–129
  clear, S131
  for concrete surfaces, S14
  exterior systems, S128, S133–134
  floor, special, S127
  glazed, high build, S128
  graffiti-resistant, S128
  interior systems, S128, S134
  liquid-applied, permeance and permeability to water vapor, 352
  on metal, S24–25
  special, S127, S128–129
  for steel, S128
  substrate conditions and, S132
  types and uses, S133–134
  wall surfaces, special, S121
Coat racks, classic, 547
Coatrooms, 796
Cobalt
  melting temperature of, S23
Cobblestone, dry-set, 137
Coffee shops, seating capacities, 798
Coin Laundry Association, 520
Coin-operated laundries, 511
Cold climate design, 714, 715
Cold Finished Steel Bar Institute, 272
Cold storage rooms, S164, 563
Cold weather construction, concrete, 172

NOTE: Page references in **boldface** preceded by **S** indicate *Supplement* pages.

Index

Collars
- flex-tube, **S91**
- framing, 298
- ties, **S52–53**

College Football Association, 700

Columns, 215
- allowable loads, 249, 281
- anchorage, 211
- anchorage, wood, 313
- angle guards for, 491
- beam connection, 249, 253
- caps, 322
- cast-in-place, 34
- cast-iron, 763
- cast plaster, two-piece, **S115**
- classical, 112, 113–114, 115
- concrete, 197, 214
- concrete-filled, 45
- concrete formwork for, **S2**, 165
- concrete reinforcement, 168
- connections, 315, 322
- construction, 215
- control joints at, 197
- corner, shelf angle at, 211
- covers, **S138–139**
- covers, plaster, 768
- covers, precast concrete connections, **S20**
- drop panels, **S2**
- equipment support, **S106**
- exterior, 315
- fireproofed, U.L.-rated, 266
- fire-resistant construction, 467
- flashing, 382
- flat drop, 173
- footings, **S2**, 165
- gas medical, 803
- glued laminated construction, 319–320
- guards, 491
- gypsum board at, 467
- gypsum plaster, glass fiber-reinforced, two-piece, **S115**
- installation, 232
- interior, 315
- lally, 266
- liquid-filled, 357
- load capacity, 249, 281
- load transfer, **S65**
- masonry anchors, 194
- metal bases, **S48**
- plaster covers, 768
- precast concrete, 183
- reinforcement, 170, 215
- roof beam, 315
- splices, 249
- steel, 50, 165, 266
- steel, anchorage, 208, 214
- steel, concrete-encased, 45
- steel, connections, 322
- steel, control joints, 197
- steel, fire protection, 45, 357
- steel, load tables, **S27**, 249
- steel, prefabricated fireproofed, 266
- steel, reinforced, 215
- for steel frames, 254
- stone, 232
- tapered, wood, 321
- tube, 265
- wood, anchored with steel baseplate, 321
- wood, load tables, 281
- wood footing, **S51**

Combination scupper and gutter, **S105**

Combustion chambers, 220

Comfort
- ASHRAE zone, 702
- climate, 702
- thermal, 65

Commission Internationale de L'Eclairage (CIE), 664

Commission of Fine Arts, 778

Communications systems, 73–74, 572, 663
- wiring, 529

Communion preparation rooms, 831

Communion rails and tables, 541–542

Community facilities, **S195**

Community planning, 75–93

Community Research Association, 854

Compass orientation, 707

Compensation guidelines forms and worksheets, 886

Composite structural elements, 45

Computer-aided design (CAD) layer guidelines, 871

Computer and Business Equipment Manufacturers Association, 558

Computer equipment, office, **S151**

Computer rooms, 492
- air conditioning, 628
- cables, 646, 647
- carrels, 537
- daylighting analysis, 58
- layout, 492
- wiring, 529
- workstation furniture, 527

Computers, building automation systems, 637

Computer workstations, **S151**

Concert Hall Research Group, 576

Concrete, 163–186
- admixtures, **S7**, **S9**
- aggregate, **S7**, **S9**, **S13**, 171, 175, 177
- aggregate, exposed, **S12**, 178
- air content, **S9**
- air-entrained, 172
- architectural, **S18**, 176–178
- bases, anchorage, 321
- beams, **S1**, **S4**, **S8**, **S16**, 49, 167, 209, 214
- bituminous, 673
- blocks, masonry, 49
- bollards, 151, 154
- bricks, pressed, 138
- bush-hammered, 178, 754
- cast-in-place, **S7–14**, 171–178, 266, 348, 380
- cement types, **S7**
- channel anchorage in, 440
- channels, 141
- coatings, **S14**
- color, integral, **S12–13**
- columns, **S1**, **S2**, 197, 214
- composite construction, 45
- connection alignment, **S20**
- connections, precast, **S19–20**, **S21**
- construction, **S7**, **S8**, 171–172
- corner details, 238
- counterflashing, **S89**, **S99**
- cracking in, **S14**
- creep, 172
- curbs, 136, 398
- curing, **S8**
- cylinder test for, **S7**, 171
- decks, **S15–16**, 262
- defect prevention, **S14**
- deflection, **S8**, 172
- diving boards, 692
- drainpipes, 140
- economy of formwork, **S1**
- encasement for fire protection, 357
- environmental impact of, 746
- extruded, high wind resistance detail, **S109**
- filled columns, 45
- filled masonry, 294
- filled steel pans, 267
- finishes, **S12–13**, **S21**, 177–178
- fireproofing of steel, 357
- flat plate, 34
- floor slabs, 168, 170
- floor systems, **S10–11**, 170, 173
- footings, **S1**, **S2**, 168, 346
- formed plastics, 177
- form liners, **S13**, 177
- formwork, **S1–5**, **S8**, 164–167, 172
- formwork hardware, **S1**, **S5**
- foundations, 174, 346
- frames, for stone stairs, 479
- gutters, 136
- historic building preservation, 752
- inserts, 178
- joints, **S13**, 175, 178
- lightweight, **S7**, 180
- lightweight, weights, 882
- minimum-strength, slabs, 168
- panels, glass fiber reinforced, 184
- panels, wall, **S17–18**, **S21**
- parapet, counterflashing, **S89**
- pavers, **S95**, 96, 136–138
- pavers on existing slab, **S126**
- permeance and permeability to water vapor, 352
- pile foundations, 135
- planter barriers, 151
- posttensioned, 35, 179
- poured-in-place formwork, 166
- precast, **S15–21**, 179–186
- precast, bumpers, 136
- precast, columns, 183
- precast, decks, 180
- precast, frame, 36
- precast, lintels, 199
- precast, panels, 226
- precast, riprap, 130
- precast, slabs, 180
- precast, systems, 45
- precast, tilt-up construction, **S1**, **S121**, 185
- pressed, unit flooring, **S126**
- pressed bricks and pavers, 138
- prestressed and pretensioned, 36, 179, 180
- properties, **S8**, 172
- proportion of structural elements, 172
- protection, **S8**, 172
- reinforced, **S6**, 35, 168–170, 184, 199, 215
- reinforced, floor systems, 166, 175, 178
- reinforced, slabs, 170
- reinforcing bars and wire, **S6**
- repairs, **S14**
- resources, 186
- retaining walls, 132
- rustication, 166
- sealants, 400
- seismic-resistant details, 49
- shoring, **S8**
- slab, mortared, **S126**
- slab, mortarless pavers on, **S126**
- slabs, **S4**, **S8**, **S10**, **S11**, **S15**, 167, 175
- slabs, floor, 168, 170
- slabs, reinforcement, 168
- slump test, **S7**
- spalled, repairs, 754
- stairs, 176, 251
- stone veneer on, 237
- strength rates, 172
- strengths, 173, 175
- structural, 168
- surfaces, **S12–14**, **S128**, 177–178
- surface texture, **S13**
- tests, cylinder, **S7**
- tests, slump, **S7**
- thermal resistance, 739
- tile roofing, **S84**
- tilt-up, **S1**, **S21**, 185
- trash receptacles, 155
- treads, 28
- tree grates, 154
- two-way, slabs, 170
- wall, single-pitch side wall detail, **S112**
- walls, **S1**, **S3**, **S17–18**, 168
- water-cement ratios, **S8**
- waterproofing, 348
- weather considerations, **S8**, 172
- weights, 171, 180, 882
- workability of, 171

Concrete masonry units (CMUs), 202, 212
- anchorage, 206
- brick veneer on, 214
- lintels, 199
- reinforced, retaining walls, 133
- types, 202
- walls, 134, 205, 207
- walls, cavity, 210
- walls, electrical outlet box in, 205
- walls, single wythe, 207

Concrete Paver Institute (CPI), 162

Concrete Reinforcing Steel Institute (CRSI), 186

Concrete Sawing and Drilling Association (CSDA), 186

Condensation
- analysis, 352
- requirements, 394
- skylights, 395

Condensers
- air conditioning, 627
- warm air heating, 632
- water pumps, 804
- water systems, 618

ConDoc modular drawing format, 870

Conductance, thermal, 738, 739

Conduction
- climate control, 716–718
- climatic design strategies, 703
- thermal comfort, 65

Conductivity, thermal, 738, 739

Conductor heads, 391

Condulets, 643

Conference furniture, **S149**, 527
- tables, 6, 531, 549, 550, 551

Conference rooms, **S149**, 794

Connections
- beam, 249, 321
- concrete, precast, **S19–20**
- glued-laminated construction, 319
- long-span structures, 44
- metal space frames, **S31**
- moment, 183
- moment-resisting, column-to-beam, 253
- open-web steel joints, 310
- pier, 185
- precast concrete, 183
- shear, 249, 254
- split ring, 323

Connectors, metal plate, **S56**

Conservation and Renewable Energy Inquiry and Referral Service (CAREIRS), 748

Construction
- concrete, **S7–8**
- heavy timber, **S67–68**
- ironwork, ornamental, **S43**
- timber frame, **S52–55**
- wood I-joist details, **S64–66**
- wood truss, **S56–57**

Construction cost estimating, 119–121
- apartments, 119
- dormitories, 119
- high schools, 120

NOTE: Page references in **boldface** preceded by **S** indicate *Supplement* pages.

Index

hospitals, 120
hotels, 120
location factors, 121
office buildings, 120
parking garages, 121
warehouses, 121
Construction Industry Manufacturers Association, 592
Construction materials
　comparison chart, 746, 747
　corrugated, 140, 141, 362, 390, 758
　embodied energy of, 743
　environmental impact of, 743, 746, 747
　fibrous, 354
　flammable, flooring, 483
　high-energy, environmental impact, 743
　historic, 750
　insulation, 354
　life-cycle analysis of, 743, 744
　metallic, 354
　movement of, 196
　nontoxic, 745
　permeance and permeability to water vapor, 352
　recyclable, 851
　recycled, 745
　thermal resistance, 739, 856
Construction Specifications Institute (CSI), 124
　documents, 888–889
　Masterformat, 888, 889
Construction Specifier, 272
Contract Furnishings Council (CFC), 558
Control and monitoring system (CMS), computerized, 637
Control joints, 193, 197, 198, 459, 460
　block, 197
　concrete slabs, 175
　gypsum wallboard, 463
　masonry, 196, 197
　masonry, horizontal, 212
　paving, 96
　pier, 197
　premolded, 175
　retaining walls, 132, 133
　strips, 472
　tongue and groove, 175
Convection
　climatic design strategies, 703
　electric heating, 624
　thermal comfort, 65
Convectors, 616
Conveying systems, 577–592
　resources, 592
Conveyor Equipment Manufacturers Association, 592
Cooking
　gas-fired equipment, 623
　kitchen layout, 783
　kitchen layout (commercial), **S154**
　residential, **S161**
Coolers, 17, 487, 610, 628
　refrigerated, 563
Cooling
　air conditioning, 627, 628, 633, 636, 640, 863, 864
　annual use, 724
　computer rooms, 628
　concepts, 725
　condensing and evaporative systems, 618
　economizer/enthalpy cycle, 720
　energy storage for, 720
　equipment interface, 723
　four-pipe systems, 629
　greenhouses, 849
　kennels and animal shelters, 846
　limited capacity devices, 723

mainframe systems, 628
natural, 722
passive solar, 725
thermal storage walls, 728
towers, 626, 627
Cooling Tower Institute, 638
Copings
　flashings, 379
　metal, 393
　stone, 236, 237–238, 239
　through wall flashing under, **S97**
Copper
　architectural metals, 757
　coated galvanized steel, 361
　dovetail slots, 194
　finishes, **S24**
　flashing, 377, 393
　gutters, 389–390
　melting temperature of, **S23**
　nails, 366
　properties of, **S22**, 244
　roofing, 373, 375
　tubing, 265, 594, 595
　weight for buildings, **S23**
　weights and gauges, **S45**
Copper Development Association (CDA), 272
Corbel, **S72**
Cork tile flooring, 480
Corners, **S75**
　blocking, **S61**
　cavity wall columns, 212
　concrete details, **S12**, 238
　connections, 315
　gravel stops, 393
　guards, **S137**, 491
　inside, **S121**
　interior stone details, 473
　ironwork, ornamental, **S43**
　outside, details, **S121**
　outside, protection for, **S50**
　wall, **S61**
　wall framing, 300
Cornices, **S74**
　classical, 113
　columns, 114
　flashings, 378
　plaster, 768
　preservation of wood, 755
　stone, 233, 235
　support detail, 302
　types, **S114**
Corridors
　accessibility, 7
　dimensions, 6
　green, 132
Corrosion, 244
　galvanic, **S23**, 195, 377, 757
Corrugated materials
　gutters, 390
　iron roofs, 758
　metal drain pipes, 140
　roofing, 362
　steel channels, 141
Cosmetic, Toiletry, and Fragrance Association, 504
Cost estimating, 118–123
Costing, life-cycle, 122, 123
Council of Educational Facility Planners (CEFP), 854
Council of Education in Landscape Architecture, 162
Council of Landscape Architecture Registration Boards, 162
Counterflashings, **S98–99**, 378, 380, 393
　concrete, **S99**
　concrete parapet, **S89**
　at existing wall, **S99**
　expansion joint, **S99**

installation, **S98**
non-masonry wall, **S99**
parapet, **S89**, **S92–93**
with receiver, **S98**
without receiver, **S98–99**
at sloped roof, **S99**
snap-in, **S98**
springlocked, **S98**
structural steel, **S99**
systems, **S98–99**
at tile roof, **S99**
Counters, 797, 798
　heights and clearances, 5
　tops, 334, 335, 471
Court construction, 673
Courthouses
　design, **S186–187**
　security, **S187**
　types, **S186**
Courtrooms, **S187–190**, 801
　accessibility, **S186**, **S189**
　design and layout, **S187–189**
　furnishings and finishes, **S189–190**
　security, **S189**
　technology needs, **S189**
Court sports, 677–681
Coverings, wall, **S135–136**
Covers
　beam, **S138–139**
　column, **S138–139**
　column, precast concrete connections, **S20**
　protective (awnings and canopies), 500–501
　protective (metal louvers), **S145–146**
Coves
　ceiling, **S116**
　light, **S116**
　moldings, **S75**
CPVC (chloropolyvinylchloride) pipe, 594
Crane Manufacturers Association of America, 592
Cranes, 591
Crawl spaces, 7, 301
　building insulation, 355
　ventilation, **S83**, 394
　walls, **S49**
Credenzas, 530
Creosote, **S69–70**
Croquet, 681
Cross bracing
　connection, 254
　docks, 111
　wood truss, 323
Crowns, masonry, 221
Crutches, 10
Cul-de-sac, 99
Cultured Marble Institute, 242
Cupboards, highboy, 507
Cupolas, 394, 755
Curbs
　concrete, 136
　continuous equipment support, **S106**
　detail, **S111**
　edge protection, 16
　equipment, **S91**
　guards, 491
　insulated, **S111**, 398
　and paving, 96, 136
　pond, 157
　radius, 90
　ramps, 14, 97
　returned, 14
　skylight, 298, 398
　stone, 233
　stops for parking lots, 103
　vertical frame, detail, **S112**
　wood, **S111**
Curling, 696

Curtain walls
　brick, 215
　functions, 449
　glass, 449
　glass, insulating, 740
　glazed, 449–455
　glazed, masonry veneer, 189
　glazed, structural sealant, 453
　insulated thermal storage, 728
　metal, 449
　metal, finishes, 245
　shop bonded stone, 240
Curves, drawing, 877, 879
Cut rock, channels, 141
Cut stonework, 239–240, 473, 479
　paving, 137
　window sills, 752
Cylinders (doors), 435
Cylinder test for concrete, 171

Daidalos, 896
Dallas Design Center, 558
Dampers, 220
　automatic intake, **S146**
　chimneys, 221–223
　dimensions, 223
　fireplaces, 218, 219
　masonry heaters, 220
　solar collection, 730
　types, 223
Dampproofing, 203, 350, 351
　of foundation walls, 204
Darkrooms, residential, 519
Dartboards, 682
Daylighting, 57–58, 717–722
Deadbolts, 405
Dead load, metal buildings, 569
Decay resistance, heartwood, **S69**
Decimal equivalents, 881
Decks, 312, 313, 316
　concrete on steel, 262
　electrified, 646
　electronic timing boxes, 689
　flat, 180
　floor, **S54**
　glued-laminated, 311
　glulam attachment, **S68**
　laminated, **S67**, 311
　laminated, loads for, 311
　longitudinal, **S67**
　long-span, precast concrete, **S16**, 181
　machine-shaped, 311
　metal, **S96**, 258–259
　metal, horizontal support for, 205
　nailable, 359
　nonnailable, 358
　non-wall-supported, base flashing for, **S89**
　panelized, nail laminated, **S67**
　plainsawed, shrinkage distortion of, 275
　plywood, 262, 310
　precast concrete, **S15–16**, 180
　roof, 258, 310
　roof, acoustical, **S120**
　roof, nailable, **S81**
　roof, non-nailable, **S81**
　steel, 50, 256
　steel base, **S126**
　steel frame, insulated, **S90**
　stemmed, **S16**, 181
　stemmed, double tee, 181
　stress-laminated, **S67**
　wall-supported, base flashing for, **S89**
　weight/insulation values, 311
　wood, 156, 311–313
　wood, tongue and groove, 311
Declination of the earth, 706, 709, 710

NOTE: Page references in **boldface** preceded by **S** indicate *Supplement* pages.

Index

Deep Foundations Institute (DFI), 162
Deflection
  concrete, **S8**, 172
  limits, beams, 282–283
  limits, planks, 314
  long-span structures, 44
Degree days, 704, 738
Demolition, 127–128
Density, residential, **S191–194**
Dental rooms, 803
Dentils, **S74**, **S114**, 341
Denver Design Center, 558
Depth ratio, long-span structures, 44
Depths
  dimension lumber, 318
  rafter spans, 326
Design
  dwelling unit, **S196–197**
  exterior space, **S195**
  landscape, **S195**
  wood frame roof, **S109**
Design and general planning data, 1–124
  accessibility, universal, 8–22
  acoustical design, 59–65
  area calculation and cost estimating, 118–124
  automobiles, roads, and parking, 98–105
  building security, 66–74
  building systems, 29–45
  classical architecture, 112–116
  egress planning, 23–28
  flood damage control, 94–95
  human dimensions, 2–7
  lighting design, 51–58
  pedestrian planning, 96–97
  resources, 124
  seismic design, 46–50
  site, community, and urban planning, 75–93
  thermal comfort design, 65
  trucks, trains, and boats, 106–111
Design Book Review, 896
Desks
  classic, 546
  library charge, 540
  office, 530
  open classroom furniture, 537
  reading/songleader, 541
  school, 536
  systems furniture, 527
Detention center rooms, 834
Dictionary stands, 540
Diffusers, 633
Dining rooms
  formal seating capacities, 798
  furniture arrangements, 780
  furniture space requirements for, 6
  table systems, 531
Dining tables
  classic, 547, 549–550
  contemporary, 551
Directories and signs, 495, 496
Disabilities, persons with
  accessibility for, 8–9
  design data for, 2
  preservation approaches for, 763
  residential bathrooms for, 20, 21
  residential kitchens for, 22
Discs, stone veneer, 238
Dishwashers, **S157**, **S160**, 516
Disposal systems
  for feminine napkins, 488
  garbage disposers, 608
  sewage, 144–146
  waste compactors, 514
Diving boards
  FINA standards, 686, 691, 692

residential pools, 683
towers, 692, 693
Diving pools, 684
Docks
  bumpers, 513
  marine, 111
  trucks, 107
Documentation
  AIA, 886, 887
  CSI, 888–889
  HABS, 777
  for restoration of interiors, 767
Domes
  gypsum, cast glass fiber-reinforced, **S115**
  laminated, 318
  long-span structures, 44
  plaster, **S114**
  skylights, 396, 397
Domus, 896
Door and Hardware Institute (DHI), 456
Door hardware, 434–441
  accessible, 15
  bevels, 437
  closers, 438
  cylinders, 435
  detectors, 73, 438
  exit devices, 439
  glossary, 434
  handles, 435, 437
  hinges, 436
  holders, 435, 438, 439
  institutional, 439
  knobs, 435, 437
  location of, 435
  locks, 435, 437
  mortise templates, 437
  mutes, 439
  pivots, 439
  push-pull bar, 435
  saddles, 15, 440
  stiles, 437
  stops, 435, 439
  types and finishes, 434
Doors, 403–456
  access, 415
  accessible, 15, 434, 761
  acoustical correction, 418
  aluminum, 421, 422
  ballistic, 419
  blast-resistant, 417
  cellar, 415
  classical, 116
  clearances, 410
  coolers and freezers, 563
  detention, 418
  dimensioning methods, 858
  double egress, 439
  elevators, 582
  emergency release, 439
  entrance, 420, 421
  environmental impact of, 747
  finishes, 410
  fire, 404
  fire, NFPA standards, 404
  fireplaces, 223
  forced entry, 419
  frames, 405, 412, 431, 435
  French, 413
  frequency of operation, 436
  functions, 72
  garages, 785
  glass, 412–414, 421
  glass, cabinet, 335
  glass, revolving, 422
  glass, sliding, 414, 423
  glazing, 433, 443–444, 446–448, 449, 453
  hands of, 434

hollow metal, 407–410, 418, 433
hollow metal, frame types and installation, 408–409
kalamen, 437
maneuvering clearances, 806
metal, 407–409, 416
openings, 295
panel, wood, 412
panels, prefabricated hinged walk-in, **S164**
performance requirements, 405
plastic, 411–412, 431
recessed, 416
resources, 456
revolving, 422
security, 405, 406, 418
sidewalk, 415
sliding, 406, 413, 414, 417, 423
sliding, wood, 414
solid molded stile, 770
special, 70, 151, 405, 415–419, 423
stairway, 26
stone surrounds, 234
swinging, 405, 417
thresholds, 15, 440, 441
trim, **S74**, 341, 770
types, 410, 412
units, 435
vinyl, 431
wood, 335, 411–414, 431, 770
wood and glass, 413
Doorways
  arched, 115
  clearances, 15
  Palladian, 304
Dormers, 297, 394, 432
  flashing, **S100**
Dormitories, construction cost estimating, 119
Dowels
  concrete, 168
  with control joints, 175
  foundation wall, 170
  grouted, 183
  kitchen cabinets, 336
  steel bar reinforcement, 207
  stone veneer, 237–238
Downlights, 657
Downspouts, 389–392
  sizing, 389
Drafting conventions, 856–858
  heating, ventilating, and air conditioning, 863
Drafting room equipment, 532, 534–535
Drains and drainage, 140–146, 612
  catch basins, 143
  closed, 141
  cold storage rooms, **S164**
  concealed, 142
  covers, 154
  fields, 146
  fittings design, 595
  graphic symbols, 859
  gravel, 132
  heavy duty, 612
  inlets, 142, 143
  kennels and animal shelters, 846
  leaders and gutters, 389
  lines cleanouts, 596
  membranes, 346
  parking lots, 104
  perforated, 140
  pipes, 140
  prefabricated panels, 737
  retaining walls, 133
  riser diagrams for apartment buildings, 604
  riser diagrams for office buildings, 605

riser diagrams for residence, 603
roof, **S91**, **S94–96**, 256, 372, 389
slot, 142
solid, 145
storm sewers, 604
subsoil, 673
subsurface, 140, 143–146
surface, 141, 142
surface details, 673
terminations, 349
trench, 143
types, 142
waterproofing, 338, 347, 349
yard, 143
Drawers, 334
  kitchen, 336
  lipped, 333
Drawings, 865–872
  CAD layer guidelines, 871
  ConDoc system, 870
  conventional, 866
  conventions and symbols, 857
  geometry, 877, 879
  measured, 774
  methods, 865–872
  paraline, 865
  perspective, 866–869
Dressage, 695
Dressing rooms, 799
  stadium, 836
Drinking fountains, 610, 859
  accessible, 17
  for handicapped, 487
Driveways, 100
  layouts, 93
  lights, 154
Drums, 510
Dry chemical systems, 575
Dryers
  automatic, 516
  laundry rooms, 511
  residential, **S160**
Drying rooms (locker rooms), 799
Drywall construction, 463–465, 468
  ceiling furring system, 475
Drywall suspension system, **S117**
Drywells, 140
Ducts
  air distribution, 631
  air velocities, 635
  bracing, 50
  branch, 634
  gas-fired furnace, 622
  insulation, 601, 602
  liners, 601
  maximum air velocities, 635
  residential buildings, 634
  sizing, **S57**, 635
  symbols, 862
  trench header, **S172**, 646
  trunk, 634
  underfloor electrical, 259
  underground banks, 649
  warm air heating, 632
  wood trusses, 326
Dumbwaiters, 579, 590
Dwelling unit design, **S196–197**

Earthquakes, 46–50
Earth shelters, 735–737
Earthwork, 129
Eaves, 301, 302
  flashings, 365
  with gutter, ice dam detail at, **S107**
  height, metal buildings, 569
  historic, 302
  and insulation, 355
  metal roofs, 374

NOTE: Page references in **boldface** preceded by **S** indicate *Supplement* pages.

Index

with panel ceiling, **S63**
with sloped ceiling, **S63**
steel framing, **S40**
strut, 253
ventilation, **S83**, 301, 394
wood, 301
Ecclesiastical equipment, 507, 541–542
Ecclesiastical facilities, 831–833
Ecologically friendly structures, 230
Economy
of concrete formwork, **S1**
of structural steel, **S26**, 248
Edges
bridge condition, **S68**
embellishments, **S55**
metal roof, **S96**
roof, at gutter, **S96**
roof, heavy metal, **S89**
roof, scupper through, **S89**
Edison Electrical Institute (EEI), 664
Egress planning, 23–28
controls, 70
Elastomeric coatings, **S128**
protective, **S96**
Elastomeric liquid flooring, **S127**
Elastomeric tape, compressible, **S92**
El Croquis, 896
Elderly
design data for, 5
group residences for, **S200**
Electrical equipment
branch circuit protection, residential, **S169**
busways, **S175**
cables, **S171**, 644
cable-supporting devices, **S171**
cable trays and racks, **S171**, 645
capacitors, **S174**
circuit breakers, **S169**, **S176**, 650, 652–653
conduits, **S171**, 642, 643, 644, 646
connection boxes, 516, 643, 644
contactors, **S174**
controls, 570, 571
disconnect switches, **S176**, 653
environmental impact of, 747
exit signs, **S184**
fuses, **S169**, **S176**, 652, 653
gang sizes, 641
lighting, **S177–182**, **S184**, 654–660
materials, 640–647
metallic tubing, 642
meter bank, **S176**
motor starters, **S175**
outlet boxes, **S170**, **S171**, 205
outlets, gang size, **S170**
outlets and plates, 641
panelboards, **S176**, 653
panelboards, small building, 652
plates, **S170**
plug-in strips, **S170**
protectors, **S174**
raceways, **S171**, 259, 642
receptacles, **S169**, **S170**
residential, **S168–169**
smoke detection, 573
switchboards, **S175**
switchboards, motor controls, generators, 651
switches, **S168**, **S169**, **S170**, **S174**, 641, 650, 653, 861
switchgears, **S173**, 649
telephone jacks, **S170**
transformers, **S173**, **S174**, 649, 650
tumblers, **S170**
wireways, 860
wiring, 640–647
wiring, environmental impact of, 747
wiring, material, 642

wiring, for open office, 529
wiring, residential, **S168–169**, 640
wiring, in wood construction, **S169**
wiring, for workstations, **S172**
Electrical systems, 639–664
circuits, 860
distribution, 646–653
emergency generators, **S184**, 651, 662
emergency power, **S183–184**, 662
emergency services, 68
floor wiring for workstations, 646–647
graphic symbols, 860–861
grounding, **S173**, 648
high-voltage distribution, 649
and insulation, 355
medium-voltage distribution, 648–649
methods, 640–641, 643, 645
modular plug-in distribution, 647
outdoor, 648
primary service, 648
requirements, child care centers, 813
requirements, commercial occupancies, 860
requirements, industrial occupancies, 860
requirements, institutional occupancies, 860
requirements, veterinary hospitals, 845
residential wiring, **S173**
resources, 664
service, 646–647, 650–653
site distribution, service, and grounding, **S173**, 648
site structures, 649
site utilities, 649
special, 661–662
standby generators and battery systems, 662
substations, **S175**
supporting devices, 644
switching, multilevel, 570
switch wiring diagrams, 641
symbols, 860, 861
uninterruptible power supply, **S183**, 661
voltage control, **S174**, 650
Electricity
annual use, 724
average load for typical office, 809
Electric plastic conduits (EPC), 643
Electric Power Research Institute, 664
Elevator buildings, **S192**, **S199**
Elevator Escalator Safety Foundation, 592
Elevator Industries Association (EIA), 592
Elevators, 578–583, 586
accessible, 9, 17
area of rescue assistance, 24
cabs, lobbies, and special design, 582
control panels, 17
electric traction, 581
flooring, 483
hydraulic, 578, 582, 583
residential, 579
selection, 580
threshold, 441
Elevator World Source, 592
Embankment stabilization, 130
Embellishments, end and edge, **S55**
Emergency access, **S191**
Emergency services, 68
Emission standards, 127
Employee entries and exits, 71
Enamels, baked polyester, **S122**
End grain box, **S78**
Energy conservation, 719–724
alternative energy systems, 719
atrium design for, 722

commercial buildings, 720–721
energy analysis, 724
historic buildings, 750
monitoring and control systems (MCS), 637
regional design for, 703
resources, 748
site factors, 705, 707
thermal storage, 723
Energy design, 714, 716–722, 745
active solar, 723, 729–731
atrium, 722
building insulation, 353–355, 741
coating for glass, 444
for commercial buildings, 720–721
compass orientation, 707
earth shelters, 735–737
for nonresidential buildings, 720
passive solar, 725–728
skylights, 395
solar angles, 709–710
solar time, 708
sun control, 705–706, 732–734
thermal transmission, 724, 738–740, 742
ventilation, 394
weather stripping, 441–442
Energy Efficient Building Association (EEBA), 748
Energy Policy Act of 1992, **S178**
Energy systems, 743
alternative, 719
analysis of, 711–712, 712, 724
calculations, 711, 712
loads, 724
low-cost, 723
management, 52, 570
remote collectors, 719
remote storage, 719
storage for cooling, 720
total annual use, 724
Entrances, 420–423
accessible, 15
commercial, 420
employee, 71
environmental factors, 420
high security, 71
historic, 761–762, 762
Palladian window and doorway, 304
retail design, 420
sports arena, 666
visitors, 71
Environmental construction, 743–747
entrances and storefronts, 420
environmental impact of materials, 743, 746–747
indoor air quality, 615
life cycle of materials, 744
resource conservation and nontoxic materials, 745
Environmental Design Research Association (EDRA), 748
Environmental impact of materials, 743, 746, 747
Environmental Protection Agency (EPA), 111, 124, 162, 748
Asbestos Hazard Emergency Response Act (AHERA), 127
National Emission Standards for Hazardous Air Pollutants (NESHAP), 127
Worker Protection Rule, 127
Environmental site analysis, 76–78
EPC (electric plastic conduits), 643
EPDM (ethylene-propylene-diene monomer)
joint fillers, 399
single-ply roofing, **S92**, 372
single-ply roofing, low-slope, **S80**

Epoxy
abrasive, 28
adhesive, 471
grout, 183
joints, preassembled stone panels, 240
joints, wood butt, 178
marble chip flooring, **S127**
mortar, 470, 471
resin, composition flooring, **S127**, 483
Equestrian facilities, 695, 847–848
Equipment, 505–520
acoustical correction, 600
airports, 822
athletic, 680, 837
audiovisual, **S149–151**
bank security, 507–508
bar, commercial, **S158–159**
checkroom, 796
cleaning, 790
computer, **S151**
darkroom, 519
ecclesiastical, 541–542
education, 538
electrical, **S168–176**, 640–647, 650–653
food service, **S152–159**
food service, commercial, **S152–157**
gardens, 792
household, 788–792
insulation, 602
laundry room, 511
library, 539–540
liturgical, 541, 542
loading dock, 513
mailroom, 795
mechanical, hot arid conditions, 717
musical instruments, 509–510
operating rooms, 803
pipe organs, 509
play, 538, 684
plumbing, 611–613
residential, **S160–162**, 516–518, 788–792
resources, 520
solid waste handling, 514
teller, 507–508
vault, 506
vending, 512
wine storage cellar, 515
Equipment rooms
air handling, 805
flooring, 483
space requirements, 804–805
stables, 847–848
Equipment support
columns, **S106**
continuous curb, **S106**
on light roofs, **S90**
on low-slope roofs, **S81**
Escalators, 584
Espaliers, 160
Ethylene-propylene-diene monomer. See EPDM
Evaporation
climatic design strategies, 703
cooling, 618, 702
cooling, greenhouses, 849
rate, plants, 160
Excavation support systems, 129
Exits, **S41**, 71, 439
exit signs, **S184**
minimum, 23
Expansion joints, **S90**, **S93–94**, 175, 196, 197, 210, 227, 459, 470, 596
ceramic tile, 470
column reinforcing bars, 170
for concrete slabs, 175
counterflashing, **S99**
covers, 271

NOTE: Page references in **boldface** preceded by **S** indicate *Supplement* pages.

Index

flooring systems, 492
glass block, 228
at gravel stop, **S104**
gutters, 390
interior stone, 473
intersection, **S104**
location of, 197
loose laid, **S92–93**
at parapet, **S104**
parapet, 387, 388
piping, 596
retaining walls, 132
roof, **S81**, **S104**, 372, 387, 388
stone veneer, 238
strips, glass blocks, 228
waterproofing, 347, 348, 349
Explosions, 575
blast resistance, 70
prevention and suppression, **S167**
venting, **S167**
Exterior insulation, 356
basement, 355
Exterior Insulation Manufacturers Association (EIMA), 402
Exterior space design, **S195**
adjacent uses, **S195**
Exterior walls, 294, 315
assemblies, 41–42, 384
bearing, 262
watertables, 384
Extruded concrete, high wind resistance detail, **S109**

Fabric
filter, **S95**, 130
geotextile, **S67**
wallcovering material, **S135**
welded wire, **S6**, 168, 180
wrapped panels, **S136**
Facing
cut stone, 239, 240
marble wall patterns, **S118**
stone, **S118**, 231, 473
stone wall patterns, **S118**
structural clay tile, 225
tile, 225
Facing Tile Institute, 484
Factory Mutual Engineering Corp. (FM), 576
Fair Housing Amendments Act, **S196**, 8, 20
kitchen standards, 22
Fair Housing Information Clearinghouse, 124
Fair housing requirements, **S196**
Fan coil units, 629
Fans, exhaust, 849
Fascia, **S63**
Fasteners, **S47–48**, 290–293, 293
anchor bolts and shields, 291
beam cover, **S139**
expansion bolts, 291
mechanical, 371
nails, 290
roofing, 359, 361, 362
rubber strips, 372
structural wood, **S48**
for wood decks, 313
wood fences, 149
Fast food service, 512
Fast-track projects, 811
Faults, seismic effects, 47
Federal Aviation Administration (FAA), 854
airport regulations and standards, 819
Federal Bureau of Prisons (FBP), Facilities Development Division (FDD), 854
Federal Emergency Management Agency (FEMA), 124
flood damage management, 94

Federation Internationale de Natation Amateur (FINA), 700
diving board standards, 686, 691, 692
Feed rooms, 847–848
Felts
asphalt glass fiber, **S86**
permeance, 352
wet ceiling units, **S123**
Feminine napkin disposal, 488
Fences, 70, 131–134, 148–149, 698–699
baseball backstop, 674
chain link, 148
foundations and setting, 148
solid, 149
transparent, 149
wood, 149
Fenestration
hot arid conditions, 717
solar gain through, 742
Fiber cement tiles, **S85**
Fiber columns, 165
Fiber forms, 167
Fiberglass
ash urns, 155
bath and shower units, 609
bolts, 292
cloth jackets, 601
flagpoles, 494
insulation, 353, 718, 739
insulation, environmental impact of, 746
interwoven mesh reinforcement layer, 356
nuts, 292
permeance and permeability to water vapor, 352
planters, 155
reinforced concrete panels, 184
reinforced plastic, 342, 343
roofing, 359
Field construction, 673
Field events, layouts, 675–676
Field hockey, 671
Field sports, 667–674
Fieldstone, uncoursed, 232
File systems, 534
cabinets, 533
modular, 535
Fillers, premolded, 136
Filter fabric, in revetment riprap, 130
Filter mats, paving, 136–137
Fine Hardwood Veneer Association (FHVA), 344, 484
Finials, **S73**
iron, 757
wood, 756
Finish carpentry, 329–330
Finishes, 457–484
aggregate, 177, 185
broached, 754
brownstone, 754
casting method, 185
concrete, **S12–14**, 177–178
conference rooms, 794
door hardware, 434
doors, 410
environmental impact of, 747
exterior systems, 356
fractured, 185
glued laminated timber, 319
interior, 767
interior, acoustical materials, 475
interior, ceiling suspension systems, 475
interior, gypsum wallboard, 463–465, 468
interior, stone, 479
interior, wood flooring, 477, 478

materials, weights, 882
mechanical, 245
on metal, **S24–25**, 245
metallic-type static-disseminating, **S127**
mortar methods, 200
nails for, 290
paving, 137
pointed, 754
precast concrete, 185
resources, 484
skylights, 395
spark resistant, **S127**
stone, 473, 479
vermiculated, 754
wall panels, 182
wood fences, 149
Fire and smoke venting, **S110**, **S113**
Fireboxes, 219, 220, 223
Firebrick, 218, 219–220, 221–222
Fire departments
NFPA 704 diamond symbols, 93
response time, 93
Fire Equipment Manufacturers Association, 504
Fireplace mantel, **S73**
Fireplaces, 218–226, 493
chimneys, **S141**, 221, 222
clearances, connections, and crowns, 221
corner, 493
designs, 218, 220, 224
dimensions, 219, 224
floor framings, 222
flues, 222
framing, 222
general information, 218
manufactured, 493
masonry, 218–224
metal solid-fuel heaters, **S140–141**
open, 224
openings, 223
Rumford, 219
single-face, 219
wood, 769
wood burning, 219
Fireproof construction, 404–406
doors, NFPA standards, 404
historic preservation, 765
steel columns, prefabricated, 266
walls, 199, 380
windows, NFPA standards, 404
Fireproofing, 357
Fire protection, 93, 357, 498–499
alarm systems, 572
apparatus, 93
detectors, 130, 438, 573, 673
escapes, 268
extinguishers, **S144**, 498, 575
extinguishing systems, **S167**
hose, racks, and cabinets, 499
hydrants, 93
metal floor and roof decks, 258
site planning for, 93
of steel, 45, 357
suppression systems, **S167**, 575
Fire ratings, 404–406
access doors, 416
ceiling grids, 475
ceilings, 468
construction, 364
doors and door frames, 404
elevators and dumbwaiters, 579
floor/roof assemblies, 257
gypsum wallboard, 464–467
insulated doors, 416
lath and plaster, 462
metal roofing, 361
staircases, 24

steel columns, 266
steel frames, 404
steel joists, **S33**
wood shingles and shakes, 364
Fire Research Section (FRS), 576
Fire-retardant treatment (FRT) standards, **S71**
Firestopping, 294, 357
noncombustible, 222
wall framing, 300
Fire Suppression Systems Association, 576
Fish pond, 157
Fittings
air boot, 634
insulation, 601
iron, 595
trunk, 634
Fixtures
fluorescent lighting, 270
high-intensity discharge, lighting, 655, 657
plumbing, 606–610
plumbing, design standards, 22
Flag football, 669
Flagpoles, **S142**, 494
flashings, 382
Flags, **S142**, 490
Flagstone, **S125**
installation, 479
Flame detectors, infrared, 573
Flame shields, 357
Flame spread index, **S71**
Flammable materials, flooring, 483
Flange
lead, **S94**
roof jack, **S106**
Flashing, **S97–103**, 377–388
apron, **S100**, 364
base, **S99**, 378, 380, 385
base, for non-wall-supported deck, **S89**
base, for wall-supported deck, **S89**
cant strips, 380
cap, **S105**, 291, 378, 379, 380
cavity walls, 212
chimneys, 381
composition, **S98–99**, **S104**
concealed, 378, 383
counter, **S98–99**
cricket, 381
door threshold, 385
dormer, **S100**
double-hung window, 431
eaves, 365
edge, 393
electrolysis, 195, 377
expansion joints, 387, 388
exposed, **S100**, 378, 383
flat pan, 381
galvanic corrosion, 195, 377
galvanized steel, 393
head, **S100**, 386
insert detail, **S98**
lap joints in, **S99**
in masonry walls, 198
membranes, 348
modified bitumen strip, **S90**
pan, **S99**
parapet, 371, 380
pediment, **S100**
pipe, prefabricated, **S92**
premolded vent pipe, 372
ridge, 383
at roof penetrations, 382
with scupper, **S100**
snap-in, 378
spandrel panel, 386
specialty details, **S100**
stone ledge, **S100**

NOTE: Page references in **boldface** preceded by **S** indicate *Supplement* pages.

Index

stone panels, 236
through wall, **S97**
through-wall, 378, 379, 381
through wall, installation, **S97**
valley, 383
walls, 199
wall-to-roof, 379, 380
wall-to-wall, 379
watertable, 384
window, **S100**
without scupper, **S100**
wood pediment ledge, **S100**
Flat Glass Marketing Association (FGMA), 456
Flat plates, 170, 173
   concrete, 34
Flexicore Manufacturers Association (FMA), 186
FlexSys Pivoting Power Column, 490
Flood damage control, 94–95
Floodproofing, 95
Flooring
   accessible, 9
Floors
   access, 30, 492, 647
   area occupant loads, 23
   asphalt plank, **S127**
   assemblies, 37, 38, 257
   brick, **S126**
   cantilever, **S39**, 300
   carpet, 481, 482
   ceramic tile, 471
   channel system, **S124**
   composite beam system, 253
   concrete, **S10–11**, 170
   conductive, 483
   construction, 256
   construction, sound and impact noise ratings, 37, 38, 468
   deck, **S54**
   decks, metal, 258, 259
   drains, 612
   environmental impact of,
   flammable materials, 483
   framing, 37–38, 300
   glued, 309
   high-impact area, 814
   hinge threshold, 440
   industrial, design, 175
   industrial, wheel loads, 175
   industrial, wood block, 269, 477, 478
   insulation, 716
   joists, **S51**, **S63**
   laboratories, 483
   latex, 483
   loads, 43
   nail-in-channel system, **S124**
   noncomposite systems, 253
   openings, 256
   plastic laminate, **S127**
   pool, movable, 687
   poured resilient, 814
   precast hollow core, 211
   pressed concrete unit, **S126**
   quartz, seamless, **S127**
   resilient, 478, 480
   resinous, **S127**
   rubber, 483
   slip-resistant treatment, **S127**
   sound criteria, 61
   sound-resistant, detail, **S55**
   special, **S127**, 483
   special coatings for, **S127**
   sprung system, **S124**
   staggered, parking garages, 105
   steel joist, 211
   stone, **S125**, 479
   strip, 477, 478
   suspended-wood, **S50**

thermal resistance, 739
tie anchor, **S48**
ties between, **S61**
tile, 480
treatment, **S127**
truss, wood, **S58**
truss, 4 x 2, **S57**
trusses, 33
trusses, cantilevered, 328
unit masonry, **S126**
wet area, 814
wiring systems, 646–647
wiring systems for workstations in, **S172**
wood, 211, 477, 478, 480
wood, installation details, 478
wood, materials and patterns, 477
wood, resilient systems, **S124**
wood, sleeper system, **S50**
Flues, 220, 221, 222
   fire clay liners, 218, 219
   furnace, boiler, and heater, 625
   linings, 381
   prefabricated, 625
Flue stack, roof penetration, **S106**
Fluting, **S72**
Foam, spray-applied roofing
   for low-slope roofs, **S80**
   polyurethane, **S96**
Foam core panels, **S55**
   nonstructural, on roof purlins, **S54**
   surface-mounted wire chases at, **S55**
   wall system, **S54**
Foam fire suppression systems, **S167**, 575
Foil, wallcovering material, **S135**
Food service, 666
   bar equipment, **S158–159**
   environmental conditio83
Football, 669
   NCAA standards, 669
   NFL standards, 669
Footcandles, 51–52, 150
Footings, 313
   bubble, 765
   column, **S2**, 165
   concrete, 168, 346
   concrete formwork, **S2**, 165
   drain, 140
   earth shelters, 737
   foundations, 346
   shallow, **S49**
   spread, 174
   step, 174
   stepped, detail, **S51**
   stone, 765
   wall, **S1**, **S2**, 165
   wood column, **S51**
   wood fences, 149
Forest Products Research Society, 344
Forklifts, 587
Form hangers, 167
Forms
   concrete surfaces, **S12–13**, 178
   flying, **S4**
   fountains, 147
   inserts, rubber, 178
   liners, concrete, 177
   liners, finishes, 182, 185
   liners, reusable plastic, **S1**, 164
   one-way joists, 173
   plyform, **S4**
   suspended, **S4**
Forum for Health Care Planning, 854
Foundation of the Wall and Ceiling Industry (FWCI), 484
Foundations, 126, 135, 262, 301, 315, 317
   basement, 716

concrete, 174
concrete walls, 170
failures, causes, 47
masonry walls, 203–204
pier, 174
pile, 135
treated wood, **S49–51**
wall anchorages, 194
waterproofing of, 346
water-resistant, 346
Fountains, 147, 157
   drinking, 17, 610
Framing, 295–300, 317, 327, 412
   anchors, 315, 327
   balloon, 716, 764
   box, 337
   cantilevered, 296, 314
   components, metal buildings, 569
   concrete, for stone stairs, 479
   details, **S60–61**
   door, 405, 412, 431, 435
   exterior walls, 316
   floors, criteria for, 37–38
   glass, 445
   glazing, 433
   hollow metal, 407–410
   hollow metal, security, 418
   in-line, **S61**
   light gauge, 260–261
   light wood, 301, 312–313
   light wood, roofs, 301
   metal, 407–409
   metal, cold-formed, 260–263
   metal, devices, 299
   metal, economy of, 248
   metal, partitions, 465, 467–468
   metal, structural, 248–255
   moment-resisting, 253
   planks and beams, 314–315
   platform, 294, 299
   preengineered, components, 569
   pre-engineered metal buildings, **S165**
   roof, **S62**
   roof headers, **S54**
   roofs, 285, 301
   roofs, criteria for, 39, 40
   roofs, details, 297
   skylight, **S66**
   space, **S31**, 255
   spiral stairs, 27
   steel, **S26–29**
   steel, cold-formed, **S34–40**
   types, 404
   walls, flashings, 380
   western, 294
   window detail, **S51**
Framing, steel, 48, 205, 255, 407–409
   beams and columns, load tables, **S27**
   cold-formed materials, **S34–35**
   details, **S36–40**
   economy of, **S26**, 248
   environmental impact of, 746
   fire protection, 357
   fire-rated, 404
   joists, **S32–33**, **S38**
   opening details, **S36–37**
   overturning forces, 48
   shapes, **S28–30**
   stone on, 237, 240
   stone panels, 235–236
   for stone stairs, 479
   systems, 253, 254
Framing, wood, 33, 49–50, 394, 404, 462
   column load tables, 281
   composite members, 45
   decks, 312–313
   design, 274–275
   details, 301, 312–313

eaves, sills, and water tables, 301
environmental impact of, 746
exterior insulation and finish systems, 356
exterior stairs, 313
fireplace floors, 218
floor joist load tables, 276–280
leaded glass, 445
mortise and tenon, 764
plywood subflooring on, 309
roof rafter load tables, 285–289
roofs, 301
single wythe masonry wall with, 205
stairs, 340
thin brick veneer on, 213
Freezers, 563
   commercial, **S154**
   residential, **S162**
Frontage types, 87
Frost heaving, 714
Frost penetration map, 126
Frost susceptibility, 714
FRT standards. *See* Fire-retardant treatment standards
Fuels
   burning equipment, automatic, 6
   ratings, 620
   types, 724
   weights, 882
Furnaces
   circuits, 640
   gas-fired, 621
   vents, 625
   warm air, 632
Furniture, 521–558
   accessible/adaptable, 522, 797
   accessories, 525, 554
   arrangements, 780
   artwork, 445
   auditorium seating, 841
   bedroom, 6, 545, 780
   classic, 546–550, 552, 553
   coatings, 245
   contemporary, 551, 552, 553
   drafting, 535
   ecclesiastical, 541–542
   educational, 536–537, 538
   folding, 524
   general use, 523–526
   information-related, 154, 155
   library, 539–540
   modular, 523
   office, 522, 523, 527–535
   outdoor, 526
   residential, 526, 531, 543–545
   resources, 558
   school, 536–538
   site, 154, 155
   space requirements, 6
   stacking, 524
   street, 93, 154, 155
   systems, 522, 524
Furring, 263, 461
   channels, **S34**, **S40**, 260
   exterior wall, **S117**
   for fire protection, 357
   foundation walls, 301
   shielded construction, 568

Gabions, 130
Gables, 297, 310, 374, 394
   decorative wood elements, 756
   edge, 303
   ventilation of, 394
Galleries
   museum, 816
   skylights, 818
Galvanic series, **S23**, 244

NOTE: Page references in **boldface** preceded by **S** indicate *Supplement* pages.

Index

Galvanized metal roofing, high wind resistance detail, **S109**
Game facilities, 665–700
    courts, 681
    resources, 700
Gantries, movable, 591
Garages, 100, 785
    concrete slab floors, 175
    doors, 785
    driveways, 100
Garbage disposers, 608
Garden apartments, **S192**
Garden city neighborhoods, towns, and villages, 80
Gardens
    common, 79
    equipment, 792
    sculpture, 815
    structures, 156, 157
    urban, 161
    walls, 131, 134
Gas
    cocks, 598
    medical columns, 803
    natural, annual use, 724
    natural, water heaters, 611
    piping, 623
    piping, hangers, 621
    piping, standard ICU outlets, 490
Gaskets
    airtight, 760
    elastomeric, 349
    glazing, 448
Gates
    chain link, 148
    crash, 151
    folding, 503
    gate valves, 598
Gazebos, 156
Geometry, 873–880
    catenary curves, 879
    double curved surfaces, 880
    ellipses, 877
    hyperbolas, 879
    irregular figures, area and volume of, 878
    parabolas, 879
    plane and solid, 873
    proportions, 872
    rotated, 880
    triangular and circular, 874
Geotextile fabric, **S67**
Geotextile filter sleeves, 140
Girders, **S26**
    aashto, 181
    concrete, 168, 170
    connections, 322
    gypsum wallboard, 467
    hybrid steel, 45
    long-span, precast concrete, **S16**, 181
    steel, **S26**, 50
    wood/steel, 299
Girts, 253
    bent, **S52**
    bent, upper, **S53**
    metal buildings, 569
    slab and beam forming, 167
Glare control, 55, 158
    with trees, 158
Glass, 443–445
    break detectors, 73
    bulletproof, 507
    coatings, 433
    corrugated, 362
    curtain walls, 449
    decorative, 445
    detention doors, 418
    doors, 412–414, 421
    doors, cabinets, 335
    doors, panel, 412
    doors, revolving, 422
    doors, sliding, 414, 423
    exterior wall assemblies, 41–42
    frames, 445
    heat loss, 740
    heat-treated, 443
    insulating, 444
    insulating, on wood doors, 444, 447
    insulating, structural sealant, 453
    insulating curtains, 740
    laminated, 433, 447
    leaded, 445
    leaded art, 234
    lights, 447
    metal windows, 425–428
    monolithic, structural sealant, 453
    panels, 270
    partitions, 433
    piping, 595
    rail system, flush-mounted, 270
    roofing, 362
    safety, 443
    security, 443
    shading devices, 732–733
    sheathed greenhouse, 849
    skylights, 395
    stained, 445
    structural sealant, 453
    sun control devices, 732–734
    tempered, 433
    thermal transmission, 740, 741
    types, 443
    unit masonry, 227–229
    wired, 430
Glass block, 227–229
    hollow units, 227
    thermal resistance, 741
Glass fiber
    asphalt felt, **S86**
    -reinforced gypsum cornice, **S114**
    -reinforced gypsum dome, cast, **S115**
    -reinforced gypsum plaster column, two-piece, **S115**
Glass Tempering Association (GTA), 456
Glazed curtain walls, 449–455
    design criteria, 449
    masonry veneer, 189
    rain screen principle, 451
    structural sealants, 453, 454
    systems, 450, 451, 452
Glazing, **S110**, **S112**, 443–448
    assemblies, 443
    daylighting, 58
    door panels, 412
    doors and windows, 433, 443–444, 446–448, 453
    double, 740
    dry, metal frame, 448
    face, 448
    frames, 433
    insulating, 445
    leaded glass, 445
    liquid-applied, permeance and permeability to water vapor, 352
    materials, thermal resistance values, 741
    methods and setting blocks, 447
    mirrors, 444
    plastic, 446
    security design, 406
    skylights, 395–398
    sliding doors, 423
    solar, 727
    solar sizing of, 727
    south, 726
    specifications, 448
    structural sealant, 453
    swimming pool, 689
    systems, 447–448
    wet, 448
Glued floors, 309
Glued-laminated construction, 318–322
    connections, 321–322
    framing, 295
Glulam deck attachment, **S68**
Gneiss
    uses and properties, 231
Gold
    melting temperature of, **S23**
Golden section, 872
Golf course design, 672
Grab bars, 18, 21, 487, 862
Grades
    glued floor systems, 309
    lumber, 305
    plywood panels, 307
    reinforcing steel, 171
Gradients, bare soils, 130
Grandstands, 837
Granite, **S118**, **S125**
    in concrete aggregate, **S13**
    curbs, 136
    edging, 136
    paving, 138
    uses and properties, 231
Graphics
    methods, 865–869, 873, 877–880
    paraline drawings, 865
    perspective drawings, 866–869
    shades and shadows, 865
    signs and directories, 496
    signs and symbols, 495
    symbols, 856–864
    symbols, architectural drawings, 857
    symbols, heat, power, and refrigeration, 863
    symbols, HVAC, 856
Grass
    paving, 138
    surface drainage, 141
Gratings, 142, 159, 269
    orientation for accessibility, 14
    structural, 343
    types, 269
Gravel
    drains, retaining walls, 132
    stops, 391, 392, 393
    stops, metal, 393
    stops, splice joints, 393
Gravel stop, **S90**, **S94**
    expansion joint at, **S104**
Gravity tanks, 93
Gravity ventilators
    gooseneck, **S106**
    roof, stationary, **S106**
Grease traps, 144, 145, 146
Greek return, **S60**
Green corridors, 79
Greenhouses, 849
    skylights, 395
    solar orientation, 849
    ventilation of, 557
Green spaces, 84
Grid strut systems, 239
Grilles and louvers, 503
    in doors, 411, 418
    supply and exhaust air, 633
Grillwork, ornamental ironwork, **S43**
Gringo blocks, 230
Grip stay insert, 237
Grooves, wood siding, 329
Groove welds, 246, 247
Ground cover, 161
Ground surface pipe insulation, 601
Ground temperature, map, 703
Group residences, **S200**
Grout, 60, 183, 470
    masonry, 191–192
    retaining walls, 133
Guardrails, 25, 270
    accessible, dimensions, 270
    vertical, 16
Guards
    wall and corner, **S137–139**, 491
Guide rails, elevators, 581, 583
Gussets
    plate, 254, 316
    T-stub, 254
Gutters, 302, 389–392, 398
    concrete, 136
    details, 758
    eaves with, ice dam detail at, **S107**
    multiple-grid section, **S113**
    pole, 758
    roof edge at, **S96**
    scupper combination, **S105**
    sizing, 389
    skylights, 395
    swimming pool, 688
    underwater lighting, 689
    wood, 758
    wood box, 302
Gymnasium equipment
    bleachers, 837
    flooring, 478
    gymnastic, 680
    lockers and shower rooms, 799–800
    sports and games, 680
Gymnastic equipment, 680
Gyms, 823
Gypsum
    cornice, glass fiber-reinforced, **S114**
    definition, 458
    dome, cast glass fiber-reinforced, **S115**
    fireproofing of steel, 357
    lathing, 458, 462
    plaster column, two-piece glass fiber-reinforced, **S115**
    wall panels, prefinished, **S117**
Gypsum Association, 484
Gypsum board, **S116–117**, 463–468, 474
    accessories, 463
    at ceiling, beams, and soffits, 468
    ceiling, with spacers, **S55**
    column enclosures, for fire protection of steel, 357
    construction at partitions, columns and ceilings, 467
    environmental impact of, 747
    metal-frame partitions, 465
    new assemblies, **S117**
    permeance and permeability to water vapor, 352
    sheathing, 308
    solid partitions and shaft walls, 466
    special conditions, **S116**
    types, 466
    wood-frame partitions, 464

Half timber, 303
Halon systems, 575
Hammer throw, 675
Handball, 671, 679
Hand dryers, electric, 488
Handicapped persons
    anthropometric data, 6
    bathroom layout, 487, 781
    curb ramp, 96
    design data, 2
    drinking fountain, 610
    kitchen layout, 783
    laundry layout, 784
    parking, 101
    parking lots, 103
    residential elevators, 579
    robe hooks, 859
    signs, 496

NOTE: Page references in **boldface** preceded by **S** indicate *Supplement* pages.

Index

stairs, 28
swimming pool access, 683
toilet layout, 486
toilet rooms, plumbing fixtures, 606
Handles
    doors, 435
    lever, 435, 437
Handrails, 27, 43
    accessible, 9, 270
    with bumper cushions, **S137**
    escalators and moving walks, 584
    lighted, 270
    metal, 270
    stair, 16, 267, 340
    steel stair, **S41**
    wall-mounted, 770
    wood, 338, 339
    wood stairs, 340
Hand tools, 791
Hangers
    acoustical ceiling suspension, 475
    beam, 321
    clevis, 621, 731
    for concrete formwork, **S4, S5**
    gas appliances, 621
    gutters, 390
    gypsum wallboard ceilings, 468
    isolation, 474
    joist, **S48, S65**
    selection, 461
    supports, 267
    suspended form, 167
    truss, 327
Hardboard, 334, 467
    core, **S76**
    permeance and permeability to water vapor, 352
Hardware
    concrete formwork, **S5**
    door, 15, 434–442
    fire door, 404
    hospitals, institutional buildings, and nursing homes, 439
    institutional door, 439
    poke-through, 646, 647
    window, 434–440
Hardwood, 333
    flooring, 477–478
Hardwood Manufacturers' Association (HMA), 484
Hardwood plywood, types, **S76**
Hardwood Plywood Manufacturers' Association (HPMA), 344
Harmonic distortion, 55
Harps, 510
Harvard Architecture Review, 896
Hatches, floor, 415, 416
Hatchways, 415
Headers
    I-joist, **S65**
    joist, **S38**
    openings, **S36**
    roof framing, **S54**
Headwalls, 142
Health care facilities, 489, 490, 827–830
    functional space programming, 829
    master facility plans, 829
Health clubs, 814
Hearing-impaired persons, considerations for, 9
Hearses, 98
    turning dimensions, 99
Hearth Products Association, 504
Hearths, 220, 477, 478
    fireplace, 218, 219
    framing, 222
Heartwood, decay resistance, **S69**
Heat detectors, 438, 573
Heat generation, 616–617, 620–625

Heating
    annual use, 724
    average monthly degree days, 704
    baseboard, 624
    concepts, 725
    degree days, U.S., 704
    electric systems, 624
    forced air, electric, 624
    gas, 622
    gas-fired, 623
    gravity vents, 622
    for greenhouses, 849
    hydronic systems, 616–617
    for kennels and animal shelters, 846
    limited capacity devices, 723
    mainless loop systems, 616
    masonry, 220
    one-pipe systems, 616
    passive solar, 722, 725
    pipes, 630
    plate-type exchangers, 630
    radiant, 624
    for saunas, 565
    solid-fuel heaters, metal, **S141–142**
    symbols, 862, 863, 864
    two-pipe systems, 617
    warm air, 632
Heat-power apparatus symbols, 863
Heat pumps
    air-to-water, 722
    ground source, 745
    operations, 627
    water loop, 630
Heat transfer, 626–630
    coefficient of, 353, 738, 741
    fluids, 723
    mechanisms of, 354
    overall, 741
    principles of, 627
    recovery systems, 630, 720
Heavy metal, roof edge, **S89**
Heavy timber
    construction, **S67–68**, 314–317
    stairs, 340
Height partition, partial, **S116**
Height standards, anthropometric data, 5
HEPA (high-efficiency particulate air), 564
Heritage Canada Foundation (HCF), 778
Highboy cupboards, banks, 507
High-efficiency particulate air (HEPA), 564
High-energy materials, environmental impact, 743
High jump, 676
    location, 675
Highways, 89, 90
High wind resistance
    for composition and asphalt shingles, **S109**
    for extruded concrete, **S109**
    for galvanized metal roofing, **S109**
    for S-type tile roofing, **S109**
Hinges, 335, 336, 436
    floor threshold, 440
Hip and ridge detail, **S84**
Historic American Buildings Survey (HABS), 750, 778
Historic buildings, 749–778
    documentation, 751, 774–777
    eaves, 302
    entrances, 761–762
    evaluating character, 751
    interiors, 766–770
    materials, 750
    measured drawings, 774
    mechanical systems, 771
    overhangs, 302
    porches, 761–762
    storefronts, 763

Historic preservation, 113–114, 749–778
    accessibility and, 9
    checklist for rehabilitation, 751
    of landscapes, 772–773
    legal requirements, 751
    materials, 750
    objectives, 750
    resources, 778
Historic Preservation Education Foundation (HPEF), 778
Hoist Manufacturers Institute, 592
Hoists, 591
Holders, door, 435, 438–439
Hollow metal doors and frames, 407–410
    anchorage and accessories, 409
    detention, 418
    frames, 407–410
    interior windows and glass partitions, 433
    security, 418
    types and installation, 408, 409
Hollow walls, 209, 215, 765
    grouted, 209
    tile, 765
Home Automation Association (HAA), 576
Home Ventilating Institute Division, Air Movement and Control Association (AMCA), 638
Hooks, stirrup, 169
Hook strips, interlocking, 441
Horizontal joints
    control, 212
    interior stone details, 473
    ladder type, 212
    metal framing, 261
    precast concrete, 181
    reinforcement, 207
    siding, 330
Horizontal loading, freestanding walls, 134
Horses
    clearances for, 847
    shows, 695
Hose racks and cabinets, 499
Hospitals, 827, 828, 829, 830
    concrete slabs, 175
    construction cost estimating, 120
    elevators, 580
    hardware, 439
    intensive care unit modules, 489, 490
    operating suite flooring, 483
    patient beds, 489, 490
    patient rooms, 489, 802
    surgical and dental rooms, 803
    veterinary, 844
Hot-air guns, electric, 755
Hot arid climate, design for, 717
Hotels, construction cost estimating, 120
Hot tubs, 566
Hot water heaters
    radiators, 617
    requirements, 611
    smoke pipe, 221
Hot water storage tanks, 612
Hot weather construction, concrete, **S8**, 172
House and Garden, 896
Household equipment, 788–792
Houses
    double, **S194**
    fourplex, **S194**
    single-family, large lot, **S193**
    single-family, small lot, **S193**
    single-family, zero lot, **S193**
    two-story attached, **S192**
House wrap, air barrier, 716

Housing, **S191–200**
    affordable, **S197**
    custom, **S197**
    elderly, **S200**
    fair, **S196**
    luxury, **S197**
    projects, **S197**
    requirements, **S196**
    single-family attached, **S192, S194**
    single-family attached, multistory variants, **S194**
    single-family detached, **S192–193**
    special needs, **S200**
    townhouses, **S194**
Human dimensions, 2–7
Humidity
    absolute, 738
    ratios, 738
    relative, 65, 738
Hurricane clips, 316
HVAC systems, 614–619
    for child care centers, 813
    controls, 636, 637
    ductwork symbols, 862
    for schools, 826
    types, 614
    variable air volume systems, 636
    for veterinary hospitals, 845
Hydrants, siamese connection, 574
Hydro massage, 566
Hydronic heating systems, 616–617
Hydronics Institute (HI), 638

Ice dam, at eave with gutter detail, **S107**
Ice hockey equipment, 696
Ice lense, 714
Ice wedge, 714
Identifying devices, **S143**, 495
IFID (intelligent field interface device), 637
Igneous rock
    uses and properties of, 231
I-joists, wood
    connection, **S65**
    construction details, **S64–66**
    headers, **S65**
    typical, **S64**
Illuminance values, 52
Illuminating Engineering Society (IES), 124, 664
    daylighting, 57
Illumination, 52–53
    daylighting, 58
    interior landscaping, 556
    lamps, 654–655
    level for offices, 809
    lighting fixtures, 657–660
Impact loads, 43
Incandescent lamps, 654–655
    circuits, 640
    light fixtures, 270, 657–660
Indiana Limestone Institute of America (ILIA), 242
Industrial Fabrics Association International (IFAI), 558, 576
Industrial Heating Equipment Association, 638
Industrial Perforators Association, 272
Inertia blocks, 600
Infiltration, 716
Infrared detectors, 73
    flame, 573
    heaters, 622, 624
Inlets, 143
INNOVA, 558
Insect protection
    masonry foundation walls, 203
    screens, 718
    wood, 275, 338

NOTE: Page references in **boldface** preceded by **S** indicate *Supplement* pages.

Index

Insect screens, **S106**
Inserts
  concrete, cavity walls, 183
  electrical supporting devices, 645
  helical, 292
Institute for Solid Wastes, 520
Institute of Business Designers (IBD), 558, 854
Institute of Electrical and Electronics Engineers (IEEE), 664
Institute of Environmental Sciences (IES), 576
Institute of Heating and Air Conditioning Industries (HACI), 638
Institute of Roofing and Waterproofing Consultants (IRWC), 402
Institutions
  furniture, stacking and folding, 524
  hardware, 439
  lavatories, 607
Insulated Steel Door Institute, 456
Insulation, **S83**, 353–355
  acoustical, **S120**, 476
  baffle, 718
  below-grade, 735
  blocking and baffle, **S83**
  bonded metal wall panels, 370, 563, 599
  buildings, 353–354, 740, 741
  compressible, **S93**
  concepts, 717
  curtain walls, 449
  earth shelters, 735, 737
  environmental impact of, 746
  exterior, 356
  exterior basement, 355
  factors affecting performance, 353
  fiber glass batt, 718
  floor, 716
  for greenhouses, 849
  hot arid conditions, 717
  mechanical, 601–602
  metal framing, 263
  metal panels, 369
  plank and beam framing, 315
  polystyrene, 137
  roof panel systems, 362
  R value, sheathing materials, 308
  slab on grade, 355
  solar, 705
  structural board, permeance and permeability to water vapor, 352
  taper, 716
  tapered roofs, 372
  thermal, 352, 354, 449, 602, 740
  weights, 882
  for wood structures, 355
Insurance Services Office (ISO), bank vault specifications, 506
Intelligent field interface device (IFID), 637
Intercolumnation, classical, 115
Interfaith Forum on Religion, Art and Architecture (IFRAA), 558, 854
Interior Design, 558
Interiors, 558
  historic, 766–770
  preservation of, 767
Interior signs, 496
Interior systems design, 29–36
  flat plate concrete, 34
  lightweight steel frame and brick veneer, 32
  posttensioned concrete, 35
  precast concrete frame, 36
  staggered steel truss, 31
  steel bar joist with bearing wall, 29
  steel frame with access floor and curtail, 30

  wood roof truss and wood floor truss, 33
International Amateur Athletic Federation (IAAF), 700
International Association of Concrete Repair Specialists, 186
International Association of Lighting Designers (IALD), 124, 558, 664
International Association of Plumbing and Mechanical Officers (IAPMO), 638
International Association of Stone Restoration & Conservation (IASRC), 242
International Center of Photography, 520
International Conference of Building Officials (ICBO), 124
International Copper Association, 272
International Design Center, N.Y. (IDCNY), 558
International District Heating and Cooling Association, 638
International Electrical Testing Association (NETA), 664
International Furnishings and Design, 558
International Institute for Lath and Plaster (IILP), 484
International Market Square, 558
International Masonry Institute (IMI), 242
International periodicals, 896
International Racquet Sports Association, 700
International Sanitary Supply Association, 504
International Society of Indoor Air Quality and Climate (ISIAQ), 748
International Solar Energy Society, 748
International Union of Elevator Constructors (IUEC), 592
Ionization detection systems, 438, 573
Iowa concrete curb, 136
Iron
  cast, architectural metals, 757
  cast, bases, 765
  cast, channels, 141
  cast, columns, 763
  cast, pipes, 595
  cast, radiators, 616
  cast, sectional type burner, 620
  construction, 764
  corrugated roofs, 758
  finials, 757
  finishes for, **S24**
  galvanized, double-hung windows, 759
  galvanized, roofing, 362
  garden wall gates, 134
  malleable, 244
  melting temperature of, **S23**
  nosings, 28
  properties of, **S22**
  roofing, 362
  wrought, 244
Ironwork
  ornamental, details, **S43**
Isogonic chart of the U.S., 707
Isolation rooms, 567
  acoustical correction, 567
  sound and vibration, 600
Isotherms, 738
Italian Marble Center (IMC), 242
Italian Tile Association (ITA), 484

Jackets, insulation, 601
Jambs
  anchors, 263
  door, 369
  freezers and coolers, 563
  glass blocks, 228
  metal frames, 407–409
  revolving, 422

  sliding metal, 414, 423
  steel framing, **S36**
  weather stripping, 442
  window, 432
  windows, metal frames, 425–428
  x-ray rooms, 568
Japan Architect, 896
Javelin throw, 675–676
Joinery, wood, **S52**
Joints
  batten, 332
  beaded, Flemish bond, 753
  beltline, 329
  brick, 192
  butt, 349
  butt, concrete slabs, 175
  butt, glazing, 433
  butt, vertical, **S121**
  butt, wood, 332
  cabinet details, 333, 335
  cold, 196
  colonial grapevine, 753
  column covers, **S138**
  concave, common bond, 753
  concrete, 175, 178
  concrete, precast, **S17**
  construction (cold), 196
  control, 96, 175, 193, 196, 198, 459, 460, 463
  control, horizontal, 212
  control, masonry, 197
  control, retaining walls, 132, 133
  control, strips, 472
  coped, **S74**
  cover, **S94**
  epoxy, stone on steel frame with, 240
  expansion, **S81**, **S90**, **S94**, 175, 196, 210, 227, 228, 459, 470, 473, 596
  expansion, column reinforcing bars, 170
  expansion, covers for, 271
  expansion, flooring systems, 492
  expansion, glass block, 228
  expansion, gutters, 390
  expansion, loose laid, **S92**
  expansion, masonry, 197
  expansion, piping, 596
  expansion, retaining walls, 132
  expansion, roof and parapet, 387–388
  expansion, stone veneer, 238
  expansion, waterproofing, 347, 348, 349
  expansion strips, glass blocks, 228
  flexible, earth shelter roof edge, 737
  flush, 753
  form, 178
  horizontal, 181, 212
  horizontal, interior stone details, 473
  horizontal, reinforcement, 207
  horizontal, siding, 330
  isolation, 196
  lap, **S53**, 473
  lap, in flashing, **S99**
  lap, interior stone details, 473
  lap, wood, 321
  masonry, 196, 197, 200
  masonry repointing, 753
  in metal roofing, 373, 375–376
  miter, wood, 332
  mortar, 192
  mortarless, 137
  mortise-and-tenon, **S53**
  movement, masonry, 196
  nestable, 260
  paving, 96
  plank ceilings, 314
  precast concrete wall panels, 182
  raked, English bond, 753
  reinforcement, 459
  reinforcement, concrete slab, 349

  reinforcement, ladder-type horizontal, 212
  reinforcement, masonry, 197
  reinforcement, masonry cavity walls, 212
  reinforcement, waterproofing, 349
  retaining walls, 132
  scarf, **S53**
  sealers, 399–401
  shoulder, beveled, **S53**
  siding, 330
  sliding, 275
  splice, 393
  spline, 473
  stone, interior, 473
  stone walls, 232
  in stonework, 239–240, 473, 479
  tolerances, 182
  vertical, 235, 330
  in wallboards, 463, 468
  wall control, **S117**
  waterproofing, 348, 349
  wood, 275, 331–332
Joists, 326
  anchors, 316
  bar, 29
  base, wood, **S126**
  bearings, **S32**, 256–257
  bevel cut, **S64**
  bracing, 261
  bridging, **S32**, **S37**
  C, 260
  ceiling, load tables, 285
  closures, 260, 263
  composite, 45
  concrete, 168
  concrete, one-way, 170
  concrete, two-way, 173
  floor, **S51**, **S63**, 317, 327
  floor, bridging, 294
  floor, concrete, 173
  floor, load tables, 276–280
  floor, trussed/residential, 326
  floor, wood rafters, 285–289
  framing details, 299
  glued floor systems, 309
  hangers, **S48**, **S65**, 328
  hangers, framing, 295, 300
  metal, 256–257
  one-way, 170, 173
  pole construction, 316
  rim, **S61**, **S64**
  roof, load tables, 286–289
  selection, 256–257
  skip, **S11**
  slab and beam forming, 167
  steel, 29, 45, 167, 260, 310, 460
  steel, allowable spans, **S34–35**
  steel, details, **S38**
  steel, long-span, **S33**, 256, 257
  steel, open-web, **S32**, 256
  timber, **S54**
  two-way, 173
  western or platform framing, 294
  wood, 45, 285–289, 299, 326, 328
  wood, allowable loads, 285
  wood, connections, 328
  wood, laminated, 282, 295
  wood, load tables, 276, 280
  wood, rafters, 285, 289
  wood floor, **S51**
Junction boxes
  shapes and sizes, 643
  zone, 646, 647
Jury rooms, 801
Justice facilities, **S186–190**
Jute Carpet Backing Council (JCBC), 484

Kakelugn (masonry heater), 220
Kennels, 846

NOTE: Page references in **boldface** preceded by **S** indicate *Supplement* pages.

Index

Keypads, 74
Kickers, slab and beam forming, 167
Kick panels, 336
Kick plates, wood stairs, 296
Kindergarten equipment, 538
Kiosks, 155
Kitchen Cabinet Manufacturers Association, 558
Kitchens
  appliance design standards, 22
  church, 831
  commercial equipment, **S152–157**
  equipment, exhaust ducts, 602
  equipment, garbage disposers, 608
  equipment, sinks, 608
  equipment, storage planning, 788, 789, 790, 791
  equipment, utensils, 788–790
  equipment, waste compactors, 514
  European-style, 336
  hoods, 623
  kitchenettes, **S162**, 518, 782
  piping, 603
  residential, 6, 782
  residential, equipment, **S160–162**, 517–518, 788–790
  residential, for persons with disabilities, 22
  work centers, 783
Kneelers, 542
Knobs, 435, 437

L. A. Mart, 558
Laboratories, flooring, 483
Lacrosse, 671
Ladders
  escape, 268
  fixed metal, **S42**
  household, 791
Lakes, on-site, 93
Lamb's tongue, end embellishment, **S55**
Laminates, decorative
  high pressure, **S76**
Laminators Safety Glass Association (LSGA), 456
Lamp and Shade Institute of America, 558
Lamps, **S177–182**, 554, 654–656
  characteristics, **S177–178**
  fluorescent, **S178**, **S179–180**
  fluorescent, thermal controls, 571
  halogen, **S181**
  HID, **S178**, **S182**
  incandescent, **S178**, **S181**
  mercury vapor, **S182**
  metal halide, **S182**
  sodium, **S182**
  types, 654, 655
Landings
  cantilevered, 296
  mats, 680
  slip-resistant, 176
  soft areas, 676
  stair, 25
Land planning, 94–95
Landscape Architecture, 162
Landscape Journal, 162
Landscaping, **S195**, 158–160, 158–161, 555–557
  earth shelters, 736
  fences, 148
  historic, 772–773
  interior, 555–557
  lights, 154
  ornamental, 161
  parking lots, 103
  paving, 96
  public, 88
  trees and shrubs, 158
  types, 88
  urban, 88
  walks, paths, and terraces, 96, 148, 479
Lap, **S104**
  joggle, **S102**
L'Arca, 896
Latches, 435
  roller, 439
Lateen, 110
Lateral loads, metal buildings, 569
Latex
  flooring, 483
  modified mortar, 137
  Portland cement mortar, 471
Latex resin flooring, **S127**
Lath and plaster, 458–462
  accessories, 459
  ceilings, 460
  ceilings, furred with radiant heating, 624
  ceilings, suspended, 461, 624
  furring for fire protection, 258, 357
  gypsum, 462
  materials, 458
  metal, 458, 462
  metal, steel bar reinforcement, 176
  metal, steel joists, 460–461
  partitions, 462
  span, 461
Laundry and Dry Cleaning International Union, 520
Laundry equipment, 516
  chutes, 590
  hot water requirements, 611
Laundry rooms, 511, 784
Lavas, 231
Lavatories, 20, 21, 603, 781, 806, 859
  accessible, 18
  accessories for, 488
  for handicapped, 6, 487
  ledge back, 607
Lawn bowling, 681
Lawn equipment, 792
  benches, 526
Lawrence Berkeley Laboratory (LBL), 664
Laws of reflection and refraction, 881
Leaching pits, 145
Leach lines, 146
Lead
  electroplated finish, radiation shielding, 568
  melting temperature of, **S23**
  properties of, **S22**, 244
Leaders, gutter and downspout, 389
Lead Industries Association, 272
League of Historic American Theaters (LHAT), 854
Lecterns, 541
Ledge
  stone, flashing, **S100**
  wood pediment, flashing, **S100**
Ledgerock pattern, 232
Ledgers, 328
  wood floor truss detail, **S58**
  wood stairs, 296
Length, thermal expansion of, 881
Libraries
  card catalogs and circulation desks, 540
  furniture, 539–540
  shelving and carrels, 539
  stack reach dimensions, 12
Library/Media Center, 826
Life cycle, of materials, 744
Life-cycle chart, 743
Life-cycle costing, 122, 123
Lifts, 585, 586
  platform, 10, 17, 586, 761
  ski, 697
  swimming pool, 687
  types, 585–586
  van, 10
  wheelchair, 10, 586
Light beam detectors, 73
Lightbulbs, electric, 654, 655
Light fixtures, 657–660
  alabaster gloss, 771
  coefficients of utilization, 658–660
  desk systems, 529
  integrated ceiling systems, 561–562
  lighting characteristics of, 658–660
  ornamental metal, 270
  pendants, 771
  racquetball courts, 679
  recessed ceiling mounted, 657
  selection, 54
Lighting, **S177–185**
  annual use, 724
  circuits, 640
  coefficients of utilization, 53
  controls, 55, 571, 720
  direct-indirect, 54
  electric, 51–54
  emergency power, **S184**, 662
  energy efficiency, **S177**
  exit signs, **S184**
  functions of, 51
  glare, 54, 55
  high-mast, 150
  indirect, 56
  integrated systems furniture, 527
  lamp characteristics, **S177–178**, 658–660
  levels, 51
  low-level, 150
  natural, 735
  outdoor, 93
  overhead flood, 689
  quality, 51
  recessed, 54
  sightlines, 56
  symbols, 860–861
  task, 51, 720
  track, integrated ceilings, 562
  underwater, 689
  uninterruptible power systems, **S183**
  walkover, 154
Lighting design, **S177**, 51–58, 150, 654–660, 720
  billiards, 682
  color issues, **S177**
  conference rooms, 794
  courtrooms, 801
  daylighting, 57–58
  drafting table lamps, 535
  drive, 154
  electronic ballasts, 656
  energy-efficient, **S177–178**
  energy management, 52
  glare control, 55
  illumination calculations, 53
  indirect, 56
  integrated, systems furniture, 527
  interior plants, 556
  kennels and animal shelters, 846
  landscape, 154
  liminaire selection parameters, 54
  malls, 150
  museums, 818
  optics and, 51
  panel boards, 652–653
  room cavity ratio, 53
  schools, 826
  site, 150
  site security, 70
  skylights, 395
  stage systems, 842–843
  workstation, 56
Lighting Design and Application (LD+A), 558
Lighting Research Center (LRC), 664
Lighting Research Institute (LRI), 664
Light loss factor (LLF), 53
Light/micro planes, 696
Lightning protection, **S185**
Lime, hydrated, 191
Limestone, **S118**, **S125**, 231
  concrete aggregate, **S13**
Linen chutes, 590
Line painting, 673
Linoleum, 480
Lintels
  ceiling soffit at, **S116**
  fireplaces, 219
  framing details, 295
  jack arch, 764
  masonry, 199
  metal, long-span, 263
  through wall flashing at, **S97**
Lips, fountains, 147
Liquefaction, soil, 47
Liquid-applied roofing, **S94**
  low-slope, **S80**
Liquid flooring, elastomeric, **S127**
Liquid weight, 882
Little League baseball and softball, 668
Liturgical equipment, 507, 541–542
Live loads
  beams, 282–283
  floor, 43
  minimum for typical offices, 809
  planks, 314
  rafter spans, 326
Living rooms
  furniture arrangements, 780
  furniture space requirements, 6
Load blocking, lateral, **S65**
Load capacity
  columns, 249
  cranes, 591
  dumbwaiters, 579
  elevators, 579, 581, 583
  steel beams, 249
Load design, column splices, 249
Loading conditions, lintels, 199
Loading Dock Equipment Manufacturers Association, 520, 592
Loading docks, 513
  flooring, 483
Loading zones, passenger, 14
Load tables
  beams, 883–885
  beams, precast concrete, **S16**, 181
  beams and columns, steel, **S27**, 249
  beams, wood floor and roof, 282–284
  ceiling joist and rafter sizes, wood, 285
  columns, steel, **S27**, 249
  columns, wood, 281
  flat deck members, 180
  floor joists, wood, 276–280
  joists, steel, **S32–33**, 256–257
  rafters and roof joists, wood, 286–289
  slabs, precast concrete, **S15**
  wood, design load tables, 276–289
Load transfer, column, **S65**
Lobbies
  elevator, 582
  modular furniture for, 523
Local area networks (LAN), **S151**
Lockboxes, mailrooms, 795
Locker rooms, 799–800, 800
  facilities checklist, 800
  flooring, 483
Lockers, 497
  gymnasium, 799–800
  ski, 697
  toilet rooms, 807

NOTE: Page references in **boldface** preceded by **S** indicate *Supplement* pages.

Index

Locks, 435
  cylinder, 437
  door, 435
  electromagnetic, 419
  metal roofing, S102
  Pittsburgh, S102
  snap, S102
  types, 435
Logs
  construction, 317
  large, sawing of, 274
  prefabricated structures, 317
  shrinkage distortions by position, 275
Long jump, 676
Long-span steel joists, 257
Long-span structures, 44, 181, 560
  creep, 138
Long-term care facilities, 828
Lotus International, 896
Lounge chairs, 523, 543
  classic, 547–550
  contemporary, 551, 552, 553
Lounges, modular furniture for, 523
Louvers, 55, 310
  metal, S145–146
  soffit and roof, 394
  storm-resistant, S146
  for sun control, 733
  wood, dadoed slats, S79
  wood, pivot pin movable slats, S79
  wood, routed slats, S79
Low-rise buildings, 31
Lug sill, stone, 234
Lumber
  column load tables, 281
  dimensional, 318
  grading of, 274
  joist and rafter load tables, 276–280, 285–289
  production of, 274
  Southern Pine preservative retentions and AWPA standards, S70
Lumen method, 52, 53
Luminaires, 654–655
  modular ceiling, 561, 562
  selection parameters, 54
Lunchrooms, seating capacities, 798
Lux, 51

Magnesium
  melting temperature of, S23
  properties of, S22
Magnesium oxychloride flooring, S127
Magnetic detectors, 73
Mailboxes, 502
Mail chutes, 590, 795
Mailrooms, 795
  apartments, 502
Major League baseball, 667
Major Soccer League, 700
Mall lighting, 150
Manholes, 143
Mantels, S73, 218–219
  historic, 769
Manufactured Housing Institute, 576
Maple Flooring Manufacturers Association, 484
Maps of the U.S.
  climatic design, 703
  deep-ground temperatures, 703, 735
  frost penetration, 126
  insulation zones, 354
  isogonic chart, 707
  passive solar heating, 703
  rainfall intensity, 389
  sun time, 708
Marble, S118, S125
  cabinet details, 333
  concrete aggregate, S13
  epoxy chip flooring, S127
  paving, 138
  uses and properties of, 231
  veneer patterns, S118
  wall facing patterns, S118
Marble Institute of America, 242
Marine development, 111
Marketplace Design Center, 558
Marking Device Association International, 504
Masking systems, electronic, 61
Mason Contractors Association of America, 242
Masonry, 187–242
  accessories, 193–199, 207
  accessory materials, 189
  acoustical units, S119
  adobe, 230
  anchors, 190, 193, 194, 207
  anchors, stone, 232
  applications, 131
  arches, 216, 217
  box-frame system, 188
  channel slots, 194
  chimneys, 365
  clay units, 201
  concrete-filled, 294
  concrete units (CMUs), 202, 212
  concrete units (CMUs), anchorage, 206
  concrete units (CMUs), brick veneer on, 214
  concrete units (CMUs), lintels, 199
  concrete units (CMUs), types, 202
  concrete units (CMUs), walls, 133, 134, 205, 207, 210
  construction, 188–190
  control joints, 197
  design, 190
  electrical outlets, 643
  enclosures for fire protection, 357
  expansion joints, 197
  exterior insulation and finish systems, 356
  fireplaces, 218–224
  flashings, 198, 380, 385
  glass block, 227–229
  grout, 191–192
  heaters, 220
  height-thickness ratios, 190
  historic, 752–754
  lintels, 199
  load-bearing, 207, 215, 765
  materials, preservation of, 753
  materials, types, 188
  mortar, 189, 191–192
  mortar, selection guide, 192
  movement joints, 196
  permeance and permeability to water vapor, 335, 352
  references, 207
  reinforced brick, S126, 215
  reinforcement, 49, 193
  reinforcement, materials selection for, 207
  reinforcement, precautions, 207
  repointing at joints, 753
  resources, 242
  rubble stone, 232
  sealants, 400
  seismic-resistant details, 49
  split-stone, 232
  stone, 216, 231–232, 235–240, 473, 479
  stoves, 220
  structural facing tile, 225
  surface cleaning, 753–754
  surfaces, S128
  temperature effects on, 753
  thermal mass, 720
  thermal resistance of materials, 739
  ties, 194
  unit, 190, 199–200, 200–226
  unit, acoustical, 476
  unit, glass, 227–229
  unit flooring, S126
  veneer, 32, 189, 213–214, 385
  wall, single-pitch back wall detail at top, S112
  walls, 188, 190, 198, 199, 207, 212, 215
  walls, bearing, 29
  walls, cavity, 197, 210–212
  walls, circular, 200
  walls, curtain veneer, 189
  walls, exterior sections, 752
  walls, foundation, 203, 204
  walls, multiwythe, 208–209
  walls, shear, 49
  walls, single wythe, 205–207
  watertables, 384
  weights, 882
Masonry Heater Association of North America, 242
Masonry Institute of America (MIA), 242
The Masonry Society (TMS), 242
Mass law, airborne sound, 62
Master facility plans, 829
Masterformat, 888, 889
Mastics, S47
  applied flooring system, S124
  environmental impact of, 747
  fills, S127
  grout, 470
  mirrors, 444
Matching patterns, wood veneer
  book, S77
  box, S78
  diamond, S78
  8-piece sunburst, S78
  end, S77
  herringbone, S78
  options, S78
  parquet, S78
  random, S77
  reverse diamond, S78
  sketch face, S78
  slip, S77
  swing, S78
  V-book, S78
Material Handling Equipment Distributors Association, 520, 592
Material Handling Institute, 592
Material handling systems, 587–589, 587–590
  conveyors, 589
  lifts, 585
Materials
  comparison chart, 746, 747
  corrugated, 140, 141, 362, 390, 758
  embodied energy of, 743
  environmental impact analysis of, 743
  environmental impact of, 746, 747
  fibrous, 354
  flammable, flooring, 483
  heat transmission resistance of, 740
  high-energy, environmental impact, 743
  historic, 750
  insulation, 354
  life-cycle analysis of, 743
  life cycle of, 744
  mechanical, 594–596, 598–600
  medium-energy, 743
  metal, properties of, S22–23
  metallic, 354
  movement of, 196
  nontoxic, 745
  permeance and permeability to water vapor, 352
  phase change, 723
  recyclable, 851
  recycled, 745
  steel framing, cold-formed, S34–35
  symbols for, 856
  thermal resistance values, 739, 740, 856
  weights of, 882
  wiring and related, S168–172
Materials and Methods Standards Association (MMSA), 484
Materials Handling and Management Society, 592
The Materials Properties Council, 272
Mathematical data, 875–876, 881
  areas and volumes, 880
  decimal equivalents, 881
  geometric construction, 877, 879
  multiplying powers, 881
  nomenclature, 883
  triangles, arcs, and chords, 874
  trigonometric functions, 875–876
Matrices, 808
Measurement
  metric units, 891
  techniques, 775
Mechanical systems
  design, 29–36
  equipment, hot arid conditions, 717
  flat plate concrete, 34
  for historic buildings, 771
  lightweight steel frame and brick veneer, 32
  materials and methods, 594–596, 598–600
  piping, 594–600
  posttensioned concrete, 35
  precast concrete frame, 36
  resources, 638
  staggered steel truss, 31
  truss and wood floor truss, 33
Medicine, environmental conditions, 564
Membranes
  drainage, 346
  earth shelters, 736
  EPDM roofing, 372
  liquid-applied, 349
  liquid-applied types, S94
  modified bitumen, roofing, S88
  PVC, 371
  reinforced, S94
  roofing, S86–96
  roofing, low-slope, S80
  roofing, protected, S95
  roofing, repair, S103
  roofs, 371, 372
  unreinforced, S94
  waterproofing, 347, 348, 349
  water-resistant, 346
Men, measurements, 2
Merchandise Mart, 558
Message boards, 155
Metal, 243–272
  anchors, glass blocks, 228
  angles, S48, S139, 264
  architectural, 757
  bucks, 405, 407–409
  buildings, pre-engineered, S165–166, 569
  cast, abrasive surface thresholds, 440
  cast, nosings, 28
  cast, saddles, 440
  cast, uses for, 154–155
  ceilings, 474–475
  chimneys, 493
  coatings, S24–25, 245
  column bases, S48

NOTE: Page references in **boldface** preceded by S indicate *Supplement* pages.

Index

coping, 208, 379, 393
coping, cavity walls, 212
corrosion, **S23**, 244
covers and column guards, 491
decks, **S96**, 258–259
decks, horizontal support for, 205
detectors, 70
doors, 407–409, 418
edge paving, 136
expanded, 458–462
fabrication, **S23**, **S41–42**, 27–28, 244, 264–269, 270
fasteners, 246–247, 291–293
ferrous, **S22**, 244
films, permeance and permeability to water vapor, 352
finishes on, **S24–25**, 245
fire escapes and escape ladders, 268
flashing, cavity walls, 183
flues, 625
flying forms, 167
foils, permeance and permeability to water vapor, 352
frames, 407–409, 418
frames, cold-formed, 260–263
frames, devices, 299
frames, economy of, 248
frames, partitions, 465, 467, 468
frames, structural, 248–255
framing, cold-formed, **S34–40**
framing, structural, **S26–31**
galvanic series, **S23**
galvanized, high wind resistance detail, **S109**
galvanized, roofs, 758
gratings, 269
gravel stops, 393
guardrails, 270
gutters, expansion, 390
halide lamps, 655
handrails, 270
heavy, roof edge, **S89**
historic, 757
hollow, doors, 407–410, 418, 433
interior thresholds, 440
joists, **S32–33**, **S38**, 256–257
ladders, **S42**
light, edges, 372
light, parapet cap, **S90**, **S94**, **S96**
light, parapet cap/aggregate ballast, **S95**
light, parapet/paver ballast, **S95**
light gauge, frame, 260–261, 404
linear ceiling system, **S122**
louvers, **S145–146**
mansard-type roofing, **S101**
materials, **S22–25**, 244–245
melting temperatures of, **S23**
muntz, **S23**
nonferrous, **S22**, 244
nosing, 28
ornamental, **S43–46**, 270
pan construction, one-way joists, 173
panels, insulated, 369
perforated, **S44–45**
pipes, 265
plate, on roof beam, 315
plate connector, **S56**
plates, **S48**
pool liner with overflow, 688
posts, 270
properties of, **S22–23**, 244
rails, 270
reglets, 377
resources, 272
risers and treads, 28
roof edge, **S96**
roofing, **S94**, 361, 362
roofing, batten and ribbed seam, 376

roofing, Bermuda type, 375
roofing, flat seam, 373
roofing, locks and seams, **S102**
roofing, standing seam, 374
roofing tiles, **S85**
roof panels, **S94**
roof panels, end laps for, **S108**
roof panels, retrofit with, **S108**
roof panels, ridge cap for, **S108**
roof panels, roof system, **S108**
roof panels, seam types for, **S108**
roof walking surface, **S107**
sheet, **S45**, **S97–103**, 373–383, 385–386, 389–390
sheet, duct insulation, 602
sheet, fabrications, 391–392
sheet, flashing, 387–388
sheet, form inserts, 178
sheet, gutters and downspouts, 389
sheet, roofing, 373–376, 758
sheet, screws, 293
shelving, 574
siding, 368, 369
stairs, **S41**, 267
strap, on roof beam, 315
studs, 462
subrails, 270
support systems, **S114–115**
surfaces, **S128**
ties, 220
ties, walls, 199
ties, wire, 190
toilet partitions, 486
treads, 269
trim, 270
tubing, 265, 642, 643
types of, 244
walls, cavity, 212
walls, curtain, 369, 449
walls, glazed curtain, 449–456
weights, **S23**, 882
windows, 424–428, 430
windows, awnings and jalousie, 428, 430
windows, casement, 425
windows, double-hung, 426
windows, pivoted, 427
windows, reversible and projected, 427
windows, sliding, 426
Metal Architecture, 272
Metal Building Manufacturers Association (MBMA), 272, 576
Metal lath, 458, 462
  furring for fire protection, 357
  steel bar reinforcement, 176
  steel joists, 460–461
Metal Lath/Steel Framing Association Division of NAMM (ML/SFA), 272
Metals & Ceramics Information Center, 272
Metal Treating Institute, 272
Metric system, 890–896
  drawing dimensions, 858, 890, 892–896
  measurements, 227, 892–896
  plane and solid angles, 891
  prefixes, 890
  rules for writing symbols and names, 890
  sample SI units and relationships, 892–895
  units and conversions, 891
Metropolis, 896
Miami International Merchandise Mart, 558
Michigan Design Center, 558
Microclimates, 16
Microcomputers, uninterruptible power supply systems, 661

Microfiche reader carrels, 539
Microprocessors, 74
Microwave detectors, 73
Microwave ovens, **S161**, 512
Millwork, flat, relieved backs in, 275
Mineral cellular materials, insulation, 354
Mineral fibrous materials, insulation, 354
Mineral Insulation Manufacturers Association (MIMA), 402
Minimum centerline radius, 90
Minitramp, 680
Mirrors, 426, 444
  bathroom cabinets, 488
  bedroom closet doors, 545
  graphic symbols, 859
  shelves for handicapped, 487
Mobility aids, 10
Modems, **S151**, 637
Modified bitumen flashing strip, **S90**
Modified bitumen membrane, **S89**, **S90**
  roofing, **S88**
  roofing, details, **S89–91**
  roofing, NRCA standards, **S91**
  three-ply, **S88**
  two-ply, **S88**
Modulus of elasticity
  lumber, 282
  wood, 318
Moisture
  curtain walls, 449
  earth shelters, 736
  logs, 317
  problems in historic buildings, 750
  removal, 65
Moisture penetration, **S132**
Moisture protection, 346–402
  resources, 402
  venting, 352
  for wood decks, 313
Moldings, 341, 459
  classical, 112
  crown, 336
  decorations and patterns, 112
  flush, 338
  mitered backhand, 770
  ogee, 341
  picture, 338
  raised, 338
  types, 113
  wood, 341, 770
Moldings, interior wood, **S74–75**
  base, **S74–75**
  bed, **S74–75**
  cap, **S74–75**
  crown, **S75**
  lap, **S74**
  panel, **S75**
  picture, **S74–75**
  rake, **S75**
  rosette, **S74**
  standard wall, **S123**
  wood, **S74**
Monel, **S45**, 244
Monitors, 74, 637
  computer, **S151**
  video, **S149**
Mop holders, 859
Mortar, 191–192
  ASTM specifications, 191
  cement, latex-Portland, 483
  ceramic tile, 471
  cover, 207
  dry-set, 470, 471
  functions, 200
  glass block, 227–228
  historic building preservation, 752
  inflexible (cement), 753
  latex-modified, 137
  masonry, 189

  placement, **S84**
  selection guide, 192
  stone walls, 232
  thick-bed, 471
  thin-set, 471
  types of, 470
  weights, 882
Mortise
  bolts, 434
  locks, 405
  templates, 437
  wood, 764
Mosques, 833
Motels, laundry rooms, 511
Motor control centers, 651
Motor operation, annual use, 724
Motor starters, 651
Mounting
  flagpoles, 494
  mailboxes, 502
  methods and materials, 496
  mirrors, 444
  plumbing fixtures, 862
  solar heat collectors, 731
Movie theaters, reverberation time, 64
Mud bricks, sundried, 230
Mudslabs, 346
Mullions
  lockstrip gasket, 452
  removable, 439
  walls, 182
Multifamily housing, mail boxes for, 502
Multi-Housing Laundry Association, 520
Multiwythe walls, 208, 209
Museums, 815–818
Music
  practice rooms, 567
  reverberation time, 64
Musical instruments, 509–510
Mutes, 439

Nailers
  horizontal wall system, **S54**
  wood, on roof purlins, **S54**
Nailing, roof slope procedures, **S84**
Nails, 290
  APA panel roofs, 310
  framing, 298
  gypsum wallboard partitions, 463–465
  roofs, 359, 361, 362, 366
  rough construction, 290
  schedules, 309–310
  shingles and shakes, 363, 364, 365
  siding, 329
  wood decking, 313, 477
National Alarm Association of America, 520
National Alliance of Preservation Commissions, 751, 778
National Alliance of Statewide Preservation Commissions, 778
National Archives and Records Service, 778
National Association of Architectural Metal Manufacturers (NAAMM), 272, 504, 576
National Association of Band Instrument Manufacturers, 520
National Association of Brick Distributors (NABD), 242
National Association of Decorative Architectural Finishes, 484, 504
National Association of Elevator Contractors (NAEC), 592
National Association of Elevator Safety Authorities, 592
National Association of Fire Equipment Distributors, 504

NOTE: Page references in **boldface** preceded by **S** indicate *Supplement* pages.

Index

National Association of Food Equipment Manufacturers, 520
National Association of Home Builders (NAHB), 344
National Association of Mirror Manufacturers, 504
National Association of Music Merchants, 520
National Association of Photographic Manufacturers, 520
National Association of Plumbing, Heating, Cooling Contractors, 638
National Association of Professional Baseball Leagues, 700
National Association of Retail Dealers of America, 520
National Association of Security and Data Vaults, 520
National Association of Service Merchandising (NASM), 504
National Association of Vertical Transportation Professionals (NAVTP), 592
National Automatic Merchandising Association, 520
National Basketball Association (NBA), 700
   basketball standards, 678
National Bulk Venders Association, 520
National Burglar and Fire Alarm Association (NBFAA), 124, 520
National Center for Preservation Law, 778
National Child Care Association, 854
National Coffee Service Association, 520
National Collegiate Athletic Association (NCAA), 700
   baseball standards, 667
   basketball standards, 674
   football standards, 669
   public swimming pools standards, 685
   water polo standards, 694
National Communications Association, 664
National Concrete Masonry Association (NCMA), 162, 242
National Conference of State Historic Preservation Officers (NCSHPO), 751, 778
National Conference of States on Building Codes and Standards (NCSBCS), 124
National Council of Acoustical Consultants (NCAC), 124, 576
National Crime Prevention Institute (NCPI), 124
National Criminal Justice Reference Service, 854
National Electrical Contractors Association (NECA), 664
National Electrical Manufacturers Association (NEMA), 504, 664
National Electric Code (NEC), 649
National Electric Sign Association, 504
National Elevator Industry, 592
National Elevator Industry Educational Program (NEIEP), 592
National Emission Standards for Hazardous Air Pollutants (NESHAP), 127
National Endowment for the Arts, 854
National Energy Specialists Association, 748
National Fenestration Rating Council (NFRC), 456
National Fire Protection Association (NFPA), 124, 456, 504, 576, 664
   diamond symbols, 93
   fire alarm systems, 572
   standards, 438
   standards for exhaust ducts, 623
   standards for explosion venting, 575
   standards for fire doors and fire windows, 404
   standards for fire escapes, 268
National Fire Sprinkler Association, 576
National Flood Insurance Program (NFIP), 94–95
National Football League (NFL), 700
   football standards, 669
National Forest Products Association (NFPA), 344
National Glass Association (NGA), 456
National Golf Association, 700
National Greenhouse Manufacturers Association, 854
National Hardwood Lumber Association (NHLA), 344
National Historical Publications and Record Commission, 778
National Hockey League, 700
National Home Furnishings Association, 558
National Independent Bank Equipment and Systems Association, 520
National Institute of Building Sciences, 344
National Institute of Corrections (NIC), 854
National Institute of Steel Detailing, 272
National Insulation and Abatement Contractors Association, 402
National Kitchen and Bath Association, 558, 854
National Landscape Association, 162
National Lighting Bureau (NLB), 664
National Lime Association (NLA), 242
National Oak Flooring Manufacturers Association, 484
National Oceanic and Atmospheric Administration (NOAA) weather data, 713
National Office Products Association, 558
National Ornamental and Miscellaneous Metals Association (NOMMA), 272
National Paint and Coatings Association (NPCA), 402
National Park Service (NPS)
   National Register of Historic Places, 751, 778
   Office of Park Historic Architecture (OPHA), 778
   Preservation Assistance Division, 778
National Particleboard Association (NPBA), 344
National Pool and Spa Institute, 576
National Precast Concrete Association (NPCA), 186
National Preservation Institute (NPI), 778
National Ready-Mixed Concrete Association (NRMCA), 186
National Recreation and Park Association (NRPA), 700
National Register of Historic Places, 751, 778
National Renewable Energy Laboratory (NREL), 748
National Research Council Canada (NRCC), Fire Research Section (FRS), 576
National Retail Hardware Association, 456
National Rifle Association of America, 700
National Roof Deck Contractors Association (NRDCA), 402
National Roofing Contractors Association (NRCA), 402
National Sanitation Foundation, 520
National Sash and Door Jobbers Association (NSDJA), 456
National School Supply Equipment Association, 558
National Shooting Sports Federation, 700
National Solid Waste Management Association (NSWMA), 520, 638, 854
National Standards Association, 124
National Stone Association (NSA), 186, 242
National Swimming Pool Foundation, 700
National Swimming Pool Institute, 700
National Terrazzo and Mosaic Association, 484
National Tile Roofing Manufacturers Association (NTRMA), 402
National Trust for Historic Preservation, 751, 778
National Wood Flooring Association, 484
National Wood Window and Door Association (NWWDA), 456
   doors standards, 412
NC (noise criteria) curves, 60
NEC (National Electric Code), 649
Neighborhoods
   garden city, 80
   mixed, **S192**
   open space, 83
   plan elements, 91
   rural, 79
   traditional design, 91, 92
   urban, 79
Neoprene
   gaskets, 737
   joint fillers, 399
   paving coats, 137
Newspaper racks, 340, 540
New York State Uniform Fire Prevention and Building Code, 110
Nickel
   melting temperature of, **S23**
   properties of, **S22**
Nickel Development Institute (NDI), 272
Nightclubs, 797
   seating for, 797, 798
Nogging, 302, 303
Noise control, 60–62
   design criteria, 63
   exterior walls, 41, 42
   floor structure, 37, 38
   kennels and animal shelters, 846
   roof structure, 39, 40
Noise criteria (NC) curves, 60
North American Telecommunications Association, 664
Northeastern Lumber Manufacturers Association, 344
Northeast Sustainable Energy Association (NSEA), 748
Nosings, 28
   accessible, 339
   ADAAG acceptable, 340
   slip-resistant, 28, 176
   stair, **S41**, 16
   stone, 479
   types, 28
Notch, roof expansion joint, **S104**
N.R.C. ratings, **S120**
NRCA built-up and modified bitumen roofing detail standards, **S91**
Nursery, 83
   church, 831
Nurses' station layout, 802
Nursing homes, 828
   hardware, 439

Obstructions, architectural, 93
Occupant loads, 23
Occupational Safety and Health Administration (OSHA), 124, 127
   construction industry asbestos standard, 127
   excavations standards, 129
   fire escape standards, 268
   sound requirements, 61
   tread covering standards, 28
Odor removal, 805
Office buildings, 808–811
   construction, 811
   construction cost estimating, 120
   core, 810
   delivery approaches, 811
   design schedule, 811
   electrical loads, average, 809
   envelope configurations, 810
   illumination level, average, 809
   interaction net, 808
   minimum live loads, 809
   postal facilities, 795
   project program, 808
   space allowance guide, 809
   support systems, 810
Office of Urban Rehabilitation, 124
Office Planners and Users Group (OPUP), 854
Office Products Manufacturers Association, 558
Offices, 808–811
   churches, 831
   conventional, 808
   cores, 810
   for facilities, 810
   flooring, 483
   furniture, 522, 527–535
   lighting, 56
   modules, 808
   open areas, 793
   open plan, 808
   planning, anthropometric data, 6
   seating, 532
   wiring systems for, **S172**, 529
Office Systems Research Association (OSRA), 854
Olgyay, Victor, bioclimatic chart, 702
Openings
   fire-rated, 404
   framing details, 295
   framing details, steel, **S36–37**
   roofs, 256
Open plan units, 537
Open space, types, 83, 84
Opera, reverberation time, 64
Operating rooms, flooring, 483
Optics, 51
Organs, 509, 510
Orientation, residences, **S191**
Oriented-strand board (OSB), **S62**
Ornamental and Miscellaneous Metal Fabricator, 272
Ornaments
   classical, 112
   frieze, **S73**
   metal, **S43**, 757
   types, 113
   wood, **S72–73**
OSB. *See* Oriented-strand board
Ottagano, 896
Outrigger, wood I-joist rafter with, **S66**
Ovens, **S155**, **S156**, **S161**
   built-in, 517
Overhangs, **S59**, **S66**, 301–302
   gable end, **S63**
   gable endwall, **S108**
   gable roof detail, **S59**
   historic, 302
   parking lot requirements, 103
   static loads for, 885
   sun shading, 732, 733
Owner-architect documents, 886
Owner-contractor documents, 886

NOTE: Page references in **boldface** preceded by **S** indicate *Supplement* pages.

Index

Pacific Design Center, 558
Painting, S130–134
Paints, S130–131
  clear, S130
  environmental impact of, 747
  finish on metal, 245
  fire-resistant, S128
  high-gloss, S130
  intumescent, S128
  opaque, S130–131
  prime coat, S130
  removal methods, 755
  semitransparent, S130
  substrate conditions, S132
  types and uses, S130, S133–134
  undercoat, S130
Panelboards, electrical, 652, 653
  symbols, 860
Panels
  absorptive, S119
  accessories, 492
  acoustical, S123, 529
  at ceiling, joint with wall, S121
  ceiling, roof eave with, S63
  ceiling, textured, S123
  ceiling-height, 528
  clips, 308
  composite, 368, 369
  concrete, fiberglass reinforced, 184
  continuous, detail at roof, S63
  curtain walls, 450
  decorative, thermally fused, S76
  desk systems, 528
  detectors, 74
  donut, 185
  door, 412
  double tee, 182
  drop, for columns, S2
  fabric-wrapped, track system, S136
  foam-core, S54–55
  glass, 270
  glass block, 227–228, 228
  hard stone, 235
  high-impact, S119, S136
  insulated metal, 369
  interior wall, S121
  interior wall details, 338
  intermediate spline, S62
  kick, 336
  leaded glass, 445
  leveling leg/toe kick, 336
  low frequency, S119
  metal roof, S94
  metal roof, end laps for, S108
  metal roof, retrofit with, S108
  metal roof, ridge cap for, S108
  metal roof, roof system, S108
  metal roof, seam types for, S108
  nail-laminated deck, S67
  non-load-bearing, connection details, 183
  panel strips, S75
  performance-rated, 306
  plenum, S136
  plywood, 306–307, 338
  plywood, minimum bending radii for, 330
  precast concrete, 182, 226
  prefabricated, cold storage room, S164
  prefabricated fabric-wrapped, S136
  prefinished gypsum wall, S117
  privacy, 528
  products, S76–78
  reflective, S119
  roof and wall, pre-engineered metal building, S166
  roof system, 364
  sandwich, 369
  sidewall, 364
  siding, 330
  sill, interior wall, S121
  splices, 374
  stone, 235, 236
  stone, preassembled, 240
  structural building, S62–63
  suspended, S120
  tackable, S119, S136
  tee, 185
  thermal break, S62
  thermal resistance, 739
  thickness, 185
  types, 306
  variations, 182
  vision, 405
  wall, precast concrete, S17–18
  wall reinforcements, 215
  wall systems, modular, S148
  widths, 185
  wood, 332, 338
Panic exit mechanisms, 439
Pantries, 782
Paper, wall coverings, S135
Paper towel dispensers, 488
Paper weights, 534
Parapets
  adobe, with extended vigas, 230
  aluminum siding, 368
  counterflashing, S89, S92–93
  edges, 393
  expansion joints, S104
  flashings, 371, 380, 387
  metal cap, light, S90, S94–96
  metal walls, insulated, 369
  roof, 235, 236
  stone, 233, 239
  wall, scupper detail at, S105
  walls, 212
  walls, scupper details, 391, 392
Parking, 98–105
  accessible, 9, 14
  commercial, 103
  garages, 100, 105
  garages, construction cost estimating, 121
  guidelines for traditional neighborhood design, 92
Parking lot design, 100, 103–104
  ADAAG specifications, 666
  drainage, 141
  lighting, 150
  required accessible spaces, 103
Parks, 83, 84
Partial loads, 43
Particleboard, S76
  environmental impact of, 746
  life cycle of, 744
Partitions, S147–148
  acoustical ratings, 464, 465
  assemblies, ceiling systems, 562
  design criteria, 61
  framing, 298
  gypsum board, 464–467
  hollow, 458
  interior glazed, 433, 439
  lath and plaster, 462
  modular wall systems, S148
  NC curves, 60
  nonbearing interior, 300
  operable, S147, 503
  partial height, S116
  piping, 597
  solid, 458
  sound-isolated, intersection, S117
  sound transmission loss, 464, 465
  terminals, 459
  toilet, 486
  wall, height tables, 261
  wire mesh, 503
Passages, 6
  accessible, 7
  locks, 435
Passive solar, 725–728
  cooling, 725
  heating, 722, 725–727
  heating, map, 703
Passive Solar Industries Council, 748
Patching, 177
Patent-hammered finishes, 754
Paths and walks, 96
Pavers
  ballast, S95, S107
  concrete, S95
  concrete, on existing slab, S126
  mortarless, on concrete slab, S126
  stone, S125
Paving, 96, 136–138
  blocks, 96, 479
  flashings, 385
  interlocking, 138
  interlocking roof tile, 367
  stone, 136–137
  surface drainage, 141
  tile, 469
  types and patterns, 138
  unit, 137
Pedestals, pavers, 137
Pedestrian areas, 91
Pedestrian crossing time, 90
Pedestrian planning, 96–97
Pediments, 114
  wood, ledge flashing, S100
Penthouses, 579
Percolation tests, 144
Pereletok, 714
Periodicals, international, 896
Perlite Institute (PI), 402
Permafrost, design conditions for, 714
Permeability and permeance, of materials to water vapor, 352, 738
Perms, thermal transmission, 738
Personnel barriers, 70
Pews, 541
Pharmaceuticals, environmental conditions, 564
Phase change materials, 723
Phenol formaldehyde metal coating, S25
Photocells, 570
Photoelectric detection systems, 438, 573
Photogrammetry, 775–776
Photographic equipment, 519
Photographic Manufacturers and Distributors Association, 520
Piano Manufacturers International, 520
Pictograms, S143
Picture moldings, S74–75
  wood, 338
Pilasters
  architrave, 770
  brick masonry, reinforced, 215
  classical, 114
  concrete, S3
  control joints, 197
  garden walls, 134
  masonry, 207, 215
  small, 166
  wall footing, 165
Piles, 135
  composite, 135
  excavations, 129
  foundations, 135
  Southern Pine preservative retentions and AWPA standards, S70
  supported foundations, 174
  types and characteristics, 135
Pipes, 594, 595
  bracing, 50
  chases, 597
  cleanouts and expansion joints, 596
  coatings, 245
  fire hydrant and standpipe connections, 93
  fire suppression systems, 574
  fittings, 595
  gas, 623
  gas, hangers, 621
  gas, standard ICU outlets, 490
  insulation, 601
  jackets, 601
  leaning, 154
  mechanical, 594–600
  metal, 265
  outlet, 145
  penetrations, 346, 348, 349
  penetrations, low-slope roofs, S81
  penetrations, multiple, S91
  penetrations, single, S91, S94, S96
  prefabricated flashing, S92
  premolded covers, 372
  roller support, S91
  smoke clearances, 221
  soil, 594, 597, 603
  steel, 266, 296
  steel, coating system for, S128
  stove, 221
  symbols, 864
  systems, 629
  tall, flashings, 382
  thermal expansions, 596
  types, 594, 595
  vitrified clay, 144
  waste and vent, 603
  water supply, 603
Pitcher's mound
  Little League baseball, 668
  Major League baseball, 667
Pitch pockets, 382
Pits, 579
Pivots, door, 439
Plan files, 535
Planks
  construction, 314
  flooring, 477, 478
  framing, 315
  staging, slab and beam forming, 167
Planning
  community, 75–93
  egress, 23–28
  general, and design data, 1–124
  general, resources for, 124
  nonresidential room, 793–811
  regional, 75, 79
  residential site, S191
  school, 823
  site, community, and urban, 75–93
  space, and building types, 779–854
  town, 75
  traditional neighborhood development, 92
Planters, 155, 557
  drains, 140
  wood, 156
Planting, 161
  details, 159
  interior, 555–557
  interior, design considerations, 557
  interior, lighting, 556
  parking areas, 104
  parking lots, 103
  plant forms and sizes, 555
  rooftops, 160
  structures, 160
Plaques, 495–496
Plaster, 458–462
  accessories, 459
  acoustical, 416
  cast, cornice, S114
  cast, two-piece column, S115
  ceilings, 460–461
  control joints, 197

NOTE: Page references in **boldface** preceded by S indicate *Supplement* pages.

Index

dome, **S114**
fire protection, 357
gypsum, two-piece, glass fiber-reinforced column, **S115**
materials, 458
ornamental, 768
ornamental fabrications, **S114–115**
partitions, 462
permeance and permeability to water vapor, 352
weights, 882
Plasterboard, gypsum, 463
Plastic
  acrylic sheets, 446
  caps, tendon installation, 179
  cushions, tendon installation, 179
  doors, 411–412, 431
  drain pipes, 140
  fiberglass-reinforced, 342, 343
  foils, permeance and permeability to water vapor, 352
  form liners, **S13**, 164
  glazing, 446
  laminates, toilet partitions, 486
  nonreinforced, 362
  permeance and permeability to water vapor, 352
  pipe and fittings, 594, 595
  pocket formers, tendon installation, 179
  resources, 344
  safety panels, posts and railings, 270
  sealants, 400
  sheathing, 308
  sheets, thermal resistance, 741
  shims, stone panels, 235–236
  skylights, 395
  structural, 342, 343
  structural, load deflection table, 343
  windows, 429–430, 431
  wire-reinforced, 362
Plastic laminate flooring, **S127**
Plastics Institute of America (PIA), 344
Plates
  concrete, **S10**
  metal, **S48**
  metal, connector, **S56**
  sill, anchors, **S48**
  sill, reduced, **S61**
  splice, **S50**
  steel, bearing shoe, **S68**
  steel framing, **S39**
  wood, double beveled, **S66**
Platform lifts, 10, 17, 761
  cylinder, 585
  wheelchair and stair, 586
Platforms
  diving facilities, 691
  materials, spiral stairs, 27
  rest, for fixed metal ladders, **S42**
Platform tennis, 681
Platonic solids, 872
Platting, 85
Play equipment, 538, 684
Playgrounds, 83, 152, 153
Playing field construction, 673–674, 674
Plexiglass, acrylic, 445
Plumbing, 603–612
  apartment building drainage, 604
  building insulation, 355
  child care centers, 813
  design standards, 22
  drainage, 604
  equipment, 611–613
  fixtures, 606–610, 859
  office building drainage, 605
  pipe chases, 597
  pipe fittings, 594
  pipe fittings, insulation, 602

residential drainage and water piping, 603
riser diagrams, 603–605
sewage disposal, 144–146
symbols, 859, 864
vent stack, **S94**
water softeners, 613
Plumbing and Drainage Institute (PDI), 638
Plumbing Manufacturers Institute, 638
Plyform for concrete formwork, **S4**
Plywood
  APA-rated, 306
  beams, framing, 295
  butt joints, 178
  cabinet details, 334, 335
  classifications, 305
  composite, 45
  decks, 262, 310
  decorative, 306
  design data, 305
  environmental impact of, 746
  exposure durability, 305
  grades, 305, 310
  hardwood types, **S76**
  marine, 295
  panels, 306, 307, 338
  panels, minimum bending radii for, 330
  permeance and permeability to water vapor, 352
  shear walls, 50
  sheathing, 50, 294, 308, 310, 315, 327
  siding, 330
  slab and beam forming, 167
  soffits, 310
  Southern Pine preservative retentions and AWPA standards, **S70**
  span ratings, 305
  stair framing, 296
  subflooring, 300, 309, 327
  thicknesses, 310
  types, 306
  underlayment application, 309
  uses, 307
  veneer core, **S76**
  walls, footings, 165
Pocket billiards, 682
Pole construction, 316
Poles, Southern Pine preservative retentions and AWPA standards, **S70**
Pole vault, 675–676
Pollution control, 620
Polo, 695
Polycarbonates, 446
Polyester enamels, baked, **S122**
Polyester metal finishes, **S25**
Polyethylene
  chlorosulfonated, metal finishes, **S25**
  foundations, 346
  sheets, 736
  vapor retarder, 716
  watershed, 737
Polyisocyanurate Insulation Manufacturers Association (PIMA), 402
Polymers
  silicone-modified, metal finishes, **S25**
Polystyrene insulation, 137
Polysulfide sealants, 399
Polyurethane foam, spray-applied roofing, **S96**
Polyurethane sealants, 399
Polyvinylchloride (PVC)
  characteristics, 371
  conduits, 689
  gutters, 390
  metal finishes, **S25**
  nosing, 28
  nosings, 28

pipe, 594
single-ply roofing, **S93**, 371
single-ply roofing, low-slope, **S80**
Pond, fish, 157
Pools
  decorative, 147
  swimming, 685–693
  wading, 684
Porcelain Enamel Institute, 504
Porches, 87
  historic, 761–762
  wood railing patterns, 756
Portland cement, 191
  based grouts, 470
  mortar, 469, 471
Portland Cement Association (PCA), 186, 242
Postal facilities, 502
  for multifamily housing, 502
  for office buildings, 795
Posts
  bumping, 108
  chain link fences, 148
  corner, framing, 298
  framing details, 298
  hammer, **S55**
  heavy timber, 765
  king, **S56**
  leaning, 154
  metal, 270
  modified queen, **S56**
  mounting, 270
  newel, 339–340
  queen, **S52**
  Southern Pine preservative retentions and AWPA standards, **S70**
  sport facilities, 674
  wood decks, 313
  wood stairs, 340
Posttensioned concrete
  construction, 179
  technology, 35
Post-Tensioning Institute (PTI), 186
Power Crane and Shovel Association, 592
Practicality, site tests, **S196**
Practice rooms, 567
Precast concrete, 179–183, 179–186, 185
  bumpers, asphalt paving, 136
  columns, 183
  decks, 180
  frame, building technology, 36
  lintels, 199
  panels, 182, 226
  riprap, 130
  slabs, 180
  systems, 45
  tilt-up construction, 185
Precast/Prestressed Concrete Institute (PCI), 186
Prefabrication
  batten roofs, 376
  chimney stacks, 625
  shower stalls, 609
  stone panels, 240
Prefilters, 805
Preservation, historic, 749–778
  accessibility, 9
  checklist for rehabilitation, 751
  documentation, 751
  of landscapes, 772–773
  legal requirements, 751
  materials, 750
  objectives, 750
  resources, 778
Preservation Action, 778
Preservatives
  oilborne, **S70**
  oilborne, organic, **S69**

waterborne, **S70**, 111
waterborne, inorganic, **S69**
wood, **S69–70**
Pressed concrete unit flooring, **S126**
Primers, 399, 401
  exterior, 245
Process Architecture, 896
Professional Archers Association, 700
Professional Rodeo Cowboys Association, 700
Progressive Architecture, 896
Protection board
  foundations, 346
  paving, 137
  waterproofing, 347, 349
Psychrometric chart, 65
Public assembly
  bleachers and grandstands, 837
  seating, 841
  theater design, 838–840
Pulpits, 541
Pumps, 599
  chilled water, 619
  fountains, 147
  for wells, 139
Purlins, **S52**, **S54**, 297, 317, 322
  beam system, 319
Push plates, doors, 435
Push-pull bars, 435
Push-pull latch, 439
PVC. *See* Polyvinylchloride
Pythagorean theorem, 872, 881

Quartz
  concrete aggregate, **S13**
  flooring, 483
  seamless flooring, **S127**
Quartzite, 231
Quirk miter, 473
  corner, 185
Quoins, stone, 233

Raceways, **S171**
  wiring for workstations, **S172**
Racquetball, 679
Radians, 881
Radiation
  climatic design strategies, 703
  fin tube, 616
  protection, 158
  shielding, 568
  thermal comfort, 65
Radiators, 616–617
  steam, 617, 771
Radon, 203
Rafters, **S66**
  building insulation, 355
  ceiling, load tables, 285
  fly, **S66**
  framing details, 297–298, 315
  jack, 298
  load tables, 286–289
  log construction, 317
  lookout, 297
  plank and beam framing, 315
  rough carpentry, 297–298, 301–302
  spans, wood truss, 326
  steel framing, bridging, **S37**
  steel framing, openings, **S38**
  ties, **S48**
  trussed, 326
  western or platform framing, 294
  wood, 285, 289
  wood, allowable loads, 286–289
  wood, trussed, 45
Railroads, 108

NOTE: Page references in **boldface** preceded by **S** indicate *Supplement* pages.

Index

Rails, 270
  accessible, 9, 270
  balcony, 27, 43
  caps, 338
  crash, **S137**
  escalators and moving walks, 584
  with extended platform, 16
  floor mounting, 270
  lighted, 270
  low, 270
  metal, 270
  newel, 339–340
  pedestrian, **S68**
  pipe, 270
  stair, 16, 25, 267, 340, 757
  systems, **S68**
  top, 270
  vehicle, **S68**
  vertical, 16
  vinyl, 270
  wood, 338, 339
  wood decks, 312
  wood porch, 756
Rain
  cap, stationary gravity roof ventilator, **S106**
  penetration, **S132**
Rainfall intensity map for U.S., 389
Rain screen principle, 451
Rain spouts, 391, 392
Rammed earth construction, 241
Ramps, 105
  accessible, 16, 313, 761
  curb, 97
  driveways, 100
  floor, 492
  moving, 584
  stairs, pitches, 7
  wood, 313
Ranges
  residential, **S161**, 517
  smoke pipe, 221
Reach dimensions, from wheelchairs, 12
Rebar positioners, 209
Receptacles, 641
  outlets, 861
Recreation facilities
  athletic equipment, 680
  flooring, 483
  sports and games, 675–676
  swimming pools, 684–686, 688, 690–693
Recycling
  materials and methods, 743–747, 851
  solid waste, spaces, 851, 852, 853
Red brass piping, 594
Redwood, 131
  paving, 136
Redwood Inspection Service (RIS) grading rules, 258
Reflectances, thermal transmission, 737
Reflection, law of, 881
Refraction, law of, 881
Refrigeration
  chilled water systems, 619–620
  coolers, 563
  cooling systems, 618
  cooling towers, 626
  cycle, 627
  equipment rooms, 804
  machines, 804
  principles, 627
  symbols for, 863
Refrigeration Service Engineers Society, 638
Refrigerators, **S162**
  commercial, **S154**, **S157**
  residential, **S162**, 518
Refuse chutes, 514

Regional planning, 75, 79
  for energy conservation, 703
  types, 80
Regional referral centers, 827
Reglets
  chimney masonry, 365
  flashings, 378
  metal, 377
  roofing, 372
Regulatory requirements, residential sites, **S191**
Rehabilitation Act of 1973, 8
Rehabilitation of historic structures
  checklist, 751
  common problems, 750
  documentation, 751
  legal requirements, 751
  standards for, 750
Reinforced concrete, **S6**, 168–170, 215
  floor systems, 166, 175, 178
  masonry lintels, 199
Reinforced Concrete Research Council, 186
Reinforcement
  of bank vaults, 506
  bars and wires, **S6**, 168, 169
  bars and wires, ASTM standard sizes, 168
  columns, 170
  concrete, **S6**, 35, 170, 184
  of entrances and porches, 762
  foundation wall, 204
  interwoven fiberglass mesh, 356
  masonry, 49, 193, 207
  panels, 227
  panel walls, 134, 215
  plates, metal deck, 258
  precautions, 207
  safe loads, 181
  single wythe walls, methods, 207
  of slab or wall openings, 170
  steel, 49, 134, 215
  steel, grades, 171
  steel, placement of, 170
  walls, 174
Relief angles
  cavity walls, 212
  stone veneer, 237
  supports, 238
Renaissance proportions, 112
Repairs
  concrete, **S14**
  spalled concrete, 754
  stone, 754
  on wood, 755
Rescue assistance, areas of, 24
Residential design
  accessibility, 9
  bathrooms, 781
  closet storage systems, 787
  landscape, 88
  neighborhood, 79–80
  for persons with disabilities, 20, 21, 22
  room planning, 780–792
  soil, waste, and vent piping, 603
  supply and drainage riser diagrams, 603
  water supply piping, 603
Residential equipment, 516–518
  garbage disposers, 608
  household, 788–792
  sinks, 608
  waste compactors, 514
Residential site planning, **S191–194**
  analysis, **S191**
  density, **S191–192**
  regulatory requirements, **S191**
Resilient Floor Covering Institute, 484

Resilient flooring, 480
  wood gymnasium floors, 478
Resource conservation, 701–748
  methods and systems, 745
  resources, 748
Resources, 896
  for building types and space planning, 854
  for concrete, 186
  for conveying systems, 592
  for doors and windows, 456
  for electrical systems, 664
  for energy and resource conservation, 748
  for equipment, 520
  for finishes, 484
  for furnishings, 558
  for general planning and design data, 124
  for historic preservation, 778
  for masonry, 242
  for mechanical systems, 638
  for metals, 272
  for sitework, 162
  for special construction, 576
  for specialties, 504
  for sports and game facilities, 700
  for thermal and moisture protection, 402
  for wood and plastics, 344
Restaurants
  chimney requirements, 221
  insulated coolers and freezers, 563
  kitchen flooring, 483
  seating for, 797, 798
Restrooms
  commercial, 806, 807
  public, ADAAG requirements, 666
  sports arena, 666
Retail design
  entrances and storefronts, 420
  shops, 666
Retrofits
  weather stripping, 759–760
  wheelchair lifts, 586
Reverberation control, acoustical design, 60
Reverberation time, 64
Ridge boards, **S40**
Ridgepole, **S52**
Ridges
  connections, **S63**
  construction, 374
  detail, **S84**
  flashings, 381, 383
  metal buildings, pre-engineered, **S166**
  roof beams, 315
  roof caps, 758
  shingles, 365
  skylights, 396, 398
Rigid plastic drain pipes, 140
Riprap, 130
  stone, **S68**
Riser diagrams, plumbing, 603–605
Risers, 28
  proportioning, 25
  stair, 16, 296, 339, 340
  stone, 479
  tables, 27
  wood, 339, 340
Rivets, 293
Roads
  nomenclature, 89
  private, 99
  types, 90
Rock
  anchors, 129
  classification of, 231
  cut, channels, 141

Rocking chairs, classic, 547
Rodeos, 695
Roof Coatings Manufacturers Association (RCMA), 402
Roof Consultants Institute (RCI), 402
Roofing Communications Network (RCN), 402
Roofing Industry Educational Institute (RIEI), 402
Roofing Products Division (RPD), 402
Roof ponds, 725
Roofs, 358–376
  access, **S74–78**, **S104–109**
  accessories, 387–388, 393
  aluminum, 362, 368
  assemblies, 39, 40, 257
  barrel tile, high wind resistance detail, **S109**
  batten, 373, 375, 376
  beams, 282–283, 319
  Bermuda, 375
  built-up, **S86–87**, 352, 358, 359, 370, 379, 380, 387, 388
  built-up, aggregate surface, **S86**
  built-up, details, **S89–91**
  built-up, mineral-surfaced cap sheet, **S87**
  built-up, smooth surface, **S87**
  clay tile, 360, 367, 758
  cold, 715
  comparative, 39, 40
  concrete tile, **S84**
  construction, 256
  continuous panel detail at, **S63**
  cresting, 758
  crimped, 362
  decks, 310
  decks, acoustical, **S120**
  decks, metal, 258, 259
  decks, nailable, **S81**, **S86–88**
  decks, non-nailable, **S81**, **S86–88**
  detail, 210
  drains, **S91**, **S93–96**, 141, 389, 604
  edge, light metal, 372
  edge, vented, 301
  edges, at gutter, **S96**
  edges, heavy metal, **S89**
  edges, metal, **S96**
  edges, scupper through, **S89**
  EPDM single-ply, **S80**, **S92**, 372
  expansion joints, **S81**, **S104**, 370, 387, 388
  factory-assembled systems, 369
  field-assembled systems, 369
  flashings, 379–380, 382–383
  flat, 297
  flat, retrofit with metal panel roof, **S108**
  flat low-pitched, 310
  flat seam, metal, 376
  flat to sloped connection detail, **S96**
  flexible sheet, 371
  framing, **S62**
  framing, criteria for, 39, 40
  framing, details, 297
  framing, light wood, 301
  framing headers, **S54**
  gable, 297, 310, 374, 394
  gable, decorative wood elements, 756
  gable, edge, 756
  gable, overhang detail, **S59**
  gable, ventilation of, 394
  galvanized metal, high wind resistance detail, **S109**
  gambrel, 297
  gambrel, framing, 285
  glass, 362
  historic, preservation of, 758
  insulated metal panels, 369

NOTE: Page references in **boldface** preceded by **S** indicate *Supplement* pages.

Index

intersecting, 297
jack flange, **S106**
lath, 317
light, equipment support on, **S90**
liquid-applied, **S94**
loads, 43, 569
louver types, 394
low slope, **S80–81**
low slope, pitched, **S82**
mansard, **S101**, 297, 302
manufactured, 368–369
materials, wind uplift design for, **S109**
membrane, **S86–96**, 370–372, 715
membrane, low slope, **S80**
membrane, repair, **S103**
metal, **S94**, 361, 362
metal, aluminum, 368
metal, batten and ribbed seam, 376
metal, Bermuda type, 375
metal, flat seam, 373
metal, locks and seams, **S102**
metal, specialty details, **S103**
metal, standing seam, 374
metal panel, retrofit with, **S108**
metal panels, **S166**
modified bitumen membrane, **S88–91**
nails for, 290
openings, 258
ornamental canopy, **S101**
overhangs, wood framing, 301, 394
overview, **S80–82**
panel system, 364
parapets, 235–236, 372
peaks, framing, 298
percentage required for skylighting, **S110**
pitched, flashings, 379
pitches, 360
planting, 557
plastic corrugated, 362
plywood sheathing for, 310
preformed, 329–330, 367–369
protected membrane, **S95**
purlins, **S52**, **S54**
PVC single-ply, **S80**, **S93**
rafter sizers and spans, 285–289
repair strategies, **S103**
ribbed seam, metal, 376
roll, 353, 358
scuttles, **S113**
sheathing, 294, 308, 327
shed, 301
shed, vent at wall for, **S83**
sheet-iron, 758
sheet metal, 373–376, 758
shingles, 360, 363, 364, 368
single membrane, 137
single-ply EPDM, 371
single-ply PVC, 371
skylights, 395
slabs, temperature reinforcement, 168
slate, 303, 360, 366
sloped, **S84**
sloped, counter flashing at, **S99**
sloped, nailing procedures on, **S84**
sloped, vent in, **S106**
special, details, **S106–107**
specialties, **S74–78**, **S104–109**, 393–394
spray-applied foam, **S80**
spray-applied polyurethane foam, **S96**
standing seam, metal, 376
steel framing, **S40**
steep slope, **S82**
steep slope, pitched, **S82**
structural member through, **S90**
ties, concrete reinforcement, 170
tile, counter flashing at, **S99**
tiles, **S84–85**, 358–367
tiles, types, **S82**

tinplate, 758
transitions, waterproofing at, **S107**
truss clips, **S48**
trusses, **S57**, **S59**
trusses, prefabricated, 33
types, 358–367
ventilation, **S83**, **S106**
ventilation of, 394
walking surfaces, **S107**
walkways, **S80**, **S81**
windows, 429
wood frame design, **S109**
zinc, 758
Room cavity ratio, 53
Room planning
  cold storage, **S164**
  nonresidential, 793–811
  office, computer furniture, **S151**
  residential, 780–792
  videoconference, **S149**
Rot damage, 317
Rough carpentry, **S49–66**, 294–304
  nails for, 290
  openings, 295
Rowing shell, 109
Rubber
  asphalt surface, 673
  chlorinated metal finish, **S25**
  fastening strips, 372
  flooring, 483
  form inserts, 178
  nosings, slip-resistant, 28
  tile, 499
Rubber Manufacturers Association (RMA), 402
Rugby, 671
Runners
  channels, 260
  metal framing, 262–263
  splices, 261
Running track layout, 675
Ruolo, **S74**
Rural neighborhood, 79
Rural roads, 88, 89, 90
Rural village design, 78
Rustication
  classical, 116
  at construction joint, 177
  exposed concrete, 166
  stone bases, 752
  wood butt joints, 178

Sabins, 64
Sacristies, 831
Saddle boots, 561
Saddles
  interior, 440
  stone, 479
Safe deposit vault, 506
Sailboats, 110
Saint Louis Design Center, 558
Sally ports, 69, 70, 71
Sandblast finishes, 185
Sand clay, 673
Sand filters, 145, 146
San Diego Design Center, 558
Sand-set bed, **S126**
Sandstone, 231
San Francisco Mart, 558
Sanitary napkin units, 859
Saunas, 565
Sauna Society of America, 576
Scabs, 167
School buses, 98
  turning dimensions, 99
Schools, 823–826
  chimney requirements, 221
  concrete slabs, 175
  construction cost estimating, 120

early learning equipment, 538
furniture, 537, 540
principals of planning & design, 823
Science cabinets, 537
Scientific notation, 881
Screeds, 459
Screens
  insect, **S106**, 718
  partitions, 503
  soffit, 310
  transparent, 149
  window, 414, 423, 426, 428, 442
  wood, **S79**
Screws, 291, 292, 293
  corrosion-resistant, 362
  roofing, 361, 362
Sculpture gardens, 815
Scuppers, **S105**, 391, 392
  assembly elevation, **S105**
  detail at parapet wall, **S105**
  and flashing, **S100**
  and gutters, **S105**
  roofs, 372
  sizing procedures, **S105**
  through roof edge, **S89**
Scuttles, **S110–113**
Sealant, Waterproofing, and Restoration Institute (SWRI), 242, 402
Sealants
  with backer rod, 235
  concrete surfaces, **S14**
  elastomeric, 371–372, 380, 399–401
  glass glazing, 448
  installation, 401
  structural, 453
  waterproofing, 347
Sealed Insulating Glass Manufacturers Association (SIGMA), 456
Sealing compound, 227
Seals, acoustical, **S120**
Seams
  butt, **S102**
  flat, **S102**
  hook, **S102**
  lap, **S102**
  lock, **S102**
  metal roofing, **S102**
  metal roofing panels, **S108**
  profiles, **S101**
  standing, **S102**
Seating
  accessible, 666, 798
  anthropometric data, 5, 6
  auditorium, 838–841
  capacities, 798, 837
  clearances for wheelchairs, 11
  courtroom, **S190**
  drafting, 535
  grandstands and bleachers, 837
  modular, 523
  office, 532
  for restaurants and bars, 797, 798
  stadium, 835, 836
Security, residential, **S191**
Security design, 66, 67
  checklist, 67
Security equipment
  access controls, 71, 836
  alarms, 74, 507, 572
  banks, 507–508
  building systems, 72
  consoles, 637
  control systems, 74
  detector types, 73
  doors, 405, 406
  file cabinets, 533
  guard booths, 70
  site barriers, 151
  skylights, 395
  systems, 73–74

vaults, 506
windows, 405, 406, 427
Security planning, 66–67, 68
  airport checkpoints, 822
  building, 66–74
  entries and exits, 71
  justice facilities, **S187**, **S188**, **S189**
  museums, 817
  public access control, 71
  site perimeters, 69
  site selection, 68
Seepage pits and beds, 145, 146
Seismic design, 46–50, 207, 534
  vibration control, 46, 600
Seminar seating, 536
Semitrailers, 106
Septic systems, 144
Septic tanks, 144, 145, 146
  drainage fields for, 146
Service chase, under floor, **S55**
Service walkways, on roofs, **S107**
Service wall systems, 489–490
Setting beds
  bituminous, 137
  stone floors, 479
Sewage disposal, 140–146, 488
  septic tanks, 144, 145, 146
  storm drainage, 604
  vitrified clay pipes, 144
Shading, 865
  coefficients, 742
  devices, 58, 732–734
Shadow construction, 706, 708
Shadow drawings, 865
Shakes, 363, 364
  wood, 360, 364
Shale
  expanded lightweight, concrete aggregate, **S13**
Shear plates, 254
  wood truss, 323
Sheathing, 305–310
  APA-rated, 306
  column clamps, 165
  double hung windows, 431
  liner joints, 178
  plywood, 50
  plywood, for roofs and soffits, 310
  rated, 305
  roof, 308
  stone panels, 235
  structural, 306
  wall, 308
  wood, 329
Sheds
  roofs, 297
  roofs, framing, 301
  skylights, 396
Sheet metal, **S97–103**
  duct insulation, 602
  fabrications, 391, 392
  flashing, 377–388
  form inserts, 178
  gutters and downspouts, 389–390
  roofing, 373–376, 758
  screws, 293
Sheet Metal and Air Conditioning Contractors National Association (SMACNA), 272, 638
  gutter standards, 390
Sheetpile, 129
Shelf angles
  brick veneer, 213
  cavity walls, 211, 212
Shelters
  civil defense, 735
  earth, 735–737
Shelves, 337
  cabinet, 334
  coated steel wire, 787

NOTE: Page references in **boldface** preceded by **S** indicate *Supplement* pages.

Index

commercial bar, **S159**
commercial food service, **S153**, **S157**
edge details, 337
fixed and semi-fixed, 337
glass block details, 228
library, 539
light, 720
parallel/side reach limits, 12
solid, 787
track, 539
wood, 337
Shields, 291
termite, **S63**, **S100**
Shims
  pads, 183
  plastic, stone panels, 235–236
Shingles, **S84–85**, 358–367
  aluminum, 360
  asphalt, 365
  asphalt, environmental impact of, 746
  asphalt, high wind resistance detail, **S109**
  asphalt, repair, **S103**
  composition, 359, 365
  composition, high wind resistance detail, **S109**
  concrete, 360
  descriptions, 359
  drip edges, 365
  hip, 365
  historic preservation of, 755
  metal, 361
  red cedar, 363
  roof flashings, 383
  for siding, 364
  slate, 360, 366
  slate, repair, **S103**
  underlayment and sheathing, 363
  wood, 360, 363–364
  wood, environmental impact of, 746
  wood, patterns, 756
  wood, roofs, 758
Shiplap, 329, 756
Shoes, bearing
  steel angle, **S68**
  steel plate, **S68**
Shoes, wall, 166
Shooting
  stalls, 698
  trap and skeet, 699
Shopfront, 87
Shoring
  concrete, **S8**, 172
  excavation support systems, 129
  floor framing, 172
Shortspans
  precast structural systems, 180
  slabs, 180
Shot landing area, 675
Shower rooms, 799–800
Showers
  accessible, 19, 20, 487
  drain receptors, 609
  drains, 612
  flooring, 483
  graphic symbols, 859
  and locker rooms, 799–800
  receptors, 470, 471
  residential, 781
  roll-in units, 21
  space requirements, 21
  toilet rooms with, 807
Shower stalls
  accessible, 19, 21, 487
  prefabricated, 609
Shredders, 514
Shrubs
  interior landscaping, 555
  planting details, 159

Shutters, 734
  interior, 433
  wood, **S79**
  wood, flat panel, **S79**
  wood, louvered, **S79**
  wood, raised panel, **S79**
Sick building syndrome, 615, 745
Sidewalks, 96
  accessible, 14
  covered, 734
  lighting, 150
  moving, 584
  network, 89
  skylights, 395
  traditional neighborhood, 91
Siding, 367–369
  aluminum, 368
  APA, 305, 314
  bevel, 756
  board-and-batten, 275, 756
  chisel, 756
  diamond, 756
  exterior, environmental impact of, 746
  face grades, 306
  factory-assembled systems, 369
  field-assembled systems, 369
  fish scale, 756
  industrial, 245
  lap, 330
  manufactured, 368–369
  metal, 368, 369
  panels, APA-rated, 306
  panels, insulated metal, 369
  panels, plywood, 306
  plywood, 330
  residential, 245
  shiplap, 756
  staggered wood, 756
  tongue and groove, 329, 756
  walls, insulated metal, 369
  wood, 329, 756
  wood, eave at, 302
  wood, profiles and patterns, 756
  wood, shingles and shakes, 360, 363, 364, 839
  wood, sliding joints, 275
Sightlines, theater, 838–840
Signs, 495, 496
  support flashings, 382
Signs and symbols, common, **S143**
Silicates, inorganic
  metal finishes, **S25**
Silicone
  glazing, 433
  rubber grout, 470
  sealants, 399, 427
Sills
  anchor bolts, 299
  anchors and wood framing details, 301, 313
  attachments, 261
  box beam, wire chase, **S55**
  door saddles, 440, 479
  flashings, 386
  frame construction, 385
  framing details, 299
  interior wall panel, **S121**
  masonry construction, 385
  metal frames, 407
  metal windows, 425–428
  plates, anchors, **S48**
  plates, reduced, **S61**
  sections, glass blocks, 228
  skylights, 398
  sliding doors, 414, 423
  steel framing, connections at jambs, **S36**
  stick frame, **S54**
  stone panels, 236
  stone veneer, 238

through wall flashing at, **S97**
timber, **S54**
timber, wire chase, **S55**
weather stripping, 442
western or platform framing, 294
windows in stone, 239
Silver
  melting temperature of, **S23**
SI metric, sample building drawings, 892–896
Single Ply Roofing Institute (SPRI), 402
Sinks, 607
  accessible, 487
  bar, **S158**
  food service, **S153**, **S157**
  graphic symbols, 862
  residential, 608
Siphon chambers, 145
Siphon tanks, sewage disposal, 146
Site analysis, residential, **S191**
Site development, 75–92
  access, 70
  analysis map, 78
  building orientation, 705, 720
  drainage, 126, 143
  electrical structures, 649
  for fire protection, 93
  furnishings, 154, 155
  improvements, 103–104, 147–157
  lighting, 70
  parking lots, 104
  plans, 75
  playing fields, 674
  security, 68, 69, 70
  security barriers, 151
  sewage disposal, 144–146
Site planning
  fair housing issues, **S196**
  residential, **S191**
Site practicality tests, **S196**
Site selection and planning, 75–93
  access considerations, 68, 69
  in cold climates, 714
  community considerations, 68
  greenhouses, 849
  process, 75
  suburban analysis, 76
Sitework, 125–162
  chemically treated wood, 131
  excavation support systems, 129
  land planning and development, 94–95
  landscaping, 158–160, 555–557
  marine, 111
  paving and surfacing, 96, 136–138
  planting, 158–159
  playing fields, 674, 675–676
  resources, 162
  sewage disposal, 144–146
  sewerage and drainage, 140–146
  sidewalks, 96
  subsurface investigation, 126
  swimming pools, 684
  walls and fences, 131–134, 148–149
SI units, 892–895
Skate sailing, 696
Skate Sailing Association of America, 700
Ski equipment, 697
Skimmers, 688
Skylights, **S110–113**, **S116**, 395–398, 455
  construction, 398
  curbs, 298
  for daylight, 720
  design, 395
  dome unit, **S111**
  double-pitch framed assembly, **S112**
  flat panel unit, **S111**
  framing, **S66**
  low slope roofs, **S80**

multiple-grid, **S113**
in museums, 818
percentage of roof area required for, **S110**
plastic glazing, 446
polygon-framed assembly, **S112**
pyramid-framed, **S111**
single-pitch framed assembly, **S112**
solar heating, 726, 727
types, 396, 397
unit section, **S111**
Skyroofs, 446
Slab on grade, **S63**
Slabs
  cavity walls, 212
  concrete, 175
  concrete, cracking in, **S14**
  concrete, floor, 168, 170
  concrete, reinforcement, 168
  concrete floor, **S10–11**
  concrete formwork for, **S4**, 167
  exposed, 210, 212
  flat, 173, 180
  floor, on grade, 175
  forming, 167
  hollow core, 180, 183
  minimum-strength concrete, 175
  mortared concrete, **S126**
  mud, 346
  one-way, 172, 173
  precast concrete, **S15–21**, 180
  reinforced concrete, 170
  thickened, 175
  thickness, 180
  two-way concrete, 34
  waterproofing under, 346
Slalom course
  skiing, 697
  water skiing, 694
Slate, **S118**, **S125**
  ceramic, **S85**
  patterns, **S125**
  paving, 479
  roofing, 366, 758
  shingles, repair, **S103**
  uses and properties of, 231
Slats
  dadoed, **S79**
  pivot pin movable, **S79**
Sleepers
  floor system, **S50**, **S124**
  wood, **S50**, **S54**
Slide projectors, 794
Slip corner, 473
Slip resistance
  finish nosings, 28
  stairs and steps, 176
Slips, marine, 111
Slopes
  analysis of, 77
  drainage, 347
  flashings, 383
  roofing, 359, 365
  runoff channels, 130
  ski, 697
  stabilization, 130
Slots, 194
Slumpstone pattern, 164
Slump test, concrete, **S7**, 171
Smart buildings, 720
Smoke chamber, 218
Smoke connections, 221
Smoke control doors, 404
Smoke detection systems, 438, 572, 573
Smoke pipes, clearances, 221
Smokeproof enclosures, 24
Smoke shelves, fireplaces, 218
Smoke venting, **S110**, **S113**
  skylights, 395

NOTE: Page references in **boldface** preceded by **S** indicate *Supplement* pages.

Index

Snooker, 682
Snow
  accumulation on building surfaces, S107
  guard, steep-slope roof, S82
Snowmaking machines, 697
Soap dispensers, 859
Soapstone slate, 333
Soccer, 670
Society for Environmental Graphic Design, 504
Society of Architectural Historians, 778
Society of Certified Kitchen Designers, 854
Society of Fire Protection Engineers (SFPE), 576
Society of Glass and Ceramic Decorators, 456
Society of the Plastics Industry (SPI), 344, 402
Socket pier foundations, 174
Sofa beds, 545
Sofas, 543
  classic, 546, 548–549
  contemporary, 551, 553
  seating systems, 523
Soffits, S63
  ceiling, at lintel, S116
  continuous vent, 716
  gypsum board at, 468
  plaster and lath ceilings, 460
  plywood, 301, 310
  stairs, 267
  stone, 473
  stone veneer, 237–238
  vented, 301
  ventilation, 394
Softball, 668, 673, 674
Software, 637
Softwood, moisture shrinkage of, 275
Soil
  bearing capacity, 126
  classes, subdrains, 140
  conditions, retaining walls, 133
  fill, 160
  gradient ratio, 130
  liquefaction, 47
  mechanics, 126
  patterns, 77
  percolation, 144
  pressure, retaining walls, 132
  surface drainage, 141
  temperature fluctuation, 160
  types, 126
  weights, 736, 882
Sol-air temperature, 717, 742
Solar absorption, 726
Solar angles, 706, 709–712
Solar collectors, 729–731
  air and photovoltaic systems, 730
  domestic water heaters, 611
  liquid systems, 729
  rooftop, 731
Solar constant, 706
Solar controls
  building orientation, 705
  energy conservation, commercial buildings, 720
  glass block, 227
  screens, 237
  shades, 732–734
  use of trees, 158
Solar cooling, passive, 725
Solar Energy Industries Association, 748
Solar Energy Research Institute (SERI)
  daylighting, 57
Solar heat gain/loss, 711–712, 717–718
  daylighting, 57
  direct systems, 725–727
  fenestration systems, 742

Solar heating
  active, 723, 729–731
  air temperature, 723
  floor area, 728
  heat exchangers, 723
  off-peak power, 723
  passive, 703, 722, 725–728
  snow considerations, 731
  storage, 723, 729
  tankless coils, 723
  of water, 611
Solar ponds, 719
Solar position, 711–712
Solar radiation, 705–712
  calculation of, 711
Solar tanks, 612
Solar time, 708
Soldier piles, 129
Solid waste
  amounts and composition, 850
  collection and recycling spaces, 851, 852, 853
Solid Waste Association of North America (SWANA), 520
Sound
  absorbing pad, 474
  absorption, and occupancies, 64
  air-borne, control, 61, 62
  attenuation, 158
  attenuation blanket, S120, 476
  control, 59, 60, 61, 62, 63, 567
  frequencies of, 59
  isolation, 567
  isolation, criteria, 61
  isolation construction, 63
  pressure levels, 59, 63
  resistance, masonry walls, 190
  transmission, 62
  transmission, ceilings, 468
  transmission, curtain walls, 449
  transmission, gypsum wallboard partitions, 464–465
Soundboard, S55
Soundproofing
  in courtrooms, S188
Sound transmission class (STC), 61–62, 190, 466
Southern Building Code Congress International (SBCCI), 124
Southern Cypress Manufacturers Association, 344
Southern Forest Products Association, 344
Southern Pine preservative retentions, S70
Space frames, S31
Space planning, 6, 779–854
  counters and seating, 797, 798
  detention centers, 834
  health club design, 814
  hospital patient rooms, 802
  kitchens, 782
  lockers, 799, 800
  resources, 854
  shower rooms, 799, 800
  solid waste collection and recycling spaces, 851–853
  vending room layout and equipment, 512
  workstation design, 793
Spacers, gypsum board ceiling with, S55
Spalling, 753
Span/depth ratio, 44
Spandrels
  beams, 164, 170, 386
  cavity walls, 211
  flashings, 235, 386
  panels, 182
  precast concrete, S17

  for steel frames, 254
  stone, 236
  through wall flashing at, S97
Span ratings
  APA panel roofs, 310
  laminated decks, 311
  plywood, 305
  sturd-i-floor, 309
Spans
  cantilevered and continuous systems, 318
  concrete, 181
  for joists and rafters, 276–280, 285–289
  live/dead loads, 256–257, 260
  long span structures, 44
  planks, 314
  rafters, 326
  for steel beams and columns, 281
Span tables
  exterior wall assemblies, 41, 42
  floor structure, 37–38
  gypsum wallboard partition height, 463
  roof structures, 39–40
Spatial definition, 86
Spatial enclosure, 86
Special coatings, S128–129
  ceiling surfaces, S122–123
  floor, S127
  types, S128
  wall surfaces, S121
Special construction, 559–576
  resources, 576
Special needs housing, S200
Special purpose rooms, 563–566
Specialties, 485–504
  resources, 504
Specifications
  CSI Masterformat, 888, 889
  metric, 890
Speech, reverberation time, 64
Speed
  angular, 881
  linear, 881
Splash pans, 390
Splices
  compression, 169, 170
  framing, 314
  moment, 314, 322
  standing seam metal roofing, 374
  steel framing, S39
Spline, intermediate panel, S62
S pocket, S102
Sports facilities, 665–700
  air, 696
  aquatics, 683–694
  arenas, accessibility checklist, 666
  boating, 109–110
  courts, 673, 677–681
  equestrian, 695, 847–848
  fields, 667–674
  gymnastics, 680
  ice and snow, 696–697
  resources, 700
  table and bar, 682
  target shooting and fencing, 698–699
  track and field, 675–676
  wrestling, 680
Sports flooring, wood, S124
Sports Turf Managers Association, 700
Spray-applied foam roofing
  for low-slope roofs, S80
  polyurethane, S96
Spray-on acoustical material, S119
Sprinkler systems, 574
  concealed ceiling, 562
Sprint boards, 691
Squash, 679
Stables, 695, 847–848

Stacks
  for boilers, 625
  offsets in, 604
  shelving, 539
Stadiums, 835, 836
  seating, 836, 837
  seating guidelines, 835
Stage lighting, 842–843
Stage rigging, counterweights, 524
Stain, S131
Stained glass windows, 445
Stainless steel
  angles, 264
  cleats, 374
  cover plate, 689
  dovetail slots, 194
  dowels, 238
  eye bolt, 689
  fasteners, 149
  flashings, 393
  flats and other shapes, 265
  gutters, 390
  helical inserts, 292
  pipes, 594–595
  properties of, 244
  roofing, 361
  split-tail anchors, 236
  stone walls, 232
Stain resistance, 245
Stair carriage connection, S65
Stairs
  accessible, 9, 16, 24
  area of rescue assistance, 24
  building code requirements, 25
  circular, 27
  closed riser, 340
  concrete, 176
  deck, 313
  design, 24–26
  design for physically handicapped, 28
  fire escapes, 268
  framing details, 296
  freestanding, 176
  heavy timber, 340
  industrial and service, S41, 267
  landings, cantilevered, 296
  lifts, 586
  moving, 584
  openings, 295
  open riser, 340
  pan type construction, S41, 267
  for persons with disabilities, 28
  proportioning graph, 26
  railings, S41, 43, 757
  risers, 28, 269
  safe, design, 28
  spiral, 27
  steel, S41, 267
  stone, 233, 479
  terrazzo, 472
  treads, 27, 28, 267, 268
  U-type, 176
  wood, 339, 340, 770
Stalls, 847–848
Standard Building Code (SBC)
  occupant loads, 23
  stairway requirements, 25
Standpipe connections, 93
Staples
  APA panel roof decking, 310
  roofing, 359
Static loads
  for cantilever beams and overhangs, 885
  for fixed beams, 884
  for simple beams, 883
STC (sound transmission class), 61–62
  gypsum wallboard, 466
  masonry walls, 190
Steel
  access doors, 415

NOTE: Page references in **boldface** preceded by **S** indicate *Supplement* pages.

Index

alloys, 248
anchor bolts, 262
anchors, 194, 236
angle bearing shoe, **S68**
angles, 219, 251, 264
angles, flashings, 382
architectural metals, 757
ash urns, 155
bank vault doors, 506
bar joist with bearing wall building system, 29
bars, masonry, 207
baseplate, wood column anchorage, 321
beam hangers, 321
beams, 45, 581
beams, load capacity, 249
beams, wall anchorage in, 214
bollards, 154
bridging, framing, 299
butt weld pipe, 594
carbon, **S22**, **S24**, **S46**
C joints, allowable loads, 260
C joists, allowable loads, 260
cleats, 374
coating systems for, **S128**
cold-formed members, 32
cold-rolled, **S46**
columns, 50, 165, 266
columns, anchorage, 208, 214
columns, concrete-encased, 45
columns, connections, 322
columns, control joints, 197
columns, fire protection, 45, 357
columns, load tables, 249
columns, prefabricated fireproofed, 266
columns, reinforced, 215
composite construction, 45
conduits, 642, 643
corrosion-resistant, **S46**
cover plate, 689
dampers, 223
deck base, **S126**
decks, concrete-topped, 45
decks, floor, 256, 259
decks, roof, 258
door jambs, 263
doors, 407–409
economy of, **S26**, 248
fasteners, 149, 238, 689
finishes, **S24**
fire protection of, 357
flagpoles, 494
flashings, 393
flats, 265
flitch plates, 295
forms, 167, 177
frames, 205, 255, 407–409
frames, economy of, **S26**, 248
frames, environmental impact of, 746
frames, fire protection, 357
frames, fire-rated, 404
frames, lightweight, **S37**
frames, overturning forces, 48
frames, stone on, 237, 240
frames, stone panels, 235–236
frames, for stone stairs, 479
frames, systems, 253, 254
framing, cold-formed, **S34–40**
galvanized, dovetail slots, 194
galvanized, flashings, 377, 393
galvanized, gauge and use, **S152**
galvanized, gutters, 390
galvanized, paving, 136
galvanizing, 245
gauges and weights, **S45**, **S152**
girders, framing, 299
grades and strengths, 168

gratings and treads, 269
gutters, 393
hatches, 415
horizontal, 207
hot-rolled, **S46**
hybrid, 45
insulated deck frame, **S90**
joist floor, 211
joists, 29, 45, 167, 260, 310, 460
joists, long-span, 257
joists, open-web, 256
leaning pipes and posts, 154
library shelving, 539
life cycle of, 744
lightweight, frame, 32
lintels, 199, 295
lockers, 497
miscellaneous shapes, 264
open web truss, 328
ornamental details, **S43**
pans, 28
for perforating applications, **S46**
perimeter channel, 262
piles, 135
pipes, 266, 296, 594–595
plate bearing shoe, **S68**
plates, 183, 296, 415
plates, compression, 314
pressed, frames, 404
properties of, 244
reinforcement, 35, 168, 170
reinforcement, concrete, **S6**, **S7**, 171
reinforcement, masonry, 197
reinforcement, one-way joist, 173
reinforcement, parapet wall, 212
reinforcement, placement of, 170
rolled shapes, 250–252
roofing, 361, 362
sealants, 400
seamless pipe, 594
seamless pressure tubing, 594
sections, 250–252, 264–265
seismic-resistant details, 49
shapes, **S28–30**, 250, 251
shelf angles, stone panels, 235
shore posts, 167
space frames, 255
stainless, 244
stainless, gauge and use, **S152**
stainless, helical inserts, 292
stairs, 267
stone veneer, 238
stone walls, 232
straps, square columns, 165
structural, 50
structural, counter flashing, **S99**
structural, economy of design, **S26**, 248
structural, fire protection, 357
structural, frames, 48, 253
structural, rolled shapes, 250–252
structural, tube, 254
structural components, 50
structural data, **S26**
structural shapes, 250–252
studs, 213, 235–236, 261–263
studs, environmental impact of, 746
subtreads, 28
trash receptacles, 155
trusses, 31, 45
tubing, 266
vertical, 207
weights for buildings, **S23**
windows, 425–427, 759
wire, 168
wire, ash urns, 155
wire, coated, 787
wire, sizes and gauges, 168
Steel Deck Institute (SDI), 272
Steel Door Institute (SDI), 456

Steel Joist Institute (SJI), 272
technical digest, 257
Steel Structures Painting Council (SSPC), 272
Steel Window Institute (SWI), 456, 576
Steps
built-in, with grab rails, 690
concrete, 176
footings, 174
stone, 233, 479
Stereophotogrammetry, 775
Stiffeners, web, **S64**
Stiles
door, 437
edge profiles, 410
wood door, 770
wood paneling, 338
Stirrups, 169
concrete reinforcement, 170
reinforced brick masonry, 215
seismic, 169
Stone, **S118**, 231–240
anchorage, 232, 235
applications, 131
arches, 216, 765
balustrades, 233
bases, rusticated, 752
bedding methods, 754
cast, for ash urns and planters, 155
classification of, 231
columns, 232
continuous coping, 236
coping, 233
cornices, 233, 235
curbs, 136, 137, 233
cut, 239–240, 473, 479
cut, paving, 137
cut, windowsills, 752
door surrounds, 234
dry stack, 134
expansion, 231
facing, **S118**, 473
finishes, 754
flooring, **S125**, 479
footings, 765
historic building preservation, 752
interior details, 473
ledge, flashing, **S100**
lug sill, 234
masonry, 216, 231–232, 235–240, 473, 479
panels, 235–236
panels, preassembled, 240
parapets, 233, 239
paving, 136, 137
properties of, 231
quoins, 233
repairs, 754
rip rap, **S68**
riprap, 130
rough, 232
rubble, 232
saddles, 479
sealants, 400
shop-bonded, 240
soffit, 473
spandrel, 236
steps, 233, 479
thresholds, 479
tiles and pavers, **S125**
treads, 28, 479
uses and finishes, 231
veneer, 237–240
wall installation, 232
wall panels, common sizes for interior use, **S118**
water absorption, 231
weatherproofing tolerances, 237
weights, 882

windowsills, 479
window surrounds, 234
Stools, **S74**, 525, 797
drafting, 532
Stoop, 87
Stops, **S75**
door, 435
gravel, **S90**, 391–393
Storage
closets, 786–787
for cooling energy, 720
drafting equipment tubes, 535
in early learning centers, 538
filing systems, 534
hot water tanks, 612
kitchen layout for handicapped, 783
overfile, 533
planning, 788–792
remote energy, 719
thermal, 723, 725–726, 728
wine cellars, 515
Storage tanks, steel
exterior coating system for, **S128**
interior coating system for, **S128**
Storefronts, 521–522
all-glass, 420
awnings, 734
canopies, 420
design, 420
environmental factors, 420
historic, 763
revolving doors, 422
sliding, 423
Stoves, 493
masonry, 220
metal solid-fuel heaters, **S140–141**
Strainer, roof drain, **S94**
Strand designation code, **S15**, 180
Strand pattern designation, **S16**, 181
Straps
diagonal steel, 261
hurricane, **S109**
ridge uplift, **S61**
ties, **S48**
Streets, 88–90
furnishings, 93, 154, 155
guidelines for traditional neighborhood design, 92
patterns, 80
sanitary sewers, 603
Strength rates, for concrete, **S6**, 172
Stress
in bending, 282–283
ranges, structural glued laminated timber, 318
Stringers, stairs, 267, 339
Strips
rustication, 166
thin-set terrazzo, 472
Strongback, **S58**
Structural building panels, **S62–63**
Structural calculations, 883–885
formula nomenclature, 883
Structural member, through roof, **S90**
Structural systems
air-supported, **S163**, 560
composite, elements, 45
design, 29–36
flat plate concrete, 34
frame construction with cold roof, 715
historic, 764–765
lightweight steel frame and brick veneer, 32
long-span, 44, 138, 181, 560
masonry box-frame, 188
post-tensioned concrete, 35
precast concrete frame, 36
preengineered, 569
pre-engineered metal, **S165–166**
preservation of, 764–765

NOTE: Page references in **boldface** preceded by **S** indicate *Supplement* pages.

Index

staggered steel truss, 31
steel bar joist with bearing wall, 29
steel frame with access floor and curtail, 30
wood roof truss and wood floor truss, 33
Struts
  eave, 253
  supports, 267
Stucco
  on adobe, 230
  half timber, 303
  historic building preservation, 752
Studio theaters, stage lighting, 843
Studs
  concrete wall, 166
  diagonal steel, 261
  lap, **S50**
  metal, **S139**
  metal framing, 260, 262
  nested, 263
  shear, 45, 258
  spacing, 462
  steel, **S34**
  ties, **S48**
  wall, 166
  western or platform framing, 294
  wood, exterior system, **S54**
  wood, infile system, **S54**
  wood framing, 300
Study carrels, 536, 539
Subdivisions, 81
  residential, 79
Subdrains, soil classes, 140
Subfloors
  APA panel, 309
  nailing schedule, 309
  plywood, 296, 300, 309
  for wood and resilient flooring, 477–478
Substrates
  concrete decks, 349
  conditions, paints and coatings, **S132**
  waterproofing, 347, 348
Subsurface drainage and filtration, 140, 143–146
Subsurface investigation, 126
Subtreads, steel, 28
Sump pans, metal roof deck, 258
Sun
  altitude, 706, 709–710
  angles, 609–712, 706
Sun control, 705–706, 732–734
Sunscreens, 237
Sun shades, 732–734
Sunspaces, 725
Sun time, 708
Support, equipment
  columns, **S106**
  continuous curb, **S106**
  on light roofs, **S90**
  on low-slope roofs, **S81**
Support systems, metal, **S114–115**
Surfaces
  areas and volumes, 873, 878, 880
  ceiling, special, **S122–123**
  complex, on low-slope roofs, **S81**
  concrete, **S12–13, S128**, 177–178
  critical factors, 177
  curved, geometry of, 880
  drainage, 141–142
  films, 354
  heat transfer coefficient, 738
  light-reflective, 720
  masonry, **S128**
  metal, **S128**
  paving, 136–138
  pipe insulation, 601

roof walking, **S107**
walls, special, **S121**
Surfing, 109
Surgical rooms, 803
Surgicenters, 828
Surveillance, 74
  systems, 507–508
Surveying, 775
Suspension, timber bridges, **S67**
Swimming pools, 685, 686
  accessibility, 687
  coatings, 245
  diving facility dimensions (FINA), 691
  diving towers, 692, 693
  edge coping, raised, 687
  gutters, 688
  ladders, platforms, end wall targets, and windows, 690
  lighting, timing panels, and float anchors, 689
  lockers and shower rooms, 799–800
  movable floors, 687
  perimeter overflows, 688
  planning, 685
  public, 684–686, 688, 690–693
  residential, 683
  shapes, 684
  skylights, 395
  steps, ladders, and targets, 690
  transfer tier, 687
  trim, 469
  wading, 684
Symbols, 495
  of accessibility, **S143**, 495
  air conditioning and heating, 863
  common, **S143**, 495
  graphic, 856–864
  materials, 856
  for plans, 856–857, 859–864
  power and refrigeration, 863
  readability, 502
Synagogues, 832
Systèm International d'Unités (SI)
  sample building drawings, 892–896
  units, 892–895

Tabernacles, 542
Tables
  audiovisual facilities, 537
  billiards, 682
  classic, 546–550
  clearances, 11
  coffee, 6
  conference, 6, 531, 549, 550, 551
  contemporary, 551, 552, 553
  dining, 547, 549–550, 551
  drafting, 535
  folding, 511, 524, 536
  food service, **S153, S154, S156, S157**
  low, 525
  mailrooms, 795
  occasional, 6, 525
  open classroom furniture, 537
  outdoor, 526
  for restaurants/bars, 797–798
  school, 536
  side, 525
  stacking, 524
  tracing, 535
Table tennis, 682
Tack rooms, 847–848
Target shooting, 698–699
Team handball, 671
Tearooms, seating capacities, 798
Tees, 252, 264
  concealed system, **S123**
  exposed system, **S123**

panel, 185
precast, 183
reveal system, **S123**
structural, **S30**
Telecommunications Association, 664
Telecommunications cabling distribution, 663
Teleconferencing, **S149**, 794
Telephones
  accessible, 17
  cables, 646–647
Television studios, flooring, 483
Tellers, 507–508
  ballistic/forced entry windows, 419
Temperatures
  air-sol, 742
  concrete reinforcement, 170
  control, 602
  deep-ground, maps, 703, 735
  dew-point, 65, 702, 738
  dry-bulb, 65, 702
  floor and roof slab reinforcement, 168
  high sol-air, 717
  indoor, 65
  for thermal comfort, 65
  two-pipe systems, 619, 629
  winter designs and averages, 704
Templates, mortise, 437
Tendons, steel reinforcing, stretching, 35
Tennis, 674, 677, 681
Termite protection, **S69**
  shields, **S63, S100**, 301
Terne, 361
Terracing, 130
Terra-cotta, 226
  brownstone, 226
  brownstone, historic building preservation, 752
  planters, 155
Terrazzo, 472
Textile Care Allied Trades Association (TCATA), 520
Theaters
  design criteria, 838–839
  sightlines, 840
  stage lighting systems, 842–843
  stage rigging counterweights, 524
Thermal construction, 721
Thermal expansion
  of area, length, and volume, 881
  of piping materials, 596
Thermal insulation, 354, 740
  curtain walls, 449
  piping and ducts, 602
Thermal mass
  climate data, 702
  hot arid conditions, 717
  masonry, 726
  time delay, 717
  utilization, 720
Thermal performance
  earth shelters, 737
  time lag, 717
Thermal protection, 346–402
  masonry, 203
  resources, 402
Thermal resistance values
  of building materials, 739, 740
  of glazing materials, 741
Thermal storage, 723
  mass, 726
  walls, 725–726, 728
Thermal transmission, 724, 738–742
  cold regions building design, 715
  hot arid region building envelope, 717
Thermometers, wells, 623
Thermopiles, 714
Thermosiphons, 725
Therms, 738

Thoroughfares, 89, 91
  types, 90
Thresholds
  assembled and cast, 440
  ceramic tile, 470
  exterior, weather stripping, 441
  interior metal, 440
  interlocking, 441
  latch track, 441
Throwing circle, construction, 676
Ticket counters, 822
Ticket windows, 666
Tiebacks, **S20**, 129
Tie holes
  exposed, 164
  treatment, **S14**, 177
Tie rods
  accessories, **S5**
Ties, 169, 212
  collar, **S40, S52–53**
  concrete, 168, 177
  concrete formwork, **S5**
  floor, **S48**
  between floors, **S61**
  hurricane, **S61**
  masonry, 194, 207, 212
  metal, 220
  pintel, 212
  rafter, **S48**
  railroad, 131
  reinforced brick masonry, 215
  spacing, column reinforcing bars, 170
  stone wall, 232
  strap, **S48**
  stud, **S48**
  typical, 166
  wall, 166
  wall, metal, 199
  wire, metal, 190
  wire, selection, 461
  Z-type, 194, 208, 212
Tile Council of America, 484
Tiles, 469–471
  acoustical, **S120, S123**
  acoustical ceiling, 474, 475
  barrel, **S109**
  carpet, 482
  ceiling, **S120**
  cement wood, **S85**
  ceramic, installation, 470–471
  clay, channels, 141
  clay, drainpipes, 140
  clay, pavers, 137
  clay, roofs, 360, 367, 758
  composite, **S85**
  concrete, **S84**
  cork, 480
  fiber cement, **S85**
  flat, **S84**
  floor, 480
  floor framing for, 300
  metal, **S85**, 361
  paving, 137
  placement of, **S84**
  ready-set, 469
  roll, **S84**
  roof, **S84–85, S109**
  roof, types, **S82**
  roofing, 358–367, 758
  rubber, 480
  shower receptors, 470
  stone, **S125**
  structural clay, 225
  S type, high wind resistance detail, **S109**
  types, shapes, and size, 469
  vinyl composition, 480
  walls, glazed, 469
  walls, hollow, 765

NOTE: Page references in **boldface** preceded by **S** indicate *Supplement* pages.

Index

Tilt-up concrete, **S1**, **S521**, 185
Tilt-Up Concrete Association (TCA), 186
Timber
  bridges, **S67–68**
  construction, heavy, **S67–68**
  curbs, 136
  frame buildings, **S52**
  frame construction, **S52–55**
  glued laminated, 318–319
  half, 303
  heavy, 314–317, 340
  lagging, 129, 346
  piles, 135
  sill and joist system, **S54**
  Southern Pine preservative retentions and AWPA standards, **S70**
  walls, 131
Time zones, 708
Tin
  melting temperature of, **S23**
  pressed, 757
  properties of, **S22**
TND (Traditional Neighborhood Development), 79, 80, 91–92
TOD (transit-oriented design), 80
Toilets
  accessories for, 488
  compartments, 486
  fixtures, 606
  grab bars, 487
  graphic symbols, 859
  for handicapped, 489
  paper holders, 488, 859
  partitions, 486
  planning, 799, 800
  rooms, 18, 807
  wet area, 799
Tooling, nonsag sealants, 401
Topiaries, 160
Topsoil, 160
Touch bar, 439
Touch football, 669
Towel bars, 488
Towel dispensers, 859
Towel racks for handicapped, 487
Townhouses, **S194**
Town planning
  block types, 82
  building types, 85
  environmental site analysis, 76–78
  frontage types, 87
  landscape types, 88
  open space types, 83–84
  plan types, 81
  process, 75
  regional types, 80
  spatial definition, 86
  thoroughfares, 89–90
  traditional neighborhood development, 91–92
Track and field, 675–676
Tracks, 673
Track splice, **S39**
Trade buildings and marts, 558
Traditional neighborhood development (TND), 79, 80, 91–92
  guidelines for, 92
Traffic control, 100
  mechanical barriers, 151
Trailers, 106
Trampolines, 680
Transformers, 649, 650
Transit-oriented design (T.O.D.), 80
Transmission rates, water vapor, 352
Transom sashes, windows, 430
Transportation, 98–99, 106–108
  airports, 819–822
  automatic systems, 588
  mobility aids and vehicles, 10

Traprock, physical properties, 231
Trap shooting, 699
Trash containers
  compactors, **S160**
  compactors and dumpsters, 514, 516
  receptacles, 155
Trash trucks, 98
  turning dimensions, 99
Travel distances, lifts, 586
Treads, 28
  accessible stairs, 16, 28
  coverings, 28
  fire escapes, 268
  landscaping, 159
  metal, 269
  proportioning, 25
  replacement of, 28
  slip-resistant, 176
  spiral stairs, 27
  stair framing, 296
  steel, **S41**, 267
  stone, 28, 479
  wood decks, 313
  wood stairs, 339, 340
Trees
  cutting and use, 160
  function and regulatory effects of, 158
  interior landscaping, 555–557
  ornamental landscaping, 161
  planting details, 159
  protection and planning, 160
  protection grates and guards, 154
Trellis, wood, 157
Trenches
  absorption, 146
  covers, 416
  drains, 142
  header ducts, 646
Trigonometric functions, 875–876, 881
Trim
  colonial, 341
  door and base, **S74**
  exterior, environmental impact of, 746
  gypsum wallboard, 463
  interior wood, **S74–75**
  special, 483
  standing and running, 341
  stone, 234
  tile, 469
  wood, 341, 770
Triple jump, construction, 676
Trowels
  notched, **S47**
  slip-resistant, 28
Truck docks, 107
Trucks, 98, 106
Trusses, **S67**, 31, 33
  anchors, **S48**
  bowstring, **S57**
  building insulation, 355
  cantilever, **S56**
  clerestory, **S56**
  concrete reinforcement bars, 170
  double fink, **S56**
  dual-pitch, **S57**
  exterior lightweight wood system, **S54**
  fabricated, 326
  fink, **S56**
  flat, 325
  floor, **S57–58**
  gypsum wallboard, 467
  Howe, **S56**
  jack, **S59**
  metal building frame, 569
  monopitch, **S57**
  monoplaner, 326
  open web, 328
  panels, 182
  parallel chord, **S57**

  pitched, **S56–57**, 323
  plywood web, 328
  prefabricated, 33
  roof, **S40**, **S57**, **S59**
  scissors, **S57**, 323, 327
  space frames, **S31**, 255
  split-ring, 323–325
  steel, 45
  step-down system, **S59**
  triple W, **S56**
  types, 327
  vaulted ceiling, **S57**
  wood, **S56–59**, 45, 323–328
  wood, exterior lightweight system, **S54**
Tubing, 594
  aluminum, 265, 595
  compressed flexible, 372
  copper, 265, 594
  electrical, 642, 643
  flexible, **S93**
  framed systems, 254
  metal, 265, 642
  metallic, 643
  seamless steel pressure, 594
Turbine pump, 147, 599
Turf, natural and synthetic, 673
Turnarounds, 11
Turnbuckles, 293, 316
Turning radius
  cars, 99
  trucks and trailers, 106
  vehicles, 99
Turnstiles, 70
2-clip, **S48**

Ultrasonic detectors, 73
Ultraviolet radiation, 58
Umbrella racks, 796
Umbrellas, outdoor furniture, 526
Underground Space Center (UGSC), 162
Underheating, design conditions for, 716
Underlayment
  carpet, 482
  low slope roofs, 365
  nailing schedule, 309
  plywood panel sheathing, 306
  roofing, 359
Underwriters Laboratories of Canada (ULC), 576
Underwriters Laboratories (UL), 257, 504, 520, 576, 664
  metal chimney system, 221
  performance vaults, 506
  rated fireproofed columns, 266
  roofing standards, 358–359
Uniform Building Code (UBC)
  occupant loads, 23
  stairway requirements, 25
Uniform capital recovery, 122
Uniform Federal Accessibility Standards (UFAS)
  kitchens, 22
  residential bathrooms, 20, 21
Uninterruptible power supply (UPS) systems, **S183**, 651, 661, 662
  battery packs, 74
  diagrams, 661
United States Department of Energy, 748
United States Department of Health and Human Services, 854
United States Department of Housing and Urban Development, 124
United States Department of Justice (USDJ), National Institute of Corrections (NIC), 854
United States Federal Asbestos Regulations 1991, 128

United States Institute for Theater Technology (USITT), 854
United States National Society for the International Society of Soil Mechanics and Foundation Engineering (USNS/ISSMFE), 162
United States Postal Service (USPS), 795
United States Professional Tennis Association, 700
United States Soccer Federation, 700
United States Tennis Association, 700
United States Tennis C (AS), 854
Unit heaters, 624
  gas-fired, 622
Unit masonry, 190, 200–230
  adobe, 230
  arches, 216–217
  brick veneer, 213–214
  cavity walls, 210–212
  ceramic veneer, 226
  clay, 201
  concrete, 202
  control and expansion joints, 197
  corner layout, 200
  fire protection, 357
  flooring, **S126**
  foundation walls, 203–204
  glass, 227–229
  multiwythe walls, 208–209
  single wythe walls, 205–207
  terra-cotta veneer, 226
  wall construction, 190
Universal accessibility, 8–22, 522
  sports arena checklist, 666
UPS (uninterruptible power supply) systems, **S183**, 651, 661, 662
  battery packs, 74
  diagrams, 661
Urban design, 75, 79–92
Urban garden, 161
Urbanism, elements of, 79
Urban Land Institute (ULI), 124, 162
Urban planning, 75–93
  contextual analysis, 76
  site analysis, 76
Urgicenters, 828
Urinals, 606, 807, 859
  accessible, 18
  for handicapped, 487
  screens, 486
Utensils, kitchen, 789, 790, 791
Utilities
  in cold climates, 714
  connection boxes, **S160**, 516
  electrical site, 649
  tables, 537
U value
  masonry walls, 190
  roofing, 361

Vacuum cleaners, 790
Valleys
  flashings, 383
  roofing, 374
  shingles, 365
Valves, 598
  gas, 623
  insulation, 601
Vanities, 21
Vans, 98
  delivery trucks, 106
  lifts, 10
Vapor
  barriers, roofing, 362
  barriers, sheathing materials, 308
  pressure, 65, 738
  retarders, 352, 355

NOTE: Page references in **boldface** preceded by **S** indicate *Supplement* pages.

Index

retarders flexible, **S89–90**
retarders, polyethylene, 716
transmission, 352
water, permeance and permeability of materials to, 352, 738
Vaults, 506
  skylights, 396
  underground, 649
Vehicles, 98
  accessible vans, 10
  automatic guided, 587
  barriers, 69, 70
  dimensions, 98, 106, 587
  forklifts, 587
  height, 106
  oversnow, 697
  track electric system, 588
  turning dimensions, 99, 106
Vending machines and rooms, 12, 512
Veneer
  brick, 32, 189, 213, 214, 301, 302, 431
  ceramic, 226
  concrete masonry backup, 237
  finishes, 185
  grades, plywood, 305
  masonry, 32, 189
  masonry, flashings, 385
  masonry anchors, 194
  plywood panels, 307
  steel frame, 237
  stone, 231–232, 237–238, 239–240
  stone, hanging systems, 473
  walls, 199
Veneers, wood, **S76–78**
  core, **S76**
  marble cutting, **S118**
  matching patterns, **S77–78**
  plain sliced, **S76**
  quarter sliced, **S76**
  rift sliced (rift cut), **S76**
  rotary cut, **S76**
Venetian blinds, 571
Ventilators and ventilation, **S63, S110–113**
  air distribution, 631–635
  applications, **S83**
  attic, **S83**, 301, 394
  climate data, 702
  cold storage rooms, **S164**
  crawl space, **S83**, 301, 394
  earth shelters, 394
  eave, **S83**, 301, 394
  electronic control systems, 636–637
  fire, skylights, 395
  fire and smoke, **S110, S113**
  flashings, 372, 382
  gravity, gooseneck, **S106**
  gravity, stationary, **S106**
  greenhouses, 849
  heat recovery, 745
  hot arid conditions, 717
  HVAC control systems, 636–637
  kennels and animal shelters, 846
  losses, 717–718
  metal solid-fuel heaters, **S141**
  natural, 713
  pipes, 597, 603
  plumbing stack, **S94**
  range hoods, **S161**
  requirements, 394
  residential, 221, 394
  ridge, **S63, S83**
  roof, **S83, S106**, 301, 310, 394, 758
  rotating, **S106**
  screened, 310
  shed roof, at wall, **S83**
  sloped roof, **S106**
  soffit, 394, 716
  space, 718
  stacks, 625
  strategies, 713
  symbols, 862
  units, 624
Vermiculite, 458
Vermiculite Association (VA), 402
Vesica Piscis, 872
Veterinary hospitals, 844, 845
Vibration, 62, 256
Vibration control, 567, 600
Video cameras, 74
Videoconference equipment, **S149–150**
Villages, 79
  garden city, 80
  rural, 78
Vinyl
  composition tile, 480
  doors and windows, 431
  insert thresholds, 441
  nosings, 28
  rails, 270
  wall coverings, **S135**
Vinyl Window and Door Institute, 456
Vision panels, 405
Visually impaired persons, considerations for, 9
Volleyball, 674, 681
Volumes
  calculation of, 118
  of solids, 873, 878
  thermal expansion of, 881

Wading pools, 684
Wainscots, 338, 341
  paneling, 769
Walers
  channels, 129
  wall, 166
Walkers, 10
Walkways, 96
  accessible, 313
  covered, 734
  lighting, 150
  low-slope roof, **S80–81**
  moving, 584
  roof, **S107**
  roof, surfaces, **S107**
  skylights, 395
  traditional neighborhood design, 91
  wood pallet-type, **S107**
Wallboard gypsum, 463–465, 468
  acoustical tile ceilings, 474
  column enclosures, 357
  environmental impact of, 747
  partitions, 463–467
  permeance and permeability to water vapor, 352
  sheathing, 308
  types, 466
Wallcovering Manufacturers Association, 484, 504
Wall expansion joints, 197
Walls
  absorptive treatment, **S119**
  acoustical treatment, **S119**, 476
  anchorage, 194, 206, 209, 211, 214
  anchorage details, **S50**
  back, single-pitch, detail at top, **S112**
  barriers, 70
  basement, **S49**, 170, 203
  basic building insulation, 355
  bearing, **S38, S65**, 29, 32
  bonded veneered, 232
  bowlock-bak, 764
  brick, 134, 190, 199, 215, 764
  brick, recess and sill details, 208
  brick, reinforced load-bearing, 208
  brick veneer, 301
  bridging, **S37**
  bullet-resistant, **S117**
  canted, with light cove, **S116**
  cavity, **S117**, 194, 198, 199, 225
  cavity, brick, 210, 212, 764
  cavity, CMU, 210
  cavity, masonry, 197, 210–212
  cavity, through wall flashing at, **S97**
  cavity, veneered, 232
  ceramic tile, 470
  circular, masonry, 200
  CMU, 134
  CMU, electrical outlet box in, 205
  combustible, clearances from, 221
  comparative assemblies, 41–42
  concrete, 168
  concrete, single-pitch side wall detail, **S112**
  concrete formwork, **S3**, 166
  concrete masonry unit, 205, 207
  construction, sandwich, **S17**
  control joint, **S117**
  corner, **S61**
  coverings, **S135–136**
  crawl space, **S49**
  curtain, 215, 240, 245, 369, 728
  curtain, brick, 215
  curtain, glazed, 449–456
  curtain, masonry, 189
  diffusive treatment, **S119**
  double loaded, parking lots, 101
  earth, 230
  end, 142
  energy-efficient, 716
  exterior, 294, 315
  exterior, assemblies, 41–42, 384
  exterior, bearing, 262
  exterior, furring, **S117**
  exterior, intersection, **S117**
  exterior, masonry, 752
  exterior, watertables, 384
  feature, with light cove, **S116**
  fire, 199, 380
  fireproof, 199
  flashings, 378, 379, 380, 383, 385, 388
  flashing through, **S97**
  floor-to-bearing connections, 183
  foam-core panel system, **S54**
  footings, **S1, S2**, 164, 165
  foundation, 170, 203, 204
  foundation, sections, 301
  foundation connections, 183
  framing details, 300
  freestanding, horizontal loading, 134
  gable end, **S108**
  garden, 131, 134
  gravity-retaining, 132
  guards, **S137–139**, 491
  heat transmission, 728
  hollow, 209, 215, 765
  hollow, grouted, 209
  hollow, tile, 765
  horizontal nailer system, **S54**
  interior, bearing, 262
  interior, foundation for, 204
  interior, paneling details, 338
  intersecting, **S61**
  intersections, 317
  intersections, control joints at, 197
  joints, 197
  knee, **S49**
  lathing and plaster systems, 462
  liquid-applied membranes, 349
  masonry, 188, 190, 198, 199, 212, 215
  masonry, single-pitch back wall detail at top, **S112**
  mass, thermal storage, 725, 728
  massive, 717
  modular systems, **S148**
  moldings, standard, **S123**
  multiwythe, 208, 209
  non-loadbearing, 204, 205
  operable, **S147**
  panels, **S166**
  panels, gypsum, prefinished, **S117**
  panels, interior, **S121**
  panels, precast concrete, **S17–18**, 182
  panels, reinforcement, 215
  parapet, scupper detail at, **S105**
  perimeter security, 69
  pilasters, concrete, 166
  pipe penetration at, 346
  purlins, **S52**
  radial, 200
  rake, **S60**
  reinforced concrete, 170
  retaining, 130–134, 131, 132, 133, 215
  sandwich, 182
  security, **S117**
  service, 489–490
  shaft, 466
  shear, **S51**, 47
  shear, masonry, 49
  shear, plywood, 50
  shear, seismic design, 46–47
  sheathing, 308
  side, single-pitch, detail, **S112**
  single wythe, 205, 206, 207
  single wythe, CMU, 207
  solid veneered, 232
  sound resistance of, 42, 567
  stone, 232
  stone, cut and veneer, 239, 240, 473
  stone, installation, 232
  structural facing tile, 225
  surfaces, special, **S121**
  thermal storage, 725
  thin veneered, 232
  ties, 194
  tile, hollow, 765
  tilt-up, **S1**
  translucent, 455
  Trombe, 727
  water, 725
  water-resistant, **S117**
  watertables, 384
  windowless, 236
  wood frame, 301
Wardrobe units, bedroom, 545
Warehouses
  construction cost estimating, 121
  flooring, 483
Warnings, detectable, 14, 97
Washers
  laundry rooms, 511
  residential, **S160**, 516
Washington Design Center, 558
Waste disposal, 850
Waste heat recovery, 630, 723
Waste management, 850–854
  chutes, 590
  collection and recycling spaces, 851, 852, 853
  compactors, 514
  containers, 514, 791
  piping, 597, 603
  receptacles, 488
Waste room plan, 853
Wastes, 743
  solid, amounts and composition, 850
Waterbeds, 545

NOTE: Page references in **boldface** preceded by **S** indicate *Supplement* pages.

Index

Water-cement ratios, 175
   concrete, 172
Water chillers, 619
   dual condenser, 630
Water closets, 20, 606, 781, 806, 807
   accessible, 18
Water coolers, 17, 487, 610, 859
Water distribution
   pipes, 597
   pipes, residential, 603
   pump capacities, 139
   pumps, 804
   residential, 139
Water fountains, 17, 487, 610
Water heaters
   circuits, 640
   domestic, 611
   domestic, annual use, 724
   gas, 611
   gas-fired, 621, 623
   instantaneous, 623
   loop pumps, 630
   solar, 611, 729
   steam, 611
Water polo, 694
Waterproofing, 346–351
   earth shelters, 735–737
   of foundations, 203, 346
   low-slope roofs, **S80**
   membranes, 347, 348, 349, 371
   paving, 137
   at roof transitions, **S107**
   under slab, 346
   stone walls, 232
Water resistance
   foundations, 346
   under slabs, 346
Water Ski Industry Association, 700
Water ski jump, 694
Water softeners, 613
Waterstops
   for concrete slabs, **S4**
   earth shelters, 736
   foundations, 346
Watertables, 301, 384, 764
Water tanks, 612
Water treatment, 613
Water vapor
   migration, **S132**, 352
   penetration, **S132**
   permeance and permeability of materials to, 352, 738
Water walls, passive solar, 725–728
Water windows, 689
Wattages
   lamps, 654–655
   residential electrical devices, 640
Watts-per-square-foot, 52
Wearing courses, waterproofing of, 347
Weather
   cold, concrete construction and, 172
   hot, concrete construction and, 172
   winter data and design conditions, 704
Weatherability, of brick joints, 192
Weatherboard, historic preservation of, 755
Weathering indexes, in U.S., 201
Weatherproofing, stone tolerances, 237
Weather stripping
   exterior thresholds, 441
   retrofitting, 759–760
   windows, 442
Weep holes
   brick masonry, 215
   cavity walls, 212
   retaining walls, 132, 133
   spandrel flashings, 386
   stone panels, 236
   stone veneer joints, 238

Weights, of materials, 882
Welding Research Council, 272
Welds, 244–245
   fillet, 246, 247, 263
   flare, 246
   joint prequalification, 246
   plug, 246, 247
   precast concrete, 183
   roofing, 362
   slot, 246, 247
   stairs, 267
   structural, 246
   symbols, 247
   wire fabric, 168, 180
Wells, pumps for, 139
Western Red Cedar Association, 344
Western Wood Products Association (WWPA), 344, 484
Wet bench (darkroom), 519
Wheelchairs, 10, 11
   clearance, 797
   handicapped bathrooms, 487, 607, 781
   lifts, 10, 586
   ramp in paving, 96
   reach dimensions from, 12
   restaurant seating arrangements for persons using, 798
   space requirements for, 11
   turning space, 806
Wheel loads, industrial floors, 175
Wheel stops
   asphalt paving, 136
   carports, 785
   parking lots, 103
Wind loads
   flagpoles, 494
   metal buildings, 569
Windows, 403–456
   awning, 428
   ballistic, 419
   bay, 297
   casement, metal, 425
   classical, 116
   combined units, 430
   custom, 430
   dimensioning methods, 858
   dormer, 432
   double-hung, 426, 429, 431, 759
   entrances and storefronts, 521–522
   environmental impact of, 747
   faceted stained glass, 445
   fire, NFPA standards, 404
   fixed glass, 430
   flashing, **S100**
   forced entry, 419
   framing detail, **S51**
   gasketed, 369
   glass for, 443–445
   glazed curtain walls, 449
   glazing, 433, 443–444, 446–448, 453
   hardware, 434–440
   heads, 236
   historic, 759–760
   historic types and construction, 759
   Hoppers, 430
   hung and sliding, 426
   interior, 433
   jalousie, 428, 430
   metal, 424–428, 430
   mill, 760
   openings, **S36**, 295
   oriel, 432
   Palladian, 304
   picture, 430
   pivoted metal, 427
   plastic glazing, 446
   projecting, 427
   rehabilitation and replacement of, 759

   replacement, wood, 760
   resources, 456
   reversible, 427
   security, 405, 406
   sills, 236, 238, 303
   sills, stone, 237, 752
   size, ventilation, 713
   sliding, metal, 426
   stained glass, 445
   steel, horizontal pivoted, 759
   steel and aluminum, 426, 427
   steel casement, 425
   stone panel heads, 236
   stone veneer, 237–238
   storefront, 420
   storm, 740, 760
   surrounds, stone, 234
   translucent wall and skylights, 455
   transom, 304
   treatment, 433
   vinyl, 431
   wall, hard stone panel at, 235
   weatherstrips for, 442
   well, 203
   wood, 429–431
   wood, double hung, 759
   wood, historic preservation of, 760
   wood and plastic, 429–433, 431, 759
Wind protection, 158
Wind resistance, high
   detail for composition and asphalt shingles, **S109**
   detail for extruded concrete, **S109**
   detail for galvanized metal roofing, **S109**
   detail for S-type tile roofing, **S109**
Windsurfing, 109
Wind tolerance, plants, 160
Wind uplift, **S109**
   design for roofing materials, **S109**
   and flashings, 378, 380
Wine Institute, 520
Wine storage cellars, 515
Winter weather data, 704
Wire
   chases, **S62**
   chases, box beam sill, **S55**
   chases, surface-mounted at foam-core panel, **S55**
   chases, timber sill, **S55**
   hangers, **S115**
Wire mesh
   baseball backstop, 674
   chain link fences, 148
   gabions, 130
   partitions, 503
Wire pulls, 335
Wire Reinforcement Institute (WRI), 186
Wires
   cables, **S171**
   cable trays, **S171**, 645
   components, 529
   electrical, 640–647
   electrical, diagrams, 641
   electrical, environmental impact of, 747
   electrical, for open office, 529
   electrical, material, 642
   fabric, welded, **S6**, 168, 180
   flat cable, 647
   glass, 443
   management, 663
   management, freestanding components, 529
   masonry ties, 194
   reinforced plastic roofing, 362
   reinforcing, **S6**, 168, 169
   sizes and gauges, 168
   steel, 168

   steel, ash urns, 155
   steel, coated, 787
   strength, 179
Wireways, 860
Wiring
   floor, for workstations, **S172**
   for open office furniture, 529
   residential electrical, **S168–169**
Witness stands, 801
Women, measurements, 2
Wood, 273–341, 341
   adhesives, **S47**
   anchorage, 313
   ash urns, 155
   beam connections, 322
   blinds, **S79**
   block pavers, 137
   bonding, **S47**
   bridging, 299
   burning fireplaces, 219
   butt joints, 178
   cabinets, 335
   cement tiles, **S85**
   chemically treated, sitework, 131
   clips, **S48**
   column footing, **S51**
   columns, anchored with steel baseplate, 321
   columns, load tables, 281
   columns, tapered, 762
   combustibility of, 275
   compression, 318
   curbs, **S111**, 398
   decay, 275
   decay-resistant, **S69**, 338
   decks, 156, 311–313, 359
   design load tables, 276–289
   deterioration, 755
   doors, 335, 411–414, 413, 431, 770
   doors, panel, 412
   doors, sliding, 414
   eaves, sills, and water tables, 301
   edge paving, 136
   exterior stairs, 313
   fences, 149
   finish, 274, 339–340
   finish, environmental impact of, 746
   fire-retardant treated, **S71**
   floors, **S124**, 211, 477–478, 580
   floors, installation details, 478
   floors, joist load tables, 276–280
   floors, materials and patterns, 477
   floors, resilient systems, **S124**
   floors, sports, **S124**
   floors, suspended, **S50**
   form inserts, 178
   formwork, 185
   foundations, system, **S49**
   foundations, treated, **S49–51**
   frames, 33, 49–50, 394, 404, 462
   frames, column load tables, 281
   frames, composite members, 45
   frames, decks, 312, 313
   frames, design, 274–275
   frames, double layer resistant, **S117**
   frames, environmental impact of, 746
   frames, exterior insulation and finish systems, 356
   frames, exterior stairs, 313
   frames, fabric-wrapped panels, **S136**
   frames, fireplace floors, 218
   frames, floor joist load tables, 276–280
   frames, leaded glass, 445
   frames, plywood subflooring on, 309
   frames, roof design, **S109**
   frames, roof rafter load tables, 285–289
   frames, roofs, 301

NOTE: Page references in **boldface** preceded by **S** indicate *Supplement* pages.

frames, single wythe masonry wall with, 205
frames, stairs, 340
frames, thin brick veneer on, 213
frames, vertical frame curb detail, **S112**
girders, 299
gutter box, 302
gutters, 758
heavy timber construction, 314–317, 321–322
historic, 755–756
I-joists, **S64–66**
insect-resistant, 338
insects, 275
interior details, 770
interior trim, **S74**
introduction to, 274, 275
joinery, **S52**
joints, 275, 331, 332
joist base, **S126**
joists, 45, 285–289, 299, 328
joists, allowable loads, 285
joists, connections, 328
joists, floor, **S51**
joists, load tables, 276, 280
laminated, joists, 282, 295
landscape lights, 154
library shelving, 539
light, decks, 312, 313
light, framing, 301, 312–313
light, rafters and joists, 45, 276–280, 285–289
lintels, 295
marine applications, 111
materials, historic, 756
moisture movement in, 275
moldings, **S74**, 770
mortise and tenon, 764
nailers, on roof purlins, **S54**
open web truss, 328
ornaments, **S72–73**
pallet-type walkways, **S107**
paneling, 338, 769
paving, 138
pediment ledge flashing, **S100**
permeance and permeability to water vapor, 352
picture molding, 338
planters, 155, 156
plate, beveled, **S66**
plywood composite, 45
prefabricated structural, 318, 319, 320, 323, 326–328
preservation of, 756
preservatives for, **S69–70**
pressure-treated, **S49**, **S69**
pressure-treated, fences, 149
pressure-treated, marine applications, 111
pressure-treated, paving, 136
rafters, 285–289
rafters, allowable loads, 286, 287, 288, 289
rafters, trussed, 45
rails, 270, 338
ramps, 313
resources, 344
retaining walls, 131
roof framing, 301
roofing, 363
rough carpentry, 294–301, 305–313
screens, **S79**
screws, 293
seismic-resistant details, 49
shakes, 360, 363–364
shelving, 337
shingles, 360, 363, 364, 758
shingles, environmental impact of, 746
shutters, **S79**
siding, 329, 756
siding, eave at, 302
siding, profiles and patterns, 756
sills, 299
sleepers, **S54**
sleepers, floor system, **S50**
sliding joints, 275
species, 318
stairs, 339–340, 340, 770
structural fasteners, **S48**
as structural material, 274
structures, insulating, 355
studs, **S54**
studs, brick veneer on, 213
tension, 318
trash receptacles, 155
treads, 269
treated, 316
treatment, **S69–71**
treatments, environmental impact of, 747
trellis, 157
trim, 341, 770
trim, interior, **S74–75**
trusses, **S56–57**, 45, 323–328
trusses, construction, 327
trusses, floor, **S58**
trusses, lightweight exterior system, **S54**
trusses, roof, **S59**
veneers, **S76–78**, **S135**
watertables, 384
windows, 429–430, 431
windows, double hung, 759
windows, historic preservation of, 760
Wood Products Center (WPI), 344
Wood Protection Council, 344
Wood & Synthetic Flooring Institute, 484
Wood Truss Council of America, 344
Woodwork
    architectural, **S72–73**, **S79**, 331–335, 331–341, 338, 341
    cabinet details, 333–336
    half timber, 303
    interior wall paneling, 338
    joints, 331–332
    molding and trim, 341
    Palladian window and doorway, 304
    shelving, 337
    stairs, 339–340
Work centers, 537
Working drawings
    dimensioning, 858
    graphic symbols, 857
    metric, 892–896
Workstations
    anthropometric data, 4, 5
    design, 793
Work triangles, kitchen layout, 782
World Forest Institute (WFI), 344
World Professional Squash Association, 700
World Sign Associates (WSA), 504
Woven Wire Products Association, 504
Wrestling equipment, 680

X-ray metal detector, 70
X-ray protection, 568
Xylophones, 510

Yield plan, 78
Yoloy steel pipe, 594
Yosemite rock pattern, 164
Young Men's Christian Association (YMCA), 700

Zamboni ice resurfacer, turning radius, 696
Zees, 264
Zinc
    architectural metals, 757
    coated steel, framing, 299
    dovetail slots, 194
    gauges and weights, **S45**
    melting temperature of, **S23**
    properties of, **S22**
    roofs, 758
    uses and properties of, 244
Zirconium
    melting temperature of, **S23**
Z-lots, **S193**
Zone junction boxes, 646, 647
Zoning
    interior, 717
    town planning, 75
Z-ties, 194, 208, 212

NOTE: Page references in **boldface** preceded by **S** indicate *Supplement* pages.